W9-BPN-490

APPLICATION BOXES

APPLETS

APPLICATION SECTIONS

STATISTICS

FOR MANAGEMENT AND ECONOMICS

DUXBURY TITLES OF RELATED INTEREST

DUXBURY

STATISTICS

FOR MANAGEMENT AND ECONOMICS

SIXTH EDITION

Gerald Keller
Wilfrid Laurier University

Brian Warrack
Wilfrid Laurier University

THOMSON

BROOKS/COLE

Australia • Canada • Mexico • Singapore • Spain • United Kingdom • United States

THOMSON

BROOKS/COLE

Publisher: Curt Hinrichs
Assistant Editor: Ann Day
Editorial Assistant: Katherine Brayton
Technology Project Manager: Burke Taft
Marketing Manager: Joseph Rogove
Marketing Assistant: Maria Salinas
Advertising Project Manager: Samantha Cabaluna
Print/Media Buyer: Jessica Reed
Permissions Editor: Bob Kauser
Production Service: Susan L. Reiland
Text and Cover Designer: Kathleen Cunningham
Photo Researcher: Pat Quest
Illustrator: Lori Heckelman
Excel and Minitab File Conversions: Wanda Lindquist @ Lori Heckelman Illustration
Cover Image: © Crowther & Carter/Getty Images/Stone
Cover Printer: Lehigh Press
Compositor: H&S Graphics
Printer: Quebecor World–Versailles

For more information about our products, contact us at:
Thomson Learning Academic Resource Center 1-800-423-0563

For permission to use material from this text, contact us by:
Phone: 1-800-730-2214
Fax: 1-800-730-2215
Web: http://www.thomsonrights.com

Brooks/Cole—Thomson Learning

511 Forest Lodge Road
Pacific Grove, CA 93950
USA

Asia
Thomson Learning
60 Albert Street, #15-01
Albert Complex
Singapore 189969

Australia
Nelson Thomson Learning
102 Dodds Street
South Melbourne, Victoria 3205
Australia

Canada
Nelson Thomson Learning
1120 Birchmount Road
Toronto, Ontario M1K 5G4
Canada

Europe/Middle East/Africa
Thomson Learning
Berkshire House
168-173 High Holborn
London WC1V 7AA
United Kingdom

Latin America
Thomson Learning
Seneca, 53
Colonia Polanco
11560 Mexico D.F.
Mexico

Spain
Paraninfo Thomson Learning
Calle/Magallanes, 25
28015 Madrid, Spain

ISBN 0-534-39186-9

Gita, Jonathan, Jeffery, Barbara, Stacey, Mitchell, and Ryan
  Gerald Keller

Karen and Cynthia
  Brian Warrack

BRIEF CONTENTS

CONTENTS

PREFACE

Statistics for Management and Economics was written for courses that emphasize applications and fundamental concepts of statistics. It is designed to be practical, flexible, and modern. This text provides a ***practical*** orientation that teaches students how to identify the correct method, calculate the statistics, and properly interpret the results in the context of the question or decision at hand. The text provides a ***flexible*** approach to instructors by consistently presenting calculations manually and with Excel and Minitab, with accompanying step-by-step instructions allowing instructors to select the method of calculation they prefer. For those who use SPSS or JMP, the same instructions are provided on the text's Web site. Accompanying the text are 814 data sets, formatted for Microsoft Excel and all major statistical software packages. The text provides a ***modern*** approach that emphasizes applications and how statistics is used in every business and economics function. Students will learn how statistics is used in their chosen major in "Applications in…" boxes and optional sections throughout the text, ranging from how probability is used in portfolio diversification to how confidence intervals are used in market segmentation. All of these optional sections are self-contained and assume the student has no background in these functional area applications.

WHY WE WROTE THIS BOOK

When we first began our careers in 1971, statistics was taught with an emphasis on manual calculations. It was believed that only by doing calculations by hand would students be able to understand the techniques and concepts. Calculations were quite time-consuming but required no more skills than the ability to add, subtract, multiply, divide, and determine square roots. The textbooks published at the time reflected this pedagogy. Ironically, a more important skill, the ability to identify the correct technique to use, was neglected. This is a skill that is needed by students in writing exams and by graduates in applying statistical analyses.

An important goal in 1988 when we published the first edition of this book was to teach students to identify the correct technique. Through the next four editions we refined our approach to equally emphasize interpretation and decision making. With our approach we divide the solution of statistical techniques into three stages and include them in every appropriate example: (1) *identify* the technique, (2) *compute* the statistics, and (3) *interpret* the results. The *compute* stage can be completed in any or all of three ways: manually (with the aid of a calculator), using Excel, and using Minitab. For those courses that wish to use the computer extensively, manual calculations can be downplayed or omitted completely. Conversely, those that wish to emphasize manual calculations may easily do so and the computer solutions can be selectively introduced or skipped entirely. Our approach leaves the decision of if and when to introduce the computer up to the instructor.

We believe that our approach offers several advantages:

- Emphasis on identification and interpretation provide students with practical skills they can apply to real problems they will face whether a course uses manual or computer calculations.

- Students learn that statistics is a method of converting data into information, With over 800 data files and corresponding problems that ask students to interpret statistical results, students are provided ample opportunities to practice data analysis and decision making.

- The optional use of the computer allows for larger and more realistic exercises and examples.

RATIONALE FOR THIS EDITION

Addressing Different Learning Styles. As we know, statistics is more than just a set of tools to process data into information. There are many valuable concepts that underlie statistics to which students should be exposed. Unfortunately, many students fear statistics because they believe that it is nothing more than a required mathematics course and they perceive themselves as being weak in these skills. In this edition, we have provided several pedagogical approaches to reflect the differing learning styles among students. New in the 6th edition are 19 Java applets centered around fundamental statistical concepts, which are integrated throughout the book. These applets allow students to "discover" various principles. For example, one applet demonstrates how the sampling distribution of the mean is created. Related applets show the effect of different populations. To focus student learning, the book includes 83 applet exercises that help students glean the appropriate conceptual understanding from each of these 19 applets.

In addition to the applets, we have several Excel workbooks that feature worksheets for confidence interval estimators and test statistics. By changing one or more inputs, students can learn, for example, the effect of increasing sample sizes on test statistics or the result of decreasing the confidence level on interval estimators. We believe that these applets and worksheets will help those students who are intimidated by statistics and provide every student with a deeper comprehension of statistical concepts.

Applications in Focus. In practice, statistical analyses are not conducted in a vacuum. Instead, statistics is used as a tool in decision making in virtually all areas of management and economics. A growing number of schools have adopted an integrated approach in business education. The integrated approach shows how the different subjects operate together to make decisions. For example, decisions about the introduction of a new product lie within the domain of marketing, finance, and operations management. Separating a decision into only one of these functional areas is practically impossible and unrealistic.

We believe that statistics properly belongs in the center of almost all business and economics decision problems. For example, statistical analysis of consumer surveys and test marketing can tell the marketing manager how large a market segment is. Statistics can play several roles in assisting the operations manager. By conducting experiments, the operations manager can determine which methods, machines, materials, and personnel to employ to produce high-quality products. Statistics can also aid in deciding the location of the production plant, planning the construction of facilities, and predicting demand.

Unfortunately, most students take their statistics courses before enrolling in the other areas of business. How can we teach the applications of statistics in marketing, finance, operations, and others if students know little about these subjects? The answer is that we teach the general context of the statistical application before showing how statistics addresses the problem.

While each of these applications is presented in an "optional" way, we have found that they provide great motivation to the student who asks, "How will I ever use this technique?" We have made their introduction easy for instructors and students. Illustrations of statistical applications in business with which students are unfamiliar are preceded by an application box, which explains the application. For example, to illustrate graphical techniques we use an example that compares the histograms of the returns on two different investments. To explain what financial analysts look for in the histograms requires an understanding that risk is measured by the amount of variation in the returns. The example is preceded by an "Applications in Finance" box that discusses how return on investment is computed and used. Later when we present the normal distribution, we feature another Application in Finance box to show why the standard deviation of the returns measures the risk of that investment. Thirty-six application boxes are scattered throughout the book.

Some applications are so large that we devote an entire section to the topic. For example, in the chapter that introduces the confidence interval estimator of a proportion, we also present market segmentation. In that section we show how the confidence interval estimate of a population proportion can yield an estimate of the size of market segments. In other chapters we illustrate various statistical techniques by showing how marketing managers can apply these techniques to determine the differences that exist between market segments. There are five such sections in this book.

KEY FEATURES OF OUR APPROACH

Teaches technique identification skills. Guides (see inside front cover), flowcharts, and review chapters develop this crucial skill. Every appropriate example in the text highlights the rationale for using a particular technique. Every technique that is introduced is accompanied by the factors that identify its use.

Offers review chapters. Exercises and cases that appear at the end of chapters naturally require the use of techniques introduced in a particular chapter. Unfortunately, students are not given such direction in future coursework or in the business world. To help further develop technique-identification skills, two review chapters (14 and 24) contain exercises and cases that require the use of techniques previously introduced. Each review chapter features a flowchart that guides students in determining the appropriate statistical method.

Uses Excel and Minitab. Both software packages are used extensively and presented consistently throughout the book to compute statistics. Most examples within chapters present manual, Excel, and Minitab solutions, allowing students to see each solution method together and to use the solution method that is preferred. This feature is provided for flexibility, allowing the instructor to decide when manual or computer calculations should be emphasized and whether a spreadsheet or statistical software is most appropriate.

Presents computer instructions. Detailed instructions for both Excel and Minitab for Windows make it easy for instructors and students to make use of the computer. They also eliminate the need for instructors to teach how to use the software and for students, the need to buy supplementary Excel or Minitab manuals. New in the 6th edition: SPSS and JMP instructions are provided on the text's Web site and directly correspond to the Excel/Minitab instructions in the text.

Provides Data Analysis Plus® 4.0. Excel macros were created to complement Excel's menu of statistical procedures. All statistical techniques introduced in this book can be computed using either Excel's Analysis ToolPak or version 4.0 of Data Analysis Plus. Data Analysis Plus® is compatible with Office 95, 97, 2000, and XP.

Data files are provided in several formats, including Excel, Minitab, JMP, SPSS, and ASCII) for most of the examples, exercises, and cases. The 6th edition includes 814 data files, some consisting of thousands of observations, which emphasize a central theme in the book—that statistical techniques convert data into information. For students who will conduct statistical analyses manually, we have provided Appendix A at the back of the book, which provides the summary statistics (e.g., means and variances) for exercises, allowing most exercises to be solved manually.

Uses realistic data in examples and exercises. Many of the examples, exercises, and cases are based on actual studies performed by statistics practitioners and published in journals, newspapers, and magazines, or presented at conferences. Many data files were recreated to produce the original results.

NEW IN THIS EDITION

- 19 Java Applets with a total of 83 applet exercises. Adapted from *Seeing Statistics*® by Gary McClelland and customized to this text, these 19 applets present statistical concepts, visually helping students gain insight. These are stored on the CD that accompanies this text.

- Chapter opening examples illustrate uses of techniques introduced in that chapter. These examples are designed to help motivate students to learn the concepts in the chapter. Examples are revisited at the chapter's conclusion, where they are solved.

- Improved and expanded Data Analysis Plus® add-ins for Excel (allows for inclusion of the names [labels] of variables). (*Note:* For a detailed listing of capabilities, see the back cover endsheet of this text.) New capabilities in version 4.0 include:
  - Stem-and-leaf display
  - Multiple box plots allow comparisons of any number of data sets.
  - Seasonal indexes
  - Separate correlation (Pearson and Spearman) add-ins
  - Allow for the inclusion of the names of variables

- New Excel spreadsheets to employ with already-computed statistics and perform what-if analyses. These are used in selected exercises and are designed to help students see how statistical output is affected by changing inputs.

- New spreadsheets that perform calculations associated with portfolio diversification and pay equity. These worksheets are referenced in two sections of the text and selected exercises and illustrate applications of statistical techniques in Finance and Human Resource Management.

- Applications in … boxes, which show fundamental applications of statistics in the following subjects:
  - 5 finance
  - 11 marketing
  - 4 human resources management
  - 13 operations management
  - 2 accounting
  - 1 economics

- 613 new exercises (in addition to many updated exercises) for a total of 1,895 exercises throughout the text (1,282 appeared in the fifth edition)

- 217 new data sets for a total of 814 data sets (597 in the fifth edition). For those who wish to solve the exercises containing data sets manually, we have provided Appendix A, which gives the corresponding summary statistics to these data sets.

- New chapter on Decision Analysis (Chapter 23)

- Updated and improved probability presentation with many new examples and exercises (Chapters 6, 7, and 8). Probability concepts are separated from discrete probability distributions to simplify the presentation. In addition, these chapters feature many new applied exercises and applets to help students visualize and understand concepts.

- Improved descriptive statistics chapters with many new examples and exercises [Chapters 2 and 4 and a review with guide and flowchart of descriptive statistics (appears between Chapters 4 and 5)]
- New CD Appendixes featuring additional techniques and concepts (e.g., index numbers, hypergeometric distribution). These are denoted in the Table of Contents as "CD Appendixes."
- Updated and streamlined forecasting and time series chapter (Chapter 21) featuring many new exercises
- Added section on operating characteristic curves and average run length in statistical process control chapter (Chapter 22)
- New Section 8.5 allows the option of introducing the Student t, chi-squared, and F distributions (Chapter 8, Continuous Distributions) earlier and alongside other continuous distributions. Those who prefer to introduce these concepts later may still do so with no loss in continuity.

TEACHING AIDS

- The Instructor's Suite CD contains solutions to every exercise (in MS Word format), over 2,800 test items containing a variety of test problems including computer exercises (authored by Mohammed El-Saidi of Ferris State University and provided in MS Word format), and Microsoft PowerPoint slides. The PowerPoint slides (authored by Zvi Goldstein of CSU Fullerton) are completely updated. Containing many animations of examples in the text, the PowerPoint slides now contain flexibility to show additional examples at the touch of a button. In addition, there are suggestions for teaching with the text such as how the computer can be used in class, assignments, and on exams.
- Instructor's Solutions Manual. Authored by Gerry Keller, this is a printout of the solutions contained on the Instructor's Suite CD.
- Test Items. A printed version of the test items on the CD.
- BCA Testing

LEARNING AIDS

- Student Solutions Manual. Contains worked solutions to the exercises containing answers in the back of the book. Available for purchase.
- Study Guide: Provided free in 6th edition in PDF form on the CD that accompanies this text. The Study Guide contains additional examples, worked problems, and student help.
- WebTutor for WebCT or Blackboard. Authored by Don St. Jean of George Brown College, the WebTutors are the perfect Web companion for traditional or distance courses. The WebTutors contain many study aids, including self-quizzing and tutoring help.
- Text Web Site. Go to *www.duxbury.com* and select "Online Book Companions"; there one can select this text and view a host of resources including software updates, typos/corrections, additional exercises, technical support, and more.

ACKNOWLEDGMENTS

Writing a statistics book requires the assistance of a large number of people. We are particularly grateful to Duxbury's statistics editor, Curt Hinrichs, who advised, guided, and encouraged us in the writing of this and previous editions, and to Hal Humphrey and Susan Reiland, who orchestrated the conversion of our manuscript into the polished textbook you're reading.

Our thanks are extended to Paul Baum, California State University, Northridge, and to Amy Puelz, Southern Methodist University, who helped find and correct errors. We also thank Zvi Goldstein, California State University, Fullerton, for the PowerPoint slides, and Mohammed El-Saidi, Ferris State University, for the test bank items.

We thank the following reviewers for their helpful comments and suggestions: Howard Clayton, Auburn University; James Hightower, California State University, Fullerton; Kenneth Klassen, California State University, Northridge; John Lawrence, California State University, Fullerton; Glenn Milligan, Ohio State University; Pin Ng, University of Illinois; and Madhu Rao, Bowling Green State University.

We also thank the survey participants: Nagraj Balakrishnan, Clemson University; Paul Baum, California State University, Northridge; Philip Cross, Georgetown University; Barry Cuffe, Wingate University; Ernest Demba, Washington University-St. Louis; Neal Duffy, State University of New York, Plattsburgh; John Dutton, North Carolina State University; Grace Esimai, University of Texas at Arlington; Abe Feinberg, California State University, Northridge; Samuel Graves, Boston College; John Hebert, Virginia Tech; Bo Honore, Princeton University; Onisforos Iordanou, Hunter College; Gordon Johnson, California State University, Northridge; Hilke Kayser, Hamilton College; Roger Kleckner, Bowling Green State University-Firelands; Harry Kypraios, Rollins College; John Lawrence, California State University, Fullerton; Neal Long, Stetson University; George Marcoulides, California State University, Fullerton; Paul Mason, University of North Florida; John McDonald, Flinders University; Richard McGrath, Bowling Green State University; Amy Miko, St. Francis College; Janis Miller, Clemson University; Kevin Murphy, Oakland University; Michael Musser, Davenport College; Des Nicholls, Australian National University; Andrew Paizis, Queens College; David Pentico, Duquesne University; Ira Perelle, Mercy College; Nelson Perera, University of Wollongong; Amy Puelz, Southern Methodist University; Colleen Quinn, Seneca College; Tony Quon, University of Ottawa; Phil Roth, Clemson University; Farhad Saboori, Albright College; Mohammed El-Saidi, Ferris State University; Don St. Jean, George Brown College; Hedayeh Samavati, Indiana-Purdue University; Sandy Shroeder, Ohio Northern University; Jineshwar Singh, George Brown College; Natalia Smirnova, Queens College; Eric Sowey, University of New South Wales; Cyrus Stanier, Virginia Tech; Steve Thorpe, University of Northern Iowa; Sheldon Vernon, Houston Baptist University; and W. F. Younkin, University of Miami.

STATISTICS
FOR MANAGEMENT AND ECONOMICS

1   WHAT IS STATISTICS?

1.1 INTRODUCTION

Statistics is a way to get information from data. That's it! Most of this textbook is devoted to describing how, when, and why managers and statistics practitioners* conduct statistical procedures. You may ask, "If that's all there is to statistics, why is this book (and most other statistics books) so large?" The answer is that there are different kinds of information and data to which students of applied statistics should be exposed. We demonstrate some of these with two cases and an example that are featured later in this book.

---

*The term *statistician* is used to describe so many different kinds of occupations that it has ceased to have any meaning. It is used, for example, to describe both a person who calculates baseball statistics and an individual educated in statistical principles. We will describe the former as a statistics practitioner and the latter as a *statistician*. A statistics practitioner is a person who uses statistical techniques properly. Examples of statistics practitioners include the following:

1. A financial analyst who develops stock portfolios based on historical rates of return

2. An economist who uses statistical models to help explain and predict

3. A market researcher who surveys consumers and converts the responses into useful information.

Our goal in this book is to convert you into one such capable individual.

The term *statistician* refers to an individual who works with the mathematics of statistics. His or her work involves research that develops techniques and concepts that in the future may help the statistics practitioner. Statisticians are also statistics practitioners, frequently conducting empirical research and consulting. The authors of this book are statisticians. If you're taking a statistics course, your instructor is probably a statistician.

CASE 12.1 PEPSI'S EXCLUSIVITY AGREEMENT WITH A UNIVERSITY

In the last few years, colleges and universities have signed exclusivity agreements with a variety of private companies. These agreements bind the university to sell that company's products exclusively on the campus. Many of the agreements involve food and beverage firms.

A large university with a total enrollment of about 50,000 students has offered Pepsi-Cola an exclusivity agreement that would give Pepsi exclusive rights to sell its products at all university facilities for the next year and an option for future years. In return, the university would receive 35% of the on-campus revenues and an additional lump sum of $200,000 per year. Pepsi has been given 2 weeks to respond.

The management at Pepsi quickly reviews what they know. The market for soft drinks is measured in terms of 12-ounce cans. Pepsi currently sells an average of 22,000 cans per week (over the 40 weeks of the year that the university operates). The cans sell for an average of 75 cents each. The costs including labor amount to 20 cents per can. Pepsi is unsure of its market share but suspects it is considerably less than 50%. A quick analysis reveals that if its current market share were 25%, then, with an exclusivity agreement, Pepsi would sell 88,000 (22,000 is 25% of 88,000) cans per week or 3,520,000 cans per year. The gross revenue would be computed as follows:

$$3,520,000 \times \$.75/\text{can} = \$2,640,000$$

This figure must be multiplied by 65% because the university would rake in 35% of the gross. Thus,

$$65\% \times \$2,640,000 = \$1,716,000$$

The total cost of 20 cents per can (or $704,000) and the annual payment to the university of $200,000 are subtracted to obtain the net profit:

$$\text{Net profit} = \$1,716,000 - \$704,000 - \$200,000 = \$812,000$$

Pepsi's current annual profit is

$$40 \text{ weeks } \times 22,000 \text{ cans/week} \times \$.55 = \$484,000$$

If the current market share is 25%, the potential gain from the agreement is

$$\$812,000 - \$484,000 = \$328,000$$

The only problem with this analysis is that Pepsi does not know how many soft drinks are sold weekly at the university. Coke is not likely to supply Pepsi with information about its sales, which together with Pepsi's line of products constitute virtually the entire market.

Pepsi assigned a recently hired university graduate to survey the university's students to supply the missing information. Accordingly, she organizes a survey that asks 500 students to keep track of the number of soft drinks they purchase in the next 7 days. The responses are stored in a file on the disk that accompanies this book.

Descriptive Statistics and Inferential Statistics

The information we would like to acquire in Case 12.1 is an estimate of annual profits from the exclusivity agreement. The data are the numbers of cans of soft drinks consumed in 7 days by the 500 students in the sample. As a first step, we need to extract information from the sample. This is the function of **descriptive statistics.**

Descriptive statistics deals with methods of organizing, summarizing, and presenting data in a convenient and informative way. One form of descriptive statistics uses graphical techniques, which allow us to draw a picture that presents the data in such a way that we can easily see what numbers the students are reporting. Chapter 2 presents a variety of graphical methods used by statistics practitioners to present data in ways that allow the reader to extract useful information.

Another form of descriptive statistics uses numerical techniques to summarize data. One such method that you have already used frequently is the average or mean. In the same way that you calculate the average age of the employees of a company, we can compute the mean number of soft drinks consumed in 7 days by the 500 students in our survey. Chapter 4 introduces several numerical statistical measures that describe different features of the data. In Case 12.1, however, we are not so much interested in what the 500 students are reporting as we are in knowing the mean number of soft drinks consumed by all 50,000 students on campus. To accomplish this goal we need another branch of statistics—**inferential statistics.**

Inferential statistics is a body of methods used to draw conclusions or inferences about characteristics of populations based on sample data. The population in question in this case is the university's 50,000 students' soft drink consumption. The cost of interviewing each student would be prohibitive and extremely time-consuming. Statistical techniques make such endeavors unnecessary. Instead, we can sample a much smaller number of students (the sample size is 500) and infer from the data the number of soft drinks consumed by all 50,000 students. We can then estimate annual profits for Pepsi.

Example 12.5 Exit Polls

When an election for political office takes place, the television networks cancel regular programming and instead provide election coverage. When the ballots are counted the results are reported. However, for important offices such as president or senator in large states, the networks actively compete to see which will be the first to predict a winner. This is done through **exit polls,** wherein a random sample of voters who exit the polling booth is asked for whom they voted. From the data the sample proportion of voters supporting the candidates is computed. A statistical technique is applied to determine whether there is enough evidence to infer that the leading candidate will garner enough votes to win. Suppose that the exit poll results from the state of Florida during the 2000 year elections are stored in a file on the disk. Although there were a number of candidates running for president, the exit pollsters recorded only the votes of the two candidates who had any chance of winning, the Republican candidate George W. Bush and the Democrat Albert Gore. Suppose that the results (there were 912 people who voted for either Bush or Gore) were stored on a file on the disk. The network analysts would like to know whether they can conclude that George W. Bush will win the state of Florida.

Example 12.5 describes a very common application of statistical inference. The population the television networks wanted to make inferences about is voting preferences of the approximately 5 million Floridians who voted for Bush or Gore. The sample consisted of the 912 people randomly selected by the polling company who voted for either of the two main candidates. The characteristic of the population that we would like to know is the proportion of the total electorate that voted for Bush. Specifically, we would like to know whether more than 50% of the electorate voted for Bush (counting only those who voted for either the Republican or Democratic candidate). It must be made clear that, because we will not ask every one of the 5 million actual voters for whom they voted, we cannot predict the outcome with 100% certainty. This is a fact that statistics practitioners and even students of statistics must understand. A sample that is only a small fraction of the size of the population can lead to correct inferences only a certain percentage of the time. You will find that statistics practitioners can control that fraction and usually set it between 90% and 99%.

Incidentally, on the night of the United States election in November 2000, the networks goofed badly. Using exit polls as well as the results of previous elections, all four networks concluded at about 8:00 P.M. that Al Gore would win the state of Florida. Shortly after 10:00 P.M., with a large percentage of the actual vote having been counted, the networks reversed course and declared that George W. Bush would win the state of Florida. By 2:00 A.M. another verdict was declared: The result was too close to call. In the future, this experience will likely be used by statistics instructors when teaching how *not* to use statistics.

CASE 14.1: HOST SELLING AND ANNOUNCER COMMERCIALS*

A study was undertaken to compare the effects of host selling commercials and announcer commercials on children. Announcer commercials are straightforward commercials in which the announcer describes to viewers why they should buy a particular product. Host selling commercials feature a children's show personality or television character who extols the virtues of the product. In 1975, the National Association of Broadcasters prohibited the use of show characters to advertise products during the same program in which the characters appear. However, this prohibition was overturned in 1982 by a judge's decree.

The objective of the study was to determine whether the two types of advertisements have different effects on children watching them. Specifically, the researchers wanted to know whether children watching host selling commercials would remember more details about the commercial and be more likely to buy the advertised product than children watching announcer commercials. The experiment consisted of two groups of children ranging in age from 6 to 10. One group of 121 children watched a program in which two host selling commercials appeared. The commercials tried to sell Canary Crunch, a breakfast cereal. A second group of 121 children watched the same program but was exposed to two announcer commercials for the same product. Immediately after the show, the children were given a questionnaire that tested their memory concerning the commercials they had watched.

Each child was tested on his or her ability to remember details of the commercial. In addition, each child was offered a free box of cereal. The children were shown four different brands of cereal—Froot Loops (FL), Boo Berries (BB), Kangaroo Hops (KH), and Canary Crunch (CC, the advertised cereal)—and asked to pick the one they wanted. The results are stored on the data disk provided with this book. (Some of the data are shown in Table 1.1.) Are there differences in memory test scores and cereal choices between the two groups of children?

In this case, we want to compare the population of memory test scores and cereal choices of children who watch host commercials with the population of memory tests scores and cereal choices of children who watch announcer commercials. The experi-

---

*Adapted from J. H. Miller, "An Empirical Evaluation of the Host Selling Commercial and the Announcer Commercial When Used on Children," *Developments in Marketing Science 9* (1985): 276–278.

Table 1.1 Memory Test Scores and Cereal Choices

Children Who Watched Host Selling Commercials		Children Who Watched Announcer Commercials	
Memory Test Scores	Cereal Choices	Memory Test Scores	Cereal Choices
6	FL	8	BB
9	CC	6	FL
7	KH	10	CC
.	.	.	.
.	.	.	.
.	.	.	.
8	BB	9	CC

ment consists of drawing samples of 121 children from each population. For each child, researchers recorded two observations. The first was the score out of 10 the child received on a test to measure his or her memory about the commercial. The second was the brand the child chose from among the four brands of breakfast cereal. Notice that, contrary to what you probably believed, data are not necessarily numbers. The test scores, of course, are numbers; however, the cereal choices are not. In Chapter 2, we will discuss the different types of data you will encounter in statistical applications and how to deal with them. The information sought by the researchers is whether there are differences in the test scores and the cereal selections between the two populations of children. By applying the appropriate statistical techniques, the researchers may be able to infer which type of commercial is more effective.

1.2 KEY STATISTICAL CONCEPTS

Statistical inference problems involve three key concepts: the population, the sample, and the statistical inference. We now discuss each of these concepts in more detail.

POPULATION

A **population** is the group of all items of interest to a statistics practitioner. It is frequently very large and may, in fact, be infinitely large. In the language of statistics, *population* does not necessarily refer to a group of people. It may, for example, refer to the population of diameters of ball bearings produced at a large plant. In Case 12.1, the population of interest consists of the 50,000 students on campus. In Case 14.1, the population consists of all children who are exposed to commercials on television.

A descriptive measure of a population is called a **parameter.** The parameter of interest in Case 12.1 is the mean number of soft drinks consumed by all the students at the university. The parameter in Example 12.5 is the proportion of the 5 million Florida voters who voted for Bush.

SAMPLE

A **sample** is a set of data drawn from the population. A descriptive measure of a sample is called a **statistic.** We use statistics to make inferences about parameters. In Case 12.1, the statistic we would compute is the mean number of soft drinks consumed in the last week by the 500 students in the sample. We would then use the sample mean to infer the value of the population mean, which is the parameter of interest in this problem. In Example 12.5, we compute the proportion of the sample of 912 Floridians who voted for each of the two principal candidates. The sample statistic is then used to make inferences about the population of all 5 million votes. That is, we predict the election results even before the actual count.

STATISTICAL INFERENCE

Statistical inference is the process of making an estimate, prediction, or decision about a population based on sample data. Because populations are almost always very large, investigating each member of the population would be impractical and expensive. It is far easier and cheaper to take a sample from the population of interest and draw conclusions or make estimates about the population on the basis of information provided by the sample. However, such conclusions and estimates are not always going to be correct. For this reason, we build into the statistical inference a measure of reliability. There are two such measures, the **confidence level** and the **significance level.** The *confidence level* is the proportion of times that an estimating procedure will be correct. For example, in Case 12.1, we will produce an estimate of the average number of soft drinks to be consumed by all 50,000 students that has a confidence level of 95%. That means that, in the long run, estimates based on this form of statistical inference will be correct 95% of the time. When the purpose of the statistical inference is to draw a conclusion about a population, the *significance level* measures how frequently the conclusion will be wrong in the long run. For example, suppose that as a result of the analysis in Example 12.5, we conclude that more than 50% of the electorate will vote for George W. Bush, and thus he will win the state of Florida. A 5% significance level means that, in the long run, this type of conclusion will be wrong 5% of the time.

1.3 STATISTICAL APPLICATIONS IN BUSINESS

We assume that most students taking their first statistics course have not taken courses in most of the other subjects in management programs such as finance, marketing, and operations management. However, to understand fully how statistics is used in these and other subjects, it is necessary to know something about them. Naturally, we cannot teach all aspects of these subjects here, but in this chapter we introduce the topics where statistics can and does play a vital supporting role.

ORGANIZATIONAL FUNCTIONS

Companies are often organized on the basis of the kind of functions performed. This is often referred to as a *functional organization.* In this formulation, organizations perform three primary functions: finance, marketing, and operations. In addition to these functions, organizations undertake several secondary functions; these include accounting, human resources, and information systems.

In this chapter we briefly introduce each of these functions and describe how statistics helps managers convert data into information and how that information plays a critical role in decision making. In later chapters we will provide more details about each of these functions as an introduction to a statistical technique that can be used in each of these topics.

Financial Management

Financial management (or simply finance) is the functional area of business that deals with the financial (money-related) decisions made by a firm in providing its products and services.

Every company must make decisions regarding what assets to acquire to produce its products, how to raise money to finance these assets, and how to manage the assets on an ongoing day-to-day basis. Corporate finance focuses on the financial aspects of these decisions.

Capital Budgeting   Capital budgeting is the process by which a firm generates, analyzes, and selects the projects that it will invest in and pursue. As we mention in the upcoming Operations Management section, the principal activity of every organization is the production and delivery of its products and services. The most important decision to be addressed, therefore, is the composition of the firm's product line. On which products, services, and markets should the company choose to focus?

Once an idea of a new product or project has been generated (often by the operations group), the financial feasibility of the project must be examined. Considerations must be given to estimating the cost of the real assets (such as land, buildings, and equipment) that must be purchased and projections must be made of the revenues and operating costs associated with the project. The probability concepts to be introduced in Chapter 6 will be helpful in dealing with the uncertainty surrounding the projected values of these future cash flows.

Capital Structure   The two primary sources of funds for a company are long-term debt (such as bonds) and equity (i.e., common shares). A company's capital structure decision refers to its choice of the proportions of long-term debt and equity to be used for long-term financing. Determining the desired capital structure for a firm requires an understanding of the basics of stock and bond valuation, which we discuss later in this book.

Working Capital Management   Once management has chosen a project to invest in and arranged for its financing, it must turn its attention to the ongoing management of its *working capital,* which refers to a firm's current assets and current liabilities. The cash position must be carefully managed, accounts receivable must be collected and bad debt avoided, short-term sources of financing such as bank loans must be arranged, and accounts payable must be paid.

Stock and Bond Valuation   A basic understanding of how financial assets, such as stocks and bonds, are valued is critical to good financial management. Understanding the basics of valuation is necessary for the capital budgeting and capital structure decisions. Moreover, understanding the basics of valuing investments such as stocks and bonds is at the heart of the huge and growing discipline known as *investment management.*

As billions upon billions of dollars have flowed into mutual funds and the stock market generally during the past decade, investors have become increasingly aware of the investment risks and returns. A central theme throughout all of finance, and the investment area in particular, is the positive relationship between risk and return. The more risky an investment, the higher should be the profit (or rate of return) one can expect to receive from the investment. (Loosely speaking, the rate of return on an investment is the profit divided by the amount of the investment.) While most of us intuitively feel that this positive relationship between risk and return should hold, a precise specification of this relationship is very difficult to state, to say the least. A model that is widely used for this analysis is the *market model,* which will be discussed in Section 18.6. This model relies heavily on the relationship between the return on an individual stock and the return on some major stock index, such as the Dow Jones Industrial Average. Another important statistical application in finance is presented in Section 7.5, where we discuss portfolio diversification and asset allocation. We introduce return on investment and the measurement of risk in Chapters 2 and 4.

Understanding Capital Markets   It is important for a financial manager to be familiar with the main characteristics of the capital markets where long-term financial assets such as stocks and bonds trade. A well-functioning capital market provides managers with useful information concerning the appropriate prices and rates of return that are required for a variety of financial securities with differing levels of risk. Statistical methods can be used to analyze capital markets and summarize their characteristics, such as the shape of the distribution of stock or bond returns.

MARKETING MANAGEMENT

Traditionally, marketing has been defined in terms of the four P's: product, price, promotion, and place. *Marketing management* is the functional area of business that focuses on the development of a product, together with its pricing, promotion, and distribution. Decisions are made in these four areas with a view to satisfying the wants and needs of consumers, while also satisfying the firm's objective.

A more contemporary view of the philosophy of marketing management, while embracing the four P's, prefers to concentrate on enhancing service and customer satisfaction, while also meeting the firm's objective.

Market Segmentation

Mass marketing refers to the mass production and marketing by a company of a single product for the entire market. Mass marketing is especially effective for commodity goods such as gasoline, which are very difficult to differentiate from the competition, except through price and convenience of availability. But generally speaking, mass marketing has given way to target marketing, which focuses on satisfying the demands of a particular segment of the entire market. For example, the Coca-Cola Company has moved from the mass marketing of a single beverage to the production of several different beverages. Among the cola products, there is Coca-Cola Classic, Diet Coke, and Caffeine-Free Diet Coke. Each product is aimed at a different market segment.

Because there is no single way to segment a market, managers must consider several different variables (or characteristics) that could be used to identify segments. Surveys of customers are used to gather data about various aspects of the market, and statistical techniques are applied to define the segments. Managers must then formulate a strategy to target these profitable segments, using the four elements of the marketing mix: product, pricing, promotion, and place. In Section 12.5 we demonstrate how statistics can be used to measure the size of one market segment. Chapters 13, 15, and 16 feature several exercises that address the problem of determining whether differences exist between market segments.

Product

The term *product* can refer to a physical good (e.g., a computer), a service (e.g., a haircut), a person (e.g., Michael Jordan), a place (e.g., Niagara Falls), or an idea (e.g., total quality management). After a new product has been conceived and some initial development has been undertaken, perhaps in conjunction with the operations management group, a marketing product planner must address such questions as the desired quality level, the special options that can be made available, the appropriate type and design of packaging, and various branding issues such as an appropriate name and logo. The objective is to select an attractive mix of features that will provide a product that appeals to consumers and that can be differentiated from those of competitors. *Test marketing*, a statistical procedure, can be used on data provided by consumer surveys or other sources to test whether one particular feature of the product is preferred over another by consumers in the target market.

Pricing

Another important decision in the overall marketing plan is the *pricing decision*, which needs to be addressed both for a new product, and from time to time for an existing product. Anyone buying a product such as a personal computer has been confronted with a wide variety of prices, accompanied by a corresponding wide variety of features. From a vendor's standpoint, establishing the appropriate price and corresponding set of attributes for a product is complicated, and must be done in the context of the overall marketing plan for the product. Here too, statistics plays a central role in the pricing decision. Chapter 2 will feature one such application.

Place

The third element of a product's marketing mix is *distribution*, otherwise known as placing the product. Having developed a product and packaged it, a manager must then make it available to potential buyers. The first decision is whether to sell directly to the consumer, as does Dell Computers with great success, or to resort to the more common approach of distributing the goods to various wholesalers and retailers. Distribution decisions involve deciding how to deliver the product to the market, including what mode of transportation to use and what use must be made of warehouses.

Promotion

The final component of the marketing mix is *promotion*, or *marketing communication*. Having produced a product, priced it, and decided how to make it available to the consumer, a company must next decide how to best promote the product. A company must communicate with consumers to inform them about the company itself and its products, and to interest them in purchasing its products. Promotional tools available to achieve these objectives include advertising, public relations, sales promotion (employing discount coupons or contests, for example), and personal selling. Statistical methods can be used to help assess how successful these tools have been in generating sales.

OPERATIONS MANAGEMENT

Operations management, production, or simply *operations* is the functional area of business that transforms inputs such as labor, material, and capital into outputs such as products and services. This is the principal activity of every organization.

The tasks undertaken by the operations management function include designing the product (henceforth we will refer to a company's "product," which includes both products and services), choosing the production process, arranging the physical plant layout, designing jobs, monitoring quality, scheduling the work, managing inventories, and planning production.

Product Design

The process that is used to design new products or improve an existing product consists of several stages.

1. **Generating ideas.** Sources of new and improved products can come from the research and development (R&D) department, customers, suppliers, and competitors. Statistics plays an important role by analyzing surveys of customers that help determine what products a firm's customers want.

2. **Feasibility study.** The concepts developed in stage 1 are modified and developed, usually by the marketing function. A market analysis can include another survey of customers as well as focus groups, which entail a small group of consumers expressing their attitudes toward a new product. This stage also examines the potential costs and profits.

3. **Preliminary design.** The description of the product developed in the feasibility study is converted into technical specifications. From these a final design can be evolved.

4. **Functional design.** This stage involves examining the way a product performs, which includes the concepts of reliability and maintainability. *Reliability* is the probability that a product or component will function properly. *Maintainability* refers to the product's capacity to be maintained or repaired. In Chapter 6 we will introduce probability and illustrate it with several examples dealing with reliability and maintainability.

5. **Form design.** This design addresses the appearance of the product. Decisions include the color, size, and shape. Marketers can analyze surveys to determine which factors are important in customers' decisions to buy or not buy.

6. **Production design.** This stage deals with the *how* of manufacturing the product. Statistical studies can be used to compare several different methods of production. The methods can be compared on the basis of cost, ease of construction, quality, reliability, and maintainability. In Chapter 13 we will provide several examples and exercises featuring this aspect of operations management. In Chapter 15 we will introduce a statistical method that is used to determine which factors most affect the quality of products. These are often referred to as the 4 M's: machines, material, methods, and manpower (the last factor has been altered to "personnel," a nonsexist term).

Process Planning

After designing or redesigning the product, management must decide how the product is to be made. The process plan converts the process design into working instructions for production. Decisions include whether the components are to be made or purchased and what equipment will be employed in the production process.

Facility Layout

Once management has determined how the product is to be produced, the next decision concerns how the manufacturing facility is to be laid out. The objective is to arrange machines and workers in such a way as to minimize costs, avoid bottlenecks, eliminate waste (of material and labor), and develop quality.

Location Analysis and Logistics

A critical decision for any firm is where to locate its production facility, storage center, or retail outlet. The circumstances that affect the location decision depend on the type of facility. For example, heavy industry requires a large amount of space so that construction and land costs must be low. The facility must be close to suppliers, and distribution links such as highways and railroads must be easily accessible. Light industries usually are located where skilled labor is plentiful. Retail and service industries must be close to their customers. A variety of statistical techniques can be employed to help make this decision. In Chapter 19 we provide a real-life application of statistics being used in selecting the site for a new motel.

Aggregate Production Planning

The aggregate production plan (APP) determines the number of units to be produced over the next 6 to 18 months. The APP begins with a forecast of demand over the planning horizon time period. It then arranges for (usually) the lowest cost method of satisfying that demand.

Several strategies can be utilized.

1. **Level production.** With this strategy we produce the same amount each day, week, or month, building inventories for times when supply exceeds demand and drawing from inventory when demand exceeds the amount produced. The key costs here are storage.

2. **Chase strategy.** Hire and lay off workers so that each period's production matches the forecasted demand. Aside from the very negative effects this strategy has on a firm's workers, the economic costs include the cost of hiring and training new workers and the costs associated with laying off workers.

3. **Overtime and undertime.** Fluctuations in periodic demand are matched by planning overtime shifts or by assigning excess workers to other (perhaps) nonproductive jobs. For example, when potential supply exceeds demand, workers can be given tasks such as cleaning the facility or be sent for more training.

4. **Subcontracting.** Additional units can be produced by other companies.

5. **Part-time workers.** Part-time workers can be hired to meet demand when the regular workforce is overwhelmed.

6. **Backordering.** For some products, it is possible to backorder to satisfy customer demands. For example, if a car dealer does not have a car with the features a customer desires, the dealer can order that car from the manufacturer and deliver it at some future date to the customer.

There are a number of management science techniques that can be used as well as a trial-and-error approach. Statistical techniques are often used to provide information as inputs to the analysis that determines the optimum strategy. (Chapter 12 offers one such application.) The process usually begins with a forecast, a statistical process that is covered in some detail in Chapter 21.

Inventory

Inventory models allow managers to determine the optimum number of units to produce in one production run. The models are usually based on balancing the costs of storage, ordering, and shortage. Probability concepts and methods are useful when making inventory decisions. In Chapters 8 and 10, we demonstrate how probability and statistics are employed to assist operations managers in managing inventory levels.

Waiting Lines (Queues)

Management scientists have developed a variety of probability-based tools to measure the lengths of waiting lines (called *queues*) and the number of people waiting for service. These techniques help managers make decisions about the size and number of service facilities (e.g., checkouts in a supermarket or tellers in a bank) and staffing. The Poisson and exponential distributions (Chapters 7 and 8) are useful in queuing analysis.

Project Management

PERT (project evaluation and review technique) and CPM (critical path method) are management science procedures that help control and plan large-scale projects (e.g., buildings, nuclear reactors, and shops). Probability distributions such as the normal distribution (Chapter 8) are applied in this topic. Chapter 7 offers another method useful in PERT/CPM.

ACCOUNTING

The functional areas of finance, operations, and marketing are directly involved with a company's production and delivery of goods and services to its customers. Although it is not directly involved in the financing, production, and marketing of a product, *accounting* is the functional area that collects, organizes, and provides information about a company's activities that helps these other areas to make decisions. Accounting information is provided both for internal use (such as for planning, control, decision making, and performance evaluation) and for external use (such as keeping investors informed). The terms *managerial accounting* and *financial accounting* are used to distinguish between the internal and external focuses, respectively, of a company's accounting activities.

The focus of managerial accounting is to provide information for internal use, to help managers make decisions regarding planning and control. For planning purposes, accountants prepare budgets, which include forecasts of sales revenues and the associated costs. The statistical forecasting methods described in Chapter 21 can be used to assist in preparing sales forecasts. Forecasting costs often make use of a cost function, which expresses the relationship between a cost and some measure of the level of activity (such as production) that creates that cost. Cost functions can be estimated using a statistical procedure described in Chapter 4.

Financial accounting typically communicates its information in the form of financial statements. Publicly held corporations are required to obtain independent external audits of the financial statements to assess their validity. Statistical sampling plays an important role in selecting samples of units (such as accounts or invoices) for inspection by auditors. In Chapter 5 we introduce the concepts and techniques of sampling.

HUMAN RESOURCES MANAGEMENT

Human resources management is the functional area of business that deals with the people-related decisions made by a firm. Companies are not simply buildings filled with desks and equipment. Human resources, or people, are needed to finance, produce, and market the products and services offered by the company. In fact, management of human resources must be practiced by managers in each of these functional areas, and is not restricted to the human resources department.

Personal or human resources management involves such activities as recruitment, training, performance appraisal, compensation, and motivation. The human resources department must periodically forecast its needs, in terms of both number of employees needed and their required skills. If additional employees are required, the recruitment process begins. Following an initial interview, prospects are usually required to take written or manual tests to determine whether their skills are suitable for the job. The firm must be prepared to provide evidence that these tests are valid selection instruments. In other words, higher-scoring applicants must be more likely to perform well than lower-scoring applicants. Statistical methods can be used to assess the validity of such tests.

Tests are often administered again at the end of a training program, to verify that an employee has benefited from the program. Once again, managers must ensure that the tests are valid measuring devices. Analysis of test results can also help to reveal deficiencies in the training program itself.

Periodic performance appraisal is necessary for the purpose of making decisions regarding retention, compensation, and promotion. Statistical methods can be used, for example, to assess the compensation program to determine whether it supports performance objectives. Statistical methods are also used to ensure that these decisions are taken without bias or discrimination. Recently, statistical procedures have been used by pay equity administrators, who attempt to judge which jobs are of "equal value" so that workers in these jobs receive equal pay.

Another aspect of compensation involves the development of severance packages for employees whose jobs become redundant as the result of a merger, or who simply lose their jobs because of a decision to reduce the size of the workforce (as happened at IBM in the late 1980s).

In the interest of raising productivity and reducing absenteeism and employee turnover, a company can use statistical methods to process the data gathered from employee interviews and surveys that seek to determine the level of employee satisfaction, as well as major areas of discontent in the workplace.

Chapters 18, 19, and 20 provide several illustrations of statistical analyses that can be performed by human resources managers.

INFORMATION SYSTEMS

Information systems is often incorrectly defined to be the use of computers in the storage and movement of information. In fact, the term refers to any process by which information is created and used. By this definition, everything we do in this book addresses information systems.

Throughout this book we describe a wide variety of statistical techniques whose goal is to provide information to financial analysts, accountants, and to marketing, operations, and human resources managers. The process starts with the demand for information. For example, in the Pepsi-Cola case described earlier, management needs to know the number of soft drinks consumed by the university's students each week. A survey of students produces the data. Statistical procedures are employed to convert the data into information, which the manager can use to make decisions. This model will be used repeatedly in describing how statistical techniques are used in business and economics.

ECONOMICS

Broadly speaking, *economics* is the study of the use of scarce resources (such as natural resources, human resources, and financial resources) to produce goods and services to satisfy the wants of consumers. Because resources are scarce and wants are unlimited, choices must be made concerning production and consumption. This in turn necessitates consideration of *opportunity costs*. (Students choosing to attend university rather than to work incur an opportunity cost: namely, the income that could have been earned if they had chosen to work.) Economists therefore study how producers choose to employ their limited resources, and how consumers choose to spend their income, giving consideration to opportunity costs.

It is conventional to view economics from two complementary perspectives: the "small picture" and the "big picture." *Microeconomics* (the "small picture") is the study of the behavior of individual economic decision makers (such as consumers and firms) and of the operation of individual markets (or industries). Economists working in this area routinely use statistical methods to provide business managers with forecasts of consumption, production, and pricing in various individual markets, such as the market for personal computers.

The focus of *macroeconomics* (the "big picture") is at a more aggregated level, concentrating on such topics as the level and growth rate in employment, income, and inflation. Economists use statistical methods to summarize and analyze the data they collect in these areas. They might, for example, use descriptive statistical methods to describe the distribution of all household incomes. Another well-known function of economists is to provide forecasts of the future level of economic variables. Economists frequently apply statistical methods to time series of data, such as the level of inflation or GDP (gross domestic product), in order to forecast their level next period. Statistical methods are also used to study relationships between variables, such as the relationship between mortgage rates and housing starts, or the relationship between consumption and disposable income. These and other applications of statistical methods in economics will be addressed throughout this book.

1.4 STATISTICS AND THE COMPUTER

In virtually all applications of statistics, the statistics practitioner must deal with large amounts of data. For example, Case 12.1 (Pepsi-Cola) involves 500 observations. To estimate annual profits, the statistics practitioner would have to perform computations on the data; although the calculations do not require any great mathematical skill, the sheer amount of arithmetic makes this aspect of the statistical method time-consuming and tedious.

Fortunately, numerous commercially prepared computer programs are available to perform the arithmetic. We have chosen to use Microsoft Excel, which is a spreadsheet program, and Minitab, which is a statistical software package. We chose Excel because we believe that it is and will continue to be the most popular spreadsheet package. One of its drawbacks is that it offers relatively few of the statistical techniques we introduce in this book. Consequently, we created add-ins that can be loaded onto your computer to enable you to use Excel for all statistical procedures introduced in this book. The add-ins are stored on the CD that accompanies the book and, when installed, will appear as Data Analysis Plus on Excel's Tools menu.

Almost all the examples, exercises, and cases will feature large data sets, also stored on the CD. We will demonstrate the solution to the statistical examples in three ways: manually, by employing Excel, and by using Minitab. Moreover, we will provide detailed instructions for all techniques. Although we used the Office XP version of Excel to produce the printouts shown in this book, the instructions, data sets, and add-ins have been tested and found to be compatible with earlier versions, including Office 95, 97, and 2000. Similarly, we employed the instructions and printouts of Release 13 of Minitab, but the instructions and data sets are consistent with earlier releases of Minitab. Brief introductions to Microsoft Excel and to Minitab are provided in the appendixes to this chapter.

The approach we prefer to take is to minimize the time spent on manual computations and to focus instead on selecting the appropriate method for dealing with a problem and on interpreting the output after the computer has performed the necessary computations. In this way, we hope to demonstrate that statistics can be as interesting and practical as any other subject in your curriculum.

APPLETS AND SPREADSHEETS

Books written for statistics courses taken by mathematics or statistics majors are considerably different from this one. Not surprisingly, such courses feature mathematical proofs of theorems and derivations of most procedures. When the material is covered in this way, the underlying concepts that support statistical inference are exposed and relatively easy to see. However, this book was created for an applied course in statistics. Consequently, we will not address directly the mathematical principles of statistics. However, as we pointed out above, one of the most important functions of statistics practitioners is to properly interpret statistical results, whether produced manually or by computer. And, to correctly interpret statistics, students require an understanding of the principles of statistics.

To help students understand the basic foundation, we offer two approaches. First, we have created several Excel spreadsheets that allow for what-if analyses. By changing some of the inputs, students can see for themselves how statistics works. (The name derives from "*What* happens to the statistics *if* I change this value?") Second, we have created applets, which are computer programs that perform similar what-if analyses or simulations. The applets and the spreadsheet applications appear in a number of chapters, where they are explained in greater detail.

1.5 WORLD WIDE WEB AND LEARNING CENTER

To assist students in the various aspects of using the computer to learn statistics, we have created a Web page. It offers useful information including additional exercises and cases, corrections to the different printings and supplements, and updates on the data sets and macros. Additionally, you can e-mail the author to make comments and ask questions about the installation of the files stored on the diskettes. The site can be accessed from the publisher's home page

http://www.duxbury.com

Click **Online Book Companions,** which will take you to a list of titles. Find and select the cover of this text.

IMPORTANT TERMS

Descriptive statistics 3	Parameter 5	Statistical inference 6
Inferential statistics 3	Sample 6	Confidence level 6
Population 5	Statistic 6	Significance level 6

REFERENCES

Berk, Kenneth N., and Patrick Carey, *Data Analysis with Microsoft Excel.* Pacific Grove, CA: Duxbury, 2001.

Carver, Robert, *Doing Data Analysis with Minitab 12.* Belmont, CA: Duxbury, 2001.

Chatfield, C., *Problem Solving: A Statistician's Guide,* 2nd edition. New York: Chapman & Hall, 1995.

Freedman, D., R. Pisani, R. Purves, and A. Adhikari, *Statistics,* 2nd edition. New York: W. W. Norton, 1991.

Middleton, Michael R., *Data Analysis Using Microsoft Excel.* Pacific Grove, CA: Duxbury, 2000.

Moore, David S., *Statistics: Concepts & Controversies,* 3rd edition. New York, W. H. Freeman, 1991.

Ramsey, F., and D. Schafer, *The Statistical Sleuth: A Course in Methods of Data Analysis.* Belmont, CA: Duxbury, 1997.

Ryan, Barbara, and Brian Joiner, *Minitab Handbook,* 4th edition, Belmont, CA: Duxbury, 2001.

Stigler, S. M., *The History of Statistics: The Measurement of Uncertainty Before 1900.* Cambridge, MA: Belknap Press, 1986.

EXERCISES

1.1 In your own words, define and give an example of each of the following statistical terms.
   a population
   b sample
   c parameter
   d statistic
   e statistical inference

1.2 Briefly describe the difference between descriptive statistics and inferential statistics.

1.3 A politician who is running for the office of mayor of a city with 25,000 registered voters commissions a survey. In the survey, 48% of the 200 registered voters interviewed say they plan to vote for her.
   a What is the population of interest?
   b What is the sample?
   c Is the value 48% a parameter or a statistic? Explain.

1.4 A manufacturer of computer chips claims that less than 10% of his products are defective. When 1,000 chips were drawn from a large production, 7.5% were found to be defective.
   a What is the population of interest?
   b What is the sample?
   c What is the parameter?
   d What is the statistic?
   e Does the value 10% refer to the parameter or to the statistic?
   f Is the value 7.5% a parameter or a statistic?
   g Explain briefly how the statistic can be used to make inferences about the parameter to test the claim.

1.5 Suppose you believe that, in general, graduates who have majored in *your* subject are offered higher salaries upon graduating than are graduates of other programs. Describe a statistical experiment that could help test your belief.

1.6 You are shown a coin that its owner says is fair in the sense that it will produce the same number of heads and tails when flipped a very large number of times.
   a Describe an experiment to test this claim.
   b What is the population in your experiment?
   c What is the sample?
   d What is the parameter?
   e What is the statistic?
   f Describe briefly how statistical inference can be used to test the claim.

1.7   Suppose that in Exercise 1.6 you decide to flip the coin 100 times.

    a What conclusion would you be likely to draw if you observed 95 heads?

    b What conclusion would you be likely to draw if you observed 55 heads?

    c Do you believe that, if you flip a perfectly fair coin 100 times, you will always observe exactly 50 heads? If you answered no, what numbers do you think are possible? If you answered yes, how many heads would you observe if you flipped the coin twice? Try it several times, and report the results.

1.8   The owner of a large fleet of taxis is trying to estimate his costs for next year's operations. One major cost is fuel purchases. To estimate fuel purchases, the owner needs to know the total distance his taxis will travel next year, the cost of a gallon of fuel, and the fuel mileage of his taxis. The owner has been provided with the first two figures (distance estimate and cost of a gallon of fuel). However, because of the high cost of gasoline, the owner has recently converted his taxis to operate on propane. He measures the propane mileage (in miles per gallon) for 50 taxis. The results are stored in file Xr01-08.

    a What is the population of interest?

    b What is the parameter the owner needs?

    c What is the sample?

    d What is the statistic?

    e Describe briefly how the statistic will produce the kind of information the owner wants.

APPENDIX 1.A: INTRODUCTION TO MICROSOFT EXCEL

The purpose of this appendix is to introduce you to Microsoft Excel and provide enough instruction to allow you to use Excel to produce statistical results. We suggest that you obtain an Excel instruction book to help you learn more about the software.

INSTALLING EXCEL

Installing Excel on your computer is easy. Simply follow the instructions in the booklet that accompanies your edition of Microsoft Excel. In most cases you will install some edition of Office, which includes Excel, Word, and PowerPoint, as well as several other programs.

After installing the software, keep the compact disk (CD) or diskettes handy; it is quite possible that you will need them again.

If the screen (called a desktop) does not show a Microsoft Excel icon, click **Start, Programs,** and **Microsoft Excel.** (Alternatively, if the desktop has an Excel icon, double-click it.) The Excel screen depicted in Figure A1.1 (page 18) will appear. (Unless otherwise stated, "clicking" refers to tapping the left button on your mouse. "Double-clicking" means tapping the left button twice quickly.) The screen that appears may be slightly different, depending on which version of Excel you have.

Figure A1.1
Blank Excel screen

EXCEL SCREEN

At this point the screen is blank except for the top, where five rows or bars appear. These are the locations of most of the commands that you will issue to Excel. Move the mouse, which in turn will move the pointer to different positions on the screen. To select a command, position the pointer over the command, and click once.

The first row is called the **Title bar.** At the left end of the title bar you see the name of the program, Microsoft Excel. At the right side there are three small boxes, which (moving left to right) minimize, restore, or close the Excel program. You can see what the box does before you execute it by placing the mouse pointer over it and waiting a second before moving or clicking.

The second row is the **Menu bar,** which contains a number of commands that open another list or menu of commands. These are called **drop-down menus.** The first menu item is **File.** Clicking this box results in a drop-down menu of other commands. For example, clicking the **Open** command asks Excel to open a file (which you must identify). Notice that this command can be issued by holding down the **Control (Ctrl)** key and hitting the letter **O.**

The next two rows are the **Toolbars.** The Toolbar contains icons that describe a number of functions that can also be executed from the **Menu bar.** The purpose of the icons is to make often-used commands easier to execute. For example, clicking the first icon opens a new workbook (described below).

The fifth row is the **Formula bar,** which displays the contents of the active cell (described below).

EXCEL WORKBOOK AND WORKSHEET

Excel files are called workbooks, which contain worksheets. A worksheet consists of rows and columns. The rows are numbered, and the columns are identified by letters. The intersection of a row and column is called a **cell,** which is a box that can store a number, word, or formula.

If you click the **New** icon (the first icon on the Toolbar) you will see Figure A1.2. Notice that the cell in row 1 column A is **active,** which means that you can type in a number, word, or formula. You can designate any cell as active by moving the mouse pointer (which now appears as a large plus sign) and clicking. Alternatively, you can use any of the four **Up**, **Down**, **Left**, or **Right** arrow keys. (These appear on your keyboard as arrows pointing up, down, left, and right, respectively.)

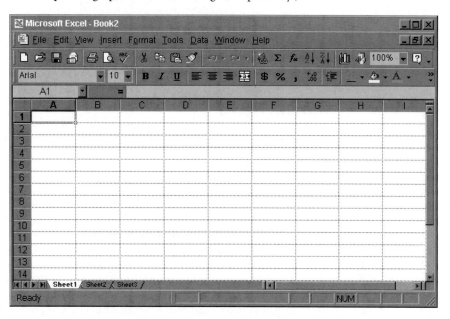

Figure A1.2
Blank Excel screen

At the bottom of the screen you will see the word **Ready**. As you begin to type something into the active cell, the word changes to **Enter**. Above this word you will find the tabs **Sheet1, Sheet2,** and **Sheet3,** the three worksheets that comprise this workbook. You can operate on any of these as well as other sheets that may be created. To change the worksheet, use your mouse pointer, and click the sheet you wish to move to.

INPUTTING DATA

To input data, open a new workbook by clicking the blank icon on the **Toolbar** or click **File** and **New**. (You may have to click ∨, which shows the commands that have been employed infrequently.) Data are usually stored in columns. Activate the cell in the first row of the column in which you plan to type the data. If you wish, you may type the name of the variable. For example, if you plan to type your assignment marks in row A you may type "Assignment Marks" in cell A1. Hit the **Enter** key, and cell A2 becomes active. Begin typing the marks, following each one by **Enter**. Use the arrow key or mouse pointer to move to a new column if you wish to enter another set of numbers.

IMPORTING DATA FILES

A data file stored on the book's CD accompanies most of the examples, exercises, and cases in this book. For example, the data set accompanying Example 2.1 (see page 31) contains 200 long-distance bills. These data are stored in a file called **Xm02-01**, which is stored in a directory (or folder) called **CH02**. (The **Xm** refers to files attached to e**Xam**ples, **Xr** is used for e**Xer**cises, and **C** refers to **C**ases.)

If you followed the instructions that accompany the CD, the Excel files will be stored in a folder called **Excel**, which in turn is in the folder **Keller6**, which is most likely on the C drive. To import a file, click the **Open** folder in the **Toolbar**, and click the yellow arrow key (**Up One Level**) repeatedly to locate the drive that stores the **Keller6** directory. Double-click each of the directories along the path until you reach the file you wish to open. For example, to import the data for Example 2.1, proceed along the following path:

C:\Keller6\Excel\CH02\Xm02-01

The file will appear in the same form that it was saved. (All the files on the CD were saved by the author.) You may save your own files (see instructions below).

EDITING DATA

Each statistical technique requires that the data be in some specific format. If the data are not in that form, it will be necessary to edit the data. As a first step, you must highlight the data you wish to edit. To do so, place the mouse pointer over the first cell of the range and hold the left button down as you move the mouse over the range. Alternatively, you can activate the first cell of the range, hold down the **Shift** key, and use the **Up, Down, Left,** or **Right** arrow keys to highlight the range.

To delete the range, hit the **Delete** key.

To move the range, place the mouse pointer at the top right corner of the range, depress the left mouse button, and move the mouse until the range is where you wish it to be. Release the button. Alternatively, click **Edit** and **Cut**. Activate the cell where the top of the range will be located, and click **Edit** and **Paste**.

You can also use similar commands to copy a range of data. Instead of **Cut**, click **Copy**.

SAVING WORKBOOKS

To save a file (either one you created or one we created that you have altered) click **File** and **Save As...**. Use the **Up One Level** key to specify the directory, and type the **File name**. Click **Save**. If the file is already saved and you wish to use the same name, click the diskette icon on the **Menu bar**, or click **File** and **Save**.

PERFORMING STATISTICAL PROCEDURES

There are several ways to conduct a statistical analysis. These are **Data Analysis, Data Analysis Plus**, the **Toolbar function** f_x, and several Excel spreadsheets that have been stored on the book's CD.

Data Analysis/Analysis ToolPak

The **Analysis ToolPak** is a group of statistical functions that comes with Excel. The **Analysis ToolPak** can be accessed through the **Menu bar**. Click **Tools** and **Data Analysis...**. If **Data Analysis...** does not appear, click **Add-Ins...** and select **Analysis ToolPak**. (Note that **Analysis ToolPak** is not the same as **Analysis ToolPak-VBA**.) If **Analysis ToolPak** is not shown, you will need to install it from the original Excel or MS Office diskettes or CD-ROM. Run the setup program and follow instructions.

There are 20 menu items in **Data Analysis...**. Click the one you wish to use, and follow the instructions described in this book. For example, the first technique in the menu **Anova: Single Factor** is described in Chapter 15.

Data Analysis Plus

Data Analysis Plus is the collection of macros we created to augment Excel's list of statistical procedures. **Data Analysis Plus** (**STATS.XLS**) is supplied on the CD that accompanies this book. The installation program that saves the data files on your computer will also save a copy of **STATS.xls** in a file called **Xlstart**. When this file is correctly saved on your computer, **Data Analysis Plus** will become a menu item in the **Tools** heading in the **Menu bar**. The instructions for **Data Analysis Plus** are also described in this book. The CD also contains a help file that is associated with **Data Analysis Plus**.

Toolbar function f_x

On the **Toolbar** you will find the f_x heading. Clicking this button produces other menus that allow you to specify functions that perform various computations.

Excel Workbooks

We created several workbooks, each containing several worksheets that perform a variety of functions that will be described in Chapters 10, 11, 12, 13, 15, and 17.

Closing the Workbook

To close a workbook, click the **Close** button (the last item) on the **Title bar**. Alternatively, click **File** and **Close**.

STATISTICS PRACTITIONERS AND STUDENTS: BEWARE

The current versions of Excel use algorithms that are not robust. This means that, under certain circumstances, Excel's calculations may be incorrect. In some extreme cases the errors can be very large. At a recent meeting (July 2001) a Microsoft representative acknowledged the problem and promised that his company would investigate further. However, until a new version of Excel becomes available, students are cautioned when using Excel on sets of data other than the ones included with this book. This advice is particularly relevant to medical researchers and other statistics practitioners whose decisions may have serious consequences. On the data sets in this book, Excel works perfectly.

APPENDIX 1.B: INTRODUCTION TO MINITAB

Minitab Release 13 for Windows is a statistical software package that is extremely easy to use and understand. This software features a wide variety of statistical methods. However, we will use only a fraction of its capabilities. Our goal in this appendix is to introduce you to the basics of Minitab. When we use this software to solve an example in this book, we will provide both the output and the specific instructions.

Within Minitab you will find a number of different windows and tools. Here is brief description of each.

MINITAB ENVIRONMENT

Windows

The **Session window** displays the statistical output requested. Most of what you command Minitab to do will appear here.

The **Data window** shows the data in the worksheet you are conducting your analysis on. Each column represents a variable.

The **History window** keeps track of all the commands you have issued.

Graph windows exhibit the graphs you requested. The maximum number of graphs that can be open at any time is 15.

The **Info window** summarizes each open worksheet.

MENUS AND TOOLS

The **menu bar** is the starting point for selecting commands.

The **Toolbar** displays buttons for functions that are used most frequently.

The **status bar** shows an explanation when you point at a menu item.

COMMANDS

There are three ways to issue commands. These are

Clicking menu items

Toolbar selections

Session commands

In this book we will describe the menu items only. For example, to produce a histogram (see page 33) from the menu bar click **Graph**. From the list that appears click **Histogram....** A dialog box will appear requesting you to identify the variable or variables you wish to describe as well as other information.

DIALOG BOXES

Among other things, you will have to identify the variable that you wish to compute statistics or graphs from. Minitab displays the **variable list**, which contains all the variables, constants, or matrices in the current worksheet. (The current worksheet is the one associated with the active Data window. You activate a data window by clicking on it.) If the variables have been named, the names will appear in the list. If the variables are unnamed, the column in which the variable is stored appears. To select a variable, type its name or column in the **Variables** box. Alternatively, click in the text box you wish to fill, highlight the variable in the variable list, and click **Select**.

DATA INPUT

Activate the Data window and start typing the data into a column starting in row 1. You can type the name of the variable in the cell immediately under the column number (e.g., C1). When finished, you may issue commands.

IMPORTING DATA

Most of the examples, exercises, and cases in this book have data sets associated with them. To import the data, you will have to install the Minitab files from the disk that accompanies this book. (Follow the instructions in the README file.)

To open a file, click **File** and **Open Worksheet....** (Do not click the file symbol. The reasons are explained below.) Select the folder containing the data files. All the data files are saved in chapter subdirectories. To open a file in Chapter 2 click **CH02**. A complete list of files will appear. The files beginning with **Xm** refer to files for examples. The data files associated with exercises begin with **Xr**, and files connected to cases begin with **C**. For example, to get the data for Example 2.2 click **Xm02-02**.

MINITAB PROJECTS AND WORKSHEETS

A Minitab project contains all the data, the output from any commands issued on the data set, and graphs. When you save the project all of this will be saved. You may have as many worksheets as you like in any project. For example, one worksheet can contain the data; a second, a graph; a third, descriptive statistics; and so on. All the data files on the disk are worksheets. If you click the file symbol on the toolbar, Minitab will attempt to open a project. The only projects you will have are the ones you yourself previously created.

MINITAB WEB SITE

For assistance you can go to Minitab's Web page

http://www.minitab.com

You can get answers to frequently asked questions as well as other information.

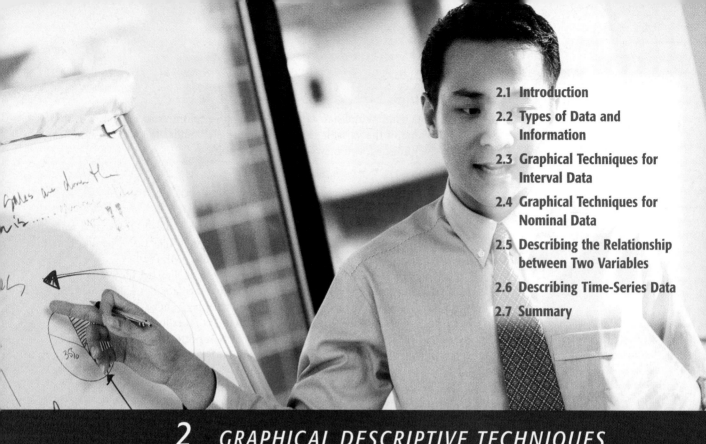

2 *GRAPHICAL DESCRIPTIVE TECHNIQUES*

TICKET PROGRAM FOR THE BARNES EXHIBIT

Several years ago the Barnes Exhibit toured major cities all over the world, with millions of people flocking to see it. Dr. Albert Barnes was a wealthy art collector who accumulated a large number of impressionist masterpieces; the total exceeds 800 paintings. When Dr. Barnes died in 1951, he stated in his will that his collection was not to be allowed to tour. However, because of the deterioration of the exhibit's home near Philadelphia, a judge ruled that the collection could go on tour to raise enough money to ren-

Factories by Vincent van Gogh

ovate the building. Because of the size and value of the collection, it was predicted (correctly) that in each city a large number of people would come to view the paintings. Because space was limited, most galleries had to sell tickets that were valid at one time (much like a play). In this way, they were able to control the number of visitors at any one time. To judge how many people to let in at any time, it was necessary to know the length of time people would spend at the exhibit; longer times would dictate smaller audiences; shorter times would allow for sale of more tickets. The manager of a gallery that will host the exhibit realized her facility can comfortably and safely hold about 250 people at any one time. Although the demand will vary throughout the day and from weekday to weekend, she believes that the demand will not drop below 500 at any time. To help make a decision about how many tickets to sell, she acquired the amount of time a sample of 400 people spent at the exhibit from another city. These data are stored in file Ch02:\Barnes. What ticket procedure should the museum management institute?

☛ *On page 45 we provide a possible answer.*

2.1 INTRODUCTION

In Chapter 1, we pointed out that statistics is divided into two basic areas: descriptive statistics and inferential statistics. The purpose of this chapter, together with the next two, is to present the principal methods that fall under the heading of descriptive statistics. In this chapter we introduce graphical statistical methods that allow managers to summarize data visually to produce useful information, often used in decision making. Chapter 3 discusses ways to use the techniques introduced in this chapter in an effective and accurate way. Another class of descriptive techniques, numerical methods, is introduced in Chapter 4.

Managers frequently have access to large masses of potentially useful data. But before the data can be used to support a decision, they must be organized and summarized. Consider, for example, the problems faced by managers who have access to the databases created by the rapidly increasing use of debit cards. The database consists of the personal information supplied by the customer when he or she applied for the debit card. This information includes age, gender, residence, and income of the cardholder. In addition, each time the card is used the database grows to include a history of the timing, price, and brand of each product so purchased. Using the appropriate statistical technique, managers can determine which segments of the market are buying their company's brands. Specialized marketing campaigns including telemarketing can be developed. Both descriptive and inferential statistics would likely be employed in the analysis.

Descriptive statistics involves arranging, summarizing, and presenting a set of data in such a way that the meaningful essentials of the data can be produced and interpreted. Its methods make use of graphical techniques and numerical descriptive measures (such as averages) to summarize and present the data, allowing managers to make decisions based on the information generated. Although descriptive statistical methods are quite straightforward, their importance should not be underestimated. Most management, business, and economics students will encounter numerous opportunities to make valuable use of graphical and numerical descriptive techniques when preparing reports and presentations in the workplace. According to a Wharton Business School study, top managers reach a consensus 25% more quickly when responding to a presentation in which graphics are used.

In Chapter 1 we introduced the distinction between a population and a sample. Recall that a **population** is the entire set of observations under study, whereas a **sample** is a subset of a population. The descriptive methods presented in this chapter and in Chapter 4 apply to both a set of data constituting a population and a set of data constituting a sample.

In both the preface and Chapter 1, we pointed out that a critical part of your education as statistics practitioners includes an understanding not only of *how* to draw graphs and calculate statistics (manually or by computer) but also *when* to use each technique that we cover. The two most important factors that determine the appropriate method to use are the type of data and the information that is needed. Both are discussed next.

2.2 TYPES OF DATA AND INFORMATION

The objective of statistics is to extract information from data. There are different types of data and information. To help explain this important principle, we need to define some terms.

A **variable** is some characteristic of a population or sample. For example, the mark on a statistics exam is a characteristic of statistics exams that certainly is of interest to readers of this book. Not all students achieve the same mark. The marks will vary from student to student, thus the name *variable*. The price of stock is another variable. The prices of most stocks vary daily. We usually represent the name of the variable using uppercase letters such as X, Y and Z.

The **values** of the variable are the possible observations of the variable. The values of statistics exam marks are the integers between 0 and 100 (assuming the exam is marked out of 100). The values of a stock price are real numbers that are usually measured in dollars and cents (sometimes in fractions of a cent). The values range from 0 to hundreds of dollars.

Data[*] are the observed values of a variable. For example, suppose that we observe the marks of 10 students, which are

67 74 71 83 93 55 48 82 68 62

These are the data from which we will extract the information we seek. Incidentally, *data* is plural for *datum*. The mark of one student is a datum.

When most people think of the terms defined above they think of sets of numbers. However, there are three types of data: interval, nominal, and ordinal data.[†]

Interval data are real numbers, such as heights, weights, incomes, and distances. We also refer to this type of data as **quantitative** or **numerical**.

The values of **nominal** data are categories. For example, responses to questions about marital status produce nominal data. The values of this variable are single, married, divorced, and widowed. Notice that the values are not numbers but instead are words describing categories. We often record nominal data by arbitrarily assigning a number to each category. For example, we could record marital status using the following codes:

Single	1	Divorced	3
Married	2	Widowed	4

---

[*]Unfortunately, the term *data*, like the term *statistician*, has taken on a number of different meanings. For example, dictionaries define data as facts, information, or statistics. In the language of computers, data may refer to any piece of information such as this textbook or an essay you have written. Such definitions make it difficult for us to present *statistics* as a method of converting *data* into *information*. In this book we carefully distinguish among the three terms.

[†]There are actually four types of data, the fourth being ratio data. However, for statistical purposes there is no difference between ratio and interval data. Consequently, we combine the two types.

However, any other numbering system is valid provided that each category has a different number assigned to it. Here is another coding system that is as valid as the one above.

Single	7	Divorced	13
Married	4	Widowed	1

Nominal data are also called **qualitative** or **categorical**.

The third type of data is ordinal. **Ordinal** data appear to be nominal, but their values are in order. For example, at the completion of most college and university courses, students are asked to evaluate the course. The variables are the ratings of various aspects of the course, including the professor. Suppose that in a particular college the values are:

Poor, fair, good, very good, and excellent

The difference between nominal and ordinal types of data is that the values of the latter are in order. Consequently, when assigning codes to the values, we should maintain the order of the values. For example, we can record the students' evaluations as

Poor	1	Very good	4
Fair	2	Excellent	5
Good	3		

Because the only constraint that we impose on our choice of codes is that the order must be maintained, we can use any set of codes that are in order. For example, we can also assign the following codes:

Poor	6	Very good	45
Fair	18	Excellent	88
Good	23		

As we discuss in Chapter 17, the use of any code that preserves the order of the data will produce exactly the same result.

Students often have difficulty distinguishing between ordinal and interval data. The critical difference between them is that the intervals or differences between values of interval data are consistent and meaningful. (That's why this type of data is called interval.) For example, the difference between marks of 85 and 80 is the same five-mark difference that exists between 73 and 68. That is, we can calculate the difference and interpret the results.

Because the codes representing ordinal data are arbitrarily assigned except for the order, we cannot calculate and interpret differences. For example, using a 1-2-3-4-5 coding system to represent poor, fair, good, very good, and excellent, we note that the difference between excellent and very good is identical to the difference between good and fair. With a 6-18-23-45-88 coding, the difference between excellent and very good is 43, and the difference between good and fair is 5. Because both coding systems are valid, we cannot use either system to compute and interpret differences.

Here is another example. Suppose that you are given the following list of the most active stocks traded on the NASDAQ in descending order of magnitude:

Order	Most active stocks
1	Microsoft
2	Cisco Systems
3	Dell Computer
4	Sun Microsystems
5	JDS Uniphase

Does this information allow you to conclude that the difference between the number of stocks traded in Microsoft and Cisco Systems is the same as the difference in the number of stocks traded between Dell Computer and Sun Microsystems? The answer is no because we have information only about the order of the numbers of trades, which are ordinal, and not the numbers of trades themselves, which are interval. That is, the difference between 1 and 2 is not necessarily the same as the difference between 3 and 4.

CALCULATIONS FOR TYPES OF DATA

Interval Data

All calculations are permitted on interval data. We often describe a set of interval data by calculating the average. For example, the average of the 10 marks listed on page 26 is 70.3. As you will discover, there are several other important statistics that we will compute.

Nominal Data

Because the codes of nominal data are completely arbitrary, we cannot perform any calculations on these codes. To understand why, consider a survey that asks people to report their marital status. Suppose that the first 10 people surveyed gave the following responses:

single, married, married, married, widowed, single, married, married, single, divorced

Using the codes

| Single | 1 | Divorced | 3 |
| Married | 2 | Widowed | 4 |

we would record these responses as

1, 2, 2, 2, 4, 1, 2, 2, 1, 3.

The average of these numerical codes is 2.0. Does this mean that the average person is married? Now suppose four more persons were interviewed, of whom three are widowed and one is divorced. The data are given here:

1, 2, 2, 2, 4, 1, 2, 2, 1, 3, 4, 4, 4, 3.

The average of these 14 codes is 2.5. Does this mean that the average person is married but halfway to getting divorced? The answer to both questions is an emphatic no. This example illustrates a fundamental truth about nominal data: Calculations based on the codes used to store this type of data are meaningless. All that we are permitted to do with nominal data is count the occurrences of each category. Thus, we would describe the 14 observations by counting the number of each marital status category and reporting the frequency, as shown in the table.

Category	Code	Frequency
Single	1	3
Married	2	5
Divorced	3	2
Widowed	4	4

Ordinal Data

The most important aspect of ordinal data is the order of the values. As a result, the only permissible calculations are ones involving a ranking process. For example, we can place all the data in order and select the code that lies in the middle. As we discuss in Chapter 4, this descriptive measurement is called the *median*.

HIERARCHY OF DATA

The data types can be placed in order of the permissible calculations. At the top of the list we place the interval data type because virtually *all* computations are allowed. The nominal data type is at the bottom because *no* calculations other than determining frequencies are permitted. (We are permitted to perform calculations using the frequencies of codes. However, this differs from performing calculations on the codes themselves.) In between interval and nominal data lies the ordinal data type. Permissible calculations are ones that rank the data.

Higher-level data types may be treated as lower-level ones. For example, in universities and colleges we convert the marks in a course, which are interval, to letter grades, which are ordinal. Some graduate courses feature only a pass or fail designation. In this case, the interval data are converted to nominal. However, we cannot treat lower-level data types as higher-level types. The definitions and hierarchy are summarized in the box.

> **TYPES OF DATA**
> - Interval
>   Values are real numbers.
>   All calculations are valid.
>   Data may be treated as ordinal or nominal.
> - Ordinal
>   Values must represent the ranked order of the data.
>   Calculations based on an ordering process are valid.
>   Data may be treated as nominal but not as interval.
> - Nominal
>   Values are the arbitrary numbers that represent categories.
>   Only calculations based on the frequencies of occurrence are valid.
>   Data may not be treated as ordinal or interval.

Interval, Ordinal, and Nominal Variables

The variables whose observations constitute our data will be given the same name as the type of data. Thus, for example, interval data are the observations of an interval variable.

PROBLEM OBJECTIVES/ INFORMATION

In presenting the different types of data, we introduced a critical factor in deciding which statistical procedure to use. A second factor is the type of information we need to produce from our data. We will discuss the different types of information in greater detail in Section 11.5 when we introduce *problem objectives*. However, in this part of the book (Chapters 2, 3, 4, and 5) we will use statistical techniques to describe a set of data and to describe the relationship between two variables. In Section 2.3 we introduce graphical techniques employed to describe a set of interval data. Section 2.4 introduces graphical methods to describe a set of nominal data. Section 2.5 presents methods to describe the relationship between two variables, and Section 2.6 introduces time-series data and line charts.

EXERCISES

2.1 Provide two examples each of nominal, ordinal, and interval data.

2.2 For each of the following examples of data, determine the type.
a the number of miles joggers run per week
b the starting salaries of graduates of MBA programs
c the months in which a firm's employees choose to take their vacations
d the final letter grades received by students in a statistics course

2.3 For each of the following examples of data, determine the type.
a the weekly closing price of the stock of Amazon.com
b the month of highest vacancy rate at a La Quinta motel
c the size of soft drink (small, medium, or large) ordered by a sample of McDonald's customers
d the number of Toyotas imported monthly by the United States over the last 5 years
e the marks achieved by the students in a statistics course final exam marked out of 100

2.4 The placement office at a university regularly surveys the graduates 1 year after graduation and asks for the following information. For each, determine the type of data.
a What is your occupation?
b What is your income?
c What degree did you obtain?
d What is the amount of your student loan?
e How would you rate the quality of instruction?

2.5 Residents of condominiums were recently surveyed and asked a series of questions. Identify the type of data for each question.
a What is your age?
b On what floor is the condominium?
c Do you own or rent?
d How many square feet?
e Does your condominium have a pool?

2.6 A sample of shoppers at a mall was asked the following questions. Identify the type of data each question would produce.

a What is your age?
b How much did you spend?
c What is your marital status?
d Rate the availability of parking: excellent, good, fair, or poor
e How many stores did you enter?

2.7 Information about a magazine's readers is of interest to both the publisher and the magazine's advertisers. A survey of readers asked respondents to complete the following:
a Age?
b Gender?
c Marital status?
d Number of magazine subscriptions?
e Annual income?
f Rate the quality of our magazine: excellent, good, fair, or poor
For each item identify the resulting data type.

2.8 Baseball fans are regularly asked to offer their opinions about various aspects of the sport. A survey asked the following questions. Identify the type of data.
a How many games do you attend annually?
b How would you rate the quality of entertainment? (excellent, very good, good, fair, poor)
c Do you have season tickets?
d How would you rate the quality of the food? (edible, barely edible, or horrible)

2.9 A survey of golfers was asked the questions below. Identify the type of data each question produces.
a How many rounds of golf do you play annually?
b Are you a member of a private club?
c What brand of clubs do you own?

2.10 At the end of the term, university and college students often complete questionnaires about their courses. Suppose that in one university, students were asked the following.
a Rate the course. (highly relevant, relevant, irrelevant)
b Rate the professor. (very effective, effective, not too effective, not at all effective)
c What was your midterm grade? (A, B, C, D, F)
Determine the type of data each question produces.

2.3 GRAPHICAL TECHNIQUES FOR INTERVAL DATA

In this section, we introduce several graphical methods that are used when the data are interval. The most important of these graphical methods is the histogram. As you will see, the histogram is not only a powerful graphical technique used to summarize interval data, but it is also used to help explain an important aspect of probability (see Chapter 8).

APPLICATIONS IN MARKETING: *PRICING*

Following deregulation of telephone service, several new companies were created to compete in the business of providing long-distance telephone service. In almost all cases these companies competed on price since the service each offered is similar. As mentioned in the introduction to marketing management in Chapter 1, **pricing** a service or product in the face of stiff competition is very difficult. Factors to be considered include supply, demand, price elasticity, and the actions of competitors. Long-distance packages may employ per-minute charges, a flat monthly rate, or some combination of the two. Determin-

ing the appropriate rate structure is facilitated by acquiring information about the behaviors of customers and in particular the size of monthly long-distance bills.

EXAMPLE 2.1

In the last decade, a number of companies have been created to compete in the long-distance telephone business. As part of a larger study, one such company wanted to acquire information about the monthly bills of new subscribers in the first month after signing with the company. The company's marketing manager conducted a survey of 200 new residential subscribers wherein the first month's bills were recorded. These data are listed below and stored in file Xm02-01. The general manager planned to present his findings to senior executives. What information can be extracted from these data?

Long-Distance Telephone Bills

42.19	39.21	75.71	8.37	1.62	28.77	35.32	13.90	114.67	15.30
38.45	48.54	88.62	7.18	91.10	9.12	117.69	9.22	27.57	75.49
29.23	93.31	99.50	11.07	10.88	118.75	106.84	109.94	64.78	68.69
89.35	104.88	85.00	1.47	30.62	0	8.40	10.70	45.81	35.00
118.04	30.61	0	26.40	100.05	13.95	90.04	0	56.04	9.12
110.46	22.57	8.41	13.26	26.97	14.34	3.85	11.27	20.39	18.49
0	63.70	70.48	21.13	15.43	79.52	91.56	72.02	31.77	84.12
72.88	104.84	92.88	95.03	29.25	2.72	10.13	7.74	94.67	13.68
83.05	6.45	3.20	29.04	1.88	9.63	5.72	5.04	44.32	20.84
95.73	16.47	115.50	5.42	16.44	21.34	33.69	33.40	3.69	100.04
103.15	89.50	2.42	77.21	109.08	104.40	115.78	6.95	19.34	112.94
94.52	13.36	1.08	72.47	2.45	2.88	.98	6.48	13.54	20.12
26.84	44.16	76.69	0	21.97	65.90	19.45	11.64	18.89	53.21
93.93	92.97	13.62	5.64	17.12	20.55	0	83.26	1.57	15.30
90.26	99.56	88.51	6.48	19.70	3.43	27.21	15.42	0	49.24

(continued)

Long-Distance Telephone Bills (Continued)

72.78	92.62	55.99	6.95	6.93	10.44	89.27	24.49	5.20	9.44
101.36	78.89	12.24	19.60	10.05	21.36	14.49	89.13	2.80	2.67
104.80	87.71	119.63	8.11	99.03	24.42	92.17	111.14	5.10	4.69
74.01	93.57	23.31	9.01	29.24	95.52	21.00	92.64	3.03	41.38
56.01	0	11.05	84.77	15.21	6.72	106.59	53.90	9.16	45.77

SOLUTION   There is little information developed by casually reading through the 200 observations. The manager can probably see that most of the bills are under $100 but that is likely to be the extent of the information garnered from browsing through the data. If he examines the data more carefully he may discover that the smallest bill is $0 and the largest is $119.63. He has now developed some information. However, his presentation to senior executives will be most unimpressive if no other information is produced. For example, someone is likely to ask how the numbers are distributed between 0 and 119.63. Are there many small bills and few large bills? What is the "typical" bill? Are the bills somewhat similar or do they vary considerably?

To help answer these questions and others like them, the marketing manager can construct a frequency distribution from which a histogram can be drawn.

A **frequency distribution** counts the number of observations that fall into each of a series of intervals, called **classes**, that cover the complete range of observations. We'll discuss how we decide the number of classes and the upper and lower limits of the intervals later. We have chosen eight classes defined in such a way that each observation falls into one and only one class. These classes are defined below.

Classes

Amounts that are less than or equal to 15

Amounts that are more than 15 but less than or equal to 30

Amounts that are more than 30 but less than or equal to 45

Amounts that are more than 45 but less than or equal to 60

Amounts that are more than 60 but less than or equal to 75

Amounts that are more than 75 but less than or equal to 90

Amounts that are more than 90 but less than or equal to 105

Amounts that are more than 105 but less than or equal to 120

Notice that the intervals do not overlap, so that there is no uncertainty about which interval to assign to any observation. Moreover, because the smallest number is 0 and the largest is 119.63, every observation will be assigned to an interval. Finally, the intervals are equally wide. Although this is not essential, it makes the task of reading and interpreting the graph easier.

To create the frequency distribution manually, we would count the number of observations that fall into each interval. These counts are called the **frequencies**, hence the name. Table 2.1 presents the frequency distribution.

Table 2.1 Frequency Distribution of the Long-Distance Bills in Example 2.1

Class Limits	Frequency	
0 to 15*	71	
15 to 30	37	
30 to 45	13	
45 to 60	9	
60 to 75	10	*(continued)*

Class Limits	Frequency
75 to 90	18
90 to 105	28
105 to 120	14
Total	200

*Classes contain observations up to and including their upper limits.

Although the frequency distribution provides information about how the numbers are distributed, the information is more easily understood and imparted by drawing a picture or graph. The graph is called a **histogram**. A histogram is created by drawing rectangles whose bases are the intervals and whose heights are the frequencies. Figure 2.1 exhibits the histogram that was drawn by hand.

Figure 2.1
Histogram for Example 2.1

As we promised in Chapter 1 (and the Preface), we will solve all examples in this book using three approaches (where feasible): manually, using Excel, and using Minitab. We not only provide the printout, but also the commands required to produce them. Moreover, we provide general instructions as well as step-by-step instructions for the specific example. We have already drawn the histogram manually. Here are the Excel and Minitab versions.

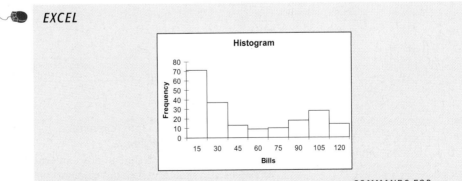

EXCEL

GENERAL COMMANDS

1. Type or import the data into one column.
2. In cell B1 type "Bins" or the name of the variable as we have done.

COMMANDS FOR EXAMPLE 2.1
Open file **Xm02-01. Times**

(continued)

3. In cell B2 type the upper limit of the first class,   **15, 30, . . ., 120**
   in B3 the upper limit of the second class,
   and so on, to complete the listing of bins.
4. Click **Tools, Data Analysis...**, and **Histogram**.
5. Type the **Input Range** of the data. Include the cell   **A1:A201**
   containing the name of the variable (if applicable).
6. Type the **Input Range** of the bins.   **B1:B9**
7. If the names of the variables have been included
   in the first row of the ranges, click **Labels**.
8. Click **Chart Output** and **OK**. This will create a chart with gaps between the
   rectangles.
9. To remove the gaps, place the cursor over one of the rectangles and click the
   right button of the mouse.
10. Click (with the left button) **Format Data Series...**.
11. Click **Options**, move the pointer to **Gap Width:** and change the number
    from 150 to 0. Click **OK**.
12. To remove the **More** class use the left button and click the cell containing
    More and the cell containing the frequency. Click the right button to
    produce a menu and click **Delete**.
13. To improve the appearance of the histogram, click inside the box containing
    the chart and click **Chart** and **Chart Options**.

Note that the numbers along the horizontal axis represent the upper limits of each
class although they appear to be placed in the centers.

It is unfortunate that the first use of Excel is the histogram, which entails more
steps than any other technique. Rest assured that all other Excel statistical techniques are conducted far more easily and quickly.

MINITAB

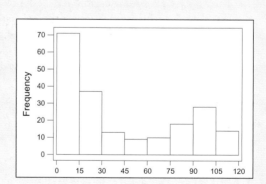

GENERAL COMMANDS

1. Type or import the data into one column.

2. Click **Graph** and **Histogram...**.

3. Type the name of the variable in box 1 of **Graph
   variables**. Alternatively, click the name of the
   variable and click **Select**.

4. Use the cursor to choose the following under **Data
   display: Bar** (under **Display**) and **Graph** (under **For
   each**). Click **OK**.

*COMMANDS FOR
EXAMPLE 2.1*
Open file **Xm02-01**.

Bills or **C1**

(continued)

Minitab will produce a histogram using its own rules to select the classes. To choose your own classes, proceed with the following steps.

5. Before clicking **OK** click **Options....**
6. Use the cursor to specify **Frequency** or **Percent**.
7. To specify midpoints, use the cursor to select **Midpoint**. Specify **Midpoint/cutpoint positions:**, hit tab, and type the midpoints you want.
8. To specify cutpoints, use the cursor to select **Cutpoint**. Specify **Midpoint/cutpoint positions:**, hit tab, and type the cutpoints you want. (The first cutpoint must be the lower limit of the first interval. For Example 2.1, begin with **0**.) Click **OK**. Click **OK**.

Note that Minitab counts the number of observations in each class that are strictly less than their upper limits.

INTERPRET

The histogram gives us a clear view of the way the bills are distributed. About half the monthly bills are small ($0 to $30), there are few bills in the middle range ($30 to $75), and there are a relatively large number of long-distance bills at the high end of the range. It would appear from this sample of first-month long-distance bills that the company's customers are split unevenly between light and heavy users of long-distance telephone service. If the company assumes that this pattern will continue, it will need to address a number of pricing issues. For example, customers who incurred large monthly bills may be targets of competitors who offer flat rates for 15-minute or 30-minute calls. The company needs to know more about these customers. With the additional information, the marketing manager may suggest an alteration of its pricing.

DETERMINING THE NUMBER OF CLASS INTERVALS

The number of class intervals we select depends entirely on the number of observations in the data set. The more observations we have, the larger the number of class intervals we need to use to draw the histogram. Table 2.2 provides guidelines on choosing the number of classes. In Example 2.1 we had 200 observations. The table tells us to use 7, 8, 9, or 10 classes.

Table 2.2 Approximate Number of Classes in Frequency Distributions

Number of Observations	Number of Classes
Less than 50	5–7
50–200	7–9
200–500	9–10
500–1,000	10–11
1,000–5,000	11–13
5,000–50,000	13–17
More than 50,000	17–20

An alternative to the guidelines listed above is to use Sturges' formula, which recommends that the number of class intervals be determined by the following:

$$\text{Number of class intervals} = 1 + 3.3 \log(n)$$

For example, if $n = 200$, Sturges' formula becomes

$$\text{Number of class intervals} = 1 + 3.3 \log(200) = 1 + 3.3(2.3) = 8.59$$

which we round to 9.

Class Interval Widths

We determine the approximate width of the classes by subtracting the smallest observation from the largest and dividing the difference by the number of classes. Thus,

$$\text{Class width} = \frac{\text{Largest observation} - \text{Smallest observation}}{\text{Number of classes}}$$

In Example 2.1 we calculated

$$\text{Class width} = \frac{119.63 - 0}{8} = 14.95$$

We often round the result to some convenient value. We then define our class limits by selecting a lower limit for the first class from which all other limits are determined. The only condition we apply is that the first class interval must contain the smallest observation. In Example 2.1, we rounded the class width to 15 and set the lower limit of the first class to 0. Thus, the first class is defined as "Amounts that are more than 0 but less than or equal to 15."

SHAPES OF HISTOGRAMS

The purpose of drawing histograms, like that of all statistical techniques, is to acquire information. Once we have the information, we frequently need to describe what we've learned to others. We describe the shape of histograms on the basis of the following characteristics.

Symmetry

A histogram is said to be **symmetric** if, when we draw a vertical line down the center of the histogram, the two sides are identical in shape and size. Figure 2.2 depicts three symmetric histograms.

Figure 2.2
Three symmetric histograms

Skewness

A skewed histogram is one with a long tail extending to either the right or left. The former is called **positively skewed**, and the latter is called **negatively skewed**. Figure 2.3 describes examples of both. Incomes of employees in large firms tend to be positively skewed, because there is a large number of relatively low-paid workers and a small number of well-paid executives. The time taken by students to write exams is frequently negatively skewed because few students hand in their exams early; most prefer to reread their papers and hand them in near the end of the scheduled test period.

Figure 2.3
Skewed histograms

Number of Modal Classes

As we discuss in Chapter 4, a *mode* is the observation that occurs with the greatest frequency. A **modal class** is the class with the largest number of observations. A **unimodal histogram** is one with a single peak. The histogram in Figure 2.4 is unimodal. A **bimodal histogram** is one with two peaks, not necessarily equal in height. Figure 2.5 depicts bimodal histograms.

Figure 2.4
A unimodal histogram

Figure 2.5
Bimodal histograms

Bell Shape

A special type of symmetric unimodal histogram is one that is bell shaped. In Chapter 8 we will explain why this type of histogram is important. Figure 2.6 exhibits a bell-shaped histogram.

Figure 2.6
Bell-shaped histogram

Now that we know what to look for, let's examine some examples of histograms and see what we can discover.

APPLICATIONS IN FINANCE: *RETURN ON INVESTMENT*

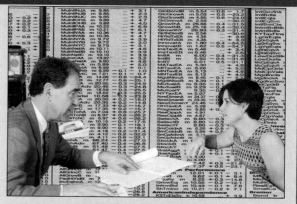

The return on an investment is calculated by dividing the gain (or loss) by the value of the investment. For example, a $100 investment that is worth $106 after 1 year has a 6% rate of return. A $100 investment that loses $20 has a −20% rate of return. For many investments, including individual stocks and stock portfolios (combinations of various stocks), the rate of return is a variable. That is, the investor does not know in advance what the rate of return will be.

Investors are torn between two goals. The first is to maximize the rate of return on investment. The second goal is to reduce risk. If we draw a histogram of the returns for a certain investment, the location of the center of the histogram gives us some information about the return one might expect from that investment. The spread or variation of the histogram provides us with guidance about the

risk. If there is little variation, an investor can be quite confident in predicting what his or her rate of return will be. If there is a great deal of variation, the return becomes much less predictable and thus riskier.

EXAMPLE 2.2

Suppose that you are facing a decision on where to invest that small fortune that remains after you have deducted the anticipated expenses for the next year from the earnings from your summer job. A friend has suggested two types of investment, and to help make the decision you acquire some annual rates of return from each type. You would like to know what you can expect by way of the return on your investment, as well as other types of information, such as whether the rates are spread out over a wide range (making the investment risky) or are grouped tightly together (indicating relatively low risk). Do the data indicate that it is possible that you can do extremely well with little likelihood of a large loss? Is it likely that you could lose money (negative rate of return)? The returns for the two types of investments are listed below and stored in file Xm02-02. Draw histograms for each set of returns and report on your findings. Which investment would you choose and why?

Returns on Investment A (%)					Returns on Investment B (%)			
30.00	6.93	13.77	−8.55		30.33	−34.75	30.31	24.30
−2.13	−13.24	22.42	−5.29		−30.37	54.19	6.06	−10.01
4.30	−18.95	34.40	−7.04		−5.61	44.00	14.73	35.24
25.00	9.43	49.87	−12.11		29.00	−20.23	36.13	40.70
12.89	1.21	22.92	12.89		−26.01	4.16	1.53	22.18
−20.24	31.76	20.95	63.00		.46	10.03	17.61	3.24
1.20	11.07	43.71	−19.27		2.07	10.51	1.20	25.10
−2.59	8.47	−12.83	−9.22		29.44	39.04	9.94	−24.24
33.00	36.08	.52	−17.00		11.00	24.76	−33.39	−38.47
14.26	−21.95	61.00	17.30		−25.93	15.28	58.67	13.44
−15.83	10.33	−11.96	52.00		8.29	34.21	.25	68.00
.63	12.68	1.94			61.00	52.00	5.23	
38.00	13.09	28.45			−20.44	−32.17	66.00	

SOLUTION   We draw the histograms of the returns on the two investments. We'll use Excel and Minitab to do the work.

EXCEL

MINITAB

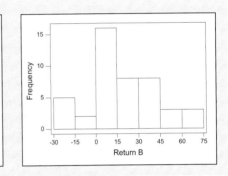

INTERPRET

Comparing the two histograms, we can extract the following information:

1. The center of the histogram of the returns of investment A is slightly lower than that for investment B.

2. The spread of returns for investment A is considerably less than that for investment B.

3. Both histograms are slightly positively skewed.

These findings suggest that investment A is superior. Although the returns on A are slightly less than those for B, the wider spread for B makes it unappealing to most investors. Both investments allow for the possibility of a relatively large return.

The interpretation of the histograms is somewhat subjective. Other viewers may not concur with our conclusion. In such cases, numerical techniques provide the detail and precision lacking in most graphs. We will redo this example in Chapter 4 to illustrate how numerical techniques compare to graphical ones.

EXAMPLE 2.3

The final marks in a statistics course that emphasized mathematical proofs and derivations both during the class and on exams are exhibited on page 40 as well as being stored in file Xm02-03. The marks obtained by students in the same course after the emphasis was changed to applications with most of the calculations performed using a computer are stored in column B of the same file. Draw histograms for both groups and interpret the results.

Marks (Manual Course)			
77	67	53	54
74	82	75	44
75	55	76	54
75	73	59	60
67	92	82	50
72	75	82	52
81	75	70	47
76	52	71	46
79	72	75	50
73	78	74	51
59	83	53	44
83	81	49	52
77	73	56	53
74	72	61	56
78	71	61	53

Marks (Computer Course)			
65	81	72	59
71	53	85	66
66	70	72	71
79	76	77	68
65	73	64	72
82	73	77	75
80	85	89	74
86	83	87	77
67	80	78	69
64	67	79	60
62	78	59	92
74	68	63	69
67	67	84	69
72	62	74	73
68	83	74	65

SOLUTION

 EXCEL

 MINITAB

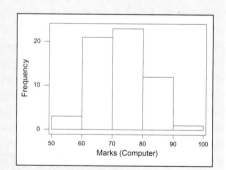

INTERPRET

The histogram of the marks in the "manual calculation" statistics course is bimodal. The larger modal class are the marks in the 70s. The smaller modal class are the marks in the 50s. There appear to be few marks in the 60s. This histogram suggests that there are two groups of students. Because of the emphasis on mathematical manipulation in the course, one may conclude that those who performed poorly in the course are weaker mathematically than those who performed well.

Contrast the first histogram with the one that describes the marks on the "computer" statistics course. This histogram is unimodal and bell shaped, and it appears that its spread is less than that of the first histogram. One possible interpretation is that this type of course allows students who are not particularly mathematical to learn statistics as well as mathematically inclined students.

STEM-AND-LEAF DISPLAY

One of the drawbacks of the histogram is that we lose potentially useful information by classifying the observations. In Example 2.1, we learned that there are 71 observations that fall between 0 and 15. By classifying the observations we did acquire useful information. However, the histogram focuses our attention on the frequency of each class and by doing so sacrifices whatever information was contained in the actual observations. A statistician named John Tukey introduced the **stem-and-leaf display**, which is a method that to some extent overcomes this loss.

The first step in developing a stem-and-leaf display is to split each observation into two parts, a stem and a leaf. There are several different ways of doing this. For example, the number 12.3 can be split so that the stem is 12 and the leaf is 3. In this definition the stem consists of the digits to the left of the decimal and the leaf is the digit to the right of the decimal. Another method can define the stem as 1 and the leaf as 2 (ignoring the 3). In this definition the stem is the number of tens and the leaf is the number of ones. We'll use this definition to create a stem-and-leaf display for Example 2.1.

The first observation is 42.19. Thus, the stem is 4 and the leaf is 2. The second observation is 38.45, which has a stem of 3 and a leaf of 8. We continue converting each number in this way. The stem-and-leaf display consists of listing the stems 0, 1, 2, . . . , 11. After each stem we list that stem's leaves, usually in ascending order. Figure 2.7 depicts the manually created stem-and-leaf display.

Stem	Leaf
0	00000000011111222222333334555555666666778888999999
1	000001111233333334455555667889999
2	00001111123446667778999
3	001335589
4	124445589
5	33566
6	3458
7	022224556789
8	334457889999
9	00112222233344555999
10	001344446699
11	0124557889

Figure 2.7
Stem-and-leaf display for Example 2.1

As you can see, the stem-and-leaf display is similar to a histogram turned on its side. The length of each line represents the frequency in the class interval defined by the stems. The stem-and-leaf's advantage over the histogram is that we can see the actual observations.

EXCEL

	A	B	C	D	E	F	G
1	Stem & Leaf Display						
2							
3	Stems	Leaves					
4	0	->000000000111112222223333334555555666666677888889999999					
5	1	->00000111123333333445555566788999 9					
6	2	->000011111234466677899999					
7	3	->001335589					
8	4	->12445589					
9	5	->33566					
10	6	->3458					
11	7	->022224556789					
12	8	->334457889999					
13	9	->00112222233344555999					
14	10	->001344446699					
15	11	->0124557889					

GENERAL COMMANDS

1. Type or import data into one column.
2. Click **Tools, Data Analysis Plus**, and **Stem and Leaf Display**.
3. Specify the **Input Range**.
4. Click one of the values of **Increment**. (The increment is the difference between stems.)
5. Click **Labels**, if appropriate. Click **OK**.

COMMANDS FOR EXAMPLE 2.1

Open file **Xm02-01**.

A1:A201

10

MINITAB

Stem-and-Leaf Display: Bills

```
Stem-and-leaf of Bills   N = 200
Leaf Unit = 1.0


    52   0 000000000111112222223333334555555666666677888889999999
    85   1 00000111123333333445555566788999 9
   (23)  2 000011111234466677899999
    92   3 001335589
    83   4 12445589
    75   5 33566
    70   6 3458
    66   7 022224556789
    54   8 334457889999
    42   9 00112222233344555999
    22  10 001344446699
    10  11 0124557889
```

The numbers in the left column are called **depths**. Each depth counts the number of observations that are on its line or beyond. For example, the second depth is 85, which means that there are 85 observations that are less than 20. The third depth is displayed in parentheses, which indicates that the third interval contains the observation that falls in the middle of all the observations, a statistic we call the *median* (to be presented in Chapter 4). For this interval the depth tells us the frequency of the interval. That is, there are 23 observations that are greater than or equal to 20 but less than 30. The fourth depth is 92, which tells us that there are 92 observations that are greater than or equal to 30. Notice that for classes below the median, the depth reports the number of observations that are less than the upper limit of that class. For classes that are above the median, the depth reports the number of observations that are greater than or equal to the lower limit of that class.   *(continued)*

	COMMANDS FOR
COMMANDS	EXAMPLE 2.1
1. Type or import the data into one column.	Open file **Xm02-01**.
2. Click **Graph**, **Character Graphs**, and **Stem-and-Leaf....**	
3. Type the name of the variable or use **Select**.	**Bills** or **C1**
4. Specify the value of the **increment**.	**10**
(Increment is the difference between the stems.)	

OGIVE

The frequency distribution lists the number of observations that fall into each class interval. We can also create a **relative frequency distribution** by dividing the frequencies by the number of observations. Table 2.3 displays the relative frequency distribution for Example 2.1.

Table 2.3 Relative Frequency Distribution for Example 2.1

Class Limits	Relative Frequency
0 to 15	71/200 = .355
15 to 30	37/200 = .185
30 to 45	13/200 = .065
45 to 60	9/200 = .045
60 to 75	10/200 = .050
75 to 90	18/200 = .090
90 to 105	28/200 = .140
105 to 120	14/200 = .070
Total	200/200 = 1.0

As you can see, the relative frequency distribution highlights the proportion of the observations that fall into each class. In some situations we may wish to highlight the proportion of observations that lie below each of the class limits. In such cases we create the **cumulative relative frequency distribution**. Table 2.4 displays this type of distribution for Example 2.1.

Table 2.4 Cumulative Relative Frequency Distribution for Example 2.1

Class Limits	Relative Frequency	Cumulative Relative Frequency
0 to 15	71/200 = .355	71/200 = .355
15 to 30	37/200 = .185	108/200 = .540
30 to 45	13/200 = .065	121/200 = .605
45 to 60	9/200 = .045	130/200 = .650
60 to 75	10/200 = .05	140/200 = .700
75 to 90	18/200 = .09	158/200 = .790
90 to 105	28/200 = .14	186/200 = .930
105 to 120	14/200 = .07	200/200 = 1.00

From Table 2.4, you can see that, for example, 54% of the bills were less than or equal to $30 and that 79% of the bills were less than or equal to $90.

Another way of presenting this information is the **ogive**, which is a graphical representation of the cumulative relative frequencies. Figure 2.8 (page 44) is the manually-drawn ogive for Example 2.1.

Figure 2.8
Ogive for Example 2.1

EXCEL

COMMANDS
Proceed through the first 7 steps to create a histogram.
   8. Click **Chart Output** and **Cumulative Percentage**.
   9. Remove the "More" category.
   10. Click on any of the rectangles and click Delete.
   11. Change the **Scale**, if necessary. (Make the **Maximum** value of **Y** equal to 1.0.)

MINITAB

COMMANDS
Proceed through the first 4 steps to create a histogram.
5. Use the cursor to specify **Cumulative Percent**.
6. Specify **Cutpoints** and type the cutpoints including 0 as the first value. Click **OK**.
7. Use the cursor to specify **Symbol** under **Display**. Click **OK**.
8. Use Tool Drawing to join the points.

We can use the ogive to estimate the cumulative relative frequencies of other values. For example, we estimate that about 62% of the bills lie below $50 and that about 48% lie below $25. See Figure 2.9.

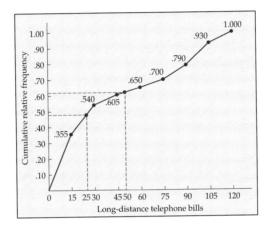

Figure 2.9
Ogive with estimated relative frequencies for Example 2.1

We're now in a position to address the question posed in the introduction to this chapter.

TICKET PROGRAM FOR THE BARNES EXHIBIT: SOLUTION

We drew the histogram displayed below. (We employed Excel; the manually-drawn histogram and Minitab's are similar to Excel's.)

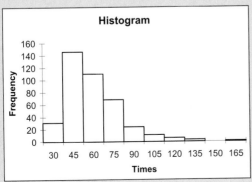

The histogram tells us that about 70% of gallery visitors stay for 60 minutes or less and most of the remainder leave within 120 minutes. Although there are other plans, the gallery director proposed the following plan. Admit 200 visitors every hour. We expect that about 140 will leave within 1 hour and about 60 will stay for an additional hour. During the next 1-hour period, 200 new visitors will be admitted. If 60 of the previous hour's admittances remain there will be a total of 260 people in the gallery. If this pattern persists during the day there will be a maximum of 260 visitors at any time. This plan should permit as many people as possible to see the exhibit and yet maintain comfort and safety.

We complete this section with a review of when to use a histogram, ogive, or stem-and-leaf display. Note that we use the term *objective* to identify the type of information produced by the statistical technique.

FACTORS THAT IDENTIFY WHEN TO USE A HISTOGRAM, OGIVE, OR STEM-AND-LEAF DISPLAY
1. **Objective:** Describe a set of data.
2. **Data type:** Interval

EXERCISES

2.11 How many classes should a histogram contain if the number of observations is 250?

2.12 Determine the number of classes of a histogram for 700 observations.

2.13 A data set consists of 125 observations that range between 37 and 188.
  a What is an appropriate number of classes to have in the histogram?
  b What class intervals would you suggest?

2.14 A statistics practitioner would like to draw a histogram of 62 observations that range from 5.2 to 6.1.
  a What is an appropriate number of class intervals?
  b Define the upper limits of the classes you would use.

2.15 The number of items rejected daily by a manufacturer because of defects was recorded for the past 30 days. The results are as follows. (The data are also stored in file Xr02-15.)
```
4  9  13  7   5   8  12  15  5  7   3   8  15  17  19
6  4  10  8  22  16   9   5  3  9  19  14  13  18   7
```
  a Construct a histogram.
  b Construct an ogive.
  c Describe the shape of the histogram.

2.16 The final exam in a third-year organizational behavior course requires students to write several essay-style answers. The numbers of pages for a sample of 25 exams were recorded. These data are shown below and stored in Xr02-16.
```
5   8  9  3  12  8  5   7  3   8  9  5  2
7  12  9  6   3  8  7  10  9  12  7  3
```
  a Draw a histogram.
  b Draw an ogive..
  c Describe what you've learned from the answers to parts **a** and **b**.

2.17 A large investment firm on Wall Street wants to review the distribution of ages of its stockbrokers. The firm believes that this information can be useful in developing plans to recruit new brokers. The ages of a sample of 40 brokers are shown here. The data are also stored in file Xr02-17.
```
46  28  51  34  29  40  38  33  41  52  53  40  50  33
36  41  25  38  37  41  36  50  46  33  61  48  32  28
30  49  41  37  26  39  35  39  46  26  31  35
```

  a Draw stem-and-leaf display.
  b Draw a histogram.
  c Draw an ogive.
  d Describe what you have learned.

2.18 The numbers of weekly sales calls by a sample of 30 telemarketers are listed below (and stored in file Xr02-18). Draw a histogram of these data and describe it.
```
14  8  6  12  21  4   9   3  25  17  9   5   8  18  16
 3  17  19  10  15  5  20  17  14  19  7  10  15  10   8
```

2.19 The amount of time (in seconds) needed to complete a critical task on an assembly line was measured for a sample of 50 assemblies. These data are stored in file Xr02-19 and listed below.

30.3	34.5	31.1	30.9	33.7
31.9	33.1	31.1	30.0	32.7
34.4	30.1	34.6	31.6	32.4
32.8	31.0	30.2	30.2	32.8
31.1	30.7	33.1	34.4	31.0
32.2	30.9	32.1	34.2	30.7
30.7	30.7	30.6	30.2	33.4
36.8	30.2	31.5	30.1	35.7
30.5	30.6	30.2	31.4	30.7
30.6	37.9	30.3	34.1	30.4

  a Draw a stem-and-leaf display.
  b Draw a histogram.
  c Describe the histogram.

2.20 A survey of individuals in a mall asked 60 people how many stores they will enter during this visit to the mall. The responses are stored in file Xr02-20 and are listed below.

3	2	4	3	3	9
2	4	3	6	2	2
8	7	6	4	5	1
5	2	3	1	1	7
3	4	1	1	4	8
0	2	5	4	4	4
6	2	2	5	3	8
4	3	1	6	9	1
4	4	1	0	4	6
5	5	5	1	4	3

  a Draw a histogram.
  b Draw an ogive.
  c Describe your findings.

2.21 A survey of 50 baseball fans asked each to report the number of games they attended last year. The results are listed below and stored in file Xr02-21. Use an appropriate graphical technique to present these data and describe what you have learned.

5	15	14	7	8
16	26	6	15	23
11	15	6	4	7
8	19	16	9	9
8	7	10	5	8
8	6	6	21	10
5	24	5	28	9
11	20	24	5	13
14	9	25	10	24
10	18	22	12	17

2.22 To help determine the need for more golf courses, a survey was undertaken. A sample of 75 self-declared golfers was asked how many rounds of golf they played last year. These data are stored in file Xr02-22 and listed below.

18	26	16	35	30
15	18	15	18	29
25	30	35	14	20
18	24	21	25	18
29	23	15	19	27
28	9	17	28	25
23	20	24	28	36
20	30	26	12	31
13	26	22	30	29
26	17	32	36	24
29	18	38	31	36
24	30	20	13	23
3	28	5	14	24
13	18	10	14	16
28	19	10	42	22

a Draw a histogram.
b Draw a stem-and-leaf display.
c Draw an ogive.
d Describe what you have learned.

The following exercises require a computer and statistical software.

2.23 The annual incomes for a sample of 200 first-year accountants were recorded and stored in file Xr02-23. Summarize these data using a graphical method. Describe your results.

2.24 The real estate board in a wealthy suburb of Los Angeles wanted to investigate the distribution of the prices (in $thousands) of homes sold during the past year. These data are stored in file Xr02-24.
a Draw a histogram.
b Draw an ogive.
c Draw a stem-and-leaf display.
d Describe what you have learned.

2.25 The number of customers entering a bank in the first hour of operation for each of the last 200 days was stored in file Xr02-25. Use a graphical technique to extract information. Describe your findings.

2.26 The lengths of time (in minutes) to serve 420 customers at a local restaurant are stored in file Xr02-26.
a How many class intervals should a histogram of these data contain?
b Draw a histogram using the number of classes specified in part **a**.
c Is the histogram symmetric or skewed?
d How many modes are there?
e Is the histogram bell shaped?

2.27 The marks of 320 students on an economics midterm test were recorded and stored in file Xr02-27. Use a graphical technique to summarize these data. What does the graph tell you?

2.28 The lengths (in inches) of 150 newborn babies were recorded and stored in file Xr02-28. Use whichever graphical technique you judge suitable to describe these data. What have you learned from the graph?

2.29 The number of copies made by an office copier was recorded for each of the past 75 days. The data are stored in file Xr02-29. Graph the data using a suitable technique. Describe what the graph tells you.

2.30 Each of a sample of 240 tomatoes grown with a new type of fertilizer was weighed (in ounces) and the data stored in file Xr02-30. Draw a histogram and describe your findings.

2.31 The volume of water used by each of a sample of 350 households was measured (in gallons) and stored in file Xr02-31. Use a suitable graphical statistical method to summarize the data. What does the graph tell you?

2.32 The number of books shipped out daily by Amazon.com was recorded for 100 days and stored in file Xr02-32. Draw a histogram and describe your findings.

APPLICATIONS IN FINANCE: *CREDIT SCORECARDS*

Credit scorecards are used by financial institutions to determine whether applicants will receive loans. The score-card is the product of a statistical technique that converts questions about income, residence, and other variables into a score. The higher the score, the higher the probability is that the applicant will repay. The scorecard is a formula produced by a statistical technique called logistic regression, which will not be presented in this book. (It is somewhat more advanced than the level of this book.) For example, a scorecard may score age categories in the following way:

Less than 25	20 points
25 to 39	24
40 to 55	30
Over 55	38

Other variables would be scored similarly. The sum for all variables would be the applicant's score. A cutoff score would be used to predict those who will repay and those who will default. Because no scorecard is perfect, it is possible to make two types of error: granting credit to those who will default and not lending money to those who would have repaid.

2.33 A small bank that heretofore did not use a scorecard wanted to determine whether a scorecard would be advantageous. The bank manager took a random sample of 300 loans that were granted and scored each on a scorecard borrowed from a similar bank. This scorecard is based on the responses supplied by the applicants to questions such as age, marital status, and household income. The cutoff is 650, which means that those scoring below are predicted to default and those scoring above are predicted to repay. Two hundred twenty of the loans were repaid; the remainder were not. The scores of those who repaid and the scores of those who defaulted are stored in columns 1 and 2, respectively, in file Xr02-33.

  a Use a graphical technique to present the scores of those who repaid.

  b Use a graphical technique to present the scores of those who defaulted.

  c What have you learned about the scorecard?

2.34 Refer to Exercise 2.33. The bank decided to try another scorecard, this one based not on the responses of the applicants, but on credit bureau reports, which list problems such as late payments and previous defaults. The scores using the new scorecard of those who repaid were stored in column 1 and the scores of those who did not repay are stored in column 2 in file Xr02-34. The cutoff score is 650.

  a Use a graphical technique to present the scores of those who repaid.

  b Use a graphical technique to present the scores of those who defaulted.

  c What have you learned about the scorecard?

  d Compare the results of this exercise with those of Exercise 2.33. Which scorecard appears to be better?

2.4 GRAPHICAL TECHNIQUES FOR NOMINAL DATA

As we discussed in Section 2.2, the only allowable calculation on nominal data is to count the frequency of each value of the variable. We can graphically display the counts in two ways: bar charts and pie charts. A **bar chart** is similar to a histogram. The bases of the rectangles are arbitrary intervals whose centers are the codes. The height of each rectangle represents the frequency of that category. A **pie chart** is a circle subdivided into slices whose areas are proportional to the frequencies. Pie charts emphasize the *proportion* of occurrences of each category. Bar charts focus the attention on the *frequency* of the occurrences of the categories. To illustrate the use of both, consider the following example.

EXAMPLE 2.4

The student placement office at a university conducted a survey of last year's business school graduates to determine the general areas in which the graduates found jobs. The placement office intended to use the resulting information to help decide where to concentrate its efforts in attracting companies to campus to conduct job interviews. Each graduate was asked in which area he or she found a job. The areas of employment are:

1. Accounting

2. Finance

3. General management

4. Marketing/Sales

5. Other

The data are stored in file Xm02-04 using the codes 1, 2, 3, 4, and 5, respectively. Summarize the data by producing an appropriate chart.

SOLUTION   The objective is to describe one set of nominal data. The data are nominal because the values of the variable, area of employment, are the five categories. The numbers (1, 2, 3, 4, and 5) used to record the responses of the university's graduates were assigned completely arbitrarily. The only legitimate statistical technique is to count the number of occurrences of each value and either use these counts in a numerical procedure (as you'll see in the rest of this book) or graphically represent these counts. The results are shown in Table 2.5.

Table 2.5 Frequencies of Categories in Example 2.4

Area	Number of Graduates	Proportion of Graduates
Accounting	73	28.9%
Finance	52	20.6
General management	36	14.2
Marketing/Sales	64	25.3
Other	28	11.1
Total	253	100

There are two graphical techniques that we can use. The first, the bar chart, shows the frequency of each area. The second technique, the pie chart, exhibits the proportion of each area.

The bar chart is created by drawing a rectangle representing each category. The height of the rectangle represents the frequency. The base is arbitrary. Figure 2.10 depicts the manually-drawn bar chart for Example 2.4.

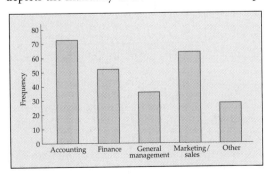

**Figure 2.10
Bar chart for Example 2.4**

EXCEL

If you have the raw data (as in file Xm02-04) follow these instructions.

COMMANDS

Proceed through the first eight steps in constructing a histogram. Use the codes representing the categories as the upper limits of the bins. The result is a bar chart.

If you or someone else has determined the frequency with which each value occurs, follow the instructions below.

1. Type or import the frequencies into a column.
2. Highlight the frequencies, click the **Chart Wizard**, and select **Column**. Click **Finish**.
3. If you wish, you can type an adjacent column with the name of the category. Highlight both columns, click the **Chart Wizard**, and select **Column**. Click **Finish**.

MINITAB

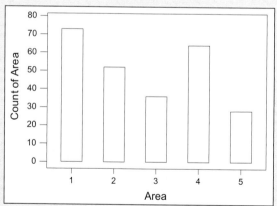

If you have the raw data (as in file Xm02-04) follow these instructions.

COMMANDS

1. Import or type the data into one column.
2. Click **Graph** and **Chart....**
3. Specify **Count** under **Function**.
4. Specify the name of the variable under both **Y** and **X**. **Area** or **C1**
5. Specify **Bar** under **Display**. Click **OK**.

COMAMNDS FOR EXAMPLE 2.4

Open file **Xm02-04**.

(continued)

If you or someone else has determined the frequency with which each value occurs, follow the instructions below.

1. Import or type the numbers into two columns. Column 1 contains the codes and column 2 contains the frequencies.
2. Click **Graph** and **Chart...**.
3. Specify **Sum** under **Function**.
4. Specify the name of the variable containing the frequencies under **Y** and the name of the variable containing the codes under **X**. You can use the names of the categories instead of the codes.
5. Specify **Bar** under **Display**. Click **OK**.

If we wish to emphasize the relative frequencies instead of drawing the bar chart, we draw the pie chart. A pie chart is simply a circle subdivided into slices that represent the categories. It is drawn so that the size of each slice is proportional to the percentage corresponding to that category. For example, since the entire circle is composed of 360 degrees, a category that contains 25% of the observations is represented by a slice of the pie that contains 25% of 360 degrees, which is equal to 90 degrees. The number of degrees for each category in Example 2.4 is shown in Table 2.6.

Figure 2.11
Pie chart for Example 2.4

Table 2.6 Proportion in Each Category in Example 2.4

Area	Proportion of Graduates	Slice of the Pie
Accounting	28.9%	104.0°
Finance	20.6	74.2
General management	14.2	51.1
Marketing/sales	25.3	91.1
Other	11.1	40.0
Total	100	360

Figure 2.11 was drawn from these results.

EXCEL

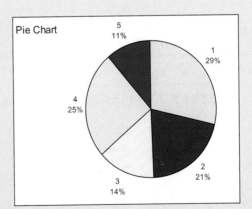

COMMANDS
1. Draw a bar chart
2. Click inside the boundaries of the bar chart and click **Chart**, **Chart Type...** and **Pie**.

MINITAB

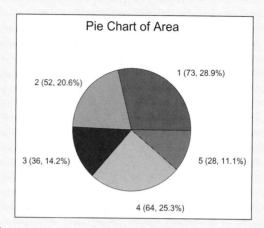

From raw data:

COMMANDS

1. Type or import the data into one column.
2. Click **Graph** and **Pie Chart...**.
3. Click **Chart data in**, and specify the name of the variable. Click **OK**.

From frequencies:

1. Type or import the data into two columns. Column 1 contains the codes and column 2 contains the frequencies.
2. Click **Graph** and **Pie Chart...**.
3. Click **Chart table**. Specify the name of the variable containing the codes (**Categories in**) and the name of the variable containing the frequencies (**Frequencies in**). Click **OK**.

COMMANDS FOR EXAMPLE 2.4

Open file **Xm02-04**.

Area or **C1**

INTERPRET

The bar chart focuses on the frequencies. As you can see, accounting is the most popular job; 73 graduates work in this area. Least popular is the "other" category. The pie chart focuses on the fraction of the total in each area. We can see, for example, that 29% of the graduates found jobs as accountants.

OTHER APPLICATIONS OF PIE CHARTS AND BAR CHARTS

Pie and bar charts are used widely in newspapers, magazines, and business and government reports. One of the reasons for this appeal is that they are eye-catching and can attract the reader's interest, whereas a table of numbers might not. Perhaps no one understands this better than the newspaper *USA Today*, which typically has a colored graph on the front page and others inside. Pie and bar charts are frequently used to simply present numbers associated with categories. The only reason to use a bar or pie chart in such a situation would be to enhance the reader's ability to grasp the substance of the data. It might, for example, allow the reader to more quickly recognize the relative sizes of the categories, as in the breakdown of a budget. Similarly, treasurers might use pie charts to show the breakdown of a firm's revenues by department, or university students might use pie charts to show the amount of time devoted to daily activities (e.g., eat, 10%; sleep, 30%; and study statistics, 60%).

EXAMPLE 2.5

Table 2.7 lists the daily oil production in millions of barrels for 10 countries around the world. Figure 2.12 depicts the same numbers using a bar chart. Notice that the chart merely shows the same numbers as the table but perhaps in a way that is more likely to attract readers.

Table 2.7 Daily Oil Production

Country	Oil Production (millions of barrels)
United States	8.1
Canada	2.3
Mexico	2.9
Venezuela	3.2
United Kingdom	2.9
Norway	3.3
Russia	5.8
China	3.2
Iran	3.7
Saudi Arabia	7.5

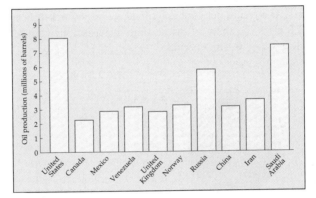

**Figure 2.12
Bar chart of daily oil production (millions of barrels)**

 EXCEL

COMMANDS
Follow the instructions to create a bar chart from frequencies.

MINITAB

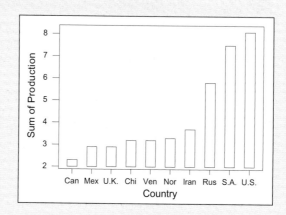

COMMANDS

Follow the instructions to create a bar chart from frequencies.

EXAMPLE 2.6

The revenues of television networks depend on the number (as well as the type) of viewers. As a result, network executives are very much concerned with these numbers. Table 2.8 gives the share of prime-time television viewing received by major U.S. networks over a specific time period.

Table 2.9 Percent Share of Television Viewers

Network	Share
ABC	20%
CBS	23%
Fox	11%
NBC	18%
Other	28%
Total	100%

Figure 2.13
Pie chart for Example 2.6

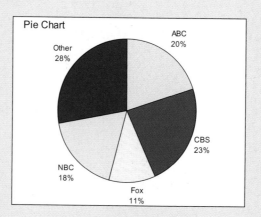 *EXCEL*

COMMANDS

Follow the instructions to create a pie chart from frequencies.

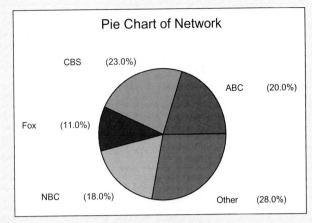

MINITAB

COMMANDS

Follow the instructions to create a pie chart from frequencies.

It should be understood that in these applications of bar and pie charts, we're simply graphing statistics already calculated, whereas in Example 2.4 we graphed *data*. The statistics may represent some interval variable such as number of barrels of oil produced daily or proportions of viewers watching the networks. We presented Examples 2.5 and 2.6 to demonstrate how bar and pie charts are often used.

We complete this section by describing when bar and pie charts are used to summarize and present data.

FACTORS THAT IDENTIFY WHEN TO USE BAR AND PIE CHARTS
1. **Objective:** Describe a set of data.
2. **Data type:** Nominal

EXERCISES

2.35 In a taste test, 220 people were asked to taste five different brands of beer and to report which one they preferred. The results are listed below.

Brand	Frequency
A	34
B	61
C	40
D	31
E	54

a Draw a bar chart.
b Draw a pie chart.
c What do the charts tell you about the sample of beer drinkers?

2.36 The vocational center at a university wanted to determine the types of jobs the graduates of the university were performing. A sample of the graduates of the university was surveyed 5 years after graduation and asked to report their occupations. The responses and their frequencies are listed here. Summarize the data with an appropriate graphical method.

Job Category	Frequency
1 Unemployed	12
2 Manager	81
3 Blue-collar worker	27
4 Clerical worker	90
5 Other	49

2.37 What are the most important characteristics of colleges and universities? This question was asked of a sample of college-bound high school seniors. The responses and the frequencies of each answer are listed below. Use a graphical technique to summarize and present the data.

Characteristic	Frequency
1 Location	59
2 Majors	33
3 Academic reputation	15
4 Career focus	25
5 Community	8
6 Number of students	12

2.38 Where do consumers get information about cars? A sample of recent car buyers was asked to identify the most useful source of information about the cars they purchased. The responses and their frequencies are listed below. Graphically depict the responses.

Source	Frequency
1 Consumer guide	172
2 Dealership	93
3 Word of mouth	40
4 Internet	26

Source: *Automotive Retailing Today*, The Gallup Organization

2.39 In 1999, 319,000 laptop computers were reported stolen. That figure rose to 387,000 in 2000. Aside from the cost of replacement (usually covered by insurance), companies may also lose corporate secrets and other sensitive information. To learn more about the problem, *TechRepublic* conducted a survey of 769 employees in corporate technology departments. The following questions were asked. The percentages of responses are also listed. Use graphical techniques to present the results of the survey.

1 Has a company laptop ever been stolen or disappeared?
    1 Yes   (64%)   2 No   (36%)

2 Was it recovered (asked of those who responded yes in Question 1)
    1 Yes   (12%)   2 No   (88%)

3 Do you use encryption to protect data on your laptop?
    1 Yes   (13%)   2 No   (87%)

2.40 After a long and distinguished career, a racehorse retired. His finishes were recorded and listed below. Use a graphical technique to summarize the data and interpret your findings.

Finish	Frequency
First	11
Second	24
Third	35
Fourth	28
Fifth	20
Sixth	6
Seventh	5
Eighth	3

2.41 A breakdown of Hewlett-Packard's sales (in $millions) for a recent 6-month period is as follows. Use a pie chart to describe the breakdown of Hewlett-Packard's sales.

Products	Sales
Computers and printers	7,401
Test and measurement equipment	1,135
Medical equipment	553
Analytical instruments	349
Electronic components	262

Source: Company reports.

2.42 Retirement savings plans [401(k)s in the United States and RRSPs in Canada] are very popular because they are used to defer income tax. A survey conducted by the Caledon Institute of Social Policy determined the percentage of different income groups that used retirement savings plans as a tax deduction last year. These figures are listed below.

Income Group	Percentage Invested in Savings Plan
Less than $10,000	3%
10,000–19,999	13
20,000–29,999	28
30,000–39,999	40
40,000–49,999	49
50,000–79,999	51
80,000–99,999	57
100,000–250,000	63
Over 250,000	68

a Which chart is better for these figures, a bar or pie chart?

b Use the chart you specified in part **a** to present the figures.

2.43 The numbers of immigrants (in thousands) to the United States from five continents during 1997 are listed below.

Continent	Number of Immigrants
Europe	119.9
Asia	265.8
North America (including Central America)	307.5
South America	52.9
Africa	47.8

Source: *Statistical Abstract of the United States*, 1999, Table 8.

a Use a bar chart to graph these numbers.
b Use a pie chart to graph these numbers.

2.44 The numbers (in thousands) of private firms that offer health insurance for their employees were categorized by the size of the firm. These figures are shown below. Use one or more graphical techniques to present these figures.

Number of Employees	Frequency	Percentage of All Firms
Fewer than 10 employees	1,311	33.2%
10 to 24 employees	583	67.1
25 to 99 employees	493	83.0
100 to 499 employees	295	93.9
500 to 999 employees	90	96.8
1,000 or more employees	473	97.7

Source: *Statistical Abstract of the United States*, 1999, Table 187.

2.45 There are a variety of consumer products that have hidden taxes. The following table lists the components of the costs of a liter of gasoline in Canada. Draw a graph to depict these numbers.

Crude oil costs (including royalties and taxes paid to various governments)	32.2 cents
Oil company costs (including refining, distribution, and administration)	7.4 cents
Dealer margin	5.2 cents
Provincial fuel taxes and federal taxes and charges	30.9 cents
Total	75.7 cents

Source: Canadian Petroleum Products Institute.

2.46 Another illustration of hidden taxes in Canada is liquor. In Canada, liquor is sold only in stores owned and operated by the provincial government. The component costs of a bottle of liquor are listed below. Draw a graph that exhibits these numbers.

Distiller's selling price (includes corporate, municipal, and employee taxes)	$3.85
Provincial markup in provincial government store	10.27
Provincial sales tax	2.09
Federal GST (goods and sales tax—7%)	1.22
Federal excise duty	3.32
Total	$20.75

Source: Association of Canadian Distillers.

2.47 In 1992 there were 5,888,883 women-owned firms in the United States. Each was categorized by industry group. The following table lists the number of women-owned firms in each industry group.

Industry	Frequency
Agriculture	82,526
Mining	37,205
Construction	183,695
Manufacturing	152,346
Transportation & public utilities	141,623
Wholesale trade	154,542
Retail trade	1,093,342
Finance, insurance, and real estate	602,802
Services	3,158,444
Other	282,358

Source: Statistical Abstract of the United States, 1999, Table 882.

a Draw a bar chart.
b Draw a pie chart.
c What information is conveyed by each chart?

The following exercises require a computer and software.

2.48 Subway train riders frequently pass the time by reading a newspaper. Toronto has a subway and four newspapers. A sample of 360 subway riders who regularly read a newspaper was asked to identify that newspaper. The responses are:
1. *Globe and Mail*
2. *National Post*
3. *Toronto Star*
4. *Toronto Sun*

The responses are stored in file Xr02-48. Draw an appropriate graph to summarize the data. What does the graph tell you?

2.49 Who applies to MBA programs? To help determine the background of the applicants, a sample of 200 applicants to the university's business school was asked to report their undergraduate degree. The degrees were recorded using the codes below.

1. BA   3. BBA
2. BSc   4. Other

The codes are stored in file Xr02-49.
a Draw a bar chart.
b Draw a pie chart.
c What do the charts tell you about the sample of MBA applicants?

2.50 Each day a restaurant lists on its menu five daily specials. Today's specials are:
1. Fried chicken
2. Meat loaf
3. Turkey pot pie
4. Fillet of sole
5. Lasagna

A sample of customers' choices is stored in file Xr02-50 (using the numerical codes). Draw a graph that describes the most important aspect of these data.

2.51 Most universities have several different kinds of residences on campus. To help long-term planning, one university surveyed a sample of graduate students and asked them to report their marital status. The possible responses are:
1. Single
2. Married
3. Divorced
4. Widowed

The responses for a sample of 250 students are stored in file Xr02-51 (using the numerical codes). Draw a graph that summarizes the information that you deem necessary.

2.52 An increasing number of business and economics courses require the use of a computer. As a result, many students buy their own. A survey asks students to identify which computer brand they have purchased. The responses are:
1. IBM
2. Compaq
3. Dell
4. Other

The results are stored in file Xr02-52.
a Draw a bar chart.
b Draw a pie chart.
c What do the charts tell you about the brands of computers used by the students?

2.53 An increasing number of statistics courses use a computer and software rather than manual calculations. A survey of statistics instructors asked each to report the software his or her course uses. The responses are:

1. Excel
2. Minitab
3. SAS
4. SPSS
5. Other

The results are stored in file Xr02-53.
a Draw a bar chart.
b Draw a pie chart.
c What do the charts tell you about the software choices?

2.54 Opinions about the economy are important measures because they can become self-fulfilling prophecies. Annual surveys are conducted to determine the level of confidence in the future prospects of the economy. A sample of 1,000 adults was asked, Compared with last year, do you think this coming year will be:
1. better?
2. the same?
3. worse?

The responses are stored in file Xr02-54. Use a suitable graphical technique to summarize these data. Describe what you have learned.

2.5 DESCRIBING THE RELATIONSHIP BETWEEN TWO VARIABLES

In Sections 2.3 and 2.4 we presented graphical techniques used to summarize single sets of data; techniques applied to single data sets are called **univariate**. There are many situations where we wish to graphically depict the relationship between variables; in such cases **bivariate** methods are required. The technique used to describe the relationship between two interval variables is the **scatter diagram**. A variation of the bar chart introduced in Section 2.4 is employed to describe the relationship between two nominal variables.

GRAPHING THE RELATIONSHIP BETWEEN TWO INTERVAL VARIABLES

Statistics practitioners frequently need to know how two interval variables are related. For example, financial analysts need to understand how the returns of individual stocks and the returns of the entire market are related. Marketing managers need to understand the relationship between sales and advertising. Economists develop statistical techniques to describe the relationship between such variables as unemployment rates and inflation.

To draw a scatter diagram we need data for two variables. In applications where one variable depends to some degree on the other variable, we label the *dependent variable* Y and the other, called the *independent variable, X*. For example, individuals' incomes depend somewhat on the number of years of education. Accordingly, we identify income as the dependent variable and label it Y, and we identify years of education as the independent variable and label it X. In other cases where there is no dependency evident, we label the variables arbitrarily.

EXAMPLE 2.7

A real estate agent wanted to know to what extent the selling price of a home is related to its size. To acquire this information he took a sample of 12 homes that had recently sold, recording the price in thousands of dollars and the size in hundreds of square feet. These data are listed in the table and are stored in file Xm02-07. Use a graphical technique to describe the relationship between size and price.

Size	Price ($000s)
23	315
18	229
26	355
20	261
22	234
14	216
33	308
28	306
23	289
20	204
27	265
18	195

SOLUTION   Using the guideline just stated, we label the price of the house Y (dependent variable) and the size X (independent variable). Figure 2.14 depicts the scatter diagram.

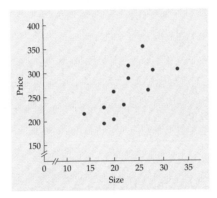

Figure 2.14
Scatter diagram for
Example 2.7

 EXCEL

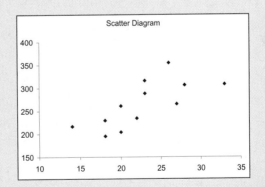

COMMANDS

1. Type or import the data into two adjacent columns. Store variable X in the first column and variable Y in the next column.
2. Click the **Chart Wizard** icon, select **XY (Scatter)** from chart type, click on the first **Chart sub-type,** and click **Next>**.
3. Click **Data Range** (if necessary) and type the input range in the **Data range** box. Click **Next>**.
4. If you wish to label the chart and axes, click **Titles** (if necessary) and fill in the boxes.

COMMANDS FOR
EXAMPLE 2.7
Open file **Xm02-07**.

A1:B13

(continued)

5. Click **Gridlines** and remove the check mark, to eliminate the horizontal lines that automatically appear. Click **Finish**.
6. If you wish to change the scale, double-click the *y*-axis, click **Scale**, and remove the check mark under **Auto** and change the **Minimum**, **Maximum**, and/or **Major** and **Minor Units**. Repeat for the *x*-axis.
7. To draw a straight line through the points, click **Chart** and **Add Trendline**. Specify **Linear** and click **OK**.

MINITAB

COMMANDS	COMMANDS FOR EXAMPLE 2.7
1. Type or import the data into two columns.	Open file **Xm02-07**.
2. Click **Graph** and **Plot...**.	
3. Type the name of the variable to appear on the *y*-axis.	**Price** or **C2**
4. Type the name of the variable to appear on the *x*-axis.	**Size** or **C1**
5. Click **OK**.	

INTERPRET

The scatter diagram reveals that, in general, the greater the size of the house, the greater the price. However, there are other variables that determine price. Further analysis may reveal what these other variables are.

PATTERNS OF SCATTER DIAGRAMS

As was the case with histograms, we frequently need to describe verbally how two variables are related. The two most important characteristics are the strength and direction of the linear relationship.

Linearity

To determine the strength of the linear relationship, we draw a straight line through the points in such a way that the line represents the relationship. If most of the points fall close to the line we say that there is a **linear relationship**. If most of the points appear to be scattered randomly with only a semblance of a straight line, there is no—or at best, a weak—linear relationship. Figure 2.15 depicts several scatter diagrams that exhibit various levels of linearity.

In drawing the line freehand, we would attempt to draw it so that it passes through the middle of the data. Unfortunately, different people drawing a straight line through the same set of data will produce somewhat different lines. Fortunately, statisticians have produced an objective way to draw the straight line. The method is called the *least squares method*, and it will be presented in Chapter 4 and employed in Chapters 18, 19, and 20.

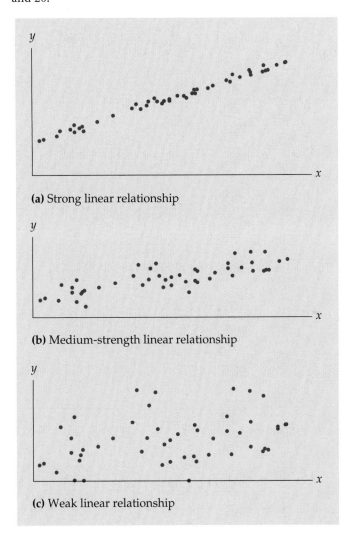

(a) Strong linear relationship

(b) Medium-strength linear relationship

(c) Weak linear relationship

Figure 2.15
Scatter diagrams describing linearity

Note that there may well be some other type of relationship, such as a quadratic or exponential one.

Direction

If, in general, when one variable increases, so does the other, we say that there is a **positive linear relationship**. When the two variables tend to move in opposite directions, we describe the nature of their association as a **negative linear relationship**. (The terms *positive* and *negative* will be explained in Chapter 4.) See Figure 2.16 for examples of scatter diagrams depicting a positive linear relationship, a negative linear relationship, no relationship, and a nonlinear relationship.

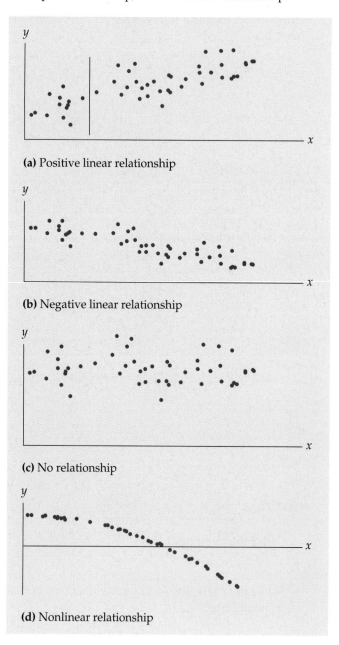

(a) Positive linear relationship

(b) Negative linear relationship

(c) No relationship

(d) Nonlinear relationship

**Figure 2.16
Scatter diagrams
describing direction**

GRAPHING THE RELATIONSHIP BETWEEN TWO NOMINAL VARIABLES

To graphically describe the relationship between two nominal variables, we must remember that we are permitted only to determine the frequency of the values.

As a first step we need to produce a **contingency table** (also called a **cross-classification table** or **cross-tabulation table**), which lists the frequency of each combination of the values of the two variables. For example, to describe the relationship between undergraduate degree and occupation, we ask university and college graduates to report both variables. We would then count the number of people for every combination of the two nominal variables. The result would be a contingency table.

To graphically represent the relationship we could draw a bar chart for each value of one variable. For example, we could draw a bar chart of the occupations for each BA graduate and do similarly for the other undergraduate degrees.

If the two variables are unrelated, the patterns exhibited in the bar charts should be approximately the same. If some relationship exists, then some bar charts would differ from others.

EXAMPLE 2.8

In a major North American city there are four competing newspapers. They are the *Globe and Mail, Post, Star,* and *Sun.* To help design advertising campaigns, the advertising managers of the newspapers need to know which segments of the newspaper market are reading their papers. A survey was conducted to analyze the relationship between newspaper read and occupation. A sample of newspaper readers was asked to report which newspaper they read and to indicate whether they were blue-collar worker, white-collar worker, or professional. The following table, which is stored in Xm02-08, was created. Use a graphical technique to describe whether occupational class and newspaper read are related.

	Blue	White	Prof.
G&M	27	29	33
Post	18	43	51
Star	38	15	24
Sun	37	21	18

SOLUTION To determine whether there is a relationship between the two variables, we draw bar charts. We have chosen to draw three, one for each occupation group. (We could have chosen instead to draw four bar charts, one for each newspaper.)

EXCEL

COMMANDS

Highlight a column (or row) of numbers, click the **Chart Wizard**, and follow the instructions on page 50 to create a bar chart. Repeat the process for the remaining columns.

MINITAB

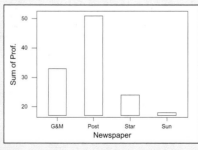

COMMANDS

Type the cross-classification table. For each column use the instructions on page 50 to create a bar chart. Repeat for the remaining columns.

Excel can draw other graphs to solve this problem.

EXCEL

COMMANDS

Highlight the entire table (including labels). Click **Column** and the first **Chart sub-type**. Alternatively, click the last **Chart sub-type**.

INTERPRET

We can see from the graphs that the patterns differ among bar graphs. Among blue-collar workers, the most commonly read newspaper is the *Star,* followed by the *Sun.* The other two papers lag behind. However, among both white-collar and professional workers, the preferred newspapers are the *Post* and the *Globe and Mail.*

Raw Data

In most circumstances we have only the data and not the contingency table. In such cases we need to create the contingency table before we apply a graphical technique. To illustrate, we created file Xm02-08a, which contains two columns. Column A lists the responses of the choice of newspaper, where 1 = *Globe and Mail,* 2 = *Post,* 3 = *Star,* and 4 = *Sun.* Column B stores the codes for the occupations, where 1 = blue-collar, 2 = white-collar, and 3 = professional.

EXCEL

	A	B	C	D	E	F
1	**Contingency Table**					
2						
3		*Newspaper*				
4	*Occupation*		1	2	3	TOTAL
5		1	27	29	33	89
6		2	18	43	51	112
7		3	38	15	24	77
8		4	37	21	18	76
9		TOTAL	120	108	126	354

COMMANDS

1. Type or import the data into two adjacent columns.
2. Click **Tools, Data Analysis Plus**, and **Contingency Table (Raw Data)**.
3. Specify the **Input Range** and click **Labels**, if appropriate. Click **OK**.

Note that part of the Excel output was deleted. It will be discussed in Chapter 16.

MINITAB

Tabulated Statistics: Newspaper, Occupation

```
   Rows: Newspaper     Columns: Occupation

                 1         2         3       All

    1           27        29        33        89
    2           18        43        51       112
    3           38        15        24        77
    4           37        21        18        76
   All         120       108       126       354

   Cell Contents --
                      Count
```

COMMANDS

1. Type or import the data into two columns.
2. Click **Stat, Tables,** and **Cross Tabulation**.
3. Specify the names of the **Classification Variables**, click **Counts**, and click **OK**.

From this contingency table (do not include the labels or the row and column totals) we can draw the graph we want.

We close this section by reviewing the factors that identify the use of the scatter diagram and the contingency table.

FACTORS THAT IDENTIFY WHEN TO USE A SCATTER DIAGRAM
1. **Objective:** Describe the relationship between two variables.
2. **Data type:** Interval

FACTORS THAT IDENTIFY WHEN TO USE A BAR CHART OF A CONTINGENCY TABLE
1. **Objective:** Describe the relationship between two variables.
2. **Data type:** Nominal

EXERCISES

2.55 To determine how the number of housing starts is affected by mortgage rates, an economist recorded the average mortgage rate and the number of housing starts in a large county for the past 10 years. These data are listed below and stored in file Xr02-55. Use a suitable graphical technique to describe the relationship between the two variables.

Rate 8.5 7.8 7.6 7.5 8.0 8.4 8.8 8.9 8.5 8.0
Starts 115 111 185 201 206 167 155 117 133 150

2.56 How are gender and choice of doctorate related? To answer this question, the doctoral graduates in the United States in 1998 were categorized by gender and by topic as listed in the accompanying table. Use a graphical technique to describe the relationship between gender and doctorate.

| | Gender | |
Doctorate	Male	Female
Engineering	5,150	769
Physical sciences	2,927	874
Earth sciences	612	226
Mathematics	883	294
Computer sciences	766	157
Biological sciences	3,722	2,924
Agriculture	858	334
Social sciences	2,002	1,392
Psychology	1,215	2,466

Source: Statistical Abstract of the United States, 2000, Table 997.

2.57 In an attempt to determine how race and gender affect company ownership among American minorities, the table below was constructed. Use a graphical technique to learn how race and gender affect ownership.

	Gender	
Race	Men	Women
Black	343,666	277,246
Hispanic	525,330	246,378
Asian, American Indian, and Alaska native	397,779	208,647

Source: *Statistical Abstract of the United States,* 1999, Table 883.

2.58 In a university where calculus is a prerequisite for the statistics course, a sample of 15 students was drawn. The marks for calculus and statistics were recorded for each student. The data are listed below.

Calculus 65 58 93 68 74 81 58 85
Statistics 74 72 84 71 68 85 63 73

Calculus 88 75 63 79 80 54 72
Statistics 79 65 62 71 74 68 73

a Draw a scatter diagram of the data.

b What does the graph tell you about the relationship between the marks in calculus and statistics?

2.59 The cost of repairing cars involved in accidents is one reason that insurance premiums are so high. In an experiment, 10 cars were driven into a wall. The speeds were varied between 2 and 20 mph. The costs of repair were estimated and are listed here. Draw an appropriate graph to analyze the relationship between the two variables. What does the graph tell you?

Speed   2   4   6   8   10
Cost of repair ($)   88 124 358 519 699

Speed   12   14   16   18   20
Cost of repair ($) 816 905 1,521 1,888 2,201

2.60 An economist wanted to determine how marital status differs between men and women in their twenties. The following table lists the relevant figures (in thousands). Use a graphical technique to describe whether gender and marital status are related in twenty-something Americans.

	Gender	
Marital Status	Male	Female
Never married	11,355	10,275
Married	5,385	7,594
Widowed	4	36
Divorced	494	698

Source: *Statistical Abstract of the United States,* 2000, Table 55.

2.61 Because inflation reduces the purchasing power of the dollar, investors seek investments that will provide higher returns when inflation is higher. It is frequently stated that common stocks provide just such a hedge against inflation. The annual percentage rates of return on common stock and annual inflation rates for a recent 10-year period are listed here.

Common Stock Return (%)	Inflation Rate (%)
25.07	4.38
8.95	4.19
5.88	4.12
11.08	3.96
21.37	5.17
−14.80	5.00
12.02	3.78
−1.43	2.14
32.55	1.70
−.18	.23

a Use a graphical technique to depict the relationship between the two variables.

b Does it appear that common stocks provide a good hedge against inflation?

The following exercises require a computer and software.

2.62 Are the marks one receives in a course related to the amount of time spent studying the subject? To analyze this mysterious possibility, a student took a random sample of 60 students who had enrolled in an accounting class last semester. She asked each to report his or her mark in the course and the total number of hours spent studying accounting. These data are stored in file Xr02-62.

a Use an appropriate graphical technique to depict the data.

b What have you learned from the graph?

2.63 The cost of smoking for individuals, companies for whom they work, and society in general is in the many billions of dollars. In an effort to reduce smoking, information campaigns about the dangers of smoking have been undertaken by various government and nongovernment organizations. Most of these have been directed at young people. This raises the question: "Are you more likely to smoke if your parents smoke?" To shed light on the issue, a sample of 20-to-40-year-old people was asked whether they smoked and whether their parents smoked. The results are stored in file Xr02-63 in the following way:

Column 1: 1 = do not smoke, 2 = smoke

Column 2: 1 = neither parent smoked,
            2 = father smoked, 3 = mother smoked,
            4 = both parents smoked

Use a graphical technique to produce the information you need.

2.64 In Chapters 17 and 18 we introduce regression analysis, which addresses the relationships between variables. One of the first applications of regression analysis was to analyze the relationship between the heights of fathers and sons. Suppose that a sample of 80 fathers and sons was drawn. The heights of the fathers and of the adult sons were measured and stored in file Xr02-64.

a Draw a scatter diagram of the data. Draw a straight line that describes the relationship.

b What is the direction of the line?

c Does it appear that there is a linear relationship between the two variables?

2.65 Most MBA students choose one of a number of areas to major in. The program coordinator wanted to know whether the undergraduate degree and choice of MBA major were related. She sampled 152 students and asked them to report their major and undergraduate degree. The data are stored in file Xr02-65 as follows:

Column 1:   1 = BA, 2 = BEng, 3 = BBA, 4 = other

Column 2:   1 = Accounting/Finance, 2 = Marketing, 3 = other

Use a graphical technique to determine whether the two appear to be related.

2.66 An increasing number of high school students hold down part-time jobs. How does this affect their performance in school? To help answer this question, a sample of 300 high school students who have part-time jobs was taken. Each student reported his or her most recent average mark and the number of hours per week at his or her job. These data are stored in file Xr02-66.

a Draw a scatter diagram of the data including a straight line.

b Does it appear that there is a linear relationship between the two variables?

2.67 Who uses the Internet? To help answer this question, a random sample of 300 adults was asked to report their age and the number of hours of Internet use weekly. These data are stored in file XR02-67.

a Employ a suitable graph to depict the data.

b Does it appear that there is a linear relationship between the two variables? If so, describe it.

2.68 Is there brand loyalty among car owners in their purchases of gasoline? To help answer the question a random sample of car owners was asked to record the brand of gasoline in their last two purchases. The data are stored in columns A (second-last purchase) and B (last purchase) in file Xr02-68, where

1 = Exxon
2 = Amoco
3 = Texaco
4 = Other

Use a graphical technique to formulate your answer.

2.69 Critics of television often refer to the detrimental effects that all the violence shown has on children. However, there may be another problem. It may be that watching television also reduces the amount of physical exercise, causing weight gains. A sample of 225 10-year-old children was taken. The number of pounds each child was overweight was recorded (a negative number indicates the child is underweight). Additionally, the number of hours of television viewing per week was also recorded. Both variables are stored in file Xr02-69.

a Draw a scatter diagram with a straight line.

b What is the direction of the line?

c What does the scatter diagram tell you?

2.70 A professor of management believes that the heights of male executives affect their incomes. He takes a random sample of 90 35-to-40-year-old male executives and records their heights in inches and their annual incomes in thousands of dollars and stores the data in file Xr02-70.

a Draw a scatter diagram of the data.

b What have you learned from the scatter diagram?

2.6 DESCRIBING TIME-SERIES DATA

Besides classifying data by type, we can also classify them according to whether the observations are measured at the same time or whether they represent measurements at successive points in time. The former are called **cross-sectional data** and the latter, **time-series data**. Marketing surveys and political opinion polls are familiar methods of collecting cross-sectional data. The data from a political survey might include, for example, the party preferences and demographic characteristics of a sample of 1,000 voters at the same point in time. Statistical techniques could be applied to the data, such as testing for differences in preferences between men and women.

To give another example, consider a real estate consultant who feels that the selling price of a house is a function of its size, age, and lot size. To estimate the specific form of the function, she samples, say, 100 homes recently sold and records the price, size, age, and lot size for each home. These data are cross-sectional, in that they all are observations at the same point in time.

The real estate consultant is also working on a separate project to forecast the monthly housing starts in the northeastern United States over the next year. To do so, she collects the monthly housing starts in this region for each of the past 5 years. These 60 values (housing starts) represent time-series data, because they are observations taken over time.

LINE CHART

Time-series data are often graphically depicted on a **line chart**, which is a plot of the variable over time. It is created by plotting the value of the variable on the vertical axis and the time periods on the horizontal axis. Line charts can be used for all three types of data.

EXAMPLE 2.9

The total amounts of income tax paid by individuals in the United States in the years 1987 to 1999 are listed below and stored in file Xm02-09. Draw a graph of these data and describe the information produced.

Year	Income Tax (in $millions)
1987	470,585
1988	480,710
1989	521,287
1990	548,198
1991	546,810
1992	564,555
1993	593,752
1994	625,483
1995	685,528
1996	754,877
1997	847,761
1998	940,402
1999	1,031,712

Source: U.S. Treasury Department.

SOLUTION

Figure 2.17 depicts the line chart.

Figure 2.17

EXCEL

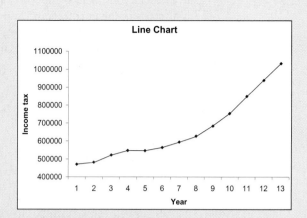

COMMANDS

1. Type or import the data into one column.
2. Highlight the column.
3. Click **Chart Wizard**, **Line**, and **Finish**.
4. Click **Chart** and **Chart Options** to make whatever changes you wish.

MINITAB

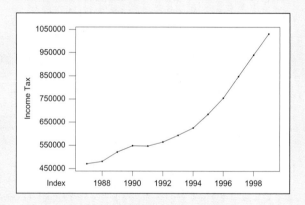

COMMANDS

1. Type or import the data into one column.
2. Click **Graph** and **Time Series Plot...**.
3. Specify the variable under **Graph**.
4. Click **Options** and specify the starting time period. Click **OK**.

INTERPRET

For the years 1987 to 1992, total tax was relatively flat. However, starting in year 7 (1993) there was a rapid increase in the annual tax revenues from individuals. This matches the improvement in the American economy as it came out of recession in the early 1990s.

When the time series is based on nominal data, we proceed as we did in the previous section. We count the number of occurrences of a category of interest to us and graph it over time.

You may also use a bar chart or a scatter diagram to depict a time series. You can experiment to see which technique provides the best view.

EXERCISES

2.71 The number of cable subscribers for each of the last 10 years is listed below. Use a graphical technique to present these figures.

Year	Cable Subscribers (in millions)
1991	51.0
1992	53.0
1993	55.0
1994	57.0
1995	58.0
1996	60.3
1997	64.1
1998	64.2
1999	65.6
2000	66.5

Source: *Statistical Abstract of the United States*, 2000, Table 925.

2.72 Because there are so many new drugs on the market, the total cost may be skyrocketing. To gauge how fast costs are increasing, the following table was produced. Graphically present these data.

Year	1990	1991	1992	1993	1994	1995	1996	1997
Cost of drugs & medical nondurable goods ($billions)	59.9	65.6	71.2	76.2	81.6	88.9	98.3	108.9

Source: *Statistical Abstract of the United States*, 2000, Table 164.

2.73 The average retail price of a gallon of gasoline for each of the past 8 weeks is listed below.

1.45, 1.48, 1.53, 1.56, 1.54, 1.50, 1.56, 1.60

a Use a graphical technique to depict these data.

b What have you learned about the price of gasoline?

2.74 The numbers of violent crimes during the years 1988 to 1998 are listed below. Use a graphical technique to present these figures.

Year	Number of Violent Crimes (thousands)
1988	13,923
1989	14,251
1990	14,476
1991	14,873
1992	14,438
1993	14,145
1994	13,990
1995	13,863
1996	13,494
1997	13,195
1998	12,476

Source: *Statistical Abstract of the United States*, 2000, Table 329.

2.75 Every month for the past two years a poll was taken to measure the perceptions of people who rate the president of the United States in his job performance. The percentages who judge that performance as satisfactory are listed here. Draw a line chart, and describe what the chart tells you.

63, 67, 69, 66, 57, 59, 64, 65, 62, 68, 66, 59, 54, 51, 54, 57, 60, 64, 61, 58, 54, 53, 50, 54

2.76 The numbers of domestic and foreign cars recalled for safety defects for the years 1989 to 1996 are listed below. Use a graphical technique to present these figures.

Year	Number of Domestic Cars (Thousands)	Number of Foreign Cars (Thousands)
1989	6,173	964
1990	4,070	1,915
1991	6,646	1,633
1992	6,545	3,577
1993	7,655	3,267
1994	4,280	1,784
1995	9,041	9,259
1996	15,104	1,980

Source: *Statistical Abstract of the United States*, 2000, Table 1047.

The following exercises require a computer and software.

2.77 The monthly value of U.S. exports to Canada (in $millions) and imports from Canada from 1974 to the present are stored in file Xr02-77. (*Source*: Federal Reserve Economic Data)

a Draw a line chart of U.S. exports to Canada.

b Draw a line chart of U.S. imports from Canada.

c Calculate the trade balance and draw a line chart.

d What do all the charts reveal?

2.78 The monthly Japanese short-term interest rates from 1990 to 2001 are stored in file Xr02-78. (*Source*: Bank of Japan)

a Draw a line chart.

b Briefly describe what the chart tells you about Japanese short-term interest rates.

2.79 The numbers (in thousands) of males and females who have earned master's degrees in the years 1980 to 1997 are stored in file Xr02-79. Provide graphs of the number of males, females, and both genders who have earned their master's. (*Source: Statistical Abstract of the United States*, 2000, Table 317)

2.80 The weekly sales at a newly opened coffee shop were recorded for the first 52 weeks of operation. The data are stored in file Xr02-80.

a Select an appropriate graphical method to present the data.

b Describe your findings.

2.81 The Gross Domestic Product (GDP) is a measure of the level of economic activity in a country. The quarterly GDP (in $billions) for the United States over the past 55 years is stored in file Xr02-81. Draw a graph that depicts these data and describe what you have learned. (*Source*: U.S. Department of Commerce, Bureau of Economic Analysis, National Accounts Data)

2.82   Deadly crashes that involve ten or more vehicles appear to be increasing across the United States. The National Highway Traffic Safety Administration recorded the number of such accidents that occurred annually from 1975 to 1999. These data are listed in chronological order in file Xr02-82. Use a suitable graphical technique to present these data.

2.83   The quarterly value (in billions of Euros) of European exports for the years 1991 to 2000 are stored in file Xr02-83. Use a graphical technique to present these data. (*Source*: European Central Bank, Monthly Bulletin)

2.84   The monthly closing prices of the Dow Jones Industrial Average (DJIA) since 1950 are stored in file Xr02-84. Draw a graph and describe what the graph tells you. (*Source: Wall Street Journal*)

2.7 SUMMARY

Descriptive statistical methods are used to summarize data sets so that we can extract the relevant information. In this chapter we presented graphical techniques.

Histograms are used to describe a single set of interval data. Statistics practitioners examine several aspects of the shapes of histograms. These are **symmetry**, number of **modes**, and its resemblance to a **bell shape**.

Bar charts and **pie charts** are employed to summarize single sets of nominal data. Because of the restrictions applied to this type of data, all that we can show is the frequency and proportion of each category.

To analyze the relationship between two interval variables, we draw a **scatter diagram**. We look for the direction and strength of the **linear relationship**. To describe the relationship between two nominal variables, we draw bar charts.

We described the difference between **time-series data** and **cross-sectional data**. Time series are graphed by line charts.

IMPORTANT TERMS

Variable 26	Symmetry 36	Univariate 58
Values 26	Positively skewed 37	Bivariate 58
Data 26	Negatively skewed 37	Scatter diagram 58
Interval 26	Modal class 37	Linearity 60
Quantitative 26	Unimodal 37	Linear relationship 61
Numerical 26	Bimodal 37	Positive linear relationship 62
Nominal 26	Return on investment 38	Negative linear relationship 62
Qualitative 27	Stem-and-leaf display 41	Contingency table 63
Categorical 27	Depths 42	Cross-classification table 63
Ordinal 27	Ogive 43	Cross-tabulation table 63
Pricing 31	Cumulative relative frequency	Cross-sectional data 68
Frequency distribution 32	distribution 43	Time-series data 68
Classes 32	Credit scorecard 48	Line chart 68
Frequencies 32	Pie chart 48	
Histogram 33	Bar chart 48	

COMPUTER OUTPUT AND INSTRUCTIONS

Graphical Technique	Excel	Minitab
Histogram	33	34
Stem-and-leaf display	42	42
Ogive	44	44
Bar chart	50	50
Pie chart	51	52
Scatter diagram	59	60
Line chart	70	70

REFERENCES

Chambers, J., W. S. Cleveland, B. Kleiner, and P. Tukey, *Graphical Methods for Data Analysis.* Boston: Duxbury Press, 1983.

Moore, David S., *Statistics: Concepts & Controversies,* 3rd edition. New York: W. H. Freeman, 1991.

Ramsey, F., and D. Schafer, *The Statistical Sleuth: A Course in Methods of Data Analysis.* Belmont, CA: Duxbury, 1997.

Tanur, Judith M., Frederick Mosteller, William H. Kruskal, Erich L. Lehmann, Richard Link, Richard S. Pieters, and Gerald R. Rising, *Statistics: A Guide to the Unknown,* 3rd edition. Belmont, CA: Duxbury, 1989.

Tukey, John, *Exploratory Data Analysis.* Reading, MA: Addison-Wesley, 1977.

Utts, Jessica, *Seeing Through Statistics,* 2nd edition. Pacific Grove, CA: Duxbury, 1999.

CHAPTER REVIEW EXERCISES

The following exercises require a computer and software.

2.85 There are several ways to teach applied statistics. The most popular approaches are
1. Emphasize manual calculations.
2. Use a computer combined with manual calculations.
3. Employ a computer exclusively with no manual calculations.

A survey of 100 statistics instructors asked each to report his or her approach. The results are stored in file Xr02-85. Use a graphical method to extract the most useful information about the teaching approaches.

2.86 Many downhill skiers eagerly look forward to the winter months and fresh snowfalls. However, winter also entails cold days. How does the temperature affect skiers' desire? To answer this question, a local ski resort recorded the temperature for 50 randomly selected days and the number of lift tickets they sold. Both variables are stored in file Xr02-86. Use a graphical technique to describe the data and interpret your results.

2.87 A Harris survey polled random samples of adults and asked each person to indicate whether he or she smoked. This survey has been repeated annually since 1985. The percentages of adults who smoke are recorded in order since 1985 in file Xr02-87. Graphically present these data.

2.88 The IQs of children born prematurely were measured when the children were 5 years old. The data are stored in file Xr02-88. Use whichever graphical technique you deem appropriate and describe what the graph tells you.

2.89 A sample of 200 people who had purchased food at the concession stand at Yankee Stadium was asked to rate the quality of the food. The responses are:
1. Poor
2. Fair
3. Good
4. Very good
5. Excellent

The responses (using the codes) were stored in Xr02-89. Draw a graph that describes the data. What does the graph tell you?

2.90 In another study conducted at Yankee Stadium, the concession manager wanted to know how the temperature affected beer sales. Accordingly, she took a sample of 50 games and recorded the number of beers sold and the mean temperature in the middle of the game. These data are stored in Xr02-90. Use a suitable graphical technique to describe the data. What conclusions can you obtain from the graph?

2.91   One hundred students who had reported that they use their computers for at least 20 hours per week were asked to keep track of the number of crashes their computers incurred during a 12-week period. The data are stored in file Xr02-91. Using an appropriate statistical method, summarize the data. Describe your findings.

2.92   Are the times of the winning runner in the New York Marathon decreasing? To answer this question, the times to complete the race for the winning male runners for the years 1978 to 1998 were recorded and stored in file Xr02-92. Draw a suitable graph and briefly comment on the results.

2.93   Refer to Exercise 2.92. Does temperature affect the race times? The answer to this question lies in the data in file Xr02-93, which stores the winning times for male runners and the temperature on the day the race was run. Use a graphical technique to present these data and describe what you have learned.

2.94   University and college students often play card games in their spare time. A survey of a university lounge identified the games that were played. The possibilities are:
1. Bridge
2. Hearts
3. Poker
4. Other
The results are stored in file Xr02-94. Use an appropriate graphical method to summarize the data. What does the graph tell you about the games students play in the lounge?

2.95   Refer to Exercise 2.94. The survey also recorded the degree program for each student. The games played and the students' degree program (1 = BA, 2 = BSc, 3 = BEng, 4 = BBA, 5 = other) are stored in file Xr02-95. Draw a graph that describes whether games played and degree program are related.

2.96   An increasing number of consumers prefer to use debit cards in place of cash or credit cards. To analyze the relationship between the amounts of purchases made with debit cards and credit cards, 240 people were interviewed and asked to report the amount of money spent on purchases using debit and credit cards during the last month. These data are stored in file Xr02-96. Draw a graph of the data and summarize your findings.

2.97   A new anti-flu vaccine has been developed, which is designed to reduce the duration of symptoms. However, the effect of the drug varies from person to person. To examine the effect of age on the effectiveness of the drug, a sample of 140 flu sufferers was drawn. Each person reported how long the symptoms of the flu persisted and his or her age. The data are stored in file Xr02-97. Draw a diagram of the data and describe your findings.

2.98   The causes of aircraft crashes are a concern to a number of government agencies. To help learn more about crashes of aircraft, their causes for the past 10 years were recorded in the following way.

When Crashes Occur	Code
Ground	1
Takeoff	2
Initial climb	3
Climb	4
Cruise	5
Descent	6
Approach	7
Landing	8

A statistics practitioner recorded the cause of crashes among small and large commercial aircraft. The data are stored in file Xr02-98. Draw a graph that depicts the relationship between the size of the aircraft and the cause of the crash.

2.99   The value of monthly U.S. exports to Japan and imports from Japan (in $millions) since 1974 are stored in file Xr02-99. (*Source:* Federal Reserve Economic Data)
   a Draw a chart that depicts exports.
   b Draw a chart that exhibits imports.
   c Compute the trade balance and graph these data.
   d What do these charts tell you?

2.100   The value of one Australian dollar measured in American dollars for the past 367 months is stored in file Xr02-100. Convert the data into the values of one American dollar measured in Australian dollars and produce a graph that shows how the exchange rate has varied over the past 30 years. (*Source:* Federal Reserve Economic Data)

2.101   A benefit of exercise is that it raises the metabolism rate. In a study to determine the effect of different durations of exercise and the metabolism rate, a sample was drawn of 100 regular exercisers. The amount of time each individual exercised and the metabolism rate 1 hour after the exercise were measured. The data are stored in Xr02-101. Draw a graph of the data and summarize your findings.

2.102   A sample of 125 university students was asked how many books they borrowed from the library over the past 12 months. Their replies are stored in file Xr02-102. Use a suitable graphical method to depict the data. What does the graph tell you?

2.103   Every March the NCAA has a basketball tournament that is televised. The annual television revenues (in $millions) for the past 30 years are listed in chronological order in file Xr02-103. Use a graphical technique to present these numbers.

2.104   The Wilfrid Laurier University bookstore conducts annual surveys of its customers. One question asks respondents to rate the prices of textbooks. The wording is "The bookstore's prices of textbooks are reasonable." The responses are:
1. Strongly disagree
2. Disagree
3. Neither agree nor disagree
4. Agree
5. Strongly agree

The responses for a group of 115 students were stored in file Xr02-104. Graphically summarize these data and report your findings.

2.105 The value of monthly U.S. exports to Mexico and imports from Mexico (in $millions) since 1974 are stored in file Xr02-105. (*Source*: Federal Reserve Economic Data)

a Draw a chart that depicts exports.

b Draw a chart that exhibits imports.

c Compute the trade balance and graph these data.

d What do these charts tell you?

2.106 Refer to Exercise 2.93. The winning times of female runners and temperatures were stored in file Xr02-106. Graph these data and report your results.

2.107 It is generally believed that one of the negative effects of quitting smoking is weight gain. To examine this issue, a group of ex-smokers who had quit 12 months earlier was asked to report their weight gain. These data are stored in file Xr02-107. Draw an appropriate graph of these data and describe what the graph tells you.

2.108 In an attempt to determine the factors that affect the amount of energy used, 200 households were analyzed. In each, the number of occupants and the amount of electricity used were measured. These data are stored in file Xr02-108.

a Draw a graph of the data.

b What have you learned from the graph?

2.109 The Red Lobster Restaurant chain conducts regular surveys of its customers to monitor the performance of individual restaurants. One of the questions asks customers to rate the overall quality of their last visit. The listed responses are: Poor (1), Fair (2), Good (3), Very good (4), Excellent (5). The survey also asks respondents whether their children accompanied them to the restaurant. The results from 220 customers are stored in file Xr02-109 (column 1 = ratings of customers without accompanying children and column 2 = rating of customers with accompanying children). Graphically depict these data and describe your findings.

2.110 The way in which most people learn to read (one word at a time) often results in slow reading. As a first step in improving the speed of reading, a group of 100 people are asked to report their number of years of education. Each person's reading speed was measured. The data are stored in file Xr02-110. Draw a graph of the data and describe how the two variables are related.

2.111 When drivers are lost, what do they do? To help answer this question, a group of drivers was asked. There were four possible responses. They are:

1. Consult a map

2. Ask someone for directions

3. Continue driving until location or direction determined

4. Other

The gender of the respondent was recorded as well as the responses, where 1 = male and 2 = female. The data are stored in file Xr02-111. Graphically depict the relationship between gender and response.

2.112 Because of the large amount of trade between Canada and the United States, the exchange rate of their currencies is an important variable. The value of one U.S. dollar measured in Canadian dollars for the past 367 months is listed in file Xr02-112. (*Source*: Federal Reserve Economic Data) Draw a chart that shows how this variable has changed over the past 30 years.

2.113 One way to judge children's development is to measure the size of their vocabulary. The vocabularies of 200 5-year-old children were measured and stored in file Xr02-113. Utilize a suitable graphical technique to present these data. What does the graph indicate about 5-year-old children's vocabularies?

2.114 Casino Windsor regularly conducts surveys of its customers. Among other questions, respondents are asked to give their opinion about "their overall impression of Casino Windsor." The responses are:

Excellent, Good, Average, Poor, Unacceptable

The responses were recorded as 5, 4, 3, 2, 1, respectively, and stored in file Xr02-114. Use a graphical procedure to summarize the data and describe your findings.

2.115 Several years ago the National Hockey League instituted a 5-minute overtime period when the game was tied after the regulation 60-minute game. The objective was to increase the excitement of the game. One way of measuring the action is to count the number of shots during the overtime period. A sample of games where the teams played the full 5 minutes was taken as well as the total number of shots. These data are stored in file Xr02-115. Use a graphical technique to summarize the data. Report your findings.

2.116 Is the value of an education worth its cost? Education costs are easy to calculate. They include tuition, books, and living expenses as well as the cost of foregone income that a job would have provided. In an effort to learn more about the value of education, a psychologist gathered data from a sample 150 30-year-old men and women. Each was asked how many years of formal education he or she had completed and his or her income ($1,000s) for the previous 12 months. These data are stored in file Xr02-116. Draw a chart that describes the relationship between years of education and income.

2.117 Most publicly traded companies have boards of directors. The rate of pay varies considerably. A survey was undertaken by the *Globe and Mail* (February 19, 2001) wherein 100 companies were surveyed and asked to report how much their directors were paid annually. The results are stored in file Xr02-117. Use a graphical technique to present these data.

2.118 Refer to Exercise 2.117. In addition to reporting the annual payment per director, the survey recorded the number of meetings last year. These data are stored in file Xr02-118. Use a graphical technique to summarize and present these data.

2.119 Is airline travel becoming safer? To help answer this question, a student recorded the number of fatal accidents and the number of deaths that occurred in the years 1987 to 1999 for scheduled airlines. These data are stored in Xr02-119. Use a graphical method to answer the question. (*Source: Statistical Abstract of the United States,* 2000, Table 1071)

2.120 How do income taxes vary from country to country? A statistics practitioner recorded the income tax rate for those individuals in the highest-income group in several countries. These data are stored in file Xr02-120. (The figures refer to the federal income tax only in the United States and in Switzerland.) Use a graphical technique to present these numbers (*Source:* Pricewaterhousecoopers)

2.121 The average monthly price-earnings ratios of all stocks on the New York Stock Exchange are stored in file Xr02-121. Use a graphical technique to present these data. What have you learned from the graph?

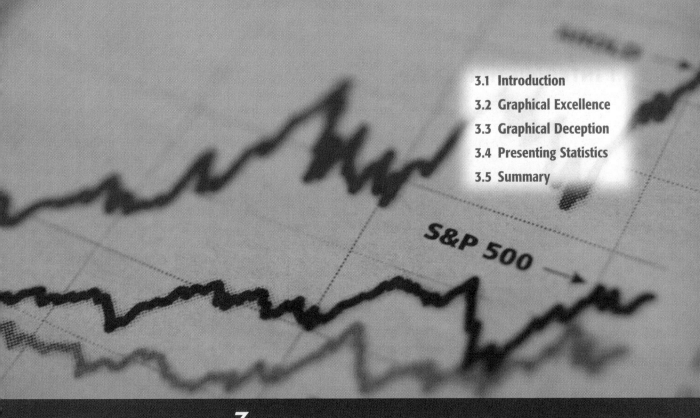

3   ART AND SCIENCE OF GRAPHICAL PRESENTATIONS

NAPOLEON'S INVASION OF AND RETREAT FROM RUSSIA

On June 21, 1812, the French Army led by Napoleon Bonaparte invaded Russia. The military campaign was a disaster; the army was virtually annihilated. A time-series chart created by Charles Joseph Minard (1781–1870), a French engineer, is considered to be one of the best graphs ever created. The chart is effective because it depicts five variables clearly and succinctly. The variables are

1. Size of the army invading
2. Size of the army retreating
3. Location on the map
4. Temperature
5. Dates

☞ *On page 84 we provide the chart.*

3.1 INTRODUCTION

In Chapter 2, we introduced a number of graphical techniques. The emphasis was on how to construct each one manually and how to command the computer to draw them. In this chapter we discuss how to use graphical techniques effectively. We introduce the concept of **graphical excellence**, which is a term we apply to techniques that are informative and concise and that impart information clearly to their viewers. Section 3.2 discusses how to achieve graphical excellence using the methods introduced in Chapter 2. In Section 3.3, we discuss an equally important concept, graphical integrity. We will demonstrate how some people use graphs and charts to purposely or inadvertently mislead readers.

3.2 GRAPHICAL EXCELLENCE

Graphical excellence is achieved when the following characteristics apply.

1 **The graph presents large data sets concisely and coherently.** Graphical techniques were created to summarize and describe large data sets. Small data sets are easily summarized with a table. One or two numbers can best be presented in a sentence.

2 **The ideas and concepts the statistics practitioner wants to deliver are clearly understood by the viewer.** The chart is designed to describe what would otherwise be described in words. An excellent chart is one that can replace a thousand words and still be clearly comprehended by its readers.

3 **The graph encourages the viewer to compare two or more variables.** Graphs displaying only one variable provide very little information. Graphs are often best used to depict relationships between two or more variables or to explain how and why the observed results occurred.

4 **The display induces the viewer to address the substance of the data and not the form of the graph.** The form of the graph is supposed to help present the substance. If the form replaces the substance, the chart is not performing its function.

5 **There is no distortion of what the data reveal.** You cannot make statistical techniques say whatever you like. A knowledgeable reader will easily see through distortions and deception. This is such an important topic that we devote Section 3.3 to its discussion.

Edward Tufte, professor of statistics at Yale University, summarized graphical excellence this way:

Graphical excellence is the well-designed presentation of interesting data—a matter of substance, of statistics, and of design.

Graphical excellence is that which gives the viewer the greatest number of ideas in the shortest time with the least ink in the smallest space.

Graphical excellence is nearly always multivariate.

And graphical excellence requires telling the truth about the data.

In attempting to demonstrate what constitutes excellence, we searched through newspapers, magazines, and financial reports. Unfortunately, we found far more examples of bad statistical applications than excellent ones. Fortunately, we can learn just as much about the proper use of graphs by examining bad ones. Here are good and bad examples.

EXAMPLES

Graphical techniques should be used when there is a large amount of data. In general, small data sets can be presented in tabular form. Examine Figure 3.1, which is a bar chart depicting the number of visitors in 1994 to Disney theme parks around the world. Does the chart provide the reader with any more information than Table 3.1 does? From both you can see that Tokyo Disneyland drew the most visitors —about 16 million— while the others drew between 8 and 11.2 million. The bar chart is completely unnecessary for two reasons. First, there are only six numbers represented; a data set this small does not need a graphical display. Second, there is no analysis associated with the attendance figures to explain why Tokyo Disneyland outdrew the others or how these figures are related to other variables, such as profits or sales. This chart also fails to address why the reader would be interested in this "information." What concept is being imparted to the reader? None that we could see.

Figure 3.1

Table 3.1 Number of People Visiting Disney Theme Parks in 1994

Park	Number of Visitors (in millions)
Tokyo Disneyland	16.0
Walt Disney World, Florida	11.2
Disneyland, California	10.3
EPCOT Center, Florida	9.7
Euro Disneyland, France	8.8
Disney-MGM Studios, Florida	8.0

Compare the amount of information contained in Figure 3.1 with that of Figure 3.2 (page 80), which describes the January effect on tax-free money funds. The January effect is a phenomenon that results in a drop in the yield of money funds during the second week of January. It is caused by investors paying their Christmas shopping bills by taking money out of their tax-free funds, which causes the yield to drop. In Figure 3.2, the concept the author wishes to describe is clear. For each of the years 1990 to 1995, the yield during the second week of January was less than the yield during the first week. However, because of the small amount of data (there are only 12 numbers shown), a table would provide at least as much information. In fact, by adding an extra column for the difference between the first-week yield and the second-week yield, Table 3.2 provides more information. We clearly can see the magnitude of the difference between the yields in weeks 1 and 2.

Figure 3.2

Table 3.2 Yields of Tax-Free Funds for First and Second Weeks in January

Year	Yield: First Week	Yield: Second Week	Difference Between First and Second Weeks
1990	5.90%	5.49%	0.41%
1991	6.21	5.29	0.92
1992	4.32	3.82	0.50
1993	2.79	1.93	0.86
1994	2.33	1.72	0.61
1995	4.09	3.26	0.83

In an article about the uneven work distribution in Canada, Figure 3.3 was drawn. A large amount of data is summarized concisely. The number of hours specified in many collective agreements had to be collected, recorded, and tabulated. The main point is clear: There is great variation in the work hours across different industries. Moreover, the reader is coaxed into analyzing the relationship between two variables: working hours and type of industry. On the negative side, a larger number of categories of working hours (e.g., 35–37.5, 37.5–40, 40–42.5, 42.5 and over) would be more useful. And, why don't the three percentages for "All Industries" add up to 100%?

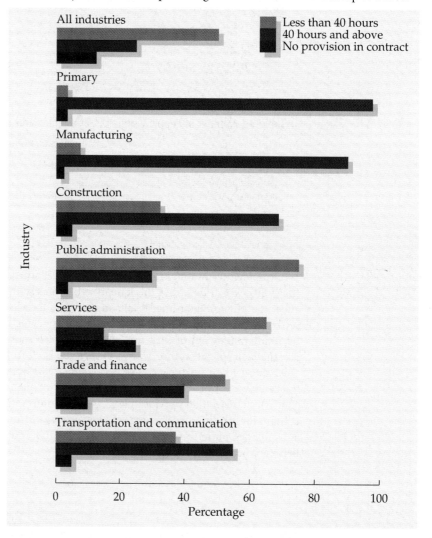

Figure 3.3
Number of working hours by industry (in major collective agreements)

Source: Creative Statistics Company.

The overwhelming majority of poorly executed charts can be attributed to the contempt most people have for statistics. It is generally believed that statistics can be manipulated to prove anything that the statistics practitioner wishes to prove. It would follow that statistics and graphs mean nothing and that there are no rules governing how they should be used. This is absolute nonsense! You cannot lie to a knowledgeable viewer. It is usually easy to detect deception in the application of statistical techniques.

It is also generally accepted that statistics are boring, and authors must resort to desperate measures to attract readers. This attitude is exemplified in Figure 3.4, which is a pie chart of the percentages of the uses of sports apparel. This is one of the worst examples of graphical techniques that we have encountered. It fails on every characteristic. It contains very little data, and hence a table would suffice. The idea that the author wants to deliver is not clear. Perhaps the creator of the chart had no ideas to impart. There is no analysis associated with the chart that would entail examining why these results were observed. When the graph appeared in the newspaper *USA Today* it was drawn to resemble a runner. (Perhaps because of the other shortcomings of the graph, the author was forced to enhance it.) Consequently, the viewer addresses the design rather than the substance. Statisticians refer to this type of graphical display as **chartjunk**. We make one request of our readers: If you ever create a chart like Figure 3.4, please don't tell anyone you learned statistics from this book.

By Sam Ward, USA TODAY

Figure 3.4
Source: USA Today (11 January, 1995).

Time lines representing time-series data are often seen in the financial sections of newspapers. However, they are often devoid of substance. For example, Figure 3.5 (page 82) is a time line of the number of basis points by which Quebec 10-year bonds exceed 10-year Canadian bonds. Since the late 1960s, the province of Quebec has threatened to secede from Canada, which has made many investors nervous about investing in Quebec. The chart depicts the degree of concern among investors—the greater the concern, the greater the premium that must be offered by the Quebec government. In its present form, the graph tells us very little. It could be improved by adding the time line of one or more related variables. Examples of related variables include Quebec's budget deficits, unemployment rates, and survey results showing support for separation. The authors could also indicate the dates of Quebec's provincial elections. They could also attempt to explain the spikes in 1975, 1977, and 1982 and the steady increase since 1984.

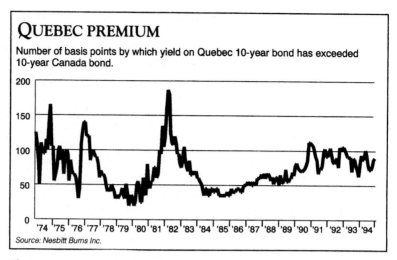

Figure 3.5

Contrast Figure 3.5 with Figure 3.6, which plots a consumer sentiment index in the United States from 1950 to 1994. The index measures how people feel about their financial prospects. The score in 1966 was arbitrarily set equal to 100. In addition to the scores, we also see the periods during which the U.S. economy underwent recessions. The years in which a new president was inaugurated as well as other key events also appear on the chart. Examining the chart provides rich details about the factors that affect Americans' perceptions of their financial circumstances. For example, recessionary periods mostly coincide with downturns in the index. From the early 1960s to 1980, there was a general downward drift. Historians would agree that this was a troubled time in the United States. The period started with the assassination of President John Kennedy, followed by the Vietnam War, the rapid increase in the price of oil, gasoline shortages, the Watergate scandal, and the Iranian hostage crisis. The inauguration of Ronald Reagan as president in 1980 marked the end of the decline, and the sharpest increase in the index took place during his 8-year stint in office, during which the greatest boom in U.S. history started. This graph is more than just a graph: It's a short story.

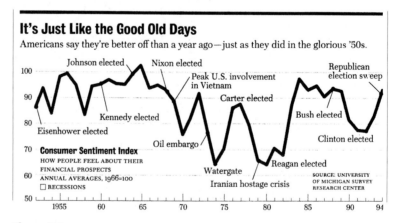

Figure 3.6
Source: *Newsweek* (30 January, 1995).

In January 1995, a financial crisis in Mexico caused many foreign investors to sell their Mexican holdings. As a result, the Mexican stock market (as measured by the Bolsa Index) fell by 6.6% on one day (January 9). In a story about the widespread effect of this event, *Time* magazine published the graphs shown in Figure 3.7, which are time lines for the stock market indexes in Mexico, Argentina, Brazil, and Chile. The story is summarized concisely and clearly by the graphs. The shock to the Mexican stock market reverberated across South America with equally disastrous consequences.

Figure 3.7
© 1995 *TIME Inc.* Reprinted by permission.

In the same section, *Time* also published an article about the fall of the Canadian dollar. Figure 3.8 depicts the time line showing the value of the Canadian dollar in U.S. dollars. It shows that in 1990 the Canadian dollar was worth about $0.86 U.S. but had dropped to about $0.71 in 1994. The article discussed several reasons for this decrease in value but pointed to Canada's rapidly increasing debt as the chief cause. The chart also included Canada's debt as a percentage of gross domestic product (GDP). As you can easily see, the debt/GDP ratio was constant between 1986 and 1989, but started a sharp increase in 1990. The argument is clear: The increasing debts produced a much lower value for the Canadian dollar.

Figure 3.8
© 1995 *TIME Inc.* Reprinted by permission.

NAPOLEON'S INVASION OF AND RETREAT FROM RUSSIA

Figure 3.9 depicts Minard's graph. The striped band is a time series depicting the size of the army at various places on the map, which is also part of the chart. When Napoleon invaded Russia by crossing the Niemen River on June 21, 1812, there were 422,000 soldiers. By the time the army reached Moscow, the number had dwindled to 100,000. At that point the army started its retreat. The black band represents the army in retreat. At the bottom of the chart we see the dates starting with October 1813. Just above the dates Minard drew another time series, this one showing the temperature. It was bitterly cold during the fall, and many soldiers died of exposure. As you can see, the temperature dipped to −30 on the 6th of December.

Figure 3.9

Source: Edward Tufte, *The Visual Display of Quantitative Information* (Cheshire, CT: Graphics Press, 1983), p. 41.

Figures 3.6–3.9 illustrate the determinants of graphical excellence. The graphs are well designed, presenting interesting data. They impart ideas concisely because they present several variables at the same time. And finally, they do not distort the data in any way.

EXERCISES

3.1 Geac is a computer company that has diversified its operations into financial services, construction, manufacturing, and hotels. In a recent annual report, the following tables were provided.

	Sales (millions of dollars) by region	
Region	Last year	Previous year
United States	67.3	40.4
Canada	20.9	18.9
Europe	37.9	35.5
Australasia	26.2	10.3
Total	152.2	105.1

	Sales (millions of dollars) by division	
Division	Last year	Previous year
Customer service	54.6	43.8
Library systems	49.3	30.5
Construction/property management	17.5	7.7
Manufacturing and distribution	15.4	8.9
Financial systems	9.4	10.9
Hotels and clubs	5.9	3.4

Create charts to present these data so that the differences between last year and the previous year are clear.

3.2 The following chart appeared in *USA Today* (11 January, 1995). Grade it A, B, C, D, or F. Explain why you graded it the way you did.

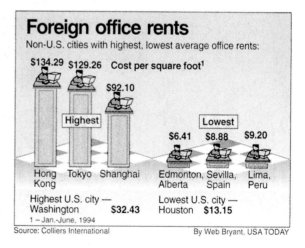

3.3 A line chart showing the value of the Canadian dollar in terms of the U.S. dollar from 1984 to 1994 is provided here.

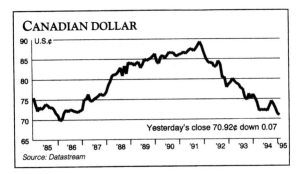

CANADIAN DOLLAR

Source: Datastream

a Write as many sentences as you need to describe the chart.

b How would you judge the amount of information that can be extracted from the chart?

c Describe how the chart could be made more informative.

3.4 The U.S. Federal Reserve Board raises interest rates during economic booms to help control inflation and produce the so-called "soft landing" when the boom eventually ends. Signs that usually indicate that the economy is overheating and likely to result in inflation are the changes in the Consumer Price Index and annual growth rates. In an article (*Globe and Mail*, 16 January, 1995) about increases in interest rates, the three charts shown appeared. Discuss the information that is imparted by the charts. Do the charts justify increases in the interest rate?

THE U.S. RECORD

3.5 The accompanying line chart graphs the number of hardcover books that appeared on the top-50 best-seller list each week during 1994. Grade it A, B, C, D, or F, and justify your grade. What have you learned from the chart?

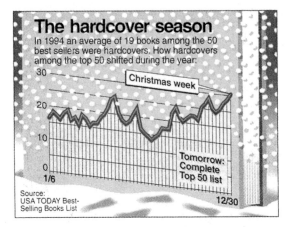

The hardcover season
In 1994 an average of 19 books among the 50 best sellers were hardcovers. How hardcovers among the top 50 shifted during the year:

Source: USA TODAY Best-Selling Books List

3.6 During 1993 and 1994, the Canadian government threatened cutbacks in university funding. Students and educators protested, arguing that higher education is critical not only to individual students but to the nation as well. The following chart was produced (*Globe and Mail*, 6 October, 1994), showing the percent changes in the number of jobs for four groups with different educational attainment levels. Grade it A, B, C, D, or F, and explain your reasons for your grade assignment.

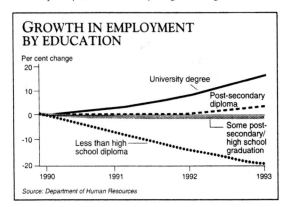

GROWTH IN EMPLOYMENT BY EDUCATION

Source: Department of Human Resources

3.7 In 1987, the U.S. government established Sematech, a federally financed consortium, to boost sales of semiconductors, a critical component of computers. Before 1987, the U.S. market share of semiconductors was decreasing while that of Japanese companies was increasing. The market shares of companies in the United States, Japan, and all other countries for the years 1981 to 1994 are listed at the top of page 86 and stored in file Xr03-07. Draw a time line of these data. Show the point at which Sematech was formed. How well does the graph describe the effect of Sematech? Grade the graph A, B, C, D, or F, and justify your grade.

Percent of Semiconductors Sold by U.S., Japanese, and Other Countries' Companies

Year	U.S.	Japan	All others
1981	73	19	8
1982	70	24	6
1983	68	28	4
1984	65	30	5
1985	61	34	5
1986	59	37	4
1987	56	39	5
1988	50	42	8
1989	48	45	7
1990	43	48	9
1991	45	46	9
1992	50	41	9
1993	52	40	8
1994	53	39	8

3.8 The stock market has survived 20 bear markets in the last 100 years. The date of the market peak, the percentage decline, and the duration (the time for the market to recover) are stored in file Xr03-08.

a Draw a graph that depicts the recovery times in chronological order.

b Manually draw a graph that depicts both the recovery time and percentage decline in chronological order.

c Draw a graph that describes the relationship between recovery times and percentage declines.

3.3 GRAPHICAL DECEPTION

The use of graphs and charts is pervasive in newspapers, magazines, business and economic reports, and seminars, in large part due to the increasing availability of computers and software that allow the storage, retrieval, manipulation, and summary of large masses of raw data. It is therefore more important than ever to be able to evaluate critically the information presented by means of graphical techniques. In the final analysis, graphical techniques merely create a visual impression, which is easy to distort. In fact, distortion is so easy and commonplace that in 1992 the Canadian Institute of Chartered Accountants found it necessary to begin setting guidelines for financial graphics, after a study of hundreds of the annual reports of major corporations found that 8% contained at least one misleading graph that covered up bad results. Although the heading for this section mentions deception, it is quite possible for an inexperienced person inadvertently to create distorted impressions with graphs. In any event, you should be aware of possible methods of graphical deception. This section illustrates a few of them.

The first thing to watch for is a graph without a scale on one axis. The time-series graph of a firm's sales in Figure 3.10 might represent a growth rate of 100% or 1% over the 5 years depicted, depending on the vertical scale. It is best simply to ignore such graphs.

**Figure 3.10
Graph without a
vertical scale**

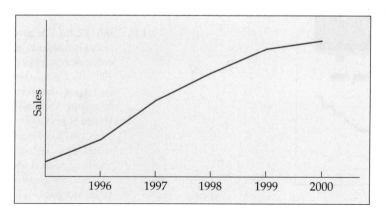

A second trap to avoid is being influenced by a graph's caption. Your impression of the trend in interest rates might be different depending on whether you read a newspaper carrying caption (a) or caption (b) in Figure 3.11.

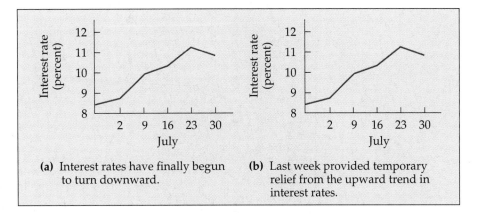

(a) Interest rates have finally begun to turn downward.

(b) Last week provided temporary relief from the upward trend in interest rates.

Figure 3.11
Different captions for the same graph

Perspective is often distorted if only absolute changes in value, rather than percentage changes, are reported. For example, a $1 drop in the price of your $2 stock is relatively more distressing than a $1 drop in the price of your $100 stock. On January 9, 1986, newspapers throughout North America displayed graphs similar to the one shown in Figure 3.12 and reported that the stock market, as measured by the Dow Jones Industrial Average (DJIA), had suffered its worst 1-day loss ever on the previous day. The loss was 39 points, exceeding even the loss of Black Tuesday—October 28, 1929. While the loss was indeed a large one, many news reports failed to mention that the 1986 level of the DJIA was much higher than the 1929 level. A better perspective on the situation could be gained by noticing that the loss on January 8, 1986, represented a 2.5% decline, while the decline in 1929 was 12.8%. As a point of interest, we note that the stock market was 12% higher within 2 months of this historic drop and 40% higher 1 year later.

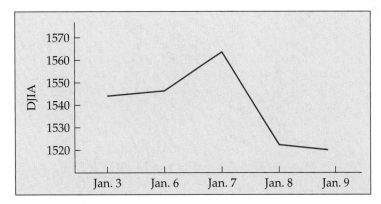

Figure 3.12
Historic drop in DJIA, 1986

We now turn to some rather subtle methods of creating distorted impressions with graphs. Consider the graph in Figure 3.13 (page 88), which depicts the growth in a firm's quarterly sales during the past year, from $100 million to $110 million. This 10% growth in quarterly sales can be made to appear more dramatic by stretching the vertical axis—a technique that involves changing the scale on the vertical axis so that a given dollar amount is represented by a greater height than before. As a result, the rise in sales appears to be greater, because the slope of the graph is visually (but not numerically) steeper. The expanded scale is usually accommodated by employing a break in the vertical axis, as in Figure 3.14(a), or by truncating the vertical axis, as in Figure 3.14(b), so that the vertical scale begins at a point greater than 0. The effect of making slopes appear steeper can also be created by shrinking the horizontal axis, in which case points on the horizontal axis are moved closer together.

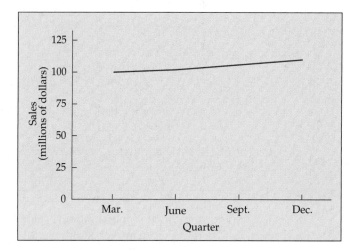

Figure 3.13
Quarterly sales for the past year

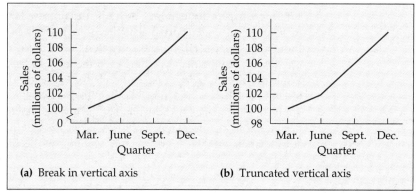

Figure 3.14
Stretching the vertical axis

(a) Break in vertical axis   **(b)** Truncated vertical axis

Just the opposite effect is obtained by stretching the horizontal axis—that is, spreading out the points on the horizontal axis to increase the distance between them so that slopes and trends will appear to be less steep. The graph of a firm's profits presented in Figure 3.15(a) shows considerable swings, both upward and downward, in the profits from one quarter to the next. However, the firm could convey the impression of reasonable stability in profits from quarter to quarter by stretching the horizontal axis, as shown in Figure 3.15(b).

Figure 3.15
Quarterly profits over two years

(a) Compressed horizontal axis   **(b)** Stretched horizontal axis

Similar illusions can be created with bar charts by stretching or shrinking the vertical or horizontal axis. Another popular method of creating distorted impressions with bar charts is to construct the bars so that their widths are proportional to their heights. The bar chart in Figure 3.16(a) correctly depicts the average weekly amount spent on food by Canadian families during three particular years. This chart correctly uses bars of equal width so that both the height and the area of each bar are proportional to the expenditures they represent. The growth in food expenditures is exaggerated in Figure 3.16(b), in which the widths of the bars increase with their heights. A quick glance at this bar chart might leave the viewer with the mistaken impression that food expenditures increased fourfold over the decade, since the 1995 bar is four times the width of the 1985 bar.

Figure 3.16
Average weekly food expenditures by Canadian families

(a) Correct bar chart

(b) Increasing bar widths to create distortion

Size distortions should be watched for particularly in pictograms, which replace the bars with pictures of objects (such as bags of money, people, or animals) to enhance the visual appeal. Figure 3.17 displays the misuse of a pictogram—the snowman grows in width as well as height. The proper use of a pictogram is shown in Figure 3.18, which effectively uses pictures of Coca-Cola bottles.

Figure 3.17
Incorrect pictogram
Source: Environment Canada, Metro Toronto Branch.

Figure 3.18
Correct pictogram
Source: Value Line Investment Survey (21 May, 1993).

The preceding examples of creating a distorted impression using graphs are not exhaustive, but they include some of the more popular methods. They should also serve to make the point that graphical techniques are used to create a visual impression and the impression you obtain may be a distorted one unless you examine the graph with care. You are less likely to be misled if you focus your attention on the numerical values that the graph represents. Begin by carefully noting the scales on both axes; graphs with unmarked axes should be ignored completely.

EXERCISES

3.9 U.S. seasonally adjusted unemployment rates from July 1993 to July 1994 are listed below.

Month		Seasonally adjusted unemployment rate
1993	July	7.6%
	August	7.6
	September	7.5
	October	7.3
	November	7.3
	December	7.2
1994	January	7.0
	February	6.7
	March	6.4
	April	6.4
	May	6.3
	June	6.0
	July	6.1

Source: U.S. Department of Labor.

a Draw a bar chart of these data with 6.0% as the lowest point on the vertical axis.
b Draw a bar chart of these data with 0% as the lowest point on the vertical axis.
c Discuss the impression given by the two charts.
d Which chart would you use? Explain.

3.10 The following table lists family incomes (in thousands 1991 dollars) and family size between 1971 and 1991. Draw time lines that describe how both variables have changed and how they appear to be related.

Year	Family income (in thousands of dollars)	Average family size
1971	39.8	3.68
1972	42.1	3.62
1973	43.5	3.60
1974	47.1	3.54
1975	48.3	3.47
1976	48.6	3.42
1977	48.2	3.40
1978	50.2	3.38
1979	50.4	3.34
1980	50.9	3.30
1981	49.2	3.27
1982	49.0	3.24
1983	48.4	3.21
1984	48.9	3.18
1985	50.2	3.17
1986	50.9	3.18
1987	52.2	3.16
1988	52.8	3.12
1989	54.2	3.10
1990	51.7	3.09
1991	51.1	3.08

Source: Creative Statistics Company.

3.11 Enerflex Systems, Inc., provides a full range of natural gas compression equipment by way of manufacturing and leasing services. In its 1993 annual report, the following data were presented.

	1993	1992	1991	1990	1989
Sales (millions of dollars)	199	69	85	88	82
Net income (millions of dollars)	7.7	3.0	4.7	4.8	1.8
Return on equity (%)	32.9	13.6	24.4	31.7	12.0
Net income per common share ($)	1.02	0.36	0.57	0.56	0.15

a Use bar charts to present these data.
b Assume that you are an unscrupulous statistics practitioner and want to make the data appear more positive than they really are. Draw the bar charts accordingly.

3.12 Are Americans reading fewer newspapers? The per capita circulation of all daily newspapers is listed in the table below.

Year	1990	1991	1992	1993	1994	1995	1996	1997	1998
Per capita daily circulation	.25	.24	.24	.23	.23	.22	.21	.21	.21

Source: Statistical Abstract of the United States, 2000, Table 942.

a Graph these data to make it look like there has been no change.
b Graph these data to make it look like there has been a large decrease.

3.4 PRESENTING STATISTICS

It is quite likely that readers of this book will be making various presentations in the near future both in other courses and in their careers. Almost as important as the ability to use statistics properly is the capability of presenting statistical results. In this section we provide some guidance. The following points were drawn from a textbook written by Janice Derr (see the References). The focus of the book is on consulting. However, much of the advice is relevant to virtually anyone who presents the results of statistical analyses.

1. **Know your audience.** Take the time to determine who is in your audience and what kind of information they will be expecting from you. Additionally, determine the level of statistical knowledge. If it is low, avoid the use of statistical terms without defining them.

2. **Restrict your main points to the objectives of the study.** Few listeners will be interested in the details of your statistical analysis. Your audience will be most interested in your conclusions and recommendations.

3. **Stay within your time limits.** If your presentation is expected to exceed your time limit, stick to the main points. Hand out additional written information if necessary.

4. **Use graphs.** It is often much easier to explain even relatively complex ideas if you provide excellent graphs.

5. **Provide handouts.** Handouts with copies of your graphs make it easier for your audience to follow your explanations.

3.5 SUMMARY

This chapter completes our discussion of graphical techniques, which began in Chapter 2. In Chapter 2, we showed how and when to construct the graphs. In this chapter, we provided guidelines for the application of graphical methods. We illustrated **graphical excellence** and **graphical deception**, and in so doing, we showed you what to do and what not to do.

IMPORTANT TERMS

Graphical excellence 78   Chartjunk 81   Graphical deception 86

REFERENCES

Chambers, J., W. S. Cleveland, B. Kleiner, and P. Tukey, *Graphical Methods for Data Analysis.* Boston: Duxbury Press, 1983.

Derr, Janice, *Statistical Consulting: A Guide to Effective Communication,* Pacific Grove, CA: Duxbury, 2000.

Huff, Darrell, *How to Lie with Statistics,* New York: W. W. Norton & Company, 1954.

Moore, David S., *Statistics: Concepts & Controversies,* 3rd edition. New York: W. H. Freeman, 1991.

Tufte, Edward, *The Visual Display of Quantitative Information.* Cheshire, CT: Graphics Press, 1983.

Tukey, John, *Exploratory Data Analysis,* Reading, MA: Addison-Wesley, 1977.

Utts, Jessica, *Seeing Through Statistics,* 2nd edition. Pacific Grove, CA: Duxbury, 1999.

Wainer, Howard, "How to Display Data Badly," *American Statistician 38,* 1984.

4 NUMERICAL DESCRIPTIVE TECHNIQUES

THE COST OF ONE MORE WIN

In the era of free agency, professional sports teams must compete for the services of the best players. In recent years, only teams whose salaries place them in the top quarter have a chance of winning the championship. Efforts have been made to provide balance by establishing salary caps or some form of equalization. To help gather information about the problem, a statistics practitioner gathered data from a recent baseball season. For each team in major league baseball, the statistics

practitioner recorded the number of wins and the team payroll ($millions). These data are stored in file Ch04:\Baseball.

To make informed decisions, we need to know how the number of wins and the team payroll are related, and, in particular, we would like an estimate of how much it costs to win one more game. After we've presented the statistical technique we will return to this problem and solve it (see page 126).

4.1 INTRODUCTION

In Chapter 2 we presented several graphical techniques that describe data. In this chapter we introduce numerical descriptive techniques, which allow the statistics practitioner to be more precise in describing various characteristics of a sample or population. They also are critical to the development of statistical inference.

As we pointed out in Chapter 2, arithmetic calculations can be applied to interval data only. Consequently, most of the techniques introduced here may be employed only to numerically describe interval data. However, some of the techniques can be used for ordinal data and one of the techniques can be employed for nominal data.

When we introduced the histogram, we commented that there are several bits of information that we look for. The first is the location of the center of the data. In Section 4.2 we will present measures of central location. Another important characteristic that we seek from a histogram is the spread of the data. The spread will be measured more precisely by measures of variability, which we'll present in Section 4.3. Section 4.4 introduces measures of relative standing and another graphical technique, the box plot.

In Section 2.5 we introduced the scatter diagram, which is a graphical method that we use to analyze the relationship between two interval variables. The numerical counterparts to the scatter diagram will be presented in Section 4.5.

In Section 4.6 we compare the information provided by graphical and numerical techniques. Finally, we complete this chapter by providing guidelines on how to explore data and retrieve information.

SAMPLE STATISTIC OR POPULATION PARAMETER

Recall the terms introduced in Chapter 1: *population, sample, parameter,* and *statistic.* A **parameter** is a descriptive measurement about a **population**, and a **statistic** is a descriptive measurement about a **sample**. In this chapter we will introduce a dozen descriptive measurements. For each we will describe how to calculate both the population parameter and the sample statistic. However, in most realistic applications, populations are very large—in fact, virtually infinite. The formulas describing the calculation of parameters are not practical and are seldom used. They are provided here primarily to teach the concept and the notation. In Chapter 7 we'll introduce probability distributions, which describe populations. At that time we'll show how parameters are calculated from probability distributions. In general, small data sets of the type we feature in this book are samples.

4.2 MEASURES OF CENTRAL LOCATION

ARITHMETIC MEAN

There are three different measures that we use to describe the center of a set of data. The first is the best known, the **arithmetic mean**, which we'll refer to simply as the mean. Students may be more familiar with its other name, the *average.* The mean is computed by summing the observations and dividing by the number of observations. We label the observations in a sample $x_1, x_2, ..., x_n$, where x_1 is the first observation, x_2 is the second, and so on until x_n, where n is the sample size. As a result, the sample mean is denoted $\bar{x}$. The number of observations in a population is labeled N. The population mean is denoted by μ (Greek letter *mu*).

MEAN

Population mean: $\mu = \dfrac{\displaystyle\sum_{i=1}^{N} x_i}{N}$ Sample mean: $\bar{x} = \dfrac{\displaystyle\sum_{i=1}^{n} x_i}{n}$

EXAMPLE 4.1

A sample of 10 adults was asked to report the number of hours they spent on the Internet the previous month. The results are listed below. Manually calculate the sample mean.

$$0 \quad 7 \quad 12 \quad 5 \quad 33 \quad 14 \quad 8 \quad 0 \quad 9 \quad 22$$

SOLUTION   Using our notation, we have $x_1 = 0$, $x_2 = 7, \ldots, x_{10} = 22$, and $n = 10$. The sample mean is

$$\bar{x} = \frac{\displaystyle\sum_{i=1}^{n} x_i}{n} = \frac{0 + 7 + 12 + 5 + 33 + 14 + 8 + 0 + 9 + 22}{10} = \frac{110}{10} = 11.0$$

EXAMPLE 4.2

Refer to Example 2.1. Find the mean long-distance telephone bill.

SOLUTION   To calculate the mean, we add the observations and divide the sum by the size of the sample. Thus,

$$\bar{x} = \frac{\displaystyle\sum_{i=1}^{n} x_i}{n} = \frac{42.19 + 38.45 + \cdots + 45.77}{200} = \frac{8,717.52}{200} = 43.59$$

There are several ways to command Excel and Minitab to compute the mean. If we simply want to compute the mean and no other statistics, we can proceed as follows.

EXCEL

COMMANDS

1. Begin by typing or importing the data.
2. Activate any empty cell.
3. Click f_x, select the category **Statistical,** select the function **Average,** and click **OK.**
4. Specify the input range of the data in **Number 1** and click **OK.**

Alternatively, type the following into any active cell:

=**AVERAGE**([Input range])

For Example 4.2, we would type into any cell

=**AVERAGE**(A2:A201)

The active cell would store the mean as 43.5876.

MINITAB

COMMANDS

1. Begin by typing or importing the data into one column.
2. Click **Calc** and **Column Statistics...**.
3. Specify **Mean** as the **Statistic**.
4. Type or select the **Input variable** and click **OK**.

The sample mean is outputted in the Session window as 43.588.

MEDIAN

The second most popular measure of central location is the *median.*

> **MEDIAN**
>
> The **median** is calculated by placing all the observations in order (ascending or descending). The observation that falls in the middle is the median. The sample and population medians are computed in the same way.

When there is an even number of observations, the median is determined by averaging the two observations in the middle.

EXAMPLE 4.3

Find the median for the data in Example 4.1.

SOLUTION   When placed in ascending order, the data appear as follows:

$$0 \quad 0 \quad 5 \quad 7 \quad 8 \quad 9 \quad 12 \quad 14 \quad 22 \quad 33$$

The median is the average of the fifth and sixth observations (the middle two), which are 8 and 9, respectively. Thus, the median is 8.5.

EXAMPLE 4.4

Find the median of the 200 observations in Example 2.1.

SOLUTION   All the observations were placed in order. We observed that the 100th and 101st observations are 26.84 and 26.97, respectively. Thus, the median is the average of these two numbers:

$$\text{Median} = \frac{26.84 + 26.97}{2} = 26.905$$

EXCEL

COMMANDS

To calculate the median, substitute **MEDIAN** in place of **AVERAGE**. That is, type into any empty cell

    =**MEDIAN**([Input Range])

The median is reported as 26.905.

MINITAB

COMMANDS

Follow the instructions above to compute the mean, except at step 3 click **Median** instead of **Mean**.

The median is outputted as 26.905 in the Session window.

INTERPRET

Half the observations are below 26.905 and half the observations are above 26.905.

MODE

The third and last measure of central location that we present here is the *mode*.

> **MODE**
> The **mode** is defined as the observation (or observations) that occurs with the greatest frequency. Both the statistic and parameter are computed in the same way.

For populations and large samples, it is preferable to report the modal class, which we defined in Chapter 2.

There are several problems with using the mode as a measure of central location. First, in a small sample it may not be a very good measure. Second, it may not be unique.

EXAMPLE 4.5

Find the mode for the data in Example 4.1.

SOLUTION   All observations except 0 occur once. There are two 0s. Thus, the mode is 0. As you can see, this is a poor measure of central location. It is nowhere near the center of the data. Compare this with the mean (11.0) and the median (8.5) and you can appreciate that in this example the mean and median are superior measures.

EXAMPLE 4.6

Determine the mode for Example 2.1.

SOLUTION   An examination of the 200 observations reveals that except for 0, it appears that each number is unique. However, there are eight 0s, which indicates that the mode is 0.

 EXCEL

COMMANDS

To compute the mode, substitute **MODE** in place of **AVERAGE** in the instructions above. Note that if there is more than one mode, Excel prints only the smallest one, without indicating whether there are other modes. In this example Excel reports that the mode is 0.

MINITAB

COMMANDS

1. Click **Stat, Tables,** and **Tally....**
2. Specify the name of the variable and **Count.** Click **OK.**

Minitab will provide a count of the frequency of each number. The mode is the observation that has the highest frequency.

EXCEL AND MINITAB: PRINTING ALL THE MEASURES OF CENTRAL LOCATION PLUS OTHER STATISTICS

Both Excel and Minitab can produce the measures of central location plus a variety of others that we will introduce in later sections.

 EXCEL

Excel Output for Examples 4.2, 4.4, and 4.6

	A	B
1	*Bills*	
2		
3	Mean	43.59
4	Standard Error	2.76
5	Median	26.91
6	Mode	0
7	Standard Deviation	38.97
8	Sample Variance	1518.64
9	Kurtosis	-1.29
10	Skewness	0.54
11	Range	119.63
12	Minimum	0
13	Maximum	119.63
14	Sum	8717.52
15	Count	200

Note: In this and other Excel printouts shown in this book, we have improved the appearance by decreasing the number of decimal places and widening some columns.

GENERAL COMMANDS

1. Type or import the data.
2. Click **Tools, Data Analysis...,** and **Descriptive Statistics**.
3. Specify the **Input Range**.
4. Click **Labels in First Row,** if applicable, click **Summary Statistics,** and click **OK.**

COMMANDS FOR EXAMPLES 4.2, 4.4, AND 4.6

Open file **Xm02-01.**

A1:A201

 MINITAB

Minitab Output for Examples 4.2 and 4.4

Descriptive Statistics: Bills

Variable	N	Mean	Median	TrMean	StDev	SE Mean
Bills	200	43.59	26.91	42.00	38.97	2.76

Variable	Minimum	Maximum	Q1	Q3		
Bills	0.00	119.63	9.28	84.94	*(continued)*	

> **MINITAB** *(continued)*
>
> **COMMANDS**
> 1. Type or import the data.
> 2. Click **Stat, Basic Statistics,** and **Display Descriptive Statistics....**
> 3. Select the variable or variables you wish to describe and click **OK**.
>
> **COMMANDS FOR EXAMPLES 4.2 AND 4.4**
> Open file **Xm02-01**.
>
> **Bills** or **C1**

MEAN, MEDIAN, MODE: WHICH IS BEST?

With three measures from which to choose, which one should we use? There are several factors to consider when making our choice of measure of central location. The mean is generally our first selection. However, there are several circumstances when the median is better. The mode is seldom the best measure of central location. One advantage the median holds is that it is not as sensitive to extreme values as is the mean. To illustrate, consider the data in Example 4.1. The mean was 11.0 and the median was 8.5. Now suppose that the respondent who reported 33 hours actually reported 133 hours (obviously an Internet addict). The mean becomes

$$\bar{x} = \frac{\sum_{i=1}^{n} x_i}{n} = \frac{0 + 7 + 12 + 5 + 133 + 14 + 8 + 0 + 9 + 22}{10} = \frac{210}{10} = 21.0$$

This value is exceeded by only two of the ten observations in the sample, making this statistic a poor measure of *central* location. The median stays the same. When there is a relatively small number of extreme observations (either very small or very large, but not both) the median usually produces a better measure of the center of the data.

To see another advantage of the median over the mean, suppose you and your classmates have written a statistics test and the instructor is returning the graded tests. What piece of information is most important to you? The answer, of course, is *your* mark. What is the next important bit of information? The answer is how well you performed relative to the class. Most students ask their instructor for the class mean. This is the wrong statistic to request. You want the *median* because it divides the class into two halves. This information allows you to identify which half of the class your mark falls into. The median provides this information; the mean does not. Nevertheless, the mean can also be useful in this scenario. If there are several sections of the course, the section means can be compared to determine whose class performed best (or worst).

MEASURES OF CENTRAL LOCATION FOR ORDINAL AND NOMINAL DATA

When the data are interval, we can use any of the three measures of central location. However, for ordinal and nominal data, the calculation of the mean is not valid. Because the calculation of the median begins by placing the data in order, this statistic is appropriate for ordinal data. The mode, which is determined by counting the frequency of each observation, is appropriate for nominal data. However, nominal data do not have a "center," so we cannot interpret the mode of nominal data in that way.

APPLICATIONS IN FINANCE: *GEOMETRIC MEAN*

The arithmetic mean is the single most popular and useful measure of central location. We noted certain situations where the median is a better measure of central location. However, there is another circumstance where neither the mean nor the median is the best measure. When the variable is a growth rate or rate of change, such as the value of an investment over periods of time, we need another measure. This will become apparent from the following illustration.

Suppose you make a 2-year investment of $1,000 and it grows by 100% to $2,000 during the first year. During the second year, however, the investment suffers a 50% loss, from $2,000 back to $1,000. The rates of return for years 1 and 2 are $R_1 = 100\%$ and $R_2 = -50\%$, respectively. The arithmetic mean (and the median) is computed as

$$\bar{R} = \frac{R_1 + R_2}{2} = \frac{100 + (-50)}{2} = 25\%$$

But this figure is misleading. Because there was no change in the value of the investment from the beginning to the end of the 2-year period, the "average" compounded rate of return is 0%. As you will see, this is the value of the *geometric mean*.

Geometric Mean

Let R_i denote the rate of return (in decimal form) in period i ($i = 1, 2, ..., n$). The **geometric mean** R_g of the returns $R_1, R_2, ..., R_n$ is defined such that

$$(1 + R_g)^n = (1 + R_1)(1 + R_2)\cdots(1 + R_n)$$

Solving for R_g, we produce the following formula:

$$R_g = \sqrt[n]{(1 + R_1)(1 + R_2)\cdots(1 + R_n)} - 1$$

The geometric mean of our investment illustration is

$$R_g = \sqrt[n]{(1 + R_1)(1 + R_2)\cdots(1 + R_n)} - 1$$
$$= \sqrt[2]{(1 + 1)(1 + [-.50])} - 1 = 1 - 1 = 0$$

The geometric mean is therefore 0%. This is the single "average" return that allows us to compute the value of the investment at the end of the investment period from the beginning value. That is, using the formula for compound interest with the rate = 0%, we find

Value at the end of the investment period
$$= 1,000(1 + R_g)^2 = 1,000(1 + 0)^2 = 1,000$$

The geometric mean is used whenever we wish to find the "average" growth rate, or rate of change, in a variable *over time*. It must be stressed, however, that the arithmetic mean of *n* returns (or growth rates) is the appropriate mean to calculate if you wish to estimate the mean rate of return (or growth rate) for any *single* period in the future. That is, in the illustration above, if we wanted to estimate the rate of return in year 3, we would use the arithmetic mean of the two annual rates of return, which we found to be 25%.

EXCEL

Excel calculates the geometric mean. Follow these instructions.

COMMANDS
1. Type or import the value of $1 + R_1$ into a column.
2. Click f_x, **Statistical,** and **GEOMEAN**.
3. Specify the input range under **Number 1** and click **OK**.
4. Subtract 1 to produce R_g.

MINITAB

Minitab does not compute the geometric mean.

Here is a summary of the numerical techniques introduced in this section and when to use them.

FACTORS THAT IDENTIFY WHEN TO COMPUTE THE MEAN
1. **Objective:** Describe a set of data.
2. **Type of data:** Interval
3. **Descriptive measurement:** Central location

FACTORS THAT IDENTIFY WHEN TO COMPUTE THE MEDIAN
1. **Objective:** Describe a set of data.
2. **Type of data:** Ordinal or interval (with extreme observations)
3. **Descriptive measurement:** Central location

FACTORS THAT IDENTIFY WHEN TO COMPUTE THE MODE
1. **Objective:** Describe a set of data.
2. **Type of data:** Interval, ordinal, or nominal

FACTORS THAT IDENTIFY WHEN TO COMPUTE THE GEOMETRIC MEAN
1. **Objective:** Describe a set of data.
2. **Type of data:** Interval; growth rates

EXERCISES

4.1 A sample of 12 people was asked how much change they had in their pockets and wallets. The responses (in cents) are

52   25   15   0   104   44   60   30   33   81   40   5

Determine the mean, median, and mode for these data.

4.2 The number of sick days due to colds and flu last year was recorded by a sample of 15 adults. The data are

5   7   0   3   15   6   5   9   3   8   10   5   2   0   12

Compute the mean, median, and mode.

4.3 A random sample of 12 joggers was asked to keep track and report the number of miles they ran last week. The responses are

5.5   7.2   1.6   22.0   8.7   2.8
5.3   3.4   12.5   18.6   8.3   6.6

a Compute the three statistics that measure central location.
b Briefly describe what each statistic tells you.

4.4 The midterm test for a statistics course has a time limit of 1 hour. However, like most statistics exams, this one was quite easy. To assess how easy, the professor recorded the amount of time taken by a sample of nine students to hand in their test papers. The times (rounded to the nearest minute) are

33   29   45   60   42   19   52   38   36

a Compute the mean, median, and mode.
b What have you learned from the three statistics calculated in part **a**?

4.5 The professors at Wilfrid Laurier University are required to submit their final exams to the registrar's office 10 days before the end of the semester. The exam coordinator sampled 20 professors and recorded the number of days before the final exam that each submitted his or her exam. The results are

14   8   3   2   6   4   9   13   10   12
7   4   9   13   15   8   11   12   4   0

a Compute the mean, median, and mode.
b Briefly describe what each statistic tells you.

4.6 Compute the geometric mean of the following rates of return:

.25   −.10   .50

4.7 What is the geometric mean of the following rates of return?

.50   .30   −.50   −.25

4.8 The following returns were realized on an investment over a 5-year period.

Year	1	2	3	4	5
Rate of Return	.10	.22	.06	−.05	.20

a Compute the mean and median of the returns.
b Compute the geometric mean.
c Which one of the three statistics computed above best describes the return over the 5-year period? Explain.

4.9 An investment you made 5 years ago has realized the following rates of return:

Year	1	2	3	4	5
Rate of Return	−.15	−.20	.15	−.08	.50

a Compute the mean and median of the rates of return.
b Compute the geometric mean.
c Which one of the three statistics computed above best describes the return over the 5-year period? Explain.

4.10 An investment of $1,000 you made 4 years ago was worth $1,200 after the first year, $1,200 after the second year, $1,500 after the third year, and $2,000 today.

a Compute the annual rates of return.
b Compute the mean and median of the rates of return.
c Compute the geometric mean.
d Discuss whether the mean, median, or geometric mean is the best measure of the performance of the investment.

4.11 Suppose that you bought a stock six years ago at $12. The stock's price at the end of each year is shown below.

Year	1	2	3	4	5	6
Price	10	14	15	22	30	25

a Compute the rate of return for each year.
b Compute the mean and median of the rates of return.
c Compute the geometric mean of the rates of return.
d Explain why the best statistic to use to describe what happened to the price of the stock over the 6-year period is the geometric mean.

The following exercises require the use of a computer and software.

4.12 The starting salaries of a sample of 125 recent MBA graduates are stored in file Xr04-12.
a Determine the mean and median of these data.
b What do these two statistics tell you about the starting salaries of MBA graduates?

4.13 To determine whether changing the color of their invoices improves the speed of payment, 200 customers were selected at random and sent their invoices on blue-colored paper. The number of days until the bills were paid was recorded and stored in file Xr04-13. Calculate the mean and median of these data. Report what you have discovered.

4.14 A survey undertaken by the U.S. Bureau of Labor Statistics, Annual Consumer Expenditure, asks American adults to report the amount of money spent on reading material last year. These data are stored in file Xr04-14. (Adapted from *Statistical Abstract of the United States*, 1999, Table 431)
a Compute the mean and median of the sample.
b What do the statistics computed in part **a** tell you about the reading materials expenditures?

4.15 The Travel Industry Association of America conducts annual surveys of travelers to develop information useful to the travel industry. One question asks business travelers and people who have taken pleasure trips to indicate the number of miles traveled. These data appear in file Xr04-15. (Adapted from *Statistical Abstract of the United States*, 1999, Table 455)
a Compute the mean and median of the distance traveled for business purposes.
b Compute the mean and median of the distance traveled for pleasure.
c Summarize your findings.

4.16 Employee training and education have become important factors in the success of many firms. An annual survey undertaken by the U.S. Bureau of Labor Statistics attempts to measure the amount of training. A survey of employers with more than 500 employees asked the personnel manager to report the number of hours of employee training for the 6-month period May to October. These data are stored in file Xr04-16. (Adapted from *Statistical Abstract of the United States*, 1999, Table 691)
a Compute the mean and median.
b Interpret the statistics you computed.

4.17 In an effort to slow drivers, traffic engineers painted a solid line 3 feet from the curb over the entire length of a road and filled the space with diagonal lines. The lines made the road look narrower. A sample of car speeds was taken after the lines were drawn. The speeds are stored in file Xr04-17.
a Compute the mean, median, and mode of these data.
b Briefly describe the information you acquired from each statistic calculated in part **a**.

4.18 How much do Americans spend on various food groups? A sample of 350 American families was surveyed and asked to report the amount of money spent annually on fruits and vegetables. These data are stored in file Xr04-18. Compute the mean and median of these data and interpret the results. (Adapted from *Statistical Abstract of the United States*, 1999, Table 738)

4.3 MEASURES OF VARIABILITY

The statistics introduced in Section 4.2 serve to provide information about the central location of the data. However, as we've already discussed in Chapter 2, there are other characteristics of data that are of interest to practitioners of statistics. One such characteristic is the spread or variability of the data. In this section we introduce four measures of variability. Let's start with the simplest.

RANGE

RANGE

Range = Largest observation − Smallest observation

The advantage of the range is its simplicity. The disadvantage is also its simplicity. Because the range is calculated from only two observations, it tells us nothing about the other observations. Consider the following two sets of data:

Set 1:   4, 4, 4, 4, 4, 50

Set 2:   4, 8, 15, 24, 39, 50

The range of both sets is 46. The two sets of data are completely different and yet their ranges are the same. To measure variability, we need other statistics that incorporate all the data and not just two observations.

VARIANCE

The variance and its related measure, the standard deviation, are arguably the most important statistics. They are used to measure variability, but as you will discover, they play a vital role in almost all statistical inference procedures.

> **VARIANCE**
>
> Population variance: $\sigma^2 = \dfrac{\sum_{i=1}^{N}(x_i - \mu)^2}{N}$
>
> Sample variance:* $s^2 = \dfrac{\sum_{i=1}^{n}(x_i - \bar{x})^2}{n - 1}$

The population variance is represented by σ^2 (Greek letter *sigma* squared).

To compute the sample variance s^2 we begin by calculating the sample mean $\bar{x}$. Next we compute the difference (also call the **deviation**) between each observation and the mean. We square the deviations and sum. Finally, we divide the sum of squared deviations by $n - 1$. It may seem strange that we divide by $n - 1$ rather than by n. However, we do so for the following reason.

Population parameters in practical settings are seldom known. One of the objectives of statistical inference is to estimate the parameter from the statistic. For example, we estimate the population mean μ from the sample mean $\bar{x}$. Although it is not logical, the statistic created by dividing $\sum (x_i - \bar{x})^2$ by $n - 1$ is a better estimator than is the one created by dividing by n. We will discuss this issue in greater detail in Section 10.2.

We'll illustrate with a simple example. Suppose that we have the following observations of the numbers of hours five students spent studying statistics last week:

$$8 \quad 4 \quad 9 \quad 11 \quad 3$$

The mean is

$$\bar{x} = \frac{8 + 4 + 9 + 11 + 3}{5} = \frac{35}{5} = 7$$

---

* Technically, the sample variance is calculated by dividing the sum of squared deviations by n. The statistic computed by dividing the sum of squared deviations by $n - 1$ is called the *sample variance corrected for the mean*. Because this statistic is used extensively, we will shorten its name to *sample variance*.

For each observation we determine its deviation from the mean.

$$8 - 7 = 1$$

$$4 - 7 = -3$$

$$9 - 7 = 2$$

$$11 - 7 = 4$$

$$3 - 7 = -4$$

Squaring the deviations yields

$$(1)^2 = 1$$

$$(-3)^2 = 9$$

$$(2)^2 = 4$$

$$(4)^2 = 16$$

$$(-4)^2 = 16$$

Summing and dividing by $n - 1$ produces

$$s^2 = \frac{1 + 9 + 4 + 16 + 16}{5 - 1} = \frac{46}{4} = 11.5$$

The calculation of this statistic raises several questions. Why do we square the deviations? If you examine the deviations, you will see that some of the deviations are positive and some are negative. When you add them together the sum is 0. This will always be the case because the sum of the positive deviations will always equal the sum of the negative deviations. Consequently, we square the deviations to avoid the "canceling effect."

Is it possible to avoid the canceling effect without squaring? We could average the *absolute value* of the deviations. In fact, such a statistic has already been invented. It is called the **mean absolute deviation** or MAD. However, this statistic has limited utility and is seldom used.

What is the unit of measurement of the variance? Because we squared the deviations, we also squared the units. In this illustration the units were hours (of study). Thus, the sample variance is 11.5 hours^2.

The calculations for larger data sets are quite time-consuming. The following shortcut for the sample variance may help lighten the load.

SHORTCUT FOR SAMPLE VARIANCE

Sample variance: $\dfrac{1}{n-1}\left[\displaystyle\sum_{i=1}^{n} x_i^2 - \dfrac{\left(\displaystyle\sum_{i=1}^{n} x_i \right)^2}{n} \right]$

EXAMPLE 4.7

The following are the number of summer jobs a sample of six students applied for. Find the mean and variance of these data.

$$17 \quad 15 \quad 23 \quad 7 \quad 9 \quad 13$$

SOLUTION The mean of the six observations is

$$\bar{x} = \frac{17 + 15 + 23 + 7 + 9 + 13}{6} = \frac{84}{6} = 14 \text{ jobs}$$

The sample variance is

$$s^2 = \frac{\sum\limits_{i=1}^{n}(x_i - \bar{x})^2}{n - 1}$$

$$= \frac{(17 - 14)^2 + (15 - 14)^2 + (23 - 14)^2 + (7 - 14)^2 + (9 - 14)^2 + (13 - 14)^2}{6 - 1}$$

$$= \frac{9 + 1 + 81 + 49 + 25 + 1}{5} = \frac{166}{5} = 33.2 \text{ jobs}^2$$

Shortcut Method

$$\sum_{i=1}^{n} x_i^2 = 17^2 + 15^2 + 23^2 + 7^2 + 9^2 + 13^2 = 1{,}342$$

$$\sum_{i=1}^{n} x_i = 17 + 15 + 23 + 7 + 9 + 13 = 84$$

$$\left(\sum_{i=1}^{n} x_i\right)^2 = 84^2 = 7{,}056$$

$$s^2 = \frac{1}{n-1}\left[\sum_{i=1}^{n} x_i^2 - \frac{\left(\sum\limits_{i=1}^{n} x_i\right)^2}{n}\right] = \frac{1}{6-1}\left[1{,}342 - \frac{7{,}056}{6}\right] = 33.2 \text{ jobs}^2$$

EXCEL

COMMANDS
Follow the instructions to compute the mean, except type VAR instead of AVERAGE.

MINITAB

COMMANDS
Minitab does not compute the variance directly.

Interpreting the Variance

We calculated the variance in Example 4.7 to be 33.2 jobs^2. What does this statistic tell us? Unfortunately, the variance provides us with only a rough idea about the amount of variation in the data. However, this statistic is useful when comparing two or more sets of data. If the variance of one data set is larger than that of a second data set, we interpret that to mean that the observations in the first set display more variation than the observations in the second set.

The problem of interpretation is caused by the way the variance is computed. Because we squared the deviations from the mean, the unit attached to the variance is the square of the unit attached to the original observations. That is, in Example 4.7, the unit of the data is jobs; the unit of the variance is jobs-squared. This contributes to the problem of interpretation. We resolve this difficulty by calculating another related measure of variability.

STANDARD DEVIATION

> ### STANDARD DEVIATION
>
> Population standard deviation: $\sigma = \sqrt{\sigma^2}$
>
> Sample standard deviation: $s = \sqrt{s^2}$

The standard deviation is simply the square root of the variance. Thus, in Example 4.7, the sample standard deviation is

$$s = \sqrt{s^2} = \sqrt{33.2} = 5.76 \text{ jobs}$$

Notice that the unit associated with the standard deviation is the unit of the original data set.

EXAMPLE 4.8

Consistency is the hallmark of a good golfer. Golf equipment manufacturers are constantly seeking ways to improve their products. Suppose that a recent innovation is designed to improve the consistency of its users. As a test, a golfer was asked to hit 150 shots using a 7-iron, 75 of which were hit with his current club and 75 with the innovative 7-iron. The distances were measured and recorded in file Xm04-08. Which 7-iron is more consistent?

SOLUTION   To gauge the consistency, we need to determine the standard deviations. (We could also compute the variances, but as we just pointed out, the standard deviation is easier to interpret.) We can get Excel and Minitab to print the sample standard deviations. Alternatively, we can calculate all the descriptive statistics, a course of action we recommend because we often need several statistics. The printouts for both 7-irons appear below.

   EXCEL

	A	B	C	D	E
1	Current			Innovation	
2					
3	Mean	150.55		Mean	150.15
4	Standard Error	0.67		Standard Error	0.36
5	Median	151		Median	150
6	Mode	150		Mode	149
7	Standard Deviation	5.79		Standard Deviation	3.09
8	Sample Variance	33.55		Sample Variance	9.56
9	Kurtosis	0.13		Kurtosis	-0.89
10	Skewness	-0.43		Skewness	0.18
11	Range	28		Range	12
12	Minimum	134		Minimum	144
13	Maximum	162		Maximum	156
14	Sum	11291		Sum	11261
15	Count	75		Count	75

MINITAB
Descriptive Statistics: Current, Innovation

Variable	N	Mean	Median	TrMean	StDev	SE Mean
Current	75	150.55	151.00	150.72	5.79	0.67
Innovati	75	150.15	150.00	150.13	3.09	0.36

Variable	Minimum	Maximum	Q1	Q3
Current	134.00	162.00	148.00	155.00
Innovati	144.00	156.00	148.00	152.00

INTERPRET

The standard deviation of the distances of the current 7-iron is 5.79 yards, whereas that of the innovative 7-iron is 3.09 yards. Based on this sample, the innovative club is more consistent. Because the mean distances are similar, it would appear that the new club is indeed superior.

Interpreting the Standard Deviation

Knowing the mean and standard deviation allows the statistics practitioner to extract useful bits of information. The information depends on the shape of the histogram. If the histogram is bell shaped, we can use the Empirical Rule.

EMPIRICAL RULE
1. Approximately 68% of all observations fall within one standard deviation of the mean.
2. Approximately 95% of all observations fall within two standard deviations of the mean.
3. Approximately 99.7% of all observations fall within three standard deviations of the mean.

EXAMPLE 4.9

After an analysis of the returns on an investment, a statistics practitioner discovered that the histogram is bell shaped and that the mean and standard deviation are 10% and 8%, respectively. What can you say about the way the returns are distributed?

SOLUTION   Because the histogram is bell shaped, we can apply the Empirical Rule. Thus,
1. Approximately 68% of the returns lie between 2% (the mean minus one standard deviation = 10 − 8) and 18% (the mean plus one standard deviation = 10 + 8).

2. Approximately 95% of the returns lie between −6% [the mean minus two standard deviations = 10 − 2(8)] and 26% [the mean plus two standard deviations = 10 + 2(8)].

3. Approximately 99.7% of the returns lie between −14% [the mean minus three standard deviations = 10 − 3(8)] and 34% [the mean plus three standard deviations = 10 + 3(8)].

A more general interpretation of the standard deviation is derived from *Chebysheff's theorem*, which applies to histograms of all shapes.

CHEBYSHEFF'S THEOREM
The proportion of observations in any sample that lie within k standard deviations of the mean is at least

$$1 - \frac{1}{k^2} \quad \text{for } k > 1$$

When $k = 2$, Chebysheff's theorem states that at least three-quarters $(1 - \frac{1}{2^2} = \frac{3}{4})$ of all observation lie within two standard deviations of the mean. With $k = 3$, Chebysheff's theorem states that at least eight-ninths $(1 - \frac{1}{3^2} = \frac{8}{9})$ of all observations lie within three standard deviations of the mean.

Note that the Empirical Rule provides approximate proportions, while Chebysheff's theorem provides lower bounds on the proportions contained in the intervals.

EXAMPLE 4.10

The annual salaries of the employees of a chain of computer stores produced a positively skewed histogram. The mean and standard deviation are \$28,000 and \$3,000, respectively. What can you say about the salaries at this chain?

SOLUTION   Because the histogram is not bell shaped, we cannot use the Empirical Rule. We must employ Chebysheff's theorem instead.

The intervals created by adding and subtracting two and three standard deviations to and from the mean are as follows:

1. At least 75% of the salaries lie between \$22,000 [the mean minus two standard deviations = 28,000 − 2(3,000)] and \$34,000 [the mean plus two standard deviations = 28,000 + 2(3,000)].

2. At least 88.9% of the salaries lie between \$19,000 [the mean minus three standard deviations = 28,000 − 3(3,000)] and \$37,000 [the mean plus three standard deviations = 28,000 + 3(3,000)].

COEFFICIENT OF VARIATION

Is a standard deviation of 10 a large number indicating great variability, or is it a small number indicating little variability? The answer depends somewhat on the magnitude of the observations in the data set. If the observations are in the millions, a standard deviation of 10 will probably be considered a small number. On the other hand, if the observations are less than 50, the standard deviation of 10 would be seen as a large number. This logic lies behind yet another measure of variability, the *coefficient of variation*.

COEFFICIENT OF VARIATION
The **coefficient of variation** of a set of observations is the standard deviation of the observations divided by their mean.

Population coefficient of variation: $CV = \dfrac{\sigma}{\mu}$

Sample coefficient of variation: $cv = \dfrac{s}{\bar{x}}$

MEASURES OF VARIABILITY FOR ORDINAL AND NOMINAL DATA

The measures of variability introduced in this section can be used only for interval data. The next section will feature a measure that can be used to describe the variability of ordinal data. There are no measures of variability for nominal data.

We complete this section by reviewing the factors that identify the use of measures of variability.

FACTORS THAT IDENTIFY WHEN TO COMPUTE THE RANGE, VARIANCE, STANDARD DEVIATION, AND COEFFICIENT OF VARIATION

1. **Objective:** Describe a set of data.
2. **Type of data:** Interval
3. **Descriptive measurement:** Variability

EXERCISES

4.19 Calculate the variance of the following sample.

9 3 7 4 1 7 5 4

4.20 Calculate the variance of the following sample.

4 5 3 6 5 6 5 6

4.21 Determine the variance and standard deviation of the following sample.

12 6 22 31 23 13 15 17 21

4.22 Find the variance and standard deviation of the following sample.

0 –5 –3 6 4 –4 1 –5 0 3

4.23 Examine the three samples listed below. Without performing any calculations, indicate which sample has the largest amount of variation and which sample has the smallest amount of variation. Explain how you produced your answer.

a 17, 29, 12, 16, 11
b 22, 18, 23, 20, 17
c 24, 37, 6, 39, 29

4.24 Refer to Exercise 4.23. Calculate the variance for each part. Was your answer in Exercise 4.23 correct?

4.25 A friend calculates a variance and reports that it is –25.0. How do you know that he has made a serious calculation error?

4.26 Create a sample of five numbers whose mean is 6 and whose standard deviation is 0.

4.27 A set of data whose histogram is bell shaped yields a sample mean and standard deviation of 50 and 4, respectively. Approximately what proportion of observations

a are between 46 and 54?
b are between 42 and 58?
c are between 38 and 62?

4.28 Refer to Exercise 4.27. Approximately what proportion of observations

a are less than 46?
b are less than 58?
c are greater than 54?

4.29 A set of data whose histogram is extremely skewed yields a sample mean and standard deviation of 70 and 12, respectively. What is the minimum proportion of observations that

a are between 46 and 94?
b are between 34 and 106?

4.30 A statistics practitioner determined that the mean and standard deviation of a sample of 500 observations were 120 and 30, respectively. What can you say about the proportions of observations that lie between

a 90 and 150?
b 60 and 180?
c 30 and 210?

The following exercises require a computer and software.

4.31 There has been much media coverage of the high cost of medicinal drugs in the United States. One concern is the large variation in costs from pharmacy to pharmacy. To investigate, a consumer advocacy group took a random sample of 100 pharmacies around the country and recorded the price of Prozac. These data (in dollars per 100 pills) are stored in file Xr04-31. Compute the range, variance, and standard deviation of the prices. Discuss what these statistics tell you.

4.32 Many traffic experts argue that the most important factor in accidents is not the average speed of cars but the amount of variation. Suppose that the speeds of a sample of 200 cars were taken over a stretch of highway that has seen numerous accidents. The data are stored in Xr04-32. Compute the variance and standard deviation of the speeds, and interpret the results.

4.33 Three men were trying to make the football team as punters. The coach had each of them punt the ball 50 times and the distances were recorded in columns 1, 2, and 3 in file Xr04-33.

a Compute the variance and standard deviation for each punter.

b What do these statistics tell you about the punters?

4.34 Variance is often used to measure quality in production-line products. Suppose that a sample of steel rods that are supposed to be exactly 100 cm long is taken. The length of each is determined, and the results are stored in Xr04-34. Calculate the variance and the standard deviation. Briefly describe what these statistics tell you.

4.35 To learn more about the size of withdrawals at a banking machine, the proprietor took a sample of 75 withdrawals and stored the amounts in file Xr04-35. Determine the mean and standard deviation of these data, and describe what these two statistics tell you about the withdrawal amounts.

4.36 Everyone is familiar with waiting lines or queues. For example, people wait in line at a supermarket to go through the checkout counter. There are two factors that determine how long the queue becomes: One is the speed of service; the other is the number of arrivals at the checkout counter. The mean number of arrivals is an important number, but so is the standard deviation. Suppose that a consultant for the supermarket counts the number of arrivals per hour during a sample of 150 hours. The data are stored in Xr04-36.

a Compute the standard deviation of the number of arrivals.

b Assuming that the histogram is bell shaped, interpret the standard deviation.

4.4 MEASURES OF RELATIVE STANDING AND BOX PLOTS

Measures of relative standing are designed to provide information about the position of particular values relative to the entire data set. We've already presented one measure of relative standing, the median, which is also a measure of central location. Recall that the median divides the data set into halves, allowing the statistics practitioner to determine which half of the data set each observation lies in. The statistics we're about to introduce will give you much more detailed information.

> **PERCENTILE**
>
> The **Pth percentile** is the value for which P percent are less than that value and $(100 - P)\%$ are greater than that value.

The scores and the percentiles of the SAT (Scholastic Achievement Test), the GMAT (Graduate Management Admission Test), as well as various other admissions tests, are reported to students writing them. Suppose, for example, that your SAT score is reported to be at the 60th percentile. This means that 60% of all the other marks are below yours and 40% are above it. You now know exactly where you stand relative to the population of SAT scores.

We have special names for the 25th, 50th, and 75th percentiles. Because these three statistics divide the set of data into quarters, these measures of relative standing are also called **quartiles**. The **first** or **lower quartile** is labeled Q_1. It is equal to the 25th percentile. The **second quartile**, Q_2, is equal to the 50th percentile, which is also the median. The **third** or **upper quartile**, Q_3, is equal to the 75th percentile. Incidentally, many people confuse the terms *quartile* and *quarter*. A common error is to state that someone is in the lower *quartile* of a group when they actually mean that someone is in the lower *quarter* of a group.

Besides quartiles, we can also convert percentiles into quintiles and deciles. **Quintiles** divide the data into fifths and **deciles** divide the data into tenths.

LOCATING PERCENTILES

The following formula allows us to approximate the location of any percentile.

> **LOCATION OF A PERCENTILE**
>
> $$L_P = (n + 1)\frac{P}{100}$$
>
> where L_p is the location of the Pth percentile.

EXAMPLE 4.11

Calculate the 25th, 50th, and 75th percentiles (first, second, and third quartiles) of the data in Example 4.1.

SOLUTION   Placing the 10 observations in ascending order, we get

$$0 \quad 0 \quad 5 \quad 7 \quad 8 \quad 9 \quad 12 \quad 14 \quad 22 \quad 33$$

The location of the 25th percentile is

$$L_{25} = (10 + 1)\frac{25}{100} = (11)(.25) = 2.75$$

The 25th percentile is three-quarters of the distance between the second (which is 0) and the third (which is 5) observations. Three-quarters of the distance is

$$(.75)(5 - 0) = 3.75$$

Because the second observation is 0, the 25th percentile is $0 + 3.75 = 3.75$.

To locate the 50th percentile, we substitute $P = 50$ into the formula and produce

$$L_{50} = (10 + 1)\frac{50}{100} = (11)(.5) = 5.5$$

which means that the 50th percentile is halfway between the fifth and sixth observations. The fifth and sixth observations are 8 and 9, respectively. The 50th percentile is 8.5. This is the median calculated in Example 4.3.

The 75th percentile's location is

$$L_{75} = (10 + 1)\frac{75}{100} = (11)(.75) = 8.25$$

Thus, it is located one-quarter of the distance between the eighth and the ninth observations, which are 14 and 22, respectively. One-quarter of the distance is

$$(.25)(22 - 14) = 2$$

which means that the 75th percentile is $14 + 2 = 16$.

EXAMPLE 4.12

Determine the quartiles for Example 2.1.

SOLUTION

 EXCEL

	A	B
1	*Bills*	
2		
3	Mean	43.59
4	Standard Error	2.76
5	Median	26.91
6	Mode	0.00
7	Standard Deviation	38.97
8	Sample Variance	1518.64
9	Kurtosis	-1.29
10	Skewness	0.54
11	Range	119.63
12	Minimum	0.00
13	Maximum	119.63
14	Sum	8717.52
15	Count	200
16	Largest(50)	85
17	Smallest(50)	9.22

COMMANDS

COMMANDS FOR EXAMPLE 4.12

1. Follow the instructions for **Descriptive Statistics**.
2. In the dialogue box click **Kth Largest** and type in the integer closest to $n/4$. **50**
3. Repeat for **Kth Smallest**, typing in the integer closest to $n/4$. **50**

Excel approximates the third and first quartiles in the following way. The **Largest(50)** is 85, which is the number such that 150 numbers are below it and 49 numbers are above it. The **Smallest(50)** is 9.22, which is the number such that 49 numbers are below it and 150 numbers are above it. The median is 26.91, a statistic we computed in Example 4.4.

 MINITAB

Descriptive Statistics: Bills

Variable	N	Mean	Median	TrMean	StDev	SE Mean
Bills	200	43.59	26.91	42.00	38.97	2.76

Variable	Minimum	Maximum	Q1	Q3		
Bills	0.00	119.63	9.28	84.94		

Minitab outputs the first and third quartiles as Q1 (9.28) and Q3 (84.94), respectively, and the median as 26.91.

We can often get an idea of the shape of the histogram from the quartiles. For example, if the first and second quartiles are closer to each other than are the second and third quartiles, the histogram is positively skewed. If the first and second quartiles are farther apart than the second and third quartiles, the histogram is negatively skewed. However, if the difference between the first and second quartiles is approximately equal to the difference between the second and third quartiles, the histogram is not necessarily symmetric. We need to examine the entire distribution to draw that conclusion.

INTERQUARTILE RANGE

The quartiles can be used to create another measure of variability, the *interquartile range*, which is defined as follows.

> **INTERQUARTILE RANGE**
>
> Interquartile range $= Q_3 - Q_1$

The interquartile range measures the spread of the middle 50% of the observations. Large values of this statistic indicate that the first and third quartiles are far apart, indicating a high level of variability.

EXAMPLE 4.13

Determine the interquartile range for Example 2.1.

SOLUTION   Using Excel's approximations of the first and third quartiles, we find

$$\text{Interquartile range } = Q_3 - Q_1 = 85 - 9.22 = 75.78$$

BOX PLOTS

Now that we have introduced quartiles, we can present one more graphical technique, the box plot. This technique graphs five statistics: the minimum and maximum observations, and the first, second, and third quartiles. It also depicts other features of a set of data. Figure 4.1 exhibits the box plot of the data in Example 4.1.

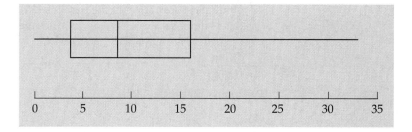

Figure 4.1
Box plot for Example 4.1

The three vertical lines of the box are the first, second, and third quartiles. The lines extending to the left and right are called **whiskers**. Any points that lie outside the whiskers are called **outliers**. The whiskers extend outward to the smaller of 1.5 times the interquartile range or to the most extreme point that is not an outlier.

Outliers

Outliers are unusually large or small observations. Because an outlier is considerably removed from the main body of the data set, its validity is suspect. Consequently, outliers should be checked to determine that they are not the result of an error in recording their values.

EXAMPLE 4.14

Draw the box plot for Example 2.1.

SOLUTION

 EXCEL

	A	B
2	Bills	
3	Smallest = 0	
4	Q1 = 9.275	
5	Median = 26.905	
6	Q3 = 84.9425	
7	Largest = 119.63	
8	IQR = 75.6675	
9	Outliers:	

COMMANDS

1. Type or import the data into one column.
2. Click **Tools, Data Analysis Plus**, and **Box Plot**.
3. Specify the **Input Range**.
4. Click **Labels** if the first row of the input range contains the name of the variable. Click **OK**.

COMMANDS FOR EXAMPLE 4.14

Open file **Xm02-01**.

A1:A201

Notice that the quartiles produced in the **Box Plot** are not exactly the same as those produced by **Descriptive Statistics**. The methods of determining these statistics vary slightly between the two methods.

 MINITAB

COMMANDS

1. Type or import the data into one column.
2. Click **Graph** and **Box Plot**....
3. Type (or use **Select**) the name of the variable under **Y**.
4. Click **Options** and click **Transpose X and Y**. Click **OK**. Click **OK**.

COMMANDS FOR EXAMPLE 4.14

Open file **Xm02-01**.

Bills or **C1**

INTERPRET

The smallest value is 0 and the largest is 119.63. The first, second, and third quartiles are 9.275, 26.905, and 84.9425, respectively. The interquartile range is 75.6675. One and one half times the interquartile range is $1.5 \times 75.6675 = 113.5013$. Outliers are defined as any observations that are less than $9.275 - 113.5013 = -104.226$ and any observations that are larger than $84.9425 + 113.5013 = 198.4438$. The whisker to the left extends to 0, which is the smallest observation that is not an outlier. The whisker to the right extends to 119.63, which is the largest observation that is not an outlier. There are no outliers.

The box plot is particularly useful when comparing two or more data sets.

EXAMPLE 4.15

There are many fast-food restaurants with drive-through windows offering drivers and their passengers the advantages of quick service. To measure how good the service is, an organization called QSR organized a study wherein the amount of time taken by a sample of drive-through customers at each of five restaurants was recorded and stored in file Xm04-15. Compare the five sets of data using a box plot and interpret the results.

SOLUTION   We'll use the computer to produce the box plots.

EXCEL

	A	B
2	*Popeyes*	
3	Smallest = 112	
4	Q1 = 156.75	
5	Median = 175	
6	Q3 = 192.75	
7	Largest = 238	
8	IQR = 36	
9	Outliers:	

15	*Wendy's*	
16	Smallest = 95	
17	Q1 = 133	
18	Median = 143.5	
19	Q3 = 155	
20	Largest = 201	
21	IQR = 22	
22	Outliers: 201, 199, 190, 97, 95,

28	*McDonald's*	
29	Smallest = 121	
30	Q1 = 136	
31	Median = 153	
32	Q3 = 177.5	
33	Largest = 223	
34	IQR = 41.5	
35	Outliers:	

41	*Hardee's*	
42	Smallest = 121	
43	Q1 = 141.25	
44	Median = 163	
45	Q3 = 207.25	
46	Largest = 338	
47	IQR = 66	
48	Outliers: 338,

54	*Jack in Box*	
55	Smallest = 190	
56	Q1 = 253.25	
57	Median = 276.5	
58	Q3 = 297.5	
59	Largest = 355	
60	IQR = 44.25	
61	Outliers:	

COMMANDS

Follow the instructions on page 113 and specify the input range as **A1:E101.**

MINITAB

COMMANDS

1. Type or import the data into two columns. One column stores the observations and the other stores codes identifying the restaurant (where 1 = Popeye's, 2 = Wendy's, 3 = McDonald's, 4 = Hardee's and 5 = Jack in the Box.
2. Click **Graph** and **Boxplot...**.

(continued)

MINITAB *(continued)*
3. Specify the observations under **Y** and the codes under **X**.
4. Click **Options...** and **Transpose X and Y**. Click **OK**. Click **OK**.

INTERPRET

Wendy's times appear to be the lowest and most consistent. The service times for Hardee's display considerably more variability. The slowest service times are provided by Jack in the Box. The service times for Popeye's, Wendy's, and Jack in the Box seem to be symmetric. However, the times for McDonald's and Hardee's are positively skewed.

MEASURES OF RELATIVE STANDING AND VARIABILITY FOR ORDINAL DATA

Because the measures of relative standing are computed by ordering the data, these statistics are appropriate for ordinal as well as for interval data. Furthermore, because the interquartile range is calculated by taking the difference between the upper and lower quartiles, it too can be employed to measure the variability of ordinal data.

Here are the factors that tell us when to use the techniques presented in this section.

> **FACTORS THAT IDENTIFY WHEN TO COMPUTE PERCENTILES AND QUARTILES**
> 1. **Objective:** Describe a set of data.
> 2. **Type of data:** Interval or ordinal
> 3. **Descriptive measurement:** Relative standing

> **FACTORS THAT IDENTIFY WHEN TO COMPUTE THE INTERQUARTILE RANGE**
> 1. **Objective:** Describe a set of data.
> 2. **Type of data:** Interval or ordinal
> 3. **Descriptive measurement:** Variability

EXERCISES

4.37 Calculate the first, second, and third quartiles of the following sample.

5 8 2 9 5 3 7 4 2 7 4 10 4 3 5

4.38 Find the third and eighth deciles (30th and 80th percentiles) of the following data set.

26 23 29 31 24 22 15 31 30 20

4.39 Find the first and second quintiles (20th and 40th percentiles) of the data below.

52 61 88 43 64 71 39 73 51 60

4.40 Determine the first, second, and third quartiles of the following data.

10.5 14.7 15.3 17.7 15.9 12.2 10.0
14.1 13.9 18.5 13.9 15.1 14.7

4.41 Calculate the 3rd and 6th deciles of the data below.

7 18 12 17 29 18 4 27
30 2 4 10 21 5 8

4.42 Refer to Exercise 4.40. Determine the interquartile range.

4.43 Refer to Exercise 4.37. Determine the interquartile range.

4.44 Compute the interquartile range from the following data.

5 8 14 6 21 11 9 10 18 2

4.45 Draw the box plot of the following set of data.

9 28 15 21 12 22 29 20
23 31 11 19 24 16 13

4.46 Given the data below, draw a box plot.

65 80 39 22 74 61 63 46 72 34
30 34 69 31 46 39 57 79 89 41

The following exercises require a computer and software.

4.47 Accountemps, a company that supplies temporary workers, sponsored a survey of 100 executives. Each was asked to report the number of minutes they spend screening each job resume they receive. The responses are stored in file Xr04-47.

a Compute the quartiles.

b What information did you derive from the quartiles? What does this suggest about writing your resume?

4.48 How much do pets cost? A random sample of dog and cat owners was asked to compute the amounts of money spent on their pets (exclusive of pet food). The responses are stored in columns 1 (dogs) and 2 (cats) in file Xr04-48. Draw a box plot for each data set and describe your findings.

4.49 The Travel Industry Association of America sponsored a poll that asked a random sample of people how much they spent in preparation for pleasure travel. The responses are stored in file Xr04-49. Determine the quartiles and describe what they tell you.

4.50 The career-counseling center at a university wanted to learn more about the starting salaries of the university's graduates. They asked each graduate to report the highest salary offer received. The survey also asked each graduate to report the degree. The starting salaries are stored in file Xr04-50; column 1 = BA, column 2 = BSc, column 3 = BBA, and column 4 = other. Draw box plots to compare the four groups of starting salaries. Report your findings.

4.51 A random sample of Boston Marathon runners was drawn and the times to complete the race were recorded and stored in file Xr04-51.
a Draw the box plot.
b What are the quartiles?

c Identify outliers.
d What information does the box plot deliver?

4.52 Do golfers who are members of private courses play faster than players on a public course? The amount of time (minutes) taken for a sample of private-course and public-course golfers was drawn. The times are stored in columns A (private course) and B (public course) in Xr04-52.
a Draw box plots for each sample.
b What do the box plots tell you?

4.53 For many restaurants, the amount of time customers linger over coffee and dessert negatively affect profits. To learn more about this variable, a sample of 200 restaurant groups was observed and the amount of time (minutes) customers spent in the restaurant was recorded and stored in file Xr04-53.
a Calculate the quartiles of these data.
b What do these statistics tell you about the amount of time spent in this restaurant?

4.54 Homeowners were surveyed and asked to report the size of their mortgage payments. These data are stored in file Xr04-54. Compute the quartiles and describe what they tell you. (Adapted from *Statistical Abstract of the United States*, 2000, Table 1209)

4.5 MEASURES OF LINEAR RELATIONSHIP

In Chapter 2 we introduced the scatter diagram, a graphical technique that describes the relationship between two interval variables. At that time we pointed out that we're particularly interested in the direction and strength of the linear relationship. We now present two numerical measures of linear relationship that provide this information. They are the *covariance* and the *coefficient of correlation*. Later in this section we discuss another related numerical technique, the *least squares line*.

COVARIANCE

As we did in Chapter 2, we label one variable X and the other Y.

> **COVARIANCE**
>
> Population covariance: $\text{COV}(X, Y) = \dfrac{\sum\limits_{i=1}^{N}(x_i - \mu_x)(y_i - \mu_y)}{N}$
>
> Sample covariance: $\text{cov}(x, y) = \dfrac{\sum\limits_{i=1}^{n}(x_i - \bar{x})(y_i - \bar{y})}{n - 1}$

The denominator in the calculation of the sample covariance is $n - 1$, not the more logical n, for the same reason we divide by $n - 1$ to calculate the sample variance (see page 102). If you plan to compute the sample covariance manually, here is a shortcut calculation.

SHORTCUT FOR SAMPLE COVARIANCE

$$\text{cov}(x, y) = \frac{1}{n-1}\left[\sum_{i=1}^{n} x_i y_i - \frac{\sum_{i=1}^{n} x_i \sum_{i=1}^{n} y_i}{n}\right]$$

To illustrate how covariance measures the linear relationship, examine the following three sets of data.

Set 1

x_i	y_i	$(x_i - \bar{x})$	$(y_i - \bar{y})$	$(x_i - \bar{x})(y_i - \bar{y})$
2	13	−3	−7	21
6	20	1	0	0
7	27	2	7	14
$\bar{x} = 5$ $\bar{y} = 20$				$\text{cov}(x, y) = 17.5$

Set 2

x_i	y_i	$(x_i - \bar{x})$	$(y_i - \bar{y})$	$(x_i - \bar{x})(y_i - \bar{y})$
2	27	−3	7	−21
6	20	1	0	0
7	13	2	−7	−14
$\bar{x} = 5$ $\bar{y} = 20$				$\text{cov}(x, y) = -17.5$

Set 3

x_i	y_i	$(x_i - \bar{x})$	$(y_i - \bar{y})$	$(x_i - \bar{x})(y_i - \bar{y})$
2	20	−3	0	0
6	27	1	7	7
7	13	2	−7	−14
$\bar{x} = 5$ $\bar{y} = 20$				$\text{cov}(x, y) = -3.5$

Notice that the values of x are the same in all three sets and that the values of y are also the same. The only difference is the order of the values of y.

In set 1 as x increases so does y. When x is larger than its mean, y is at least as large as its mean. Thus $(x_i - \bar{x})$ and $(y_i - \bar{y})$ have the same sign or 0. Their product is also positive or 0. Consequently, the covariance is a positive number. Generally, when two variables move in the same direction (both increase or both decrease) the covariance will be a large positive number.

If you examine set 2 you will discover that as x increases, y decreases. When x is larger than its mean, y is less than or equal to its mean. As a result, when $(x_i - \bar{x})$ is positive, $(y_i - \bar{y})$ is negative or 0. Their products are either negative or 0. It follows that the covariance is a negative number. In general, when two variables move in opposite directions, the covariance is a large negative number.

In set 3 as x increases y does not exhibit any particular direction. One of the products $(x_i - \bar{x})(y_i - \bar{y})$ is 0, one is positive, and one is negative. The resulting covariance is a small number. In general, when there is no particular pattern, the covariance is a small number.

We would like to extract two pieces of information. The first is the sign of the co-variance, which tells us the direction of the linear relationship. The second is the magnitude, which describes the strength of the linear relationship. Unfortunately, the magnitude may be difficult to judge. For example, if you're told that the covariance between two variables is 500, does this mean that there is a strong linear relationship? The answer is that it is impossible to judge without additional statistics. Fortunately, we can improve upon the information produced by this statistic by creating another one.

COEFFICIENT OF CORRELATION

The **coefficient of correlation** is defined as the covariance divided by the standard deviations of the variables.

> **COEFFICIENT OF CORRELATION**
>
> Population coefficient of correlation: $\rho = \dfrac{COV(X, Y)}{\sigma_x \sigma_y}$
>
> Sample coefficient of correlation: $r = \dfrac{cov(x, y)}{s_x s_y}$

The population parameter is denoted by the Greek letter *rho*.

The advantage that the coefficient of correlation has over the covariance is that the former has a set lower and upper limit. The limits are −1 and +1, respectively. That is,

$$-1 \le r \le +1 \quad \text{and} \quad -1 \le \rho \le +1$$

When the coefficient of correlation equals −1, there is a negative linear relationship and the scatter diagram exhibits a straight line. When the coefficient of correlation equals +1, there is a perfect positive linear relationship. When the coefficient of correlation equals 0, there is no linear relationship. All other values of correlation are judged in relation to these three values.

COMPARING THE SCATTER DIAGRAM, COVARIANCE, AND COEFFICIENT OF CORRELATION

The scatter diagram depicts relationships graphically; the covariance and the coefficient of correlation describe the linear relationship numerically. Figures 4.2, 4.3, and 4.4 depict three scatter diagrams. To show how the graphical and numerical techniques compare, we calculated the covariance and the coefficient of correlation for each. (The data are stored in files Fig04-02, Fig04-03, and Fig04-04.) As you can see, Figure 4.2 depicts a strong positive relationship between the two variables. The sample covariance is 38.81 and the coefficient of correlation is .9641. The variables in Figure 4.3 produced a relatively strong negative linear relationship; the sample covariance and coefficient of correlation are −35.97 and −.8791, respectively. The sample covariance and coefficient of correlation for the data in Figure 4.4 are 2.18 and .1206, respectively. There is no apparent linear relationship in this figure.

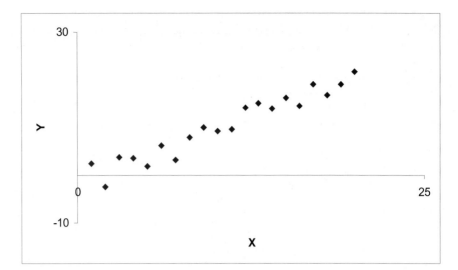

Figure 4.2
Strong positive linear relationship

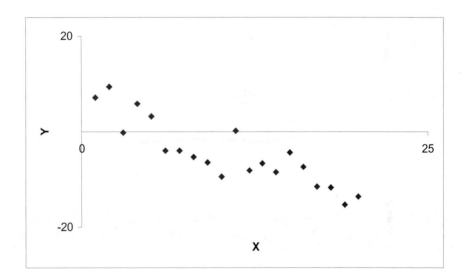

Figure 4.3
Strong negative linear relationship

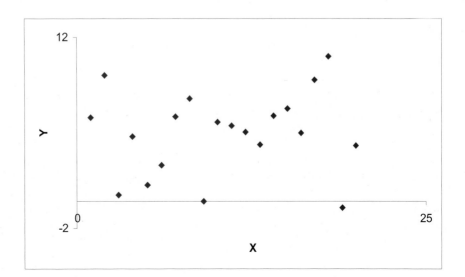

Figure 4.4
No linear relationship

S e e i n g   S t a t i s t i c s

APPLET 1
SCATTER DIAGRAMS AND CORRELATION

In Section 1.4 we introduced applets as a method to allow students of applied statistics to see how statistical techniques work and to gain insights into the underlying principles. The applets are stored on the CD that accompanies this book. See the Readme file for instructions on how to use them.

Instructions for Applet 1

Use your mouse to move the slider in the graph. As you move the slider, observe how the coefficient of correlation changes as the points become more "organized" in the scatter diagram. If you click "Switch sign" you can see the difference between positive and negative coefficients. The figure below displays the applet for two values of *r*.

Applet Exercises

1.1 Drag the slider to the right until the correlation coefficient is *r* = 1.0. Describe the pattern of the data points.

1.2 Drag the slider to the left until the correlation coefficient is *r* = −1.0. Describe the pattern of the data points. In what way does it differ from the case where *r* = 1.0?

1.3 Drag the slider toward the center until the correlation coefficient is *r* = 0 (approximately). Describe the pattern of the data points. Is there a pattern? Or do the points appear to be scattered randomly?

1.4 Drag the slider until the correlation coefficient is *r* = .5 (approximately). Can you detect a pattern? Now click on the "Switch Sign" button to change the correlation coefficient *r* to −.5. How does the pattern change when the sign switches? Switch back and forth several times so that you can see the changes.

S e e i n g   S t a t i s t i c s

APPLET 2
SCATTER PATTERNS AND CORRELATION

This applet allows you to place points on a graph and see the resulting value of the coefficient of correlation.

Instructions

Click on the graph to place a point. As you add points, the correlation coefficient is recalculated. Click to add

points in various patterns to see how the correlation does (or does not) reflect those patterns. Click on the "Reset" button to clear all points. The figure shown to the left depicts a scatter diagram and its coefficient of correlation.

Applet Exercises

2.1 Create a scatter diagram where *r* is approximately 0. Describe how you did it.

2.2 Create a scatter diagram with a pattern where *r* is approximately 1. Describe how this was done.

2.3 Plot points such that *r* is approximately .5. How would you describe the resulting scatter diagram?

2.4 Plot the points on a scatter diagram where *r* is approximately 1. Now, add one more point, decreasing *r* by as much as possible. What does this tell you about extreme points?

2.5 Repeat Applet Exercise 2.4 adding two points. How close to *r* = 0 did you get?

EXAMPLE 4.16

Students who apply to MBA programs must write the Graduate Management Admission Test (GMAT). University admissions committees use the GMAT score as one of the critical indicators of how well a student is likely to perform in the MBA program. However, the GMAT may not be a very strong indicator for all MBA programs. Suppose that an MBA program designed for middle managers who wish to upgrade their skills was launched 3 years ago. To judge how well the GMAT score predicts MBA performance, a sample of 12 graduates was taken. Their grade point average in the MBA program (values from 0 to 12) and the GMAT score (values from 200 to 800) are listed in the table below and stored in file Xm04-16. Compute the covariance and the coefficient of correlation, and interpret your findings.

GMAT and GPA Scores for 12 MBA Students

GMAT	GPA
599	9.6
689	8.8
584	7.4
631	10.0
594	7.8
643	9.2
656	9.6
594	8.4
710	11.2
611	7.6
593	8.8
683	8.0

SOLUTION We believe that the GMAT score affects the GPA. Accordingly, we label the former X and the latter Y. We'll employ the shortcut to compute the sample covariance (including the shortcut for the variances presented in Section 4.3 on page 103). The required summations can be obtained from the following table.

Student	x	y	xy	x^2	y^2
1	599	9.6	5750.4	358801	92.16
2	689	8.8	6063.2	474721	77.44
3	584	7.4	4321.6	341056	54.76
4	631	10.0	6310.0	398161	100.00
5	594	7.8	4633.2	352836	60.84
6	643	9.2	5915.6	413449	84.64
7	656	9.6	6297.6	430336	92.16
8	594	8.4	4989.6	352836	70.56
9	710	11.2	7952.0	504100	125.44
10	611	7.6	4643.6	373321	57.76
11	593	8.8	5218.4	351649	77.44
12	683	8.0	5464.0	466489	64.00
Total	7,587	106.4	67,559.2	4,817,755	957.2

$$\text{cov}(x, y) = \frac{1}{n-1}\left[\sum_{i=1}^{n} x_i y_i - \frac{\sum_{i=1}^{n} x_i \sum_{i=1}^{n} y_i}{n}\right] = \frac{1}{12-1}\left[67,559.2 - \frac{(7,587)(106.4)}{12}\right] = 26.16$$

$$s_x^2 = \frac{1}{n-1}\left[\sum_{i=1}^{n} x_i^2 - \frac{\left(\sum_{i=1}^{n} x_i\right)^2}{n}\right] = \frac{1}{12-1}\left[4,817,755 - \frac{(7,587)^2}{12}\right] = 1,897.7$$

$$s_x = \sqrt{s_x^2} = \sqrt{1,897.7} = 43.56$$

$$s_y^2 = \frac{1}{n-1}\left[\sum_{i=1}^{n} y_i^2 - \frac{\left(\sum_{i=1}^{n} y_i\right)^2}{n}\right] = \frac{1}{12-1}\left[957.2 - \frac{(106.4)^2}{12}\right] = 1.25$$

$$s_y = \sqrt{s_y^2} = \sqrt{1.25} = 1.12$$

$$r = \frac{\text{cov}(x, y)}{s_x s_y} = \frac{26.16}{(43.56)(1.12)} = .5362$$

  EXCEL

	A	B	C
1		GMAT	GPA
2	GMAT	1739.52	
3	GPA	23.98	1.15

COVARIANCE

Excel produces the variance–covariance matrix, which yields the variance for both variables and the covariance. Note, however, that Office 2000 and Office XP produce the population parameters COV(X, Y), σ_x^2, and σ_y^2. (Office 97 produces the sample statistics.) We computed the sample statistics cov(x, y), s_x^2, and s_y^2 by multiplying each by $[n/(n-1)] = [12/11]$.

	A	B	C
1		GMAT	GPA
2	GMAT	1897.66	
3	GPA	26.16	1.25

COMMANDS

1. Type or import the data into two adjacent columns.
2. Click **Tools, Data Analysis**, and **Covariance**.
3. Type the **Input Range**.
4. Click **Labels in First Row** if applicable and click **OK**.

COMMANDS FOR EXAMPLE 4.16

Open file **XM04-16.**

A1:B13

CORRELATION

Excel produces a matrix of sample correlation coefficients.

Correlation Matrix

	A	B	C
1		*GMAT*	*GPA*
2	GMAT	1	
3	GPA	0.5365	1

The sample coefficient of correlation between GPA and GMAT is .5365. (The other entries in the matrix are 1s, representing the coefficients of correlation between GPA and GPA and between GMAT and GMAT, both meaningless statistics.)

COMMANDS

   1. Click **Correlation** instead of **Covariance** in the instructions above.

MINITAB

VARIANCE–COVARIANCE MATRIX

Covariances: GMAT, GPA

```
                       GMAT          GPA
        GMAT     1897.6591
        GPA        26.1636       1.2533
```

COMMANDS

   1. Type the data into two columns.
   2. Click **Stat, Basic Statistics**, and **Covariance....**
   3. Specify the names of the variables.
   4. Click **OK.**

COEFFICIENT OF CORRELATION

Correlations: GMAT, GPA

```
        Pearson correlation of GMAT and GPA = 0.536
```

COMMANDS

Click **Correlation** instead of **Covariance** at step 2 above.

INTERPRET

The covariance is 26.16 and the coefficient of correlation is .536. These two statistics tell us that there is a positive linear relationship between GMAT score and GPA. The coefficient of correlation tells us that the linear relationship is not very strong.

LEAST SQUARES METHOD

When we presented the scatter diagram in Section 2.5, we pointed out that we're interested in measuring the strength and direction of the linear relationship. Both can be more easily judged by drawing a straight line through the data. However, if different people draw a line through the same data set it is likely that each person's line would differ from all the others. Moreover, we often need to know the equation of the line. Consequently, we need an objective method of producing a straight line. Such a method has been developed; it is called the **least squares method**.

The least squares method produces a straight line drawn through the points so that the sum of squared deviations between the points and the line is minimized. The line is represented by the equation

$$\hat{y} = b_0 + b_1 x$$

where b_0 is the y-intercept (where the line intersects the y-axis), b_1 is the slope (defined as rise/run), and $\hat{y}$ is the value of y determined by the line. The coefficients b_0 and b_1 are derived using calculus so that we minimize the sum of squared deviations

$$\sum_{i=1}^{n} (y_i - \hat{y}_i)^2$$

LEAST SQUARES LINE COEFFICIENTS

$$b_1 = \frac{\text{cov}(x, y)}{s_x^2}$$

$$b_0 = \bar{y} - b_1 \bar{x}$$

EXAMPLE 4.17

Determine the least squares line for Example 4.16.

SOLUTION   In Example 4.16 we determined that $\text{cov}(x, y) = 26.16$ and $s_x^2 = 1,897.7$. Thus,

$$b_1 = \frac{\text{cov}(x, y)}{s_x^2} = \frac{26.16}{1,897.7} = .0138$$

To compute the y-intercept, we find

$$\bar{x} = \frac{\sum x_i}{n} = \frac{7,587}{12} = 632.25$$

$$\bar{y} = \frac{\sum y_i}{n} = \frac{106.4}{12} = 8.87$$

Thus,

$$b_0 = \bar{y} - b_1 \bar{x} = 8.87 - (.0138)(632.25) = .145$$

The least squares line is

$$\hat{y} = .145 + .0138x$$

EXCEL

COMMANDS

1. Follow the instructions to draw a scatter diagram. Highlight the columns containing the variables. The first column should store the independent variable and the second column, the dependent variable.
2. Click **Chart** and **Add Trendline...**.
3. Select **Linear** and click **Options**. Select **Display equation on chart** and click **OK**.

MINITAB

Regression Plot

GPA = 0.149633 + 0.0137873 GMAT

S = 0.990892   R-Sq = 28.8 %   R-Sq(adj) = 21.7 %

COMMANDS

1. Click **Stat, Regression**, and **Fitted Line Plot**.
2. Specify variables Y and X (**Response [Y] and Predictor [X]**).
3. Specify **Linear** and click **OK**.

INTERPRET

The least squares line produced by computer is

$$\hat{y} = .1496 + .0138x$$

(It differs from the manually computed line because of rounding.) The y-intercept is .1496, which means that, if we extend the least squares line backward to $x = 0$, it would intersect the y-axis at .1496. In most cases this value has little actual meaning.

The slope is defined as rise/run, which means that it is the change in y (rise) for a 1-unit increase in x (run). Put less mathematically, the slope measures the *marginal* rate of change in the dependent variable. The marginal rate of change refers to the effect of increasing the independent variable by 1 additional unit. In this example the slope is .0138, which means that in this sample for each 1-unit increase in the GMAT score the marginal increase in the GPA is .0138. Stated another way, if we compare two students in our sample whose GMAT scores differ by 100 points the student with the higher GMAT score will have a GPA that is, on average, larger by 100(.0138) = 1.38.

COST OF ONE MORE WIN: SOLUTION

We use the least squares method to produce a straight line through the data. Because we believe that the number of games a baseball teams wins depends to some extent on its team payroll, we label Games won as the dependent variable and Payroll as the independent variable.

EXCEL

MINITAB

INTERPRET

The least squares line is

$$\hat{y} = 72.63 + .1477x$$

The slope is equal to .1477, which is the marginal rate of change for each 1-unit increase in payroll. Because payroll is measured in millions of dollars, we estimate that for each 1-million-dollar increase in the payroll, the number of games won increases on average by .1477. Thus, to win one more game requires an additional expenditure of an incredible $6,770,000 (calculated as 1 million/.1477).

We complete this section with a review of when to use the techniques introduced in this section.

> **FACTORS THAT IDENTIFY WHEN TO COMPUTE COVARIANCE, COEFFICIENT OF CORRELATION, AND LEAST SQUARES LINE**
> 1. **Objective:** Describe the relationship between two variables.
> 2. **Type of data:** Interval

EXERCISES

4.55 Calculate the covariance and coefficient of correlation for the following sample.

X	3	5	2	9	6	3	9	1
Y	8	4	9	2	4	7	3	7

4.56 Calculate the covariance and coefficient of correlation for the following sample.

X	45	22	16	50	44	31	48	27	30	28
Y	77	31	28	49	63	84	40	92	72	67

4.57 The selling price ($thousands) and the size (square feet) were recorded for a sample of 10 houses that were recently sold. The data are:

Price	153	202	199	315	148
Size	1,526	1,849	1,906	2,460	1,602

Price	194	250	167	305	258
Size	1,731	2,208	2,041	2,595	2,008

a Calculate the covariance of the two variables.
b Determine the coefficient of correlation.
c What do these statistics tell you about the relationship between price and size?

4.58 Attempting to analyze the relationship between advertising and sales, the owner of a furniture store recorded the monthly advertising budget ($thousands) and the sales ($millions) for a sample of 12 months. The data are listed here.

Advertising	23	46	60	54	28	33
Sales	9.6	11.3	12.8	9.8	8.9	12.5

Advertising	25	31	36	88	90	99
Sales	12.0	11.4	12.6	13.7	14.4	15.9

a Calculate the covariance of the two variables.

b Determine the coefficient of correlation.

c What do these statistics tell you about the relationship between advertising and sales?

4.59 The covariance of two variables has been calculated to be −150. What does the statistic tell you about the relationship between the two variables?

4.60 Refer to Exercise 4.59. You've now learned that the two sample standard deviations are 16 and 12. Calculate the coefficient of correlation. What does this statistic tell you about the relationship between the two variables?

The following exercises require a computer and software.

4.61 Studies of twins may reveal more about the "nature or nurture" debate. The issue being debated is whether nature or the environment has more effect on individual traits such as intelligence. Suppose that a sample of identical twins was selected and their IQs measured. These data are stored in file Xr04-61. Compute the coefficient of correlation and describe what it tells you about the relationship between the IQs of identical twins.

4.62 Besides the known long-term effects of smoking, do cigarettes also cause short-term illnesses such as colds? To help answer this question, a sample of smokers was drawn. Each person was asked to report the average number of cigarettes smoked per day and the number of sick days due to colds last year. The data are stored in file Xr04-62.

a Calculate the covariance of the two variables.

b Determine the coefficient of correlation.

c What do these statistics tell you about the relationship between smoking cigarettes and the incidence of colds?

4.63 Refer to Exercise 2.62.

a Calculate the coefficient of correlation.

b Describe what this statistic tells you about the relationship between marks and study time.

4.64 Refer to Exercise 2.67.

a Calculate the coefficient of correlation.

b Briefly discuss the relationship between Internet use and age.

4.65 Do better golfers play faster than poorer ones? To determine whether a relationship exists, a sample of 125 foursomes was selected. Their total scores and the amount of time taken to complete the 18 holes were recorded and stored in file Xr04-65. Calculate the coefficient of correlation and describe what this statistic tells you about the relationship between score and time.

4.66 Refer to Exercise 2.70. Calculate the coefficient of correlation and describe what this statistic tells you about the relationship between the incomes and heights of male executives.

APPLICATIONS IN MANAGERIAL ACCOUNTING: *FIXED AND VARIABLE COSTS*

A firm's operating costs can be classified as fixed, variable, or mixed. *Variable costs* are those costs that vary in direct proportion to changes in the level of activity. For example, in some firms sales representatives are paid a commission, which is a percentage of the sales the representative makes. *Fixed costs* are those costs that do not change with changes in the level of activity. An example of fixed costs is the salaries of managers. Costs for items such as telephone, electrical power, and maintenance are often *mixed costs,* meaning they have both a fixed-cost and a variable-cost component.

For planning purposes, companies prepare budgets, which include forecasts of future sales revenues and costs. The associated costs are often estimated by a *cost function,* which expresses the relationship between a cost and some measure of the level of activity creating that cost. A total cost function is estimated from historical data and is assumed to take the linear form $y = b_0 + b_1 x$. The coefficient b_0 estimates the fixed cost and b_1 estimates the variable cost over the range of activity. Managerial accountants need to determine both fixed and variable costs from data. The next three exercises are based on this technique.

4.67 A retailer wanted to estimate the monthly fixed and variable selling expenses. As a first step, she collected data from the past 18 months. The total selling expenses (in $1,000) and the total sales (in $1,000) were stored in file Xr04-67.

a Compute the covariance and the coefficient of correlation, and describe what these statistics tell you.

b Determine the least squares line and use it to produce the estimates the retailer wants.

4.68   A manufacturing firm produces its products in batches using sophisticated machines and equipment. The general manager wanted to investigate the relationship between direct labor costs and the number of units produced per batch. He recorded the data from the last 30 batches; the results are stored in file Xr04-68. Determine the fixed and variable labor costs.

4.69   A manufacturer has recorded its cost of electricity and the total number of hours of machine time for each of 52 weeks and stored the results in file Xr04-69. Estimate the fixed and variable electricity costs.

4.70   File Xr04-70 contains the number of wins and the team payrolls for the National Basketball Association. Determine an estimate for the cost of an additional win.

4.71   File Xr04-71 contains the number of wins and the team payrolls for the National Hockey League. Determine an estimate for the cost of an additional win.

4.6 COMPARING GRAPHICAL AND NUMERICAL TECHNIQUES

As we mentioned before, graphical techniques are useful in producing a quick picture of the data. For example, you learn something about the location, spread, and shape of a set of interval data when you examine its histogram. Numerical techniques provide the same approximate information. We have measures of central location, measures of variability, and measures of relative standing that do what the histogram does. The scatter diagram graphically describes the relationship between two interval variables. But so do the numerical measures covariance, coefficient of correlation, and least squares line. Why then do we need to learn both categories of techniques? The answer is that they differ in the information each provides. We'll illustrate the difference between graphical and numerical methods by redoing three examples we used to illustrate graphical techniques in Chapter 2.

EXAMPLE 2.2

In Example 2.2 we wanted to judge which investment appeared to be better. As the Applications in Finance: Return on Investment summary (page 38) discussed, we judge investments in terms of the return we can expect and its risk. We drew histograms and attempted to interpret them. The centers of the histograms provided us with information about the expected return, and their spreads gauged the risk. However, the histograms were not clear. Fortunately, we can use numerical measures. The mean and median provide us with information about the return we can expect, and the variance or standard deviation tells us about the risk associated with each investment.

Here are the descriptive statistics produced by Excel. Minitab's are similar.

	A	B	C	D	E
1	Return A			Return B	
2					
3	Mean	10.95		Mean	12.76
4	Standard Error	3.10		Standard Error	3.97
5	Median	9.88		Median	10.755
6	Mode	12.89		Mode	#N/A
7	Standard Deviation	21.89		Standard Deviation	28.05
8	Sample Variance	479.35		Sample Variance	786.62
9	Kurtosis	-0.32		Kurtosis	-0.62
10	Skewness	0.54		Skewness	0.01
11	Range	84.95		Range	106.47
12	Minimum	-21.95		Minimum	-38.47
13	Maximum	63		Maximum	68
14	Sum	547.27		Sum	638.01
15	Count	50		Count	50

We can now see that investment B has a larger mean and median, but that investment A has a smaller variance and standard deviation. If an investor were interested in low-risk investments, he or she would choose investment A. If you reexamine the histograms from Example 2.2 (page 39) you will see that the precision provided by the numerical techniques (mean, median, and standard deviation) provides more useful information than did the histograms.

EXAMPLE 2.3

In Example 2.3 we wanted to see what differences existed between the marks in the two statistics classes. Here are the descriptive statistics.

	A	B	C	D	E
1	Marks (Manual)			Marks (Computer)	
2					
3	Mean	66.40		Mean	72.67
4	Standard Error	1.61		Standard Error	1.07
5	Median	71.50		Median	72.00
6	Mode	75.00		Mode	67.00
7	Standard Deviation	12.47		Standard Deviation	8.29
8	Sample Variance	155.50		Sample Variance	68.77
9	Kurtosis	-1.24		Kurtosis	-0.36
10	Skewness	-0.22		Skewness	0.16
11	Range	48		Range	39
12	Minimum	44		Minimum	53
13	Maximum	92		Maximum	92
14	Sum	3984		Sum	4360
15	Count	60		Count	60
16	Largest(15)	76		Largest(15)	79
17	Smallest(15)	53		Smallest(15)	67

The statistics tell us that the mean and median of the marks in the computer statistics course are higher than in the course that emphasizes manual calculation. Moreover, the standard deviation is lower. However, the histograms (on page 40) also provided important information. We found that the histogram of the manual statistics marks was bimodal, which we interpreted to mean that this type of approach created differences between students. The unimodal histogram of the computer statistics marks informed us that this approach eliminated those differences.

EXAMPLE 2.7

The scatter diagram in this example graphically described the relationship between the size and price of a house. To do the same numerically, we produced the coefficient of correlation and the least squares line below. The coefficient of correlation is .7265, which tells us that there is a moderately strong positive linear relationship between the two variables. The scatter diagram provides the same information. We can estimate the slope of the line from the graph. However, using the least squares method allows us to produce a slope coefficient that is based on the least squares criterion. The least squares line is

$$\hat{y} = 105.3 + 7.03x$$

The slope coefficient tells us that, on average, for each additional square foot the price increases by $7.03. As in Examples 2.2 and 2.3, the precision of the numerical techniques provides information not available from the graphs.

	A	B	C
2		Size	Price
3	Size	1	
4	Price	0.7265	1

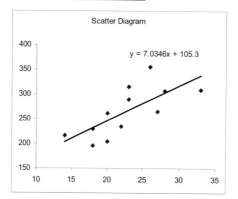

Excel Output for
Example 2.7

EXERCISES

4.72 Refer to Exercise 2.16. Calculate the mean and standard deviation. Discuss the difference between the information produced by the graphical method and by the statistics.

4.73 Refer to Exercise 2.17. Compute measures of central location and variability. Briefly describe the difference in information derived from the histogram and from the statistics.

4.74 Refer to Exercise 2.20. Compute the mean, median, and standard deviation. What information did you produce from these statistics that the histogram did not supply?

The following exercises require a computer and statistical software.

4.75 Compute the mean and standard deviation of the data in Exercise 2.23. Compare the information produced from the histogram and from the statistics.

4.76 Refer to Exercise 2.26.
  a Calculate the standard deviation.
  b What does this statistic tell you about the variability of the data?
  c How does the information you gained from the standard deviation compare to what you learned from the graphical technique?

4.77 Refer to Exercise 2.27. Compute any statistics you believe will produce useful information. Compare this information with that produced from the histogram.

4.78 Refer to Exercise 2.30. Compute the mean, median, and standard deviation. Describe what you have learned from the statistics compared to the information generated from the graphical method.

4.7 GENERAL GUIDELINES FOR EXPLORING DATA

The purpose of applying graphical and numerical techniques is to describe and summarize data. Statistics practitioners usually apply graphical techniques as a first step because we need to know the shape of the distribution. The shape of the distribution helps answer the following questions:

1. Where is the approximate center of the distribution?

2. Are the observations close to one another, or are they widely dispersed?

3. Is the distribution unimodal, bimodal, or multimodal? If there is more than one mode, where are the peaks, and where are the valleys?

4. Is the distribution symmetric? If not, is it skewed? If symmetric, is it bell shaped?

Histograms and box plots provide most of the answers. We can frequently make several inferences about the nature of the data from the shape. For example, we can assess the relative risk of investments by noting their spreads. We can attempt to improve the teaching of a course by examining whether the distribution of final grades is bimodal and whether they are skewed.

The shape can also provide some guidance on which numerical techniques to use. As we noted in this chapter, the central location of highly skewed data may be more appropriately measured by the median. We may also choose to use the interquartile range instead of the standard deviation to describe the spread of skewed data.

When we have an understanding of the structure of the data, we may proceed to further analysis. For example, we often want to determine how one variable, or several variables, affects another. Scatter diagrams, covariance, and the coefficient of correlation are useful techniques for detecting relationships between variables. A number of techniques to be introduced later in this book will help uncover the nature of these associations.

4.8 SUMMARY

This chapter extended our discussion of descriptive techniques, which deal with methods of summarizing and presenting the essential information contained in a set of data. After constructing a frequency distribution to obtain a general idea about the distribution of a data set, we can use numerical measures to describe the **central location** and **variability** of interval data. Three popular measures of central location are the **mean**, the **median**, and the **mode**. Taken by themselves, these measures provide an inadequate description of the data because they say nothing about the extent to which the data vary. Information regarding the variability of interval data is conveyed by such numerical measures as the **range**, **variance**, and **standard deviation**.

For the special case in which a sample of measurements has a mound-shaped distribution, the **Empirical Rule** provides a good approximation of the percentages of measurements that fall within one, two, or three standard deviations of the mean. **Chebysheff's theorem** applies to all sets of data no matter the shape of the histogram.

Measures of relative standing that were presented in this chapter are **percentiles** and **quartiles**. The **box plot** graphically depicts these measures as well as several others. The linear relationship between two interval variables is measured by the **covariance**, the **coefficient of correlation**, and the **least squares line.**

IMPORTANT TERMS

Measures of central location 93
Mean 93
Median 95
Mode 96
Modal class 96
Geometric mean 99
Measures of variability 101
Range 101
Variance 102
Standard deviation 105
Empirical Rule 106

Chebysheff's theorem 107
Percentiles 109
Quartiles 109
Interquartile range 112
Box plots 112
Outlier 112
Measures of linear relationship 116
Covariance 116
Coefficient of correlation 118
Least squares method 124
Least squares line 124

SYMBOLS

Symbol	Pronounced	Represents
μ	*mu*	Population mean
σ^2	*sigma-squared*	Population variance
σ	*sigma*	Population standard deviation
ρ	*rho*	Population coefficient of correlation
$\sum$	*sum of*	Summation
$\sum_{i=1}^{n} x_i$	*Sum of x_i from 1 to n*	Summation of n numbers
$\hat{y}$	*y-hat*	Fitted or calculated value of y
b_0	*b-zero*	y-intercept
b_1	*b-one*	Slope coefficient

FORMULAS

Population mean

$$\mu = \frac{\sum_{i=1}^{N} x_i}{N}$$

Sample mean

$$\bar{x} = \frac{\sum_{i=1}^{n} x_i}{n}$$

Range

Largest observation − Smallest observation

Population variance

$$\sigma^2 = \frac{\sum_{i=1}^{N} (x_i - \mu)^2}{N}$$

Sample variance

$$s^2 = \frac{\sum_{i=1}^{n} (x_i - \bar{x})^2}{n - 1}$$

Population standard deviation

$$\sigma = \sqrt{\sigma^2}$$

Sample standard deviation

$$s = \sqrt{s^2}$$

Population covariance

$$\text{COV}(X, Y) = \frac{\sum (x_i - \mu_x)(y_i - \mu_y)}{N}$$

Sample covariance

$$\text{cov}(x, y) = \frac{\sum (x_i - \bar{x})(y_i - \bar{y})}{n - 1}$$

Population coefficient of correlation

$$\rho = \frac{\text{COV}(X, Y)}{\sigma_x \sigma_y}$$

Sample coefficient of correlation

$$r = \frac{\text{cov}(x, y)}{s_x s_y}$$

Slope coefficient

$$b_1 = \frac{\text{cov}(x, y)}{s_x^2}$$

y-intercept

$$b_0 = \bar{y} - b_1 \bar{x}$$

COMPUTER OUTPUT AND INSTRUCTIONS

Technique	Excel	Minitab
Mean	94	95
Median	95	96
Mode	96	97
Geometric mean	99	
Variance	104	
Standard deviation	105	106
Descriptive statistics	105	106
Quartiles	111	111
Box plot	113	113
Covariance	122	123
Correlation	123	123
Least squares coefficients	125	125

REFERENCES

Chatfield, C., *Problem Solving: A Statistician's Guide*, 2nd edition. New York: Chapman & Hall, 1995.

Freedman, D., R. Pisani, R. Purves, and A. Adhikari, *Statistics*, 2nd edition., New York: W. W. Norton, 1991.

Moore, David S., *Statistics: Concepts & Controversies*, 3rd edition. New York: W. H. Freeman, 1991.

Ramsey, F., and D. Schafer, *The Statistical Sleuth: A Course in Methods of Data Analysis*. Belmont, CA: Duxbury, 1997.

Tanur, Judith M., Frederick Mosteller, William H. Kruskal, Erich L. Lehmann, Richard Link, Richard S. Pieters, and Gerald R. Rising, *Statistics: A Guide to the Unknown*. 3rd edition. Belmont, CA: Duxbury, 1989.

Utts, Jessica, *Seeing Through Statistics*, 2nd edition. Pacific Grove, CA: Duxbury, 1999.

CHAPTER REVIEW EXERCISES

4.79 Osteoporosis is a condition wherein bone density decreases, often resulting in broken bones. Bone density usually peaks at age 30 and decreases thereafter. To understand more about the condition, a random sample of women aged 50 and over were recruited. Each woman's bone density loss was recorded. These data are stored in file Xr04-79.
 a Compute the mean and median of these data.
 b Compute the standard deviation of the bone density losses.
 c Describe what you have learned from the statistics.

4.80 The temperature in December in Buffalo, New York, is often below 40 degrees Fahrenheit (4 degrees Celsius). Not surprisingly, when the National Football League Buffalo Bills play at home in December, coffee is a popular item at the concession stand. The concession manager would like to acquire more information so that he can manage inventories more efficiently. The number of cups of coffee sold during 50 games played in December in Buffalo were recorded and stored in Xr04-80.
 a Determine the mean and median.
 b Determine the variance and standard deviation.
 c Draw a box plot.
 d Briefly describe what you have learned from your statistical analysis.

4.81 Refer to Exercise 4.79. In addition to the bone density losses, the ages of the women were also recorded. These data are stored in file Xr04-81. Compute the coefficient of correlation and describe what this statistic tells you.

4.82 Refer to Exercise 4.80. Suppose that in addition to recording the coffee sales, the manager also recorded the average temperature (measured in degrees Fahrenheit) during the game. These data together with the number of cups of coffee sold are stored in columns A and B in Xr04-82.
 a Compute the covariance and coefficient of correlation.
 b Determine the coefficients of the least squares line.

 c What have you learned about the relationship between the number of cups of coffee sold and the temperature from the statistics calculated above?
 d Discuss the information obtained here and in Exercise 4.80. Which is more useful to the manager?

4.83 Chris Golfnut loves the game of golf. Chris also loves statistics. Combining both passions, Chris records a sample of 100 scores and stores the data in Xr04-83.
 a What statistics should Chris compute to describe the scores?
 b Calculate the mean and standard deviation of the scores.
 c Briefly describe what the statistics computed in part **b** divulge.

4.84 The Internet is growing rapidly with an increasing number of regular users. However, among people older than 50, Internet use is still relatively low. To learn more about this issue, a sample of 250 men and women older than 50 who had used the Internet at least once were selected. The number of hours on the Internet during the past month was recorded and stored in Xr04-84.
 a Calculate the mean and median.
 b Calculate the variance and standard deviation.
 c Draw a box plot.
 d Briefly describe what you have learned from the statistics you calculated.

4.85 Refer to Exercise 4.83. For each score Chris recorded the number of putts and stored these data in Xr04-85. Conduct an analysis of both sets of data. What conclusions can be achieved from the statistics?

4.86 Refer to Exercise 4.84. In addition to Internet use, suppose that we have also recorded the number of years of education. These two variables are stored in Xr04-86.
 a Compute the covariance and coefficient of correlation.
 b Determine the coefficients of the least squares line.
 c Describe what these statistics tell you about the relationship between Internet use and education.
 d Discuss the information obtained here and in Exercise 4.84.

4.87 A sample was drawn of 1-acre plots of land planted with corn. The crop yields were recorded and stored in Xr04-87. Calculate the descriptive statistics you judge to be useful. Interpret these statistics.

4.88 Refer to Exercise 4.87. For each plot we recorded the amount of rainfall and stored it and the crop yields in Xr04-88.
  a Compute the covariance and coefficient of correlation.
  b Determine the coefficients of the least squares line.
  c Describe what these statistics tell you about the relationship between crop yield and rainfall.
  d Discuss the information obtained here and in Exercise 4.87.

4.89 Refer to Exercise 4.87. For each plot we recorded the amount of fertilizer and stored it and the crop yields in Xr04-89.
  a Compute the covariance and coefficient of correlation.
  b Determine the coefficients of the least squares line.
  c Describe what these statistics tell you about the relationship between crop yield and the amount of fertilizer.
  d Discuss the information obtained here and in Exercise 4.87.

4.90 Refer to Exercise 2.113.
  a Calculate the mean and median. What do these statistics tell you about the vocabularies of 5-year-old children?
  b Calculate the variance and standard deviation. What information can be obtained from these statistics?

  c Determine the three quartiles. What do they tell you about the size of the vocabularies?

4.91 Refer to Exercise 2.93.
  a Calculate the coefficient of correlation.
  b What does this statistic tell you about temperature and winning times among male runners of the New York Marathon?
  c Compare the information you obtained from the scatter diagram in Exercise 2.93 and the statistic above.

4.92 Refer to Exercise 2.106.
  a Calculate the coefficient of correlation.
  b What does this statistic tell you about temperature and winning times among female runners of the New York Marathon?
  c Compare the information you obtained from the scatter diagram in Exercise 2.106 and the statistic above.

4.93 Refer to Exercise 2.116. Calculate a number of descriptive statistics and report your findings.

4.94 Increasing tuition has resulted in some students being saddled with large debts upon graduation. To examine this issue, a random sample of recent graduates was asked to report whether they had student loans and, if so, how much was the debt at graduation. The amounts of debt were stored in file Xr04-94.
  a Compute all three measures of central location.
  b What do these statistics reveal about student loan debt at graduation?

◈ CASE 4.1
CADILLAC'S LAGGING SALES

For many years the top-selling luxury car in North America was the Cadillac. It reigned from 1950 to 1998. In 2000 it sank to sixth, behind Lexus, BMW, and Mercedes. Cadillac's sales during 2000 were half that of 1978, Cadillac's peak year. The problem is that Cadillac appears to appeal mainly to older males. Younger people seeking luxury cars shop elsewhere. Although Cadillac made $700 million in 2000, if the company doesn't pick up sales among younger shoppers, profits will go the way of fins. To put Cadillac back on top, it is necessary to understand who is buying. A survey of luxury car buyers was undertaken. The following information was gathered from random samples of recent buyers of the luxury cars.

Column 1	Luxury Car
1	BMW
2	Cadillac
3	Lexus
4	Lincoln
5	Mercedes-Benz

File C04-01a contains the ages of the buyers, C04-01b stores their household incomes, and C04-01c stores the number of years of education. (*Source*: Company reports and *Newsweek* magazine, May 28, 2001)

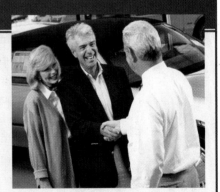

a Use statistics to describe the ages, household incomes, and education of the five groups of car buyers.

b Use box plots to compare the ages, household incomes, and education of the five groups of car buyers.

c Write a brief report describing your findings.

REVIEW OF DESCRIPTIVE TECHNIQUES

Here is a list of the statistical techniques introduced in Chapters 2 and 4. This is followed by a flowchart designed to help you select the most appropriate method to use to address any problem requiring a descriptive method.

To provide practice in identifying the correct descriptive method to use, we have created a number of review exercises. These are stored on the CD that accompanies this book.

GRAPHICAL TECHNIQUES

Histogram

Stem-and-leaf display

Ogive

Bar chart

Pie chart

Scatter diagram

Bar chart of a contingency table

Line chart (time series)

Box plot

NUMERICAL TECHNIQUES

Measures of central location

    Mean

    Median

    Mode

    Geometric mean (growth rates)

Measures of variability

    Range

    Variance

    Standard deviation

    Coefficient of variation

    Interquartile range

Measures of relative standing

    Percentiles

    Quartiles

Measure of linear relationship

    Covariance

    Coefficient of correlation

    Least squares line

FLOWCHART: GRAPHICAL AND NUMERICAL TECHNIQUES

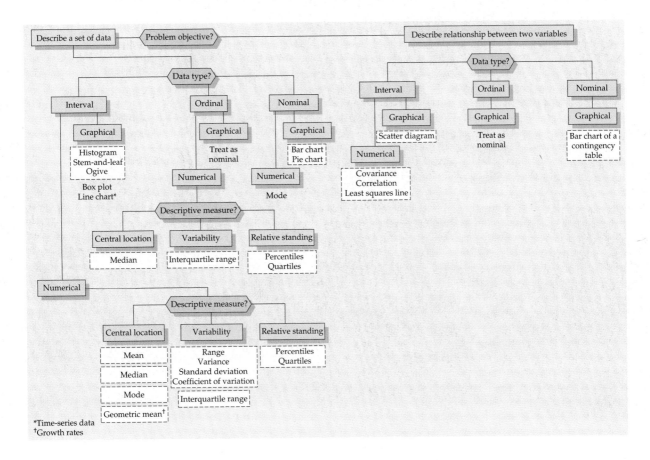

*Time-series data
†Growth rates

5 DATA COLLECTION AND SAMPLING

SAMPLING AND THE CENSUS

The census, which is conducted every 10 years in the United States, is an important function. It is the basis for deciding how many congressional representatives and how many votes in the electoral college each state will have. Businesses often use the information derived from the census to help make decisions about products, advertising, and plant locations.

One of the problems with the census is the issue of undercounting, which occurs when some people are not included. For example, the 1990 census reported that 12.05% of adults were African-American; the true value was 12.41%. To address undercounting, the Census Bureau adjusts the numbers it gets from the census. The adjustment is based on another survey. The

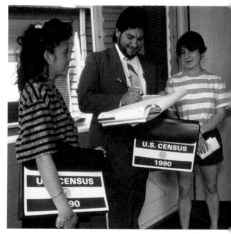

mechanism is called the Accuracy and Coverage Evaluation. Using sampling methods described in this chapter, the Census Bureau is able to adjust the numbers in American subgroups. For example, the Bureau may discover that the number of Hispanics has been undercounted or that the number of people living in California has not been accurately counted.

Later in this chapter (page 148) we'll discuss how the sampling is conducted and how the adjustments are made.

5.1 INTRODUCTION

In Chapter 1, we briefly introduced the concept of statistical inference—the process of inferring information about a population from a sample. Because information about populations can usually be described by parameters, the statistical technique used generally deals with drawing inferences about population parameters from sample statistics. (Recall that a *parameter* is a measurement about a population, and a *statistic* is a measurement about a sample.)

Working within the covers of a statistics textbook, we can assume that population parameters are known. In real life, however, calculating parameters is virtually impossible because populations tend to be very large. As a result, most population parameters are not only unknown but also unknowable. The problem that motivates the subject of statistical inference is that we often need information about the value of parameters in order to make decisions. For example, to make decisions about whether to expand a line of clothing, we may need to know the mean annual expenditure on clothing by North American adults. Because the size of this population is approximately two hundred million, determining the mean annual expenditure is prohibitive. However, if we are willing to accept less than 100% accuracy, we can use statistical inference to obtain an estimate. Rather than investigating the entire population, we select a sample of people, determine the annual expenditures on clothing in this group, and calculate the sample mean. Although the probability that the sample mean will equal the population mean is very small, we would expect them to be close. For many decisions we need to know how close. We postpone that discussion until Chapters 10 and 11. In this chapter we will discuss the basic concepts and techniques of sampling itself. But first we take a look at various methods for collecting data.

5.2 METHODS OF COLLECTING DATA

Most of this book addresses the problem of converting data into information. The question arises, Where do data come from? The answer is that there is a large number of methods that produce data. Before we proceed, however, we'll remind you of the definition of data introduced in Section 2.2. Data are the observed values of a variable. That is, we define a variable or variables that are of interest to us and then proceed to collect observations of those variables.

DIRECT OBSERVATION

The simplest method of obtaining data is by direct observation. When data are gathered in this way, they are said to be **observational**. For example, suppose that a researcher for a pharmaceutical company wants to determine whether aspirin does reduce the incidence of heart attacks. Observational data may be gathered by selecting a sample of men and women and asking each whether they have taken aspirin regularly over the past 2 years. Each person would be asked whether they had suffered a heart attack over the same period. The proportions reporting heart attacks would be compared and a statistical technique that is introduced in Chapter 13 would be used to determine whether aspirin is effective in reducing the likelihood of heart attacks. There are many drawbacks to this method. One of the most critical is that it is difficult to produce useful information in this way. For example, if the statistics practitioner concludes that people who take aspirin suffer fewer heart attacks, can we conclude that aspirin is effective? It may be that people who take aspirin tend to be more heath-conscious, and health-conscious people tend to have fewer heart attacks. The one advantage to direct observation is that it is relatively inexpensive.

EXPERIMENTS

A more expensive but better way to produce data is through experiments. Data produced in this manner are called **experimental**. In the aspirin illustration above, a statistics practitioner can randomly select men and women. The sample would be divided into two groups. One group would take aspirin regularly and the other would not. After 2 years the statistics practitioner would determine the proportion of people in each group who had suffered a heart attack, and again statistical methods would be employed to determine whether aspirin works. If we find that the aspirin group suffered fewer heart attacks, we may more confidently conclude that taking aspirin regularly is a healthy decision.

SURVEYS

One of the most familiar methods of collecting data is the **survey**, which solicits information from people concerning such things as their income, family size, and opinions on various issues. We're all familiar, for example, with opinion polls that accompany each political election. The Gallup Poll and the Harris Survey are two well-known surveys of public opinion whose results are often reported by the media. But the majority of surveys are conducted for private use. Private surveys are used extensively by market researchers to determine the preferences and attitudes of consumers and voters. The results can be used for a variety of purposes, from helping to determine the target market for an advertising campaign to modifying a candidate's platform in an election campaign. As an illustration, consider a television network that has hired a market research firm to provide the network with a profile of owners of luxury automobiles, including what they watch on television and at what times. The network could then use this information to develop a package of recommended time slots for Cadillac commercials, including costs, which it would present to General Motors. It is quite likely that many students reading this book will one day be marketing executives who will "live and die" by such market research data.

An important aspect of surveys is the response rate. The **response rate** is the proportion of all people who were selected who complete the survey. As we discuss in the next section, a low response rate can destroy the validity of any conclusion resulting from the statistical analysis. Statistics practitioners need to ensure that data are reliable.

Personal Interview

Many researchers feel that the best way to survey people is by means of a **personal interview**, which involves an interviewer soliciting information from a respondent by asking prepared questions. A personal interview has the advantage of having a higher expected response rate than other methods of data collection. In addition, there will probably be fewer incorrect responses resulting from respondents misunderstanding some questions, because the interviewer, if asked, can clarify misunderstandings. But the interviewer must also be careful not to say too much, for fear of biasing the response. To avoid introducing such biases, as well as to reap the potential benefits of a personal interview, the interviewer must be well trained in proper interviewing techniques and well informed on the purpose of the study. The main disadvantage of personal interviews is that they are expensive, especially when travel is involved.

Telephone Interview

A **telephone interview** is usually less expensive, but it is also less personal and has a lower expected response rate. Unless the issue is of interest, many people will refuse to respond to telephone surveys. This problem is exacerbated by telemarketers trying to sell something.

Self-Administered Survey

A third popular method of data collection is the **self-administered questionnaire**, which is usually mailed to a sample of people. This is an inexpensive method of conducting a survey and is therefore attractive when the number of people to be surveyed is large. But self-administered questionnaires usually have a low response rate and may have a relatively high number of incorrect responses due to respondents misunderstanding some questions.

Questionnaire Design

Whether a questionnaire is self-administered or completed by an interviewer, it must be well designed. Proper questionnaire design takes knowledge, experience, time, and money. Some basic points to consider regarding questionnaire design follow.

1. First and foremost, the questionnaire should be kept as short as possible to encourage respondents to complete it. Most people are unwilling to spend much time filling out a questionnaire.

2. The questions themselves should also be short, as well as simply and clearly worded, to enable respondents to answer quickly, correctly, and without ambiguity. Even familiar terms, such as "unemployed" and "family," must be defined carefully because several interpretations are possible.

3. Questionnaires often begin with simple demographic questions to help respondents get started and become comfortable quickly.

4. Dichotomous questions (questions with only two possible responses, such as "yes" and "no") and multiple-choice questions are useful and popular because of their simplicity, but they, too, have possible shortcomings. For example, a respondent's choice of yes or no to a question may depend on certain assumptions not stated in the question. In the case of a multiple-choice question, a respondent may feel that none of the choices offered is suitable.

5. Open-ended questions provide an opportunity for respondents to express opinions more fully, but they are time-consuming and more difficult to tabulate and analyze.

6. Avoid using leading questions, such as, "Wouldn't you agree that the statistics exam was too difficult?" These types of questions tend to lead the respondent to a particular answer.

7. Time permitting, it is useful to pretest a questionnaire on a small number of people in order to uncover potential problems, such as ambiguous wording.

8. Finally, when preparing the questions, think about how you intend to tabulate and analyze the responses. First determine whether you are soliciting values (i.e., responses) for an interval, ordinal, or nominal variable. Then consider which type of statistical techniques—descriptive or inferential—you intend to apply to the data to be collected, and note the requirements of the specific techniques to be used. Thinking about these questions will help to ensure that the questionnaire is designed to collect the data you need.

Whatever method is used to collect primary data, we need to know something about sampling, the subject of the next section.

EXERCISES

5.1 Briefly describe the difference between observational and experimental data.

5.2 A soft-drink manufacturer has been supplying its cola drink in bottles to grocery stores and in cans to small convenience stores. The company is analyzing sales of this cola drink to determine which type of packaging is preferred by consumers.

a Is this study observational or experimental? Explain your answer.

b Outline a better method for determining whether a store will be supplied with cola in bottles or in cans so that future sales data will be more helpful in assessing the preferred type of packaging.

5.3 **a** Briefly describe how you might design a study to investigate the relationship between smoking and lung cancer.

b Is your study in part **a** observational or experimental? Explain why.

5.4 **a** List three methods of conducting a survey of people.

b Give an important advantage and disadvantage of each of the methods listed in part **a**.

5.5 List five important points to consider when designing a questionnaire.

5.3 SAMPLING

The chief motive for examining a sample rather than a population is cost. Statistical inference permits us to draw conclusions about a population parameter based on a sample that is quite small in comparison to the size of the population. For example, television executives want to know the proportion of television viewers who watch a network's programs. Because 100 million people may be watching television in the United States on a given evening, determining the actual proportion of the population that is watching certain programs is impractical and prohibitively expensive. The Nielsen ratings provide approximations of the desired information by observing what is watched by a sample of 1,000 television viewers. The proportion of households watching a particular program can be calculated for the households in the Nielsen sample. This sample proportion is then used as an **estimate** of the proportion of all households (the population proportion) that watched the program.

Another illustration of sampling can be taken from the field of quality management. To ensure that a production process is operating properly, the operations manager needs to know what proportion of items being produced is defective. If the quality technician must destroy the item in order to determine whether it is defective, then there is no alternative to sampling: A complete inspection of the product population would destroy the entire output of the production process.

We know that the sample proportion of television viewers or of defective items is probably not exactly equal to the population proportion we want to estimate. Nonetheless, the sample statistic can come quite close to the parameter it is designed to estimate if the **target population** (the population about which we want to draw inferences) and the **sampled population** (the actual population from which the sample has been taken) are the same. In practice, these may not be the same. One of statistics' most famous failures illustrates this phenomenon.

The *Literary Digest* was a popular magazine of the 1920s and 1930s that had correctly predicted the outcomes of several presidential elections. In 1936, the *Digest* predicted that the Republican candidate, Alfred Landon, would defeat the Democratic incumbent, Franklin D. Roosevelt, by a 3 to 2 margin. But in that election, Roosevelt defeated Landon in a landslide victory, garnering the support of 62% of the electorate. The source of this blunder was the sampling procedure, and there were two distinct mistakes.* First, the *Digest* sent out 10 million sample ballots to prospective voters. However, most of the names of these people were taken from the *Digest's* subscription list and from telephone directories. Subscribers to the magazine and people who owned telephones tended to be wealthier than average and such people then, as today, tended to vote Republican. Additionally, only 2.3 million ballots were returned, resulting in a self-selected sample.

Self-selected samples are almost always biased, because the individuals who participate in them are more keenly interested in the issue than are the other members of the population. You often find similar surveys conducted today when radio and television stations ask people to call and give their opinion on an issue of interest. Again, only listeners who are concerned about the topic and have enough patience to get through to the station will be included in the sample. Hence, the sampled population is comprised entirely of people who are interested in the issue, whereas the target population is made up of all the people within the listening radius of the radio station. As a result, the conclusions drawn from such surveys are frequently wrong.

An excellent example of this phenomenon occurred on ABC's *Nightline* in 1984. Viewers were given a 900 telephone number (cost: 50 cents) and asked to phone in their responses to the question of whether the United Nations should continue to be located in the United States. More than 186,000 people called, with 67% responding "no." At the same time, a (more scientific) market research poll of 500 people revealed that 72% wanted the United Nations to remain in the United States. In general, because the true value of the parameter being estimated is never known, these surveys give the impression of providing useful information. In fact, the results of such surveys are likely to be no more accurate than the results of the 1936 *Literary Digest* poll or *Nightline's* phone-in show. Statisticians have coined two terms to describe these polls: SLOP (self-selected opinion poll) and "*oy vey*" (from the Yiddish lament), both of which convey the contempt that statisticians have for such data-gathering processes.

EXERCISES

5.6 For each of the following sampling plans, indicate why the target population and the sampled population are not the same.

a To determine the opinions and attitudes of customers who regularly shop at a particular mall, a surveyor stands outside a large department store in the mall and randomly selects people to participate in the survey.

b A library wants to estimate the proportion of its books that have been damaged. The librarians

---

*Many statisticians ascribe the *Literary Digest's* statistical debacle to the wrong causes. For an understanding of what really happened, read Maurice C. Bryson, "The *Literary Digest* Poll: Making of a Statistical Myth," *American Statistician* 30(4) (November 1976): 184–185.

decide to select one book per shelf to sample by measuring 12 inches from the left edge of each shelf and selecting the book in that location.

c Political surveyors visit 200 residences during one afternoon to ask eligible voters present in the house at the time whom they intend to vote for.

5.7 **a** Describe why the *Literary Digest* poll of 1936 has become infamous.

b What caused this poll to be so wrong?

5.8 **a** What is meant by a self-selected sample?

b Give an example of a recent poll that involved a self-selected sample.

c Why are self-selected samples not desirable?

5.9 A regular feature in a newspaper asks readers to respond via e-mail to a survey that requires a yes or no response. In the following day's newspaper, the percentages of yes and no responses are reported. Discuss why we should ignore these statistics.

5.10 Suppose your statistics professor distributes a questionnaire about the course. One of the questions asks, "Would you recommend this course to a friend?" Can the professor use the results to infer something about all statistics courses? Explain.

5.4 SAMPLING PLANS

Our objective in this section is to introduce three different sampling plans: simple random sampling, stratified random sampling, and cluster sampling. We begin our presentation with the most basic design.

SIMPLE RANDOM SAMPLING

> **SIMPLE RANDOM SAMPLE**
> A **simple random sample** is a sample selected in such a way that every possible sample with the same number of observations is equally likely to be chosen.

One way to conduct a simple random sample is to assign a number to each element in the population, write these numbers on individual slips of paper, toss them into a hat, and draw the required number of slips (the sample size, n) from the hat. This is the kind of procedure that occurs in raffles, when all the ticket stubs go into a large rotating drum from which the winners are selected.

Sometimes the elements of the population are already numbered. For example, virtually all adults have Social Security numbers (in the United States) or Social Insurance numbers (in Canada); all employees of large corporations have employee numbers; many people have driver's license numbers, medical plan numbers, student numbers, and so on. In such cases, choosing which sampling procedure to use is simply a matter of deciding how to select from among these numbers.

In other cases, the existing form of numbering has built-in flaws that make it inappropriate as a source of samples. Not everyone has a phone number, for example, so the telephone book does not list all the people in a given area. Many households have two (or more) adults, but only one phone listing. Couples often list the phone number under the man's name, so telephone listings are likely to be disproportionately male. Some people do not have phones, some have unlisted phone numbers, and some have more than one phone; these differences mean that each element of the population does not have an equal probability of being selected.

After each element of the chosen population has been assigned a unique number, sample numbers can be selected at random. A random number table can be used to select these sample numbers. [See, for example, *CRC Standard Management Tables*, W. H. Beyer (Ed.), Boca Raton, FL: CRC Press.] Alternatively, we can use a computer to perform this function.

EXAMPLE 5.1

A government income tax auditor has been given responsibility for 1,000 tax returns. A computer is used to check the arithmetic of each return. However, to determine whether the returns have been completed honestly, the auditor must check each entry and confirm its veracity. Because it takes, on average, 1 hour to completely audit a return and she has only 1 week to complete the task, the auditor has decided to randomly select 40 returns. The returns are numbered from 1 to 1,000. Use a computer random number generator to select the sample for the auditor.

SOLUTION

We generated 50 numbers between 1 and 1,000 even though we needed only 40 numbers. We did so because it is likely that there will be some duplicates. We will use the first 40 unique random numbers to select our sample. The following numbers were generated by Excel. The instructions for both Excel and Minitab are provided below. (Notice that the 24th and 36th [counting down the columns] numbers generated were the same—467.)

Computer-Generated Random Numbers

383	246	372	952	75
101	46	356	54	199
597	33	911	706	65
900	165	467	817	359
885	220	427	973	488
959	18	304	467	512
15	286	976	301	374
408	344	807	751	986
864	554	992	352	41
139	358	257	776	231

 EXCEL

GENERAL COMMANDS

COMMANDS FOR EXAMPLE 5.1

1. Click **Tools, Data Analysis...,** and **Random Number Generation.**
2. Specify the **Number of Variables.** **1**
3. Specify the **Number of Random Numbers.** **50**
4. Select **Uniform Distribution.**
5. Specify the range of the uniform distribution (**Parameters**). Click **OK**. Column A will fill with 50 numbers that range between 0 and 1. **0 and 1**
6. Multiply column A by 1,000 and store the products in column B.
7. Make cell C1 active, and click f_x, **Math & Trig, ROUNDUP,** and **OK**.
8. Specify the first number to be rounded. **B1**
9. Type the **number of digits** (decimal places). Click **OK**. **0**
10. Complete column C.

The first five steps command Excel to generate 50 uniformly distributed random numbers between 0 and 1 to be stored in column A. Steps 6 through 10 convert these random numbers to integers between 1 and 1,000. Each number has the same probability (1/1,000 = .001) of being selected. Thus, each member of the population is equally likely to be included in the sample.

MINITAB

COMMANDS	COMMANDS FOR EXAMPLE 5.1
1. Click **Calc**, **Random Data**, and **Integer....**	
2. Type the number of random numbers you wish.	**50**
3. Specify where the numbers are to be stored.	**C1**
4. Specify the **Minimum value**.	**1**
5. Specify the **Maximum value**. Click **OK**.	**1000**

INTERPRET

The auditor would examine the tax returns selected by the computer. Each of these returns would be audited to determine whether they are fraudulent. If the objective is to audit these 40 returns, no statistical procedure would be employed. However, if the objective is to estimate the proportion of all 1,000 returns that are dishonest, she would use one of the inferential techniques presented later in this book.

STRATIFIED RANDOM SAMPLING

In making inferences about a population, we attempt to extract as much information as possible from a sample. The basic sampling plan, simple random sampling, often accomplishes this goal at low cost. Other methods, however, can be used to increase the amount of information about the population. One such procedure is *stratified random sampling*.

STRATIFIED RANDOM SAMPLE

A **stratified random sample** is obtained by separating the population into mutually exclusive sets, or strata, and then drawing simple random samples from each stratum.

Examples of criteria for separating a population into strata follow.

1 Gender
     male
     female

2 Age
     under 20
     20–30
     31–40
     41–50
     51–60
     over 60

3 Occupation
     professional
     clerical
     blue-collar
     other

4 Household income
     under $25,000
     $25,000–$39,999
     $40,000–$60,000
     over $60,000

To illustrate, suppose a public opinion survey is to be conducted in order to determine how many people favor a tax increase. A stratified random sample could be obtained by selecting a random sample of people from each of the four income groups described above. We usually stratify in a way that enables us to obtain particular kinds of information. In this example, we would like to know whether people in the different income categories differ in their opinions about the proposed tax increase, because the tax increase will affect the strata differently. We avoid stratifying when there is no connection between the survey and the strata. For example, little purpose is served in trying to determine whether people within religious strata have divergent opinions about the tax increase.

One advantage of stratification is that, besides acquiring information about the entire population, we can also make inferences within each stratum or compare strata. For instance, we can estimate what proportion of the lowest income group favors the tax increase, or we can compare the highest and lowest income groups to determine whether they differ in their support of the tax increase.

Any stratification must be done in such a way that the strata are mutually exclusive: Each member of the population must be assigned to exactly one stratum. After the population has been stratified in this way, we can employ simple random sampling to generate the complete sample. There are several ways to do this. For example, we can draw random samples from each of the four income groups according to their proportions in the population. Thus, if in the population the relative frequencies of the four groups are as listed below, our sample will be stratified in the same proportions. If a total sample of 1,000 is to be drawn, we will randomly select 250 from stratum 1, 400 from stratum 2, 300 from stratum 3, and 50 from stratum 4.

Stratum	Income Categories	Population Proportions
1	under $25,000	25%
2	$25,000–$39,999	40
3	$40,000–$60,000	30
4	over $60,000	5

The problem with this approach, however, is that if we want to make inferences about the last stratum, a sample of 50 may be too small to produce useful information. In such cases, we usually increase the sample size of the smallest stratum to ensure that the sample data provide enough information for our purposes. An adjustment must then be made before we attempt to draw inferences about the entire population. The required procedure is beyond the level of this book. We recommend that anyone planning such a survey consult an expert statistician or a reference book on the subject. Better still, become an expert statistician yourself by taking additional statistics courses.

CLUSTER SAMPLING

> **CLUSTER SAMPLE**
> A **cluster sample** is a simple random sample of groups or clusters of elements.

Cluster sampling is particularly useful when it is difficult or costly to develop a complete list of the population members (making it difficult and costly to generate a simple random sample). It is also useful whenever the population elements are widely dispersed geographically. For example, suppose we wanted to estimate the average annual household income in a large city. To use simple random sampling, we would need a complete list of households in the city from which to sample. To use stratified random sampling, we would need the list of households, and we would also need to have each household categorized by some other variable (such as age of household head) in order to develop the strata. A less expensive alternative would be to let each block within the city represent a cluster. A sample of clusters could then be randomly selected, and every household within these clusters could be questioned to determine income. By reducing the distances the surveyor must cover to gather data, cluster sampling reduces the cost.

But cluster sampling also increases sampling error (see Section 5.5), because households belonging to the same cluster are likely to be similar in many respects including household income. This can be partially offset by using some of the cost savings to choose a larger sample than would be used for a simple random sample.

SAMPLE SIZE

Whichever type of sampling plan you select, you still have to decide what size sample to use. Determining the appropriate sample size will be addressed in detail in Chapters 10 and 12. Until then, we can rely on our intuition, which tells us that the larger the sample size is, the more accurate we can expect the sample estimates to be.

SAMPLING AND THE CENSUS

To adjust for undercounting, the Census Bureau conducts cluster sampling. The clusters are geographic blocks. For the year 2000 census, the Bureau randomly sampled 11,800 blocks, which contained 314,000 housing units. Each unit was intensively revisited to ensure that all residents were counted. From the results of this survey, the Census Bureau estimated the number of people missed by the first census in various subgroups, defined by several variables including gender, race, and age. Because of the importance of determining state populations, adjustments were made to state totals. For

example, by comparing the results of the census and of the sampling, the Bureau determined that the undercount in the state of Texas was 1.7087%. The official census produced a state population of 20,851,820. Taking 1.7087% of this total produced an adjustment of 356,295. Using this method changed the population of the state of Texas to 21,208,115.

It should be noted that this process is contentious. The controversy centers on the way in which subgroups are defined. Changing the definition alters the undercounts, making this statistical technique subject to politicking.

EXERCISES

5.11 A statistics practitioner would like to conduct a survey to ask people their views on a proposed new shopping mall in their community. According to the latest census, there are 500 households in the community. The practitioner has numbered each household (from 1 to 500), and he would like to randomly select 25 of these households to participate in the study. Use Excel or Minitab to generate the sample.

5.12 A safety expert wants to determine the proportion of cars in his state with worn tire treads. The state license plate contains six digits. Use Excel or Minitab to generate a sample of 20 cars to be examined.

5.13 A large university campus has 60,000 students. The president of the students' association wants to conduct a survey of the students to determine their views on an increase in the student activity fee. She would like to acquire information about all the students but would also like to compare the school of business, the faculty of arts and sciences, and the graduate school. Describe a sampling plan that accomplishes these goals.

5.14 A telemarketing firm has recorded the households that have purchased one or more of the company's products. These number in the millions. They would like to conduct a survey of purchasers to acquire information about their attitude concerning the timing of the telephone calls. The president of the company would like to know the views of all purchasers but would also like to compare the attitudes of people in the West, South, North, and East. Describe a suitable sampling plan.

5.15 The operations manager of a large plant with four departments wants to estimate the person-hours lost per month due to accidents. Describe a sampling plan that would be suitable for estimating the plantwide loss and for comparing departments.

5.16 A statistics practitioner wants to estimate the mean age of children in his city. Unfortunately, he does not have a complete list of households. Describe a sampling plan that would be suitable for his purposes.

5.5 SAMPLING AND NONSAMPLING ERRORS

Two major types of error can arise when a sample of observations is taken from a population: *sampling error* and *nonsampling error*. Anyone reviewing the results of sample surveys and studies, as well as statistics practitioners conducting surveys and applying statistical techniques, should understand the sources of these errors.

SAMPLING ERROR

Sampling error refers to differences between the sample and the population that exists only because of the observations that happened to be selected for the sample. Sampling error is an error that we expect to occur when we make a statement about a population that is based only on the observations contained in a sample taken from the population. To illustrate, suppose that we wish to determine the mean annual income of North American blue-collar workers. To determine this parameter, we would have to ask each North American blue-collar worker what his or her income is and then calculate the mean of all the responses. Because the size of this population is several million, the task is both expensive and impractical. We can use statistical inference to estimate the mean income μ of the population if we are willing to accept less than 100% accuracy. We record the incomes of a sample of the workers and find the mean $\bar{x}$ of this sample of incomes. This sample mean is an estimate of the desired population mean. But the value of the sample mean will deviate from the population mean simply by chance, because the value of the sample mean depends on which incomes just happened to be selected for the sample. The difference between the true (unknown) value of the population mean and its estimate (the sample mean) is the sampling error. The size of this deviation may be large simply due to bad luck—bad luck that a particularly unrepresentative sample happened to be selected. The only way we can reduce the expected size of this error is to take a larger sample.

Given a fixed sample size, the best we can do is to state the probability that the sampling error is less than a certain amount (as we will discuss in Chapter 10). It is common today for such a statement to accompany the results of an opinion poll. If an opinion poll states that, based on sample results, the incumbent candidate for mayor has the support of 54% of eligible voters in an upcoming election, that statement may be accompanied by the following explanatory note: This percentage is correct to within three percentage points, 19 times out of 20. This statement means that we estimate that the actual level of support for the candidate is between 51% and 57%, and that, in the long run, this type of procedure is correct 95% of the time.

S e e i n g   S t a t i s t i c s

APPLET 3: SAMPLING

When you select this applet you will see 100 circles. Imagine that each of the circles represents a household. You want to estimate the proportion of households having high-speed Internet access (DSL, cable modem, etc.). You may collect data from a sample of 10 households by clicking on a household's circle. If the circle turns red, then the household has high-speed Internet access. If the circle turns green, then the household does not have high-speed access. After collecting your sample and obtaining your estimate, click on the "Show All" button to see information for all the households. How well did your sample estimate the true proportion? Click the "Reset" button to try again. (*Note:* This page uses a randomly determined base proportion each time this page is loaded/reloaded.)

APPLET EXERCISES

3.1 Run the applet 25 times. How many times did the sample proportion equal the population proportion?

3.2 Run the applet 20 times. For each simulation, record the sample proportion of homes with high-speed Internet access as well as the population proportion. Compute the average sampling error.

NONSAMPLING ERROR

Nonsampling error is more serious than sampling error, because taking a larger sample won't diminish the size, or the possibility of occurrence, of this error. Even a census can (and probably will) contain nonsampling errors. **Nonsampling errors** are due to mistakes made in the acquisition of data or due to the sample observations being selected improperly.

1. *Errors in data acquisition.* This type of error arises from the recording of incorrect responses. Incorrect responses may be the result of incorrect measurements being taken because of faulty equipment, mistakes made during transcription to a computer file, inaccurate recording of data due to misinterpretation of terms, or inaccurate responses to questions concerning sensitive issues such as sexual activity or possible tax evasion.

2. *Nonresponse error.* **Nonresponse error** refers to error (or **bias**) introduced when responses are not obtained from some members of the sample. When this happens, the sample observations that are collected may not be representative of the target population, resulting in biased results (as was discussed in Section 5.3). Nonresponse can occur for a number of reasons. An interviewer may be unable to contact a person listed in the sample, or the sampled person may refuse to respond for some reason. In either case, responses are not obtained from a selected person, and bias is introduced. The problem of nonresponse is even greater when self-administered questionnaires are used rather than an interviewer, who can attempt to reduce the nonresponse rate by means of callbacks. As noted earlier, the *Literary*

Digest fiasco was partly due to a high nonresponse rate, resulting in a biased, self-selected sample.

3 *Selection bias.* **Selection bias** occurs when the sampling plan is such that some members of the target population cannot possibly be selected for inclusion in the sample. Together with nonresponse error, selection bias played a role in the *Literary Digest* poll being so wrong, as voters without telephones or without a subscription to *Literary Digest* were excluded from possible inclusion in the sample taken.

EXERCISES

5.17 **a** Explain the difference between sampling error and nonsampling error.
b Which type of error in part **a** is more serious? Why?

5.18 Briefly describe three types of nonsampling error.

5.19 Is it possible for a sample to yield better results than a census? Explain.

5.6 SUMMARY

Because most populations are very large, it is extremely costly and impractical to investigate each member of the population to determine the values of the parameters. As a practical alternative, we take a sample from the population and use the sample statistics to draw inferences about the parameters. Care must be taken to ensure that the **sampled population** is the same as the **target population**.

We can choose from among several different sampling plans, including **simple random sampling**, **stratified random sampling**, and **cluster sampling**. Whatever sampling plan is used, it is important to realize that both **sampling error** and **nonsampling error** will occur and to understand what the sources of these errors are.

IMPORTANT TERMS

Estimate 142
Target population 143
Sampled population 143
Self-selected sample 143

Simple random sample 144
Stratified random sample 146
Cluster sample 147
Sampling error 149

Nonsampling error 150
Nonresponse error (bias) 150
Selection bias 151

REFERENCES

Cochran, William G., *Sampling Techniques,* 3rd edition. New York: John Wiley & Sons, 1977.

Cooper, Donald R., and Pamela S. Schindler, *Business Research Methods,* 7th edition. Burr Ridge, IL: McGraw Hill, 2001.

Lohr, Sharon, *Sampling: Design & Analysis.* Pacific Grove, CA: Duxbury, 1999.

Scheaffer, Richard L., William Mendenhall, and R. Lyman Ott, *Elementary Survey Sampling,* 5th edition. Belmont, CA: Duxbury, 1996.

6   PROBABILITY

AUDITING TAX RETURNS

Government auditors routinely check tax returns to determine whether calculation errors were made. They also attempt to detect fraudulent returns. There are several methods that dishonest taxpayers use to evade income tax. One method is not to declare various sources of income. Auditors have several detection methods, including spending patterns. Another form of tax fraud is to invent deductions that are not real. Auditors are constantly seeking methods to detect such fraud. Suppose that auditors believe that 10% of the returns of self-employed individuals contain significant fraud. After analyzing the returns of several thousand self-employed taxpayers, an auditor has determined that 24% of fraudulent returns contain a certain type of expense deduction, and that only 3% of honest returns contain the expense deduction. An auditor has just received a tax return for a self-employed individual with this type of expense deduction. What is the probability that this tax return contains significant fraud? (See page 176 for the answer.)

6.1 INTRODUCTION

In Chapters 2, 3, and 4 we introduced graphical and numerical descriptive methods. While the methods are useful on their own, we are particularly interested in developing statistical inference. As we pointed out in Chapter 1, statistical inference is the process by which we acquire information about populations from samples. A critical component of inference is *probability* because it provides the link between the population and the sample.

Our primary objective in this and the following two chapters is to develop the probability-based tools that are at the basis of statistical inference. However, probability can also play a critical role in decision making, a subject we explore in Chapter 23.

6.2 ASSIGNING PROBABILITY TO EVENTS

To introduce probability we need to first define a *random experiment*.

> **RANDOM EXPERIMENT**
> A **random experiment** is an action or process that leads to one of several possible outcomes.

Here are six illustrations of random experiments and their outcomes.

Illustration 1. *Experiment*: Flip a coin.
  Outcomes: Heads and tails

Illustration 2. *Experiment*: Record marks on a statistics test (out of 100).
  Outcomes: Numbers between 0 and 100

Illustration 3. *Experiment*: Record grade on a statistics test.
  Outcomes: A, B, C, D, and F

Illustration 4. *Experiment*: Record student evaluations of a course
  Outcomes: Poor, fair, good, very good, and excellent

Illustration 5. *Experiment*: Measure the time to assemble a computer.
  Outcomes: Numbers whose smallest possible value is 0 seconds with no predefined upper limit

Illustration 6. *Experiment*: Record the party that a voter will vote for in an upcoming election.
  Outcomes: Party A, Party B, . . .

The first step in assigning probabilities is to produce a list of the outcomes. The listed outcomes must be **exhaustive**, which means that all possible outcomes must be included. Additionally, the outcomes must be **mutually exclusive**, which means that no two outcomes can occur at the same time.

To illustrate the concept of exhaustive outcomes, consider this list of the outcomes of the toss of a die:

1, 2, 3, 4, and 5

This list is not exhaustive, because we have omitted 6.

The concept of mutual exclusiveness can be seen by listing the following outcomes in illustration 2 above:

$0 - 50$, $50 - 60$, $60 - 70$, $70 - 80$,   and $80 - 100$

These outcomes are not mutually exclusive because two outcomes can occur for some students. For example, if a student receives a mark of 70, both the third and fourth outcomes occur.

It should be noted that we could produce more than one list of exhaustive and mutually exclusive outcomes. For example, here is another list of outcomes for illustration 3 above:

Pass and fail

A list of exhaustive and mutually exclusive outcomes is called a *sample space* and is denoted by *S*. The outcomes are denoted by $O_1, O_2, ..., O_k$.

> **SAMPLE SPACE**
> A **sample space** of a random experiment is a list of all possible outcomes of the experiment. The outcomes must be exhaustive and mutually exclusive.

Using set notation, we represent the sample space and its outcomes as

$$S = \{O_1, O_2, ..., O_k\}$$

Once a sample space has been prepared, we begin the task of assigning probabilities to the outcomes. There are three ways to assign probability to outcomes. However it is done, there are two rules governing probabilities, as stated in the next box.

> **REQUIREMENTS OF PROBABILITIES**
> Given a sample space $S = \{O_1, O_2, ..., O_k\}$, the probabilities assigned to the outcomes must satisfy two requirements:
> 1. The probability of any outcome must lie between 0 and 1. That is,
> $$0 \leq P(O_i) \leq 1 \quad \text{for each } i$$
>   [*Note*: $P(O_i)$ is the notation we employ to represent the probability of outcome *i*.]
> 2. The sum of the probabilities of all the outcomes in a sample space must be 1.
>   That is, $\sum_{i=1}^{k} P(O_i) = 1$

THREE APPROACHES TO ASSIGNING PROBABILITIES

The **classical approach** is used by mathematicians to help determine probability associated with games of chance. For example, the classical approach specifies that the probabilities of heads and tails in the flip of a balanced coin are equal to each other. Because the sum of the probabilities must be 1, the probability of heads and the probability of tails are both 50%. Similarly, the six possible outcomes of the toss of a balanced die have the same probability; each is assigned a probability of $\frac{1}{6}$. In some experiments it is necessary to develop mathematical ways to count the number of outcomes. For example, to determine the probability of winning a lottery, we need to determine the number of possible combinations.

The **relative frequency** approach defines probability as the long-run relative frequency with which an outcome occurs. For example, suppose that we know that of the last 1,000 students who took the statistics course you're now taking, 200 received a grade of A. The relative frequency of A's is then $\frac{200}{1,000}$ or 20%. This figure represents an estimate of the probability of obtaining a grade of A in the course. It is only an estimate because the relative frequency approach defines probability as the "long-run" relative frequency. One thousand students do not constitute the long run. The larger the number of students whose grades we have observed, the better the estimate becomes. In theory, we would have to observe an infinite number of grades to determine the exact probability.

When it is not reasonable to use the classical approach and there is no history of the outcomes, we have no alternative but to employ the **subjective approach**. In the subjective approach, we define probability as the degree of belief that we hold in the occurrence of an event. An excellent example is derived from the field of investment. Here an investor would like to know the probability that a particular stock will increase in value. Using the subjective approach, the investor would analyze a number of factors associated with the stock and the stock market in general and, using his or her judgment, assign a probability to the outcomes of interest.

DEFINING EVENTS

An individual outcome of a sample space is called a **simple event.**

> **EVENT**
> An **event** is a collection or set of one or more simple events in a sample space.

In illustration 2 we can define the event, achieve a grade of A, as the set of marks that lie between 80 and 100, inclusive. Using set notation, we have

$$A = \{80, 81, 82, \ldots, 99, 100\}$$

Similarly, the event, receive an F, is defined as

$$F = \{0, 1, 2, \ldots, 48, 49\}$$

PROBABILITY OF EVENTS

We can now define the *probability* of any event.

> **PROBABILITY OF AN EVENT**
> The **probability of an event** is the sum of the probabilities of the simple events that constitute the event.

For example, suppose that in illustration 3, we employed the relative frequency approach to assign probabilities to the simple events as follows:

$$P(A) = .20$$
$$P(B) = .30$$
$$P(C) = .25$$
$$P(D) = .15$$
$$P(F) = .10$$

The probability of the event, pass the course, is

$$P(\text{Pass the course})$$

$$= P(A) + P(B) + P(C) + P(D)$$

$$= .20 + .30 + .25 + .15 = .90$$

INTERPRETING PROBABILITY

No matter what method was used to assign probability, we interpret it using the relative frequency approach for an infinite number of experiments. For example, an investor may have used the subjective approach to determine that there is a 65% probability that a particular stock's price will increase over the next month. However, we interpret the 65% figure to mean that if we had an infinite number of stocks with exactly the same economic and market characteristics as the one the investor will buy, 65% of them will increase in price over the next month. Similarly, we can determine that the probability of throwing a 5 with a balanced die is $\frac{1}{6}$. We may have used the classical approach to determine this probability. However, we interpret the number as the proportion of times that a 5 is observed on a balanced die thrown an infinite number of times.

This relative frequency approach is useful to interpret probability statements such as those heard from weather forecasters or scientists. You will also discover that this is the way we link the population and the sample in statistical inference.

EXERCISES

6.1 The weather forecaster reports that the probability of rain tomorrow is 10%.
  a Which approach was used to arrive at this number?
  b How do you interpret the probability?

6.2 A sportscaster states that he believes that the probability that the New York Yankees will win the World Series this year is 25%.
  a Which method was used to assign that probability?
  b How would you interpret the probability?

6.3 A quiz contains a multiple-choice question with five possible answers, only one of which is correct. A student plans to guess the answer because he knows absolutely nothing about the subject.
  a Produce the sample space for this experiment.
  b Assign probabilities to the simple events in the sample space you produced.
  c Which approach did you use to answer part **b**?
  d Interpret the probabilities you assigned in part **b**.

6.4 An investor tells you that in her estimation there is a 60% probability that the Dow Jones Industrial Index will increase tomorrow.
  a Which approach was used to produce this figure?
  b Interpret the 60% probability.

6.5 The sample space of the toss of a fair die is
  $$S = \{1, 2, 3, 4, 5, 6\}$$
  If the die is balanced, each simple event has the same probability. Find the probability of the following events:
  a An even number
  b A number less than or equal to 4
  c A number greater than or equal to 5

6.6 Four candidates are running for mayor. The four candidates are Adams, Brown, Collins, and Dalton. Determine the sample space of the results of the election.

6.7 Refer to Exercise 6.6. Employing the subjective approach, a political scientist has assigned the following probabilities

  $P(\text{Adams wins}) = .42$
  $P(\text{Brown wins}) = .09$
  $P(\text{Collins wins}) = .27$
  $P(\text{Dalton wins}) = .22$

  Determine the probabilities of the following events:
  a Adams loses.
  b Either Brown or Dalton wins.
  c Either Adams, Brown, or Collins wins.

6.8 The manager of a computer store has kept track of the number of computers sold per day. On the basis of this information, the manager produced the following list of the number of daily sales.

Number of computers sold	Probability
0	.08
1	.17
2	.26
3	.21
4	.18
5	.10

  a If we define the experiment as observing the number of computers sold tomorrow, determine the sample space.
  b Use set notation to define the event, sell more than 3 computers.
  c What is the probability of selling 5 computers?
  d What is the probability of selling 2, 3, or 4 computers?
  e What is the probability of selling 6 computers?

6.9   Three contractors (call them contractors 1, 2, and 3) bid on a project to build a new bridge. What is the sample space?

6.10 Refer to Exercise 6.9. Suppose that you believe that contractor 1 is twice as likely to win as contractor 3 and that contractor 2 is three times as likely to win as contractor 3. What are the probabilities of winning for each contractor?

6.11 Shoppers can pay for their purchases with cash, a credit card, or a debit card. Suppose that the proprietor of a shop determines that 60% of her customers use a credit card, 30% pay with cash, and the rest use a debit card.
  a Determine the sample space for this experiment.
  b Assign probabilities to the simple events.
  c Which method did you use in part **b**?

6.12 Refer to Exercise 6.11.
  a What is the probability that a customer does not use a credit card?
  b What is the probability that a customer pays in cash or with a credit card?

6.13 A survey asks adults to report their marital status. The sample space is $S = \{$single, married, divorced, widowed$\}$. Use set notation to represent the event the adult is not married.

6.14 Refer to Exercise 6.13. Suppose that in the city in which the survey is conducted, 50% of adults are married, 15% are single, 25% are divorced, and 10% are widowed.
  a Assign probabilities to each simple event in the sample space.
  b Which approach did you use in part **a**?

6.15 Refer to Exercises 6.13 and 6.14. Find the probability of each of the following events:
  a The adult is single.
  b The adult is not divorced.
  c The adult is either widowed or divorced.

6.3 JOINT, MARGINAL, AND CONDITIONAL PROBABILITY

In the previous section we described how to produce a sample space and assign probabilities to the simple events in the sample space. Although this method of determining probability is useful, we need to develop more sophisticated methods. In this section we discuss how to calculate the probability of more complicated events from the probability of related events. Here is an illustration of the process.

The sample space for the toss of a die is

$$S = \{1, 2, 3, 4, 5, 6\}$$

If the die is balanced, the probability of each simple event is $\frac{1}{6}$. In most parlor games and casinos, players toss two dice. To determine playing and wagering strategies, players need to compute the probabilities of various totals of the two dice. For example, the probability of tossing a total of 3 with two dice is $\frac{2}{36}$. This probability was derived by creating combinations of the simple events. There are several different types of combinations. One of the most important types is the *intersection* of two events.

INTERSECTION

INTERSECTION OF EVENTS A AND B
The **intersection** of events A and B is the event that occurs when both A and B occur. It is denoted as

A and B

The probability of the intersection is called the **joint probability**.

For example, one way to toss a 3 with two dice is to toss a 1 on the first die *and* a 2 on the second die, which is the intersection of two simple events. Incidentally, to compute the probability of a total of 3, we need to combine this intersection with another intersection—namely, a 2 on the first die and a 1 on the second die. This type of combination is called a *union* of two events and it will be described later in this section. Here is another illustration.

APPLICATIONS IN FINANCE: *MUTUAL FUNDS*

A **mutual fund** is a pool of investments made on behalf of people who share similar objectives. In most cases, a professional manager who has been educated in finance and statistics manages the fund. He or she makes decisions to buy and sell individual stocks and bonds in accordance with a specified investment philosophy. For example, there are funds that concentrate on other publicly traded mutual fund companies. Other mutual funds specialize in Internet (so-called "dot-coms") stocks while others buy stocks of biotech firms. Surprisingly, most mutual funds do not outperform the market. That is, the increase in the net asset value (NAV) of the mutual fund is often less than the increase in the value of stock indexes that represent their stock markets. One reason for this is the management expense ratio (MER), which is a measure of the costs charged to the fund by the manager to cover expenses, including the salary and bonus of the managers. The MERs for most funds range from .5% to more than 4%. The ultimate success of the fund depends on the skill and knowledge of the fund manager. This raises the question, Which managers do best?

EXAMPLE 6.1

Why are some mutual fund managers more successful than others? One possible factor is where the manager earned his or her MBA. Suppose that a potential investor examined the relationship between how well the mutual fund performs and where the fund manager earned his or her MBA. After the analysis, Table 6.1, the table of joint probabilities, was developed. Analyze these probabilities and interpret the results.

Table 6.1 Probabilities Associated with Mutual Fund Managers

	Mutual fund outperforms market	Mutual fund does not outperform market
Top-20 MBA program	.11	.29
Not top-20 MBA program	.06	.54

Table 6.1 tells us that the joint probability that a mutual fund outperforms the market *and* that its manager graduated from a top-20 MBA program is .11. That is, 11% of all mutual funds outperform the market and their managers graduated from a top-20 MBA program. The other three joint probabilities are defined similarly. That is,

The probability that a mutual fund outperforms the market and its manager did not graduate from a top-20 MBA program is .06.

The probability that a mutual fund does not outperform the market and its manager graduated from a top-20 MBA program is .29.

The probability that a mutual fund does not outperform the market and its manager did not graduate from a top-20 MBA program is .54.

To help make our task easier, we'll use notation to represent the events. Let

A_1 = Fund manager graduated from a top-20 MBA program
A_2 = Fund manager did not graduate from a top-20 MBA program
B_1 = Fund outperforms the market
B_2 = Fund does not outperform the market

Thus,

$$P(A_1 \text{ and } B_1) = .11$$
$$P(A_2 \text{ and } B_1) = .06$$
$$P(A_1 \text{ and } B_2) = .29$$
$$P(A_2 \text{ and } B_2) = .54$$

MARGINAL PROBABILITY

The joint probabilities in Table 6.1 allow us to compute various probabilities. **Marginal probabilities**, computed by adding across rows and down columns, are so named because they are calculated in the margins of the table.

Adding across the first row produces

$$P(A_1) = P(A_1 \text{ and } B_1) + P(A_1 \text{ and } B_2) = .11 + .29 = .40$$

Notice that both intersections state that the manager graduated from a top-20 MBA program (represented by A_1). Thus, for a randomly selected mutual fund, the probability that its manager graduated from a top-20 MBA program is .40. Expressed as a relative frequency, 40% of all mutual fund managers graduated from a top-20 MBA program.

Adding across the second row:

$$P(A_2) = P(A_2 \text{ and } B_1) + P(A_2 \text{ and } B_2) = .06 + .54 = .60$$

This probability tells us that 60% of all mutual fund managers did not graduate from a top-20 MBA program (represented by A_2). Notice that the probability that a mutual fund manager graduated from a top-20 MBA program and the probability that the manager did not graduate from a top-20 MBA program add to 1.

Adding down the columns produces the following marginal probabilities:

Column 1:

$$P(B_1) = P(A_1 \text{ and } B_1) + P(A_2 \text{ and } B_1) = .11 + .06 = .17$$

Column 2:

$$P(B_2) = P(A_1 \text{ and } B_2) + P(A_2 \text{ and } B_2) = .29 + .54 = .83$$

These marginal probabilities tell us that 17% of all mutual funds outperform the market and that 83% of mutual funds do not outperform the market.

The following table lists all the joint and marginal probabilities.

Table 6.2 Joint and Marginal Probabilities

	Mutual fund outperforms market	Mutual fund does not outperform market	Totals
Top-20 MBA program	$P(A_1 \text{ and } B_1) = .11$	$P(A_1 \text{ and } B_2) = .29$	$P(A_1) = .40$
Not top-20 MBA program	$P(A_2 \text{ and } B_1) = .06$	$P(A_2 \text{ and } B_2) = .54$	$P(A_2) = .60$
Totals	$P(B_1) = .17$	$P(B_2) = .83$	1.00

CONDITIONAL PROBABILITY

We frequently need to know how two events are related. In particular, we would like to know the probability of one event given the occurrence of another related event. For example, we would certainly like to know the probability that a fund managed by a top-20 MBA program graduate will outperform the market. Such a probability will allow us to make an informed decision about where to invest our money. This probability is called a **conditional probability** because we want to know the probability that a fund will outperform the market *given* the condition that the manager graduated from a top-20 MBA program. The conditional probability that we seek is represented by

$$P(B_1 \mid A_1)$$

where the "|" represents the word *given*. Here is how we compute this conditional probability.

The marginal probability that a manager graduated from a top-20 MBA program is .40, which is the sum of two joint probabilities, .11 and .29. We can interpret these numbers in the following way. On average, for every 100 mutual funds, 40 will be managed by a top-20 MBA program graduate. Of these 40 managers, on average 11 of them will manage a mutual fund that will outperform the market. Thus, the conditional probability is $\frac{11}{40} = .275$. Notice that this ratio is the same as the ratio of the joint probability $P(A_1 \text{ and } B_1)$ to the marginal probability $P(A_1)$. All conditional probabilities can be computed this way.

CONDITIONAL PROBABILITY

The probability of event *A* given event *B* is

$$P(A|B) = \frac{P(A \text{ and } B)}{P(B)}$$

The probability of event *B* given event *A* is

$$P(B|A) = \frac{P(A \text{ and } B)}{P(A)}$$

EXAMPLE 6.2

Suppose that in Example 6.1 we select one mutual fund at random and discover that it did not outperform the market. What is the probability that a top-20 MBA program graduate manages it?

SOLUTION   We wish to find a conditional probability. The condition is that the fund did not outperform the market (event B_2) and the event whose probability we seek is that the fund is managed by a top-20 MBA program graduate (event A_1). Thus, we want to compute the following probability:

$$P(A_1|B_2)$$

Using the conditional probability formula, we find

$$P(A_1 | B_2) = \frac{P(A_1 \text{ and } B_2)}{P(B_2)} = \frac{.29}{.83} = .3494$$

Thus, 34.94% of all mutual funds that do not outperform the market are managed by top-20 MBA program graduates.

The calculation of conditional probabilities raises the question of whether the two events, the fund outperformed the market and the manager graduated from a top-20 MBA program, are related, a subject we tackle next.

INDEPENDENCE

One of the objectives of calculating conditional probability is to determine whether two events are related. In particular, we would like to know whether they are *independent*.

INDEPENDENT EVENTS
Two events A and B are said to be **independent** if

$$P(A|B) = P(A)$$

or

$$P(B|A) = P(B)$$

Put another way, two events are independent if the probability of one event is not affected by the occurrence of the other event.

EXAMPLE 6.3

Determine whether the fund outperforming the market and whether the manager graduated from a top-20 MBA program are independent events.

SOLUTION We can solve this problem in any one of four ways (using any one of the four combinations of events). We arbitrarily choose the events A_1 and B_2.

The marginal probability that a manager graduated from a top-20 MBA program is

$$P(A_1) = .40$$

In Example 6.2 we determined the conditional probability

$$P(A_1 | B_2) = .3494$$

Since the two probabilities are not equal, we conclude that the two events are dependent.

Note that we would draw the same conclusion by using any of the other combinations. For example, the probability that a fund does not outperform the market is

$$P(B_2) = .83$$

We compute the conditional probability

$$P(B_2 | A_2) = \frac{P(A_2 \text{ and } B_2)}{P(A_2)} = \frac{.54}{.60} = .90$$

Once again, the inequality of the two probabilities informs us that whether the fund does or does not outperform the market is dependent upon whether the manager graduated from a top-20 MBA program.

UNION

Another event that is the combination of other events is the *union.*

> **UNION OF EVENTS A AND B**
> The **union** of events A and B is the event that occurs when either A or B or both occur. It is denoted as
>
> A or B

EXAMPLE 6.4

Determine the probability that a randomly selected fund outperforms the market or the manager graduated from a top-20 MBA program.

SOLUTION We want to compute the probability of the union of two events

$$P(A_1 \text{ or } B_1)$$

The union A_1 or B_1 consists of three events. That is, the union occurs whenever any of the following joint events occurs:

1. Fund outperforms the market and the manager graduated from a top-20 MBA program
2. Fund outperforms the market and the manager did not graduate from a top-20 MBA program
3. Fund does not outperform the market and the manager graduated from a top-20 MBA program

Their probabilities are

$$P(A_1 \text{ and } B_1) = .11$$
$$P(A_2 \text{ and } B_1) = .06$$
$$P(A_1 \text{ and } B_2) = .29$$

Thus the probability of the union, the fund outperforms the market or the manager graduated from a top-20 MBA program, is the sum of the three probabilities. That is,

$$P(A_1 \text{ or } B_1) = P(A_1 \text{ and } B_1) + P(A_2 \text{ and } B_1) + P(A_1 \text{ and } B_2)$$

$$= .11 + .06 + .29 = .46$$

Notice that there is another way to produce this probability. Of the four probabilities in Table 6.1, the only one representing an event that is *not* part of the union is the probability of the event the fund does not outperform the market and the manager did not graduate from a top-20 MBA program. That probability is

$$P(A_2 \text{ and } B_2) = .54$$

which is the probability that the union *does not* occur. Thus, the probability of the union is

$$P(A_1 \text{ or } B_1) = 1 - P(A_2 \text{ and } B_2) = 1 - .54 = .46$$

Thus, we determined that 46% of mutual funds either outperform the market or are managed by a top-20 MBA program graduate or both.

EXERCISES

6.16 Given the following table of joint probabilities, calculate the marginal probabilities.

	A_1	A_2	A_3
B_1	.1	.3	.2
B_2	.2	.1	.1

6.17 Calculate the marginal probabilities from the following table of joint probabilities.

	A_1	A_2
B_1	.4	.3
B_2	.2	.1

6.18 Refer to Exercise 6.17.
a Determine $P(A_1|B_1)$.
b Determine $P(A_2|B_1)$.
c Did your answers to parts **a** and **b** sum to 1? Is this a coincidence? Explain.

6.19 Refer to Exercise 6.17. Calculate the following probabilities.
a $P(A_1|B_2)$
b $P(B_2|A_1)$
c Did you expect the answers to parts **a** and **b** to be reciprocals? That is, did you expect that $P(A_1|B_2) = 1/P(B_2|A_1)$? Why is this impossible (unless both probabilities are 1)?

6.20 Are the events in Exercise 6.17 independent? Explain.

6.21 Refer to Exercise 6.17. Compute the following.
a $P(A_1 \text{ or } B_1)$
b $P(A_1 \text{ or } B_2)$
c $P(A_1 \text{ or } A_2)$

6.22 Suppose that you have been given the following joint probabilities. Are the events independent? Explain.

	A_1	A_2
B_1	.20	.60
B_2	.05	.15

6.23 Determine whether the events are independent from the following joint probabilities.

	A_1	A_2
B_1	.20	.15
B_2	.60	.05

6.24 Suppose we have the following joint probabilities.

	A_1	A_2	A_3
B_1	.15	.20	.10
B_2	.25	.25	.05

Compute the marginal probabilities.

6.25 Refer to Exercise 6.24.
a Compute $P(A_2|B_2)$.
b Compute $P(B_2|A_2)$.
c Compute $P(B_1|A_2)$.

6.26 Refer to Exercise 6.24.
a Compute $P(A_1 \text{ or } A_2)$.
b Compute $P(A_2 \text{ or } B_2)$.
c Compute $P(A_3 \text{ or } B_1)$.

6.27 The female instructors at a large university recently lodged a complaint about the most recent round of promotions from assistant professor to associate professor. An analysis of the relationship between gender and promotion was undertaken with the joint probabilities in the following table being produced.

	Promoted	Not promoted
Female	.03	.12
Male	.17	.68

a What is the rate of promotion among female assistant professors?
b What is the rate of promotion among male assistant professors?
c Is it reasonable to accuse the university of gender bias?

6.28 A department store analyzed its most recent sales and determined the relationship between the way the customer paid for the item and the price category of the item. The joint probabilities in the following table were calculated.

	Cash	Credit card	Debit card
Under $20	.09	.03	.04
$20–$100	.05	.21	.18
Over $100	.03	.23	.14

a What proportion of purchases was paid by debit card?
b Find the probability that a credit card purchase was over $100.
c Determine the proportion of purchases made by credit card or by debit card.

6.29 An analysis of the relationship between gender and whether a vote was cast in last mayoral election in Miami Beach produced the probabilities shown at the top of page 164.

	Female	Male
Voted in last mayoral election	.25	.18
Did not vote in last mayoral election	.33	.24

a What proportion of the electorate voted in the last election?

b Are gender and whether a vote was cast in the last mayoral election in Miami Beach independent? Explain how you arrived at your conclusion.

6.30 The following table lists the joint probabilities associated with smoking and lung disease among 60-to-65 year-old men.

	He is a smoker	He is a nonsmoker
He has lung disease	.12	.03
He does not have lung disease	.19	.66

One 60-to-65 year-old man is selected at random. What is the probability of the following events?

a He is a smoker

b He does not have lung disease

c He has lung disease given that he is a smoker

d He has lung disease given that he does not smoke

6.31 Refer to Exercise 6.30. Are smoking and lung disease among 60-to-65 year-old men related?

6.32 The method of instruction in college and university applied statistics courses is changing. Historically, most courses were taught with an emphasis on manual calculation. The alternative is to employ a computer and a software package to perform the calculations. An analysis of applied statistics courses investigated whether the instructor's educational background is primarily mathematics (or statistics) or some other field. The result of this analysis is the accompanying table of joint probabilities.

	Statistics course emphasizes manual calculations	Statistics course employs computer and software
Mathematics or Statistics education	.23	.36
Other education	.11	.30

a What is the probability that a randomly selected applied statistics course instructor whose education was in statistics emphasizes manual calculations?

b What proportion of applied statistics courses employ a computer and software?

c Are the educational background of the instructor and the way his or her course is taught independent?

6.33 A restaurant chain routinely surveys customers and, among other questions, asks each customer whether he or she would return and to rate the quality of food. Summarizing hundreds of thousands of questionnaires produced the table of joint probabilities below.

Rating	Customer will return	Customer will not return
Poor	.02	.10
Fair	.08	.09
Good	.35	.14
Excellent	.20	.02

a What proportion of customers say that they will return and rate the restaurant's food as good?

b What proportion of customers who say that they will return rate the restaurant's food as good?

c What proportion of customers who rate the restaurant's food as good say that they will return?

d Discuss the differences in your answers to parts **a**, **b**, and **c**.

6.34 To determine whether drinking alcoholic beverages has an effect on the bacteria that cause ulcers, researchers developed the following table of joint probabilities.

Number of alcoholic drinks per day	Ulcer	No ulcer
None	.01	.22
One	.03	.19
Two	.03	.32
More than two	.04	.16

a What proportion of people have ulcers?

b What is the probability that a teetotaler (no alcoholic beverages) develops an ulcer?

c What is the probability that someone who has an ulcer does not drink alcohol?

d Are ulcers and the drinking of alcohol independent? Explain.

6.35 When male and female drivers are lost, what do they do? After a thorough analysis, the following joint probabilities were developed.

Action	Male	Female
Consult a map	.25	.14
Ask someone for directions	.12	.28
Continue driving until direction or location determined	.13	.08

a What is the probability that a man would ask for directions?

b What proportion of drivers consult a map?

c Are gender and consulting a map independent? Explain.

6.36 Many critics of television claim that there is too much violence and that it has a negative impact on society. However, there may also be a negative effect on advertisers. To examine this issue, researchers developed two versions of a cops-and-robbers made-for-television movie. One version depicted several violent crimes, and the other removed these scenes. In the middle of the movie, one 60-second commercial was shown advertising a new product and brand name. At the end of the movie, viewers were asked to name the brand. After observing the results, the researchers produced the following table of joint probabilities.

	Watch violent movie	Watch nonviolent movie
Remember the brand name	.15	.18
Do not remember the brand name	.35	.32

a What proportion of viewers remember the brand name?

b What proportion of viewers who watch the violent movie remember the brand name?

c Does watching a violent movie affect whether the viewer will remember the brand name? Explain.

6.37 Is there a relationship between the male hormone testosterone and criminal behavior? To answer this question, medical researchers measured the testosterone level of penitentiary inmates and recorded whether they were convicted of murder. After analyzing the results, they produced the following table of joint probabilities.

Testosterone level	Murderer	Other felon
Above average	.27	.24
Below average	.21	.28

a What proportion of murderers have above average testosterone levels?

b Are level of testosterone and the crime committed independent? Explain.

6.38 According to the U.S. National Center for Education Statistics, there are more than 63 million American workers 18 years and over who use computers at work. From this study, which was conducted in 1994 and 1998 (*Source: Statistical Abstract of the United States*, 2000, Table 690), the following table of joint probabilities was developed.

	Computer usage	
Gender	Uses a spreadsheet	Does not use spreadsheet
Female	.298	.228
Male	.209	.265

a What proportion of workers use a spreadsheet?

b What proportion of male workers use a spreadsheet?

c What proportion of spreadsheet users are female?

6.39 Refer to Exercise 6.38. Are gender and use of a spreadsheet independent events?

6.40 The annual report of the U.S. Bureau of Labor Statistics (*Source: Statistical Abstract of the United States*, 2000, Table 703) lists the number of employees who receive various types of benefits. From the information in the January 1999 report, the following probabilities were derived.

	Dental Care	
Type of worker	Provided by employer	Not provided by employer
Professional/technical	.166	.094
Clerical/sales	.195	.135
Blue-collar/services	.230	.180

a What proportion of workers are provided with dental care?

b What proportion of professional/technical workers are provided with dental care?

c Is the type of worker related to whether the employer provides dental care?

6.41 A firm has classified its customers in two ways: according to whether the account is overdue and whether the account is new (less than 12 months) or old. An analysis of the firm's records provided the input for the following table of joint probabilities.

	Overdue	Not overdue
New	.06	.13
Old	.52	.29

One account is randomly selected.

a If the account is overdue, what is the probability that it is new?

b If the account is new, what is the probability that it is overdue?

c Is the age of the account related to whether it is overdue? Explain.

6.42 How are the size of a firm (measured in terms of the number of employees) and the type of firm related? To help answer the question an analyst referred to the U.S. Census (*Source: Statistical Abstract of the United States*, 2000, Table 868) and developed the following table of joint probabilities.

Number of employees	Industry		
	Construction	Manufacturing	Retail
Under 20	.2307	.0993	.5009
20 to 99	.0189	.0347	.0876
100 or more	.0019	.0147	.0113

If one firm is selected at random, find the probability of the following events.

a The firm employs fewer than 20 employees

b The firm is in the retail industry

c A firm in the construction industry employs between 20 and 99 workers

6.43 Credit scorecards are used by financial institutions to help decide to whom loans should be granted (see the Applications in Finance: Credit Scorecards summary on page 48). An analysis of the records of one bank produced the following probabilities.

	Score	
Loan performance	Under 400	400 or more
Fully repaid	.19	.64
Defaulted	.13	.04

a What proportion of loans are fully repaid?

b What proportion of loans given to scorers of less than 400 fully repay?

c What proportion of loans given to scorers of 400 or more fully repay?

d Are score and whether the loan is fully repaid independent? Explain.

6.44 A retail outlet wanted to know whether its weekly advertisement in the daily newspaper works. To acquire this critical information, the store manager surveyed the people who entered the store and determined whether each individual saw the ad and whether a purchase was made. From the information developed, the manager produced the table of joint probabilities below. Are the ads effective? Explain.

	Purchase	No purchase
See ad	.18	.42
Do not see ad	.12	.28

6.45 To gauge the relationship between education and unemployment, an economist turned to the U.S. census (*Source: Statistical Abstract of the United States,* 2000, Table 251). The table enabled the economist to develop the following table of joint probabilities.

Education	Employed	Unemployed
Not a high school graduate	.0975	.0080
High school graduate	.3108	.0128
Some college, no degree	.1785	.0062
Associate's degree	.0849	.0023
Bachelor's degree	.1959	.0041
Advanced degree	.0975	.0015

a What is the probability that a high school graduate is unemployed?

b Determine the probability that a randomly selected individual is employed

c Find the probability that an unemployed person possesses an advanced degree.

d What is the probability that a randomly selected person did not finish high school?

6.46 The decision about where to build a new plant is a major one for most companies. One of the factors that is often considered is the education level of the location's residents. Census information may be useful in this regard. (*Source: Statistical Abstract of the United States,* 2000, Table 251) After analyzing a recent census, a company produced the following joint probabilities.

Education	Region Northwest	Midwest	South	West
Not a high school graduate	.0301	.0318	.0683	.0359
High school graduate	.0711	.0843	.1174	.0608
Some college, no degree	.0262	.0410	.0605	.0456
Associate's degree	.0143	.0180	.0248	.0181
Bachelor's degree	.0350	.0368	.0559	.0418
Advanced degree	.0190	.0184	.0269	.0180

a Determine the probability that a person living in the West has a bachelor's degree.

b Find the probability that a high school graduate with no college education lives in the Northwest.

c What is the probability that a person selected at random lives in the South?

d Are education and region independent? Explain.

6.4 PROBABILITY RULES AND TREES

In Section 6.3 we introduced intersection and union and described how to determine the probability of the intersection and the union of two events. In this section we present other methods of determining these probabilities. We introduce three rules that enable us to calculate the probability of more complex events from the probability of simpler events.

COMPLEMENT RULE

The **complement** of event A is the event that occurs when event A does not occur. The complement of event A is denoted by A^C. The complement rule defined below derives from the fact that the probability of an event and the probability of the event's complement must sum to 1.

COMPLEMENT RULE

$$P(A^C) = 1 - P(A)$$

for any event A.

We will demonstrate the use of this rule after we introduce the next rule.

MULTIPLICATION RULE

The **multiplication rule** is used to calculate the joint probability of two events. It is based on the formula for conditional probability supplied in the previous section. That is, from the following formula

$$P(A|B) = \frac{P(A \text{ and } B)}{P(B)}$$

we derive the multiplication rule simply by multiplying both sides by $P(B)$.

> **MULTIPLICATION RULE**
> The joint probability of any two events A and B is
>
> $$P(A \text{ and } B) = P(A|B)\,P(B)$$
>
> or, altering the notation,
>
> $$P(A \text{ and } B) = P(B|A)\,P(A)$$

If A and B are independent events, $P(A|B) = P(A)$ and $P(B|A) = P(B)$. It follows that the joint probability of two independent events is simply the product of the probabilities of the two events. We can express this as a special form of the multiplication rule.

> **MULTIPLICATION RULE FOR INDEPENDENT EVENTS**
> The joint probability of any two independent events A and B is
>
> $$P(A \text{ and } B) = P(A)\,P(B)$$

EXAMPLE 6.5

A graduate statistics course has seven male and three female students. The professor wants to select two students at random to help her conduct a research project. What is the probability that the two students chosen are female?

SOLUTION   Let A represent the event that the first student chosen is female and B represent the event that the second student chosen is also female. We want the joint probability $P(A \text{ and } B)$. Consequently, we apply the multiplication rule:

$$P(A \text{ and } B) = P(B|A)P(A)$$

Because there are three female students in a class of ten, the probability that the first student chosen is female is

$$P(A) = \frac{3}{10}$$

After the first student is chosen, there are only nine students left. Given that the first student chosen was female, there are only two female students left. It follows that

$$P(B|A) = \frac{2}{9}$$

Thus the joint probability is

$$P(A \text{ and } B) = P(B|A)P(A) = \left(\frac{2}{9}\right)\left(\frac{3}{10}\right) = \frac{6}{90} = .067$$

EXAMPLE 6.6

Refer to Example 6.5. The professor who teaches the course is suffering from the flu and will be unavailable for two classes. The professor's replacement will teach the next two classes. His style is to select one student at random and pick on him or her to answer questions during that class. What is the probability that the two students chosen are female?

SOLUTION The form of the question is the same as in Example 6.5; we wish to compute the probability of choosing two female students. However, the experiment is slightly different. It is now possible to choose the same student in each of the two classes the replacement teaches. Thus A and B are independent events, and we apply the multiplication rule for independent events:

$$P(A \text{ and } B) = P(A)P(B)$$

The probability of choosing a female student in each of the two classes is the same. That is,

$$P(A) = \frac{3}{10} \quad \text{and} \quad P(B) = \frac{3}{10}$$

Hence,

$$P(A \text{ and } B) = P(A)P(B) = \left(\frac{3}{10}\right)\left(\frac{3}{10}\right) = \frac{9}{100} = .09$$

ADDITION RULE

The **addition rule** enables us to calculate the probability of the union of two events.

> **ADDITION RULE**
> The probability that event A, or event B, or both occur is
> $$P(A \text{ or } B) = P(A) + P(B) - P(A \text{ and } B)$$

If you're like most students, you're wondering why we subtract the joint probability from the sum of the probabilities of A and B. To understand why this is necessary, examine Table 6.2 (page 159), which we have reproduced here as Table 6.3.

Table 6.3 Joint and Marginal Probabilities

	B_1	B_2	Totals
A_1	$P(A_1 \text{ and } B_1) = .11$	$P(A_1 \text{ and } B_2) = .29$	$P(A_1) = .40$
A_2	$P(A_2 \text{ and } B_1) = .06$	$P(A_2 \text{ and } B_2) = .54$	$P(A_2) = .60$
Totals	$P(B_1) = .17$	$P(B_2) = .83$	

This table summarizes how the marginal probabilities were computed. For example, the marginal probability of A_1 and the marginal probability of B_1 were calculated as:

$$P(A_1) = P(A_1 \text{ and } B_1) + P(A_1 \text{ and } B_2) = .11 + .29 = .40$$

$$P(B_1) = P(A_1 \text{ and } B_1) + P(A_2 \text{ and } B_1) = .11 + .06 = .17$$

If we now attempt to calculate the probability of the union of A_1 and B_1 by summing their probabilities, we find

$$P(A_1) + P(B_1) = .11 + .29 + .11 + .06$$

Notice that we added the joint probability of A_1 and B_1 (which is .11) twice. To correct the double counting, we subtract the joint probability from the sum of the probabilities of A_1 and B_1. Thus,

$$P(A_1 \text{ or } B_1) = P(A_1) + P(B_1) - P(A_1 \text{ and } B_1)$$

$$= [.11 + .29] + [.11 + .06] - .11$$

$$= .40 + .17 - .11 = .46$$

Notice that this is the probability of the union of A_1 and B_1, which we calculated in Example 6.4 (page 162).

As was the case with the multiplication rule, there is a special form of the addition rule. When two events are mutually exclusive (which means that the two events cannot occur together), their joint probability is 0.

ADDITION RULE FOR MUTUALLY EXCLUSIVE EVENTS

The probability of the union of two mutually exclusive events A and B is

$$P(A \text{ or } B) = P(A) + P(B)$$

EXAMPLE 6.7

In a large city, two newspapers are published, the *Sun* and the *Post*. The circulation departments report that 22% of the city's households have a subscription to the *Sun* and 35% subscribe to the *Post*. A survey reveals that 6% of all households subscribe to both newspapers. What proportion of the city's households subscribe to at least one newspaper?

SOLUTION We can express this question as: What is the probability of selecting a household at random that subscribes to the *Sun*, the *Post*, or both? It is now clear that we seek the probability of the union, and we must apply the addition rule. Let A = event the household subscribes to the *Sun* and B = event the household subscribes to the *Post*. We perform the following calculation:

$$P(A \text{ or } B) = P(A) + P(B) - P(A \text{ and } B) = .22 + .35 - .06 = .51$$

The probability that a randomly selected household subscribes to at least one newspaper is .51. Expressed as relative frequency, 51% of the city's households subscribe to at least one newspaper.

PROBABILITY TREES

An effective and simpler method of applying the probability rules is the probability tree, wherein the events in an experiment are represented by lines. The resulting figure resembles a tree, hence the name. We will illustrate the probability tree with several examples, including two that we addressed using the probability rules alone.

In Example 6.5 we wanted to find the probability of choosing two female students, where the two choices had to be different. The tree diagram in Figure 6.1 describes this experiment. Notice that the first two branches represent the two possibilities, female and male students, on the first choice. The second set of branches represents the two possibilities on the second choice. The probabilities of female and male student chosen first are 3/10 and 7/10, respectively. The probabilities for the second set of branches are conditional probabilities based on the choice of the first student selected.

We calculate the joint probabilities by multiplying the probabilities on the linked branches. Thus, the probability of choosing two female students is $P(F \text{ and } F) = \left(\frac{3}{10}\right)\left(\frac{2}{9}\right) = \frac{6}{90}$. The remaining joint probabilities are computed similarly.

**Figure 6.1
Probability tree for
Example 6.5**

In Example 6.6, the experiment was similar to that of Example 6.5. However, the student selected on the first choice was returned to the pool of students and was eligible to be chosen again. Thus, the probabilities on the second set of branches remain the same as the probabilities on the first set, and the probability tree is drawn with these changes, as shown in Figure 6.2.

**Figure 6.2
Probability tree for
Example 6.6**

The advantage of a probability tree on this type of problem is that it restrains its users from making the wrong calculation. Once the tree is drawn and the probabilities of the branches inserted, virtually the only allowable calculation is the multiplication of the probabilities of linked branches. An easy check on those calculations is available. The joint probabilities at the ends of the branches must sum to 1, because all possible events are listed. Notice in both figures that the joint probabilities do indeed sum to 1.

The special form of the addition rule for mutually exclusive events can be applied to the joint probabilities. In both probability trees, we can compute the probability that one student chosen is female and one is male simply by adding the joint probabilities. For the tree in Example 6.5, we have

$$P(F \text{ and } M) + P(M \text{ and } F) = \frac{21}{90} + \frac{21}{90} = \frac{42}{90}$$

In the probability tree in Example 6.6, we find

$$P(F \text{ and } M) + P(M \text{ and } F) = \frac{21}{100} + \frac{21}{100} = \frac{42}{100}$$

EXAMPLE 6.8

Students who graduate from law schools must still pass a bar exam before becoming lawyers. Suppose that in a particular jurisdiction the pass rate for first-time test takers is 72%. Candidates who fail the first exam may take it again several months later. Of those who fail their first test, 88% pass their second attempt. Find the probability that a randomly selected law school graduate becomes a lawyer. Assume that candidates cannot take the exam more than twice.

SOLUTION   The probability tree in Figure 6.3 is employed to describe the experiment. Note that we use the complement rule to determine the probability of failing each exam.

**Figure 6.3
Probability tree for
Example 6.8**

First exam	Second exam	Joint probability
Pass .72		Pass .72
Fail .28	Pass|Fail .88	Fail and Pass (.28)(.88) = .2464
	Fail|Fail .12	Fail and Fail (.28)(.12) = .0336

We apply the multiplication rule to calculate $P(\text{fail and pass})$, which we find to be .2464. We then apply the addition rule for mutually exclusive events to find the probability of passing the first or second exam:

$$P(\text{Pass [on first exam]}) + P(\text{Fail [on first exam] and Pass [on second exam]})$$

$$= .72 + .2464 = .9664$$

Thus, 96.64% of applicants become lawyers by passing the first or second exam.

EXERCISES

6.47   Given the following probabilities, compute all joint probabilities.
$P(A) = .9$ $P(A^C) = .1$
$P(B|A) = .4$ $P(B|A^C) = .7$

6.48   Determine all joint probabilities from the following.
$P(A) = .8$ $P(A^C) = .2$
$P(B|A) = .4$ $P(B|A^C) = .7$

6.49 Draw a probability tree to compute the joint probabilities from the following probabilities.

$$P(A) = .5 \qquad P(A^C) = .5$$
$$P(B|A) = .4 \qquad P(B|A^C) = .7$$

6.50 Given the following probabilities, draw a probability tree to compute the joint probabilities.

$$P(A) = .8 \qquad P(A^C) = .2$$
$$P(B|A) = .3 \qquad P(B|A^C) = .3$$

6.51 Given the following probabilities, find the joint probability $P(A \text{ and } B)$.

$$P(A) = .7 \qquad P(B|A) = .3$$

6.52 Approximately 10% of people are left-handed. If two people are selected at random, what is the probability of the following events?
  a Both are right-handed
  b Both are left-handed
  c One is right-handed and the other is left-handed
  d At least one is right-handed

6.53 Refer to Exercise 6.52. Suppose that three people are selected at random.
  a Draw a probability tree to depict the experiment.
  b If we use the notation *RRR* to describe the selection of three right-handed people, similarly describe the remaining seven events. (Use *L* for left-hander.)
  c How many of the events yield no right-handers, one right-hander, two right-handers, three right-handers?
  d Find the probability of no right-handers, one right-hander, two right-handers, three right-handers.

6.54 Suppose that there are 100 students in your accounting class, of whom 10 are left-handed. Two students are selected at random.
  a Draw a probability tree and insert the probabilities for each branch.
  What is the probability of the following events?
  b Both are right-handed
  c Both are left-handed
  d One is right-handed and the other is left-handed
  e At least one is right-handed

6.55 Refer to Exercise 6.54. Suppose that three people are selected at random.
  a Draw a probability tree and insert the probabilities of each branch.
  b What is the probability of no right-handers, one right-hander, two right-handers, three right-handers?

6.56 An aerospace company has submitted bids on two separate federal government defense contracts. The company president believes that there is a 40% probability of winning the first contract. If they win the first contract, the probability of winning the second is 70%. However, if they lose the first contract, the president thinks that the probability of winning the second contract decreases to 50%.
  a What is the probability that they win both contracts?
  b What is the probability that they lose both contracts?
  c What is the probability that they win only one contract?

6.57 A telemarketer calls people and tries to sell them a subscription to a daily newspaper. On 20% of her calls, there is no answer or the line is busy. She sells subscriptions to 5% of the remaining calls. For what proportion of calls does she make a sale?

6.58 A foreman for an injection-molding firm admits that on 10% of his shifts, he forgets to shut off the injection machine on his line. This causes the machine to overheat, increasing the probability that a defective molding will be produced during the early morning run from 2% to 20%. What proportion of moldings from the early morning run is defective?

6.59 Refer to Exercise 6.29. Suppose that, instead of providing the joint probabilities, the analysis yielded the following information.
  1. Proportion of males in the electorate = 42%
  2. Gender and voting record are independent.
  3. Proportion of eligible voters who voted in the last election = 43%
  Use a probability tree or the probability laws to compute the following probabilities.
  a P(voted in last election and male)
  b P(voted in last election and female)

6.60 In early 2001, the United States Census Bureau started releasing the results of the latest census. Among many other pieces of information, the bureau recorded the race or ethnicity of the residents of every county in every state. From these results the bureau calculated a "diversity index," which measures the probability that two people chosen at random are of different races or ethnicities. The census determined that in a county in Wisconsin, 80% of its residents are White, 15% are Black, and 5% are Asian. Calculate the diversity index for this county.

6.61 A survey of middle-aged men reveals that 28% of them are balding at the crown of their head. Moreover, it is known that such men have an 18% probability of suffering a heart attack in the next 10 years. Men who are not balding in this way have an 11% probability of a heart attack. Find the probability that a middle-aged man will suffer a heart attack sometime in the next 10 years.

6.62 The chartered financial analyst (CFA) is a designation earned after taking three annual exams (CFA I, II, and III). The exams are taken in early June. Candidates who pass an exam are eligible to take the exam for the next level in the following year. The pass rates for levels I, II, and III are .57, .73, and .85, respectively. Suppose that 3,000 candidates take the level I exam, 2,500 take the level II exam, and 2,000 take the level III exam. Suppose that one student is selected at random. What is the probability that he or she has passed the exam? (*Source*: Institute of Financial Analysts)

6.63 The Nickels restaurant chain regularly conducts surveys of its customers. Respondents are asked to assess food quality, service, and price. The responses are

Excellent   Good   Fair

They are also asked whether they would come back. After analyzing the responses, an expert in probability determined that 87% of customers say that they will return. Of those who so indicate, 57% rate the restaurant as excellent, 36% rate it as good, and the remainder rate it as fair. Of those who say that they won't return, the probabilities are 14%, 32%, and 54%, respectively. What proportion of customers rate the restaurant as good?

6.64 Researchers at the University of Pennsylvania School of Medicine have determined that children under 2 years old who sleep with the lights on have a 36% chance of becoming myopic before they are 16. Children who sleep in darkness have a 21% probability of becoming myopic. A survey indicates that 28% of children under 2 sleep with some light on. Find the probability that a child under 16 is myopic.

6.65 All printed circuit boards (PCBs) that are manufactured at a certain plant are inspected. An analysis of the company's records indicates that 22% of all PCBs are flawed in some way. Of those that are flawed, 84% are reparable and the rest must be discarded. If a newly produced PCB is randomly selected, what is the probability that it does not have to be discarded?

6.66 A financial analyst has determined that there is a 22% probability that a mutual fund will outperform the market over a 1-year period provided that it outper-

formed the market the previous year. If only 15% of mutual funds outperform the market during any year, what is the probability that a mutual fund will outperform the market 2 years in a row?

6.67 An investor believes that on a day when the Dow Jones Industrial Average (DJIA) increases, the probability that the NASDAQ also increases is 77%. If the investor believes that there is a 60% probability that the DJIA will increase tomorrow, what is the probability that the NASDAQ will increase as well?

6.68 The controls of an airplane have several backup systems or redundancies, so that if one fails the plane will continue to operate. Suppose that the mechanism that controls the flaps has two backups. If the probability that the main control fails is .0001 and the probability that each backup will fail is .01, what is the probability that all three fail to operate?

6.69 According to *TNS Intersearch,* 69% of wireless Web users use it primarily for receiving and sending e-mail. Suppose that three wireless Web users are selected at random. What is the probability that all of them use it primarily for e-mail?

6.70 A financial analyst estimates that the probability that the economy will experience a recession in the next 12 months is 25%. She also believes that if the economy encounters a recession, the probability that her mutual fund will increase in value is 20%. If there is no recession, the probability that the mutual fund will increase in value is 75%. Find the probability that the mutual fund's value will increase.

6.5 BAYES' LAW

Conditional probability is often used to gauge the relationship between two events. In many of the examples and exercises you've already encountered, conditional probability measures the probability that an event occurs given that a possible cause of the event has occurred. In Example 6.2 we calculated the probability that a mutual fund outperforms the market (the effect) given that the fund manager graduated from a top-20 MBA program (the possible cause). There are problems, however, where we witness a particular event and we need to compute the probability of one of its possible causes. The following examples illustrate one important form of this type of problem.

EXAMPLE 6.9

Physicians routinely perform medical tests on their patients when they suspect various diseases. However, few tests are 100% accurate. Most can produce false-positive or false-negative results. (A false-positive result is one in which the patient does not have the disease, but the test shows positive. False-negative results are ones where the patient does have the disease, but the test produces a negative result.) Many people misinterpret medical test results. When the disease can be fatal, such misconceptions are themselves serious and need to be corrected. Moreover, incorrect medical tests often lead to additional costs to both the individual and to insurance companies. To help control these costs, it is necessary to properly interpret the probabilities associated with the tests.

A particular test correctly identifies those with a certain serious disease 94% of the time and correctly diagnoses those without the disease 98% of the time. A male friend has just informed you that he has received a positive result and asks for your advice about how to interpret these probabilities. He knows nothing about probability, but he feels that because the test is quite accurate, the probability that he does have the disease is quite high, likely in the 95% range. Before attempting to address your friend's concerns, you research the illness and discover that 4% of men have this disease. There is now enough information to draw a probability tree (see Figure 6.4). Let

$$D = \text{Has the disease}$$

$$D^C = \text{Does not have the disease}$$

$$PT = \text{Positive test result}$$

$$NT = \text{Negative test result}$$

Figure 6.4
Probability tree for Example 6.9

The tree allows you to determine the probability of obtaining a positive test result. It is

$$P(PT) = P(D \text{ and } PT) + P(D^C \text{ and } PT) = .0376 + .0192 = .0568$$

Your friend has been given a positive test result. Thus, the probability that you now calculate is the conditional probability that your friend has the disease given that he has a positive test result:

$$P(D|PT) = \frac{P(D \text{ and } PT)}{P(PT)} = \frac{.0376}{.0568} = .6620$$

There is a 66.2% probability that he has the disease. The probability is high, but considerably lower than your friend feared.

Thomas Bayes first employed the calculation of conditional probability performed above in the eighteenth century. Accordingly, it is called Bayes' law. Although there is a formula defining Bayes' law, we will not offer it here, preferring instead to use a probability tree to conduct all such calculations.

The probabilities $P(D)$ and $P(D^C)$ are called **prior probabilities** because they are determined *prior* to the test results. The conditional probabilities are called **likelihood probabilities** for reasons that are beyond the mathematics in this book. Finally, the conditional probability $P(D|PT)$, and similar conditional probabilities $P(D^C|PT)$, $P(D|NT)$, and $P(D^C|NT)$ are called **posterior probabilities**, because these probabilities are determined *after* the test is conducted.

DEVELOPING AN UNDERSTANDING OF PROBABILITY CONCEPTS

If you review the computations made above, you'll realize that the prior probabilities are as important as the probabilities associated with the test results (the likelihood probabilities) in determining the posterior probabilities. To understand this point, suppose that additional research indicates that age is a factor in the disease and that only 1% of men your friend's age contract the disease. Recalculating the probabilities from the tree produces the following:

$$P(PT) = P(D \text{ and } PT) + P(D^C \text{ and } PT) = (.01)(.94) + (.99)(.02)$$

$$= .0094 + .0198$$

$$= .0292$$

$$P(D|PT) = \frac{P(D \text{ and } PT)}{P(PT)} = \frac{.0094}{.0292} = .3219$$

As you can see, the probability that your friend has the disease has decreased by about half.

Now suppose that more research tells us that 40% of men of the same ethnic group and age have the disease. What is the posterior probability? Repeating the calculations with the new prior probabilities produces these probabilities:

$$P(PT) = P(D \text{ and } PT) + P(D^C \text{ and } PT) = (.40)(.94) + (.60)(.02)$$

$$= .3760 + .0120$$

$$= .3880$$

$$P(D|PT) = \frac{P(D \text{ and } PT)}{P(PT)} = \frac{.3760}{.3880} = .9691$$

Notice that as the prior probability increases, so does the posterior probability.

There is a wide range of applications of Bayes' law. We have featured just one. In the exercise set that accompanies this section, we offer several more.

AUDITING TAX RETURNS: SOLUTION

We need to revise the prior probability that this return contains significant fraud. The tree shown in Figure 6.5 details the calculation.

F = Tax return is fraudulent

F^C = Tax return is honest

ED = Tax return contains expense deduction

ED^C = Tax return does not contain expense deduction

Figure 6.5 Probability Tree for Auditing Tax Returns

Tax return status	Expense deduction	Joint probability
F .10	$ED\|F$ .24	F and ED: (.10)(.24) = .024
	$ED^C\|F$ .76	F and ED^C: (.10)(.76) = .076
F^C .90	$ED\|F^C$ .03	F^C and ED: (.90)(.03) = .027
	$ED^C\|F^C$ .97	F^C and ED^C: (.90)(.97) = .873

$$P(ED) = P(F \text{ and } ED) + P(F^C \text{ and } ED) = .024 + .027 = .051$$

$$P(F|ED) = \frac{P(F \text{ and } ED)}{P(ED)} = \frac{.024}{.051} = .471$$

The probability that this return is fraudulent is .471.

EXERCISES

6.71 Refer to Exercise 6.47. Determine $P(A|B)$.

6.72 Refer to Exercise 6.48. Find the following.
  a $P(A|B)$
  b $P(A^C|B)$
  c $P(A|B^C)$
  d $P(A^C|B^C)$

6.73 Refer to Example 6.9.
  a Find the probability that your friend has the disease when the false-positive and false-negative rates are .01 and .02, respectively.
  b Find the probability that your friend has the disease when the false-positive and false-negative rates are .15 and .30, respectively.

6.74 Refer to Exercise 6.58. The plant manager randomly selects a molding from the early morning run and discovers it is defective. What is the probability that the foreman forgot to shut off the machine the previous night?

6.75 The U.S. National Highway Traffic Safety Administration gathers data concerning the causes of highway crashes where at least one fatality has occurred. From the 1998 annual study, the following probabilities were determined (BAC is blood-alcohol content):
$P(\text{BAC} = 0|\text{Crash with fatality}) = .616$
$P(\text{BAC is between .01 and .09}|\text{Crash with fatality}) = .300$
$P(\text{BAC is greater than .09}|\text{Crash with fatality}) = .084$

Source: Statistical Abstract of the United States, 2000 Table 1042.

Suppose over a certain stretch of highway during a 1-year period, the probability of being involved in a crash that results in at least one fatality is .01. It has been estimated that 12% of all drivers on this highway drive while their BAC is greater than .09. Determine the probability of a crash with at least one fatality if a driver drives while legally intoxicated (BAC greater than .09).

6.76 Refer to Exercise 6.62. A randomly selected candidate who took a CFA exam tells you that he has passed the exam. What is the probability that he took the CFA I exam?

6.77 Bad gums may mean a bad heart. Researchers discovered that 85% of people who have suffered a heart attack had periodontal disease, an inflammation of the gums. Only 29% of healthy people have this disease. Suppose that in a certain community heart attacks are quite rare, occurring with only 10% probability. If someone has periodontal disease, what is the probability that he or she will have a heart attack?

6.78 Refer to Exercise 6.77. If 40% of the people in a community will have a heart attack, what is the probability that a person with periodontal disease will have a heart attack?

6.79 Transplant operations have become routine. One common transplant operation is for kidneys. The most dangerous aspect of the procedure is the possibility that the body may reject the new organ. There are several new drugs available for such circumstances. And the earlier the drug is administered, the higher the probability of averting rejection. The *New England Journal of Medicine* recently reported the development of a new urine test to detect early warning signs that the body is rejecting a transplanted kidney. However, like most other tests, the new test is not perfect. Approximately one in five negative tests are erroneous and 8% of positive tests prove to be incorrect. Physicians know that in about 35% of kidney transplants the body tries to reject the organ. If the new test has a positive result (indicating early warning of rejection), what is the probability that the body is attempting to reject the kidney?

6.80 Data from the Office on Smoking and Health, Centers for Disease Control and Prevention, indicate that 40% of adults who did not finish high school, 34% of high school graduates, 24% of adults who completed some college, and 14% of college graduates smoke. Suppose that one individual is selected at random and it is discovered that the individual smokes. Use the probabilities in Exercise 6.45 to calculate the probability that the individual is a college graduate.

6.81 Three airlines serve a small town in Ohio. Airline A has 50% of all the scheduled flights, airline B has 30%, and airline C has the remaining 20%. Their on-time rates are 80%, 65%, and 40% respectively. A plane has just left on time. What is the probability that it was airline A?

6.82 Your favorite team is in the final playoffs. You have assigned a probability of 60% that they will win the championship. Past records indicate that when teams win the championship, they win the first game of the series 70% of the time. When they lose the series, they win the first game 25% of the time. The first game is over; your team has lost. What is the probability that they will win the series?

6.6 IDENTIFYING THE CORRECT METHOD

As we've previously pointed out, one of the emphases in this book will be on identifying the correct statistical technique to use. In Chapters 2 and 4 we showed how to summarize data by first identifying the appropriate method to use. Although it is difficult to offer strict rules on which probability method to use, nevertheless we can provide some general guidelines.

In the examples and exercises in this text (and most other introductory statistics books), the key issue is whether joint probabilities are provided or are required.

JOINT PROBABILITIES ARE GIVEN

In Section 6.3 we addressed problems where the joint probabilities were given. In these problems, we can compute marginal probabilities by adding across rows and down columns. We can use the joint and marginal probabilities to compute conditional probabilities, for which a formula is available. This allows us to determine whether the events described by the table are independent or dependent.

We can also apply the addition rule to compute the probability that either of two events occurs.

JOINT PROBABILITIES ARE REQUIRED

The previous section introduced three probability rules and probability trees. We need to apply some or all of these rules in circumstances where one or more joint probabilities are required. We apply the multiplication rule (either by formula or through a probability tree) to calculate the probability of intersections. In some problems we're interested in adding several joint probabilities. We're actually applying the addition rule for mutually exclusive events here. We also frequently use the complement rule. We can also calculate new conditional probabilities using Bayes' law.

6.7 SUMMARY

The first step in assigning probability is to create an **exhaustive** and **mutually exclusive** list of outcomes. The second step is to use the **classical**, **relative frequency**, or **subjective approach** and assign probability to the outcomes. There are a variety of methods available to compute the probability of other events. These methods include **probability rules** and **trees**.

An important application of these rules is **Bayes' law**, which allows us to compute **conditional probabilities** from other forms of probability.

IMPORTANT TERMS

Exhaustive 153
Mutually exclusive 153
Classical approach 154
Sample space 155
Relative frequency approach 154
Subjective approach 155
Simple event 155

Event 155
Intersection 157
Joint probability 157
Marginal probability 159
Conditional probability 160
Independent events 161
Union 162

Complement rule 166
Multiplication rule 167
Addition rule 168
Bayes' law 173
Prior probability 175
Likelihood probability 175
Posterior probability 175

FORMULAS

Conditional probability

$$P(A|B) = \frac{P(A \text{ and } B)}{P(B)}$$

Complement rule

$$P(A^C) = 1 - P(A)$$

Multiplication rule

$$P(A \text{ and } B) = P(A|B)P(B)$$

Addition rule

$$P(A \text{ or } B) = P(A) + P(B) - P(A \text{ and } B)$$

REFERENCES

Alexander, G. J., W. F. Sharpe, and J. V. Bailey, *Fundamentals of Investing*, 2nd edition. Englewood Cliffs, NJ: Prentice Hall, 1993.

Bernstein, Peter L., *Against the Gods*. New York: John Wiley and Sons, 1996.

Berry, Donald A., *Statistics: A Bayesian Perspective*. Belmont, CA: Duxbury, 1996.

Durrett, Richard, *Probability: Theory and Examples*, 2nd edition. Belmont, CA: Duxbury, 1995.

Feller, William, *An Introduction to Probability Theory, Vol. 1*, 3rd edition. New York: John Wiley and Sons, 1968.

Gelman, Andrew, J. B. Carlin, H. S. Stern, and D. B. Rubin, *Bayesian Data Analysis*. New York: Chapman & Hall, 1995.

Ross, Sheldon M., *A First Course in Probability*, 5th edition. Englewood Cliffs, NJ: Prentice Hall, 1997.

Ross, Sheldon M., *Introduction to Probability Models*, 4th edition. New York: Academic Press, 1989.

CHAPTER REVIEW EXERCISES

6.83 The following table lists the joint probabilities of achieving grades of A and not in two MBA courses.

	Achieve a grade of A in marketing	Does not achieve a grade of A in marketing
Achieve a grade of A in statistics	.06	.13
Does not achieve a grade of A in statistics	.23	.58

a What is the probability that a student achieves a grade of A in marketing?

b What is the probability that a student achieves a grade of A in marketing, given that he or she does not achieve a grade of A in statistics?

c Are achieving grades of A in marketing and statistics independent events? Explain.

6.84 A construction company has bid on two contracts. The probability of winning contract A is .3. If the company wins contract A, the probability of winning contract B is .4. If the company loses contract A, the probability of winning contract B decreases to .2. You've just been informed that the company lost contract B. What is the probability that they also lost contract A?

6.85 Laser surgery to fix short-sightedness is becoming more popular. However, for some people, a second procedure is necessary. The following table lists the joint probability of needing a second procedure and whether the patient has a corrective lens with a factor (diopter) of minus 8 or less.

	Vision corrective factor of more than minus 8	Vision corrective factor of minus 8 or less
First procedure is successful	.66	.15
Second procedure is required	.05	.14

a Find the probability that a second procedure is required.

b Determine the probability that someone whose corrective lens factor is minus 8 or less does not require a second procedure.

c Are the events independent? Explain your answer.

6.86 The effect of an antidepressant drug varies from person to person. Suppose that the drug is effective on 80% of women and 65% of men. It is known that 66% of the people who take the drug are women. What is the probability that the drug is effective?

6.87 Refer to Exercise 6.86. Suppose that you are told that the drug is effective. What is the probability that the drug-taker is a man?

6.88 In a four-cylinder engine there are four spark plugs. If any one of them malfunctions, the car will idle roughly, and power will be lost. Suppose that for a certain brand of spark plugs, the probability that a spark plug will function properly after 5,000 miles is .90.

Assuming that the spark plugs operate independently, what is the probability that the car will idle roughly after 5,000 miles?

6.89 A telemarketer sells magazine subscriptions over the telephone. The probability of a busy signal or no answer is 65%. If the telemarketer does make contact, the probability of 0, 1, 2, or 3 magazine subscriptions is .50, .25, .20, and .05, respectively. Find the probability that in one call she sells no magazines.

6.90 A statistics professor believes that there is a relationship between the number of missed classes and the grade on his midterm test. After examining his records, he produced the following table of joint probabilities.

	Student fails the test	Student passes the test
Student misses fewer than 5 classes	.02	.86
Student misses 5 or more classes	.09	.03

a What is the pass rate on the midterm test?

b What proportion of students who miss 5 or more classes pass the midterm test?

c What proportion of students who miss fewer than 5 classes pass the midterm test?

d Are the events independent?

6.91 In Canada, criminals are entitled to parole after serving only one-third of their sentence. Virtually all prisoners, with several exceptions including murderers, are released after serving two-thirds of their sentence. The government has proposed a new law that would create a special category of inmates based on whether they had committed crimes involving violence or drugs. Such criminals would be subject to additional detention if the Correction Service judges them highly likely to reoffend. Currently, 27% of prisoners who are released commit another crime within 2 years of release. Among those who have reoffended, 41% would have been detained under the new law, whereas 31% of those who have not reoffended would have been detained.

a What is the probability that a prisoner who would have been detained under the new law does commit another crime within 2 years?

b What is the probability that a prisoner who would not have been detained under the new law does commit another crime within 2 years?

6.92 Casino Windsor conducts surveys to determine the opinions of its customers. Among other questions, respondents are asked to give their opinion about "Your overall impression of Casino Windsor." The responses are:

Excellent   Good   Average   Poor

Additionally, the gender of the respondent is noted. After analyzing the results, the following table of joint probabilities was produced.

Rating	Women	Men
Excellent	.27	.22
Good	.14	.10
Average	.06	.12
Poor	.03	.06

a What proportion of customers rate Casino Windsor as excellent?

b Determine the probability that a male customer rates Casino Windsor as excellent.

c Find the probability that a customer who rates Casino Windsor as excellent is a man.

d Are gender and rating independent? Explain your answer.

6.93 A customer service supervisor regularly conducts a survey of customer satisfaction. The results of the latest survey indicate that 8% of customers were not satisfied with the service they received at their last visit to the store. Of those who are not satisfied, only 22% return to the store within a year. Of those who are satisfied, 64% return within the year. A customer has just entered the store. In response to your question, he informs you that it is less than 1 year since his last visit to the store. What is the probability that he was satisfied with the service he received?

6.94 How does level of affluence affect health care? To address one dimension of the problem, a group of heart attack victims was drawn. Each was categorized as a low-, medium-, or high-income earner. Each was also categorized as having survived or died. A demographer notes that in our society 21% fall into the low-income group, 49% are in the medium-income group, and 30% are in the high-income group. Furthermore, an analysis of heart attack victims reveals that 12% of low-income people, 9% of medium-income people, and 7% of high-income people die of heart attacks. Find the probability that a survivor of a heart attack is in the low-income group.

6.95 A statistics professor and his wife are planning to take a 2-week vacation in Hawaii, but they can't decide whether to spend 1 week on each of the islands of Maui and Oahu, 2 weeks on Maui, or 2 weeks on Oahu. Placing their faith in random chance, they insert two Maui brochures in one envelope, two Oahu brochures in a second envelope, and one brochure from each island in a third envelope. The professor's wife will select one envelope at random, and their vacation schedule will be based on the brochures of the islands so selected. After his wife randomly selects an envelope, the professor removes one brochure from the envelope (without looking at the second brochure) and observes that it is a Maui brochure. What is the probability that the other brochure in the envelope is a Maui brochure? (*Hint:* Proceed with caution; the problem is more difficult than it appears.)

6.96 The owner of an appliance store is interested in the relationship between the price at which an item is sold (regular or sale price) and the customer's decision on whether to purchase an extended warranty. After analyzing her records, she produced the following joint probabilities.

	Purchased extended warranty	Did not purchase extended warranty
Regular price	.21	.57
Sale price	.14	.08

a What is the probability that a customer who bought an item at the regular price purchased the extended warranty?

b What proportion of customers buy an extended warranty?

c Are the events independent? Explain.

6.97 Researchers have developed statistical models based on financial ratios that predict whether a company will go bankrupt over the next 12 months. In a test of one such model, the model correctly predicted the bankruptcy of 85% of firms that did in fact fail, and it correctly predicted nonbankruptcy for 74% of firms that did not fail. Suppose that we expect 8% of the firms in a particular city to fail over the next year. Suppose that the model predicts bankruptcy for a firm that you own. What is the probability that your firm will fail within the next 12 months?

6.98 A union's executive conducted a survey of its members to determine what the membership felt were the important issues to be resolved during upcoming negotiations with management. The results indicate that 74% felt that job security was an important issue, while 65% identified pension benefits as an important issue. Of those who felt that pension benefits were important, 60% also felt that job security was an important issue. One member is selected at random.

a What is the probability that he or she felt that both job security and pension benefits were important?

b What is the probability that the member felt that at least one of these two issues was important?

6.99 In a class on probability, a statistics professor flips two balanced coins. Both fall to the floor and roll under his desk. A student in the first row informs the professor that he can see both coins. He reports that at least one of them shows tails. What is the probability that the other coin is also tails? (Beware the obvious.)

6.100 Refer to Exercise 6.99. Suppose the student informs the professor that he can see only one coin and it shows tails. What is the probability that the other coin is also tails?

◈ CASE 6.1
PSA TEST FOR PROSTATE CANCER*

Prostate cancer is the most common form of cancer found in men. The probability of developing prostate cancer over a lifetime is 11.2%. Many physicians perform a PSA test, particularly for men over age 50. Prostate-specific antigen (PSA) is a protein produced only by the prostate gland and thus is fairly easy to detect. Normally, men have PSA levels between 0 and 4 mg/ml. Readings above 20 are considered high and potentially indicative of cancer. Studies have shown that the test is not very accurate. In fact, the probability of having an elevated PSA level given that the man does not have cancer is .135. If the man does

have cancer, the probability of an elevated level of PSA is almost double at .268. Suppose physicians have examined four men of differing ages and medical histories. On the basis of these two factors, scientists have determined the probability that each has prostate cancer as follows.

1. Age 29; grandfather died of prostate cancer
$$P(cancer) = .08$$

2. Age 71; no history of cancer
$$P(cancer) = .15$$

3. Age 56; mother developed breast cancer, father lung cancer
$$P(cancer) = .19$$

4. Age 62; father had prostate cancer
$$P(cancer) = .21$$

Each man took the PSA test, which indicated PSA levels in excess of 20. For each, determine the probability that he has prostate cancer.

* The authors are grateful to Joe Whitney for tracking down the relevant probabilities.
Source: Canada Cancer Statistics 2001: Probability of Developing Cancer by Age and Lifetime Probability of Developing and Dying of Cancer.

◈ CASE 6.2
LET'S MAKE A DEAL

A number of years ago, there was a popular television game show called "Let's Make a Deal." The host, Monty Hall, would randomly select contestants from the audience and, as the title suggests, he would make deals for prizes. Contestants would be given relatively modest prizes and then would be offered the opportunity to risk those prizes to win better ones.

Suppose that you are a contestant on this show. Monty has just given you a free trip touring toxic waste sites around the country. He now offers you a trade: Give up the trip in exchange for a gamble. On the stage are three curtains, A, B, and C.

Behind one of them is a brand new car worth $20,000. Behind the other two curtains, the stage is empty. You decide to gamble and select curtain A. In an attempt to make things more interesting, Monty then exposes an empty stage by opening curtain C (he knows there is nothing behind curtain C). Monty then offers you the following choices:

1. Quit now and take the free trip.
2. Keep whatever is behind curtain A.
3. Switch to curtain B.

What do you do?

To help you answer that question, try first answering these questions.

1. Before Monty shows you what's behind curtain C, what is the probability that the car is behind curtain A? What is the probability that the car is behind curtain B?

2. After Monty shows you what's behind curtain C, what is the probability that the car is behind curtain A? What is the probability that the car is behind curtain B?

♦ CASE 6.3
TO BUNT OR NOT TO BUNT, THAT IS THE QUESTION

No sport generates as many statistics as baseball. Reporters, managers, and fans argue and discuss strategies on the basis of these statistics. An article in *Chance* ("A Statistician Reads the Sports Page," Hal S. Stern, Vol. 1, Winter 1997) offers baseball lovers another opportunity to analyze numbers associated with the game. Table 1 lists the probabilities of scoring at least one run in situations that are defined by the number of outs and the bases occupied. For example, the probability of scoring at least one run when there are no outs and a man is on first base is .39. If the bases are loaded with one out, the probability of scoring any runs is .67. (Probabilities are based on results from the American League during the 1989 season. The results for the National League are also shown in the article and are similar.) Table 1

allows us to determine the best strategy in a variety of circumstances. This case will concentrate on the strategy of the sacrifice bunt. The purpose of the sacrifice bunt is to sacrifice the batter to move base runners to the next base. It can be employed when there are fewer than two outs and men on base. Ignoring the suicide squeeze, any of four outcomes can occur:

1 The bunt is successful. The runner (or runners) advances one base, and the batter is out.

2 The batter is out but fails to advance the runner.

3 The batter bunts into a double play.

4 The batter is safe (hit or error), and the runner advances.

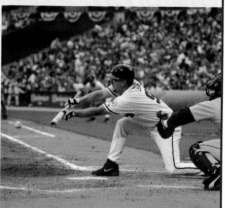

Suppose that you are an American League manager. The game is tied in the middle innings of a game, and there is a runner on first base with no one out. Given the following probabilities of the four outcomes of a bunt for the batter at the plate, should you signal the batter to sacrifice bunt?

P(outcome 1) = .75

P(outcome 2) = .10

P(outcome 3) = .10

P(outcome 4) = .05

Assume for simplicity that after the hit or error in outcome 4, there will be men on first and second base and no one out.

Table 1 Probability of Scoring Any Runs

Bases Occupied	0 Outs	1 Out	2 Outs
Bases empty	.26	.16	.07
First base	.39	.26	.13
Second base	.57	.42	.24
Third base	.72	.55	.28
First base and second base	.59	.45	.24
First base and third base	.76	.61	.37
Second base and third base	.83	.74	.37
Bases loaded	.81	.67	.43

7 *RANDOM VARIABLES AND DISCRETE PROBABILITY DISTRIBUTIONS*

INVESTING TO MAXIMIZE RETURNS AND MINIMIZE RISK

An investor has $100,000 to invest in the stock market. She is interested in developing a stock portfolio made up of Intel, Motorola, General Motors, and Gillette. However, she doesn't know how much to invest in each one. She wants to maximize her return but she would also like to minimize the risk. She has computed the monthly returns for all four stocks during a 48-month period. These data are stored in file Ch 7:\Invest. After some consideration, she narrowed her choices down to the following three. What should she do?

1. $25,000 in each stock

2. Intel: $10,000;
   Motorola: $40,000;
   General Motors: $30,000;
   Gillette: $20,000

3. Intel: $70,000;
   Motorola: $10,000;
   General Motors: $10,000;
   Gillette: $10,000

We will provide our answer after we've developed the necessary tools in Section 7.5.

7.1 INTRODUCTION

In this chapter, we extend the concepts and techniques of probability introduced in Chapter 6. We present random variables and probability distributions, which are essential in the development of statistical inference.

Here is a brief glimpse into the wonderful world of statistical inference. Suppose that you flip a coin 100 times and count the number of heads. The objective is to determine whether we can infer from the count that the coin is not balanced. It is reasonable to believe that observing a large number of heads (say, 90) or a small number (say, 15) would be a statistical indication of an unbalanced coin. However, where do we draw the line? At 75 or 65 or 55? Without knowing the probability of the frequency of the number of heads from a balanced coin, we cannot draw any conclusions from the sample of 100 coin flips.

The concepts and techniques of probability introduced in this chapter will allow us to calculate the probability we seek. As a first step, we introduce random variables and probability distributions.

7.2 RANDOM VARIABLES AND PROBABILITY DISTRIBUTIONS

Consider an experiment where we flip two balanced coins and observe the results. We can represent the events as

Heads on the first coin and heads on the second coin

Heads on the first coin and tails on the second coin

Tails on the first coin and heads on the second coin

Tails on the first coin and tails on the second coin

However, we can list the events in a different way. Instead of defining the events by describing the outcome of each coin, we can count the number of heads (or, if we wish, the number of tails). Thus, the events are now

2 heads

1 head

1 head

0 heads

The number of heads is called the **random variable**. We often label the random variable X, and we're interested in the probability of each value of X. Thus, in this illustration the values of X are 0, 1, and 2.

Here is another example. In many parlor games as well as in the game of craps played in casinos, the player tosses two dice. One way of listing the events is to describe the number on the first die and the number on the second die, as follows:

1, 1	1, 2	1, 3	1, 4	1, 5	1, 6
2, 1	2, 2	2, 3	2, 4	2, 5	2, 6
3, 1	3, 2	3, 3	3, 4	3, 5	3, 6
4, 1	4, 2	4, 3	4, 4	4, 5	4, 6
5, 1	5, 2	5, 3	5, 4	5, 5	5, 6
6, 1	6, 2	6, 3	6, 4	6, 5	6, 6

However, in almost all games the player is primarily interested in the total. Accordingly, we can list the total of the two dice instead of the individual numbers:

2	3	4	5	6	7
3	4	5	6	7	8
4	5	6	7	8	9
5	6	7	8	9	10
6	7	8	9	10	11
7	8	9	10	11	12

If we define the random variable X as the total of the two dice, X can equal 2, 3, 4, 5, 6, 7, 8, 9, 10, 11, and 12.

RANDOM VARIABLE

A **random variable** is a function or rule that assigns a number to each outcome of an experiment.

In some experiments the outcomes are numbers. For example, when we observe the return on an investment or measure the amount of time to assemble a computer, the experiment produces events that are numbers. Put simply, the value of a random variable is a numerical event.

There are two types of random variables, *discrete* and *continuous*. A **discrete random variable** is one that can take on a countable number of values. For example, if we define X as the number of heads observed in an experiment that flips a coin 10 times, the values of X are 0, 1, 2, . . ., 10. There is a total of 11 values that X can assume. Obviously, we counted the number of values; hence X is discrete.

A **continuous random variable** is one whose values are uncountable. An excellent example of a continuous random variable is the amount of time to complete a task. For example, let X = time to write a statistics exam in a university where the time limit is 3 hours and students cannot leave before 30 minutes. The smallest value of X is 30 minutes. If we attempt to count the number of values that X can take on, we need to identify the next value. Is it 30.1 minutes? 30.01 minutes? 30.001 minutes? None of these is the second possible value of X because there exist numbers larger than 30 and smaller than 30.001. It becomes clear that we cannot identify the second, or third, or any other values of X (except for the largest value, 180 minutes). Thus, we cannot count the number of values and X is continuous.

A **probability distribution** is a table, formula, or graph that describes the values of a random variable and the probability associated with these values. We will address discrete probability distributions in the rest of this chapter and cover continuous distributions in Chapter 8.

As we noted above, an uppercase letter will represent the *name* of the random variable, usually X. Its lowercase counterpart will represent the value of the random variable. Thus, we represent the probability that the random variable X will equal x as

$$P(X = x)$$

or, more simply,

$$p(x)$$

DISCRETE PROBABILITY DISTRIBUTIONS

The probabilities of the values of a discrete random variable may be derived by means of probability tools such as tree diagrams or by applying one of the definitions of probability. However, two fundamental requirements apply. They are stated in the box.

> **REQUIREMENTS FOR A DISTRIBUTION OF A DISCRETE RANDOM VARIABLE**
> For a discrete random variable X that can assume values x_i,
>   1. $0 \le p(x_i) \le 1$ for all x_i
>
>   2. $\displaystyle\sum_{\text{all } x_i} p(x_i) = 1$

These requirements are equivalent to the rules of probability provided in Chapter 6. To illustrate, consider the following example.

EXAMPLE 7.1

The *Statistical Abstract of the United States* is published annually. It contains a wide variety of information based on the census as well as other sources. The objective is to provide information about a variety of different aspects of the lives of the country's residents. One of the questions asked households to report the number of color televisions in the household. The following table summarizes the data. Develop the probability distribution of the random variable defined as the number of color televisions per household.

Number of Color Televisions	Number of Households (thousands)
0	1,218
1	32,379
2	37,961
3	19,387
4	7,714
5	2,842
Total	101,501

Source: Statistical Abstract of the United States, 2000, Table 1221.

SOLUTION The probability of each value of X, the number of color televisions per household, is computed as the relative frequency. We divide the frequency for each value of X by the total number of households, producing the following probability distribution.

x	$p(x)$
0	1,218/101,501 = .012
1	32,379/101,501 = .319
2	37,961/101,501 = .374
3	19,387/101,501 = .191
4	7,714/101,501 = .076
5	2,842/101,501 = .028
Total	1.000

As you can see, the requirements are satisfied. Each probability lies between 0 and 1 and the total is 1.

We interpret the probabilities in the same way we did in Chapter 6. For example, if we select one household at random, the probability that it owns three color televisions is

$$P(X = 3) = p(3) = .191$$

We can also apply the addition rule for mutually exclusive events. (The values of X are mutually exclusive; a household can own 0, 1, 2, 3, 4, or 5 color televisions.) The probability that a randomly selected household owns two or more color televisions is

$$P(X \geq 2) = p(2) + p(3) + p(4) + p(5) = .374 + .191 + .076 + .028 = .669$$

In Example 7.1, we calculated the probabilities using census information about the entire population. The next example illustrates the use of the techniques introduced in Chapter 6 to develop a probability distribution.

EXAMPLE 7.2

A mutual fund salesperson has arranged to call on three people tomorrow. Based on past experience, the salesperson knows that there is a 20% chance of closing a sale on each call. Determine the probability distribution of the number of sales the salesperson will make.

SOLUTION We can use the probability rules and trees introduced in Section 6.4. Figure 7.1 displays the probability tree for this example. Let $X =$ the number of sales.

Figure 7.1 Probability tree for Example 7.2

The tree exhibits each of the eight possible outcomes and their probabilities. We see that there is one outcome that represents no sales, and its probability is $p(0) = .512$. There are three outcomes representing one sale, each with probability .128. Thus,

$$p(1) = 3(.128) = .384$$

The probability of two sales is computed similarly:

$$p(2) = 3(.032) = .096$$

There is one outcome where there are three sales:

$$p(3) = .008$$

The probability distribution of X is listed in Table 7.1 on page 188.

Table 7.1 Probability Distribution of the Number of Sales in Example 7.2

x	p(x)
0	.512
1	.384
2	.096
3	.008

PROBABILITY DISTRIBUTIONS AND POPULATIONS

The importance of probability distributions derives from their use as representatives of populations. In Example 7.1 the distribution provided us with information about the population of numbers of color televisions per household. In Example 7.2 the population was the number of sales made in three calls by the salesperson. And, as we noted before, statistical inference deals with inference about populations.

EXERCISES

7.1 The number of accidents that occur on a busy stretch of highway is a random variable.
  a What are the possible values of this random variable?
  b Are the values countable? Explain.
  c Is there a finite number of values? Explain.
  d Is the random variable discrete or continuous? Explain.

7.2 The distance a car travels on a tank of gasoline is a random variable.
  a What are the possible values of this random variable?
  b Are the values countable? Explain.
  c Is there a finite number of values? Explain.
  d Is the random variable discrete or continuous? Explain.

7.3 The amount of money students earn on their summer jobs is a random variable.
  a What are the possible values of this random variable?
  b Are the values countable? Explain.
  c Is there a finite number of values? Explain.
  d Is the random variable discrete or continuous? Explain.

7.4 The mark on a statistics exam that consists of 100 multiple-choice questions is a random variable.
  a What are the possible values of this random variable?
  b Are the values countable? Explain.
  c Is there a finite number of values? Explain.
  d Is the random variable discrete or continuous? Explain.

7.5 Determine whether each of the following is a valid probability distribution.

  a

x	0	1	2	3
p(x)	.1	.3	.4	.1

  b

x	5	−6	10	0
p(x)	.01	.01	.01	.97

  c

x	14	12	−7	13
p(x)	.25	.46	.04	.24

7.6 Let X be the random variable designating the number of spots that turn up when a balanced die is rolled. What is the probability distribution of X?

7.7 The recent census in a large county revealed the following information about the number of children under 18 per household.

Number of children	0	1	2
Number of households	24,750	37,950	59,400

Number of children	3	4	5
Number of households	29,700	9,900	3,300

Determine the following probabilities.
$$P(X \le 2) \qquad P(X > 2) \qquad P(X \ge 4)$$

7.8 Using historical records, the personnel manager of a plant has determined the probability distribution of X, the number of employees absent per day. It is

x	0	1	2	3	4	5	6	7
p(x)	.005	.025	.310	.340	.220	.080	.019	.001

Find the following probabilities.
  a $P(2 \le X \le 5)$
  b $P(X > 5)$
  c $P(X < 4)$

7.9 Second-year business students at many universities are required to take 10 one-semester courses. The number of courses that result in a grade of A is a discrete random variable. Suppose that each value of this random variable has the same probability. Determine the probability distribution.

7.10 The random variable X has the following probability distribution.

x	−3	2	6	8
p(x)	.2	.3	.4	.1

Find the following probabilities.
  a $P(X > 0)$
  b $P(X \ge 1)$
  c $P(X \ge 2)$
  d $P(2 \le X \le 5)$

7.11 The number of pizzas delivered to university students each month is a random variable with the following probability distribution.

x	0	1	2	3
p(x)	.1	.3	.4	.2

Find the probability that a student has received delivery of two or more pizzas this month.

7.12 The probability that a university graduate will be offered no jobs within a month of graduation is estimated to be 5%. The probability of receiving one, two, and three job offers has similarly been estimated to be 43%, 31%, and 21%, respectively. Determine the following probabilities.

a A graduate is offered fewer than two jobs
b A graduate is offered more than one job

7.13 Use a probability tree to compute the probability of the following events when flipping two fair coins.

a Heads on the first coin and heads on the second coin
b Heads on the first coin and tails on the second coin
c Tails on the first coin and heads on the second coin
d Tails on the first coin and tails on the second coin

7.14 Refer to Exercise 7.13. Find the following probabilities.

a No heads
b One head
c Two heads
d At least one head

7.15 Draw a probability tree to describe the flipping of three fair coins.

7.16 Refer to Exercise 7.15. Find the following probabilities.

a Two heads
b One head
c At least one head
d At least two heads

7.17 After watching a number of children playing games at a video arcade, a statistics practitioner estimated the following probability distribution of X, the number of games played per visit.

x	1	2	3	4	5	6	7
p(x)	.05	.15	.15	.25	.20	.10	.10

a What is the probability that a child will play more than four games?
b What is the probability that a child will play at least two games?

7.18 A survey of Amazon.com shoppers reveals the following probability distribution of the number of books purchased per hit.

x	0	1	2	3	4	5	6	7
p(x)	.35	.25	.20	.08	.06	.03	.02	.01

a What is the probability that an Amazon.com visitor will buy four books?
b What is the probability that an Amazon.com visitor will buy eight books?
c What is the probability that an Amazon.com visitor will not buy any books?
d What is the probability that an Amazon.com visitor will buy at least one book?

7.19 A university librarian produced the following probability distribution of the number of times a student walks into the library over the period of a semester.

x	0	5	10	15	20	25	30	40	50	75	100
p(x)	.22	.29	.12	.09	.08	.05	.04	.04	.03	.03	.01

Find the following probabilities.

a $P(X \geq 20)$
b $P(X = 60)$
c $P(X > 50)$
d $P(X > 100)$

7.20 After analyzing the frequency with which cross-country skiers participate in their sport, a sportswriter created the following probability distribution for X = number of times per year cross-country skiers ski.

x	0	1	2	3	4	5	6	7	8
p(x)	.04	.09	.19	.21	.16	.12	.08	.06	.05

Find the following.

a $P(X = 3)$
b $P(X \geq 5)$
c $P(5 \leq X \leq 7)$

7.21 The natural remedy echinacea is reputed to boost the immune system, which will reduce flu and colds. A 6-month study was undertaken to determine whether the remedy works. From this study, the following probability distribution of the number of respiratory infections per year (X) for echinacea users was produced.

x	0	1	2	3	4
p(x)	.45	.31	.17	.06	.01

Find the following probabilities.

a An echinacea user has more than one infection per year
b An echinacea user has no infections per year
c An echinacea user has between one and three (inclusive) infections per year

7.3   DESCRIBING THE POPULATION/PROBABILITY DISTRIBUTION

In Chapter 4, we showed how to calculate the mean, variance, and standard deviation of a population. The formulas we provided were based on knowing the value of the random variable for each member of the population. For example, if we want to know the mean and variance of the annual income of all North American blue-collar workers, we would record each of their incomes and use the formulas introduced in Chapter 4:

$$\mu = \frac{\sum_{i=1}^{N} x_i}{N}$$

$$\sigma^2 = \frac{\sum_{i=1}^{N} (x_i - \mu)^2}{N}$$

where x_1 is the income of the first blue-collar worker, x_2 is the second worker's income, and so on. It is likely that N equals several million. As you can appreciate, these formulas are seldom used in practical applications because populations are so large. It is unlikely that we would be able to record all the incomes in the population of North American blue-collar workers. As we noted in the previous section, probability distributions represent populations. Rather than record each of the many observations in a population, we list the values and their associated probabilities as we did in deriving the probability distribution of the number of color televisions per household in Example 7.1 and the number of successes in three calls by the mutual fund salesperson in Example 7.2. These can be used to compute the mean and variance of the population.

The **population mean** is the weighted average of all of its values. The weights are the probabilities. This parameter is also called the **expected value** of X and is represented by $E(X)$.

POPULATION MEAN

$$E(X) = \mu = \sum_{\text{all } x} x p(x)$$

The **population variance** is calculated similarly. It is the weighted average of the squared deviations from the mean.

POPULATION VARIANCE

$$V(X) = \sigma^2 = \sum_{\text{all } x} (x - \mu)^2 p(x)$$

There is a shortcut calculation that simplifies the calculations for the population variance. This formula is not an approximation; it will yield the same value as the formula above.

SHORTCUT CALCULATION FOR POPULATION VARIANCE

$$V(X) = \sigma^2 = \sum_{\text{all } x} x^2 p(x) - \mu^2$$

The standard deviation is defined as in Chapter 4.

POPULATION STANDARD DEVIATION

$$\sigma = \sqrt{\sigma^2}$$

EXAMPLE 7.3

Find the mean, variance, and standard deviation for the population of the number of color televisions per household in Example 7.1.

SOLUTION   The mean of X is

$$E(X) = \mu = \sum_{\text{all } x} xp(x) = 0p(0) + 1p(1) + 2p(2) + 3p(3) + 4p(4) + 5p(5)$$

$$= 0(.012) + 1(.319) + 2(.374) + 3(.191) + 4(.076) + 5(.028)$$

$$= 2.084$$

Notice that the random variable can assume integer values only, yet the mean is 2.084. The variance of X is

$$V(X) = \sigma^2 = \sum_{\text{all } x} (x - \mu)^2 p(x)$$

$$= (0 - 2.084)^2(.012) + (1 - 2.084)^2(.319) + (2 - 2.084)^2(.374)$$

$$+ (3 - 2.084)^2(.191) + (4 - 2.084)^2(.076) + (5 - 2.084)^2(.028)$$

$$= 1.107$$

To demonstrate the shortcut method, we'll use it to recompute the variance:

$$\sum_{\text{all } x} x^2 p(x) = 0^2(.012) + 1^2(.319) + 2^2(.374) + 3^2(.191) + 4^2(.076) + 5^2(.028) = 5.450$$

and

$$\mu = 2.084$$

Thus,

$$\sigma^2 = \sum_{\text{all } x} x^2 p(x) - \mu^2 = 5.450 - (2.084)^2 = 1.107$$

The standard deviation is

$$\sigma = \sqrt{\sigma^2} = \sqrt{1.107} = 1.052$$

These parameters tell us that the mean and standard deviation of the number of color televisions per household are 2.084 and 1.052, respectively.

LAWS OF EXPECTED VALUE AND VARIANCE

As you will discover, we often create new variables that are functions of other random variables. The formulas given in the next two boxes allow us to quickly determine the expected value and variance of these new variables. In the notation used here, X is the random variable and c is a constant.

LAWS OF EXPECTED VALUE

1. $E(c) = c$
2. $E(X + c) = E(X) + c$
3. $E(cX) = cE(X)$

LAWS OF VARIANCE

1. $V(c) = 0$
2. $V(X + c) = V(X)$
3. $V(cX) = c^2 V(X)$

EXAMPLE 7.4

The monthly sales at a computer store have a mean of $25,000 and a standard deviation of $4,000. Profits are calculated by multiplying sales by 30% and subtracting fixed costs of $6,000. Find the mean and standard deviation of monthly profits.

SOLUTION We can describe the relationship between profits and sales by the following equation:

$$\text{Profit} = .30(\text{Sales}) - 6{,}000$$

The expected or mean profit is

$$E(\text{Profit}) = E[.30(\text{Sales}) - 6{,}000]$$

Applying the second law of expected value, we produce

$$E(\text{Profit}) = E[.30(\text{Sales})] - 6{,}000$$

Applying law 3 yields

$$E(\text{Profit}) = .30E(\text{Sales}) - 6{,}000 = .30(25{,}000) - 6{,}000 = 1{,}500$$

Thus, the mean monthly profit is $1,500.
The variance is

$$V(\text{Profit}) = V[.30(\text{Sales}) - 6{,}000]$$

The second law of variance states that

$$V(\text{Profit}) = V[.30(\text{Sales})]$$

and law 3 yields

$$V(\text{Profit}) = (.30)^2 V(\text{Sales}) = .09(4,000)^2 = 1,440,000$$

Thus, the standard deviation of monthly profits is

$$\sigma_{\text{Profit}} = \sqrt{1,440,000} = \$1,200$$

EXERCISES

7.22 Find the mean, variance, and standard deviation for the probability distribution below.

x	−2	5	7	8
$p(x)$	.59	.15	.25	.01

7.23 Given the following probability distribution, calculate the mean, variance, and standard deviation.

x	0	1	2	3
$p(x)$	.4	.3	.2	.1

7.24 Refer to Exercise 7.23. Suppose that $Y = 3X + 2$. For each value of X, determine the value of Y. What is the probability distribution of Y?

7.25 Refer to Exercise 7.24. Calculate the mean, variance, and standard deviation from the probability distribution of Y.

7.26 Refer to Exercises 7.23 and 7.24. Use the laws of expected value and variance to calculate the mean, variance, and standard deviation of Y from the mean, variance, and standard deviation of X. Compare these answers to those obtained in Exercise 7.25. Are they the same (except for rounding)?

7.27 Refer to Exercise 7.7. Determine the mean, variance, and standard deviation of the number of children per household.

7.28 Refer to Exercise 7.11. Compute the mean and standard deviation of the number of pizzas delivered each month to university students.

7.29 Refer to Exercise 7.28. If the pizzeria makes a profit of $3 per pizza, determine the mean and standard deviation of the profits per student.

7.30 Refer to Exercise 7.17. Suppose that each game costs the player 25 cents. Determine the probability distribution of the amount of money the arcade takes in per child.

7.31 Refer to Exercise 7.30. Use the definitions of expected value and variance to calculate the mean and standard deviation of the amount of money the arcade makes per child.

7.32 Refer to Exercise 7.17. Use the laws of expected value and variance to calculate the mean and standard deviation of the amount of money the arcade makes per child. (Each game costs the player 25 cents.)

7.33 A shopping mall estimates the probability distribution of the number of stores mall customers actually enter, as shown in the table.

x	0	1	2	3	4	5	6
$p(x)$	.04	.19	.22	.28	.12	.09	.06

Find the mean and standard deviation of the number of stores entered.

7.34 Refer to Exercise 7.33. Suppose that, on average, customers spend 10 minutes in each store they enter. Find the mean and standard deviation of the total amount of time customers spend in stores.

7.35 Refer to Exercise 7.18. Find the expected value and standard deviation of the number of books sold per hit.

7.36 When parking a car in a downtown parking lot, drivers pay according to the number of hours or fraction thereof. The probability distribution of the number of hours cars are parked has been estimated as follows.

x	1	2	3	4	5	6	7	8
$p(x)$	.24	.18	.13	.10	.07	.04	.04	.20

Find the mean and standard deviation of the number of hours cars are parked in the lot.

7.37 Refer to Exercise 7.36. The cost of parking is $2.50 per hour. Calculate the mean and standard deviation of the amount of revenue each car generates.

7.38 You have been given the choice of receiving $500 in cash or receiving a gold coin that has a face value of $100. However, the actual value of the gold coin depends on its gold content. You are told that the coin has a 40% probability of being worth $400, a 30% probability of being worth $900, and a 30% probability of being worth its face value. Basing your decision on expected value, should you choose the coin?

7.39 To examine the effectiveness of its four annual advertising promotions, a mail-order company has sent a questionnaire to each of its customers, asking how many of the previous year's promotions prompted orders that would not have otherwise been made. The accompanying table lists the probabilities that were derived from the questionnaire, where X is the random variable representing the number of promotions that prompted orders. If we assume that overall customer behavior next year will be the same as last year, what is the expected number of promotions that each customer will take advantage of next year by ordering goods that otherwise would not be purchased?

x	0	1	2	3	4
$p(x)$	.10	.25	.40	.20	.05

7.40 Refer to Exercise 7.39. A previous analysis of historical records found that the mean value of orders for promotional goods is $20, with the company earning a gross profit of 20% on each order. Calculate the expected value of the profit contribution next year.

7.41 Refer to Exercises 7.39 and 7.40. The fixed cost of conducting the four promotions is estimated to be $15,000 with a variable cost of $3.00 per customer for mailing and handling costs. How large a customer base does the company need in order to cover the cost of promotions?

7.42 The owner of a small firm has just purchased a personal computer, which she expects will serve her for the next 2 years. The owner has been told that she "must" buy a surge suppressor to provide protection for her new hardware against possible surges or variations in the electrical current, which have the capacity to damage the computer. The amount of damage to the computer depends on the strength of the surge. It has been estimated that there is a 1% chance of incurring $400 damage, 2% chance of incurring $200 damage, and 10% chance of $100 damage. An inexpensive suppressor, which would provide protection for only one surge, can be purchased. How much should the owner be willing to pay if she makes decisions on the basis of expected value?

7.4 BIVARIATE DISTRIBUTIONS

Thus far, we have dealt with the distribution of a *single* variable. However, there are circumstances where we need to know about the relationship between two variables. Recall that we have addressed this problem statistically in Chapter 2 by drawing the scatter diagram and in Chapter 4 by calculating the covariance and the coefficient of correlation. In this section we present the **bivariate distribution**, which provides probabilities of combinations of two variables. Incidentally, when we need to distinguish between the bivariate distributions and the distributions of one variable, we'll refer to the latter as **univariate distributions**.

The joint probability that two variables X and Y will assume the values of x and y, respectively, is denoted $p(x, y)$ where

$$p(x, y) = P(X = x \text{ and } Y = y)$$

A **bivariate** (or **joint**) **probability distribution** of X and Y is a table or formula that lists the joint probabilities $p(x, y)$ for all pairs of values of x and y. As was the case with univariate distributions, the joint probability must satisfy two requirements.

REQUIREMENTS FOR A DISCRETE BIVARIATE DISTRIBUTION

1. $0 \leq p(x, y) \leq 1$ for all pairs of values (x, y)

2. $\displaystyle\sum_{\text{all } x} \sum_{\text{all } y} p(x, y) = 1$

EXAMPLE 7.5

Xavier and Yvette are real estate agents. Let X denote the number of houses that Xavier will sell in a month and let Y denote the number of houses Yvette will sell in a month. An analysis of their past monthly performances has the following joint probabilities.

Bivariate Probability Distribution

		X		
		0	1	2
	0	.12	.42	.06
Y	1	.21	.06	.03
	2	.07	.02	.01

We interpret these joint probabilities in the same way we did in Chapter 6. For example, the probability that Xavier sells 0 houses and Yvette sells 1 house in the month is $P(X = 0$ and $Y = 1) = p(0, 1) = .21$.

MARGINAL PROBABILITIES

As we did in Chapter 6, we can calculate the marginal probabilities by summing across rows and down columns.

Marginal Probability Distribution of X in Example 7.5

$$P(X = 0) = p(0, 0) + p(0, 1) + p(0, 2) = .12 + .21 + .07 = .4$$

$$P(X = 1) = p(1, 0) + p(1, 1) + p(1, 2) = .42 + .06 + .02 = .5$$

$$P(X = 2) = p(2, 0) + p(2, 1) + p(2, 2) = .06 + .03 + .01 = .1$$

The marginal probability distribution of X is

x	$p(x)$
0	.4
1	.5
2	.1

Marginal Probability Distribution of Y in Example 7.5

$$P(Y = 0) = p(0, 0) + p(1, 0) + p(2, 0) = .12 + .42 + .06 = .6$$

$$P(Y = 1) = p(0, 1) + p(1, 1) + p(2, 1) = .21 + .06 + .03 = .3$$

$$P(Y = 2) = p(0, 2) + p(1, 2) + p(2, 2) = .07 + .02 + .01 = .1$$

The marginal probability distribution of Y is

y	$p(y)$
0	.6
1	.3
2	.1

Notice that both marginal probability distributions meet the requirements; the probabilities are between 0 and 1, and they add to 1.

DESCRIBING THE BIVARIATE DISTRIBUTION

As we did with the univariate distribution, we often describe the bivariate distribution by computing the mean, variance, and standard deviation of each variable. We do so by utilizing the marginal probabilities.

Expected Value, Variance, and Standard Deviation of X in Example 7.5

$$E(X) = \mu_x = \sum xp(x) = 0(.4) + 1(.5) + 2(.1) = .7$$

$$V(X) = \sigma_x^2 = \sum (x - \mu_x)^2\, p(x) = (0-.7)^2(.4) + (1-.7)^2(.5) + (2-.7)^2(.1) = .41$$

$$\sigma_x = \sqrt{\sigma_x^2} = \sqrt{.41} = .64$$

Expected Value, Variance, and Standard Deviation of Y in Example 7.5

$$E(Y) = \mu_y = \sum yp(y) = 0(.6) + 1(.3) + 2(.1) = .5$$

$$V(Y) = \sigma_y^2 = \sum (y - \mu_y)^2\, p(y) = (0-.5)^2(.6) + (1-.5)^2(.3) + (2-.5)^2(.1) = .45$$

$$\sigma_y = \sqrt{\sigma_y^2} = \sqrt{.45} = .67$$

There are two more parameters we can and need to compute. Both deal with the relationship between the two variables. They are the covariance and the coefficient of correlation. Recall that both were introduced in Chapter 4, where the formulas were based on the assumption that we knew each of the N observations of the population. In this chapter we compute parameters like the covariance and the coefficient of correlation from the bivariate distribution.

COVARIANCE

The covariance of two discrete variables is defined as

$$COV(X,\,Y) = \sum_{\text{all } x} \sum_{\text{all } y} (x - \mu_x)(y - \mu_y)p(x,\,y)$$

Notice that we multiply the deviations from the mean for both X and Y and then multiply by the joint probability.

The calculations are simplified by the following shortcut method.

SHORTCUT CALCULATION FOR COVARIANCE

$$COV(X,\,Y) = \sum_{\text{all } x} \sum_{\text{all } y} xyp(x,\,y) - \mu_x \mu_y$$

The coefficient of correlation is calculated in the same way as in Chapter 4.

COEFFICIENT OF CORRELATION

$$\rho = \frac{COV(X, Y)}{\sigma_x \sigma_y}$$

EXAMPLE 7.6

Compute the covariance and the coefficient of correlation between the numbers of houses sold by the two agents in Example 7.5.

SOLUTION   We start by computing the covariance.

$$COV(X, Y) = \sum_{\text{all } x} \sum_{\text{all } y} (x - \mu_x)(y - \mu_y)p(x, y)$$

$$= (0 - .7)(0 - .5)(.12) + (1 - .7)(0 - .5)(.42) + (2 - .7)(0 - .5)(.06)$$

$$+ (0 - .7)(1 - .5)(.21) + (1 - .7)(1 - .5)(.06) + (2 - .7)(1 - .5)(.03)$$

$$+ (0 - .7)(2 - .5)(.07) + (1 - .7)(2 - .5)(.02) + (2 - .7)(2 - .5)(.01)$$

$$= -.15$$

As we did with the shortcut method for the variance, we'll recalculate the covariance using its shortcut method.

$$\sum_{\text{all } x} \sum_{\text{all } y} xyp(x, y) = (0)(0)(.12) + (1)(0)(.42) + (2)(0)(.06)$$

$$+ (0)(1)(.21) + (1)(1)(.06) + (2)(1)(.03)$$

$$+ (0)(2)(.07) + (1)(2)(.02) + (2)(2)(.01)$$

$$= .2$$

Using the expected values computed above, we find

$$COV(X, Y) = \sum_{\text{all } x} \sum_{\text{all } y} xyp(x, y) - \mu_x\mu_y = .2 - (.7)(.5) = -.15$$

We also computed the standard deviations above. Thus, the coefficient of correlation is

$$\rho = \frac{COV(X, Y)}{\sigma_x \sigma_y} = \frac{-.15}{(.64)(.67)} = -.35$$

There is a weak negative relationship between the two variables.

SUM OF TWO VARIABLES

The bivariate distribution allows us to develop the probability distribution of any combination of the two variables. Of particular interest to us is the sum of two variables. The analysis of this type of distribution leads to an important statistical application in finance, which we present in the next section.

To demonstrate how to develop the probability distribution of the sum of two variables from their bivariate distribution, return to Example 7.5. The sum of the two variables X and Y is the total number of houses sold per month. The possible values of $X + Y$ are 0, 1, 2, 3, and 4. The probability that $X + Y = 2$, for example, is obtained by summing the joint probabilities of all pairs of values of X and Y that sum to 2:

$$P(X + Y = 2) = p(0, 2) + p(1, 1) + p(2, 0) = .07 + .06 + .06 = .19$$

We calculate the probabilities of the other values of $X + Y$ similarly, producing the following table.

Probability Distribution of $X + Y$ in Example 7.5

$x + y$	0	1	2	3	4
$p(x + y)$	.12	.63	.19	.05	.01

We can compute the expected value, variance, and standard deviation of $X + Y$ in the usual way:

$$E(X + Y) = 0(.12) + 1(.63) + 2(.19) + 3(.05) + 4(.01) = 1.2$$

$$V(X + Y) = \sigma^2_{X+Y} = (0 - 1.2)^2(.12) + (1 - 1.2)^2(.63) + (2 - 1.2)^2(.19)$$

$$+ (3 - 1.2)^2(.05) + (4 - 1.2)^2(.01)$$

$$= .56$$

$$\sigma_{X+Y} = \sqrt{.56} = .75$$

We can derive a number of laws that enable us to compute the expected value and variance of the sum of two variables.

LAWS OF EXPECTED VALUE AND VARIANCE OF THE SUM OF TWO VARIABLES

1. $E(X + Y) = E(X) + E(Y)$

2. $V(X + Y) = V(X) + V(Y) + 2COV(X, Y)$

If X and Y are independent, $COV(X, Y) = 0$ and thus $V(X + Y) = V(X) + V(Y)$.

EXAMPLE 7.7

Use the laws of expected value and variance of the sum of two variables to calculate the mean and variance of the total number of houses sold per month in Example 7.5.

SOLUTION   Using law 1, we compute the expected value of $X + Y$:

$$E(X + Y) = E(X) + E(Y) = .7 + .5 = 1.2$$

which is the same value we produced directly from the probability distribution of $X + Y$.

We apply law 3 to determine the variance:

$$V(X + Y) = V(X) + V(Y) + 2COV(X, Y) = .41 + .45 + 2(-.15) = .56$$

This is the same value we obtained from the probability distribution of $X + Y$.

We will encounter several applications where we need the laws of expected value and variance for the sum of two variables. Additionally, we will demonstrate an important application in operations management where we need the formulas for the expected value and variance of the sum of more than two variables. See Exercises 7.57–7.60 below.

EXERCISES

7.43   The table below lists the bivariate distribution of X and Y.

y	x 1	2
1	.5	.1
2	.1	.3

a   Find the marginal probability distribution of X.
b   Find the marginal probability distribution of Y.
c   Compute the mean and variance of X.
d   Compute the mean and variance of Y.

7.44   Refer to Exercise 7.43. Compute the covariance and the coefficient of correlation.

7.45   Refer to Exercise 7.43. Use the laws of expected value and variance of the sum of two variables to compute the mean and variance of $X + Y$.

7.46   Refer to Exercise 7.43.
a   Determine the distribution of $X + Y$.
b   Determine the mean and variance of $X + Y$.
c   Does your answer to part **b** equal the answer to Exercise 7.45?

7.47   The bivariate distribution of X and Y is described below.

y	x 1	2
1	.28	.42
2	.12	.18

a   Find the marginal probability distribution of X.
b   Find the marginal probability distribution of Y.
c   Compute the mean and variance of X.
d   Compute the mean and variance of Y.

7.48   Refer to Exercise 7.47. Compute the covariance and the coefficient of correlation.

7.49   Refer to Exercise 7.47. Use the laws of expected value and variance of the sum of two variables to compute the mean and variance of $X + Y$.

7.50   Refer to Exercise 7.47.
a   Determine the distribution of $X + Y$.
b   Determine the mean and variance of $X + Y$.
c   Does your answer to part **b** equal the answer to Exercise 7.49?

7.51   The joint probability distribution of X and Y is shown in the table below.

y	x 1	2	3
1	.42	.12	.06
2	.28	.08	.04

a   Determine the marginal distributions of X and Y.
b   Compute the covariance and coefficient of correlation between X and Y.
c   Develop the probability distribution of $X + Y$.

7.52   The following distributions of X and of Y have been developed. If X and Y are independent, determine the joint probability distribution of X and Y.

x	0	1	2
$p(x)$	.6	.3	.1

y	1	2
$p(y)$	.7	.3

7.53   The distributions of X and of Y are described below. If X and Y are independent, determine the joint probability distribution of X and Y.

x	0	1
$p(x)$	.2	.8

y	1	2	3
$p(y)$	.2	.4	.4

7.54 After analyzing several months of sales data, the owner of an appliance store produced the following joint probability distribution of the number of refrigerators and stoves sold daily.

Refrigerators

Stoves	0	1	2
0	.08	.14	.12
1	.09	.17	.13
2	.05	.18	.04

a Find the marginal probability distribution of the number of refrigerators sold daily.
b Find the marginal probability distribution of the number of stoves sold daily.
c Compute the mean and variance of the number of refrigerators sold daily.
d Compute the mean and variance of the number of stoves sold daily.
e Compute the covariance and the coefficient of correlation.

7.55 Canadians who visit the United States often buy liquor and cigarettes, which are much cheaper in the United States. However, there are limitations. Canadians visiting in the United States for more than 2 days are allowed to bring into Canada one bottle of liquor and one carton of cigarettes. A Canada Customs agent has produced the following joint probability distribution of the number of bottles of liquor and the number of cartons of cigarettes imported by Canadians who have visited the United States for 2 or more days.

Bottles of Liquor

Cartons of Cigarettes	0	1
0	.63	.18
1	.09	.10

a Find the marginal probability distribution of the number of bottles imported.
b Find the marginal probability distribution of the number of cigarette cartons imported.
c Compute the mean and variance of the number of bottles imported.
d Compute the mean and variance of the number of cigarette cartons imported.
e Compute the covariance and the coefficient of correlation.

7.56 Refer to Exercise 7.54. Find the following conditional probabilities.
a $P(1 \text{ refrigerator} \mid 0 \text{ stoves})$
b $P(0 \text{ stoves} \mid 1 \text{ refrigerator})$
c $P(2 \text{ refrigerators} \mid 2 \text{ stoves})$

APPLICATIONS IN OPERATIONS MANAGEMENT: PERT/CPM

PERT (Project Evaluation and Review Technique) and **CPM** (Critical Path Method) are related management science techniques that help operations managers control the activities and the amount of time it takes to complete a project. Both techniques are based on the order in which the activities must be performed. For example, in building a house, the excavation of the foundation must precede the pouring of the foundation, which in turn precedes the framing. A **path** is defined as a sequence of related activities that leads from the starting point to the completion of a project. In most projects there are several paths with differing amounts of time needed for their completion. The longest path is called the **critical path** because any delay in the activities along this path will result in a delay in the completion of the project. In some versions of PERT/CPM, the activity completion times are fixed and the chief task of the operations manager is to determine the critical path. In other versions, each activity's completion time is considered to be a random variable, where the mean and variance can be estimated. By extending the laws of expected value and variance for the sum of two variables to more than two variables, we produce the following, where $X_1, X_2, ..., X_k$ are the times

for the completion of critical path activities 1, 2, ..., k, respectively. These times are independent random variables.

Laws of Expected Value and Variance for the Sum of More Than Two Independent Variables

1. $E\left(\sum_{i=1}^{k} X_i\right) = \sum_{i=1}^{k} E(X_i)$

2. $V\left(\sum_{i=1}^{k} X_i\right) = \sum_{i=1}^{k} V(X_i)$

Using these laws, we can then produce the expected value and variance for the complete project. Exercises 7.57–7.60 address this problem.

EXERCISES

7.57 There are four activities along the critical path for a project. The expected values and variances of the completion times of the activities are listed below. Determine the expected value and variance of the completion time of the project.

Activity	Expected Completion Time (Days)	Variance
1	18	8
2	12	5
3	27	6
4	8	2

7.58 The operations manager of a large plant wishes to overhaul a machine. After conducting a PERT/CPM analysis, he has developed the following critical path:
1. Disassemble machine
2. Determine parts that need replacing
3. Find needed parts in inventory
4. Reassemble machine
5. Test machine

He has estimated the means and standard deviations (in minutes) of the completion times as follows.

Activity	Mean	Variance
1	35	8
2	20	5
3	20	4
4	50	12
5	20	2

Determine the mean and standard deviation of the completion time of the project.

7.59 In preparing to launch a new product, a marketing manager has determined the critical path for her department. The activities and the mean and variance of the completion time for each activity along the critical path are shown in the table. Determine the mean and variance of the completion time of the project.

Activity	Expected Completion Time (Days)	Variance
Develop survey questionnaire	8	2
Pretest the questionnaire	14	5
Revise the questionnaire	5	1
Hire survey company	3	1
Conduct survey	30	8
Analyze data	30	10
Prepare report	10	3

7.60 A professor of business statistics is about to begin work on a new research project. Because his time is quite limited, he has developed a PERT/CPM critical path, which consists of the following activities:
1. Conduct a search for relevant research articles
2. Write proposal for a research grant
3. Perform the analysis
4. Write the article and send to journal
5. Wait for reviews
6. Revise on the basis of the reviews and resubmit

The mean and standard deviation (in days) of the completion times are as follows:

Activity	Mean	Standard deviation
1	10	3
2	3	0
3	30	10
4	5	1
5	100	20
6	20	8

Compute the mean and standard deviation of the completion time of the entire project.

7.5 (OPTIONAL) APPLICATIONS IN FINANCE: PORTFOLIO DIVERSIFICATION AND ASSET ALLOCATION

In this section we introduce an important application in finance that is based on the previous section.

In Chapters 2 (page 38) and 4 (page 128), we described how the variance or standard deviation can be used to measure the risk associated with an investment. Most investors tend to be risk averse, which means that they prefer to have lower risk associated with their investments. One of the ways in which financial analysts lower the risk that is associated with the stock market is through **diversification**. This strategy was first mathematically developed by Harry Markowitz in 1952. His model paved the way to the development of modern portfolio theory (MPT), which is the concept underlying mutual funds (see page 158).

To illustrate the basics of portfolio diversification, consider an investor who forms a portfolio, consisting of only two stocks, by investing $4,000 in one stock and $6,000 in a second stock. Suppose that the results after 1 year are as listed below. (We've previously defined return on investment. See Applications in Finance: Return on Investment on page 38.)

One-Year Results

Stock	Initial Investment	Value of Investment After 1 Year	Rate of Return on Investment
1	$4,000	$5,000	$R_1 = .25$ (25%)
2	$6,000	$5,400	$R_2 = -.10$ (−10%)
Total	$10,000	$10,400	$R_p = .04$ (4%)

Another way of calculating the portfolio return R_p is to compute the weighted average of the individual stock returns R_1 and R_2, where the weights w_1 and w_2 are the proportions of the initial $10,000 invested in stocks 1 and 2, respectively. In this illustration $w_1 = .4$ and $w_2 = .6$. (Note that w_1 and w_2 must always sum to 1 because the two stocks constitute the entire portfolio.) The weighted average of the two returns is

$$R_p = w_1 R_1 + w_2 R_2$$

$$= (.4)(.25) + (.6)(-.10) = .04$$

This is how portfolio returns are calculated. However, when the initial investments are made, the investor does not know what the returns will be. In fact, the returns are random variables. We are interested in determining the expected value and variance of the portfolio. The formulas below were derived from the laws of expected value and variance introduced in the two previous sections.

MEAN AND VARIANCE OF A PORTFOLIO OF TWO STOCKS

$$E(R_p) = w_1 E(R_1) + w_2 E(R_2)$$

$$V(R_p) = w_1^2 V(R_1) + w_2^2 V(R_2) + 2w_1 w_2 \, COV(R_1, R_2)$$

$$= w_1^2 \sigma_1^2 + w_2^2 \sigma_2^2 + 2w_1 w_2 \, \rho \sigma_1 \sigma_2$$

where w_1 and w_2 are the proportions or weights of investments 1 and 2, $E(R_1)$ and $E(R_2)$ are their expected values, σ_1 and σ_2 are their standard deviations, and ρ is the coefficient of correlation.

EXAMPLE 7.8

An investor has decided to form a portfolio by putting 25% of his money into McDonald's stock and 75% into Cisco Systems stock. The investor assumes that the expected returns will be 8% and 15%, respectively, and that the standard deviations will be 12% and 22%, respectively.
  a Find the expected return on the portfolio.
  b Compute the standard deviation of the returns on the portfolio assuming that
        (i) the two stocks' returns are perfectly positively correlated
        (ii) the coefficient of correlation is .5
        (iii) the two stocks' returns are uncorrelated

SOLUTION   a The expected values of the two stocks are

$$E(R_1) = .08 \quad \text{and} \quad E(R_2) = .15$$

The weights are $w_1 = .25$ and $w_2 = .75$. Thus,

$$E(R_p) = w_1 E(R_1) + w_2 E(R_2) = .25(.08) + .75(.15) = .1325$$

b The standard deviations are

$$\sigma_1 = .12 \quad \text{and} \quad \sigma_2 = .22$$

Thus,

$$V(R_p) = w_1^2 \sigma_1^2 + w_2^2 \sigma_2^2 + 2w_1 w_2 \rho \sigma_1 \sigma_2$$

$$= (.25^2)(.12^2) + (.75^2)(.22^2) + 2(.25)(.75)\,\rho(.12)(.22)$$

$$= .0281 + .0099\rho$$

When $\rho = 1$,

$$V(R_p) = .0281 + .0099(1) = .0380$$

When $\rho = .5$,

$$V(R_p) = .0281 + .0099(.5) = .0331$$

When $\rho = 0$,

$$V(R_p) = .0281 + .0099(0) = .0281$$

Notice that the variance of the portfolio returns decreases as the coefficient of correlation decreases.

PORTFOLIO DIVERSIFICATION IN PRACTICE

The formulas introduced in this section require that we know the expected values, variances, and covariance (or coefficient of correlation) of the investments we're interested in. The question arises: How do we determine these parameters? (Incidentally, this question is rarely addressed in finance textbooks!) The most common procedure is to estimate the parameters from historical data, using sample statistics.

PORTFOLIOS WITH MORE THAN TWO STOCKS

We can extend the formulas that describe the mean and variance of the returns of a portfolio of two stocks to a portfolio of any number of stocks.

MEAN AND VARIANCE OF A PORTFOLIO OF k STOCKS

$$E(R_p) = \sum_{i=1}^{k} w_i E(R_i)$$

$$V(R_p) = \sum_{i=1}^{k} w_i^2 \sigma_i^2 + 2 \sum_{i=1}^{k} \sum_{j=i+1}^{k} w_i w_j \operatorname{COV}(R_i, R_j)$$

where R_i is the return of the ith stock, w_i is the proportion of the portfolio invested in stock i, and k is the number of stocks in the portfolio.

When k is greater than 2, the calculations can be tedious and time-consuming. For example, when $k = 3$, we need to know the values of the three weights, three expected values, three variances, and three covariances. When $k = 4$, there are four expected values, four variances, and six covariances. [The number of covariances required in general is $k(k-1)/2$.] To assist you, we have created an Excel worksheet to perform the computations when $k = 2$, 3, or 4. (For larger values of k, see the reference at the end of the chapter.) To demonstrate, we'll return to the problem described in this chapter's introduction.

INVESTING TO MINIMIZE RISK AND MAXIMIZE RETURNS: SOLUTION

Because of the large amount of calculations, we will solve this problem using only Excel. From the file we compute the means of each stock's returns.

Excel Means

	A	B	C	D
1	0.04510	0.01996	0.01921	0.02336

Next we compute the variance–covariance matrix. (The commands are the same as those described in Chapter 4—simply include all the columns of the returns of the investments you wish to include in the portfolio.)

Excel Variance-Covariance Matrix

	A	B	C	D	E
1		INTEL	MOTOROLA	GM	GILLETTE
2	INTEL	0.00946			
3	MOTOROLA	0.00162	0.00695		
4	GM	-0.00128	0.00011	0.00353	
5	GILLETTE	0.00106	0.00033	-0.00029	0.00263

Notice that the variances of the returns are listed on the diagonal. Thus, for example, the variance of the 48 monthly returns of Intel is .00946. The covariances appear below the diagonal. The covariance between the returns of Intel and Motorola is .00162.

The means and the variance–covariance matrix are copied to the spreadsheet using the commands described below. The weights are typed, producing the output below.

The expected return on the portfolio is .0269 and the variance is .0016.

COMMANDS

1. Open the file containing the returns. In this example open file **Ch7:\ Invest**.
2. Compute the means of the columns containing the returns of the stocks in the portfolio.
3. Using the commands described in Chapter 4 (page 122), compute the variance–covariance matrix.
4. Open the **Portfolio Diversification** workbook. Use the tab to select the 4 Stocks worksheet. DO NOT CHANGE ANY CELLS THAT APPEAR IN BOLD PRINT. DO NOT SAVE ANY WORKSHEETS.
5. Copy the means into cells C8 to F8. (Use **Copy, Paste Special** with **Values and number formats**.)
6. Copy the variance–covariance matrix (including row and column labels) into columns B, C, D, E, and F.
7. Type the weights into cells C10 to F10.

The mean, variance, and standard deviation of the portfolio will be printed. Use similar commands for 2-stock and 3-stock portfolios.

Excel Worksheet: Portfolio Diversification-Plan # 1

	A	B	C	D	E	F
1	Portfolio of 4 Stocks					
2			INTEL	MOTOROLA	GM	GILLETTE
3	Variance-Covariance Matrix	INTEL	0.00946			
4		MOTOROLA	0.00162	0.00695		
5		GM	-0.00128	0.00011	0.00353	
6		GILLETTE	0.00106	0.00033	-0.00029	0.00263
7						
8	Expected Returns		0.04510	0.01996	0.01921	0.02336
9						
10	Weights		0.25	0.25	0.25	0.25
11						
12	Portfolio Return					
13	Expected Value	0.0269				
14	Variance	0.0016				
15	Standard Deviation	0.0400				

(continued)

INVESTING TO MINIMIZE RISK AND MAXIMIZE RETURNS: SOLUTION   (continued)

The results for Plan #2 are

	A	B
1	**Portfolio Return**	
2	**Expected Value**	**0.0229**
3	**Variance**	**0.0018**
4	**Standard Deviation**	**0.0421**

The output for Plan #3 is

	A	B
1	**Portfolio Return**	
2	**Expected Value**	**0.0378**
3	**Variance**	**0.0050**
4	**Standard Deviation**	**0.0705**

Plan 1 is better than plan 2 because its expected value is larger and its variance is smaller. Plan 3's expected value is larger than that of plan 1. However, plan 3's variance is much larger than plan 1's variance. To minimize risk, the investor should choose plan 1.

In this example we showed how to compute the expected return, variance, and standard deviation from a sample of returns on the investments for any combination of weights. (We illustrated the process with three sets of weights. It is possible to determine the "optimal" weights that minimize risk for a given expected value or maximize expected return for a given standard deviation. This is an extremely important function of financial analysts and investment advisors. Solutions can be determined using a management science technique called *linear programming*, a subject taught by most schools of business and faculties of management.

EXERCISES

7.61 A portfolio is composed of two stocks. Given the following parameters associated with the returns of the two stocks, determine the mean and standard deviation of the return on the portfolio.

Stock	1	2
Proportion of portfolio	.30	.70
Mean	.12	.25
Standard deviation	.02	.15
Coefficient of correlation:	.5	

7.62 Repeat Exercise 7.61 assuming that the coefficient of correlation is .25.

7.63 Repeat Exercise 7.61 assuming that the coefficient of correlation is 0.

7.64 Describe what happens to the expected value and standard deviation of the portfolio returns when the coefficient of correlation decreases.

7.65 An investor is given the following information about the returns on two stocks.

	Stock	
	1	2
Mean	.09	.13
Standard deviation	.15	.21

   a If she is most interested in maximizing her returns, which stock should she choose?

   b If she is most interested in minimizing her risk, which stock should she choose?

7.66 Refer to Exercise 7.65. Compute the expected value and variance of the portfolio composed of 60%

stock 1 and 40% stock 2. The coefficient of correlation is .4.

7.67 Refer to Exercise 7.65. Compute the expected value and variance of the portfolio composed of 30% stock 1 and 70% stock 2.

7.68 The semiannual returns for three stocks over an 18-year-period are stored in file Xr07-68.

   a Calculate the mean and variance of each of the three stocks.

   b If you wish to construct a portfolio that maximizes the expected return, what should you do?

   c If you wish to construct a portfolio that minimizes the risk, what should you do?

7.69 Refer to Exercise 7.68.

   a Find the expected value and variance of a portfolio composed of equal investments in the three stocks.

   b How do the expected value and variance of the portfolio compare with those of Exercise 7.68 part **a**?

7.70 Refer to Exercise 7.68.

   a Find the expected value and variance of the following portfolio:

      Stock 1   50%

      Stock 2   30%

      Stock 3   20%

   b How do the expected value and variance of the portfolio compare with those of Exercise 7.68 part **a** and Exercise 7.69?

7.71   A financial analyst recorded the quarterly returns on investment for three stocks. These data are stored in file Xr07-71.

  a Calculate the mean and variance of each of the three stocks.

  b If you wish to construct a portfolio that maximizes the expected return, what should you do?

  c If you wish to construct a portfolio that minimizes the risk, what should you do?

7.72   Refer to Exercise 7.71.

  a Find the expected value and variance of the following portfolio:

>   Stock 1   30%
>
>   Stock 2   40%
>
>   Stock 3   30%

  b How do the expected value and variance of the portfolio compare with those of Exercise 7.71 part **a**?

7.73   Refer to Exercise 7.71.

  a Find the expected value and variance of the following portfolio:

>   Stock 1   10%
>
>   Stock 2   10%
>
>   Stock 3   80%

  b How do the expected value and variance of the portfolio compare with those of Exercise 7.71 part **a** and Exercise 7.72?

7.74   The quarterly rates of return for four stocks are stored in file Xr07-74.

  a Calculate the mean and variance of each of the four stocks.

  b If you wish to construct a portfolio that maximizes the expected return, what should you do?

  c If you wish to construct a portfolio that minimizes the risk, what should you do?

7.75   Refer to Exercise 7.74.

  a Find the expected value and variance of the following portfolio:

>   Stock 1   25%
>
>   Stock 2   25%
>
>   Stock 3   25%
>
>   Stock 4   25%

  b How do the expected value and variance of the portfolio compare with those of Exercise 7.74 part **a**?

7.76   Refer to Exercise 7.74.

  a Find the expected value and variance of the following portfolio:

>   Stock 1   20%
>
>   Stock 2   20%
>
>   Stock 3   10%
>
>   Stock 4   50%

  b How do the expected value and variance of the portfolio compare with those of Exercise 7.74 part **a** and Exercise 7.75?

7.77   The monthly returns on investment for General Electric, Seagram, Coca-Cola, and McDonald's are stored in file Xr07-77.

  a Compute the mean and variance for each stock.

  b If an investor wishes to maximize his expected return, which stock would you recommend?

  c If an investor wishes to minimize his risk, which stock would you recommend?

7.78   Refer to Exercise 7.77.

  a Determine the variance–covariance matrix.

  b Which stocks would you suggest the investor include in his portfolio to lower risk?

7.79   Refer to Exercise 7.77. Find the expected value and variance of the following portfolio:

>   General Electric   40%
>
>   Seagram   25%
>
>   Coca-Cola   20%
>
>   McDonald's   15%

7.80   Refer to Exercise 7.77. Produce your own portfolio and compute the expected value and variance.

7.6 BINOMIAL DISTRIBUTION

Now that we've introduced probability distributions in general, we need to introduce several specific probability distributions. In this section we present the *binomial distribution.*

The binomial distribution is the result of a *binomial experiment.*

> **BINOMIAL EXPERIMENT**
>
> 1 The **binomial experiment** consists of a fixed number of trials. We represent the number of trials by n.
>
> 2 On each trial there are two possible outcomes. We label one outcome a *success*, and the other a *failure*.
>
> 3 The probability of success is p. The probability of failure is $1 - p$.
>
> 4 The trials are independent, which means that the outcome of one trial does not affect the outcomes of any other trials.

The random variable is defined as the number of successes in the n trials. It is called the **binomial random variable**. Here are several examples of binomial experiments.

1. Flip a coin 10 times. The two outcomes per trial are heads and tails. The terms "success" and "failure" are arbitrary. We can label either outcome success. However, generally, we call success anything we're looking for. For example, if we were betting on heads, we would label heads a success. If the coin is fair, the probability of heads is 50%. Thus, $p = .5$. Finally, we can see that the trials are independent, because the outcome of one coin flip cannot possibly affect the outcomes of other flips.

2. Draw five cards out of a shuffled deck. We can label as success whatever card we seek. For example, if we wish to know the probability of receiving five clubs, a club is labeled a success. On the first draw, the probability of a club is 13/52 = 25%. However, if we draw a second card without replacing the first card and shuffling, the trials are not independent. To see why, suppose that the first draw is a club. If we draw again without replacement, the probability of drawing a second club is 12/51, which is not 25%. In this experiment, the trials are *not* independent.* Hence, this is not a binomial experiment. However, if we replace the card and shuffle before drawing again, the experiment is binomial. Note that in most card games, we do not replace the card, and as a result the experiment is not binomial.

3. A political survey asks 1,500 voters whom they intend to vote for in an approaching election. In most elections in the United States, there are only two candidates, the Republican and Democratic nominees. Thus, we have two outcomes per trial. The trials are independent, because the choice of one voter does not affect the choice of other voters. In Canada, and in other countries with a parliamentary system of government, there are usually several candidates in the race. However, we can label a vote for our favored candidate (or the party that is paying us to do the survey) a success and all the others are failures.

As you will discover, the third example is a very common application of statistical inference. The actual value of p is unknown, and the job of the statistics practitioner is to estimate its value. By understanding the probability distribution that uses p, we will be able to develop the statistical tools to estimate p.

BINOMIAL RANDOM VARIABLE

The binomial random variable is the number of successes in the experiment's n trials. It can take on values $0, 1, 2, \ldots, n$. Thus, the random variable is discrete. In order to proceed, we need to be capable of calculating the probability associated with each value.

---

*The *hypergeometric distribution* (see CD Appendix 7.1) is used to calculate probabilities in such cases.

Using a probability tree, we draw a series of branches as depicted in Figure 7.2. The stages represent the outcomes for each of the n trials. At each stage there are two branches, representing success and failure. To calculate the probability that there are x successes in n trials, we note that for each success in the sequence we must multiply by p. And, if there are x successes there must be $n - x$ failures. For each failure in the sequence we multiply by $1 - p$. Thus, the probability for each sequence of branches that represent x successes and $n - x$ failures is

$$p^x(1 - p)^{n - x}$$

Figure 7.2
Probability tree for a binomial experiment

There are a number of branches that yield x successes and $n - x$ failures. For example, there are two ways to produce exactly one success and one failure in two trials—SF and FS. To count the number of branch sequences that produce x successes and $n - x$ failures, we use the combinatorial formula

$$C_x^n = \frac{n!}{x!(n - x)!}$$

where

$$n! = n(n - 1)(n - 2) \cdots (2)(1)$$

For example,

$$3! = 3(2)(1) = 6$$

Incidentally, although it may not appear to be logical, $0! = 1$.

Pulling together the two components of the probability distribution yields the following.

> **BINOMIAL PROBABILITY DISTRIBUTION**
> The probability of x successes in a binomial experiment with n trials and probability of success $= p$ is
>
> $$P(X = x) = p(x) = \frac{n!}{x!(n - x)!} p^x(1 - p)^{n-x} \quad \text{for } x = 0, 1, 2, \dots, n$$

EXAMPLE 7.9

Pat Statsdud is a student taking a statistics course. Unfortunately, Pat is not a good student. Pat does not read the textbook before class, does not do homework, and regularly misses class. Pat intends to rely on luck to pass the next quiz. The quiz consists of 10 multiple-choice questions. Each question has five possible answers, only one of which is correct. Pat plans to guess the answer to each question.

a What is the probability that Pat gets no answers correct?

b What is the probability that Pat gets two answers correct?

SOLUTION   The experiment consists of 10 identical trials, each with two possible outcomes and where success is defined as a correct answer. Because Pat intends to guess, the probability of success is $\frac{1}{5}$ or .2. Finally, the trials are independent because the outcome of any of the questions does not affect the outcomes of any other questions. These four properties tell us that the experiment is binomial with $n = 10$ and $p = .2$.

a The probability of no successes is computed from

$$P(X = x) = \frac{n!}{x!(n - x)!} p^x(1 - p)^{n-x}$$

where

$$n = 10, \quad p = .2, \quad \text{and } x = 0$$

Hence,

$$P(X = 0) = \frac{10!}{0!(10 - 0)!} (.2)^0(1 - .2)^{10-0}$$

The combinatorial part of the formula is $\dfrac{10!}{0!10!}$ which is 1. This is the number of ways to get 0 correct and 10 incorrect answers. Obviously, there is only one way to produce $X = 0$. And because $(.2)^0 = 1$,

$$P(X = 0) = 1(1)(.8)^{10}$$

$$= .1074$$

b The probability of two correct answers is computed similarly by substituting $n = 10$, $p = .2$, and $x = 2$.

$$P(X = x) = \frac{n!}{x!(n! - x)!} p^x(1 - p)^{n - x}$$

$$P(X = 2) = \frac{10!}{2!(10 - 2)!} (.2)^2(1 - .2)^{10 - 2}$$

$$= \frac{(10)(9)(8)(7)(6)(5)(4)(3)(2)(1)}{(2)(1)(8)(7)(6)(5)(4)(3)(2)(1)} (.04)(.1678)$$

$$= 45(.006711)$$

$$= .3020$$

In this calculation, we discovered that there are 45 ways to get exactly two correct and eight incorrect answers, and that each such outcome has probability .006711. Multiplying the two numbers produces a probability of .3020.

CUMULATIVE PROBABILITY

The formula of the binomial distribution allows us to determine the probability that X equals individual values. In Example 7.9, the values of interest were 0 and 2. There are many circumstances where we wish to find the probability that a random variable is less than or equal to a value. That is, we want to determine $P(X \leq x)$. Such a probability is called a **cumulative probability**.

EXAMPLE 7.10

Find the probability that Pat fails the quiz. A mark is considered a failure if it is less than 50%.

SOLUTION   In this quiz, a mark of less than 5 is a failure. Because the marks must be integers, a mark of 4 or less is a failure. We wish to determine $P(X \leq 4)$.

$$P(X \leq 4) = p(0) + p(1) + p(2) + p(3) + p(4)$$

From Example 7.9, we know $p(0) = .1074$ and $p(2) = .3020$. Using the binomial formula, we find $p(1) = .2684$, $p(3) = .2013$, and $p(4) = .0881$. Thus

$$P(X \leq 4) = .1074 + .2684 + .3020 + .2013 + .0881 = .9672$$

There is a 96.72% probability that Pat will fail the quiz by guessing the answer for each question.

BINOMIAL TABLE

There is another way to determine binomial probabilities. Table 1 in Appendix B provides cumulative binomial probabilities for selected values of n and p. We can use this table to answer the question in Example 7.10, where we need $P(X \leq 4)$. Refer to Table 1, find $n = 10$, and in that table find $p = .20$. The values in that column are $P(X \leq k)$ for $k = 0, 1, 2, \ldots , 10$, which are shown in Table 7.2.

Table 7.2 Cumulative Binomial Probabilities with $n = 10$ and $p = .2$

k	$P(X \leq k)$
0	.107
1	.376
2	.678
3	.879
4	.967
5	.994
6	.999
7	1.000
8	1.000
9	1.000
10	1.000

The first cumulative probability is $P(X \leq 0)$, which is $p(0) = .107$. The probability we need for Example 7.10 is $P(X \leq 4) = .967$, which is the same value we obtained manually using four decimal places.

We can use the table and the complement rule to determine probabilities of the type $P(X \geq x)$. For example, to find the probability that Pat will pass the quiz, we note that

$$P(X \leq 4) + P(X \geq 5) = 1$$

Thus,

$$P(X \geq 5) = 1 - P(X \leq 4) = 1 - .967 = .033$$

USING TABLE 1 TO FIND THE BINOMIAL PROBABILITY P(X ≥ x)

$$P(X \geq x) = 1 - P(X \leq [x - 1])$$

The table is also useful in determining the probability of an individual value of X. For example, to find the probability that Pat will get exactly two right answers we note that

$$P(X \leq 2) = p(0) + p(1) + p(2)$$

and

$$P(X \leq 1) = p(0) + p(1)$$

The difference between these two cumulative probabilities is $p(2)$. Thus

$$p(2) = P(X \leq 2) - P(X \leq 1) = .678 - .376 = .302$$

USING TABLE 1 TO FIND THE BINOMIAL PROBABILITY P(X = x)

$$p(x) = P(X \leq x) - P(X \leq [x - 1])$$

USING THE COMPUTER

 ### EXCEL

We can employ Excel to compute cumulative probabilities and the probability of individual values of a binomial random variable.

COMMANDS

1. Click f_x, **Function category: Statistical**, and **Function name: BINOMDIST**. Click **OK**.
2. Type the value of x (**Number_s**), the number of trials, n (**Trials**), the probability of success, p (**Probability_s**), and **true** (**Cumulative**) to yield a cumulative probability or **false** for an individual probability. The probability appears on the right side of the dialog box. Clicking **OK** will print the probability in the active cell.

 ### MINITAB

COMMANDS

1. Click **Calc**, **Probability Distributions**, and **Binomial....**
2. Select either **Probability** or **Cumulative probability**.
3. Specify the **Number of trials** and the **Probability of success**.
4. If you wish to make a probability statement about one value of x, specify **Input constant** and type the value of x. Click **OK**.
5. If you wish to make probability statements about several values of x from the same binomial distribution, type the values of x into a column before clicking **Calc**. At step 4 specify **Input column**, type the name of the column, and click **OK**.

MEAN AND VARIANCE OF A BINOMIAL DISTRIBUTION

Statisticians have developed general formulas for the mean, variance, and standard deviation of a binomial random variable. They are

$$\mu = np$$

$$\sigma^2 = np(1-p)$$

$$\sigma = \sqrt{np(1-p)}$$

EXAMPLE 7.11

Suppose that a professor has a class full of students like Pat (a nightmare!). What is the mean mark? What is the standard deviation?

SOLUTION The mean mark for a class of Pat Statsduds is

$$\mu = np = 10(.2) = 2$$

The standard deviation is

$$\sigma = \sqrt{np(1-p)} = \sqrt{10(.2)(1-.2)} = 1.26$$

EXERCISES

7.81 Given a binomial random variable with $n = 10$ and $p = .3$. Use the formula to find the following probabilities.
  a $P(X = 3)$
  b $P(X = 5)$
  c $P(X = 8)$

7.82 Repeat Exercise 7.81 using Table 1 in Appendix B.

7.83 Repeat Exercise 7.81 using Excel or Minitab.

7.84 X is a binomial random variable with $n = 5$ and $p = .4$. Use the formula to find the following probabilities.
  a $P(X = 0)$
  b $P(X = 2)$
  c $P(X \leq 3)$
  d $P(X \geq 2)$

7.85 Repeat Exercise 7.84 using Table 1 in Appendix B.

7.86 Repeat Exercise 7.84 using Excel or Minitab.

7.87 X is a binomial random variable with $n = 25$ and $p = .7$. Use Table 1 to find the following.
  a $P(X = 18)$
  b $P(X = 15)$
  c $P(X \leq 20)$
  d $P(X \geq 16)$

7.88 Repeat Exercise 7.87 using Excel or Minitab.

7.89 X is a binomial random variable with $n = 100$ and $p = .22$. Use Excel or Minitab to find the following.
  a $P(X = 24)$
  b $P(X \leq 25)$
  d $P(X \geq 20)$

7.90 A sign on the gas pumps of a chain of gasoline stations encourages customers to have their oil checked, claiming that one out of four cars needs to have oil added. If this is true, what is the probability of the following events?
  a One out of the next four cars needs oil
  b Two out of the next eight cars need oil
  c 10 out of the next 40 cars need oil

7.91 The probability of winning a game of craps (a dice-throwing game played in casinos) is 244/495.
  a What is the probability of winning 5 or more times in 10 games?
  b What is the expected number of wins in 100 games?

7.92 In the game of blackjack as played in casinos in Las Vegas, Atlantic City, Niagara Falls, as well as many other cities, the dealer has the advantage. Most players do not play very well. As a result, the probability that the average player wins a hand is about 45%. Find the probability that an average player wins
  a twice in 5 hands.
  b 10 or more times in 25 hands.

7.93 There are several books that teach blackjack players the "basic strategy," which increases the probability of winning any hand to 50%. Repeat Exercise 7.92 assuming the player plays the basic strategy.

7.94 The best way of winning at blackjack is to "case the deck," which involves counting tens, non-tens, and aces. For card counters, the probability of winning a hand may increase to 52%. Repeat Exercise 7.92 for a card counter.

7.95 In the game of roulette, a steel ball is rolled onto a wheel that contains 18 red, 18 black, and 2 green slots. If the ball is rolled 25 times, find the probabilities of the following events.
  a The ball falls into the green slots two or more times
  b The ball does not fall onto any green slots
  c The ball falls into black slots 15 or more times
  d The ball falls into red slots 10 or fewer times

7.96 The leading brand of dishwasher detergent has a 30% market share. A sample of 25 dishwasher detergent customers was taken. What is the probability that ten or fewer customers chose the leading brand?

7.97 A certain type of tomato seed germinates 90% of the time. A backyard farmer planted 25 seeds.
  a What is the probability that exactly 20 germinate?
  b What is the probability that 20 or more germinate?
  c What is the probability that 24 or fewer germinate?
  d What is the expected number of seeds that germinate?

7.98 According to the American Academy of Cosmetic Dentistry, 75% of adults believe that an unattractive smile hurts career success. Suppose that 25 adults are randomly selected. What is the probability that 15 or more of them would agree with the claim?

7.99 According to a Gallup Poll conducted March 5–7, 2001, 52% of American adults think that protecting the environment should be given priority over developing U.S. energy supplies, 36% think that developing energy supplies is more important, and 6% believe the two are equally important. The rest had no opinion. Suppose that a sample of 100 American adults is quizzed on the subject. What is the probability of the following events?
  a 50 or more think that protecting the environment should be given priority
  b 30 or fewer think that developing energy supplies is more important
  c 5 or fewer have no opinion

7.100 A student majoring in accounting is trying to decide on the number of firms to which he should apply. Given his work experience and grades, he can expect to receive a job offer from 70% of the firms to which he applies. The student decides to apply to only four firms. What is the probability that he receives no job offers?

7.101   In a *Bon Appetit* poll, 38% of people said that chocolate was their favorite flavor of ice cream. A sample of 20 people was asked to name their favorite flavor of ice cream. What is the probability that half or more of them prefer chocolate?

7.102   In the United States, voters who are neither Democrat nor Republican are called Independent. It is believed that 10% of all voters are Independent. A survey asked 25 people to identify themselves as Democrat, Republican, or Independent.
   a What is the probability that none of the people are Independent?
   b What is the probability that fewer than five people are Independent?
   c What is the probability that more than two people are Independent?

7.103   Most Internet service providers (ISPs) attempt to provide a large enough service so that customers seldom encounter a busy signal. Suppose that the customers of one ISP encounter busy signals 8% of the time.

During the week a customer of this ISP called 25 times. What is the probability that she did not encounter any busy signals?

7.104   Major software manufacturers offer a help line that allows customers to call and receive assistance in solving their problems. However, because of the volume of calls, customers frequently are put on hold. One software manufacturer claims that only 20% of callers are put on hold. Suppose that 100 customers call. What is the probability that more than 40 of them are put on hold?

7.105   A study of drivers reveals that, when lost, 45% will stop and ask for directions, 30% will consult a map, and 25% will continue driving until the location has been determined. Suppose that a sample of 200 drivers was asked to report what they do when lost. Find the following probabilities.
   a At least 100 stop and ask directions
   b At most 55 continue driving
   c Between 50 and 75 (inclusive) consult a map

7.7 POISSON DISTRIBUTION

Another useful discrete probability distribution is the **Poisson distribution**, named after its French creator. Like the binomial random variable, the **Poisson random variable** is the number of occurrences of events, which we'll continue to call successes. The difference between the two random variables is that a binomial random variable is the number of successes in a set number of trials, whereas a Poisson random variable is the number of successes in an interval of time or specific region of space. Here are several examples of Poisson random variables.

1. The number of cars arriving at a service station in 1 hour. (The interval of time is 1 hour.)

2. The number of flaws in a bolt of cloth. (The specific region is a bolt of cloth.)

3. The number of accidents in 1 day on a particular stretch of highway. (The interval is defined by both time, 1 day, and space, the particular stretch of highway.)

The *Poisson experiment* is described below.

POISSON EXPERIMENT

A **Poisson experiment** is characterized by the following properties.

1. The number of successes that occur in any interval is independent of the number of successes that occur in any other interval.

2. The probability of a success in an interval is the same for all equal-sized intervals.

3. The probability of a success is proportional to the size of the interval.

4. The probability of more than one success in an interval approaches 0 as the interval becomes smaller.

As a general rule, a Poisson random variable is the number of occurrences of a *relatively rare* event that occurs *randomly* and *independently*. The number of hits on an active Web site is not a Poisson random variable, because the hits are not rare. The number of people arriving at a restaurant is not Poisson, because restaurant patrons usually arrive in groups, which violates the independence property.

POISSON RANDOM VARIABLE

The **Poisson random variable** is the number of successes that occur in a period of time or an interval of space in a Poisson experiment.

There are several ways to derive the probability distribution of a Poisson random variable. However, all are beyond the mathematical level of this book. We simply provide the formula and illustrate how it is used.

POISSON PROBABILITY DISTRIBUTION

If X is a Poisson random variable, the probability that it assumes a value of x is

$$P(X = x) = p(x) = \frac{e^{-\mu}\mu^x}{x!} \quad \text{for } x = 0, 1, 2, \ldots$$

where μ is the mean number of successes in the interval or region and e is the base of the natural logarithm (approximately 2.71828).

EXAMPLE 7.12

A statistics instructor has observed that the number of typographical errors in new editions of textbooks varies considerably from book to book. After some analysis, he concludes that the number of errors is Poisson distributed with a mean of 1.5 per 100 pages. The instructor randomly selects 100 pages of a new book. What is the probability that there are no typos?

SOLUTION We want to determine the probability that a Poisson random variable with a mean of 1.5 is equal to 0. Thus, we substitute $x = 0$ and $\mu = 1.5$ into the formula for the Poisson distribution.

$$P(X = 0) = \frac{e^{-\mu}\mu^x}{x!} = \frac{e^{-1.5}1.5^0}{0!} = \frac{(2.71828)^{-1.5}(1)}{1} = .2231$$

The probability that in the 100 pages selected there are no errors is .2231.

Notice that in Example 7.12 we wanted to find the probability of 0 typos in *100 pages* given a mean of 1.5 typos in *100 pages*. The next example illustrates how we calculate the probability of events where the intervals or regions do not match.

EXAMPLE 7.13

Refer to Example 7.12. Suppose that the instructor has just received a copy of a new statistics book. He notices that there are 400 pages.

a What is the probability that there are no typos?

b What is the probability that there are five or fewer typos?

SOLUTION The specific region that we're interested in is 400 pages. To calculate Poisson probabilities associated with this region, we need to determine the mean number of typos per 400 pages. Because the mean is specified as 1.5 per 100 pages, we multiply this figure by 4 to convert to 400 pages. Thus $\mu = 6$ typos per 400 pages.

a The probability of no typos is

$$P(X = 0) = \frac{e^{-\mu}\mu^x}{x!}$$

$$= \frac{e^{-6}6^0}{0!}$$

$$= \frac{(2.71828)^{-6}(1)}{1}$$

$$= .002479$$

b We want to determine the probability that a Poisson random variable with a mean of 6 is 5 or less. That is, we want to calculate

$$P(X \le 5) = p(0) + p(1) + p(2) + p(3) + p(4) + p(5)$$

From part **a**, we know $p(0) = .002479$. Substituting $x = 1, 2, 3, 4,$ and 5 into

$$p(x) = \frac{e^{-\mu}\mu^x}{x!}$$

we find $p(1) = .01487$, $p(2) = .04462$, $p(3) = .08924$, $p(4) = .1339$, and $p(5) = .1606$.

Thus,

$$P(X \le 5) = .002479 + .01487 + .04462 + .08924 + .1339 + .1606$$

$$= .4457$$

The probability of observing 5 or fewer typos in this book is .4457.

POISSON TABLE

As was the case with the binomial distribution, a table is available that makes it easier to compute Poisson probabilities of individual values of X as well as cumulative and related probabilities.

Table 2 in Appendix B provides cumulative Poisson probabilities for selected values of μ. This table makes it easy to find cumulative probabilities like that in Example 7.13, part 2, where we found $P(X \leq 5)$. To do so, find $\mu = 6$ in Table 2. The values in that column are $P(X \leq k)$ for $k = 0, 1, 2, \ldots$, which are shown in Table 7.3.

Table 7.3 Cumulative Poisson Probabilities for $\mu = 6$

k	$P(X \leq k)$
0	.002
1	.017
2	.062
3	.151
4	.285
5	.446
6	.606
7	.744
8	.847
9	.916
10	.957
11	.980
12	.991
13	.996
14	.999
15	.999
16	1.000

Theoretically, a Poisson random variable has no upper limit. The table provides cumulative probabilities until the sum is 1.000 (using three decimal places).

The first cumulative probability is $P(X \leq 0)$, which is $p(0) = .002$. The probability we need for Example 7.13, part 2, is $P(X \leq 5) = .446$, which is the same value (using three decimal places) we obtained manually.

Like Table 1 for binomial probabilities, Table 2 can be used to determine probabilities of the type $P(X \geq x)$. For example, to find the probability that in Example 7.13 there are 6 or more typos, we note that $P(X \leq 5) + P(X \geq 6) = 1$. Thus,

$$P(X \geq 6) = 1 - P(X \leq 5) = 1 - .446 = .554$$

USING TABLE 2 TO FIND THE POISSON PROBABILITY P(X ≥ x)

$$P(X \geq x) = 1 - P(X \leq [x - 1])$$

We can also use the table to determine the probability of an individual value of X. For example, to find the probability that the book contains exactly 10 typos, we note that

$$P(X \leq 10) = p(0) + p(1) + \cdots + p(9) + p(10)$$

and

$$P(X \leq 9) = p(0) + p(1) + \cdots + p(9)$$

The difference between these two cumulative probabilities is p(10). Thus

$$p(10) = P(X \leq 10) - P(X \leq 9) = .957 - .916 = .041$$

USING TABLE 2 TO FIND THE POISSON PROBABILITY P(X = x)

$$p(x) = P(X \leq x) - P(X \leq [x-1])$$

USING THE COMPUTER

EXCEL

We can employ Excel to compute cumulative probabilities and the probability of individual values of a Poisson random variable.

COMMANDS

1. Click f_x, **Function category: Statistical**, and **Function name: POISSON**. Click **OK**.
2. Type the value of x (**X**), the mean (**Mean**), and **true** (**Cumulative**) to yield a cumulative probability or **false** for an individual probability. The probability appears on the right side of the dialog box. Clicking **OK** will print the probability in the active cell.

MINITAB

COMMANDS

1. Click **Calc**, **Probability Distributions**, and **Poisson....**
2. Select either **Probability** or **Cumulative probability**.
3. Specify the **Mean**.
4. If you wish to make a probability statement about one value of x, specify **Input constant** and type the value of x. Click **OK**.
5. If you wish to make probability statements about several values of x from the same Poisson distribution, type the values of x into a column before clicking **Calc**. At step 4 specify **Input column**, type the name of the column, and click **OK**.

EXERCISES

7.106 Given a Poisson random variable with $\mu = 2$. Use the formula to find the following probabilities.
   a $P(X = 0)$
   b $P(X = 3)$
   c $P(X = 5)$

7.107 Repeat Exercise 7.106 using Table 2 in Appendix B.

7.108 Repeat Exercise 7.106 using Excel or Minitab.

7.109 X is a Poisson random variable with $\mu = .5$. Use the formula to determine the following probabilities.
   a $P(X = 0)$
   b $P(X = 1)$
   c $P(X = 2)$

7.110 Repeat Exercise 7.109 using Table 2 in Appendix B.

7.111 Repeat Exercise 7.109 using Excel or Minitab.

7.112 The number of accidents that occur at a busy intersection is Poisson distributed with a mean of 3.5 per week. Find the probability of the following events.
   a No accidents in one week
   b Five or more accidents in a week
   c One accident today

7.113 Snowfalls occur randomly and independently over the course of winter in a Minnesota city. The average is one snowfall every 3 days.
   a What is the probability of five snowfalls in 2 weeks?
   b Find the probability of a snowfall today.

7.114 The number of students who seek assistance with their statistics assignments is Poisson distributed with a mean of two per day.
  a What is the probability that no students seek assistance tomorrow?
  b Find the probability that 10 students seek assistance in a week (7 days).

7.115 Hits on a personal Web site occur quite infrequently. They occur randomly and independently with an average of five per week.
  a Find the probability that the site gets 10 or more hits in a week.
  b Determine the probability that the site gets 20 or more hits in 2 weeks.

7.116 The author's computer has a variety of software including Office XP as well as several other packages. Additionally, there are numerous Word and Excel files. As a result, the computer crashes on average once per week. If the number of crashes is Poisson distributed, find the probability

that the computer will not crash at all over the next 2 weeks.

7.117 The number of bank robberies that occur in a large North American city is Poisson distributed with a mean of 1.8 per day. Find the probabilities of the following events.
  a Three or more bank robberies in a day
  b Between 10 and 15 (inclusive) robberies during a 5-day period

7.118 Flaws in a carpet tend to occur randomly and independently at a rate of one every 200 square feet. What is the probability that a carpet that is 8 feet by 10 feet contains no flaws?

7.119 Complaints about an Internet brokerage firm occur at a rate of five per day. The number of complaints appears to be Poisson distributed.
  a Find the probability that the firm receives 10 or more complaints in a day.
  b Find the probability that the firm receives 25 or more complaints in a 5-day period.

APPLICATIONS IN OPERATIONS MANAGEMENT: *WAITING LINES*

Everyone is familiar with waiting lines. We wait in line at banks, groceries, and fast-food restaurants. There are also waiting lines in firms where trucks wait to load and unload and on assembly lines where stations wait for new subassemblies. Management scientists have developed mathematical models that allow managers to determine the operating characteristics of waiting lines. Some of the operating characteristics are

  The probability that there are no units in the system
  The average number of units in the waiting line
  The average time a unit spends in the waiting line
  The probability that an arriving unit must wait for service

The Poisson probability distribution is used extensively in waiting line (also called *queuing*) models. Many models

assume that the arrival of units for service is Poisson distributed with a specific value of μ. In the next chapter we will discuss the distribution of service times. Exercises 7.120–7.122 require the calculation of the probability of a number of arrivals.

7.120 The number of trucks crossing at the Ambassador Bridge connecting Detroit, Michigan, and Windsor, Ontario is Poisson distributed with a mean of 1.5 per minute.
  a What is the probability that in any 1-minute time span two or more trucks will cross the bridge?
  b What is the probability that fewer than four trucks will cross the bridge over the next 4 minutes?

7.121 Cars arriving for gasoline at a Shell station follow a Poisson distribution with a mean of 5 per hour.

  a Determine the probability that over the next hour only one car will arrive.
  b Compute the probability that in the next 3 hours more than 20 cars will arrive.

7.122 The number of users of an automatic banking machine is Poisson distributed. The mean number of users per 5-minute interval is 1.5. Find the probability of the following events.
  a No users in the next 5 minutes
  b 5 or fewer users in the next 15 minutes
  c 3 or more users in the next 10 minutes

7.8 SUMMARY

There are two types of random variable. A **discrete random variable** is one whose values are countable. A **continuous random variable** can assume an uncountable number of values. In this chapter we discussed discrete random variables and their **probability distributions**. We defined the **expected value**, **variance**, and **standard deviation** of a population represented by a discrete probability distribution. Also introduced in this chapter were bivariate discrete distributions, on which an important application in finance was based. Finally, the two most important discrete distributions, the **binomial** and the **Poisson**, were presented.

IMPORTANT TERMS

Random variable 184
Discrete random variable 185
Continuous random variable 185
Probability distribution 185
Expected value 190
Variance 190
Standard deviation 191
Bivariate distribution 194
Univariate distribution 194
Binomial experiment 207
Binomial random variable 207
Binomial probability distribution 209
Cumulative probability 210
Poisson experiment 214
Poisson random variable 214
Poisson probability distribution 215

SYMBOLS

Symbol	Pronounced	Represents
$\displaystyle\sum_{\text{all } x} x$	Sum of x for all values of x	Summation
C_x^n	n-choose-x	Number of combinations
$n!$	n-factorial	$n(n-1)(n-2)\cdots(3)(2)(1)$
e		2.71828...

FORMULAS

Expected value (mean)

$$E(X) = \mu = \sum_{\text{all } x} xp(x)$$

Variance

$$V(x) = \sigma^2 = \sum_{\text{all } x} (x - \mu)^2 \, p(x)$$

Standard deviation

$$\sigma = \sqrt{\sigma^2}$$

Covariance

$$\text{COV}(X, Y) = \sum (x - \mu_x)(y - \mu_y)p(x, y)$$

Coefficient of correlation

$$\rho = \frac{\text{COV}(X, Y)}{\sigma_x \sigma_y}$$

Laws of expected value

1. $E(c) = c$
2. $E(X + c) = E(X) + c$
3. $E(cX) = cE(X)$

Laws of variance

1. $V(c) = 0$
2. $V(X + c) = V(X)$
3. $V(cX) = c^2 V(X)$

Laws of expected value and variance of the sum of two variables

1. $E(X + Y) = E(X) + E(Y)$
2. $V(X + Y) = V(X) + V(Y) + 2\text{COV}(X, Y)$

Laws of expected value and variance of the sum of more than two independent variables

1. $E\left(\sum_{i=1}^{k} X_i\right) = \sum_{i=1}^{k} E(X_i)$

2. $V\left(\sum_{i=1}^{k} X_i\right) = \sum_{i=1}^{k} V(X_i)$

Mean and variance of a portfolio of two stocks

$$E(R_p) = w_1 E(R_1) + w_2 E(R_2)$$

$$V(R_p) = w_1^2 V(R_1) + w_2^2 V(R_2) + 2w_1 w_2 \text{COV}(R_1, R_2)$$

$$= w_1^2 \sigma_1^2 + w_2^2 \sigma_2^2 + 2w_1 w_2 \rho \sigma_1 \sigma_2$$

Mean and variance of a portfolio of k stocks

$$E(R_p) = \sum_{i=1}^{k} w_i E(R_i)$$

$$V(R_p) = \sum_{i=1}^{k} w_i^2 \sigma_i^2 + 2 \sum_{i=1}^{k} \sum_{j=i+1}^{k} w_i w_j \text{COV}(R_i, R_j)$$

Binomial probability

$$P(X = x) = \frac{n!}{x!(n - x)!} p^x (1 - p)^{n - x}$$

$$\mu = np$$

$$\sigma^2 = np(1 - p)$$

$$\sigma = \sqrt{np(1 - p)}$$

Poisson probability

$$P(X = x) = \frac{e^{-\mu} \mu^x}{x!}$$

COMPUTER INSTRUCTIONS

Probability Distribution	Excel	Minitab
Binomial	212	213
Poisson	218	218

REFERENCES

Benninga, Simon, and Benjamin Czaczkes, *Financial Modeling*, 2nd edition. Cambridge, MA: MIT Press, 2000.

Bodie, Zvi, Alex Kane, and Alan Marcus, *Investments*. Homewood, IL: Irwin 1989.

Cox, J., and M. Rubinstein, *Option Pricing: A Simplified Approach*. Englewood Cliffs, NJ: Prentice Hall, 1985.

Gelman, Andrew, J. B. Carlin, H. S. Stern, and D. B. Rubin, *Bayesian Data Analysis*. New York: Chapman & Hall, 1995.

Hull, J., *Options, Futures and Other Derivative Securities*, 2nd edition. Englewood Cliffs, NJ: Prentice Hall, 1993.

Luenberger, David, *Investment Science*. Oxford: Oxford University Press, 1997.

Markowitz, Harry M., "Portfolio Selection," *Journal of Finance*, Vol. VII, No. 1, 77–91, 1952.

Ross, Sheldon M., *A First Course in Probability*, 5th edition. Englewood Cliffs, NJ: Prentice Hall, 1997.

Ross, Sheldon M., *Introduction to Probability Models*, 4th edition. New York: Academic Press, 1989.

Stampfli, Joseph, and Victor Goodman, *The Mathematics of Finance: Modeling and Hedging*. Pacific Grove, CA: Brooks/Cole, 2001.

Winston, Wayne, L., *Financial Models Using Simulation and Optimization*. Newfield, NY: Palisade Corp, 1998.

Winston, Wayne L., and S. Christian Albright, *Practical Management Science: Spreadsheet Modeling and Applications*, 2nd edition. Pacific Grove, CA: Duxbury, 2001.

CHAPTER REVIEW EXERCISES

7.123 In 2000, Northwest Airlines boasted that 77.4% of its flights were on time. (*Source:* Department of Transportation) If we select five Northwest flights at random, what is the probability that all five are on time?

7.124 The final exam in a one-term statistics course is taken in the December exam period. Students who are sick or have other legitimate reasons for missing the exam are allowed to write a deferred exam scheduled for the first week in January. A statistics professor has observed that only 2% of all students legitimately miss the December final exam. Suppose that the professor has 40 students registered this term.
  a How many students can the professor expect to miss the December exam?
  b What is the probability that the professor will not have to create a deferred exam?

7.125 The number of magazine subscriptions per household is represented by the following probability distribution.

Magazine subscriptions per household 0 1 2 3 4
Probability   .48 .35 .08 .05 .04
  a Calculate the mean number of magazine subscriptions per household.
  b Find the standard deviation.

7.126 The number of arrivals at a car wash is Poisson distributed with a mean of eight per hour.
  a What is the probability that 10 cars will arrive in the next hour?
  b What is the probability that more than 5 cars will arrive in the next hour?
  c What is the probability that fewer than 12 cars will arrive in the next hour?

7.127 The percentage of customers who enter a restaurant and ask to be seated in a smoking section is 15%. Suppose that 100 people enter the restaurant.
  a What is the expected number of people who request a smoking table?
  b What is the standard deviation of the number of requests for a smoking table?
  c What is the probability that 20 or more people request a smoking table?

7.128 Lotteries are an important source for various governments around the world. However, the availability of lotteries and other forms of gambling have created a social problem—gambling addicts. A critic of government-controlled gambling contends that 30% of people who regularly buy lottery tickets are gambling addicts. If we randomly select 10 people among those who report that they regularly buy lottery tickets, what is the probability that more than five of them are addicts?

7.129 The number of 60-minute cassettes that can be played on a Walkman before the battery expires is a variable. The distribution is shown below.

Number of 60-minute cassettes on a Walkman before battery expires	5	6	7	8	9	10
Probability	.05	.16	.41	.27	.07	.04

  a Calculate the mean number of cassettes.

  b Find the standard deviation.

7.130 An auditor is preparing for a physical count of inventory as a means of verifying its value. Items counted are reconciled with a list prepared by the storeroom supervisor. In one particular firm, 20% of the items counted cannot be reconciled without reviewing invoices. The auditor selects 10 items. Find the probability that 6 or more items cannot be reconciled.

7.131 Shutouts in the National Hockey League occur randomly and independently at a rate of 1 every 20 games. Calculate the probability of the following events.

  a 2 shutouts in the next 10 games

  b 25 shutouts in 400 games

  c a shutout in tonight's game

7.132 Most Miami Beach restaurants offer "early-bird" specials. These are lower-priced meals that are available only from 4:00 to 6:00. However, not all customers who arrive between 4:00 and 6:00 order the special. In fact, only 70% do.

  a Find the probability that of 80 customers between 4:00 and 6:00, more than 65 order the special.

  b What is the expected number of customers who order the special?

  c What is the standard deviation?

7.133 Psychologists generally believe that women who work and have children lead stressful lives. To investigate, a research project was undertaken. A random sample of working mothers was selected. Respondents were asked how many times in the past week they experienced depression. After examining the results, the researchers produced the probability distribution below. The random variable X is the number of times per week working mothers suffer bouts of depression.

x	0	1	2	3	4
$p(x)$	.35	.25	.18	.13	.09

Find the mean and standard deviation of this distribution.

7.134 Researchers at the University of Pennsylvania School of Medicine theorized that children under 2 years old who sleep in rooms with the light on have a 40% probability of becoming myopic by age 16. Suppose that researchers found 25 children who slept with the light on before they were 2.

  a What is the probability that 10 of them will become myopic before the age of 16?

  b What is the probability that fewer than five of them will become myopic before the age of 16?

  c What is the probability that more than 15 of them will become myopic before the age of 16?

7.135 A pharmaceutical researcher working on a cure for baldness noticed that middle-aged men who are balding at the crown of their head have a 45% probability of suffering a heart attack over the next decade. In a sample of 100 middle-aged balding men, what are the following probabilities?

  a More than 50 will suffer a heart attack in the next decade

  b Fewer that 44 will suffer a heart attack in the next decade

  c Exactly 45 will suffer a heart attack in the next decade

7.136 Advertising researchers have developed a theory that states that commercials that appear in violent television shows are less likely to be remembered and thus will be less effective. After examining samples of viewers who watch violent and nonviolent programs and asking them a series of five questions about the commercials, the researchers produced the following probability distributions of the number of correct answers.

Viewers of violent shows

x	0	1	2	3	4	5
$p(x)$	.36	.22	.20	.09	.08	.05

Viewers of nonviolent shows

x	0	1	2	3	4	5
$p(x)$	.15	.18	.23	.26	.10	.08

  a Calculate the mean and standard deviation of the number of correct answers among viewers of violent television programs.

  b Calculate the mean and standard deviation of the number of correct answers among viewers of nonviolent television programs.

  c What can you conclude from parts **a** and **b**?

7.137 According to the U.S. census, one-third of all businesses are owned by women. If we select 25 businesses at random, what is the probability that 10 or more of them are owned by women?

7.138 It is recommended that women over 40 have a mammogram annually. A recent report indicated that if a woman has annual mammograms over a 10-year period, there is a 60% probability that there will be at least one false-positive result. (A false-positive mammogram test result is one that indicates the presence of cancer when in fact there is no cancer.) If the annual test results are independent, what is the probability that in any one year a mammogram will produce a false-positive result? (*Hint:* Find the value of p such that the probability that a binomial random variable with $n = 10$ is greater than or equal to 1 is .60.)

7.139 In a recent election the mayor received 60% of the vote. Last week a survey was undertaken that asked 100 people whether they would vote for the mayor. Assuming that her popularity has not changed, what is the probability that more than 50 people in the sample would vote for the mayor?

7.140 When Earth traveled through the storm of meteorites trailing the comet Tempel-Tuttle on November 17, 1998, the storm was 1,000 times as intense as the average meteor storm. Before the comet arrived, telecommunication companies worried about the potential damage that might be inflicted on the approximately 650 satellites in orbit. It was estimated that each satellite had a 1% chance of being hit, causing damage to the satellite's electronic system. One company had five satellites in orbit at the time. Determine the probability distribution of the number of the company's satellites that would be damaged.

✦ CASE 7.1
TO BUNT OR NOT TO BUNT, THAT IS THE QUESTION—PART II

In Case 6.3, we presented the probabilities of scoring at least one run and asked you to determine whether the manager should signal for the batter to sacrifice bunt. The decision was made on the basis of comparing the probability of scoring at least one run when the manager signaled for the bunt and when he signaled the batter to swing away. Another factor that should be incorporated into the decision is the number of runs the manager expects his team to score. In the same article referred to in Case 6.3, the author also computed the expected number of runs scored for each situation. Table 1 lists the expected number of runs in situations that are defined by the number of outs and the bases occupied.

Table 1 Expected Number of Runs Scored

Bases Occupied	0 Outs	1 Out	2 Outs
Bases empty	.49	.27	.10
First base	.85	.52	.23
Second base	1.06	.69	.34
Third base	1.21	.82	.38
First base and second base	1.46	1.00	.48
First base and third base	1.65	1.10	.51
Second base and third base	1.94	1.50	.62
Bases loaded	2.31	1.62	.82

Assume that the manager wishes to score as many runs as possible. Using the same probabilities of the four outcomes of a bunt listed in Case 6.3, determine whether the manager should signal the batter to sacrifice bunt.

8 CONTINUOUS PROBABILITY DISTRIBUTIONS

MINIMUM GMAT SCORE TO ENTER EXECUTIVE MBA PROGRAM

A university has just approved a new Executive MBA Program. The new director believes that in order to maintain the prestigious image of the business school, the new program must be seen as having high standards. Accordingly, the Faculty Council decides that one of the entrance requirements will be that applicants must score in the top 1% of GMAT (Graduate Management Admission Test) scores. The director knows that GMAT scores are normally distributed with a mean of 490 and a standard deviation of 61. The only thing she doesn't know is what the minimum GMAT score for admission should be. After introducing the normal distribution, we will return to this question and answer it. (See page 243.)

8.1 INTRODUCTION

This chapter completes our presentation of probability by introducing continuous random variables and their distributions. Recall from Section 7.6 that the binomial distribution allows us to determine the probability of the number of times one particular value of a nominal variable (which we call a success) occurs. In this way we connect the population represented by the probability distribution with a sample of nominal data. In this chapter we introduce continuous probability distributions, which are used to calculate the probability associated with an interval variable. By doing so, we develop the link between a population and a sample of interval data.

Section 8.2 introduces probability density functions and demonstrates with the uniform density function how probability is calculated. In Section 8.3 we focus on the normal distribution, one of the most important distributions because of its role in the development of statistical inference. Section 8.4 introduces the exponential distribution, a distribution that has proven to be useful in various management science applications. Finally, in Section 8.5 we introduce three additional continuous distributions. They will be used in statistical inference throughout the book.

8.2 PROBABILITY DENSITY FUNCTIONS

A continuous random variable is one that can assume an uncountable number of values. Because this type of random variable is so different from a discrete variable, we need to treat it completely differently. First, we cannot list the possible values because there is an infinite number of them. Second, because there is an infinite number of values, the probability of each individual value is virtually 0. Consequently, we can only determine the probability of a range of values. To illustrate how this is done, consider the histogram we created for the long-distance telephone bills (Example 2.1), which is depicted in Figure 8.1.

Figure 8.1
Histogram for Example 2.1

We found, for example, that the relative frequency of the interval 15 to 30 was 37/200. Using the relative frequency approach, we estimate that the probability that a randomly selected long-distance bill will fall between $15 and $30 is 37/200 = 18.5%. We can similarly estimate the probabilities of the other intervals in the histogram.

Interval	Relative frequency	Interval	Relative frequency
$0 < X \leq 15$	71/200	$60 < X \leq 75$	10/200
$15 < X \leq 30$	37/200	$75 < X \leq 90$	18/200
$30 < X \leq 45$	13/200	$90 < X \leq 105$	28/200
$45 < X \leq 60$	9/200	$105 < X \leq 120$	14/200

Notice that the sum of the probabilities equals 1. To proceed, we set the values along the vertical axis so that the *area* in all the rectangles together adds to 1. We accomplish this by dividing each relative frequency by the width of the interval, which is 15. The result is a rectangle over each interval whose *area* equals the probability that the random variable will fall into that interval.

To determine probabilities of ranges other than the ones created when we drew the histogram, we apply the same approach. For example, the probability that a long-distance bill will fall between $50 and $80 is equal to the area between 50 and 80, as shown in Figure 8.2.

Figure 8.2
Histogram for Example 2.1: Relative frequencies divided by interval width

The areas in the rectangles are calculated and added together as follows.

Interval	Height of rectangle	Base multiplied by height
$50 < X \leq 60$	$9/(200 \times 15) = .00300$	$(60 - 50) \times .00300 = .030$
$60 < X \leq 75$	$10/(200 \times 15) = .00333$	$(75 - 60) \times .00333 = .050$
$75 < X \leq 80$	$18/(200 \times 15) = .00600$	$(80 - 75) \times .00600 = .030$
		Total $= .110$

We estimate that the probability that a randomly selected long-distance bill falls between $50 and $80 is 11%.

If the histogram is drawn with a large number of small intervals, we can smooth the edges of the rectangles to produce a smooth curve, as shown in Figure 8.3 on page 228. In many cases it is possible to determine a function $f(x)$ that approximates the curve. The function is called a **probability density function**. Its requirements are stated in the box.

REQUIREMENTS FOR A PROBABILITY DENSITY FUNCTION
The following requirements apply to a probability density function $f(x)$ whose range is $a \leq x \leq b$.

1. $f(x) \geq 0$ for all x between a and b.

2. The total area under the curve between a and b is 1.0.

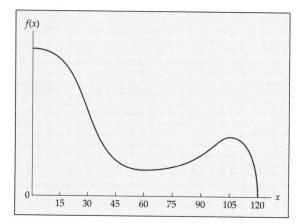

Figure 8.3
Density function for
Example 2.1

Integral calculus can often be used to calculate the area under a curve. Fortunately, the continuous probability distributions that we deal with do not require this mathematical tool to compute probability. The distributions will be either simple or too complex for calculus. Let's start with the simplest continuous distribution.

UNIFORM DISTRIBUTION

To illustrate how we find the area under the curve that describes a probability density function, consider the **uniform probability distribution**, also called the **rectangular probability distribution**.

UNIFORM PROBABILITY DENSITY FUNCTION
The uniform distribution is described by the function

$$f(x) = \frac{1}{b-a} \quad \text{where } a \le x \le b$$

The function is graphed in Figure 8.4. You can see why the distribution is called *rectangular*.

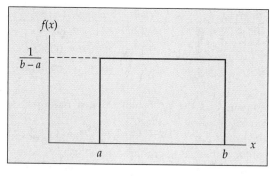

Figure 8.4
Uniform distribution

To calculate the probability of any interval, simply find the area under the curve. For example, to find the probability that X falls between x_1 and x_2, determine the area in the rectangle whose base is $x_2 - x_1$ and whose height is $1/(b - a)$. Figure 8.5 depicts the area we wish to find. As you can see, it is a rectangle and the area of a rectangle is found by multiplying the base times the height.

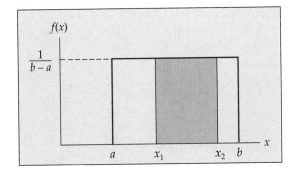

Figure 8.5
$P(x_1 < X < x_2)$

Thus,

$$P(x_1 < X < x_2) = \text{Base} \times \text{Height} = (x_2 - x_1) \times \frac{1}{b - a}$$

EXAMPLE 8.1

The amount of gasoline sold daily at a service station is uniformly distributed with a minimum of 2,000 gallons and a maximum of 5,000 gallons.

a Find the probability that daily sales will fall between 2,500 and 3,000 gallons.
b What is the probability that the service station will sell at least 4,000 gallons?
c What is the probability that the station will sell exactly 2,500 gallons?

SOLUTION   The probability density function is

$$f(x) = \frac{1}{5,000 - 2,000} = \frac{1}{3,000}, \quad 2,000 \le x \le 5,000$$

a The probability that X falls between 2,500 and 3,000 is the area under the curve between 2,500 and 3,000, as depicted in Figure 8.6(a). The area of a rectangle is the base times the height. Thus,

$$P(2,500 \le X \le 3,000) = (3,000 - 2,500) \times \left(\frac{1}{3,000}\right) = .1667$$

b $P(X \ge 4,000) = (5,000 - 4,000) \times \left(\frac{1}{3,000}\right) = .3333$ [See Figure 8.6(b).]

(a) $P(2,500 < X < 3,000)$

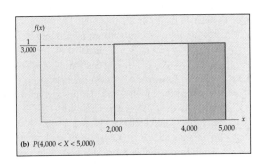

(b) $P(4,000 < X < 5,000)$

Figure 8.6

c $P(X = 2,500) = 0$ Because there is an uncountable infinite number of values of X, the probability of each individual value is 0. Moreover, as you can see from Figure 8.6(c), the area of a line is 0.

Figure 8.6 continued

(c) $P(X = 2,500)$

USING A CONTINUOUS DISTRIBUTION TO APPROXIMATE A DISCRETE DISTRIBUTION

In our definition of discrete and continuous random variables, we distinguish between them by noting whether the number of possible values is countable or uncountable. However, in practice, we frequently use a continuous distribution to approximate a discrete one when the number of values the variable can assume is countable but large. For example, the number of possible values of weekly income is countable. The values of weekly income expressed in dollars are 0, .01, .02, ... Although there is no set upper limit, we can easily identify (and thus, count) all the possible values. Consequently, weekly income is a discrete random variable. However, because it can assume such a large number of values, we prefer to employ a continuous probability distribution to determine the probability associated with such variables. In the next section we introduce the normal distribution, which is often used to describe discrete random variables that can assume a large number of values.

EXERCISES

8.1 Refer to the Barnes exhibit histogram on page 45. Estimate the following probabilities.
a $P(30 < X < 45)$ **b** $P(90 < X < 120)$
c $P(40 < X < 80)$ **d** $P(X > 100)$

8.2 Refer to Example 2.2. Estimate the following from the histogram of the returns on investment A.
a $P(X > 45)$ **b** $P(10 < X < 40)$
c $P(X < 25)$ **d** $P(35 < X < 65)$

8.3 Refer to Example 2.3. From the histogram of the marks in the manual-calculations statistics course, estimate the following probabilities.
a $P(55 < X < 80)$ **b** $P(X > 65)$
c $P(X < 85)$ **d** $P(75 < X < 85)$

8.4 A random variable is uniformly distributed between 5 and 25.
a Draw the density function.

b Find $P(X > 25)$.
c Find $P(10 < X < 15)$.
d Find $P(5.0 < X < 5.1)$.

8.5 A uniformly distributed random variable has minimum and maximum values of 20 and 60, respectively.
a Draw the density function.
b Determine $P(35 < X < 45)$.
c Draw the density function, including the calculation of the probability in part **b**.

8.6 The amount of time it takes for a student to complete a statistics quiz is uniformly distributed between 30 and 60 minutes. One student is selected at random. Find the probability of the following events.
a The student requires more than 55 minutes to complete the quiz

b The student completes the quiz in a time between 30 and 40 minutes

c The student completes the quiz in exactly 37.23 minutes

8.7 Refer to Exercise 8.6. The professor wants to reward (with bonus marks) students who are in the lowest quarter of completion times. What completion time should she use for the cutoff of the awarding of bonus marks?

8.8 Refer to Exercise 8.6. The professor would like to track (and possibly help) students who are in the top 10% of completion times. What completion time should she use?

8.9 The weekly output of a steel mill is a uniformly distributed random variable that lies between 110 and 175 metric tons.

a Compute the probability that the steel mill will produce more than 150 metric tons next week.

b Determine the probability that the steel mill will produce between 120 and 160 metric tons next week.

8.10 Refer to Exercise 8.9. The operations manager labels any week that is in the bottom 20% of production a "bad week." How many metric tons should be used to define a bad week?

8.11 A random variable has the following density function.
$$f(x) = 1 - .5x, \quad 0 < x < 2$$
a Graph the density function.

b Verify that $f(x)$ is a density function.

c Find $P(X > 1)$.

d Find $P(X < .5)$.

e Find $P(X = 1.5)$.

8.12 The following function is the density function for the random variable X.
$$f(x) = \frac{x - 1}{8}, \quad 1 < x < 5$$
a Graph the density function.

b Find the probability that X lies between 2 and 4.

c What is the probability that X is less than 3?

8.13 The following density function describes the random variable X.
$$f(x) = \begin{cases} \dfrac{x}{25} & 0 < x < 5 \\[2ex] \dfrac{10 - x}{25} & 5 < x < 10 \end{cases}$$
a Graph the density function.

b Find the probability that X lies between 1 and 3.

c What is the probability that X lies between 4 and 8?

d Compute the probability that X is less than 7.

e Find the probability that X is greater than 3.

8.14 The following is a graph of a density function.

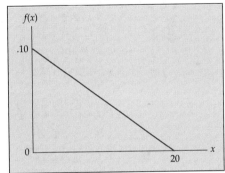

a Determine the density function.

b Find the probability that X is greater than 10.

c Find the probability that X lies between 6 and 12.

8.3 NORMAL DISTRIBUTION

The normal distribution is the most important of all probability distributions because of its crucial role in statistical inference.

NORMAL PROBABILITY DENSITY FUNCTION

The probability density function of a **normal random variable** is

$$f(x) = \frac{1}{\sigma\sqrt{2\pi}} e^{-\frac{1}{2}\left(\frac{x - \mu}{\sigma}\right)^2} \qquad -\infty < x < \infty$$

where $e = 2.71828\ldots$ and $\pi = 3.14159\ldots$

Figure 8.7 depicts a normal distribution. Notice that the curve is symmetric about its mean and the random variable ranges between $-\infty$ and ∞.

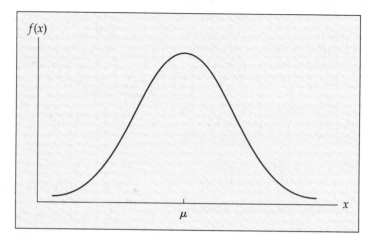

Figure 8.7
Symmetrical, bell-shaped normal distribution

The normal distribution is described by two parameters, the mean μ and the standard deviation σ. In Figure 8.8, we demonstrate the effect of changing the value of μ. Obviously, increasing μ shifts the curve to the right and decreasing μ shifts it to the left.

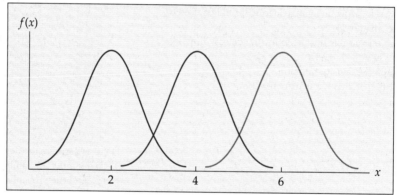

Figure 8.8
Normal distributions with the same variance but different means

Figure 8.9 describes the effect of σ. Larger values of σ widen the curve and smaller ones narrow it.

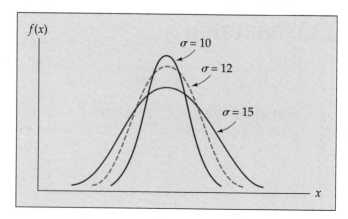

Figure 8.9
Normal distributions with the same mean but different standard deviations

S e e i n g   S t a t i s t i c s

APPLET 4:
NORMAL DISTRIBUTION PARAMETERS

This applet can be used to see the effect of changing the values of the mean and standard deviation of a normal distribution.

Move the top slider left or right to decrease or increase the mean of the distribution. Notice that when you change the value of the mean, the shape stays the same; only the location changes. Move the second slider to change the standard deviation. The shape of the bell curve is changed when you increase or decrease the standard deviation.

Applet Exercises

4.1 Move the slider bar for the standard deviation so that the standard deviation of the red distribution is greater than 1. What does this do to the spread of the normal distribution? Does it squeeze it or stretch it?

4.2 Move the slider bar for the standard deviation so that the standard deviation of the red distribution is less than 1. What does this do to the spread of the normal distribution? Does it squeeze it or stretch it?

4.3 Move both the mean and standard deviation sliders so that the red distribution is different from the blue distribution. What would you need to subtract from the red values to slide the red distribution back (forward) so that the centers of the red and blue distributions would overlap? By what would you need to divide the red values to squeeze or stretch the red distribution so that it would have the same spread as the blue distribution?

CALCULATING NORMAL PROBABILITIES

To calculate the probability that a normal random variable falls into any interval, we need to compute the area in the interval under the curve. Unfortunately, the function is not as simple as the uniform, precluding the use of simple mathematics or even integral calculus. Instead we will resort to using a probability table much as we did in determining binomial and Poisson probabilities in Chapter 7. Recall that to determine binomial probabilities from Table 1 we needed a table for each value of n and a separate column for selected values of p. Similarly, to find Poisson probabilities we needed a separate column for each value of μ that we chose to include in Table 2. It would appear then that we will need a separate table for normal probabilities for a selected set of values of μ and σ. Fortunately, this won't be necessary. Instead we reduce the number of tables needed to one by standardizing the random variable. We standardize a random variable by subtracting its mean and dividing by its standard deviation. When the variable is normal, the transformed variable is called a **standard normal random variable** and denoted by Z. That is,

$$Z = \frac{X - \mu}{\sigma}$$

The probability statement about X is transformed by this formula into a statement about Z. To illustrate how we proceed, consider the following problem.

Suppose that the amount of time to assemble a computer is normally distributed with a mean of 50 minutes and a standard deviation of 10 minutes. We would like to know the probability that a computer is assembled in a time between 45 and 60 minutes.

We want to find the probability

$$P(45 < X < 60)$$

Figure 8.10 describes a normal curve with mean 50 and standard deviation 10, and the area we want to find.

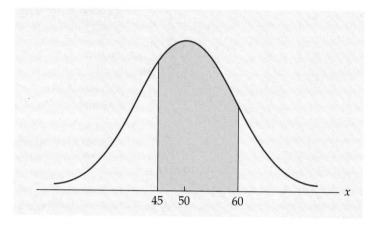

Figure 8.10
P(45 < X < 60)

The first step is to standardize X. However, if we perform any operations on X we must perform the same operations on 45 and 60. Thus

$$P(45 < X < 60) = P\left(\frac{45 - 50}{10} < \frac{X - \mu}{\sigma} < \frac{60 - 50}{10}\right) = P(-.5 < Z < 1)$$

Figure 8.11 describes the transformation that has taken place. Notice that the variable X was transformed into Z, 45 was transformed into −.5, and 60 was transformed into 1. However, the area has not changed. That is, the probability that we wish to compute, $P(45 < X < 60)$, is identical to $P(-.5 < Z < 1)$.

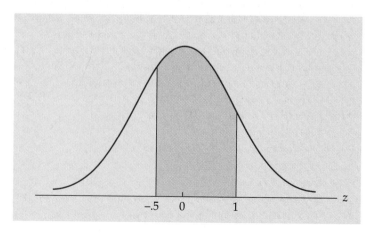

Figure 8.11
P(−.5 < Z < 1)

The values of Z specify the locations of the corresponding values of X. A value $Z = -.5$ corresponds to a value of X, 45, that is one-half a standard deviation below the mean. A value of $Z = 1$ corresponds to a value of X, 60, that is 1 standard deviation above the mean. Notice as well that the mean of Z, which is 0, corresponds to the mean of X.

If we know the mean and standard deviation of a normally distributed random variable, we can always transform the probability statement about X into a probability statement about Z. Consequently, we need only one table, Table 3 in Appendix B, the standard normal probability table, which is reproduced here as Table 8.1.

TABLE 8.1 Normal Probabilities (from Appendix B, Table 3)

z	.00	.01	.02	.03	.04	.05	.06	.07	.08	.09
0.0	.0000	.0040	.0080	.0120	.0160	.0199	.0239	.0279	.0319	.0359
0.1	.0398	.0438	.0478	.0517	.0557	.0596	.0636	.0675	.0714	.0753
0.2	.0793	.0832	.0871	.0910	.0948	.0987	.1026	.1064	.1103	.1141
0.3	.1179	.1217	.1255	.1293	.1331	.1368	.1406	.1443	.1480	.1517
0.4	.1554	.1591	.1628	.1664	.1700	.1736	.1772	.1808	.1844	.1879
0.5	.1915	.1950	.1985	.2019	.2054	.2088	.2123	.2157	.2190	.2224
0.6	.2257	.2291	.2324	.2357	.2389	.2422	.2454	.2486	.2517	.2549
0.7	.2580	.2611	.2642	.2673	.2704	.2734	.2764	.2794	.2823	.2852
0.8	.2881	.2910	.2939	.2967	.2995	.3023	.3051	.3078	.3106	.3133
0.9	.3159	.3186	.3212	.3238	.3264	.3289	.3315	.3340	.3365	.3389
1.0	.3413	.3438	.3461	.3485	.3508	.3531	.3554	.3577	.3599	.3621
1.1	.3643	.3665	.3686	.3708	.3729	.3749	.3770	.3790	.3810	.3830
1.2	.3849	.3869	.3888	.3907	.3925	.3944	.3962	.3980	.3997	.4015
1.3	.4032	.4049	.4066	.4082	.4099	.4115	.4131	.4147	.4162	.4177
1.4	.4192	.4207	.4222	.4236	.4251	.4265	.4279	.4292	.4306	.4319
1.5	.4332	.4345	.4357	.4370	.4382	.4394	.4406	.4418	.4429	.4441
1.6	.4452	.4463	.4474	.4484	.4495	.4505	.4515	.4525	.4535	.4545
1.7	.4554	.4564	.4573	.4582	.4591	.4599	.4608	.4616	.4625	.4633
1.8	.4641	.4649	.4656	.4664	.4671	.4678	.4686	.4693	.4699	.4706
1.9	.4713	.4719	.4726	.4732	.4738	.4744	.4750	.4756	.4761	.4767
2.0	.4772	.4778	.4783	.4788	.4793	.4798	.4803	.4808	.4812	.4817
2.1	.4821	.4826	.4830	.4834	.4838	.4842	.4846	.4850	.4854	.4857
2.2	.4861	.4864	.4868	.4871	.4875	.4878	.4881	.4884	.4887	.4890
2.3	.4893	.4896	.4898	.4901	.4904	.4906	.4909	.4911	.4913	.4916
2.4	.4918	.4920	.4922	.4925	.4927	.4929	.4931	.4932	.4934	.4936
2.5	.4938	.4940	.4941	.4943	.4945	.4946	.4948	.4949	.4951	.4952
2.6	.4953	.4955	.4956	.4957	.4959	.4960	.4961	.4962	.4963	.4964
2.7	.4965	.4966	.4967	.4968	.4969	.4970	.4971	.4972	.4973	.4974
2.8	.4974	.4975	.4976	.4977	.4977	.4978	.4979	.4979	.4980	.4981
2.9	.4981	.4982	.4982	.4983	.4984	.4984	.4985	.4985	.4986	.4986
3.0	.4987	.4987	.4987	.4988	.4988	.4989	.4989	.4989	.4990	.4990

Source: Abridged from Table 1 of A. Hald, *Statistical Tables and Formulas* (New York: Wiley & Sons, Inc.), 1952. Reported by permission of A. Hald and the publisher, John Wiley & Sons, Inc.

The table provides the probability that a standard normal random variable falls between 0 and values of z. For example, the probability $P(0 < Z < 2.00)$ is found by finding 2.0 in the left margin and under the heading .00 finding .4772. The probability $P(0 < Z < 2.01)$ is found in the same row but under the heading .01. It is .4778.

Because the normal curve is symmetric about its mean and the total area under the curve is 1, we can state the following:

$$P(Z > 0) = P(Z < 0) = .5$$

Notice that the largest value of z in the table is 3.09, and that $P(0 < Z < 3.09) = .4990$. This means that

$$P(Z > 3.09) = P(Z > 0) - P(0 < Z < 3.09) = .5 - .4990 = .001$$

However, because the table lists no values beyond 3.09, we approximate any area beyond 3.10 as 0. That is,

$$P(Z > 3.10) = P(Z < -3.10) \approx 0$$

Returning to our example, we note that the probability that we seek is actually the sum of two probabilities:

$$P(-.5 < Z < 1) = P(-.5 < Z < 0) + P(0 < Z < 1)$$

The second probability on the right is easily determined from the table. It is $P(0 < Z < 1.00) = .3413$. The first probability, $P(-.5 < Z < 0)$, is equal to $P(0 < Z < .5)$, which is found in the table to be .1915. Thus,

$$P(-.5 < Z < 1) = .1915 + .3413 = .5328$$

Figure 8.12 shows how this calculation is performed.

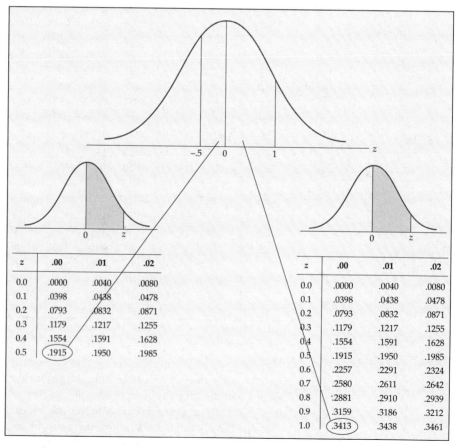

Figure 8.12
Calculating
$P(-.5 < Z < 1)$

Therefore, the probability that a randomly selected computer takes between 45 and 60 minutes to assemble is .5328.

Seeing Statistics

APPLET 5:
NORMAL DISTRIBUTION AREAS

This applet can be used to show the calculation of the probability of any interval for any values of μ and σ. Click or drag anywhere in the graph to move the nearest end to that point. Adjust the ends to correspond to either z-scores or actual scores. The area under the normal curve between the two endpoints is highlighted in red. The size of this area corresponds to the probability of obtaining a score between the two endpoints. You can change the mean and standard deviation of the actual scores by changing the numbers in the text boxes. After changing a number, press the Enter or Return key to update the graph. When this page first loads, the mean and standard deviation correspond to a mean of 50 and a standard deviation of 10.

Applet Exercises

The graph is initially set with mean 50 and standard deviation 10. Change it so that it represents the distribution of IQs, which are normally distributed with a mean of 100 and a standard deviation of 16.

5.1 About what proportion of people have IQ scores equal to or less than 116?

5.2 About what proportion of people have IQ scores between 100 and 116?

5.3 About what proportion have IQ scores greater than 120?

5.4 About what proportion of the scores are within one standard deviation of the mean?

5.5 About what proportion of the scores are within two standard deviations of the mean?

5.6 About what proportion of the scores are within three standard deviations of the mean?

APPLICATIONS IN FINANCE *MEASURING RISK*

In previous chapters we discussed several probability and statistical applications in finance where we wanted to measure and perhaps reduce the risk associated with investments. In Example 2.2 we drew histograms to gauge the spread of the histogram of the returns on two investments. We repeated this example in Chapter 4 where we computed the standard deviation and variance as numerical measures of risk. In Section 7.5 we developed an important application in finance where the emphasis was placed on reducing the variance of the returns on a portfolio. However, we have not demonstrated why risk is measured by the variance and standard deviation. The following example corrects this deficiency.

EXAMPLE 8.2

Consider an investment whose return is normally distributed with a mean of 10% and a standard deviation of 5%.

a Determine the probability of losing money.

b Find the probability of losing money when the standard deviation is equal to 10%.

SOLUTION

a The investment loses money when the return is negative. Thus we wish to determine

$$P(X < 0)$$

The first step is to standardize both X and 0 in the probability statement.

$$P(X < 0) = P\left(\frac{X - \mu}{\sigma} < \frac{0 - 10}{5}\right) = P(Z < -2)$$

Because of symmetry the area (probability) to the left of -2 is equal to the area to the right of 2. That is,

$$P(Z < -2) = P(Z > 2)$$

Table 3 provides probabilities of the range 0 to z. Thus, from Table 3, we determine that

$$P(0 < Z < 2) = .4772$$

Because the area under the curve is 1 and half the area is above 0 (and half below), it follows that

$$P(Z > 0) = .5$$

Thus

$$P(Z > 2) = .5 - P(0 < Z < 2)$$

$$= .5 - .4772$$

$$= .0228$$

Therefore the probability of losing money is .0228. Figure 8.13(a) depicts this calculation.

b If we increase the standard deviation to 10%, the probability of suffering a loss becomes

$$P(X < 0) = P\left(\frac{X - \mu}{\sigma} < \frac{0 - 10}{10}\right)$$

$$= P(Z < -1)$$
$$= P(Z > 1)$$

$$= .5 - P(0 < Z < 1)$$

$$= .5 - .3413$$

$$= .1587$$

As you can see, increasing the standard deviation increases the probability of losing money. [Figure 8.13(b) on page 240 displays this calculation.] It should be noted that increasing the standard deviation will also increase the probability that the return will exceed some relatively large amount. However, because investors tend to be risk averse, we emphasize the increased probability of negative returns when discussing the effect of increasing the standard deviation.

z	.00	.01	.02
0.0	.0000	.0040	.0080
0.1	.0398	.0438	.0478
0.2	.0793	.0832	.0871
0.3	.1179	.1217	.1255
0.4	.1554	.1591	.1628
0.5	.1915	.1950	.1985
0.6	.2257	.2291	.2324
0.7	.2580	.2611	.2642
0.8	.2881	.2910	.2939
0.9	.3159	.3186	.3212
1.0	.3413	.3438	.3461
1.1	.3643	.3665	.3686
1.2	.3849	.3869	.3888
1.3	.4032	.4049	.4066
1.4	.4192	.4207	.4222
1.5	.4332	.4345	.4357
1.6	.4452	.4463	.4474
1.7	.4554	.4564	.4573
1.8	.4641	.4649	.4656
1.9	.4713	.4719	.4726
2.0	.4772	.4778	.4783

Figure 8.13
(a) $P(X < 0)$ with $\sigma = 5$

z	.00	.01	.02
0.0	.0000	.0040	.0080
0.1	.0398	.0438	.0478
0.2	.0793	.0832	.0871
0.3	.1179	.1217	.1255
0.4	.1554	.1591	.1628
0.5	.1915	.1950	.1985
0.6	.2257	.2291	.2324
0.7	.2580	.2611	.2642
0.8	.2881	.2910	.2939
0.9	.3159	.3186	.3212
1.0	.3413	.3438	.3461

Figure 8.13
(b) $P(X < 0)$ with $\sigma = 10$

FINDING VALUES OF z

There is a family of problems that require us to determine the value of z given a probability. We use the notation z_A to represent the value of z such that the area to its right under the standard normal curve is A. That is, z_A is a value of a standard normal random variable such that

$$P(Z > z_A) = A$$

Figure 8.14 depicts this notation.

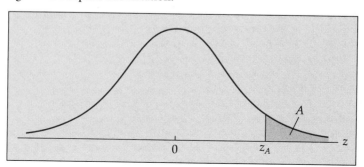

Figure 8.14
$P(Z > z_A) = A$

To find z_A for any value of A requires us to use the standard normal table backward. As you saw in Example 8.2, to find a probability about Z we must find the value of z in the table and determine the probability associated with it. To use the table backward we need to specify a probability and then determine the z-value associated with it. We'll demonstrate by finding $z_{.025}$. Figure 8.15 depicts the standard normal curve and $z_{.025}$. Because of the format of the standard normal table, we begin by determining the area between 0 and $z_{.025}$, which is $.5 - .025 = .4750$. (Notice that we expressed this probability with four decimal places to make it easier for you to see what you need to do.) We now search through the probability part of the table looking for .4750. When we locate it, we see that the z-value associated with it is 1.96.

Thus, $z_{.025} = 1.96$, which means that $P(Z > 1.96) = .025$.

Figure 8.15
Finding $z_{.025}$

z	.00	.01	.02	.03	.04	.05	.06	.07	.08	.09
0.0	.0000	.0040	.0080	.0120	.0160	.0199	.0239	.0279	.0319	.0359
0.1	.0398	.0438	.0478	.0517	.0557	.0596	.0636	.0675	.0714	.0753
0.2	.0793	.0832	.0871	.0910	.0948	.0987	.1026	.1064	.1103	.1141
0.3	.1179	.1217	.1255	.1293	.1331	.1368	.1406	.1443	.1480	.1517
0.4	.1554	.1591	.1628	.1664	.1700	.1736	.1772	.1808	.1844	.1879
0.5	.1915	.1950	.1985	.2019	.2054	.2088	.2123	.2157	.2190	.2224
0.6	.2257	.2291	.2324	.2357	.2389	.2422	.2454	.2486	.2517	.2549
0.7	.2580	.2611	.2642	.2673	.2704	.2734	.2764	.2794	.2823	.2852
0.8	.2881	.2910	.2939	.2967	.2995	.3023	.3051	.3078	.3106	.3133
0.9	.3159	.3186	.3212	.3238	.3264	.3289	.3315	.3340	.3365	.3389
1.0	.3413	.3438	.3461	.3485	.3508	.3531	.3554	.3577	.3599	.3621
1.1	.3643	.3665	.3686	.3708	.3729	.3749	.3770	.3790	.3810	.3830
1.2	.3849	.3869	.3888	.3907	.3925	.3944	.3962	.3980	.3997	.4015
1.3	.4032	.4049	.4066	.4082	.4099	.4115	.4131	.4147	.4162	.4177
1.4	.4192	.4207	.4222	.4236	.4251	.4265	.4279	.4292	.4306	.4319
1.5	.4332	.4345	.4357	.4370	.4382	.4394	.4406	.4418	.4429	.4441
1.6	.4452	.4463	.4474	.4484	.4495	.4505	.4515	.4525	.4535	.4545
1.7	.4554	.4564	.4573	.4582	.4591	.4599	.4608	.4616	.4625	.4633
1.8	.4641	.4649	.4656	.4664	.4671	.4678	.4686	.4693	.4699	.4706
1.9	.4713	.4719	.4726	.4732	.4738	.4744	.4750	.4756	.4761	.4767
2.0	.4772	.4778	.4783	.4788	.4793	.4798	.4803	.4808	.4812	.4817

EXAMPLE 8.3

Find the value of a standard normal random variable such that the probability that the random variable is greater than it is 5%.

SOLUTION We wish to determine $z_{.05}$. Figure 8.16 (page 242) depicts the normal curve and $z_{.05}$. If .05 is the area in the tail, then the area between 0 and $z_{.05}$ must be .45. To find $z_{.05}$ we search the table looking for the probability .4500. We don't find this probability but we find two values that are close: .4495 and .4505. The z-values associated with these probabilities are 1.64 and 1.65, respectively. The average is taken as $z_{.05}$. Thus, $z_{.05} = 1.645$.

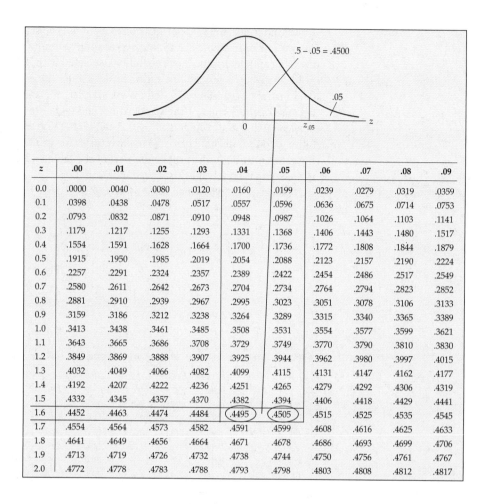

Figure 8.16
Finding $z_{.05}$

EXAMPLE 8.4

Find the value of a standard normal random variable such that the probability that the random variable is less than it is 5%.

SOLUTION   Because the standard normal curve is symmetric about 0, we wish to find $-z_{.05}$. In Example 8.3 we found $z_{.05} = 1.645$. Thus, $-z_{.05} = -1.645$. See Figure 8.17.

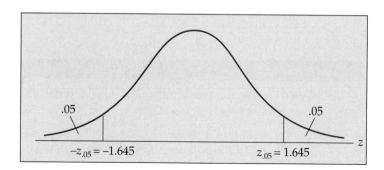

Figure 8.17
$-z_{.05}$

MINIMUM GMAT SCORE TO ENTER EXECUTIVE MBA PROGRAM: SOLUTION

Figure 8.18 depicts the distribution of GMAT scores. We've labeled the minimum score needed to enter the new Executive MBA Program $x_{.01}$ such that $P(X > x_{.01}) = .01$.

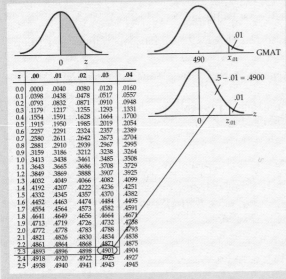

Figure 8.18 Minimum GMAT Score

z	.00	.01	.02	.03	.04
0.0	.0000	.0040	.0080	.0120	.0160
0.1	.0398	.0438	.0478	.0517	.0557
0.2	.0793	.0832	.0871	.0910	.0948
0.3	.1179	.1217	.1255	.1293	.1331
0.4	.1554	.1591	.1628	.1664	.1700
0.5	.1915	.1950	.1985	.2019	.2054
0.6	.2257	.2291	.2324	.2357	.2389
0.7	.2580	.2611	.2642	.2673	.2704
0.8	.2881	.2910	.2939	.2967	.2995
0.9	.3159	.3186	.3212	.3238	.3264
1.0	.3413	.3438	.3461	.3485	.3508
1.1	.3643	.3665	.3686	.3708	.3729
1.2	.3849	.3869	.3888	.3907	.3925
1.3	.4032	.4049	.4066	.4082	.4099
1.4	.4192	.4207	.4222	.4236	.4251
1.5	.4332	.4345	.4357	.4370	.4382
1.6	.4452	.4463	.4474	.4484	.4495
1.7	.4554	.4564	.4573	.4582	.4591
1.8	.4641	.4649	.4656	.4664	.4671
1.9	.4713	.4719	.4726	.4732	.4738
2.0	.4772	.4778	.4783	.4788	.4793
2.1	.4821	.4826	.4830	.4834	.4838
2.2	.4861	.4864	.4868	.4871	.4875
2.3	.4893	.4896	.4898	.4901	.4904
2.4	.4918	.4920	.4922	.4925	.4927
2.5	.4938	.4940	.4941	.4943	.4945

Below the normal curve, we depict the standard normal curve and $z_{.01}$. We can determine the value of $z_{.01}$ as we did in Example 8.3. In the standard normal table we find $.5 - .01 = .4900$ (its closest value in the table is .4901) and the z-value 2.33. Thus, the standardized value of $x_{.01}$ is $z_{.01} = 2.33$. To find $x_{.01}$ we must *unstandardize* $z_{.01}$. We do so by solving for $x_{.01}$ in the equation

$$z_{.01} = \frac{x_{.01} - \mu}{\sigma}$$

Substituting $z_{.01} = 2.33$, $\mu = 490$, and $\sigma = 61$, we find

$$2.33 = \frac{x_{.01} - 490}{61}$$

Solving, we get

$$x_{.01} = 2.33(61) + 490 = 632.13$$

Rounding up (GMAT scores are integers), we find that the minimum GMAT score to enter the Executive MBA Program is 633.

Z_A AND PERCENTILES

In Chapter 4 we introduced percentiles, which are measures of relative standing. The values of z_A are the $100(1 - A)$th percentiles of a standard normal random variable. For example, $z_{.05} = 1.645$, which means that 1.645 is the 95th percentile; 95% of all values of z are below it and 5% are above it. We interpret other values of z_A similarly.

USING THE COMPUTER

EXCEL

We can employ Excel to compute probabilities and values of X and Z. To compute cumulative normal probabilities $P(X < x)$, proceed as follows.

COMMANDS
1. Click f_x, **Function category: Statistical**, and **Function name: NORMDIST**. Click **OK**.
2. Type the value of x (**X**), the mean (**Mean**), the standard deviation (**Standard_dev**), and **true** (**Cumulative**) to yield a cumulative probability. (Typing **false** will produce the value of the density function, a number with little meaning.) The probability appears on the right side of the dialog box. Clicking **OK** will print the probability in the active cell.
3. Alternatively, type (in any cell)

= NORMDIST([X],[Mean],[Standard_dev],TRUE)

If you type 0 for **Mean** and 1 for **Standard_dev** you will obtain standard normal probabilities. Alternatively, click **NORMSDIST** instead of **NORMDIST**. Type the value of z (**Z**) and click **OK**.

For example, we determined

$$\text{NORMDIST}(60,50,10,\text{TRUE}) = .8413$$

and

$$\text{NORMDIST}(1.0,1,0,\text{TRUE}) = \text{NORMSDIST}(1.0) = .8413$$

To determine a value of X given a cumulative probability, follow these instructions.

COMMANDS

1. Click f_x, **Function category: Statistical**, and **Function name: NORMINV**. Click **OK**.
2. Type the cumulative probability (**Probability**), the mean (**Mean**), and the standard deviation (**Standard_dev**).
3 Alternatively, type

   $$=\text{NORMINV}([\text{probability}],[\text{Mean}],[\text{Standard\_dev}])$$

If you type 0 for **Mean** and 1 for **Standard_dev** you will obtain the standard normal random variable. Alternatively, click **NORMSINV** instead of **NORMINV**. Type the cumulative probability (**Probability**).

For example,

$$\text{NORMINV}(.99,490,61) = 631.91$$

and

$$\text{NORMSINV}(.99) = 2.326$$

 MINITAB

COMMANDS

1. Click **Calc**, **Probability Distributions**, and **Normal....**
2. Select either **Cumulative probability** [to determine [$P(X < x)$] or **Inverse cumulative probability** [to find the value of x or z].
3. Specify the **Mean** and **Standard deviation**.
4. If you wish to compute the probability for one value of x or determine the value of x for one probability, specify **Input constant** and type the value of x or the probability. Click **OK**.
5. If you wish to make probability statements about several values of x from the same normal distribution, or determine the value of x for several cumulative probabilities, type the values into a column before clicking **Calc**. At step 4 specify **Input column**, type the name of the column, and click **OK**.

EXERCISES

In Exercises 8.15 – 8.30 find the following probabilities.

8.15 $P(0 < Z < 1.5)$
8.16 $P(0 < Z < 1.51)$
8.17 $P(0 < Z < 1.55)$
8.18 $P(0 < Z < 1.59)$
8.19 $P(0 < Z < 1.6)$

8.20 $P(0 < Z < 2.3)$
8.21 $P(-1.4 < Z < .6)$
8.22 $P(Z > -1.44)$
8.23 $P(Z < 2.03)$
8.24 $P(Z > 1.67)$
8.25 $P(Z < 2.84)$

8.26 $P(1.14 < Z < 2.43)$

8.27 $P(-.91 < Z < -.33)$

8.28 $P(Z > 3.09)$

8.29 $P(Z > 0)$

8.30 $P(Z > 4.0)$

8.31 Find $z_{.02}$.

8.32 Find $z_{.045}$.

8.33 Find $z_{.20}$.

8.34 X is normally distributed with mean 100 and standard deviation 20. What is the probability that X is greater than 145?

8.35 X is normally distributed with mean 250 and standard deviation 40. What value of X does only the top 15% exceed?

8.36 X is normally distributed with mean 1,000 and standard deviation 250. What is the probability that X lies between 800 and 1,100?

8.37 X is normally distributed with mean 50 and standard deviation 8. What value of X is such that only 8% of values are below it?

8.38 The long-distance calls made by the employees of a company are normally distributed with a mean of 6.3 minutes and a standard deviation of 2.2 minutes. Find the probability that a call

   a Lasts between 5 and 10 minutes.

   b Lasts more than 7 minutes.

   c Last less than 4 minutes.

8.39 Refer to Exercise 8.38. How long do the longest 10% of calls last?

8.40 The lifetimes of lightbulbs that are advertised to last for 5,000 hours are normally distributed with a mean of 5,100 hours and a standard deviation of 200 hours. What is the probability that a bulb lasts longer than the advertised figure?

8.41 Refer to Exercise 8.40. If we wanted to be sure that 98% of all bulbs last longer than the advertised figure, what figure should be advertised?

8.42 Travelbyus is an Internet-based travel agency wherein customers can see videos of the cities they plan to visit. The number of hits daily is a normally distributed random variable with a mean of 10,000 and a standard deviation of 2,400.

   a What is the probability of getting more than 12,000 hits?

   b What is the probability of getting fewer than 9,000 hits?

8.43 Refer to Exercise 8.42. Some Internet sites have bandwidths that are not sufficient to handle all their traffic, often causing the system to crash. Bandwidth can be measured by the number of hits it can handle. How large a bandwidth should Travelbyus have in order to handle 99.9% of daily traffic?

8.44 A new car that is a gas- and electric-powered hybrid has recently hit the market. The distance traveled on 1 gallon of fuel is normally distributed with a mean of 65 miles and a standard deviation of 4 miles. Find the probability of the following events.

   a The car travels more than 70 miles per gallon.

   b The car travels less than 60 miles per gallon.

   c The car travels between 55 and 70 miles per gallon.

8.45 The top-selling Red and Voss tire is rated 70,000 miles, which means nothing. In fact, the distance the tires can run until wear-out is a normally distributed random variable with a mean of 82,000 miles and a standard deviation of 6,400 miles.

   a What is the probability that the tire wears out before 70,000 miles?

   b What is the probability that a tire lasts more than 100,000 miles?

8.46 The heights of children 2 years old are normally distributed with a mean of 32 inches and a standard deviation of 1.5 inches. Pediatricians regularly measure the heights of toddlers to determine whether there is a problem. There may be a problem when a child is in the top or bottom 5% of heights. Determine the heights of 2-year-old children that could be a problem.

8.47 Refer to Exercise 8.46. Find the probability of these events.

   a A 2-year-old child is taller than 36 inches.

   b A 2-year-old child is shorter than 34 inches.

   c A 2-year-old child is between 30 and 33 inches tall.

8.48 University and college students average 7.2 hours of sleep per night with a standard deviation of 40 minutes. If the amount of sleep is normally distributed, what proportion of university and college students sleep for more than 8 hours?

8.49 Refer to Exercise 8.48. Find the amount of sleep that is exceeded by only 25% of students.

8.50 The amount of time devoted to studying statistics each week by students who achieve a grade of A in the course is a normally distributed random variable with a mean of 7.5 hours and a standard deviation of 2.1 hours.

   a What proportion of A students study for more than 10 hours per week?

   b Find the probability that an A student spends between 7 and 9 hours studying.

   c What proportion of A students spend less than 3 hours studying?

   d What is the amount of time below which only 5% of all A students spend studying?

8.51 The number of pages printed before replacing the cartridge in a laser printer is normally distributed with a mean of 11,500 pages and a standard deviation of 800 pages. A new cartridge has just been installed.

   a What is the probability that the printer produces more than 12,000 pages before this cartridge needs to be replaced?

   b What is the probability that the printer produces fewer than 10,000 pages?

8.52 Refer to Exercise 8.51. The manufacturer wants to provide guidelines to potential customers advising them the minimum number of pages they can expect from each cartridge. How many pages should it advertise if the company wants to be correct 99% of the time?

8.53 Battery manufacturers compete on the basis of the amount of time their products last in cameras and toys. A manufacturer of alkaline batteries has observed that its batteries last for an average of 26 hours when used in a toy racing car. The amount of time is normally distributed with a standard deviation of 2.5 hours.

   a What is the probability that the battery lasts between 24 and 28 hours?

   b What is the probability that the battery lasts longer than 28 hours?

   c What is the probability that the battery lasts less than 24 hours?

8.54 Because of the relatively high interest rates, most consumers attempt to pay off their credit card bills promptly. However, this is not always possible. An analysis of the amount of interest paid monthly by a bank's Visa cardholders reveals that the amount is normally distributed with a mean of $27 and a standard deviation of $7.

   a What proportion of the bank's Visa cardholders pay more than $30 in interest?

   b What proportion of the bank's Visa cardholders pay more than $40 in interest?

   c What proportion of the bank's Visa cardholders pay less than $15 in interest?

   d What interest payment is exceeded by only 20% of the bank's Visa cardholders?

8.55 It is said that sufferers of a cold virus experience symptoms for 7 days. However, the amount of time is actually a normally distributed random variable whose mean is 7.5 days and whose standard deviation is 1.2 days.

   a What proportion of cold sufferers experiences less than 4 days of symptoms?

   b What proportion of cold sufferers experiences symptoms for between 7 and 10 days?

8.56 How much money does a typical family of four spend at McDonald's restaurants per visit? The amount is a normally distributed random variable whose mean is $16.40 and whose standard deviation is $2.75.

   a Find the probability that a family of four spends less than $10.

   b What is the amount below which only 10% of families of four spend at McDonald's?

8.57 The final marks in a statistics course are normally distributed with a mean of 70 and a standard deviation of 10. The professor must convert all marks to letter grades. She decides that she wants 10% A's, 30% B's, 40% C's, 15% D's, and 5% F's. Determine the cutoffs for each letter grade.

8.58 *Mensa* is an organization whose members possess IQs that are in the top 2% of the population. It is known that IQs are normally distributed with a mean of 100 and a standard deviation of 16. Find the minimum IQ needed to be a Mensa member.

8.59 The lifetimes of televisions produced by the Hishobi Company are normally distributed with a mean of 75 months and a standard deviation of 8 months. If the manufacturer wants to have to replace only 1% of its televisions, what should its warranty be?

APPLICATIONS IN OPERATIONS MANAGEMENT: *INVENTORY MODELS*

Every organization maintains some inventory, which is defined as a stock of items. For example, grocery stores hold inventories of almost all the products they sell. When the total number of products drops to a specified level, the manager arranges for the delivery of more product. An automobile repair shop keeps an inventory of a large number of replacement parts. A school keeps a stock of items that it uses regularly, including chalk, pens, envelopes, file folders, and paper clips. There are costs associated with inventories. These include cost of capital, losses (theft and obsolescence), warehouse space, as well as maintenance and record keeping. Management scientists have developed many models to help determine the optimum inventory level that balances the cost of inventory with the cost of shortages and the cost of making many small orders. Several of these models are deterministic—that is, they assume that the demand for the product is constant. However, in most realistic situations the demand is a random variable. One commonly applied probabilistic model assumes that the demand during lead time is a normally distributed random variable. *Lead time* is defined as the amount of time between when the order is placed and when it is delivered.

8.60 A retailer of computing products sells a variety of computer-related products. One of her most popular products is an HP Laser Printer. The average weekly demand is 200. Lead time for a new order from the manufacturer to arrive is 1 week. If the demand for printers were constant, the retailer would order exactly 200 printers every week. However, the demand is a random variable. An analysis of previous weeks reveals that the weekly demand standard deviation is 30. The retailer knows that if a customer wants to buy an HP Laser Printer but she has none available, she will lose that sale plus possibly additional sales. She wants the probability of running short in any week to be no more than 6%. How many HP Laser Printers should she order?

8.61 The demand for a daily newspaper at a newsstand at a busy intersection is known to be normally distributed with a mean of 150 and a standard deviation of 25. How many newspapers should the newsstand operator order to ensure that he runs short on no more than 20% of days?

8.62 Every day a bakery prepares its famous marble rye. A statistically savvy customer determined that daily demand is normally distributed with a mean of 850 and a standard deviation of 90. How many loaves should the bakery make if it wants the probability of running short on any day to be no more than 30%?

8.63 Refer to Exercise 8.62. Any marble ryes that are unsold at the end of the day are marked down and sold for half price. How many loaves should the bakery prepare so that the proportion of days that result in unsold loaves is no more than 60%?

APPLICATIONS IN OPERATIONS MANAGEMENT: *PERT/CPM*

In the Application box on page 200 we introduced PERT/CPM. The purpose of this powerful management science procedure is to determine the critical path of a project. The expected value and variance of the completion time of the project are based on the expected values and variances of the completion times of the activities on the critical path. Once we have the expected value and variance of the completion time of the project, we can use these figures to determine the probability that the project, will be completed by a certain date. Statisticians have established that the completion time of the project is approximately normally distributed, enabling us to compute the needed probabilities.

8.64 Refer to Exercise 7.57. Find the probability that the project will take more than 60 days to complete.

8.65 Refer to Exercise 7.58. What is the probability that it will take less than 2.5 hours to overhaul the machine?

8.66 Refer to Exercise 7.59. The manager has been given 110 days to complete the report. What is the probability that the report will be completed before the deadline?

8.67 Refer to Exercise 7.60. The research project must be completed within 180 days. Determine the probability that the project will not be completed by this time.

The following exercises deal with the risk and return associated with investments.

8.68 The annual rate of return on a mutual fund is normally distributed with a mean of 14% and a standard deviation of 18%.
  a What is the probability that the fund returns more than 25% next year?
  b What is the probability that the fund loses money next year?

8.69 Repeat Exercise 8.68 when the standard deviation is 9%.

8.70 Refer to Exercise 7.61.
  a What is the probability that stock 1 loses money?
  b Calculate the probability that the return on stock 1 is greater than 20%.

  c Find the probability that stock 2 loses money.
  d What is the probability that the return on stock 2 is greater than 20%?

8.71 Refer to Exercise 7.62.
  a Determine the probability that the portfolio loses money.
  b What is the probability that the return on the portfolio is greater than 20%?

8.72 What do your answers to Exercises 8.70 and 8.71 tell you about the advantages and disadvantages of diversification?

8.73 Refer to Exercise 7.65.
  a What is the probability that stock 1 loses money?
  b Calculate the probability that the return on stock 1 is greater than 15%.
  c Find the probability that stock 2 loses money.
  d What is the probability that the return on stock 2 is greater than 15%?

8.74 Refer to Exercise 7.66.
  a Determine the probability that the portfolio loses money.
  b What is the probability that the return on the portfolio is greater than 15%?

8.75   What do your answers to Exercises 8.73 and 8.74 tell you about the advantages and disadvantages of diversification?

8.76   Refer to Exercise 7.69.
  a Find the probability of losing money with the portfolio.
  b What is the probability that the return on the portfolio is greater than 20%?

8.77   Refer to Exercise 7.70.
  a Find the probability of losing money with the portfolio.
  b What is the probability that the return on the portfolio is greater than 20%?

8.78   Refer to Exercise 7.72.
  a Find the probability of losing money with the portfolio.
  b What is the probability that the return on the portfolio is greater than 40%?

8.79   Refer to Exercise 7.73.
  a Find the probability of losing money with the portfolio.
  b What is the probability that the return on the portfolio is greater than 40%?

8.4 (OPTIONAL) EXPONENTIAL DISTRIBUTION

Another important continuous distribution is the **exponential distribution.**

> **EXPONENTIAL PROBABILITY DENSITY FUNCTION**
> A random variable X is exponentially distributed if its probability density function is given by
>
> $$f(x) = \lambda e^{-\lambda x}, \quad x \geq 0$$
>
> where $e = 2.71828...$ and λ is the parameter of the distribution.

Statisticians have shown that the mean and standard deviation of an exponential random variable are equal to each other:

$$\mu = \sigma = \frac{1}{\lambda}$$

Recall that the normal distribution is a two-parameter distribution. The distribution is completely specified once the values of the two parameters μ and σ are known. In contrast, the exponential distribution is a one-parameter distribution. The distribution is completely specified once the value of the parameter λ is known. Figure 8.19 depicts three exponential distributions, corresponding to three different values of the parameter λ. Notice that for any exponential density function $f(x), f(0) = \lambda$ and $f(x)$ approaches 0 as x approaches infinity.

Figure 8.19
Exponential distributions

The exponential density function is easier to work with than the normal and, as a result, we can develop formulas for the calculation of the probability of any ranges of values. Using integral calculus, we can determine the following probability statements.

> **PROBABILITY ASSOCIATED WITH AN EXPONENTIAL RANDOM VARIABLE**
>
> If X is an exponential random variable,
>
> $$P(X > x) = e^{-\lambda x}$$
>
> $$P(X < x) = 1 - e^{-\lambda x}$$
>
> $$P(x_1 < X < x_2) = P(X < x_2) - P(X < x_1) = e^{-\lambda x_1} - e^{-\lambda x_2}$$

The value of $e^{-\lambda x}$ can be obtained with the aid of a calculator.

EXAMPLE 8.5

The lifetime of an alkaline battery (measured in hours) is exponentially distributed with $\lambda = .05$.

a   What are the mean and standard deviation of the battery's lifetime?
b   Find the probability that a battery will last between 10 and 15 hours.
c   What is the probability that a battery will last for more than 20 hours?

SOLUTION

a   The mean and standard deviation are equal to $1/\lambda$. Thus,

$$\mu = \sigma = \frac{1}{\lambda} = \frac{1}{.05} = 20 \text{ hours}$$

b   Let X denote the lifetime of a battery. The required probability is

$$P(10 \le X \le 15) = e^{-.05(10)} - e^{-.05(15)}$$

$$= e^{-.5} - e^{-.75}$$

$$= .6065 - .4724$$

$$= .1341$$

c $$P(X > 20) = e^{-.05(20)} = e^{-1} = .3679$$

Figure 8.20 depicts these probabilities.

(a) $P(10 < X < 15)$

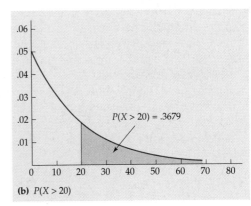

(b) $P(X > 20)$

Figure 8.20

USING THE COMPUTER

EXCEL

COMMANDS

1. Click f_x, **Function category: Statistical,** and **Function name: EXPONDIST.** Click **OK.**
2. Type the value of x (**X**), λ (**Lambda**), and **true** (**Cumulative**) to yield a cumulative probability. (Typing **false** will produce the value of the density function, a number with little meaning.) The probability appears on the right side of the dialog box. Clicking **OK** will print the probability in the active cell.
3. Alternatively, type (in any cell)

   $= \text{EXPONDIST}([X],[\lambda],\text{TRUE})$

MINITAB

COMMANDS

1. Click **Calc, Probability Distributions,** and **Exponential....**
2. Select either **Cumulative probability** [to determine $P(X < x)$] or **Inverse cumulative probability** [to find the value of x].
3. Specify the **Mean,** which is $1/\lambda$.
4. If you wish to compute the probability for one value of x or determine the value of x for one probability, specify **Input constant** and type the value of x or the probability. Click **OK.**
5. If you wish to make probability statements about several values of x from the same exponential distribution, or determine the value of x for several cumulative probabilities, type the values into a column before clicking **Calc.** At step 4 specify **Input column,** type the name of the column, and click **OK.**

APPLICATIONS IN OPERATIONS MANAGEMENT: *WAITING LINES*

In Section 7.7 we described waiting line models and described how the Poisson distribution is used to calculate the probabilities of the number of arrivals per time period. In order to calculate the operating characteristics of waiting lines, management scientists often assume that the times to complete a service are exponentially distributed. In this application the parameter λ is the service rate, which is defined as the mean number of service completions per time period. For example, if service times are exponentially distributed with $\lambda = 5$/hour, this tells us that the service rate is 5 units per hour or 5 per 60 minutes. Recall that the mean of an exponential distribution is $\mu = 1/\lambda$. In this case the service facility can complete a service in an average of 12 minutes. This was calculated as

We can use this distribution to make a variety of probability statements.

$$\mu = \frac{1}{\lambda} = \frac{1}{5/\text{hr.}} = \frac{1}{5/60 \text{ min.}} = \frac{60 \text{ min.}}{5} = 12 \text{ min.}$$

EXAMPLE 8.6

A checkout counter at a supermarket completes the process according to an exponential distribution with a service rate of 15 per hour. A customer arrives at the checkout counter. Find the probability of the following events.
  a The service is completed in less than 5 minutes
  b The customer leaves the checkout counter more than 10 minutes after arriving
  c The service is completed in a time between 5 and 8 minutes

SOLUTION   One way to solve this problem is to convert the service rate so that the time period is 1 minute. (Alternatively, we can solve by converting the probability statements so that the time periods are measured in fractions of an hour.)
Let the service rate $= \lambda = .25$/minute.

  a $P(X < 5) = 1 - e^{-\lambda x} = 1 - e^{-.25(5)} = 1 - e^{-1.25} = 1 - .2865 = .7135$

  b $P(X > 10) = e^{-\lambda x} = e^{-.25(10)} = e^{-2.5} = .0821$

  c $P(5 < X < 8) = e^{-.25(5)} - e^{-.25(8)} = e^{-1.25} - e^{-2} = .2865 - .1353 = .1512$

EXERCISES

8.80 The random variable X is exponentially distributed with $\lambda = 3$. Sketch the graph of the distribution of X by plotting and connecting the points representing $f(x)$ for $x = 0, .5, 1, 1.5,$ and 2.

8.81 X is an exponential random variable with $\lambda = .25$. Sketch the graph of the distribution of X by plotting and connecting the points representing $f(x)$ for $x = 0,$ $2, 4, 6, 8, 10, 15, 20$.

8.82 X is an exponential random variable with $\lambda = .5$. Find the following probabilities.
  a $P(X > 1)$
  b $P(X > .4)$
  c $P(X < .5)$
  d $P(X < 2)$

8.83 The random variable X is exponentially distributed with $\lambda = 1.5$. Find the following probabilities.
  a $P(X > 1)$
  b $P(X < 3)$
  c $P(2 < X < 4)$
  d $P(X > .5)$

8.84 X is an exponential random variable with $\lambda = .3$. Find the following probabilities.
  a $P(X > 2)$
  b $P(X < 4)$
  c $P(1 < X < 2)$
  d $P(X = 3)$

8.85 The production of a complex chemical needed for anticancer drugs is exponentially distributed with $\lambda = 6$ kilograms per hour. What is the probability that the production process requires more than 15 minutes to produce the next kilogram of drugs?

8.86 The time between breakdowns of aging machines is known to be exponentially distributed with a mean of 25 hours. The machine has just been repaired. Determine the probability that the next breakdown occurs more than 50 hours from now.

8.87 Refer to Exercise 7.120, where we described the arrival rate of trucks at the Ambassador Bridge. Each truck must be checked by customs agents. The times are exponentially distributed with a service rate of 10 per hour. What is the probability that a truck requires more than 15 minutes to be checked?

8.88 A bank wishing to increase its customer base advertises that it has the fastest service and that virtually all of its customers are served in less than 10 minutes. A management scientist has studied the service times and concluded that service times are exponentially distributed with a mean of 5 minutes. Determine what the bank means when it claims "virtually all" its customers are served in under 10 minutes.

8.89 Toll booths on the New York Throughway are often congested because of the large number of cars waiting to pay. A consultant working for the state concluded that if service times are measured from the time a car stops in line until it leaves, service times are exponentially distributed with a mean of 2.7 minutes. What proportion of cars can get through the toll booth in less than 3 minutes?

8.90 Refer to Exercise 7.121. The manager of the gas station has observed that the times required by drivers to fill their car's tank and pay are quite variable. In fact, the times are exponentially distributed with a mean of

7.5 minutes. What is the probability that a car can complete the transaction in less than 5 minutes?

8.91 Refer to Exercise 7.122. Because automatic banking machine (ABM) customers can perform a number of transactions, the times to complete them can be quite variable. A banking consultant has noted that the times are exponentially distributed with a mean of 125 seconds. What proportion of the ABM customers take more than 3 minutes to do their banking?

8.92 The manager of a supermarket tracked the amount of time needed for customers to be served by the cashier. After checking with his statistics professor, he concluded that the checkout times are exponentially distributed with a mean of 6 minutes. What proportion of customers require more than 10 minutes to check out?

8.5 OTHER CONTINUOUS DISTRIBUTIONS

In this section we introduce three more continuous distributions. We will employ them extensively in statistical inference.

STUDENT *t* DISTRIBUTION

The Student *t* distribution was first derived by William S. Gosset in 1908. (Gosset published his findings under the pseudonym "Student" and used the letter *t* to represent the random variable, hence the **Student *t* distribution** — also called the Student's *t* distribution.) It is very commonly used in statistical inference, where its applications will be introduced in Chapters 12, 13, 15, 18, 19, and 20.

STUDENT *t* PROBABILITY DENSITY FUNCTION

The density function of the Student *t* distribution is as follows:

$$f(t) = \frac{[(\nu - 1)/2]!}{\sqrt{\nu\pi}[(\nu - 2)/2]!}\left[1 + \frac{t^2}{\nu}\right]^{-(\nu + 1)/2}$$

where $\pi = 3.14159...$ and ν (Greek letter *nu*) is the parameter of the Student *t* distribution called the **degrees of freedom.**

The mean and variance of a Student *t* random variable are

$$E(t) = 0$$

and

$$V(t) = \frac{\nu}{\nu - 2} \quad \text{for } \nu > 2$$

Figure 8.21 depicts the Student *t* distribution. As you can see, this distribution is similar to the standard normal distribution. Both are symmetrical about 0. (Both random variables have a mean of 0.) We describe the Student *t* distribution as mound shaped, whereas the normal distribution is bell shaped.

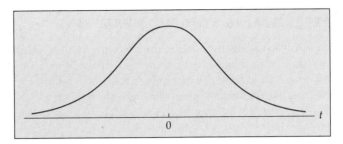

Figure 8.21
Student *t* distribution

Figure 8.22 shows both a Student *t* and the standard normal distributions. The former is more widely spread out than the latter. (The variance of a standard normal random variable is 1, whereas the variance of a Student *t* random variable is $v/(v-2)$, which is greater than 1 for all v.)

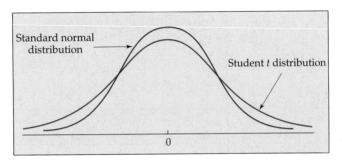

Figure 8.22
Student *t* and normal distributions

Figure 8.23 depicts Student *t* distributions with several different degrees of freedom. Notice that for larger degrees of freedom the Student *t* distribution's dispersion is smaller. For example, when $v = 10$, $V(t) = 1.25$, when $v = 50$, $V(t) = 1.042$, and when $v = 200$, $V(t) = 1.010$. As v grows larger, the Student *t* distribution approaches the standard normal distribution.

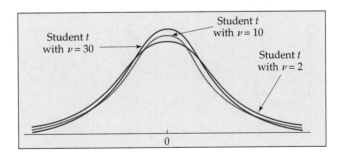

Figure 8.23
Student *t* distributions with different degrees of freedom

STUDENT *t* PROBABILITIES

For each value of v (the number of degrees of freedom) there is a different Student *t* distribution. If we wanted to calculate probabilities of the Student *t* random variable manually as we did for the normal random variable, we would need a different table for each v, which is not feasible. Alternatively, we can use Microsoft Excel or Minitab. The instructions appear later in this section.

DETERMINING STUDENT *t* VALUES

As you will discover later in this book, the Student *t* distribution is employed extensively in statistical inference. And for inferential methods, we often need to find values of the random variable. To determine values of a normal random variable we used Table 3 backward. Finding values of a Student *t* random variable is considerably easier. Table 4 in Appendix B (reproduced here as Table 8.2) lists values of $t_{A,v}$, which are the values of a Student *t* random variable with v degrees of freedom such that

$$P(t > t_{A,v}) = A \qquad \text{(Figure 8.24 depicts this notation.)}$$

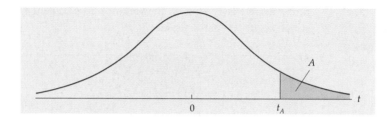

**Figure 8.24
Student *t*
distribution
with t_A**

TABLE 8.2 Critical Values of *t*

Degrees of Freedom	$t_{.10}$	$t_{.05}$	$t_{.025}$	$t_{.01}$	$t_{.005}$	Degrees of Freedom	$t_{.10}$	$t_{.05}$	$t_{.025}$	$t_{.01}$	$t_{.005}$
1	3.078	6.314	12.706	31.821	63.657	24	1.318	1.711	2.064	2.492	2.797
2	1.886	2.920	4.303	6.965	9.925	25	1.316	1.708	2.060	2.485	2.787
3	1.638	2.353	3.182	4.541	5.841	26	1.315	1.706	2.056	2.479	2.779
4	1.533	2.132	2.776	3.747	4.604	27	1.314	1.703	2.052	2.473	2.771
5.	1.476	2.015	2.571	3.365	4.032	28	1.313	1.701	2.048	2.467	2.763
6	1.440	1.943	2.447	3.143	3.707	29	1.311	1.699	2.045	2.462	2.756
7	1.415	1.895	2.365	2.998	3.499	30	1.310	1.697	2.042	2.457	2.750
8	1.397	1.860	2.306	2.896	3.355	35	1.306	1.690	2.030	2.438	2.724
9	1.383	1.833	2.262	2.821	3.250	40	1.303	1.684	2.021	2.423	2.705
10	1.372	1.812	2.228	2.764	3.169	45	1.301	1.679	2.014	2.412	2.690
11	1.363	1.796	2.201	2.718	3.106	50	1.299	1.676	2.009	2.403	2.678
12	1.356	1.782	2.179	2.681	3.055	60	1.296	1.671	2.000	2.390	2.660
13	1.350	1.771	2.160	2.650	3.012	70	1.294	1.667	1.994	2.381	2.648
14	1.345	1.761	2.145	2.624	2.977	80	1.292	1.664	1.990	2.374	2.639
15	1.341	1.753	2.131	2.602	2.947	90	1.291	1.662	1.987	2.369	2.632
16	1.337	1.746	2.120	2.583	2.921	100	1.290	1.660	1.984	2.364	2.626
17	1.333	1.740	2.110	2.567	2.898	120	1.289	1.658	1.980	2.358	2.617
18	1.330	1.734	2.101	2.552	2.878	140	1.288	1.656	1.977	2.353	2.611
19	1.328	1.729	2.093	2.539	2.861	160	1.287	1.654	1.975	2.350	2.607
20	1.325	1.725	2.086	2.528	2.845	180	1.286	1.653	1.973	2.347	2.603
21	1.323	1.721	2.080	2.518	2.831	200	1.286	1.653	1.972	2.345	2.601
22	1.321	1.717	2.074	2.508	2.819	∞	1.282	1.645	1.960	2.326	2.576
23	1.319	1.714	2.069	2.500	2.807						

Source: From M. Merrington, "Table of Percentage Points of the *t*-Distribution," *Biometrika 32* (1941): 300. Reproduced by permission of the Biometrika Trustees.

Observe that $t_{A,v}$ is provided for degrees of freedom ranging from 1 to 200 and ∞. To read this table, simply identify the degrees of freedom and find that value or the closest number to it if it is not listed. Then locate the column representing the t_A value you wish. For example, if we want the value of t with 10 degrees of freedom such that the area to its right under the Student t curve is .05, we locate 10 in the first column and move across this row until we locate the number under the heading $t_{.05}$. We find (see Table 8.3)

$$t_{.05,10} = 1.812$$

If the number of degrees of freedom is 25, we determine (see Table 8.4)

$$t_{.05,25} = 1.708$$

If the number of degrees of freedom is 74, we find the number of degrees of freedom closest to 74 listed in the table, which is 70, and determine (see Table 8.5)

$$t_{.05,74} \approx t_{.05,70} = 1.667$$

Table 8.3 Finding $t_{.05,10}$

Degrees of Freedom	$t_{.10}$	$t_{.05}$	$t_{.025}$	$t_{.01}$	$t_{.005}$
1	3.078	6.314	12.706	31.821	63.657
2	1.886	2.920	4.303	6.965	9.925
3	1.638	2.353	3.182	4.541	5.841
4	1.533	2.132	2.776	3.747	4.604
5	1.476	2.015	2.571	3.365	4.032
6	1.440	1.943	2.447	3.143	3.707
7	1.415	1.895	2.365	2.998	3.499
8	1.397	1.860	2.306	2.896	3.355
9	1.383	1.833	2.262	2.821	3.250
10	1.372	1.812	2.228	2.764	3.169
11	1.363	1.796	2.201	2.718	3.106
12	1.356	1.782	2.179	2.681	3.055

Table 8.4 Finding $t_{.05,25}$

Degrees of Freedom	$t_{.10}$	$t_{.05}$	$t_{.025}$	$t_{.01}$	$t_{.005}$
1	3.078	6.314	12.706	31.821	63.657
2	1.886	2.920	4.303	6.965	9.925
3	1.638	2.353	3.182	4.541	5.841
4	1.533	2.132	2.776	3.347	4.604
5	1.476	2.015	2.571	3.365	4.032
⋮					
21	1.323	1.721	2.080	2.518	2.831
22	1.321	1.717	2.074	2.508	2.819
23	1.319	1.714	2.069	2.500	2.807
24	1.318	1.711	2.064	2.492	2.797
25	1.316	1.708	2.060	2.485	2.787
26	1.315	1.706	2.056	2.479	2.779

Table 8.5 Finding $t_{.05,70}$

Degrees of Freedom	$t_{.10}$	$t_{.05}$	$t_{.025}$	$t_{.01}$	$t_{.005}$
1	3.078	6.314	12.706	31.821	63.657
2	1.886	2.920	4.303	6.965	9.925
3	1.638	2.353	3.182	4.541	5.841
4	1.533	2.132	2.776	3.747	4.604
5	1.476	2.015	2.571	3.365	4.032
⋮					
45	1.301	1.679	2.014	2.412	2.690
50	1.299	1.676	2.009	2.403	2.678
60	1.296	1.671	2.000	2.390	2.660
70	1.294	1.667	1.994	2.381	2.648
80	1.292	1.664	1.990	2.374	2.639
90	1.291	1.662	1.987	2.369	2.632
100	1.290	1.660	1.984	2.364	2.626
120	1.289	1.658	1.980	2.358	2.617
140	1.288	1.656	1.977	2.353	2.611
160	1.287	1.654	1.975	2.350	2.607
180	1.286	1.653	1.973	2.347	2.603
200	1.286	1.653	1.972	2.345	2.601
∞	1.282	1.645	1.960	2.326	2.576

Because the Student t distribution is symmetric about 0, the value of t such that the area to its *left* is A is $-t_{A,v}$. For example, the value of t with 10 degrees of freedom such that the area to its left is .05 is

$$-t_{.05,10} = -1.812$$

Notice the last row in the Student t table. The number of degrees of freedom is infinite and the t values are identical (except for the number of decimal places) to the values of z. For example,

$$t_{.10,\infty} = 1.282$$

$$t_{.05,\infty} = 1.645$$

$$t_{.025,\infty} = 1.960$$

$$t_{.01,\infty} = 2.326$$

$$t_{.005,\infty} = 2.576$$

In the previous section we showed (or showed how we determine) that

$$z_{.10} = 1.28$$

$$z_{.05} = 1.645$$

$$z_{.025} = 1.96$$

$$z_{.01} = 2.33$$

$$z_{.005} = 2.575$$

USING THE COMPUTER

EXCEL

To compute Student *t* probabilities, proceed as follows.

COMMANDS

1. Click f_x, **Function category: Statistical**, and **Function name: TDIST**. Click **OK**.
2. Type the value of *x*, where *x* must be positive (**X**), the degrees of freedom (**Deg_freedom**), and the number of tails (**Tails**). Typing **1** for **Tails** produces the area to the right of *x*. Typing **2** for **Tails** produces the area to the right of *x* plus the area to the left of $-x$.
3. Alternatively, type into any cell

    = TDIST([X], [degrees of freedom], [Tails])

For example,

    TDIST(2,50,1) = .025474

and

    TDIST(2,50,2) = .050947

To determine a value of a Student *t* random variable follow these instructions.

COMMANDS

1. Click f_x, **Function category: Statistical**, and **Function name: TINV**. Click **OK**.
2. Type the two-tail probability (**Probability**) and the degrees of freedom (**Deg_freedom**).
3. Alternatively, type into any cell

    = TINV([Probability], [Degrees of freedom])

The result is the value of *t* such that the area to its right is half the probability. The other half of the probability is located to the left of $-t$. For example,

    TINV(.05,200) = 1.972

which means that $P(t > 1.972) + P(t < -1.972) = .025 + .025 = .05$

MINITAB

We can employ Minitab to compute probabilities and values of a Student *t* random variable.

COMMANDS

1. Click **Calc, Probability Distributions,** and **t....**
2. Select either **Cumulative probability** [to determine $P(X < x)$] or **Inverse cumulative probability** [to find the value of *x* such that $P(X < x) =$ cumulative probability].
3. Specify the **Degrees of freedom**.
4. If you wish to compute the probability for one value of *x* or determine the value of *x* for one probability, specify **Input constant**, and type the value of *x* or the probability. Click **OK**.
5. If you wish to make probability statements about several values of *x* from the same *t* distribution, or determine the value of *x* for several cumulative probabilities, type the values into a column before clicking **Calc**. At step 4 specify **Input column**, type the name of the column, and click **OK**.

S e e i n g   S t a t i s t i c s

APPLET 6:
STUDENT *t* DISTRIBUTION

The Student *t* Distribution applet allows you to see for yourself the shape of the distribution, how the degrees of freedom change the shape, and its resemblance to the standard normal curve. The first graph shows the comparison of the normal distribution (red curve) to Student *t* distribution (blue curve). Use the right slider to change the degrees of freedom for the *t* distribution. Use the text boxes to change either the value of *t* or the two-tail probability. Remember to press the Return key in the text box to record the change.

The second graph is the same as the one above except the comparison to the normal distribution has been removed. This graph is a little easier to use to find critical values of *t* or to find the probability of specific values of *t*.

Applet Exercises
The following exercises employ Graph 1.

6.1 Set the degrees of freedom equal to 2. For values (on the horizontal axis) near 0, which curve is higher? The higher curve is more likely to have observations in that region.

6.2 Again for df = 2, for values around either +4 or −4, which curve is higher? In other words, which distribution is more likely to have extreme values—the normal (red) or Student *t* (blue) distribution?

The following exercises employ Graph 2.

6.3 As you use the scrollbar to increase (slowly) the degrees of freedom, what happens to the value of $t_{.025}$ and $-t_{.025}$?

6.4 When the degrees of freedom = 100, is there still a small difference between the critical values of $t_{.025}$ and $z_{.025}$? How large do you think the degrees of freedom would have to be before the two sets of critical values were identical?

CHI-SQUARED DISTRIBUTION

The density function of another very useful random variable is exhibited next.

CHI-SQUARED PROBABILITY DENSITY FUNCTION
The chi-squared density function is

$$f(\chi^2) = \frac{1}{[(\nu/2) - 1]!} \frac{1}{2^{\nu/2}} (\chi^2)^{(\nu/2)-1} e^{-\chi^2/2} \qquad \chi^2 > 0$$

The parameter ν is the number of degrees of freedom, which like the degrees of freedom of the Student *t* distribution, affects the shape.

Figure 8.25 depicts a chi-squared distribution. As you can see, it is positively skewed, ranging between 0 and ∞. Like that of the Student t distribution, its shape depends on its number of degrees of freedom. The effect of increasing the degrees of freedom is seen in Figure 8.26.

Figure 8.25
Chi-squared distribution

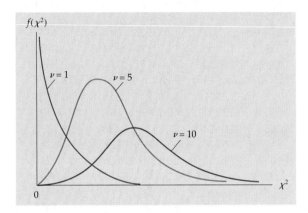

Figure 8.26
Chi-squared distributions

Determining Chi-Squared Values

The value of χ^2 with ν degrees of freedom such that the area to its right under the chi-squared curve is equal to A is denoted $\chi^2_{A,\nu}$. We cannot use $-\chi^2_{A,\nu}$ to represent the point such that the area to its *left* is A (as we did with the standard normal and Student t values) because χ^2 is always greater than 0. To represent left-tail critical values, we note that if the area to the left of a point is A, the area to its right must be $1 - A$ because the entire area under the chi-squared curve (as well as all continuous distributions) must equal 1. Thus $\chi^2_{1-A,\nu}$ denotes the point such that the area to its left is A. See Figure 8.27.

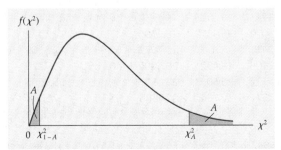

Figure 8.27
χ^2_A **and** χ^2_{1-A}

Table 5 in Appendix B (reproduced here as Table 8.6) lists critical values of the chi-squared distribution for degrees of freedom equal to 1 to 30, 40, 50, 60, 70 , 80, 90, and 100. For example, to find the point in a chi-squared distribution with 8 degrees of freedom such that the area to its right is .05, locate 8 degrees of freedom in the left column and $\chi^2_{.050}$ across the top. The intersection of the row and column contains the number we seek, as shown in Table 8.7. That is,

$$\chi^2_{.050,8} = 15.5073$$

To find the point in the same distribution such that the area to its *left* is .05, find the point such that the area to its *right* is .95. Locate $\chi^2_{.950}$ across the top row and 8 degrees of freedom down the left column (also shown in Table 8.7). You should see that

$$\chi^2_{.950,8} = 2.73264$$

Table 8.6 Critical Values of χ^2

Degrees of freedom	$\chi^2_{.995}$	$\chi^2_{.990}$	$\chi^2_{.975}$	$\chi^2_{.950}$	$\chi^2_{.900}$	$\chi^2_{.100}$	$\chi^2_{.050}$	$\chi^2_{.025}$	$\chi^2_{.010}$	$\chi^2_{.005}$
1	0.0000393	0.0001571	0.0009821	0.0039321	0.0157908	2.70554	3.84146	5.02389	6.63490	7.87944
2	0.0100251	0.0201007	0.0506356	0.102587	0.210720	4.60517	5.99147	7.37776	9.21034	10.5966
3	0.0717212	0.114832	0.215795	0.351846	0.584375	6.25139	7.81473	9.34840	11.3449	12.8381
4	0.206990	0.297110	0.484419	0.710721	1.063623	7.77944	9.48773	11.1433	13.2767	14.8602
5	0.411740	0.55430	0.831211	1.145476	1.61031	9.23635	11.0705	12.8325	15.0863	16.7496
6	0.675727	0.872085	1.237347	1.63539	2.20413	10.6446	12.5916	14.4494	16.8119	18.5476
7	0.989265	1.239043	1.68987	2.16735	2.83311	12.0170	14.0671	16.0128	18.4753	20.2777
8	1.344419	1.646482	2.17973	2.73264	3.48954	13.3616	15.5073	17.5346	20.0902	21.9550
9	1.734926	2.087912	2.70039	3.32511	4.16816	14.6837	16.9190	19.0228	21.6660	23.5893
10	2.15585	2.55821	3.24697	3.94030	4.86518	15.9871	18.3070	20.4831	23.2093	25.1882
11	2.60321	3.05347	3.81575	4.57481	5.57779	17.2750	19.6751	21.9200	24.7250	26.7569
12	3.07382	3.57056	4.40379	5.22603	6.30380	18.5494	21.0261	23.3367	26.2170	28.2995
13	3.56503	4.10691	5.00874	5.89186	7.04150	19.8119	22.3621	24.7356	27.6883	29.8194
14	4.07468	4.66043	5.62872	6.57063	7.78953	21.0642	23.6848	26.1190	29.1413	31.3193
15	4.60094	5.22935	6.26214	7.26094	8.54675	22.3072	24.9958	27.4884	30.5779	32.8013
16	5.14224	5.81221	6.90766	7.96164	9.31223	23.5418	26.2962	28.8454	31.9999	34.2672
17	5.69724	6.40776	7.56418	8.67176	10.0852	24.7690	27.5871	30.1910	33.4087	35.7185
18	6.26481	7.01491	8.23075	9.39046	10.8649	25.9894	28.8693	31.5264	34.8053	37.1564
19	6.84398	7.63273	8.90655	10.1170	11.6509	27.2036	30.1435	32.8523	36.1908	38.5822
20	7.43386	8.26040	9.59083	10.8508	12.4426	28.4120	31.4104	34.1696	37.5662	39.9968
21	8.03366	8.89720	10.28293	11.5913	13.2396	29.6151	32.6705	35.4789	38.9321	41.4010
22	8.64272	9.54249	10.9823	12.3380	14.0415	30.8133	33.9244	36.7807	40.2894	42.7956
23	9.26042	10.19567	11.6885	13.0905	14.8479	32.0069	35.1725	38.0757	41.6384	44.1813
24	9.88623	10.8564	12.4011	13.8484	15.6587	33.1963	36.4151	39.3641	42.9798	45.5585
25	10.5197	11.5240	13.1197	14.6114	16.4734	34.3816	37.6525	40.6465	44.3141	46.9278
26	11.1603	12.1981	13.8439	15.3791	17.2919	35.5631	38.8852	41.9232	45.6417	48.2899
27	11.8076	12.8786	14.5733	16.1513	18.1138	36.7412	40.1133	43.1944	46.9630	49.6449
28	12.4613	13.5648	15.3079	16.9279	18.9392	37.9159	41.3372	44.4607	48.2782	50.9933
29	13.1211	14.2565	16.0471	17.7083	19.7677	39.0875	42.5569	45.7222	49.5879	52.3356
30	13.7867	14.9535	16.7908	18.4926	20.5992	40.2560	43.7729	46.9792	50.8922	53.6720
40	20.7065	22.1643	24.4331	26.5093	29.0505	51.8050	55.7585	59.3417	63.6907	66.7659
50	27.9907	29.7067	32.3574	34.7642	37.6886	63.1671	67.5048	71.4202	76.1539	79.4900
60	35.5346	37.4848	40.4817	43.1879	46.4589	74.3970	79.0819	83.2976	88.3794	91.9517
70	43.2752	45.4418	48.7576	51.7393	55.3290	85.5271	90.5312	95.0231	100.425	104.215
80	51.1720	53.5400	57.1532	60.3915	64.2778	96.5782	101.879	106.629	112.329	116.321
90	59.1936	61.7541	65.6466	69.1260	73.2912	107.565	113.145	118.136	124.116	128.299
100	67.3276	70.0648	74.2219	77.9295	82.3581	118.498	124.342	129.561	135.807	140.169

Source: From C. M. Thompson, "Tables of the Percentage Points of the χ^2-Distribution," *Biometrika* 32 (1941): 188–89. Reproduced by permission of the Biometrika trustees.

Table 8.7 Finding $\chi^2_{.050,8}$ and $\chi^2_{.950,8}$

Degrees of Freedom	$\chi^2_{.995}$	$\chi^2_{.990}$	$\chi^2_{.975}$	$\chi^2_{.950}$	$\chi^2_{.900}$	$\chi^2_{.100}$	$\chi^2_{.050}$	$\chi^2_{.025}$	$\chi^2_{.010}$	$\chi^2_{.005}$
1	0.0000393	0.0001571	0.0009821	0.0039321	0.0157908	2.70554	3.84146	5.02389	6.63490	7.87944
2	0.0100251	0.0201007	0.0506356	0.102587	0.210720	4.60517	5.99147	7.37776	9.21034	10.5966
3	0.0717212	0.114832	0.215795	0.351846	0.584375	6.25139	7.81473	9.34840	11.3449	12.8381
4	0.206990	0.297110	0.484419	0.710721	1.063623	7.77944	9.48773	11.1433	13.2767	14.8602
5	0.411740	0.55430	0.831211	1.145476	1.61031	9.23635	11.0705	12.8325	15.0863	16.7496
6	0.675727	0.872085	1.237347	1.63539	2.20413	10.6446	12.5916	14.4494	16.8119	18.5476
7	0.989265	1.239043	1.68987	2.16735	2.83311	12.0170	14.0671	16.0128	18.4753	20.2777
8	1.344419	1.646482	2.17973	2.73264	3.48954	13.3616	15.5073	17.5346	20.0902	21.9550
9	1.734926	2.087912	2.70039	3.32511	4.16816	14.6837	16.9190	19.0228	21.6660	23.5893
10	2.15585	2.55821	3.24697	3.94030	4.86518	15.9871	18.3070	20.4831	23.2093	25.1882
11	2.60321	3.05347	3.81575	4.57481	5.57779	17.2750	19.6751	21.9200	24.7250	26.7569

USING THE COMPUTER

EXCEL

To compute the probability to the right of any chi-squared value, proceed as follows.

COMMANDS

1. Click f_x, **Function category: Statistical**, and **Function name: CHIDIST**. Click **OK**.
2. Type the value of x (**X**) and the degrees of freedom (**Deg_freedom**).
3. Alternatively, type into any cell

$$= \text{CHIDIST}([X], [\text{Degrees of freedom}])$$

For example, CHIDIST(6.25139,3) $= .1000$.

To determine a value of a chi-squared random variable, follow these instructions.

COMMANDS

1. Click f_x, **Function category: Statistical**, and **Function name: CHIINV**. Click **OK**.
2. Type the cumulative probability (**Probability**) and the degrees of freedom (**Deg_freedom**).
3. Alternatively, type into any cell

$$= \text{CHIINV}([\text{Probability}], [\text{Degrees of freedom}])$$

For example, CHIINV(.10,3) $= 6.25139$.

MINITAB

We can employ Minitab to compute probabilities and values of a chi-squared random variable.

COMMANDS

1. Click **Calc**, **Probability Distributions**, and **Chi-square....**
2. Select either **Cumulative probability** [to determine $P(X < x)$] or **Inverse cumulative probability** [to find the value of x such that $P(X < x) =$ cumulative probability].
3. Specify the **Degrees of freedom**.
4. If you wish to compute the probability for one value of x or determine the value of x for one probability, specify **Input constant** and type the value of x or the probability. Click **OK**.
5. If you wish to make probability statements about several values of x from the same t distribution, or determine the value of x for several cumulative probabilities, type the values into a column before clicking **Calc**. At step 4 specify **Input column**, type the name of the column, and click **OK**.

Seeing Statistics

APPLET 7:
CHI-SQUARED DISTRIBUTION

Like the Student t applet, this applet allows you to see how the degrees of freedom affect the shape of the chi-squared distribution. Additionally, you can use the applet to determine probabilities and values of the chi-squared random variable.

Use the right slider to change the degrees of freedom. Use the text boxes to change either the value of ChiSq or the probability. Remember to press the Return key in the text box to record the change.

Applet Exercises

7.1 What happens to the shape of the chi-squared distribution as the degrees of freedom increase?

7.2 Describe what happens to $\chi^2_{.05}$ when the degrees of freedom increase.

7.3 Describe what happens to $\chi^2_{.95}$ when the degrees of freedom increase.

F DISTRIBUTION

The density function of the F distribution is given in the next box.

F PROBABILITY DENSITY FUNCTION

$$f(F) = \frac{\left(\dfrac{\nu_1 + \nu_2 - 2}{2}\right)!}{\left(\dfrac{\nu_1 - 2}{2}\right)!\left(\dfrac{\nu_2 - 2}{2}\right)!}\left(\dfrac{\nu_1}{\nu_2}\right)^{\frac{\nu_1}{2}}\frac{F^{\frac{\nu_1 - 2}{2}}}{\left(1 + \dfrac{\nu_1 F}{\nu_2}\right)^{\frac{\nu_1 + \nu_2}{2}}} \qquad F > 0$$

where F ranges from 0 to ∞, and ν_1 and ν_2 are the parameters of the distribution called degrees of freedom. For reasons that are clearer in Chapter 13, we call ν_1 the *numerator degrees of freedom* and ν_2 the *denominator degrees of freedom*.

Figure 8.28 describes the density function when it is graphed. As you can see, the F distribution is positively skewed. Its actual shape depends on the two numbers of degrees of freedom.

Figure 8.28
F distribution

Determining Values of F

We define F_{A,ν_1,ν_2} as the value of F with ν_1 and ν_2 degrees of freedom such that the area to its right under the curve is A. That is,

$$P(F > F_{A,\nu_1,\nu_2}) = A$$

Because the F random variable, like the chi-squared, can equal only positive values, we define F_{1-A,ν_1,ν_2} as the value such that the area to its left is A. Figure 8.29 depicts this notation. Table 6 in Appendix B provides values of F_{A,ν_1,ν_2} for $A = .05, .025,$ and $.01$. Part of Table 6 is reproduced on page 264 as Table 8.8.

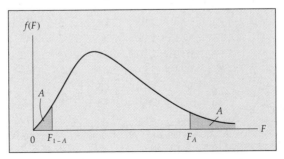

Figure 8.29
F_A and F_{1-A}

Values of F_{1-A,ν_1,ν_2} are unavailable. However, we do not need them because we can determine F_{1-A,ν_1,ν_2} from F_{A,ν_1,ν_2}. That is, statisticians can show that

$$F_{1-A,\nu_1,\nu_2} = \frac{1}{F_{A,\nu_2,\nu_1}}$$

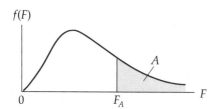

$f(F)$

A

0 F_A F

Table 8.8 Critical Values of F: $A = .05$

v_1				Numerator Degrees of Freedom				
v_2	1	2	3	4	5	6	7	8	9
1	161.4	199.5	215.7	224.6	230.2	234.0	236.8	238.9	240.5
2	18.51	19.00	19.16	19.25	19.30	19.33	19.35	19.37	19.38
3	10.13	9.55	9.28	9.12	9.01	8.94	8.89	8.85	8.81
4	7.71	6.94	6.59	6.39	6.26	6.16	6.09	6.04	6.00
5	6.61	5.79	5.41	5.19	5.05	4.95	4.88	4.82	4.77
6	5.99	5.14	4.76	4.53	4.39	4.28	4.21	4.15	4.10
7	5.59	4.74	4.35	4.12	3.97	3.87	3.79	3.73	3.68
8	5.32	4.46	4.07	3.84	3.69	3.58	3.50	3.44	3.39
9	5.12	4.26	3.86	3.63	3.48	3.37	3.29	3.23	3.18
10	4.96	4.10	3.71	3.48	3.33	3.22	3.14	3.07	3.02
11	4.84	3.98	3.59	3.36	3.20	3.09	3.01	2.95	2.90
12	4.75	3.89	3.49	3.26	3.11	3.00	2.91	2.85	2.80
13	4.67	3.81	3.41	3.18	3.03	2.92	2.83	2.77	2.71
14	4.60	3.74	3.34	3.11	2.96	2.85	2.76	2.70	2.65
15	4.54	3.68	3.29	3.06	2.90	2.79	2.71	2.64	2.59
16	4.49	3.63	3.24	3.01	2.85	2.74	2.66	2.59	2.54
17	4.45	3.59	3.20	2.96	2.81	2.70	2.61	2.55	2.49
18	4.41	3.55	3.16	2.93	2.77	2.66	2.58	2.51	2.46
19	4.38	3.52	3.13	2.90	2.74	2.63	2.54	2.48	2.42
20	4.35	3.49	3.10	2.87	2.71	2.60	2.51	2.45	2.39
21	4.32	3.47	3.07	2.84	2.68	2.57	2.49	2.42	2.37
22	4.30	3.44	3.05	2.82	2.66	2.55	2.46	2.40	2.34
23	4.28	3.42	3.03	2.80	2.64	2.53	2.44	2.37	2.32
24	4.26	3.40	3.01	2.78	2.62	2.51	2.42	2.36	2.30
25	4.24	3.39	2.99	2.76	2.60	2.49	2.40	2.34	2.28
26	4.23	3.37	2.98	2.74	2.59	2.47	2.39	2.32	2.27
27	4.21	3.35	2.96	2.73	2.57	2.46	2.37	2.31	2.25
28	4.20	3.34	2.95	2.71	2.56	2.45	2.36	2.29	2.24
29	4.18	3.33	2.93	2.70	2.55	2.43	2.35	2.28	2.22
30	4.17	3.32	2.92	2.69	2.53	2.42	2.33	2.27	2.21
40	4.08	3.23	2.84	2.61	2.45	2.34	2.25	2.18	2.12
60	4.00	3.15	2.76	2.53	2.37	2.25	2.17	2.10	2.04
120	3.92	3.07	2.68	2.45	2.29	2.17	2.09	2.02	1.96
∞	3.84	3.00	2.60	2.37	2.21	2.10	2.01	1.94	1.88

Denominator Degrees of Freedom (left label)

Source: From M. Merrington and C. M. Thompson, "Tables of Percentage Points of the Inverted Beta (F)-Distribution," *Biometrika 33* (1943): 73–88. Reproduced by permission of the Biometrika trustees.

To determine any critical value, find the numerator degrees of freedom v_1 across the top of Table 6 and the denominator degrees of freedom v_2 down the left column. The intersection of the row and column contains the number we seek. To illustrate, suppose that we want to find $F_{.05,5,7}$. Table 8.9 shows how this point is found. Locate the numerator degrees of freedom, 5, across the top and the denominator degrees of freedom, 7, down the left column. The intersection is 3.97. Thus, $F_{.05,5,7} = 3.97$.

Note that the order in which the degrees of freedom appear is important. To find $F_{.05,7,5}$ (numerator degrees of freedom = 7 and denominator degrees of freedom = 5), we locate 7 across the top and 5 down the side. The intersection is $F_{.05,7,5} = 4.88$.

Suppose that we want to determine the point in an F distribution with $v_1 = 4$ and $v_2 = 8$ such that the area to its left is .05, which means the area to its right is .95.

$$F_{.95,4,8} = \frac{1}{F_{.05,8,4}} = \frac{1}{6.04} = .166$$

Table 8.9 Finding $F_{.05,5,7}$

v_1	Numerator Degrees of Freedom								
v_2	1	2	3	4	5	6	7	8	9
1	161.4	199.5	215.7	224.6	230.2	234.0	236.8	238.9	240.5
2	18.51	19.00	19.16	19.25	19.30	19.33	19.35	19.37	19.38
3	10.13	9.55	9.28	9.12	9.01	8.94	8.89	8.85	8.81
4	7.71	6.94	6.59	6.39	6.26	6.16	6.09	6.04	6.00
5	6.61	5.79	5.41	5.19	5.05	4.95	4.88	4.82	4.77
6	5.99	5.14	4.76	4.53	4.39	4.28	4.21	4.15	4.10
7	5.59	4.74	4.35	4.12	3.97	3.87	3.79	3.73	3.68
8	5.32	4.46	4.07	3.84	3.69	3.58	3.50	3.44	3.39
9	5.12	4.26	3.86	3.63	3.48	3.37	3.29	3.23	3.18
10	4.96	4.10	3.71	3.48	3.33	3.22	3.14	3.07	3.02
11	4.84	3.98	3.59	3.36	3.20	3.09	3.01	2.95	2.90
12	4.75	3.89	3.49	3.26	3.11	3.00	2.91	2.85	2.80
13	4.67	3.81	3.41	3.18	3.03	2.92	2.83	2.77	2.71
14	4.60	3.74	3.34	3.11	2.96	2.85	2.76	2.70	2.65
15	4.54	3.68	3.29	3.06	2.90	2.79	2.71	2.64	2.59

Denominator Degrees of Freedom

USING THE COMPUTER

EXCEL

To compute the probability to the right of any F value, proceed as follows.

COMMANDS
1. Click f_x, **Function category: Statistical**, and **Function name: FDIST**. Click **OK**.
2. Type the value of x (**X**), numerator degrees of freedom (**Deg_freedom1**), and denominator degrees of freedom (**Deg_freedom2**).
3. Alternately, type

   = FDIST([X], [Numerator degrees of freedom],[Denominator degrees of freedom])

For example, FDIST(3.97,5,7) = .05.

To determine a value of an F random variable, follow these instructions.

COMMANDS
1. Click f_x, **Function category: Statistical**, and **Function name: FINV**. Click **OK**.

2. Type the probability to the right of the value (**Probability**) the numerator degrees of freedom (**Deg_freedom1**), and the denominator degrees of freedom (**Deg_freedom2**).
3. Alternatively, type

   = FINV([Probability],[Numerator degrees of freedom],[Denominator degrees of freedom])

   For example, FINV(.05,5,7) = 3.97.

MINITAB

We can employ Minitab to compute probabilities and values of an *F* random variable.

COMMANDS

1. Click **Calc**, **Probability Distributions**, and **F...**.
2. Select either **Cumulative probability** [to determine $P(X < x)$] or **Inverse cumulative probability** [to find the value of *x* such that $P(X < x) =$ cumulative probability].
3. Specify the **Numerator degrees of freedom** and the **Denominator degrees of freedom**.
4. If you wish to compute the probability for one value of *x* or determine the value of *x* for one probability, specify **Input constant** and type the value of *x* or the probability. Click **OK**.
5. If you wish to make probability statements about several values of *x* from the same *t* distribution, or determine the value of *x* for several cumulative probabilities, type the values into a column before clicking **Calc**. At step 4 specify **Input column**, type the name of the column, and click **OK**.

S e e i n g   S t a t i s t i c s

APPLET 8:
F DISTRIBUTION

The graph shows the *F* distribution. Use the left and right sliders to change the numerator and denominator, respectively, degrees of freedom. Use the text boxes to change either the value of *F* or the probability. Remember to press the Return key in the text box to record the change.

Applet Exercises

8.1 Set the numerator degrees of freedom equal to 1. What happens to the shape of the *F* distribution as the denominator degrees of freedom increase?

8.2 Set the numerator degrees of freedom equal to 10. What happens to the shape of the *F* distribution as the denominator degrees of freedom increase?

8.3 Describe what happens to $F_{.05}$ when either the numerator or denominator degrees of freedom increase.

8.4 Describe what happens to $F_{.95}$ when either the numerator or denominator degrees of freedom increase.

EXERCISES

Some of the following exercises require the use of a computer and software.

8.93 Use the *t* table (Table 4) to find the following values of *t*.

a $t_{.10,15}$ **b** $t_{.10,23}$ **c** $t_{.025,83}$ **d** $t_{.05,195}$

8.94 Use the *t* table (Table 4) to find the following values of *t*.

a $t_{.005,33}$ **b** $t_{.10,600}$ **c** $t_{.05,4}$ **d** $t_{.01,20}$

8.95 Use a computer to find the following values of *t*.

a $t_{.10,15}$ **b** $t_{.10,23}$ **c** $t_{.025,83}$ **d** $t_{.05,195}$

8.96 Use a computer to find the following values of *t*.

a $t_{.05,143}$ **b** $t_{.01,12}$ **c** $t_{.025,\infty}$ **d** $t_{.05,100}$

8.97 Use a computer to find the following probabilities.

a $P(t_{64} > 2.12)$

b $P(t_{27} > 1.90)$

c $P(t_{159} > 1.33)$

d $P(t_{550} > 1.85)$

8.98 Use a computer to find the following probabilities.

a $P(t_{141} > .94)$

b $P(t_{421} > 2.00)$

c $P(t_{1000} > 1.96)$

d $P(t_{82} > 1.96)$

8.99 Use the χ^2 table (Table 5) to find the following values of χ^2.

a $\chi^2_{.10,5}$ **b** $\chi^2_{.01,100}$ **c** $\chi^2_{.95,18}$ **d** $\chi^2_{.99,60}$

8.100 Use the χ^2 table (Table 5) to find the following values of χ^2.

a $\chi^2_{.90,26}$ **b** $\chi^2_{.01,30}$ **c** $\chi^2_{.10,1}$ **d** $\chi^2_{.99,78}$

8.101 Use a computer to find the following values of χ^2.

a $\chi^2_{.25,66}$ **b** $\chi^2_{.40,100}$ **c** $\chi^2_{.50,17}$ **d** $\chi^2_{.10,17}$

8.102 Use a computer to find the following values of χ^2.

a $\chi^2_{.99,55}$ **b** $\chi^2_{.05,800}$ **c** $\chi^2_{.99,43}$ **d** $\chi^2_{.10,233}$

8.103 Use a computer to find the following probabilities.

a $P(\chi^2_{73} > 80)$

b $P(\chi^2_{200} > 125)$

c $P(\chi^2_{88} > 60)$

d $P(\chi^2_{1000} > 450)$

8.104 Use a computer to find the following probabilities.

a $P(\chi^2_{250} > 250)$

b $P(\chi^2_{36} > 25)$

c $P(\chi^2_{600} > 500)$

d $P(\chi^2_{120} > 100)$

8.105 Use the *F* table (Table 6) to find the following values of *F*.

a $F_{.05,3,7}$ **b** $F_{.05,7,3}$ **c** $F_{.025,5,20}$ **d** $F_{.01,12,60}$

8.106 Use the *F* table (Table 6) to find the following values of *F*.

a $F_{.025,8,22}$ **b** $F_{.05,20,30}$ **c** $F_{.01,9,18}$ **d** $F_{.025,24,10}$

8.107 Use a computer to find the following values of *F*.

a $F_{.05,70,70}$ **b** $F_{.01,45,100}$ **c** $F_{.025,36,50}$ **d** $F_{.05,500,500}$

8.108 Use a computer to find the following values of *F*.

a $F_{.01,100,150}$ **b** $F_{.05,25,125}$ **c** $F_{.01,11,33}$ **d** $F_{.05,300,800}$

8.109 Use a computer to find the following probabilities.

a $P(F_{7,20} > 2.5)$

b $P(F_{18,63} > 1.4)$

c $P(F_{34,62} > 1.8)$

d $P(F_{200,400} > 1.1)$

8.110 Use a computer to find the following probabilities.

a $P(F_{600,800} > 1.1)$

b $P(F_{35,100} > 1.3)$

c $P(F_{66,148} > 2.1)$

d $P(F_{17,37} > 2.8)$

8.6 SUMMARY

This chapter dealt with **continuous random variables** and their distributions. Because a continuous random variable can assume an infinite number of values, the probability that the random variable equals any single value is 0. Consequently, we address the problem of computing the probability of a range of values. We showed that the probability of any interval is the area in the interval under the curve representing the **density function**.

We introduced the most important distribution in statistics and showed how to compute the probability that a **normal random variable** falls into any interval. Additionally, we demonstrated how to use the normal table backward to find values of a normal random variable given a probability. Next we introduced the **exponential distribution**, a distribution that is particularly useful in several management science applications. Finally, we presented three more continuous random variables and their probability density functions. The **Student *t*, chi-squared**, and *F* **distributions** will be employed extensively in statistical inference.

IMPORTANT TERMS

Probability density function 227
Uniform probability distribution 228
Rectangular probability distribution 228
Normal distribution 231
Normal random variable 231
Standard normal random variable 233

Exponential distribution 248
Student t distribution 252
Degrees of freedom 252
Chi-squared distribution 258
F distribution 262

SYMBOLS

Symbol	Pronounced	Represents
π	*pi*	3.14159...
z_A	*z-sub-A* or *z-A*	Value of Z such that area to its right is A
ν	*nu*	Degrees of freedom
t_A	*t-sub-A* or *t-A*	Value of t such that area to its right is A
χ^2_A	*chi-squared-sub-A* or *chi-squared-A*	Value of chi-squared such that area to its right is A
F_A	*F-sub-A* or *F-A*	Value of F such that area to its right is A
ν_1	*nu-sub-one* or *nu-one*	Numerator degrees of freedom
ν_2	*nu-sub-two* or *nu-two*	Denominator degrees of freedom

COMPUTER OUTPUT AND INSTRUCTIONS

Probability/ Random Variable	Excel	Minitab
Normal probability	243	244
Normal random variable	244	244
Exponential probability	250	250
Exponential random variable		250
Student t probability	257	257
Student t random variable	257	257
Chi-squared probability	261	262
Chi-squared random variable	261	262
F probability	265	266
F random variable	265	266

REFERENCES

Durrett, Richard, *Probability: Theory and Examples,* 2nd edition. Belmont, CA: Duxbury, 1995.

Feller, William, *An Introduction to Probability Theory,* Vol. 1, 3rd edition. New York: John Wiley and Sons, 1968.

Ross, Sheldon M., *A First Course in Probability,* 5th edition. Englewood Cliffs, NJ: Prentice Hall, 1997.

Ross, Sheldon M., *Introduction to Probability Models,* 4th edition. New York: Academic Press, 1989.

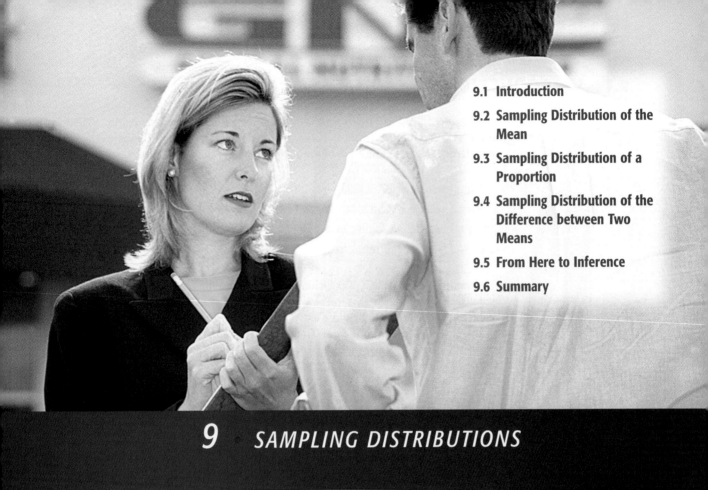

9 · *SAMPLING DISTRIBUTIONS*

MCDONALD'S DAILY SALES OF HAMBURGER

The amount of hamburger beef sold per hour from 11:30 A.M. to 8:30 P.M. by the McDonald's restaurants across a large city is normally distributed. It is known that the mean is 2,100 pounds and the standard deviation is 450 pounds. What is the probability that in a given day the restaurants sell more than 20,000 pounds? (See page 281 for the solution.)

9.1   INTRODUCTION

This chapter introduces the *sampling distribution*, a fundamental element in statistical inference. We remind you that statistical inference is the process of converting data into information. Here are the parts of the process we have thus far discussed:

1. Parameters describe populations.
2. Parameters are almost always unknown.
3. We take a random sample of a population to obtain the necessary data.
4. We calculate one or more statistics from the data.

For example, to estimate a population mean, we compute the sample mean. Although there is very little chance that the sample mean and the population mean are identical, we would expect them to be quite close. However, for the purposes of statistical inference, we need to be able to measure how close. The sampling distribution provides this service. It plays a crucial role in the process, because the measure of proximity it provides is the key to statistical inference.

9.2 SAMPLING DISTRIBUTION OF THE MEAN

To grasp the idea of a sampling distribution, consider the population created by throwing a fair die infinitely many times, with the random variable X indicating the number of spots showing on any one throw. The probability distribution of the random variable X is as follows.

x	1	2	3	4	5	6
$p(x)$	1/6	1/6	1/6	1/6	1/6	1/6

The population is infinitely large, because we can throw the die infinitely many times (or at least imagine doing so). From the definitions of expected value and variance presented in Section 7.3, we calculate the population mean, variance, and standard deviation.

Population mean:

$$\mu = \sum xp(x)$$

$$= 1\left(\tfrac{1}{6}\right) + 2\left(\tfrac{1}{6}\right) + 3\left(\tfrac{1}{6}\right) + 4\left(\tfrac{1}{6}\right) + 5\left(\tfrac{1}{6}\right) + 6\left(\tfrac{1}{6}\right)$$

$$= 3.5$$

Population variance:

$$\sigma^2 = \sum (x - \mu)^2 \, p(x)$$

$$= (1 - 3.5)^2\left(\tfrac{1}{6}\right) + (2 - 3.5)^2\left(\tfrac{1}{6}\right) + (3 - 3.5)^2\left(\tfrac{1}{6}\right) + (4 - 3.5)^2\left(\tfrac{1}{6}\right)$$

$$+ (5 - 3.5)^2\left(\tfrac{1}{6}\right) + (6 - 3.5)^2\left(\tfrac{1}{6}\right)$$

$$= 2.92$$

Population standard deviation:

$$\sigma = \sqrt{\sigma^2} = \sqrt{2.92} = 1.71$$

Now suppose that μ is unknown and that we want to estimate its value by using the sample mean $\bar{X}*$ calculated from a sample of size $n = 2$. In actual practice, only one sample would be drawn, and hence there would be only one value of $\bar{X}$, but to assess how closely $\bar{X}$ estimates the value of μ we will develop the sampling distribution of $\bar{X}$ by evaluating every possible sample of size 2.

Consider all the different possible samples of size 2 that could be drawn from the population of die tosses. Figure 9.1 depicts this process. For each sample, we compute the mean. Because the value of the sample mean varies randomly from sample to sample, we can regard $\bar{X}$ as a new random variable created by sampling. Table 9.1 lists all the possible samples and their corresponding values of $\bar{x}$.

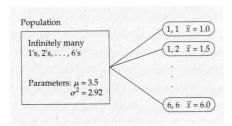

Figure 9.1
Drawing samples of size 2 from a population

Table 9.1 All Samples of Size 2 and Their Means

Sample	$\bar{x}$	Sample	$\bar{x}$	Sample	$\bar{x}$
1, 1	1.0	3, 1	2.0	5, 1	3.0
1, 2	1.5	3, 2	2.5	5, 2	3.5
1, 3	2.0	3, 3	3.0	5, 3	4.0
1, 4	2.5	3, 4	3.5	5, 4	4.5
1, 5	3.0	3, 5	4.0	5, 5	5.0
1, 6	3.5	3, 6	4.5	5, 6	5.5
2, 1	1.5	4, 1	2.5	6, 1	3.5
2, 2	2.0	4, 2	3.0	6, 2	4.0
2, 3	2.5	4, 3	3.5	6, 3	4.5
2, 4	3.0	4, 4	4.0	6, 4	5.0
2, 5	3.5	4, 5	4.5	6, 5	5.5
2, 6	4.0	4, 6	5.0	6, 6	6.0

There are 36 different possible samples of size 2; because each sample is equally likely, the probability of any one sample being selected is 1/36. However, $\bar{X}$ can assume only 11 different possible values: 1.0, 1.5, 2.0, ..., 6.0, with certain values of $\bar{x}$ occurring more frequently than others. The value $\bar{X} = 1.0$ occurs only once, so its probability is 1/36. The value $\bar{X} = 1.5$ can occur in two ways; hence, $p(1.5) = 2/36$. The probabilities of the other values of $\bar{X}$ are determined in similar fashion, and the resulting sampling distribution of $\bar{X}$ is shown in Table 9.2.

---

*Recall our convention introduced in Chapter 7. Uppercase letters represent the random variables and their lowercase counterparts represent their values. In this chapter we introduce the sampling distribution of the sample mean. When we refer to the random variable we will use $\bar{X}$; the values of this random variable are represented by $\bar{x}$.

Table 9.2 Sampling Distribution of $\overline{X}$

$\overline{x}$	$p(\overline{x})$
1.0	1/36
1.5	2/36
2.0	3/36
2.5	4/36
3.0	5/36
3.5	6/36
4.0	5/36
4.5	4/36
5.0	3/36
5.5	2/36
6.0	1/36

The most interesting aspect of the sampling distribution of $\overline{X}$ is how different it is from the distribution of X, as can be seen in Figure 9.2.

Figure 9.2
Distributions of X and $\overline{X}$

(a) Distribution of X

(b) Sampling distribution of $\overline{X}$

We can also compute the mean, variance, and standard deviation of the sampling distribution. Once again using the definitions of expected value and variance, we determine the following parameters of the sampling distribution.

Mean of the sampling distribution of $\overline{X}$:

$$\mu_{\overline{x}} = \sum \overline{x}p(\overline{x})$$

$$= 1.0\left(\tfrac{1}{36}\right) + 1.5\left(\tfrac{2}{36}\right) + \cdots + 6.0\left(\tfrac{1}{36}\right)$$

$$= 3.5$$

Notice that the mean of the sampling distribution of $\overline{X}$ is equal to the mean of the population of the toss of a die computed above.

Variance of the sampling distribution of $\overline{X}$:

$$\sigma_{\overline{x}}^2 = \sum (\overline{x} - \mu_{\overline{x}})^2 p(\overline{x})$$

$$= (1.0 - 3.5)^2\left(\tfrac{1}{36}\right) + (1.5 - 3.5)^2\left(\tfrac{2}{36}\right) + \cdots + (6.0 - 3.5)^2\left(\tfrac{1}{36}\right)$$

$$= 1.46$$

It is no coincidence that the variance of the sampling distribution of $\overline{X}$ is exactly half of the variance of the population of the toss of a die (computed above as $\sigma^2 = 2.92$).

Standard deviation of the sampling distribution of $\overline{X}$:

$$\sigma_{\overline{x}} = \sqrt{\sigma_{\overline{x}}^2} = \sqrt{1.46} = 1.21$$

It is important to recognize that the distribution of $\overline{X}$ is different from the distribution of X as depicted in Figure 9.2. However, the two random variables are related. Their means are the same ($\mu_{\bar{x}} = \mu = 3.5$) and their variances are related ($\sigma_{\bar{x}}^2 = \sigma^2/2$).

Don't get lost in the terminology and notation. Remember that μ and σ^2 are the parameters of the population of X. To create the sampling distribution of $\overline{X}$, we repeatedly drew samples of size 2 from the population and calculated $\bar{x}$ for each sample. Thus, we treat $\overline{X}$ as a brand-new random variable, with its own distribution, mean, and variance. The mean is denoted $\mu_{\bar{x}}$ and the variance is denoted $\sigma_{\bar{x}}^2$.

If we now repeat the sampling process with the same population but with other values of n, we produce somewhat different sampling distributions of $\overline{X}$. Figure 9.3 shows the sampling distributions of $\overline{X}$ when $n = 5$, 10, and 25.

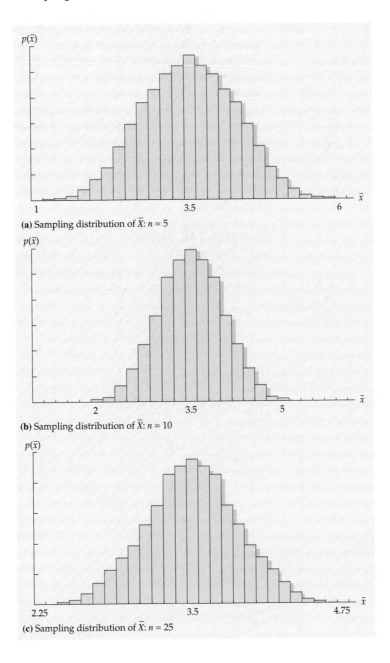

(a) Sampling distribution of $\overline{X}$: $n = 5$

(b) Sampling distribution of $\overline{X}$: $n = 10$

(c) Sampling distribution of $\overline{X}$: $n = 25$

Figure 9.3
Sampling distributions of $\overline{X}$ for different sample sizes

For each value of n, the mean* of the sampling distribution of $\overline{X}$ is the mean of the population from which we're sampling. That is,

$$\mu_{\overline{x}} = \mu = 3.5$$

The variance of the sampling distribution of the sample mean is the variance of the population divided by the sample size. That is,

$$\sigma_{\overline{x}}^2 = \frac{\sigma^2}{n}$$

This means that for all values of n, the variance of the sampling distribution of $\overline{X}$ is less than the variance of the population we're sampling from. Thus, a randomly selected value of $\overline{X}$ (the mean of the number of spots observed in, say, five throws of the die) is likely to be closer to the mean value of 3.5 than is a randomly selected value of X (the number of spots observed in one throw). Indeed, this is what you would expect, because in five throws of the die you are likely to get some 5's and 6's and some 1's and 2's, which will tend to offset one another in the averaging process and produce a sample mean reasonably close to 3.5. As the number of throws of the die increases, the probability that the sample mean will be close to 3.5 also increases. Thus, we observe in Figure 9.3 that the sampling distribution of $\overline{X}$ becomes narrower (or more concentrated about the mean) as n increases.

Another thing that happens as n gets larger is that the sampling distribution of $\overline{x}$ becomes increasingly bell shaped. This phenomenon is summarized in the **central limit theorem.**

CENTRAL LIMIT THEOREM

The sampling distribution of the mean of a random sample drawn from any population is approximately normal for a sufficiently large sample size. The larger the sample size, the more closely the sampling distribution of $\overline{X}$ will resemble a normal distribution.

The accuracy of the approximation alluded to in the central limit theorem depends on the probability distribution of the parent population and on the sample size. If the population is normal, then $\overline{X}$ is normally distributed for all values of n. If the population is nonnormal, then $\overline{X}$ is approximately normal only for larger values of n. In many practical situations, a sample size of 30 may be sufficiently large to allow us to use the normal distribution as an approximation for the sampling distribution of $\overline{X}$. However, if the population is extremely nonnormal (examples of extremely nonnormal populations include bimodal and highly skewed distributions), the sampling distribution will also be nonnormal even for moderately large values of n.

We can now summarize what we know about the sampling distribution of the sample mean.

---

*In CD Appendix 9.1 we use the laws of expected value and variance (page 200) to derive the parameters of sampling distributions.

SAMPLING DISTRIBUTION OF THE SAMPLE MEAN

1. $\mu_{\bar{x}} = \mu$

2. $\sigma_{\bar{x}}^2 = \sigma^2 / n,$* and $\sigma_{\bar{x}} = \sigma / \sqrt{n}$ (The standard deviation of $\bar{X}$ is called the **standard error of the mean**.)

3. If X is normal, $\bar{X}$ is normal. If X is nonnormal, $\bar{X}$ is approximately normal for sufficiently large sample sizes. The definition of "sufficiently large" depends on the extent of nonnormality of x.

$S\ e\ e\ i\ n\ g$ $S\ t\ a\ t\ i\ s\ t\ i\ c\ s$

APPLET 9:
FAIR DICE 1

This applet has two parts. The first part simulates the tossing of one fair die. You can toss one at a time, 10 at a time, or 100 at a time. The histogram of the cumulative results is shown. The second part allows you to simulate tossing 2 dice one set at a time, 10 sets a time, or 100 sets a time. The histogram of the means of the cumulative results is exhibited. To start again, click Refresh or Reload on the browser menu. The value N represents the number of sets. The larger the value of N, the closer the histogram approximates the theoretical distribution.

Applet Exercises
Simulate 2,500 tosses of one fair die and 2,500 tosses of two fair dice.

9.1 Does the simulated probability distribution of one die look like the theoretical distribution displayed in Figure 9.2? Discuss the reason for the deviations.

9.2 Does the simulated sampling distribution of the mean of two dice look like the theoretical distribution displayed in Figure 9.2? Discuss the reason for the deviations.

9.3 Do the distribution of one die and the sampling distribution of the mean of two dice have the same or different shapes? How would you characterize the difference?

9.4 Do the centers of the distribution of one die and the sampling distribution of the mean of two dice appear to be about the same?

9.5 Do the spreads of the distribution of one die and the sampling distribution of the mean of two dice appear to be about the same? Which one has the smaller spread?

---

*The variance of $\bar{X}$ is σ^2 / n if the population from which we're sampling is infinitely large. If the population is finite, the variance of $\bar{X}$ is

$$\sigma_{\bar{x}}^2 = \left(\frac{\sigma^2}{n}\right)\left(\frac{N - n}{N - 1}\right)$$

where N is the population size and $(N - n)/(N - 1)$ is the **finite population correction factor**. In most practical situations (including all examples and exercises in this book), the target population is finite but very large relative to the sample size (e.g., the population of television viewers in North America). In such cases the finite population correction factor is so close to 1 that we can ignore it. As a general rule, include the finite population correction factor only if the sample size is greater than 1% of the population size.

S e e i n g   S t a t i s t i c s

APPLET 10:
FAIR DICE 2

This applet allows you to simulate tossing 12 fair dice and drawing the sampling distribution of the mean. As was the case with the previous applet, you can toss one set, 10 sets, or 100 sets. To start again, click Refresh or Reload on the browser menu.

Applet Exercises
Simulate 2,500 tosses of 12 fair dice.

10.1 Does the simulated sampling distribution of $\bar{X}$ appear to be bell shaped?

10.2 Does it appear that the simulated sampling distribution of the mean of 12 fair dice is narrower than that of 2 fair dice? Explain why this is so.

S e e i n g   S t a t i s t i c s

APPLET 11:
LOADED DICE

This applet has two parts. The first part simulates the tossing of a loaded die. "Loaded" refers to the inequality of the probabilities of the six outcomes. You can toss one at a time, 10 at a time, or 100 at a time. The second part allows you to simulate tossing 12 loaded dice one set at a time, 10 sets at a time, or 100 sets at a time.

Applet Exercises
Simulate 2,500 tosses of one loaded die.

11.1 Estimate the probability of each value of X.

11.2 Use the estimated probabilities to compute the expected value, variance, and standard deviation of X.

Simulate 2,500 tosses of 12 loaded dice.

11.3 Does it appear that the mean of the simulated sampling distribution of $\bar{X}$ is equal to 3.5?

11.4 Does it appear that the standard deviation of the simulated sampling distribution of the mean of 12 loaded dice is greater than that for 12 fair dice? Explain why this is so.

11.5 Does the simulated sampling distribution of the mean of 12 loaded dice appear to be bell shaped? Explain why this is so.

Seeing Statistics

APPLET 12:
SKEWED DICE

This applet has two parts. The first part simulates the tossing of a skewed die. You can toss it one at a time, 10 at a time, or 100 at a time. The second part allows you to simulate tossing 2 dice one set at a time, 10 sets at a time, or 100 sets at a time.

Applet Exercises

Simulate 2,500 tosses of one skewed die.

12.1 Estimate the probability of each value of X.

12.2 Use the estimated probabilities to compute the expected value, variance, and standard deviation of X.

Simulate 2,500 tosses of 12 skewed dice.

12.3 Does it appear that the mean of the simulated sampling distribution of $\overline{X}$ is less than 3.5?

12.4 Does the simulated sampling distribution of the mean of 12 skewed dice appear to be bell shaped? Explain why this is so.

EXAMPLE 9.1

The foreman of a bottling plant has observed that the amount of soda in each "32-ounce" bottle is actually a normally distributed random variable, with a mean of 32.2 ounces and a standard deviation of .3 ounce.

a If a customer buys one bottle, what is the probability that the bottle will contain more than 32 ounces?

b If a customer buys a carton of four bottles, what is the probability that the mean amount of the four will be greater than 32 ounces?

SOLUTION

a Because the random variable is the amount of soda in one bottle, we want to find $P(X > 32)$, where X is normally distributed, $\mu = 32.2$, and $\sigma = .3$. Hence,

$$P(X > 32) = P\left(\frac{X - \mu}{\sigma} > \frac{32 - 32.2}{.3}\right)$$

$$= P(Z > -.67)$$

$$= .5 + .2486 = .7486$$

b Now we want to find the probability that the mean amount of four filled bottles exceeds 32 ounces. That is, we want $P(\overline{X} > 32)$. From our previous analysis and from the central limit theorem, we know the following:

1. $\overline{X}$ is normally distributed.
2. $\mu_{\bar{x}} = \mu = 32.2$
3. $\sigma_{\bar{x}} = \sigma/\sqrt{n} = .3/\sqrt{4} = .15$

Hence,

$$P(\overline{X} > 32) = P\left(\frac{\overline{X} - \mu_{\bar{x}}}{\sigma_{\bar{x}}} > \frac{32 - 32.2}{.15}\right)$$

$$= P(Z > -1.33)$$

$$= .5 + .4082$$

$$= .9082$$

Figure 9.4 illustrates the distributions used in this example.

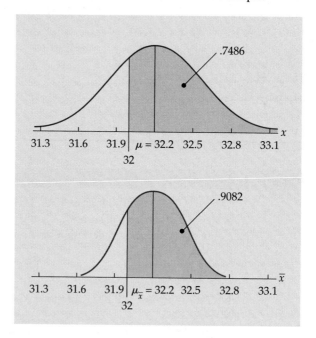

Figure 9.4
Distribution of X and
sampling distribution of X̄
in Example 9.1

In Example 9.l(b), we began with the assumption that both μ and σ were known. Then, using the sampling distribution, we made a probability statement about $\overline{X}$. Unfortunately, the values of μ and σ are not usually known, so an analysis such as that in Example 9.1 cannot usually be conducted. However, we can use the sampling distribution to infer something about an unknown value of μ on the basis of a sample mean.

EXAMPLE 9.2

The dean of a business school claims that the average weekly income of his school's BBA graduates 1 year after graduation is $600.

a If the dean's claim is correct, and if the distribution of weekly incomes has a standard deviation of $100, what is the probability that 25 randomly selected graduates have an average weekly income of less than $550?

b If a random sample of 25 graduates had an average weekly income of $550, what would you conclude about the validity of the dean's claim?

SOLUTION

a We want to find $P(\overline{X} < 550)$. The distribution of X, the weekly income, is likely to be positively skewed, but not sufficiently to make the distribution of $\overline{X}$ nonnormal. As a result, we may assume that $\overline{X}$ is normal with mean $\mu_{\bar{x}} = \mu = 600$ and standard deviation $\sigma_{\bar{x}} = \sigma/\sqrt{n} = 100/\sqrt{25} = 20$. Thus,

$$P(\overline{X} < 550) = P\left(\frac{\overline{X} - \mu_{\bar{x}}}{\sigma_{\bar{x}}} < \frac{550 - 600}{20}\right)$$

$$= P(Z < -2.5)$$

$$= .5 - .4938$$

$$= .0062$$

Figure 9.5 describes this calculation.

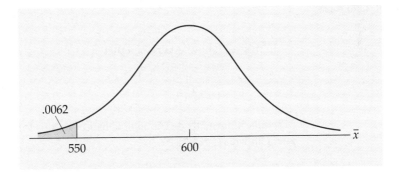

Figure 9.5
$P(\overline{X} < 550)$

b The probability of observing a sample mean as low as $550 when the population mean is $600 is extremely small. Because this event is quite unlikely, we would have to conclude that the dean's claim is not justified.

USING THE SAMPLING DISTRIBUTION FOR INFERENCE

Our conclusion in part (b) of Example 9.2 illustrates how the sampling distribution can be used to make inferences about population parameters. The first form of inference is estimation, which we introduce in the next chapter. In preparation for this momentous occasion, we'll present another way of expressing the probability associated with the sampling distribution.

Recall the notation introduced in Section 8.3 (see page 240). We defined z_A to be the value of z such that the area to the right of z_A under the standard normal curve is equal to A. We also showed that $z_{.025} = 1.96$. Because the standard normal distribution is symmetric about 0, the area to the left of -1.96 is also .025. The area between -1.96 and 1.96 is .95. Figure 9.6 depicts this notation. We can express the notation algebraically as

$$P(-1.96 < Z < 1.96) = .95$$

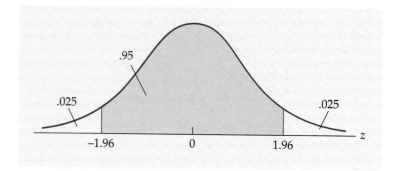

Figure 9.6
$P(-1.96 < Z < 1.96) = .95$

In this section we established that

$$Z = \frac{\overline{X} - \mu}{\sigma/\sqrt{n}}$$

is standard normally distributed. Substituting this form of Z into the probability statement above, we produce

$$P\left(-1.96 < \frac{\overline{X} - \mu}{\sigma/\sqrt{n}} < 1.96\right) = .95$$

With a little algebraic manipulation (multiply all three terms by $\sigma/\sqrt{n}$ and add μ to all three terms), we determine

$$P\left(\mu - 1.96\frac{\sigma}{\sqrt{n}} < \overline{X} < \mu + 1.96\frac{\sigma}{\sqrt{n}}\right) = .95$$

Returning to Example 9.2, where $\mu = 600$, $\sigma = 100$, and $n = 25$, we compute

$$P\left(600 - 1.96\frac{100}{\sqrt{25}} < \overline{X} < 600 + 1.96\frac{100}{\sqrt{25}}\right) = .95$$

Thus, we can say that

$$P(560.8 < \overline{X} < 639.2) = .95$$

This tells us that there is a 95% probability that a mean of a sample of size 25 drawn from a population whose mean is 600 and whose standard deviation is 100 will fall between 560.8 and 639.2. Because the sample mean was computed to be $550, we would have to conclude that the dean's claim is not supported by the statistic.

Changing the probability from .95 to .90 changes the probability statement to

$$P\left(\mu - 1.645\frac{\sigma}{\sqrt{n}} < \overline{X} < \mu + 1.645\frac{\sigma}{\sqrt{n}}\right) = .90$$

We can also produce a general form of this statement:

$$P\left(\mu - z_{\alpha/2}\frac{\sigma}{\sqrt{n}} < \overline{X} < \mu + z_{\alpha/2}\frac{\sigma}{\sqrt{n}}\right) = 1 - \alpha$$

In this formula, α (Greek letter *alpha*) is the probability that $\overline{X}$ does not fall into the interval. To apply this formula all we need do is substitute the values for μ, σ, n, and α. For example, with $\mu = 600$, $\sigma = 100$, $n = 25$ and $\alpha = .01$, we produce

$$P\left(\mu - z_{.005}\frac{\sigma}{\sqrt{n}} < \overline{X} < \mu + z_{.005}\frac{\sigma}{\sqrt{n}}\right) = 1 - .01$$

$$P\left(600 - 2.575\frac{100}{\sqrt{25}} < \overline{X} < 600 + 2.575\frac{100}{\sqrt{25}}\right) = .99$$

$$P(548.5 < \overline{X} < 651.5) = .99$$

which is another probability statement about $\overline{X}$. In Section 10.3, we will use a similar type of probability statement to derive the first statistical inference technique.

MCDONALD'S DAILY SALES OF HAMBURGER

We would like to compute the probability that the total amount sold of hamburger over a 9-hour period is greater than 20,000 pounds. However, the information we have describes the distribution of *hourly* sales. Fortunately, it is easy to convert the probability statement about the total to one about hourly sales. That is,

$$P(\text{Total} > 20,000) = P\left(\text{Hourly Mean} > \frac{20,000}{9} = 2,222.2\right)$$

$$P(\overline{X} > 2,222.2) = P\left(\frac{\overline{X} - \mu}{\sigma/\sqrt{n}} > \frac{2,222.2 - 2,100}{450/\sqrt{9}}\right)$$

$$= P(Z > .81) = .5 - .2910 = .2090$$

The probability that total sales of hamburger between 11:30 A.M. and 8:30 P.M. exceeds 20,000 pounds is .2090.

EXERCISES

9.1 Let X represent the result of the toss of a fair die. Find the following probabilities.
   a $P(X = 3)$
   b $P(X = 4)$
   c $P(X = 1)$
   d $P(X = 6)$

9.2 Let $\overline{X}$ represent the mean of the toss of two fair dice. Find the following probabilities.
   a $P(\overline{X} = 3)$
   b $P(\overline{X} = 4)$
   c $P(\overline{X} = 1)$
   d $P(\overline{X} = 6)$

9.3 Refer to Exercises 9.1 and 9.2. What do the probabilities tell you about the variances of X and of $\overline{X}$?

9.4 An experiment consists of tossing five balanced dice. Find the following probabilities.
   a $P(\overline{X} = 1)$
   b $P(\overline{X} = 6)$

9.5 A normally distributed population has a mean of 40 and a standard deviation of 12. What does the central limit theorem say about the sampling distribution of the mean if samples of size 100 are drawn from this population?

9.6 Refer to Exercise 9.5. Suppose that the population is not normally distributed. Does this change your answer? Explain.

9.7 A sample of $n = 16$ observations is drawn from a normal population with $\mu = 1,000$ and $\sigma = 200$. Find the following.

  a $P(\overline{X} > 1,050)$
  b $P(\overline{X} < 960)$
  c $P(\overline{X} > 1,100)$

9.8 Repeat Exercise 9.7 with $n = 25$.

9.9 Repeat Exercise 9.7 with $n = 100$.

9.10 Given a normal population whose mean is 50 and whose standard deviation is 5.

  a Find the probability that a random sample of 4 has a mean between 49 and 52.
  b Find the probability that a random sample of 16 has a mean between 49 and 52.
  c Find the probability that a random sample of 25 has a mean between 49 and 52.

9.11 Repeat Exercise 9.10 for a standard deviation of 10.

9.12 Repeat Exercise 9.10 for a standard deviation of 20.

9.13 The heights of North American women are normally distributed with a mean of 64 inches and a standard deviation of 2 inches.

  a What is the probability that a randomly selected woman is taller than 66 inches?
  b A random sample of four women is selected. What is the probability that the sample mean height is greater than 66 inches?
  c What is the probability that the mean height of a random sample of 100 women is greater than 66 inches?

9.14 Refer to Exercise 9.13. If the population of women's heights is not normally distributed, which, if any, of the questions can you answer? Explain.

9.15 An automatic machine in a manufacturing process is operating properly if the lengths of an important subcomponent are normally distributed with mean of 117 cm and standard deviation of 5.2 cm.

  a Find the probability that one selected subcomponent is longer than 120 cm.
  b Find the probability that if four subcomponents are randomly selected, their mean length exceeds 120 cm.
  c Find the probability that if four subcomponents are randomly selected, all four have lengths that exceed 120 cm.

9.16 The amount of time that university professors devote to their jobs per week is normally distributed with a mean of 52 hours and a standard deviation of 6 hours.

  a What is the probability that a professor works for more than 60 hours per week?
  b Find the probability that the mean amount of work per week for three randomly selected professors is more than 60 hours.
  c Find the probability that if three professors are randomly selected, all three work for more than 60 hours per week.

9.17 The number of pizzas consumed per month by university students is normally distributed with a mean of 10 and a standard deviation of 3.

  a What proportion of students consume more than 12 pizzas per month?
  b What is the probability that in a random sample of 25 students, more than 275 pizzas are consumed? (*Hint:* What is the mean number of pizzas consumed by the sample of 25 students?)

9.18 The marks on a statistics midterm test are normally distributed with a mean of 78 and a standard deviation of 6.

  a What proportion of the class has a midterm mark of less than 75?
  b What is the probability that a class of 50 has an average midterm mark that is less than 75?

9.19 The amount of time spent by North American adults watching television per day is normally distributed with a mean of 6 hours and a standard deviation of 1.5 hours.

  a What is the probability that a randomly selected North American adult watches television for more than 7 hours per day?
  b What is the probability that the average time watching television by a random sample of five North American adults is more than 7 hours?
  c What is the probability that in a random sample of five North American adults, all watch television for more than 7 hours per day?

9.20 The manufacturer of cans of salmon that are supposed to have a net weight of 6 ounces tells you that the net weight is actually a normal random variable with a mean of 6.05 ounces and a standard deviation of .18 ounce. Suppose that you draw a random sample of 36 cans.

  a Find the probability that the mean weight of the sample is less than 5.97 ounces.
  b Suppose your random sample of 36 cans of salmon produced a mean weight that is less than 5.97 ounces. Comment on the statement made by the manufacturer.

9.21 The number of customers who enter a supermarket each hour is normally distributed with a mean of 600 and a standard deviation of 200. The supermarket is open 16 hours per day. What is the probability that the total number of customers who enter the supermarket in one day is greater than 10,000? (*Hint:* Calculate the average hourly number of customers necessary to exceed 10,000 in one 16-hour day.)

9.22 The sign on the elevator in the Peters Building, which houses the School of Business and Economics at Wilfrid Laurier University, states, "Maximum Capacity 1,140 kilograms (2500 pounds) or 16 Persons." A professor of statistics wonders what the probability is that 16 persons would weigh more than 1,140 kilograms. Discuss what the professor needs (besides the ability to perform the calculations) in order to satisfy his curiosity.

9.23 Refer to Exercise 9.22. Suppose that the professor discovers that the weights of people who use the elevator are normally distributed with an average of 75 kilograms and a standard deviation of 10 kilograms. Calculate the probability that the professor seeks.

9.24 The time it takes for a statistics professor to mark his midterm test is normally distributed with a mean of 4.8 minutes and a standard deviation of 1.3 minutes. There are 60 students in the professor's class. What is the probability that he needs more than 5 hours to mark all the midterm tests?

9.25 Refer to Exercise 9.24 Does your answer change if you discover that the times needed to mark a midterm test are not normally distributed?

9.26 The dean of a business school claims that the average MBA graduate is offered a starting salary of $55,000. The standard deviation of the offers is $4,600. What is the probability that in a random sample of 38 MBA graduates, the mean starting salary is less than $53,000?

9.27 Refer to Exercise 9.26. Suppose that a random sample of 38 MBA graduates report that their mean starting salary is $53,000. What does this tell you about the dean's claim?

9.3 SAMPLING DISTRIBUTION OF A PROPORTION

In Section 7.6 we introduced the binomial distribution, whose parameter is p, the probability of success in any trial. In order to compute binomial probabilities, we assumed that p was known. However, in reality p is unknown, requiring the statistics practitioner to estimate its value from a sample. The estimator of a population proportion of successes is the *sample proportion.* That is, we count the number of successes in a sample and compute

$$\hat{P} = \frac{X}{n}$$

($\hat{P}$ is read as *p-hat*) where X is the number of successes and n is the sample size. When we take a sample of size n we're actually conducting a binomial experiment and as a result X is binomially distributed. Thus, the probability of any value of $\hat{P}$ can be calculated from its value of X. For example, suppose that we have a binomial experiment with $n = 10$ and $p = .4$. To find the probability that the sample proportion $\hat{P}$ is less than or equal to .50, we find the probability that X is less than or equal to 5 (because 5/10 = .50). From Table 1 in Appendix B we find with $n = 10$ and $p = .4$

$$P(\hat{P} \le .50) = P(X \le 5) = .834$$

We can calculate the probability associated with other values of $\hat{P}$ similarly.

Discrete distributions like the binomial do not lend themselves easily to the kinds of calculation needed for inference. And, inference is the reason we need sampling distributions. Fortunately, we can approximate the binomial distribution using the normal distribution.

NORMAL APPROXIMATION TO THE BINOMIAL DISTRIBUTION

Recall how we introduced continuous probability distributions in Chapter 8. We developed the density function by converting a histogram so that the total area in the rectangles equaled 1. We can do the same for a binomial distribution. To illustrate, let X be a binomial random variable with $n = 20$ and $p = .5$. We can easily determine the probability of each value of X, where $X = 0, 1, 2, ..., 19, 20$. A rectangle representing a value of x is drawn so that its area equals the probability. We accomplish this by letting the height of the rectangle equal the probability and the base of the rectangle equal 1. Thus the base of each rectangle for x is the interval $x - .5$ to $x + .5$. Figure 9.7 depicts this graph. As you can see, the rectangle representing $x = 10$ is the rectangle whose base is the interval 9.5 to 10.5 and whose height is $P(X = 10)$, which is calculated to be .176.

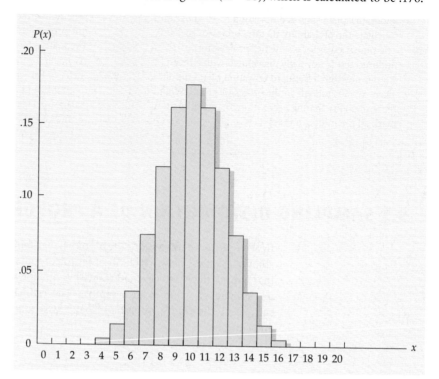

Figure 9.7
Binomial distribution with
$n = 20$ and $p = .5$

If we now smooth the ends of the rectangles, we produce a bell-shaped curve as seen in Figure 9.8. Thus to use the normal approximation, all we need do is find the area under the *normal* curve between 9.5 and 10.5. To find normal probabilities requires us to first standardize X by subtracting the mean and dividing by the standard deviation. The values for μ and σ are derived from the binomial distribution being approximated. In Section 7.6 we pointed out that

$$\mu = np$$

and

$$\sigma = \sqrt{np(1 - p)}$$

For $n = 20$ and $p = .5$ we have

$$\mu = np = 20(.5) = 10$$

and

$$\sigma = \sqrt{np(1 - p)} = \sqrt{20(.5)(1 - .5)} = 2.24$$

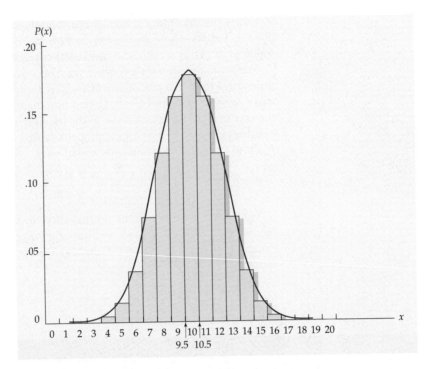

Figure 9.8
Binomial distribution with
$n = 20$ and $p = .5$ and
normal approximation

To calculate the probability that $X = 10$ using the normal distribution requires that we find the area under the normal curve between 9.5 and 10.5. That is,

$$P(X = 10) \approx P(9.5 < Y < 10.5)$$

where Y is a normal random variable approximating the binomial random variable X. We standardize Y and employ Table 3.

$$P(9.5 < Y < 10.5) = P\left(\frac{9.5 - 10}{2.24} < \frac{Y - \mu}{\sigma} < \frac{10.5 - 10}{2.24}\right)$$

$$= P(-.22 < Z < .22)$$

$$= 2(.0871)$$

$$= .1742$$

The actual probability that X equals 10 is

$$P(X = 10) = .176$$

As you can see, the approximation is quite good.

Notice that to draw a binomial distribution, which is discrete, it was necessary to draw rectangles whose bases were constructed by adding and subtracting .5 to the values of X. The .5 is called the **continuity correction factor**.

The approximation for any other value of X would proceed in the same manner. In general, the binomial probability $P(X = x)$ is approximated by the area under a normal curve between $x - .5$ and $x + .5$. To find the binomial probability $P(X \le x)$, we calculate the area under the normal curve to the left of $x + .5$. For the same binomial random variable ($n = 20$ and $p = .5$), the probability that its value is less than or equal to 8 is $P(X \le 8) = .252$. The normal approximation is

$$P(X \le 8) \approx P(Y < 8.5) = P\left(\frac{Y - \mu}{\sigma} < \frac{8.5 - 10}{2.24}\right) = P(Z < -.67) = .2514$$

We find the area under the normal curve to the right of $x - .5$ to determine the binomial probability $P(X \ge x)$. To illustrate, the probability that the binomial random variable (with $n = 20$ and $p = .5$) is greater than or equal to 14 is $P(X \ge 14) = .058$. The normal approximation is

$$P(X \ge 14) \approx P(Y > 13.5) = P\left(\frac{Y - \mu}{\sigma} > \frac{13.5 - 10}{2.24}\right) = P(Z > 1.56) = .0594$$

Seeing Statistics

APPLET 13:

NORMAL APPROXIMATION TO BINOMIAL PROBABILITIES

This applet shows how well the normal distribution approximates the binomial distribution. Select values for n and p, which will specify a binomial distribution. Then set a value for k. The applet calculates and graphs both the binomial and normal probabilities for $P(X \le k)$.

Applet Exercises

13.1 Given a binomial distribution with $n = 5$ and $p = .2$, use the applet to compute the actual and normal approximations of the following.

a $P(X \le 0)$
b $P(X \le 1)$

c $P(X \le 2)$
d $P(X \le 3)$

Describe how well the normal distribution approximates the binomial when n is small and when p is small.

13.2 Repeat Exercise 13.1 with $p = .5$. Describe how well the normal distribution approximates the binomial when n is small and when p is .5.

13.3 Suppose that X is a binomial random variable with $n = 10$ and $p = .2$. Use the applet to calculate the actual and normal approximations of the following.

a $P(X \le 2)$
b $P(X \le 3)$
c $P(X \le 4)$
d $P(X \le 5)$

Describe how well the normal distribution approximates the binomial when $n = 10$ and when p is small.

13.4 Repeat Exercise 13.3 with $p = .5$. Describe how well the normal distribution approximates the binomial when $n = 10$ and when p is .5.

13.5 Describe the effect on the normal approximation to the binomial as n increases.

OMITTING THE CORRECTION FACTOR FOR CONTINUITY

When calculating the probability of *individual* values of X, as we did when we computed the probability that X equals 10 above, the correction factor *must* be used. If we don't, we are left with finding the area in a line, which is 0. When computing the probability of a *range* of values of X, we can omit the correction factor. However, the omission of the correction factor will decrease the accuracy of the approximation. For example, if we approximate $P(X \leq 8)$ as we did above except without the correction factor, we find

$$P(X \leq 8) \approx P(Y < 8) = P\left(\frac{Y - \mu}{\sigma} < \frac{8 - 10}{2.24}\right) = P(Z < -.89) = .1867$$

The absolute size of the error between the actual cumulative binomial probability and its normal approximation is quite small when the values of x are in the tail regions of the distribution. For example, the probability that a binomial random variable with $n = 20$ and $p = .5$ is less than or equal to 3 is

$$P(X \leq 3) = .0013 \quad \text{(using Excel)}$$

The normal approximation with the correction factor is

$$P(X \leq 3) \approx P(Y < 3.5) = P\left(\frac{Y - \mu}{\sigma} < \frac{3.5 - 10}{2.24}\right) = P(Z < -2.90) = .0019$$

The normal approximation without the correction factor is (using Excel)

$$P(X \leq 3) \approx P(Y < 3) = P\left(\frac{Y - \mu}{\sigma} < \frac{3 - 10}{2.24}\right) = P(Z < -3.13) = .0009$$

For larger values of *n*, the differences between the normal approximation with and without the correction factor are small even for values of *x* near the center of the distribution. For example, the probability that a binomial random variable with $n = 1{,}000$ and $p = .3$ is less than or equal to 260 is

$$P(X \leq 260) = .0029 \quad \text{(using Excel)}$$

The normal approximation with the correction factor is

$$P(X \leq 260) \approx P(Y < 260.5) = P\left(\frac{Y - \mu}{\sigma} < \frac{260.5 - 300}{14.49}\right) = P(Z < -2.73) = .0032$$

The normal approximation without the correction factor is

$$P(X \leq 260) \approx P(Y < 260) = P\left(\frac{Y - \mu}{\sigma} < \frac{260 - 300}{14.49}\right) = P(Z < -2.76) = .0029$$

As we pointed out, the normal approximation of the binomial distribution is made necessary by the needs of statistical inference. As you will discover, statistical inference generally involves the use of large values of *n* and the part of the sampling distribution that is of greatest interest lies in the tail regions. The correction factor was a temporary tool that allowed us to convince you that a binomial distribution can be approximated by a normal distribution. Now that we have done so, we will use the normal approximation of the binomial distribution to approximate the sampling distribution of a sample proportion and in such applications the correction factor will be omitted.

APPROXIMATE SAMPLING DISTRIBUTION OF A SAMPLE PROPORTION

Using the laws of expected value and variance (see CD Appendix 9.1), we can determine the mean, variance, and standard deviation of $\hat{P}$. (The standard deviation of $\hat{P}$ is called the **standard error of the proportion**.) That is,

$$E(\hat{P}) = p$$

$$V(\hat{P}) = \sigma_{\hat{p}}^2 = \frac{p(1 - p)}{n}$$

$$\sigma_{\hat{p}} = \sqrt{p(1 - p)/n}$$

Thus, the variable

$$Z = \frac{\hat{P} - p}{\sqrt{p(1 - p)/n}}$$

is approximately standard normally distributed provided that the sample size is large. The theoretical sample size requirements are that np and $n(1 - p)$ are both greater than or equal to 5. We refer to this requirement as *theoretical* because in practice much larger sample sizes are needed for the inference to be useful.

EXAMPLE 9.3

In the last election, a state representative received 52% of the votes cast. One year after the election the representative organized a survey that asked a random sample of 300 people whether they would vote for him in the next election. Assuming that his popularity has not changed, what is the probability that more than half of the sample would vote for him?

SOLUTION The number of respondents who would vote for the representative is a binomial random variable with $n = 300$ and $p = .52$. We want to determine the probability that the sample proportion is greater than 50%. That is, we want to find $P(\hat{P} > .50)$.

We now know that the sample proportion $\hat{P}$ is approximately normally distributed with mean $p = .52$ and standard deviation $\sqrt{p(1 - p)/n} = \sqrt{(.52)(.48)/300} = .0288$. Thus we calculate

$$P(\hat{P} > .50) = P\left(\frac{\hat{P} - p}{\sqrt{p(1 - p)/n}} > \frac{.50 - .52}{.0288}\right) = P(Z > -.69) = .5 + .2549 = .7549$$

Assuming that the level of support remains at 52%, the probability that more than half the sample of 300 people would vote for the representative is 75.49%.

EXERCISES

Use the normal approximation without the correction factor to find the probabilities in the following exercises.

9.28 In a binomial experiment with $n = 300$ and $p = .5$, find the probability that $\hat{P}$ is greater than 60%.

9.29 Repeat Exercise 9.28 with $p = .55$.

9.30 Repeat Exercise 9.28 with $p = .6$.

9.31 The probability of success on any trial of a binomial experiment is 25%. Find the probability that the proportion of successes in a sample of 500 is less than 22%.

9.32 Repeat Exercise 9.31 given $n = 800$.

9.33 Repeat Exercise 9.31 given $n = 1,000$.

9.34 The proportion of eligible voters in the next election who will vote for the incumbent is assumed to be 55%. What is the probability that in a random sample of 500 voters, less than 49% say they will vote for the incumbent?

9.35 The assembly line that produces an electronic component of a missile system has historically resulted in a 2% defective rate. A random sample of 800 components is drawn. What is the probability that the defective rate is greater than 4%? Suppose that in the random sample the defective rate is 4%. What does that suggest about the assembly line defective rate?

9.36 A manufacturer of aspirin claims that the proportion of headache sufferers who get relief with just two aspirins is 53%. What is the probability that in a random sample of 400 headache sufferers, less than 50% obtain relief? If 50% of the sample actually obtained relief, what does this suggest about the manufacturer's claim?

9.37 Repeat Exercise 9.36 using a sample of 1,000.

9.38 A commercial for a household appliances manufacturer claims that less than 5% of all its products require a service call in the first year. A consumer protection association wants to check the claim by surveying 400 households that recently purchased one of the company's appliances. What is the probability that more than 10% require a service call within the first year? What would you say about the commercial's

honesty if in a random sample of 400 households, 10% report at least one service call?

9.39 The Laurier Company's brand has a market share of 30%. Suppose that in a survey, 1,000 consumers of the product are asked which brand they prefer. What is the probability that more than 32% of the respondents say they prefer Laurier brand?

9.40 A university bookstore claims that 50% of its customers are satisfied with the service and prices.

a If this claim is true, what is the probability that in a random sample of 600 customers, less than 45% are satisfied?

b Suppose that in a random sample of 600 customers, 270 express satisfaction with the bookstore. What does this tell you about the bookstore's claim?

9.41 A psychologist believes that 80% of male drivers when lost continue to drive, hoping to find the location they seek rather than ask directions. To examine this belief, he took a random sample of 350 male drivers and asked each what they did when lost. If the belief is true, determine the probability that less than 75% said they continue driving.

9.42 The Red Lobster restaurant chain regularly surveys its customers. On the basis of these surveys, the management of the chain claims that 75% of its customers rate the food as excellent. A consumer testing service wants to examine the claim by asking 460 customers to rate the food. What is the probability that less that 70% rate the food as excellent?

9.43 An accounting professor claims that no more than one quarter of undergraduate business students will major in accounting. What is the probability that in a random sample of 1,200 undergraduate business students, 336 or more will major in accounting?

9.44 Refer to Exercise 9.43. A survey of a random sample of 1,200 undergraduate business students indicates that there are 336 students who plan to major in accounting. What does this tell you about the professor's claim?

9.4 SAMPLING DISTRIBUTION OF THE DIFFERENCE BETWEEN TWO MEANS

Another sampling distribution that you will soon encounter is that of the **difference between two sample means**. The sampling plan calls for independent random samples drawn from each of two normal populations. The samples are said to be *independent* if the selection of the members of one sample is independent of the selection of the members of the second sample. We will expand upon this discussion in Chapter 13. We are interested in the sampling distribution of the difference between the two sample means.

In Section 9.2 we introduced the central limit theorem, which states that in repeated sampling from a normal population whose mean is μ and whose standard deviation is σ, the sampling distribution of the sample mean is normal with mean μ and standard deviation $\sigma/\sqrt{n}$. Statisticians have shown that the difference between two independent normal random variables is also normally distributed. Thus, the difference between two sample means $\overline{X}_1 - \overline{X}_2$ is normally distributed if both populations are normal.

Through the use of the laws of expected value and variance (see CD Appendix 9.1), we derive the expected value and variance of the sampling distribution of $\overline{X}_1 - \overline{X}_2$:

$$\mu_{\overline{x}_1 - \overline{x}_2} = \mu_1 - \mu_2$$

and

$$\sigma_{\overline{x}_1 - \overline{x}_2}^2 = \frac{\sigma_1^2}{n_1} + \frac{\sigma_2^2}{n_2}$$

Thus, it follows that in repeated independent sampling from two populations with means μ_1 and μ_2 and standard deviations σ_1 and σ_2, respectively, the sampling distribution of $\overline{X}_1 - \overline{X}_2$ is normal with mean

$$\mu_{\overline{x}_1 - \overline{x}_2} = \mu_1 - \mu_2$$

and standard deviation (which is the **standard error of the difference between two means**)

$$\sigma_{\overline{x}_1 - \overline{x}_2} = \sqrt{\frac{\sigma_1^2}{n_1} + \frac{\sigma_2^2}{n_2}}$$

If the populations are nonnormal then the sampling distribution is only approximately normal for large sample sizes. The required sample sizes depend on the extent of nonnormality. However, for most populations, sample sizes of 30 or more are sufficient.

Figure 9.9 depicts the sampling distribution of the difference between two means.

**Figure 9.9
Sampling Distribution
of $\bar{x}_1 - \bar{x}_2$**

EXAMPLE 9.4

Suppose that the starting salaries of MBAs at Wilfrid Laurier University (WLU) are normally distributed with a mean of $62,000 and a standard deviation of $14,500. The starting salaries of MBAs at the University of Western Ontario (UWO) are normally distributed with a mean of $60,000 and a standard deviation of $18,300. If a random sample of 50 WLU MBAs and a random sample of 60 UWO MBAs are selected, what is the probability that the sample mean starting salary of WLU graduates will exceed that of the UWO graduates?

SOLUTION   We want to determine $P(\bar{X}_1 - \bar{X}_2 > 0)$. We know that $\bar{X}_1 - \bar{X}_2$ is normally distributed with mean $\mu_1 - \mu_2 = 62{,}000 - 60{,}000 = 2{,}000$ and standard deviation

$$\sqrt{\frac{\sigma_1^2}{n_1} + \frac{\sigma_2^2}{n_2}} = \sqrt{\frac{14{,}500^2}{50} + \frac{18{,}300^2}{60}} = 3{,}128$$

We can standardize the variable and refer to Table 3:

$$P(\bar{X}_1 - \bar{X}_2 > 0) = P\left(\frac{(\bar{X}_1 - \bar{X}_2) - (\mu_1 - \mu_2)}{\sqrt{\dfrac{\sigma_1^2}{n_1} + \dfrac{\sigma_2^2}{n_2}}} > \frac{0 - 2{,}000}{3{,}128} \right) = P(Z > -.64) = .5 + .2389 = .7389$$

There is a 73.89% probability that for a sample of size 50 from the WLU graduates and a sample of size 60 of UWO graduates, the sample mean starting salary of WLU graduates will exceed the sample mean of UWO graduates. Note that this means that even though the population mean of WLU graduates is $2,000 more than that of the UWO graduates, there is a 26.11% probability (calculated from $1 - .7389$) that the sample mean starting salary of UWO graduates would be greater than that of WLU graduates.

Seeing Statistics

APPLET 14:

DISTRIBUTION OF THE DIFFERENCES BETWEEN MEANS

This first part of this applet depicts two graphs. The first graph shows the distribution of the random variable of two populations. Moving the top slider shifts the first distribution left or right. The right slider controls the value of the population standard deviations, which are assumed to be equal. By moving each slider, you can see the relationship between the two populations.

The second graph describes the sampling distribution of the mean of each population in the first graph. Moving the right slider increases or decreases the sample size, which is the same for both samples.

The second part of the applet has three graphs. The first two graphs are identical to the graphs in the first part. The third graph depicts the sampling distribution of the difference between the two sample means from the populations described above.

Moving the sliders allows you to see the effect on the sampling distribution of $\bar{x}_1 - \bar{x}_2$ of changing the relationship between the two population means, the common population standard deviation, and the sample size.

Applet Exercises

14.1 Describe the effect of changing the difference between the population means from −5.0 to 4.5 on the population random variables, the sampling distribution of $\bar{X}_1$, the sampling distribution of $\bar{X}_2$, and the sampling distribution of $\bar{X}_1 - \bar{X}_2$.

14.2 Describe the effect of changing the standard deviations from $\sigma_1 = \sigma_2 = 1.1$ to $\sigma_1 = \sigma_2 = 3.0$ on the population random variables, the sampling distribution of $\bar{X}_1$, the sampling distribution of $\bar{X}_2$, and the sampling distribution of $\bar{X}_1 - \bar{X}_2$.

14.3 Describe the effect of changing the sample sizes from $n_1 = n_2 = 2$ to $n_1 = n_2 = 20$ on the sampling distribution of $\bar{X}_1$, the sampling distribution of $\bar{X}_2$, and the sampling distribution of $\bar{X}_1 - \bar{X}_2$.

EXERCISES

9.45 Independent random samples of 10 observations each are drawn from normal populations. The parameters of these populations are

Population 1: $\mu = 280, \sigma = 25$

Population 2: $\mu = 270, \sigma = 30$

Find the probability that the mean of sample 1 is greater than the mean of sample 2 by more than 25.

9.46 Repeat Exercise 9.45 with samples of size 50.

9.47 Repeat Exercise 9.45 with samples of size 100.

9.48 Suppose that we have two normal populations with means and standard deviations listed below. If random samples of size 25 are drawn from each population, what is the probability that the mean of sample 1 is greater than the mean of sample 2?

Population 1: $\mu = 40, \sigma = 6$

Population 2: $\mu = 38, \sigma = 8$

9.49 Repeat Exercise 9.48 assuming that the standard deviations are 12 and 16, respectively.

9.50 Repeat Exercise 9.48 assuming that the means are 140 and 138, respectively.

9.51 A factory's worker productivity is normally distributed. One worker produces an average of 75 units per day with a standard deviation of 20. Another worker produces at an average rate of 65 per day with a standard deviation of 21.
   a What is the probability that in any single day worker 1 will outproduce worker 2?
   b What is the probability that during one week (5 working days), worker 1 will outproduce worker 2?

9.52 A professor of statistics noticed that the marks in his course are normally distributed. He has also noticed that his morning classes average 73% with a standard deviation of 12% on their final exams. His afternoon classes average 77% with a standard deviation of 10%.
   a What is the probability that a randomly selected student in the morning class has a higher final exam mark than a randomly selected student from an afternoon class?
   b What is the probability that the mean mark of four randomly selected students from a morning class is greater than the average mark of four randomly selected students from an afternoon class?

9.53 The manager of a restaurant believes that waiters and waitresses who introduce themselves by telling customers their names will get larger tips than those who don't. In fact, she claims that the average tip for the former group is 18% while that of the latter is only 15%. If tips are normally distributed with a standard deviation of 3%, what is the probability that in a random sample of 10 tips recorded from waiters and waitresses who introduce themselves and 10 tips from waiters and waitresses who don't, the mean of the former will exceed that of the latter?

9.54 The average North American loses an average of 15 days per year due to colds and flu. The natural remedy echinacea is reputed to boost the immune system. One manufacturer of echinacea pills claims that consumers of its product will reduce the number of days lost to colds and flu by one-third. To test the claim, a random sample of 50 people was drawn. Half took echinacea, and the other half took placebos. If we assume that the standard deviation of the number of days lost to colds and flu with and without echinacea is 3 days, find the probability that the mean number of days lost for echinacea users is less than that for nonusers.

9.5 FROM HERE TO INFERENCE

The primary function of the sampling distribution is statistical inference. To see how the sampling distribution contributes to the development of inferential methods, we need to briefly review how we got to this point.

In Chapters 7 and 8 we introduced probability distributions, which allowed us to make probability statements about values of the random variable. A prerequisite of this calculation is knowledge of the distribution and the relevant parameters. In Example 7.9, we needed to know that the probability that Pat Statsdud guesses the correct answer is 20% ($p = .2$) and that the number of correct answers (successes) in 10 questions (trials) is a binomial random variable. We then could compute the probability of any number of successes. In Example 8.2, we needed to know that the return on investment is normally distributed with a mean of 10% and a standard deviation of 5%. These three bits of information allowed us to calculate the probability of various values of the random variable.

Figure 9.10 symbolically represents the use of probability distributions. Simply put, knowledge of the population and its parameter(s) allows us to use the probability distribution to make probability statements about individual members of the population. The direction of the arrows indicates the direction of the flow of information.

Figure 9.10
Probability distribution

In this chapter, we developed the sampling distribution, wherein knowledge of the parameter(s) and some information about the distribution allow us to make probability statements about a sample statistic. In Example 9.2, knowing the population mean and standard deviation and assuming that the population is not extremely nonnormal enabled us to calculate a probability statement about a sample mean. Figure 9.11 describes the application of sampling distributions.

Figure 9.11
Sampling distribution

Notice that in applying both probability distributions and sampling distributions, we need to know the value of the relevant parameters, a highly unlikely circumstance. In the real world, parameters are almost always unknown because they represent descriptive measurements about extremely large populations. Statistical inference addresses this problem. It does so by reversing the direction of the flow of knowledge in Figure 9.11. In Figure 9.12 we display the character of statistical inference. Starting in Chapter 10, we will assume that most population parameters are unknown. The statistics practitioner will sample from the population and compute the required statistic. The sampling distribution of that statistic will enable us to draw inferences about the parameter.

Figure 9.12
Sampling distribution in inference

You may be surprised to learn that, by and large, that is all we do in the remainder of this book. Why then do we need another 15 chapters? They are needed because there are many more parameter and sampling distribution combinations that define the inferential procedures to be presented in an introductory statistics course. However, they all work in the same way. If you understand how one procedure is evolved, you will likely understand all of them. Our task in the next two chapters is to ensure that you understand the first inferential method. Your job is identical.

9.6 SUMMARY

The **sampling distribution** of a statistic is created by repeated sampling from a population. In this chapter we introduced the sampling distribution of the mean, the proportion, and the difference between two means. We described how these distributions are created theoretically and empirically.

IMPORTANT TERMS

Sampling distribution 270
Central limit theorem 274
Sampling distribution of the sample mean 275
Standard error of the mean 275
Normal approximation of the binomial distribution 283
Continuity correction factor 286
Sampling distribution of a sample proportion 288
Standard error of the proportion 288
Sampling distribution of the difference between two sample means 290
Standard error of the difference between two means 290

SYMBOLS

Symbol	Pronounced	Represents
$\mu_{\bar{x}}$	mu-x-bar	Mean of the sampling distribution of the sample mean
$\sigma_{\bar{x}}^2$	sigma-squared-x-bar	Variance of the sampling distribution of the sample mean
$\sigma_{\bar{x}}$	sigma-x-bar	Standard deviation (standard error) of the sampling distribution of the sample mean
α	alpha	Probability
$\hat{P}$	p-hat	Sample proportion
$\sigma_{\hat{p}}^2$	sigma-squared-p-hat	Variance of the sampling distribution of the sample proportion
$\sigma_{\hat{p}}$	sigma-p-hat	Standard deviation (standard error) of the sampling distribution of the sample proportion
$\mu_{\bar{x}_1 - \bar{x}_2}$	mu-x-bar-1-minus x-bar-2	Mean of the sampling distribution of the difference between two sample means
$\sigma_{\bar{x}_1 - \bar{x}_2}^2$	sigma-squared-x-bar-1-minus-x-bar-2	Variance of the sampling distribution of the difference between two sample means
$\sigma_{\bar{x}_1 - \bar{x}_2}$	sigma-x-bar-1-minus x-bar-2	Standard deviation (standard error) of the sampling distribution of the difference between two sample means

FORMULAS

Expected value of the sample mean

$$E(\overline{X}) = \mu_{\bar{x}} = \mu$$

Variance of the sample mean

$$V(\overline{X}) = \sigma_{\bar{x}}^2 = \frac{\sigma^2}{n}$$

Standard error of the sample mean

$$\sigma_{\bar{x}} = \frac{\sigma}{\sqrt{n}}$$

Standardizing the sample mean

$$Z = \frac{\overline{X} - \mu}{\sigma/\sqrt{n}}$$

Expected value of the sample proportion

$$E(\hat{P}) = \mu_{\hat{p}} = p$$

Variance of the sample proportion

$$V(\hat{P}) = \sigma_{\hat{p}}^2 = \frac{p(1 - p)}{n}$$

Standard error of the sample proportion

$$\sigma_{\hat{p}} = \sqrt{\frac{p(1 - p)}{n}}$$

Standardizing the sample proportion

$$Z = \frac{\hat{P} - p}{\sqrt{p(1 - p)/n}}$$

Expected value of the difference between two means

$$E(\overline{X}_1 - \overline{X}_2) = \mu_{\bar{x}_1 - \bar{x}_2} = \mu_1 - \mu_2$$

Variance of the difference between two means

$$V(\overline{X}_1 - \overline{X}_2) = \sigma_{\bar{x}_1 - \bar{x}_2}^2 = \frac{\sigma_1^2}{n_1} + \frac{\sigma_2^2}{n_2}$$

Standard error of the difference between two means

$$\sigma_{\bar{x}_1 - \bar{x}_2} = \sqrt{\frac{\sigma_1^2}{n_1} + \frac{\sigma_2^2}{n_2}}$$

Standardizing the difference between two sample means

$$Z = \frac{(\overline{X}_1 - \overline{X}_2) - (\mu_1 - \mu_2)}{\sqrt{\frac{\sigma_1^2}{n_1} + \frac{\sigma_2^2}{n_2}}}$$

REFERENCES

Feller, William, *An Introduction to Probability Theory*, Vol. 1, 3rd edition. New York: John Wiley and Sons, 1968.
Ross, Sheldon M., *A First Course in Probability*, 5th edition. Englewood Cliffs, NJ: Prentice Hall, 1997.
Ross, Sheldon M., *Introduction to Probability Models*, 4th edition. New York: Academic Press, 1989.

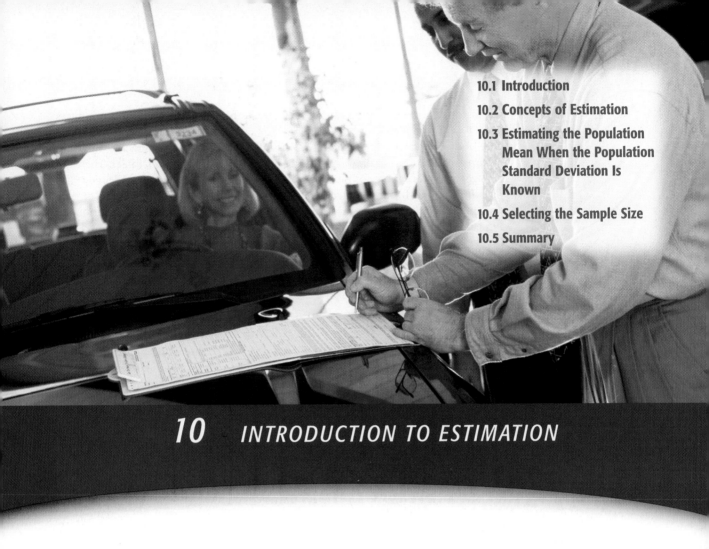

10 INTRODUCTION TO ESTIMATION

ESTIMATING A MEAN ASSEMBLY TIME

The supervisor of a production line that assembles computer keyboards has been experiencing problems since a new process was instituted. He notes that there has been an increase in the number of defective units and occasional backlogs when the productivity of a station does not match that of the others. Upon reviewing the operation of the assembly line, he discovered that there have been a number of changes in the sequence and times of the operation's stations. To redo the setup he needs an accurate estimate of the mean assembly time for all the stations. He starts by drawing a sample of 75 completion times (in seconds) of the operation

at the point where problems have been occurring. These data are stored in Ch10:\Assemblyline. See page 310 for the solution.

10.1 INTRODUCTION

Having discussed descriptive statistics (Chapter 4), probability distributions (Chapters 7 and 8), and sampling distributions (Chapter 9), we are ready to tackle statistical inference. As we explained in Chapter 1, *statistical inference* is the process by which we acquire information and draw conclusions about populations from samples. There are two general procedures for making inferences about populations: *estimation* and *hypothesis testing*. In this chapter, we introduce the concepts and foundations of estimation and demonstrate them with simple examples. In Chapter 11, we describe the fundamentals of hypothesis testing. Because most of what we do in the remainder of this book applies the concepts of estimation and hypothesis testing, understanding Chapters 10 and 11 is vital to your development as a statistics practitioner.

10.2 CONCEPTS OF ESTIMATION

As its name suggests, the objective of estimation is to determine the approximate value of a population parameter on the basis of a sample statistic. For example, the sample mean is employed to estimate the population mean. We refer to the sample mean as the *estimator* of the population mean. Once the sample mean has been computed, its value is called the *estimate*. In this chapter we will introduce the statistical process whereby we estimate a population mean using sample data. In the rest of the book we use the concepts and techniques introduced here for other parameters.

POINT AND INTERVAL ESTIMATORS

We can use sample data to estimate a population parameter in two ways. First, we can compute the value of the estimator and consider that value as the estimate of the parameter. Such an estimator is called a *point estimator*.

> **POINT ESTIMATOR**
> A **point estimator** draws inferences about a population by estimating the value of an unknown parameter using a single value or point.

In drawing inferences about a population, it is intuitively reasonable to expect that a large sample will produce more accurate results, because it contains more information than a smaller sample does. But point estimators don't have the capacity to reflect the effects of larger sample sizes. The second way of estimating a population parameter is to use an *interval estimator*.

> **INTERVAL ESTIMATOR**
> An **interval estimator** draws inferences about a population by estimating the value of an unknown parameter using an interval.

As you will see, the interval estimator is affected by the sample size; because it possesses this feature, we will deal mostly with interval estimators in this text.

To illustrate the difference between point and interval estimators, suppose that a statistics professor wants to estimate the mean summer income of his second-year business students. Selecting 25 students at random, he calculates the sample mean weekly income to be $400. The point estimate is the sample mean. That is, he estimates the mean weekly summer income of all second-year business students to be $400. Using the technique described below, he may instead use an interval estimate; he estimates the mean weekly summer income of second-year business students to lie between $380 and $420.

Numerous applications of estimation occur in the real world. For example, television network executives want to know the proportion of television viewers who are tuned in to their networks; an economist wants to know the mean income of university graduates; a medical researcher wishes to estimate the recovery rate of heart attack victims treated with a new drug. In each of these cases, in order to accomplish the objective exactly, the statistics practitioner would have to examine each member of the population and then calculate the parameter of interest. For instance, network executives would have to ask each person in the country what he or she is watching to determine the proportion of people who are watching their shows. Since there are millions of television viewers, the task is both impractical and prohibitively expensive. An alternative would be to take a random sample from this population, calculate the sample proportion, and use that as an estimator of the population proportion. The use of the sample proportion to estimate the population proportion seems logical. The selection of the sample statistic to be used as an estimator, however, depends on the characteristics of that statistic. Naturally, we want to use the statistic with the most desirable qualities for our purposes.

One desirable quality of an estimator is *unbiasedness*.

UNBIASED ESTIMATOR

An **unbiased estimator** of a population parameter is an estimator whose expected value is equal to that parameter.

This means that, if you were to take an infinite number of samples, calculate the value of the estimator in each sample, the average value of the estimators would equal the parameter. This amounts to saying that, on average, the sample statistic is equal to the parameter.

We know that the sample mean $\overline{X}$ is an unbiased estimator of the population mean μ. In presenting the sampling distribution of $\overline{X}$ in Section 9.2, we stated that $E(\overline{X}) = \mu$. We also know that the sample proportion is an unbiased estimator of the population proportion because $E(\hat{P}) = p$ and that the difference between two sample means is an unbiased estimator of the difference between two population means because $E(\overline{X}_1 - \overline{X}_2) = \mu_1 - \mu_2$.

Recall that in Chapter 4 we defined the sample variance as

$$s^2 = \sum \frac{(x_i - \overline{x})^2}{n - 1}$$

At the time, it seemed odd that we divided by $n - 1$ rather than by n. The reason for choosing $n - 1$ was to make $E(S^2) = \sigma^2$ so that this definition makes the sample variance an unbiased estimator of the population variance. (The proof of this statement requires about a page of algebraic manipulation, which is more than we would be comfortable in presenting here.) Had we defined the sample variance using n in the denominator, the resulting statistic would be a biased estimator of the population variance, one whose expected value is less than the parameter.

Knowing that an estimator is unbiased only assures us that its expected value equals the parameter; it does not tell us how close the estimator is to the parameter. Another desirable quality is that as the sample size grows larger, the sample statistic should come closer to the population parameter. This quality is called *consistency*.

> **CONSISTENCY**
>
> An unbiased estimator is said to be **consistent** if the difference between the estimator and the parameter grows smaller as the sample size grows larger.

The measure we use to gauge closeness is the variance (or the standard deviation). Thus, $\overline{X}$ is a consistent estimator of μ, because the variance of $\overline{X}$ is σ^2 / n. This implies that as n grows larger, the variance of $\overline{X}$ grows smaller. As a consequence, an increasing proportion of sample means falls close to μ.

Figure 10.1 depicts two sampling distributions of $\overline{X}$ when samples are drawn from a population whose mean is 0 and whose standard deviation is 10. One sampling distribution is based on samples of size 25, and the other is based on samples of size 100. The former is more spread out than the latter.

Figure 10.1
Sampling distributions of
$\overline{X}$ with $n = 25$ and $n = 100$

Similarly, $\hat{P}$ is a consistent estimator of p because it is unbiased and the variance of $\hat{P}$ is $p(1 - p)/n$, which grows smaller as n grows larger.

A third desirable quality is *relative efficiency*, which compares two unbiased estimators of a parameter.

> **RELATIVE EFFICIENCY**
>
> If there are two unbiased estimators of a parameter, the one whose variance is smaller is said to be **relatively efficient**.

We have already seen that the sample mean is an unbiased estimator of the population mean and that its variance is σ^2 / n. Statisticians have established that several other statistics are unbiased and consistent when estimating the population mean. However, the variance of the sampling distribution of the mean will be smaller than the variance of the sampling distribution of any of these statistics. (See Exercises 10.34 to 10.40.) As a consequence, the sample mean will be our first choice in drawing inferences about a population mean.

Over the remaining chapters of this book, we will present the statistical inference of a number of different population parameters. In each case, we will select a sample statistic that is unbiased and consistent, and where there is more than one such statistic we will choose the one that is relatively efficient to serve as the estimator.

DEVELOPING AN UNDERSTANDING OF STATISTICAL CONCEPTS

In this section we described three desirable characteristics of estimators: unbiasedness, consistency, and relative efficiency. An understanding of statistics requires that you know that there are several potential estimators for each parameter, but that we choose the estimators used in this book because they possess these characteristics.

EXERCISES

10.1 Define unbiasedness.

10.2 Draw a sampling distribution of an unbiased estimator.

10.3 Draw a sampling distribution of a biased estimator.

10.4 Define consistency.

10.5 Is the sample mean a consistent estimator of the population mean? Explain.

10.6 Draw diagrams representing what happens to the sampling distribution of a consistent estimator when the sample size increases.

10.7 Define relative efficiency.

10.8 Draw a diagram representing the sampling distribution representing two unbiased estimators, one of which is relatively efficient.

10.3 ESTIMATING THE POPULATION MEAN WHEN THE POPULATION STANDARD DEVIATION IS KNOWN

We now describe how an interval estimator is produced from a sampling distribution. We choose to demonstrate estimation with an example that is unrealistic. However, this liability is offset by the example's simplicity. When you understand more about estimation, you will be able to apply the technique to more realistic situations.

Suppose we have a population with mean μ and standard deviation σ. The population mean is assumed to be unknown, and our task is to estimate its value. As we just discussed, the estimation procedure requires the statistics practitioner to draw a random sample of size n and calculate the sample mean $\bar{x}$.

The central limit theorem presented in Section 9.2 stated that $\bar{X}$ is normally distributed if X is normally distributed, or approximately normally distributed if X is nonnormal and n is sufficiently large. This means that the variable

$$Z = \frac{\bar{X} - \mu}{\sigma/\sqrt{n}}$$

is standard normally distributed (or approximately so). In Section 9.2 (page 281) we developed the following probability statement associated with the sampling distribution of the mean:

$$P\left(\mu - z_{\alpha/2}\frac{\sigma}{\sqrt{n}} < \bar{X} < \mu + z_{\alpha/2}\frac{\sigma}{\sqrt{n}}\right) = 1 - \alpha$$

which was derived from

$$P\left(-z_{\alpha/2} < \frac{\bar{X} - \mu}{\sigma/\sqrt{n}} < z_{\alpha/2}\right) = 1 - \alpha$$

Using a similar algebraic manipulation, we can express the probability in a slightly different form. That is,

$$P\left(\bar{X} - z_{\alpha/2}\frac{\sigma}{\sqrt{n}} < \mu < \bar{X} + z_{\alpha/2}\frac{\sigma}{\sqrt{n}}\right) = 1 - \alpha$$

Notice that in this form the population mean is in the center of the interval created by adding and subtracting $z_{\alpha/2}$ standard errors to the sample mean. It is important for you to understand that this is merely another form of probability statement about the sample mean. This equation says that, with repeated sampling from this population, the proportion of values of $\bar{X}$ for which the interval

$$\overline{X} - z_{\alpha/2}\frac{\sigma}{\sqrt{n}}, \quad \overline{X} + z_{\alpha/2}\frac{\sigma}{\sqrt{n}}$$

includes the population mean μ is equal to $1 - \alpha$. However, this form of probability statement is very useful to us because it is the **confidence interval estimator of μ**.

CONFIDENCE INTERVAL ESTIMATOR OF μ*

$$\bar{x} - z_{\alpha/2}\frac{\sigma}{\sqrt{n}}, \quad \bar{x} + z_{\alpha/2}\frac{\sigma}{\sqrt{n}}$$

The probability $1 - \alpha$ is called the **confidence level**.

$\bar{x} - z_{\alpha/2}\sigma/\sqrt{n}$ is called the **lower confidence limit (LCL).**

$\bar{x} + z_{\alpha/2}\sigma/\sqrt{n}$ is called the **upper confidence limit (UCL).**

We often represent the confidence interval estimator as

$$\bar{x} \pm z_{\alpha/2}\sigma/\sqrt{n}$$

where the minus sign defines the lower confidence limit and the plus sign defines the upper confidence limit.

To apply this formula we specify the confidence level $1 - \alpha$, from which we determine α, $\alpha/2$, and $z_{\alpha/2}$ (from Table 3 in Appendix B). Because the confidence level is the probability that the interval includes the actual value of μ, we generally set $1 - \alpha$ close to 1 (usually between .90 and .99).

In Table 10.1, we list four commonly used confidence levels and their associated values of $z_{\alpha/2}$. For example, if the confidence level is $1 - \alpha = .95$, then $\alpha = .05$, $\alpha/2 = .025$, and $z_{\alpha/2} = z_{.025} = 1.96$. The resulting confidence interval estimator is then called the **95% confidence interval estimator of μ.**

Table 10.1 Four Commonly Used Confidence Levels and $z_{\alpha/2}$

$1 - \alpha$	α	$\alpha/2$	$z_{\alpha/2}$
.90	.10	.05	$z_{.05} = 1.645$
.95	.05	.025	$z_{.025} = 1.96$
.98	.02	.01	$z_{.01} = 2.33$
.99	.01	.005	$z_{.005} = 2.575$

As an illustration, suppose we want to estimate the mean value of the distribution resulting from the throw of a fair die. Because we know the distribution, we also know that $\mu = 3.5$ and $\sigma = 1.71$. Pretend now that we know only that $\sigma = 1.71$, that μ is unknown, and that we want to estimate its value. To estimate μ we draw a sample of size $n = 100$ and calculate $\bar{x}$. The confidence interval estimator of μ is

$$\bar{x} \pm z_{\alpha/2}\frac{\sigma}{\sqrt{n}}$$

---

*Since Chapter 7 we've been using the convention whereby an uppercase letter (usually X) represents a random variable and a lowercase letter (usually x) represents one of its values. However, in the formulas used in statistical inference, the distinction between the variable and its value becomes blurred. Accordingly, we will discontinue the notational convention and simply use lowercase letters except when we wish to make a probability statement.

The 90% confidence interval estimator is

$$\bar{x} \pm z_{\alpha/2} \frac{\sigma}{\sqrt{n}} = \bar{x} \pm 1.645 \frac{1.71}{\sqrt{100}} = \bar{x} \pm .28$$

This notation means that, if we repeatedly draw samples of size 100 from this population, 90% of the values of $\bar{x}$ will be such that μ would lie somewhere between $\bar{x} - .28$ and $\bar{x} + .28$, and 10% of the values of $\bar{x}$ will produce intervals that would not include μ. To illustrate this point, imagine that we draw 40 samples of 100 observations each. The values of $\bar{x}$ and the resulting confidence interval estimates of μ are shown in Table 10.2. Notice that not all the intervals include the true value of the parameter. Samples 5, 16, 22, and 34 produce values of $\bar{x}$ that in turn produce intervals that exclude μ.

Table 10.2 90% Confidence Interval Estimates of μ

Sample	$\bar{x}$	LCL = $\bar{x}$ − .28	UCL = $\bar{x}$ + .28	Does Interval Include μ = 3.5?
1	3.55	3.27	3.83	Yes
2	3.61	3.33	3.89	Yes
3	3.47	3.19	3.75	Yes
4	3.48	3.20	3.76	Yes
5	3.80	3.52	4.08	No
6	3.37	3.09	3.65	Yes
7	3.48	3.20	3.76	Yes
8	3.52	3.24	3.80	Yes
9	3.74	3.46	4.02	Yes
10	3.51	3.23	3.79	Yes
11	3.23	2.95	3.51	Yes
12	3.45	3.17	3.73	Yes
13	3.57	3.29	3.85	Yes
14	3.77	3.49	4.05	Yes
15	3.31	3.03	3.59	Yes
16	3.10	2.82	3.38	No
17	3.50	3.22	3.78	Yes
18	3.55	3.27	3.83	Yes
19	3.65	3.37	3.93	Yes
20	3.28	3.00	3.56	Yes
21	3.40	3.12	3.68	Yes
22	3.88	3.60	4.16	No
23	3.76	3.48	4.04	Yes
24	3.40	3.12	3.68	Yes
25	3.34	3.06	3.62	Yes
26	3.65	3.37	3.93	Yes
27	3.45	3.17	3.73	Yes
28	3.47	3.19	3.75	Yes
29	3.58	3.30	3.86	Yes
30	3.36	3.08	3.64	Yes
31	3.71	3.43	3.99	Yes
32	3.51	3.23	3.79	Yes
33	3.42	3.14	3.70	Yes
34	3.11	2.83	3.39	No
35	3.29	3.01	3.57	Yes
36	3.64	3.36	3.92	Yes
37	3.39	3.11	3.67	Yes
38	3.75	3.47	4.03	Yes
39	3.26	2.98	3.54	Yes
40	3.54	3.26	3.82	Yes

Students often react to this situation by asking, "What went wrong with samples 5, 16, 22, and 34?" The answer is nothing. Statistics does not promise 100% certainty. In fact, in this illustration, we expected 90% of the intervals to include μ and 10% to exclude μ. Since we produced 40 intervals, we expected that 4.0 (10% of 40) intervals would not contain $\mu = 3.5.^{*}$ It is important to understand that, even when the statistics practitioner performs experiments properly, a certain proportion (in this example, 10%) of the experiments will produce incorrect estimates by random chance.

We can improve the confidence associated with the interval estimate. If we let the confidence level $1 - \alpha$ equal .95, the 95% confidence interval estimator is

$$\bar{x} \pm z_{\alpha/2} \frac{\sigma}{\sqrt{n}} = \bar{x} \pm 1.96 \frac{1.71}{\sqrt{100}} = \bar{x} \pm .34$$

Because this interval is wider, it is more likely to include the value of μ. If you redo Table 10.2, this time using a 95% confidence interval estimator, only samples 16, 22, and 34 will produce intervals that do not include μ. (Notice that we expected 5% of the intervals to exclude μ and that we actually observed $3/40 = 7.5\%$.) The 99% confidence interval estimator is

$$\bar{x} \pm z_{\alpha/2} \frac{\sigma}{\sqrt{n}} = \bar{x} \pm 2.575 \frac{1.71}{\sqrt{100}} = \bar{x} \pm .44$$

Applying this interval estimator to the sample means listed in Table 10.2 would result in having all 40 interval estimates include the population mean $\mu = 3.5$. (We expected 1% of the intervals to exclude μ; we observed $0/40 = 0\%$.)

In actual practice, only one sample will be drawn and thus only one value of $\bar{x}$ will be calculated. The resulting interval estimate will either correctly include the parameter or incorrectly exclude it. Unfortunately, statistics practitioners do not know whether in each case they are correct; they know only that, in the long run, they will incorrectly estimate the parameter some of the time. Statistics practitioners accept that as a fact of life.

The following example illustrates how estimation techniques are applied. It also illustrates how we intend to solve problems in the rest of this book. The solution process that we advocate and use throughout this book is by and large the same one that statistics practitioners use to apply their skills in the real world. The process is divided into three stages. The first step is to identify the correct statistical technique. Of course, for this example you will have no difficulty identifying the technique, since at this point you know only one.

The second step is to perform the calculations. We will do this in three ways. To illustrate how the computations are completed, we will do the arithmetic manually with the assistance of a calculator. Solving problems by hand often provides insights into the statistical inference technique. We will also use Excel and Minitab. The choice of which one to use is left to the instructor and student.

In the third and last step of the solution, we intend to interpret the results and deal with the question that began the problem. To be capable of properly interpreting statistical results, one needs to have an understanding of the fundamental principles underlying statistical inference.

---

*In this illustration, exactly 10% of the sample means produced interval estimates that excluded the value of μ, but this will not always be the case. Remember, we expect 10% of the sample means in the long run to result in intervals excluding μ. This group of 40 sample means does not constitute "the long run."

APPLICATIONS IN OPERATIONS MANAGEMENT: *INVENTORY MANAGEMENT*

Operations managers use inventory models to determine the stock level that minimizes total costs. In Section 8.3 we showed how a probabilistic model is used to make the inventory level decision. (See page 246.) One component of that model is the mean demand during lead time. Recall that lead time refers to the interval between the time an order is made and when it is delivered. Demand during lead time is a random variable that is often assumed to be normally distributed. There are several ways to determine mean demand during lead time, but the simplest is to estimate that quantity from a sample.

EXAMPLE 10.1

The Doll Computer Company makes its own computers and delivers them directly to customers who order them via the Internet. Doll competes primarily on price and speed of delivery. To achieve its objective of speed, Doll makes each of its five most popular computers and transports them to warehouses across the country. The computers are stored in the warehouses from which it generally takes 1 day to deliver a computer to the customer. This strategy requires high levels of inventory that add considerably to the cost. To lower these costs, the operations manager wants to employ an inventory model. He notes that both daily demand and lead time are random variables. He concludes that demand during lead time is normally distributed and he needs to know the mean in order to compute the optimum inventory level. He observes 25 lead time periods and records the demand during each period. These data are stored in file Xm10-01 and listed below. The manager would like a 95% confidence interval estimate of the mean demand during lead time. Assume that the manager knows that the standard deviation is 75 computers.

Demand During Lead Time

235	374	309	499	253	421	361	514	462	369
394	439	348	344	330	261	374	302	466	535
386	316	296	332	334

SOLUTION

IDENTIFY

To ultimately determine the optimum inventory level, the manager needs to know the mean demand during lead time. Thus, the parameter to be estimated is μ. At this point, we have described only one estimator. Thus, the confidence interval estimator that we intend to employ is

$$\bar{x} \pm z_{\alpha/2} \frac{\sigma}{\sqrt{n}}$$

The next step is to perform the calculations. As we discussed above, we will perform the calculations in three ways: manually, using Excel, and using Minitab.

COMPUTE

 MANUALLY

We need four values to construct the confidence interval estimate of μ. They are

$$\bar{x}, \quad z_{\alpha/2}, \quad \sigma, \quad \text{and} \quad n$$

Using a calculator, we determine the summation $\sum x_i = 9{,}254$. From this we find

$$\bar{x} = \frac{\sum x_i}{n} = \frac{9{,}254}{25} = 370.16$$

The confidence level is set at 95%; thus $1 - \alpha = .95$, $\alpha = 1 - .95 = .05$, and $\alpha/2 = .025$. From Table 3 in Appendix B or from Table 10.1 we find

$$z_{\alpha/2} = z_{.025} = 1.96$$

The population standard deviation is $\sigma = 75$, and the sample size is 25. Substituting $\bar{x}$, $z_{\alpha/2}$, σ, and n into the confidence interval estimator, we find

$$\bar{x} \pm z_{\alpha/2} \frac{\sigma}{\sqrt{n}} = 370.16 \pm z_{.025} \frac{75}{\sqrt{25}} = 370.16 \pm 1.96 \frac{75}{\sqrt{25}} = 370.16 \pm 29.40$$

The lower and upper confidence limits are LCL = 340.76 and UCL = 399.56, respectively.

EXCEL

	A	B	C
1	**z-Estimate: Mean**		
2			
3			*Demand*
4	Mean		370.16
5	Standard Deviation		80.78
6	Observations		25
7	SIGMA		75
8	LCL		340.76
9	UCL		399.56

COMMANDS
1. Type or import the data into one column.
2. Click **Tools, Data Analysis Plus,** and **Z-Estimate: Mean.**
3. Specify the **Input Range.** (Either highlight the data before clicking **Tools** or type the input range.)
4. Type in the value of the **Standard Deviation (SIGMA).**
5. Click **Labels** if the input range includes the name of the variable in the first row.
6. Specify the confidence level by typing the value of **Alpha.** Click **OK.**

COMMANDS FOR EXAMPLE 10.1
Open file **Xm10-01.**

A1:A26

75

.05

There is another way to produce the interval estimate for this problem. If you have already calculated the sample mean and know the sample size and population standard deviation, you need not employ the data set and the macro described above. Instead, open the file **Estimators** (it will be in the **Excel Workbooks** folder, which is in the same directory as the chapter directories). This workbook contains eight sheets, each showing a confidence interval estimator that is presented in this book. Using the tabs, find and click **z-Estimate_Mean.** The worksheet that will be opened represents the solution to Example 10.1. We typed the values of $\bar{x}$ (370.16), σ (75), and n (25) in cells B3, B4, and B5, respectively, and the confidence level (.95) in cell B6. The confidence interval estimator is automatically computed. The completed worksheet is shown here. As you can see, we produce the same result as above.

	A	B	C	D	E
1	z-Estimate of a Mean				
2					
3	Sample mean	370.160	Confidence Interval Estimate		
4	Population standard deviation	75	370.16	±	29.40
5	Sample size	25	Lower confidence limit		340.76
6	Confidence level	0.95	Upper confidence limit		399.56

There are several ways to use this sheet. First, to solve other problems simply type in the new values of $\bar{x}$, σ, n, and $1 - \alpha$ in cells B3, B4, B5, and B6, respectively. Do not change any other cells. We recommend that you *not* save any of these files in order to avoid altering the calculations.

Second, you can perform a "what-if" analysis. That is, this worksheet provides you the opportunity to learn how changing some of the inputs affects the estimate. For example, type 0.99 in cell B6 to see what happens to the width of the interval when you increase the confidence level. Type 1000 in cell B5 to examine the effect of increasing the sample size. Type 10 in cell B4 and see what happens when the population standard deviation is smaller.

In the next three chapters we will describe the other seven sheets in this workbook as well as other workbooks. They are all designed in the same way. They can complete the calculation of various techniques from summary statistics and perform what-if analyses.

MINITAB

One-Sample Z: Demand

```
The assumed sigma = 75

Variable        N      Mean    StDev    SE Mean       95.0% CI
Demand         25     370.2     80.8      15.0  (   340.8,    399.6)
```

The output includes the value of σ (**The assumed sigma**), the sample size (**N**), the sample mean (**Mean**), and the sample standard deviation (**StDev** = 80.8, which is not needed for this interval estimate). Also printed is the standard error **SE Mean** = $\sigma / \sqrt{n}$ = 15.0) and last, but not least, the 95% confidence interval estimate of the population mean. To produce this output, see the commands below.

COMMANDS	COMMANDS FOR EXAMPLE 10.1
1. Type or import the data into one column.	Open file **Xm10-01**.
2. Click **Stat, Basic Statistics,** and **1-Sample Z....**	
3. Type or **Select** the variable name.	**Demand** or **C1**
4. Type the value of the population standard deviation σ (**Sigma**).	**75**
5. Click **Options....** Type the value for the **Confidence interval**.	**95.0**
6. In the **Alternative** box select **not equal**; click **OK**. Click **OK**.	

INTERPRET

The operations manager estimates that the mean demand during lead time lies between 340.76 and 399.56. He can use this estimate as an input in developing an inventory policy. The model discussed in Section 8.3 computes the number of units to order assuming a particular value of the mean demand during lead time. In this example he could have used the sample mean as a point estimator of the mean demand, from which the inventory policy could be determined. However, the use of the confidence interval estimator allows the manager to use both the lower and upper limits so that he can understand the possible outcomes.

INTERPRETING THE CONFIDENCE INTERVAL ESTIMATE

Some people erroneously interpret the confidence interval estimate in Example 10.1 to mean that there is a 95% probability that the population mean lies between 340.76 and 399.56. This interpretation is wrong because it implies that the population mean is a variable about which we can make probability statements. In fact, the population mean is a fixed but unknown quantity. Consequently, we cannot interpret the confidence interval estimate of μ as a probability statement about μ. To translate the confidence interval estimate properly, we must remember that the confidence interval estimator was derived from the sampling distribution of the *sample mean*. In Section 9.2, we used the sampling distribution to make probability statements about the sample mean. Although the form has changed, the confidence interval estimator is also a probability statement about the sample mean. It states that there is $1 - \alpha$ probability that the sample mean will be equal to a value such that the interval $\bar{x} - z_{\alpha/2}\sigma / \sqrt{n}$ to $\bar{x} + z_{\alpha/2}\sigma / \sqrt{n}$ will include the population mean. Once the sample mean is computed, the interval acts as the lower and upper limits of the interval estimate of the population mean.

We summarize our calculations in Example 10.1 as follows. We estimate that the mean demand during lead time falls between 340.76 and 399.56, and this type of estimator is correct 95% of the time. Incidentally, the media often refer to the 95% figure as "19 times out of 20," which emphasizes the long-run aspect of the confidence level.

S e e i n g   S t a t i s t i c s

APPLET 15:
CONFIDENCE INTERVAL ESTIMATES OF A MEAN

The simulations used in the applets introduced in Chapter 9 can be used here to demonstrate how confidence interval estimates are interpreted. This applet generates samples of size 100 from the population of the toss of a die. We know that the population mean is $\mu = 3.5$ and that the standard deviation is 1.71. The 95% confidence interval estimator is

$$\bar{x} \pm z_{\alpha/2}\frac{\sigma}{\sqrt{n}} = \bar{x} \pm 1.96\frac{1.71}{\sqrt{100}} = \bar{x} \pm .335$$

The applet will generate one sample, 10 samples, or 100 samples at a time. The resulting confidence inter-

val is displayed as a horizontal line between the upper and lower ends of the confidence interval. The true mean of 3.5 is the green vertical line. If the confidence interval includes the true population mean of 3.5 (i.e., if the confidence interval line overlaps the green vertical line), it is displayed in blue. If it does not include the true mean, it is displayed in red.

After you understand the basics, click the "Sample 10" button a few times to see ten confidence intervals (but not their calculations) at once. Then click on the "Sample 100" button to generate 100 samples and confidence intervals.

S e e i n g   S t a t i s t i c s

APPLET 15:
CONFIDENCE INTERVAL ESTIMATES OF A MEAN *(continued)*

95% Confidence Interval for the Mean, n = 100

Applet Exercises

Simulate 100 samples.

15.1 Are all the confidence interval estimates identical?

15.2 Count the number of confidence interval estimates that include the true value of the mean.

15.3 How many intervals did you expect to see that correctly included the mean?

15.4 What do these exercises tell you about the proper interpretation of a confidence interval estimate?

INFORMATION AND THE WIDTH OF THE INTERVAL

Interval estimation, like all other statistical techniques, is designed to convert data into information. However, a wide interval provides little information. For example, suppose that as a result of a statistical study we estimate with 95% confidence that the average starting salary of an accountant lies between $15,000 and $100,000. This interval is so wide that very little information was derived from the data. Suppose, however, that the interval estimate was $42,000 to $45,000. This interval is much narrower, providing accounting students more precise information about starting salaries.

The width of the confidence interval estimate is a function of the population standard deviation, the confidence level, and the sample size. Consider Example 10.1, where σ was assumed to be 75. The interval estimate was 370.16 ± 29.40. If σ equaled 150, the 95% confidence interval estimate would become

$$\bar{x} \pm z_{\alpha/2}\frac{\sigma}{\sqrt{n}} = 370.16 \pm z_{.025}\frac{150}{\sqrt{25}} = 370.16 \pm 1.96\frac{150}{\sqrt{25}} = 370.16 \pm 58.80$$

Thus, doubling the population standard deviation has the effect of doubling the width of the confidence interval estimate. This result is quite logical. If there is a great deal of variation in the random variable (reflected by a large standard deviation), it is more difficult to accurately estimate the population mean. That difficulty is translated into a wider interval.

While we have no control over the value of σ, we do have the power to select values for the other two elements. In Example 10.1, we chose a 95% confidence level. If we had chosen 99% instead, the interval estimate would have been

$$\bar{x} \pm z_{\alpha/2}\frac{\sigma}{\sqrt{n}} = 370.16 \pm z_{.005}\frac{75}{\sqrt{25}} = 370.16 \pm 2.575\frac{75}{\sqrt{25}} = 370.16 \pm 38.63$$

A 90% confidence level results in this interval estimate:

$$\bar{x} \pm z_{\alpha/2}\frac{\sigma}{\sqrt{n}} = 370.16 \pm z_{.05}\frac{75}{\sqrt{25}} = 370.16 \pm 1.645\frac{75}{\sqrt{25}} = 370.16 \pm 24.68$$

As you can see, decreasing the confidence level will narrow the interval; increasing it widens the interval. However, a large confidence level is generally desirable since that means a larger proportion of confidence interval estimates that will be correct in the long run. There is a direct relationship between the width of the interval and the confidence level. This is because in order to be more confident in the estimate we need to widen the interval. (The analogy is that to be more likely to capture a butterfly, we need a larger butterfly net.) The tradeoff between increased confidence and the resulting wider confidence interval estimates must be resolved by the statistics practitioner. As a general rule, however, 95% confidence is considered "standard."

The third element is the sample size. Had the sample size been 100 instead of 25, the 95% confidence interval estimate would become

$$\bar{x} \pm z_{\alpha/2} \frac{\sigma}{\sqrt{n}} = 370.16 \pm z_{.025} \frac{75}{\sqrt{100}} = 370.16 \pm 1.96 \frac{75}{\sqrt{100}} = 370.16 \pm 14.70$$

Increasing the sample size fourfold decreases the width of the interval by half. A larger sample size provides more potential information. The increased amount of information is reflected in a narrower interval. However, there is another tradeoff: Increasing the sample size increases the sampling cost. We will discuss these issues when we present sample size selection in Section 10.4.

Now that we have the tools for the job, we can return to the problem that opened this chapter.

APPLICATIONS IN OPERATIONS MANAGEMENT: *ASSEMBLY LINE BALANCING*

An important operations management function is line balancing an assembly line. This ensures that operations at different stations take approximately the same amount of time. If the line is not balanced, there will be points where operators will be idle and other points where bottlenecks will occur. The result is that the product piles up at the operation that is more time-consuming than at least one of its predecessors. Often the assembly line is set up using a variety of management science tools. One of the inputs to this process is an estimate of the mean amount of time to perform operations on the assembly line.

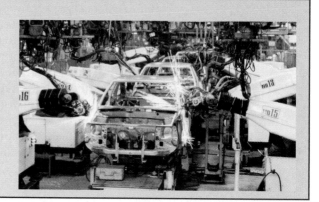

ESTIMATING A MEAN ASSEMBLY TIME: SOLUTION

IDENTIFY

We need to produce an estimate of the mean assembly time. Assume that we know that the population standard deviation is $\sigma = 10$ and that a 90% confidence level is adequate for our purposes. The confidence interval estimator that we intend to employ is

$$\bar{x} \pm z_{\alpha/2} \frac{\sigma}{\sqrt{n}}$$

COMPUTE

MANUALLY
We need four values to construct the confidence interval estimate of μ. They are

$$\bar{x}, \quad z_{\alpha/2}, \quad \sigma, \quad \text{and} \quad n$$

Using a calculator, we determine the summation $\sum x_i = 6,860.6$. From this we find

ESTIMATING A MEAN ASSEMBLY TIME: SOLUTION (continued)

$$\bar{x} = \frac{\sum x_i}{n} = \frac{6,860.6}{75} = 91.47$$

The confidence level is set at 90%; thus $1 - \alpha = .90$, $\alpha = 1 - .90 = .10$, and $\alpha/2 = .05$. Hence,

$$z_{\alpha/2} = z_{.05} = 1.645$$

The 90% confidence interval estimate of the mean assembly time is

$$\bar{x} \pm z_{\alpha/2} \frac{\sigma}{\sqrt{n}} = 91.47 \pm z_{.05} \frac{10}{\sqrt{75}}$$

$$= 91.47 \pm 1.645 \frac{10}{\sqrt{75}} = 91.47 \pm 1.90$$

$$\text{LCL} = 89.57 \quad \text{and} \quad \text{UCL} = 93.37$$

EXCEL

	A	B	C
1	z-Estimate: Mean		
2			
3			Time
4	Mean		91.47
5	Standard Deviation		11.06
6	Observations		75
7	SIGMA		10
8	LCL		89.58
9	UCL		93.37

MINITAB

One-Sample Z: Time

```
The assumed sigma = 10

Variable        N      Mean    StDev   SE Mean         90.0% CI
Time           75     91.47    11.06      1.15  (  89.58,   93.37)
```

INTERPRET

We estimate that the mean assembly time lies between 89.58 and 93.37 seconds. The operations manager can use this estimate to help balance the assembly line.

EXERCISES

Developing an Understanding of Statistical Concepts

*Exercises 10.9 to 10.33 are "what-if analyses" designed to determine what happens to the interval estimate when the confidence level, sample size, and standard deviation change. These problems can be solved manually or using Excel's **z-Estimate_Mean** worksheet in the **Estimators** workbook.*

10.9 A statistics practitioner took a random sample of 50 observations from a population whose standard deviation is 25 and computed the sample mean to be 100. Estimate the population mean with 95% confidence.

10.10 Repeat Exercise 10.9 using a 90% confidence level.

10.11 Repeat Exercise 10.9 using a 99% confidence level.

10.12 Describe the effect on the confidence interval estimate of increasing the confidence level in Exercises 10.9 to 10.11.

10.13 Repeat Exercise 10.9 changing the population standard deviation to 10.

10.14 Repeat Exercise 10.9 changing the population standard deviation to 50.

10.15 Based on Exercises 10.9, 10.13, and 10.14, describe what happens to the confidence interval estimate when the standard deviation is increased.

10.16 Repeat Exercise 10.9 assuming a sample size of 25.

10.17 Repeat Exercise 10.9 assuming a sample size of 400.

10.18 Summarize Exercises 10.9, 10.16, and 10.17 by describing what happens to the confidence interval estimate when the sample size increases.

10.19 Repeat Exercise 10.9 when the sample mean is 30.

10.20 Repeat Exercise 10.9 when the sample mean is 200.

10.21 Describe the effect on the width of the confidence interval estimate of increasing the sample mean in Exercises 10.9, 10.19, and 10.20.

10.22 Given the information below, determine the 90% confidence interval estimate of the population mean:
$$\bar{x} = 500, \quad \sigma = 12, \quad \text{and} \quad n = 50$$

10.23 Repeat Exercise 10.22 using a 95% confidence level.

10.24 Repeat Exercise 10.22 using a 99% confidence level.

10.25 Review Exercises 10.22 to 10.24 and discuss the effect on the confidence interval estimator of decreasing the confidence level.

10.26 Repeat Exercise 10.22 changing the population standard deviation to 10.

10.27 Repeat Exercise 10.22 changing the population standard deviation to 14.

10.28 From Exercises 10.22, 10.26, and 10.27, indicate what happens to the confidence interval estimator when the standard deviation decreases.

10.29   Repeat Exercise 10.22 with a sample size of 100.

10.30   Repeat Exercise 10.22 with a sample size of 200.

10.31   Summarize Exercises 10.22, 10.29, and 10.30 by describing what happens to the confidence interval estimator when the sample size decreases.

10.32   Repeat Exercise 10.22 with a sample mean of 100.

10.33   Summarize Exercises 10.22 and 10.32 by describing what happens to the width of the confidence interval estimator when the sample mean decreases.

Exercises 10.34–10.40 are based on the following discussion. Statisticians have shown that when the population is normal, the sample median is normally distributed. The expected value and variance of the sampling distribution of the sample median are

$$E(\text{Sample median}) = \mu$$

and

$$V(\text{Sample median}) = \frac{\pi}{2} \frac{\sigma^2}{n}$$

where $\pi = 3.14159\ldots$, μ is the population mean, and σ^2 is the population variance. Thus the standard error of the sample median is

$$\sigma_{\text{median}} = \sqrt{\frac{3.14519}{2} \frac{\sigma^2}{n}} = \frac{1.2533\sigma}{\sqrt{n}}$$

Exercises 10.34–10.40 assume that the population is normal.

10.34   Is the sample median an unbiased estimator of the population mean? Explain.

10.35   Is the sample median a consistent estimator of the population mean? Explain.

10.36   Show that the sample mean is relatively more efficient than the sample median when estimating the population mean.

10.37   Develop the confidence interval estimator of the population mean using the sample median.

10.38   Given the information below, determine the 90% confidence interval estimate of the population mean using the sample median.

Sample median = 500, $\sigma = 12$,   and $n = 50$

10.39   Compare your answers to Exercises 10.22 and 10.38. Explain why the confidence interval estimate in Exercise 10.38 was wider.

10.40   Bearing in mind how the sample mean and sample median are calculated, discuss why the confidence interval estimator of the mean using the sample median is wider than the confidence interval estimator of the mean using the sample mean (for the same sample size, confidence level, and population standard deviation).

Applications

10.41   The following data represent a random sample of 9 marks (out of 10) on a statistics quiz. The marks are normally distributed with a standard deviation of 2. Estimate the population mean with 90% confidence.

7,   9,   7,   5,   4,   8,   3,   10,   9

10.42   The following observations are the ages of a random sample of 8 men in a bar. It is known that the ages are normally distributed with a standard deviation of 10.

Determine the 95% confidence interval estimate of the population mean. Interpret the interval estimate.

52,   68,   22,   35,   30,   56,   39,   48

10.43   How many rounds of golf do physicians (who play golf) play per year? A survey of 12 physicians revealed the following numbers:

3,   41,   17,   1,   33,   37,
18,   15,   17,   12,   29,   51

Estimate with 95% confidence the mean number of rounds per year played by physicians, assuming that the number of rounds is normally distributed with a standard deviation of 7.

10.44   Among the most exciting aspects of a university professor's life are the departmental meetings where such critical issues as the color the walls will be painted and who gets a new desk are decided. A sample of 20 professors was asked how many hours per year are devoted to these meetings. The responses are listed below. Assuming that the variable is normally distributed with a standard deviation of 8 hours, estimate the mean number of hours spent at departmental meetings by all professors. Use a confidence level of 90%.

14,   17,   3,   6,   17,   3,   8,   4,   20,   15,
7,   9,   0,   5,   11,   15,   18,   13,   8,   4

10.45   The number of cars sold annually by used car salespeople is normally distributed with a standard deviation of 15. A random sample of 400 salespeople was taken and the mean number of cars sold annually was found to be 75. Find the 95% confidence interval estimate of the population mean. Interpret the interval estimate.

10.46   It is known that the amount of time needed to change the oil on a car is normally distributed with a standard deviation of 5 minutes. A random sample of 100 oil changes yielded a sample mean of 22 minutes. Compute the 99% confidence interval estimate of the mean of the population.

10.47   Suppose that the amount of time teenagers spend weekly at part-time jobs is normally distributed with a standard deviation of 20 minutes. A random sample of 100 observations is drawn and the sample mean is computed as 125 minutes. Determine the 95% confidence interval estimate of the population mean.

10.48   One of the few negative side effects of quitting smoking is weight gain. Suppose that the weight gain in the 12 months following a cessation in smoking is normally distributed with a standard deviation of 6 pounds. To estimate the mean weight gain, a random sample of 50 quitters was drawn and the sample mean was found to be 25 pounds. Determine the 90% confidence interval estimate of the mean 12-month weight gain for all quitters.

10.49   Because of different sales ability, experience, and devotion, the incomes of real estate agents vary considerably. Suppose that in a large city the annual income is normally distributed with a standard deviation of $7,500. A random sample of 16 real estate agents reveals that the mean annual income is $52,000.

Determine the 99% confidence interval estimate of the mean annual income of all real estate agents in the city.

The following exercises require the use of a computer and software. The answers may be calculated manually. See Appendix A for the sample statistics.

10.50 A survey of 400 statistics professors was undertaken. Each was asked how much time was devoted to teaching graphical techniques. We believe that the times are normally distributed with a standard deviation of 30 minutes. The data are stored in file Xr10-50. Estimate the population mean with 95% confidence.

10.51 In a survey conducted to determine, among other things, the cost of vacations, 64 individuals were randomly sampled. Each person was asked to compute the cost of her or his most recent vacation. The data are stored in file Xr10-51. Assuming that the standard deviation is $400, estimate with 95% confidence the average cost of all vacations.

10.52 In an article about *disinflation*, various investments were examined. The investments included stocks, bonds, and real estate. Suppose that a random sample of 200 rates of return on real estate investments were computed and stored in file Xr10-52. Assuming that the standard deviation of all rates of return on real estate investments is 2.1%, estimate the mean rate of return on all real estate investments with 90% confidence. Interpret the estimate.

10.53 A statistics professor is in the process of investigating how many classes university students miss each semester. To help answer this question, she took a random sample of 100 university students and asked each to report how many classes he or she had missed in the previous semester. These data are stored in file Xr10-53. Estimate the mean number of classes missed by all students at the university. Use a 99% confidence level and assume that the population standard deviation is known to be 2.2 classes.

10.54 As part of a project to develop better lawn fertilizers, a research chemist wanted to determine the mean weekly growth rate of Kentucky bluegrass, a common type of grass. A sample of 250 blades of grass was measured, and the amount of growth in 1 week was recorded. These data are stored in file Xr10-54. Assuming that weekly growth is normally distributed with a standard deviation of .10 inch, estimate with 99% confidence the mean weekly growth of Kentucky bluegrass. Briefly describe what the interval estimate tells you about the growth of Kentucky bluegrass.

10.55 A time study of a large production facility was undertaken to determine the mean time required to assemble a cell phone. A random sample of the times to assemble 50 cell phones was recorded and stored in file Xr10-55. An analysis of the assembly times reveals that they are normally distributed with a standard deviation of 1.3 minutes. Estimate with 95% confidence the mean assembly time for all cell phones. What do your results tell you about the assembly times?

10.56 The image of the Japanese manager is that of a workaholic with little or no leisure time. In a survey, a random sample of 250 Japanese middle managers was asked how many hours per week they spent in leisure activities (e.g., sports, movies, television). The results of the survey are stored in file Xr10-56. Assuming that the population standard deviation is 6 hours, estimate with 90% confidence the mean leisure time per week for all Japanese middle managers. What do these results tell you?

10.57 One measure of physical fitness is the amount of time it takes for the pulse rate to return to normal after exercise. A random sample of 100 women aged 40–50 exercised on stationary bicycles for 30 minutes. The amount of time it took for their pulse rates to return to pre-exercise levels was measured and recorded. The data are stored in file Xr10-57. If the times are normally distributed with a standard deviation of 2.3 minutes, estimate with 99% confidence the true mean pulse-recovery time for all 40–50-year-old women. Interpret the results.

10.58 A survey of 80 randomly selected companies asked them to report the annual income of their presidents. These data are stored in file Xr10-58. Assuming that incomes are normally distributed with a standard deviation of $30,000, determine the 90% confidence interval estimate of the mean annual income of all company presidents. Interpret the statistical results.

10.59 To help make a decision about expansion plans, the president of a music company needs to know how many compact discs teenagers buy annually. Accordingly, he commissions a survey of 250 teenagers. Each is asked to report how many CDs he or she purchased in the previous 12 months. The responses are stored in file Xr10-59. Estimate with 90% confidence the mean annual number of CDs purchased by all teenagers. Assume that the population standard deviation is 3 CDs.

STATISTICAL APPLICATIONS IN MARKETING: *ADVERTISING*

As mentioned in the introduction to marketing management, one of the major tools in the promotion mix is advertising. One of the many important decisions to be made by the advertising manager is how to allocate the company's total advertising budget among the various competing media types, including television, radio, and newspapers. Ultimately the manager wants to know, for example, which television programs are most watched by potential customers, and how effective it is to sponsor these programs through advertising. But first the manager must assess the size of the audience, which involves estimating the amount of exposure potential customers have to the various media types, such as television.

10.60 The sponsors of television shows targeted at the children's market wanted to know the amount of time children spend watching television, since the types and number of programs and commercials are greatly influenced by this information. As a result, it was decided to survey 100 North American children and ask them to keep track of the number of hours of television they watch each week. The data are stored in file Xr10-60. From past experience, it is known that the population standard deviation of the weekly amount of television watched is $\sigma = 8.0$ hours. The television sponsors want an estimate of the amount of television watched by the average North American child. A confidence level of 95% is judged to be appropriate.

10.4 SELECTING THE SAMPLE SIZE

As we discussed in the previous section, if the interval estimate is too wide it provides little information. In Example 10.1 the interval estimate was 340.76 to 399.56. If the manager is to use this estimate as input for an inventory model, he needs greater precision. Fortunately, statistics practitioners can control the width of the interval by determining the sample size necessary to produce narrow intervals. Suppose that before gathering the data, the manager had decided that he needed to estimate the mean demand to within 5 units of the true value. The phrase "to within 5 units" means that the interval estimate is to be of the form

$$\bar{x} \pm 5$$

That is, the manager has specified the quantity following the plus/minus sign to be 5. The formula for the confidence interval estimate of μ is

$$\bar{x} \pm z_{\alpha/2} \frac{\sigma}{\sqrt{n}}$$

It follows therefore that

$$z_{\alpha/2} \frac{\sigma}{\sqrt{n}} = 5$$

After some algebra, the equation becomes

$$n = \left(\frac{z_{\alpha/2}\sigma}{5}\right)^2$$

We have specified the confidence level to be 95%, thus $z_{\alpha/2} = 1.96$. The value of σ is 75. Thus,

$$n = \left(\frac{(1.96)(75)}{5}\right)^2 = 865$$

To produce the 95% confidence interval estimate of the mean $\bar{x} \pm 5$ we need to sample 865 lead time periods. Notice that all that is left to be done is to take the sample and calculate the sample mean. If the sample mean is (say) 350, the interval estimate becomes 350 ± 5.

To derive a general formula for the sample size needed to estimate a population mean, let W represent the quantity following the $\pm$ sign. With the same algebraic performance we derive the formula for the sample size.

SAMPLE SIZE TO ESTIMATE A MEAN

$$n = \left(\frac{z_{\alpha/2}\sigma}{W}\right)^2$$

In this chapter we have assumed that we know the value of the population standard deviation. In practice this is seldom the case. (In Chapter 12 we introduce a more realistic confidence interval estimator of the population mean.) To use the formula above, it is frequently necessary to "guesstimate" the value of σ. That is, we must use our knowledge of the variable with which we're dealing to assign some value to σ. Unfortunately, we cannot be very precise in this guess. However, in guesstimating the value of σ, we prefer to err on the high side. To understand why, consider the following example.

EXAMPLE 10.2

Lumber companies need to be able to estimate the amount of lumber that they can harvest in a tract of land to determine whether the effort will be profitable. To do so, they must estimate the mean diameter of the trees. It has been decided to estimate that parameter to within 1 inch with 99% confidence. A forester familiar with the territory guesses that the diameters of the trees are normally distributed with a standard deviation of 6 inches. How large a sample should be taken?

SOLUTION The confidence level is 99% ($1 - \alpha = .99$). Thus $\alpha = .01$ and $\alpha/2 = .005$. It follows that $z_{\alpha/2} = 2.575$. Substituting this quantity, $W = 1$, and $\sigma = 6$, we compute

$$n = \left(\frac{z_{\alpha/2}\sigma}{W}\right)^2 = \left(\frac{2.575 \times 6}{1}\right)^2 = 239$$

To estimate with 99% confidence the mean of a normal population whose standard deviation is assumed to be 6 requires a random sample of 239 trees. From the data the sample mean will be computed and ultimately the confidence interval estimator will be produced. If the standard deviation is actually 6 inches the interval estimate will be $\bar{x} \pm 1$.

However, if the standard deviation is actually a number larger than 6, the confidence interval estimator will be wider than planned and thus less precise and useful. To illustrate, suppose that after sampling the trees we discover that σ is actually 12 inches. The confidence interval estimator becomes

$$\bar{x} \pm z_{\alpha/2} \frac{\sigma}{\sqrt{n}} = \bar{x} \pm 2.575 \frac{12}{\sqrt{239}} = \bar{x} \pm 2$$

which is twice the width we had planned.

If we discover that the standard deviation is less than we assumed when we determined the sample size, the confidence interval estimator will be narrower, and therefore more precise. In the example above if σ is actually 3 inches, the confidence interval estimator becomes

$$\bar{x} \pm z_{\alpha/2} \frac{\sigma}{\sqrt{n}} = \bar{x} \pm 2.575 \frac{3}{\sqrt{239}} = \bar{x} \pm .5$$

Although this means that we have sampled more trees than needed, the additional cost is relatively low when compared to the value of the information derived.

EXERCISES

Developing an Understanding of Statistical Concepts

10.61 Determine the sample size required to estimate a population mean to within 10 units given that the population standard deviation is 50. A confidence level of 90% is judged to be appropriate.

10.62 Redo Exercise 10.61 changing the standard deviation to 100.

10.63 Redo Exercise 10.61 using a 95% confidence level.

10.64 Redo Exercise 10.61 wherein we wish to estimate the population mean to within 20 units.

10.65 Review the results of Exercises 10.61 to 10.64. Describe what happens to the sample size when
a the population standard deviation increases
b the confidence level increases
c the width of the interval increases

10.66 A statistics practitioner would like to estimate a population mean to within 50 units with 99% confidence given that the population standard deviation is 250. What sample size should be used?

10.67 Redo Exercise 10.66 changing the standard deviation to 50.

10.68 Redo Exercise 10.66 using a 95% confidence level.

10.69 Redo Exercise 10.66 wherein we wish to estimate the population mean to within 10 units.

10.70 Review the results of Exercises 10.66 to 10.69. Describe what happens to the sample size when
a the population standard deviation decreases
b the confidence level decreases
c the width of the interval decreases

10.71 Determine the sample size necessary to estimate a population mean to within 1 with 90% confidence given that the population standard deviation is 10.

10.72 Refer to Exercise 10.71. Suppose that the sample mean was calculated as 150. Estimate the population mean with 90% confidence.

10.73 Repeat Exercise 10.72 after discovering that the population standard deviation is actually 5.

10.74 Repeat Exercise 10.72 after discovering that the population standard deviation is actually 20.

10.75 Review Exercises 10.71 to 10.74. Describe what happens to the confidence interval estimate when
a the standard deviation is equal to the value used to determine the sample size
b the standard deviation is smaller than the one used to determine the sample size
c the standard deviation is larger than the one used to determine the sample size

10.76 A statistics practitioner would like to estimate a population mean to within 10 units. The confidence level has been set at 95% and $\sigma = 200$. Determine the sample size.

10.77 Refer to Exercise 10.76. Suppose that the sample mean was calculated as 500. Estimate the population mean with 95% confidence.

10.78 Repeat Exercise 10.77 after discovering that the population standard deviation is actually 100.

10.79 Repeat Exercise 10.77 after discovering that the population standard deviation is actually 400.

10.80 Review Exercises 10.76 to 10.79. Describe what happens to the confidence interval estimate when
a the standard deviation is equal to the value used to determine the sample size
b the standard deviation is smaller than the one used to determine the sample size
c the standard deviation is larger than the one used to determine the sample size

Applications

10.81 A medical statistician wants to estimate the average weight loss of people who are on a new diet plan. In a preliminary study, he guesses that the standard deviation of the population of weight losses is about 10 pounds. How large a sample should he take to estimate the mean weight loss to within 2 pounds, with 90% confidence?

10.82 The operations manager of a large production plant would like to estimate the average amount of time workers take to assemble a new electronic component. After observing a number of workers assembling similar devices, she guesses that the standard deviation is 6 minutes. How large a sample of workers should she take if she wishes to estimate the mean assembly time to within 20 seconds? Assume that the confidence level is to be 99%.

10.83 A statistics professor wants to compare today's students with those 25 years ago. All of his current students' marks are stored on a computer so that he can easily determine the population mean. However, the marks 25 years ago reside only in his musty files. He does not want to retrieve all the marks and will be satisfied with a 95% confidence interval estimate of the mean mark 25 years ago. If he assumes that the population standard deviation is 12, how large a sample should he take to estimate the mean to within 2 marks?

10.84 A medical researcher wants to investigate the amount of time it takes for patients' headache pain to be relieved after taking a new prescription painkiller. She plans to use statistical methods to estimate the mean of the population of relief times. She believes that the population is normally distributed with a standard deviation of 20 minutes. How large a sample should she take to estimate the mean time to within 1 minute with 90% confidence?

10.85 The label on 1-gallon cans of paint states that the amount of paint in the can is sufficient to paint 400 square feet. However, this number is quite variable. In fact, the amount of coverage is known to be approximately normally distributed with standard deviation of 25 square feet. How large a sample should be taken to estimate the true mean coverage of all 1-gallon cans to within 5 square feet with 95% confidence?

10.86 The operations manager of a plant making cellular telephones has proposed rearranging the production process to be more efficient. She wants to estimate the time to assemble the telephone using the new arrangement. She believes that the population standard deviation is 15 seconds. How large a sample of workers should she take to estimate the mean assembly time to within 2 seconds with 95% confidence?

10.5 SUMMARY

This chapter introduced the concepts of **estimation** and the **estimator** of a population mean when the population variance is known. It also presented a formula to calculate the sample size necessary to estimate a population mean.

IMPORTANT TERMS

Estimator 298
Point estimator 298
Interval estimator 298
Unbiased estimator 299
Consistency 300
Relative efficiency 300

Confidence interval estimator of μ 302
Confidence level 302
Lower confidence limit (LCL) 302
Upper confidence limit (UCL) 302
Sample size to estimate μ 314

SYMBOLS

Symbol	Pronounced	Represents
$1 - \alpha$	One-minus-alpha	Confidence level
W		Half-width of confidence interval estimator
$z_{\alpha/2}$	z-alpha-by-2	Value of Z such that the area to its right is equal to $\alpha/2$

FORMULAS

Confidence interval estimator of μ

$$\bar{x} \pm z_{\alpha/2} \frac{\sigma}{\sqrt{n}}$$

Sample size to estimate μ

$$n = \left(\frac{z_{\alpha/2}\sigma}{W} \right)^2$$

COMPUTER OUTPUT AND INSTRUCTIONS

Technique	Excel	Minitab
Confidence interval estimate of μ	306	307

REFERENCES

Casella, George, and Roger L. Berger, *Statistical Inference.* Belmont, CA: Duxbury, 1990.

Gaither, Norman, and Gregory Frazier, *Production and Operations Management*, 8th edition. Cincinnati, OH: Southwestern, 1999.

Gastwirth, Joseph L., *Statistical Reasoning in Law and Public Policy*, San Diego, CA: Academic Press, 1988.

Hogg, Robert V., and Allan T. Craig, *Introduction to Mathematical Statistics*, 5th edition. Englewood Cliffs, NJ: Prentice Hall, 1995.

Kotler, Phillip, *Marketing Management*, 8th edition. Englewood Cliffs, NJ: Prentice Hall, 1994.

Mood, A. M., F. A. Graybill, and D. L. Boes, *Introduction to the Theory of Statistics*, 3rd edition. New York: McGraw Hill, 1974.

Nahmias, Steven, *Production and Operations Analysis*, 4th edition. Burr Ridge, IL: McGraw Hill, 2001.

Rice, John A., *Mathematical Statistics and Data Analysis*, 2nd edition. Belmont, CA: Duxbury, 1995.

11 INTRODUCTION TO HYPOTHESIS TESTING

SSA ENVELOPE PLAN

Federal Express (FedEx) sends invoices to customers requesting payment within 30 days. The bill lists an address, and customers are expected to use their own envelopes to return their payments. Currently the mean and standard deviation of the amount of time taken to pay bills are 24 days and 6 days, respectively. The chief financial officer (CFO) believes that including a stamped self-addressed (SSA) envelope would decrease the amount of time. She calculates that the improved cash flow from a 2-day decrease in the payment period would pay for the costs of the envelopes and stamps. Any further

decrease in the payment period would generate a profit. To test her belief, she randomly selects 220 customers and includes a stamped self-addressed envelope with their invoices. The numbers of days until payment is received are stored in file Ch11:\SSA. Can the CFO conclude that the plan will be profitable?

After we've introduced the required tools, we'll return to this question and answer it (see page 333).

11.1 INTRODUCTION

In Chapter 10, we introduced estimation and showed how it is used. Now we're going to present the second general procedure of making inferences about a population—hypothesis testing. The purpose of this type of inference is to determine whether enough statistical evidence exists to enable us to conclude that a belief or hypothesis about a parameter is supported by the data. You will discover that hypothesis testing has a wide variety of applications in business and economics, as well as many other fields. This chapter will lay the foundation upon which the rest of the book is based. As such it represents a critical contribution to your development of a statistics practitioner.

In the next section, we will introduce the concepts of hypothesis testing, and in Section 11.3 we will develop the method employed to test a hypothesis about a population mean when the population standard deviation is known. The rest of the chapter deals with related topics.

11.2 CONCEPTS OF HYPOTHESIS TESTING

The term *hypothesis testing* is likely new to most readers, but the concepts underlying hypothesis testing are quite familiar. There are a variety of nonstatistical applications of hypothesis testing, the best known of which is a criminal trial.

When a person is accused of a crime, he or she faces a trial. The prosecution presents its case and a jury must make a decision on the basis of the evidence presented. In fact, the jury conducts a test of hypothesis. There are actually two hypotheses that are tested. The first is called the **null hypothesis** and is represented by H_0 (pronounced *H-nought: nought* is a British term for zero). It is

H_0: The defendant is innocent.

The second is called the **alternative** or **research hypothesis** and is denoted H_1. In a criminal trial it is

H_1: The defendant is guilty.

Of course, the jury does not know which hypothesis is correct. They must make a decision on the basis of evidence presented by both the prosecution and defense. There are only two possible decisions—convict or acquit the defendant. In statistical parlance, convicting the defendant is equivalent to *rejecting the null hypothesis in favor of the alternative*. Acquitting a defendant is phrased as *not rejecting the null hypothesis in favor of the alternative*. Notice that we do *not* say that we *accept* the null hypothesis. In a criminal trial, that would be interpreted as finding the defendant innocent. Our justice system does not allow this decision.

When testing hypotheses there are two possible errors. A **Type I error** occurs when we reject a true null hypothesis. A **Type II error** is defined as not rejecting a false null hypothesis. In the criminal trial, a Type I error is made when an innocent person is wrongly convicted. A Type II error occurs when a guilty defendant is acquitted. The probability of a Type I error is denoted by α, which is also called the **significance level**. The probability of a Type II error is denoted by β (Greek letter *beta*). The error probabilities α and β are inversely related, meaning that any attempt to reduce one will increase the other.

In our justice system, Type I errors are regarded as more serious. As a consequence, the system is set up so that the probability of a Type I error is small. This is arranged by placing the burden of proof on the prosecution (the prosecution must prove guilt—the defense need not prove anything) and by having judges instruct the jury to find the defendant guilty only if there is "evidence beyond a reasonable doubt." In the absence of enough evidence, the jury must acquit even though there may be some evidence of guilt. The consequence of this arrangement is that the probability of acquitting guilty people is relatively large. Oliver Wendell Holmes, a United States Supreme Court justice, once phrased the relationship between the probabilities of Type I and Type II errors in the following way: "Better to acquit 100 guilty men than convict one innocent one." In Justice Holmes's opinion, the probability of a Type I error should be 1/100 of the probability of a Type II error.

The critical concepts are these.

1. There are two hypotheses. One is called the null hypothesis and the other the alternative or research hypothesis.

2. The testing procedure begins with the assumption that the null hypothesis is true.

3. The goal of the process is to determine whether there is enough evidence to infer that the alternative hypothesis is true.

4. There are two possible decisions:
   Reject the null hypothesis in favor of the alternative.
   Do not reject the null hypothesis in favor of the alternative.

5. Two possible errors can be made in any test. A Type I error occurs when we reject a true null hypothesis, and a Type II error occurs when we don't reject a false null hypothesis. The probabilities of Type I and Type II errors are:

$$P(\text{Type I error}) = \alpha$$

$$P(\text{Type II error}) = \beta$$

Let's extend these concepts to statistical hypothesis testing.

In statistics we frequently test hypotheses about parameters. (It is too early in the pedagogy to discuss variations that do not involve parameters.) The hypotheses we test are generated by questions that managers need to answer. To illustrate, suppose that in Example 10.1 the operations manager did not want to estimate the mean demand during lead time, but instead wanted to know whether the mean is greater than 350, which may be the point at which the current inventory policy needs to be altered. That is, the manager wants to determine whether he can infer that $\mu > 350$. As was the case with the criminal trial, whatever we're investigating is specified as the alternative (research) hypothesis. Thus,

$$H_1: \quad \mu > 350$$

Had the manager wanted to determine whether the mean is *less than* 350, he would have set up the alternative hypothesis as

$$H_1: \quad \mu < 350$$

If he wanted to know whether the mean *differs from* 350, the alternative hypothesis would be

$$H_1: \quad \mu \neq 350$$

To test the alternative hypothesis, we employ the sampling distribution of the mean. We do so by assuming that the mean lead time demand is equal to 350. (In the criminal trial we assume that the defendant is innocent.) This is represented by the null hypothesis. That is,

$$H_0: \quad \mu = 350$$

Why do we need the null hypothesis if we want to know whether the alternative hypothesis is true? The reason is that the sampling distribution requires us to assume that μ is a specific value. In this illustration we would assume its value is 350.

The next element in the procedure is to randomly sample the population and calculate the sample mean. This is called the *test statistic*. The test statistic is the criterion upon which we base our decision about the hypotheses. (In the criminal trial analogy, this is equivalent to the evidence presented in the case.) The test statistic is based on the best estimator of the parameter. In Chapter 10 we stated that the best estimator of a population mean is the sample mean.

If the test statistic's value is inconsistent with the null hypothesis, we reject the null hypothesis and infer that the alternative hypothesis is true. For example, if we're trying to decide whether the mean is greater than 350, a large value of $\bar{x}$ (say, 550) would provide evidence that the null hypothesis is false and that the alternative is true. If the test statistic value is consistent with the null hypothesis, we do not reject the null. For instance, if $\bar{x}$ is close to 350 (say, 355) we could not say that this provides a great deal of evidence to infer that the mean is greater than 350. In the absence of sufficient evidence, we do not reject the null hypothesis in favor of the alternative. (In the absence of sufficient evidence of guilt, a jury finds the defendant not guilty.)

In a criminal trial "sufficient evidence" is defined as "evidence beyond a reasonable doubt." In statistics we need to use the test statistic's sampling distribution to define "sufficient evidence." We will do so in the next section.

| EXERCISES

Exercises 11.1–11.5 feature nonstatistical applications of hypothesis testing. For each, identify the hypotheses, define Type I and Type II errors, and discuss the consequences of each error. In setting up the hypotheses, you will have to consider where to place the "burden of proof."

11.1   It is the responsibility of the federal government to judge the safety and effectiveness of new drugs. There are two possible decisions: approve the drug or disapprove the drug.

11.2   You are contemplating a Ph.D. in business or economics. If you succeed, a life of fame, fortune, and happiness awaits you. If you fail, you've wasted 5 years of your life. Should you go for it?

11.3   You are the center fielder of the New York Yankees. It is the bottom of the ninth inning of the seventh game of the World Series. The Yanks lead by 2 with 2 outs and men on second and third. The batter is known to hit for high average, runs very well, but with mediocre

power. A single will tie the game and a hit over your head will likely result in the Yanks losing. Do you play shallow?

11.4   You are faced with two investments. One is very risky but the potential returns are high. The other is safe but the potential is quite limited. Pick one.

11.5   You are the pilot of a jumbo jet. You smell smoke in the cockpit. The nearest airport is less than 5 minutes away. Should you land the plane immediately?

11.6   Several years ago in a high-profile case, a defendant was acquitted in a double-murder trial but was subsequently found responsible for the deaths in a civil trial. (Guess the name of the defendant—the answer is in Appendix C.) In a civil trial the plaintiff (the victims' relatives) are required only to show that the preponderance of evidence points to the guilt of the defendant. Aside from the other issues in the cases, discuss why these results are logical.

11.3 TESTING THE POPULATION MEAN WHEN THE POPULATION STANDARD DEVIATION IS KNOWN

To illustrate the process, consider the following example.

EXAMPLE 11.1

The manager of a department store is thinking about establishing a new billing system for the store's credit customers. After a thorough financial analysis, she determines that the new system will be cost effective only if the mean monthly account is more than $170. A random sample of 400 monthly accounts is drawn, for which the sample mean is $178. (The data are stored in file Xm11-01.) The manager knows that the accounts are approximately normally distributed with a standard deviation of $65. Can the manager conclude from this that the new system will be cost effective?

SOLUTION

IDENTIFY

This example deals with the population of the credit accounts at the store. To conclude that the system will be cost effective requires the manager to show that μ, the mean account for all customers, is greater than $170. Consequently, we set up the alternative hypothesis to express this circumstance:

$$H_1: \quad \mu > 170$$

The null hypothesis must specify a single value for the parameter. Thus the null hypothesis is

$$H_0: \quad \mu = 170$$

As we previously pointed out, the test statistic is the best estimator of the parameter. In Chapter 10, we used the sample mean to estimate the population mean. To conduct this test we ask and answer the following question: "Is a sample mean of 178 sufficiently greater than 170 to allow us to confidently infer that the population mean is greater than 170?"

There are two approaches to answering this question. The first is called the *rejection region method*. It can be used in conjunction with the computer but it is mandatory for those computing statistics manually. The second is the *p-value approach*, which in general can be employed only in conjunction with a computer and statistical software. We recommend, however, that users of statistical software be familiar with both approaches.

REJECTION REGION

It seems reasonable to reject the null hypothesis if the value of the sample mean is large relative to 170. If we had calculated the sample mean to be, say, 500, it would be quite apparent that the null hypothesis is false and we would reject it. On the other hand, values of $\bar{x}$ close to 170, such as 171, do not allow us to reject the null hypothesis because it is entirely possible to observe a sample mean of 171 from a population whose mean is 170. Unfortunately, the decision is not always so obvious. In this example, the sample mean was calculated to be 178, a value apparently neither very far away from nor very close to 170. In order to make a decision about this sample mean, we set up the *rejection region*.

> **REJECTION REGION**
> The **rejection region** is a range of values such that if the test statistic falls into that range, we decide to reject the null hypothesis in favor of the alternative hypothesis.

Suppose we define the value of the sample mean that is just large enough to reject the null hypothesis as $\bar{x}_L$. The rejection region is

$$\bar{x} > \bar{x}_L$$

Since a Type I error is defined as rejecting a true null hypothesis, and the probability of committing a Type I error is α, it follows that

$$\alpha = P(\text{rejecting } H_0 \text{ given that } H_0 \text{ is true})$$
$$= P(\bar{x} > \bar{x}_L \text{ given that } H_0 \text{ is true})$$

Figure 11.1 depicts the sampling distribution and the rejection region.

Figure 11.1
Sampling distribution for Example 11.1

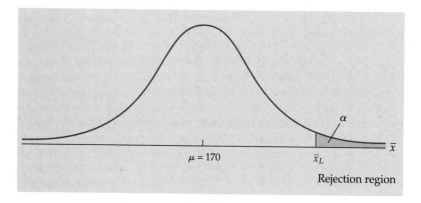

From Section 9.2, we know that the sampling distribution of $\bar{x}$ is normal or approximately normal, with mean μ and standard deviation $\sigma/\sqrt{n}$. As a result, we can standardize $\bar{x}$ and obtain the following probability:

$$P\left(\frac{\bar{x} - \mu}{\sigma/\sqrt{n}} > \frac{\bar{x}_L - \mu}{\sigma/\sqrt{n}}\right) = P\left(Z > \frac{\bar{x}_L - \mu}{\sigma/\sqrt{n}}\right) = \alpha$$

From Section 8.3, we defined z_α to be the value of a standard normal random variable such that

$$P(Z > z_\alpha) = \alpha$$

Since both probability statements involve the same distribution (standard normal) and the same probability (α), it follows that the limits are identical. Thus,

$$\frac{\bar{x}_L - \mu}{\sigma/\sqrt{n}} = z_\alpha$$

We know that $\sigma = 65$ and $n = 400$. Because the probabilities defined above are conditional upon the null hypothesis being true, we have $\mu = 170$. To calculate the rejection region we need a value of α, the significance level. Suppose that the manager chose α to be 5%. It follows that $z_\alpha = z_{.05} = 1.645$. We can now calculate the value of $\bar{x}_L$:

$$\frac{\bar{x}_L - \mu}{\sigma/\sqrt{n}} = z_\alpha$$

$$\frac{\bar{x}_L - 170}{65/\sqrt{400}} = 1.645$$

$$\bar{x}_L = 175.34$$

Therefore the rejection region is

$$\bar{x} > 175.34$$

The sample mean was computed to be 178. Since the test statistic (sample mean) is in the rejection region (it is greater than 175.34), we reject the null hypothesis. Thus, there is sufficient evidence to infer that the mean monthly account is greater than $170.

Our calculations determined that any value of $\bar{x}$ above 175.34 represents an event that is quite unlikely when sampling (with $n = 400$) from a population whose mean is 170 (and whose standard deviation is 65). This suggests that the assumption that the null hypothesis is true is incorrect, and consequently we reject the null hypothesis in favor of the alternative hypothesis.

STANDARDIZED TEST STATISTIC

The preceding test used the test statistic $\bar{x}$; as a result, the rejection region had to be set up in terms of $\bar{x}$. An easier method specifies that the test statistic be the standardized value of $\bar{x}$. That is, we use the *standardized test statistic*

$$z = \frac{\bar{x} - \mu}{\sigma/\sqrt{n}}$$

and the rejection region consists of all values of z that are greater than z_α. Algebraically, the rejection region is

$$z > z_\alpha$$

We can redo Example 11.1 using the standardized test statistic.
The rejection region is

$$z > z_\alpha = z_{.05} = 1.645$$

The value of the test statistic is calculated next.

$$z = \frac{\bar{x} - \mu}{\sigma/\sqrt{n}} = \frac{178 - 170}{65/\sqrt{400}} = 2.46$$

Because 2.46 is greater than 1.645, reject the null hypothesis and conclude that there is enough evidence to infer that the mean monthly account is greater than $170.

As you can see, the conclusions we draw from using the test statistic $\bar{x}$ and the standardized test statistic z are identical. Figures 11.2 and 11.3 depict the two sampling distributions, highlighting the equivalence of the two tests.

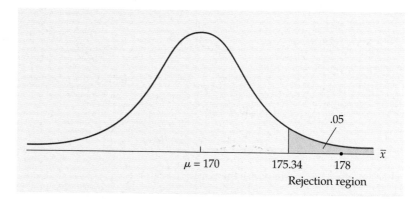

Figure 11.2
Sampling distribution of $\bar{x}$ for Example 11.1

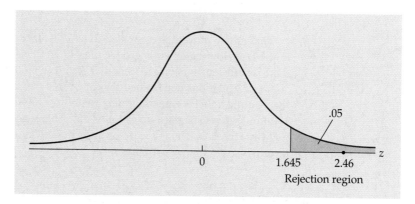

Figure 11.3
Sampling distribution of z for Example 11.1

Because of the convenience and because statistical software packages employ them, the standardized test statistic will be used throughout this book. For simplicity we will refer to the *standardized test statistic* simply as the *test statistic*.

Incidentally, when a null hypothesis is rejected, the test is said to be *statistically significant* at whatever significance level the test was conducted. Summarizing Example 11.1, we would say that the test was significant at the 5% significance level.

P-VALUE

There are several drawbacks to the rejection region method. Foremost among them is the type of information provided by the result of the test. The rejection region method produces a yes or no response to the question, "Is there sufficient statistical evidence to infer that the alternative hypothesis is true?" The implication is that the result of the test of hypothesis will be converted automatically into one of two possible courses of action: one action as a result of rejecting the null hypothesis in favor of the alternative or another as a result of not rejecting the null hypothesis in favor of the alternative. In Example 11.1 the rejection of the null hypothesis seems to imply that the new billing system will be installed.

In fact, this is not the way in which the result of a statistical analysis is utilized. The statistical procedure is only one of several factors considered by a manager when making a decision. In Example 11.1 the manager discovered that there was enough statistical evidence to conclude that the mean monthly account is greater than $170. However, before taking any action, the manager would like to consider a number of factors including the cost and feasibility of restructuring the billing system and the possibility of making an error—in this case, a Type I error.

What is needed to take full advantage of the information available from the test result and make a better decision is a measure of the amount of statistical evidence supporting the alternative hypothesis so that it can be weighed in relation to the other factors, especially the financial ones. The *p-value of a test* provides this measure.

> ### p-VALUE
> The **p-value** of a test is the probability of observing a test statistic at least as extreme as the one computed given that the null hypothesis is true.

In Example 11.1 the *p*-value is the probability of observing a sample mean at least as large as 178 when the population mean is 170. Thus,

$$p\text{-value} = P(\bar{x} > 178) = P\left(\frac{\bar{x} - \mu}{\sigma/\sqrt{n}} > \frac{178 - 170}{65/\sqrt{400}}\right) = P(Z > 2.46) = .0069$$

Figure 11.4 describes this calculation.

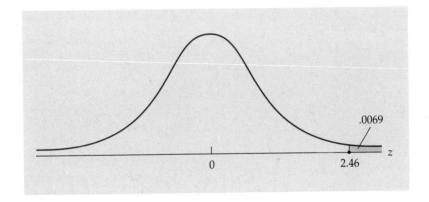

Figure 11.4
_p_-value for Example 11.1

Interpreting the _p_-Value

To properly interpret the results of an inferential procedure, you must remember that the technique is based on the sampling distribution. The sampling distribution allows us to make probability statements about a sample statistic assuming knowledge of the population parameter. Thus, the probability of observing a sample mean at least as large as 178 from a population whose mean is 170 is .0069, which is very small. In other words, we have just observed an unlikely event—an event so unlikely that we must doubt the assumption that began the process. Recall that we assume that the null hypothesis is true in order to calculate the value of the test statistic. Consequently, we have reason to reject the null hypothesis and support the alternative hypothesis.

Students may be tempted to simplify the interpretation by stating that the *p*-value is the probability that the null hypothesis is true. Don't! As was the case with interpreting the confidence interval estimator, you cannot make a probability statement about a parameter. It is not a random variable.

The *p*-value of a test provides valuable information because it measures the amount of statistical evidence that supports the alternative hypothesis. To understand this interpretation fully, refer to Table 11.1, where we list several values of $\bar{x}$, their *z* statistics, and *p*-values for Example 11.1. Notice that the closer $\bar{x}$ is to the hypothesized mean, 170, the larger the *p*-value is. The farther $\bar{x}$ is above 170, the smaller the *p*-value is. Values of $\bar{x}$ far above 170 tend to indicate that the alternative hypothesis is true. Thus, the smaller the *p*-value, the more statistical evidence exists to support the alternative hypothesis. Figure 11.5 graphically depicts the information in Table 11.1.

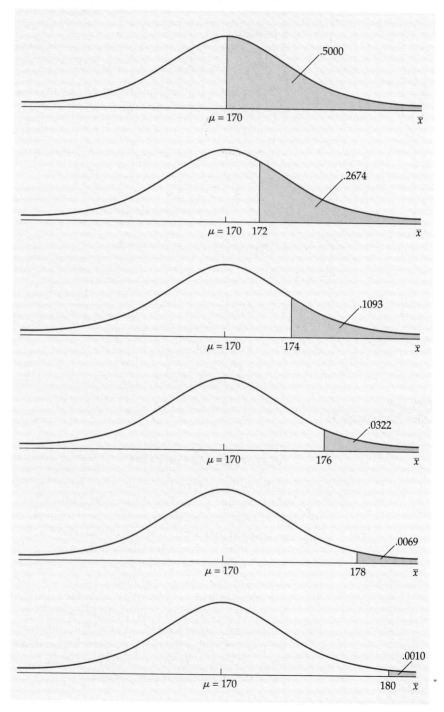

Figure 11.5
***p*-values for Example 11.1**

Table 11.1 Test Statistics and *p*-Values for Example 11.1

Sample Mean	Test Statistic $z = \dfrac{\bar{x} - \mu}{\sigma/\sqrt{n}} = \dfrac{\bar{x} - 170}{65/\sqrt{400}}$	*p*-Value
170	0	.5000
172	0.62	.2674
174	1.23	.1093
176	1.85	.0322
178	2.46	.0069
180	3.08	.0010

This raises the question, How small does the *p*-value have to be to infer that the alternative hypothesis is true? In general, the answer depends on a number of factors, including the costs of making Type I and Type II errors. In Example 11.1, a Type I error would occur if the manager adopts the new billing system when it is not cost effective. If the cost of this error is high, we attempt to minimize its probability. In the rejection region method, we do so by setting the significance level quite low—say, 1%. Using the *p*-value method, we would insist that the *p*-value be quite small, providing sufficient evidence to infer that the mean monthly account is greater than $170 before proceeding with the new billing system.

Describing the *p*-Value

Statistics practitioners often translate *p*-values using the following descriptive terms:

If the *p*-value is less than 1%, we say that there is *overwhelming* evidence to infer that the alternative hypothesis is true. We also say that the test is *highly significant*.

If the *p*-value lies between 1% and 5%, there is *strong* evidence to infer that the alternative hypothesis is true. The result is deemed to be *significant*.

If the *p*-value is between 5% and 10%, we say that there is *weak* evidence to indicate that the alternative hypothesis is true. When the *p*-value is greater than 5%, we say that the result is *not statistically significant*.

When the *p*-value exceeds 10%, we say that there is no evidence to infer that the alternative hypothesis is true.

Figure 11.6 summarizes these terms.

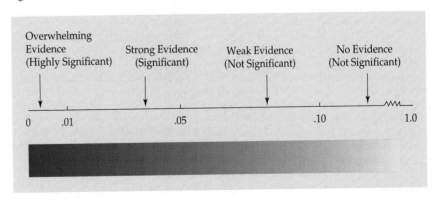

Figure 11.6
Describing the *p*-value of a test

THE *p*-VALUE AND REJECTION REGION METHODS

If we so choose, we can use the *p*-value to make the same type of decisions we make in the rejection region method. The rejection region method requires the decision maker to select a significance level, from which the rejection region is constructed. We then decide to reject or not reject the null hypothesis. Another way of making that type of decision is to compare the *p*-value with the selected value of the significance level. If the *p*-value is less than α, we judge the *p*-value to be small enough to reject the null hypothesis. If the *p*-value is greater than α, we do not reject the null hypothesis.

SOLVING MANUALLY, USING EXCEL, AND USING MINITAB

As you have already seen, we offer three ways to solve statistical problems. When we perform the calculations manually, we will use the rejection region approach. We will set up the rejection region using the test statistic's sampling distribution and associated table (in Appendix B). The calculations will be performed manually and a reject/don't reject decision will be made. In this chapter it is possible to compute the *p*-value of the test manually. However, in later chapters we will be using test statistics that are not normally distributed, making it impossible to calculate the *p*-values manually. In these instances manual calculations require the decision to be made via the rejection region method only.

Most software packages used to compute statistics, including the two used in this book, Excel and Minitab, print the *p*-value of the test. When we employ the computer we will not set up the rejection region. Instead, we will focus on the interpretation of the *p*-value.

EXCEL

	A	B	C	D
1	Z-Test: Mean			
2				
3				*Accounts*
4	Mean			178.00
5	Standard Deviation			68.37
6	Observations			400
7	Hypothesized Mean			170
8	SIGMA			65
9	z Stat			2.46
10	P(Z<=z) one-tail			0.0069
11	z Critical one-tail			1.6449
12	P(Z<=z) two-tail			0.0138
13	z Critical two-tail			1.96

COMMANDS
1. Type or import the data into one column.
2. Click **Tools, Data Analysis Plus,** and **Z-Test: Mean.**
3. Specify the **Input Range.**
4. Specify the **Hypothesized Mean.**
5. Specify the **Standard Deviation (SIGMA).**
6. Click **Labels** if appropriate.
7. Specify a value for **Alpha** and click **OK.**

COMMANDS FOR
EXAMPLE 11.1
Open file **Xm11-01.**

A1:A401

170

65

.05

The first part of the printout reports the statistics and the details of the test. As you can see, the test statistic is $z = 2.46$. The p-value[*] of the test is $P(z > 2.46) = .0069$. Excel reports this probability $P(z > 2.46)$ as

P(Z<=z) one-tail

Don't take Excel's notation literally. It is *not* giving us the probability that Z is less than or equal to the value of the z statistic. We'll discuss the terms *one-tail* and *two-tail* later. Also printed is the critical value of the rejection region, shown as

Z Critical one-tail

The printout shown above was produced from the raw data. That is, we input the 400 observations in the data set, and the computer calculated the value of the test statistic and the p-value. As was the case with estimation, if you have calculated the value of the sample mean, you can use an Excel worksheet we created for this book.

EXCEL

Open the **Test Statistics** workbook and find the worksheet **z-Test_Mean**. Input the components of the test: $\bar{x}$, σ, n, and the hypothesized value of μ. The value of z (z Stat), the p-value, and various other quantities (to be discussed subsequently) will be output. You can also conduct a what-if analysis. Try changing any of the inputs to discover their effects. The worksheet for Example 11.1 is shown next.

	A	B	C	D
1	z-Test of a Mean			
2				
3	Sample mean	178	z Stat	2.46
4	Population standard deviation	65	P(Z<=z) one-tail	0.0069
5	Sample size	400	z Critical one-tail	1.6449
6	Hypothesized mean	170	P(Z<=z) two-tail	0.0138
7	Alpha	0.05	z Critical two-tail	1.9600

MINITAB

One-Sample Z: Accounts

```
Test of mu = 170 vs mu > 170
The assumed sigma = 65

Variable            N       Mean      StDev    SE Mean
Accounts          400     178.00      68.37       3.25

Variable     95.0% Lower Bound          Z        P
Accounts                172.65       2.46    0.007
```

GENERAL COMMANDS
1. Type or import the data into one column.
2. Click **Stat, Basic Statistics,** and **1-Sample Z....**
3. Type or **Select** the variable (**Variables**).
4. Type the value of **Sigma** under the null hypothesis.
5. Type the value of μ (**Test mean**) under the null hypothesis.
6. Click **Options...** and specify the **Alternative** Hypothesis. Click **OK.** Click **OK.**

COMMANDS FOR EXAMPLE 11.1
Open file **Xm11-01.**

Accounts
65

170

greater than

---

[*]Excel provides two probabilities in its printout. The way in which we determine the p-value of the test from the printout is somewhat complicated. Interested students are advised to read CD Appendix 11.1.

INTERPRETING THE RESULTS OF A TEST

In Example 11.1, we rejected the null hypothesis. Does this prove that the alternative hypothesis is true? The answer is no; because our conclusion is based on sample data (and not on the entire population), we can never *prove* anything by using statistical inference. Consequently, we summarize the test by stating that there is enough statistical evidence to infer that the null hypothesis is false and that the alternative hypothesis is true.

Now suppose that $\bar{x}$ had equaled 174 instead of 178. We would then have calculated $z = 1.23$ (*p*-value $= .1093$), which is not in the rejection region. Could we conclude on this basis that there is enough statistical evidence to infer that the null hypothesis is true and hence that $\mu = 170$? Again the answer is no because it is absurd to suggest that a sample mean of 174 provides enough evidence to infer that the population mean is 170. (If it *proved* anything, it would prove that the population mean is 174.) Because we're testing a single value of the parameter under the null hypothesis, we can never have enough statistical evidence to establish that the null hypothesis is true (unless we sample the entire population).

Consequently, if the value of the test statistic does not fall into the rejection region (or the *p*-value is large), rather than say we accept the null hypothesis (which implies that we're stating that the null hypothesis is true), we state that we do not reject the null hypothesis, and we conclude that not enough evidence exists to show that the alternative hypothesis is true. Although it may appear to be the case, we are not being overly technical. Your ability to set up tests of hypotheses properly and to interpret their results correctly very much depends on your understanding of this point. The point is that the conclusion is based on the alternative hypothesis. In the final analysis, there are only two possible conclusions of a test of hypothesis.

CONCLUSIONS OF A TEST OF HYPOTHESIS

If we reject the null hypothesis, we conclude that there is enough statistical evidence to infer that the alternative hypothesis is true.

If we do not reject the null hypothesis, we conclude that there is not enough statistical evidence to infer that the alternative hypothesis is true.

Observe that the alternative hypothesis is the focus of the conclusion. It represents what we are investigating. That is why it is also called the research hypothesis. Whatever you're trying to show statistically must be represented by the alternative hypothesis (bearing in mind that you have only three choices for the alternative hypothesis—the parameter is greater than, less than, or not equal to the value specified in the null hypothesis).

When we introduced statistical inference in Chapter 10, we pointed out that the first step in the solution is to identify the technique. Part of this process when the problem involves hypothesis testing is the specification of the hypotheses. Because the alternative hypothesis represents the condition we're researching, we will identify it first. The null hypothesis automatically follows because the null hypothesis must specify equality. However, by tradition, when we list the two hypotheses, the null hypothesis comes first, followed by the alternative hypothesis. All examples in this book will follow that format.

SSA ENVELOPE PLAN: SOLUTION

IDENTIFY

The objective of the study is to draw a conclusion about the mean payment period. Thus, the parameter to be tested is the population mean μ. We want to know whether there is enough statistical evidence to show that the population mean is less than 22 days. Thus, the alternative hypothesis is

$$H_1: \mu < 22$$

The null hypothesis automatically follows:

$$H_0: \mu = 22$$

The test statistic is the only one we've presented thus far. It is

$$z = \frac{\bar{x} - \mu}{\sigma/\sqrt{n}}$$

COMPUTE

 MANUALLY

To solve this problem manually, we need to define the rejection region, which requires us to specify a significance level. A 10% significance level is deemed to be appropriate. (We'll discuss our choice later.)

We wish to reject the null hypothesis in favor of the alternative only if the sample mean and hence the value of the test statistic is small enough. As a result, we locate the rejection region in the left tail of the sampling distribution. To understand why, remember that we're trying to decide whether there is enough statistical evidence to infer that the mean is less than 22 (which is the alternative hypothesis). If we observe a large sample mean (and hence a large value of z), do we want to reject the null hypothesis in favor of the alternative? The answer is an emphatic no. It is illogical to think that if the sample mean is, say, 30, there is enough evidence to conclude that the mean payment period for all customers would be less than 22. Consequently, we want to reject the null hypothesis only if the sample mean (and hence the value of the test statistic z) is small. How small is small enough? The answer is determined by the significance level and the rejection region. Thus, we set up the rejection region as

$$z < -z_\alpha = -z_{.10} = -1.28$$

Note that the direction of the inequality in the rejection region ($z < -z_\alpha$) matches the direction of the inequality in the alternative hypothesis ($\mu < 22$). Also note the negative sign, since the rejection region is in the left tail (containing values of z less than 0) of the sampling distribution.

From the data, we compute the sum and the sample mean. They are

$$\sum x_i = 4{,}759$$

$$\bar{x} = \frac{\sum x_i}{220} = \frac{4{,}759}{220} = 21.63$$

We will assume that the standard deviation of the payment periods for the SSA plan is unchanged from its current value of $\sigma = 6$. The sample size is $n = 220$, and the value of μ is hypothesized to be 22. We compute the value of the test statistic as

$$z = \frac{\bar{x} - \mu}{\sigma/\sqrt{n}} = \frac{21.63 - 22}{6/\sqrt{220}} = -.91$$

Because the value of the test statistic, $z = -.91$, is not less than -1.28, we do not reject the null hypothesis in favor of the alternative hypothesis. There is insufficient evidence to infer that the mean is less than 22 days. We can determine the p-value of the test. It is

$$p\text{-value} = P(Z < -.91) = .5 - .3186 = .1814$$

In this type of one-tail (left-tail) test of hypothesis, we calculate the p-value as $P(Z < z)$ where z is the actual value of the test statistic. Figure 11.7 depicts the sampling distribution, rejection region, and p-value.

Figure 11.7 Sampling distribution for SSA Envelope example

SSA ENVELOPE PLAN: SOLUTION (CONT.)

 EXCEL

	A	B	C
1	Z-Test: Mean		
2			
3			*Payment*
4	Mean		21.63
5	Standard Deviation		5.84
6	Observations		220
7	Hypothesized Mean		22
8	SIGMA		6
9	z Stat		-0.91
10	P(Z<=z) one-tail		0.1814
11	z Critical one-tail		1.2816
12	P(Z<=z) two-tail		0.3628
13	z Critical two-tail		1.6449

 MINITAB

One-Sample Z: Payment

```
Test of mu = 22 vs mu < 22
The assumed sigma = 6

Variable          N      Mean    StDev   SE Mean
Payment         220    21.632    5.835     0.405

Variable      95.0% Upper Bound       Z      P
Payment                  22.297    -0.91  0.181
```

INTERPRET

The value of the test statistic is −.91 and its *p*-value is .1814, a figure that does not allow us to reject the null hypothesis. Because we were not able to reject the null hypothesis, we say that there is not enough evidence to infer that the mean payment period is less than 22 days. Note that there was *some* evidence to indicate that the mean of the entire population of payment periods is less than 22 days. We did calculate the sample mean to be 21.63. However, to reject the null hypothesis we need *enough* statistical evidence, and in this case we simply did not have enough reason to reject the null hypothesis in favor of the alternative. In the absence of evidence to show that the mean payment period for all customers sent a stamped self-addressed envelope would be less than 22 days, we cannot infer that the plan would be profitable.

A Type I error occurs when we conclude that the plan works when it actually does not. The cost of this mistake is not high. A Type II error occurs when we don't adopt the SSA envelope plan when it would reduce costs. The cost of this mistake can be high. As a consequence, we would like to minimize the probability of a Type II error. Thus we chose a large value for the probability of a Type I error; we set $\alpha = .10$.

ONE- AND TWO-TAIL TESTS

The statistical tests conducted in Example 11.1 and the SSA Envelope example are called *one-tail tests* because the rejection region is located in only one tail of the sampling distribution. The *p*-value is also computed by finding the area in one tail of the sampling distribution. The right tail in Example 11.1 is the important one because the alternative hypothesis specifies that the mean is *greater than* 170. In the SSA Envelope example, the left tail is emphasized because the alternative hypothesis specifies that the mean is *less than* 22.

We'll now present an example that requires a two-tail test.

EXAMPLE 11.2

In recent years, a number of companies have been formed that offer competition to AT&T in long-distance calls. All advertise that their rates are lower than AT&T's, and as a result their bills will be lower. AT&T has responded by arguing that for the average consumer there will be no difference in billing. Suppose that a statistics practitioner working for AT&T determines that the mean and standard deviation of monthly long-distance bills for all its residential customers are $17.09 and $3.87, respectively. He then takes a random sample of 100 customers and recalculates their last month's bill using the rates quoted by a leading competitor. These data are stored in file Xm11-02. Assuming that the standard deviation of this population is the same as for AT&T, can we conclude at the 5% significance level that there is a difference between AT&T's bills and those of the leading competitor?

SOLUTION

IDENTIFY

In this problem we want to know whether the mean monthly long-distance bill is different from $17.09. Consequently, we set up the alternative hypothesis to express this condition:

$$H_1: \quad \mu \neq 17.09$$

The null hypothesis specifies that the mean is equal to the value specified under the alternative hypothesis. Hence

$$H_0: \quad \mu = 17.09$$

COMPUTE

MANUALLY

To set up the rejection region, we need to realize that we can reject the null hypothesis when the test statistic is large or when it is small. That is, we must set up a *two-tail rejection region*. Because the total area in the rejection region must be α we divide this probability by 2. Thus, the rejection region[*] is

$$z < -z_{\alpha/2} \text{ or } z > z_{\alpha/2}$$

For $\alpha = .05$, $\alpha/2 = .025$, and $z_{\alpha/2} = z_{.025} = 1.96$. The rejection region is then

$$z < -1.96 \text{ or } z > 1.96$$

From the data we compute

$$\sum x_i = 1{,}754.99$$

$$\bar{x} = \frac{\sum x_i}{n} = \frac{1{,}754.99}{100} = 17.55$$

The value of the test statistic is

$$z = \frac{\bar{x} - \mu}{\sigma/\sqrt{n}} = \frac{17.55 - 17.09}{3.87/\sqrt{100}} = 1.19$$

Since 1.19 is not greater than 1.96 or less than -1.96, we cannot reject the null hypothesis.

---

[*]Statistics practitioners often represent this rejection region as $|z| > z_{\alpha/2}$, which reads, "the *absolute* value of z is greater than $z_{\alpha/2}$." We prefer our method because it is clear that we are performing a two-tail test.

We can also calculate the p-value of the test. Because it is a two-tail test, we determine the p-value by finding the area in both tails. That is,

$$p\text{-value} = P(Z < -1.19) + P(Z > 1.19) = .1170 + .1170 = .2340$$

Or, more simply, multiply the probability in one tail by 2.

In general, the p-value in a two-tail test is determined by

$$p\text{-value} = 2P(Z > |z|)$$

where z is the actual value of the test statistic and $|z|$ is its absolute value.

EXCEL

	A	B	C
1	Z-Test: Mean		
2			
3			Bills
4	Mean		17.55
5	Standard Deviation		3.94
6	Observations		100
7	Hypothesized Mean		17.09
8	SIGMA		3.87
9	z Stat		1.19
10	P(Z<=z) one-tail		0.1173
11	z Critical one-tail		1.6449
12	P(Z<=z) two-tail		0.2346
13	z Critical two-tail		1.96

MINITAB

One-Sample Z: Bills

```
Test of mu = 17.09 vs mu not = 17.09
The assumed sigma = 3.87

Variable          N          Mean        StDev      SE Mean
Bills            100        17.550        3.938       0.387

Variable               95.0% CI                   Z      P
Bills         (  16.791,    18.308)            1.19  0.235
```

There is not enough evidence to infer that the mean long-distance bill is different from AT&T's mean of $17.09. Figure 11.8 depicts the sampling distribution for this example.

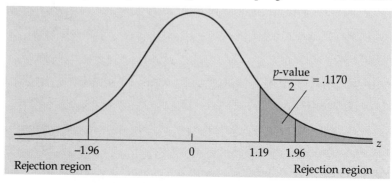

Figure 11.8
Sampling distribution for Example 11.2

WHEN DO WE CONDUCT ONE- AND TWO-TAIL TESTS?

A two-tail test is conducted whenever the alternative hypothesis specifies that the mean is *not equal* to the value stated in the null hypothesis—that is, when the hypotheses assume the following form:

$$H_0: \quad \mu = \mu_0$$
$$H_1: \quad \mu \neq \mu_0$$

There are two one-tail tests. We conduct a one-tail test that focuses on the right tail of the sampling distribution whenever we want to know whether there is enough evidence to infer that the mean is greater than the quantity specified by the null hypothesis—that is, when the hypotheses are

$$H_0: \quad \mu = \mu_0$$
$$H_1: \quad \mu > \mu_0$$

The second one-tail test involves the left tail of the sampling distribution. It is used when the statistics practitioner wants to determine whether there is enough evidence to infer that the mean is less than the value of the mean stated in the null hypothesis. The resulting hypotheses appear in this form:

$$H_0: \quad \mu = \mu_0$$
$$H_1: \quad \mu < \mu_0$$

The techniques introduced in Chapters 12, 13, 17, 18, 19, and 20 require you to decide which of the three forms of the test to employ. The decision is made in the same way as described here.

TESTING HYPOTHESES AND CONFIDENCE INTERVAL ESTIMATORS

As you've seen, the test statistic and the confidence interval estimator are both derived from the sampling distribution. It shouldn't be a surprise then that we can use the confidence interval estimator to test hypotheses. To illustrate, consider Example 11.2. The 95% confidence interval estimate of the population mean is

$$\bar{x} \pm z_{\alpha/2}\frac{\sigma}{\sqrt{n}} = 17.55 \pm 1.96\frac{3.87}{\sqrt{100}} = 17.55 \pm .76$$

$$\text{LCL} = 16.79 \quad \text{and} \quad \text{UCL} = 18.31$$

We estimate that μ lies between $16.79 and $18.31. Because this interval includes 17.09, we cannot conclude that there is sufficient evidence to infer that the population mean differs from 17.09.

In Example 11.1, the 95% confidence interval estimate is LCL = 171.63 and UCL = 184.37. The interval estimate excludes 170, allowing us to conclude that the population mean account is not equal to $170.

As you can see, the confidence interval estimator can be employed to conduct tests of hypotheses. This process is equivalent to the rejection region approach. However, instead of finding the critical values of the rejection region and determining whether the test statistic falls into the rejection region, we compute the interval estimate and determine whether the hypothesized value of the mean falls into the interval.

Using the interval estimator to test hypotheses has the advantage of simplicity. Apparently, we don't need the formula for the test statistic; we need only the interval estimator. However, there are two serious drawbacks.

First, when conducting a one-tail test, our conclusion may not answer the original question. In Example 11.1 we wanted to know whether there was enough evidence to infer that the mean is *greater than* 170. The estimate concludes that the mean *differs from* 170. You may be tempted to say that since the entire interval is greater than 170, there is enough statistical evidence to infer that the population mean is greater than 170. However, in attempting to draw this conclusion we run into the problem of determining the procedure's significance level. Is it 5% or is it 2.5%? We may be able to overcome this problem through the use of **one-sided confidence interval estimators**. However, if the purpose of using confidence interval estimators instead of test statistics is simplicity, one-sided estimators are a contradiction.

Second, the confidence interval estimator does not yield a *p*-value, which we have argued is the better way to draw inferences about a parameter. Using the confidence interval estimator to test hypotheses forces the decision maker into making a reject/don't reject decision rather than providing information about how much statistical evidence exists to be judged with other factors in the decision process. Furthermore, we only postpone the point in time when a test of hypothesis must be used. In later chapters we will present problems where only a test produces the information we need to make decisions.

DEVELOPING AN UNDERSTANDING OF STATISTICAL CONCEPTS 1

As is the case with the confidence interval estimator, the test of hypothesis is based on the sampling distribution of the sample statistic. The result of a test of hypothesis is a probability statement about the sample statistic. We assume that the population mean is equal to the value specified by the null hypothesis. We then compute the test statistic and determine how likely it is to observe this large (or small) a value when the null hypothesis is true. If the probability is small, we conclude that the assumption that the null hypothesis is true is unfounded and we reject it.

DEVELOPING AN UNDERSTANDING OF STATISTICAL CONCEPTS 2

When we (or the computer) calculate the value of the test statistic

$$z = \frac{\bar{x} - \mu}{\sigma/\sqrt{n}}$$

we're also measuring the difference between the sample statistic $\bar{x}$ and the hypothesized value of the parameter μ. The unit of measurement of the difference is the standard error $\sigma/\sqrt{n}$. In Example 11.2 we found that the value of the test statistic was $z = 1.19$. This means that the sample mean was 1.19 standard errors above the hypothesized value of μ. The standard normal probability table told us that this value is not considered unlikely. As a result, we did not reject the null hypothesis.

The concept of measuring the difference between the sample statistic and the hypothesized value of the parameter in terms of the standard error is one that will be used frequently throughout this book.

EXERCISES

Developing an Understanding of Statistical Concepts

For each of the next six exercises, calculate the value of the test statistic, set up the rejection region, determine the p-value, interpret the result, and draw the sampling distribution.

11.7 H_0: $\mu = 1,000$
H_1: $\mu \neq 1,000$
$\sigma = 200$, $n = 100$, $\bar{x} = 980$, $\alpha = .01$

11.8 H_0: $\mu = 50$
H_1: $\mu > 50$
$\sigma = 5$, $n = 9$, $\bar{x} = 51$, $\alpha = .03$

11.9 H_0: $\mu = 15$
H_1: $\mu < 15$
$\sigma = 2$, $n = 25$, $\bar{x} = 14.3$, $\alpha = .10$

11.10 H_0: $\mu = 100$
H_1: $\mu \neq 100$
$\sigma = 10$, $n = 100$, $\bar{x} = 100$, $\alpha = .05$

11.11 H_0: $\mu = 70$
H_1: $\mu > 70$
$\sigma = 20$, $n = 100$, $\bar{x} = 80$, $\alpha = .01$

11.12 H_0: $\mu = 50$
H_1: $\mu < 50$
$\sigma = 15$, $n = 100$, $\bar{x} = 48$, $\alpha = .05$

Exercises 11.13 to 11.41 are "what-if analyses" designed to determine what happens to the test statistic and p-value when the sample size, standard deviation, and sample mean change. These problems can be solved manually or using the **Test Statistics** *workbook.*

11.13 Compute the *p*-value in order to test the hypotheses below given that
$\bar{x} = 52$, $n = 9$, $\sigma = 5$, $\alpha = .05$
H_0: $\mu = 50$
H_1: $\mu > 50$

11.14 Repeat Exercise 11.13 with $n = 25$.

11.15 Repeat Exercise 11.13 with $n = 100$.

11.16 Refer to Exercises 11.13 to 11.15. Describe what happens to the value of the test statistic and *p*-value when the sample size increases.

11.17 Repeat Exercise 11.13 with $\sigma = 10$.

11.18 Repeat Exercise 11.13 with $\sigma = 20$.

11.19 Review Exercises 11.13, 11.17, and 11.18, and discuss what happens to the value of the test statistic and its *p*-value when the standard deviation increases.

11.20 Repeat Exercise 11.13 with $\bar{x} = 54$.

11.21 Repeat Exercise 11.13 with $\bar{x} = 56$.

11.22 Summarize Exercises 11.13, 11.20, and 11.21 by describing what happens to the value of the test statistic and its *p*-value when the value of $\bar{x}$ increases.

11.23 Test the hypotheses below by calculating the *p*-value given that
$\bar{x} = 99$, $n = 100$, $\sigma = 8$, $\alpha = .05$
H_0: $\mu = 100$
H_1: $\mu < 100$

11.24 Repeat Exercise 11.23 with $n = 50$.

11.25 Repeat Exercise 11.23 with $n = 20$.

11.26 From Exercises 11.23 to 11.25 discuss the effect on the value of the test statistic and the *p*-value of the test when the sample size decreases.

11.27 Repeat Exercise 11.23 with $\sigma = 12$.

11.28 Repeat Exercise 11.23 with $\sigma = 15$.

11.29 Refer to Exercises 11.23, 11.27, and 11.28. Describe what happens to the value of the test statistic and its *p*-value when the standard deviation decreases.

11.30 Repeat Exercise 11.23 with $\bar{x} = 98$.

11.31 Repeat Exercise 11.23 with $\bar{x} = 96$.

11.32 Summarize Exercises 11.23, 11.30, and 11.31 by describing what happens to the value of the test statistic and the *p*-value of the test when the value of $\bar{x}$ decreases.

The following three exercises refer to Example 11.1.

11.33 Redo Example 11.1 with
a $n = 200$
b $n = 100$
Describe the effect on the test statistic and the *p*-value when *n* increases.

11.34 Redo Example 11.1 with
a $\sigma = 35$
b $\sigma = 100$
Describe the effect on the test statistic and the *p*-value when σ increases.

11.35 Perform a what-if analysis to calculate the *p*-values in Table 11.1.

The following three exercises refer to the SSA Envelope example.

11.36 Redo the example with
a $n = 100$
b $n = 500$
Describe the effect on the test statistic and the *p*-value when *n* increases.

11.37 Redo the example with
a $\sigma = 3$
b $\sigma = 12$
Describe the effect on the test statistic and the *p*-value when σ increases.

11.38 Create a table that shows the effect on the test statistic and the *p*-value of decreasing the value of the sample mean. Use $\bar{x} = 22.0, 21.8, 21.6, 21.4, 21.2, 21.0, 20.8, 20.6$, and 20.4.

The following three exercises refer to Example 11.2.

11.39 Redo Example 11.2 with
a $n = 50$
b $n = 400$
Describe the effect on the test statistic and the *p*-value when *n* increases.

11.40 Redo Example 11.2 with
a $\sigma = 2$
b $\sigma = 10$
Describe the effect on the test statistic and the *p*-value when σ increases.

11.41 Create a table that shows the effect on the test statistic and the *p*-value of changing the value of the sample mean. Use $\bar{x} = 15.0, 15.5, 16.0, 16.5, 17.0, 17.5, 18.0, 18.5$, and 19.0.

Applications

11.42 A random sample of 18 young adult men (20–30 years old) was sampled. Each person was asked how many minutes of sports they watched on television daily. The responses are listed below. It is known that $\sigma = 10$. Test to determine at the 5% significance level whether there is enough statistical evidence to infer that the mean amount of television watched daily by all young adult men is greater than 50 minutes.

50, 48, 65, 74, 66, 37, 45, 68, 64,
65, 58, 55, 52, 63, 59, 57, 74, 65

11.43 A random sample of 12 second-year university students enrolled in a business statistics course was drawn. At the course's completion, each student was asked how many hours he or she spent doing homework in statistics. The data are listed below. It is known that the population standard deviation is $\sigma = 8.0$. The instructor has recommended that students devote 3 hours per week for the duration of the 12-week semester, for a total of 36 hours. Test to determine whether there is evidence that the average student spent less than the recommended amount of time. Compute the *p*-value of the test.

31, 40, 26, 30, 36, 38,
29, 40, 38, 30, 35, 38

11.44 A machine that produces ball bearings is set so that the average diameter is .50 inch. A sample of 10 ball bearings was measured with the results shown below. Assuming that the standard deviation is .05 inch, can we conclude at the 5% significance level that the mean diameter is not .50 inch?

.48, .50, .49, .52, .53,
.48, .49, .47, .46, .51

The following exercises require the use of a computer and software. The answers may be calculated manually. See Appendix A for the sample statistics.

11.45 A manufacturer of lightbulbs advertises that, on average, its long-life bulb will last more than 5,000 hours. To test the claim, a statistician took a random sample of 100 bulbs and measured the amount of time until each bulb burned out. The data are stored in file Xr11-45. If we assume that the lifetime of this type of bulb has a standard deviation of 400 hours, can we conclude at the 5% significance level that the claim is true?

11.46 In the midst of labor–management negotiations, the president of a company argues that the company's blue-collar workers, who are paid an average of $30,000 per year, are well paid because the mean annual income of all blue-collar workers in the country is less than $30,000. That figure is disputed by the union, which does not believe that the mean blue-collar income is less than $30,000. To test the company president's belief, an arbitrator draws a random sample of 350 blue-collar workers from across the country and asks each to report his or her annual income. The results are stored in file Xr11-46. If the arbitrator assumes that the blue-collar incomes are distributed with a standard deviation of $8,000, can it be inferred at the 5% significance level that the company president is correct?

11.47 A dean of a business school claims that the GMAT scores of applicants to the school's MBA program have increased during the past 5 years. Five years ago, the mean and standard deviation of GMAT scores of MBA applicants were 560 and 50, respectively. Twenty applications for this year's program were randomly selected and the GMAT scores recorded. These are stored in file Xr11-47. If we assume that the distribution of GMAT scores of this year's applicants is the same as that of 5 years ago, with the possible exception of the mean, can we conclude at the 5% significance level that the dean's claim is true?

11.48 Past experience indicates that the monthly long-distance telephone bill is normally distributed with a mean of $17.85 and a standard deviation of $3.87. After an advertising campaign aimed at increasing long-distance telephone usage, a random sample of 25 household bills was taken. The results are stored in file Xr11-48.
a Do the data allow us to infer at the 10% significance level that the campaign was successful?
b What assumption must you make to answer part **a**?

11.49 In an attempt to reduce the number of person-hours lost as a result of industrial accidents, a large production plant installed new safety equipment. In a test of the effectiveness of the equipment, a random sample of 50 departments was chosen. The number of person-hours lost in the month prior to and the month after the installation of the safety equipment was recorded. The percentage change was calculated, and the data stored in file Xr11-49. Assume that the population standard deviation is $\sigma = 5$. Can we infer at the 10% significance level that the new safety equipment is effective?

11.50 A highway patrol officer believes that the average speed of cars traveling over a certain stretch of highway exceeds the posted limit of 55 mph. The speeds of a random sample of 200 cars were recorded and stored in file Xr11-50. Do these data provide sufficient evidence at the 1% significance level to support the officer's belief? What is the *p*-value of the test? (Assume that the standard deviation is known to be 5.)

11.51 An automotive expert claims that the large number of self-serve gasoline stations has resulted in poor automobile maintenance, and that the average tire pressure is more than 4 pounds per square inch (psi) below its manufacturer's specification. As a quick test, 50 tires are examined, and the number of psi each tire is below specification is recorded and stored in file Xr11-51. If we assume that tire pressure is normally distributed with $\sigma = 1.5$ psi, can we infer at the 10% significance level that the expert is correct? What is the *p*-value?

11.52   For the past few years, the number of customers of a drive-up bank in New York has averaged 20 per hour, with a standard deviation of 3 per hour. This year, another bank 1 mile away opened a drive-up window. The manager of the first bank believes that this will result in a decrease in the number of customers. The number of customers who arrived during 36 randomly selected hours was recorded and stored in file Xr11-52. Can we conclude at the 5% significance level that the manager is correct? What is the p-value?

11.53   A fast-food franchiser is considering building a restaurant at a certain location. Based on financial analyses, a site is acceptable only if the number of pedestrians passing the location averages more than 100 per hour. The number of pedestrians observed for each of 40 hours was recorded and stored in file Xr11-53. Assuming that the population standard deviation is known to be 12, can we conclude that the site is acceptable? (Set your own significance level.)

11.54   Many Alpine ski centers base their projections of revenues and profits on the assumption that the average Alpine skier skis 4 times per year. To investigate the validity of this assumption, a random sample of 63 skiers is drawn and each is asked to report the number of times they skied the previous year. The responses are stored in file Xr11-54. If we assume that the standard deviation is 2, can we infer at the 10% significance level that the assumption is wrong?

11.55   The golf professional at a private course claims that members who have taken lessons from him lowered their handicap by more than 5 strokes. The club manager decides to test the claim by randomly sampling 25

members who have had lessons and asking each to report the reduction in handicap. These data are stored in file Xr11-55, where a negative number indicates an increase in the handicap. Assuming that the reduction in handicap is approximately normally distributed with a standard deviation of 2 strokes, test the golf professional's claim using a 10% significance level.

11.56   The current no-smoking regulations in office buildings require workers who smoke to take breaks and leave the building in order to satisfy their habits. A study indicates that such workers average 32 minutes per day taking smoking breaks. The standard deviation is 6 minutes. To help reduce the average, break rooms with powerful exhausts were installed in the buildings. To see whether these rooms serve their designed purpose, a random sample of 110 smokers was taken. The total amount of time away from their desks was measured for 1 day. These data are stored in file Xr11-56. Test to determine whether there has been a decrease in the mean time away from their desks. Compute the p-value and judge it relative to the costs of Type I and Type II errors.

11.57   A low-handicap golfer who uses Titleist brand golf balls observed that his average drive is 230 yards and the standard deviation is 10 yards. Nike has just introduced a new ball, which has been endorsed by Tiger Woods. Nike claims that the ball will travel further than Titleist. To test the claim the golfer hits 100 drives with a Nike ball and measures the distances. These data are stored in file Xr11-57. Conduct a test to determine whether Nike is correct. Compute the p-value and interpret it relative to the costs of Type I and Type II errors.

11.4 CALCULATING THE PROBABILITY OF A TYPE II ERROR

To properly interpret the results of a test of hypothesis requires that you be able to specify an appropriate significance level or to judge the p-value of a test. However, it also requires that you have an understanding of the relationship between Type I and Type II errors. In this section, we describe how the probability of a Type II error is computed and interpreted.

Recall Example 11.1, where we conducted the test using the sample mean as the test statistic and we computed the rejection region (with $\alpha = .05$) as

$$\bar{x} > 175.34$$

A Type II error occurs when a false null hypothesis is not rejected. Thus, in Example 11.1, if $\bar{x}$ is less than 175.34, we will not reject the null hypothesis. If we do not reject the null hypothesis we will not install the new billing system. Thus, the consequence of a Type II error in this example is that we will not install the new system when it would be cost effective. The probability of this occurring is the probability of a Type II error. It is defined as

$$\beta = P(\bar{x} < 175.34 \text{ given that the null hypothesis is false})$$

The condition that the null hypothesis is false tells us only that the mean is not equal to 170. If we want to compute β, we need to specify a value for μ. Suppose that when the mean account is at least \$180, the new billing system's savings become so attractive that the manager would hate to make the mistake of not installing it. As a result, she would like to determine the probability of not installing the new system when it would produce large cost savings. Because calculating probability from an approximately normal sampling distribution requires a value of μ (as well as σ and n), we will calculate the probability of not installing the new system when μ is *equal* to 180:

$$\beta = P(\overline{X} < 175.34, \text{ given that } \mu = 180)$$

We know that $\overline{X}$ is approximately normally distributed with mean μ and standard deviation $\sigma/\sqrt{n}$. To proceed, we standardize $\overline{X}$ and use the standard normal table (Table 3 in Appendix B):

$$\beta = P\left(\frac{\overline{X} - \mu}{\sigma/\sqrt{n}} < \frac{175.34 - 180}{65/\sqrt{400}}\right) = P(Z < -1.43) = .0764$$

This tells us that when the mean account is actually \$180, the probability of incorrectly not rejecting the null hypothesis is .0764. Figure 11.9 graphically depicts how the calculation was performed. Notice that in order to calculate the probability of a Type II error, we had to express the rejection region in terms of the unstandardized test statistic $\overline{x}$, and we had to specify a value for μ other than the one shown in the null hypothesis. In this illustration, the value of μ used was based on a financial analysis indicating that when μ is at least \$180 the cost savings would be very attractive.

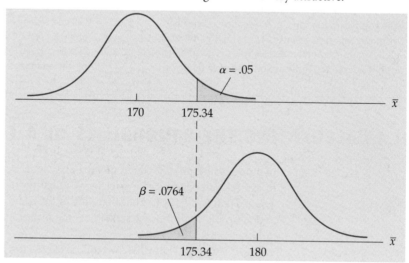

Figure 11.9
Calculating β for $\mu = 180$, $\alpha = .05$, and $n = 400$

EFFECT ON β OF CHANGING α

Suppose that in the illustration above we had used a significance level of 1% instead of 5%. The rejection region expressed in terms of the standardized test statistic would be

$$z > z_{.01} = 2.33$$

or

$$\frac{\overline{x} - 170}{65/\sqrt{400}} > 2.33$$

Solving for $\bar{x}$, we find the rejection region in terms of the unstandardized test statistic:

$$\bar{x} > 177.57$$

The probability of a Type II error when $\mu = 180$ is

$$\beta = P\left(\frac{\overline{X} - \mu}{\sigma/\sqrt{n}} < \frac{177.57 - 180}{65/\sqrt{400}}\right) = P(Z < -.75) = .2266$$

Figure 11.10 depicts this calculation. Compare this figure with Figure 11.9. As you can see, by decreasing the significance level from 5% to 1% we have shifted the critical value of the rejection region to the right and thus enlarged the area where the null hypothesis is not rejected. The probability of a Type II error increases from .0764 to .2266.

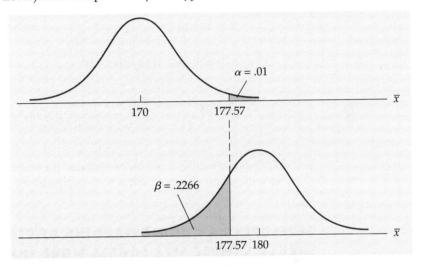

Figure 11.10
Calculating β for $\mu = 180$,
$\alpha = .01$, and $n = 400$

This calculation illustrates the inverse relationship between the probabilities of Type I and Type II errors alluded to in Section 11.2. It is important to understand this relationship. From a practical point of view, it tells us that if you want to decrease the probability of a Type I error (by specifying a small value of α), you increase the probability of a Type II error. In applications where the cost of a Type I error is considerably larger than the cost of a Type II error, this is appropriate. In fact, a significance level of 1% or less is probably justified. However, when the cost of a Type II error is relatively large, a significance level of 5% or more may be appropriate.

Unfortunately, there is no simple formula to determine what the significance level should be. It is necessary for the manager to consider the costs of both mistakes in deciding what to do. Judgment and knowledge of the factors in the decision are crucial.

JUDGING THE TEST

There is another important concept to be derived from this section. A statistical test of hypothesis is effectively defined by the significance level and the sample size, both of which are selected by the statistics practitioner. We can judge how well the test functions by calculating the probability of a Type II error at some value of the parameter. To illustrate, in Example 11.1 the manager chose a sample size of 400 and a 5% significance level on which to base her decision. With those selections we found β to be .0764 when the actual mean is 180. If we believe that the cost of a Type II error is high and thus that the probability is too large, we have two ways to reduce the probability. We can increase the value of α; however, this would result in an increase in the chance of making a Type I error, which is very costly. Or, we can increase the sample size.

Suppose that the manager chose a sample size of 1,000. We'll now recalculate β with $n = 1,000$ (and $\alpha = .05$). The rejection region is

$$z > z_{.05} = 1.645$$

or

$$\frac{\bar{x} - 170}{65/\sqrt{1,000}} > 1.645$$

which yields

$$\bar{x} > 173.38$$

The probability of a Type II error is

$$\beta = P\left(\frac{\bar{X} - \mu}{\sigma/\sqrt{n}} < \frac{173.38 - 180}{65/\sqrt{1,000}}\right) = P(Z < -3.22) = 0 \text{ (approximately)}$$

In this case we left $\alpha = .05$ but we reduced the probability of not installing the system when the actual mean account is $180 to virtually 0.

DEVELOPING AN UNDERSTANDING OF STATISTICAL CONCEPTS: LARGER SAMPLE SIZE EQUALS MORE INFORMATION EQUALS BETTER DECISIONS

Figure 11.11 displays the previous calculation. When compared with Figure 11.9, the sampling distribution of the mean is narrower because the standard error of the mean $\sigma/\sqrt{n}$ becomes smaller as n increases. Narrower distributions represent more information. The increased information is reflected in a smaller probability of a Type II error.

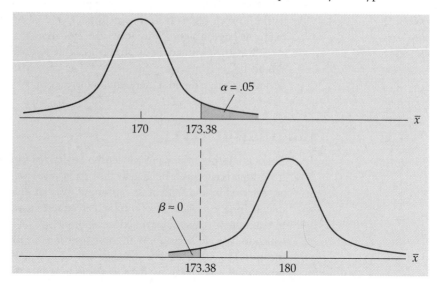

Figure 11.11
Calculating β for $\mu = 180$, $\alpha = .05$, and $n = 1,000$

The calculation of the probability of a Type II error for $n = 400$ and for $n = 1,000$ illustrates a concept whose importance cannot be overstated. By increasing the sample size we reduce the probability of a Type II error. By reducing the probability of a Type II error we make this type of error less frequently. And hence, we make better decisions in the long run. This finding lies at the heart of applied statistical analysis and reinforces the book's first sentence, "Statistics is a way to get information from data."

Throughout this book we introduce a variety of applications in finance, marketing, operations management, human resources management, and economics. In all such applications the statistics practitioner must make a decision, which involves converting data into information. The more information, the better the decision. Without such information decisions must be based on guesswork, instinct, and luck. A famous statistician, W. Edwards Deming, said it best: "Without data you're just another person with an opinion."

POWER OF A TEST

Another way of expressing how well a test performs is to report its *power*—the probability of its leading us to rejecting the null hypothesis when it is false. Thus, the power of a test is $1 - \beta$.

When more than one test can be performed in a given situation, we would naturally prefer to use the test that is correct more frequently. If (given the same alternative hypothesis, sample size, and significance level) one test has a higher power than a second test, the first test is said to be more powerful.

USING THE COMPUTER

EXCEL

We have made it possible to utilize Excel to calculate β for any test of hypothesis.

	A	B	C	D
1	Type II Error			
2				
3	H0: MU	170	Critical value	175.35
4	SIGMA	65	Prob(Type II error)	0.0761
5	Sample size	400	Power of the test	0.9239
6	ALPHA	0.05		
7	H1: MU	180		

Open the **Beta-mean** workbook. There are three worksheets. They are **Right-tail test, Left-Tail test,** and **Two-tail test**. Find the appropriate worksheet for the test of hypothesis you are analyzing and type values for μ (under the null hypothesis), σ, n, α, and μ (actual value under the alternative hypothesis).

The accompanying printout was produced by selecting the **Right-tail Test** worksheet and substituting $\mu = 170$ (under the null hypothesis), $\sigma = 65$, $n = 400$, $\alpha = .05$, and $\mu = 180$ (under the alternative hypothesis).

You can use the **Left-tail Test** worksheet to compute the probability of Type II errors when the alternative hypothesis states that the mean is less than a specified value (e.g., the SSA Envelope example). The **Two-tail Test** worksheet is used to compute β for two-tail tests (e.g., Example 11.2).

MINITAB

Minitab computes the power of the test.

Power and Sample Size

```
1-Sample Z Test

Testing mean = null (versus > null)
Calculating power for mean = null + difference
Alpha = 0.05   Sigma = 65

                Sample
Difference       Size    Power
       10         400   0.9239
```

COMMANDS

1. Click **Stat, Power and Sample Size**, and **1-Sample Z....**
2. Specify the value or values of the **Sample sizes**. (You can specify more than one value of n. Minitab will compute the power for each value.)
3. Specify the **Differences** between the actual value of μ and the value of μ under the null hypothesis. (You can specify more than one value.)
4. Specify the value of **Sigma**.
5. Click **Options**... and specify the **Alternative Hypothesis** and the **Significance level**.

For Example 11.1, we typed **400** to select the **Sample sizes**, **Differences** was **10** (= 180 − 170), **Sigma** was **65**, the **Alternative Hypothesis** was **Greater than**, and the **Significance level** was **0.05**.

OPERATING CHARACTERISTIC CURVE

To compute the probability of a Type II error, we need to specify the significance level, the sample size, and an alternative value of the population mean. One way to keep track of all these components is to draw the **operating characteristic (OC) curve**, which plots the values of β versus the values of μ. Because of the time-consuming nature of these calculations, the computer is a virtual necessity. To illustrate, we'll draw the OC curve for Example 11.1. We used Excel (we could have used Minitab instead) to compute the probability of a Type II error in Example 11.1 for $\mu = 170, 171, ..., 185$, with $n = 400$. Figure 11.12 depicts this curve. Notice that as the alternative value of μ increases, the value of β decreases. This tells us that as the alternative value of μ moves farther from the value of μ under the null hypothesis, the probability of a Type II error decreases. In other words, it becomes easier to distinguish between $\mu = 170$ and other values of μ when μ is farther from 170.

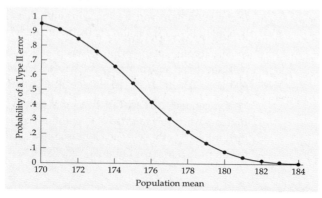

Figure 11.12
Operating characteristic curve for Example 11.1

The OC curve can also be useful in selecting a sample size. Figure 11.13 shows the OC curve for Example 11.1 with $n = 100, 400, 1,000$, and $2,000$. An examination of this chart sheds some light concerning the effect of increasing the sample size on how well the test performs at different values of μ. For example, we can see that smaller sample sizes will work well to distinguish between 170 and values of μ larger than 180. However, to distinguish between 170 and smaller values of μ requires larger sample sizes. Although the information is imprecise, it does allow us to select a sample size that is suitable for our purposes.

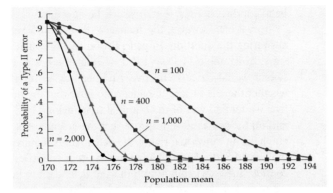

Figure 11.13
Operating characteristic curve for Example 11.1 for *n* = 100, 400, 1,000, and 2,000

Seeing   Statistics

APPLET 16:
POWER OF z TEST

We are given the following hypotheses to test:

H_0: $\mu = 10$
H_1: $\mu \neq 10$

The applet allows you to choose the actual value of μ (bottom slider), the value of α (left slider), and the

sample size (right slider). The graph shows the effect of changing any of the three values on the two sampling distributions.

Applet Exercises

16.1 Use the left and right sliders to depict the test when $n = 50$ and $\alpha = .10$. Describe what happens to the power of the test (Power $= 1 - \beta$) when the actual value of μ approximately equals the following values:

9.0,   9.4,   9.8,   10.2,   10.6,   11.0

16.2 Use the bottom and right sliders to depict the test when $\mu = 11$ and $n = 25$. Describe the effect on the test's power when α approximately equals the following:

.01,   .03,   .05,   .10,   .20,
.30,   .40,   .50

16.3 Use the bottom and left sliders to depict the test when $\mu = 11$ and $\alpha = .10$. Describe the effect on the test's power when n equals the following:

2,   5,   10,   25,   50,   75,   100

SETTING UP THE ALTERNATIVE HYPOTHESIS TO DEFINE TYPE I AND TYPE II ERRORS

We've already discussed how the alternative hypothesis is set up. It represents the condition we're investigating. In Example 11.1 we wanted to know whether there was sufficient statistical evidence to infer that the new billing system would be cost effective—that is, whether the mean monthly account is greater than $170. In this textbook you will encounter many problems using similar phraseology. Your job will be to conduct the test that answers the question.

In real life, however, the manager (that's you 5 years from now) will be asking and answering the question. In general, you will find that the question can be posed in two ways. In Example 11.1 we asked whether there was evidence to conclude that the new system would be cost effective. Another way of investigating the issue is to determine whether there is sufficient evidence to infer that the new system would *not* be cost effective. We remind you of the criminal trial analogy. In a criminal trial the burden of proof falls on the prosecution to prove that the defendant is guilty. In other countries with less emphasis on individual rights, the defendant is required to prove his or her innocence. In the United States and Canada (and in other countries) we chose the former because we consider the conviction of an innocent defendant to be the greater error. Thus the test is set up with the null and alternative hypotheses as described in Section 11.2.

In a statistical test where we are responsible for asking the question, as well as answering it, we must ask the question so that we directly control the error that is more costly. As you have already seen, we control the probability of a Type I error by specifying its value (the significance level). Consider Example 11.1 once again. There are two possible errors: conclude that the billing system is cost effective when it isn't and conclude that the system is not cost effective when it is. If the manager concludes that the billing plan is cost effective the company will install the new system. If, in reality, the system is not cost effective the company will incur a loss. On the other hand, if the manager concludes that the billing plan is not going to be cost effective, the company will not install the system. However, if the system is actually cost effective the company will lose the potential gain from installing it. Which cost is greater?

Suppose we believe that the cost of installing a system that is not cost effective is higher than the potential loss of not installing an effective system. The error we wish to avoid is the erroneous conclusion that the system is cost effective. We define this as a Type I error. As a result, the burden of proof is placed on the system to deliver sufficient statistical evidence that the mean account is greater than $170. The null and alternative hypotheses are as formulated previously. That is,

$$H_0: \quad \mu = 170$$
$$H_1: \quad \mu > 170$$

However, if we believe that the potential loss of not installing the new system when it would be cost effective is the larger cost, we would place the burden of proof on the manager to infer that the mean monthly account is less than $170. Consequently, the hypotheses would be

$$H_0: \quad \mu = 170$$
$$H_1: \quad \mu < 170$$

This discussion emphasizes the need in practice to examine the costs of making both types of error before setting up the hypotheses. However, it is important for readers to understand that the questions posed in exercises throughout this book have already considered these costs. Accordingly, your task is to set up the hypotheses to answer the questions.

EXERCISES

11.58 Calculate the probability of a Type II error for the following test of hypothesis, given that $\mu = 203$.

$$H_0: \quad \mu = 200$$
$$H_1: \quad \mu \neq 200$$
$$\alpha = .05, \quad \sigma = 10, \quad n = 100$$

11.59 Find the probability of a Type II error for the following test of hypothesis, given that $\mu = 1,050$.

$$H_0: \quad \mu = 1,000$$
$$H_1: \quad \mu > 1,000$$
$$\alpha = .01, \quad \sigma = 50, \quad n = 25$$

11.60 Determine β for the following test of hypothesis, given that $\mu = 48$.

$$H_0: \quad \mu = 50$$
$$H_1: \quad \mu < 50$$
$$\alpha = .05, \quad \sigma = 10, \quad n = 40$$

11.61 Draw a figure similar to Figure 11.9 depicting the calculation in Exercise 11.58.

11.62 Using a graph to Figure 11.9 to describe how you solved Exercise 11.59.

11.63 Refer to Excercise 11.60. Graphically depict your calculations.

Exercises 11.64–11.66 *refer to the SSA Envelope example.*

11.64 **a** Calculate the probability of a Type II error when $\mu = 21.5$.

b Calculate the probability of a Type II error when $\mu = 21.0$.

c Discuss the effect on β when μ decreases.

11.65 **a** Calculate the probability of a Type II error when $\mu = 21.0$ and $\alpha = .05$.

b Calculate the probability of a Type II error when $\mu = 21.0$ and $\alpha = .01$.

c Discuss the effect on β when α decreases.

11.66 **a** Calculate the probability of a Type II error when $\mu = 21.0$ and $n = 300$.

b Calculate the probability of a Type II error when $\mu = 21.0$ and $n = 400$.

c Discuss the effect on β when n increases.

Exercises 11.67–11.69 *refer to Example* 11.2.

11.67 **a** Calculate the probability of a Type II error when $\mu = 17.80$.

b Calculate the probability of a Type II error when $\mu = 18.00$.

c Discuss the effect on β when μ increases.

11.68 **a** Calculate the probability of a Type II error when $\mu = 18.00$ and $\alpha = .075$.

b Calculate the probability of a Type II error when $\mu = 18.00$ and $\alpha = .10$.

c Discuss the effect on β when α increases.

11.69 **a** Calculate the probability of a Type II error when $\mu = 18.00$ and $n = 150$.

b Calculate the probability of a Type II error when $\mu = 18.00$ and $n = 200$.

c Discuss the effect on β when n increases.

11.70 For the test of hypothesis

$$H_0: \quad \mu = 1,000$$
$$H_1: \quad \mu \neq 1,000$$
$$\alpha = .05, \quad \sigma = 200$$

draw the operating characteristic curve for $n = 25$, 100, and 200.

11.71 Draw the operating characteristic curve for $n = 10$, 50, and 100 for the following test:

$$H_0: \quad \mu = 400$$
$$H_1: \quad \mu > 400$$
$$\alpha = .05, \quad \sigma = 50$$

11.72 Find the probability of erroneously concluding that there is not enough evidence to infer that the claim is true in Exercise 11.45 when the mean is 5,100.

11.73 Refer to Excercise 11.46. What is the probability that the test is unable to allow us to infer that the population mean differs from $30,000 when in fact the mean is $28,500?

11.74 Refer to Excercise 11.47. Find the probability of erroneously concluding that there is not enough evidence to support the claim when, in fact, the true mean GMAT score is 600.

11.75 Refer to Exercise 11.48. Draw the operating characteristic curve for $\alpha = .01$, .05, and .10.

11.76 Draw the operating characteristic curve for Exercise 11.48 using sampling sizes of 25, 250, and 100.

11.77 Find the probability that the test conducted in Exercise 11.49 is unable to conclude that the new safety equipment is effective when the mean percent reduction is 3%.

11.78 Refer to Exercise 11.50. Find the probability if a Type II error when the actual mean speed is 57 mph.

11.79 Refer to Exercise 11.51. Find the probability of making a Type II error when the actual tire underinflation is 5 psi.

11.80 Refer to Exercise 11.52. What is the probability of not concluding that there has been a decrease when in fact the mean number of customers is 18.5?

11.81 Draw the operating characteristic curve with $\alpha = .05$ for Example 11.53.

11.82 Refer to Exercise 11.55. Draw the operating characteristic curve for $n = 25$ and 100.

11.83 Using a significance level of 5%, draw the operating characteristic curve for Exercise 11.56.

11.84 Suppose that in Example 11.1 we wanted to determine whether there was sufficient evidence to conclude that the new system would *not* be cost effective. Set up the null and alternative hypotheses and discuss the consequences of Type I and Type II errors. Conduct the test. Is your conclusion the same as the one reached in Example 11.1? Explain.

11.85 A school board administrator believes that the average number of days absent per year among students is less than 10 days. From past experience, he knows that the population standard deviation is 3 days. In testing to determine whether his belief is true, he could use either of the following plans.

i $n = 100$, $\alpha = .01$
ii $n = 75$, $\alpha = .05$
iii $n = 50$, $\alpha = .10$

Which plan has the lowest probability of a Type II error, given that the true population average is 9 days?

11.5 THE ROAD AHEAD

We had two principal goals to accomplish in Chapters 10 and 11. First, we wanted to present the concepts of estimation and hypothesis testing. Second, we wanted to show how to produce confidence interval estimates and conduct tests of hypotheses. The importance of both of these goals should not be underestimated. Almost everything that follows this chapter will involve either estimating a parameter or testing a set of hypotheses. Consequently, Sections 10.3 and 11.3 set the pattern for the way in which statistical techniques are applied. It is no exaggeration to state that if you understand how to produce and use confidence interval estimates and how to conduct and interpret hypothesis tests, then you are well on your way to the ultimate goal of being competent at analyzing, interpreting, and presenting data. It is fair for you to ask what more you must accomplish to achieve this goal. The answer, simply put, is much more of the same.

In the chapters that follow, we plan to present about three dozen different statistical techniques that can be (and frequently are) employed by statistics practitioners. To calculate the value of test statistics or confidence interval estimates requires nothing more than the ability to add, subtract, multiply, divide, and compute square roots. If you intend to use the computer, all you need to know are the commands. The key, then, to applying statistics is knowing which formula to calculate or which set of commands to issue. Thus, the real challenge of the subject lies in being able to define the problem and identify which statistical method is the most appropriate one to use.

Most students have some difficulty recognizing the particular kind of statistical problem they are addressing unless, of course, the problem appears among the exercises at the end of a section that just introduced the technique needed. Unfortunately, in practice, statistical problems do not appear already so identified. Consequently, we have adopted an approach to teaching statistics that is designed to help identify the statistical technique.

A number of factors determine which statistical method should be used, but two are especially important: the type of data and the purpose of the statistical inference. In Chapter 2, we pointed out that there are effectively three types of data—interval, ordinal, and nominal. Recall that nominal data represent categories such as marital status, occupation, and gender. Statistics practitioners often record nominal data by assigning numbers to the responses (e.g., 1 = single; 2 = married; 3 = divorced; 4 = widowed). Because these numbers are assigned completely arbitrarily, any calculations performed on them are meaningless. All that we can do with nominal data is count the number of times each category is observed. Ordinal data are obtained from questions whose answers represent a rating or ranking system. For example, if students are asked to rate a university professor, the responses may be excellent, good , fair, or poor. To draw inferences about such data, we convert the responses to numbers. Any numbering system is valid as long as the order of the responses is preserved. Thus "4 = excellent; 3 = good; 2 = fair; 1 = poor" is just as valid as "15 = excellent; 8 = good; 5 = fair; 2 = poor." Because of this feature, the most appropriate statistical procedures for ordinal data are ones based on a ranking process.

Interval data are real numbers such as those representing income, age, height, weight, and volume. Computation of means and variances is permissible.

The second key factor in determining the statistical technique is the purpose of doing the work. Every statistical method has some specific objective. There are five such objectives addressed in this book.

PROBLEM OBJECTIVES

1. **Describe a population.** Our objective here is to describe some property of a population of interest. The decision about which property to describe is generally dictated by the type of data. For example, suppose the population of interest consists of all purchasers of home computers. If we are interested in the purchasers' incomes (for which the data are interval), we may calculate the mean or the variance to describe that aspect of the population. But if we are interested in the brand of computer that has been bought (for which the data are nominal), all we can do is compute the proportion of the population that purchases each brand.

2. **Compare two populations.** In this case, our goal is to compare a property of one population with a corresponding property of a second population. For example, suppose the populations of interest are male and female purchasers of computers. We could compare the means of their incomes, or we could compare the proportion of each population that purchases a certain brand. Once again, the data type generally determines what kinds of properties we compare.

3. **Compare two or more populations.** We might want to compare the average income in each of several locations in order (for example) to decide where to build a new shopping center. Or we might want to compare the proportions of defective items in a number of production lines in order to determine which line is the best. In each case, the problem objective involves comparing two or more populations.

4. **Analyze the relationship between two variables.** There are numerous situations in which we want to know how one variable is related to another. Governments need to know what effect rising interest rates have on the unemployment rate. Companies want to investigate how the sizes of their advertising budgets influence sales volume. In most of the problems in this introductory text, the two variables to be analyzed will be of the same type; we will not attempt to cover the fairly large body of statistical techniques that has been developed to deal with two variables of different types.

5. **Analyze the relationship among two or more variables.** Our objective here is usually to forecast one variable (called the dependent variable) on the basis of several other variables (called independent variables). We will deal with this problem only in situations in which all variables are interval.

Table 11.2 lists the types of data and the five problem objectives. For each combination, the table specifies the chapter and/or section where the appropriate statistical technique is presented. For your convenience, a more detailed version of this table is reproduced inside the front cover of this book.

Table 11.2 Guide to Statistical Inference Showing Where Each Technique Is Introduced

Problem Objective	Data Type		
	Nominal	*Ordinal*	*Interval*
Describe a population	Sec 12.4. 16.2	Not covered	Sec 12.2, 12.3
Compare two populations	Sec 13.6, 16.3	Sec 17.2, 17.3	Sec 13.2, 13.4, 13.5, 17.2, 17.3
Compare two or more populations	Sec 16.3	Sec 17.4, 17.5	Chapter 15; Sec 17.4, 17.5
Analyze the relationship between two variables	Sec 16.3	Sec 18.8	Chapter 18
Analyze the relationship among two or more variables	Not covered	Not covered	Chapters 19, 20

DERIVATIONS

Because this book is about statistical applications, we assume that our readers have little interest in the mathematical derivations of the techniques described. However, it might be helpful for you to have some understanding about the process that produces the formulas.

As described above, factors such as the problem objective and the type of data determine the parameter to be estimated and tested. For each parameter, statisticians have determined which statistic to use. That statistic has a sampling distribution that can usually be expressed as a formula. For example, in this chapter, the parameter of interest was the population mean μ, whose best estimator is the sample mean $\bar{x}$. Assuming that the population standard deviation σ is known, the sampling distribution of $\bar{x}$ is normal (or approximately so) with mean μ and standard deviation $\sigma/\sqrt{n}$. The sampling distribution can be described by the formula

$$z = \frac{\bar{x} - \mu}{\sigma/\sqrt{n}}$$

This formula also describes the test statistic for μ with σ known. With a little algebra, we were able to derive (in Section 10.3) the confidence interval estimator of μ.

In future chapters, we will repeat this process, which in several cases involves the introduction of a new sampling distribution. Although its shape and formula will differ from the sampling distribution used in this chapter, the pattern will be the same. In general, the formula that expresses the sampling distribution will describe the test statistic. Then some algebraic manipulation (which we will not show) produces the interval estimator. Consequently, we will reverse the order of presentation of the two techniques. That is, we will present the test of hypothesis first, followed by the confidence interval estimator.

11.6 SUMMARY

In this chapter, we introduced the concepts of hypothesis testing and applied them to testing hypotheses about a population mean. We showed how to specify the null and alternative hypotheses, set up the rejection region, compute the value of the test statistic, and finally, to make a decision. Equally as important, we discussed how to interpret the test results. This chapter also demonstrated another way to make decisions—by calculating and using the p-value of the test. To help interpret test results, we showed how to calculate the probability of a Type II error. Finally, we provided a road map of how we plan to present statistical techniques.

IMPORTANT TERMS

Hypothesis testing 320
Null hypothesis 320
Alternative or research
    hypothesis 320
Type I error 320
Type II error 320

Significance level 320
Test statistic 323
Rejection region 323
Standardized test statistic 325
p-value of the test 326
Highly significant 329

Significant 329
One-tail test 334
Two-tail test 334
One-sided interval estimator 338
Problem objective 351

SYMBOLS

Symbol	Pronounced	Represents
H_0	*H-nought*	Null hypothesis
H_1	*H-one*	Alternative (research) hypothesis
α	*alpha*	Probability of a Type I error
β	*beta*	Probability of a Type II error
$\bar{x}_L$	*X-bar-sub L* or *X-bar-L*	Critical value of $\bar{x}$
$\lvert z \rvert$	*Absolute z*	Absolute value of z
z_α	*z-sub-alpha* or *z-alpha*	Critical value of z (one-tail test)
$z_{\alpha/2}$	*z-sub-alpha-by-2* or *z-alpha-by-2*	Critical value of z (two-tail test)

FORMULA

Test statistic for μ

$$z = \frac{\bar{x} - \mu}{\sigma/\sqrt{n}}$$

COMPUTER OUTPUT AND INSTRUCTIONS

Technique	Excel	Minitab
Test of μ	330	331
Probability of a Type II error (and Power)	345	346

REFERENCES

Casella, George, and Roger L. Berger, *Statistical Inference.* Belmont, CA: Duxbury, 1990.

Gastwirth, Joseph L., *Statistical Reasoning in Law and Public Policy.* San Diego, CA: Academic Press, 1988.

Hogg, Robert V., and Allan T. Craig, *Introduction to Mathematical Statistics,* 5th edition. Englewood Cliffs, NJ: Prentice Hall, 1995.

Lehmann, E. L., *Testing Statistical Hypotheses,* 2nd edition. New York: Chapman & Hall, 1991.

Mood, A. M., F. A. Graybill, and D. L. Boes, *Introduction to the Theory of Statistics,* 3rd edition. New York: McGraw Hill, 1974.

Rice, John A., *Mathematical Statistics and Data Analysis,* 2nd edition, Belmont, CA: Duxbury, 1995.

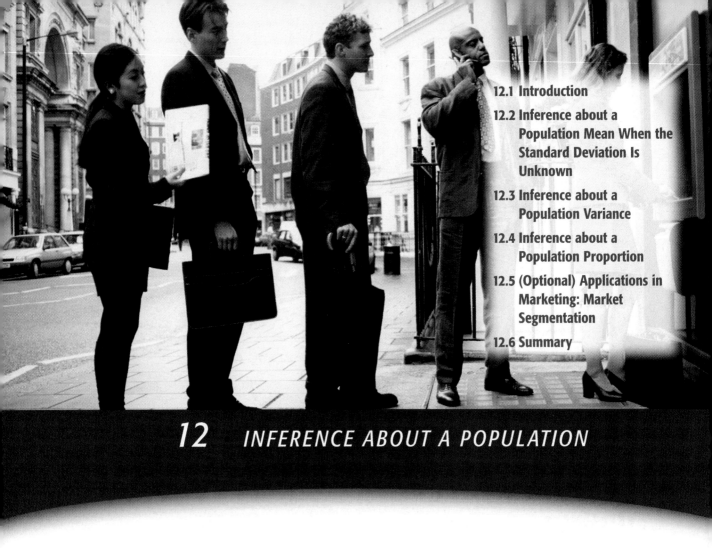

12 INFERENCE ABOUT A POPULATION

NIELSEN RATINGS

Statistical techniques play a vital role in helping advertisers determine how many viewers watch the shows that they sponsor. Although several companies sample television viewers to determine what shows they watch, the best known is the A. C. Nielsen firm. The Nielsen ratings are based on a sample of between 1,000 and 2,000 randomly selected families. A device attached to the family television keeps track of the channels the television receives. The ratings then produce the proportions of viewers whose televisions are tuned to each show, from which sponsors can determine the number of viewers and the potential value of any commercials.

Suppose that the results of a survey of 2,000 television viewers at 11:40 P.M. on Monday, September 28, 1998,

were stored in file CH12:\Nielsen using the following codes.

1. "Tonight Show" with Jay Leno (NBC)

2. "The Late Show with David Letterman" (CBS)

3. "Nightline" (ABC)

4. Other

5. Television turned off

CBS would like to use the data to estimate how many of the 100 million potential television sets in the population are tuned to the "Tonight Show." On page 377 we provide a solution to this problem.

12.1 INTRODUCTION

In the previous two chapters, we introduced the concepts of statistical inference and showed how to estimate and test a population mean. However, the illustration we chose is unrealistic because the techniques require us to use the population standard deviation σ, which, in general, is unknown. The purpose, then, of Chapters 10 and 11 was to set the pattern for the way in which we plan to present other statistical techniques. That is, we will begin by identifying the parameter to be estimated or tested. We will then specify the parameter's estimator (each parameter has an estimator chosen because of the characteristics we discussed at the beginning of Chapter 10) and its sampling distribution. Using simple mathematics, statisticians have derived the interval estimator and the test statistic. This pattern will be used repeatedly as we introduce new techniques.

In Section 11.5, we described the five problem objectives addressed in this book, and we laid out the order of presentation of the statistical methods. In this chapter, we will present techniques employed when the problem objective is to describe a population. When the data are interval, the parameters of interest are the population mean μ and the population variance σ^2. In Section 12.2, we describe how to make inferences about the population mean under the more realistic assumption that the population standard deviation is unknown. In Section 12.3, we continue to deal with interval data, but our parameter of interest becomes the population variance.

In Chapter 2 and in Section 11.5, we pointed out that when the data are nominal, the only computation that makes sense is determining the proportion of times each value occurs. Section 12.4 discusses inference about the proportion p.

12.2 INFERENCE ABOUT A POPULATION MEAN WHEN THE STANDARD DEVIATION IS UNKNOWN

In Sections 10.3 and 11.3, we demonstrated how to estimate and test the population mean when the population standard deviation is known. The interval estimator and the test statistic were derived from the sampling distribution of the sample mean with σ known, expressed as

$$z = \frac{\bar{x} - \mu}{\sigma/\sqrt{n}}$$

In this section, we take a more reasonable approach by acknowledging that if the population mean is unknown, so is the population standard deviation. Consequently, the sampling distribution above cannot be used. Instead, we substitute the sample standard deviation s in place of the unknown population standard deviation σ. The result is called a t statistic because that is what mathematician William S. Gosset called it. In 1908, Gosset showed that the t statistic defined as

$$t = \frac{\bar{x} - \mu}{s/\sqrt{n}}$$

is Student t distributed when the sampled population is normal. (Gosset published his findings under the pseudonym "Student," hence the **Student t distribution**.) The number of degrees of freedom is $\nu = n - 1$. Recall that we introduced the Student t distribution in Section 8.5.

With exactly the same logic used to develop the test statistic in Section 11.3 and the confidence interval estimator in Section 10.3, we derive the following inferential methods.

TEST STATISTIC FOR μ WHEN σ IS UNKNOWN

When the population standard deviation is unknown and the population is normal, the test statistic for testing hypotheses about μ is

$$t = \frac{\bar{x} - \mu}{s/\sqrt{n}}$$

which is Student t distributed with $\nu = n - 1$ degrees of freedom.

CONFIDENCE INTERVAL ESTIMATOR OF μ WHEN σ IS UNKNOWN

$$\bar{x} \pm t_{\alpha/2}\frac{s}{\sqrt{n}} \qquad \nu = n - 1$$

These formulas now make obsolete the test statistic and interval estimator employed in Chapters 10 and 11 to estimate and test a population mean. Although we continue to use the concepts developed in Chapters 10 and 11 (as well as all the other chapters), we will no longer use the z statistic and the z estimator of μ. All future inferential problems involving a population mean will be solved using the t statistic and t estimator of μ shown in the preceding boxes.

APPLICATIONS IN *OPERATIONS MANAGEMENT*

Aggregate Production Planning

In Chapter 1 we discussed the operations management function, aggregate production planning. We pointed out that there are several strategies that can be used to meet the demand for a company's product. These include level production, chase strategy, scheduling overtime and undertime, subcontracting, hiring part-time workers, and backordering when demand exceeds supply. Using the chase strategy, the company will hire and lay off workers so that each period's production matches the forecasted demand. However, the productivity of new workers tends to be quite variable, making it difficult for managers to know how many units they will produce. One way to get the information managers require is to employ statistical analyses.

EXAMPLE 12.1

Couriers such as UPS and FedEx compete on service and price. One way to reduce costs is to keep labor costs low by hiring and laying off workers to meet demand. This strategy requires managers to hire and train new workers. But newly hired and trained workers are not as productive as more experienced ones. Thus, determining the number of workers required and the work schedule is difficult. The current work schedule is based on the belief that trainees will achieve more than 90% of the level of experienced workers within 1 week of hiring. To determine the accuracy of this number, an operations manager conducted an experiment. Fifty trainees were observed for 1 hour and the numbers of packages processed and routed were recorded. These data appear here and are stored in file Xm12-01. It is known that experienced workers process an average of 500 packages per hour. The manager is concerned that if he concludes that the mean is greater than 450 when it isn't, the result will be some late deliveries. Can the manager conclude from the data that the belief is correct?

Number of Packages

505	480	487	482	409
400	466	373	442	501
499	477	416	465	440
415	445	424	449	444
418	413	471	523	485
467	537	427	488	475
551	484	509	508	470
444	418	410	432	485
481	465	515	405	469
429	496	435	440	450

SOLUTION

IDENTIFY

The problem objective is to describe the population of the numbers of packages processed in 1 hour by trainees. The data are interval, indicating that the parameter to be tested is the population mean. Because the manager wants to know whether the belief that trainees' productivity is more than 90% of that of experienced workers, who process an average of 500 packages per hour, the alternative hypothesis is

$$H_1: \quad \mu > 450$$

The null hypothesis automatically follows:

$$H_0: \quad \mu = 450$$

The test statistic is

$$t = \frac{\bar{x} - \mu}{s/\sqrt{n}} \qquad \nu = n - 1$$

COMPUTE

 MANUALLY

The manager believes that the cost of a Type I error (concluding that the mean is greater than 450 when it isn't) is not excessively high. Consequently, he sets the significance level at 5%. The rejection region is

$$t > t_{\alpha, n-1} = t_{.05, 49} \approx t_{.05, 50} = 1.676$$

To calculate the value of the test statistic, we need to calculate the sample mean $\bar{x}$ and the sample standard deviation s. From the data we determine

$$\sum x_i = 23{,}019 \quad \text{and} \quad \sum x_i^2 = 10{,}671{,}357$$

Thus,

$$\bar{x} = \frac{\sum x_i}{n} = \frac{23{,}019}{50} = 460.38$$

$$s^2 = \frac{\sum x_i^2 - \dfrac{\left(\sum x_i\right)^2}{n}}{n - 1} = \frac{10{,}671{,}357 - \dfrac{(23{,}019)^2}{50}}{50 - 1} = 1{,}507.55$$

and

$$s = \sqrt{s^2} = \sqrt{1{,}507.55} = 38.83$$

The value of μ is to be found in the null hypothesis. It is 450. The value of the test statistic is

$$t = \frac{\bar{x} - \mu}{s/\sqrt{n}} = \frac{460.38 - 450}{38.83/\sqrt{50}} = 1.89$$

Because 1.89 is greater than 1.676, we reject the null hypothesis in favor of the alternative.

EXCEL

	A	B	C	D
1	t-Test: Mean			
2				
3				*Packages*
4	Mean			460.38
5	Standard Deviation			38.83
6	Hypothesized Mean			450
7	df			49
8	t Stat			1.89
9	P(T<=t) one-tail			0.0323
10	t Critical one-tail			1.6766
11	P(T<=t) two-tail			0.0646
12	t Critical two-tail			2.0096

COMMANDS   COMMANDS FOR EXAMPLE 12.1

1. Type or import the data into one column.   Open file **Xm12-01.**
2. Click **Tools, Data Analysis Plus**, and
   t-test: Mean.
3. Specify the **Input Range.**   **A1:A51**
4. Specify the value of the **Hypothesized Mean**. **450**
5. Click **Labels**, if appropriate.
6. Specify a value of α (**Alpha**) and click **OK**.   **.05**

To conduct this test from statistics or to perform a what-if analysis, open the **Test Statistics** workbook and find the **t-Test_Mean** worksheet. Substitute values for the sample mean, sample standard deviation, sample size, and hypothesized value of the population mean.

MINITAB

One-Sample T: Packages

```
Test of mu = 450 vs mu > 450

Variable          N       Mean      StDev    SE Mean
Packages         50     460.38      38.83       5.49

Variable      95.0% Lower Bound         T        P
Packages                  451.17      1.89    0.032
```

COMMANDS   COMMANDS FOR EXAMPLE 12.1

1. Type or import the data into one column.   Open file **Xm12-01.**
2. Click **Stat, Basic Statistics**, and **1-Sample t ….**
3. Type the variable name.   **Packages** or **C1**
4. Use the cursor to choose **Test mean**.
5. Type the value of μ under the null hypothesis.   **450**
6. Click **Options ...** and specify the **Alternative**   **greater than**
   hypothesis. Click **OK**. Click **OK**.

The value of the test statistic is $t = 1.89$ and its p-value is .0323. There is enough evidence to infer that the mean number of parcels processed by trainees is more than 90% of that of experienced workers. Thus, the number of workers hired to meet demand under the chase strategy appears to be valid and the resulting aggregate production plan should be satisfactory. Figure 12.1 exhibits the sampling distribution for this example.

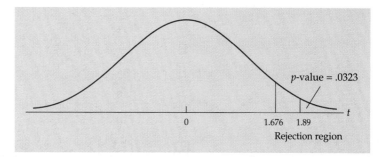

Figure 12.1
Sampling distribution of the test statistic for Example 12.1

EXAMPLE 12.2

During the last decade a number of institutions dedicated to improving the quality of products and services in the United States have been formed. Many of these groups annually give awards to companies that produce high-quality goods and services. An investor believes that publicly traded companies that win awards are likely to out-perform companies that do not win such awards. To help determine his return on investment in such companies, he took a random sample of 83 firms that won quality awards the previous year and computed the annual return had he invested. These data are listed below and stored in file Xm12-02. The investor would like an estimate of the returns he can expect. A 95% confidence level is deemed appropriate.

16.2	0.58	25.47	11.42	16.34	−1.06	15.52	5.14	15.45
15.34	16.65	27.25	28.26	22.69	22.45	16.82	14.3	21.58
19.55	24.6	25.46	21.45	−0.21	7.23	17.52	24.77	14.15
13.53	−2.27	18.07	21.36	7.76	26.2	29.68	23.33	
6.76	−0.67	2.62	23.8	2.28	21.93	18.02	9.88	
13.9	12.8	13.45	9.01	6.89	21.02	22.37	18.41	
11.72	26.01	9.45	26.58	23.94	17.85	25.32	2.26	
17.63	15.46	12.74	6.51	9.62	7.9	22.78	16.52	
10.97	−1.16	13.6	18.63	13.72	12.54	14.65	5.66	
22.1	7.41	−3.6	24.69	21.39	20.95	21.15	6.39	

SOLUTION

The problem objective is to describe the population of annual returns from buying shares of quality-award winners. The data are interval and, hence, the parameter is the population mean μ. The question asks us to estimate this parameter. The confidence interval estimator is

$$\bar{x} \pm t_{\alpha/2} \frac{s}{\sqrt{n}}$$

COMPUTE

 MANUALLY

From the data we determine

$$\sum x_i = 1{,}246.43 \quad \text{and} \quad \sum x_i^2 = 24{,}374.22$$

Thus,

$$\bar{x} = \frac{\sum x_i}{n} = \frac{1{,}246.43}{83} = 15.02$$

and

$$s^2 = \frac{\sum x_i^2 - \dfrac{\left(\sum x_i\right)^2}{n}}{n-1} = \frac{24{,}374.22 - \dfrac{(1{,}246.43)^2}{83}}{83-1} = 68.98$$

Thus

$$s = \sqrt{s^2} = \sqrt{68.98} = 8.31$$

Because we want a 95% confidence interval estimate, $1 - \alpha = .95, \alpha = .05, \alpha/2 = .025,$ and $t_{\alpha/2,n-1} = t_{.025,83-1} = t_{.025,82} \approx t_{.025,80} = 1.990.$ Thus, the 95% confidence interval estimate of μ is

$$\bar{x} \pm t_{\alpha/2}\frac{s}{\sqrt{n}} = 15.02 \pm 1.990\frac{8.31}{\sqrt{83}} = 15.02 \pm 1.82$$

or

$$\text{LCL} = 13.20 \quad \text{UCL} = 16.84$$

EXCEL

	A	B	C	D
1	t-Test: Estimate			
2				
3				*Returns*
4	Mean			15.02
5	Standard Deviation			8.31
6	LCL			13.20
7	UCL			16.83

COMMANDS   COMMANDS FOR EXAMPLE 12.2

1. Type or import the data into one column.   Open file **Xm12-02.**
2. Click **Tools, Data Analysis Plus**, and
   t-Estimate: Mean.
3. Specify the **Input Range**.   **A1:A84**
4. Click **Labels**, if appropriate.
5. Specify a value of α (**Alpha**) and click **OK**.   **.05**

If you know the sample mean, sample standard deviation, and sample size, you can use the **t-Estimate_Mean** worksheet in the **Estimators** workbook, which can also be employed for what-if analyses.

MINITAB

One-Sample T: Returns

```
Variable        N     Mean    StDev   SE Mean        95.0% CI
Returns        83    15.017   8.305    0.912   ( 13.204,  16.831)
```

COMMANDS   *COMMANDS FOR EXAMPLE 12.2*

1. Type or import the data into one column.   Open file **Xm12-02**.
2. Click **Stat, Basic Statistics,** and **1-Sample t…**.
3. Type the variable name.   **Returns** or **C1**
4. Click **Options…**, specify the **Confidence level**,
   Alternative: not equal, click **OK**, and click **OK**.   **.95**

INTERPRET

We estimate that the mean return lies between 13.20% and 16.83% (Excel's figures). We can use this estimate to help decide whether to invest in quality-award winners and, if so, what return on investment we can expect.

CHECKING THE REQUIRED CONDITIONS

When we introduced the Student t distribution, we pointed out that the t statistic is Student t distributed if the population from which we've sampled is normal. However, statisticians have shown that the mathematical process that derived the Student t distribution is **robust**, which means that if the population is nonnormal, the results of the t test and confidence interval estimate are still valid provided that the population is not *extremely* nonnormal. To check this requirement, we draw the histogram and determine whether it is far from bell shaped. Figures 12.2 and 12.3 depict the Excel histograms for Examples 12.1 and 12.2, respectively. (The Minitab histograms are similar.) Both histograms suggest that the variables are not extremely nonnormal.

Figure 12.2   **Figure 12.3**

MISSING DATA

In real statistical applications, we occasionally find that the data set is incomplete. In some instances the statistics practitioner may have failed to properly record some observations or some data may have been lost. In other cases, respondents may refuse to answer. For example, in political surveys where the statistics practitioner asks voters for whom they intend to vote in the next election, some people will answer that they haven't decided or that their vote is confidential and refuse to answer. In surveys where respondents are asked to report their income, people often refuse to divulge this information. This is a troublesome issue for statistics practitioners. We can't force people to answer our questions. However, if the number of nonresponses is high, the results of our analysis may be invalid because the sample is no longer truly random. To understand why, suppose that people who are in the top quarter of household incomes regularly refuse to answer questions about their incomes. The estimate of the population household income mean will be lower than the actual value.

The issue can be complicated. There are several ways to compensate for nonresponses. The simplest method is simply to eliminate them. To illustrate, suppose that in a political survey, respondents are asked for whom they intend to vote in a two-candidate race. Surveyors record the results as 1 = Candidate A, 2 = Candidate B, 3 = "Don't know," and 4 = "Refuse to say." If we wish to infer something about the proportion of decided voters who will vote for Candidate A, we can simply omit codes 3 and 4. If we're doing the work manually, we will count the number of voters who prefer Candidate A and the number who prefer Candidate B. The sum of these two numbers is the total sample size.

In the language of statistical software, nonresponses that we wish to eliminate are collectively called "missing data." Software packages deal with missing data in different ways.

EXCEL

Excel (the techniques listed under **Data Analysis...**) addresses the problem inconsistently. Some functions recognize blank cells as missing data; others, as well as the add-ins in **Data Analysis Plus**, do not. The safest and easiest way to omit missing data is to simply delete all blank cells. Sort the data (Click **Data** and **Sort...**) in order, highlight the cells you wish to delete, and with one keystroke delete the missing data.

MINITAB

Minitab treats an asterisk as missing data. You can record the data in this way. However, in most cases you will have to recode the data. We now describe how to do so.

RECODING DATA

EXCEL

To recode data we employ a logical function. Click f_x, **Logical** (**Function category**), and **IF** (**Function name**). To illustrate, suppose that in column A you have stored data consisting of codes 1 through 6 and you wish to convert all 4's, 5's, and 6's to 9's. Activate cell B1 and type

=IF(A1>=4,9,A1)

This logical function determines whether the value in cell A1 is greater than or equal to 4. If so, Excel places a 9 in cell B1. If A1 is less than 4, then B1 = A1. Dragging to fill in column B converts all 4's, 5's, and 6's to 9's and stores the results in column B.

If 4's, 5's, and 6's represent nonresponses, you can replace these codes with a blank. Type in cell B1

=IF(A1>=4," ",A1)

MINITAB
To recode data in Minitab follow these instructions.
1. Click **Manip** and **Code**.
2. Specify **Numeric to Numeric....**.
3. Type the variable name of the **Code data from columns**.
4. Type variable name where the new codes are to be placed (**Into columns:**).
5. Specify the **Original values:** you wish to recode and their **New:** values. Click **OK**.

We have purposely "lost" some data in several exercises scattered throughout the book to give you opportunities to practice addressing the problem of missing data.

DEVELOPING AN UNDERSTANDING OF STATISTICAL CONCEPTS 1

This section introduced the term *degrees of freedom*. We will encounter this term many times in this book, so a brief discussion of its meaning is warranted. The Student t distribution is based on using the sample variance to estimate the unknown population variance. The sample variance is defined as

$$s^2 = \frac{\sum (x_i - \bar{x})^2}{n-1}$$

To compute s^2, we must first determine $\bar{x}$. Recall that sampling distributions are derived by repeated sampling from the same population. To repeatedly take samples to compute s^2, we can choose any numbers for the first $n-1$ observations in the sample. However, we have no choice on the nth value because the sample mean must be calculated first. To illustrate, suppose that $n = 3$ and we find $\bar{x} = 10$. We can have x_1 and x_2 assume any values without restriction. However, x_3 must be such that $\bar{x} = 10$. For example, if $x_1 = 6$ and $x_2 = 8$, then x_3 must equal 16. Therefore, there are only 2 degrees of freedom in our selection of the sample. We say that we lose 1 degree of freedom because we had to calculate $\bar{x}$.

Notice that the denominator in the calculation of s^2 is equal to the number of degrees of freedom. This is not a coincidence and will be repeated throughout this book.

DEVELOPING AN UNDERSTANDING OF STATISTICAL CONCEPTS 2

The t statistic, like the z statistic, measures the difference between the sample mean $\bar{x}$ and the hypothesized value of μ in terms of the number of standard errors. However, when the population standard deviation σ is unknown, we estimate the standard error as $s/\sqrt{n}$.

DEVELOPING AN UNDERSTANDING OF STATISTICAL CONCEPTS 3

When we introduced the Student t distribution in Section 8.5, we pointed out that it is more widely spread out than the standard normal. This circumstance is logical. The only variable in the z statistic is the sample mean $\bar{x}$, which will vary from sample to sample. The t statistic has two variables, the sample mean $\bar{x}$ and the sample standard deviation s, both of which will vary from sample to sample. Because of this feature, the t statistic will display greater variability. Exercises 12.21–12.29 address this concept.

Let's complete this section with a review of how we identify the techniques introduced in this section.

FACTORS THAT IDENTIFY THE *t* TEST AND ESTIMATOR OF μ
1. **Problem objective:** Describe a population.
2. **Data type:** Interval
3. **Type of descriptive measurement:** Central location

EXERCISES

Developing an Understanding of Statistical Concepts

*The following exercises are "what-if analyses" designed to determine what happens to the test statistics and interval estimates when elements of the statistical inference change. These problems can be solved manually or using Excel's **Test Statistics** or **Estimators** workbooks.*

12.1 A random sample of 50 was drawn from a population. The sample mean and standard deviation are $\bar{x} = 510$ and $s = 125$. Estimate μ with 95% confidence.

12.2 Repeat Exercise 12.1 with $n = 100$.

12.3 Repeat Exercise 12.1 with $n = 25$.

12.4 Refer to Exercises 12.1 to 12.3. Describe what happens to the confidence interval estimate when the sample size increases.

12.5 Repeat Exercise 12.1 with $s = 200$.

12.6 Repeat Exercise 12.1 with $s = 75$.

12.7 Using the results of Exercises 12.1, 12.5, and 12.6, discuss the effect on the confidence interval estimate of decreasing the standard deviation *s*.

12.8 Repeat Exercise 12.1 with a 90% confidence level.

12.9 Repeat Exercise 12.1 with a 99% confidence level.

12.10 Review the results of Exercises 12.1, 12.8, and 12.9. What is the effect on the confidence interval estimate of increasing the confidence level?

12.11 The sample mean and standard deviation from a random sample of 20 observations from a normal population were computed as $\bar{x} = 23$ and $s = 9$. Calculate the *t* statistic (and for Excel users, the *p*-value) of the test required to determine whether there is enough evidence to infer at the 5% significance level that the population mean is greater than 20.

12.12 Repeat Exercise 12.11 with $n = 10$.

12.13 Repeat Exercise 12.11 with $n = 50$.

12.14 Refer to Exercises 12.11 to 12.13. Describe the effect on the *t* statistic (and for Excel users, the *p*-value) of increasing the sample size.

12.15 Repeat Exercise 12.11 with $s = 5$.

12.16 Repeat Exercise 12.11 with $s = 20$.

12.17 Refer to Exercises 12.11, 12.15, and 12.16. Discuss what happens to the *t* statistic (and for Excel users, the *p*-value) when the standard deviation decreases.

12.18 Repeat Exercise 12.11 with $\bar{x} = 21$.

12.19 Repeat Exercise 12.11 with $\bar{x} = 26$.

12.20 Review the results of Exercises 12.11, 12.18, and 12.19. What happens to the *t* statistic (and for Excel users, the *p*-value) when the sample mean increases?

12.21 A random sample of 10 observations was drawn from a normal population. The sample mean and sample standard deviation are $\bar{x} = 50$ and $s = 15$. Estimate the population mean with 95% confidence.

12.22 Repeat Exercise 12.21 assuming that you know that the population standard deviation is $\sigma = 15$.

12.23 Review Exercises 12.21 and 12.22. Explain why the interval estimate produced in Exercise 12.22 is narrower than that in Exercise 12.21.

12.24 A random sample of 8 observations was taken from a normal population. The sample mean and standard deviation are $\bar{x} = 75$ and $s = 50$. Can we infer at the 10% significance level that the population mean is less than 100?

12.25 Repeat Exercise 12.24 assuming that you know that the population standard deviation is $\sigma = 50$.

12.26 Review Exercises 12.24 and 12.25. Explain why the test statistics differed.

12.27 After sampling 1,000 members of a normal population you find $\bar{x} = 15,500$ and $s = 9,950$. Estimate the population mean with 90% confidence.

12.28 Repeat Exercise 12.27 assuming that you know that the population standard deviation is $\sigma = 9,950$.

12.29 Review Exercises 12.27 and 12.28. Explain why the interval estimates were virtually identical.

Applications

12.30 A courier service advertises that its average delivery time is less than 6 hours for local deliveries. A random sample of times for 12 deliveries to an address across town was recorded. These data are shown below. Is this sufficient evidence to support the courier's advertisement, at the 5% level of significance?

3.03, 6.33, 6.50, 5.22, 3.56, 6.76, 7.98, 4.82, 7.96, 4.54, 5.09, 6.46

12.31 How much money do winners go home with from the television quiz show "Jeopardy"? To determine an answer, a random sample of winners was drawn and the amount of money each won was recorded and listed below. Estimate with 95% confidence the mean winnings for all the show's players.

26,650	6,060	52,820	8,490	13,660
25,840	49,840	23,790	51,480	18,960
990	11,450	41,810	21,060	7,860

12.32 A diet doctor claims that the average North American is more than 20 pounds overweight. To test his claim, a random sample of 20 North Americans was weighed, and the difference between their actual weight and their ideal weight was calculated. The data are listed below. Do these data allow us to infer at the 5% significance level that the doctor's claim is true?

16,   23,   18,   41,   22,   18,   23,   19,   22,   15,
18,   35,   16,   15,   17,   19,   23,   15,   16,   26

12.33 A federal agency responsible for enforcing laws governing weights and measures routinely inspects packages to determine whether the weight of the contents is at least as great as that advertised on the package. A random sample of 18 containers whose packaging states that the contents weigh 8 ounces was drawn. The contents were weighed and the results listed below. Can we conclude that on average the containers are mislabeled? (Use $\alpha = .10$.)

7.80,   7.91,   7.93,   7.99,   7.94,   7.75,
7.97,   7.95,   7.79,   8.06,   7.82,   7.89,
7.92,   7.87,   7.92,   7.98,   8.05,   7.91

The following exercises require the use of a computer and software. The answers may be calculated manually. See Appendix A for the sample statistics. **Use a 5% significance level unless specified otherwise.**

12.34 A growing concern for educators in the United States is the number of teenagers who have part-time jobs while they attend high school. To investigate this problem, a school guidance counselor took a random sample of 200 15-year-old high school students and asked how many hours per week each worked at a part-time job. The results were recorded and stored in file Xr12-34. Estimate with 95% confidence the mean amount of time all 15-year-old high school students devote per week to part-time jobs.

12.35 A company that produces universal remote controls wanted to determine the number of remote control devices American homes contain. The company hired a statistician to survey 240 randomly selected homes and determine the number of remote controls. These data are stored in file Xr12-35. If there are 100 million households, estimate with 99% confidence the total number of remote controls in the United States.

12.36 How much time do executives spend each day reading and sending e-mail? A survey was conducted by *Accountemps* (reported in *USA TODAY*, March 12, 2001). The responses (in minutes) were stored in file Xr12-36. Can we infer from these data that the mean amount of time spent by all executives reading and sending e-mail daily exceeds 60 minutes? (*Caution*: Missing data)

12.37 The American Medical Association conducts surveys of its member each year. A sample of physicians is selected and asked to report the amount of time each devotes to patient care each week. The results for the 1997 survey are stored in file Xr12-37. Can we infer that the mean amount of time devoted to patient care per week by all physicians exceeds 45 hours? (Adapted from the American Medical Association, *Socioeconomic Characteristics of Medical Practice 1997/1998* and the *Statistical Abstract of the United States*, 2000, Table 190)

12.38 An increasing number of North Americans regularly take vitamin or herbal remedies daily. To gauge this phenomenon, a random sample of Americans was asked to report the number of vitamin and herbal supplements they take daily. The results are stored in file Xr12-38. Estimate with 95% confidence the mean number of vitamin and herbal supplements Americans take daily.

12.39 Refer to Exercise 12.38. Assuming that there are 200 million adults, estimate with 95% confidence the total size of the annual market for vitamin and herbal supplements.

12.40 A manufacturer of a brand of designer jeans has pitched her advertising to develop an expensive and classy image. The suggested retail price is $75. However, she is concerned that retailers are undermining her image by offering the jeans at discount prices. To better understand what is happening, she randomly samples 30 retailers who sell her product and determines the price. The results are stored in file Xr12-40. She would like an estimate of the mean selling price of the jeans at all retail stores. (*Caution*: Missing data)

a Determine the 95% confidence interval estimate.

b What assumption must be made to be sure that the estimate produced in part **a** is valid? Use a graphical technique to check the required condition.

12.41 Schools are often judged on the basis of how well their students perform academically. But what about school lunches? According to USDA rules, the maximum percentage of calories from fat is 30%. To judge how well they are doing, a sample of schools was drawn and for each school the percentage of calories from fat for their lunches was measured and recorded in file Xr12-41. Estimate with 95% confidence the mean percentage of calories from fat in school lunches.

12.42 To help estimate the size of the disposable razor market, a random sample of men was asked to count the number of shaves they used each razor for. The responses are stored in file Xr12-42. If we assume that each razor is used once per day, estimate with 95% confidence the number of days a pack of 10 razors will last.

12.43 Because of the enormity of the viewing audience, firms that advertise during the Super Bowl create special commercials that tend to be quite entertaining. Thirty-second commercials cost $2.3 million during the 2001 Super Bowl game. A random sample of people who watched the game was asked how many commercials they watched in their entirety. The responses are stored in file Xr12-43. Do these data allow us to infer that the mean number of commercials watched is greater than 15? (*Caution:* Missing data)

12.44 On a per capita basis, the United States spends far more on health than any other country. To help assess the costs, annual surveys are undertaken. One such survey asks a sample of Americans to report the number of times they visited a health care professional in the year. The data for 1998 are stored in file Xr12-44. In 1998 the United States population was 270,509,000. Estimate with 95% confidence the total number of visits to a health care professional. (Adapted from U.S. National Center for Health Statistics, United States, 2000)

12.45 Companies that sell groceries over the Internet are called e-grocers. Customers enter their orders, pay by credit card, and receive delivery by truck. A potential e-grocer analyzed the market and determined that to be profitable the average order would have to exceed $85. To determine whether an e-grocery would be profitable in one large city, she offered the service and recorded the size of the order for a random sample of customers. These data are stored in file Xr12-45. Can we infer from these data that an e-grocery will be profitable in this city?

12.46 Ecologists have long advocated recycling newspapers as a way of saving trees and reducing landfills. In recent years a number of companies have gone into the business of collecting used newspapers from households and recycling them. A financial analyst for one such company has recently computed that the firm would make a profit if the mean weekly newspaper collection from each household exceeded 2 pounds. In a study to determine the feasibility of a recycling plant, a random sample of 100 households was drawn, and the weekly weight of newspapers discarded for recycling for each household was recorded and stored in file Xr12-46. Do these data provide sufficient evidence at the 1% significance level to allow the analyst to conclude that a recycling plant would be profitable?

12.3 INFERENCE ABOUT A POPULATION VARIANCE

In Section 12.2, where we presented the inferential methods about a population mean, we were interested in acquiring information about the central location of the population. As a result, we tested and estimated the population mean. If we are interested instead in drawing inferences about a population's variability, the parameter we need to investigate is the population variance σ^2. Inference about the variance can be used to make decisions in a variety of problems.

In an example illustrating the use of the normal distribution in Section 8.3, we showed why variance is a measure of risk. In Section 7.5 we described an important application in finance wherein stock diversification was shown to reduce the variance of a portfolio and in so doing, reduce the risk associated with that portfolio. In both sections we assumed that the population variances were known. In this section we take a more realistic approach and acknowledge that we need to use statistical techniques to draw inferences about a population variance.

Another application of the use of variance comes from operations management. Quality technicians attempt to ensure that their company's products consistently meet specifications. One way of judging the consistency of a production process is to compute the variance of the size, weight, or volume of the product. That is, if the variation in product size, weight, or volume is large, it is likely that an unsatisfactorily large number of products will lie outside the specifications for that product. We will return to this subject later in this book. In Section 15.6 we discuss how operations managers search for and reduce the variation in production processes.

The task of deriving the test statistic and the interval estimator provides us with another opportunity to show how statistical techniques in general are developed. We begin by identifying the best estimator. That estimator has a sampling distribution, from which we produce the test statistic and the interval estimator.

STATISTIC AND SAMPLING DISTRIBUTION

The estimator of σ^2 is the sample variance introduced in Section 4.3. The statistic s^2 has the desirable characteristics presented in Section 10.2; that is, s^2 is an unbiased, consistent estimator of σ^2.

Statisticians have shown that the sum of squared deviations from the mean $\sum(x_i - \bar{x})^2$ [which is equal to $(n - 1)s^2$] divided by the population variance is chi-squared distributed with $\nu = n - 1$ degrees of freedom provided that the sampled population is normal. The statistic

$$\chi^2 = \frac{(n - 1)s^2}{\sigma^2}$$

is called the **chi-squared statistic** (χ^2 *statistic*). The chi-squared distribution was introduced in Section 8.5.

TESTING AND ESTIMATING A POPULATION VARIANCE

As we discussed in Section 11.5, the formula that describes the sampling distribution is the formula of the test statistic.

TEST STATISTIC FOR σ^2

The test statistic used to test hypotheses about σ^2 is

$$\chi^2 = \frac{(n - 1)s^2}{\sigma^2}$$

which is chi-squared distributed with $\nu = n - 1$ degrees of freedom when the population random variable is normally distributed with variance equal to σ^2.

Using the notation introduced in Section 8.5, we can make the following probability statement:

$$P(\chi^2_{1-\alpha/2} < \chi^2 < \chi^2_{\alpha/2}) = 1 - \alpha$$

Substituting

$$\chi^2 = \frac{(n - 1)s^2}{\sigma^2}$$

and with some algebraic manipulation we derive the estimator of a population variance.

CONFIDENCE INTERVAL ESTIMATOR OF σ^2

Lower confidence limit (LCL) $= \dfrac{(n - 1)s^2}{\chi^2_{\alpha/2}}$

Upper confidence limit (UCL) $= \dfrac{(n - 1)s^2}{\chi^2_{1-\alpha/2}}$

APPLICATIONS IN *OPERATIONS MANAGEMENT*

Quality

A critical aspect of production is quality. The quality of a final product is a function of the quality of the product's components. If the components don't fit, the product will not function as planned and it will likely cease functioning before its customers expect it to. For example, if a car door is not made to its specifications it will not fit. As a result, the door will leak both water and air.

Operations managers attempt to maintain and improve the quality of products by ensuring that all components are made so that there is as little variation as possible.

As you have already seen, statisticians measure variation by computing the variance. Incidentally, an entire chapter (Chapter 22) is devoted to the topic of quality.

EXAMPLE 12.3

Container-filling machines are used to package a variety of liquids, including milk, soft drinks, and paint. Ideally, the amount of liquid should vary only slightly, since large variations will cause some containers to be underfilled (cheating the customer) and some to be overfilled (resulting in costly waste). The president of a company that developed a new type of machine boasts that this machine can fill 1-liter (1,000 cubic centimeters) containers so consistently that the variance of the fills will be less than $1 \; (cc)^2$. To examine the veracity of the claim, a random sample of 25 l-liter fills was taken and the results recorded. These data are listed below and also stored in file Xm12-03. Do these data allow the president to make this claim at the 5% significance level?

1,000.3	999.8	1,001.0	999.6	998.1
1,001.0	998.7	999.4	999.8	1,000.7
999.5	1,000.6	999.5	1,000.0	999.1
999.7	999.4	998.5	998.5	1,000.1
999.3	999.4	1,001.3	1,001.4	1,000.7

SOLUTION

IDENTIFY

The problem objective is to describe the population of l-liter fills from this machine. The data are interval, and we're interested in the variability of the fills. It follows that the parameter of interest is the population variance. Because we want to determine whether there is enough evidence to support the claim, the alternative hypothesis is

$$H_1: \quad \sigma^2 < 1$$

The null hypothesis is

$$H_0: \quad \sigma^2 = 1$$

and the test statistic we will employ is

$$\chi^2 = \frac{(n-1)s^2}{\sigma^2}$$

COMPUTE

MANUALLY

Using a calculator, we find

$$\sum x_i = 24{,}996.4 \quad \text{and} \quad \sum x_i^2 = 24{,}992{,}821.3$$

Thus,

$$s^2 = \frac{\sum x_i^2 - \dfrac{\left(\sum x_i\right)^2}{n}}{n-1} = \frac{24{,}992{,}821.3 - \dfrac{(24{,}996.4)^2}{25}}{25-1} = .8659$$

The value of the test statistic is

$$\chi^2 = \frac{(n-1)s^2}{\sigma^2} = \frac{(25-1)(.8659)}{1} = 20.78$$

The rejection region is

$$\chi^2 < \chi^2_{1-\alpha,\,n-1} = \chi^2_{1-.05,\,25-1} = \chi^2_{.95,\,24} = 13.8484$$

Since 20.78 is not less than 13.8484, we cannot conclude that the variance of the new machine will be less than 1 $(cc)^2$.

 EXCEL

	A	B	C	D
1	**Chi Squared Test: Variance**			
2				
3				*Fills*
4	Sample Variance			0.8659
5	Hypothesized Variance			1
6	df			24
7	chi-squared Stat			20.78
8	P (CHI<=chi) one-tail			0.3484
9	chi-squared Critical one tail	Left-tail		13.8484
10		Right-tail		36.4150
11	P (CHI<=chi) two-tail			0.6969
12	chi-squared Critical two tail	Left-tail		12.4011
13		Right-tail		39.3641

The value of the test statistic is 20.78. P(CHI<=chi) one-tail is the probability $P(\chi^2 < 20.78)$, which is equal to .3484. Because this is a one-tail test, the *p*-value is .3484.

<table>
<tr><td>COMMANDS</td><td>COMMANDS FOR EXAMPLE 12.3</td></tr>
<tr><td>1. Type or import the data into one column.</td><td>Open file Xm12-03.</td></tr>
<tr><td>2. Click Tools, Data Analysis Plus, and
Chi-squared Test: Variance.</td><td></td></tr>
<tr><td>3. Specify the Input Range.</td><td>A1:A26</td></tr>
<tr><td>4. Specify the Hypothesized Variance.</td><td>1</td></tr>
<tr><td>5. Click Labels if appropriate.</td><td></td></tr>
<tr><td>6. Specify the value of α (Alpha) and click OK.</td><td>.05</td></tr>
</table>

We can also use the worksheet **Chi-squared Test_Variance** in the **Test Statistics** workbook to perform the calculations as well as to conduct what-if analyses.

MINITAB

Minitab does not conduct this procedure. However, you can use Minitab to compute the sample variance, from which the test statistic can be determined.

INTERPRET

There is not enough evidence to infer that the claim is true. As we discussed before, the result does not say that the variance is greater than 1; it merely states that we are unable to show that the variance is less than 1. Figure 12.4 depicts the sampling distribution of the test statistic.

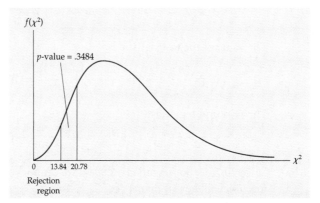

Figure 12.4
Sampling distribution for
Example 12.3

EXAMPLE 12.4

Estimate with 99% confidence the variance of fills in Example 12.3.

SOLUTION

COMPUTE

 MANUALLY

In the solution to Example 12.3, we found $(n-1)s^2$ to be 20.8. From Table 5 in Appendix B we find

$$\chi^2_{\alpha/2,n-1} = \chi^2_{.005,24} = 45.5585 \quad \text{and} \quad \chi^2_{1-\alpha/2,n-1} = \chi^2_{.995,24} = 9.88623$$

Thus,

$$\text{LCL} = \frac{(n-1)s^2}{\chi^2_{\alpha/2}} = \frac{20.8}{45.5585} = .46 \quad \text{and} \quad \text{UCL} = \frac{(n-1)s^2}{\chi^2_{1-\alpha/2}} = \frac{20.8}{9.88623} = 2.10$$

We estimate that the variance of fills is a number that lies between .46 and 2.10.

 EXCEL

	A	B
1	Chi Squared Estimate: Variance	
2		
3		Fills
4	Sample Variance	0.8659
5	Observations	24
6	LCL	0.4562
7	UCL	2.1021

COMMANDS
1. Type or import the data into one column.
2. Click **Tools, Data Analysis Plus**, and **Chi-squared Estimate: Variance**.

COMMANDS FOR EXAMPLE 12.4
Open file **Xm12-03**.

> 3. Specify the **Input Range**.   A1:A26
> 4. Click **Labels** if appropriate.
> 5. Specify the value of α (**Alpha**) and click **OK**.   .01
>
> If you know the sample variance and sample size, you can employ the **Chi-squared Estimate_Variance** worksheet in the **Estimators** workbook to perform the calculations. This spreadsheet can be used to conduct what-if analyses.

MINITAB

> Minitab does not compute the interval estimator of a variance. But, as was the case with the test statistic, the sample variance can be outputted and the interval estimate produced manually.

INTERPRET

In Example 12.3, we saw that there was not sufficient evidence to infer that the population variance is less than 1. Here we see that σ^2 is estimated to lie between .46 and 2.10. Part of this interval is above 1, which tells us that the variance may be larger than 1, confirming the conclusion we reached in Example 12.3. We may be able to use the estimate to predict the percentage of overfilled and underfilled bottles. This may allow us to choose among competing machines.

CHECKING THE REQUIRED CONDITION

Like the t test and estimator of μ introduced in Section 12.2, the chi-squared test and estimator of σ^2 theoretically require that the sample population be normal. In practice, however, the technique is valid so long as the population is not extremely nonnormal. We can gauge the extent of nonnormality by drawing the histogram. Figure 12.5 depicts Excel's version of this histogram. The fills do not appear to be extremely nonnormal, which supports the validity of the conclusions drawn in Examples 12.3 and 12.4.

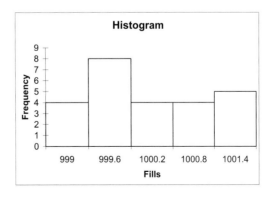

Figure 12.5

Let's review how we recognize when to use the techniques introduced in this section.

FACTORS THAT IDENTIFY THE CHI-SQUARED TEST AND ESTIMATOR OF σ^2
1. **Problem objective:** Describe a population.
2. **Data type:** Interval
3. **Type of descriptive measurement:** Variability

EXERCISES

Developing an Understanding of Statistical Concepts

*The following exercises are "what-if analyses" designed to determine what happens to the test statistics and interval estimates when elements of the statistical inference change. These problems can be solved manually or using Excel's **Test Statistics** or **Estimators** workbook.*

12.47 A random sample of 100 observations was drawn from a normal population. The sample variance was calculated to be $s^2 = 220$. Test with $\alpha = .05$ to determine whether we can infer that the population variance differs from 300.

12.48 Repeat Exercise 12.47, changing the sample size to 50. What is the effect of decreasing the sample size?

12.49 The sample variance of a random sample of 50 observations from a normal population was found to be $s^2 = 80$. Can we infer at the 1% significance level that σ^2 is less than 100?

12.50 Repeat Exercise 12.49, increasing the sample size to 100. What is the effect of the change?

12.51 Estimate σ^2 with 90% confidence given that $n = 15$ and $s^2 = 12$.

12.52 Repeat Exercise 12.51 with $n = 30$. What is the effect of this change?

Applications

12.53 The weights of a random sample of cereal boxes that are supposed to weigh 1 pound are listed below. Estimate the variance of the entire population of cereal box weights with 90% confidence.

1.05,   1.03,   .98,   1.00,   .99,   .97,   1.01,   .96

12.54 Refer to Exercise 12.53. Can we infer at the 5% significance level that the population variance is less than .001?

12.55 Refer to Exercise 12.33. Estimate with 95% confidence the variance in contents' weights.

12.56 Refer to Exercise 12.30. In addition to concern about the mean delivery time, we are also concerned about variation in delivery times. Estimate the population variance with 95% confidence.

The following exercises require the use of a computer and software. The answers may be calculated manually. See Appendix A for the sample statistics.

12.57 Refer to Exercise 12.37. Estimate the variance in the amount of time physicians spend with patients. Use a 95% confidence level.

12.58 One important factor in inventory control is the variance of the daily demand for the product. A management scientist has developed the optimal order quantity and reorder point, assuming that the variance is equal to 250. Recently, the company has experienced some inventory problems, which induced the operations manager to doubt the assumption. To examine the problem, the manager took a sample of 25 daily demands and stored them in file Xr12-58.

a Do these data provide sufficient evidence at the 5% significance level to infer that the management scientist's assumption about the variance is wrong?

b What is the required condition for the statistical procedure in part **a**?

c Does it appear that the required condition is not satisfied?

12.59 Refer to Example 12.58. What are the smallest and largest values that σ^2 is likely to assume? (Define "likely" as 95% confidence.)

12.60 Refer to Exercise 12.34.

a Estimate with 90% confidence the variance in the time spent at part-time jobs.

b Check to determine whether the required condition appears to be satisfied.

12.61 Some traffic experts believe that the major cause of highway collisions is the differing speeds of cars. That is, when some cars are driven slowly while others are driven at speeds well in excess of the speed limit, cars tend to congregate in bunches, increasing the probability of accidents. Thus, the greater the variation in speeds, the greater the number of collisions that occur. Suppose that one expert believes that when the variance exceeds 18 $(mph)^2$, the number of accidents will be unacceptably high. A random sample of the speeds of 245 cars on a highway with one of the highest accident rates in the country is taken. These data are stored in file Xr12-61. Can we conclude at the 10% significance level that the variance in speeds exceeds 18 $(mph)^2$?

12.62 One problem facing the manager of maintenance departments is when to change the bulbs in streetlamps. If bulbs are changed only when they burn out, it is quite costly to send crews out to change only one bulb at a time. This method also requires someone to report the problem and, in the meantime, the light is off. If each bulb lasts approximately the same amount of time, they can all be replaced periodically, producing significant cost savings in maintenance. Suppose that a financial analysis of the lights at Yankee Stadium has concluded that it will pay to replace all of the lightbulbs at the same time if the variance of the lives of the bulbs is less than 200 $hours^2$. The lengths of life of the last 100 bulbs were recorded and stored in file Xr12-62. What conclusion can be drawn from these data? Use a 5% significance level.

12.4 INFERENCE ABOUT A POPULATION PROPORTION

In this section we continue to address the problem of describing a population. However, we shift our attention to populations of nominal data, which means that the population consists of nominal or categorical values. For example, in a brand preference survey where the statistics practitioner asks consumers of a particular product which brand they purchase, the values of the random variable are the brands. If there are five brands, the values could be represented by their names, letters (A, B, C, D, and E), or by numbers (1, 2, 3, 4, and 5). When numbers are used, it should be understood that the numbers only represent the name of the brand, are completely arbitrarily assigned, and cannot be treated as real numbers. That is, we cannot calculate means and variances.

PARAMETER

Recall the discussion of types of data in Chapter 2. When the data are nominal, all that we are permitted to do to describe the population or sample is count the number of occurrences of each value. From the counts we calculate proportions. Thus, the parameter of interest in describing a population of nominal data is the population proportion p. In Section 7.6 this parameter was used to calculate probabilities based on the binomial experiment. One of the characteristics of the binomial experiment is that there are only two possible outcomes per trial. Most practical applications of inference about p involve more than two outcomes. However, in most cases we're interested in only one outcome, which we label a "success." All other outcomes are labeled as "failures." For example, in brand preference surveys we are interested in our company's brand. In political surveys we wish to estimate or test the proportion of voters who will vote for one particular candidate—likely the one who has paid for the survey.

STATISTIC AND SAMPLING DISTRIBUTION

The logical statistic employed to estimate and test the population proportion is the sample proportion, defined as

$$\hat{p} = \frac{x}{n}$$

where x is the number of successes in the sample and n is the sample size. In Section 9.3 we presented the approximate sampling distribution of $\hat{p}$. (The actual distribution is based on the binomial distribution, which does not lend itself to statistical inference.) The sampling distribution of $\hat{p}$ is approximately normal with mean p and standard deviation $\sqrt{p(1-p)/n}$ [provided that np and $n(1-p)$ are greater than 5]. We express this sampling distribution as

$$z = \frac{\hat{p} - p}{\sqrt{p(1-p)/n}}$$

TESTING AND ESTIMATING A PROPORTION

As you have already seen, the formula that summarizes the sampling distribution also represents the test statistic.

TEST STATISTIC FOR p

$$z = \frac{\hat{p} - p}{\sqrt{p(1 - p)/n}}$$

which is approximately normal for np and $n(1 - p)$ greater than 5.

Using the same algebra employed in Sections 10.3 and 12.2, we attempt to derive the confidence interval estimator of p from the sampling distribution. The result is

$$\hat{p} \pm z_{\alpha/2}\sqrt{p(1 - p)/n}$$

This formula, although technically correct, is useless. To understand why, examine the standard error of the sampling distribution, $\sqrt{p(1 - p)/n}$. To produce the interval estimate we must compute the standard error, which requires us to know the value of p, which is the parameter we wish to estimate. This is the first of several statistical techniques where we face the same problem—how to determine the value of the standard error. In this application the problem is easily and logically solved: Simply estimate the value of p with $\hat{p}$. Thus, we estimate the standard error with $\sqrt{\hat{p}(1 - \hat{p})/n}$.

CONFIDENCE INTERVAL ESTIMATOR OF p

$$\hat{p} \pm z_{\alpha/2}\sqrt{\hat{p}(1 - \hat{p})/n}$$

which is valid provided that $n\hat{p}$ and $n(1 - \hat{p})$ are greater than 5.

EXAMPLE 12.5

After the polls close on election day, networks compete to be the first to predict which candidate will win. The predictions are based on counts in certain precincts and on exit polls. Exit polls are conducted by asking random samples of voters who have just exited from the polling booth (hence the name) for which candidate they voted. In American presidential elections, the candidate who receives the most votes in a state receives the state's entire Electoral College vote. In practice, this means that either the Democrat or the Republican candidate will win. Suppose that the results of an exit poll in one state are stored in file Xm12-05, where 1 = Democrat and 2 = Republican. The polls close at 8:00. Can the networks conclude from these data that the Republican candidate will win the state? Should the network announce at 8:01 that the Republican candidate will win?

SOLUTION

IDENTIFY

The problem objective is to describe the population of votes in the state. The data are nominal since the values are "Democrat" and "Republican." Thus the parameter to be tested is the proportion of votes in the entire state that are for the Republican candidate. Because we want to determine whether the network can declare the Republican to be the winner at 8:01, the alternative hypothesis is

$$H_1: \quad p > .5$$

which makes the null hypothesis

$$H_0: \quad p = .5$$

The test statistic is

$$z = \frac{\hat{p} - p}{\sqrt{p(1 - p)/n}}$$

COMPUTE

MANUALLY

It appears that this is a "standard" problem, which requires a 5% significance level. Thus, the rejection region is

$$z > z_\alpha = z_{.05} = 1.645$$

From the file we count the number of "successes," which is the number of votes cast for the Republican (code = 2) and find $x = 407$. The sample proportion is

$$\hat{p} = \frac{x}{n} = \frac{407}{765} = .532$$

The value of the test statistic is

$$z = \frac{\hat{p} - p}{\sqrt{p(1 - p)/n}} = \frac{.532 - .5}{\sqrt{.5(1 - .5)/765}} = 1.77$$

Since the test statistic is (approximately) normally distributed we can determine the p-value. It is

$$p\text{-value} = P(Z > 1.77) = .5 - .4616 = .0384$$

There is enough evidence at the 5% significance level that the Republican candidate has won.

EXCEL

	A	B	C	D
1	**z-Test: Proportion**			
2				
3				*Votes*
4	Sample Proportion			0.532
5	Observations			765
6	Hypothesized Proportion			0.5
7	z Stat			1.77
8	P(Z<=z) one-tail			0.0382
9	z Critical one-tail			1.6449
10	P(Z<=z) two-tail			0.0764
11	z Critical two-tail			1.96

COMMANDS   COMMANDS FOR EXAMPLE 12.5

1. Type or import the data.   Open file **Xm12-05**.
2. Click **Tools, Data Analysis Plus**, and **Z-Test: Proportion**.
3. Specify the **Input Range**.   **A1:A766**
4. Specify the **Code for Success**.   **2**
5. Type the **Hypothesized Proportion**.   **.5**
6. Click **Labels**, if appropriate.
7. Specify the value of α (**Alpha**) and click **OK**.   **.05**

To complete the technique from the sample proportion or to conduct a what-if analysis, open the **Test Statistics** workbook and the **z-Test-_Proportion** worksheet.

MINITAB
Test and CI for One Proportion: Votes

```
Test of p = 0.5 vs p > 0.5

Success = 2

Variable        X      N  Sample p  95.0% Lower Bound  Z-Value  P-Value
Votes         407    765  0.532026           0.502352     1.77    0.038
```

Besides computing the *z* statistic and *p*-value, and because we're conducting a one-tail test, Minitab calculates a one-sided confidence interval estimate.

COMMANDS

The data must represent successes and failures. The codes can be numbers or text. There can be only two kinds of entries, one representing success and the other representing failure. If numbers are used, Minitab will interpret the larger one as a success.

	COMMANDS FOR EXAMPLE 12.5
1. Type or import the data.	Open file **Xm12-05**.
2. Click **Stat, Basic Statistics**, and **1 Proportion…**.	
3. Use the cursor to select **Samples in columns** and type the name of the variable.	**Votes** or **C1**
4. Click **Options…** and **Test proportion**. Type the value of *p* under the null hypothesis.	**.5**
5. Specify the **Alternative** hypothesis.	**greater than**
6. To use the normal approximation of the binomial, specify **Use test and interval based on normal approximation**. Click **OK**. Click **OK**.	

There are two variations on the instructions above.

1. If, instead of the raw data, you know the number of successes (and the sample size) you can specify **Summarized data** (at step 3 above) and type the **Number of trials** and the **Number of successes**.

2. You can use the exact distribution (binomial) of the number of successes instead of the normal distribution. Simply omit step 6 above.

INTERPRET

One of the key issues to consider here is the cost of Type I and Type II errors. A Type I error occurs if we conclude that the Republican will win when in fact he has lost. Such an error would mean that a network would announce at 8:01 that the Republican has won and then later in the evening would have to admit to a mistake. If a particular network were the only one that made this error it would cast doubt on their integrity and possibly affect the number of viewers.

This is exactly what happened on the evening of the U.S. presidential elections in November 2000. Shortly after the polls closed at 8:00, all the networks declared that the Democratic candidate Albert Gore would win in the state of Florida. A couple of hours later, the networks admitted that a mistake had been made and the Republican candidate George W. Bush had won. Several hours later they again admitted a mistake and finally declared the race too close to call. Fortunately for each network, all the networks made the same mistake. However, if one network had not done this it would have developed a better track record, which could have been used in future advertisements for news shows and likely drawn more viewers.

To reduce Type I errors the networks should set the significance at 1%. The *p*-value in this example, .0384, is not small enough to declare that the Republican has won.

NIELSEN RATINGS: SOLUTION

IDENTIFY

The problem objective is to describe the population of television shows watched by viewers across the country. The data are nominal. The combination of problem objective and data type make the parameter to be estimated the proportion of the entire population that watched the "Tonight Show." The confidence interval estimator is

$$\hat{p} \pm z_{\alpha/2}\sqrt{\frac{\hat{p}(1 - \hat{p})}{n}}$$

COMPUTE

MANUALLY

To solve manually we count the number of 1's in the (Nielsen) file. We find this value to be 226. Thus,

$$\hat{p} = \frac{x}{n} = \frac{226}{2,000} = .113$$

The confidence level is $1 - \alpha = .95$. It follows that $\alpha = .05$, $\alpha/2 = .025$, and $z_{\alpha/2} = z_{.025} = 1.96$. The 95% confidence interval estimate of p is

$$\hat{p} \pm z_{\alpha/2}\sqrt{\frac{\hat{p}(1 - \hat{p})}{n}} = .113 \pm 1.96\sqrt{\frac{(.113)(1 - .113)}{2,000}} = .113 \pm .014$$

$$LCL = .099 \qquad UCL = .127$$

EXCEL

	A	B
1	**z-Estimate: Proportion**	
2		*Shows*
3	Sample Proportion	0.113
4	Observations	2000
5	LCL	0.099
6	UCL	0.127

COMMANDS

1. Type or import the data into one column.
2. Click **Tools, Data Analysis Plus**, and **Z-Estimate: Proportion**.
3. Specify the **Input Range**.
4. Specify the **Code for Success.**
5. Click **Labels**, if appropriate.
6. Specify the value of α (**Alpha**) and click **OK**.

COMMANDS FOR EXAMPLE

Open file **Nielsen**.

A1:A2001

1

.05

To complete the technique from the sample proportion or to conduct a what-if analysis, open the **Estimators** workbook and the **z-Estimate_Proportion** worksheet.

MINITAB

Test and CI for One Proportion: Shows

```
Test of p = 0.5 vs p not = 0.5

Success = 1

Variable        X     N   Sample p        95.0% CI
Shows         226  2000   0.113000  (0.099125, 0.126875)
```

Minitab both performs a test of hypothesis and computes the confidence interval estimate. Ignore the test output. (We have deleted that part of the printout.)

COMMANDS

Minitab requires that there be only two possible codes. If the codes are numerical, Minitab reads the larger value as the code for success. Therefore the data must be recoded so that 1 = "Tonight Show" and 0 = Other. (See Section 12.2 for a discussion on how to recode data.) Follow the instructions to test a proportion. After clicking **Options...** type the **Confidence level**. To produce a two-sided confidence interval estimate, specify the **Alternative** hypothesis as **not equal**.

INTERPRET

We estimate that between 9.9% and 12.7% of all television sets had received the "Tonight Show." If we multiply these figures by the total number of televisions, 100 million, we produce an interval estimate of the number of televisions tuned to the "Tonight Show." Thus, the 95% confidence interval estimate of the number of televisions tuned to the "Tonight Show" lies between

$$LCL = .099 \times 100 \text{ million} = 9.9 \text{ million}$$

and

$$UCL = .127 \times 100 \text{ million} = 12.7 \text{ million}$$

Sponsoring companies can then determine the value of any commercials that appeared on the show.

SELECTING THE SAMPLE SIZE TO ESTIMATE THE PROPORTION

When we introduced the sample size selection method to estimate a mean in Section 10.4, we pointed out that the sample size depends on the confidence level and the size of the interval the statistics practitioner wants to produce. When the parameter to be estimated is a proportion, the confidence interval estimator is

$$\hat{p} \pm z_{\alpha/2}\sqrt{\frac{\hat{p}(1 - \hat{p})}{n}}$$

When we specify the confidence level, we can determine the value of $z_{\alpha/2}$. The width of the interval is determined by the value of the quantity that follows the plus/minus sign. Thus, if we wish to estimate a proportion to within W we need to solve the following equation to find the sample size:

$$W = z_{\alpha/2}\sqrt{\frac{\hat{p}(1 - \hat{p})}{n}}$$

Solving for n, we produce the required sample size as indicated in the box.

> **SAMPLE SIZE TO ESTIMATE A PROPORTION**
>
> $$n = \left(\frac{z_{\alpha/2}\sqrt{\hat{p}(1 - \hat{p})}}{W}\right)^2$$

To illustrate the use of this formula, suppose that in a brand preference survey we want to estimate the proportion of consumers who prefer our company's brand to within .03 with 95% confidence. This means that when the sample is taken and the calculations completed, the interval estimate is to be $\hat{p} \pm .03$. Thus, $W = .03$. Since $1 - \alpha = .95$, $\alpha = .05$, $\alpha/2 = .025$, and $z_{\alpha/2} = z_{.025} = 1.96$. Therefore

$$n = \left(\frac{1.96\sqrt{\hat{p}(1 - \hat{p})}}{.03}\right)^2$$

To solve for n, we need to know $\hat{p}$. Unfortunately, this value is unknown, because the sample has not yet been taken. At this point, we can use either of two methods to solve for n.

Method 1

If we have no knowledge of even the approximate value of $\hat{p}$, we let $\hat{p} = .5$. We choose $\hat{p} = .5$ because the product $\hat{p}(1 - \hat{p})$ equals its maximum value at $\hat{p} = .5$. (Figure 12.6 illustrates this point.) This, in turn, results in a conservative value of n and, as a result, the confidence interval will be no wider than the interval $\hat{p} \pm .03$.

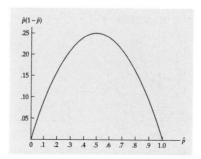

Figure 12.6
Plot of $\hat{p}$ versus $\hat{p}(1 - \hat{p})$

If, when the sample is drawn, $\hat{p}$ does not equal .5, the confidence interval estimate will be better (that is, narrower) than planned. Thus,

$$n = \left(\frac{1.96 \sqrt{(.5)(.5)}}{.03} \right)^2 = (32.67)^2 = 1{,}068$$

If it turns out that $\hat{p} = .5$, the interval estimate is $\hat{p} \pm .03$. If not, the interval estimate will be narrower. For instance, if it turns out that $\hat{p} = .2$, the estimate is $\hat{p} \pm .024$, which is better than we had planned.

Method 2

If we have some idea about the value of $\hat{p}$, we can use that quantity to determine n. For example, if we believe that $\hat{p}$ will turn out to be approximately .2, we can solve for n as follows:

$$n = \left(\frac{1.96 \sqrt{(.2)(.8)}}{.03} \right)^2 = (26.13)^2 = 683$$

Notice that this produces a smaller value of n (thus reducing sampling costs) than does method 1. If $\hat{p}$ actually lies between .2 and .8, however, the estimate will not be as good as we wanted, because the interval will be wider than desired.

Method 1 is often used to determine the sample size used in public opinion surveys reported by newspapers, magazines, television, and radio. These polls usually estimate proportions to within 3%, with 95% confidence. (The media often state the confidence level as "19 times out of 20.") If you've ever wondered why opinion polls almost always estimate proportions to within 3%, consider the sample size required to estimate a proportion to within 1%:

$$n = \left(\frac{1.96 \sqrt{(.5)(.5)}}{.01} \right)^2 = (98)^2 = 9{,}604$$

The sample size 9,604 is 9 times the sample size needed to estimate a proportion to within 3%. Thus, to divide the width of the interval by 3 requires multiplying the sample size by 9. The cost would also increase considerably. For most applications, the increase in accuracy (created by decreasing the width of the confidence interval estimate) does not overcome the increased cost. Confidence interval estimates with W equal to 5% or 10% (sample sizes 385 and 97, respectively) are generally considered too wide to be useful. Thus, the 3% figure is the happy compromise between cost and accuracy.

We complete this section by reviewing the factors that tell us when to test and estimate a population proportion.

FACTORS THAT IDENTIFY THE *z* TEST AND ESTIMATOR OF *p*
1. **Problem objective:** Describe a population.
2. **Data type:** Nominal

EXERCISES

Developing an Understanding of Statistical Concepts

*Exercises 12.63 to 12.76 are "what-if analyses" designed to determine what happens to the test statistics and interval estimates when elements of the statistical inference change. These problems can be solved manually or using Excel's **Test Statistics** or **Estimators** workbooks.*

12.63 In a random sample of 500 observations, we found the proportion of successes to be 48%. Estimate with 95% confidence the population proportion of successes.

12.64 Repeat Exercise 12.63 with $n = 200$.

12.65 Repeat Exercise 12.63 with $n = 1,000$.

12.66 Refer to Exercises 12.63 to 12.65. Describe the effect on the confidence interval estimate of increasing the sample size.

12.67 Repeat Exercise 12.63 with $\hat{p} = 33\%$.

12.68 Repeat Exercise 12.63 with $\hat{p} = 10\%$.

12.69 Review Exercises 12.63, 12.67, and 12.68. Discuss the effect on the width of the confidence interval estimate of reducing the sample proportion.

12.70 Calculate the *p*-value of the test of the following hypotheses given that $\hat{p} = .63$ and $n = 100$.

$$H_0: \quad p = .60$$
$$H_1: \quad p > .60$$

12.71 Repeat Exercise 12.70 with $n = 200$.

12.72 Repeat Exercise 12.70 with $n = 400$.

12.73 Refer to Exercises 12.70 to 12.72. Describe the effect on the *z* statistic and its *p*-value of increasing the sample size.

12.74 Repeat Exercise 12.70 with $\hat{p} = .62$.

12.75 Repeat Exercise 12.70 with $\hat{p} = .61$.

12.76 Refer to Exercises 12.70, 12.74, and 12.75. Describe the effect on the *z* statistic and its *p*-value of decreasing the sample proportion.

12.77 Determine the sample size necessary to estimate a population proportion to within .03 with 90% confidence, assuming you have no knowledge of the approximate value of the sample proportion.

12.78 Suppose that you used the sample size calculated in Exercise 12.77 and found $\hat{p} = .5$.
  a Estimate the population proportion with 90% confidence.
  b Is this the result you expected? Explain.

12.79 Suppose that you used the sample size calculated in Exercise 12.77 and found $\hat{p} = .75$.
  a Estimate the population proportion with 90% confidence.
  b Is this the result you expected? Explain.
  c If you were hired to conduct this analysis, would the person who hired you be satisfied with the interval estimate you produced? Explain.

12.80 Redo Exercise 12.77, assuming that you know that the sample proportion will be no less than .75.

12.81 Suppose that you used the sample size calculated in Exercise 12.80 and found $\hat{p} = .75$.
  a Estimate the population proportion with 90% confidence.
  b Is this the result you expected? Explain.

12.82 Suppose that you used the sample size calculated in Exercise 12.80 and found $\hat{p} = .92$.
  a Estimate the population proportion with 90% confidence.
  b Is this the result you expected? Explain.
  c If you were hired to conduct this analysis, would the person who hired you be satisfied with the interval estimate you produced? Explain.

12.83 Suppose that you used the sample size calculated in Exercise 12.80 and found $\hat{p} = .5$.
  a Estimate the population proportion with 90% confidence.
  b Is this the result you expected? Explain.
  c If you were hired to conduct this analysis, would the person who hired you be satisfied with the interval estimate you produced? Explain.

12.84 Given that $\hat{p} = .84$ and $n = 600$, estimate *p* with 90% confidence.

12.85 In a random sample of 250, we found 75 successes. Estimate the population proportion of success, with 99% confidence.

12.86 If $\hat{p} = .59$ and $n = 100$, can we conclude at the 5% level of significance that the population proportion *p* is greater than .50?

12.87 Suppose that, in a sample of 200, we observe 140 successes. Is this sufficient evidence at the 1% significance level to indicate that the population proportion of successes is greater than 65%?

12.88 Find the *p*-value of the test in Exercise 12.87.

Applications

The following exercises require the use of a computer and software. The answers may be calculated manually. See Appendix A for the sample statistics. Use a 5% significance level unless specified otherwise.

12.89 To determine how many Americans smoke, annual surveys are conducted by the U.S. National Center for Health Statistics. The survey asks a random sample of Americans whether they smoke on some days. The responses (1 = No and 2 = Yes) are stored in file Xr12-89. Estimate with 95% confidence the proportion of Americans who smoke. (Adapted from the *Statistical Abstract of the United States*, 2000, Table 226)

12.90 The results of an annual Claimant Satisfaction Survey of policyholders who have had a claim with State Farm Insurance Company revealed a 90% satisfaction rate for claim service. To check the accuracy of this claim, a random sample of State Farm claimants was asked to rate whether they were satisfied with the quality of the service. The responses (1 = Satisfied and 2 = Unsatisfied) are stored in file

Xr12-90. Can we infer that the satisfaction rate is less than 90%?

12.91 A random sample of Americans was asked whether they had ever been bitten by a dog. (Gallup Poll, February 19–21, 2001) The responses (1 = Yes and 2 = No) are stored in file Xr12-91. If there are currently 280 million Americans, estimate with 95% confidence the total number of Americans who have been bitten by a dog.

12.92 In a television commercial, the manufacturer of a toothpaste claims that more than four out of five dentists recommend the ingredients in its product. To test that claim, a consumer protection group randomly samples 400 dentists and asks each one whether he or she would recommend toothpaste that contained the ingredients. The responses are 1 = No and 2 = Yes. The responses are stored in file Xr12-92. Can the consumer group infer that the claim is true?

12.93 In 1997, 56.7% of all students attending public schools had access to a computer at school. To determine whether private schools were as fortunate, a random sample of 226 private school students were asked to report whether each had access to a computer at school. The responses (1 = Yes and 2 = No) are stored in file Xr12-93. Can we infer from these data that private school students have less access to computers at school than public school students? (Adapted from the *Statistical Abstract of the United States*, 2000, Table 278)

12.94 A professor of business statistics recently adopted a new textbook. At the completion of the course, 100 randomly selected students were asked to assess the book. The responses are as follows:

Excellent (1), Good (2), Adequate (3), Poor (4)

The results are stored in file Xr12-94 using the codes in parentheses. Do the data allow us to conclude at the 10% significance level that more than 50% of all business students would rate it as excellent?

12.95 Refer to Exercise 12.94. Do the data allow us to conclude at the 10% significance level that more than 90% of all business students would rate it as at least adequate?

12.96 Refer to the file CH12:\Nielsen. Estimate with 95% confidence the number of televisions that had received the "Late Show with David Letterman."

12.97 The wine industry is an important part of the economy of western New York State and of Southern Ontario. The wine is made from grapes grown on vines. During the winter, some of the grape vines die from the extreme cold that is common in this part of the continent. In the spring the vines are pruned. If the vine is brown, it means that the plant is dead; green indicates a healthy vine. To test how well a vineyard has survived the winter, a random sample of vines is selected. The results of the latest pruning are stored in file Xr12-97 (2 = Dead and 1 = Alive). Estimate with 90% confidence the degree of winter kill for this vineyard.

APPLICATIONS IN *MARKETING*

Consumer Surveys

Consumer surveys are used extensively by marketing managers to assess the attitudes of consumers toward various characteristics of a product, such as its convenience, quality, and price. Although information obtained from a survey is very useful to managers comtemplating changes to an existing product, such information is absolutely invaluable to managers about to introduce a new, untested product to the market. Of utmost impor-tance is whether the new product will capture sufficient market share to reach the breakeven level of profit-ability within a reasonable period of time.

12.98 In the fall of 1998, a newspaper publisher launched a new "national" newspaper in Canada. It was believed that the new newspaper would have to capture at least 12% of the Toronto market in order to be financially viable. During the planning stages of this new newspaper, a market survey was conducted of a sample of 400 Toronto readers. The survey provided a brief description of the proposed newspaper, and then asked whether the survey participant would subscribe to the newspaper if the cost did not exceed $20 per month. The responses (1 = No and 2 = Yes) are stored in file Xr12-98. Can the publisher conclude that the proposed newspaper will be financially viable?

12.99 Obesity is not only a health problem, but also an economic one. Obesity has been related to a wide variety of medical problems including heart attacks, strokes, and cancer. To help gauge the extent of the problem, the U.S. Center for Health Statistics took a survey of Americans and determined whether each was obese. The results for 1997 are stored in file Xr12-99 (1 = Obese and 2 = Not obese). Assuming a total population of 270 million people, estimate with 90% confidence the total number of Americans who are obese. (Adapted from the *Statistical Abstract of the United States*, 2000, Table 231)

12.100 Chlorofluorocarbons (CFCs) are used in air conditioners. However, CFCs damage the ozone layer, which protects us from the sun's harmful rays. As a result, many jurisdictions have banned the production and use of CFCs. The latest jurisdiction to do so is the province of Ontario, which has banned the use of CFCs in car and truck air conditioners effective January 1, 2002. However, it is not known how many vehicles will be affected by the new legislation. A survey of 650 vehicles was undertaken. Each vehicle was identified as either using CFCs (code = 2) or not (code = 1). The data are stored in file Xr12-100. If there are 5 million vehicles registered in Ontario, estimate with 95% confidence the number of vehicles affected by the new law.

12.5 (OPTIONAL) APPLICATIONS IN MARKETING: MARKET SEGMENTATION

Market segmentation separates consumers of a product into different groups in such a way that members of each group are similar to each other and there are differences between groups. Market segmentation grew out of the realization that a single product can seldom satisfy the needs and wants of all consumers. For example, the market for new cars must be segmented because there is a wide variety of needs that a car must satisfy. There are often identifiable segments of the market to which specifically designed products can be directed.

There are many ways to segment a market. Table 12.1 lists several different segmentation variables and their market segments. For example, car manufacturers can use education levels to segment the market. It is likely that high school graduates would be quite similar to others in this group and that members of this group would differ from university graduates. We would expect those differences to include the types and brands of cars each group would choose to buy. However, it is likely that income level would differentiate more clearly between segments. Statistical techniques can be used to help determine the best way to segment the market. These statistical techniques are more advanced than this textbook. Consequently, we will focus our attention on other statistical applications.

Table 12.1 Market Segmentation

Segmentation variable	*Segments*
Geographic	
Countries	Brazil, Canada, China, France, United States
Country regions	Midwest, Northeast, Southwest, Southeast
Demographic	
Age	Under 5, 5–12, 13–19, 20–29, 30–50, over 50
Education	Some high school, high school graduate, some college, college or university graduate
Income	Under $20,000, 20,000–29,999, 30,000–50,000, over $50,000
Marital status	Single, married, divorced, widowed
Social	
Religion	Catholic, Protestant, Jewish, Islam, Buddhist
Class	Upper class, middle class, working class, lower class
Behavior	
Media usage	TV, Internet, newspaper, magazine
Payment method	Cash, check, Visa, Mastercard

In Example 12.6 below we demonstrate how statistical methods can be used to determine the size of a segment, which is used to determine its profitability. This aspect is crucial because not all segments are worth pursuing. In some instances the size of the segment is too small or the costs of satisfying a segment may be too high. The size of a segment can be determined in several ways. The census can provide useful information. For example, we can determine the number of Americans in various age categories. For other segments we may need to survey members of a population and use the inferential techniques introduced in this chapter.

EXAMPLE 12.6

In segmenting the breakfast cereal market, a food manufacturer uses health and diet consciousness as the segmentation variable. Four segments are developed:

1. Concerned about eating healthy foods
2. Concerned primarily about weight
3. Concerned about health because of illness
4. Unconcerned

To distinguish between groups, surveys are conducted. On the basis of a questionnaire, people are categorized as belonging to one of these groups. A recent survey asked a random sample of 1,250 American adults (20 and over) to complete the questionnaire. The results are stored in file Xm12-06. The most recent census reveals that there are 194,506,000 Americans who are 20 and over. Estimate with 95% confidence the number of American adults who are concerned about eating healthy foods.

SOLUTION

IDENTIFY

The problem objective is to describe the population of American adults. The data are nominal. Consequently, the parameter we wish to estimate is the proportion p of American adults who classify themselves as concerned about eating healthy. The confidence interval estimator we need to employ is

$$\hat{p} \pm z_{\alpha/2}\sqrt{\frac{\hat{p}(1 - \hat{p})}{n}}$$

COMPUTE

 MANUALLY

To solve manually, we count the number of 1's in the file. We find this value to be 269. Thus,

$$\hat{p} = \frac{x}{n} = \frac{269}{1,250} = .2152$$

The confidence level is $1 - \alpha = .95$. It follows that $\alpha = .05$, $\alpha/2 = .025$, and $z_{\alpha/2} = z_{.025} = 1.96$. The 95% confidence interval estimate of p is

$$\hat{p} \pm z_{\alpha/2}\sqrt{\frac{\hat{p}(1 - \hat{p})}{n}} = .2152 \pm .196\sqrt{\frac{(.2152)(1 - .2152)}{1,250}} = .2152 \pm .0228$$

$$\text{LCL} = .1924 \qquad \text{UCL} = .2380$$

EXCEL

	A	B
1	z-Estimate: Proportion	
2		Group
3	Sample Proportion	0.2152
4	Observations	1250
5	LCL	0.1924
6	UCL	0.2380

MINITAB

Test and CI for One Proportion: Group

```
Test of p = 0.5 vs p not = 0.5

Success = 1

Variable        X      N  Sample p         95.0% CI        Z-Value  P-Value
Group         269   1250  0.215200  (0.192418, 0.237982)   -20.14    0.000
```

Note: It was necessary to recode the data. We did so in such a way that group 1 is represented by code = 1 and the other groups are represented by code = 0.

INTERPRET

We estimate that the proportion of American adults who are in group 1 lies between .1924 and .2380. Because there are 194,506,000 adults in the population, we estimate that the number of adults who belong to group 1 falls between

$$LCL = 194,506,000 \,(.1924) = 37,422,954$$

and

$$UCL = 194,506,000 \,(.2380) = 46,292,428$$

We will return to the subject of market segmentation in other chapters where we demonstrate how statistics can be employed to determine whether differences actually exist between segments.

EXERCISES

The following exercises require the use of a computer and software. The answers may be solved manually. See Appendix A for the sample statistics.

12.101 A new credit card company is investigating various market segments to determine whether it is profitable to direct its advertising specifically at each one. One of the market segments is composed of Hispanic people. The latest census indicates that there are 19,108,000 Hispanic people in the United States. A survey of 475 Hispanics asked each how they usually pay for products that they purchase. The responses are

    1. Cash
    2. Check
    3. Visa
    4. Mastercard
    5. Other credit card

The responses are stored in file Xr12-101. Estimate with 95% confidence the number of Hispanics in the United States who usually pay by credit card.

12.102 A California university is investigating expanding its evening programs. It wants to target people between 25 and 55 years old who have completed high school but did not complete college or university. To help determine the extent and type of offerings, the university needs to know the size of its target market. A survey of 320 California adults was drawn and each person was asked to identify his or her highest educational attainment. The responses are

    1. Did not complete high school
    2. Completed high school only
    3. Some college or university
    4. College or university graduate

The responses are stored in file Xr12-102. The *Statistical Abstract of the United States*, 2000, Table 24, indicates that there are 14,814,000 Californians between the ages of 25 and 55. Estimate with 95% confidence the number of Californians between 25 and 55 years of age who are in the market segment the university wishes to target.

12.103 The J. C. Penney department store chain segments the market for women's apparel by its identification of values. The three segments are

    1. Conservative
    2. Traditional
    3. Contemporary

Questionnaires about personal and family values are used to identify which segment a woman falls into. Suppose that the questionnaire was sent to a random sample of 1,836 women. Each woman was classified using the codes 1, 2, and 3. These data are stored in file Xr12-103. The latest census reveals that there are 101,282,000 adult women in the United States. (*Statistical Abstract of the United States*, 2000, Table 13)

a Estimate with 95% confidence the proportion of adult American women who are classified as traditional.

b Estimate the size of the traditional market segment.

12.6 SUMMARY

The inferential methods presented in this chapter address the problem of describing a population. When the data are interval, the parameters of interest are the population mean μ and the population variance σ^2. The Student t distribution is used to test and estimate the mean when the population standard deviation is unknown. The chi-squared distribution is used to make inferences about a population variance. When the data are nominal, the parameter to be tested and estimated is the population proportion p. The sample proportion follows an approximate normal distribution, which produces the test statistic and the interval estimator. We also discussed how to determine the sample size required to estimate a population proportion. Finally, we introduced market segmentation and described how statistical techniques presented in this chapter can be used to estimate the size of a segment.

IMPORTANT TERMS

Student t distribution 355
Degrees of freedom 355
Robust 361

Missing data 361
Chi-squared statistic 367
Exit polls 374

SYMBOLS

Symbol	Pronounced	Represents
ν	*nu*	Degrees of freedom
χ^2	*chi-squared*	Chi-squared statistic
$\hat{p}$	*p-hat*	Sample proportion

FORMULAS

Test statistic for μ

$$t = \frac{\bar{x} - \mu}{s/\sqrt{n}}$$

Interval estimator of μ

$$\bar{x} \pm t_{\alpha/2} \frac{s}{\sqrt{n}}$$

Test statistic for σ^2

$$\chi^2 = \frac{(n-1)s^2}{\sigma^2}$$

Interval estimator of σ^2

$$LCL = \frac{(n-1)s^2}{\chi^2_{\alpha/2}}$$

$$UCL = \frac{(n-1)s^2}{\chi^2_{1-\alpha/2}}$$

Test statistic for p

$$z = \frac{\hat{p} - p}{\sqrt{p(1-p)/n}}$$

Interval estimator of p

$$\hat{p} \pm z_{\alpha/2}\sqrt{\hat{p}(1-\hat{p})/n}$$

Sample size to estimate p

$$n = \left(\frac{z_{\alpha/2}\sqrt{\hat{p}(1-\hat{p})}}{W} \right)^2$$

COMPUTER OUTPUT AND INSTRUCTIONS

Technique	Excel	Minitab
t test of μ	358	358
t estimator of μ	360	361
Recoding data	362	363
Chi-squared test of σ^2	369	
Chi-squared estimator of σ^2	370	
z test of p	375	376
z estimator of p	377	377

REFERENCES

Fuerderer, R., A. Herrmann, and G. Wuebker, *Optimal Bundling: Marketing Strategies to Improve Economic Performance*. New York: Springer Verlag, 1999.

Gaither, Norman, and Gregory Frazier, *Production and Operations Management*, 8th edition. Cincinnati, OH: Southwestern, 1999.

Hogg, Robert V., and Allan T. Craig, *Introduction to Mathematical Statistics*, 5th edition. Englewood Cliffs, NJ: Prentice Hall, 1995.

Kotler, Phillip, *Marketing Management*, 8th edition. Englewood Cliffs, NJ: Prentice Hall, 1994.

Lehmann, E. L., *Testing Statistical Hypotheses*, 2nd edition. New York: Chapman & Hall, 1991.

Lillien, Gary L., and Arvind Rangaswamy, *Marketing Engineering: Computer Assisted Marketing Analysis and Planning*, Reading, MA: Addison Wesley, 1998.

Mood, A. M., F. A. Graybill, and D. L. Boes, *Introduction to the Theory of Statistics*, 3rd edition, New York: McGraw Hill, 1974.

Nahmias, Steven, *Production and Operations Analysis*, 4th edition. Burr Ridge, IL: McGraw Hill, 2001.

Peter, J. Paul, and James H. Donnely, Jr., *A Preface to Marketing Management*, 8th edition. Boston, MA: Irwin/McGraw-Hill, 2000.

CHAPTER REVIEW EXERCISES

The following exercises require the use of a computer and soft-ware. **Use a 5% significance level unless specified otherwise.**

12.104 One of the issues that came up in a recent municipal election was the high cost of housing. A candidate seeking to unseat an incumbent claimed that the average family spends more than 30% of its annual income on housing. A housing expert was asked to investigate the claim. A random sample of 125 households was drawn, and each household was asked to report the percentage of household income spent on housing costs. The data are stored in file Xr12-104.

    a Is there enough evidence to infer that the candidate is correct?

    b Using a confidence level of 95%, estimate the mean percentage of household income spent on housing by all households.

    c What is the required condition for the techniques used in parts **a** and **b**?

12.105 The "just-in-time" policy of inventory control (developed by the Japanese) is growing in popularity. For example, General Motors recently spent $2 billion on its Oshawa, Ontario, plant so that it will be less than 1 hour from most suppliers. Suppose that an automobile parts supplier claims to deliver parts to any manufacturer in an average time of less than 1 hour. In an effort to test the claim, a manufacturer recorded the times (in minutes) of 24 deliveries from this supplier. These data are stored in file Xr12-105. Can we conclude that the supplier's assertion is correct?

12.106 Robots are being used with increasing frequency on production lines to perform monotonous tasks. To determine whether a robot welder should replace human welders in producing automobiles, an experiment was performed. The time for the robot to complete a series of welds was found to be 38 seconds. A random sample of 20 workers was taken, and the time for each worker to complete the welds was measured and stored in file Xr12-106. The mean was calculated to be 38 seconds, the same as the robot's time. However, the robot's time did not vary, whereas there was variation among the workers' times. An analysis of the production line revealed that if the variance exceeds 17 seconds^2, there will be problems. Perform an analysis of the data, and determine whether problems using human welders are likely.

12.107 Opinion Research International surveyed people whose household incomes exceed $50,000 and asked each for their top money-related new year's resolutions. The responses are

    1. Get out of credit card debt
    2. Retire before age 65
    3. Die broke
    4. Make do with current finances
    5. Look for higher-paying job

The responses are stored in file Xr12-107. Estimate with 90% confidence the proportion of people whose household incomes exceed $50,000 whose top money-related resolution is to get out of credit card debt.

12.108 Suppose that, in a large state university (with numerous campuses), the marks in an introductory statistics course are normally distributed with a mean of 68%. To determine the effect of requiring students to pass a calculus test (which at present is not a prerequisite), a random sample of 50 students who have taken calculus is given a statistics course. The marks out of 100 are stored in file Xr12-108.

    a Estimate with 95% confidence the mean statistics mark for all students who have taken calculus.

    b Do these data provide evidence to infer that students with a calculus background would perform better in statistics than students with no calculus?

12.109 Duplicate bridge is a game in which players compete for master points. When a player receives 300 master points, he or she becomes a life master. Since that title comes with a year's free subscription to the American Contract Bridge League's (ACBL) monthly bulletin, the ACBL is interested in knowing the status of non–life masters. Suppose that a random sample of 80 non–life masters was asked how many master points they have. The results are stored in file Xr12-109. The ACBL would like an estimate of the mean number of master points held by all non–life masters. A confidence level of 90% is considered adequate in this case.

12.110 A national health care system was an issue in the 1992 presidential election campaign and is likely to be a subject of debate for many years. The issue arose because of the large number of Americans who have no health insurance. Under the present system, free health care is available to poor people, while relatively well-off Americans buy their own health insurance. Those who are considered working poor and who are in the lower-middle-class economic stratum appear to be most unlikely to have adequate medical insurance. To investigate this problem, a statistics practitioner surveyed 250 families whose gross income last year was between $10,000 and $15,000. Family heads were asked whether they have medical insurance coverage. The answers were stored in file Xr12-110 (2 = Has medical insurance and 1 = Doesn't have medical insurance). The statistics practitioner wanted an estimate of the fraction of all families whose incomes are in the range of $10,000 to $15,000 who have medical insurance. Perform the necessary calculations to produce an interval estimate with 90% confidence.

12.111 The routes of postal deliverers are carefully planned so that each deliverer works between 7 and 7.5 hours per shift. The planned routes assume an average walking speed of 2 miles per hour and no shortcuts across lawns. In an experiment to examine the amount of time deliverers actually spend completing their shifts, a random sample of 75 postal deliverers was secretly timed. The data from the survey are stored in file Xr12-111.

a Estimate with 99% confidence the mean shift time for all postal deliverers.

b Check to determine whether the required condition for this statistical inference is satisfied.

c Is there enough evidence at the 10% significance level to conclude that postal workers are on average spending less than 7 hours per day doing their jobs?

12.112 As you can easily appreciate, the number of Internet users is rapidly increasing. A recent survey reveals that there are about 30 million Internet users in North America. Suppose that a survey of 200 of these people asked them to report the number of hours they spent on the Internet last week. The results are stored in file Xr12-112. Estimate with 95% confidence the annual total amount of time spent by all North Americans on the Internet.

12.113 The manager of a branch of a major bank wants to improve service. She is thinking about giving $1 to any customer who waits in line for a period of time that is considered excessive. (The bank ultimately decided that more than 8 minutes is excessive.) However, to get a better idea about the level of current service, she undertakes a survey of customers. A student is hired to measure the time spent waiting in line by a random sample of 50 customers. Using a stopwatch, the student determined the amount of time between the time the customer joined the line and the time he or she reached the teller. The times were recorded and are stored in file Xr12-113. Construct a 90% confidence interval estimate of the mean waiting time for the bank's customers.

12.114 In an examination of consumer loyalty in the travel business, 72 first-time visitors to a tourist attraction were asked whether they planned to return. The responses were stored in file Xr12-114 where 2 = Yes and 1 = No. Estimate with 95% confidence the proportion of all first-time visitors who planned to return to the same destination.

12.115 Engineers who are in charge of the production of springs used to make car seats are concerned about the variability in the length of the springs. The springs are designed to be 500 mm long. When the springs are too long they will loosen and fall out. When they are too short they will not fit into the frames. The springs that are too long and too short must be reworked at considerable additional cost. The engineers have calculated that a standard deviation of 2 mm will result in an acceptable number of springs that must be reworked. A random sample of 100 springs was measured. The data are stored in file Xr12-115. Can we infer at the 10% significance level that the number of springs requiring reworking is unacceptably large?

12.116 Refer to Exercise 12.115. Suppose the engineers recoded the data so that springs that were the correct length were recorded as 1, springs that were too long were recorded as 2, and springs that were too short were recorded as 3. These data are stored in file Xr12-116. Can we infer at the 10% significance level that less than 90% of the springs are the correct length?

12.117 An advertisement for a major home appliance manufacturer claims that its repair personnel are the loneliest in the world because its appliances require the smallest number of service calls. To examine this claim, a researcher drew a random sample of 100 owners of 5-year-old washing machines. The number of service calls made in the 5-year period were recorded and stored in file Xr12-117. Find the 90% confidence interval estimate of the mean number of service calls for all 5-year-old washing machines.

12.118 An oil company sends out monthly statements to its customers who purchased gasoline and other items using the company's credit card. Until now, the company has not included a preaddressed envelope for returning payments. The average and the standard deviation of the number of days before payment is received are 9.8 and 3.2, respectively. As an experiment to determine whether enclosing preaddressed envelopes speeds up payment, 150 customers selected at random were sent preaddressed envelopes with their bills. The number of days to payment was recorded and stored in file Xr12-118.

a Do the data provide sufficient evidence at the 10% level of significance to establish that enclosure of preaddressed envelopes improves the average speed of payments?

b Can we conclude at the 10% significance level that the variability in payment speeds decreases when a preaddressed envelope is sent?

12.119 A rock promoter is in the process of deciding whether to book a new band for a rock concert. He knows that this band appeals almost exclusively to teenagers. According to the latest census, there are 400,000 teenagers in the area. The promoter decides to do a survey to try to estimate the proportion of teenagers who will attend the concert. How large a sample should be taken in order to estimate the proportion to within .02 with 99% confidence?

12.120 In Exercise 12.119, suppose that the promoter decided to draw a sample of size 600 (because of financial considerations). Each teenager was asked whether he or she would attend the concert. The answers were stored in file Xr12-120 using the following codes: 2 = Yes, I will attend; 1 = No, I will not attend. Estimate with 95% confidence the number of teenagers who will attend the concert.

12.121 The owner of a downtown parking lot suspects that the person she hired to run the lot is stealing some money. The receipts as provided by the employee indicate that the average number of cars parked in the lot is 125 per day and that, on average, each car is parked for 3.5 hours. In order to determine whether the employee is stealing, the owner watches the lot for 5 days. On those days, the number of cars parked were as follows:

$$120, \quad 130, \quad 124, \quad 127, \quad 128$$

The time spent on the lot for the 629 cars that the owner observed during the 5 days was stored in file Xr12-121. Can the owner conclude at the 1% level of significance that the employee is stealing? (*Hint:* Since there are two ways to steal, two tests should be performed.)

✧ *CASE 12.1*
PEPSI'S EXCLUSIVITY AGREEMENT WITH A UNIVERSITY

In the last few years, colleges and universities have signed exclusivity agreements with a variety of private companies. These agreements bind the university to sell that company's products exclusively on the campus. Many of the agreements involve food and beverage firms.

A large university with a total enrollment of about 50,000 students has offered Pepsi-Cola an exclusivity agreement, which would give Pepsi exclusive rights to sell its products at all university facilities for the next year and an option for future years. In return, the university would receive 35% of the on-campus revenues and an additional lump sum of $200,000 per year. Pepsi has been given 2 weeks to respond.

The management at Pepsi quickly reviews what it knows. The market for soft drinks is measured in terms of the equivalent of 12-ounce cans. Pepsi currently sells an average of 22,000 cans or their equivalents per week (over the 40 weeks of the year that the university operates). The cans sell for an average of $.75 each. The costs including labor amount to $.20 per can. Pepsi is unsure of its market share but suspects it is considerably less than 50%. A quick analysis reveals that if its current market share were 25%, then with an exclusivity agreement Pepsi would sell 88,000 cans per week. Thus, annual sales would be 3,520,000 cans per year (calculated as 88,000 cans per week × 40 weeks). The gross revenue would be computed as follows:

Gross revenue = 3,520,000 cans × $.75 revenue/can = $2,640,000

This figure must be multiplied by 65% because the university would rake in 35% of the gross. Thus,

65% × $2,640,000 = $1,716,000

The total cost of $.20 per can (or $704,000) and the annual payment to the university of $200,000 are subtracted to obtain the net profit:

Net profit = $1,716,000 − $704,000 − $200,000 = $812,000

Pepsi's current annual profit is

Current profit = 40 weeks × 22,000 cans/week × $.55/can = $484,000

If the current market share is 25%, the potential gain from the agreement is

$812,000 − $484,000 = $328,000

The only problem with this analysis is that Pepsi does not know how many soft drinks are sold weekly at the university. In addition, Coke is not likely to supply Pepsi with information about its sales, which together with Pepsi's line of products constitute virtually the entire market.

Pepsi assigned a recent university graduate to survey the university's students to supply the missing information. Accordingly, she organizes a survey that asks 500 students to keep track of the number of soft drinks they purchase on campus over the next 7 days. The responses are stored in file C12-01. Perform a statistical analysis to extract the needed information from the data. Estimate with 95% confidence the parameter that is at the core of the decision problem. Use the estimate to compute estimates of the annual profit. Assume that Coke and Pepsi drinkers would be willing to buy either product in the absence of their first choice.

On the basis of maximizing profits from sales of soft drinks at the university, should Pepsi agree to the exclusivity agreement?

◈ CASE 12.2
PEPSI'S EXCLUSIVITY AGREEMENT WITH A UNIVERSITY: THE COKE SIDE OF THE EQUATION

While the executives of Pepsi-Cola are trying to decide what to do, the university informs them that a similar offer has gone out to the Coca-Cola Company. Furthermore, if both companies want exclusive rights, then a bidding war will take place. The executives at Pepsi would like to know how likely it is that Coke will want

exclusive rights under the conditions outlined by the university.

Perform a similar analysis to the one you did in Case 12.1, but this time from Coke's point of view. Is it likely that Coke will want to conclude an exclusivity agreement with the university? Discuss the reasons for your conclusions.

◈ CASE 12.3
NUMBER OF UNINSURED MOTORISTS*

A number of years ago, the Michigan legislature passed a law requiring insurance for all drivers. Prior to this event, drivers did not have to be covered by insurance. The law was challenged on the grounds that it discriminated against poor people who would not be able legally to drive. At issue at the trial was the number of Michigan motorists who would be coerced by the law into buying insurance. To support the challenge, it was necessary to count the number of uninsured motorists. (These would be the people who would be forced by law to buy insurance.) There were a total of 4,505,665 license plates for passenger vehicles registered in Michigan at the time. An investigation of each one of these to determine whether they had insurance coverage would be prohibitively expensive and time-consuming. It was decided that the state would draw a random

sample of motorists and estimate the number of Michigan's driving population who were uninsured from the sample data. A random sample of 249 license plates was drawn using statistically sound sampling methods. Each was investigated to determine its insurance status. Each license plate sampled was placed in one of three categories. The categories and the codes on the disk are as follows:

1. Insured

2. Not insured

3. Missing

(License plates that were drawn for the sample but where investigators were unable to find the car or its owner were classified as missing.) The data are stored in column 1 of file C12-03.

Your job is to estimate the proportion of all Michigan passenger vehicles that are not insured. Provide two methods for dealing with the missing data. From each method determine the upper and lower limits for the estimated number of motorists who would have been forced by law to buy insurance. Discuss which method is more reasonable.

---

*Adapted from L. Katz, "Presentation of a Confidence Interval Estimate as Evidence in a Legal Proceeding," Department of Statistics, Michigan State University (1974).

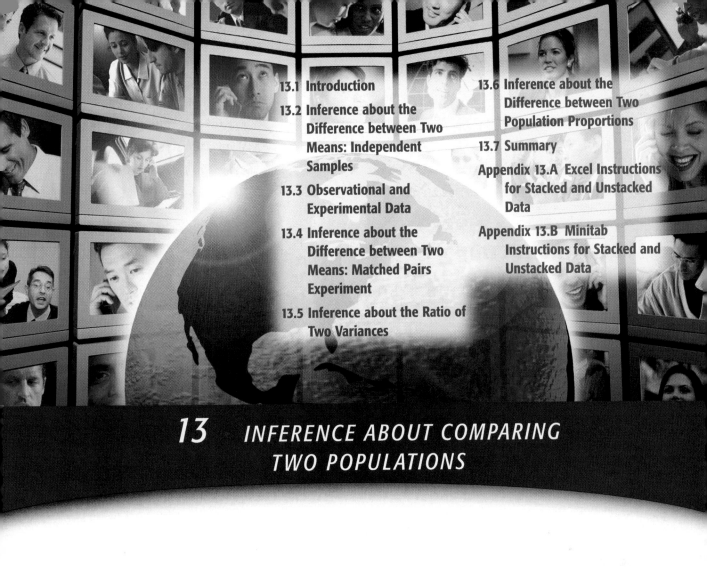

13 INFERENCE ABOUT COMPARING TWO POPULATIONS

ESTIMATING THE COST OF A LIFE SAVED

Two drugs are used to treat heart attack victims. Streptokinase, which has been available since 1959, costs about $460. The second drug is t-PA, a genetically engineered product that sells for about $2,900 per dose. Both streptokinase and t-PA work by opening the arteries and dissolving blood clots, which are the cause of heart attacks. Several previous studies have failed to reveal any differences between the effects of the two drugs. Consequently, in many countries where health care is funded by governments, physicians are required to use the less expensive streptokinase. However, t-PA's maker, Genentech Inc., contended that in the earlier studies showing no difference between the two drugs, t-PA was not used in the right way. Genentech decided to sponsor a more thorough experiment. The experiment was organized in 15 countries, including the United States and Canada, and involved a total of

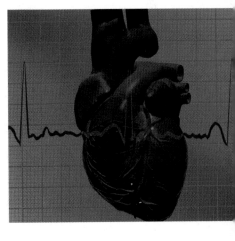

41,000 patients. In this study, t-PA was given to patients in 90 minutes instead of 3 hours as in previous trials. Half of the sample of 41,000 patients was treated by a rapid injection of t-PA with intravenous heparin, while the other half received streptokinase along with heparin. The number of deaths in each sample was recorded. A total of 1,497 patients treated with streptokinase died, while 1,292 patients who received t-PA died. Estimate the cost per life saved by using t-PA instead of streptokinase. The solution is shown on page 441.

13.1 INTRODUCTION

We can compare learning how to employ statistical techniques to learning how to drive a car. We began by describing what you are going to do in this course (Chapter 1), and then presented the essential background material (Chapters 2 through 9). Learning the concepts of statistical inference and applying them the way we did in Chapters 10 and 11 is akin to driving a car in an empty parking lot. You're driving, but it's not a realistic experience. Learning Chapter 12 is like driving on a quiet side street with little traffic. The experience represents real driving, but much of the difficulties have been eliminated. In this chapter, you begin to drive for real, with many of the actual problems faced by licensed drivers, and the experience prepares you to tackle the next difficulty.

In this chapter, we present a variety of techniques whose objective is to compare two populations. In Sections 13.2 and 13.4, we deal with interval variables; the parameter of interest is the difference between two means. The difference between these two sections introduces yet another factor that determines the correct statistical method—the design of the experiment used to gather the data. In Section 13.2, the samples are independently drawn, whereas in Section 13.4, the samples are taken from a matched pairs experiment. In Section 13.3, we discuss the difference between observational and experimental data, a distinction that is critical to the way in which we interpret statistical results.

Section 13.5 presents the procedures employed to infer whether two population variances differ. The parameter is the ratio σ_1^2/σ_2^2. (When comparing two variances, we use the ratio rather than the difference because of the nature of the sampling distribution.)

Section 13.6 addresses the problem of comparing two populations of nominal data. The parameter to be tested and estimated is the difference between two proportions.

13.2 INFERENCE ABOUT THE DIFFERENCE BETWEEN TWO MEANS: INDEPENDENT SAMPLES

In order to test and estimate the difference between two population means, the statistics practitioner draws random samples from each of two populations. In this section, we discuss independent samples. In Section 13.4, where we present the matched pairs experiment, the distinction between independent samples and matched pairs will be made clear. For now, we define independent samples as samples completely unrelated to one another.

Figure 13.1 depicts the sampling process. Observe that we draw a sample of size n_1 from population 1 and a sample of size n_2 from population 2. For each sample, we compute the sample means and sample variances.

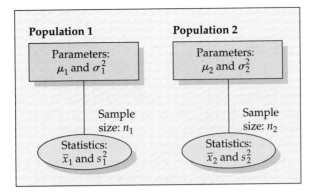

Figure 13.1
Independent samples from two populations

The best estimator of the difference between two population means, $\mu_1 - \mu_2$, is the difference between two sample means, $\bar{x}_1 - \bar{x}_2$. In Section 9.4 we presented the sampling distribution of $\bar{x}_1 - \bar{x}_2$.

SAMPLING DISTRIBUTION OF $\bar{x}_1 - \bar{x}_2$

1. $\bar{x}_1 - \bar{x}_2$ is normally distributed if the populations are normal and approximately normal if the populations are nonnormal and the sample sizes are large.
2. The expected value of $\bar{x}_1 - \bar{x}_2$ is

$$E(\bar{x}_1 - \bar{x}_2) = \mu_1 - \mu_2$$

3. The variance of $\bar{x}_1 - \bar{x}_2$ is

$$V(\bar{x}_1 - \bar{x}_2) = \frac{\sigma_1^2}{n_1} + \frac{\sigma_2^2}{n_2}$$

The standard error of $\bar{x}_1 - \bar{x}_2$ is

$$\sqrt{\frac{\sigma_1^2}{n_1} + \frac{\sigma_2^2}{n_2}}$$

Thus,
$$z = \frac{(\bar{x}_1 - \bar{x}_2) - (\mu_1 - \mu_2)}{\sqrt{\dfrac{\sigma_1^2}{n_1} + \dfrac{\sigma_2^2}{n_2}}}$$

is a standard normal (or approximately normal) random variable. It follows that the test statistic is

$$z = \frac{(\bar{x}_1 - \bar{x}_2) - (\mu_1 - \mu_2)}{\sqrt{\dfrac{\sigma_1^2}{n_1} + \dfrac{\sigma_2^2}{n_2}}}$$

The interval estimator is

$$(\bar{x}_1 - \bar{x}_2) \pm z_{\alpha/2}\sqrt{\frac{\sigma_1^2}{n_1} + \frac{\sigma_2^2}{n_2}}$$

However, these formulas are rarely used because the population variances σ_1^2 and σ_2^2 are virtually always unknown. Consequently, it is necessary to estimate the standard error of the sampling distribution. (We've encountered this problem before; when we derived the confidence interval estimator of a population proportion in Section 12.4, it was necessary to estimate the standard error of $\hat{p}$.) The way to do this depends on whether the two unknown population variances are equal. When they are equal, the test statistic is defined in the following way.

TEST STATISTIC FOR $\mu_1 - \mu_2$ WHEN $\sigma_1^2 = \sigma_2^2$

$$t = \frac{(\bar{x}_1 - \bar{x}_2) - (\mu_1 - \mu_2)}{\sqrt{s_p^2\left(\frac{1}{n_1} + \frac{1}{n_2}\right)}} \qquad \nu = n_1 + n_2 - 2$$

where

$$s_p^2 = \frac{(n_1 - 1)s_1^2 + (n_2 - 1)s_2^2}{n_1 + n_2 - 2}$$

The quantity s_p^2 is called the **pooled variance estimator**. It is the weighted average of the two sample variances. The requirement that the population variances be equal makes this calculation feasible, since we need only one estimate of the common value of σ_1^2 and σ_2^2. It makes sense for us to use the pooled variance estimator because, in combining both samples, we produce a better estimate.

The test statistic is Student t distributed with $n_1 + n_2 - 2$ degrees of freedom, provided that the two populations are normal. The confidence interval estimator is derived by mathematics that by now has become routine.

CONFIDENCE INTERVAL ESTIMATOR OF $\mu_1 - \mu_2$ WHEN $\sigma_1^2 = \sigma_2^2$

$$(\bar{x}_1 - \bar{x}_2) \pm t_{\alpha/2}\sqrt{s_p^2\left(\frac{1}{n_1} + \frac{1}{n_2}\right)} \qquad \nu = n_1 + n_2 - 2$$

We will refer to the above formulas as the **equal-variances test statistic** and **confidence interval estimator**, respectively.

The question naturally arises of "How do we know when the population variances are equal?" The answer is that since σ_1^2 and σ_2^2 are unknown, we can't know for certain whether they're equal. However, we can use the sample variances s_1^2 and s_2^2 to make inferences about the population variances. In Section 13.5, we will present a statistical technique that will allow us to test for the equality of variances. However, for now we will simply examine the sample variances and informally judge their relative values to determine whether we can assume that the population variances are equal.

When the population variances are unequal, we cannot use the pooled variance estimate. Instead, we estimate each population variance with its sample variance. Unfortunately, the sampling distribution of the resulting statistic

$$\frac{(\bar{x}_1 - \bar{x}_2) - (\mu_1 - \mu_2)}{\sqrt{\dfrac{s_1^2}{n_1} + \dfrac{s_2^2}{n_2}}}$$

is neither normally nor Student t distributed. However, it can be approximated by a Student t distribution with degrees of freedom equal to

$$\nu = \frac{(s_1^2/n_1 + s_2^2/n_2)^2}{\left(\dfrac{(s_1^2/n_1)^2}{n_1 - 1} + \dfrac{(s_2^2/n_2)^2}{n_2 - 1}\right)}$$

The test statistic and confidence interval estimator are easily derived from the sampling distribution.

TEST STATISTIC FOR $\mu_1 - \mu_2$ WHEN $\sigma_1^2 \neq \sigma_2^2$

$$t = \frac{(\bar{x}_1 - \bar{x}_2) - (\mu_1 - \mu_2)}{\sqrt{\left(\dfrac{s_1^2}{n_1} + \dfrac{s_2^2}{n_2}\right)}} \qquad \nu = \frac{(s_1^2/n_1 + s_2^2/n_2)^2}{\left(\dfrac{(s_1^2/n_1)^2}{n_1 - 1} + \dfrac{(s_2^2/n_2)^2}{n_2 - 1}\right)}$$

CONFIDENCE INTERVAL ESTIMATOR OF $\mu_1 - \mu_2$ WHEN $\sigma_1^2 \neq \sigma_2^2$

$$(\bar{x}_1 - \bar{x}_2) \pm t_{\alpha/2}\sqrt{\left(\dfrac{s_1^2}{n_1} + \dfrac{s_2^2}{n_2}\right)} \qquad \nu = \frac{(s_1^2/n_1 + s_2^2/n_2)^2}{\left(\dfrac{(s_1^2/n_1)^2}{n_1 - 1} + \dfrac{(s_2^2/n_2)^2}{n_2 - 1}\right)}$$

We will refer to the above formulas as the **unequal-variances test statistic** and **confidence interval estimator**, respectively.

DECISION RULE: EQUAL-VARIANCES OR UNEQUAL-VARIANCES t TESTS AND ESTIMATORS

Statisticians have shown that the number of degrees of freedom associated with the equal-variances test statistic and confidence interval estimator is always greater than or equal to the number of degrees of freedom associated with the unequal-variances test statistic and confidence interval estimator for given sample sizes n_1 and n_2. That is,

$$n_1 + n_2 - 2 \geq \frac{(s_1^2/n_1 + s_2^2/n_2)^2}{\left(\dfrac{(s_1^2/n_1)^2}{n_1 - 1} + \dfrac{(s_2^2/n_2)^2}{n_2 - 1}\right)}$$

(See Exercises 13.25 and 13.26.) Larger numbers of degrees of freedom have the same effect as having larger sample sizes. And we have seen that larger sample sizes yield more information by producing more powerful tests (lower Type II error probabilities) and narrower confidence interval estimators. As a result, we would prefer that population variances be equal when conducting statistical inference about the difference between two means. Accordingly, we adopt the following rule: We will use the equal-variances test statistic and confidence interval estimator unless there is evidence (based on the sample variances) to indicate that the population variances are unequal, in which case we will apply the unequal-variances test statistic and confidence interval estimator.

EXAMPLE 13.1

Despite some controversy, scientists generally agree that high-fiber cereals reduce the likelihood of various forms of cancer. However, one scientist claims that people who eat high-fiber cereal for breakfast will consume, on average, fewer calories for lunch than people who don't eat high-fiber cereal for breakfast. If this is true, high-fiber cereal manufacturers will be able to claim another advantage of eating their product—potential weight reduction for dieters. As a preliminary test of the claim, 150 people were randomly selected and asked what they regularly eat for breakfast and lunch. Each person was identified as either a consumer or a nonconsumer of high-fiber cereal, and the number of calories consumed at lunch was measured and recorded. These data are listed below and stored in columns 1 and 2 of file Xm13-01. Can the scientist conclude at the 5% significance level that his belief is correct?

Calories Consumed at Lunch by Consumers of High-Fiber Cereal

568	646	607	555	530	714	593	647	650
498	636	529	565	566	639	551	580	629
589	739	637	568	687	693	683	532	651
681	539	617	584	694	556	667	467	
540	596	633	607	566	473	649	622	

Calories Consumed at Lunch by Nonconsumers of High-Fiber Cereal

705	754	740	569	593	637	563	421	514	536
819	741	688	547	723	553	733	812	580	833
706	628	539	710	730	620	664	547	624	644
509	537	725	679	701	679	625	643	566	594
613	748	711	674	672	599	655	693	709	596
582	663	607	505	685	566	466	624	518	750
601	526	816	527	800	484	462	549	554	582
608	541	426	679	663	739	603	726	623	788
787	462	773	830	369	717	646	645	747	
573	719	480	602	596	642	588	794	583	
428	754	632	765	758	663	476	490	573	

SOLUTION

IDENTIFY

To assess the claim, the scientist needs to compare the population of consumers of high-fiber cereal to the population of nonconsumers. The data are obviously interval (we've recorded real numbers). This problem objective/data type combination tells us that the parameter to be tested is the difference between two means, $\mu_1 - \mu_2$. The claim to be tested is that the mean caloric intake of consumers (μ_1) is less than that of nonconsumers (μ_2) of high-fiber cereal. Hence the alternative hypothesis is

$$H_1: \quad (\mu_1 - \mu_2) < 0$$

As usual, the null hypothesis automatically follows:

$$H_0: \quad (\mu_1 - \mu_2) = 0$$

To identify the test statistic, the scientist instructs the computer to output the sample variances. They are

$$s_1^2 = 4{,}103 \quad \text{and} \quad s_2^2 = 10{,}670$$

There is reason to believe that the population variances are unequal. Consequently, we use the unequal-variances test statistic.

COMPUTE

 MANUALLY

From the data we calculated the following statistics.

$$\bar{x}_1 = 604.02$$

$$\bar{x}_2 = 633.23$$

$$s_1^2 = 4{,}103$$

$$s_2^2 = 10{,}670$$

The number of degrees of freedom of the test statistic is

$$\nu = \frac{\left(s_1^2/n_1 + s_2^2/n_2\right)^2}{\left(\dfrac{\left(s_1^2/n_1\right)^2}{n_1 - 1} + \dfrac{\left(s_2^2/n_2\right)^2}{n_2 - 1}\right)}$$

$$= \frac{\left(4{,}103/43 + 10{,}670/107\right)^2}{\left(\dfrac{\left(4{,}103/43\right)^2}{43 - 1} + \dfrac{\left(10{,}670/107\right)^2}{107 - 1}\right)}$$

$$= 122.60 \text{ (rounded to 123)}$$

The rejection region is

$$t < -t_{\alpha,\nu} = -t_{.05,123} \approx -1.658$$

We determine that the value of the test statistic is

$$t = \frac{(\bar{x}_1 - \bar{x}_2) - (\mu_1 - \mu_2)}{\sqrt{\left(\dfrac{s_1^2}{n_1} + \dfrac{s_2^2}{n_2}\right)}}$$

$$= \frac{(604.02 - 633.23) - (0)}{\sqrt{\left(\dfrac{4{,}103}{43} + \dfrac{10{,}670}{107}\right)}}$$

$$= -2.09$$

EXCEL

	A	B	C
1	t-Test: Two-Sample Assuming Unequal Variances		
2			
3		Consumers	Nonconsumers
4	Mean	604.02	633.23
5	Variance	4102.98	10669.77
6	Observations	43	107
7	Hypothesized Mean Difference	0	
8	df	123	
9	t Stat	-2.09	
10	P(T<=t) one-tail	0.0193	
11	t Critical one-tail	1.6573	
12	P(T<=t) two-tail	0.0386	
13	t Critical two-tail	1.9794	

COMMANDS

1. Type or import the data into two columns.
2. Click **Tools, Data Analysis...,** and **t-Test: Two-Sample Assuming Unequal Variances.**
3. Specify the **Variable 1 Range.**
4. Specify the **Variable 2 Range.**
5. Type the value of the **Hypothesized Mean Difference.***
6. Click **Labels** (if appropriate).
7. Specify a value for α (**Alpha**) and click **OK.**

COMMANDS FOR
EXAMPLE 13.1
Open file **Xm13-01.**

A1:A44
B1:B108
0

.05

To conduct this test from means and variances or to perform a what-if analysis, activate the **t-Test_2 Means (Uneq-Var)** worksheet in the **Test Statistics** workbook.

---

*This term is technically incorrect. Because we're testing $\mu_1 - \mu_2$, Excel should ask for and output the "Hypothesized Difference between Means." We hope this will be fixed in the next version of Excel.

MINITAB

Two-Sample T-Test and CI: Consumers, Nonconsumers

```
Two-sample T for Consumers vs Nonconsumers

            N      Mean    StDev   SE Mean
Consumer   43     604.0     64.1       9.8
Nonconsu  107      633      103        10

Difference = mu Consumers - mu Nonconsumers
Estimate for difference:  -29.2
95% upper bound for difference: -6.1
T-Test of difference = 0 (vs <): T-Value = -2.09  P-Value = 0.019  DF = 122
```

COMMANDS

1. Type or import the data.
2. **Click Stat, Basic Statistics,** and **2-Sample t....**
3. Use the cursor to select **Samples in one column** (stacked data) or **Samples in different columns** (unstacked data).
(See the discussion on Data Formats on page 405 for a discussion of stacked and unstacked data.)
4. Select the variable names or columns.

5. Indicate that the population variances are not equal (leave the box empty).
6. Click **Options...** and specify the hypothesized difference (**Test Mean**).

7. Specify the **Alternative**. Click **OK**. Click **OK**.

COMMANDS FOR EXAMPLE 13.1
Open file **Xm13-01**.

Samples in different columns

Consumers Nonconsumers or **C1 C2**

0

less than

INTERPRET

The value of the test statistic is –2.09. The one-tail *p*-value is .0193. We observe that the *p*-value of the test is small (and the test statistic falls into the rejection region). As a result, we conclude that there is sufficient evidence to infer that consumers of high-fiber cereal do eat fewer calories at lunch than do nonconsumers. However, there are two reasons to be cautious about concluding that high-fiber cereals constitute an effective contribution to weight loss. First, the data were likely self-reported, which means that each person determined the number of calories recorded that he or she consumed. Such data are often unreliable. Ideally, a less subjective method of counting calories should be used. Second, the way in which the experiment was performed may lead to several interpretations of the data. We will discuss this important issue in the next section.

In addition to testing a value of the difference between two population means, we can also estimate the difference between means. Below we compute the 95% confidence interval estimate of the difference between mean caloric intake for consumers and nonconsumers of high-fiber cereals.

COMPUTE

MANUALLY

The confidence interval estimator of the difference between two means with unequal population variances is

$$(\bar{x}_1 - \bar{x}_2) \pm t_{\alpha/2}\sqrt{\frac{s_1^2}{n_1} + \frac{s_2^2}{n_2}}$$

The 95% confidence interval estimate of the difference between the mean caloric intake of those who eat and those who do not eat high-fiber cereal for breakfast is

$$(\bar{x}_1 - \bar{x}_2) \pm t_{\alpha/2}\sqrt{\frac{s_1^2}{n_1} + \frac{s_2^2}{n_2}} = (604.02 - 633.23) \pm 1.980\sqrt{\frac{4{,}103}{43} + \frac{10{,}670}{107}}$$

$$= -29.21 \pm 27.65$$

The lower and upper limits are −56.86 and −1.56.

EXCEL

	A	B	C	D	E	F
1	t-Estimate of the Difference Between Two Means (Unequal-Variances)					
2						
3		Sample 1	Sample 2	Confidence Interval Estimate		
4	Mean	604.02	633.2	-29.21	±	27.65
5	Variance	4102	10671	Lower confidence limit		-56.86
6	Sample size	43	107	Upper confidence limit		-1.56
7	Degrees of freedom	122.62				
8	Confidence level	0.95				

COMMANDS

The Excel output does not include the interval estimator. However, you can use the **t-Estimate_2 Means** (**Uneq-Var**) worksheet in the **Estimators** workbook. Simply plug in the values of the sample means, sample variances, and sample sizes, as well as the confidence level. If you've already tested the means, simply copy and paste the six cells containing the statistics you need (use **Copy, Paste Special,** and **Values**).

MINITAB

Two-Sample T-Test and CI: Consumers, Nonconsumers

```
Two-sample T for Consumers vs Nonconsumers

              N      Mean     StDev    SE Mean
Consumer     43     604.0      64.1        9.8
Nonconsu    107       633       103         10

Difference = mu Consumers - mu Nonconsumers
Estimate for difference:   -29.2
95% CI for difference: (-56.9, -1.6)
T-Test of difference = 0 (vs not =): T-Value = -2.09   P-Value = 0.039
```

COMMANDS

To produce a confidence interval estimate, follow the instructions for the test, but specify the **Confidence level** and **not equal** for the **Alternative**. Minitab will conduct a two-tail test and produce the confidence interval estimate.

INTERPRET

We estimate that nonconsumers of high-fiber cereal eat on average between 1.56 and 56.86 calories more than do consumers.

APPLICATIONS IN OPERATIONS MANAGEMENT: *PRODUCTION DESIGN*

In Chapter 1 we discussed production design wherein an operations manager determines how a product is to be manufactured. The objective is to produce the highest-quality product at a reasonable cost. This objective is achieved by choosing the machines, materials, methods, and "manpower" (personnel), the so-called 4 M's. The manager can often employ statistical tools to help make this decision. Various experiments can be conducted to determine the lowest cost or fastest production schedule. The experiments use different materials, machines, methods, or personnel. There are several ways to judge differences in processes. The manager can determine whether differences in quality exist, or differences in cost. If no differences exist, the manager may decide on the basis of some other criterion, such as the process that requires the least new training of workers.

EXAMPLE 13.2

The plant manager of a company that manufactures office equipment is attempting to determine the process that will be used to assemble a new ergonomic chair. The material, machines, and workforce have already been decided. However, there are two methods under consideration. The methods differ by the order in which the separate operations are performed. To help decide which should be used, an experiment was performed. Twenty-five randomly selected workers each assembled the chair using method A, and 25 workers each assembled the chair using method B. The assembly times in minutes were recorded and are exhibited below and stored in file Xm13-02. The plant manager would like to know whether the assembly times of the two methods differ. A 5% significance level is judged to be appropriate.

Assembly Times for Method A

6.8	5.0	7.9	5.2	7.6	5.0	5.9	5.2	6.5	7.4	6.1	6.2	7.1
4.6	6.0	7.1	6.1	5.0	6.3	7.0	6.4	6.1	6.6	7.7	6.4	

Assembly Times for Method B

5.2	6.7	5.7	6.6	8.5	6.5	5.9	6.7	6.6	4.2	4.2	4.5	5.3
7.9	7.0	5.9	7.1	5.8	7.0	5.7	5.9	4.9	5.3	4.2	7.1	

SOLUTION

IDENTIFY

The data are interval, and the objective of the experiment is to compare the two populations of assembly times. The parameter of interest is the difference between two population means, $\mu_1 - \mu_2$. The plant manager wants to determine whether a difference between the two methods exists. As a result, the alternative hypothesis is

$$H_1: \quad (\mu_1 - \mu_2) \neq 0$$

and the null hypothesis is

$$H_0: \quad (\mu_1 - \mu_2) = 0$$

To identify the correct test statistic, we need to calculate the sample variances. They are

$$s_1^2 = .848 \quad \text{and} \quad s_2^2 = 1.303$$

Because the sample variances are similar, we will assume that the population variances are equal and use the equal-variances test statistic.

COMPUTE

 MANUALLY

From the data we calculated the following statistics:

$$\bar{x}_1 = 6.288$$

$$\bar{x}_2 = 6.016$$

$$s_1^2 = .848$$

$$s_2^2 = 1.303$$

$$s_p^2 = \frac{(n_1 - 1)s_1^2 + (n_2 - 1)s_2^2}{n_1 + n_2 - 2}$$

$$= \frac{(25 - 1)(.848) + (25 - 1)(1.303)}{25 + 25 - 2}$$

$$= 1.076$$

The number of degrees of freedom of the test statistic is

$$\nu = n_1 + n_2 - 2 = 25 + 25 - 2 = 48$$

The rejection region is

$$t < -t_{\alpha/2,\nu} = -t_{.025,48} \approx -2.009 \quad \text{or} \quad t > t_{\alpha/2,\nu} = t_{.025,48} \approx 2.009$$

The value of the test statistic is computed next.

$$t = \frac{(\bar{x}_1 - \bar{x}_2) - (\mu_1 - \mu_2)}{\sqrt{s_p^2 \left(\dfrac{1}{n_1} + \dfrac{1}{n_2} \right)}}$$

$$= \frac{(6.288 - 6.016)}{\sqrt{1.076 \left(\dfrac{1}{25} + \dfrac{1}{25} \right)}}$$

$$= .93$$

EXCEL

	A	B	C
1	t-Test: Two-Sample Assuming Equal Variances		
2			
3		Method A	Method B
4	Mean	6.288	6.016
5	Variance	0.8478	1.3031
6	Observations	25	25
7	Pooled Variance	1.0754	
8	Hypothesized Mean Difference	0	
9	df	48	
10	t Stat	0.93	
11	P(T<=t) one-tail	0.1792	
12	t Critical one-tail	1.6772	
13	P(T<=t) two-tail	0.3584	
14	t Critical two-tail	2.0106	

COMMANDS

Follow the instructions for Example 13.1 except at step 2 click **Tools, Data Analysis...,** and **t-Test: Two-Sample Assuming Equal Variances.**

Use the **t-Test_2 Means (Eq-Var)** worksheet in the **Test Statistics** workbook to complete this test from the sample statistics and to perform a what-if analysis.

MINITAB

Two-Sample T-Test and CI: Method A, Method B

```
Two-sample T for Method A vs Method B

            N    Mean    StDev   SE Mean
Method A   25    6.288   0.921    0.18
Method B   25    6.02    1.14     0.23


Difference = mu Method A - mu Method B
Estimate for difference:  0.272
95% CI for difference: (-0.318, 0.862)
T-Test of difference = 0 (vs not =): T-Value = 0.93   P-Value = 0.358   DF = 48
Both use Pooled StDev = 1.04
```

COMMANDS

Follow the instructions for Example 13.1 except at step 5 indicate that the population variances are equal.

INTERPRET

The t statistic is .93 and its p-value is .3584. Accordingly, we conclude that there is little evidence to infer that the mean times differ. Once again, the manager should determine that all of the required conditions are satisfied (see the following subsection) and that there are no other factors that need to be considered. For example, is the quality of the finished product identical using the two designs? Is it possible that one method is better than another, but this experiment failed to demonstrate it because it takes longer to adapt to the new production design than this experiment allowed? If the conclusion stands, however, the manager should choose the method using some other criterion, such as worker preference.

We can also draw inferences about the difference between the two population means by calculating the confidence interval estimator. We use the equal-variances confidence interval estimator of $\mu_1 - \mu_2$ and a 95% confidence level.

COMPUTE

MANUALLY

From the calculation of the test statistic above we found

$$\bar{x}_1 = 6.288$$

$$\bar{x}_2 = 6.016$$

$$s_p^2 = 1.076$$

The number of degrees of freedom of the test statistic is

$$\nu = n_1 + n_2 - 2 = 25 + 25 - 2 = 48$$

and

$$t_{\alpha/2,\nu} = t_{.025,48} \approx 2.009$$

The 95% confidence interval estimate is

$$(\bar{x}_1 - \bar{x}_2) \pm t_{\alpha/2}\sqrt{s_p^2\left(\frac{1}{n_1} + \frac{1}{n_2}\right)}$$

$$= (6.288 - 6.016) \pm 2.009\sqrt{1.076\left(\frac{1}{25} + \frac{1}{25}\right)}$$

$$= .272 \pm .589$$

$$\text{LCL} = -.317 \quad \text{and} \quad \text{UCL} = .861$$

EXCEL

	A	B	C	D	E	F
1	t-Estimate of the Difference Between Two Means (Equal-Variances)					
2						
3		Sample 1	Sample 2	Confidence Interval Estimate		
4	Mean	6.288	6.0160	0.2720	±	0.5897
5	Variance	0.8478	1.3031	Lower confidence limit		-0.3177
6	Sample size	25	25	Upper confidence limit		0.8617
7	Pooled Variance	1.075				
8	Confidence level	0.95				

COMMANDS

To estimate the difference between two means with equal population variances, activate the **t-Estimate_2 Means (Eq-Var)** worksheet in the **Estimators** workbook and substitute the sample statistics and confidence level.

MINITAB

Minitab prints the confidence interval estimate as part of the output of the test statistic. However, you must specify the **Alternative** hypothesis as **not equal** to produce a two-sided interval.

INTERPRET

We estimate that the difference in mean assembly times between method A and method B lies between −.318 and .862 minute.

CHECKING THE REQUIRED CONDITION

Both the equal-variances and unequal-variances techniques require that the populations be normally distributed. As before, we can check to see whether the requirement is satisfied by drawing the histograms of the data. To illustrate, we used Excel (Minitab histograms are almost identical) to create the histograms for Examples 13.1 (Figures 13.2 and 13.3) and 13.2 (Figures 13.4 and 13.5). Although the histograms are not perfectly bell shaped, it appears that in both examples the data are at least approximately normal. Because this technique is robust, we can be confident in the validity of the results.

Figure 13.2

Figure 13.3

Figure 13.4

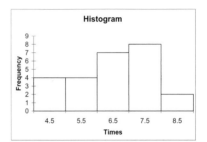

Figure 13.5

VIOLATION OF THE REQUIRED CONDITION

When the normality requirement is unsatisfied, we can use a nonparametric technique—the Wilcoxon rank sum test for independent samples (Chapter 17)—to replace the equal-variances test of $\mu_1 - \mu_2$. We have no alternative to the unequal-variances test of $\mu_1 - \mu_2$ when the populations are very nonnormal.

DATA FORMATS

There are two formats for storing the data when drawing inferences about the difference between two means. The first, which you have seen demonstrated in both Examples 13.1 and 13.2, is called **unstacked**, wherein the observations from sample 1 are stored in one column and the observations from sample 2 are stored in a second column. We may also store the data in **stacked** format. In this format all the observations are stored in one column. A second column contains the codes, usually 1 and 2, that indicate from which sample the corresponding observation was drawn. Here is an example of unstacked data.

Column 1 (Sample 1)	Column 2 (Sample 2)
12	18
19	23
13	25

Here are the same data in stacked form.

Column 1	Column 2
12	1
19	1
13	1
18	2
23	2
25	2

It should be understood that the data need not be in order. Hence, they could have been stored in this way.

Column 1	Column 2
18	2
25	2
13	1
12	1
23	2
19	1

If there are two populations to compare and only one variable, it is probably better to record the data in unstacked form. However, it is frequently the case that we want to observe several variables and compare them. For example, suppose that we survey male and female MBAs and ask each to report his or her age, income, and number of years of experience. These data are usually stored in stacked form using the following format.

Column 1: Code identifying female (1) and male (2)

Column 2: Age

Column 3: Income

Column 4: Years of experience

To compare ages, we would use columns 1 and 2. Columns 1 and 3 are used to compare incomes, and columns 1 and 4 are used to compare experience levels.

Most statistical software requires one format or the other. Excel demands that the data be unstacked. Some of Minitab's procedures allow either format, whereas others specify only one. Fortunately, both of our software packages allow the statistics practitioner to alter the format. (See Appendixes 13.A and 13.B for details.) We say "fortunately" because this allowed us to store the data in either form on the data disk provided with this book. In fact, we've used both forms to allow you to practice your ability to manipulate the data as necessary. You will need this ability to perform statistical techniques in this and other chapters in this book.

DEVELOPING AN UNDERSTANDING OF STATISTICAL CONCEPTS 1

The formulas in this section are relatively complicated. However, conceptually both test statistics are based on the techniques we introduced in Chapter 11 and repeated in Chapter 12. That is, the value of the test statistic is the difference between the statistic $\bar{x}_1 - \bar{x}_2$ and the hypothesized value of the parameter $\mu_1 - \mu_2$ measured in terms of the standard error.

DEVELOPING AN UNDERSTANDING OF STATISTICAL CONCEPTS 2

As was the case with the interval estimator of p, the standard error must be estimated from the data for all inferential procedures introduced here. The method we use to compute the standard error of $\bar{x}_1 - \bar{x}_2$ depends on whether the population variances are equal. When they are equal, we calculate and use the pooled variance estimator s_p^2. An important principle is being applied here and will be again in this chapter (Section 13.6) and in later chapters. The principle can be loosely stated as follows: Where possible, it is advantageous to pool sample data to estimate the standard error. In the application above, we are able to pool because we assume that the two samples were drawn from populations with a common variance. Combining both samples increases the accuracy of the estimate. Thus, s_p^2 is a better estimator of the common variance than either s_1^2 or s_2^2 separately. When the two population variances are unequal, we cannot pool the data and produce a common estimator. We must compute s_1^2 and s_2^2 and use them to estimate σ_1^2 and σ_2^2, respectively.

Here is a summary of how we recognize the techniques presented in this section.

FACTORS THAT IDENTIFY THE EQUAL-VARIANCES t TEST AND ESTIMATOR OF $\mu_1 - \mu_2$

1. **Problem objective:** Compare two populations.
2. **Data type:** Interval
3. **Descriptive measurement:** Central location
4. **Experimental design:** Independent samples
5. **Population variances:** Equal

FACTORS THAT IDENTIFY THE UNEQUAL-VARIANCES t TEST AND ESTIMATOR OF $\mu_1 - \mu_2$

1. **Problem objective:** Compare two populations.
2. **Data type:** Interval
3. **Descriptive measurement:** Central location
4. **Experimental design:** Independent samples
5. **Population variances:** Unequal

EXERCISES

Developing an Understanding of Statistical Concepts

*Exercises 13.1 to 13.26 are "what-if analyses" designed to determine what happens to the test statistics and interval estimates when elements of the statistical inference change. These problems can be solved manually or using Excel's **Test Statistics** or **Estimators** workbooks.*

Exercises 13.1 to 13.5 are based on the following problem.

In random samples of 25 from each of two normal populations, we found the following statistics.

$$\bar{x}_1 = 524 \qquad s_1 = 129$$

$$\bar{x}_2 = 469 \qquad s_2 = 141$$

13.1 Estimate the difference between the two population means with 95% confidence.

13.2 Repeat Exercise 13.1, increasing the standard deviations to $s_1 = 255$ and $s_2 = 307$.

13.3 Review Exercises 13.1 and 13.2. Describe what happens when the sample standard deviations get larger.

13.4 Repeat Exercise 13.1 with samples of size 100.

13.5 Review Exercises 13.1 and 13.4. Discuss the effects of increasing the sample size.

Exercises 13.6 to 13.12 are based on the following problem.

In random samples of 12 from each of two normal populations, we found the following statistics.

$$\bar{x}_1 = 74 \qquad s_1 = 18$$

$$\bar{x}_2 = 71 \qquad s_2 = 15$$

13.6 Test with $\alpha = .05$ to determine whether we can infer that the population means differ.

13.7 Repeat Exercise 13.6, increasing the standard deviations to $s_1 = 210$ and $s_2 = 198$.

13.8 Review Exercises 13.6 and 13.7. Describe what happens when the sample standard deviations get larger.

13.9 Repeat Exercise 13.6 with samples of size 150.

13.10 Review Exercises 13.6 and 13.9. Discuss the effects of increasing the sample size.

13.11 Repeat Exercise 13.6, changing the mean of sample 1 to $\bar{x}_1 = 76$.

13.12 Review Exercises 13.6 and 13.11. Discuss the effect of increasing $\bar{x}_1$.

Exercises 13.13 to 13.17 are based on the following problem.

Random sampling from two normal populations produced the following results.

$$\bar{x}_1 = 63 \qquad s_1 = 18 \qquad n_1 = 50$$

$$\bar{x}_2 = 60 \qquad s_2 = 7 \qquad n_2 = 45$$

13.13 Estimate with 90% confidence the difference between the two population means.

13.14 Repeat Exercise 13.13, changing the sample standard deviations to 41 and 15, respectively.

13.15 Review Exercises 13.13 and 13.14. What happens when the sample standard deviations increase?

13.16 Repeat Exercise 13.13, doubling the sample sizes.

13.17 Review Exercises 13.11 and 13.16. Describe the effects of increasing the sample sizes.

Exercises 13.18 to 13.24 are based on the following problem.

Random sampling from two normal populations produced the following results.

$$\bar{x}_1 = 412 \qquad s_1 = 128 \qquad n_1 = 150$$

$$\bar{x}_2 = 405 \qquad s_2 = 54 \qquad n_2 = 150$$

13.18 Can we infer at the 5% significance level that μ_1 is greater than μ_2?

13.19 Repeat Exercise 13.18, decreasing the standard deviations to $s_1 = 31$ and $s_2 = 26$.

13.20 Review Exercises 13.18 and 13.19. Describe what happens when the sample standard deviations get smaller.

13.21 Repeat Exercise 13.18 with samples of size 20.

13.22 Review Exercises 13.18 and 13.21. Discuss the effects of decreasing the sample size.

13.23 Repeat Exercise 13.18, changing the mean of sample 1 to $\bar{x}_1 = 409$.

13.24 Review Exercises 13.18 and 13.23. Discuss the effect of decreasing $\bar{x}_1$.

13.25 For each of the following, determine the number of degrees of freedom assuming equal population variances and unequal population variances.

    a $n_1 = 15, \quad n_2 = 15, \quad s_1^2 = 25, \quad s_2^2 = 15$
    b $n_1 = 10, \quad n_2 = 16, \quad s_1^2 = 100, \quad s_2^2 = 15$
    c $n_1 = 50, \quad n_2 = 50, \quad s_1^2 = 8, \quad s_2^2 = 14$
    d $n_1 = 60, \quad n_2 = 45, \quad s_1^2 = 75, \quad s_2^2 = 10$

13.26 Refer to Exercise 13.25.

    a Confirm that in each case the number of degrees of freedom for the equal-variances test statistic and confidence interval estimator is larger than that for the unequal-variances test statistic and confidence interval estimator.

    b Try various combinations of sample sizes and sample variances to illustrate that the number of degrees of freedom for the equal-variances test statistic and confidence interval estimator is larger than that for the unequal-variances test statistic and confidence interval estimator.

13.27 Samples of size 8 were drawn independently from two normal populations. These data are listed below and stored in file Xr13-27. Test to determine whether the means of the two populations differ. (Use $\alpha = .05$.)
Sample 1: 7, 4, 6, 3, 7, 5, 8, 7
Sample 2: 6, 4, 5, 3, 6, 5, 7, 5

13.28 Samples of size 6 were drawn independently from two normal populations. These data are listed below and stored in file Xr13-28. Test to determine whether the means of the two populations differ. (Use $\alpha = .05$.)
Sample 1: 12, 6, 5, 8, 11, 5
Sample 2: 7, 11, 13, 5, 8, 7

*The following exercises require the use of a computer and software. The answers may be calculated manually. See Appendix A for the sample statistics. **Use a 5% significance level unless specified otherwise.***

13.29 The data obtained from sampling from two populations are stored in file Xr13-29. (*Caution:* Missing data)

    a Conduct a test to determine whether the population means differ.

    b Estimate the difference in population means with 95% confidence.

    c What is the required condition(s) of the techniques employed in parts **a** and **b**?

    d Is the required condition(s) satisfied?

13.30 Random samples were drawn from each of two populations. The data are stored in stacked format in file Xr13-30.

    a Is there sufficient evidence at the 10% significance level to infer that the mean of population 1 is greater than the mean of population 2?

    b Estimate with 90% confidence the difference between the two population means.

    c What is the required condition(s) of the techniques employed in parts **a** and **b**?

    d Is the required condition(s) satisfied?

13.31 Samples of 40 observations were taken from each of two populations. The data are stored in columns 1 (all observations) and 2 (code specifying the sample) in file Xr13-31. Do these data provide sufficient evidence at the 1% significance level to infer that the mean of population 2 is less than the mean of population 1?

13.32 A statistics practitioner gathered data from two populations and stored them in columns 1 (sample 1) and 2 (sample 2) in file Xr13-32. Can the statistics practitioner infer at the 10% significance level that the mean of population 1 is less than the mean of population 2?

Applications

13.33 The president of Tastee Inc., a baby-food producer, claims that her company's product is superior to that of her leading competitor, because babies gain weight faster with her product. (This is a good thing for babies.) To test the claim, a survey was undertaken. Mothers of newborn babies were asked which baby food they intended to feed their babies. Those who responded Tastee or the leading competitor were asked to keep track of their babies' weight gains over the next 2 months. There were 15 mothers who indicated that they would feed their babies Tastee and 25 who responded that they would feed their babies the product of the leading competitor. Each baby's weight gain (in ounces) was recorded and stored in file Xr13-33.

   a Can we conclude, using weight gain as our criterion, that Tastee baby food is indeed superior?

   b Estimate with 95% confidence the difference between the mean weight gains of the two products.

   c Check to ensure that the required condition(s) is satisfied.

13.34 Medical experts advocate the use of vitamin and mineral supplements to help fight infections. A study undertaken by Dr. Ranjit Schneider of Memorial University (reported in the British journal *Lancet*, November 1992) recruited 96 men and women age 65 and older. One half of them received daily supplements of vitamins and minerals, while the other half received placebos. The supplements contained the daily recommended amounts of 18 vitamins and minerals, including vitamins B-6, B-12, C, and D, thiamine, riboflavin, niacin, calcium, copper, iodine, iron, selenium, magnesium, and zinc. The doses of vitamins A and E were slightly less than the daily requirements. The supplements included four times the amount of beta-carotene that the average person ingests daily. The number of days of illness from infections (ranging from colds to pneumonia) was recorded for each person. The data are stored in stacked format in file Xr13-34 (code 1 = Supplements and code 2 = Placebo). Can we infer that taking vitamin and mineral supplements daily increases the body's immune system?

13.35 In assessing the value of radio advertisements, sponsors consider not only the total number of listeners, but also their ages. The 18-to-34 age group is considered to spend the most money. To examine the issue, the manager of an FM station commissioned a survey. One objective was to measure the difference in listening habits between the 18-to-34 and 35-to-50 age groups. The survey asked 250 people in each age category how much time they spent listening to FM radio per day. The results (in minutes) were recorded and stored in file Xr13-35 (column 1 = Listening times; column 2 identifies the age group: 1 = 18-to-34 and 2 = 35-to-50).

   a Can we conclude that a difference exists between the two groups?

   b Estimate with 95% confidence the difference in mean time listening to FM radio between the two age groups.

   c Are the required conditions satisfied for the techniques you used in parts **a** and **b**?

13.36 Is the number of visits to a health care professional growing in the United States? To help answer this question, a health insurance researcher studied the results of surveys conducted by the U.S. National Center for Health Statistics. The numbers of visits in 1997 and 1998 are recorded in file Xr13-36. Can we infer that the answer to the question is yes when comparing 1997 and 1998 figures? (Adapted from the U.S. National Center for Health Statistics, United States, 2000)

13.37 Automobile insurance companies take many factors into consideration when setting rates. These factors include age, marital status, and miles driven per year. In order to determine the effect of gender, a random sample of male and female drivers was surveyed. Each was asked how many miles he or she drove in the past year. The distances (in thousands of miles) are stored in stacked format (code 1 = Male and code 2 = Female) in file Xr13-37.

   a Can we conclude that male and female drivers differ in the numbers of miles driven per year?

   b Estimate with 95% confidence the difference in mean distance driven by male and female drivers.

   c Check to ensure that the required condition(s) of the techniques used in parts **a** and **b** is satisfied.

13.38 The president of a company that manufactures automobile air conditioners is considering switching his supplier of condensers. Supplier A, the current producer of condensers for the manufacturer, prices its product 5% higher than supplier B does. Since the president wants to maintain his company's reputation for quality he wants to be sure that supplier B's condensers last at least as long as supplier A's. After a careful analysis, the president decided to retain supplier A if there is sufficient statistical evidence that supplier A's condensers last longer on the average than supplier B's condensers. In an experiment, 30 midsize cars were equipped with air conditioners using type A condensers while another 30 midsize cars were equipped with type B condensers. The number of miles (in thousands) driven by each car before the condenser broke down was recorded, and the data stored in unstacked format in file Xr13-38. Should the president retain supplier A? (*Caution:* Missing data)

13.39 High blood pressure (hypertension) is a leading cause of strokes. Medical researchers are constantly seeking ways to treat patients suffering from this condition. A specialist in hypertension claims that regular aerobic exercise can reduce high blood pressure just as successfully as drugs, with none of the adverse side effects. To test the claim, 50 patients who suffer from high blood pressure were chosen to participate in an experiment. For 60 days, half the sample exercised three times per week for 1 hour; the other half took the standard medication. The percentage reduction in blood pressure was recorded for each individual, and the resulting data are stored (column 1 = Exercise and column 2 = Drug) in file Xr13-39.

a Can we conclude at the 1% significance level that exercise is more effective than medication in reducing hypertension?

b Estimate with 95% confidence the difference in mean percentage reduction in blood pressure between drugs and exercise programs.

c Check to ensure that the required condition(s) of the techniques used in parts **a** and **b** is satisfied.

13.40 A statistics professor is about to select a statistical software package for her course. One of the most important features, according to the professor, is the ease with which students learn to use the software. She has narrowed the selection to two possibilities: software A, a menu-driven statistical package with some high-powered techniques, and software B, a spreadsheet that has the capability of performing most techniques. She asks 40 statistics students selected at random to choose one of the two packages. She gives each student a statistics problem to solve by computer and the appropriate manual. The amount of time (in minutes) each student needs to complete the assignment was recorded and stored (column 1 = package A and column 2 = package B) in file Xr13-40. (*Caution:* Missing data)

a Can the professor conclude from these data that the two software packages differ in the amount of time needed to learn how to use them? (Use a 1% significance level.)

b Estimate with 95% confidence the difference in the mean amount of time needed to learn to use the two packages.

c What are the required conditions for the techniques used in parts **a** and **b**?

d Check to see whether the required conditions are satisfied.

13.41 One factor in low productivity is the amount of time wasted by workers. Wasted time includes time spent cleaning up mistakes, waiting for more material and equipment, and performing any other activity not related to production. In a project designed to examine the problem, an operations management consultant took a survey of 200 workers in companies that were classified as successful (on the basis of their latest annual profits) and another 200 workers from unsuccessful companies. The amount of time (in hours) wasted during a standard 40-hour workweek was recorded for each worker. These data are stored in columns 1 (successful companies) and 2 (unsuccessful companies) in file Xr13-41.

a Do these data provide enough evidence at the 1% significance level to infer that the amount of time wasted in unsuccessful firms exceeds that of successful ones?

b Estimate with 95% confidence how much more time is wasted in unsuccessful firms than in successful ones.

13.42 Recent studies seem to indicate that using a cell phone while driving is dangerous. One reason for this is that a driver's reaction times may slow while he or she is talking on the phone. Researchers at the Miami (Ohio) University measured the reaction times of a sample of drivers who owned a car phone. Half the sample was tested while on the phone and the other half was not on the phone. The reaction times are stored in file Xr13-42. Can we conclude that reaction times are slower for drivers using cell phones?

13.43 Refer to Exercise 13.42. To determine whether the type of phone usage affects reaction times, another study was launched. A group of drivers was asked to participate in a discussion. Half the group engaged in simple chitchat and the other half participated in a political discussion. Once again, reaction times were measured and stored in file Xr13-43. Can we infer that the type of telephone discussion affects reaction times?

13.44 Most consumers who require someone to perform various professional services undertake research before making their selection. A random sample of people who recently selected a financial planner and a random sample of individuals who chose a stockbroker were asked to report the amount of time they spent researching before deciding. (*Source:* Yankelovich Partners) The responses are stored in file Xr13-44. Can we infer that people spend more time researching for a financial planner than they do for a stockbroker?

13.45 A recent study by researchers at North Carolina State University found thousands of errors in 12 of the most widely used middle school science texts. For example, the Statue of Liberty is left-handed; volume is equal to length multiplied by depth. (*Time Magazine*, February 12, 2001) The books are so bad that Philip Sadler, director of science education at the Harvard-Smithsonian Center for Astrophysics, decided to conduct a study of their effects. He recorded the college physics marks of students who had used a textbook in high school and the marks of students who did not have a high school textbook. These data are stored in file Xr13-45. Do these data allow us to infer that students without high school textbooks in science outperform students who used textbooks?

13.46 Between Wendy's and McDonald's, which fast-food drive-through window is faster? To answer the question, a random sample of service times (in seconds) for each restaurant was measured and stored in file Xr13-46. (*Source: 2000 QSR Drive-Thru Time Study*) Can we infer from these data that there are differences in service times between the two chains?

13.47 The American Medical Association tracks the amount of time physicians devote to patient care per week. An insurance executive wanted to determine whether different specialties differ in the amounts of time. She acquired the results of the survey in 1997 (the most recent year available). She recorded the amount of time for physicians who are in general/family practice and those whose specialty is pediatrics. These data are stored in file Xr13-47. Can we infer that the two types of physicians differ in the time devoted to patient care per week? (Adapted from the American Medical Association, *Socioeconomic Characteristics of Medical Practice* 1997/1998 and the *Statistical Abstract of the United States,* 2000, Table 190)

13.48 It is often useful for companies to know who their customers are and how they became customers. In a study of credit card use, a random sample of cardholders who applied for the credit card and a random sample of credit cardholders who were contacted by telemarketers were drawn. The total purchases made by each last month were recorded and stored in file Xr13-48. Can we conclude from these data that differences exist between the two types of customers?

13.49 Tire manufacturers are constantly researching ways to produce tires that last longer. New innovations are tested by professional drivers on racetracks. However, any promising inventions are also test-driven by ordinary drivers. The latter tests are closer to what the tire company's customers will actually experience. Suppose that to determine whether a new steel-belted radial tire lasts longer than the company's current model, two new-design tires were installed on the rear wheels of 20 randomly selected cars and two existing-design tires were installed on the rear wheels of another 20 cars. All drivers were told to drive in their usual way until the tires wore out. The number of miles (in 1,000s) driven by each driver was recorded and stored in file Xr13-49. Can the company infer that the new tire will last longer than the existing tire?

13.50 Slow play of golfers is a serious problem for golf clubs. Slow play results in fewer rounds of golf and less profits for public course owners. To examine this problem, a random sample of British and American golf courses was selected. The amount of time taken (in minutes) was recorded for random samples of British and American golfers. These data are stored in file Xr13-50. Can we conclude that British golfers play golf in less time than do American golfers? (*Source: Golf Magazine,* July 2001)

13.51 In an effort to explain the results of Exercise 13.50, a researcher recorded the distances (in yards) for a random sample of British and American courses. These data are stored in file Xr13-51. Can we infer that British courses are shorter than American courses?

13.52 In another effort to analyze the results of Exercise 13.50, the researcher recorded the total travel length of the course. This variable measures the total distance golfers must walk to play a round of golf. It is the sum of the golf course playing distance plus the distance golfers must walk from the green to the next tee. These data are stored in file Xr13-52. What can you conclude from these data?

13.3 OBSERVATIONAL AND EXPERIMENTAL DATA

As we've pointed out several times, the ability to properly interpret the results of a statistical technique is a crucial skill for students to develop. This ability is dependent on your understanding of Type I and Type II errors and the fundamental concepts that are part of statistical inference. However, there is another component that needs to be understood: the difference between **observational data** and **experimental data**. To explain this difference, we will reexamine Examples 13.1 and 13.2 and analyze the way the data were obtained in each example.

In Example 13.1, we randomly selected 150 people and on the basis of their responses, assigned them to one of two groups: high-fiber consumers and nonconsumers. We then recorded the number of calories consumed at lunch for the members of each group. Such data are called *observational.* Now examine Example 13.2, where the data were gathered by randomly assigning 25 workers to assemble chairs using method A and 25 workers to assemble chairs using method B. Data produced in this manner are said to be *experimental* or *controlled*. The statistical technique to be applied is not affected by whether the data are observational or experimental. However, the interpretation of the results may be affected.

In Example 13.1, we found that there was evidence to infer that people who eat high-fiber cereal for breakfast consume fewer calories at lunch than do nonconsumers of high-fiber cereal. From this result, we're inclined to believe that eating a high-fiber cereal at breakfast may be a way to reduce weight. However, other interpretations are possible. For example, people who eat fewer calories are probably more health conscious, and such people are more likely to eat high-fiber cereal as part of a healthy breakfast. In this interpretation, high-fiber cereals do not necessarily lead to fewer calories at lunch. Instead, another factor, general health consciousness, leads to both fewer calories at lunch and high-fiber cereal for breakfast. Notice that the conclusion of the statistical procedure is unchanged. On average, people who eat high-fiber cereal consume fewer calories at lunch. However, because of the way the data were gathered, we have more difficulty interpreting this result.

Suppose that we redo Example 13.1 using the experimental approach. We randomly select 150 people to participate in the experiment. We randomly assign 75 to eat high-fiber cereal for breakfast and the other 75 to eat something else. We then record the number of calories each person consumes at lunch. Ideally, in this experiment both groups will be similar in all other dimensions, including health consciousness. (Larger sample sizes increase the likelihood that the two groups will be similar.) If the statistical result is about the same as in Example 13.1, we may have some valid reason to believe that high-fiber cereal at breakfast leads to a decrease in caloric intake at lunch.

Experimental data are usually more expensive to obtain because of the planning required to set up the experiment; observational data usually require less work to gather. Furthermore, in many situations it is impossible to conduct a controlled experiment. For example, suppose that we want to determine whether an undergraduate degree in engineering better prepares students for an MBA than does an arts degree. In a controlled experiment, we would randomly assign some students to achieve a degree in engineering and other students to obtain an arts degree. We would then make them sign up for an MBA program, where we would record their grades. Unfortunately for statistical despots (and fortunately for the rest of us), we live in a democratic society, which makes the coercion necessary to perform this controlled experiment impossible.

To answer our question about the relative performance of engineering and arts students, we have no choice but to obtain our data by observational methods. We would take a random sample of engineering students and arts students who have already entered MBA programs and record their grades. If we find that engineering students do better, we may tend to conclude that an engineering background better prepares students for an MBA program. However, it may be true that better students tend to choose engineering as their undergraduate major, and that better students achieve higher grades in all programs, including the MBA program.

Although we've discussed observational and experimental data in the context of the test of the difference between two means, you should be aware that the issue of how the data are obtained is relevant to the interpretation of all the techniques that follow.

EXERCISES

13.53 Are the data in Exercise 13.33 observational or experimental? Explain. If the data are observational, describe a method of producing experimental data.

13.54 Refer to Exercise 13.53. If the data are observational, describe another conclusion besides the one that infers that Tastee is better for babies.

13.55 Are the data in Exercise 13.34 observational or experimental? Explain. If the data are observational, describe a method of producing experimental data.

13.56 Refer to Exercise 13.40.
   a Are the data observational or experimental? Explain.
   b If the data are observational, describe a method of answering the question with experimental data.
   c If the data are observational, produce another explanation for the statistical outcome.

13.57 Suppose that you wish to test to determine whether one method of teaching statistics is better than another.
   a Describe a data-gathering process that produces observational data.
   b Describe a data-gathering process that produces experimental data.

13.58 You wish to determine whether MBA graduates who majored in finance attract higher starting salaries than MBA graduates who majored in marketing.

   a Describe a data-gathering process that produces observational data.
   b Describe a data-gathering process that produces experimental data.
   c If observational data indicate that finance majors attract higher salaries than do marketing majors, provide two explanations for this result.

13.59 Suppose that you are analyzing one of the hundreds of statistical studies linking smoking with lung cancer. The study analyzed thousands of randomly selected people, some of whom had lung cancer. The statistics indicate that those who have lung cancer smoked on average significantly more than those who did not have lung cancer.
   a Explain how you know that the data are observational.
   b Is there another interpretation of the statistics besides the obvious one that smoking causes lung cancer? If so, what is it? (Students who produce the best answers will be eligible for a job in the public relations department of a tobacco company.)
   c Is it possible to conduct a controlled experiment to produce data that address the question of the relationship between smoking and lung cancer? If so, describe the experiment.

13.4 INFERENCE ABOUT THE DIFFERENCE BETWEEN TWO MEANS: MATCHED PAIRS EXPERIMENT

We continue our presentation of statistical techniques that address the problem of comparing two populations of interval data. In Section 13.2, the parameter of interest was the difference between two population means, where the data were generated from independent samples. In this section, the data are gathered from a matched pairs experiment. To illustrate why matched pairs experiments are needed and how we deal with data produced in this way, consider the following example.

EXAMPLE 13.3

In the last few years a number of Web-based companies that offer job placement services have been created. The manager of one such company wanted to investigate the job offers recent MBAs were obtaining. In particular, she wanted to know whether finance majors were being offered higher salaries than marketing majors. In a preliminary study, she randomly sampled 50 recently graduated MBAs, half of whom majored in finance and half in marketing. From each she obtained the highest salary (including benefits) offer. These data are stored in file Xm13-03 and listed at the top of page 414. Can we infer that finance majors obtain higher salary offers than do marketing majors among MBAs?

Highest salary offer made to Finance majors

61,228 51,836 20,620 73,356 84,186 79,782 29,523 80,645 76,125 62,531 77,073
86,705 70,286 63,196 64,358 47,915 86,792 75,155 65,948 29,392 96,382 80,644
51,389 61,955 63,573

Highest salary offer made to Marketing majors

73,361 36,956 63,627 71,069 40,203 97,097 49,442 75,188 59,854 79,816 51,943
35,272 60,631 63,567 69,423 68,421 56,276 47,510 58,925 78,704 62,553 81,931
30,867 49,091 48,843

SOLUTION

IDENTIFY

The objective is to compare two populations of interval data. The parameter is the difference between two means, $\mu_1 - \mu_2$ (where μ_1 = mean highest salary offer to finance majors, and μ_2 = mean highest salary offer to marketing majors). Because we want to determine whether finance majors are offered higher salaries, the alternative hypothesis will specify that μ_1 is greater than μ_2. Calculation of the sample variances allows us to use the equal-variances test statistic.

$$H_0: \quad (\mu_1 - \mu_2) = 0$$

$$H_1: \quad (\mu_1 - \mu_2) > 0$$

Test statistic: $\quad t = \dfrac{(\bar{x}_1 - \bar{x}_2) - (\mu_1 - \mu_2)}{\sqrt{s_p^2 \left(\dfrac{1}{n_1} + \dfrac{1}{n_2} \right)}}$

COMPUTE

 MANUALLY

From the data we calculated the following statistics.

$$\bar{x}_1 = 65{,}624$$

$$\bar{x}_2 = 60{,}423$$

$$s_1^2 = 360{,}433{,}294$$

$$s_2^2 = 262{,}228{,}559$$

$$s_p^2 = \frac{(n_1 - 1)s_1^2 + (n_2 - 1)s_2^2}{n_1 + n_2 - 2}$$

$$= \frac{(25 - 1)(360{,}433{,}294) + (25 - 1)(262{,}228{,}559)}{25 + 25 - 2}$$

$$= 311{,}330{,}926$$

The value of the test statistic is computed next.

$$t = \frac{(\bar{x}_1 - \bar{x}_2) - (\mu_1 - \mu_2)}{\sqrt{s_p^2\left(\dfrac{1}{n_1} + \dfrac{1}{n_2}\right)}}$$

$$= \frac{(65{,}624 - 60{,}423) - (0)}{\sqrt{311{,}330{,}926\left(\dfrac{1}{25} + \dfrac{1}{25}\right)}}$$

$$= 1.04$$

The number of degrees of freedom of the test statistic is

$$\nu = n_1 + n_2 - 2 = 25 + 25 - 2 = 48$$

The rejection region for a 5% significance level is

$$t > t_{\alpha,\nu} = t_{.05,48} \approx 1.676$$

 EXCEL

	A	B	C
1	t-Test: Two-Sample Assuming Equal Variances		
2			
3		*Finance*	*Marketing*
4	Mean	65624	60423
5	Variance	360433294	262228559
6	Observations	25	25
7	Pooled Variance	311330926	
8	Hypothesized Mean Difference	0	
9	df	48	
10	t Stat	1.04	
11	P(T<=t) one-tail	0.1513	
12	t Critical one-tail	1.6772	
13	P(T<=t) two-tail	0.3026	
14	t Critical two-tail	2.0106	

MINITAB

Two-Sample T-Test and CI: Finance, Marketing

```
Two-sample T for Finance vs Marketing

            N       Mean     StDev    SE Mean
Finance    25      65624     18985      3797
Marketin   25      60423     16193      3239

Difference = mu Finance - mu Marketing
Estimate for difference:  5201
95% lower bound for difference: -3169
T-Test of difference = 0 (vs >): T-Value = 1.04   P-Value = 0.151   DF = 48
Both use Pooled StDev =  17645
```

INTERPRET

The value of the test statistic ($t = 1.04$) and its p-value (.1513) indicate that there is very little evidence to support the hypothesis that finance majors attract higher salary offers than marketing majors.

As was the case with some earlier examples, we have some evidence to support the alternative hypothesis, but not enough. Note that the difference in sample means is

$$(\bar{x}_1 - \bar{x}_2) = (65{,}624 - 60{,}423) = 5{,}201$$

However, we judge the difference in sample means in relation to the standard error of $\bar{x}_1 - \bar{x}_2$. As we've already calculated,

$$s_p^2 = 311{,}330{,}926$$

and

$$\sqrt{s_p^2 \left(\frac{1}{n_1} + \frac{1}{n_2} \right)} = 4{,}991$$

Consequently, the value of the test statistic is $t = 5{,}201/4{,}991 = 1.04$, a value that does not allow us to reject the null hypothesis. We can see that although the difference between the sample means was quite large, the variability of the data, as measured by s_p^2, was also large, resulting in a small test statistic value.

EXAMPLE 13.4

Suppose now that we redo the experiment in the following way. We examine the transcripts of finance and marketing MBA majors. We randomly sample a finance and a marketing major whose grade point average (GPA) falls between 3.92 and 4 (based on a maximum of 4.0). We then randomly sample a finance and a marketing major whose GPA is between 3.84 and 3.92. We continue this process until the 25th pair of finance and marketing majors are selected whose GPA fell between 2.0 and 2.08. (The minimum GPA required for graduation is 2.0.) As we did in Example 13.3, we record the highest salary offer. These data, together with the GPA group, are stored in file Xm13-04 and listed below. Can we conclude from these data that finance majors draw larger salary offers than do marketing majors?

Group	Finance	Marketing
1	95,171	89,329
2	88,009	92,705
3	98,089	99,205
4	106,322	99,003
5	74,566	74,825
6	87,089	77,038
7	88,664	78,272
8	71,200	59,462
9	69,367	51,555
10	82,618	81,591
11	69,131	68,110
12	58,187	54,970
13	64,718	68,675
14	67,716	54,110
15	49,296	46,467
16	56,625	53,559
17	63,728	46,793
18	55,425	39,984
19	37,898	30,137
20	56,244	61,965
21	51,071	47,438
22	31,235	29,662
23	32,477	33,710
24	35,274	31,989
25	45,835	38,788

SOLUTION   The experiment described in Example 13.3 is one in which the samples are independent. That is, there is no relationship between the observations in one sample and the observations in the second sample. However, in this example the experiment was designed in such a way that each observation in one sample is matched with an observation in the other sample. The matching is conducted by selecting finance and marketing majors with similar GPAs. Thus, it is logical to compare the salary offers for finance and marketing majors in each group. This type of experiment is called **matched pairs**. We now describe how we conduct the test.

For each GPA group, we calculate the matched pair difference between the salary offers for finance and marketing majors.

Group	Finance	Marketing	Difference
1	95,171	89,329	5,842
2	88,009	92,705	−4,696
3	98,089	99,205	−1,116
4	106,322	99,003	7,319
5	74,566	74,825	−259
6	87,089	77,038	10,051
7	88,664	78,272	10,392
8	71,200	59,462	11,738
9	69,367	51,555	17,812
10	82,618	81,591	1,027
11	69,131	68,110	1,021
12	58,187	54,970	3,217
13	64,718	68,675	−3,957
14	67,716	54,110	13,606
15	49,296	46,467	2,829
16	56,625	53,559	3,066
17	63,728	46,793	16,935
18	55,425	39,984	15,441
19	37,898	30,137	7,761
20	56,244	61,965	−5,721
21	51,071	47,438	3,633
22	31,235	29,662	1,573
23	32,477	33,710	−1,233
24	35,274	31,989	3,285
25	45,835	38,788	7,047

The experimental design tells us that the parameter of interest is the **mean of the population of differences**, which we label μ_D. Note that $\mu_1 - \mu_2 = \mu_D$ but that we test μ_D because of the way the experiment was performed. The hypotheses to be tested are

$$H_0: \quad \mu_D = 0$$

$$H_1: \quad \mu_D > 0$$

We have already presented inferential techniques about a population mean. Recall that in Chapter 12 we introduced the t test of μ. Thus, to test hypotheses about μ_D, we use the following test statistic.

TEST STATISTIC FOR μ_D

$$t = \frac{\bar{x}_D - \mu_D}{s_D/\sqrt{n_D}}$$

which is Student t distributed with $\nu = n_D - 1$ degrees of freedom, provided that the differences are normally distributed.

Aside from the subscript D, this test statistic is identical to the one presented in Chapter 12. We conduct the test in the usual way.

COMPUTE

 MANUALLY

Using the differences computed above, we find the following statistics:

$$\bar{x}_D = 5{,}065$$

$$s_D = 6{,}647$$

from which we calculate the value of the test statistic

$$t = \frac{\bar{x}_D - \mu_D}{s_D/\sqrt{n_D}} = \frac{5{,}065 - 0}{6{,}647/\sqrt{25}} = 3.81$$

The rejection region is

$$t > t_{\alpha,\nu} = t_{.05,24} = 1.711$$

 EXCEL

	A	B	C
1	t-Test: Paired Two Sample for Means		
2			
3		Finance	Marketing
4	Mean	65438	60374
5	Variance	444981810	469441785
6	Observations	25	25
7	Pearson Correlation	0.9520	
8	Hypothesized Mean Difference	0	
9	df	24	
10	t Stat	3.81	
11	P(T<=t) one-tail	0.0004	
12	t Critical one-tail	1.7109	
13	P(T<=t) two-tail	0.0009	
14	t Critical two-tail	2.0639	

Excel prints the sample means, variances, and sample sizes for each sample (as well as the coefficient of correlation), which implies that the procedure uses these statistics. It doesn't. The technique is based on computing the paired differences from which the mean, variance, and sample size are determined. Excel should have printed these statistics. Again we hope this will be fixed soon. In the meantime, ignore the first four lines of the output.

COMMANDS

1. Type or import the data into two columns.
2. Click **Tools, Data Analysis...,** and **t-Test: Paired Two- Sample for Means**.

COMMANDS FOR EXAMPLE 13.4

Open file **Xm13-04**.

3. Specify the **Variable 1 Range**.	**A1:A21**
4. Specify the **Variable 2 Range**.	**B1:B21**
5. Type the value of the **Hypothesized Mean Difference**.	**0**
6. Click **Labels** (if appropriate).	
7. Specify a value for (**Alpha**) and click **OK**.	**.05**

MINITAB

Paired T-Test and CI: Finance, Marketing

```
Paired T for Finance - Marketing

                N      Mean     StDev   SE Mean
Finance        25     65438     21095      4219
Marketing      25     60374     21667      4333
Difference     25      5065      6647      1329

95% lower bound for mean difference: 2790
T-Test of mean difference = 0 (vs > 0): T-Value = 3.81  P-Value = 0.000
```

COMMANDS

1. Type or import the data.
2. **Click Stat, Basic Statistics, and Paired t....**
3. Select the variable name of the **First sample**.
4. Select the variable name of the **Second sample**.
5. Click **Options....**
6. Use the cursor to specify **Test mean** and type the hypothesized paired difference.
7. Specify the **Alternative**. Click **OK**. Click **OK**.

COMMANDS FOR EXAMPLE 13.4

Open file **Xm13-04**.

Finance or **C1**
Marketing or **C2**

0

greater than

INTERPRET

The value of the test statistic is $t = 3.81$ with a *p*-value of .0004. There is now overwhelming evidence to infer that finance majors obtain higher salary offers than marketing majors. By redoing the experiment as matched pairs, we were able to extract this information from the data.

ESTIMATING THE MEAN DIFFERENCE

Applying the usual algebra, we derive the confidence interval estimator of μ_D.

CONFIDENCE INTERVAL ESTIMATOR OF μ_D

$$\bar{x}_D \pm t_{\alpha/2} \frac{s_D}{\sqrt{n_D}}$$

EXAMPLE 13.5

Compute the 95% confidence interval estimate of the mean difference in salary offers between finance and marketing majors.

SOLUTION

COMPUTE

 MANUALLY

The 95% confidence interval estimate of the mean difference is

$$\bar{x}_D \pm t_{\alpha/2} \frac{s_D}{\sqrt{n_D}} = 5{,}065 \pm 2.064 \frac{6{,}647}{\sqrt{25}} = 5{,}065 \pm 2{,}744$$

$$\text{LCL} = 2{,}321 \quad \text{and} \quad \text{UCL} = 7{,}809$$

 EXCEL

	A	B	C	D
1	t-Estimate: Mean			
2				
3				Difference
4	Mean			5065
5	Standard Deviation			6647
6	LCL			2321
7	UCL			7808

COMMANDS

To estimate the mean difference, employ the *t* estimate of the mean of the differences. (See Section 12.2.) You must first instruct Excel to calculate the differences.

 MINITAB

Paired T-Test and CI: Finance, Marketing

```
Paired T for Finance - Marketing

                 N      Mean     StDev    SE Mean
Finance         25     65438     21095       4219
Marketing       25     60374     21667       4333
Difference      25      5065      6647       1329

95% CI for mean difference: (2321, 7808)
T-Test of mean difference = 0 (vs not = 0): T-Value = 3.81   P-Value = 0.001
```

COMMANDS

Follow the instructions to test the paired difference. However, you must specify **not equal** for the **Alternative** hypothesis to produce the two-sided confidence interval estimate of the mean difference.

INTERPRET

We estimate that the mean salary offer to finance majors exceeds the mean salary offer to marketing majors by an amount that lies between $2,321 and $7,808 (using the computer output).

INDEPENDENT SAMPLES OR MATCHED PAIRS: WHICH EXPERIMENTAL DESIGN IS BETTER?

Examples 13.3 and 13.4 demonstrated that the experimental design is an important factor in statistical inference. However, these two examples raise several questions about experimental designs:

1. Why does the matched pairs experiment result in rejecting the null hypothesis, whereas the independent samples experiment could not?

2. Should we always use the matched pairs experiment? In particular, are there disadvantages to its use?

3. How do we recognize when a matched pairs experiment has been performed?

Here are our answers.

1. The matched pairs experiment worked in Example 13.4 by reducing the variation in the data. To understand this point, examine the statistics from both examples. In Example 13.3, we found $\bar{x}_1 - \bar{x}_2 = 5,201$. In Example 13.4, we computed $\bar{x}_D = 5,065$. Thus, the numerators of the two test statistics were quite similar. However, the test statistic in Example 13.4 was much larger than the test statistic in Example 13.3 because of the standard errors. In Example 13.3, we calculated

$$s_p^2 = 311{,}330{,}926 \quad \text{and} \quad \sqrt{s_p^2\left(\frac{1}{n_1} + \frac{1}{n_2}\right)} = 4{,}991$$

Example 13.4 produced

$$s_D = 6{,}647 \quad \text{and} \quad \frac{s_D}{\sqrt{n_D}} = 1{,}329$$

As you can see, the difference in the test statistics was caused not by the numerator but by the denominator. This raises another question: Why was the variation in the data of Example 13.3 so much greater than the variation in the data of Example 13.4? If you examine the data and statistics from Example 13.3, you will find that there was a great deal of variation *between* the salary offers in each sample. That is, some MBA graduates received high salary offers and others, relatively low ones. This high level of variation made the difference between the sample means appear to be small. As a result, we could not conclude that finance majors attract higher salary offers.

Looking at the data from Example 13.4, we see that there is very little variation between the observations of the paired differences. The variation caused by different GPAs has been markedly decreased. The smaller variation causes the value of the test statistic to be larger. Consequently, we conclude that finance majors obtain higher salary offers.

2. Will the matched pairs experiment always produce a larger test statistic than the independent samples experiment? The answer is "Not necessarily." Suppose that in our example we found that companies did not consider grade point averages when making decisions about how much to offer the MBA graduates. In such circumstances, the matched pairs experiment would result in no significant decrease in variation when compared to independent samples. It is possible that the matched pairs experiment may be less likely to reject the null hypothesis than the independent samples experiment. The reason can be seen by calculating the degrees of

freedom. In Example 13.3, the number of degrees of freedom was 48, whereas in Example 13.4, it was 24. Even though we had the same number of observations (25 in each sample), the matched pairs experiment had half the number of degrees of freedom as the equivalent independent samples experiment. For exactly the same value of the test statistic, a smaller number of degrees of freedom in a Student t distributed test statistic yields a larger p-value. What this means is that if there is little reduction in variation to be achieved by the matched pairs experiment, the statistics practitioner should choose instead to conduct the experiment with independent samples.

3. As you've seen, in this book we deal with questions arising from experiments that have already been conducted. Thus, one of your tasks is to determine the appropriate test statistic. In the case of comparing two populations of interval data, you must decide whether the samples are independent (in which case the parameter is $\mu_1 - \mu_2$) or matched pairs (in which case the parameter is μ_D) in order to select the correct test statistic. To help you do so, we suggest you ask and answer the following question: "Does some natural relationship exist between each *pair* of observations that provides a logical reason to compare the first observation of sample 1 with the first observation of sample 2, the second observation of sample 1 with the second observation of sample 2, and so on?" If so, the experiment was conducted by matched pairs. If not, it was conducted using independent samples.

OBSERVATIONAL AND EXPERIMENTAL DATA

The points we made in Section 13.3 are also valid in this section. That is, we can design a matched pairs experiment where the data are gathered using a controlled experiment or by observation. The data in Examples 13.3 and 13.4 are observational. As a consequence, when the statistical result provided evidence that finance majors attracted higher salary offers, it did not necessarily mean that students educated in finance are more attractive to prospective employers. It may be, for example, that better students major in finance and better students achieve higher starting salaries.

CHECKING THE REQUIRED CONDITION

The validity of the results of the t test and estimator of μ_D depends on the normality of the differences. The histogram of the differences (Figure 13.6) confirms that the normality requirement in this example is satisfied.

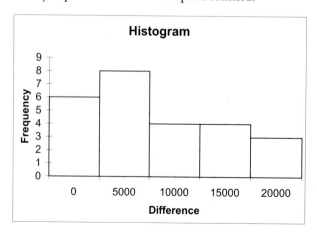

Figure 13.6

VIOLATION OF REQUIRED CONDITION

If the differences are very nonnormal, we cannot use the t test of μ_D. We can, however, employ a nonparametric technique—the Wilcoxon signed rank sum test for matched pairs, which we present in Chapter 17.

DEVELOPING AN UNDERSTANDING OF STATISTICAL CONCEPTS 1

Two of the most important principles in statistics were applied in this section. The first is the concept of analyzing sources of variation. In Examples 13.3 and 13.4, we showed that by reducing the variation between salary offers in each sample, we were able to detect a real difference between the two majors. This was an application of the more general procedure of analyzing data and attributing some fraction of the variation to several sources. In Example 13.4, the two sources of variation were the GPA and the MBA major. However, we were not interested in the variation between graduates with differing GPAs. Instead, we only wanted to eliminate that source of variation, making it easier to determine whether finance majors draw larger salary offers.

In Chapter 15, we will introduce a technique called the *analysis of variance*, which does what its name suggests; it analyzes sources of variation in an attempt to detect real differences. In most applications of this procedure, we will be interested in each source of variation and not simply in reducing one source. We refer to the process as *explaining the variation*. The concept of explained variation also will be applied in Chapters 18, 19, and 20.

DEVELOPING AN UNDERSTANDING OF STATISTICAL CONCEPTS 2

The second principle demonstrated in this section is that statistics practitioners can design data-gathering procedures in such a way that they can analyze sources of variation. Before conducting the experiment in Example 13.4, the statistics practitioner suspected that there were large differences between graduates with different GPAs. Consequently, the experiment was organized so that the effects of those differences were mostly eliminated. It is also possible to design experiments that allow for easy detection of real differences and minimize the costs of data gathering. Unfortunately, we will not present this topic. However, you should understand that the entire subject of the design of experiments is an important one, because statistics practitioners often need to be able to analyze data to detect differences, and the cost is almost always a factor.

Here is a summary of how we determine when to use these techniques.

FACTORS THAT IDENTIFY THE t TEST AND ESTIMATOR OF μ_D
1. **Problem objective:** Compare two populations.
2. **Data type:** Interval
3. **Descriptive measurement:** Central location
4. **Experimental design:** Matched pairs

EXERCISES

Developing an Understanding of Statistical Concepts

13.60 Given the following data generated from a matched pairs experiment, test to determine whether we can infer that the mean of population 1 exceeds the mean of population 2. (Use $\alpha = .01$.)

Pair	1	2	3	4	5
Sample 1	20	23	15	18	19
Sample 2	17	16	9	19	15

13.61 The data below and stored in file Xr13-61 were produced from a matched pairs experiment. Determine whether these data are sufficient to infer at the 10% significance level that the two population means differ.

Pair	1	2	3	4	5	6	7	8	9	10
Sample 1	7	12	19	17	22	18	30	33	40	48
Sample 2	10	13	18	21	25	19	31	31	44	47

13.62 The following data were generated from a matched pairs experiment. (The data are stored in columns 1 and 2 of file Xr13-62.)

Pair	1	2	3	4	5	6	7	8	9	10
Sample 1	3	12	15	10	17	14	10	9	16	8
Sample 2	7	13	14	14	23	13	12	12	18	9

a Estimate with 90% confidence the mean difference.
b Briefly describe what the interval estimate in part **a** tells you.

13.63 Refer to Exercise 13.27. Suppose that instead of independently sampling from the two populations, a statistics practitioner conducts a matched pairs experiment. The data are shown below.

Pair	1	2	3	4	5	6	7	8
Sample 1	7	4	6	3	7	5	8	7
Sample 2	6	4	5	3	6	5	7	5

a Test to determine whether the population means differ. (Use $\alpha = .05$.)
b Discuss why you obtained a different conclusion from the one in Exercise 13.27.

13.64 Refer to Exercise 13.28. Suppose that instead of independently sampling from the two populations, a statistics practitioner conducts a matched pairs experiment. The data are shown below.

Pair	1	2	3	4	5	6
Sample 1	12	6	5	8	11	5
Sample 2	7	11	13	5	8	7

a Test to determine whether the population means differ. (Use $\alpha = .05$.)
b Discuss why you obtained the same conclusion as the one in Exercise 13.28.

Applications

13.65 In an effort to determine whether a new type of fertilizer is more effective than the type currently in use, researchers took 12 two-acre plots of land scattered throughout the county. Each plot was divided into two equal-sized subplots, one of which was treated with the current fertilizer and the other of which was treated with the new fertilizer. Wheat was planted, and the crop yields were measured. These data are stored in file Xr13-65 and listed below.

Plot	1	2	3	4	5	6	7	8	9	10	11	12
Current fertilizer	56	45	68	72	61	69	57	55	60	72	75	66
New fertilizer	60	49	66	73	59	77	61	60	58	75	72	71

a Can we conclude at the 5% significance level that the new fertilizer is more effective than the current one?
b Estimate with 95% confidence the difference in mean crop yields between the two fertilizers.
c What is the required condition(s) for the validity of the results obtained in parts **a** and **b**?
d Is the required condition(s) satisfied?
e Are these data experimental or observational?
f How should the experiment be conducted if the researchers believed that the land throughout the county was essentially the same?

13.66 The president of a large company is in the process of deciding whether to adopt a lunchtime exercise program. The purpose of such programs is to improve the health of workers and, in so doing, reduce medical expenses. To get more information, she instituted an exercise program for the employees in one office. The president knows that during the winter months, medical expenses are relatively high because of the incidence of colds and flu. Consequently, she decides to use a matched pairs design by recording medical expenses for the 12 months before the program and for 12 months after the program. The "before" and "after" expenses (in thousands of dollars) are compared on a month-to-month basis and shown below. (These data are stored in file Xr13-66.)

Month	Jan	Feb	Mar	Apr	May	Jun
Before program	68	44	30	58	35	33
After program	59	42	20	62	25	30
Month	Jul	Aug	Sep	Oct	Nov	Dec
Before program	52	69	23	69	48	30
After program	56	62	25	75	40	26

a Do the data indicate that exercise programs reduce medical expenses? (Test with $\alpha = .05$.)
b Estimate with 95% confidence the mean savings produced by exercise programs.
c Was it appropriate to conduct a matched pairs experiment? Explain.

The following exercises require the use of a computer and software. The answers may be calculated manually. See Appendix A for the sample statistics. **Use a 5% significance level unless specified otherwise.**

13.67 One measure of the state of the economy is the amount of money homeowners pay on their mortgage each month. To determine the extent of change between this year and 5 years ago, a random sample of 150 homeowners was drawn. The monthly mortgage payments for each homeowner for this year and for 5 years ago are stored in file Xr13-67. (The amounts have been adjusted so that we're comparing constant dollars.) Can we infer that mortgage payments have risen over the past 5 years?

13.68 Do waiters or waitresses earn larger tips? To answer this question, a restaurant consultant undertook a preliminary study. The study involved measuring the percentage of the total bill left as a tip for one randomly selected waiter and one randomly selected waitress in each of 50 restaurants during a 1-week period. The data are stored in columns 1 and 2 of file Xr13-68. What conclusions can be drawn from these data?

13.69 To determine the effect of advertising in the Yellow Pages, Bell Telephone took a sample of 40 retail stores that did not advertise in the Yellow Pages last year but did so this year. The annual sales (in thousands of dollars) for each store in both years were recorded and stored in file Xr13-69.

  a Estimate with 90% confidence the improvement in sales between the two years.

  b Can we infer that advertising in the Yellow Pages improves sales?

  c Check to ensure that the required condition(s) of the techniques used in parts **a** and **b** is satisfied.

  d Would it be advantageous to perform this experiment with independent samples? Explain why or why not.

13.70 Research scientists at a pharmaceutical company have recently developed a new nonprescription sleeping pill. They decide to test its effectiveness by measuring the time it takes for people to fall asleep after taking the pill. Preliminary analysis indicates that the time to fall asleep varies considerably from one person to another. Consequently, they organize the experiment in the following way. A random sample of 100 volunteers who regularly suffer from insomnia is chosen. Each person is given one pill containing the newly developed drug and one placebo. (A placebo is a pill that contains absolutely no medication.) Participants are told to take one pill one night and the second pill one night a week later. (They do not know whether the pill they are taking is the placebo or the real thing, and the order of use is random.) Each participant is fitted with a device that measures the time until sleep occurs. The data are stored in file Xr13-70. Can we conclude that the new drug is effective?

13.71 The cost of health care is rising faster than most other items. To learn more about the problem, a survey was undertaken to determine whether differences in health care expenditures exist between men and women. The survey randomly sampled men and women aged 21, 22, ..., 65 and determined the total amount spent on health care. These data are stored in file Xr13-71. Do these data allow us to infer that men and women spend different amounts on health care? (*Source: Bureau of Labor Statistics, Consumer Expenditure Survey*)

13.72 The fluctuations in the stock market induce some investors to sell and move their money into more stable investments. To determine the degree to which recent fluctuations affected ownership, a random sample of 170 people who confirmed that they owned some stock were surveyed. The values of the holdings were recorded at the end of last year and at the end of the year before. These data are stored in file Xr13-72. Can we infer that the value of the stock holdings has decreased?

13.73 Are Americans more deeply in debt this year compared to last year? To help answer this question, a statistics practitioner randomly sampled Americans this year and last year. The sampling was conducted so that the samples were matched by the age of the head of the household. For each, the ratio of debt payments to household income was recorded and stored in file Xr13-73. Can we infer that the ratios are higher this year than last?

13.74 Every April, Americans and Canadians fill out their tax return forms. Many turn to tax preparation companies to do this tedious job. The question arises, "Are there differences between companies?" In an experiment, two of the largest companies were asked to prepare the tax returns of a sample of 55 taxpayers. The amounts of tax payable were recorded and stored in file Xr13-74. Can we conclude that company 1's service results in higher tax payable?

13.75 Refer to Exercise 13.49. Suppose now we redo the experiment in the following way. On 20 randomly selected cars, one of each type of tire is installed on the rear wheels and, as before, the cars are driven until the tires wear out. The number of miles (in 1,000s) until wear-out occurred is stored in file Xr13-75. Can we conclude from these data that the new tire is superior?

13.76 Refer to Exercises 13.49 and 13.75. Explain why the matched pairs experiment produced significant results whereas the independent samples t test did not.

13.77 Refer to Examples 13.3 and 13.4. Suppose that another experiment is conducted. Finance and marketing MBA majors were matched according to their undergraduate GPA. As in the previous examples, the highest starting salary offers were recorded. These data are stored in file Xr13-77. Can we infer from these data that finance majors attract higher salary offers than marketing majors?

13.5 INFERENCE ABOUT THE RATIO OF TWO VARIANCES

In Sections 13.2 and 13.4, we dealt with statistical inference concerning the difference between two population means. The problem objective in each case was to compare two populations of interval data, and our interest was in comparing measures of central location. This section discusses the statistical technique to use when the problem objective and the data type are the same as in Sections 13.2 and 13.4, but our interest is in comparing variability. Here we will study the ratio of two population variances. We make inferences about the ratio because the sampling distribution features ratios rather than differences.

In the previous chapter, we presented the procedures used to draw inferences about a single population variance. We pointed out that variance can be used to address problems where we need to judge the consistency of a production process. We also use variance to measure the risk associated with a portfolio of investments. In this section we compare two variances, enabling us to compare the consistency of two production processes. We can also compare the relative risks of two sets of investments.

There is another important use of the statistical methods to be presented in this section. One of the factors that determines the correct technique when testing or estimating the difference between two means from independent samples is whether the two unknown population variances are equal. Statistics practitioners often test for the equality of σ_1^2 and σ_2^2 before deciding which of the two procedures introduced in Section 13.2 is to be used.

We will proceed in a manner that is probably becoming quite familiar.

PARAMETER

As you will see shortly, we compare two population variances by determining the ratio. Consequently, the parameter is σ_1^2 / σ_2^2.

STATISTIC AND SAMPLING DISTRIBUTION

We have previously noted that the sample variance (defined in Chapter 4) is an unbiased and consistent estimator of the population variance. Not surprisingly, the estimator of the parameter σ_1^2 / σ_2^2 is the ratio of the two sample variances drawn from their respective populations, s_1^2 / s_2^2.

The sampling distribution of s_1^2 / s_2^2 is said to be F distributed provided that we have independently sampled from two normal populations. (The F distribution was introduced in Section 8.5.)

Statisticians have shown that the ratio of two independent chi-squared variables divided by their degrees of freedom is F distributed. The degrees of freedom of the F distribution are identical to the degrees of freedom for the two chi-squared distributions. In Section 12.3, we pointed out that $(n - 1)s^2/\sigma^2$ is chi-squared distributed provided that the sampled population is normal. If we have independent samples drawn from two normal populations, then both $(n_1 - 1)s_1^2/\sigma_1^2$ and $(n_2 - 1)s_2^2/\sigma_2^2$ are chi-squared distributed. If we divide each by its respective number of degrees of freedom and take the ratio, we produce

$$\frac{\dfrac{(n_1 - 1)s_1^2/\sigma_1^2}{(n_1 - 1)}}{\dfrac{(n_2 - 1)s_2^2/\sigma_2^2}{(n_2 - 1)}}$$

which simplifies to

$$\frac{s_1^2/\sigma_1^2}{s_2^2/\sigma_2^2}$$

This statistic is F distributed with $v_1 = n_1 - 1$ and $v_2 = n_2 - 1$ degrees of freedom. Recall that v_1 is called the **numerator degrees of freedom** and v_2 is called the **denominator degrees of freedom**.

TESTING AND ESTIMATING A RATIO OF TWO VARIANCES

In this book, our null hypothesis will always specify that the two variances are equal. As a result, the ratio will equal 1. Thus, the null hypothesis will always be expressed as

$$H_0: \quad \frac{\sigma_1^2}{\sigma_2^2} = 1$$

The alternative hypothesis can state that the ratio σ_1^2/σ_2^2 is either not equal to 1, greater than 1, or less than 1. Technically, the test statistic is

$$F = \frac{s_1^2/\sigma_1^2}{s_2^2/\sigma_2^2}$$

However, under the null hypothesis, which states that $\sigma_1^2/\sigma_2^2 = 1$, the test statistic becomes as follows.

TEST STATISTIC FOR σ_1^2/σ_2^2

The test statistic employed to test that σ_1^2/σ_2^2 is equal to 1 is

$$F = \frac{s_1^2}{s_2^2}$$

which is F distributed with $v_1 = n_1 - 1$ and $v_2 = n_2 - 1$ degrees of freedom provided that the populations are normal.

With the usual algebraic manipulation, we can derive the confidence interval estimator of the ratio of two population variances.

CONFIDENCE INTERVAL ESTIMATOR OF σ_1^2/σ_2^2

$$\text{LCL} = \left(\frac{s_1^2}{s_2^2}\right)\frac{1}{F_{\alpha/2,v_1,v_2}}$$

$$\text{UCL} = \left(\frac{s_1^2}{s_2^2}\right)F_{\alpha/2,v_2,v_1}$$

where $v_1 = n_1 - 1$ and $v_2 = n_2 - 1$

EXAMPLE 13.6

In Example 13.1, we applied the unequal-variances t test of $\mu_1 - \mu_2$. We chose that test statistic after computing the variance of the sample of consumers of high-fiber cereal to be 4,103 and the variance of the sample of nonconsumers of high-fiber cereal to be 10,670. The difference between the two sample variances appears to indicate that the population variances differ. Test to determine whether that decision was correct.

SOLUTION

IDENTIFY

We need to conduct the F test of σ_1^2/σ_2^2 to determine whether the two population variances differ. The test proceeds as follows.

$$H_0: \quad \sigma_1^2/\sigma_2^2 = 1$$

$$H_1: \quad \sigma_1^2/\sigma_2^2 \neq 1$$

COMPUTE

 MANUALLY

The rejection region (assuming that $\alpha = .05$) is

$$F > F_{\alpha/2,\nu_1,\nu_2} = F_{.025,42,106} \approx F_{.025,40,120} = 1.61$$

or

$$F < F_{1-\alpha/2,\nu_1,\nu_2} = F_{.975,42,106} = \frac{1}{F_{.025,106,42}} \approx \frac{1}{F_{.025,120,40}} = \frac{1}{1.72} = .58$$

The value of the test statistic is

$$F = \frac{s_1^2}{s_2^2} = \frac{4,103}{10,670} = .3845$$

Since the value of the test statistic is less than .58, we reject the null hypothesis.

 EXCEL

	A	B	C
1	F-Test Two-Sample for Variances		
2			
3		Consumers	Nonconsumers
4	Mean	604.02	633.23
5	Variance	4102.98	10669.77
6	Observations	43	107
7	df	42	106
8	F	0.3845	
9	P(F<=f) one-tail	0.0004	
10	F Critical one-tail	0.6371	

The value of the test statistic is $F = .3845$. Excel outputs the one-tail p-value. Because we're conducting a two-tail test, we double that value. Thus, the p-value of the test we're conducting is $2 \times .0004 = .0008$.

COMMANDS FOR
EXAMPLE 13.5
Open file **Xm13-01**.

COMMANDS
 1. Type or import the data into two columns.
 2. Click **Tools, Data Analysis...**, and **F-Test
    Two-Sample for Variances**.
 3. Specify the **Variable 1 Range**.   **A1:A44**
 4. Specify the **Variable 2 Range**.   **B1:B108**
 5. Click **Labels** (if appropriate).
 6. Specify a value for α (**Alpha**) and click **OK**.   **.05**

Use the **F-Test_2 Variances** worksheet to complete this test from the sample variances and to perform a what-if analysis.

MINITAB

Test for Equal Variances

```
F-Test (normal distribution)


Test Statistic: 0.385
P-Value       : 0.001
```

(*Note:* Some of the printout has been omitted.)

COMMANDS FOR
EXAMPLE 13.5
Open file **Xm13-01**.

COMMANDS
 1. Type or import the data.
 2. Click **Stat, Basic Statistics**, and **2 Variances...**.
 3. Specify **Samples in different columns** if
    appropriate.
 4. Specify the names of variables (**First** and **Second**).   **C1, C2** or **Consumers,**
    Click **OK**.   **Nonconsumers**

INTERPRET

There is enough evidence to infer that the population variances differ. It follows that we were justified in using the unequal-variances *t* test in Example 13.1. We're confident that the normality requirement for this test is satisfied. It is the same requirement for the *t* test, which we checked when we drew the histograms. (See Figures 13.2 and 13.3.)

EXAMPLE 13.7

Determine the 95% confidence interval estimate of the ratio of the two population variances in Example 13.1.

SOLUTION

COMPUTE

 MANUALLY

We find

$$F_{\alpha/2, \nu_1, \nu_2} = F_{.025, 42, 106} \approx F_{.025, 40, 120} = 1.61$$

and

$$F_{\alpha/2, \nu_2, \nu_1} = F_{.025, 106, 42} \approx F_{.025, 120, 40} = 1.72$$

Thus,

$$\text{LCL} = \left(\frac{s_1^2}{s_2^2}\right)\frac{1}{F_{\alpha/2,\nu_1,\nu_2}} = \left(\frac{4{,}102.98}{10{,}669.77}\right)\frac{1}{1.61} = .2388$$

$$\text{UCL} = \left(\frac{s_1^2}{s_2^2}\right)\frac{1}{F_{\alpha/2,\nu_2,\nu_1}} = \left(\frac{4{,}102.98}{10{,}669.77}\right)1.72 = .6614$$

We estimate that σ_1^2/σ_2^2 lies between .2388 and .6614.

 EXCEL

	A	B	C	D	E
1	F-Estimate of the Ratio of Two Variances				
2					
3		Sample 1	Sample 2	Confidence Interval Estimate	
4	Sample variance	4103	10670	Lower confidence limit	0.2374
5	Sample size	43	107	Upper confidence limit	0.6594
6	Confidence level	0.95			

COMMANDS

Open the **F-Estimator_2 Variances** worksheet in the **Estimators** workbook and substitute sample variances, samples sizes, and the confidence level.

 MINITAB

Minitab does not compute the estimate of the ratio of two variances.

INTERPRET

As we pointed out in Chapter 11, we can often use a confidence interval estimator to test hypotheses. In this example the interval estimate excludes the value of 1. Consequently, we can draw the same conclusion as we did in Example 13.5; the appropriate technique to test the data in Example 13.1 was the unequal-variances t test of $\mu_1 - \mu_2$.

> *FACTORS THAT IDENTIFY THE F TEST AND ESTIMATOR OF σ_1^2/σ_2^2*
> 1. **Problem objective**: Compare two populations.
> 2. **Data type**: Interval
> 3. **Descriptive measurement**: Variability

EXERCISES

Developing an Understanding of Statistical Concepts

*Exercises 13.78 to 13.83 are "what-if analyses" designed to determine what happens to the test statistics and interval estimates when elements of the statistical inference change. These problems can be solved manually or using Excel's **Test Statistics** or **Estimators** workbooks.*

13.78 Random samples from two normal populations produced the following statistics:
$$s_1^2 = 350 \qquad n_1 = 30$$
$$s_2^2 = 700 \qquad n_2 = 30$$

Can we infer at the 5% significance level that the two population variances differ?

13.79 Repeat Exercise 13.78, changing the sample sizes to $n_1 = 15$ and $n_2 = 15$.

13.80 Refer to Exercises 13.78 and 13.79. Describe what happens to the test statistic when the sample sizes decrease.

13.81 Random samples from two normal populations produced the following statistics:

$s_1^2 = 28 \qquad n_1 = 10$

$s_2^2 = 19 \qquad n_2 = 10$

Estimate with 95% confidence the ratio of the two population variances.

13.82 Repeat Exercise 13.81, changing the sample sizes to $n_1 = 25$ and $n_2 = 25$.

13.83 Refer to Exercises 13.81 and 13.82. Describe what happens to the width of the confidence interval estimate when the sample sizes increase.

13.84 Given the following statistics, test to determine whether the variance of population 1 is larger than the variance of population 2. (Use $\alpha = .05$.)

$s_1^2 = 60 \qquad n_1 = 20$

$s_2^2 = 25 \qquad n_2 = 20$

13.85 Given the data below, test the following hypotheses with $\alpha = .10$.

$H_0: \quad \sigma_1^2 / \sigma_2^2 = 1$

$H_1: \quad \sigma_1^2 / \sigma_2^2 \neq 1$

Sample 1:   7   4   9   12   8   6   9   14

Sample 2:   10   7   13   18   4   8   21   20   5   8

13.86 Random samples from two normal populations produced the following results. Is there enough evidence at the 5% significance level to infer that the population variances differ?

Sample 1:   27   52   41   20   33   59   41   28   29   51

Sample 2:   18   15   19   31   49   12   48   29   45   50

The following exercises require the use of a computer and software. The answers may be calculated manually. See Appendix A for the sample statistics.

13.87 Can we conclude from the data stored in columns 1 and 2 of file Xr13-87 that the variance of population 1 is less than that of population 2? Use a 1% significance level.

13.88 Refer to Exercise 13.87. Estimate the ratio of population variances with 95% confidence.

Applications

13.89 Test at the 5% significance level to determine whether the t test of $\mu_1 - \mu_2$ that you applied in Exercise 13.39 was justified.

13.90 Determine whether the test you used to answer Exercise 13.47 was appropriate. Conduct a test with $\alpha = .10$.

13.91 Did you use the correct technique when you answered the question posed in Exercise 13.48? Answer by conducting a test with $\alpha = .05$.

13.92 The weekly returns of two portfolios were recorded for 1 year with the results stored in file Xr13-92. Can we conclude at the 5% significance level that portfolio 2 is riskier than portfolio 1?

13.93 An important statistical measurement in service facilities (such as restaurants and banks) is the variability in service times. As an experiment, two bank tellers were observed, and the service times for each of 100 customers were recorded and stored in columns 1 and 2 of file Xr13-93. Do these data allow us to infer at the 10% significance level that the variance in service times differs between the two tellers?

13.6 INFERENCE ABOUT THE DIFFERENCE BETWEEN TWO POPULATION PROPORTIONS

In this section, we present the procedures for drawing inferences about the difference between populations whose data are nominal. The number of applications of these techniques is almost limitless. For example, pharmaceutical companies test new drugs by comparing the new and old or the new versus a placebo. Marketing managers compare market shares before and after advertising campaigns. Operations managers compare defective rates between two machines. Political pollsters measure the difference in popularity before and after an election.

PARAMETER

When data are nominal, the only meaningful computation is to count the number of occurrences of each type of outcome and calculate proportions. Consequently, the parameter to be tested and estimated in this section is the difference between two population proportions, $p_1 - p_2$.

STATISTIC AND SAMPLING DISTRIBUTION

To draw inferences about $p_1 - p_2$, we take a sample of size n_1 from population 1 and a sample of size n_2 from population 2 (Figure 13.7 depicts the sampling process). For each sample, we count the number of successes (recall that we call anything we're looking for a success), which we label x_1 and x_2, respectively. The sample proportions are then computed:

$$\hat{p}_1 = \frac{x_1}{n_1} \quad \text{and} \quad \hat{p}_2 = \frac{x_2}{n_2}$$

Statisticians have proved that the statistic $\hat{p}_1 - \hat{p}_2$ is an unbiased, consistent estimator of the parameter $p_1 - p_2$.

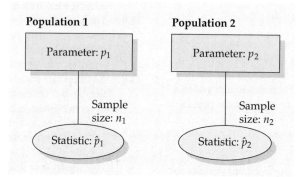

Figure 13.7
Sampling from two populations of nominal data

Using the same mathematics as in Chapter 9 to derive the sampling distribution of the sample proportion $\hat{p}$, we determine the sampling distribution of the difference between two sample proportions.

SAMPLING DISTRIBUTION OF $\hat{p}_1 - \hat{p}_2$

1. The statistic $\hat{p}_1 - \hat{p}_2$ is approximately normally distributed provided that the sample sizes are large enough so that $n_1 p_1$, $n_1(1 - p_1)$, $n_2 p_2$, and $n_2(1 - p_2)$ are all greater than or equal to 5. [Because p_1 and p_2 are unknown, we express the sample size requirement as $n_1 \hat{p}_1$, $n_1(1 - \hat{p}_1)$, $n_2 \hat{p}_2$, and $n_2(1 - \hat{p}_2)$ are greater than or equal to 5.]

2. The mean of $\hat{p}_1 - \hat{p}_2$ is

$$E(\hat{p}_1 - \hat{p}_2) = p_1 - p_2$$

3. The variance of $\hat{p}_1 - \hat{p}_2$ is

$$V(\hat{p}_1 - \hat{p}_2) = \frac{p_1(1 - p_1)}{n_1} + \frac{p_2(1 - p_2)}{n_2}$$

The standard error is

$$\sigma_{\hat{p}_1 - \hat{p}_2} = \sqrt{\frac{p_1(1 - p_1)}{n_1} + \frac{p_2(1 - p_2)}{n_2}}$$

Thus, the variable

$$z = \frac{(\hat{p}_1 - \hat{p}_2) - (p_1 - p_2)}{\sqrt{\dfrac{p_1(1 - p_1)}{n_1} + \dfrac{p_2(1 - p_2)}{n_2}}}$$

is approximately standard normally distributed.

TESTING AND ESTIMATING THE DIFFERENCE BETWEEN TWO PROPORTIONS

We would like to use the z statistic just described as our test statistic; however, the standard error of $\hat{p}_1 - \hat{p}_2$, which is

$$\sigma_{\hat{p}_1 - \hat{p}_2} = \sqrt{\frac{p_1(1 - p_1)}{n_1} + \frac{p_2(1 - p_2)}{n_2}}$$

is unknown, since both p_1 and p_2 are unknown. As a result, the standard error of $\hat{p}_1 - \hat{p}_2$ must be estimated from the sample data. There are two different estimators of this quantity, and the determination of which one to use depends on the null hypothesis. If the null hypothesis states that $p_1 - p_2 = 0$, the hypothesized equality of the two population proportions allows us to pool the data from the two samples to produce an estimate of the common value of the two proportions p_1 and p_2. The **pooled proportion estimator** is defined as

$$\hat{p} = \frac{x_1 + x_2}{n_1 + n_2}$$

Thus, the estimated standard error of $\hat{p}_1 - \hat{p}_2$ is

$$\sqrt{\frac{\hat{p}(1 - \hat{p})}{n_1} + \frac{\hat{p}(1 - \hat{p})}{n_2}} = \sqrt{\hat{p}(1 - \hat{p})\left(\frac{1}{n_1} + \frac{1}{n_2}\right)}$$

The principle used in estimating the standard error of $\hat{p}_1 - \hat{p}_2$ is analogous to that applied in Section 13.2 to produce the pooled variance estimate s_p^2, which is used to test $\mu_1 - \mu_2$ with σ_1^2 and σ_2^2 unknown but equal. That principle roughly states that, where possible, pooling data from two samples produces a better estimate of the standard error. Here, pooling is made possible by hypothesizing (under the null hypothesis) that $p_1 = p_2$. (In Section 13.2, we used the pooled variance estimate because we assumed that $\sigma_1^2 = \sigma_2^2$.) We will call this application Case 1.

TEST STATISTIC FOR $p_1 - p_2$: CASE 1

If the null hypothesis specifies

$$H_0: \ (p_1 - p_2) = 0$$

the test statistic is

$$z = \frac{(\hat{p}_1 - \hat{p}_2) - (p_1 - p_2)}{\sqrt{\hat{p}(1 - \hat{p})\left(\dfrac{1}{n_1} + \dfrac{1}{n_2}\right)}}$$

(continued)

Because we hypothesize that $p_1 - p_2 = 0$, we simplify the test statistic to

$$z = \frac{(\hat{p}_1 - \hat{p}_2)}{\sqrt{\hat{p}(1 - \hat{p})\left(\dfrac{1}{n_1} + \dfrac{1}{n_2}\right)}}$$

The second case applies when, under the null hypothesis, we state that $p_1 - p_2 = D$, where D is some value other than 0. Under such circumstances, we cannot pool the sample data to estimate the standard error of $\hat{p}_1 - \hat{p}_2$. The appropriate test statistic is described next as Case 2.

TEST STATISTIC FOR $p_1 - p_2$: CASE 2

If the null hypothesis specifies

$$H_0: \quad (p_1 - p_2) = D \quad (D \neq 0)$$

the test statistic is

$$z = \frac{(\hat{p}_1 - \hat{p}_2) - (p_1 - p_2)}{\sqrt{\dfrac{\hat{p}_1(1 - \hat{p}_1)}{n_1} + \dfrac{\hat{p}_2(1 - \hat{p}_2)}{n_2}}}$$

which can also be expressed as

$$z = \frac{(\hat{p}_1 - \hat{p}_2) - D}{\sqrt{\dfrac{\hat{p}_1(1 - \hat{p}_1)}{n_1} + \dfrac{\hat{p}_2(1 - \hat{p}_2)}{n_2}}}$$

Notice that this test statistic is determined by simply substituting the sample statistics $\hat{p}_1$ and $\hat{p}_2$ in the standard error of $\hat{p}_1 - \hat{p}_2$.

You will find that, in most practical applications (including the exercises in this book), Case 1 applies—in most problems, we want to know whether the two population proportions differ; that is,

$$H_1: \quad (p_1 - p_2) \neq 0$$

or whether one proportion exceeds the other; that is,

$$H_1: \quad (p_1 - p_2) > 0 \quad \text{or} \quad H_1: \quad (p_1 - p_2) < 0$$

In some other problems, however, the objective is to determine whether one proportion exceeds the other by a specific nonzero quantity. In such situations, Case 2 applies.

We derive the interval estimator of $p_1 - p_2$ in the same manner we have been using since Chapter 10.

CONFIDENCE INTERVAL ESTIMATOR OF $p_1 - p_2$

$$(\hat{p}_1 - \hat{p}_2) \pm z_{\alpha/2}\sqrt{\dfrac{\hat{p}_1(1 - \hat{p}_1)}{n_1} + \dfrac{\hat{p}_2(1 - \hat{p}_2)}{n_2}}$$

This formula is valid when $n_1\hat{p}_1$, $n_1(1 - \hat{p}_1)$, $n_2\hat{p}_2$, and $n_2(1 - \hat{p}_2)$ are greater than or equal to 5.

Notice that the standard error is estimated using the individual sample proportions rather than the pooled proportion. In this procedure we cannot assume that the population proportions are equal as we did in the Case 1 test statistic.

APPLICATIONS IN MARKETING: *TEST MARKETING*

Marketing managers frequently make use of test marketing to assess consumer reaction to a change in a characteristic (such as price or packaging) of an existing product, or to assess consumers' preferences regarding a proposed new product. *Test marketing* involves experimenting with changes to the marketing mix in a small, limited test market and assessing consumers' reaction in the test market before undertaking costly changes in production and distribution for the entire market.

EXAMPLE 13.8

The Johnson Brothers Company produces and sells a variety of household products. Because of stiff competition, one of its products—a bath soap—is not selling well. Hoping to improve sales, Johnson Brothers decided to introduce more attractive packaging. The company's advertising agency developed two new designs. The first design features several bright colors to distinguish it from other brands. The second design is light green in color with just the company's logo on it. As a test to determine which design is better, the marketing manager selected two supermarkets. In one supermarket the soap was packaged in a box using the first design, and in the second supermarket the second design was used. The product scanner at each supermarket tracked every buyer of soap over a 1-week period. The supermarkets recorded a 1 if some other soap product was purchased and a 2 if the Johnson Brothers brand was purchased. After the trial period, the scanner data were transferred to file Xm13-08, where column 1 contains the results for supermarket 1 and column 2 stores the data for supermarket 2. Because the first design is more expensive, management has decided to use this design only if there is sufficient evidence to allow them to conclude that it is better. Should management switch to the brightly colored design or the simple green one?

SOLUTION

IDENTIFY

The problem objective is to compare two populations. The first is the population of soap sales in supermarket 1 and the second is the population of soap sales in supermarket 2. The data are nominal because the values are "buy Johnson Brothers soap" and "buy other companies' soap." These two factors tell us that the parameter to be tested is the difference between two population proportions $p_1 - p_2$ (where p_1 and p_2 are the proportions of soap sales that are a product of the Johnson Brothers Company in supermarkets 1 and 2, respectively). Because we want to know whether there is enough evidence to adopt the brightly colored design, the alternative hypothesis is

$$H_1: \quad (p_1 - p_2) > 0$$

The null hypothesis must be

$$H_0: \quad (p_1 - p_2) = 0$$

which tells us that this is an application of Case 1. Thus, the test statistic is

$$z = \frac{(\hat{p}_1 - \hat{p}_2)}{\sqrt{\hat{p}(1 - \hat{p})\left(\dfrac{1}{n_1} + \dfrac{1}{n_2}\right)}}$$

COMPUTE

 MANUALLY

To compute the test statistic manually requires the statistics practitioner to tally the number of successes in each sample, where success is represented by the code 2. Reviewing all the sales reveals that

$$x_1 = 180, \quad n_1 = 904, \quad x_2 = 155, \quad n_2 = 1{,}038$$

The sample proportions are

$$\hat{p}_1 = \frac{180}{904} = .1991$$

and

$$\hat{p}_2 = \frac{155}{1{,}038} = .1493$$

The pooled proportion is

$$\hat{p} = \frac{180 + 155}{904 + 1{,}038} = \frac{335}{1{,}942} = .1725$$

The value of the test statistic is

$$z = \frac{(\hat{p}_1 - \hat{p}_2)}{\sqrt{\hat{p}(1 - \hat{p})\left(\dfrac{1}{n_1} + \dfrac{1}{n_2}\right)}} = \frac{(.1991 - .1493)}{\sqrt{(.1725)(1 - .1725)\left(\dfrac{1}{904} + \dfrac{1}{1{,}038}\right)}} = 2.90$$

A 5% significance level seems to be appropriate. Thus, the rejection region is

$$z > z_\alpha = z_{.05} = 1.645$$

EXCEL

	A	B	C	D
1	z-Test: Two Proportions			
2				
3			Supermarket 1	Supermarket 2
4	Sample Proportions		0.1991	0.1493
5	Observations		904	1038
6	Hypothesized Difference		0	
7	z Stat		2.90	
8	P(Z<=z) one tail		0.0019	
9	z Critical one-tail		1.6449	
10	P(Z<=z) two-tail		0.0038	
11	z Critical two-tail		1.96	

COMMANDS

1. Type or import the data into two adjacent columns.
2. Click **Tools, Data Analysis Plus,** and **Z-Test: 2 Proportions**.
3. Specify the **Variable 1 Range** and the **Variable 2 Range**.
4. Specify the **Code for Success.**
5. Specify the **Hypothesized Difference.**
6. Click **Labels**, if appropriate.
7. Type a value for α (**Alpha**) and click **OK.**

COMMANDS FOR EXAMPLE 13.8

Open file **Xm13-08**.

A1:A905 and B1: B1039

2

0

.05

To conduct this procedure from the sample proportions, activate the **z-Test_2 Proportions (Case 1)** worksheet in the **Test Statistics** workbook.

MINITAB

Test and CI for Two Proportions: Supermarket 1, Supermarket 2

```
Success = 2

Variable          X      N   Sample p
Supermarket     180    904   0.199115
Supermarket     155   1038   0.149326

Estimate for p(Supermarket) - p(Supermarket):  0.0497894
95% lower bound for p(Supermarket) - p(Supermarket):  0.0213577
Test for p(Supermarket) - p(Supermarket) = 0 (vs > 0):
  Z = 2.90  P-Value = 0.002
```

COMMANDS

The data must represent successes and failures. The codes can be numbers or text. There can be only two kinds of entries, one representing success and the other, failure. If numbers are used, Minitab will interpret the larger one as a success.

COMMANDS FOR EXAMPLE 13.8

Open file **Xm13-08**.

1. Type or import the data.
2. Click **Stat, Basic Statistics,** and **2 Proportions....**
3. Specify **Samples in different columns.**
4. Specify the **First** and **Second** samples.

C1 and **C2** or **Supermarket 1** and **Supermarket 2**

5. Click **Options...** and type the value of the **Test difference**.

0

6. Specify the **Alternative** hypothesis.

greater than

7. Click **Use pooled estimate of p for test**. Click **OK.** Click **OK.**

(continued)

If the data are stacked, click **Samples in one column** at step 3.

The test can also be completed from statistics. At step 3 click **Summarized data**, specify the sample sizes (**Trials**) and the number of **Successes** for the **First sample** and the **Second sample**.

INTERPRET

The value of the test statistic is $z = 2.90$; its p-value is .0019. There is enough evidence to infer that the brightly colored design is more popular than the simple design. As a result, it is recommended that management switch to the first design.

EXAMPLE 13.9

Suppose that in Example 13.8 the additional cost of the brightly colored design requires that it outsell the simple design by more than 3%. Should management switch to the brightly colored design?

SOLUTION

IDENTIFY

The alternative hypothesis is

$$H_1: \quad (p_1 - p_2) > .03$$

and the null hypothesis follows as

$$H_0: \quad (p_1 - p_2) = .03$$

Because the null hypothesis specifies a nonzero difference, we would apply the Case 2 test statistic.

COMPUTE

 MANUALLY

The value of the test statistic is

$$z = \frac{(\hat{p}_1 - \hat{p}_2) - (p_1 - p_2)}{\sqrt{\dfrac{\hat{p}_1(1 - \hat{p}_1)}{n_1} + \dfrac{\hat{p}_2(1 - \hat{p}_2)}{n_2}}} = \frac{(.1991 - .1493) - (.03)}{\sqrt{\dfrac{.1991(1 - .1991)}{904} + \dfrac{.1493(1 - .1493)}{1,038}}} = 1.15$$

 EXCEL

	A	B	C	D
1	**z-Test: Two Proportions**			
2				
3			*Supermarket 1*	*Supermarket 2*
4	Sample Proportions		0.1991	0.1493
5	Observations		904	1038
6	Hypothesized Difference		0.03	
7	z Stat		1.14	
8	P(Z<=z) one tail		0.1261	
9	z Critical one-tail		1.6449	
10	P(Z<=z) two-tail		0.2522	
11	z Critical two-tail		1.96	

COMMANDS

Use the same commands as above, except specify that the **Hypothesized Difference** is .03. Excel will apply the Case 2 test statistic when a nonzero value is typed.

MINITAB

Test and CI for Two Proportions: Supermarket 1, Supermarket 2

```
Success = 2

Variable          X      N   Sample p
Supermarket      180    904   0.199115
Supermarket      155   1038   0.149326

Estimate for p(Supermarket) - p(Supermarket):  0.0497894
95% lower bound for p(Supermarket) - p(Supermarket):  0.0213577
Test for p(Supermarket) - p(Supermarket) = 0.03 (vs > 0.03):
   Z = 1.14  P-Value = 0.126
```

COMMANDS

Use the commands detailed above, except at step 6, specify that the **Test difference is .03** and a step 7 do not click **Use pooled estimate of p for test.**

INTERPRET

There is not enough evidence to infer that the proportion of soap customers who buy the product with the brightly colored design is more than 3% higher than the proportion of soap customers who buy the product with the simple design. In the absence of sufficient evidence, the analysis suggests that the product should be packaged using the simple design.

EXAMPLE 13.10

To help estimate the difference in profitability, the marketing manager in Exercises 13.8 and 13.9 would like to estimate the difference between the two proportions. A confidence level of 95% is suggested.

SOLUTION

IDENTIFY

The parameter is $p_1 - p_2$, which is estimated by the following confidence interval estimator:

$$(\hat{p}_1 - \hat{p}_2) \pm z_{\alpha/2}\sqrt{\frac{\hat{p}_1(1 - \hat{p}_1)}{n_1} + \frac{\hat{p}_2(1 - \hat{p}_2)}{n_2}}$$

COMPUTE

 MANUALLY

The sample proportions have already been computed. They are

$$\hat{p}_1 = \frac{180}{904} = .1991$$

and

$$\hat{p}_2 = \frac{155}{1,038} = .1493$$

The 95% confidence interval estimate of $p_1 - p_2$ is

$$(\hat{p}_1 - \hat{p}_2) \pm z_{\alpha/2}\sqrt{\frac{\hat{p}_1(1 - \hat{p}_1)}{n_1} + \frac{\hat{p}_2(1 - \hat{p}_2)}{n_2}}$$

$$= (.1991 - .1493) \pm 1.96\sqrt{\frac{.1991(1 - .1991)}{904} + \frac{.1493(1 - .1493)}{1,038}}$$

$$= .0498 \pm .0339$$

$$\text{LCL} = .0159 \quad \text{and} \quad \text{UCL} = .0837$$

EXCEL

	A	B	C	D
1	z-Estimate: Two Proportions			
2				
3			Supermarket 1	Supermarket 2
4	Sample Proportions		0.1991	0.1493
5	Observations		904	1038
6				
7	LCL		0.0159	
8	UCL		0.0837	

COMMANDS

1. Type or import the data into two adjacent columns.
2. Click **Tools, Data Analysis Plus,** and **Z-Estimate: 2 Proportions**.
3. Specify the **Variable 1 Range** and the **Variable 2 Range**.
4. Specify the **Code for Success**.
5. Click **Labels**, if appropriate.
6. Type a value for α (**Alpha**) and click **OK**.

COMMANDS FOR EXAMPLE 13.10
Open file **Xm13-08**.

A1:A905 and **B1: B1039**

2

.05

To produce the confidence interval estimate of the difference between two proportions or to perform a what-if analysis, activate the **z-Estimate_2 Proportions** worksheet in the **Estimators** workbook.

MINITAB

Test and CI for Two Proportions: Supermarket 1, Supermarket 2

```
Success = 2

Variable          X      N    Sample p
Supermarket      180    904   0.199115
Supermarket      155   1038   0.149326

Estimate for p(Supermarket) - p(Supermarket):  0.0497894
95% CI for p(Supermarket) - p(Supermarket):  (0.0159109, 0.0836679)
Test for p(Supermarket) - p(Supermarket) = 0 (vs not = 0):
  Z = 2.90  P-Value = 0.004
```

COMMANDS

Follow the commands to test hypotheses about two proportions. Specify the alternative hypothesis as **not equal**.

INTERPRET

We estimate that the market share for the brightly colored design is between 1.6% and 8.4% larger than the market share for the simple design.

ESTIMATING THE COST OF A LIFE SAVED: SOLUTION

IDENTIFY

The problem objective is to compare two populations, the outcomes of the treatments with t-PA and with streptokinase. The data are nominal because we record only whether the patient lived or died. Thus, the parameter is $p_1 - p_2$, where p_1 = death rate with t-PA and p_2 = death rate with streptokinase. Because we wish to estimate the cost per life saved, we first must estimate the difference in death rates between the two drugs. We'll use a 95% confidence level.

COMPUTE

 MANUALLY

The sample proportions are

$$\hat{p}_1 = \frac{1497}{20,500} = .0730$$

and

$$\hat{p}_2 = \frac{1292}{20,500} = .0630$$

The 95% confidence interval estimate of the difference between death rates is

$$(\hat{p}_1 - \hat{p}_2) \pm z_{\alpha/2}\sqrt{\frac{\hat{p}_1(1 - \hat{p}_1)}{n_1} + \frac{\hat{p}_2(1 - \hat{p}_2)}{n_2}}$$

$$= (.0730 - .0630) \pm 1.96\sqrt{\frac{.0730(1-.0730)}{20,500} + \frac{.0630(1-.0630)}{20,500}}$$

$$= .0100 \pm .0049$$

$$\text{LCL} = .0051 \quad \text{and} \quad \text{UCL} = .0149$$

 EXCEL

	A	B	C	D	E	F
1	z-Estimate of the Difference Between Two Proportions					
2						
3		Sample 1	Sample 2	Confidence Interval Estimate		
4	Sample proportion	0.0730	0.0630	0.0100	±	0.0049
5	Sample size	20500	20500	Lower confidence limit		0.0051
6	Confidence level	0.95		Upper confidence limit		0.0149

COMMANDS

Open the **z-Estimate_2 Proportions** worksheet in the **Estimators** workbook and substitute the sample proportions, sample sizes, and confidence level.

MINITAB

Test and CI for Two Proportions

```
Sample      X       N   Sample p
1         1497   20500  0.073024
2         1292   20500  0.063024

Estimate for p(1) - p(2):  0.01
95% CI for p(1) - p(2):  (0.00512657, 0.0148734)
Test for p(1) - p(2) = 0 (vs not = 0):   Z = 4.02   P-Value = 0.000
```

COMMANDS

1. Click **Stat, Basic Statistics,** and 2 **Proportions**...
2. Click **Summarized data** and type the sample
   sizes (**Trials**) and the values of x_1 and x_2
   (**Successes**).
3. Click **Options...,** type the value of the
   Confidence level.
4. Specify the **Alternative** as **not equal.** Click **OK.** Click **OK.**

COMMANDS FOR
EXAMPLE

20500 1497
20500 1292

.95

INTERPRET

We estimate that between .51% and 1.49% more heart attack victims will survive
because of the use of t-PA instead of streptokinase. However, the difference in cost is
$2,900 – $460 = $ 2,440. The cost per life saved by switching to t-PA is estimated to fall
between

$$LCL = 2,440/.0149 = \$163,758$$

and

$$UCL = 2,440/.0051 = \$478,431$$

The factors that identify the inference about the difference between two proportions
are listed in the box.

FACTORS THAT IDENTIFY THE z-TEST AND ESTIMATOR OF $p_1 - p_2$
1. **Problem objective:** Compare two populations.
2. **Data type:** Nominal

EXERCISES

Developing an Understanding of Statistical Concepts

*Exercises 13.94 to 13.103 are "what-if analyses" designed to deter-
mine what happens to the test statistics and interval estimates
when elements of the statistical inference change. These problems
can be solved manually, using Excel's **Test Statistics** or **Estimators**
workbooks, or using Minitab.*

13.94   Random samples from two binomial populations

yielded the following statistics:

$\hat{p}_1 = .45$ $n_1 = 100$
$\hat{p}_2 = .40$ $n_2 = 100$

Calculate the *p*-value of a test to determine whether
we can infer that the population proportions differ.

13.95   Repeat Exercise 13.94, increasing the sample sizes to
400.

13.96 Review Exercises 13.94 and 13.95. Describe what happens to the p-value when the sample sizes increase.

13.97 Repeat Exercise 13.94, with $\hat{p}_1 = .95$ and $\hat{p}_2 = .90$.

13.98 Review Exercises 13.94 and 13.97. Describe the effect on the p-value of increasing the sample proportions.

13.99 Repeat Exercise 13.94 with $\hat{p}_1 = .05$ and $\hat{p}_2 = .10$.

13.100 Review Exercises 13.94 and 13.99. Describe the effect on the p-value of decreasing the sample proportions.

13.101 After sampling from two binomial populations, we found the following.

$$\hat{p}_1 = .18 \qquad n_1 = 100$$
$$\hat{p}_2 = .22 \qquad n_2 = 100$$

Estimate with 90% confidence the difference in population proportions.

13.102 Repeat Exercise 13.101, increasing the sample proportions to .48 and .52, respectively.

13.103 Review Exercises 13.101 and 13.102. Describe the effects of increasing the sample proportions.

Applications

13.104 Cold and allergy medicines have been available for a number of years. One serious side effect of these medications is that they cause drowsiness, which makes them dangerous for industrial workers. In recent years, a nondrowsy cold and allergy medicine has been developed. One such product, Hismanal, is claimed by its manufacturer to be the first, once-a-day, nondrowsy allergy medicine. The nondrowsy part of the claim is based on a clinical experiment in which 1,604 patients were given Hismanal and 1,109 patients were given a placebo. Of the first group, 7.1% reported drowsiness; of the second group, 6.4% reported drowsiness. Do these results allow us to infer at the 5% significance level that Hismanal's claim is false?

13.105 Surveys have been widely used by politicians around the world as a way of monitoring the opinions of the electorate. Six months ago, a survey was undertaken to determine the degree of support for a national party leader. Of a sample of 1,100, 56% indicated that they would vote for this politician. This month, another survey of 800 voters revealed that 46% now support the leader.

a At the 5% significance level, can we infer that the national leader's popularity has decreased?

b At the 5% significance level, can we infer that the national leader's popularity has decreased by more than 5%?

c Estimate with 95% confidence the decrease in percentage support between now and 6 months ago.

13.106 The process that is used to produce a complex component used in medical instruments typically results in defective rates in the 40% range. Recently, two innovative processes have been developed to replace the existing process. Process 1 appears to be more promising, but it is considerably more expensive to purchase and operate than process 2. After a thorough analysis of the costs, management decides that it will adopt process 1 only if the proportion of defective components it produces is more than 8% smaller than that produced by process 2. In a test to guide the decision, both processes were used to produce 300 components. Of the 300 components produced by process 1, 33 were found to be defective, whereas 84 out of the 300 produced by process 2 were defective. Using a significance level of 1%, conduct a test to help management make a decision.

13.107 Plavix is a drug that is given to angioplasty patients to help prevent blood clots. A researcher at McMaster University organized a study that involved 12,562 patients in 482 hospitals in 28 countries. All the patients had acute coronary syndrome, which produces mild heart attacks or unstable angina, chest pain that may precede a heart attack. The patients were divided into two equal groups. Group 1 received daily Plavix pills, while group 2 received a placebo. After 1 year, 9.3% of patients on Plavix suffered a stroke or new heart attack, or had died of cardiovascular disease, compared with 11.5% of those who took the placebo. Can we infer at the 5% significance level that Plavix is effective?

The following exercises require the use of a computer and software. The answers may be calculated manually. See Appendix A for the sample statistics. **Use a 5% significance level unless specified otherwise.**

13.108 Telemarketers obtain names and telephone numbers from several sources. To determine whether one particular source is better than a second, a random sample of names and numbers from the two different sources was obtained. For each potential customer, a statistics practitioner recorded whether that individual made a purchase (code = 2) or not (code = 1). These data are stored in stacked format in file Xr13-108. Can we infer that differences exist between the two sources?

13.109 The image of westerners is that they are more active physically. To examine the truth of the image, a random sample of Californians and New Yorkers was asked whether they take part in physical activities. The responses (2 = yes and 1 = no) are stored in file Xr13-109. Can we infer that New Yorkers are more likely to respond no than Californians?

13.110 The cost of cigarette smoking to smokers and to society in general is high. To determine whether various antismoking campaigns have been successful, annual surveys are conducted. Randomly selected individuals are asked whether they smoke on some days. The responses (1 = no and 2 = yes) for this year and 10 years ago are stored in file Xr13-110. Can we infer that the proportion of smokers has declined in the last 10 years? (*Caution:* Missing data) (Adapted from the U.S. National Center for Health Statistics)

13.111 An insurance company is thinking about offering discounts on its life insurance policies to nonsmokers. As part of its analysis, it randomly selects 200 men who are 60 years old and asks them whether they smoke at least one pack of cigarettes per day and whether they have ever suffered from heart disease. The results are stored in file Xr13-111, where 2 = suffer from heart disease and 1 = do not suffer from heart disease.

a Can the company conclude at the 10% significance level that smokers have a higher incidence of heart disease than nonsmokers?

b Estimate with 90% confidence the difference in the fractions of men suffering from heart disease between smokers and nonsmokers.

13.112 The impact of the accumulation of carbon dioxide in the atmosphere caused by burning fossil fuels such as oil, coal, and natural gas has been hotly debated for more than a decade. Some environmentalists and scientists have predicted that the excess carbon dioxide will increase the earth's temperature over the next 50 to 100 years with disastrous consequences. This belief is often called the "greenhouse effect." Other scientists claim that we don't know what the effect will be, and yet others believe that the earth's temperature is likely to decrease. Given the debate among scientists, it is not surprising that the general population is confused. To gauge the public's opinion on the subject, a random sample of 400 people was asked 2 years ago whether they believed in the greenhouse effect. This year, 500 people were asked the same question. The results are stored in file Xr13-112 using the following codes: 2 = believe in greenhouse effect; 1 = do not believe in greenhouse effect.

a Can we infer at the 10% significance level that there has been a decrease in belief in the greenhouse effect?

b Estimate the real change in the public's opinion about the subject. Use a 90% confidence level.

13. 113 Has the illicit use of drugs decreased over the past ten years? Government agencies have undertaken surveys of Americans 12 years of age and older. Each was asked whether he or she used drugs at least once in the previous month. The responses (1 = no and 2 = yes) this year and 10 years ago are stored in file Xr13-113. Can we infer that the use of illicit drugs in the United States has increased in the past decade? (Adapted from the U.S. Substance Abuse and Mental Health Services Administration, National Household Survey on Drug Abuse)

13.114 An operations manager of a computer chip maker is in the process of selecting a new machine to replace several older ones. Although technological innovations have improved the production process, it is quite common for the machines to produce defective chips. The operations manager must choose between two machines. The cost of machine A is several thousand dollars greater than the cost of machine B. After an analysis of the costs, it was determined that machine A is warranted provided that its defective rate is more than 2% less than that of machine B. To help decide, both machines are used to produce 200 chips each. Each chip was examined and whether it was defective (code = 2) or not (code = 1) was recorded. These data for machines A and B are stored in file Xr13-114. Should the operations manager select machine A?

APPLICATIONS IN MARKETING: *MARKET SEGMENTATION*

In Section 12.5 we introduced market segmentation and described how the size of market segments can be estimated. Once the segments have been defined, we can use statistical techniques to determine whether members of the segments differ in their purchases of a firm's products.

13.115 The market for breakfast cereals has been divided into several segments related to health. One company identified a segment as those adults who are health conscious. The marketing manager would like to know whether this segment is more likely to purchase its Special X cereal that is pitched toward the health-conscious segment. A survey of adults classified each as either a member of the health-conscious group or not. Each respondent was also asked whether he or she buys Special X (1 = no, 2 = yes). The responses for the health-conscious group and the others were stored in file Xr13-115. Can we infer from these data that health-conscious adults are more likely to buy Special X?

13.116 Quik Lube is a company that offers oil change service while the customer waits. Its market has been segmented by income. The company would like to determine whether those in the low-income group use the company's service more frequently than do members of the high-income group. Surveys identified a random sample of individuals as either low-income or high-income. Each person was asked whether they buy the company's service. The responses (1 = no, 2 = yes) are stored in file Xr13-116. Can we infer that low-income individuals are more likely to use the company's services? (*Caution:* Missing data)

APPLICATIONS IN OPERATIONS MANAGEMENT: *PHARMACEUTICAL AND MEDICAL EXPERIMENTS*

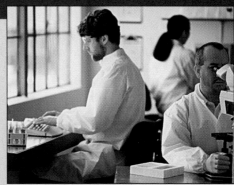

When new products are developed, they are tested in several ways. First, does the new product work? Second, is it better than the existing product? Third, will customers buy it at a price that is profitable? Performing a customer survey or some other experiment that yields the information needed often tests the last question. This experiment is usually the domain of the marketing manager.

The other two questions are dealt with by the developers of the new product, which usually means the research department or the operations manager. When the product is a new drug, there are particular ways in which the data are gathered. The sample is divided into two groups. One group is assigned the new drug and the other is assigned a placebo, a pill that contains no medication. The experiment is often called "double-blind" because neither the subjects who take the drug nor the physician/scientist who provides the drug knows whether any individual is taking the drug or the placebo. At the end of the experiment the data are produced that allow statistics practitioners to do their work.

13.117 In a study that was highly publicized, doctors discovered that aspirin seems to help prevent heart attacks. The research project, which was scheduled to last for 5 years, employed 22,000 American physicians (all male). Half took an aspirin tablet three times per week, while the other half took a placebo on the same schedule. The researchers tracked each of the volunteers and updated the records regularly. File Xr13-117 stores the code numbers for each physician, which group he belonged to, and whether he suffered a heart attack (1 = no, 2 = yes). Determine whether these results indicate that aspirin is effective in reducing the incidence of heart attacks.

13.7 SUMMARY

In this chapter, we presented a variety of techniques that allow statistics practitioners to compare two populations. When the data are interval and we are interested in measures of central location, we encountered two more factors that must be considered when choosing the appropriate technique. When the samples are **independent**, we can use either the **equal-variances** or **unequal-variances** formulas. When the samples are **matched pairs**, we have only one set of formulas. We introduced the *F* statistic, which is used to make inferences about two population variances. When the data are nominal, the parameter of interest is the difference between two proportions. For this parameter we had two test statistics and one interval estimator. Finally, we discussed **observational** and **experimental data**, important concepts in attempting to interpret statistical findings.

IMPORTANT TERMS

Pooled variance estimator 394
Equal-variances test statistic
    and interval estimator 394
Unequal-variances test statistic
    and interval estimator 395

Observational data 411
Experimental data 411
Matched pairs experiment 417
Mean of the population of
    differences 417

Numerator degrees of
    freedom 427
Denominator degrees of
    freedom 427
Pooled proportion estimator 433

SYMBOLS

Symbol	Pronounced	Represents
s_p^2	s-sub-p-squared	Pooled variance estimator
μ_D	mu-sub-D or mu-D	Mean of the paired differences
$\bar{x}_D$	x-bar-sub-D or x-bar-D	Sample mean of the paired differences
s_D	s-sub-D or s-D	Sample standard deviation of the paired differences
n_D	n-sub-D or n-D	Sample size of the paired differences
$\hat{p}$	p-hat	Pooled proportion

FORMULAS

Equal-variances t test of $\mu_1 - \mu_2$

$$t = \frac{(\bar{x}_1 - \bar{x}_2) - (\mu_1 - \mu_2)}{\sqrt{s_p^2\left(\dfrac{1}{n_1} + \dfrac{1}{n_2}\right)}} \qquad \nu = n_1 + n_2 - 2$$

Equal-variances interval estimator of $\mu_1 - \mu_2$

$$(\bar{x}_1 - \bar{x}_2) \pm t_{\alpha/2}\sqrt{s_p^2\left(\frac{1}{n_1} + \frac{1}{n_2}\right)} \qquad \nu = n_1 + n_2 - 2$$

Unequal-variances t test of $\mu_1 - \mu_2$

$$t = \frac{(\bar{x}_1 - \bar{x}_2) - (\mu_1 - \mu_2)}{\sqrt{\left(\dfrac{s_1^2}{n_1} + \dfrac{s_2^2}{n_2}\right)}} \qquad \nu = \frac{(s_1^2/n_1 + s_2^2/n_2)^2}{\left(\dfrac{(s_1^2/n_1)^2}{n_1 - 1} + \dfrac{(s_2^2/n_2)^2}{n_2 - 1}\right)}$$

Unequal-variances interval estimator of $\mu_1 - \mu_2$

$$(\bar{x}_1 - \bar{x}_2) \pm t_{\alpha/2}\sqrt{\frac{s_1^2}{n_1} + \frac{s_2^2}{n_2}} \qquad \nu = \frac{(s_1^2/n_1 + s_2^2/n_2)^2}{\left(\dfrac{(s_1^2/n_1)^2}{n_1 - 1} + \dfrac{(s_2^2/n_2)^2}{n_2 - 1}\right)}$$

t test of μ_D

$$t = \frac{\bar{x}_D - \mu_D}{s_D/\sqrt{n_D}} \qquad \nu = n_D - 1$$

Interval estimator of μ_D

$$\bar{x}_D \pm t_{\alpha/2}\frac{s_D}{\sqrt{n_D}} \qquad \nu = n_D - 1$$

F test of σ_1^2/σ_2^2

$$F = \frac{s_1^2}{s_2^2} \qquad \nu_1 = n_1 - 1 \text{ and } \nu_2 = n_2 - 1$$

Interval estimator of σ_1^2/σ_2^2

$$\text{LCL} = \left(\frac{s_1^2}{s_2^2}\right)\frac{1}{F_{\alpha/2,\nu_1,\nu_2}}$$

$$\text{UCL} = \left(\frac{s_1^2}{s_2^2}\right)F_{\alpha/2,\nu_2,\nu_1}$$

z test of $p_1 - p_2$

Case 1: $z = \dfrac{(\hat{p}_1 - \hat{p}_2)}{\sqrt{\hat{p}(1-\hat{p})\left(\dfrac{1}{n_1} + \dfrac{1}{n_2}\right)}}$

Case 2: $z = \dfrac{(\hat{p}_1 - \hat{p}_2) - (p_1 - p_2)}{\sqrt{\dfrac{\hat{p}_1(1-\hat{p}_1)}{n_1} + \dfrac{\hat{p}_2(1-\hat{p}_2)}{n_2}}}$

Interval estimator of $p_1 - p_2$

$$(\hat{p}_1 - \hat{p}_2) \pm z_{\alpha/2}\sqrt{\frac{\hat{p}_1(1-\hat{p}_1)}{n_1} + \frac{\hat{p}_2(1-\hat{p}_2)}{n_2}}$$

COMPUTER OUTPUT AND INSTRUCTIONS

Technique	Excel	Minitab
Unequal-variances t test of $\mu_1 - \mu_2$	398	399
Unequal-variances estimator of $\mu_1 - \mu_2$	400	400
Equal-variances t test of $\mu_1 - \mu_2$	403	403
Equal-variances estimator of $\mu_1 - \mu_2$	404	403
t test of μ_D	418	419
t estimator of μ_D	420	420
F test of σ_1^2/σ_2^2	428	429
F estimator of σ_1^2/σ_2^2	430	
z test of $p_1 - p_2$ (Case 1)	437	437
z test of $p_1 - p_2$ (Case 2)	438	438
z estimator of $p_1 - p_2$	440	440

REFERENCES

Fuerderer, R., A. Herrmann, and G. Wuebker, *Optimal Bundling: Marketing Strategies to Improve Economic Performance.* New York: Springer Verlag, 1999.

Gaither, Norman, and Gregory Frazier, *Production and Operations Management,* 8th edition. Cincinnati, OH: Southwestern, 1999.

Hogg, Robert V., and Allan T. Craig, *Introduction to Mathematical Statistics,* 5th edition. Englewood Cliffs, NJ: Prentice Hall, 1995.

Kotler, Phillip, *Marketing Management,* 8th edition. Englewood Cliffs, NJ: Prentice Hall, 1994.

Lehmann, E. L., *Testing Statistical Hypotheses,* 2nd edition. New York: Chapman & Hall, 1991.

Lillien, Gary L., and Arvind Rangaswamy, *Marketing Engineering: Computer Assisted Marketing Analysis and Planning.* Reading, MA: Addison Wesley, 1998.

Mood, A. M., F. A. Graybill, and D. L. Boes, *Introduction to the Theory of Statistics,* 3rd edition. New York: McGraw Hill, 1974.

Nahmias, Steven, *Production and Operations Analysis,* 4th edition. Burr Ridge, IL: McGraw Hill, 2001.

Peter, J. Paul, and James H. Donnely, Jr., *A Preface to Marketing Management,* 8th edition. Boston, MA: Irwin/ McGraw-Hill, 2000.

CHAPTER REVIEW EXERCISES

The following exercises require the use of a computer and software. **Use a 5% significance level unless specified otherwise.**

13.118 Is eating oat bran an effective way to reduce cholesterol? Early studies indicated that eating oat bran daily reduces cholesterol levels by 5% to 10%. Reports of this study resulted in the introduction of many new breakfast cereals with various percentages of oat bran as an ingredient. However, an experiment performed by medical researchers in Boston, Massachusetts, cast doubt on the effectiveness of oat bran. In that study, 120 volunteers ate oat bran for breakfast, and another 120 volunteers ate another grain cereal for breakfast. At the end of 6 weeks, the percentage of cholesterol reduction was computed for both groups. These data are stored in file Xr13-118. Can we infer that oat bran is different from other cereals in terms of cholesterol reduction?

13.119 An inspector for the Atlantic City Gaming Commission suspects that a particular blackjack dealer may be cheating (in favor of the casino) when he deals at expensive tables. To test her belief, she observed 500 hands each at the $100-limit table and the $3,000-limit table. For each hand, she recorded whether the dealer won (code = 2) or lost (code = 1). When a tie occurs, there is no winner or loser. These data are stored in file Xr13-119. (Column 1 stores the outcomes for the $100-limit table, and column 2 stores the outcomes for the $3,000-limit table.) Can the inspector conclude at the 10% significance level that the dealer is cheating at the more expensive table?

13.120 A restaurant located in an office building decides to adopt a new strategy for attracting customers to the restaurant. Every week it advertises in the city newspaper. To assess how well the advertising is working, the restaurant owner recorded the weekly gross sales for the 15 weeks after the campaign began and the weekly gross sales for the 24 weeks immediately prior to the campaign. These data are stored in columns 1 (during campaign) and 2 (before campaign) in file Xr13-120. Can the restaurateur conclude that the advertising campaign is successful?

13.121 Refer to Exercise 13.120. Assume that the profit is 20% of the gross. If the ads cost $50 per week, can the restaurateur conclude that the ads are profitable?

13.122 How important to your health are regular vacations? In a study, a random sample of men and women were asked how frequently they take vacations. The men and women were divided into two groups each. The members of group 1 had suffered a heart attack; the members of group 2 had not. The number of days of vacation last year was recorded for each person. The data are stored in file Xr13-122. Can we infer that men and women who suffer heart attacks vacation less than those who did not suffer a heart attack?

13.123 Because of the high cost of energy, homeowners in northern climates need to find ways to cut their heating costs. A building contractor wanted to investigate the effect on heating costs of increasing the insulation. As an experiment, he located a large subdevelopment built around 1970 with minimal insulation. His plan was to insulate some of the houses and compare the heating costs in the insulated homes with those that remained uninsulated. However, it was clear to him that the size of the house was a critical factor in determining heating costs. Consequently, he found 16 pairs of identical-sized houses ranging from about 1,200 to 2,800 square feet. He insulated one house in each pair (levels of R20 in the walls and R32 in the attic) and left the other house unchanged. The heating cost for the following winter season was recorded for each house. The data are stored in file Xr13-123 (column 1 = size of the house, column 2 = heating cost of uninsulated house, column 3 = heating cost of insulated house).

a Do these data allow the contractor to infer at the 10% significance level that the heating cost for insulated houses is less than that for uninsulated houses?

b Estimate with 95% confidence the mean savings due to insulating.

c What is the required condition for the use of the techniques in parts **a** and **b**?

13.124 The city of Toronto boasts four daily newspapers. Not surprisingly, competition is keen. To help learn more about newspaper readers, and advertiser selected a random sample of people who bought their newspapers from a street vendor and people who had the newspaper delivered to their homes. Each was asked how many minutes they spent reading their newspapers. These data are stored in columns 1 and 2 in file Xr13-124. Can we infer that the amount of time reading differs between the two groups?

13.125 In recent years, a number of state governments have passed mandatory seat-belt laws. Although the use of seat belts is known to save lives and reduce serious injuries, compliance with seat-belt laws is not universal. In an effort to increase the use of seat belts, a government agency sponsored a 2-year study. Among its objectives was to determine whether there was enough evidence to infer that seat-belt usage increased between last year and this year. To test this belief, random samples of drivers last year and this year were asked whether they always use their seat belts. The responses (2 = wear seat belt; 1 = do not wear seat belt) were stored in file Xr13-125. Can we infer that seat-belt usage has increased over the last year?

13.126 An important component of the cost of living is the amount of money spent on housing. Housing costs include rent (for tenants), mortgage payments and property tax (for homeowners), heating, electricity, and water. An economist undertook a 5-year study to determine how housing costs have changed. Five years ago, he took a random sample of 200 households and recorded the percentage of total income spent on housing. This year, he took another sample of 200 households. The data are stored in columns 1 (5 years ago) and 2 (this year) in file Xr13-126.

a Conduct a test (with $\alpha = .10$) to determine whether the economist can infer that housing cost as a percentage of total income has increased over the last 5 years.

b Use whatever statistical method you deem appropriate to check the required condition(s) of the test used in part **a**.

13.127 In designing advertising campaigns to sell magazines, it is important to know how much time each of a number of demographic groups spends reading magazines. In a preliminary study, 40 people were randomly selected. Each was asked how much time per week he or she spends reading magazines; additionally, each was categorized by gender and by income level (high or low). The data are stored in file Xr13-127 in the following way: column 1 = time spent reading magazines per week in minutes for all respondents; column 2 = gender (1 = male, 2 = female); column 3 = income level (1 = low, 2 = high).

a Is there sufficient evidence at the 10% significance level to conclude that men and women differ in the amount of time spent reading magazines?

b Is there sufficient evidence at the 10% significance level to conclude that high-income individuals devote more time to reading magazines than low-income people?

13.128 In a study to determine whether gender affects salary offers for graduating MBA students, 25 pairs of students were selected. Each pair consisted of a female and a male student who were matched according to their grade point averages, courses taken, ages, and previous work experience. The highest salary offered (in thousands of dollars) to each graduate was recorded and stored in file Xr13-128 (column 1 = salary offer for females, column 2 = salary offer for males).

a Is there enough evidence at the 10% significance level to infer that gender is a factor in salary offers?

b Discuss why the experiment was organized in the way it was.

c Is the required condition for the test in part **a** satisfied?

13.129 Have North Americans grown to distrust television and newspaper journalists? A study was conducted this year to compare what Americans currently think of the press versus what they said 3 years ago. The survey asked respondents whether they agree that the press tends to favor one side when reporting on political and social issues. A random sample of people was asked to participate in this year's survey. The results of a survey of another random sample taken 3 years ago are also available. The responses (2 = agree; 1 = disagree) are stored in file Xr13-129. Can we conclude at the 10% significance level that Americans have become more distrustful of television and newspaper reporting this year than they were 3 years ago?

13.130 Before deciding which of two types of stamping machines should be purchased, the plant manager of an automotive parts manufacturer wants to determine the number of units that each produces. The two machines differ in cost, reliability, and productivity. The firm's accountant has calculated that machine A must produce 25 more nondefective units per hour than machine B to warrant buying machine A. To help decide, both machines were operated for 24 hours. The total number of units and the number of defective units produced by each machine per hour were recorded. These data are stored in file Xr13-130 (column 1 = total number of units produced by machine A; column 2 = number of defectives produced by machine A; column 3 = total number of units produced by machine B; column 4 = number of defectives produced by machine B). Determine which machine should be purchased.

13.131 Refer to Exercise 13.130. Can we conclude that the defective rate differs between the two machines?

13.132 The growing use of bicycles to commute to work has caused many cities to create exclusive bicycle lanes. These lanes are usually created by disallowing parking on streets that formerly allowed curbside parking. Merchants on such streets complain that the removal of parking will cause their businesses to suffer. To examine this problem, the mayor of a large city decided to launch an experiment on one busy street that had 1-hour parking meters. The meters were removed and a bicycle lane was created. The mayor asked the three businesses (a dry cleaner, a doughnut shop, and a convenience store) in one block to record daily sales for two complete weeks (Sunday to Saturday) prior to the change and two complete weeks after the change. The data are stored in file Xr13-132 (column 1 = day of the week, column 2 = sales before change for dry cleaner, column 3 = sales after change for dry cleaner, column 4 = sales before change for doughnut shop, column 5 = sales after change for doughnut shop, column 6 = sales before change for convenience store, and column 7 = sales after change for convenience store). What conclusions can you draw from these data?

13.133 There may be a new health concern—too much iron in our bodies. An article in the *Wall Street Journal* (17 January 1992) reported that some scientists have implicated iron as a factor in various diseases, including cancer. Part of the problem, it is believed, is that iron builds up in the body over many years. To examine the issue, a random sample of 20-year-old men and women and 40-year-old men and women was drawn. The amount of iron in their bodies was measured and recorded. The results are stored in file Xr13-133 in the following way: Column 1 shows the amount of stored iron in men (in milligrams); column 2 indicates the men's ages; column 3 shows the amount of stored iron in women; column 4 lists the women's ages.

a Conduct a test at the 10% significance level to determine whether we can infer that 40-year-old men have more iron in their bodies than do 20-year-old men.

b Repeat part **a** for women.

13.134 It is known that clinical depression is linked to several other diseases. Scientists at Johns Hopkins University undertook a study to determine whether heart disease is one of these. A group of 1,190 male medical students was tracked over a 40-year period. Of these, 132 had suffered clinically diagnosed depression. For each student the scientists recorded whether the student died of a heart attack (code = 2) or did not (code = 1). These data are stored in columns 1 (clinically depressed) and 2 (not clinically depressed) in file Xr13-134.

a Can we infer at the 1% significance level that men who are clinically depressed are more likely to die from heart diseases?

b If the answer to part **a** is yes, can you interpret this to mean that depression causes heart disease? Explain.

13.135 An important function of a firm's human resources manager is to track worker turnover. As a general rule, companies prefer to retain workers. New workers often need to be trained and it often takes time for new workers to learn how to perform their jobs. In order to investigate nationwide results, a human resources manager organized a survey wherein a random sample of men and women were asked how long they have worked for their current employer. The responses (in years) are stored in file Xr13-135. Can we infer that men and women have different job tenures? (Adapted from the *Statistical Abstract of the United States*, 2000, Table 664)

13.136 Most people exercise in order to lose weight. To determine better ways to lose weight, a random sample of male and female exercisers was divided into groups. The first group exercised vigorously twice a week. The second group exercised moderately four times per week. The weight loss for each individual was recorded and stored in file Xr13-136. Can we infer that people who exercise moderately more frequently lose weight faster?

13.137 After observing the results of the test in Exercise 13.136, a statistics practitioner organized another experiment. People were matched according to gender, height, and weight. One member of each matched pair then exercised vigorously twice a week and the other member exercised moderately four times per week. The weight losses are stored in file Xr13-137. Can we infer that people who exercise moderately more frequently lose weight faster?

13.138 Pass the Lotion, a long-running television commercial for Special K cereal, features a flabby sunbather who asks his wife to smear sun lotion on his back. A random sample of Special K customers and a random sample of people who do not buy Special K were asked to indicate whether they liked or disliked the ad. The responses (1 = yes, 2 = no) were stored in file Xr13-138. Can we infer that Special K buyers like the ad more than nonbuyers?

13.139 Refer to Exercise 13.138. The respondents were also asked whether they thought the ad would be effective in selling the product. The responses (1 = yes, 2 = no) are stored in file Xr13-139. Can we infer that Special K buyers are more likely to respond yes than nonbuyers?

13.140 Most English professors complain that students don't write very well. In particular, they point out that students often confuse quality and quantity. A study at the University of Texas examined this claim. In the study, undergraduate students were asked to compare the cost benefits of Japanese and American cars. All wrote their analyses on computers. Unbeknownst to the students, the computers were rigged so that some students would have to type twice as many words to fill a single page. The number of words used by each student was recorded and stored in file Xr13-140. (Column 1 contains the number of words written by students who were allotted a small space and column 2 contains the number of words written by students who were allotted a large space.) Can we conclude at the 10% significance level that students write in such a way as to fill the allotted space?

13.141 Approximately 20 million Americans work for themselves. Most run single-person businesses out of their homes. One-quarter of these individuals use personal computers in their businesses. A market research firm, Computer Intelligence InfoCorp, wanted to know whether single-person businesses that use personal computers are more successful than those with no computer. They surveyed 150 single-person firms and recorded their annual incomes. These data are stored in file Xr13-141. (Column 1 stores the incomes of businesses that use a computer and column 2 stores the incomes of businesses that do not.) Can we infer at the 10% significance level that single-person businesses that use a personal computer earn more than those that do not?

13.142 Many small retailers advertise in their neighborhoods by sending out flyers. People deliver these to homes and are paid according to the number of flyers delivered. Each deliverer is given several streets whose homes become their responsibility. One of the ways retailers use to check the performance of deliverers is to randomly sample some of the homes and ask the homeowner whether he or she received the flyer. Recently university students started a new delivery service. They have promised better service at a competitive price. A retailer wanted to know whether the new company's delivery rate is better than that of the existing firm. She had both companies deliver her flyers. Random samples of homes were drawn and each was asked whether he or she received the flyer (2 = yes and 1 = no). These data are stored in file Xr13-142. Can the retailer conclude that the new company is better? (Test with $\alpha = .10$)

13.143 Is marriage good for your health? To answer this question, researchers at the University of Toronto Medical School followed 103 couples, each with one spouse who was slightly hypertensive (mild high blood pressure). Participants also completed a questionnaire about their marriages. Three years later, the blood pressure of the previously hypertensive mate was measured. The reduction in blood pressure for those in happy marriages was stored in column 1 in file Xr13-143. The reduction of those in unhappy marriages was stored in column 2. Can we infer that spouses in happy marriages have a greater reduction in blood pressure than those in unhappy marriages?

APPLICATIONS IN MARKETING: *MARKET SEGMENTATION*

In Section 12.5 we introduced market segmentation. The following exercise addresses the problem of determining whether two market segments differ in their pattern of purchases of a particular product or service.

13.144 Movie studios segment their markets by age. Two segments that are particularly important to this industry are teenagers and 20-to-30-year-olds. In order to assess markets and guide the making of movies, a random sample of teenagers and 20-to-30-year-olds was drawn. Each was asked to report the number of movies they saw in theaters last year. These data are stored in file Xr13-144. Do these data allow us to infer that teenagers see more movies than 20-to-30-year-olds?

✦ CASE 13.1
ACCOUNTING COURSE EXEMPTIONS*

One of the problems encountered in teaching accounting in a business program is the issue of what to do with students who have taken one or more accounting courses in high school. Should these students be exempted from the introductory accounting course usually offered in the first or second year of the business program? Some professors have argued that high school courses do not have the breadth or depth of university courses, and that as a consequence, high school accounting students should not be exempted. Others think that the high school accounting course coverage is sufficiently close to that of the university course, and that forcing students with high school accounting to "retake" the course is a waste of time and resources.

*Adapted from E. Morass, G. Walsh, and N. M. Young, "Accounting for Performance: An Analysis of the Relationship Between Success in Introductory Accounting in University and Prior Study of Accounting in High School," *Proceedings of the 14th Annual Atlantic Schools of Business Conference* (1984): 13–44.

In order to examine the problem, students who were enrolled in the third year of the Bachelor of Commerce program at St. Mary's University were sampled. In the third year of this program, two introductory accounting half-credits are required: ACT 241 and ACT 242. Of the 638 students enrolled in ACT 241 in the fall semester, 374 were elected because of the similarities in their educational backgrounds (excluding high school accounting). Student files were examined for all 374 students, of whom 275 continued on to ACT 242 in the winter semester. For each student, researchers recorded the mark (out of 100) in ACT 241 and the mark in ACT 242 (if it was taken), as well as the number of high school accounting courses (either 0, 1, or 2). The results are stored in the file C13-01. Columns A, B, and C contain

the marks in ACT 241 for students who have taken 0, 1, and 2 high school accounting courses, respectively. Columns D, E, and F contain the marks in ACT 242 for students who have taken 0, 1, and 2 high school accounting courses, respectively.

The researchers would like to know whether students with one high school accounting course outperform those with no high school accounting and whether students with two high school accounting courses outperform those with no high school accounting. What exemption policy should be adopted?

APPENDIX 13.A EXCEL INSTRUCTIONS FOR STACKED AND UNSTACKED DATA

Most Excel statistical techniques require unstacked data. Suppose that the data are stacked in the following way: Column A stores the observations, and column B stores the codes representing the samples. If the data are scrambled (not in order), proceed with steps 1, 2, and 3 below. Otherwise, go to step 4.

1. Highlight columns A and B.
2. Click **Data** and **Sort...** .
3. Specify column B and **Ascending**. Click **OK**.

The data will now be unscrambled—all the observations from the first sample will occupy the top rows of column A, and the observations from the second sample will occupy the bottom rows of column A. To unstack, issue the following commands. (The following commands assume that there are only two samples.)

4. Highlight the rows of column A that were taken from sample 2.
5. Click **Edit** and **Cut**.
6. Make cell C1 active.
7. Click **Edit** and **Paste**.
8. Delete column B.

Columns A and B will now store the unstacked data.
   If the data are unstacked in columns A and B and you wish to stack them in column A, proceed as follows.

1. Highlight the cells in column B.
2. Click **Edit** and **Cut**.
3. Make the first empty cell in column A active. Click **Edit** and **Paste**.
4. Type the codes in column B.

Column A and B will now contain the stacked data—all the observations in column A and the codes identifying the sample in column B.

APPENDIX 13.B MINITAB INSTRUCTIONS FOR STACKED AND UNSTACKED DATA

MANIPULATING DATA

Minitab can perform a number of statistical analyses when the data are stacked or unstacked. However, some techniques require one format only. In this part of the appendix, we discuss how to change the format of the data.
   To stack unstacked data:

1. Click **Manip, Stack,** and **Stack Columns...** .
2. Specify the variables to be stacked (**Stack the following columns**).
3. Specify the variable where the data are to be stored (**Column of current worksheet**).
4. Specify where the codes are to be stored (**Store subscripts in**), if needed.

To unstack stacked data:

1. Click **Manip** and **Unstack Columns...** .
2. Specify the variable to be unstacked (**Unstack the data in**).
3. Specify the variable representing the codes (**Using subscripts in**).
4. Specify the variable where the data are to be stored (**Store unstacked data**) by clicking **After last column in use**.

DESCRIPTIVE STATISTICS AND GRAPHS FOR STACKED DATA

When the data are stacked, you can unstack the data before instructing Minitab to calculate the descriptive statistics or draw various graphs. Alternatively, you can use the following commands.

1. Click **Stat, Basic Statistics,** and **Display Descriptive Statistics...** .
2. Specify the **Variables** to be described.
3. Use the cursor to click **By variable:** and specify the codes.

To draw histograms and stem-and-leaf displays, proceed as above.

1. Click **Graph, Character Graphs,** and any one of **Histogram..., Box-plot...,** or **Stem-and-Leaf...** .
2. Specify the **Variables** to be described.
3. Use the cursor to click **By variable** and specify the variable representing the codes.

14 STATISTICAL INFERENCE: REVIEW OF CHAPTERS 12 AND 13

14.1 INTRODUCTION

This chapter is more than just a review of the previous two chapters. It is a critical part of your development as a statistics practitioner. When you solved problems at the end of each section in the preceding chapters (you *have* been solving problems at the end of each section covered, haven't you?), you probably had no great difficulty identifying the correct technique to use. You used the statistical technique introduced in that section. While those exercises provided practice in setting up hypotheses, producing computer output of tests of hypothesis and confidence interval estimators, and interpreting the results, you did not address a fundamental question faced by statistics practitioners: which technique to use. If you still do not appreciate the dimension of this problem, consider the following, which lists all the inferential methods covered thus far.

t test and estimator of μ

χ^2 test and estimator of σ^2

z test and estimator of p

t test and estimator of $\mu_1 - \mu_2$ (equal-variances formulas)

t test and estimator of $\mu_1 - \mu_2$ (unequal-variances formulas)

t test and estimator of μ_D

F test and estimator of σ_1^2/σ_2^2

z test (Cases 1 and 2) and estimator of $p_1 - p_2$

Counting tests and confidence interval estimators of a parameter as two different techniques, a total of 17 statistical procedures have been presented thus far, and there is much left to be done. Faced with statistical problems that require the use of some of these techniques (such as in real-world applications or on a midterm test), most students need some assistance in identifying the appropriate method. In the next section, we discuss in greater detail how to make this decision. At the end of this chapter you will have the opportunity to practice your decision skills; we've provided exercises and cases that require all of the inferential techniques introduced in Chapters 12 and 13. Solving these problems will require you to do what statistics practitioners must do: You must analyze the problem, identify the technique or techniques, employ statistical software and a computer to yield the required statistics, and interpret the results.

14.2 GUIDE TO IDENTIFYING THE CORRECT TECHNIQUE: CHAPTERS 12 AND 13

As you've probably already discovered, the two most important factors in determining the correct statistical technique are the problem objective and the data type. In some situations, once these have been recognized, the technique automatically follows. In other cases, however, several additional factors must be identified before you can proceed. For example, when the problem objective is to compare two populations and the data are interval, three other significant issues must be addressed: the descriptive measurement (central location or variability), if central location, whether the samples are independently drawn, and, if so, whether the unknown population variances are equal.

The flowchart in Figure 14.1 represents the logical process that leads to the identification of the appropriate method. We've also included a more detailed guide (Table 14.1) to the statistical techniques that lists the formulas of the test statistics, the confidence interval estimators, and the required conditions.

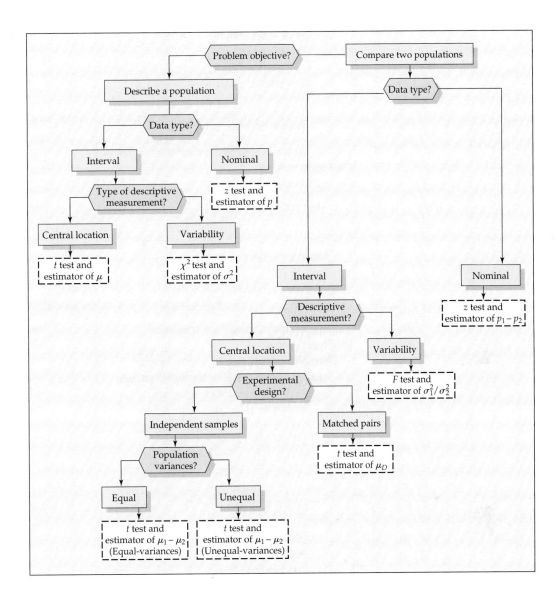

**Figure 14.1
Flowchart of
techniques:
Chapters 12
and 13**

Table 14.1 Summary of Statistical Inference: Chapters 12 and 13

Problem objective: Describe a population.

Data type: Interval

Descriptive measurement: Central location

Parameter: μ

Test statistic: $t = \dfrac{\bar{x} - \mu}{s/\sqrt{n}}$

Interval estimator: $\bar{x} \pm t_{\alpha/2}\dfrac{s}{\sqrt{n}}$

Required condition: Population is normal.

Descriptive measurement: Variability

Parameter: σ^2

Test statistic: $\chi^2 = \dfrac{(n-1)s^2}{\sigma^2}$

Interval estimator: LCL $= \dfrac{(n-1)s^2}{\chi^2_{\alpha/2}}$ UCL $= \dfrac{(n-1)s^2}{\chi^2_{1-\alpha/2}}$

Required condition: Population is normal.

Data type: Nominal

Parameter: p

Test statistic: $z = \dfrac{\hat{p} - p}{\sqrt{p(1-p)/n}}$

Interval estimator: $\hat{p} \pm z_{\alpha/2}\sqrt{\dfrac{\hat{p}(1-\hat{p})}{n}}$

Required condition: $np \geq 5$ and $n(1-p) \geq 5$ (for test)

$n\hat{p} \geq 5$ and $n(1-\hat{p}) \geq 5$ (for estimate)

Problem objective: Compare two populations.

Data type: Interval

Descriptive measurement: Central location

Experimental design: Independent samples

Population variances: $\sigma^2_1 = \sigma^2_2$

Parameter: $\mu_1 - \mu_2$

Test statistic: $t = \dfrac{(\bar{x}_1 - \bar{x}_2) - (\mu_1 - \mu_2)}{\sqrt{s^2_p\left(\dfrac{1}{n_1} + \dfrac{1}{n_2}\right)}}$

Interval estimator: $(\bar{x}_1 - \bar{x}_2) \pm t_{\alpha/2}\sqrt{s^2_p\left(\dfrac{1}{n_1} + \dfrac{1}{n_2}\right)}$

Required condition: Populations are normal.

Population variances: $\sigma^2_1 \neq \sigma^2_2$

Parameter: $\mu_1 - \mu_2$

Test statistic: $t = \dfrac{(\bar{x}_1 - \bar{x}_2) - (\mu_1 - \mu_2)}{\sqrt{\dfrac{s^2_1}{n_1} + \dfrac{s^2_2}{n_2}}}$

Interval estimator: $(\bar{x}_1 - \bar{x}_2) \pm t_{\alpha/2}\sqrt{\dfrac{s^2_1}{n_1} + \dfrac{s^2_2}{n_2}}$

Required condition: Populations are normal.

Experimental design: Matched pairs

Parameter: μ_D

Test statistic: $t = \dfrac{\bar{x}_D - \mu_D}{s_D/\sqrt{n_D}}$

Interval estimator: $\bar{x}_D \pm t_{\alpha/2}\dfrac{s_D}{\sqrt{n_D}}$

Required condition: Differences are normal.

Descriptive measurement: Variability

Parameter: σ_1^2/σ_2^2

Test statistic: $F = s_1^2/s_2^2$

Interval estimator: $\text{LCL} = \left(\dfrac{s_1^2}{s_2^2}\right)\dfrac{1}{F_{\alpha/2,\nu_1,\nu_2}}$

$\text{UCL} = \left(\dfrac{s_1^2}{s_2^2}\right)F_{\alpha/2,\nu_2,\nu_1}$

Required condition: Populations are normal.

Data type: Nominal

Parameter: $p_1 - p_2$

Test statistic:

Case 1: $H_0: (p_1 - p_2) = 0$

$$z = \dfrac{(\hat{p}_1 - \hat{p}_2)}{\sqrt{\hat{p}(1-\hat{p})\left(\dfrac{1}{n_1} + \dfrac{1}{n_2}\right)}}$$

Case 2: $H_0: (p_1 - p_2) = D\ (D \neq 0)$

$$z = \dfrac{(\hat{p}_1 - \hat{p}_2) - (p_1 - p_2)}{\sqrt{\dfrac{\hat{p}_1(1-\hat{p}_1)}{n_1} + \dfrac{\hat{p}_2(1-\hat{p}_2)}{n_2}}}$$

Interval estimator: $(\hat{p}_1 - \hat{p}_2) \pm z_{\alpha/2}\sqrt{\dfrac{\hat{p}_1(1-\hat{p}_1)}{n_1} + \dfrac{\hat{p}_2(1-\hat{p}_2)}{n_2}}$

Required conditions: $n_1\hat{p}_1,\ n_1(1-\hat{p}_1),\ n_2\hat{p}_2,$ and $n_2(1-\hat{p}_2) \geq 5$

EXAMPLE 14.1

Is the antilock braking system (ABS), now available as a standard feature on many cars, really effective? The ABS works by automatically pumping brakes extremely quickly on slippery surfaces so the brakes do not lock, avoiding an uncontrollable skid. If ABS is effective, we would expect that cars equipped with ABS would have fewer accidents, and the costs of repairs for the accidents that do occur would be smaller. To investigate the effectiveness of ABS, the Highway Loss Data Institute gathered data on a random sample of 500 1991 General Motors cars that did not have ABS and 500 1992 GM cars that were equipped with ABS. For each year, the institute recorded whether the car was involved in an accident and, if so, the cost of making repairs. Forty-two 1991 cars and 38 1992 cars were involved in accidents. The costs of repairs were stored in columns 1 (1991 cars) and 2 (1992 cars) in file Xm14-01. Using frequency of accidents and cost of repairs as measures of effectiveness, can we conclude that ABS is effective? If so, estimate how much better are cars equipped with ABS compared to cars without ABS.

SOLUTION   This is a typical illustration of the work that statistics practitioners perform and the way they do it. The Highway Loss Data Institute wants to determine whether ABS is effective. Even before the data are gathered, the statistics practitioner must decide which techniques to apply. To do so requires the statistics practitioner to frame the questions so that tests of hypotheses or interval estimators can be specified. Simply asking whether ABS works is not sufficiently well defined. Because there are several ways to measure the effectiveness of ABS, the following questions were posed.

  a. Is there sufficient evidence to infer that the accident rate is lower in ABS-equipped cars than in cars without ABS? (If ABS is effective, we would expect a lower accident rate in ABS-equipped cars.)

b. Is there sufficient evidence to infer that the cost of repairing accident damage in ABS-equipped cars is less than that of cars without ABS? (When accidents do occur, we expect the severity of accidents to be lower in ABS-equipped cars, assuming that ABS is effective.)

c. Assuming that we discover that ABS-equipped cars suffer less damage in accidents, estimate how much cheaper they are to repair on average than cars without ABS.

These questions allow the statistics practitioner to select the appropriate techniques. We will proceed through the flowchart to illustrate how this is done. When the data are gathered and stored in the computer, the statistics practitioner executes the commands to output the results. The results are interpreted to answer the central question: Is ABS effective?

Question (a)

IDENTIFY

The first factor to identify in the flowchart is the problem objective. In question (a), the problem objective is to compare two populations: 1991 model results and 1992 model results. Next, we're asked to determine the data type. The data are nominal. (The values of the random variable are "accident occurred" and "no accident occurred.") The flowchart (Figure 14.1) identifies the technique as the z test and estimator of $p_1 - p_2$. We define

p_1 = proportion of 1991 model cars without ABS involved in an accident
p_2 = proportion of 1992 model cars with ABS involved in an accident

Because we want to know whether ABS brakes are effective in reducing accidents, we specify the alternative hypothesis as

$$H_1: \ (p_1 - p_2) > 0$$

The null hypothesis automatically becomes

$$H_0: \ (p_1 - p_2) = 0$$

which indicates the use of the Case 1 test statistic:

$$\text{Test statistic:} \quad z = \frac{(\hat{p}_1 - \hat{p}_2)}{\sqrt{\hat{p}(1 - \hat{p})\left(\dfrac{1}{n_1} + \dfrac{1}{n_2}\right)}}$$

COMPUTE

The sample proportion of accidents for 1991 cars is

$$\hat{p}_1 = \frac{42}{500} = .084$$

The accident rate for 1992 cars is

$$\hat{p}_2 = \frac{38}{500} = .076$$

EXCEL

	A	B	C	D	E
1	z-Test of the Difference Between Two Proportions (Case 1)				
2					
3		Sample 1	Sample 2	z Stat	0.47
4	Sample proportion	0.084	0.076	P(Z<=z) one-tail	0.3205
5	Sample size	500	500	z Critical one-tail	1.6449
6	Alpha	0.05		P(Z<=z) two-tail	0.6410
7				z Critical two-tail	1.9600

MINITAB

Test and CI for Two Proportions

```
Sample      X       N   Sample p
1          42     500   0.084000
2          38     500   0.076000

Estimate for p(1) - p(2):  0.008
95% lower bound for p(1) - p(2):  -0.0202195
Test for p(1) - p(2) = 0 (vs > 0):   Z = 0.47   P-Value = 0.320
```

INTERPRET

The value of the test statistic and its *p*-value are .47 and .3205, respectively. There is not enough evidence to infer that ABS-equipped cars have fewer accidents than cars without ABS.

Question (b)

IDENTIFY

The problem objective is to compare two populations. The data are interval; we measured and recorded the costs of repairs, which are real numbers. The flowchart now asks about the descriptive measurement, which we identify as central location. (We want to know whether the repair costs in one population are in general larger than the repair costs in the second population.) The next question asks us to identify the experimental design. Because there is no relationship between the two samples, we know that the samples are independent. The next factor we need to specify is whether the population variances are equal. To make this decision, we apply the F test of σ_1^2/σ_2^2. The results (see the printout below), $F = 1.15$ and *p*-value (Excel: $2 \times .3313$) = .6626, indicate that there is not enough evidence to infer that the variances differ. Putting all the factors together, we identify the equal-variances t test of $\mu_1 - \mu_2$.

μ_1 = mean cost of repairing 1991 model cars damaged in accidents
μ_2 = mean cost of repairing 1992 model cars damaged in accidents

Because we want to know whether μ_1 is greater than μ_2, we specify the alternative hypothesis as

$$H_1: \ (\mu_1 - \mu_2) > 0$$

and the null hypothesis is

$$H_0: \quad (\mu_1 - \mu_2) = 0$$

The test statistic is

$$t = \frac{(\bar{x}_1 - \bar{x}_2) - (\mu_1 - \mu_2)}{\sqrt{s_p^2\left(\dfrac{1}{n_1} + \dfrac{1}{n_2}\right)}}$$

COMPUTE

EXCEL

	A	B	C
1	F-Test Two-Sample for Variances		
2			
3		*Cost 1991*	*Cost 1992*
4	Mean	2075	1714
5	Variance	450343	390409
6	Observations	42	38
7	df	41	37
8	F	1.15	
9	P(F<=f) one-tail	0.3313	
10	F Critical one-tail	1.7129	

	A	B	C
1	t-Test: Two-Sample Assuming Equal Variances		
2			
3		*Cost 1991*	*Cost 1992*
4	Mean	2075	1714
5	Variance	450343	390409
6	Observations	42	38
7	Pooled Variance	421913	
8	Hypothesized Mean Difference	0	
9	df	78	
10	t Stat	2.48	
11	P(T<=t) one-tail	0.0077	
12	t Critical one-tail	1.6646	
13	P(T<=t) two-tail	0.0153	
14	t Critical two-tail	1.9908	

MINITAB

Test for Equal Variances

```
F-Test (normal distribution)


Test Statistic: 1.154
P-Value       : 0.663
```

Two-Sample T-Test and CI: Cost 1991, Cost 1992

```
Two-sample T for Cost 1991 vs Cost 1992

             N     Mean    StDev   SE Mean
Cost 1991   42     2075      671       104
Cost 1992   38     1714      625       101

Difference = mu Cost 1991 - mu Cost 1992
Estimate for difference:   360
95% lower bound for difference: 118
T-Test of difference = 0 (vs >): T-Value = 2.48   P-Value = 0.008   DF = 78
Both use Pooled StDev =   650
```

INTERPRET

The value of the test statistic is $z = 2.48$. The p-value is .0077. The t test of $\mu_1 - \mu_2$ indicates that the cost of repairs is less for ABS-equipped cars than for cars without ABS.

Question (c)

IDENTIFY

To measure how much better off a car owner is with ABS, we determine the 95% confidence interval estimator of the difference between the two mean costs. The confidence interval estimator is

$$(\bar{x}_1 - \bar{x}_2) \pm t_{\alpha/2}\sqrt{s_p^2\left(\frac{1}{n_1} + \frac{1}{n_2}\right)}$$

COMPUTE

 EXCEL

	A	B	C	D	E	F
1	t-Estimate of the Difference Between Two Means (Equal-Variances)					
2						
3		Sample 1	Sample 2	Confidence Interval Estimate		
4	Mean	2075	1714	361	±	290
5	Variance	450343	390409	Lower confidence limit		71
6	Sample size	42	38	Upper confidence limit		651
7	Pooled Variance	421913				
8	Confidence level	0.95				

MINITAB

Two-Sample T-Test and CI: Cost 1991, Cost 1992

```
Two-sample T for Cost 1991 vs Cost 1992

              N      Mean     StDev   SE Mean
Cost 1991    42      2075       671       104
Cost 1992    38      1714       625       101

Difference = mu Cost 1991 - mu Cost 1992
Estimate for difference:  360
95% CI for difference: (71, 650)
T-Test of difference = 0 (vs not =): T-Value = 2.48   P-Value = 0.015   DF = 78
Both use Pooled StDev =   650
```

INTERPRET

The 95% confidence interval estimate of $\mu_1 - \mu_2$ is

$$\text{LCL} = 71 \quad \text{and} \quad \text{UCL} = 651$$

CHECKING THE REQUIRED CONDITIONS

Figures 14.2 and 14.3 depict the histograms of the costs of repairs of the 1991 and 1992 cars, respectively. Although the histograms are not bell shaped, it appears that costs of repairs in both years are not extremely nonnormal. The conclusions we reached in the statistical procedures above are valid.

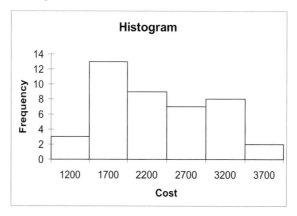

Figure 14.2
Histogram of Repair Costs of 1991 Cars

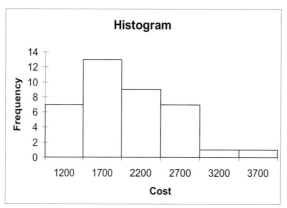

Figure 14.3
Histogram of Repair Costs of 1992 Cars

INTERPRETING ALL THE STATISTICAL RESULTS

The data indicate that the accident rate in ABS-equipped cars may be no lower than that of cars without ABS. However, the cost of repairing the accident damage is less for the former group. We estimate that the average repair bill for an ABS-equipped car is between $71 and $651 less than for a car not equipped with ABS. Can we now say conclusively that ABS is effective? Unfortunately, this is only one interpretation of the results.

Because the experiment uses observational data, we must be careful about the meaning of the tests. It is possible that poor drivers will buy ABS-equipped cars and better drivers will not. If so, the results would tend to indicate that ABS is either ineffective, as in part (a), or not as effective as it really is, as in parts (b) and (c). Experimental data may have been able to overcome this problem. Experimental data could be gathered by randomly selecting people to drive either ABS-equipped cars or cars without ABS for 1 year and recording the data. In this way the drivers in both groups should be quite similar, making the comparison more definitive.

Another problem in interpreting the results to proclaim that ABS is effective is that it is possible that driving ABS-equipped cars changes the behavior of the drivers. They may drive more dangerously in the mistaken belief that ABS will save them. It may be possible to remedy this problem by not telling the drivers which type they have been assigned to drive. However, most drivers will likely know from the feel and performance of the brakes. Another experiment can be undertaken to determine whether driving behavior is indeed altered by ABS. (See Exercise 14.23.)

Yet another difficulty arose because the experiment was performed using different model years. The ABS-equipped cars were all 1992 models, and the cars without ABS were all 1991 models. The results we observed may be due to differences either in the repair costs or the performance of the models between 1991 and 1992 cars. Undoubtedly, it would have been better to compare 1992 cars with and without ABS. (Note that we are merely reporting the way the Highway Loss Data Institute actually conducted the study; we are not endorsing their methods. We may have gathered the data in a different way.)

Besides teaching you how to identify the appropriate statistical technique, this example also highlights the issues that must be considered when interpreting the results.

EXERCISES

The purpose of the exercises that follow is twofold. First, the exercises provide you with practice in the critical skill of identifying the correct technique. Second, they allow you to improve your ability to determine the statistics needed to answer the question and interpret the results. We believe that the first skill is underdeveloped, because up to now you have had little practice. The exercises you've worked on have appeared at the end of sections and chapters where the correct techniques have just been presented. Determining the correct technique should not have been difficult. Because the exercises that follow were selected from the types that you have already encountered at the ends of Chapters 12 and 13, they will help you develop your technique-identification skills.

You will note that in the exercises that require a test of hypothesis, we do not specify a significance level. We have left this decision to you. After analyzing the issues raised in the exercise, use your own judgment to determine whether the p-value is small enough to reject the null hypothesis.

14.1   Shopping malls are more than places where we buy things. We go to malls to watch movies; buy breakfast, lunch, and dinner; exercise; meet friends; and, in general, to socialize. To study the trends, a sociologist took a random sample of 100 mall shoppers and asked a variety of questions. This survey was first conducted 3 years ago with another sample of 100 shoppers. In both surveys, respondents were asked to report the number of hours they spend in malls during an average week. The results are stored in file Xr14-01. Can we conclude that the amount of time spent at malls has decreased over the past 3 years?

14.2   It is often useful for retailers to determine why their potential customers choose to visit their store. Possible reasons include advertising, advice from a friend, or previous experience. To determine the effect of full-page advertisements in the local newspaper, the owner of an electronic-equipment store asked 200 randomly selected people who visited the store whether they had seen the ad. He also determined whether the customers had bought anything, and, if so, how much they spent. There were 113 respondents who saw the ad. Of these, 49 made a purchase. Of the 87 respondents who did not see the ad, 21 made a purchase. The amounts spent were stored in file Xr14-02.

a Can the owner conclude that customers who see the ad are more likely to make a purchase than those who do not see the ad?

b Can the owner conclude that customers who see the ad spend more than those who do not see the ad (among those who make a purchase)?

c Estimate with 95% confidence the proportion of all customers who see the ad who then make a purchase.

d Estimate with 95% confidence the mean amount spent by customers who see the ad and make a purchase.

14.3 In an attempt to reduce the number of person-hours lost as a result of industrial accidents, a large multiplant corporation installed new safety equipment in all departments and all plants. To test the effectiveness of the equipment, a random sample of 25 plants was drawn. The number of person-hours lost in the month prior to installation of the safety equipment and in the month after installation was recorded. The results are stored in file Xr14-03. Can we conclude that the equipment is effective?

14.4 The United States Postal Service (USPS) offers a service called Priority Mail that originally promised 2-day delivery. At that time, it cost about $3.00 to send a letter by Priority Mail within the United States. A spokesperson for the USPS claimed that it had a success rate of more than 95% in delivering letters within the 2-day deadline. Station WARY in Miami (as reported in their newscast of December 24, 1992) decided to conduct an experiment to determine whether the $3.00 cost is worthwhile. Letters were sent by Priority Mail and by ordinary mail (at that time, a 29-cent stamp) from New York City to Cleveland, Ohio. Letters that arrived within the deadline were recorded with a 2; letters that were late were recorded with a 1. The data are stored in file Xr14-04.

a Do these data provide sufficient evidence to support the spokesperson's claim?

b Do these data provide sufficient evidence to infer that Priority Mail delivered letters within 2 days more frequently than did ordinary mail?

14.5 The electric company is considering an incentive plan to encourage its customers to pay their bills promptly. The plan is to discount the bills 1% if the customer pays within 5 days, as opposed to the usual 25 days. As an experiment, 50 customers are offered the discount on their September bill. The amount of time each

takes to pay his or her bill is recorded. The amount of time a random sample of 50 customers not offered the discount take to pay their bills is also recorded. Both sets of data are stored in file Xr14-05. Do these data allow us to infer that the discount plan works?

14.6 Traffic experts are always looking for ways to control automobile speeds. Some communities have experimented with "traffic-calming" techniques. These include speed bumps and various obstructions that force cars to slow to drive around them. Critics point out that the techniques are counterproductive because they cause drivers to speed on other parts of these roads. In an analysis of the effectiveness of speed bumps, a statistics practitioner organized a study over a 1-mile stretch of city road that had ten stop signs. He then took a random sample of 100 cars and recorded their average speed (the speed limit was 30 mph) and the number of proper stops at the stop signs. He repeated the observations for another sample of 100 cars after speed bumps were placed on the road. These data were stored in file Xr14-06. Do these data allow the statistics practitioner to conclude that the speed bumps are effective?

14.7 The proliferation of self-serve pumps at gas stations has generally resulted in poorer automobile maintenance. One feature of poor maintenance is low tire pressure, which results in shorter tire life and higher gasoline consumption. To examine this problem, an automotive expert took a random sample of cars across the country and measured the tire pressure. The difference between the recommended tire pressure and the observed tire pressure was recorded and stored in file Xr14-07. (A recording of 8 means that the pressure of the tire is 8 pounds per square inch [psi] less than the amount recommended by the tire manufacturer.) Suppose that for each psi below recommendation, tire life decreases by 100 miles and gasoline consumption increases by .1 gallon per mile. Estimate with 95% confidence the effect of under-inflation on tire life and gasoline consumption.

14.8 Many North American cities encourage the use of bicycles as a way to reduce pollution and traffic congestion. So many people now regularly use the bicycle to get to work and for exercise that some jurisdictions have enacted bicycle helmet laws, which specify that all bicycle riders must wear helmets to protect against head injuries. Critics of these laws complain that it is a violation of individual freedom and that helmet laws tend to discourage bicycle usage. To examine this issue, a researcher randomly sampled 50 bicycle users and asked each to record the number of miles he or she rode weekly. Several weeks later the helmet law was enacted. The number of miles each of the 50 bicycle riders rode weekly was recorded for the week after the law was passed. These data are stored in file Xr14-08. Can we infer from these data that the law discourages bicycle usage?

14.9 Cardizem CD is a prescription drug that is used to treat high blood pressure and angina. One common side effect of such drugs is the occurrence of headaches and dizziness. To determine whether its drug has the same side effects, the drug's manufacturer, Marion Merrell Dow, Inc., undertook a study. A random sample of 908 high blood pressure sufferers was recruited; 607 took Cardizem CD and 301 took a placebo. Each reported whether they suffered from headaches and/ or dizziness (2 = yes, 1 = no). The responses were recorded in file Xr14-09. Can the pharmaceutical company scientist infer that Cardizem CD users are more likely to suffer headache and dizziness side effects than nonusers?

14.10 A fast-food franchiser is considering building a restaurant at a downtown location. Based on a financial analysis, a site is acceptable only if the number of pedestrians passing the location during the work day averages more than 200 per hour. To help decide whether to build on the site, a statistics practitioner observes the number of pedestrians who pass the site each hour over a 40-hour workweek. These data are stored in file Xr14-10. Should the franchiser build on this site?

14.11 There has been much debate about the effects of secondhand smoke. A U.S. government study (*Globe and Mail*, 20 June 1991) observed samples of households with children living with at least one smoker and households with children living with no smokers. Each child's health was assessed. The data from this study are stored in file Xr14-11, where 1 = child is healthy and 2 = child is in fair to poor health.
  a Can we infer that children in smoke-free households are less likely to be in fair to poor health than children in households with at least one smoker?
  b Assuming that there are 10 million children living in homes with at least one smoker, estimate with 95% confidence the number of these children who are in fair to poor health.

14.12 The presidential election in November 2000 was a cliff-hanger whose ultimate conclusion was dependent on the count in the state of Florida. Have Floridians accepted the result? Random samples of 625 registered voters statewide were surveyed in November 2000 and again in February 2001. Each person was asked "who won the Florida vote?" The results are stored in file Xr14-12, where 1 = Bush and 2 = Gore. Can we infer that there are more Floridians who believe that Mr. Bush won the election than there are Floridians who believe that Mr. Gore won?

14.13 Most automobile repair shops now charge according to a schedule that is claimed to be based on average times. This means that instead of determining the actual time to make a repair and multiplying this value by their hourly rate, repair shops determine the cost from a schedule that is calculated from average times. A critic of this policy is examining how closely this schedule adheres to the actual time to complete a job. He randomly selects five jobs. According to the schedule, these jobs should take 45 minutes, 60 minutes, 80 minutes, 100 minutes, and 125 minutes, respectively. The critic then takes a random sample of repair shops and records the actual times for each of 20 cars for each job. The times are stored in file Xr14-13. For each job, can we infer that the time specified by the schedule is greater than the actual time?

14.14 Most people who quit smoking cigarettes do so for health reasons. However, some quitters find that they gain weight after quitting, and scientists estimate that the health risks of smoking two packs of cigarettes per day and of carrying 65 extra pounds of weight are about equivalent. In an attempt to learn more about the effects of quitting smoking, the U.S. Centers for Disease Control conducted a study (reported in *Time*, 25 March 1991). A sample of 1,885 smokers was taken. During the course of the experiment, some of the smokers quit their habit. The amount of weight gained by all of the subjects was recorded and stored in file Xr14-14. Do these data allow us to conclude that quitting smoking results in weight gains?

14.15 Golf equipment manufacturers compete against one another by offering a bewildering array of new products and innovations. Oversized clubs, square grooves, and graphite shafts are examples of such innovations. The effect of these new products on the average golfer is, however, much in doubt. One product, a perimeter-weighted iron, was designed to increase the consistency of distance and accuracy. The most important aspect of irons is consistency, which means that ideally there should be no variation in distance from shot to shot. To examine the relative merits of two brands of perimeter-weighted irons, an average golfer used the 7-iron, hitting 100 shots using each of two brands. The distance in yards was recorded and stored in file Xr14-15. Can the golfer conclude that brand B is superior to brand A?

14.16 No one disputes the value of physical exercise. Regular exercise has been proven to prolong life and decrease the incidence of certain diseases. But what about exercises for the mind? Are there ways in which one can exercise one's intellect without resorting to the mental equivalent of boring calisthenics? The answer may lie in the game of bridge. In a study undertaken at Scripps College in California, researchers tested 50 bridge players and 50 nonplayers aged between 55 and 91 (as reported in the *ACBL Bulletin*, July 1992). The test measured working memory, reasoning, reaction time, and vocabulary. The results of the tests are stored in file Xr14-16 (columns A and B = working memory for players and nonplayers; columns C and D = reasoning for players and nonplayers; columns E and F = reaction time for players and nonplayers; columns G and H = vocabulary for players and nonplayers). Bearing in mind that the game of bridge places demands on memory and reasoning but requires only 15 words and can be played quite slowly, can we infer that playing bridge improves the memory and reasoning of seniors but does not affect their reaction time and vocabulary?

14.17 Advertising is critical in the residential real estate industry. Agents are always seeking ways to increase sales through improved advertising methods. A particular agent believes that he can increase the number of inquiries (and thus the probability of making a sale) by describing the house for sale without indicating its asking price. To support his belief, he conducted an experiment in which 100 houses for sale were advertised in two ways—with and without the asking price. The number of inquiries for each house was recorded as well as whether the customer saw the ad with or without the asking price shown. The number of inquiries for each house is stored in file Xr14-17. Do these data allow the real estate agent to infer that ads with no price shown are more effective in generating interest in a house?

14.18 In most offices, the copier is the most frequently used and abused machine. Consequently, buyers of copiers need to know how frequently service will be required before a decision to buy is made. Prior to making a major purchase, the general manager of a large company asks 150 recent buyers of this copier whether they required maintenance in the first year and, if so, how frequently. The number of service calls is stored in file Xr14-18. If the president plans to buy 1,000 copiers, estimate with 95% confidence the number of service calls he expects in the first year.

14.19 Throughout the day there are a number of exercise shows appearing on television. These usually feature attractive and fit men and women performing various exercises and urging viewers to duplicate the activity at home. Some viewers are exercisers. However, some people like to watch the shows without exercising (which explains why they use attractive people as demonstrators). Various companies sponsor the shows and there are commercial breaks. One sponsor wanted to determine whether there are differences between exercisers and nonexercisers in terms of how well they remember the sponsor's name. A random sample of viewers was selected and called after the exercise show was over. Each was asked to report whether they exercised or only watched. They were also asked to name the sponsor's brand name (2 = yes, they could; 1 = no, they couldn't). These results are stored in file Xr14-19. Can the sponsor conclude that exercisers are more likely to remember the sponsor's brand name than those who only watch?

14.20 A professor of statistics hands back his graded midterms in class by calling out the name of each student and personally handing the exam over to its owner. At the end of the process he notes that there are several exams left over, the result of students missing that class. He forms the theory that the absence is caused by a poor performance by those students on the test. If the theory is correct, the leftover papers will have lower marks than those papers handed back. He stored the marks (out of 100) for the leftover papers and the marks of the returned papers in file Xr14-20. Do the data support the professor's theory?

14.21 Periodically, coupons that can be used to purchase products at discount prices appear in newspapers. The goal is to persuade shoppers to take advantage of the coupon to visit the store and buy other products. The manager of a supermarket chain wonders whether the coupons actually work. As part of her analysis, she places 25-cent coupons for bread in the newspaper. Over the next 2 days, she randomly samples 500 shoppers and determines whether they used the coupon and how much they spent on groceries, not including bread. These data are stored in file Xr14-21. Can the manager conclude that coupon users spend more money on groceries than do non-users?

14.22 According to the latest census, the number of households in a large metropolitan area is 425,000. The home delivery department of the local newspaper reports that 104,320 households receive daily home delivery. To increase home delivery sales, the marketing department launches an expensive advertising campaign. A financial analyst tells the publisher that for the campaign to be successful, home delivery sales must increase to more than 110,000 households. Anxious to see whether the campaign is working, the publisher authorizes a telephone survey of 400 households within 1 week of the beginning of the campaign and asks each household head whether he or she has the newspaper delivered. The responses are stored in file Xr14-22 (2 = yes; 1 = no).
  a Do these data indicate that the campaign will increase home delivery sales?
  b Do these data allow the publisher to conclude that the campaign will be successful?

14.23 Does driving an ABS-equipped car change the behavior of drivers? To help answer this question, the following experiment was undertaken. A random sample of 200 drivers who currently operate cars without ABS was selected. Each person was given an identical car to drive for 1 year. Half the sample were given cars that had ABS, and the other half were given cars with standard-equipment brakes. Computers on the cars recorded the average speed (in miles per hour) during the year. These data are stored in file Xr14-23. Can we infer that operating an ABS-equipped car changes the behavior of the driver?

14.24 Health care costs in the United States and Canada are concerns for citizens and politicians. The question is, How can we devise a system wherein people's medical bills are covered but yet individuals attempt to reduce costs? An American company has come up with a possible solution. Golden Rule is an insurance company in Indiana with 1,300 employees. The company offered its employees a choice of programs. One choice was a medical savings account (MSA) plan. Here's how it works. To ensure that a major illness or accident does not financially destroy an employee, Golden Rule offers catastrophic insurance—a policy that covers all expenses above $2,000 per year. At the beginning of the year, the company deposits $1,000 (for a single employee) and $2,000 (for an employee with a family) into the MSA. For minor expenses, the employee pays from his or her MSA. As an incentive for the employee to spend wisely, any money left in the MSA at the end of the year can be withdrawn by the employee. To determine how well it works, a

random sample of employees who opted for the medical savings account plan was compared to employees who chose the regular plan. At the end of the year, the medical expenses for each employee were recorded and stored in columns A (MSA plan) and B (regular plan) in file Xr14-24. Critics of MSA say that the plan leads to poorer health care, and as a result employees are less likely to be in excellent health. To address this issue, each employee was examined. The results of the examination are stored in columns C (MSA plan) and D (regular plan) where 1 = excellent health and 2 = not in excellent health.

a Can we infer from these data that MSA is effective in reducing costs?

b Can we infer that the critics of MSA are correct?

◈ CASE 14.1
*HOST SELLING AND ANNOUNCER COMMERCIALS**

A study was undertaken to compare the effects of host selling commercials and announcer commercials on children. Announcer commercials are straightforward commercials in which the announcer describes to viewers why they should buy a particular product. Host selling commercials feature a children's show personality or television character who extols the virtues of the product. In 1975, the National Association of Broadcasters prohibited using show characters to advertise products during the same program in which the characters appear. However, this prohibition was overturned in 1982 by a judge's decree.

The objective of the study was to determine whether the two types of advertisements have different effects on children watching them. Specifically, the researchers wanted to know whether children watching host selling commercials would remember more details about the commercial and would be more likely to buy the advertised product than children watching announcer commercials.

The experiment consisted of two groups of children ranging in age from 6 to 10. One group of 121 children watched a program in which two host selling commercials appeared. The commercials tried to sell Canary Crunch, a breakfast cereal. A second group of 121 children watched the same program but was exposed to two announcer commercials for the same product. Immediately after the show, the children were given a questionnaire that tested their memory concerning the commercials they had watched. Each child was marked (out of 10) on his or her ability to remember details of the commercial. In addition, each child was offered a free box of cereal. The children were shown four different brands of cereal—Froot Loops, Boo Berries, Kangaroo Hops, and Canary Crunch (the advertised cereal)—and asked to pick the one they wanted. The results are stored in file C14-01 in the following way.

Column A: Recall test mark for the children who watched the host selling commercial

Column B: Recall test mark for the children who watched the announcer commercial

Column C: Children's choice of cereal where 1 = Froot Loops, 2 = Boo Berries, 3 = Kangaroo Hops, and 4 = Canary Crunch for children who watched the host commercial

Column D: Children's choice of cereal for children who watched the announcer commercial

Are there differences in memory test marks and children's choice of advertised cereal between the two groups of children?

---

* Adapted from J. H. Miller, "An Empirical Evaluation of the Host Selling Commercial and the Announcer Commercial When Used on Children," *Developments in Marketing Science* 8 (1985): 276-278.

✧ CASE 14.2
QUEBEC SEPARATION? OUI OU NON

Since the 1960s, there has been an ongoing campaign among Quebecers to separate from Canada and form an independent nation. Should Quebec separate, the ramifications for the rest of Canada, American states that border Quebec, the North American Free Trade Agreement, and numerous multinational corporations would be enormous. In the 1993 federal election, the prosovereigntist *Bloc Quebecois* won 54 of Quebec's 75 seats in the House of Commons. In 1994, the separatist *Parti Quebecois* formed the provincial government in Quebec and promised to hold a referendum on separation. As with most political issues, polling plays an important role in trying to influence voters and to predict the outcome of the referendum vote. Shortly after the 1993 federal election, *The Financial Post Magazine*, in cooperation with several polling companies, conducted a survey of Quebecers.

A total of 641 adult Quebecers were interviewed. They were asked the following question. (Francophones were asked the questions in French.) The pollsters also recorded the language (English or French) in which the respondent answered.

> If a referendum were held today on Quebec's sovereignty with the following question, "Do you want Quebec to separate from Canada and become an independent country?" would you vote yes or no?
>   2 Yes
>   1 No

The responses are stored in columns A (planned referendum vote for Francophones) and B (planned referendum vote for Anglophones) in file C14-02.

Infer from the data:

a If the referendum were held on the day of the survey, would Quebec vote to remain in Canada?
b Estimate with 95% confidence the difference between French- and English-speaking Quebecers in their support for separation.

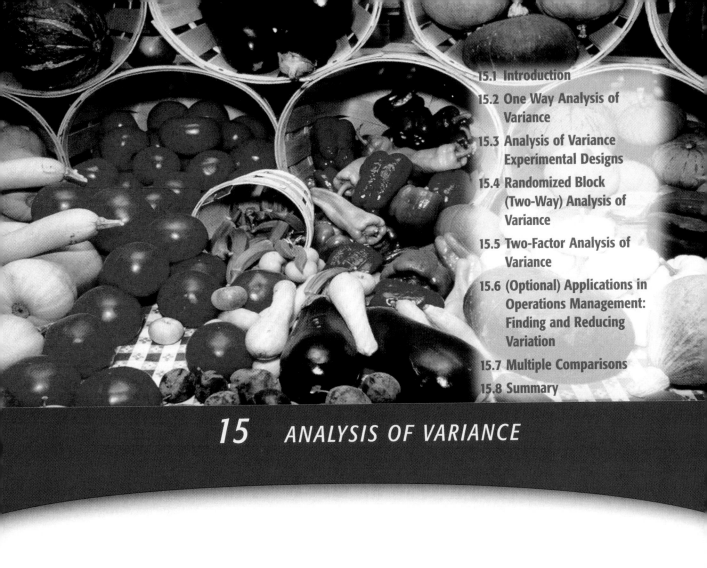

15 ANALYSIS OF VARIANCE

CAUSES OF VARIATION

A critical component in an aircraft engine is a steel rod that must be 41.387 cm long. The operations manager has noted that there has been some variation in the lengths. In some cases the steel rods had to be discarded or reworked because they were either too short or too long. The operations manager believes that some of the variation is caused by the way the production process has been designed. Specifically, he believes that the rods vary from machine to machine and from operator to operator. To help unravel the truth, he organizes an experiment.

Each of the three operators produces five rods on each of the four machines. The lengths are measured and recorded in the following way. Columns 1 through 4 store the data for machines 1 to 4, respectively. In each column, the first five rows represent operator 1, the next five rows represent operator 2, and the last five rows represent operator 3. The data are stored in file Ch15:\Variation. Determine whether the machines and/or the operators are indeed sources of variation. See page 514 for the solution.

15.1 INTRODUCTION

The technique presented in this chapter allows statistics practitioners to compare two or more populations of interval data. The technique is called the *analysis of variance*, and it is an extremely powerful and commonly used procedure. The analysis of variance technique determines whether differences exist between population means. Ironically, the procedure works by analyzing the sample variance, hence the name. We will examine several different forms of the technique.

One of the first applications of the analysis of variance was conducted in the 1920s to determine whether different treatments of fertilizer produced different crop yields. The terminology of that original experiment is still used. No matter what the experiment, the procedure is designed to determine whether there are significant differences between the *treatment* means.

15.2 ONE-WAY ANALYSIS OF VARIANCE

The analysis of variance is a procedure that tests to determine whether differences exist between two or more population means. The name of the technique derives from the way in which the calculations are performed. That is, the technique analyzes the variance of the data to determine whether we can infer that the population means differ. As in Chapter 13, the experimental design is a determinant in identifying the proper method to use. In this section, we describe the procedure to apply when the samples are independently drawn. Figure 15.1 depicts the sampling process for drawing independent samples. The mean and variance of population j ($j = 1, 2, ..., k$) are labeled μ_j and σ_j^2, respectively. Both parameters are unknown. For each population, we draw independent random samples. For each sample, we can compute the mean $\bar{x}_j$ and the variance s_j^2.

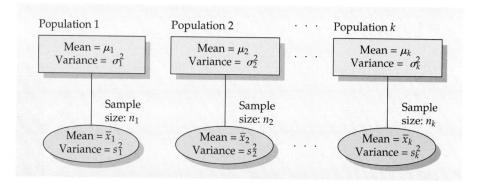

Figure 15.1
Sampling scheme for independent samples

APPLICATIONS IN *MARKETING*

Test Marketing
In Chapter 13 we described test marketing, which is often used to assess consumer reaction to changes in one or more elements of the marketing mix. Marketing managers will conduct experiments to determine whether differences in sales exist between different prices for the product, different package designs, or different advertising strategies. Some of these experiments are carried out in small communities where it is easy to vary particular elements that the manager wishes to investigate.

EXAMPLE 15.1

An apple juice manufacturer has developed a new product—a liquid concentrate that, when mixed with water, produces 1 liter of apple juice. The product has several attractive features. First, it is more convenient than canned apple juice, which is the way apple juice is currently sold. Second, because the apple juice that is sold in cans is actually made from concentrate, the quality of the new product is at least as high as that of canned apple juice. Third, the cost of the new product is slightly lower than that of canned apple juice. The marketing manager has to decide how to market the new product. She can create advertising that emphasizes convenience, quality, or price. To facilitate a decision, she conducts an experiment in three different small cities. In one city, she launches the product with advertising stressing the convenience of the liquid concentrate (e.g., easy to carry from store to home and takes up less room in the freezer). In the second city, the advertisements emphasize the quality of the product ("average" shoppers are depicted discussing how good the apple juice tastes). Advertising that highlights the relatively low cost of the liquid concentrate is used in the third city. The number of packages sold weekly is recorded for the 20 weeks following the beginning of the campaign. These data are stored in file Xm15-01 and are listed in the accompanying table. The marketing manager wants to know whether differences in sales exist between the three advertising strategies. (We will assume that except for the type of advertising, the three cities are identical.)

City 1 (Convenience)	City 2 (Quality)	City 3 (Price)
529	804	672
658	630	531
793	774	443
514	717	596
663	679	602
719	604	502
711	620	659
606	697	689
461	706	675
529	615	512
498	492	691
663	719	733
604	787	698
495	699	776
485	572	561
557	523	572
353	584	469
557	634	581
542	580	679
614	624	532

SOLUTION   You should confirm that the data are interval and that the problem objective is to compare three populations (sales of the liquid concentrate in the three cities). Following the pattern that we have used repeatedly in this book, we introduce the statistical technique by specifying the null and alternative hypotheses. The null hypothesis will state that there are no differences between the population means. Hence,

$$H_0: \quad \mu_1 = \mu_2 = \mu_3$$

The analysis of variance determines whether there is enough statistical evidence to show that the null hypothesis is false. Consequently, the alternative hypothesis will always specify the following:

H_1:   At least two means differ.

The next step is to determine the test statistic, which is somewhat more involved than the test statistics we have introduced thus far. The process of performing the analysis of variance is facilitated by the notation in Table 15.1.

Table 15.1 Notation for the One-Way Analysis of Variance

	Treatment				
	1	2	j		k
	x_{11}	x_{12}	$\cdots$	x_{1j}	$\cdots$	x_{1k}
	x_{21}	x_{22}	$\cdots$	x_{2j}	$\cdots$	x_{2k}
	.	.		.		.
	.	.		.		.
	.	.		.		.
	$x_{n_1 1}$	$x_{n_2 2}$		$x_{n_j j}$		$x_{n_k k}$
Sample size	n_1	n_2		n_j		n_k
Sample mean	$\bar{x}_1$	$\bar{x}_2$		$\bar{x}_j$		$\bar{x}_k$

$x_{ij} = i$th observation of the jth sample

$n_j =$ Number of observations in the sample taken from the jth population

$$\bar{x}_j = \text{Mean of the } j\text{th sample} = \frac{\sum\limits_{i=1}^{n_j} x_{ij}}{n_j}$$

$\bar{\bar{x}} =$ Grand mean of all the observations

$$= \frac{\sum\limits_{j=1}^{k} \sum\limits_{i=1}^{n_j} x_{ij}}{n} \qquad \text{where } n = n_1 + n_2 + \cdots + n_k \text{ and } k \text{ is the number of populations.}$$

The variable x is called the **response variable**, and its values are called **responses**. The unit that we measure is called an **experimental unit**. In this example, the response variable is weekly sales, and the experimental units are the weeks in the three cities when we record sales figures. The sales figures are the responses. The criterion by which we classify the populations is called a **factor**. Each population is called a factor **level**. The factor in Example 15.1 is the advertising strategy and there are three levels. Later in this chapter we'll discuss an experiment where the populations are classified using two factors. In this section we deal with single-factor experiments only.

TEST STATISTIC

The test statistic is computed in accordance with the following rationale. If the null hypothesis is true, the population means would all be equal. We would then expect that the sample means would be close to one another. If the alternative hypothesis is true, however, there would be large differences between some of the sample means. The statistic that measures the proximity of the sample means to each other is called the **between-treatments variation**, denoted **SST**, which stands for **sum of squares for treatments**.

SUM OF SQUARES FOR TREATMENTS

$$SST = \sum_{j=1}^{k} n_j (\bar{x}_j - \bar{\bar{x}})^2$$

As you can deduce from this formula, if the sample means are close to each other, all of the sample means would be close to the grand mean, and, as a result, SST would be small. In fact, SST achieves its smallest value (zero) when all the sample means are equal. That is, if

$$\bar{x}_1 = \bar{x}_2 = \cdots = \bar{x}_k$$

then

$$\text{SST} = 0$$

It follows that a small value of SST supports the null hypothesis. In this example, we compute the sample means and the grand mean as

$$\bar{x}_1 = 577.55$$

$$\bar{x}_2 = 653.00$$

$$\bar{x}_3 = 608.65$$

$$\bar{\bar{x}} = 613.07$$

Then

$$\text{SST} = \sum_{j=1}^{k} n_j \left(\bar{x}_j - \bar{\bar{x}} \right)^2$$

$$= 20(577.55 - 613.07)^2 + 20(653.00 - 613.07)^2 + 20(608.65 - 613.07)^2$$

$$= 57{,}512.23$$

If large differences exist between the sample means, at least some sample means differ considerably from the grand mean, producing a large value of SST. It is then reasonable to reject the null hypothesis in favor of the alternative hypothesis. The key question to be answered in this test (as in all other statistical tests) is, "How large does the statistic have to be for us to justify rejecting the null hypothesis?" In our example, SST = 57,512.23. Is this value large enough to indicate that the population means differ? To answer this question, we need to know how much variation exists in the weekly sales, which is measured by the **within-treatments variation**, which is denoted by **SSE** (**sum of squares for error**). The within-treatments variation provides a measure of the amount of variation we can expect from the random variable we've observed.

SUM OF SQUARES FOR ERROR

$$\text{SSE} = \sum_{j=1}^{k} \sum_{i=1}^{n_j} (x_{ij} - \bar{x}_j)^2$$

When SSE is partially expanded, we get

$$SSE = \sum_{i=1}^{n_1} (x_{i1} - \bar{x}_1)^2 + \sum_{i=1}^{n_2} (x_{i2} - \bar{x}_2)^2 + \cdots + \sum_{i=1}^{n_k} (x_{ik} - \bar{x}_k)^2$$

If you examine each of the k components of SSE, you'll see that each is a measure of the variability of that sample. If we divide each component by $n_j - 1$, we obtain the sample variances. We can express this by rewriting SSE as

$$SSE = (n_1 - 1)s_1^2 + (n_2 - 1)s_2^2 + \cdots + (n_k - 1)s_k^2$$

where s_j^2 is the sample variance of sample j. SSE is thus the combined or pooled variation of the k samples. This is an extension of a calculation we made in Section 13.2, where we tested and estimated the difference between two means using the pooled estimate (denoted s_p^2) of the common population variance. One of the required conditions for that statistical technique is that the population variances are equal. That same condition is now necessary for us to use SSE. That is, we require that

$$\sigma_1^2 = \sigma_2^2 = \cdots = \sigma_k^2$$

Returning to our example, we calculate the sample variances as follows:

$$s_1^2 = 10{,}775.00$$

$$s_2^2 = 7{,}238.11$$

$$s_3^2 = 8{,}670.24$$

Thus,

$$SSE = (n_1 - 1)s_1^2 + (n_2 - 1)s_2^2 + (n_3 - 1)s_3^2$$

$$= 19(10{,}775.00) + 19(7{,}238.11) + 19(8{,}670.24)$$

$$= 506{,}983.50$$

The next step is to compute quantities called the **mean squares**. The **mean square for treatments** is computed by dividing SST by the number of treatments minus 1.

MEAN SQUARE FOR TREATMENTS

$$MST = \frac{SST}{k - 1}$$

The **mean square for error** is determined by dividing SSE by the total sample size (labeled n) minus the number of treatments.

MEAN SQUARE FOR ERROR

$$MSE = \frac{SSE}{n - k}$$

Finally, the test statistic is defined as the ratio of the two mean squares.

TEST STATISTIC

$$F = \frac{MST}{MSE}$$

SAMPLING DISTRIBUTION OF THE TEST STATISTIC

The test statistic is F distributed with $k - 1$ and $n - k$ degrees of freedom, provided that the response variable is normally distributed. In Section 8.5, we introduced the F distribution and in Section 13.5 we used it to test and estimate the ratio of two population variances. The test statistic in that application was the ratio of two sample variances, s_1^2 and s_2^2. If you examine the definitions of SST and SSE, you will see that both measure sample variation similar to the numerator in the formula used to calculate the sample variance s^2 used throughout this book. When we divide SST by $k - 1$ and SSE by $n - k$ to calculate MST and MSE, respectively, we're actually computing unbiased estimators of the common population variance. Thus, the ratio $F = MST/MSE$ is the ratio of two sample variances. The degrees of freedom for this application are the denominators in the mean squares. That is, $\nu_1 = k - 1$, and $\nu_2 = n - k$. For Example 15.1, the degrees of freedom are

$$\nu_1 = k - 1 = 3 - 1 = 2$$

$$\nu_2 = n - k = 60 - 3 = 57$$

In our example, we found

$$MST = \frac{SST}{k - 1} = \frac{57,512.23}{2} = 28,756.12$$

$$MSE = \frac{SSE}{n - 1} = \frac{506,983.50}{57} = 8,894.45$$

$$F = \frac{MST}{MSE} = \frac{28,756.12}{8,894.45} = 3.23$$

REJECTION REGION AND *p*-VALUE

The purpose of calculating the F statistic is to determine whether the value of SST is large enough to reject the null hypothesis. As you can see, if SST is large, F will be large. Hence, we reject the null hypothesis only if

$$F > F_{\alpha, k-1, n-k}$$

If we let $\alpha = .05$, the rejection region for Example 15.1 is

$$F > F_{\alpha,k-1,n-k} = F_{.05,2,57} \approx 3.15$$

We found the value of the test statistic to be $F = 3.23$. Thus, there is enough evidence to infer that the mean weekly sales differ between the three cities.

The p-value of this test is

$$P(F > 3.23)$$

A computer is required to calculate this value.

Figure 15.2 depicts the sampling distribution for Example 15.1.

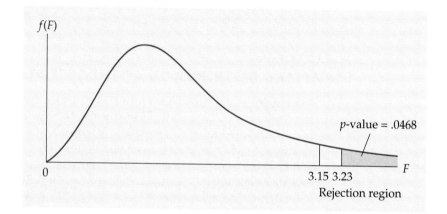

Figure 15.2
Sampling distribution for Example 15.1

The results of the analysis of variance are usually reported in an **analysis of variance (ANOVA) table**. Table 15.2 shows the general organization of the ANOVA table, while Table 15.3 shows the ANOVA table for Example 15.1.

Table 15.2 ANOVA Table for the One-Way Analysis of Variance

Source of Variation	Degrees of Freedom	Sum of Squares	Mean Square	F-Statistic
Treatments	$k - 1$	SST	MST = SST/($k - 1$)	F = MST/MSE
Error	$n - k$	SSE	MSE = SSE/($n - k$)	
Total	$n - 1$	SS(Total)		

Table 15.3 ANOVA Table for Example 15.1

Source of Variation	Degrees of Freedom	Sum of Squares	Mean Square	F-Statistic
Treatments	2	57,512.23	28,756.12	3.23
Error	57	506,983.50	8,894.45	
Total	59	564,495.73		

The terminology used in the ANOVA table (and for that matter, in the test itself) is based on the partitioning of the sum of squares. Such partitioning is derived from the following equation (whose validity can be demonstrated by using the rules of summation):

$$\sum_{j=1}^{k} \sum_{i=1}^{n_j} (x_{ij} - \bar{\bar{x}})^2 = \sum_{j=1}^{k} n_j(\bar{x}_j - \bar{\bar{x}})^2 + \sum_{j=1}^{k} \sum_{i=1}^{n_j} (x_{ij} - \bar{x}_j)^2$$

The term on the left represents the total variation of all the data. This expression is denoted SS(Total). If we divide SS(Total) by the total sample size minus 1 (that is, by $n-1$), we would obtain the sample variance (assuming that the null hypothesis is true). The first term on the right of the equal sign is SST, and the second term is SSE. As you can see, the total variation SS(Total) is partitioned into two sources of variation. The sum of squares for treatments (SST) is the variation attributed to the differences between the treatment means, while the sum of squares for error (SSE) measures the variation within the samples. The preceding equation can be restated as

$$SS(Total) = SST + SSE$$

The test is then based on the comparison of SST and SSE.

Recall that in discussing the advantages and disadvantages of the matched pairs experiment in Section 13.4, we pointed out that statistics practitioners frequently seek ways to reduce or explain the variation in a random variable. In the analysis of variance introduced in this section, the sum of squares for treatments explains the variation attributed to the treatments (advertising strategies). The sum of squares for error measures the amount of variation that is unexplained. If SST explains a significant portion of the total variation, we conclude that the population means differ. In Sections 15.4 and 15.5, we will introduce other experimental designs of the analysis of variance—ones that attempt to reduce or explain even more of the variation.

If you've felt some appreciation of the computer and statistical software sparing you the need to manually perform the statistical techniques in earlier chapters, your appreciation should now grow, because the computer will allow you to avoid the incredibly time-consuming and boring task of performing the analysis of variance by hand. As usual, we've solved Example 15.1 using Excel and Minitab, whose outputs are shown below.

COMPUTE

  EXCEL

	A	B	C	D	E	F	G
1	Anova: Single Factor						
2							
3	SUMMARY						
4	*Groups*	*Count*	*Sum*	*Average*	*Variance*		
5	Convenience	20	11551	577.55	10775		
6	Quality	20	13060	653	7238.11		
7	Price	20	12173	608.65	8670.24		
8							
9							
10	ANOVA						
11	*Source of Variation*	*SS*	*df*	*MS*	*F*	*P-value*	*F crit*
12	Between Groups	57512.2	2	28756	3.23	0.0468	3.16
13	Within Groups	506983.5	57	8894			
14							
15	Total	564495.7	59				

COMMANDS   *COMMANDS FOR EXAMPLE 15.1*

1. Type or import the data into adjacent columns.   Open file **Xm15-01.**
2. Click **Tools, Data Analysis...**, and **Anova: Single Factor.**
3. Specify the **Input Range.**   **A1:C21**
4. Click **Labels in First Row** (if appropriate).
5. Specify a value for α (**Alpha**). Click **OK.**   **.05**

MINITAB

One-way ANOVA: Convenience, Quality, Price

```
Analysis of Variance
Source      DF        SS        MS        F        P
Factor       2     57512     28756     3.23    0.047
Error       57    506984      8894
Total       59    564496
```

```
                                    Individual 95% CIs For Mean
                                    Based on Pooled StDev
Level       N      Mean     StDev   ---+---------+---------+---------+---
Convenie    20    577.55   103.80   (--------*-------)
Quality     20    653.00    85.08                   (--------*-------)
Price       20    608.65    93.11          (--------*-------)
                                    ---+---------+---------+---------+---
Pooled StDev =   94.31             550       600       650       700
```

COMMANDS

1. Type or import the data.
   If the data are unstacked:
2. Click **Stat**, **ANOVA**, and **Oneway (Unstacked)**.
3. Specify the variable names of the treatments.
   Click **OK**.
   If the data are stacked:
2. Click **Stat**, **ANOVA**, and **Oneway**.
3. Type the variable name of the response variable
   and the name of the factor variable. Click **OK**.

COMMANDS FOR EXAMPLE 15.1

Open file **Xm15-01**.

**Convenience, Quality,
Price or C1, C2, C3**

INTERPRET

The value of the test statistic is $F = 3.23$ and its p-value is .0468, which means there is evidence to infer that mean weekly sales of the apple juice concentrate are different in at least two of the cities. Can we conclude that the effects of the advertising strategies differ? Recall that it is easier to answer this type of question when the data are obtained through a controlled experiment. In this example, the marketing manager randomly assigned an advertising strategy to each city. Thus, the data are experimental. As a result, we are quite confident that the strategy used to advertise the product will produce different sales figures.

Incidentally, when the data are obtained through a controlled experiment in the single-factor analysis of variance, we call the experimental design the **completely randomized design of the analysis of variance**.

CHECKING THE REQUIRED CONDITIONS

The F test of the analysis of variance requires that the random variable be normally distributed with equal variances. The normality requirement is easily checked graphically by producing the histograms for each sample. From the Excel histograms in Figure 15.3, we can see that there is no reason to believe that the requirement is not satisfied.

The equality of variances is examined by printing the sample standard deviations or variances. Excel output includes the variances, and Minitab calculates the standard deviations. The similarity of sample variances allows us to assume that the population variances are equal. In CD Appendix 15.1, we present Bartlett's test, a statistical procedure designed to test for the equality of variances.

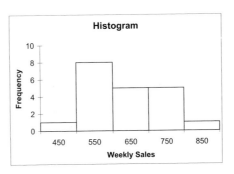

Figure 15.3
Histogram of sales, city 1 (convenience)

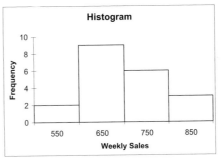

Figure 15.3
Histogram of sales, city 2 (quality)

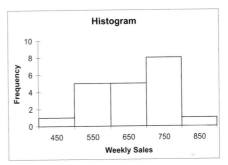

Figure 15.3
Histogram of sales, city 3 (price)

VIOLATION OF THE REQUIRED CONDITIONS

If the data are not normally distributed we can replace the one-way analysis of variance with its nonparametric counterpart, which is the Kruskal-Wallis test. (See Section 17.4.) If the population variances are unequal, we can use several methods to correct the problem. However, these corrective measures are beyond the level of this book.

CAN WE USE *t* TEST OF THE DIFFERENCE BETWEEN TWO MEANS INSTEAD OF THE ANALYSIS OF VARIANCE?

The analysis of variance tests to determine whether there is evidence of differences between two or more population means. The *t* test of $\mu_1 - \mu_2$ determines whether there is evidence of a difference between two population means. The question arises: Can we use *t* tests instead of the analysis of variance? That is, instead of testing all the means in one test as in the analysis of variance, why not test each pair of means? In Example 15.1, we would test $\mu_1 - \mu_2$, $\mu_1 - \mu_3$, and $\mu_2 - \mu_3$. If we found no evidence of a difference in each test, we would conclude that none of the means differ. If there was evidence of a difference in at least one test, we would conclude that some of the means differ.

There are two reasons why we don't use multiple t tests instead of one F test. First, we would have to perform many more calculations. Even with a computer, this extra work is tedious. Second, and more important, conducting multiple tests increases the probability of making Type I errors. To understand why, consider a problem where we want to compare six populations, all of which are identical. If we conduct an analysis of variance where we set the significance level at 5%, there is a 5% chance that we would reject the true null hypothesis. That is, there is a 5% chance that we would conclude that differences exist when in fact they don't.

To replace the F test, we would perform 15 t tests. [This number is derived from the number of combinations of pairs of means to test, which is $C_2^6 = (6 \times 5)/2 = 15$.] Each test would have a 5% probability of erroneously rejecting the null hypothesis. The probability of committing one or more Type I errors is about 54%.*

One remedy for this problem is to decrease the significance level. In this illustration, we would perform the t tests with $\alpha = .05/15$, which is equal to .0033. (We will use this procedure in Section 15.7 when we discuss multiple comparisons.) Unfortunately, this would increase the probability of a Type II error. Regardless of the significance level, performing multiple t tests increases the likelihood of making mistakes. Consequently, when we want to compare more than two populations of interval data, we use the analysis of variance.

Now that we've argued that the t tests cannot replace the analysis of variance, we need to argue that the analysis of variance cannot replace the t test.

CAN WE USE THE ANALYSIS OF VARIANCE INSTEAD OF THE t TEST OF $\mu_1 - \mu_2$?

The analysis of variance is the first of several techniques that allow us to compare two or more populations. Most of the examples and exercises deal with more than two populations. However, it should be noted that like all other techniques whose objective is to compare two or more populations, the analysis of variance can be used to compare only two populations. If that's the case, why do we need techniques to compare exactly two populations? Specifically, why do we need the t test of $\mu_1 - \mu_2$ when the analysis of variance can be used to test two population means?

To understand why we still need the t test to make inferences about $\mu_1 - \mu_2$, suppose that we plan to use the analysis of variance to test two population means. The null and alternative hypotheses are

$$H_0: \quad \mu_1 = \mu_2$$

$$H_1: \quad \text{At least two means differ.}$$

Of course, the alternative hypothesis specifies that $\mu_1 \neq \mu_2$. However, if we want to determine whether μ_1 is greater than μ_2 (or vice versa), we cannot use the analysis of variance because this technique only allows us to test for a difference. Thus, if we want to test to determine whether one population mean exceeds the other, we must use the t test of $\mu_1 - \mu_2$ (with $\sigma_1^2 = \sigma_2^2$). Moreover, the analysis of variance requires that the population variances are equal. If they are not, we must use the unequal-variances test statistic.

---

*The probability of committing at least one Type I error is computed from a binomial distribution with $n = 15$ and $p = .05$. Thus,

$$P(X \geq 1) = 1 - P(X = 0) = 1 - .463 = .537$$

RELATIONSHIP BETWEEN THE *F* STATISTIC AND THE *t* STATISTIC

It is probably useful for you to understand the relationship between the *t* statistic and the *F* statistic. The test statistic for testing hypotheses about $\mu_1 - \mu_2$ with equal variances is

$$t = \frac{(\bar{x}_1 - \bar{x}_2) - (\mu_1 - \mu_2)}{\sqrt{s_p^2\left(\frac{1}{n_1} + \frac{1}{n_2}\right)}}$$

If we square this quantity, the result is the *F* statistic. That is, $F = t^2$. To illustrate this point, we'll redo Example 13.2 using the analysis of variance.

If you reexamine Example 13.2, you'll see that the null and alternative hypotheses were

$$H_0: \quad \mu_1 = \mu_2$$

$$H_1: \quad \mu_1 \neq \mu_2$$

Because we were able to assume that the population variances were equal, the test statistic was

$$t = \frac{(\bar{x}_1 - \bar{x}_2) - (\mu_1 - \mu_2)}{\sqrt{s_p^2\left(\frac{1}{n_1} + \frac{1}{n_2}\right)}}$$

The value of the test statistic was $t = .93$ with a *p*-value of .3584. Using the analysis of variance (the Excel output is shown below; Minitab's is similar), we find that the value of the test statistic is $F = .860$, which is $(.93)^2$, and that the *p*-value is .3584. Thus, we draw exactly the same conclusion using the analysis of variance as we did when we applied the *t* test of $\mu_1 - \mu_2$.

Excel Analysis of Variance Output for Example 13.2

	A	B	C	D	E	F	G
1	Anova: Single Factor						
2							
3	SUMMARY						
4	*Groups*	*Count*	*Sum*	*Average*	*Variance*		
5	Method A	25	157.2	6.288	0.8478		
6	Method B	25	150.4	6.016	1.3031		
7							
8							
9	ANOVA						
10	*Source of Variation*	*SS*	*df*	*MS*	*F*	*P-value*	*F crit*
11	Between Groups	0.92	1	0.925	0.860	0.3584	4.04
12	Within Groups	51.62	48	1.075			
13							
14	Total	52.54	49				

DEVELOPING AN UNDERSTANDING OF STATISTICAL CONCEPTS

Conceptually and mathematically, the *F* test of the independent samples single-factor analysis of variance is an extension of the *t* test of $\mu_1 - \mu_2$. Moreover, if we simply want to determine whether a difference between two means exists, we can use the analysis of variance. The advantage of using the analysis of variance is that we can partition the total sum of squares, which enables us to measure how much variation is attributable to differences between populations and how much variation is attributable to differences within populations. As we pointed out in Section 13.4, explaining the variation is an extremely important topic, one that will be seen again in other experimental designs of the analysis of variance and in regression analysis (Chapters 18, 19, and 20).

Let's review how we recognize the need to use the technique introduced in this section.

FACTORS THAT IDENTIFY THE ONE-WAY ANALYSIS OF VARIANCE
1. **Problem objective:** Compare two or more populations.
2. **Data type:** Interval
3. **Experimental design:** Independent samples

EXERCISES

Developing an Understanding of Statistical Concepts

Exercises 15.1 to 15.11 are "what-if analyses" designed to determine what happens to the test statistic when the means, variances, and sample sizes change. These problems can be solved manually or using the **ANOVA** *worksheet in the* **Test Statistics** *workbook.*

15.1 A statistics practitioner calculated the following statistics. Complete the ANOVA table.

Statistic	Treatment		
	1	2	3
n	5	5	5
$\bar{x}$	10	15	20
s^2	50	50	50

15.2 Repeat Exercise 15.1, changing the sample sizes to 10 each.

15.3 Review Exercises 15.2 and 15.3. Describe what happens to the F statistic when the sample sizes increase.

15.4 Repeat Exercise 15.1, changing the variances to 25 each.

15.5 Examine Exercises 15.1 and 15.4. Describe the effect on the F statistic of decreasing the sample variances.

15.6 Repeat Exercise 15.1, changing the means to 110, 115, and 120, respectively.

15.7 From the results of Exercises 15.1 and 15.6, discuss what happens to the F statistic when we add 100 to each sample mean.

15.8 Repeat Exercise 15.1 changing the means to 5, 15, and 25, respectively.

15.9 Review Exercises 15.1 and 15.8. Describe the effect on the F statistic of doubling the differences between the sample means.

15.10 Repeat Example 15.1, changing all three sample means to 15. What is the effect on the F statistic?

15.11 Repeat Example 15.1, changing all three sample variances to 0. What is the effect on the F statistic?

Exercises 15.12 to 15.14 can be solved manually or through the use of the **ANOVA** *worksheet in the* **Test Statistics** *workbook.*

15.12 The following statistics were calculated. Determine the ANOVA table.

Statistic	Treatment		
	1	2	3
n	10	14	11
$\bar{x}$	14.7	11.6	19.3
s	5.3	7.1	6.8

15.13 Using the following statistics, test to determine whether differences exist between the population means. (Use $\alpha = .01$.)

$n_1 = 49$ $n_2 = 45$ $n_3 = 29$
$\bar{x}_1 = 8.36$ $\bar{x}_2 = 7.91$ $\bar{x}_3 = 9.02$
$s_1 = 2.98$ $s_2 = 3.15$ $s_3 = 3.62$

15.14 Test to discover whether differences exist between the population means given the statistics below. (Use $\alpha = .05$.)

$n_1 = 9$ $n_2 = 13$ $n_3 = 8$
$\bar{x}_1 = 35.0$ $\bar{x}_2 = 47.3$ $\bar{x}_3 = 40.2$
$s_1 = 8.3$ $s_2 = 6.4$ $s_3 = 7.7$

Applications

The following exercises require the use of a computer and software. Some answers may be calculated manually. See Appendix A for the sample statistics. **Use a 5% significance level unless specified otherwise.**

15.15 Because there are no national or regional standards, it is difficult for university admission committees to compare graduates of different high schools. University administrators have noted that an 80% average at a high school with low standards may be equivalent to a 70% average at another school with higher standards of grading. In an effort to more equitably compare applications, a pilot study was initiated. Random samples of students who were admitted the previous year from four local high schools were drawn. All of the students entered the business program with averages between 70% and 80%. Their average grades in the first year at the university were computed and stored in file Xr15-15.

a Can the university admissions officer conclude that there are differences in grading standards between the four high schools?

b What are the required conditions for the test conducted in part **a**?

c Does it appear that the required conditions of the test in part **a** are satisfied?

15.16 The friendly folks at the Internal Revenue Service (IRS) are always looking for ways to improve the wording and format of its tax return forms. Three new forms have been developed recently. To determine which, if any, are superior to the current form, 120 individuals were asked to participate in an experiment. Each of the three new forms and the currently used form were filled out by 30 different people. The amount of time (in minutes) taken by each person to complete the task was recorded and stored in file Xr15-16.

a What conclusions can be drawn from these data?

b What are the required conditions for the test conducted in part **a**?

c Does it appear that the required conditions of the test in part **a** are satisfied?

15.17 Are proficiency test scores affected by the education of the child's parents? (Proficiency tests are administered to a sample of students in private and public schools. Test scores can range from 0 to 500.) To answer this question, a random sample of 9-year-old children was drawn. Each child's test score and the educational level of the parent with the higher level were recorded. The education categories are less than high school, high school graduate, some college, and college graduate. The test scores are stored in file Xr15-17. Can we infer that there are differences in test scores between children whose parents have different educational levels? (Adapted from the *Statistical Abstract of the United States*, 2000, Table 286)

15.18 A manufacturer of outdoor brass lamps and mailboxes has received numerous complaints about premature corrosion. The manufacturer has identified the cause of the problem as the low-quality lacquer used to coat the brass. He decides to replace his current lacquer supplier with one of five possible alternatives. In order to judge which is best, he uses each of the five lacquers to coat 25 brass mailboxes and puts all 125 mailboxes outside. He records, for each, the number of days until the first sign of corrosion is observed. The results are stored in file Xr15-18. (*Caution:* Missing data)

a Is there sufficient evidence at the 1% significance level to allow the manufacturer to conclude that differences exist between the five lacquers?

b What are the required conditions for the test conducted in part **a**?

c Does it appear that the required conditions of the test in part **a** are satisfied?

15.19 In early 2001 the economy was slowing down and companies were laying off workers. A Gallup poll conducted February 9–11, 2001, asked a random sample of workers how long it would be before they had significant financial hardships if they lost their jobs and couldn't find new ones. They also classified their income. The classifications are

> Over $50,000
>
> $30,000 to $50,000
>
> $20,000 to $30,000
>
> Less than $20,000

The responses (in weeks) are stored in file Xr15-19. Can we infer that differences exist between the four groups?

15.20 In the introduction to this chapter, we mentioned that the first use of the analysis of variance was in the 1920s. It was employed to determine whether different amounts of fertilizer yielded different amounts of crop. Suppose that a scientist at an agricultural college wanted to redo the original experiment using three different types of fertilizer. Accordingly, he applied fertilizer A to 20 1-acre plots of land, fertilizer B to another 20 plots, and fertilizer C to yet another 20 plots of land. At the end of the growing season, the crop yields were recorded and stored in file Xr15-20. Can the scientist infer that differences exist among the crop yields?

15.21 A study performed by a Columbia University professor (described in *Report on Business*, August 1991) counted the number of times per minute professors from three different departments said "uh" or "ah" during lectures to fill gaps between words. The data derived from observing 100 minutes from each of the three departments are stored in file Xr15-21 of the data disk. If we assume that the more frequent use of "uh" and "ah" results in more boring lectures, can we conclude that some departments' professors are more boring than others?

15.22 Does the level of success of publicly traded companies affect the way their board members are paid? Publicly traded companies were divided into four quarters using the rate of return in their stocks to differentiate among the companies. The annual payment (in $1,000s) to their board members was stored in file Xr15-22. Can we infer that the amount of payment differs among the four groups of companies?

15.23 In 1994 the chief executive officers of the major tobacco companies testified before a Senate subcommittee. One of the accusations made was that tobacco firms added nicotine to their cigarettes, which made them even more addictive to smokers. Company scientists argued that the amount of nicotine in cigarettes depended completely on the size of the tobacco leaf. That is, during poor growing seasons the tobacco leaves would be smaller than in normal or good growing seasons. However, since the amount of nicotine in a leaf is a fixed quantity, smaller leaves would result in cigarettes having more nicotine (since a greater fraction of the leaf would be used to make a cigarette). To examine the issue, a university chemist took random samples of tobacco leaves that were grown in greenhouses where the amount of water was allowed to vary. Three different groups of tobacco leaves were grown. Group 1 leaves were grown with about an average season's rainfall. Group 2 leaves were given about 67% of group 1's water, and group 3 leaves were given 33% of group 1's water. The size of the leaf (in grams) and the amount of nicotine in each leaf were measured and stored in file Xr15-23.

  a Test to determine whether the leaf sizes differ between the three groups.

  b Test to determine whether the amounts of nicotine differ in the three groups.

15.24 There is a bewildering number of breakfast cereals on the market. Each company produces several different products in the belief that there are distinct markets. For example, there is a market composed primarily of children, another for diet-conscious adults, and another for health-conscious adults. Each cereal the companies produce has at least one market as its target. However, consumers make their own decisions, which may or may not match the target predicted by the cereal maker. In an attempt to distinguish between consumers, a survey of adults between the ages of 25 and 65 was undertaken. Each was asked several questions including age, income, and years of education, as well as which brand of cereal they consumed most frequently. The cereal choices are

  1. Sugar Smacks, a children's cereal
  2. Special K, a cereal aimed at dieters
  3. Fiber One, a cereal that is designed and advertised as healthy
  4. Cheerios, a combination of healthy and tasty

The results of the survey are stored in file Xr15-24 using the following format:

Column 1:   Cereal choice

Column 2:   Age of respondent

Column 3:   Annual household income

Column 4:   Years of education

  a Determine whether there are differences between the ages of the consumers of the four cereals.

  b Determine whether there are differences between the incomes of the consumers of the four cereals.

  c Determine whether there are differences between the educational levels of the consumers of the four cereals.

  d Summarize your findings in parts **a** through **c** and prepare a report describing the differences between the four groups of cereal consumers.

APPLICATIONS IN *MARKETING*

Test Marketing

In Example 15.1 we illustrated test marketing, which allows us to determine whether changing some of the elements of the marketing mix yields different sales. The technique was applied to determine whether there were differences in the advertising strategies. We can also apply the technique to discover the effect of different prices.

15.25 A manufacturer of novelty items is undecided about the price to charge for a new product. The marketing manager knows that it should sell for about $10, but is unsure of whether sales will vary significantly if it is priced at either $9 or $11. To conduct a pricing experiment, she distributes the new product to a sample of 60 stores belonging to a certain chain of variety stores. These 60 stores are all located in similar neighborhoods. The manager randomly selects 20 stores in which to sell the item at $9, 20 stores to sell it at $10, and the remaining 20 stores to sell it at $11. Sales at the end of the trial period are stored in file Xr15-25. What should the manager conclude?

APPLICATIONS IN *MARKETING*

Marketing Segmentation

Section 12.5 introduced market segmentation. In Chapter 13 we demonstrated how to use statistical analyses to determine whether two segments differ in their buying behavior. The next two exercises require you to apply the analysis of variance to determine whether several segments differ.

15.26 Refer to Exercise 13.144. Teenagers were further segmented into three age groups; 12 to 14, 15 to 16, and
17 to 19. Random samples were drawn from each
segment and the number of movies each teenager saw
last year was recorded in file Xr15-26. Do these data
allow a marketing manager of a movie studio to conclude that differences exist between the three segments?

15.27 In Exercise 12.103 marketing managers for J. C.
Penney's department store chain segmented the

market for women's apparel on the basis of personal
and family values. The segments are Conservative,
Traditional, and Contemporary. Recall that the classification was done on the basis of questionnaires.
Suppose that in addition to identifying the segment,
the questionnaire also asked each woman to report
family income (in $1,000s). These data are stored in
file Xr15-27. Do these data allow us to infer that family
incomes differ between the three market segments?

15.3 ANALYSIS OF VARIANCE EXPERIMENTAL DESIGNS

Since we introduced the matched pairs experiment in Section 13.4, the experimental
design has been one of the factors that determines which technique we use. Statistics
practitioners often design experiments to help extract the information they need to
assist them in making decisions. The one-way analysis of variance introduced in
Section 15.2 is only one of many different experimental designs of the analysis of
variance. For each type of experiment, we can describe the behavior of the response
variable using a mathematical expression or model. Although we will not exhibit the
mathematical expressions (we introduce models in Chapter 18) in this chapter, we
think it is useful for you to be aware of the elements that distinguish one experimental
design or model from another. In this section, we present some of these elements, and
in so doing, we introduce two of the experimental designs that will be presented later
in this chapter.

SINGLE-FACTOR AND MULTIFACTOR EXPERIMENTAL DESIGNS

As we pointed out in Section 15.2, the criterion by which we identify populations is
called a *factor*. The experiment described in Section 15.2 is a single-factor analysis of
variance, because it addresses the problem of comparing two or more populations
defined on the basis of only one factor. A **multifactor experiment** is one where there
are two or more factors that define the treatments. The experiment described in
Example 15.1 is a single-factor design because the treatments were the three advertising strategies. That is, the factor is the advertising strategy, and the three levels are
advertising that emphasizes convenience, advertising that emphasizes quality, and
advertising that emphasizes price.

Suppose that in another study, the medium used to advertise also varied: We can
advertise on television or in newspapers. We would then develop a two-factor analysis
of variance where the first factor, advertising strategy, has three levels, and the second
factor, advertising medium, has two levels. We will discuss two-factor experiments in
Section 15.5.

INDEPENDENT SAMPLES AND BLOCKS

In Section 13.4, we introduced statistical techniques where the data were gathered
from a matched pairs experiment. This type of experimental design reduces the variation within the samples, making it easier to detect differences between the two
populations. When the problem objective is to compare more than two populations,

the experimental design that is the counterpart of the matched pairs experiment is called the randomized block design. The term **block** refers to a matched group of observations from each population. Here is an example.

To determine whether incentive pay plans are effective, a statistics practitioner selected three groups of five workers who assemble electronic equipment. Each group will be offered a different incentive plan. The treatments are the incentive plans, the response variable is the number of units produced in one day, and the experimental units are the workers. If we obtain data from independent samples, we may not be able to detect differences between the pay plans because of variation between workers. If there are differences between workers, we need to identify the source of the differences. Suppose, for example, that we know that more experienced workers produce more units no matter what the pay plan. We could improve the experiment if we were to block the workers into five groups of three according to their experience. The three workers with the most experience will represent block 1, the next three will constitute block 2, and so on. As a result, the workers in each block will have approximately the same amount of experience. By designing the experiment in this way, the statistics practitioner removes the effect of different amounts of experience on the response variable. By doing so, we improve the chances of detecting real differences between pay incentives.

We can also perform a blocked experiment by using the same subject (person, plant, and store) for each treatment. For example, we can determine whether sleeping pills are effective by giving three brands of pills to the same group of people to measure the effects. Such experiments are called **repeated measures designs**. Technically, this is a different design than the randomized block. However, the data are analyzed in the same way for both designs. Hence, we will treat repeated measures designs as randomized block designs.

The randomized block experiment is also called the *two-way analysis of variance*. In Section 15.4, we introduce the technique used to calculate the test statistic for this type of experiment.

FIXED AND RANDOM EFFECTS

If our analysis includes all possible levels of a factor, the technique is called a **fixed-effects analysis of variance**. If the levels included in the study represent a random sample of all the levels that exist, the technique is called a **random-effects analysis of variance**. In Example 15.1, there were only three possible advertising strategies. Consequently, the study is a fixed-effects experiment. However, if there were other advertising strategies besides the three described in the example, and we wanted to know whether there were differences in sales between all the advertising strategies, the application would be a random-effects experiment. Here's another example.

To determine whether there is a difference in the number of units produced by the machines in a large factory, four machines out of 50 in the plant are randomly selected for study. The number of units each produces per day for 10 days will be recorded. This experiment is a random-effects experiment because we selected a random sample of four machines, and therefore the statistical results will allow us to determine whether there are differences between the 50 machines.

In some experimental designs, there are no differences in calculations of the test statistic between fixed- and random-effects analysis of variance. However, in others, including the two-factor experiment presented in Section 15.5, the calculations are different.

15.4 RANDOMIZED BLOCK (TWO-WAY) ANALYSIS OF VARIANCE

The purpose of designing a randomized block experiment is to reduce the within-treatments variation to more easily detect differences between the treatment means. In the one-way analysis of variance, we partitioned the total variation into the between-treatments and the within-treatments variation. That is,

$$SS(Total) = SST + SSE$$

In the randomized block design of the analysis of variance, we partition the total variation into three sources of variation:

$$SS(Total) = SST + SSB + SSE$$

where SSB, the sum of squares for blocks, measures the variation between the blocks. When the variation associated with the blocks is removed, SSE is reduced, making it easier to determine whether differences exist between the treatment means.

At this point in our presentation of statistical inference, we will deviate from our usual procedure of solving examples in three ways: manually, using Excel, and using Minitab. The calculations for this experimental design and for the experiment presented in the next section are so time-consuming that solving them by hand is pointless. Consequently, although we will continue to present the concepts by discussing how the statistics are calculated, we will solve the problems only by computer.

To help you understand the formulas, we will use the following notation.

$$\bar{x}[T]_j = \text{Mean of the observations in the } j\text{th treatment } (j = 1, 2, ..., k)$$

$$\bar{x}[B]_i = \text{Mean of the observations in the } i\text{th block } (i = 1, 2, ..., b)$$

$$b = \text{Number of blocks}$$

Table 15.4 summarizes the notation we use in this experimental design.

Table 15.4 Notation for the Randomized Block Analysis of Variance

	Treatments				
Block	1	2	$\cdots$	k	Block Mean
1	x_{11}	x_{12}	$\cdots$	x_{1k}	$\bar{x}[B]_1$
2	x_{21}	x_{22}	$\cdots$	x_{2k}	$\bar{x}[B]_2$
.	.	.		.	.
.	.	.		.	.
.	.	.		.	.
b	x_{b1}	x_{b2}	$\cdots$	x_{bk}	$\bar{x}[B]_b$
Treatment mean	$\bar{x}[T]_1$	$\bar{x}[T]_2$	$\cdots$	$\bar{x}[T]_k$	

The definitions of SS(Total) and SST in the randomized block design are identical to those in the independent samples design. SSE in the independent samples design is equal to the sum of SSB and SSE in the randomized block design.

SUMS OF SQUARES IN THE RANDOMIZED BLOCK EXPERIMENT

$$SS(Total) = \sum_{j=1}^{k} \sum_{i=1}^{b} (x_{ij} - \bar{\bar{x}})^2$$

$$SST = \sum_{j=1}^{k} b(\bar{x}[T]_j - \bar{\bar{x}})^2$$

$$SSB = \sum_{i=1}^{b} k(\bar{x}[B]_i - \bar{\bar{x}})^2$$

$$SSE = \sum_{j=1}^{k} \sum_{i=1}^{b} (x_{ij} - \bar{x}[T]_j - \bar{x}[B]_i + \bar{\bar{x}})^2$$

The test is conducted by determining the mean squares, which are computed by dividing the sums of squares by their respective degrees of freedom.

MEAN SQUARES FOR THE RANDOMIZED BLOCK EXPERIMENT

$$MST = \frac{SST}{k-1}$$

$$MSB = \frac{SSB}{b-1}$$

$$MSE = \frac{SSE}{n-k-b+1}$$

Finally, the test statistic is the ratio of mean squares, as described in the box.

TEST STATISTIC FOR THE RANDOMIZED BLOCK EXPERIMENT

$$F = \frac{MST}{MSE}$$

which is F distributed with $\nu_1 = k - 1$ and $\nu_2 = n - k - b + 1$ degrees of freedom.

An interesting, and sometimes useful, by-product of the test of the treatment means is that we can also test to determine whether the block means differ. This will allow us to determine whether the experiment should have been conducted as a randomized block design. (If there are no differences between the blocks, the randomized block design is less likely to detect real differences between the treatment means.) Such a discovery could be useful in future similar experiments. The test of the block means is almost identical to that of the treatment means except the test statistic is

$$F = \frac{MSB}{MSE}$$

which is F distributed with $\nu_1 = b - 1$ and $\nu_2 = n - k - b + 1$ degrees of freedom.

As with the one-way experiment, the statistics generated in the randomized block experiment are summarized in an ANOVA table, whose general form is exhibited in Table 15.5.

Table 15.5 ANOVA Table for the Randomized Block Analysis of Variance

Source of Variation	Degrees of Freedom	Sums of Squares	Mean Square	F Statistic
Treatments	$k-1$	SST	$MST = SST/(k-1)$	$F = MST/MSE$
Blocks	$b-1$	SSB	$MSB = SSB/(b-1)$	$F = MSB/MSE$
Error	$n-k-b+1$	SSE	$MSE = SSE/(n-k-b+1)$	
Total	$n-1$	SS(Total)		

EXAMPLE 15.2

Many North Americans suffer from high levels of cholesterol, which can lead to heart attacks. For those with very high levels (over 280), doctors prescribe drugs to reduce cholesterol levels. A pharmaceutical company has recently developed four such drugs. To determine whether any differences exist in their benefits, an experiment was organized. The company selected 25 groups of four men, each of whom had cholesterol levels in excess of 280. In each group, the men were matched according to age and weight. The drugs were administered over a 2-month period, and the reduction in cholesterol was recorded. The data are listed below and stored in file Xm15-02. Do these results allow the company to conclude that differences exist between the four new drugs?

Group	Drug 1	Drug 2	Drug 3	Drug 4
1	6.6	12.6	2.7	8.7
2	7.1	3.5	2.4	9.3
3	7.5	4.4	6.5	10.0
4	9.9	7.5	16.2	12.6
5	13.8	6.4	8.3	10.6
6	13.9	13.5	5.4	15.4
7	15.9	16.9	15.4	16.3
8	14.3	11.4	17.1	18.9
9	16.0	16.9	7.7	13.7
10	16.3	14.8	16.1	19.4
11	14.6	18.6	9.0	18.5
12	18.7	21.2	24.3	21.1
13	17.3	10.0	9.3	19.3
14	19.6	17.0	19.2	21.9
15	20.7	21.0	18.7	22.1
16	18.4	27.2	18.9	19.4
17	21.5	26.8	7.9	25.4
18	20.4	28.0	23.8	26.5
19	21.9	31.7	8.8	22.2
20	22.5	11.9	26.7	23.5
21	21.5	28.7	25.2	19.6
22	25.2	29.5	27.3	30.1
23	23.0	22.2	17.6	26.6
24	23.7	19.5	25.6	24.5
25	28.4	31.2	26.1	27.4

SOLUTION

IDENTIFY

The problem objective is to compare four populations, and the data are interval. Because the researchers recorded the cholesterol reduction for each drug for each member of the similar groups of men, we identify the experimental design as randomized block. The response variable is the cholesterol reduction, the treatments are the drugs, and the blocks are the 25 similar groups of men. The hypotheses to be tested are as follows:

$$H_0: \quad \mu_1 = \mu_2 = \mu_3 = \mu_4$$

$$H_1: \quad \text{At least two means differ.}$$

COMPUTE

 EXCEL

	A	B	C	D	E	F	G
1	Anova: Two-Factor Without Replication						
2							
3	ANOVA						
4	*Source of Variation*	*SS*	*df*	*MS*	*F*	*P-value*	*F crit*
5	Rows	3848.7	24	160.361	10.11	0.0000	1.67
6	Columns	196.0	3	65.318	4.12	0.0094	2.73
7	Error	1142.6	72	15.869			
8							
9	Total	5187.2	99				

The output includes block and treatment statistics (sums, averages, and variances, which are not shown here), and the ANOVA table. The *F* statistic to determine whether differences exist between the four drugs (**Columns**) is 4.12. Its *p*-value is .0094. The other *F* statistic, 10.11 (*p*-value = 0) indicates that there are differences between the groups of men (**Rows**).

COMMANDS	*COMMANDS FOR EXAMPLE 15.2*
1. Type or import the data into adjacent columns.	Open file **Xm15-02**.
2. Click **Tools, Data Analysis . . .**, and **Anova: Two-Factor Without Replication**.	
3. Specify the **Input Range**.	**A1:E26**
4. Click **Labels** if applicable. If you do, both the treatments and blocks must be labeled (as in Xm15-02).	
5. Specify the value of α (**Alpha**) and click **OK**.	**.05**

 MINITAB

Two-way ANOVA: Reduction versus Group, Drug

```
Analysis of Variance for Reductio
Source       DF        SS        MS        F        P
Group        24    3848.7     160.4    10.11    0.000
Drug          3     196.0      65.3     4.12    0.009
Error        72    1142.6      15.9
Total        99    5187.2
```

The *F* statistic for **Drug** is 4.12 with a *p*-value of .009. The *F* statistic for the blocks (**Group**) is 10.11, with a *p*-value of 0. *(continued)*

MINITAB (*continued*)

COMMANDS	COMMANDS FOR EXAMPLE 15.2
1. Type or import the data in stacked format in three columns. One column contains the responses, another contains codes for the levels of the blocks, and a third column contains codes for the levels of the treatments.	Open file **Xm15-02**. Stack the data into **C5.** Type block codes into **C6** and treatment codes into **C7**.
2. Click **Stat, ANOVA,** and **Twoway…**.	
3. Specify the **Responses, Row factor,** and **Column factor**. Click **OK**.	**Reduction** or **C5** **Group** or **C6** **Drug** or **C7**

INTERPRET

A Type I error occurs when you conclude that differences exist when, in fact, they do not. A Type II error is committed when the test reveals no difference when at least two means differ. It would appear that both errors are equally costly. Accordingly, we judge the *p*-value against a standard of 5%. Because the *p*-value = .0094, we conclude that there is sufficient evidence to infer that at least two of the drugs differ. An examination reveals that cholesterol reduction is greatest using drugs 2 and 4. Further testing is recommended to determine which is best.

CHECKING THE REQUIRED CONDITIONS

The *F* test of the randomized block design of the analysis of variance has the same requirements as the independent samples design. That is, the random variable must be normally distributed and the population variances must be equal. The histograms (not shown) appear to support the validity of our results; the reductions appear to be normal. The equality of variances requirement also appears to be met.

VIOLATION OF THE REQUIRED CONDITIONS

When the response is not normally distributed, we can replace the randomized block analysis of variance with the Friedman test, which is introduced in Section 17.5.

CRITERIA FOR BLOCKING

In Section 13.4, we listed the advantages and disadvantages of performing a matched pairs experiment. The same comments are valid when we discuss performing a blocked experiment. The purpose of blocking is to reduce the variation caused by differences between the experimental units. By grouping the experimental units into homogeneous blocks with respect to the response variable, the statistics practitioner increases the chances of detecting actual differences between the treatment means. Hence, we need to find criteria for blocking that significantly affect the response variable. For example, suppose that a statistics professor wants to determine which of four methods of teaching statistics is best. In a one-way experiment, he might take four samples of 10 students, teach each sample by a different method, grade the students at the end of the course, and perform an *F* test to determine whether differences exist. However, it is likely that there are very large differences between the students within each class that may hide differences between classes. To reduce this variation, the statistics professor needs to identify variables that are linked to a student's grade in statistics. For example, overall ability of the student, completion of mathematics courses, and exposure to other statistics courses are all related to performance in a statistics course.

The experiment could be performed in the following way. The statistics professor selects four students at random whose average grade before statistics is 95–100. He then randomly assigns the students to one of the four classes. He repeats the process with students whose average is 90–95, 85–90, ..., and 50–55. The final grades would be used to test for differences between the classes.

Any characteristics that are related to the experimental units are potential blocking criteria. For example, if the experimental units are people, we may block according to age, gender, income, work experience, intelligence, residence (country, county, or city), weight, or height. If the experimental unit is a factory and we're measuring number of units produced hourly, blocking criteria include workforce experience, age of the plant, and quality of suppliers.

DEVELOPING AN UNDERSTANDING OF STATISTICAL CONCEPTS

As we explained above, the randomized block experiment is an extension of the matched pairs experiment discussed in Section 13.4. In the matched pairs experiment, we simply remove the effect of the variation caused by differences between the experimental units. The effect of this removal is seen in the decrease in the value of the standard error (compared to the standard error in the test statistic produced from independent samples) and the increase in the value of the t statistic. In the randomized block experiment of the analysis of variance, we actually measure the variation between the blocks by computing SSB. The sum of squares for error is reduced by SSB, making it easier to detect differences between the treatments. Additionally, we can test to determine whether the blocks differ—a procedure we were unable to perform in the matched pairs experiment.

To illustrate, let's return to Examples 13.3 and 13.4, which were experiments to determine whether there was a difference in starting salaries offered to finance and marketing MBA majors. (In fact, we tested to determine whether finance majors draw higher salary offers than do marketing majors. However, the analysis of variance can only test for differences.) In Example 13.3 (independent samples), there was insufficient evidence to infer a difference between the two types of majors. In Example 13.4 (matched pairs experiment), there was enough evidence to infer a difference. As we pointed out in Section 13.4, matching by grade point average allowed the statistics practitioner to more easily discern a difference between the two types of majors. If we repeat Examples 13.3 and 13.4 using the analysis of variance, we come to the same conclusion. The Excel outputs are shown below. (Minitab's printouts are similar.)

Excel Analysis of Variance Output for Example 13.3

	A	B	C	D	E	F	G
1	Anova: Single Factor						
2							
3	SUMMARY						
4	*Groups*	*Count*	*Sum*	*Average*	*Variance*		
5	Finance	25	1640595	65624	360433294		
6	Marketing	25	1510570	60423	262228559		
7							
8							
9	ANOVA						
10	*Source of Variation*	*SS*	*df*	*MS*	*F*	*P-value*	*F crit*
11	Between Groups	338130013	1	338130013	1.09	0.3026	4.04
12	Within Groups	14943884470	48	311330926			
13							
14	Total	15282014483	49				

	A	B	C	D	E	F	G
1	Anova: Two-Factor Without Replication						
2							
3	ANOVA						
4	*Source of Variation*	*SS*	*df*	*MS*	*F*	*P-value*	*F crit*
5	Rows	21415991654	24	892332986	40.39	0.0000	1.98
6	Columns	320617035	1	320617035	14.51	0.0009	4.26
7	Error	530174605	24	22090609			
8							
9	Total	22266783295	49				

Excel Analysis of Variance Output for Example 13.4

In Example 13.3, we partition the total sum of squares [SS(Total) = 15,282,014,483] into two sources of variation: SST = 338,130,013 and SSE = 14,943,884,470. In Example 13.4, the total sum of squares is SS(Total) = 22,266,783,295, SST (sum of squares for majors) = 320,617,035, SSB (sum of squares for GPA) = 21,415,991,654, and SSE = 530,174,605. As you can see, the sums of squares for treatments are approximately equal (338,130,013 and 320,617,035). However, where the two calculations differ is in the sums of squares for error. SSE in Example 13.4 is much smaller than SSE in Example 13.3 because the randomized block experiment allows us to measure and remove the effect of the variation between MBA students with the same majors. The sum of squares for blocks (sum of squares for GPA groups) is 21,415,991,654, a statistic that measures how much variation exists between the salary offers within majors. As a result of removing this variation, SSE is small. Thus, we conclude in Example 13.4 that the salary offers differ between majors whereas there was not enough evidence in Example 13.3 to draw the same conclusion.

Notice that in both examples the square of the t statistic equals the F statistic. That is, in Example 13.3, $t = 1.04$, which when squared equals 1.09, which is the F statistic (rounded). In Example 13.4 $t = 3.81$, which when squared equals 14.51, the F statistic for the test of the treatment means. Moreover the p-values are also the same.

We'll complete this section by listing the factors that we need to recognize to use this experiment of the analysis of variance.

FACTORS THAT IDENTIFY THE RANDOMIZED BLOCK (TWO-WAY) ANALYSIS OF VARIANCE
1. **Problem objective:** Compare two or more populations.
2. **Data type:** Interval
3. **Experimental design:** Blocked samples

EXERCISES

Developing an Understanding of Statistical Concepts

15.28 The following statistics were generated from a randomized block experiment with $k = 3$ and $b = 7$.

SST = 100   SSB = 50   SSE = 25

a Test to determine whether the treatment means differ. (Use $\alpha = .05$.)

b Test to determine whether the block means differ. (Use $\alpha = .05$.)

15.29 A randomized block experiment produced the following statistics.

$k = 5$ $b = 12$ SST = 1,500   SSB = 1,000

SS(Total) = 3,500

a Test to determine whether the treatment means differ. (Use $\alpha = .01$.)

b Test to determine whether the block means differ. (Use $\alpha = .01$.)

15.30 Suppose the following statistics were calculated from data gathered from a randomized block experiment with $k = 4$ and $b = 10$.

SS(Total) = 1,210   SST = 275   SSB = 625

a Can we conclude from these statistics that the treatment means differ? (Use $\alpha = .01$.)

b Can we conclude from these statistics that the block means differ? (Use $\alpha = .01$.)

15.31 The following data were generated from a randomized block experiment.

  a Test at the 5% significance level to determine whether the treatment means differ.

  b Test at the 5% significance level to determine whether the block means differ.

Block	Treatment 1	2	3
1	7	12	8
2	10	8	9
3	12	16	13
4	9	13	6
5	12	10	11

15.32 A randomized block experiment produced the accompanying data.

Block	Treatment 1	2	3	4
1	6	5	4	4
2	8	5	5	6
3	7	6	5	6

  a Can we infer at the 5% significance level that the treatment means differ?

  b Can we infer at the 5% significance level that the block means differ?

The following exercises require the use of a computer and software. The answers may be calculated manually. See Appendix A for the sample statistics. **Use a 5% significance level unless specified otherwise.**

15.33 Data from a randomized block experiment (three treatments and 10 blocks) are stored in file Xr15-33. Can we conclude at the 1% significance level that the treatment means differ?

15.34 The data from a randomized block experiment with $k = 4$ and $b = 25$ are stored in file Xr15-34.

  a Can we conclude that the treatment means differ?

  b Is there enough evidence to infer that the block means differ?

  c What are the required conditions for the procedure used in part **a**?

  d Are the conditions listed in part **c** satisfied?

Applications

15.35 In recent years, lack of confidence in the Postal Service has led many companies to send all of their correspondence by private courier. A large company is in the process of selecting one of three possible couriers to act as its sole delivery method. To help in making the decision, an experiment was performed whereby letters were sent using each of the three couriers at 12 different times of the day to a delivery point across town. The number of minutes required for delivery was recorded and stored in file Xr15-35.

  a Can we conclude that there are differences in delivery times between the three couriers?

  b Did the statistics practitioner choose the correct design? Explain.

15.36 Refer to Exercise 15.20. Despite failing to show that differences in the three types of fertilizer exist, the scientist continued to believe that there were differences, and that the differences were masked by the variation between the plots of land. Accordingly, he conducted another experiment. In the second experiment he found 20 3-acre plots of land scattered across the county. He divided each into three plots and applied the three types of fertilizer on each of the 1-acre plots. The crop yields were recorded and stored in file Xr15-36.

  a Can the scientist infer that there are differences between the three types of fertilizer?

  b What do these test results reveal about the variation between the plots?

15.37 A recruiter for a computer company would like to determine whether there are differences in sales ability between business, arts, and science graduates. She takes a random sample of 20 business graduates who have been working for the company for the past 2 years. Each is then matched with an arts graduate and a science graduate with similar educational and working experience. The commission earned by each (in thousands of dollars) in the last year was recorded and stored in file Xr15-37.

  a Is there sufficient evidence to allow the recruiter to conclude that there are differences in sales ability between the holders of the three types of degrees?

  b Conduct a test to determine whether an independent samples design would have been a better choice.

  c What are the required conditions for the test in part **a**?

  d Are the required conditions satisfied?

15.38 Exercise 15.16 described an experiment that involved comparing the completion times associated with four different income tax forms. Suppose the experiment is redone in the following way. Thirty people are asked to fill out all four forms. The completion times (in minutes) are recorded and stored in file Xr15-38.

  a Is there sufficient evidence at the 1% significance level to infer that differences in the completion times exist between the four forms?

  b Comment on the suitability of this experimental design in this problem.

15.39 The advertising revenues commanded by a radio station depend on the number of listeners it has. The manager of a station that plays mostly hard rock music wants to learn more about its listeners—mostly teenagers and young adults. In particular, he wants to know whether the amount of time they spend listening to radio music varies by the day of the week. If the manager discovers that the mean time per day is about the same, he will schedule the most popular music evenly throughout the week. Otherwise, the top hits will be played mostly on the days that attract the greatest audience. An opinion survey company is hired, and it randomly selects 200 teenagers and asks them to record the amount of time spent listening to music on the radio for each day of the previous week. The data are stored in file Xr15-39. What can the manager conclude from these data?

15.40 Do medical specialists differ in the amount of time they devote to patient care? In order to answer this question, a statistics practitioner organized a study. The numbers of hours of patient care per week were recorded for five specialists. The experimental design was randomized blocks. The physicians were blocked by age. These data are stored in file Xr15-40.

   a Can we infer that there are differences in the amount of patient care between medical specialties?

   b Can we infer that blocking by age was appropriate? (Adapted from the *Statistical Abstract of the United States*, 2000, Table 190)

15.41 Refer to Exercise 15.15. Another study was conducted in the following way. Students from each of the high schools who were admitted to the business program were matched according to their high school averages. The average grades in the first year were recorded and stored in file Xr15-41. Can the university admissions officer conclude that there are differences in grading standards between the four high schools?

15.5 TWO-FACTOR ANALYSIS OF VARIANCE

In Section 15.2, we addressed problems where the data were generated from single-factor experiments. In Example 15.1, the treatments were the three different marketing strategies. Thus, there were three levels of the factor advertising strategy. In this section, we address the problem where the experiment features two factors. The general term for such data-gathering procedures is **factorial experiments**. In factorial experiments, we can examine the effect on the random variable of two or more factors, although we address the problem of only two factors in this book. We can use the analysis of variance to determine whether the levels of each factor are different from one another.

We will present the technique for the fixed effects only. That means we will address problems where all the levels of the factors are included in the experiment. As was the case with the randomized block design, calculation of the test statistic in this type of experiment is quite time-consuming. As a result, we will use Excel and Minitab to produce our statistics.

EXAMPLE 15.3

Suppose that in Example 15.1, in addition to varying the marketing strategy, the manufacturer also decided to advertise in one of the two media that are available: television and newspapers. As a consequence, the experiment was repeated in the following way. Six different small cities were selected. In city 1, the marketing emphasized convenience, and all the advertising was conducted on television. In city 2, marketing also emphasized convenience, but all the advertising was conducted in the daily newspaper. Quality was emphasized in cities 3 and 4. City 3 learned about the product from television commercials, and city 4 saw newspaper advertising. Price was the marketing emphasis in cities 5 and 6. City 5 saw television commercials, and city 6 saw newspaper advertisements. In each city, the weekly sales for each of 10 weeks were recorded. These data are listed in the accompanying table and in file Xm15-03 (columns 1 to 6 store the 10 observations for each of the cities). What conclusions can be drawn from these results? (As we did in Example 15.1, we assume that except for the advertising, the cities are identical.)

City 1	City 2	City 3	City 4	City 5	City 6
491	464	677	689	575	803
712	559	627	650	614	584
558	759	590	704	706	525
447	557	632	652	484	498
479	528	683	576	478	812
624	670	760	836	650	565
546	534	690	628	583	708
444	657	548	798	536	546
582	557	579	497	579	616
672	474	644	841	795	587

SOLUTION

IDENTIFY

Notice that there are six treatments. However, the treatments are defined by two different factors. One factor is the marketing strategy, which has three levels (convenience, quality, and price). The second factor is the advertising medium, which has two levels (television and newspaper). If we assume that there are only three advertising strategies and only two advertising media, we identify this experiment as a fixed-effects design. We can proceed to solve this problem in the same way we did in Section 15.2. That is, we test the following hypotheses:

$$H_0: \quad \mu_1 = \mu_2 = \mu_3 = \mu_4 = \mu_5 = \mu_6$$

$H_1:$ At least two means differ.

COMPUTE

 EXCEL

	A	B	C	D	E	F	G
1	Anova: Single Factor						
2							
3	SUMMARY						
4	*Groups*	*Count*	*Sum*	*Average*	*Variance*		
5	City-1	10	5555	555.5	8641.39		
6	City-2	10	5759	575.9	8545.88		
7	City-3	10	6430	643.0	3884.67		
8	City-4	10	6871	687.1	12558.54		
9	City-5	10	6000	600.0	9527.56		
10	City-6	10	6244	624.4	12523.82		
11							
12							
13	ANOVA						
14	*Source of Variation*	*SS*	*df*	*MS*	*F*	*P-value*	*F crit*
15	Between Groups	113620	5	22724	2.45	0.0452	2.39
16	Within Groups	501137	54	9280			
17							
18	Total	614757	59				

MINITAB

One-way ANOVA: City-1, City-2, City-3, City-4, City-5, City-6

```
Analysis of Variance
Source      DF        SS        MS        F        P
Factor       5    113620     22724     2.45    0.045
Error       54    501137      9280
Total       59    614757
                                    Individual 95% CIs For Mean
                                    Based on Pooled StDev
Level        N      Mean     StDev    ----------+---------+---------+------
City-1      10    555.50     92.96    (-------*--------)
City-2      10    575.90     92.44    (-------*--------)
City-3      10    643.00     62.33              (--------*--------)
City-4      10    687.10    112.06                     (--------*--------)
City-5      10    600.00     97.61        (--------*-------)
City-6      10    624.40    111.91           (--------*--------)
                                    ----------+---------+---------+------
Pooled StDev =     96.33                    560       630       700
```

INTERPRET

The value of the test statistic is $F = 2.45$ with a p-value of .0452. We conclude that there are differences in sales between the six cities.

This statistical result raises more questions. Namely, can we conclude that the differences in weekly sales between the cities are caused by differences between the marketing strategies? Or are they caused by differences between television and newspaper advertising? Or, perhaps, are there combinations of marketing strategy and advertising medium that result in especially high or low sales? To show how we test for each type of difference, we need to develop some terminology.

A **complete factorial experiment** is an experiment in which the data for all possible combinations of the levels of the factors are gathered. That means that in Example 15.3 we measured the sales for all six combinations. This experiment is called a complete 3×2 factorial experiment. Had we omitted gathering sales figures for (say) emphasizing price with advertising on television, we would not have a complete factorial experiment.

In general, we will refer to one of the factors as factor A (arbitrarily chosen). The number of levels of this factor will be denoted by a. The other factor is called factor B, and its number of levels is denoted by b. This terminology becomes clearer when we present the data from Example 15.3 in another format. Table 15.6 depicts the layout for a *two-way classification*, which is another name for the complete factorial experiment. The number of observations for each combination is called a **replicate**. The number of replicates is denoted by r. In this book, we address only problems in which the number of replicates is the same for each treatment. Such a design is called **balanced**.

Table 15.6 Two-Way Classification for Example 15.3

Factor B: Medium	Factor A: Strategy		
	Convenience	Quality	Price
Television	491	677	575
	712	627	614
	558	590	706
	447	632	484
	479	683	478
	624	760	650
	546	690	583
	444	548	536
	582	579	579
	672	644	795

(continued)

Table 15.6 Two-Way Classification for Example 15.3 *(continued)*

Factor B: Medium	Factor A: Strategy		
	Convenience	*Quality*	*Price*
Newspaper	464	689	803
	559	650	584
	759	704	525
	557	652	498
	528	576	812
	670	836	565
	534	628	708
	657	798	546
	557	497	616
	474	841	587

Thus, we use a complete factorial experiment where the number of treatments is ab with r replicates per treatment. In Example 15.3, $a = 3$, $b = 2$, and $r = 10$. As a result, we have 10 observations for each of the six treatments.

If there are differences between the treatment means, we would like to know whether both factors affect the response. That is, are there differences between the levels of A and differences between the levels of B? If only one factor affects the response, is it A or is it B? If both A and B affect the response, do they do so independently, or do they interact (a term we explain below)? Figures 15.4 to 15.7 graphically depict the possible differences.

Figure 15.4
Differences between the levels of factor A and differences between the levels of factor B; no interaction

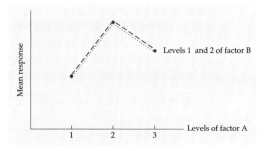

Figure 15.5
Differences between the levels of factor A and no difference between the levels of factor B; no interaction

Figure 15.6
No differences between the levels of factor A and differences between the levels of factor B; no interaction

**Figure 15.7
Interaction between
factors A and B**

Figure 15.4 graphs the mean weekly sales when there are differences between the levels of A as well as differences between the levels of B. However, the factors affect sales independently, which means there is no interaction. Figure 15.5 describes the case where there are differences between the levels of A, but no difference between the levels of B. Figure 15.6 depicts differences between the levels of B but no differences between the levels of A. Figure 15.7 shows the levels of A and B interacting.

To understand what is meant by the term *interaction*, examine Figures 15.4 and 15.5. In both figures there are differences between the means of the three levels of factor A. However, the size of the differences between the means is not affected by the levels of factor B. In Figure 15.4, the differences between the means of the three levels of factor A for level 1 of factor B are the same as the differences between the means of the three levels of factor A for level 2 of factor B. Now examine Figure 15.7. Once again there are differences between the means of the levels of factor A. However, the difference between each pair of means is affected by factor B. For example, for level 1 of factor B the mean of level 1 of factor A is greater than the mean of level 2. For level 2 of factor B the mean of level 1 of factor A is less than the mean of level 2. Thus, the levels of factor B interact with the levels of factor A.

To test for each possibility, we conduct several *F* tests similar to the one performed in Section 15.2. Figure 15.8 illustrates the partitioning of the total sum of squares that leads to the *F* tests. We've included in this figure the partitioning used in the one-way study. This part of the analysis of variance has already been performed in Example 15.3. When the one-way analysis of variance allows us to infer that differences between the treatment means exist, we continue our analysis by partitioning the treatment sum of squares into three sources of variation. The first is sum of squares for factor A, which we label SS(A), which measures the variation between the levels of factor A. Its degrees of freedom are $a - 1$. The second is the sum of squares for factor B, whose degrees of freedom are $b - 1$. SS(B) is the variation between the levels of factor B. The interaction sum of squares is labeled SS(AB), which is a measure of the amount of variation between the combinations of factors A and B; its degrees of freedom are $(a - 1) \times (b - 1)$. The sum of squares for error is SSE, and its degrees of freedom are $n - ab$. (Recall that n is the total sample size, which in this experiment is $n = abr$.) Notice that SSE and its number of degrees of freedom are identical in both partitions. As in the previous experiment, SSE is the variation within the treatments.

**Figure 15.8
Partitioning SS(Total) in
single-factor and two-
factor analyses of variance**

Seeing Statistics

APPLET 17:
PLOTS OF TWO-WAY ANOVA EFFECTS

This applet provides a graph similar to those seen in Figures 15.4 to 15.7. There are three sliders—one for rows, one for columns, and one for interaction. Moving the top slider changes the difference between the row means. The second slider changes the difference between the column means. The third slider allows us to see the effects of interaction.

Applet Exercises

Label the columns factor A and the rows factor B. Move the sliders to arrange for each of the following differences. Describe what the resulting figure tells you about differences between levels of factor A, levels of factor B, and interaction.

	Row	Column	$R \times C$
17.1	-30	0	0
17.2	0	25	0
17.3	0	0	-20
17.4	25	-30	0
17.5	30	0	30
17.6	30	0	-30
17.7	0	20	20
17.8	0	20	-20
17.9	30	30	30
17.10	30	30	-30

For those whose mathematical confidence is high, we have provided a listing of the notation and the definitions of the sums of squares below. (See Table 15.7.) Learning how the sums of squares are calculated is useful but hardly essential to your ability to conduct the tests.

We then perform three F tests to determine whether the differences between the treatment means are caused by differences between levels of A, levels of B, or interaction. We call this analysis the two-factor or two-way analysis of variance. These tests are summarized below.

To help you understand the formulas, we will use the following notation.

$$\bar{x}[AB]_{ij} = \text{Mean of the response variable in the } ij\text{th treatment (mean of the}$$
$$\text{treatment when the factor A level is } i \text{ and the factor B level is } j)$$

$$\bar{x}[A]_i = \text{Mean of the observations when the factor A level is } i$$

$$\bar{x}[B]_j = \text{Mean of the observations when the factor B level is } j$$

$$\bar{\bar{x}} = \text{Mean of all the observations}$$

$$a = \text{Number of factor A levels}$$

$$b = \text{Number of factor B levels}$$

$$r = \text{Number of replicates}$$

TABLE 15.7 Notation for Two-Factor Model

Factor B	Factor A 1		Factor A 2		. . .	Factor A a		
1	$\begin{matrix}x_{111}\\x_{112}\\.\\.\\.\\x_{11r}\end{matrix}$	$\bar{x}[AB]_{11}$	$\begin{matrix}x_{211}\\x_{212}\\.\\.\\.\\x_{21r}\end{matrix}$	$\bar{x}[AB]_{21}$		$\begin{matrix}x_{a11}\\x_{a12}\\.\\.\\x_{a1r}\end{matrix}$	$\bar{x}[AB]_{a1}$	$\bar{x}[B]_1$
2	$\begin{matrix}x_{121}\\x_{122}\\.\\.\\.\\x_{12r}\end{matrix}$	$\bar{x}[AB]_{12}$	$\begin{matrix}x_{221}\\x_{222}\\.\\.\\x_{22r}\end{matrix}$	$\bar{x}[AB]_{22}$		$\begin{matrix}x_{a21}\\x_{a22}\\.\\.\\x_{a2r}\end{matrix}$	$\bar{x}[AB]_{a2}$	$\bar{x}[B]_2$
. . .								
b	$\begin{matrix}x_{1b1}\\x_{1b2}\\.\\.\\.\\x_{1br}\end{matrix}$	$\bar{x}[AB]_{1b}$	$\begin{matrix}x_{2b1}\\x_{2b2}\\.\\.\\x_{2br}\end{matrix}$	$\bar{x}[AB]_{2b}$		$\begin{matrix}x_{ab1}\\x_{ab2}\\.\\.\\x_{abr}\end{matrix}$	$\bar{x}[AB]_{ab}$	$\bar{x}[B]_b$
	$\bar{x}[A]_1$		$\bar{x}[A]_2$			$\bar{x}[A]_a$		$\bar{\bar{x}}$

In this notation, $\bar{x}[AB]_{11}$ is the mean of the responses for factor A level 1 and factor B level 1. The mean of the responses for factor A level 1 is $\bar{x}[A]_1$. The mean of the responses for factor B level 1 is $\bar{x}[B]_1$. The sums of squares are defined as follows.

SUMS OF SQUARES IN THE TWO-FACTOR ANALYSIS OF VARIANCE

$$\text{SS(Total)} = \sum_{i=1}^{a} \sum_{j=1}^{b} \sum_{k=1}^{r} (x_{ijk} - \bar{x})^2$$

$$\text{SS(A)} = rb \sum_{i=1}^{a} (\bar{x}[A]_i - \bar{x})^2$$

$$\text{SS(B)} = ra \sum_{j=1}^{b} (\bar{x}[B]_j - \bar{x})^2$$

$$\text{SS(AB)} = r \sum_{i=1}^{a} \sum_{j=1}^{b} (\bar{x}[AB]_{ij} - \bar{x}[A]_i - \bar{x}[B]_j + \bar{x})^2$$

$$\text{SSE} = \sum_{i=1}^{a} \sum_{j=1}^{b} \sum_{k=1}^{r} (x_{ijk} - \bar{x}[AB]_{ij})^2$$

To compute SS(A), we calculate the sum of the squared differences between the factor A level means, which are denoted $\bar{x}[A]_i$, and the grand mean, $\bar{\bar{x}}$. The sum of squares for factor B, SS(B), is defined similarly. The interaction sum of squares, SS(AB), is calculated by taking each treatment mean (a treatment consists of a combination of a level of factor A and a level of factor B), subtracting the factor A level mean, subtracting the factor B level mean, adding the grand mean, squaring this quantity, and adding. The sum of squares for error, SSE, is calculated by subtracting the treatment means from the observations, squaring, and adding.

F TESTS CONDUCTED IN TWO-FACTOR ANALYSIS OF VARIANCE

Test for Differences between the Levels of Factor A

H_0: The means of the a levels of factor A are equal.

H_1: At least two means differ.

Test statistic: $F = \dfrac{\text{MS(A)}}{\text{MSE}}$

Test for Differences between the Levels of Factor B

H_0: The means of the b levels of factor B are equal.

H_1: At least two means differ.

Test statistic: $F = \dfrac{\text{MS(B)}}{\text{MSE}}$

Test for Interaction between Factors A and B

H_0: Factors A and B do not interact to affect the mean responses.

H_1: Factors A and B do interact to affect the mean responses.

Test statistic: $F = \dfrac{\text{MS(AB)}}{\text{MSE}}$

Required Conditions

1. The distribution of the response is normally distributed.
2. The variance for each treatment is identical.
3. The samples are independent.

As in the two previous experimental designs of the analysis of variance, we summarize the results in an ANOVA table. Table 15.8 depicts the general form of the table for the complete factorial experiment.

Table 15.8 ANOVA Table for the Two-Factor Experiment

Source of Variation	Degrees of Freedom	Sums of Squares	Mean Square	F Statistic
Factor A	$a-1$	SS(A)	$MS(A) = SS(A)/(a-1)$	$F = MS(A)/MSE$
Factor B	$b-1$	SS(B)	$MS(B) = SS(B)/(b-1)$	$F = MS(B)/MSE$
Interaction	$(a-1)(b-1)$	SS(AB)	$MS(AB) = SS(AB)/[(a-1)(b-1)]$	$F = MS(AB)/MSE$
Error	$n-ab$	SSE	$MSE = SSE/(n-ab)$	
Total	$n-1$	SS(Total)		

We'll illustrate the techniques using the data in Example 15.3. All calculations will be performed by Excel and Minitab.

Test of Differences in Mean Weekly Sales between Three Marketing Strategies

H_0: The means of the three levels of factor A are equal.

H_1: At least two means differ.

Test statistic: $F = \dfrac{MS(A)}{MSE}$

Value of the test statistic: From the computer output, we have $MS(A) = 49,419$, $MSE = 9,280$, and $F = 49,419/9,280 = 5.33$ (p-value = .0077).

There is evidence at the 5% significance level to infer that differences in weekly sales exist between the different marketing strategies.

Test for Differences in Mean Weekly Sales between Advertising Media

H_0: The means of the two levels of factor B are equal.

H_1: At least two means differ.

Test statistic: $F = \dfrac{MS(B)}{MSE}$

Value of the test statistic: From the computer output, we find $MS(B) = 13,172$ and $MSE = 9,280$. Thus, $F = 13,172/9,280 = 1.42$ (p-value = .2387).

There is insufficient evidence at the 5% significance level to infer that differences in weekly sales exist between television and newspaper advertising.

Test for Interaction between Factors A and B

H_0:   Factors A and B do not interact to affect mean weekly sales.

H_1:   Factors A and B do interact to affect mean weekly sales.

Test statistic: $F = \dfrac{MS(AB)}{MSE}$

Value of the test statistic: From the printouts, MS(AB) = 805, MSE = 9,280, and $F = 805/9,280 = .087$ (p-value = .9171).

There is not enough evidence to conclude that there is an interaction between marketing strategy and advertising medium that affects mean weekly sales.

EXCEL

	A	B	C	D	E	F	G
1	Anova: Two-Factor With Replication						
2							
3	ANOVA						
4	*Source of Variation*	*SS*	*df*	*MS*	*F*	*P-value*	*F crit*
5	Sample	13172	1	13172.0	1.42	0.2387	4.02
6	Columns	98839	2	49419.3	5.33	0.0077	3.17
7	Interaction	1610	2	804.8	0.09	0.9171	3.17
8	Within	501137	54	9280.3			
9							
10	Total	614757	59				

The actual output includes a variety of statistics, which we have omitted. In the ANOVA table, **Sample** refers to factor B (medium) and **Columns** refers to factor A (advertising strategy). Thus, MS(B) = 13,172.0, MS(A) = 49,419.3, MS(AB) = 804.8, and MSE = 9,280.3. The F statistics are 1.42 (medium), 5.33 (advertising strategy), and .09 (interaction).

COMMANDS   *COMMANDS FOR EXAMPLE 15.3*

1. Type or import the data. (See Sheet2 in file   Open file **Xm15-03 (Sheet 2)**.
   Xm15-03 for the correct format.)
2. Click **Tools, Data Analysis…**, and
   Anova:Two-Factor with Replication.
3. Specify the **Input Range.**   **A1:D21**
4. Type the number of replications r (**Rows   **10**
   per sample**).
5. Click **Labels** (if appropriate). If you do,
   you must label the rows and columns as we
   did in Sheet 2 of file Xm15-03.
6. Specify a value for α (**Alpha**) and click **OK.**   **.05**

MINITAB

Two-way ANOVA: Sales versus Strategy, Medium

```
Analysis of Variance for Sales
Source         DF        SS        MS        F        P
Strategy        2     98839     49419     5.33    0.008
Medium          1     13172     13172     1.42    0.239
Interaction     2      1610       805     0.09    0.917
Error          54    501137      9280
Total          59    614757
```

The *F* statistics are 5.33 for the advertising strategy, 1.42 for the medium, and .09 for interaction.

COMMANDS	*COMMANDS FOR EXAMPLE 15.3*
1. Type or import the data in stacked format in three columns. One column contains the responses, another contains codes for the levels of factor A, and a third column contains codes for the levels of factor B.	Open file **XM15-03.** Stack the data into **C4.** Type factor A codes into **C5** and factor B codes into **C6.**
2. Click **Stat, ANOVA,** and **Twoway....**	
3. Specify the **Responses, Row factor,** and **Column factor**. Click **OK.**	**Sales** or **C4** **Strategy** or **C5** **Medium** or **C6**

INTERPRET

Figure 15.9 graphs the mean sales for each factor. As you can see, there are differences between the levels of factor A, no difference between the levels of factor B, and no interaction is apparent. These results indicate that emphasizing quality produces the highest sales and that television and newspapers are equally effective.

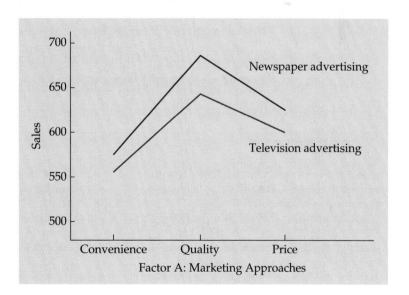

Figure 15.9
Mean responses for factors A and B: Example 15.3

CONDUCTING THE ANALYSIS OF VARIANCE FOR THE COMPLETE FACTORIAL EXPERIMENT

In addressing the problem outlined in Example 15.3, we began by conducting a one-way analysis of variance to determine whether differences existed between the six treatment means. This was done primarily for pedagogical reasons to enable you to see that when the treatment means differ, we need to analyze the reasons for the differences. However, in practice, we generally do not conduct this test in the complete factorial experiment (although it should be noted that some statistics practitioners prefer this "two-stage" strategy). We recommend that you proceed directly to the two-factor analysis of variance.

DEVELOPING AN UNDERSTANDING OF STATISTICAL CONCEPTS

You may have noticed that there are similarities between the two-factor experiment and the randomized block experiment. In fact, when the number of replicates is 1, the calculations are identical. (Minitab uses the same command.) This raises the question: What is the difference between a factor in a multifactor study and a block in a randomized block experiment? In general, the difference between the two experimental designs is that in the randomized block experiment, blocking is performed specifically to reduce variation, whereas in the two-factor model the effect of the factors on the response variable is of interest to the statistics practitioner. The criteria that define the blocks are always characteristics of the experimental units. Consequently, factors that are characteristics of the experimental units will be treated not as factors in a multifactor study but as blocks in a randomized block experiment.

Let's review how we recognize the need to use the procedure described in this section.

FACTORS THAT IDENTIFY THE INDEPENDENT SAMPLES TWO-FACTOR ANALYSIS OF VARIANCE

1. **Problem Objective:** Compare two or more populations (populations are defined as combinations of levels of two factors).
2. **Data type:** Interval
3. **Experimental design:** Independent samples

EXERCISES

15.42 A two-factor analysis of variance experiment was performed with $a = 3$, $b = 4$, and $r = 20$. The following sums of squares were computed.

$$SS(Total) = 42,450 \quad SS(A) = 1,560$$
$$SS(B) = 2,880 \quad SS(AB) = 7,605$$

a Test at the 1% significance level to determine whether differences exist between the levels of factor A.

b Test at the 1% significance level to determine whether differences exist between the levels of factor B.

c Test at the 1% significance level to determine whether factors A and B interact.

15.43 A statistics practitioner conducted a two-factor analysis of variance experiment with $a = 4$, $b = 3$, and $r = 8$. The sums of squares are listed below.

$$SS(Total) = 9,420 \quad SS(A) = 203$$
$$SS(B) = 859 \quad SS(AB) = 513$$

a Test at the 5% significance level to determine whether differences exist between the levels of factor A.

b Test at the 5% significance level to determine whether differences exist between the levels of factor B.

c Test at the 5% significance level to determine whether factors A and B interact.

15.44 The following data were generated from a 2×2 factorial experiment with 3 replicates.

FACTOR A	FACTOR B	
	1	2
1	6	12
	9	10
	7	11
2	9	15
	10	14
	5	10

a Test at the 5% significance level to determine whether factors A and B interact.

b Test at the 5% significance level to determine whether differences exist between the levels of factor A.

c Test at the 5% significance level to determine whether differences exist between the levels of factor B.

15.45 The data shown below were taken from a 2×3 factorial experiment with 4 replicates.

FACTOR A	FACTOR B	
	1	2
1	23	20
	18	17
	17	16
	20	19
2	27	29
	23	23
	21	27
	28	25
3	23	27
	21	19
	24	20
	16	22

a Test at the 5% significance level to determine whether factors A and B interact.

b Test at the 5% significance level to determine whether differences exist between the levels of factor A.

c Test at the 5% significance level to determine whether differences exist between the levels of factor B.

Applications

15.46 Headaches are one of the most common, but least understood, ailments. Most people get headaches several times per month; over-the-counter medication is usually sufficient to eliminate their pain. However, for a significant proportion of people, headaches are debilitating and make their lives almost unbearable.

Many such people have investigated a wide spectrum of possible treatments, including narcotic drugs, hypnosis, biofeedback, and acupuncture, with little or no success. In the last few years, a promising new treatment has been developed. Simply described, the treatment involves a series of injections of a local anesthetic to the occipital nerve (located in the back of the neck). The current treatment procedure is to schedule the injections once a week for 4 weeks. However, it has been suggested that another procedure may be better, one that features one injection every other day for a total of four injections. Additionally, some physicians recommend other combinations of drugs that may increase the effectiveness of the injections. To analyze the problem, an experiment was organized. It was decided to test for a difference between the two schedules of injection and to determine whether there are differences between four drug mixtures. Because of the possibility of an interaction between the schedule and the drug, a complete factorial experiment was chosen. Five headache patients were randomly selected for each combination of schedule and drug. Forty patients were treated and each was asked to report the frequency, duration, and severity of his or her headache prior to treatment and for the 30 days following the last injection. An index ranging from 0 to 100 was constructed for each patient, where 0 indicates no headache pain and 100 specifies the worst headache pain. The improvement in the headache index for each patient was recorded and reproduced in the accompanying table. (A negative value indicates a worsening condition.) (The authors are grateful to Dr. Lorne Greenspan for his help in writing this example.)

Improvement in Headache Index

Schedule	Drug Mixture			
	1	2	3	4
One injection	17	24	14	10
every week	6	15	9	−1
(4 weeks)	10	10	12	0
	12	16	0	3
	14	14	6	−1
One injection	18	−2	20	−2
every 2 days	9	0	16	7
(4 days)	17	17	12	10
	21	2	17	6
	15	6	18	7

a What are the factors in this experiment?

b What is the response variable?

c Identify the levels of each factor.

d Can we conclude at the 5% significance level that differences exist between the two schedules?

e Can we conclude at the 5% significance level that differences exist between the four drug mixtures?

f Conduct a test to determine whether the two factors interact.

15.47 Most college instructors prefer to have their students participate actively in class. Ideally, students will ask their professor questions and answer their professor's questions, making the classroom experience more interesting and useful. Many professors seek ways to encourage their students to participate in class. A statistics professor at a community college in upper New York state believes that there are a number of external factors that affect student participation. He believes that the time of day and the configuration of seats are two such factors. Consequently, he organized the following experiment. Six classes of about 60 students each were scheduled for one semester. Two classes were scheduled at 9:00 A.M., two at 1:00 P.M., and two at 4:00 P.M. At each of the three times, one of the classes was assigned to a room where the seats were arranged in rows of 10 seats. The other class was a U-shaped, tiered room, where students not only face the instructor, but face their fellow students as well. In each of the six classrooms, over five days, student participation was measured by counting the number of times students asked and answered questions. These data are displayed in the accompanying table and stored in file Xr15-47 in exactly the same format as the table.

	Time		
Class Configuration	9:00 A.M.	1:00 P.M.	4:00 P.M.
Rows	10	9	7
	7	12	12
	9	12	9
	6	14	20
	8	8	7
U-shape	15	4	7
	18	4	4
	11	7	9
	13	4	8
	13	6	7

a How many factors are there in this experiment? What are they?

b What is the response variable?

c Identify the levels of each factor.

d What conclusions (with $\alpha = .05$) can the professor draw from these data?

The following exercises require the use of a computer and software.

15.48 Refer to Exercise 15.16. Suppose that the experiment is redone in the following way. Thirty taxpayers fill out each of the four forms. However, 10 taxpayers in each group are in the lowest income bracket, 10 are in the next income bracket, and the remaining 10 are in the highest bracket. The amount of time needed to complete the returns is recorded and stored in file Xr15-48 using the following format:

Column 1:   Group number

Column 2:   times to complete form 1 (first 10 rows = low income, next 10 rows = next income bracket, and last 10 rows = highest bracket)

Column 3:   times to complete form 2 (same format as column 2)

Column 4:   times to complete form 3 (same format as column 2)

Column 5:   times to complete form 4 (same format as column 2)

a How many treatments are there in this experiment?

b How many factors are there? What are they?

c What are the levels of each factor?

d Can we conclude at the 5% significance level that differences exist between the 4 forms?

e Can we conclude at the 5% significance level that taxpayers in different brackets require different amounts of time to complete their tax forms?

f Is there evidence at the 5% significance level of interaction between the two factors?

15.49 Detergent manufacturers frequently make claims about the effectiveness of their products. A consumer protection service decided to test the five best-selling brands of detergent, each of whose manufacturer claims that its product produces the "whitest whites" in all water temperatures. The experiment was conducted in the following way. One hundred fifty white sheets were equally soiled. Thirty sheets were washed in each brand—10 with cold water, 10 with warm water, and 10 with hot water. After washing, the "whiteness" scores for each sheet were measured with laser equipment. The results are stored in file Xr15-49 using the following format:

Column 1:   Water temperature

Column 2:   scores for detergent 1 (first 10 rows = cold water, middle 10 rows warm, and last 10 rows = hot)

Column 3:   scores for detergent 2 (same format as column 2)

Column 4:   scores for detergent 3 (same format as column 2)

Column 5:   scores for detergent 4 (same format as column 2)

Column 6:   scores for detergent 5 (same format as column 2)

a What are the factors in this experiment?

b What is the response variable?

c Identify the levels of each factor.

d Can we conclude at the 5% significance level that differences exist between the five detergents?

e Can we conclude at the 5% significance level that differences exist between the three water temperatures?

f Test at the 5% significance level to determine whether the two factors interact.

15.6 (OPTIONAL) APPLICATIONS IN OPERATIONS MANAGE-MENT: FINDING AND REDUCING VARIATION

In the introduction to Example 12.3, we pointed out that variation in the size, weight, or volume of a product's components cause the product to fail or not function properly. Unfortunately, it is impossible to eliminate all variation. Designers of products and the processes that make the products understand this phenomenon. Consequently, when they specify the length, weight, or some other measurable characteristic of the product, they allow for some variation, called the **tolerance**. For example, the diameters of the piston rings of a car are supposed to be .826 millimeter (mm) with a tolerance of .006 (mm). That is, the product will function provided that the diameter is between .826 − .006 = .820 and .826 + .006 = .832 mm. These quantities are called the **lower** and **upper specification limits** (**LSL** and **USL**), respectively.

Suppose that the diameter of the piston rings is actually a random variable that is normally distributed with a mean of .826 and a standard deviation of .003 mm. We can compute the probability that a piston ring's diameter is between the specification limits. Thus,

$$P(.820 < X < .832) = P\left(\frac{.820 - .826}{.003} < \frac{X - \mu}{\sigma} < \frac{.832 - .826}{.003}\right)$$

$$= P(-2.0 < Z < 2.0)$$

$$= 2(.4772)$$

$$= .9544$$

The probability that the diameter does not meet specifications is 1 − .9544 = .0456. This probability is a measure of the **process capability**.

If we can decrease the standard deviation, a greater proportion of piston rings will have diameters that meet specification. Suppose that the operations manager has decreased the diameter's standard deviation to .002. The proportion of piston rings that do not meet specifications is .0026. When the probabilities are quite low, we express the probabilities as the number of defective units per million or per billion. Thus, if the standard deviation is .002, the number of defective piston rings is expected to be 2,600 per million. The goal of many firms is to reduce the standard deviation so that the lower specification and upper specification limits are at least 6 standard deviations away from the mean. If the standard deviation is .001, the proportion of nonconforming piston rings is $1 - P(-6 < Z < 6)$, which is 2 per billion. (Incidentally, this figure is often erroneously quoted as 3.4 per million.) The goal is called **six sigma**. Figure 15.10 on page 512 depicts the proportion of conforming and nonconforming piston rings for $\sigma = .003, .002,$ and .001.

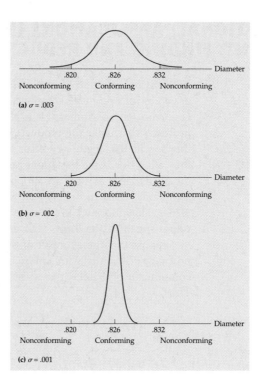

Figure 15.10
Proportion of conforming and nonconforming piston rings

Another way to measure how well the process works is the **process capability index**, denoted by C_p, which is defined as

$$C_p = \frac{\text{USL} - \text{LSL}}{6\sigma}$$

In the illustration above, USL = .832 and LSL = .820. If the standard deviation is .002, then

$$C_p = \frac{\text{USL} - \text{LSL}}{6\sigma} = \frac{.832 - .820}{6(.002)} = 1.0$$

The larger the process capability index, the more capable is the process in meeting specifications. A C_p value of 1.0 describes a production process where the specification limits are equal to 3 standard deviations above and below the mean. A C_p value of 2.0 means that the upper and lower limits are 6 standard deviations above and below the mean. This is the goal for many firms.

In practice, the standard deviation must be estimated from the data. We will address this issue again in Chapter 22.

TAGUCHI LOSS FUNCTION

Historically, operations managers applied the "goalpost" philosophy, a name derived from the game of football. If the ball is kicked *anywhere* between the goalposts, the kick is equally as successful as one that perfectly splits the goalposts. Under this philosophy, a piston ring that has a diameter of .821 works as well as one that is exactly .826. That is, the company sustains a loss only when the product falls outside the goalposts. Products that lie between the goalposts suffer no financial loss. For many firms this philosophy has now been replaced by the Taguchi loss function (named for Genichi Taguchi, a Japanese statistician whose ideas and techniques permeate any discussion of statistical applications in quality management).

Products whose length or weight fall within the tolerances of their specifications do not all function in exactly the same way. There is a difference between a product that barely falls between the goalposts and ones that are in the exact center. The Taguchi loss function recognizes that any deviation from the specification results in a financial loss. In addition, the farther the product's variable is from the specification, the greater the loss. The piston ring described above is specified to have a diameter of exactly .826 mm, an amount specified by the manufacturer to work at the optimum level. Any deviation will cause that and perhaps other parts to wear out prematurely. Although customers will not know the reason for the problem, they will know that the unit had to be replaced. The greater the deviation, the more quickly the part will wear and need replacing. If the part is under warranty, the company will incur a loss in replacing it. If the warranty has expired, customers will have to pay to replace the unit, causing some degree of displeasure, which may cause them to buy another company's product in the future. In either case, the company loses money. Figure 15.11 depicts the loss function. As you can see, any deviation from the specification results in some loss, with large deviations resulting in larger losses.

Management scientists have shown that the loss function can be expressed as a function of the production process mean and variance. In Figure 15.12 we describe a normal distribution of the diameter of the machined part specified to be .826 mm. When the mean of the distribution is .826, any loss is caused by the variance. The statistical techniques introduced in Chapter 22 are usually employed to center the distribution at its specification. However, reducing the variance is considerably more difficult. To reduce variation it is necessary to first find the sources of variation. We do so by conducting experiments. The principles are quite straightforward, drawing on the concepts developed in the previous section.

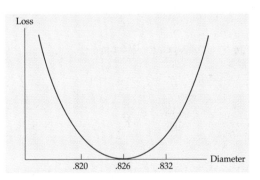

Figure 15.11
Taguchi loss function

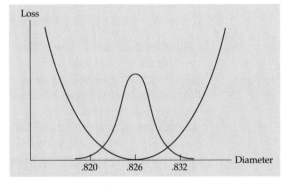

Figure 15.12
Taguchi loss function and the distribution of piston rings

There are several factors that can affect the final product. In the introduction to operations management (see page 10) we discussed the four Ms: machines, materials, methods, and personnel (manpower). By altering some or all of these elements, the operations manager can alter the size, weight, or volume and ultimately, the quality of the product.

The Causes of Variation example that opened this chapter illustrates this strategy. Because we have limited our discussion to the two-factor model, the example features this experimental design. It should be understood, however, that more complicated models are needed to fully investigate sources of variation.

CAUSES OF VARIATION: SOLUTION

IDENTIFY

The two factors are the operators and the machines. There are three levels of operators and four levels of machines. The model we employ is the two-factor model with interaction. The computer output is shown below.

COMPUTE

EXCEL

	A	B	C	D	E	F	G
1	Anova: Two-Factor With Replication						
2							
3	ANOVA						
4	Source of Variation	SS	df	MS	F	P-value	F crit
5	Sample	0.0151	2	0.0076	6.98	0.0022	3.19
6	Columns	0.0034	3	0.0011	1.04	0.3856	2.80
7	Interaction	0.0046	6	0.0008	0.71	0.6394	2.29
8	Within	0.0520	48	0.0011			
9							
10	Total	0.0751	59				

MINITAB

Two-way ANOVA: Length versus Operator, Machine

```
Analysis of Variance for Length
Source         DF        SS         MS         F         P
Operator        2     0.01513    0.00757      6.98     0.002
Machine         3     0.00336    0.00112      1.04     0.386
Interaction     6     0.00465    0.00077      0.71     0.639
Error          48     0.05199    0.00108
Total          59     0.07514
```

We first test for interaction. The F statistic for interaction is .71 and its p-value is .6394. There is no evidence to infer that there is interaction between the machines and the operators. Next, we test to determine whether there are differences between the levels of each factor. The F statistic for the operator factor is 6.98 (p-value = .0022). The F statistic for the machine factor is 1.04 (p-value = .3856).

INTERPRET

We conclude that there are differences only between the levels of the operators. Thus, the only source of variation here is the different operators. The operations manager can now focus on reducing or eliminating this variation. For example, the manager may use only one operator in the future or investigate why the operators differ.

DESIGN OF EXPERIMENTS AND TAGUCHI METHODS

In the example just discussed, the experiment employed only two factors. In practice, there are frequently many more factors. The problem is that the total number of treatments or combinations can be quite high, making any experimentation both time-consuming and expensive. For example, if there are 10 factors, each with two levels, the number of treatments is $2^{10} = 1,024$. If we measure each treatment with 10 replicates, the number of observations, 10,240, makes this experiment prohibitive. Fortunately, it is possible to reduce this number considerably. Through the use of *orthogonal arrays*, we can conduct *fractional factorial experiments* that can produce useful results at a small fraction of the cost. The experimental designs and statistical analyses are beyond the level of this book. Interested readers can find a variety of books at different levels of mathematical and statistical sophistication to learn more about this application.

EXERCISES

Applications

The following exercises require the use of a computer and software.
Use a 5% significance level.

15.50 The headrest on a car's front seats are designed to protect the driver and front-seat passenger from whiplash when the car is hit from behind. The frame of the headrest is made from metal rods. A machine is used to bend the rod into a U-shape exactly 440 millimeters wide. The width is critical—too wide or too narrow and it won't fit into the holes drilled into the car seat frame. The company has experimented with different metal alloys in the hope of finding a material that will result in more headrest frames that fit. Another possible source of variation is the machines used. To learn more about the process, the operations manager conducts an experiment. Both of the machines are used to produce 10 headrests from each of the two metal alloys now being used. Each frame is measured and the data (in millimeters) are stored in file Xr15-50 using the format below. Analyze the data to determine whether the alloys, machines, or both are sources of variation.

Column 1:   Machine 1; rows 1–10, alloy A;
rows 11–20, alloy B

Column 2:   Machine 2; rows 1–10, alloy A;
rows 11–20, alloy B

15.51 A paint manufacturer is attempting to improve the process that fills the 1-gallon containers. The foreperson has suggested that the nozzle can be made from several different alloys. Furthermore, the way that the process "knows" when to stop the flow of paint can be accomplished in two ways—by setting a predetermined amount or by measuring the amount of paint already in the can. To determine what factors lead to variation, an experiment is conducted. For each of the four alloys that could be used to make the nozzles and

the two measuring devices, five cans are filled. The amount of paint in each container is precisely measured. The data in liters are stored in file Xr15-51 in the following way:

Column 1:   Device 1; rows 1–5, alloy A;
rows 6–10, alloy B; etc.

Column 2:   Device 2; rows 1–5, alloy A;
rows 6–10, alloy B; etc.

Can we infer that the alloys, the measuring devices, or both are sources of variation?

15.52 In Example 13.2, the operations manager wanted to know whether the two methods used to assemble a new ergonomic chair were different with respect to the amount of time taken to assemble the chair. The manager was now faced with another problem. The marketing department of the firm has ascertained that there is a growing market for a specialized desk that houses the various parts of a computer system. The operations manager is summoned to put together a plan that will produce high-quality desks at low cost. The characteristics of the desk have been dictated by the marketing department, which has specified the material that the desk will be made from and the machines used to produce the parts. However, there are three methods that can be utilized. Moreover, because of the complexity of the operation, the manager realizes that it is possible that different skill levels of the workers can yield different results. Accordingly, he organized an experiment. Workers from each of three skill levels were chosen. These groups were further divided into two subgroups. Each subgroup assembled the desks using methods A and B. The amount of time taken to assemble each of eight desks was recorded and stored in file Xr15-52. (Columns 1 and 2 contain the times for methods A and B; rows 1–8, 9–16, and 17–24 store the times for the three skill levels.) What can we infer from these data?

15.7 MULTIPLE COMPARISONS

When we conclude from the one-way analysis of variance that at least two treatment means differ, we often need to know which treatment means are responsible for these differences. For example, if an experiment is undertaken to determine whether different locations within a store produce different mean sales, the manager would be keenly interested in determining which locations result in higher sales and which locations result in lower sales. Similarly, a stockbroker would like to know which one of several mutual funds outperforms the others, and a television executive would like to know which television commercials hold the viewers' attention and which are ignored.

Although it may appear that all we need to do is examine the sample means and identify the largest or the smallest to determine which population means are largest or smallest, this is not the case. To illustrate, suppose that in a five-treatment analysis of variance, we discover that differences exist and that the sample means are as follows.

$$\bar{x}_1 = 20 \qquad \bar{x}_2 = 19 \qquad \bar{x}_3 = 35 \qquad \bar{x}_4 = 22 \qquad \bar{x}_5 = 17$$

The statistics practitioner wants to know which of the following conclusions are valid:

1. μ_3 is larger than the other means.
2. μ_3 and μ_4 are larger than the other means.
3. μ_5 is smaller than the other means.
4. μ_5 and μ_2 are smaller than the other means.
5. μ_3 is larger than the other means, and μ_5 is smaller than the other means.

From the information we have, it is impossible to determine which, if any, of the statements are true. We need a statistical method to make this determination.

There are several statistical inference procedures that deal with this problem. We will present three methods that allow us to determine which population means differ. All three methods apply to the one-way experiment only.

FISHER'S LEAST SIGNIFICANT DIFFERENCE (LSD) METHOD

This method was briefly introduced in Section 15.2 (page 482). To determine which population means differ, we could perform a series of t tests of the difference between two means on all pairs of population means to determine which are significantly different. In Chapter 13, we introduced the equal-variances t test of the difference between two means. The test statistic and confidence interval estimator are, respectively,

$$t = \frac{(\bar{x}_1 - \bar{x}_2) - (\mu_1 - \mu_2)}{\sqrt{s_p^2\left(\dfrac{1}{n_1} + \dfrac{1}{n_2}\right)}}$$

$$(\bar{x}_1 - \bar{x}_2) \pm t_{\alpha/2}\sqrt{s_p^2\left(\dfrac{1}{n_1} + \dfrac{1}{n_2}\right)}$$

with degrees of freedom $\nu = n_1 + n_2 - 2$.

Recall that s_p^2 is the pooled variance estimate, which is an unbiased estimator of the variance of the two populations. (Recall that the use of these techniques requires that the population variances are equal.) In this section we modify the test statistic and interval estimator.

Earlier in this chapter we pointed out that MSE is an unbiased estimator of the common variance of the populations we're testing. Since MSE is based on all the observations in the k samples, it will be a better estimator than s_p^2 (which is based on only two samples). Thus, we could draw inferences about every pair of means by substituting MSE in place of s_p^2 in the test statistic and confidence interval estimator above. The number of degrees of freedom would also change to $\nu = n - k$ (where n is the total sample size). The test statistic to determine whether μ_i and μ_j differ is

$$t = \frac{(\bar{x}_i - \bar{x}_j) - (\mu_i - \mu_j)}{\sqrt{\text{MSE}\left(\dfrac{1}{n_i} + \dfrac{1}{n_j}\right)}}$$

The confidence interval estimator is

$$(\bar{x}_i - \bar{x}_j) \pm t_{\alpha/2}\sqrt{\text{MSE}\left(\frac{1}{n_i} + \frac{1}{n_j}\right)}$$

and $\nu = n - k$.

We define the least significant difference LSD as

$$\text{LSD} = t_{\alpha/2}\sqrt{\text{MSE}\left(\frac{1}{n_i} + \frac{1}{n_j}\right)}$$

A simple way of determining whether differences exist between each pair of population means is to compare the absolute value of the difference between their two sample means and LSD. That is, we will conclude that μ_i and μ_j differ if

$$|\bar{x}_i - \bar{x}_j| > \text{LSD}$$

LSD will be the same for all pairs of means if all k sample sizes are equal. If some sample sizes differ, LSD must be calculated for each combination.

In Section 15.2 we argued that this method is flawed because it will increase the probability of committing a Type I error. That is, it is more likely than the analysis of variance to conclude that a difference exists in some of the population means when in fact none differ. On page 482 we calculated that if $k = 6$ and all population means are equal, the probability of erroneously inferring at the 5% significance level that at least two means differ is about 54%. The 5% figure is now referred to as the *comparisonwise Type I error rate*. The true probability of making at least one Type I error is called the *experimentwise Type I error rate*, denoted α_E. The experimentwise Type I error rate can be calculated as

$$\alpha_E = 1 - (1 - \alpha)^C$$

where C is the number of pairwise comparisons. That is, $C = k(k-1)/2$. Mathematicians have proven that

$$\alpha_E \leq C\alpha$$

which means that if we want the probability of making at least one Type I error to be no more than α_E, we simply specify $\alpha = \alpha_E/C$. The resulting procedure is called the **Bonferroni adjustment.**

BONFERRONI ADJUSTMENT TO LSD METHOD

The adjustment is made by dividing the specified experimentwise Type I error rate by the number of combinations of pairs of population means. For example if, $k = 6$, then

$$C = \frac{k(k-1)}{2} = \frac{6(5)}{2} = 15$$

If we want the true probability of a Type I error to be no more than 5%, we divide this probability by C. Thus,

$$\alpha = \frac{\alpha_E}{C} = \frac{.05}{15} = .0033$$

To illustrate Fisher's LSD method and the Bonferroni adjustment, consider Example 15.1, where we tested to determine whether three population means differ using a 5% significance level. The three sample means are 577.55, 653.00, and 608.65. The pairwise absolute differences are

$$|\bar{x}_1 - \bar{x}_2| = |577.55 - 653.00| = |-75.45| = 75.45$$

$$|\bar{x}_1 - \bar{x}_3| = |577.55 - 608.65| = |-31.10| = 31.10$$

$$|\bar{x}_2 - \bar{x}_3| = |653.00 - 608.65| = |44.35| = 44.35$$

If we conduct the LSD procedure with $\alpha = .05$, we find $t_{\alpha/2, n-k} = t_{.025, 57} = 2.002$. (This figure was determined from Excel. If you find the critical value manually from Table 4 in Appendix B, you will have to approximate the degrees of freedom with 60 and find $t_{.025, 57} \approx t_{.025, 60} = 2.000$.) Thus,

$$t_{\alpha/2}\sqrt{\text{MSE}\left(\frac{1}{n_i} + \frac{1}{n_j}\right)} = 2.002\sqrt{8,894\left(\frac{1}{20} + \frac{1}{20}\right)} = 59.71$$

We can see that only one pair of sample means differ by more than 59.71. That is, $|\bar{x}_1 - \bar{x}_2| = 75.45$; the other two differences are less than LSD. Consequently, we conclude that only μ_1 and μ_2 differ.

If we perform the LSD procedure with the Bonferroni adjustment, the number of pairwise comparisons is 3 [calculated as $C = k(k-1)/2 = 3(2)/2$]. We set $\alpha = .05/3 = .0167$. Thus, $t_{\alpha/2} = 2.467$ (available from Excel and difficult to approximate manually) and

$$t_{\alpha/2}\sqrt{\text{MSE}\left(\frac{1}{n_i} + \frac{1}{n_j}\right)} = 2.467\sqrt{8,894\left(\frac{1}{20} + \frac{1}{20}\right)} = 73.54$$

Again we conclude that only μ_1 and μ_2 differ. Notice, however, that LSD is larger in the second calculation, reflecting the higher hurdle dictated by the smaller probability.

The drawback to the LSD procedure is that we increase the probability of at least one Type I error. The Bonferroni adjustment corrects this problem. However, recall that the probabilities of Type I and Type II errors are inversely related. The Bonferroni adjustment uses a smaller value of α, which results in an increased probability of a Type II error. A Type II error occurs when a difference between population means exists yet we cannot detect it. The next multiple comparison method addresses this problem.

TUKEY'S MULTIPLE COMPARISON METHOD

A more powerful test is Tukey's multiple comparison method. This technique determines a critical number such that, if any pair of sample means has a difference greater than this critical number, we conclude that the pair's two corresponding population means are different.

The test is based on the Studentized range, which is defined as the variable

$$q = \frac{\bar{x}_{\max} - \bar{x}_{\min}}{s/\sqrt{n}}$$

where $\bar{x}_{\max}$ and $\bar{x}_{\min}$ are the largest and smallest sample means, respectively, assuming that there are no differences between the population means. We can find a critical number ω (Greek letter *omega*) such that if the difference between any pair of sample means exceeds ω, we can take this as sufficient evidence that the pair's corresponding population means differ. We define the number ω as follows.

CRITICAL NUMBER

$$\omega = q_\alpha(k, \nu)\sqrt{\frac{\text{MSE}}{n_g}}$$

where

$$n = \text{Number of observations } (n = n_1 + n_2 + \cdots + n_k)$$

$$\nu = \text{Number of degrees of freedom association with MSE } (\nu = n - k)$$

$$n_g = \text{Number of observations in each of } k \text{ samples}$$

$$\alpha = \text{Significance level}$$

$$q_\alpha(k, \nu) = \text{Critical value of the Studentized range}$$

Theoretically, this procedure requires that all sample sizes be equal. However, if the sample sizes are different, we can still use this technique provided that the sample sizes are at least similar. The value of n_g used above is the *harmonic mean* of the sample sizes. That is,

$$n_g = \frac{k}{\dfrac{1}{n_1} + \dfrac{1}{n_2} + \cdots + \dfrac{1}{n_k}}$$

Table 7 in Appendix B provides values of $q_\alpha(k, \nu)$ for a variety of values of k and ν, and for $\alpha = .01$ and $.05$. To illustrate the table's use, suppose that $k = 3$, $\nu = 15$, and $\alpha = .05$. From the table we find $q_{.05}(3, 15) = 3.67$.

Applying Tukey's method to Example 15.1, we find

$$k = 3$$

$$n_1 = n_2 = n_3 = n_g = 20$$

$$\nu = n - k = 60 - 3 = 57$$

$$\text{MSE} = 8,894$$

Thus,

$$\omega = q_\alpha(k, \nu)\sqrt{\frac{\text{MSE}}{n_g}} = q_{.05}(3, 57)\sqrt{\frac{8,894}{20}} = 3.40 \times 21.09 = 71.70$$

[We approximated $q_{.05}(3, 57)$ with $q_{.05}(3, 60) = 3.40$.]

EXCEL
Tukey's and Fisher's LSD Method ($\alpha = .05$)

	A	B	C	D	E
1	Multiple Comparisons				
2					
3				LSD	Omega
4	Treatment	Treatment	Difference	Alpha = 0.05	Alpha = 0.05
5	Convenience	Quality	-75.45	59.721	71.701
6		Price	-31.1	59.721	71.701
7	Quality	Price	44.35	59.721	71.701

Tukey and Fisher's LSD with the Bonferroni Adjustment ($\alpha = .05/3 = .0167$)

	A	B	C	D	E
1	Multiple Comparisons				
2					
3				LSD	Omega
4	Treatment	Treatment	Difference	Alpha = 0.0167	Alpha = 0.05
5	Convenience	Quality	-75.45	73.542	71.701
6		Price	-31.1	73.542	71.701
7	Quality	Price	44.35	73.542	71.701

The printout includes Fisher's LSD, ω (Tukey's method), and the differences between sample means for each combination of populations. (The Bonferroni adjustment is made by specifying another value for α.)

COMMANDS	COMMANDS FOR EXAMPLE 15.1
1. Type or import the data into adjacent columns.	Open file **Xm15-01**.
2. Click **Tools, Data Analysis Plus**, and **Multiple Comparisons**.	
3. Specify the **Input Range**.	**A1:C21**
4. Click **Labels** (if appropriate).	
5. Type the value of α (**Alpha**). To use the Bonferroni adjustment, divide α by $C = k(k-1)/2$. For Tukey, Excel computes ω only for $\alpha = .05$.	**.05** (for Fisher's LSD and **.0167** (for Bonferroni adjustment)

MINITAB

One-way ANOVA: Convenience, Quality, Price

```
Analysis of Variance
Source    DF         SS         MS        F        P
Factor     2      57512      28756     3.23    0.047
Error     57     506984       8894
Total     59     564496

                                    Individual 95% CIs For Mean
                                    Based on Pooled StDev
Level      N       Mean      StDev   ---+---------+---------+---------+---
Convenie  20     577.55     103.80   (--------*-------)
Quality   20     653.00      85.08                    (--------*-------)
Price     20     608.65      93.11            (--------*-------)
                                    ---+---------+---------+---------+---
Pooled StDev =    94.31              550       600       650       700


Tukey's pairwise comparisons

    Family error rate = 0.0500
Individual error rate = 0.0195

Critical value = 3.40

Intervals for (column level mean) - (row level mean)

                  1          2

       2      -147.2
                -3.7

       3      -102.8      -27.4
                40.6      116.1
```

(continued)

```
Fisher's pairwise comparisons

    Family error rate = 0.121
Individual error rate = 0.0500

Critical value = 2.002

Intervals for (column level mean) - (row level mean)

                        1              2

        2        -135.2
                 -15.7

        3        -90.8        -15.4
                 28.6         104.1
```

The printout includes the ANOVA table and the multiple comparison statistics. For Tukey's method, Minitab prints the critical value $q_\alpha(k, \nu) = 3.40$, from which you may calculate ω. (We calculated $\omega = 71.70$.) You need not, however, because Minitab prints the difference between each pair of sample means $\pm\omega$. For example, to determine whether μ_1 and μ_2 differ, Minitab prints

$$(\bar{x}_1 - \bar{x}_2) \pm \omega = (577.55 - 653.00) \pm 71.70 = -75.45 \pm 71.70 = (-147.2, -3.7)$$

We estimate that $\mu_1 - \mu_2$ falls between −147.2 and −3.7. Because this interval excludes 0, we infer that there is a difference between μ_1 and μ_2. Notice that the other two intervals, (−102.8, 40.6) and (−27.4, 116.1) include 0, indicating that μ_1 and μ_3, and μ_2 and μ_3 may not differ.

For Fisher's LSD, Minitab prints the difference between each pair of sample means $\pm$ LSD. The interpretation is the same as for Tukey's method. In the printout above we used $\alpha = .05$ for both Tukey's and Fisher's procedures.

COMMANDS	*COMMANDS FOR EXAMPLE 15.1*
1. Type or import the data. The data must be stacked. (We stacked the data into column 4 (Sales) and the subscript in column 5 (City).	Open file **Xm15-01**.
2. Click **Stat, ANOVA**, and **Oneway…**.	
3. Specify the **Response**.	**Sales**
4. Specify the **Factor**.	**City**
5. Click **Comparisons…**.	
6. Use the cursor to select **Tukey**'s method and specify α.	**.05 or 5**
7. Use the cursor to select **Fisher**'s method and specify α. Click **OK**. Click **OK**.	**.05 or 5**
For the Bonferroni adjustment, divide α by $C = k(k-1)/2$.	**.0167 or 1.67**

INTERPRET

Using any of the three multiple comparison methods, we discover that only μ_1 and μ_2 differ and no other pairs differ. This tells the marketing manager that advertising emphasizing quality (city 2) outsells advertising stressing convenience (city 1), and that there is no evidence to infer that advertising emphasizing price (city 3) is any different from the other two. It would appear that the company should launch an advertising campaign that features various ways of describing the high quality of the product. It may also advertise stressing the price of the product.

WHICH MULTIPLE COMPARISON METHOD TO USE

In Example 15.1, all three multiple comparison methods yielded the same results. This will not always be the case. When the results differ, the statistics practitioner must choose which one to use. Bear in mind as well that there are other techniques besides the ones described here. Unfortunately, no one procedure works best in all types of problems. Most statisticians agree with the following guideline.

If you have identified two or three pairwise comparisons that you wish to make before conducting the analysis of variance, use the Bonferroni method. This means that if in a problem there are 10 populations but you're particularly interested in comparing, say, populations 3 and 7, and populations 5 and 9, use Bonferroni with $C = 2$.

If you plan to compare all possible combinations, use Tukey.

When do we use Fisher's LSD? If the purpose of the analysis is to point to areas that should be investigated further, Fisher's LSD method is indicated.

Incidentally, to employ Fisher's LSD or the Bonferroni adjustment, you must perform the analysis of variance first. Tukey's method can be employed instead of the analysis of variance.

EXERCISES

Developing an Understanding of Statistical Concepts

15.53 Use Fisher's LSD method with $\alpha = .05$ to determine which population means differ in the following problem.

$$k = 3 \quad n_1 = 10 \quad n_2 = 10 \quad n_3 = 10$$
$$MSE = 700 \quad \bar{x}_1 = 128.7 \quad \bar{x}_2 = 101.4 \quad \bar{x}_3 = 133.7$$

15.54 Repeat Exercise 15.53, using the Bonferroni adjustment.

15.55 Repeat Exercise 15.53, using Tukey's multiple comparison method.

15.56 Use Fisher's LSD procedure with $\alpha = .05$ to determine which population means differ given the following statistics.

$$k = 5 \quad n_1 = 5 \quad n_2 = 5 \quad n_3 = 5 \quad n_4 = 5 \quad n_5 = 5$$
$$MSE = 125 \quad \bar{x}_1 = 227 \quad \bar{x}_2 = 205 \quad \bar{x}_3 = 219 \quad \bar{x}_4 = 248 \quad \bar{x}_5 = 202$$

15.57 Repeat Exercise 15.56, using the Bonferroni adjustment.

15.58 Repeat Exercise 15.56, using Tukey's multiple comparison method

Applications

15.59 Apply Fisher's LSD method with the Bonferroni adjustment to determine which schools differ in Exercise 15.15. Use $\alpha = .05$.

15.60 Repeat Exercise 15.59, applying Tukey's method instead.

15.61 Apply Tukey's multiple comparison method to determine which forms differ in Exercise 15.16. (Use $\alpha = .05$.)

15.62 Repeat Exercise 15.61, applying the Bonferroni adjustment.

15.63 Use Tukey's multiple comparison method with $\alpha = .05$ to determine which lacquers differ in Exercise 15.18. (*Caution:* Missing data)

15.64 Repeat Exercise 15.63, using the Bonferroni adjustment with $\alpha = .10$.

The following exercises require the use of a computer and software. The answers may be calculated manually. See Appendix A for the sample statistics.

15.65 Police cars, ambulances, and other emergency vehicles are required to carry road flares. One of the most important features of flares is their burning times. To help decide which of four brands on the market to use, a police laboratory technician measured the burning time for a random sample of 10 flares of each brand. The results, recorded to the nearest minute, are stored in file Xr15-65.

a Can we conclude at the 5% significance level that differences exist between the burning times of the four brands of flares?

b Apply Fisher's LSD method with the Bonferroni adjustment to determine which flares are better.

c Repeat part **b** using Tukey's method.

15.66 An engineering student who is about to graduate decided to survey various firms in Silicon Valley to see which offered the best chance for early promotion and career advancement. He surveyed 30 small firms (size level is based on gross revenues), 30 medium-size firms, and 30 large firms and determined how much time must elapse before an average engineer can receive a promotion. These data are stored in file Xr15-66.

a Can the engineering student conclude at the 5% significance level that speed of promotion varies between the three sizes of engineering firms?

b If differences exist, which of the following is true? Use Tukey's method.

i   Small firms differ from the other two.

ii Medium-size firms differ from the other two.

iii Large firms differ from the other two.

iv All three firms differ from one another.

v   Small firms differ from large firms.

15.8 SUMMARY

The **analysis of variance** allows us to test for differences between populations when the data are interval. The analyses of the results of three different experimental designs were presented in this chapter. The first is the **one-way analysis of variance**. The second experimental design, **randomized block**, uses data gathered by observing the results of a matched or blocked experiment (**two-way analysis of variance**). The third design is the **two-factor experiment**, wherein the treatments are defined as the combinations of the levels of two factors. All the analyses of variance are based on partitioning the total sum of squares into sources of variation from which the mean squares and F statistics are computed.

We described an important application in operations management that employs the analysis of variance. Finally, we introduced three **multiple comparison methods**, which allow us to determine which means differ in the one-way analysis of variance.

IMPORTANT TERMS

Analysis of variance 472	Random effects 488
Treatment means 472	Block means 489
One-way analysis of variance 472	Between-blocks variation 490
Between treatments variation 474	Sum of squares for blocks (SSB) 490
Sum of squares for treatments (SST) 474	Factorial experiment 497
Response variable 474	Complete factorial experiment 499
Responses 474	Two-way classification 499
Experimental units 474	Replicate 499
Factor 474	Balanced 499
Level 474	Tolerance 511
Within-treatments variation 475	Lower specification limit 511
Sum of squares for error (SSE) 475	Upper specification limit 511
Mean squares 476	Process capability 511
ANOVA table 478	Six sigma 511
Total sum of squares 479	Process capability index 512
Completely randomized design 480	Taguchi loss function 512
Single factor 487	Fisher's Least Significant Difference 516
Two factor 487	Bonferroni procedure 517
Repeated measures 488	Tukey's multiple comparison method 518
Fixed effects 488	

SYMBOLS

Symbol	Pronounced	Represents
$\bar{\bar{x}}$	x-double-bar	Overall or grand mean
$\bar{x}[T]_j$	x-bar-T-sub-j	Mean of the jth treatment
$\bar{x}[B]_i$	x-bar-B-sub-i	Mean of the ith block
$\bar{x}[AB]_{ij}$	x-bar-A-B-sub-i-j	Mean of the ijth treatment
$\bar{x}[A]_i$	x-bar-A-sub-i	Mean of the observations when the factor A level is i
$\bar{x}[B]_j$	x-bar-B-sub-j	Mean of the observations when the factor B level is j
q		Studentized range
ω	omega	Critical value of Tukey's multiple comparison method
$q_\alpha(k, \nu)$	q-sub-alpha-k-ν	Critical value of the Studentized range
n_g		Number of observations in each of k samples

FORMULAS

One-way analysis of variance

$$\text{SST} = \sum_{j=1}^{k} n_j(\bar{x}_j - \bar{\bar{x}})^2$$

$$\text{SSE} = \sum_{j=1}^{k} \sum_{i=1}^{n_j} (x_{ij} - \bar{x}_j)^2$$

$$\text{MST} = \frac{\text{SST}}{k-1}$$

$$\text{MSE} = \frac{\text{SSE}}{n-k}$$

$$F = \frac{\text{MST}}{\text{MSE}}$$

Two-way analysis of variance (randomized block design of experiment)

$$\text{SS(Total)} = \sum_{j=1}^{k} \sum_{i=1}^{b} (x_{ij} - \bar{\bar{x}})^2$$

$$\text{SST} = \sum_{j=1}^{k} b(\bar{x}[T]_j - \bar{\bar{x}})^2$$

$$\text{SSB} = \sum_{i=1}^{b} k(\bar{x}[B]_i - \bar{\bar{x}})^2$$

$$\text{SSE} = \sum_{j=1}^{k} \sum_{i=1}^{b} (x_{ij} - \bar{x}[T]_j - \bar{x}[B]_i + \bar{\bar{x}})^2$$

$$\text{MST} = \frac{\text{SST}}{k-1}$$

$$\text{MSB} = \frac{\text{SSB}}{b-1}$$

$$\text{MSE} = \frac{\text{SSE}}{n-k-b+1}$$

$$F = \frac{\text{MST}}{\text{MSE}}$$

$$F = \frac{\text{MSB}}{\text{MSE}}$$

Two-factor experiment

$$\text{SS(Total)} = \sum_{i=1}^{a} \sum_{j=1}^{b} \sum_{k=1}^{r} (x_{ijk} - \bar{\bar{x}})^2$$

$$\text{SS(A)} = rb \sum_{i=1}^{a} (\bar{x}[A]_i - \bar{\bar{x}})^2$$

$$\text{SS(B)} = ra \sum_{j=1}^{b} (\bar{x}[B]_j - \bar{\bar{x}})^2$$

$$\text{SS(AB)} = r \sum_{i=1}^{a} \sum_{j=1}^{b} (\bar{x}[AB]_{ij} - \bar{x}[A]_i - \bar{x}[B]_j + \bar{\bar{x}})^2$$

$$\text{SSE} = \sum_{i=1}^{a} \sum_{j=1}^{b} \sum_{k=1}^{r} (x_{ijk} - \bar{x}[AB]_{ij})^2$$

$$F = \frac{\text{MS(A)}}{\text{MSE}}$$

$$F = \frac{\text{MS(B)}}{\text{MSE}}$$

$$F = \frac{\text{MS(AB)}}{\text{MSE}}$$

Least significant difference comparison method

$$\text{LSD} = t_{\alpha/2}\sqrt{\text{MSE}\left(\frac{1}{n_i} + \frac{1}{n_j}\right)}$$

Tukey's multiple comparison method

$$\omega = q_\alpha(k, \nu)\sqrt{\frac{\text{MSE}}{n_g}}$$

COMPUTER OUTPUT AND INSTRUCTIONS

Technique	Excel	Minitab
One-way ANOVA	479	480
Two-way (randomized block) ANOVA	492	492
Two-factor ANOVA	506	507
Multiple comparisons (LSD, Bonferroni adjustment, and Tukey)	520	520

REFERENCES

Berger, Paul D., and Robert Maurer, *Experimental Design with Applications in Management, Engineering & Sciences.* Belmont, CA: Duxbury, 2002.

Box, George E. P., William G. Hunter, and J. Stuart Hunter, *Statistics for Experimenters: An Introduction to Design, Data Analysis and Model Building.* New York: John Wiley & Sons, 1978.

Cochran, W. G., and G. M. Cox, *Experimental Design*, 2nd edition. New York: John Wiley and Sons, 1957.

Deming, W. Edwards, *Out of the Crisis*, Cambridge, MA: MIT Center for Advanced Engineering Study, 1986.

Gaither, Norman, and Gregory Frazier, *Production and Operations Management*, 8th edition. Cincinnati, OH: Southwestern, 1999.

Juran, J. M., and Frank M. Gryna, *Quality Planning and Analysis*, 3rd edition. New York: McGraw Hill, 1993.

Lillien, Gary L., and Arvind Rangaswamy, *Marketing Engineering: Computer Assisted Marketing Analysis and Planning.* Reading, MA: Addison Wesley, 1998.

Mendenhall, William, *Introduction to Linear Models and the Design and Analysis of Experiments*, Belmont, CA: Duxbury, 1968.

Montgomery, Douglas C., *Design and Analysis of Experiments*, 4th edition. New York: John Wiley and Sons, 1997.

Nahmias, Steven, *Production and Operations Analysis*, 4th edition. Burr Ridge, IL: McGraw Hill, 2001.

Neter, John, Michael H. Kutner, Christopher J. Nachtsheim, and William Wasserman, *Applied Linear Statistical Models*, 4th edition. Chicago: Irwin, 1996.

Ryan, T. D., *Statistical Methods for Quality Improvement.* New York: John Wiley and Sons, 1989.

Scheffé, H., *The Analysis of Variance.* New York: John Wiley and Sons, 1959.

Snedecor, George W., and William G. Cochran, *Statistical Methods*, 7th edition. Ames, IA: Iowa State University Press, 1980.

CHAPTER REVIEW EXERCISES

The following exercises require the use of a computer and software.
Use a 5% significance level.

15.67 The possible imposition of a residential property tax has been a sensitive political issue in a large city that consists of five boroughs. Currently, property tax is based on an assessment system that dates back to 1950. This system has produced numerous inequities whereby newer homes tend to be assessed at higher values than older homes. A new system based on the market value of the house has been proposed. Opponents of the plan argue that residents of some boroughs would have to pay considerably more on the average, while residents of other boroughs would pay less. As part of a study examining this issue, several homes in each borough were assessed under both plans. The percentage increase (a decrease is represented by a negative increase) in each case was recorded and stored in file Xr15-67.

a Can we conclude that there are differences in the effect the new assessment system would have on the five boroughs?

b If differences exist, which boroughs differ? Use Tukey's multiple comparison method.

c What are the required conditions for your conclusions to be valid?

d Are the required conditions satisfied?

15.68 The editor of the student newspaper was in the process of making some major changes in the newspaper's layout. He was also contemplating changing the typeface of the print used. To help make a decision, he set up an experiment in which 20 individuals were asked to read four newspaper pages, with each page printed in a different typeface. If the reading speed differed, then the typeface that was read fastest would be used. However, if there was not enough evidence to conclude that such differences existed, the current typeface would be continued. The times (in seconds) to completely read one page were stored in file Xr15-68. What should the editor do?

15.69 Each year billions of dollars are lost because of worker injuries on the job. Costs can be decreased if injured workers can be rehabilitated quickly. As part of an analysis of the amount of time taken for workers to return to work, a sample of male blue-collar workers aged 35 to 45 who suffered a common wrist fracture was taken. The researchers believed that the mental and physical condition of the individual affects recovery time. Each man was given a questionnaire to complete, which measured whether he tended to be optimistic or pessimistic. Their physical condition was also evaluated and categorized as very physically fit, average, or in poor condition. The number of days until the wrist returned to full function was measured for each individual. These data are stored in file Xr15-69 in the following way:

Column 1: time to recover for optimists (columns 1 to 10) = very fit, rows 11 to 20 = in average condition, rows 21 to 30 = poor condition)

Column 2: time to recover for pessimists (same format as column 1)

a What are the factors in this experiment? What are the levels of each factor?

b Can we conclude that pessimists and optimists differ in their recovery times?

c Can we conclude that physical condition affects recovery times?

15.70 In the past decade, American companies have spent nearly $1 trillion on computer systems. However, productivity gains have been quite small. During the 1980s, productivity in U.S. service industries (where most computers are used) grew by only 0.7% annually. In the 1990s, this figure rose to 1.5%. (Source: *New York Times Service*, 22 February 1995) The problem of small productivity increases may be caused by employee difficulty in learning how to use the computer. Suppose that in an experiment to examine the problem, 100 firms were studied. Each company had bought a new computer system 5 years ago. The companies reported their increase in productivity over the 5-year period and were also classified as offering extensive employee training, some employee training, little employee training, or no formal employee training in the use of computers. (There were 25 firms in each group.) The results are stored in file Xr15-70.

a Can we conclude that differences in productivity gain exist between the four groups of companies?

b If there are differences, what are they?

15.71 The marketing manager of a large ski resort wants to advertise that his ski resort has the shortest lift lines of any resort in the area. To avoid the possibility of a false advertising liability suit, he collects data on the average wait in line at his resort and at each of two competing resorts on each of 14 days. These results are stored in file Xr15-71.

a Can he conclude that there are differences in waiting times between the three resorts?

b What are the required conditions for the techniques above?

c Does it appear that the required conditions are satisfied?

15.72 A popularly held belief about university professors is that they don't work very hard, and that the higher their rank, the less work they do. A statistics student decided to determine whether the belief is true. She took a random sample of 20 university instructors in each of the faculties of business, engineering, arts, and sciences. In each sample of 20, five were instructors, five were assistant professors, five were associate professors, and five were full professors. Each professor was surveyed and asked to report confidentially the number of weekly hours of work. These data are stored in file Xr15-72 in the following way:

Column 1: hours of work for business professors (first 5 rows = instructors, next 5 rows = assistant professors, next 5 rows = associate professors, and last 5 rows = full professors)

Column 2: hours of work for engineering professors (same format as column 1)

Column 3: hours of work for arts professors (same format as column 1)

Column 4: hours of work for science professors (same format as column 1)

a If we conduct the test under the single-factor analysis of variance, how many levels are there? What are they?

b Test to determine whether differences exist using a single-factor analysis of variance.

c If we conduct tests using the two-factor analysis of variance, what are the factors? What are their levels?

d Are there differences between the four ranks of instructor?

e Are there differences between the four faculties?

f Is there evidence of interaction?

15.73 In marketing children's products, it's extremely important to produce television commercials that hold the attention of the children who view them. A psychologist hired by a marketing research firm wants to determine whether differences in attention span exist between children watching advertisements for different types of products. One hundred fifty children under 10 years of age were recruited for an experiment. One third watched a 60-second commercial for a new computer game, one third watched a commercial for a breakfast cereal, and another third watched a commercial for children's clothes. Their attention spans were measured. The results (in seconds) were stored in file Xr15-73. Do these data provide enough evidence to conclude that there are differences in attention span between the three products advertised?

15.74 Upon reconsidering the experiment in Exercise 15.73, the psychologist decides that the age of the child may influence the attention span. Consequently, the experiment is redone in the following way. Three 10-year-olds, three 9-year-olds, three 8-year-olds,

three 7-year-olds, three 6-year-olds, three 5-year-olds, and three 4-year-olds are randomly assigned to watch one of the commercials, and their attention spans are measured. The data are stored in file Xr15-74. Do the results indicate that there are differences in the abilities of the products advertised to hold children's attention?

15.75 North American automobile manufacturers have become more concerned with quality because of foreign competition. One aspect of quality is the cost of repairing damage caused by accidents. A manufacturer is considering several new types of bumpers. In order to test how well they react to low-speed collisions, 40 bumpers of each of five different types were installed on midsize cars, which were then driven into a wall at 5 miles per hour. The cost of repairing the damage in each case was assessed, and the relevant data stored in file Xr15-75.

a Is there sufficient evidence to infer that the bumpers differ in their reactions to low-speed collisions?

b If differences exist, which bumpers differ?

15.76 It is important for salespeople to be knowledgeable about how people shop for certain products. Suppose that a new car salesman believes that the age and sex of a car shopper affect the way he or she makes an offer on a car. He records the initial offers made by a group of men and women shoppers on a $20,000 Mercury Sable. Besides the sex of the shopper, the salesman also notes the age category. The amount of money below the asking price that each person offered initially for the car was recorded and stored in file Xr15-76 using the following format. Column 1 contains the data for the under-30 group; the first 25 rows store the results for female shoppers and the last 25 rows represent the male shoppers. Columns 2 and 3 store the data for the 30–45 age category and over 45 category, respectively. What can we conclude from these data?

15.77 Many of you reading this page probably learned how to read using the whole-language method. This strategy maintains that the natural and effective way is to be exposed to whole words in context. Students learn how to read by recognizing words they have seen before. In the past generation this has been the dominant teaching strategy throughout North America. It replaced phonics, wherein children were taught to sound out the letters to form words. The whole-language method was instituted with little or no research and has been severely criticized in the past. A recent study may have resolved the question of which method should be employed. Barbara Foorman, an educational psychologist at the University of Houston, described the experiment at the annual meeting of the American Association for the Advancement of Science. The subjects were 375 low-achieving, poor, grade 1 students in Houston schools. The students were divided into three groups. One was educated according to the whole-language philosophy, a second group was taught using a pure phonics strategy, and the third was taught employing a mixed or embedded phonics technique. At the end of the term, students were asked to read words on a list of 50 words. The number of words each child could read are stored in file Xr15-77.

a Can we infer that differences exist between the effects of the three teaching strategies?

b If differences exist, identify which method appears to be best.

15.78 Are babies who are exposed to music before their birth smarter than those who are not? And, if so, what kind of music is best? Researchers at the University of Wisconsin conducted an experiment with rats. The researchers selected a random sample of pregnant rats and divided the sample into three groups. Mozart works were played to one group, a second group was exposed to white noise (a steady hum with no musical elements), and the third group listened to Philip Glass music, which are very simple compositions. The researchers then trained the young rats to run a maze in search of food. The amount of time for the rats to complete the maze was measured for all three groups. These data are stored in file Xr15-78.

a Can we infer from these data that there are differences between the three groups?

b If there are differences, determine which group is best.

15.79 Increasing tuition has resulted in some students being saddled with large debts upon graduation. To examine this issue, a random sample of recent graduates was asked to report whether they had student loans, and if so, how much was the debt at graduation. Each person who reported that they owed money was also asked whether their degree was a BA, BSc, BBA, or other. The amounts of debt were stored in file Xr15-79. Can we conclude that debt levels differ among the four types of degree?

15.80 Studies indicate that single male investors tend to take the most risk, whereas married female investors tend to be conservative. This raises the question, "Which does best?" The risk-adjusted returns for single and married men, and for single and married women were recorded and stored in columns A through D, respectively, in file Xr15-80. Can we infer that differences exist among the four groups of investors?

15.81 Like many fine restaurants, Ye Olde Steak House in Windsor, Ontario, attempts to have three "seatings" on weekend nights. Three seatings means that each table gets three different customers. Obviously, any group

that lingers over dessert and coffee may result in the loss of one seating and profit for the restaurant. In an effort to determine which types of groups tend to linger, a random sample of 150 groups was drawn. For each group, the number of members and the length of time that the group stayed were recorded. These data are stored in file Xr15-81 in the following way:

Column A: length of time for 2 people

Column B: length of time for 3 people

Column C: length of time for 4 people

Column D: length of time for more than 4 people

Do these data allow us to infer that the length of time in the restaurant depends on the size of the party?

15.82 When the stock market has a large 1-day decline, does it bounce back the next day or does the bad news endure? To answer this question, an economist examined a random sample of daily changes to the Toronto Stock Index (TSE). He recorded the percent change. He classified declines as

Down by less than .5%

Down by .5% to 1.5%

Down by 1.5% to 2.5%

Down by more than 2.5%

For each of these days, he recorded the percent loss the following day. These data are stored in file Xr15-82. Do these data allow us to infer that there are differences in changes to the TSE depending on the loss the previous day? (This exercise is based on a study undertaken by Tim Whitehead, an economist for Left Bank Economics, a consulting firm near Paris, Ontario.)

15.83 Stock market investors are always seeking the "Holy Grail," a sign that tells them the market has bottomed out or achieved its highest level. There are several indicators. One is the buy signal developed by Gerald Appel. Appel says that a bottom has been reached when the difference between the weekly close of the NYSE index and the 10-week moving average (see Chapter 21) is −4.0 points or more. Another bottom indicator is based on identifying a certain pattern in the line chart of the stock market index. As an experiment, a financial analyst randomly selected 100 weeks. For each week, he determined whether there was an Appel buy, a chart buy, or no indication. For each type of week, he recorded the percentage change over the next 4 weeks. These data are stored in file Xr15-83. Can we infer that the two buy indicators are not useful?

❖ CASE 15.1
EFFECTS OF FINANCIAL PLANNING

In the United States, approximately one-half million small businesses fail annually.

Many researchers have investigated small businesses in order to determine the factors distinguishing those that succeed from those that fail. One set of researchers suggested that a potential factor is the degree of planning. They identified three different levels of planning:

1. *Structured strategic planning*—this involves producing a formalized written description of long-term plans with a 3- to 15-year horizon.
2. *Structured operational planning*—this type of planning deals with short-term issues such as action plans for the current fiscal year.
3. *Unstructured planning*—this covers arrangements in which there is no formal or informal planning.

A random sample of 73 firms participated in the study. The mean age of the firms was 9.2 years, mean annual revenues were $4.25 million, and mean net income was $300,000. On average, 71 people were employed.

These statistics suggest that the 73 participating companies are fairly representative of the population to be investigated.

The companies were analyzed over a five-year period, and the following four measures of performance were used:

1. *Revenue growth*—average sales growth in percent over the 5 years
2. *Net income growth*—growth in percent average net income (before taxes) over the 5 years
3. *Present value growth*—average book value growth in percent over the 5 years
4. *CEO cash compensation growth*—percent average growth in the cash payments to chief executive officers over the 5 years

The data are stored in file C15-01 using the following format:

Column 1: revenue growth for all companies
Column 2: income growth for all companies
Column 3: present value growth for all companies

Column 4: compensation growth for all companies
Column 5: index 1 = companies with structured strategic planning;
2 = companies with structured operational planning;
3 = companies with unstructured planning

Can we infer that for each of the performance measures, there are differences between firms at each planning level?

*Adapted from T. S. Bracker, B. W. Keats, and J. N. Pearson, "Planning and Financial Performance between Small Firms in a Growth Industry," *Strategic Management Journal* 9 (1988): 591–603.

◈ *CASE 15.2*
DIVERSIFICATION STRATEGY FOR MULTINATIONAL FIRMS

One of the many goals of management researchers is to identify factors that differentiate between success and failure and between different levels of success in businesses. In this way, it may be possible to help more businesses become successful. Among multinational enterprises (MNEs), two factors to be examined are the degree of product diversification and the degree of internationalization. *Product diversification* refers to efforts by companies to increase the range and variety of the products they produce. The more unrelated the products are, the greater is the degree of diversification created. *Internationalization* is a term that expresses geographic diversification. Companies that sell their products to many countries are said to employ a high degree of internationalization.

Three management researchers set out to examine these issues. In particular, they wanted to test two hypotheses:

1. MNEs employing strategies that result in more product diversification outperform those with less product diversification.
2. MNEs employing strategies that result in more internationalization outperform those with less internationalization.

Company performance was measured in two ways.

1. Profit-to-sales is the ratio of profit to total sales, expressed as a percentage.
2. Profit-to-assets is the ratio of profit to total assets, expressed as a percentage.

A random sample of 189 companies was selected. For each company, the profit-to-sales and profit-to-assets ratios were measured. In addition, each company was judged to have a low (1), medium (2), or high (3) level of diversification. The degree of internationalization was measured on a 5-point scale where 1 = lowest level and 5 = highest level.

The results are stored in file C15-02 on the data disk, using the following format:

Column 1: profit-to-sales ratio

Column 2: profit-to-assets ratio

Column 3: level of diversification

Column 4: degree of internationalism

What do these data tell you about the researchers' hypotheses?

*Adapted from J. M. Geringer, P. W. Beamish, and R. C. da Costa, "Diversification Strategy and Internationalization: Implication for MNE Performance," *Strategic Management Journal* 10 (1989): 109–119.

16   CHI-SQUARED TESTS

EXIT POLLS IN OHIO

After the polls close on Election Day, networks compete to be the first to predict which candidate will win. The predictions are based on counts in certain precincts and on exit polls. Exit polls are conducted by asking random samples of voters who have just exited from the polling booth for which candidate they voted. In addition to asking for whom the respondents voted, pollsters ask a variety of other questions that provide information to politicians, journalists, and other citizens. The responses to questions about gender, age, education, and the vote cast (Gore or Bush) in the state of Ohio during the 2000 elections were collected and the tables in file Ch16:\Exit were created. What do these results tell about the vote in Ohio? On page 544 we answer this question.

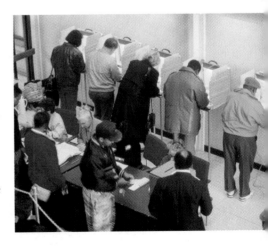

16.1 INTRODUCTION

This chapter develops two statistical techniques that involve nominal data. The first is a *goodness-of-fit test* applied to data produced by a *multinomial experiment,* a generalization of a binomial experiment. The second uses data arranged in a table (called a *contingency table*) to determine whether two classifications of a population of nominal data are statistically independent; this test can also be interpreted as a comparison of two or more populations. The sampling distribution of the test statistics in both tests is the chi-squared distribution introduced in Chapter 8.

16.2 CHI-SQUARED GOODNESS-OF-FIT TEST

This section presents another test designed to describe a population of nominal data. The first such test was introduced in Section 12.4, where we discussed the statistical procedure employed to test hypotheses about a population proportion. In that case, the nominal variable could assume one of only two possible values, success or failure. Our tests dealt with hypotheses about the proportion of successes in the entire population. Recall that the experiment that produces the data is called a *binomial experiment.* In this section, we introduce the *multinomial experiment,* which is an extension of the binomial experiment, wherein there are two or more possible outcomes per trial.

> **MULTINOMIAL EXPERIMENT**
> A **multinomial experiment** is one possessing the following properties:
> 1. The experiment consists of a fixed number n of trials.
> 2. The outcome of each trial can be classified into one of k categories, called *cells*.
> 3. The probability p_i that the outcome will fall into cell i remains constant for each trial. Moreover, $p_1 + p_2 + \cdots + p_k = 1$.
> 4. Each trial of the experiment is independent of the other trials.

When $k = 2$, the multinomial experiment is identical to the binomial experiment. Just as we count the number of successes (recall that we label the number of successes x) and failures in a binomial experiment, we count the number of outcomes falling into each of the k cells in a multinomial experiment. In this way, we obtain a set of observed frequencies $f_1, f_2, \ldots, f_k$ where f_i is the observed frequency of outcomes falling into cell i, for $i = 1, 2, \ldots, k$. Because the experiment consists of n trials and an outcome must fall into some cell,

$$f_1 + f_2 + \cdots + f_k = n$$

Just as we used the number of successes x (by calculating the sample proportion $\hat{p}$, which is equal to x/n to draw inferences about p, so do we use the observed frequencies to draw inferences about the cell probabilities. We'll proceed in what by now has become a standard procedure. We will set up the hypotheses and develop the test statistic and its sampling distribution. We'll demonstrate the process with the following example.

EXAMPLE 16.1

Two companies, A and B, have recently conducted aggressive advertising campaigns in order to maintain and possibly increase their respective shares of the market for fabric softener. These two companies enjoy a dominant position in the market. Before the advertising campaigns began, the market share of company A was 45%, whereas that of company B was 40%. Other competitors accounted for the remaining 15%. To determine whether these market shares changed after the advertising campaigns, a marketing analyst solicited the preferences of a random sample of 200 customers of fabric softener. Of the 200 customers, 102 indicated a preference for company A's product, 82 preferred company B's fabric softener, and the remaining 16 preferred the products of one of the competitors. Can the analyst infer at the 5% significance level that customer preferences have changed from their levels before the advertising campaigns were launched?

SOLUTION The population in question is composed of the brand preferences of the fabric softener customers. The data are nominal because each respondent will choose one of three possible answers—product A, product B, or other. If there were only two categories, or if we were interested only in the proportion of one company's customers (which we would label as successes and label the others as failures), we would identify the technique as the z test of p. However, in this problem we're interested in the proportions of all three categories. We recognize this experiment as a multinomial experiment, and we identify the technique as the chi-squared goodness-of-fit test.

Because we want to know whether the market shares have changed, we specify those precampaign market shares in the null hypothesis:

$$H_0: \quad p_1 = .45, \quad p_2 = .40, \quad p_3 = .15$$

The alternative hypothesis attempts to answer our question, "Have the proportions changed?" Thus,

$$H_1: \quad \text{At least one } p_i \text{ is not equal to its specified value.}$$

TEST STATISTIC

If the null hypothesis is true, we would expect the number of customers selecting brand A, brand B, and other to be 200 times the proportions specified under the null hypothesis. That is,

$$e_1 = 200(.45) = 90$$

$$e_2 = 200(.40) = 80$$

$$e_3 = 200(.15) = 30$$

In general, the expected frequency for each cell is given by

$$e_i = np_i$$

This expression is derived from the formula for the expected value of a binomial random variable, first seen in Section 7.6.

If the expected frequencies e_i and the observed frequencies f_i are quite different, we would conclude that the null hypothesis is false, and we would reject it. However, if the expected and observed frequencies are similar, we would not reject the null hypothesis. The test statistic defined in the box measures the difference between the expected and observed frequencies.

CHI-SQUARED GOODNESS-OF-FIT TEST STATISTIC

$$\chi^2 = \sum \frac{(f_i - e_i)^2}{e_i}$$

The sampling distribution of the test statistic is approximately chi-squared with $v = k - 1$ degrees of freedom, provided that the sample size is large. We will discuss this required condition later. (The chi-squared distribution was introduced in Section 8.5.)

The table below demonstrates the calculation of the test statistic. Thus, the value of chi-squared for this example is $\chi^2 = 8.18$. As usual, we judge the size of this test statistic by specifying the rejection region or by determining the p-value.

Company	Observed Frequency f_i	Expected Frequency e_i	$(f_i - e_i)$	$\dfrac{(f_i - e_i)^2}{e_i}$
A	102	90	12	1.60
B	82	80	2	0.05
Other	16	30	−14	6.53
Total	200	200		$\chi^2 = 8.18$

When the null hypothesis is true, the observed and expected frequencies should be similar, in which case the test statistic will be small. Thus, a small test statistic supports the null hypothesis. If the null hypothesis is untrue, some of the observed and expected frequencies will differ and the test statistic will be large. Consequently, we want to reject the null hypothesis when χ^2 is greater than $\chi^2_{\alpha,k-1}$. That is, the rejection region is

$$\chi^2 > \chi^2_{\alpha,k-1}$$

In Example 16.1, $k = 3$; the rejection region is

$$\chi^2 > \chi^2_{\alpha,k-1} = \chi^2_{.05,2} = 5.99147$$

Since the test statistic is $\chi^2 = 8.18$, we reject the null hypothesis. The p-value of the test is

$$p\text{-value} = P(\chi^2 > 8.18)$$

Unfortunately, Table 5 in Appendix B does not allow us to perform this calculation (except for approximation by interpolation). The p-value must be produced by computer. Figure 16.1 depicts the sampling distribution, rejection region, and p-value.

Figure 16.1
Sampling distribution for Example 16.1

EXCEL

The output from the commands listed below is the *p*-value of the test. It is .016711.

	COMMANDS FOR
COMMANDS	*EXAMPLE 16.1*

1. Type the observed values into one column and the expected values into another column. (If you wish, you can type the cell probabilities specified in the null hypothesis and let Excel convert these into expected values by multiplying by the sample size.)

102	90
82	80
16	30

2. Activate some empty cell and click *f_x*, **Statistical**, and **CHITEST**.
3. Specify the range of the observed values (**Actual_range**).   **A1:A3**
4. Specify the range of the expected values (**Expected_range**). Click **OK**.   **B1:B3**

You can also perform what-if analyses to determine for yourself the effect of changing some of the observed values and the sample size.

If we have the raw data representing the nominal responses, we must first determine the frequency of each category (the observed values). To do so proceed as follows:

1. Activate any empty cell.
2. Click *f_x*, **Statistical**, and **COUNTIF**.
3. Specify the **Range** of the data (do not include the cell containing the name of the variable) and the category you wish to count (**Criteria**). Click **OK**.

MINITAB

Minitab does not conduct this procedure. However, it is relatively easy to program Minitab to do so. See CD Appendix 16.2 for details.

If we have the raw data representing the nominal responses, we can instruct Minitab to determine the frequencies of each value. Click **Stat**, **Tables**, and **Tally**. Specify the variable and click **Counts**. The frequency of each nominal value will be output.

INTERPRET

There is sufficient evidence to infer that the proportions have changed since the advertising campaigns. If the sampling was conducted properly, we can be quite confident in our conclusion. This technique has only one required condition, which is satisfied. (See the next subsection.) It is probably a worthwhile exercise to determine the nature and causes of the changes. The results of this analysis will determine the design and timing of other advertising campaigns.

REQUIRED CONDITION

The actual sampling distribution of the test statistic defined above is discrete, but can be approximated by the chi-squared distribution provided that the sample size is large. This requirement is similar to the one we imposed when we used the normal approximation to the binomial in the sampling distribution of a proportion. In that approximation, we needed np and $n(1 - p)$) to be 5 or more. A similar rule is imposed for the chi-squared test statistic. That is, the sample size must be large enough so that the expected value for each cell must be 5 or more. Where necessary, cells should be combined in order to satisfy this condition. We discuss this required condition and provide more details on its application in CD Appendix 16.1.

FACTORS THAT IDENTIFY THE CHI-SQUARED GOODNESS-OF-FIT TEST
1. **Problem objective:** Describe a population
2. **Data type:** Nominal
3. **Number of categories:** 2 or more

EXERCISES

Developing an Understanding of Statistical Concepts

*Exercises 16.1 to 16.6 are "what-if analyses" designed to determine what happens to the goodness-of-fit test when elements of the statistical inference change. These problems can be solved manually or using Excel's **CHITEST**.*

16.1 Consider a multinomial experiment involving $n = 300$ trials and $k = 5$ cells. The observed frequencies resulting from the experiment are shown in the accompanying table, and the null hypothesis to be tested is as follows:

H_0: $p_1 = .1, p_2 = .2, p_3 = .3, p_4 = .2, p_5 = .2$

Test the hypothesis at the 1% significance level.

Cell	1	2	3	4	5
Frequency	24	64	84	72	56

16.2 Repeat Exercise 16.1, with $n = 150$ and the following frequencies:

Cell	1	2	3	4	5
Frequency	12	32	42	36	28

16.3 Repeat Exercise 16.1, with $n = 75$ and the following frequencies:

Cell	1	2	3	4	5
Frequency	6	16	21	18	14

16.4 Review the results of Exercises 16.1–16.3. What is the effect of decreasing the sample size?

16.5 Consider a multinomial experiment involving $n = 150$ trials and $k = 4$ cells. The observed frequencies resulting from the experiment are shown in the accompanying table, and the null hypothesis to be tested is

H_0: $p_1 = .3, p_2 = .3, p_3 = .2, p_4 = .2$

Cell	1	2	3	4
Frequency	38	50	38	24

Test the hypotheses, using $\alpha = .05$.

16.6 For Exercise 16.5, retest the hypotheses, assuming that the experiment involved twice as many trials ($n = 300$) and that the observed frequencies were twice as high as before, as shown below.

Cell	1	2	3	4
Frequency	76	100	76	48

The following exercises require the use of a computer and software. The answers may be calculated manually. See Appendix A for the sample statistics.

16.7 The results of a multinomial experiment with $k = 5$ are stored in file Xr16-07. The outcomes are identified by the numbers 1 through 5. Test to determine whether there is enough evidence at the 10% significance level to infer that the proportion of each outcome is the same.

16.8 A multinomial experiment was conducted with $k = 4$. Each outcome is stored as an integer from 1 to 4, and the results of a survey are stored in file Xr16-08. Test the following hypotheses with a 5% significance level.

H_0: $p_1 = .15, p_2 = .40, p_3 = .35, p_4 = .10$

H_1: At least one p_i is not equal to its specified value.

16.9 To determine whether a single die is balanced, or fair, the die was rolled 600 times. The outcomes are stored in file Xr16-09. Is there sufficient evidence at the 5% significance level to allow you to conclude that the die is not fair?

Applications

16.10 Grades assigned by an economics instructor have historically followed a symmetrical distribution: 5% A's, 25% B's, 40% C's, 25% D's, and 5% F's. This year, a sample of 150 grades was drawn. The grades (1 = A, 2 = B, 3 = C, 4 = D, and 5 = F) are stored in file Xr16-10. Can you conclude, at the 5% level of significance, that this year's grades are distributed differently from grades in the past?

16.11 Pat Statsdud is about to write a multiple-choice exam but, as usual, knows absolutely nothing. Pat plans to guess one of the five choices. Pat has been given one of the professor's previous exams with the correct answers marked. The correct choices are stored in file Xr16-11 where 1 = (a), 2 = (b), 3 = (c), 4 = (d), and 5 = (e). Help Pat determine whether this professor does not randomly distribute the correct answer over the five choices? (Use a 10% significance level.) If this is true, how does it affect Pat's strategy?

16.12 Financial managers are interested in the speed with which customers who make purchases on credit pay their bills. In addition to calculating the average number of days that unpaid bills (called *accounts receivable*) remain outstanding, they often prepare an aging schedule. An *aging schedule* classifies outstanding accounts receivable according to the time that has elapsed since billing and records the proportion of accounts receivable belonging to each classification. A large firm has determined its aging schedule for the past 5 years. These results are shown in the accompanying table. During the past few months, however, the economy has taken a downturn. The company would like to know whether the recession has affected the aging schedule. A random sample of 250 accounts receivable was drawn and each account was classified (and stored in file Xr16-12) as follows:

1 = 0–14 days outstanding
2 = 15–29 days outstanding
3 = 30–59 days outstanding
4 = 60 or more days outstanding

Number of Days Outstanding	Proportion of Accounts Receivable Past 5 Years
0–14	.72
15–29	.15
30–59	.10
60 and over	.03

Determine whether the aging schedule has changed. (Use $\alpha = .05$.)

16.13 License records in a county reveal that 15% of cars are subcompacts (1), 25% are compacts (2), 40% are midsize (3), and the rest are an assortment of other styles and models (4). A random sample of accidents involving cars licensed in the county was drawn. The type of car was stored in file Xr16-13 using the codes in parentheses. Can we infer at the 5% significance level that certain sizes of cars are involved in a higher than expected percentage of accidents?

16.14 In an election held last year that was contested by three parties, party A captured 31% of the vote, party B garnered 51%, and party C received the remaining votes. A survey of 1,200 voters asked each to identify the party that they would vote for in the next election. These results are stored in file Xr16-14 where 1 = party A, 2 = party B, and 3 = party C. Can we infer at the 10% significance level that voter support has changed since the election?

16.15 In a number of pharmaceutical studies, volunteers who take placebos (but are told they have taken a cold remedy) report the following side effects.

Headache (1)   5%
Drowsiness (2)   7%
Stomach upset (3)   4%
No side effect (4)   84%

A random sample of 250 people who were given a placebo (but who thought they had taken an anti-inflammatory) reported whether they had experienced each of the side effects. These data are stored in file Xr16-15 using the codes in parentheses. Can we infer at the 5% significance level that the reported side effects of the placebo for an anti-inflammatory differ from those of a cold remedy?

APPLICATIONS IN MARKETING: *MARKET SEGMENTATION*

Market segmentation was introduced in Section 12.5, where a statistical technique was used to estimate the size of a segment. In Chapters 13 and 15, statistical procedures were applied to determine whether market segments differ in their purchases of products and services. Exercise 16.16 requires you to apply the chi-squared goodness-of-fit test to determine whether the relative sizes of segments have changed.

16.16 Refer to Exercise 12.102, where the statistics practitioner estimated the size of market segments based on education achievement among California adults. Suppose that census figures from 10 years ago showed the education levels and the proportions of California adults. These are

Level	Proportion
1. Did not complete high school	.23
2. Completed high school only	.40
3. Some college or university	.15
4. College or university graduate	.22

Using the data in file Xr12-102, determine whether there has been a change in these proportions. (Use $\alpha = .05$.)

16.3 CHI-SQUARED TEST OF A CONTINGENCY TABLE

In this section, we introduce another chi-squared test, this one designed to satisfy two different problem objectives. The chi-squared test of a contingency table is used to determine whether there is enough evidence to infer that two nominal variables are related and to infer that differences exist among two or more populations of nominal variables. Completing both objectives entails classifying items according to two different criteria. To see how this is done, consider the following example.

EXAMPLE 16.2

The MBA program was experiencing problems scheduling courses. The demand for the program's optional courses and majors was quite variable from one year to the next. In one year, students seem to want marketing courses and in other years accounting or finance are the rage. In desperation, the dean of the business school turned to a statistics professor for assistance. The statistics professor believed that the problem may be the variability in the academic background of the students and that the undergraduate degree affects the choice of major. As a start, he took a random sample of last year's MBA students and recorded the undergraduate degree and the major selected in the graduate program. The undergraduate degrees were BA, BEng, BBA, as well as several others. There are three possible majors for the MBA students: accounting, finance, and marketing. The results were summarized in a table called a *contingency* or *cross-classification table*, shown below. Can the statistics professor conclude that the undergraduate degree affects the choice of major?

	MBA Major			
Undergraduate Degree	Accounting	Finance	Marketing	Total
BA	31	13	16	60
BEng	8	16	7	31
BBA	12	10	17	39
Other	10	5	7	22
Total	61	44	47	152

SOLUTION One way to solve the problem is to consider that there are two variables represented by the contingency table. The variables are the undergraduate degree and the MBA major. Both are nominal. The values of the undergraduate degree are BA, BEng, BBA, and other. The values of MBA major are accounting, finance, and marketing. The problem objective is to analyze the relationship between the two variables. Specifically, we want to know whether one variable affects the other.

Another way of addressing the problem is to determine whether differences exist among BA's, BEng's, BBA's, and others. In other words, we treat the earners of each undergraduate degree as a separate population. Each population has three possible values represented by the MBA major. (We can also answer the question by treating the MBA majors as populations and the undergraduate degrees as the values of the random variable.) Here the problem objective is to compare four populations.

As you will shortly discover, both objectives lead to the same test. Consequently, we address both objectives at the same time.

The null hypothesis will specify that there is no relationship between the two variables. We state this in the following way:

H_0:   The two variables are independent.

The alternative hypothesis specifies that one variable affects the other, expressed as

H_1:   The two variables are dependent.

If the null hypothesis is true, undergraduate degree and MBA major are independent of one another. This means that whether an MBA student earned a BA, BEng, BBA, or other degree does not affect his or her choice of major program in the MBA. Consequently, there is no difference in major choice among the graduates of the undergraduate programs. If the alternative hypothesis is true, undergraduate degree does affect the choice of MBA major. Thus, there are differences among the four undergraduate degree categories.

TEST STATISTIC

The test statistic is the same as the one employed to test proportions in the goodness-of-fit test. That is, the test statistic is

$$\chi^2 = \sum_{i=1}^{k} \frac{(f_i - e_i)^2}{e_i}$$

where k is the number of cells in the contingency table. If you examine the null hypothesis described in the goodness-of-fit test and the one described above, you will discover a major difference. In the goodness-of-fit test, the null hypothesis lists values for the probabilities p_i. The null hypothesis for the chi-squared test of a contingency table states only that the two variables are independent. However, we need the probabilities to compute the expected values e_i, which in turn are needed to calculate the value of the test statistic. (The entries in the table are the observed values f_i.) The question immediately arises: From where do we get the probabilities? The answer is that they must come from the data after we assume that the null hypothesis is true.

If we consider each undergraduate degree as a separate population, each row represents a multinomial experiment with three cells. If the null hypothesis is true, the four multinomial populations should have similar proportions in each cell. We can estimate the cell probabilities by calculating the total in each column and dividing by the sample size. Thus,

$$P(\text{Accounting}) = \frac{61}{152} = .401$$

$$P(\text{Finance}) = \frac{44}{152} = .289$$

$$P(\text{Marketing}) = \frac{47}{152} = .309$$

We can calculate the expected values for each cell in the four multinomial experiments by multiplying these probabilities by the total number of MBA students from each undergraduate program. By adding across each row, we find there were 60 BA's, 31 BEng's, 39 BBA's, and 22 MBA students with other undergraduate degrees.

Expected Values of the MBA Majors of BA's

MBA Major	Expected Value
Accounting	$60 \times \dfrac{61}{152} = 24.08$
Finance	$60 \times \dfrac{44}{152} = 17.37$
Marketing	$60 \times \dfrac{47}{152} = 18.55$

Expected Values of the MBA Majors of BEng's

MBA Major	Expected Value
Accounting	$31 \times \dfrac{61}{152} = 12.44$
Finance	$31 \times \dfrac{44}{152} = 8.97$
Marketing	$31 \times \dfrac{47}{152} = 9.59$

Expected Values of the MBA Majors of BBA's

MBA Major	Expected Value
Accounting	$39 \times \dfrac{61}{152} = 15.65$
Finance	$39 \times \dfrac{44}{152} = 11.29$
Marketing	$39 \times \dfrac{47}{152} = 12.06$

Expected Values of the MBA Majors of Others

MBA Major	Expected Value
Accounting	$22 \times \dfrac{61}{152} = 8.83$
Finance	$22 \times \dfrac{44}{152} = 6.37$
Marketing	$22 \times \dfrac{47}{152} = 6.80$

Notice that the expected values are computed by multiplying the row total by the column total and dividing by the sample size.

EXPECTED FREQUENCIES FOR A CONTINGENCY TABLE

The expected frequency of the cell in row i and column j is

$$e_{ij} = \frac{\text{Row } i \text{ total} \times \text{Column } j \text{ total}}{\text{Sample size}}$$

The expected cell frequencies are shown in parentheses in the table below. As in the case of the goodness-of-fit test, the expected cell frequencies should satisfy the requirement that the expected frequency in every cell is at least 5.

	MBA Major		
Undergraduate Degree	*Accounting*	*Finance*	*Marketing*
BA	31 (24.08)	13 (17.37)	16 (18.55)
BEng	8 (12.44)	16 (8.97)	7 (9.59)
BBA	12 (15.65)	10 (11.29)	17 (12.06)
Other	10 (8.83)	5 (6.37)	7 (6.80)

We can now calculate the value of the test statistic.

$$\chi^2 = \sum_{i=1}^{k} \frac{(f_i - e_i)^2}{e_i}$$

$$= \frac{(31 - 24.08)^2}{24.08} + \frac{(13 - 17.37)^2}{17.37} + \frac{(16 - 18.55)^2}{18.55} + \frac{(8 - 12.44)^2}{12.44}$$

$$+ \frac{(16 - 8.97)^2}{8.97} + \frac{(7 - 9.59)^2}{9.59} + \frac{(12 - 15.65)^2}{15.65} + \frac{(10 - 11.29)^2}{11.29}$$

$$+ \frac{(17 - 12.06)^2}{12.06} + \frac{(10 - 8.33)^2}{8.33} + \frac{(5 - 6.37)^2}{6.37} + \frac{(7 - 6.80)^2}{6.80}$$

$$= 14.70$$

Notice that we continue to use a single subscript in the formula of the test statistic when we should use two subscripts, one for the rows and one for the columns. We believe it is clear that for each cell, we need to calculate the squared difference between the observed and expected frequencies divided by the expected frequency. We don't believe that the satisfaction of using the mathematically correct notation overcomes the unnecessary complication.

REJECTION REGION AND *p*-VALUE

To determine the rejection region, we need to know the number of degrees of freedom associated with the chi-squared statistic. The number of degrees of freedom for a contingency table with r rows and c columns is $\nu = (r - 1)(c - 1)$. For this example, the number of degrees of freedom is $\nu = (r - 1)(c - 1) = (4 - 1)(3 - 1) = 6$.

If we employ a 5% significance level, the rejection region is

$$\chi^2 > \chi^2_{\alpha,\nu} = \chi^2_{.05,6} = 12.5916$$

Because $\chi^2 = 14.70$, we reject the null hypothesis and conclude that there is evidence of a relationship between undergraduate degree and MBA major.

The *p*-value of the test statistic is

$$P(\chi^2 > 14.70)$$

Unfortunately, we cannot determine the *p*-value manually.

USING THE COMPUTER

Excel and Minitab can produce the chi-squared statistic from either a contingency table whose frequencies have already been calculated or from raw data. The respective print-outs are almost identical.

For the raw data we created file Xm16-02 that contains the raw data using the following codes:

Column 1 (Undergraduate Degree)	Column 2 (MBA Major)
1 = BA	1 = Accounting
2 = BEng	2 = Finance
3 = BBA	3 = Marketing
4 = Other	

 EXCEL

	A	B	C	D	E
1	Contingency Table				
2					
3		Column 1	Column 2	Column 3	TOTAL
4	Row 1	31	13	16	60
5	Row 2	8	16	7	31
6	Row 3	12	10	17	39
7	Row 4	10	5	7	22
8	TOTAL	61	44	47	152
9					
10	chi-squared Stat			14.7019	
11	df			6	
12	p-value			0.0227	
13	chi-squared Critical			12.5916	

COMMANDS (COMPLETED TABLE)

1. Type the frequencies into adjacent columns.
2. Click **Tools**, **Data Analysis Plus**, and **Contingency Table**.
3. Specify the **Input Range**.
4. Click **Labels** if the first row and first column of the input range contain the names of the categories.
5. Specify the value for α (**Alpha**) and click **OK**.

COMMANDS (RAW DATA)

1. Type or import the data where one column represents the codes for one variable and a second column stores the codes for the second variable. The codes must be positive integers.
2. Click **Tools**, **Data Analysis Plus**, and **Contingency Table** (**Raw Data**).
3. Specify the **Input Range**.
4. Click **Labels** if appropriate.
5. Specify the value of α (**Alpha**) and click **OK**.

COMMANDS FOR EXAMPLE 16.2

31	**13**	**16**
8	**16**	**7**
12	**10**	**17**
10	**5**	**7**

A1:C4

.05

COMMANDS FOR EXAMPLE 16.2

Open file **Xm16-02**.

A1:B153

.05

MINITAB

Chi-Square Test: C1, C2, C3

```
Expected counts are printed below observed counts

               C1       C2       C3    Total
     1         31       13       16       60
             24.08    17.37    18.55

     2          8       16        7       31
             12.44     8.97     9.59

     3         12       10       17       39
             15.65    11.29    12.06

     4         10        5        7       22
              8.83     6.37     6.80

  Total        61       44       47      152

Chi-Sq =   1.989 +   1.099 +   0.351 +
           1.585 +   5.502 +   0.697 +
           0.852 +   0.147 +   2.024 +
           0.155 +   0.294 +   0.006 = 14.702
DF = 6, P-Value = 0.023
```

COMMANDS (COMPLETE TABLE)

1. Type the observed frequencies into adjacent columns.
2. Click **Stat**, **Tables**, and **Chisquare Test....**

3. Select the **columns containing the table**. Click **OK**.

COMMANDS (RAW DATA)

1. Type or import the data where one column represents the codes for one variable and a second column stores the codes for the second variable. The codes must be positive integers.
2. Click **Stat**, **Tables**, and **Cross Classification....**
3. Select the **Classification variables**.

4. Specify **Chisquare analysis** and **Above and Expected Count**. Click **OK**.

COMMANDS
FOR EXAMPLE 16.2

31	**13**	**16**
8	**16**	**7**
12	**10**	**17**
10	**5**	**7**

C1–C3

COMMANDS
FOR EXAMPLE 16.2

Open file **Xm16-02**.

Degree, **Major** or
C1, C2

INTERPRET

There is enough evidence to infer that the undergraduate degree and MBA major are related. This suggests that the dean can predict the number of optional courses by counting the number of MBA students with each type of undergraduate degree. We can see that BA's favor accounting courses, BEng's prefer finance, BBA's drift to marketing, and others lean toward accounting.

REQUIRED CONDITION

In the previous section, we pointed out that the expected values should be at least 5 to ensure that the chi-squared distribution provides an adequate approximation of the sampling distribution. In a contingency table where one or more cells have expected values of less than 5, we need to combine rows or columns to satisfy the rule of five. This subject is discussed in CD Appendix 16.1.

EXIT POLLS IN OHIO: SOLUTION

For each of the three tables, we conduct the chi-squared test of a contingency table. The Excel printouts appear below. (Minitab's are similar.)

	A	B	C	D
1	Contingency Table			
2				
3		Gore	Bush	TOTAL
4	Men	109	138	247
5	Women	152	112	264
6	TOTAL	261	250	511
7				
8	chi-squared Stat			9.233
9	df			1
10	p-value			0.0024
11	chi-squared Critical			3.8415

	A	B	C	D
1	Contingency Table			
2				
3		Gore	Bush	TOTAL
4	18-29	44	120	164
5	30-44	86	128	214
6	45-59	73	128	201
7	60+	61	123	184
8	TOTAL	264	499	763
9				
10	chi-squared Stat			7.761
11	df			3
12	p-value			0.0512
13	chi-squared Critical			7.8147

	A	B	C	D
1	Contingency Table			
2				
3		Gore	Bush	TOTAL
4	No HS	16	99	115
5	HS	55	128	183
6	Some college	78	133	211
7	College	59	133	192
8	Post-grad	51	115	166
9	TOTAL	259	608	867
10				
11	chi-squared Stat			19.1786
12	df			4
13	p-value			0.0007
14	chi-squared Critical			9.4877

INTERPRET

There is enough evidence at the 5% significance level to infer that gender and education affect the way people voted in the presidential election of 2000. However, there is only weak evidence to infer that age and presidential vote are related.

Here is a summary of the factors that tell us when to apply the chi-squared test of a contingency table. Note that there are two problem objectives satisfied by this statistical procedure.

FACTORS THAT IDENTIFY THE CHI-SQUARED TEST OF A CONTINGENCY TABLE

1. **Problem objectives:** Analyze the relationship between two variables and compare two or more populations.
2. **Data type:** Nominal

EXERCISES

Developing an Understanding of Statistical Concepts

16.17 Conduct a test to determine whether the two classifications L and M are independent, using the data in the accompanying contingency table. (Use $\alpha = .05$.)

	M_1	M_2
L_1	28	68
L_2	56	36

16.18 Repeat Exercise 16.17, using the following table.

	M_1	M_2
L_1	14	34
L_2	28	18

16.19 Repeat Exercise 16.17, using the following table.

	M_1	M_2
L_1	7	17
L_2	14	9

16.20 Review the results of Exercises 16.17–16.19. What is the effect of decreasing the sample size?

16.21 Conduct a test to determine whether the two classifications R and C are independent, using the data in the accompanying contingency table. (Use $\alpha = .10$.)

	C_1	C_1	C_3
R_1	40	32	48
R_2	30	48	52

Applications

16.22 The trustee of a company's pension plan has solicited the opinions of a sample of the company's employees about a proposed revision of the plan. A breakdown of the responses is shown in the accompanying table. Is there evidence at the 10% significance level to infer that the responses differ among the three groups of employees?

Responses	Blue-collar workers	White-collar workers	Managers
For	67	32	11
Against	63	18	9

16.23 The operations manager of a company that manufactures shirts wants to determine whether there are differences in the quality of workmanship among the three daily shifts. She randomly selects 600 recently made shirts and carefully inspects them. Each shirt is classified as either perfect or flawed, and the shift that produced it is also recorded. The accompanying table summarizes the number of shirts that fell into each cell. Do these data provide sufficient evidence at the 5% significance level to infer that there are differences in quality among the three shifts?

Shirt Condition	Shift 1	2	3
Perfect	240	191	139
Flawed	10	9	11

16.24 One of the issues that came up in a recent national election (and is likely to arise in many future elections) is how to deal with a sluggish economy. Specifically, should governments cut spending, raise taxes, inflate the economy (by printing more money), or do none of the above and let the deficit rise? And like most issues, politicians need to know which parts of the electorate support these options. Suppose that a random sample of 1,000 people was asked which option they support and their political affiliation. The possible responses to the question about political affiliation were Democrat, Republican, and Independent (which included a variety of political persuasions). The responses were summarized in the table below. Do these results allow us to conclude at the 5% significance level that political affiliation affects support for the economic options?

Economic Options	Political Affiliation Democrat	Republican	Independent
Cut spending	101	282	61
Raise taxes	38	67	25
Inflate the economy	131	88	31
Let deficit increase	61	90	25

The following exercises require the use of a computer and software. The answers may be calculated manually. See Appendix A for the sample statistics. ***Use a 5% significance level.***

16.25 To determine whether commercials viewed during happy television programs are more effective than those viewed during sad television programs, a study was conducted in which a random sample of students viewed an upbeat segment from "Real People" with commercials, while another random sample of students viewed a very sad segment from "Sixty Minutes" with commercials. The students were then asked what they were thinking during the final commercial. From their responses, they were categorized as thinking primarily about the commercial (1), thinking primarily about the program (2), or thinking about both (3). The results were stored in file Xr16-25. (Column 1 lists the program: 1 = "Real People" and 2 = "Sixty Minutes"; column 2 lists the responses.) Do commercials viewed during happy television programs appear to have a different effect than those viewed during sad television programs? (*Source:* Marvin E. Goldberg and Gerald J. Corn, "Happy and Sad TV Programs: How They Affect Reactions to Commercials," *Journal of Consumer Research* 14 (1987): 387–403)

16.26 Acute otitis media, an infection of the middle ear, is a very common childhood illness. Although it is normally treated with amoxicillin, emerging resistance to the antibiotic has promoted the search for an alternative. A recent article discussed the efficacy of one such alternative: trimethoprim-sulfamethoxazole. In this study, 203 "patients were randomly assigned to receive either amoxicillin (1) or trimethoprim-sulfamethoxazole (2) by means of a computer-generated table of random numbers." Each patient was judged to be cured (1), improved (2), or to have no improvement (3). The data are stored in file Xr16-26. Can we conclude from these data that there are differences in outcomes for children treated with amoxicillin and for children treated with trimethoprim-sulfamethoxazole? (*Source:* William Feldman, Joanne Momy, and Corinne Dulberg, "Trimethoprim-Sulfamethoxazole v. Amoxicillin in the Treatment of Acute Otitis Media," *Canadian Medical Association Journal* 139 (1988): 961–964)

16.27 An antismoking group recently had a large advertisement published in local newspapers throughout Florida. Several statistical facts and medical details were included, in the hope that the ad would have meaningful impact on smokers. The antismoking group is concerned, however, that smokers might have read less of the advertisement than did nonsmokers. This concern is based on the belief that a reader tends to spend more time reading articles that agree with his or her predisposition. The antismoking group has conducted a survey asking those who saw the advertisement whether they read the headline only (1), some detail (2), or most of the advertisement (3). The questionnaire also asks respondents to identify themselves as either a heavy smoker—more than two packs per day (1), a moderate smoker—between one and two packs per day (2), a light smoker—less than one pack per day (3), or a nonsmoker (4). The results are stored in file Xr16-27. Do the data indicate that level of smoking affects how much one reads of an anti-smoking advertisement?

16.28 An investor who can correctly forecast the direction and size of changes in foreign currency exchange rates is able to reap huge profits in the international currency markets. A knowledgeable reader of the *Wall Street Journal* (in particular, of the currency futures market quotations) can determine the direction of change in various exchange rates that is predicted by all investors, viewed collectively. Predictions from 216 investors, together with the subsequent actual directions of change, are stored in file Xr16-28. (Column 1: predicted change where 1 = positive and 2 = negative; column 2: actual change where 1 = positive and 2 = negative.)

   a Test the hypothesis that a relationship exists between the predicted and actual directions of change.

   b To what extent would you make use of these predictions in formulating your forecasts of future exchange rate changes?

16.29 During the past decade many cigarette smokers have attempted to quit. Unfortunately, nicotine is highly addictive. There is a large number of different methods that smokers employ to help them quit. These include nicotine patches, hypnosis, and various forms of therapy. A researcher for the Addiction Research Council wanted to determine why some people quit while others attempted to quit, but failed. He surveyed 1,000 people who planned to quit smoking. He determined their educational level and whether, 1 year later they continued to smoke. Educational level was recorded in the following way:

   1 = did not finish high school
   2 = high school graduate
   3 = university or college graduate
   4 = completed a postgraduate degree

A continuing smoker was recorded as 1; a quitter was recorded as 2. These data are stored in file Xr16-28. Can we infer that the amount of education is a factor in determining whether a smoker will quit?

APPLICATIONS IN MARKETING: *MARKET SEGMENTATION*

In Section 12.5 and in Chapters 13 and 15, we described how marketing managers use statistical analyses to estimate the size of market segments, and to determine whether there are differences between segments.

The following exercises require the application of the chi-squared test of a contingency table to determine whether market segments differ with respect to some nominal variable.

16.30 Exercise 12.103 described the market segments defined by J. C. Penney's. One of the questions included in the questionnaire that classified the women surveyed asked whether each worked outside the home. The responses were
   1. No
   2. Part-time job
   3. Full-time job
   These data plus the classifications (1 = Conservative, 2 = Traditional, and 3 = Contemporary) are stored in file Xr16-30. Can we infer from these data that there are differences in employment status between the three market segments?

16.31 Refer to Exercise 12.103. The women in the survey were also asked to define value by identifying what they considered to be the most important attribute of value. The responses are
   1. Price
   2. Quality
   3. Fashion
   The responses and the classifications of segments (1 = Conservative, 2 = Traditional, and 3 = Contemporary) are stored in file Xr16-31. Do these data allow us to infer that there are differences in the definition of value between the three market segments?

16.32 Refer to Example 12.6. In segmenting the breakfast cereal market, a food manufacturer uses health and diet consciousness as the segmentation variable. Four segments are developed:
   1. Concerned about eating healthy foods
   2. Concerned primarily about weight
   3. Concerned about health because of illness
   4. Unconcerned
   A survey was undertaken and each person was asked to report their educational level. The responses are
   1. Did not finish high school
   2. High school graduate
   3. Some college
   4. College graduate
   The responses and the market segments of each respondent are stored in file Xr16-32. Can we infer that there are differences in educational levels between the market segments?

16.33 After a thorough analysis of the market, a publisher of business and economics statistics books has divided the market into three general approaches to teach applied statistics. These are (1) use of a computer and statistical software with no manual calculations, (2) traditional teaching of concepts and solution of problems by hand, (3) mathematical approach with emphasis on derivations and proofs. The publisher wanted to know whether this market could be segmented on the basis of the educational background of the instructor. As a result, the statistics editor organized a survey that asked 200 professors of business and economics statistics to report their approach to teaching and which one of the following categories represents their highest degree:

1. Business (MBA or Ph.D. in business)

2. Economics
3. Mathematics or engineering
4. Other

The responses are stored in columns 1 (teaching approach) and 2 (degree) in file Xr16-33. Can the editor infer that there are differences in type of degree among the three teaching approaches? If so, how can the editor use this information?

16.4 SUMMARY OF TESTS ON NOMINAL DATA

At this point in the textbook, we've described four tests that are used when the data are nominal:

z test of p (Section 12.4)

z test of $p_1 - p_2$ (Section 13.6)

Chi-squared goodness-of-fit test (Section 16.2)

Chi-squared test of a contingency table (Section 16.3)

In the process of presenting these techniques, we concentrated on one technique at a time and focused on the kinds of problems each addresses. However, this approach tends to conflict somewhat with our promised goal of emphasizing the "when" of statistical inference. In this section, we summarize the statistical tests on nominal data to ensure that you are capable of selecting the correct method.

There are two critical factors in identifying the technique used when the data are nominal. The first, of course, is the problem objective. The second is the number of categories that the nominal variable can assume. Table 16.1 provides a guide to help select the correct technique.

Table 16.1 Statistical Techniques for Nominal Data

Problem Objective	Number of Categories	Statistical Technique
Describe a population	2	z test of p or the chi-squared goodness of-fit test
Describe a population	More than 2	Chi-squared goodness-of-fit test
Compare two populations	2	z test of $p_1 - p_2$ or chi-squared test of a contingency table
Compare two populations	More than 2	Chi-squared test of a contingency table
Compare two or more populations	2 or more	Chi-squared test of a contingency table
Analyze the relationship between two variables	2 or more	Chi-squared test of a contingency table

Notice that when we describe a population of nominal data with exactly two categories, we can use either of two techniques. We can employ the z test of p or the chi-squared goodness-of-fit test. These two tests are equivalent because if there are only two categories, the multinomial experiment is actually a binomial experiment (one of the categorical outcomes is labeled success and the other is labeled failure). Mathematical statisticians have established that if we square the value of z, the test statistic for the test of p, we produce the χ^2 statistic. That is, $z^2 = \chi^2$. Thus, if we want to conduct a two-tail test of a population proportion, we can employ either technique. However, the chi-squared goodness-of-fit test can only test to determine whether the hypothesized values of p_1 (which we can label p) and p_2 (which we call $1 - p$) are not equal to their specified values. Consequently, to perform a one-tail test of a population proportion, we must use the z test of p. (This issue was discussed in Chapter 15 when we pointed out that we can use either the t test of $\mu_1 - \mu_2$ or the analysis of variance to conduct a test to determine whether two population means differ.)

When we test for differences between two populations of nominal data with two categories, we can also use either of two techniques: the z test of $p_1 - p_2$ (Case 1) or the chi-squared test of a contingency table. Once again, we can use either technique to perform a two-tail test about $p_1 - p_2$. (Squaring the value of the z statistic yields the value of the χ^2 statistic.) However, one-tail tests must be conducted by the z test of $p_1 - p_2$. The rest of the table is quite straightforward. Notice that when we want to compare two populations when there are more than two categories, we use the chi-squared test of a contingency table.

Figure 16.2 offers another summary of the tests that deal with nominal data introduced in this book. There are two groups of tests: those that test hypotheses about single populations and those that test either for differences between populations or for independence. In the first set, we have the z test of p, which can be replaced by the chi-squared goodness-of-fit test. The latter test is employed when there are more than two categories.

To test for differences between two proportions, we apply the z test of $p_1 - p_2$. We can use instead the chi-squared test of a contingency table, which can be applied to a variety of other problems.

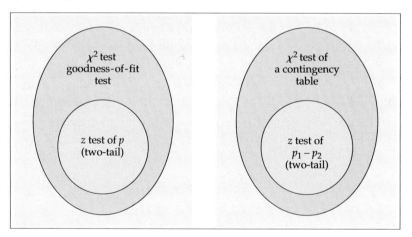

Figure 16.2
Tests on nominal data

DEVELOPING AN UNDERSTANDING OF STATISTICAL CONCEPTS

Table 16.1 and Figure 16.2 summarize how we deal with nominal data. We determine the frequency of each category and use these frequencies to compute test statistics. We can then compute proportions to calculate z statistics or use the frequencies to calculate χ^2 statistics. Because squaring a standard normal random variable produces a chi-squared variable, we can employ either statistic to test for differences. As a consequence, when you encounter nominal data in the problems described in this book (and other introductory applied statistics books), the most logical starting point in selecting the appropriate technique will be either a z statistic or a χ^2 statistic. However, you should know that there are other statistical procedures that can be applied to nominal data—techniques that are not included in this book.

16.5 (OPTIONAL) CHI-SQUARED TEST FOR NORMALITY

We can use the goodness-of-fit test presented in Section 16.2 in another way. We can test to determine whether data were drawn from any distribution. The most common application of this procedure is a test of normality.

In the examples and exercises shown in Section 16.2, the probabilities specified in the null hypothesis were derived from the question. In Example 16.1, the probabilities p_1, p_2, and p_3 were the market shares before the advertising campaign. To test for normality (or any other distribution), the probabilities must first be calculated using the hypothesized distribution. To illustrate, consider Example 12.1, where we tested the mean productivity of new workers using the Student t distribution. The required condition for this procedure is that the data must be normally distributed. To determine whether the 50 observations in our sample were indeed taken from a normal distribution, we must calculate the theoretical probabilities assuming a normal distribution. To do so, we must first calculate the sample mean and standard deviation. They are $\bar{x} = 460.38$ and $s = 38.83$. Next we find the probabilities of an arbitrary number of intervals. For example, we can find the probabilities of the following intervals:

Interval 1: $X \leq 421.55$
Interval 2: $421.55 < X \leq 460.38$
Interval 3: $460.38 < X \leq 499.21$
Interval 4: $X > 499.21$

We will discuss the reasons for our choices of intervals later.

The probabilities are computed using the normal distribution and the values of $\bar{x}$ and s as estimators of μ and σ. Thus,

$$P(X \leq 421.55) = P\left(\frac{X - \mu}{\sigma} \leq \frac{421.55 - 460.38}{38.83}\right) = P(Z \leq -1) = .1587$$

$$P(421.55 < X \leq 460.38) = P\left(\frac{421.55 - 460.38}{38.83} < \frac{X - \mu}{\sigma} \leq \frac{460.38 - 460.38}{38.83}\right) = P(-1 < Z \leq 0) = .3413$$

$$P(460.38 < X \leq 499.21) = P\left(\frac{460.38 - 460.38}{38.83} < \frac{X - \mu}{\sigma} \leq \frac{499.21 - 460.38}{38.83}\right) = P(0 < Z \leq 1) = .3413$$

$$P(X > 499.21) = P\left(\frac{X - \mu}{\sigma} > \frac{499.21 - 460.38}{38.83}\right) = P(Z > 1) = .1587$$

To test for normality is to test the following hypotheses:

H_0: $p_1 = .1587, p_2 = .3413, p_3 = .3413, p_4 = .1587$

H_1: At least one p_i is not equal to its specified value.

We complete the test as we did in Section 16.2, except that the number of degrees of freedom associated with the chi-squared statistic is the number of intervals minus 1, minus the number of parameters estimated, which in this illustration is 2. (We estimated the population mean μ and the population standard deviation σ.) Thus, in this case the number of degrees of freedom is $4 - 1 - 2 = 1$.

The expected values are

$$e_1 = np_1 = 50(.1587) = 7.94$$

$$e_2 = np_2 = 50(.3413) = 17.07$$

$$e_3 = np_3 = 50(.3413) = 17.07$$

$$e_4 = np_4 = 50(.1587) = 7.94$$

The observed values are determined manually by counting the number of values in each interval. Thus,

$$f_1 = 10$$

$$f_2 = 13$$

$$f_3 = 19$$

$$f_4 = 8$$

The chi-squared statistic is

$$\chi^2 = \sum_{i=1}^{k} \frac{(f_i - e_i)^2}{e_i} = \frac{(10 - 7.94)^2}{7.94} + \frac{(13 - 17.07)^2}{17.07} + \frac{(19 - 17.07)^2}{17.07} + \frac{(8 - 7.94)^2}{7.94}$$

$$= 1.72$$

The rejection region for a 5% significance level is

$$\chi^2 > \chi^2_{\alpha,k-3} = \chi^2_{.05,1} = 3.84146$$

There is no evidence to conclude that these data are not normally distributed.

CLASS INTERVALS

In practice, you can use any intervals you like. We chose the intervals we did to facilitate the calculation of the normal probabilities. The number of intervals was chosen to comply with the rule of five, which requires that all expected values be at least equal to 5. Because the number of degrees of freedom is $k - 3$, the minimum number of intervals is $k = 4$.

USING THE COMPUTER

 EXCEL

	A	B	C	D
1	**Chi-Squared Test of Normality**			
2				
3		*Packages*		
4	Mean	460.38		
5	Standard deviation	38.8271		
6	Observations	50		
7				
8	Intervals	Probability	Expected	Observed
9	(z <= -1)	0.158655	7.93275	10
10	(-1 < z <= 0)	0.341345	17.06725	13
11	(0 < z <= 1)	0.341345	17.06725	19
12	(z > 1)	0.158655	7.93275	8
13				
14				
15				
16	chi-squared Stat	1.7274		
17	df	1		
18	p-value	0.1887		
19	chi-squared Critical	3.8415		

We programmed Excel to calculate the value of the test statistic so that the expected values are at least 5 (where possible) and the minimum number of intervals is 4. Hence, if the number of observations is more than 220, the intervals and probabilities are

Interval	Probability
$Z \leq -2$	.0228
$-2 < Z \leq -1$	.1359
$-1 < Z \leq 0$	.3413
$0 < Z \leq 1$	.3413
$1 < Z \leq 2$	.1359
$Z > 2$	.0228

If the sample size is less than or equal to 220 and greater than 80, the intervals are

Interval	Probability
$Z \leq -1.5$	.0668
$-1.5 < Z \leq -.5$	.2417
$-.5 < Z \leq .5$	.3829
$.5 < Z \leq 1.5$	.2417
$Z > 1.5$	.0668

If the sample size is less than or equal to 80, we employ the minimum number of intervals, 4. When the sample size is less than 32, at least one expected value will be less than 5. The intervals are

Interval	Probability
$Z \leq -1$	.1587
$-1 < Z \leq 0$	.3413
$0 < Z \leq 1$	.3413
$Z > 1$	.1587

COMMANDS

1. Type or import the data into one column.
2. Click **Tools, Data Analysis Plus,** and **Chi-Squared Test of Normality**.
3. Specify the **Input Range**.
4. Click **Labels** if appropriate.
5. Specify the value of α (**Alpha**) and click **OK**.

COMMANDS FOR EXAMPLE 12.1

Open file **Xm12-01**.

A1:A51

.05

MINITAB

Minitab does not conduct this procedure. However, you can use Minitab to perform several parts of the statistical procedure. See CD Appendix 16.2.

EXERCISES

16.34 Suppose that a random sample of 100 observations was drawn from a population, after which the mean and standard deviation were calculated. Each observation was standardized and the number of observations in each of the intervals below was counted. Can we infer at the 5% significance level that the data were not drawn from a normal population?

Interval	Frequency
$Z \le -1.5$	10
$-1.5 < Z \le -.5$	18
$-.5 < Z \le .5$	48
$.5 < Z \le 1.5$	16
$Z > 1.5$	8

16.35 A random sample of 50 observations yielded the following frequencies for the standardized intervals:

Interval	Frequency
$Z \le -1$	6
$-1 < Z \le 0$	27
$0 < Z \le 1$	14
$Z > 1$	3

Can we infer that the data are not normal? (Use $\alpha = .10$.)

The following exercises require the use of a computer and soft-ware.

16.36 Refer to Exercise 12.34. Test at the 10% significance level to determine whether the amount of time spent working at part-time jobs is normally distributed.

16.37 The test in Exercise 12.46 requires that the weight of discarded newspaper is normally distributed. Conduct a test with $\alpha = .05$ to determine whether the required condition is unsatisfied.

16.38 Exercise 13.41 required you to conduct a t test of the difference between two means. Each sample's productivity data are required to be normally distributed. Is that required condition violated? Test with $\alpha = .05$.

16.39 In Exercise 13.69 you performed a test of the mean matched pairs difference. The test result depends on the requirement that the differences are normally distributed. Test with a 10% significance level to determine whether the requirement is violated.

16.6 SUMMARY

This chapter introduced three statistical techniques. The first is the **chi-squared goodness-of-fit test,** which is applied when the problem objective is to describe a single population of nominal data with two or more categories. The second is the **chi-squared test of a contingency table.** There are two objectives of this test: to analyze the relationship between two nominal variables and to compare two or more populations of nominal data. The last procedure is designed to **test for normality.**

IMPORTANT TERMS

Multinomial experiment 532
Chi-squared goodness-of-
fit test 532

Expected frequency 533
Contingency table 538
Cross-classification table 538

Chi-squared test of a
contingency table 538

SYMBOLS

Symbol	Pronounced	Represents
f_i	f-sub-i	Frequency of the ith category
e_i	e-sub-i	Expected value of the ith category
χ^2	Chi-squared	Test statistic

FORMULA

Test statistic for all procedures

$$\chi^2 = \sum_{i=1}^{k} \frac{(f_i - e_i)^2}{e_i}$$

COMPUTER OUTPUT AND INSTRUCTIONS

Technique	Excel	Minitab
Chi-squared goodness-of-fit test	535	
Chi-squared test of a contingency table	542	543
Chi-squared test of a contingency table (raw data)	542	543
Chi-squared test of normality	551	

REFERENCES

Agresti, Alan, *Categorical Data Analysis.* New York: John Wiley and Sons, 1990.

Kotler, Phillip, *Marketing Management,* 8th edition. Englewood Cliffs, NJ: Prentice Hall, 1994.

Lillien, Gary L., and Arvind Rangaswamy, *Marketing Engineering: Computer Assisted Marketing Analysis and Planning.* Reading, MA: Addison Wesley, 1998.

CHAPTER REVIEW EXERCISES

16.40 An organization dedicated to ensuring fairness in television game shows is investigating "Wheel of Fortune." In this show, three contestants are required to solve puzzles by selecting letters. Each contestant gets to select the first letter and continues selecting until he or she chooses a letter that is not in the hidden word, phrase, or name. The order of contestants is random. However, contestant 1 gets to start game 1, contestant 2 starts game 2, and so on. The contestant who wins the most money is declared the winner and he or she is given an opportunity to win a grand prize. Usually, more than three games are played per show, and as a result it appears that contestant 1 has an advantage: contestant 1 will start two games, whereas contestant 3 will usually start only one game. To see whether this is the case, a random sample of 30 shows was taken and the starting position of the winning contestant for each show was recorded. These are shown in the following table.

Starting Position	Number of Winners
1	14
2	10
3	6

Do the tabulated results allow us to conclude at the 10% significance level that the game is unfair?

16.41 Econetics Research Corporation, a well-known Montreal-based consulting firm, wants to test how it can influence the proportion of questionnaires returned from surveys. Believing that the inclusion of an inducement to respond may be important, it sends out 1,000 questionnaires: 200 promise to send respondents a summary of the survey results, 300 indicate that 20 respondents (selected by lottery) will be awarded gifts, and 500 are accompanied by no inducements. Of these, 80 questionnaires promising a summary, 100 questionnaires offering gifts, and 120 questionnaires offering no inducements are returned. What can you conclude from these results? (Use

$\alpha = .05.$) (*Hint:* The sample size is 1,000 and your analysis must include the complete sample.)

16.42 It has been estimated that employee absenteeism costs North American companies more than $100 billion per year. As a first step in addressing the rising cost of absenteeism, the personnel department of a large corporation recorded the weekdays during which individuals in a sample of 362 absentees were away over the past several months. Do these data suggest that absenteeism is higher on some days of the week than on others? (Use $\alpha = .05$.)

Day of the Week	Mon.	Tues.	Wed.	Thurs.	Fri.
Number Absent	87	62	71	68	74

16.43 Suppose that the personnel department in Exercise 16.42 continued its investigation by categorizing absentees according to the shift on which they worked, as shown in the accompanying table. Is there sufficient evidence (at the 10% significance level) of a relationship between the days on which employees are absent and the shift on which the employees work?

Shift	Mon.	Tues.	Wed.	Thurs.	Fri.
Day	52	28	37	31	33
Evening	35	34	34	37	41

16.44 A management behavior analyst has been studying the relationship between male/female supervisory structures in the workplace and the level of employees' job satisfaction. The results of a recent survey are shown in the table. Conduct a test with $\alpha = .05$ to determine whether the level of job satisfaction depends on the boss/employee gender relationship.

Level of Satisfaction	Boss/Employee			
	Female/ Male	Female/ Female	Male/ Male	Male/ Female
Satisfied	21	25	54	71
Neutral	39	49	50	38
Dissatisfied	31	48	10	11

The following exercises require the use of a computer and software. **Use a 5% significance level.**

16.45 During the decade of the 1980s, professional baseball thrived in North America. Attendance rose continuously from 45 million in 1984 to 58 million in 1991. However, in 1992, attendance dropped by about 2 million. In addition, the number of television viewers also decreased. In order to examine the popularity of baseball relative to other sports, surveys were performed. In 1985 and in 1993, a Harris Poll asked a random sample of 500 people to name their favorite sport. The results, which were published in the *Wall Street Journal* (6 July 1993), are stored in file Xr16-45 in the following way. Column 1: results from 1985; 1 = professional football, 2 = baseball, 3 = professional basketball, 4 = college basketball, 5 = college football, and 6 = other. Column 2 contains the results from 1993 using the same codes.

a Do these results indicate that North Americans changed their favorite sport between 1985 and 1993? (*Hint:* Stack the data.)

b Do these results indicate that the popularity of baseball has changed between 1985 and 1993?

16.46 According to NBC News (11 March 1994), more than 3,000 Americans quit smoking each day. (Unfortunately, more than 3,000 Americans start smoking each day.) Because nicotine is one of the most addictive drugs, quitting smoking is a difficult and frustrating task. It usually takes several tries before success is achieved. There are various methods, including cold turkey, nicotine patch, hypnosis, and group therapy sessions. In an experiment to determine how these methods differ, a random sample of smokers who have decided to quit is selected. Each smoker has chosen one of the methods listed above. After 1 year the respondents report whether they have quit (1= yes, 2 = no) and which method they used (1 = cold turkey; 2 = nicotine patch; 3 = hypnosis; 4 = group therapy sessions). These data are stored in file Xr16-46. Is there sufficient evidence to conclude that the four methods differ in their success?

16.47 A newspaper publisher, trying to pinpoint his market's characteristics, wondered whether the way people read a newspaper is related to the reader's educational level. A survey asked adult readers to report which section of the paper they read first and their highest educational level. These data were recorded (column 1 = first section read, where 1 = front page, 2 = sports, 3 = editorial, and 4 = other; column 2 = educational level, where 1 = did not complete high school, 2 = high school graduate, 3 = university or college graduate, and 4 = postgraduate degree) and stored in file Xr16-47. What do these data tell the publisher about how educational level affects the way adults read the newspaper?

16.48 Every week the Florida Lottery draws 6 numbers between 1 and 49. Lottery ticket buyers are naturally interested in whether certain numbers are drawn more frequently than others. To assist players, the *Sun-Sentinel* publishes the number of times each of the 49 numbers has been drawn in the past 52 weeks. The numbers and the frequency with which each occurred are stored in file Xr16-48. These data are from the Sunday, January 5, 1997, edition.

a If the numbers are drawn randomly, what is the expected frequency for each number?

b Can we infer that the data were not generated randomly?

16.49 Canadians have the option of investing income in registered retirement savings plans (RRSPs). Subject to limits calculated on the basis of income, employer retirement plans, and previous RRSPs, money invested in RRSPs is not taxable. (Money withdrawn from retirement plans is taxable.) Critics argue that RRSPs are a tax loophole for the rich because only wealthier people are in a position to take advantage of the tax provisions. In a study to determine who uses RRSPs, the Caledon Institute of Social Policy randomly sampled Canadians in different tax brackets. (Survey results were published in the *Globe and Mail*, 5 February 1994.) For each respondent, the researchers recorded the tax bracket (1 = less than $20,000; 2 = $20,000–40,000; 3 = $40,000–$60,000; 4 = $60,000–100,000; 5 = over $100,000), and whether they invested in an RRSP this year (2 = yes; 1 = no). These data are stored in file Xr16-49. Can we infer from these data that there are differences in RRSP positions among the income groups?

16.50 In Section 16.5, we showed how to test for normality. However, we can use the same process to test for any other distribution.

A scientist believes that the gender of a child is a binomial random variable with probability = .5 for a boy and .5 for a girl. To help test her belief, she randomly samples 100 families with 5 children. She records the number of boys and stores the results in file Xr16-50. Can the scientist infer that the number of boys in families with 5 children is not a binomial random variable with $p = .5$? (*Hint:* Find the probabilities of $X = 0, 1, 2, 3 , 4$, and 5 from a binomial distribution with $n = 5$ and $p = .5$.)

16.51 Given the high cost of medical care, research that points the way to avoid illness is welcome. Previously performed research tells us that stress affects the immune system. Two scientists at Carnegie Mellon Hospital in Pittsburgh asked 114 healthy adults about their social circles; they were asked to list every group they had contact with at least once every two weeks— family, coworkers, neighbors, friends, religious, and community groups. Participants also reported negative life events over the past year—events such as death of a friend or relative, divorce, or job-related problems. The participants were divided into four groups:

Group 1: Highly social and highly stressed
Group 2: Not highly social and highly stressed
Group 3: Highly social and not highly stressed
Group 4: Not highly social and not highly stressed

Each individual was classified in this way. In addition, whether each person contracted a cold over the next 12 weeks was recorded (1 = cold, 2 = no cold). The data are stored in file Xr16-51. Can we infer that there are differences between the four groups in terms of contracting a cold?

16.52 The relationship between drug companies and medical researchers is under scrutiny because of possible conflict of interest. The issue that started the controversy was a 1995 case–control study that suggested that the use of calcium-channel blockers to treat hypertension led to an increased risk of heart disease.

This led to an intense debate both in technical journals and in the press. Researchers writing in the *New England Journal of Medicine* ("Conflict of Interest in the Debate over Calcium-Channel Antagonists," 8 January 1998, p. 101) looked at the 70 reports that appeared during 1996–1997, classifying them as favorable, neutral, or critical toward the drugs. The researchers then contacted the authors of the reports and questioned them about financial ties to drug companies. The results are stored in file Xr16-52 in the following way:

Column 1: Results of the scientific study;
           1 = favorable, 2 = neutral, 3 = critical
Column 2: 1 = financial ties to drug companies,
           2 = no ties to drug companies

Do these data allow us to infer that the research findings for calcium-channel blockers are affected by whether the research is funded by drug companies?

16.53 In October 1998, the *National Post* began publishing across Canada. The biggest market in Canada is Toronto, which now has four daily newspapers—the *National Post*, the *Globe and Mail*, the *Sun*, and the *Toronto Star*. A marketing consultant wanted to determine the demographic characteristics of the readers of each newspaper. Accordingly, he organized a survey that asked newspaper readers in Toronto to indicate which paper they regularly read and their occupation. The data were stored in file Xr16-53 in the following way:

Column 1: Newspaper, where 1 = *National Post*,
           2 = *Globe and Mail*, 3 = the *Sun*,
           4 = *Toronto Star*
Column 2: Occupation, where 1 = managerial,
           2 = blue-collar, 3 = professional,
           4 = other

Can we infer that the readerships of the four daily newspapers differ in terms of the occupations of their readers?

16.54 Clinical depression is a serious and sometimes debilitating disease. It is often treated by antidepressants such as Prozac and Zoloft. Recent studies may indicate another possible remedy. Researchers took a random sample of people who are clinically depressed and divided them into three groups. The first group was treated with antidepressants and light therapy, the second was treated with a placebo and light therapy, and the third group was treated with a placebo. Whether the patient showed improvement (code = 1) or not (code = 2) and the group number are stored in file Xr16-54. Can we infer that there are differences between the three groups?

✦ CASE 16.1

PREDICTING THE OUTCOMES OF BASKETBALL, BASEBALL, FOOTBALL, AND HOCKEY GAMES FROM INTERMEDIATE RESULTS*

Some basketball fans generally believe that it doesn't pay to watch an entire game because the outcome is determined in the last few minutes (some say the last 2 minutes) of the game. Is this really true, and, if so, is basketball different in this respect from other professional sports played in North America? For example, is it true that the team that leads a baseball game after seven innings almost always wins the game? To address these questions, three researchers tracked basketball, baseball, football, and hockey games. The results (whether the early-game leader and whether the late-game leader won) of games during the 1990 season (for baseball and football) and during the 1990–1991 season (for basketball and hockey) were recorded. Early-game leaders are defined as the teams that are ahead after one quarter of basketball

and football, one period of hockey, or three innings of baseball. Late-game leaders are defined as the teams that are ahead after three quarters of basketball and football, two periods of hockey, or seven innings of baseball.

The data are stored in file C16-01 in the following way:

Column 1: Results of games where 2 = early-game leader wins and 1 = early-game leader loses

Column 2: Early-game leader game where 1 = basketball, 2 = baseball, 3 = football, and 4 = hockey game

Column 3: Results of games where 2 = late-game leader wins and 1 = late-game leader loses

Column 4: Late-game leader game where 1 = basketball, 2 = baseball, 3 = football, and 4 = hockey

Can we infer from these data that all four professional sports experience the same proportion of early-game leaders winning the game? Can we infer from these data that all four professional sports experience the same proportion of late-game leaders winning the game?

*Adapted from H. Cooper, K. M. DeNeve, and E. Mosteller, "Predicting Professional Sports Game Outcomes from Intermediate Game Scores," *Chance* 5, Nos. 3–4 (1992): 18–22.

◈ CASE 16.2
CAN EXPOSURE TO A CODE OF PROFESSIONAL ETHICS HELP MAKE MANAGERS MORE ETHICAL?*

In many North American business schools, the issue of whether a course on ethics should be compulsory has been hotly debated. The empirical evidence appears to be far from consistent on the effects of such courses. To help shed more light on the issue, two researchers organized a study in which they took a random sample of 68 accounting students and 132 non-accounting students. As part of their curriculum, the accounting students were exposed to the American Institute of Certified Public Accountants' code of professional ethics. The non-accounting business students did not take any course that dealt with issues of ethical behavior.

All 200 students in the study were taking a required senior-level policy course. As part of the course, they were assigned to read the article "Crisis in Conscience at Quasar" by A. Fendrock (*Harvard Business Review*, March-April 1968, 112–120). In the case, Universal, the parent company, learned that the senior managers of one of its subsidiaries, Quasar, deliberately lied about financial conditions in its monthly report to corporate headquarters. Quasar's president, John Kane, and its controller, Hugh Kay, were forced to resign. Universal wanted to know why no one at Quasar provided any information about the true financial conditions, whether any other executives were

accomplices to the phony reports, and what could be done to avert such occurrences in the future. Universal sent a fact finder to interview other executives at Quasar—George Kessler, vice president, manufacturing; William Heller, vice president, engineering; Peter Loomis, vice president, marketing; Donald Morgan, chief accountant; and Paul Brown, vice president, industrial relations.

After studying the case, students completed the questionnaire shown below. The results are stored in file C16-02. [The responses to questions 1 to 6 for all students are stored in columns 1 to 6; column 7 indicates whether the student was an accounting student (1) or a non-accounting business student (2).] Does it appear that accounting students exposed to a code of ethics answer the questionnaire differently from non-accounting business students not exposed to the same code?

1. If you had been John Kane, president of Quasar, do you think you would have been tempted to withhold the bad news from corporate management at the parent company?
   2 Yes   1 No
2. Do you think that under the circumstances you would have withheld the bad news?
   2 Yes   1 No

3. Do you think you would have gone around the president and reported the bad news to corporate headquarters at Universal?
   2 Yes   1 No
4. Do you think Kane's withholding the bad news was (check one)...
   1 practical_____ ?
   2 unethical_____?
   3 poor judgment_____?
5. Do you think the blame lies with (check just one)...
   1 Universal's corporate management_____ ?
   2 Quasar's president _____?
   3 Quasar's controller_____?
   4 other_____?
6. Is the problem one of (check just one)...
   1 poor organization_____?
   2 lack of communication_____?
   3 excessive personal loyalty_____?
   4 inadequate supervision_____?
   5 other_____?

*Adapted from W. E. Fulmer and B. R. Cargile, "Ethical Perceptions of Accounting Students: Does Exposure to a Code of Professional Ethics Help?" *Issues in Accounting Education* (Fall 1987): 207–219.

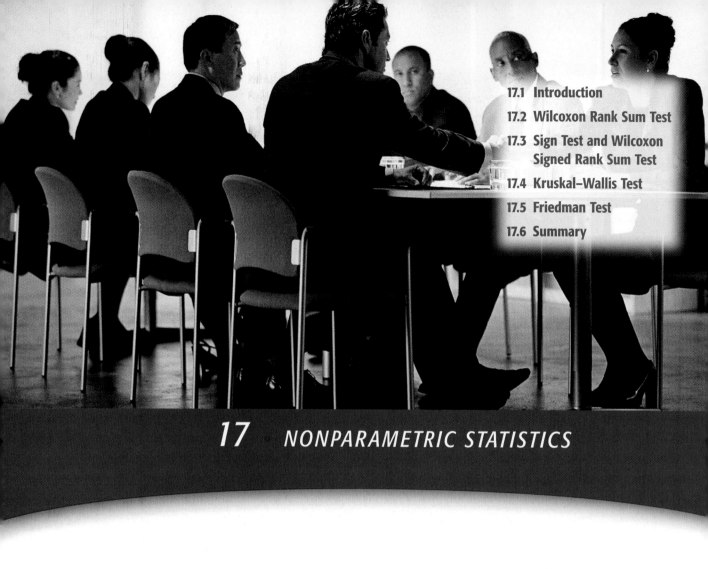

17 · NONPARAMETRIC STATISTICS

RETAINING WORKERS

Because of the high cost of hiring and training new employees, employers would like to ensure that they retain highly qualified workers. To help develop a hiring program, the human resources manager of a large company wanted to compare how long business and nonbusiness university graduates worked for the company before quitting to accept a position elsewhere. The manager selected a random sample of 25 business and 20 nonbusiness graduates who had been hired 5 years ago. The number of months each had worked for the company was recorded. (Those who had not quit were recorded as having worked for 60 months.) The data are stored in file CH17:\Workers and are listed on page 559. Can the human resources manager conclude at the 5% significance level that a difference in duration of employment exists between business and nonbusiness graduates? On page 567 we provide our answer.

Duration of Employment (Months)

Business Graduates												*Nonbusiness Graduates*									
60	11	18	19	5	25	60	7	8	17	37	4 8	25	60	22	24	23	36	39	15	35	16
28	27	11	60	25	5	13	22	11	17	9	4	28	9	60	29	16	22	60	17	60	32

17.1 INTRODUCTION

Throughout this book we have presented statistical techniques that are used when the data are either interval or nominal. In this chapter, we introduce statistical techniques that deal with ordinal data. We will introduce three methods that compare two populations and two procedures used to compare two or more populations. As you've seen, when we compare two or more populations of interval data, we measure the difference between means. However, as we discussed in Chapter 2, when the data are ordinal, the mean is not an appropriate measure of location. As a result, the methods in this chapter do not enable us to test the difference in population means; instead, we will test characteristics of populations without referring to specific parameters. For this reason, these techniques are called **nonparametric techniques**. Rather than testing to determine whether the population means differ, we will test to determine whether the *population locations* differ.

Although nonparametric methods are designed to test ordinal data, they have another area of application. The statistical tests described in Sections 13.2 and 13.4, and Chapter 15 require that the populations be normally distributed. If the data are extremely nonnormal, the t tests and F test are invalid. Fortunately, nonparametric techniques can be used instead. For this reason, nonparametric procedures are often (perhaps more accurately) called **distribution-free statistics**. The techniques presented here can be used when the data are interval and the required condition of normality is unsatisfied. In such circumstances we will treat the interval data as if they were ordinal. For this reason, even when the data are interval and the mean is the appropriate measure of location, we will choose instead to test population locations.

Figure 17.1 depicts the distributions of two populations when their locations are the same. Notice that, since we don't know (or care) anything about the shape of the distributions, we represent them as nonnormal. Figure 17.2 describes a circumstance when the location of population 1 is to the right of the location of population 2. The location of population 1 is to the left of the location of population 2 in Figure 17.3.

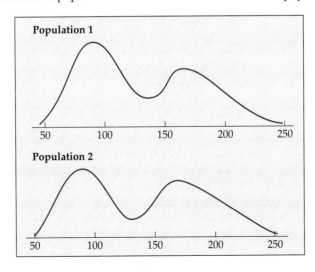

Figure 17.1
Population locations are the same

Figure 17.2
Location of population 1 is to the right of the location of population 2

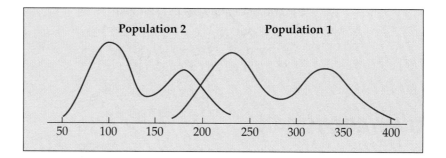

Figure 17.3
Location of population 1 is to the left of the location of population 2

When the problem objective is to compare two populations, the null hypothesis will state

H_0:   The two population locations are the same.

The alternative hypothesis can take on any one of the following three forms.

1. If we want to know whether there is sufficient evidence to infer that there is a difference between the two populations, the alternative hypothesis is

   H_1:   The location of population 1 is different from the location of population 2.

2. If we want to know whether we can conclude that the random variable in population 1 is larger in general than the random variable in population 2 (see Figure 17.2), the alternative hypothesis is

   H_1:   The location of population 1 is to the right of the location of population 2.

3. If we want to know whether we can conclude that the random variable in population 1 is smaller in general than the random variable in population 2 (see Figure 17.3), the alternative hypothesis is

   H_1:   The location of population 1 is to the left of the location of population 2.

As you will see, nonparametric tests utilize a ranking procedure as an integral part of the calculations. You've actually dealt with such a process already in this book. In Chapter 4, we introduced the median as a measure of central location. The median is computed by placing the observations in order and selecting the observation that falls in the middle. Thus, the appropriate measure of central location of ordinal data is the median, a statistic that is the product of a ranking process.

In the next section, we present the Wilcoxon rank sum test employed when we wish to test for the differences between population locations when the data are generated from independent samples. Section 17.3 introduces the sign test and the Wilcoxon signed rank sum test, both of which are applied to the matched pairs experiment. Sections 17.4 and 17.5 introduce the Kruskal–Wallis test and the Friedman test, respectively, procedures that are employed when the objective is to compare two or more populations.

17.2 WILCOXON RANK SUM TEST

The test we introduce in this section deals with problems with the following characteristics:

1. The problem objective is to compare two populations.
2. The data are either ordinal or interval where the normality requirement necessary to perform the equal-variances t test of $\mu_1 - \mu_2$ is unsatisfied.
3. The samples are independent.

To illustrate how to compute the test statistic for the Wilcoxon rank sum test for independent samples, we offer the following example.

EXAMPLE 17.1

Suppose that we want to determine whether the following observations drawn from two populations allow us to conclude at the 5% significance level that the location of population 1 is to the left of the location of population 2.

Sample 1: 22   23   20

Sample 2: 18   27   26

We want to test the following hypotheses:

H_0: The two population locations are the same.
H_1: The location of population 1 is to the left of the location of population 2.

TEST STATISTIC

The first step is to rank all six observations with rank 1 assigned to the smallest observation and rank 6 to the largest.

Sample 1	Rank	Sample 2	Rank
22	3	18	1
23	4	27	6
20	2	26	5
	$T_1 = 9$		$T_2 = 12$

Observe that 18 is the smallest number, so it receives a rank of 1; 20 is the second-smallest number, and it receives a rank of 2. We continue until rank 6 is assigned to 27, which is the largest of the observations. In case of ties, we average the ranks of the tied observations. The second step is to calculate the sum of the ranks of each sample. The rank sum of sample 1, denoted T_1, is 9. The rank sum of sample 2, denoted T_2, is 12. (Note that T_1 plus T_2 must equal the sum of the integers from 1 to 6, which is 21.) We can use either rank sum as the test statistic. We arbitrarily select T_1 as the test statistic and label it T. The value of the test statistic in this example is $T = T_1 = 9$.

SAMPLING DISTRIBUTION OF THE TEST STATISTIC

A small value of T indicates that most of the smaller observations are in sample 1 and that most of the larger observations are in sample 2. This would imply that the location of population 1 is to the left of the location of population 2. Therefore, in order for us to conclude statistically that this is the case, we need to show that T is small. The definition of "small" comes from the sampling distribution of T. As we did in Section 9.2 when we derived the sampling distribution of the sample mean, we can derive the sampling distribution of T by listing all possible values of T. In Table 17.1 we show all possible rankings of two samples of size 3.

Table 17.1 All Possible Ranks and Rank Sums of Two Samples of Size 3

Ranks of Sample 1	Rank Sum	Ranks of Sample 2	Rank Sum
1, 2, 3	6	4, 5, 6	15
1, 2, 4	7	3, 5, 6	14
1, 2, 5	8	3, 4, 6	13
1, 2, 6	9	3, 4, 5	12
1, 3, 4	8	2, 5, 6	13
1, 3, 5	9	2, 4, 6	12
1, 3, 6	10	2, 4, 5	11
1, 4, 5	10	2, 3, 6	11
1, 4, 6	11	2, 3, 5	10
1, 5, 6	12	2, 3, 4	9
2, 3, 4	9	1, 5, 6	12
2, 3, 5	10	1, 4, 6	11
2, 3, 6	11	1, 4, 5	10
2, 4, 5	11	1, 3, 6	10
2, 4, 6	12	1, 3, 5	9
2, 5, 6	13	1, 3, 4	8
3, 4, 5	12	1, 2, 6	9
3, 4, 6	13	1, 2, 5	8
3, 5, 6	14	1, 2, 4	7
4, 5, 6	15	1, 2, 3	6

If the null hypothesis is true and the two population locations are identical, then it follows that each possible ranking is equally likely. Since there are 20 different possibilities, each value of T has the same probability, namely, 1/20, Notice that there is one value of 6, one value of 7, two values of 8, and so on. Table 17.2 summarizes the values of T and their probabilities, and Figure 17.4 depicts this sampling distribution.

Table 17.2 Sampling Distribution of T with Two Samples of Size 3

T	$P(T)$
6	1/20
7	1/20
8	2/20
9	3/20
10	3/20
11	3/20
12	3/20
13	2/20
14	1/20
15	1/20
Total	1

From this sampling distribution we can see that $P(T \le 6) = P(T = 6) = 1/20 = .05$. Because we're trying to determine whether the value of the test statistic is small enough for us to reject the null hypothesis at the 5% significance level, we specify the rejection region as $T \le 6$. Since $T = 9$, we cannot reject the null hypothesis.

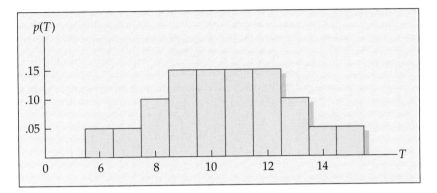

Figure 17.4
**Sampling distribution of *T*
with two samples of size 3**

Statisticians have generated the sampling distribution of T for various combinations of sample sizes. The critical values are provided in Table 8 in Appendix B and reproduced here as Table 17.3. Table 17.3 provides values of T_L and T_U for sample sizes between 3 and 10 (n_1 is the size of sample 1 and n_2 is the size of sample 2). The values of T_L and T_U in part (a) of the table are such that

$$P(T \le T_L) = P(T \ge T_U) = .025$$

TABLE 17.3 Critical Values of the Wilcoxon Rank Sum Test

(a) $\alpha = .025$ one-tail; $\alpha = .05$ two-tail

n_2 \ n_1	3		4		5		6		7		8		9		10	
	T_L	T_U	T_L	T_U	T_L	T_U	T_L	T_U	T_L	T_U	T_L	T_U	T_L	T_U	T_L	T_U
4	6	18	11	25	17	33	23	43	31	53	40	64	50	76	61	89
5	6	21	12	28	18	37	25	47	33	58	42	70	52	83	64	96
6	7	23	12	32	19	41	26	52	35	63	44	76	55	89	66	104
7	7	26	13	35	20	45	28	56	37	68	47	81	58	95	70	110
8	8	28	14	38	21	49	29	61	39	73	49	87	60	102	73	117
9	8	31	15	41	22	53	31	65	41	78	51	93	63	108	76	124
10	9	33	16	44	24	56	32	70	43	83	54	98	66	114	79	131

(b) $\alpha = .05$ one-tail; $\alpha = .10$ two-tail

n_2 \ n_1	3		4		5		6		7		8		9		10	
	T_L	T_U	T_L	T_U	T_L	T_U	T_L	T_U	T_L	T_U	T_L	T_U	T_L	T_U	T_L	T_U
3	6	15	11	21	16	29	23	37	31	46	39	57	49	68	60	80
4	7	17	12	24	18	32	25	41	33	51	42	62	52	74	63	87
5	7	20	13	27	19	36	26	46	35	56	45	67	55	80	66	94
6	8	22	14	30	20	40	28	50	37	61	47	73	57	87	69	101
7	9	24	15	33	22	43	30	54	39	66	49	79	60	93	73	107
8	9	27	16	36	24	46	32	58	41	71	52	84	63	99	76	114
9	10	29	17	39	25	50	33	63	43	76	54	90	66	105	79	121
10	22	31	18	42	26	54	35	67	46	80	57	95	69	111	83	127

Source: From F. Wilcoxon and R.A. Wilcox, "Some Rapid Approximate Statistical Procedures" (1964), p. 28. Reproduced with the permission of American Cyanamid Company.

The values of T_L and T_U in part (b) of the table are such that

$$P(T \leq T_L) = P(T \geq T_U) = .05$$

Part (a) is used either in a two-tail test with $\alpha = .05$ or in a one-tail test with $\alpha = .025$. Part (b) is employed either in a two-tail test with $\alpha = .10$ or in a one-tail test with $\alpha = .05$. Because no other values are provided, we are restricted to those values of α.

Although it is possible to derive the sampling distribution of the test statistic for any other sample sizes, the process can be quite tedious. Fortunately, it is also unnecessary. Statisticians have shown that when the sample sizes are larger than 10, the test statistic is approximately normally distributed with mean $E(T)$ and standard deviation σ_T, where

$$E(T) = \frac{n_1(n_1 + n_2 + 1)}{2}$$

and

$$\sigma_T = \sqrt{\frac{n_1 n_2(n_1 + n_2 + 1)}{12}}$$

Thus, the standardized test statistic is

$$z = \frac{T - E(T)}{\sigma_T}$$

EXAMPLE 17.2

A pharmaceutical company is planning to introduce a new painkiller. In a preliminary experiment to determine its effectiveness, 30 people were randomly selected, of whom 15 were given the new painkiller and 15 were given aspirin. All 30 were told to use the drug when headaches or other minor pains occurred and to indicate which of the following statements most accurately represented the effectiveness of the drug they took.

$\quad$ 5 = The drug was extremely effective.

$\quad$ 4 = The drug was quite effective.

$\quad$ 3 = The drug was somewhat effective.

$\quad$ 2 = The drug was slightly effective.

$\quad$ 1 = The drug was not at all effective.

The responses are listed below using the codes. (The data are also stored in file Xm17-02.) Can we conclude at the 5% significance level that the new painkiller is perceived to be more effective?

$\quad$ New painkiller:$\quad$ 3, 5, 4, 3, 2, 5, 1, 4, 5, 3, 3, 5, 5, 5, 4

$\quad$ Aspirin:$\quad$ 4, 1, 3, 2, 4, 1, 3, 4, 2, 2, 2, 4, 3, 4, 5

SOLUTION

IDENTIFY

The objective is to compare two populations: the perceived effectiveness of the new painkiller and of aspirin. We recognize that the data are ordinal, because except for the order of the codes, the numbers used to record the results are arbitrary. Finally, the samples are independent. These factors tell us that the appropriate technique is the Wilcoxon rank sum test. We denote the effectiveness scores of the new painkiller as sample 1 and the effectiveness scores of aspirin as sample 2. Because we want to know whether the new painkiller is better than aspirin, the alternative hypothesis is

H_1: The location of population 1 is to the right of the location of population 2.

We specify the null hypothesis as

H_0: The two population locations are the same.

COMPUTE

 MANUALLY

If the alternative hypothesis is true, the location of population 1 will be located to the right of the location of population 2. It follows that T and z would be large. Our job is to determine whether z is large enough to reject the null hypothesis in favor of the alternative hypothesis. Thus, the rejection region is

$$z > z_\alpha = z_{.05} = 1.645$$

We compute the test statistic by ranking all of the observations.

New Pain Killer	Rank	Aspirin	Rank
3	12	4	19.5
5	27	1	2
4	19.5	3	12
3	12	2	6
2	6	4	19.5
5	27	1	2
1	2	3	12
4	19.5	4	19.5
5	27	2	6
3	12	2	6
3	12	2	6
5	27	4	19.5
5	27	3	12
5	27	4	19.5
4	19.5	5	27
	$T_1 = 276.5$		$T_2 = 188.5$

Notice that there are three "ones" that occupy ranks 1, 2, and 3. The average is 2. Thus, each "one" is assigned a rank of 2. There are five "twos" whose ranks are 4, 5, 6, 7, and 8, the average of which is 6. We continue until all the observations have been similarly ranked. The rank sums are computed with $T_1 = 276.5$ and $T_2 = 188.5$. The unstandardized test statistic is $T = T_1 = 276.5$. To standardize, we determine $E(T)$ and σ_T:

$$E(T) = \frac{n_1(n_1 + n_2 + 1)}{2} = \frac{15(31)}{2} = 232.5$$

$$\sigma_T = \sqrt{\frac{n_1 n_2 (n_1 + n_2 + 1)}{12}} = \sqrt{\frac{(15)(15)(31)}{12}} = 24.1$$

The standardized test statistic is calculated next.

$$z = \frac{T - E(T)}{\sigma_T} = \frac{276.5 - 232.5}{24.1} = 1.83$$

The p-value of the test is

$$p\text{-value} = P(Z > 1.83) = .5 - .4664 = .0336$$

EXCEL

	A	B	C
1	Wilcoxon Rank Sum Test		
2			
3		Rank Sum	Observations
4	*New*	276.5	15
5	*Aspirin*	188.5	15
6	z Stat	1.83	
7	P(Z<=z) one-tail	0.034	
8	z Critical one-tail	1.6449	
9	P(Z<=z) two-tail	0.068	
10	z Critical two-tail	1.96	

COMMANDS

1. Type or import the data into two adjacent columns.
2. Click **Tools, Data Analysis Plus,** and **Wilcoxon Rank Sum Test.**
3. Specify the **Input Range.**
4. Click **Labels** if appropriate.
5. Specify the value of α (**Alpha**) and click **OK.**

COMMANDS FOR
EXAMPLE 17.2
Open file **Xm17-02.**

A1:B16

.05

MINITAB

Mann-Whitney Test and CI: New, Aspirin

```
New        N =  15      Median =       4.000
Aspirin    N =  15      Median =       3.000
Point estimate for ETA1-ETA2 is        1.000
95.4 Percent CI for ETA1-ETA2 is (0.001,2.000)
W = 276.5
Test of ETA1 = ETA2  vs  ETA1 > ETA2 is significant at 0.0356
The test is significant at 0.0321 (adjusted for ties)
```

Minitab performs the **Mann–Whitney test** rather than the Wilcoxon test. However, the tests are equivalent. In the output above, **ETA** represents the population median. The test statistic, **W = 276.5**, is the value of the Wilcoxon rank sum statistic. That is, $T = W = 276.5$. The output includes the p-value (**0.0356**) and another p-value calculated by adjusting for tied observations (**0.0321**). We will report the first p-value only.

COMMANDS FOR
EXAMPLE 17.2
Open file **Xm17-02.**

COMMANDS
1. Type or import the data into two columns.
2. Click **Stat, Nonparametrics,** and **Mann-Whitney….**
3. Type the variable name for the **First Sample**.
4. Type the variable name of the **Second Sample**.
5. Specify one of **less than, not equal to,** or **greater than.** Click **OK.**

New or **C1**

Aspirin or **C2**
greater than

INTERPRET

The data provide sufficient evidence to infer that the new painkiller is perceived to be more effective than aspirin. We note that the data were generated from a controlled experiment. That is, the subjects were assigned to take either the new painkiller or aspirin. (When subjects decide for themselves which medication to take, the data are observational.) This factor helps support the claim that the new painkiller is indeed more effective than aspirin. Factors that weaken the argument are small sample sizes and the inexactness of the responses. There may be methods to measure the effectiveness less subjectively. Additionally, a double-blind experiment should have been employed.

As we pointed out in the introduction to this chapter, the Wilcoxon rank sum test is used to compare two populations when the data are either ordinal or interval. Example 17.2 illustrated the use of the Wilcoxon rank sum test when the data are ordinal. In the example that opened this chapter we demonstrate its use when the data are interval.

RETAINING WORKERS: SOLUTION

IDENTIFY

The problem objective is to compare two populations whose data are interval. The samples are independent. Thus, the appropriate parametric technique is the t test of $\mu_1 - \mu_2$, which requires that the populations be normally distributed. However, when the histograms are drawn (see Figures 17.5 and 17.6), it becomes clear that this requirement is unsatisfied. It follows that the correct statistical procedure is the Wilcoxon rank sum test. The null and alternative hypotheses are

H_0: The two population locations are the same.

H_1: The location of population 1 (business graduates) is different from the location of population 2 (nonbusiness graduates)

COMPUTE

🐭 *MANUALLY*

The rejection region is

$z < -z_{\alpha/2} = -z_{.025} = -1.96$ or

$z > z_{\alpha/2} = z_{.025} = 1.96$

We calculate the value of the test statistic in the following way.

Business	Rank	Nonbusiness	Rank
60	42	25	28
11	11	60	42
18	20	22	23
19	21	24	26
5	3.5	23	25
25	28	36	36
60	42	39	38
7	5	15	14
8	6.5	35	35
17	18	16	15.5
37	37	28	31.5
4	1.5	9	8.5
8	6.5	60	42
28	31.5	29	33
27	30	16	15.5
11	11	22	23
60	42	60	42
25	28	17	18

(continued)

RETAINING WORKERS: SOLUTION (continued)

Business	Rank	Nonbusiness	Rank
5	3.5	60	42
13	13	32	34
22	23		$T_2 = 572$
11	11		
17	18		
9	8.5		
4	1.5		
	$T_1 = 463$		

The unstandardized test statistic is $T = T_1 = 463$. To calculate z, we first determine the mean and standard deviation of T. Note that $n_1 = 25$ and $n_2 = 20$.

$$E(T) = \frac{n_1(n_1 + n_2 + 1)}{2} = \frac{25(46)}{2} = 575$$

$$\sigma_T = \sqrt{\frac{n_1 n_2(n_1 + n_2 + 1)}{12}} = \sqrt{\frac{(25)(20)(46)}{12}} = 43.8$$

The standardized test statistic is

$$z = \frac{T - E(T)}{\sigma_T} = \frac{463 - 575}{43.8} = -2.56$$

p-value $= 2P(Z < -2.56) = 2(.5 - .4948) = .0104$

EXCEL

	A	B	C
1	**Wilcoxon Rank Sum Test**		
2			
3		Rank Sum	Observations
4	*Business*	463	25
5	*Non-Bus*	572	20
6	z Stat	-2.56	
7	P(Z<=z) one-tail	0.0053	
8	z Critical one-tail	1.6449	
9	P(Z<=z) two-tail	0.0106	
10	z Critical two-tail	1.96	

MINITAB

Mann-Whitney Test and CI: Business, Non-Bus

```
Business   N = 25   Median =    17.00
Non-Bus    N = 20   Median =    26.50
Point estimate for ETA1-ETA2 is    -11.00
95.2 Percent CI for ETA1-ETA2 is (-19.00,-3.00)
W = 463.0
Test of ETA1 = ETA2  vs ETA1 not = ETA2 is significant at 0.0109
The test is significant at 0.0107 (adjusted for ties)
```

Figure 17.5 Histogram of Length of Employment of Business Graduates in Example 17.3

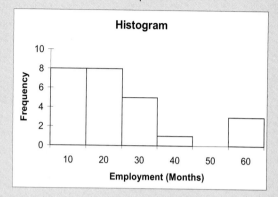

Figure 17.6 Histogram of Length of Employment of Nonbusiness Graduates in Example 17.3

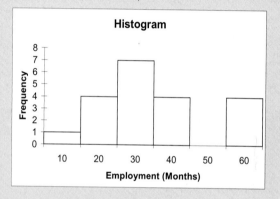

INTERPRET

There is enough evidence to infer that the duration of employment is different for business and nonbusiness graduates. The data cannot tell us the cause of this conclusion. For example, we don't know whether business graduates are in greater demand, making it more likely that such employees will leave for better jobs, or that nonbusiness graduates are more satisfied with their jobs and thus remain longer. Moreover, we don't know what the results would have been had we surveyed employees 10 years after they were employed.

REQUIRED CONDITIONS

The Wilcoxon rank sum test (like the other nonparametric tests presented in this chapter) actually tests to determine whether the population *distributions* are identical. This means that it tests not only for identical locations, but for identical spreads (variances) and shapes (distributions) as well. Unfortunately, this means that the rejection of the null hypothesis may not necessarily signify a difference in population locations. The rejection of the null hypothesis may be due instead to a difference in distribution shapes and/or spreads. To avoid this problem, we will require that the two probability distributions be identical except with respect to location, which then becomes the sole focus of the test. This requirement is made for the tests introduced in the next three sections (sign test and Wilcoxon signed rank sum test, Kruskal–Wallis test, and Friedman test).

The histograms in Figures 17.5 and 17.6 appear to confirm that the required condition for the use of the Wilcoxon rank sum test is satisfied in Example 17.3.

DEVELOPING AN UNDERSTANDING OF STATISTICAL CONCEPTS

When applying nonparametric techniques, we do not perform any calculations using the original data. Instead, we perform computations only on the ranks. (We determine the rank sums and use them to make our decision.) As a result, we do not care about the actual distribution of the data (hence the name *distribution-free techniques*), and we do not specify parameters in the hypotheses (hence the name *nonparametric techniques*). Although there are other techniques that do not specify parameters in the hypotheses, we use the term *nonparametric* for procedures that feature these concepts.

Here is a summary of how to identify the Wilcoxon rank sum test.

FACTORS THAT IDENTIFY THE WILCOXON RANK SUM TEST
1. **Problem objective:** Compare two populations.
2. **Data type:** Ordinal or interval but nonnormal
3. **Experimental design:** Independent samples

EXERCISES

Developing an Understanding of Statistical Concepts

Exercises 17.1–17.6 are "what-if analyses" designed to determine what happens to the test statistics and p-values when elements of the statistical inference change. These problems can be solved manually or using the **Wilcoxon Rank Sum Test** *worksheet in the* **Test Statistics** *workbook.*

17.1 Given the following statistics, calculate the *p*-value of the test to determine whether the population locations differ.

$$T_1 = 250 \quad n_1 = 15$$
$$T_2 = 215 \quad n_2 = 15$$

17.2 Repeat Exercise 17.1 with $T_1 = 275$ and $T_2 = 190$.

17.3 Review Exercises 17.1 and 17.2. Describe the effect of increasing T_1 to 275.

17.4 From the following statistics, test (with $\alpha = .01$) to determine whether the location of population 1 is to the right of the location of population 2.

$$T_1 = 1,205 \quad n_1 = 30$$
$$T_2 = 1,280 \quad n_2 = 40$$

17.5 Repeat Exercise 17.4 with $T_1 = 1,065$.

17.6 From your answers to Exercises 17.4 and 17.5, discuss the effect of decreasing T_1 to 1,065.

17.7 Use the Wilcoxon rank sum test on the following data to determine whether the location of population 1 is to the left of the location of population 2. (Use $\alpha = .05$.)

Sample 1: 75 60   73 66   81
Sample 2: 90 72 103 82   78

17.8 Use the Wilcoxon rank sum test on the data below (which are also stored in file Xr17-08) to determine whether the two population locations differ. (Use a 10% significance level.)

Sample 1: 15   7 22 20 32 18 26 17 23 30
Sample 2: 8 27 17 25 20 16 21 17 10 18

Exercises 17.9 to 17.25 require the use of a computer and software.
Use a 5% significance level.

17.9 In a taste test of a new beer, 25 people rated the new beer and another 25 rated the leading brand on the market. The possible ratings were Poor, Fair, Good, Very good, and Excellent. The responses for the new beer and the leading beer were stored in file Xr17-09 using a 1–2–3–4–5 coding system. Can we infer that the new beer is less highly rated than the leading brand?

17.10 Refer to Exercise 17.9. The responses were recoded so that 3 = Poor, 8 = Fair, 22 = Good, 37 = Very good, and 55 = Excellent. These data are stored in file Xr17-10. Can we infer that the new beer is less highly rated than the leading brand?

17.11 Review Exercises 17.9 and 17.10. What do these exercises tell you about ordinal data?

17.12 To determine whether the satisfaction rating of an airline differs between business class and economy class, a survey was performed. Random samples of both groups were asked to rate their satisfaction with the quality of service using the following responses:

Very satisfied
Quite satisfied
Somewhat satisfied
Neither satisfied nor dissatisfied
Somewhat dissatisfied
Quite dissatisfied
Very dissatisfied

Using a 7–6–5–4–3–2–1 coding system, the results were stored in file Xr17-12. Can we infer that business and economy class differ in their degree of satisfaction with the service?

17.13 Refer to Exercise 17.12. The responses were recoded using the values 88–67–39–36–25–21–18. These data are stored in file Xr17-13. Can we infer that business and economy class differ in their degree of satisfaction with the airline?

17.14 What is the effect of changing the codes in Exercises 17.12 and 17.13? Why was this expected?

17.15 Refer to Example 17.2. Suppose that the responses were coded as follows:

100 = The drug was extremely effective.
60 = The drug was quite effective.
40 = The drug was somewhat effective.
35 = The drug was slightly effective.
10 = The drug was not at all effective.

These data are stored in file Xr17-15. Determine whether we can infer that the new painkiller is more effective than aspirin.

17.16 Why are the results of Example 17.2 and Exercise 17.15 identical?

Applications

Exercises 17.17 to 17.25 may be solved manually. See Appendix A for the sample statistics. **Use a 5% significance level unless specified otherwise.**

17.17 A survey of statistics professors asked them to rate the importance of teaching nonparametric techniques. The possible responses are

Very important
Quite important
Somewhat important
Not too important
Not important at all

The professors were classified as either a member of the Mathematics Department or a member of some other department. The responses (codes 5, 4, 3, 2, and 1, respectively) were stored in file Xr17-17. Can we infer that members of the Mathematics Department rate nonparametric techniques as more important than do members of other departments?

17.18 In recent years, insurance companies offering medical coverage have given discounts to companies that are committed to improving the health of their employees. To help determine whether this policy is reasonable, the general manager of one large insurance company organized a study of a random sample of 30 workers who regularly participate in their company's lunchtime exercise program and 30 workers who do not. Over a 2-year period, he observed the total dollar amount of medical expenses for each individual. These data are stored in file Xr17-18. Can the manager conclude that companies that provide exercise programs should be given discounts?

17.19 Feminist organizations often use the issue of who does the housework in two-career families as a gauge of equality. Suppose that a study was undertaken and a random sample of 125 two-career families was selected. The wives were asked to report the number of hours of housework they performed the previous week. The results together with the responses from a survey performed last year (with a different sample of two-career families) are stored in Xr17-19. Can we conclude that women are doing less housework today than last year?

17.20 The American public's support for the space program is important for the program's continuation and for the financial health of the aerospace industry. In a poll conducted by the Gallup organization last year, a random sample of 100 Americans were asked, "Should the amount of money being spent on the space program be increased or kept at current levels (3), decreased (2), or ended altogether (1)?" The survey was conducted again this year. The results are stored in file Xr17-20 using the codes in parentheses. Can we conclude at the 10% significance level that public support decreased between last year and this year?

17.21 Certain drugs differ in their side effects depending on the gender of the patient. In a study to determine whether men or women suffer more serious side effects when taking a powerful penicillin substitute, 50 men and 50 women were given the drug. Each was asked to evaluate the level of stomach upset on a 4-point scale, where 4 = extremely upset, 3 = somewhat upset, 2 = not too upset, and 1 = not upset at all. The results are stored in file Xr17-21. Can we conclude that men and women experience different levels of stomach upset from the drug?

17.22 The president of Tastee Inc., a baby-food producer, claims that her company's product is superior to that of her leading competitor because babies gain weight faster with her product. As an experiment, 40 healthy newborn infants are randomly selected. For two months, 15 of the babies are fed Tastee baby food and the other 25 are fed the competitor's product. Each baby's weight gain (in ounces) is stored in file Xr17-22. Can we conclude that if we use weight gain as our criterion, Tastee baby food is indeed superior? This exercise is identical to Exercise 13.33 (except for the data).

17.23 Do the ways that women dress influence the ways that other women judge them? This question was addressed by a researcher at Ohio State University (*Working Mother*, April 1992). The experiment consisted of asking women to rate how professional two women looked. One woman wore a size 6 dress, and the other wore a size 14. Suppose that the researcher asked 20 women to rate the woman wearing the size 6 dress and another 20 to rate the woman wearing the size 14 dress. The ratings were as follows:

    4 = highly professional
    3 = somewhat professional
    2 = not very professional
    1 = not at all professional

The results are stored in file Xr17-23. Do these data provide sufficient evidence at the 10% significance level to infer that women perceive another woman wearing a size 6 dress as more professional than one wearing a size 14 dress?

17.24 The image of the lowly prune is not very good. It is perceived as a product used by seniors to help avoid constipation. However, in reality it is a nutritious and (for many) a tasty treat. To help improve the image of the prune, a company that produces the product decided to see the effect of changing its name to dried plums (which is what a prune is). To gauge the effect, a random sample of shoppers was asked how likely it was that they would purchase the product. Half the sample was shown a package that identified its contents as prunes. The other half was shown packages labeled dried plums. The responses are

    Highly unlikely (1)
    Somewhat unlikely (2)
    Somewhat likely (3)
    Highly likely (4)

The responses are stored in file Xr17-24. Can we infer from these data that changing the name of prunes to dried plums increases the likelihood that shoppers will buy?

17.25 Burger King Restaurants regularly survey customers to determine how well they are doing. Suppose that a survey asked customers to rate (among other things) the speed of service. The responses are

    1 = Poor
    2 = Good
    3 = Very good
    4 = Excellent

The responses for the day shift and night shift are stored in file Xr17-25. Can we infer that night shift customers rate the service differently than the day shift?

17.3 SIGN TEST AND WILCOXON SIGNED RANK SUM TEST

In the preceding section, we discussed the nonparametric technique for comparing two populations of data that are either ordinal or interval and where the data are independently drawn. In this section, the problem objective and data type remain as they were in Section 17.2, but we will be working with data generated from a matched pairs experiment. We have dealt with this type of experiment before. In Section 13.4, we dealt with the mean of the paired differences represented by the parameter μ_D. In this section, we introduce two nonparametric techniques that test hypotheses in problems with the following characteristics:

1. The problem objective is to compare two populations.
2. The data are either ordinal or interval (where the normality requirement necessary to perform the parametric test is unsatisfied).
3. The samples are matched pairs.

    To extract all the potential information from a matched pairs experiment, we must create the matched pair differences. Recall that we did so when conducting the *t* test and estimate of μ_D. We then calculated the mean and standard deviation of these differences and determined the test statistic and confidence interval estimator. The first step in both nonparametric methods presented here is the same: Compute the differences for each pair of observations. However, if the data are ordinal, we cannot perform any calculations on those differences because differences between ordinal values have no meaning.

To understand this point, consider comparing two populations of responses of people rating a product or service. The responses are "excellent," "good," "fair," and "poor." Recall that we can assign any numbering system so long as the order is maintained. The simplest system is 4–3–2–1. However, any other system such as 66–38–25–11 (a set of numbers randomly selected except for maintaining the order) is equally valid. Now suppose that in one matched pair the sample 1 response was "excellent" and the sample 2 response was "good." Calculating the matched pairs difference under the 4–3–2–1 system gives a difference of $4 - 3 = 1$. Using the 66–38–25–11 system gives a difference of $66 - 38 = 28$. If we treat this and other differences as real numbers, we are likely to produce different results, depending on which numbering system we used. Thus, we cannot use any method that uses the actual differences. However, we can use the sign of the differences. In fact, when the data are ordinal, that is the only method that is valid. That is, no matter what numbering system is employed, we know that "excellent" is better than "good." In the 4–3–2–1 system, the difference between "excellent" and "good" is $+1$. In the 66–38–25–11 system, the difference is $+28$. If we ignore the magnitude of the number and record only the sign, the two numbering systems (and all other systems where the rank order is maintained) will produce exactly the same result.

As you will shortly discover, the sign test uses only the sign of the differences. That's why it's called the *sign test*.

When the data are interval, however, differences have real meaning. Although we can use the sign test when the data are interval, doing so results in a loss of potentially useful information. For example, knowing that the difference in sales between two matched used car salespeople is 25 cars is much more informative than simply knowing that the first salesperson sold more cars than the second salesperson. As a result, when the data are interval but not normal we will use the *Wilcoxon signed rank sum test*, which incorporates not only the sign of the difference (hence the name), but the magnitude as well.

SIGN TEST

The sign test is employed in the following situations:

1. The problem objective is to compare two populations.

2. The data are ordinal.

3. The experimental design is matched pairs

TEST STATISTIC AND SAMPLING DISTRIBUTION

The sign test is quite simple. For each matched pair, we calculate the difference between the observation in sample 1 and the related observation in sample 2. We then count the number of positive differences and the number of negative differences. If the null hypothesis is true, we expect the number of positive differences to be approximately equal to the number of negative differences. Expressed another way, we expect the number of positive differences and the number of negative differences each to be approximately equal to half the total sample size. If either number is too large or too small, we reject the null hypothesis. By now you know that the determination of what is too large or too small comes from the sampling distribution of the test statistic. We will arbitrarily choose the test statistic to be the number of positive differences, which we denote x. The test statistic x is a binomial random variable, and under the null hypothesis, the binomial proportion is $p = .5$. Thus, the sign test is none other than the z test of p introduced in Section 12.4.

Recall from Sections 7.6 and 9.3 that x is binomially distributed and that, for sufficiently large n, x is approximately normally distributed with mean $\mu = np$ and standard deviation $\sqrt{np(1 - p)}$. Thus, the standardized test statistic is

$$z = \frac{x - np}{\sqrt{np(1 - p)}}$$

The null hypothesis

H_0:   The two population locations are the same.

is equivalent to

H_0: $p = .5$

Assuming that the null hypothesis is true, the test statistic becomes

$$z = \frac{x - np}{\sqrt{np(1 - p)}} = \frac{x - .5n}{\sqrt{n(.5)(.5)}} = \frac{x - .5n}{.5\sqrt{n}}$$

The normal approximation of the binomial distribution is valid when $np \geq 5$ and $n(1 - p) \geq 5$. When $p = .5$,

$$np = n(.5) \geq 5$$

and

$$n(1 - p) = n(.5) \geq 5$$

implies that n must be greater than or equal to 10. Thus, this is one of the required conditions of the sign test. However, the quality of the inference with so small a sample size is poor. Larger sample sizes are recommended and will be used in the examples and exercises that follow.

It is common practice in this type of test to eliminate the matched pairs of observations when the differences equal 0. Consequently, n equals the number of nonzero differences in the sample.

EXAMPLE 17.3

In an experiment to determine which of two cars is perceived to have the more comfortable ride, 25 people rode (separately) in the back seat of an expensive European model and also in the back seat of a North American midsize car. Each of the 25 people was asked to rate the ride on the following 5-point scale:

1 = Ride is very uncomfortable.
2 = Ride is quite uncomfortable.
3 = Ride is neither uncomfortable nor comfortable.
4 = Ride is quite comfortable.
5 = Ride is very comfortable.

The results are stored in file Xm17-03 and are shown on page 574. Do these data allow us to conclude at the 5% significance level that the European car is perceived to be more comfortable than the North American car?

	Comfort Ratings	
Respondent	European Car	North American Car
1	4	5
2	2	1
3	5	4
4	3	2
5	2	1
6	5	3
7	1	3
8	4	2
9	4	2
10	2	2
11	3	2
12	4	3
13	2	1
14	3	4
15	2	1
16	4	3
17	2	1
18	4	3
19	5	4
20	3	1
21	4	2
22	3	3
23	3	4
24	5	2
25	2	3

SOLUTION

IDENTIFY

The problem objective is to compare two populations of ordinal data. Because the same 25 people rated both cars, we recognize the experimental design as matched pairs. The sign test is applied, with the following results:

H_0: The two population locations are the same.

H_1: The location of population 1 (European car rating) is to the right of the location of population 2 (North American car rating).

COMPUTE

 MANUALLY

The rejection region is

$$z > z_\alpha = z_{.05} = 1.645$$

To calculate the value of the test statistic, we calculate the paired differences and count the number of positive, negative, and zero differences. The matched pairs differences are

$$-1, 1, 1, 1, 1, 2, -2, 2, 2, 0, 1, 1, 1, -1, 1, 1, 1, 1, 1, 2, 2, 0, -1, 3, -1$$

There are 18 positive, 5 negative, and 2 zero differences. Thus, $x = 18$ and $n = 23$. The value of the test statistic is

$$z = \frac{x - .5n}{.5\sqrt{n}} = \frac{18 - .5(23)}{.5\sqrt{23}} = 2.71$$

Because the test statistic is normally distributed we can calculate the p-value of the test:

$$p\text{-value} = P(Z > 2.71) = .5 - .4966 = .0034$$

EXCEL

	A	B	C
1	**Sign Test**		
2			
3	Difference	*European - American*	
4			
5	Positive Differences	18	
6	Negative Differences	5	
7	Zero Differences	2	
8	z Stat	2.71	
9	P(Z<=z) one-tail	0.0034	
10	z Critical one-tail	1.6449	
11	P(Z<=z) two-tail	0.0068	
12	z Critical two-tail	1.96	

COMMANDS
1. Type or import the data into two adjacent columns.
2. Click **Tools, Data Analysis Plus,** and **Sign Test.**
3. Specify the **Input Range.**
4. Click **Labels** if appropriate.
5. Specify the value of α (**Alpha**) and click **OK.**

COMMANDS FOR
EXAMPLE 17.3
Open file **Xm17-03.**

A1:B26

.05

MINITAB

Sign Test for Median: Diff

```
Sign test of median = 0.00000 versus  >  0.00000

              N  Below  Equal  Above        P    Median
Diff         25      5      2     18   0.0053     1.000
```

Minitab prints the number of differences that are negative (**Below**), the number of zero differences (**Equal**), and the number of positive differences (**Above**). The p-value .0053 is based on the actual distribution of the number of positive differences, which is binomial.

COMMANDS
1. Type or import the data into two columns.
2. Create a new variable, the paired difference. Click **Calc** and **Calculator**. Specify the name of the new variable.
3. Type the mathematical expression.

COMMANDS FOR
EXAMPLE 17.3
Open file **Xm17-03.**

Diff or **C3**
European-American or **C1-C2**

4. Click **Stat, Nonparametrics,** and **1-Sample Sign....**
5. Specify the new variable.   **Diff** or **C3**
6. Select **Test median** and type **0**.
7. Select one of **less than, not equal,** or **greater than.**   **greater than**
   Click **OK**.

INTERPRET

There is relatively strong evidence to indicate that people perceive the European car to provide a more comfortable ride than the North American car. There are, however, two aspects of the experiment that may detract from the conclusion that European cars provide a more comfortable ride. First, did the respondents know in which car they were riding? If so, they may have answered on their preconceived bias that European cars are more expensive and therefore better. If the subjects were blindfolded, we would be more secure in our conclusion. Second, was the order in which each subject rode the two cars varied? If all of the subjects rode the North American car first and the European car second, that may have influenced their ratings. The experiment should have been conducted so that the car each subject rode in first was randomly determined.

CHECKING THE REQUIRED CONDITIONS

As we noted in Section 17.2, the sign test requires that the populations be identical in shape and spread. The histograms (Figures 17.7 and 17.8) confirm that these conditions are satisfied in this example. The other condition is that the sample size exceeds 10.

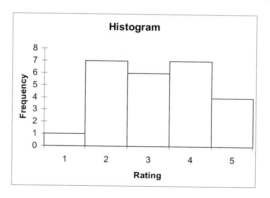

Figure 17.7
Histogram of ratings of European car in Example 17.3

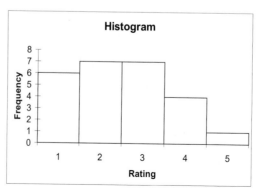

Figure 17.8
Histogram of ratings of North American car in Example 17.3

WILCOXON SIGNED RANK SUM TEST

The Wilcoxon signed rank sum test is used under the following circumstances:

1. The problem objective is to compare two populations.
2. The data are interval but not normally distributed.
3. The samples are matched pairs.

The Wilcoxon signed rank sum test is the nonparametric counterpart of the t test of μ_D. Because the data are interval, we can refer to the Wilcoxon signed rank sum test as a test of μ_D. However, to be consistent with the other nonparametric techniques and to avoid confusion, we will express the hypotheses to be tested in the same way as in Section 17.2.

TEST STATISTIC AND SAMPLING DISTRIBUTION

We begin by computing the paired differences. As we did in the sign test, we eliminate all differences that are equal to 0. Next we rank the absolute values of the nonzero differences where 1 = smallest value and n = largest value, with n = number of nonzero differences. (We average the ranks of tied observations.) The sum of the ranks of the positive differences (denoted T^+) and the sum of the ranks of the negative differences (denoted T^-) are then calculated. We arbitrarily select T^+, which we label T, as our test statistic.

For relatively small samples, which we define as $n \leq 30$, the critical values of T can be determined from Table 9 in Appendix B (reproduced below as Table 17.4). This table lists values of T_L and T_U for sample sizes between 6 and 30. The values of T_L and T_U in part (a) of the table are such that

$$P(T \leq T_L) = P(T \geq T_U) = .025$$

The values of T_L and T_U in part (b) of the table are such that

$$P(T \leq T_L) = P(T \geq T_U) = .05$$

Part (a) is used either in a two-tail test with $\alpha = .05$ or in a one-tail test with $\alpha = .025$. Part (b) is employed either in a two-tail test with $\alpha = .10$ or in a one-tail test with $\alpha = .05$.

Table 17.4   Critical Values for the Wilcoxon Signed Rank Sum Test

n	(a) $\alpha = .025$ One-Tail $\alpha = .05$ Two-Tail		(b) $\alpha = .05$ One-Tail $\alpha = .10$ Two-Tail	
	T_L	T_U	T_L	T_U
6	1	20	2	19
7	2	26	4	24
8	4	32	6	30
9	6	39	8	37
10	8	47	11	44
11	11	55	14	52
12	14	64	17	61
13	17	74	21	70
14	21	84	26	79
15	25	95	30	90
16	30	106	36	100

(continued)

n	T_L	T_U	T_L	T_U
17	35	118	41	112
18	40	131	47	124
19	46	144	54	136
20	52	158	60	150
21	59	172	68	163
22	66	187	75	178
23	73	203	83	193
24	81	219	92	208
25	90	235	101	224
26	98	253	110	241
27	107	271	120	258
28	117	289	130	276
29	127	308	141	294
30	137	328	152	313

For relatively large sample sizes (we will define this to mean $n > 30$), T is approximately normally distributed with mean

$$E(T) = \frac{n(n+1)}{4}$$

and standard deviation

$$\sigma_T = \sqrt{\frac{n(n+1)(2n+1)}{24}}$$

Thus, the standardized test statistic is

$$z = \frac{T - E(T)}{\sigma_T}$$

EXAMPLE 17.4

Traffic congestion on roads and highways costs industry billions of dollars annually as workers struggle to get to and from work. Several suggestions have been made about how to improve this situation, one of which is called *flextime*, which involves allowing workers to determine their own schedules (provided they work a full shift). Such workers will likely choose an arrival and departure time to avoid rush-hour traffic. In a preliminary experiment designed to investigate such a program, the general manager of a large company wanted to compare the times it took workers to travel from their homes to work at 8:00 A.M. with travel time under the flextime program. A random sample of 32 workers was selected. The employees recorded the time (in minutes) it took to arrive at work at 8:00 A.M. on Wednesday of one week. The following week, the same employees arrived at work at times of their own choosing. The travel time on Wednesday of that week was recorded. These results are stored in columns 1 (arrive at 8:00 A.M.) and 2 (flextime) in file Xm17-04 and are listed in the following table. Can we conclude at the 5% significance level that travel times under the flextime program are different from travel times to arrive at work at 8:00 A.M.?

Worker	Travel Time: Arrival at 8:00 A.M.	Travel Time: Flextime Program
1	34	31
2	35	31
3	43	44
4	46	44
5	16	15
6	26	28
7	68	63
8	38	39
9	61	63
10	52	54
11	68	65
12	13	12
13	69	71
14	18	13
15	53	55
16	18	19
17	41	38
18	25	23
19	17	14
20	26	21
21	44	40
22	30	33
23	19	18
24	48	51
25	29	33
26	24	21
27	51	50
28	40	38
29	26	22
30	20	19
31	19	21
32	42	38

SOLUTION

IDENTIFY

The objective is to compare two populations; the data are interval and were produced from a matched pairs experiment. If matched pair differences are normally distributed, we should apply the t test of μ_D. To judge whether the data are normal, we computed the paired differences and drew the histogram (actually Excel did). Figure 17.9 depicts

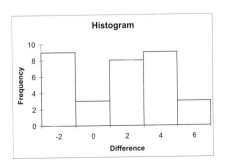

Figure 17.9
Histogram of the differences for Example 17.4

this histogram. Apparently, the normality requirement is not satisfied, indicating that we should employ the Wilcoxon signed rank sum test.

Because we want to know whether the two groups of times differ, we perform a two-tail test whose hypotheses are

H_0: The two population locations are the same.

H_1: The location of population 1 (travel times for current work schedule) is different from the location of population 2 (travel times for flextime program).

COMPUTE

 MANUALLY

For each worker, we compute the difference between travel time with arrival at 8:00 A.M. and travel time under flextime.

Worker	Travel Time: Arrival at 8:00 A.M.	Flextime Program	Difference	|Difference|	Rank	
1	34	31	3	3	21.0	
2	35	31	4	4	27.0	
3	43	44	−1	1		4.5
4	46	44	2	2	13.0	
5	16	15	1	1	4.5	
6	26	28	−2	2		13.0
7	68	63	5	5	31.0	
8	38	39	−1	1		4.5
9	61	63	−2	2		13.0
10	52	54	−2	2		13.0
11	68	65	3	3	21.0	
12	13	12	1	1	4.5	
13	69	71	−2	2		13.0
14	18	13	5	5	31.0	
15	53	55	−2	2		13.0
16	18	19	−1	1		4.5
17	41	38	3	3	21.0	
18	25	23	2	2	13.0	
19	17	14	3	3	21.0	
20	26	21	5	5	31.0	
21	44	40	4	4	27.0	
22	30	33	−3	3		21.0
23	19	18	1	1	4.5	
24	48	51	−3	3		21.0
25	29	33	−4	4		27.0
26	24	21	3	3	21.0	
27	51	50	1	1	4.5	
28	40	38	2	2	13.0	
29	26	22	4	4	27.0	
30	20	19	1	1	4.5	
31	19	21	−2	2		13.0
32	42	38	4	4	27.0	

The differences and the absolute values of the differences are calculated. We rank the absolute differences. (If there were any zero differences, we would eliminate them before ranking the absolute differences.) Ties are resolved by calculating the averages. The ranks of the negative differences are offset to facilitate the summing of the ranks. The rank sums of the positive and negative differences are

$$T^+ = 367.5 \quad \text{and} \quad T^- = 160.5$$

The test statistic is

$$z = \frac{T - E(T)}{\sigma_T}$$

where

$$T = T^+ = 367.5$$
$$E(T) = \frac{n(n + 1)}{4} = \frac{32(33)}{4} = 264$$
$$\sigma_T = \sqrt{\frac{n(n + 1)(2n + 1)}{24}} = \sqrt{\frac{32(33)(65)}{24}} = 53.48$$

Thus,

$$z = \frac{T - E(T)}{\sigma_T} = \frac{367.5 - 264}{53.48} = 1.94$$

The rejection region is

$$z < -z_{\alpha/2} = -z_{.025} = -1.96 \quad \text{or} \quad z > z_{\alpha/2} = z_{.025} = 1.96$$

 EXCEL

	A	B	C
1	**Wilcoxon Signed Rank Sum Test**		
2			
3	Difference	*8:00-Arr - Flextime*	
4			
5	T+	367.5	
6	T-	160.5	
7	Observations (for test)	32	
8	z Stat	1.94	
9	P(Z<=z) one-tail	0.0265	
10	z Critical one-tail	1.6449	
11	P(Z<=z) two-tail	0.0530	
12	z Critical two-tail	1.96	

COMMANDS

1. Type or import the data into two adjacent columns.
2. Click **Tools, Data Analysis Plus,** and **Wilcoxon Signed Rank Sum Test.**
3. Specify the **Input Range.**
4. Click **Labels** if appropriate.
5. Specify the value of α (**Alpha**) and click **OK.**

COMMANDS FOR EXAMPLE 17.4
Open file **Xm17-04.**

A1:B33

.05

MINITAB
Wilcoxon Signed Rank Test: Diff

```
Test of median = 0.000000 versus median not = 0.000000

                 N for    Wilcoxon                 Estimated
           N     Test     Statistic        P        Median
Diff       32     32        367.5        0.054       1.000
```

The output includes the original sample size, the number of nonzero differences (**N for Test**), the value of T^+ (**Wilcoxon Statistic 367.5**), and the *p*-value (**0.054**).

COMMANDS
Follow the same steps as in the sign test. At step 4, click **Stat, Nonparametrics,** and **1-Sample Wilcoxon....**

INTERPRET

There is not enough evidence to infer that flextime commutes are different from the commuting times under the current schedule. This conclusion may be due primarily to the way in which this experiment was performed. All of the drivers recorded their travel time with 8:00 A.M. arrival on the first Wednesday and their flextime travel time on the second Wednesday. If the second day's traffic was heavier than usual, that may account for the conclusion reached. As we pointed out in Example 17.4, the order of schedules should have been randomly determined for each employee. In this way, the effect of varying traffic conditions could have been minimized.

Here is how we recognize when to use the two techniques introduced in this section.

FACTORS THAT IDENTIFY THE SIGN TEST
1. **Problem objective:** Compare two populations.
2. **Data type:** Ordinal
3. **Experimental design:** Matched pairs

FACTORS THAT IDENTIFY THE WILCOXON SIGNED RANK SUM TEST
1. **Problem objective:** Compare two populations.
2. **Data type:** Interval
3. **Distribution of differences:** Nonnormal
4. **Experimental design:** Matched pairs

EXERCISES

17.26 If in a matched pairs experiment, we find 30 negative, 5 zero, and 15 positive differences, perform the sign test to determine whether the two population locations differ. (Use a 5% significance level.)

17.27 Suppose that in a matched pairs experiment, we find 28 positive differences, 7 zero differences, and 41 negative differences. Can we infer at the 10% significance level that the location of population 1 is to the left of the location of population 2?

17.28 A matched pairs experiment yielded these results:
Positive differences: 18
Zero differences: 0

Negative differences: 12
Can we infer at the 5% significance level that the location of population 1 is to the right of the location of population 2?

17.29 Use the sign test on the following data, which are also stored in file Xr17-29, to determine whether the location of population 1 is to the right of the location of population 2. (Use $\alpha = .01$.)

Pair:	1	2	3	4	5	6	7	8	9	10	11	12	13	14	15	16
Sample 1:	5	3	4	2	3	4	3	5	4	3	4	5	4	5	3	2
Sample 2:	3	2	4	3	3	1	3	4	2	5	1	2	2	3	1	2

17.30 Given the following statistics from a matched pairs experiment, perform the Wilcoxon signed rank sum test to determine whether we can infer at the 5% significance level that the two population locations differ.
$$T^+ = 660 \qquad T^- = 880 \qquad n = 55$$

17.31 A matched pairs experiment produced the statistics below. Conduct a Wilcoxon signed rank sum test to determine whether the location of population 1 is to the right of the location of population 2. (Use $\alpha = .01$.)
$$T^+ = 3,457 \qquad T^- = 2,429 \qquad n = 108$$

17.32 Perform the Wilcoxon signed rank sum test for the following matched pairs to determine whether the two population locations differ. (Use $\alpha = .10$.)

Pair:	1	2	3	4	5	6
Sample 1:	9	12	13	8	7	10
Sample 2:	5	10	11	9	3	9

17.33 Perform the Wilcoxon signed rank sum test to determine whether the location of population 1 differs from the location of population 2 given the data below (also stored in file Xr17-33). (Use $\alpha = .05$.)

Pair:	1	2	3	4	5	6	7	8	9	10	11	12
Sample 1:	18.2	14.1	24.5	11.9	9.5	12.1	10.9	16.7	19.6	8.4	21.7	23.4
Sample 2:	18.2	14.1	23.6	12.1	9.5	11.3	9.7	17.6	19.4	8.1	21.9	21.6

Exercises 17.34 to 17.57 require the use of a computer and software. Use a 5% significance level unless specified otherwise.

Developing an Understanding of Statistical Concepts

17.34 In a taste test of a new beer, 100 people rated the new beer and the leading brand on the market. The possible ratings were Poor, Fair, Good, Very good, and Excellent. The responses for the new beer and the leading beer were stored in file Xr17-34 using a 1–2–3–4–5 coding system. Can we infer that the new beer is more highly rated than the leading brand?

17.35 Refer to Exercise 17.34. The responses were recoded so that 3 = Poor, 8 = Fair, 22 = Good, 37 = Very good, and 55 = Excellent. These data are stored in file Xr17-34. Can we infer that the new beer is less highly rated than the leading brand?

17.36 Compare your answers in Exercises 17.34 and 17.35. Why are they identical?

17.37 A random sample of 50 people was asked to rate two brands of ice cream using the following responses:

  Delicious

  OK

  Not bad

  Terrible

The responses were converted to codes 4, 3, 2, and 1, respectively, and stored in file Xr17-37. Can we infer that brand A is preferred?

17.38 Refer to Exercise 17.37. The responses were recoded using the values 28, 25, 16, and 3. These data are stored in file Xr17-38. Can we infer that brand A is preferred?

17.39 Compare your answers for Exercises 17.37 and 17.38. Are they identical? Explain why.

17.40 Refer to Example 17.3. Suppose that the responses have been recoded in the following way:

  6 = Ride is very uncomfortable.

  24 = Ride is quite uncomfortable.

  28 = Ride is neither uncomfortable nor comfortable.

  53 = Ride is quite comfortable.

  95 = Ride is very comfortable.

The results are stored in file Xr17-40. Do these data allow us to conclude that the European car is perceived to be more comfortable than the North American car?

17.41 Compare your answer for Exercise 17.40 with that obtained in Example 17.3. Explain why the results are identical.

17.42 Data from a matched pairs experiment were stored in file Xr17-42. Use the sign test to determine whether the population locations differ.

17.43 Repeat Exercise 17.42, using the Wilcoxon signed rank sum test.

17.44 Compare Exercises 17.42 and 17.43. Why do they differ?

17.45 Data from a matched pairs experiment were stored in file Xr17-45. Use the sign test to determine whether the population locations differ.

17.46 Repeat Exercise 17.45, using the Wilcoxon signed rank sum test.

17.47 Why do the results of Exercises 17.45 and 17.46 differ?

Applications

Exercises 17.48 to 17.57 may be solved manually. See Appendix A for the sample statistics.

17.48 Research scientists at a pharmaceutical company have recently developed a new nonprescription sleeping pill. They decide to test its effectiveness by measuring the time it takes for people to fall asleep after taking the pill. Preliminary analysis indicates that the time to fall asleep varies considerably from one person to another. Consequently, they organize the experiment in the following way. A random sample of 100 volunteers who regularly suffer from insomnia is chosen. Each person is given one pill containing the newly developed drug and one placebo. (A placebo is a pill that contains absolutely no medication.) Participants are told to take one pill one night and the second pill one night a week later. (They do not know whether the pill they are taking is the placebo or the new drug, and the order of use is random.) Each participant is fitted with a device that measures the time until sleep occurs. The data are stored in file Xr17-48. Can we conclude that the new drug is effective? (This exercise is identical to Exercise 13.70 except for the data.)

17.49 Suppose the housework study referred to in Exercise 17.19 was repeated with some changes. In the revised experiment, 60 women were asked last year and again this year how many hours of housework they perform weekly. The results are stored in file Xr17-49. Can we conclude at the 1% significance level that women as a group are doing less housework now than 5 years ago?

17.50 At the height of the energy shortage during the 1970s, governments were actively seeking ways to persuade consumers to reduce their energy consumption. Among other efforts undertaken, several advertising campaigns were launched. To provide input on how to design effective advertising messages, a poll was taken in which people were asked how concerned they were about shortages of gasoline and electricity. There were four possible responses to the questions:

> Not concerned at all (1)
> Not too concerned (2)
> Somewhat concerned (3)
> Very concerned (4)

A poll of 150 individuals produced the results stored in file Xr17-50. Do these data provide enough evidence to allow us to infer that concern about a gasoline shortage exceeded concern about an electricity shortage?

17.51 A locksmith is in the process of selecting a new key-cutting machine. If there is a difference in key-cutting speed between the two machines under consideration, he will purchase the faster one. If there is no difference, he will purchase the cheaper machine. The times (in seconds) required to cut each of the 24 most common types of keys are stored in file Xr17-51. What should he do?

17.52 A large sporting-goods store located in Florida is planning a renovation that will result in an increase in the floor space for one department. The manager of the store has narrowed her choice about which department's floor space to increase to two possibilities: the tennis equipment department or the swimming accessories department. The manager would like to enlarge the tennis equipment department because she believes that this department improves the overall image of the store. She decides, however, that if the swimming accessories department can be shown to have higher gross sales, she will choose that department. She has collected each of the two departments' weekly gross sales data for the past 6 months; these are stored in file Xr17-52. Which department should be enlarged?

17.53 Does the brand name of an ice cream affect consumers' perceptions of it? The marketing manager of a major dairy pondered this question. She decided to ask 60 randomly selected people to taste the same flavor of ice cream in two different dishes. The dishes contained exactly the same ice cream but were labeled differently. One was given a name that suggested that its maker was European and sophisticated; the other was given a name that implied that the product was domestic and inexpensive. The tasters were asked to rate each ice cream on a 5-point scale, where 1 = poor, 2 = fair, 3 = good, 4 = very good, 5 = excellent. The responses are stored in file Xr17-53. Do the results allow the manager to conclude at the 10% significance level that the European brand is preferred?

17.54 Do children feel less pain than adults? That question was addressed by nursing professors at the Universities of Alberta and Saskatchewan. Suppose that in a preliminary study, 50 8-year-old children and their mothers were subjected to moderately painful pressure on their hands. Each was asked to rate the level of pain as very severe (4), severe (3), moderate (2), or weak (1). The data were stored in file Xr17-54 using the codes in parentheses. Can we conclude at the 1% significance level that children feel less pain than adults?

17.55 In a study to determine whether gender affects salary offers for graduating MBA students, 25 pairs of students were selected. Each pair consisted of a male and a female student who had almost identical grade-point averages, courses taken, ages, and previous work experience. The highest salary offered to each student upon graduation was recorded and stored in file Xr17-55. Is there sufficient evidence to allow us to conclude that the salary offers differ between men and women? (This exercise is identical to Exercise 13.128 except for the data.)

17.56 Admissions officers at universities and colleges face the problem of comparing grades achieved at different high schools. As a step toward developing a more informed interpretation of such grades, an admissions officer at a large state university conducts the following experiment. The records of 100 students from the same local high school who just completed their first year at the university were selected. Each of these students was paired (according to average grade in the last year of high school) with a student from another local high school who also just completed the first year at the university. For each matched pair, the average letter grades (4 = A, 3 = B, 2 = C, 1 = D, or 0 = F) in the first year of university study were recorded. The results are stored in file Xr17-56. Do these results allow us to conclude that, in comparing two students with the same high-school average (one from high school 1 and the other from high school 2), preference in admissions should be given to the student from high school 1?

17.57 Some movie studios believe that by adding sexually explicit scenes to the home video version of a movie they can increase the movie's appeal and profitability (*Wall Street Journal*, 14 October 1988). A studio executive decided to test this belief. She organized a study that involved 40 movies that were rated PG-13. Versions of each movie were created by adding scenes that changed the rating to R. The two versions of the movies were then made available to rental shops. For each of the 40 pairs of movies, the total number of rentals in one major city during a 1-week period was recorded and stored in file Xr17-57. Do these data provide enough evidence to support the belief?

17.4 KRUSKAL–WALLIS TEST

In this section we introduce the first of two statistical procedures designed to compare two or more populations. The *Kruskal–Wallis test* is applied to problems with the following characteristics:

1. The problem objective is to compare two or more populations.

2. The data are either ordinal or interval but nonnormal.

3. The samples are independent.

When the data are interval and normal, we used the analysis of variance F test presented in Chapter 15 to determine whether differences exist. When the data are not normal, we will treat the data as if they were ordinal and employ the Kruskal–Wallis test.

The null and alternative hypotheses for this test are similar to those we specified in the analysis of variance. Because the data are ordinal or are treated as ordinal, however, we test population locations instead of population means. In all applications of the Kruskal–Wallis test, the null and alternative hypotheses are

H_0: The locations of all k populations are the same.
H_1: At least two population locations differ.

Here, k represents the number of populations to be compared.

TEST STATISTIC

The test statistic is calculated in a way that closely resembles the way in which the Wilcoxon rank sum test was calculated. The first step is to rank all the observations. As before, 1 = smallest observation and n = largest observation, where $n = n_1 + n_2 + \cdots + n_k$. In case of ties, average the ranks.

If the null hypothesis is true, the ranks should be evenly distributed among the k samples. The degree to which this is true is judged by calculating the rank sums (labeled $T_1, T_2, \ldots, T_k$). The last step is to calculate the test statistic, which is denoted H.

> ### TEST STATISTIC FOR KRUSKAL–WALLIS TEST
>
> $$H = \left[\frac{12}{n(n + 1)} \sum_{j=1}^{k} \frac{T_j^2}{n_j} \right] - 3(n + 1)$$

Although it is impossible to see from this formula, if the rank sums are similar, the test statistic will be small. As a result, a small value of H supports the null hypothesis. Conversely, if considerable differences exist between the rank sums, the test statistic will be large. To judge the value of H, we need to know its sampling distribution.

SAMPLING DISTRIBUTION OF THE TEST STATISTIC

The distribution of the test statistic can be derived in the same way we derived the sampling distribution of the test statistic in the Wilcoxon rank sum test. That is, we can list all possible combinations of ranks and their probabilities to yield the sampling distribution. A table of critical values can then be determined. However, this is necessary only for small sample sizes. For sample sizes greater than or equal to 5, the test statistic H is approximately chi-squared distributed with $k - 1$ degrees of freedom. Recall that we introduced the chi-squared distribution in Section 8.5.

REJECTION REGION AND *p*-VALUE

As we noted above, large values of H are associated with different population locations. Consequently, we want to reject the null hypothesis if H is sufficiently large. Thus, the rejection region is

$$H > \chi^2_{\alpha, k-1}$$

and the *p*-value is

$$P(\chi^2 > H)$$

Figure 17.10 describes this sampling distribution and the *p*-value.

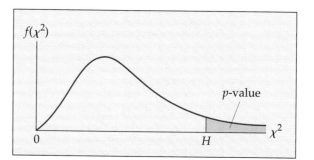

Figure 17.10
Sampling distribution of *H*

EXAMPLE 17.5

The management of fast-food restaurants is extremely interested in knowing how their customers rate the quality of food and service and the cleanliness of the restaurants. Customers are given the opportunity to fill out customer comment cards. Suppose that one franchise wanted to compare how customers rate the three shifts (4:00 P.M. to midnight, midnight to 8:00 A.M., and 8:00 A.M. to 4:00 P.M.). In a preliminary study, 10 customer cards were randomly selected from each shift. The responses to the question concerning speed of service were stored in columns 1 to 3, respectively, in file Xm17-05 (4 = excellent, 3 = good, 2 = fair, and 1 = poor) and are listed here. Do these data provide sufficient evidence at the 5% significance level to indicate whether customers perceive the speed of service to be different between the three shifts?

4:00 P.M. to Midnight	Midnight to 8:00 A.M.	8:00 A.M. to 4:00 P.M.
4	3	3
4	4	1
3	2	3
4	2	2
3	3	1
3	4	3
3	3	4
3	3	2
2	2	4
3	3	1

SOLUTION

IDENTIFY

The problem objective is to compare three populations of ordinal data (the ratings of the three shifts), and the samples are independent. These factors are sufficient to determine the use of the Kruskal–Wallis test. The null and alternative hypotheses are

H_0: The locations of all three populations are the same.

H_1: At least two population locations differ.

COMPUTE

 MANUALLY

The data are ranked in the same way as we ranked the data in the Wilcoxon rank sum test. Ties are resolved by assigning the average rank. When all the data have been ranked, the rank sums are computed.

Sample 1	Rank	Sample 2	Rank	Sample 3	Rank
4	27.0	3	16.5	3	16.5
4	27.0	4	27.0	1	2.0
3	16.5	2	6.5	3	16.5
4	27.0	2	6.5	2	6.5
3	16.5	3	16.5	1	2.0
3	16.5	4	27.0	3	16.5
3	16.5	3	16.5	4	27.0
3	16.5	3	16.5	2	6.5
2	6.5	2	6.5	4	27.0
3	16.5	3	16.5	1	2.0
	$T_1 = 186.5$		$T_2 = 156.0$		$T_3 = 122.5$

The value of the test statistic is

$$H = \left[\frac{12}{n(n+1)} \sum_{j=1}^{k} \frac{T_j^2}{n_j} \right] - 3(n+1)$$

$$= \frac{12}{n(n+1)} \left(\frac{T_1^2}{n_1} + \frac{T_2^2}{n_2} + \frac{T_3^2}{n_3} \right) - 3(n+1)$$

$$= \frac{12}{30(30+1)} \left(\frac{186.5^2}{10} + \frac{156^2}{10} + \frac{122.5^2}{10} \right) - 3(30+1)$$

$$= 2.64$$

The rejection region is

$$H > \chi^2_{\alpha, k-1} = \chi^2_{.05, 2} = 5.99147$$

EXCEL

	A	B	C
1	**Kruskal-Wallis Test**		
2			
3	Group	Rank Sum	Observations
4	*4:00-mid*	186.5	10
5	*Mid-8:00*	156	10
6	*8:00-4:00*	122.5	10
7			
8	H Stat		2.6445
9	df		2
10	p-value		0.2665
11	chi-squared Critical		5.9915

COMMANDS

1. Type or import the data into k adjacent columns.
2. Click **Tools, Data Analysis Plus,** and **Kruskal–Wallis Test**.
3. Specify the **Input Range**.
4. Click **Labels**, if applicable.
5. Specify the value of α (**Alpha**) and click **OK**.

COMMANDS FOR EXAMPLE 17.5

Open file **Xm17-05**.

A1:C11

.05

MINITAB

Kruskal-Wallis Test: Service versus Shift

```
Kruskal-Wallis Test on Service

Shift      N    Median    Ave Rank         Z
1         10     3.000        18.7      1.39
2         10     3.000        15.6      0.04
3         10     2.500        12.3     -1.43
Overall   30                  15.5

H = 2.64   DF = 2   P = 0.267
H = 3.01   DF = 2   P = 0.222  (adjusted for ties)
```

COMMANDS

1. Type or import the data. The data must be stacked.

COMMANDS FOR EXAMPLE 17.5

Open file **Xm17-05**. The data are stacked in column 4, codes in column 5.

2. Click **Stat, Nonparametrics,** and **Kruskal-Wallis....**
3. Select the name of the **Response** variable.
4. Select the name of **Factor** variable. Click **OK**.

Service or **C4**

Shift or **C5**

INTERPRET

There is not enough evidence to infer that a difference in speed of service exists between the three shifts. Management should assume that all three of the shifts are equally rated, and any action to improve service should be applied to all three shifts. Management should also bear in mind that the data were generated from a self-selected sample. (See the story of the *Literary Digest* presented in Chapter 5.)

KRUSKAL–WALLIS TEST AND THE WILCOXON RANK SUM TEST

The Kruskal–Wallis test can be used to test for a difference between two populations only. It will produce the same outcome as the two-tail Wilcoxon rank sum test. However, the Kruskal–Wallis test can determine only whether a difference exists. To determine whether one population is larger than another, we must apply the Wilcoxon rank sum test.

We complete this section with a review of how to recognize the use of the Kruskal–Wallis test.

FACTORS THAT IDENTIFY THE KRUSKAL–WALLIS TEST
1. **Problem objective:** Compare two or more populations
2. **Data type:** Ordinal or interval but not normal
3. **Experimental design:** Independent samples

EXERCISES

17.58 Conduct the Kruskal–Wallis test on the statistics below. Use a 5% significance level.

$T_1 = 984$ $n_1 = 23$
$T_2 = 1,502$ $n_2 = 36$
$T_3 = 1,430$ $n_3 = 29$

17.59 From the following statistics, test (with $\alpha = .01$) to determine whether the population locations differ.

$T_1 = 1,207$ $n_1 = 25$
$T_2 = 1,088$ $n_2 = 25$
$T_3 = 1,310$ $n_3 = 25$
$T_4 = 1,445$ $n_4 = 25$

17.60 Use the following statistics to determine whether there is enough statistical evidence at the 10% significance level to infer that the population locations differ.

$T_1 = 3,741$ $n_1 = 47$
$T_2 = 1,610$ $n_2 = 29$
$T_3 = 4,945$ $n_3 = 67$

17.61 Use the Kruskal–Wallis test on the following data to determine whether the population locations differ. (Use $\alpha = .05$.)

Sample 1: 27   33   18   29   41   52   75
Sample 2: 37   12   17   22   30
Sample 3: 19   12   33   41   28   18

17.62 Using the Kruskal–Wallis test, determine whether there is enough evidence provided by the accompanying data to enable us to infer that at least two population locations differ. (Use $\alpha = .05$.)

Sample 1: 25   15   20   22   23
Sample 2: 19   21   23   22   28
Sample 3: 27   25   22   29   28

17.63 Apply the Kruskal–Wallis test to determine whether there is enough evidence at the 5% significance level to infer that at least two population locations differ, given the following data. (The data are stored in file Xr17-63.)

Sample 1: 39   8   7   21   14   40   42   15
Sample 2: 31   43   50   57   54   46   26   29
Sample 3: 13   58   16   26   44   17   15   19
Sample 4: 50   51   55   28   57   37   41   37

Exercises 17.64 to 17.76 require the use of a computer and software. Use a 5% significance level.

Developing an Understanding of Statistical Concepts

17.64 Random samples of 50 people each were asked to rate four different computer printers in terms of their ease of use. The responses are

Very easy to use
Easy to use
Difficult to use
Very difficult to use

The responses were coded using a 4–3–2–1 system and stored in file Xr17-64. Do these data yield enough evidence to infer that differences in ratings exist among the four printers?

17.65 Refer to Exercise 17.64. The responses were recoded using a 25–22–5–2 system. Do these data yield enough evidence to infer that differences in ratings exist among the four printers?

17.66 Compare your answers in Exercises 17.64 and 17.65. Why are they identical?

17.67 Refer to Example 17.5. The responses were recoded using a 100–90–55–25 system and stored in file Xr17-67. Do these data yield enough evidence to infer that differences in ratings exist among the three shifts?

17.68 Why are the answers to Example 17.5 and Exercise 17.67 identical?

Applications

Exercises 17.69 to 17.76 may be solved manually. See Appendix A for the sample statistics.

17.69 In an effort to determine whether differences exist among three methods of teaching statistics, a professor of business taught his course differently in each of three large sections. In the first section, he taught by lecturing; in the second, he taught by the case method; and in the third, he used a computer software package extensively. At the end of the semester, each student was asked to evaluate the course on a 7-point scale, where 1 = atrocious, 2 = poor, 3 = fair, 4 = average, 5 = good, 6 = very good, and 7 = excellent. From each section, the professor chose 25 evaluations at random. The data are in file Xr17-69. Is there evidence that differences in student satisfaction exist with respect to at least two of the three teaching methods?

17.70 Applicants to MBA programs must write the Graduate Management Admission Test (GMAT). There are several companies that offer assistance in preparing for the test. To determine whether they work, and if so, which one is best, an experiment was conducted. Several hundred MBA applicants were surveyed and asked to report their GMAT score and which, if any, GMAT preparation course they took. The responses are course A, course B, course C, or no preparatory course. The scores are stored in file Xr17-70. Do these data allow us to infer that there are differences among the four groups of GMAT scores?

17.71 Because there are no national or regional standards, it is difficult for university admission committees to compare graduates of different high schools. University administrators have noted that an 80% average at a high school with low standards may be equivalent to a 70% average at another school with higher standards of grading. In an effort to more equitably compare applications, a pilot study was initiated. Random samples of students who were admitted the previous year from four local high schools were drawn. All of the students entered the business program with averages between 70% and 80%. Their average grades in the first year at the university were computed and stored in file Xr17-71. Can the university admissions officer conclude that there are differences in grading standards between the four high schools? (This exercise is identical to Exercise 15.15 except for the data.)

17.72 A consumer testing service is comparing the effectiveness of four different brands of drain cleaner. The experiment consists of using each product on 50 different clogged sinks and measuring the amount of time that elapsed until each drain became unclogged. The recorded times, measured in minutes, are stored in file Xr17-72.

    a Which techniques should be considered as possible procedures to apply to determine whether differences exist? What are the required conditions? How do you decide?

    b If a statistical analysis has shown that the times are not normally distributed, can the service conclude that differences exist between the speeds at which the four brands perform?

17.73 During the last presidential campaign, the Gallup organization surveyed a random sample of 30 registered Democrats in January, another 30 in February, and yet another 30 in March. All 90 Democrats were asked to "rate the chances of the Democrats winning the presidential race in your state." The responses and their numerical codes were excellent (4), good (3), fair (2), and poor (1). The results of the surveys are stored in file Xr17-73. Do these data allow us to infer that Democrats' ratings of their chances of winning the presidency changed over the 3-month period?

17.74 It is common practice in the advertising business to create several different advertisements and then ask a random sample of potential customers to rate the ads on several different dimensions. Suppose that an advertising firm developed four different ads for a new breakfast cereal and asked a sample of 400 shoppers to rate the believability of the advertisements. One hundred people viewed ad 1, another 100 viewed ad 2, another 100 saw ad 3, and another 100 saw ad 4. The ratings were very believable (4), quite believable (3), somewhat believable (2), and not believable at all (1). The responses are stored in file Xr17-74. Can the firm's management conclude that differences exist in believability between the four ads?

17.75 Do university students become more supportive of their varsity teams as they progress through their 4-year stint? To help answer this question, a sample of students was drawn. Each was asked their class standing (freshman, sophomore, junior, or senior) and to what extent they supported the university's football team, the Hawks. The responses to the latter question are

    Wildly fanatic
    Support the Hawks wholeheartedly
    Support the Hawks, but not that enthusiastically
    Who are the Hawks?

The responses were coded using a 4–3–2–1 numbering system. The data were stored in file Xr17-75. Can we conclude that the four levels of students differ in their support for the Hawks?

17.76 In anticipation of buying a new scanner, a student turned to a Web site that reported the results of surveys of users of the different scanners. A sample of 133 responses was listed, showing the ease of use of five different brands. The survey responses were

    Very easy
    Easy
    Not easy
    Difficult
    Very difficult

The responses were assigned numbers from 1 to 5 and stored in file Xr17-76. Can we infer that there are differences in perceived ease of use among the five brands of scanners?

17.5 FRIEDMAN TEST

This section introduces another statistical technique whose objective is to compare two or more populations of ordinal or interval data. In Section 15.4, we presented the randomized block experimental design of the analysis of variance. In this section, we present its nonparametric counterpart. The *Friedman test* is applied to problems with the following characteristics:

1. The problem objective is to compare two or more populations.

2. The data are either ordinal or interval but not normal.

3. The data are generated from a randomized block experiment.

The null and alternative hypotheses are identical to the ones tested in the Kruskal-Wallis test:

H_0: The locations of all k populations are the same.

H_1: At least two population locations differ.

TEST STATISTIC

To calculate the test statistic, we first rank each observation within each block, where 1 = smallest observation and k = largest observation, averaging the ranks of ties. Then we compute the rank sums, which we label $T_1, T_2, \ldots, T_k$. The test statistic is defined as follows. (Recall that b = number of blocks.)

> **TEST STATISTIC FOR THE FRIEDMAN TEST**
>
> $$F_r = \left[\frac{12}{b(k)(k+1)} \sum_{j=1}^{k} T_j^2 \right] - 3b(k+1)$$

SAMPLING DISTRIBUTION OF THE TEST STATISTIC

The test statistic is approximately chi-squared distributed with $k - 1$ degrees of freedom, provided that either k or b is greater than or equal to 5. As was the case with the Kruskal–Wallis test, we reject the null hypothesis when the test statistic is large. Hence, the rejection region is

$$F_r > \chi^2_{\alpha, k-1}$$

and the p-value is

$$P(\chi^2 > F_r)$$

Figure 17.11 depicts the sampling distribution and p-value.

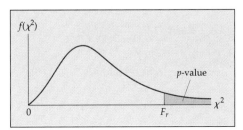

Figure 17.11
Sampling distribution of F_r

This test, like all the other nonparametric tests, requires that the populations being compared are identical in shape and spread.

EXAMPLE 17.6

The personnel manager of a national accounting firm has been receiving complaints from senior managers about the quality of recent hirings. All new accountants are hired through a process whereby four managers interview the candidate and rate her or him on several dimensions, including academic credentials, previous work experience, and personal suitability. Each manager then summarizes the results and produces an evaluation of the candidate. There are five possibilities:

1. The candidate is in the top 5% of applicants.
2. The candidate is in the top 10% of applicants, but not in the top 5%.
3. The candidate is in the top 25% of applicants, but not in the top 10%.
4. The candidate is in the top 50% of applicants, but not in the top 25%.
5. The candidate is in the bottom 50% of applicants.

The evaluations are then combined in making the final decision. The personnel manager believes that the quality problem is caused by the evaluation system. However, she needs to know whether there is general agreement or disagreement between the interviewing managers in their evaluations. To test for differences between the managers, she takes a random sample of the evaluations of eight applicants. The results are shown below and are stored in file Xm17-06. What conclusions can the personnel manager draw from these data? Employ a 5% significance level.

	Manager			
Applicant	1	2	3	4
1	2	1	2	2
2	4	2	3	2
3	2	2	2	3
4	3	1	3	2
5	3	2	3	5
6	2	2	3	4
7	4	1	5	5
8	3	2	5	3

SOLUTION

IDENTIFY

The problem objective is to compare the four populations of managers' evaluations, which we can see are ordinal data. This experiment is identified as a randomized block design because the eight applicants were evaluated by all four managers. (The treatments are the managers, and the blocks are the applicants.) The appropriate statistical technique is the Friedman test. The null and alternative hypotheses are as follows:

H_0: The locations of all four populations are the same.
H_1: At least two population locations differ.

COMPUTE

 MANUALLY

The rejection region is

$$F_r > \chi^2_{\alpha, k-1} = \chi^2_{.05, 3} = 7.81473$$

The following table demonstrates how the ranks are assigned and the rank sums calculated. Notice how the ranks are assigned by moving across the rows (blocks) and the rank sums computed by adding down the columns (treatments).

			Manager				
Applicant	*1 (Rank)*		*2 (Rank)*		*3 (Rank)*		*4 (Rank)*
1	2	(3)	1	(1)	2	(3)	2 (3)
2	4	(4)	2	(1.5)	3	(3)	2 (1.5)
3	2	(2)	2	(2)	2	(2)	3 (4)
4	3	(3.5)	1	(1)	3	(3.5)	2 (2)
5	3	(2.5)	2	(1)	3	(2.5)	5 (4)
6	2	(1.5)	2	(1.5)	3	(3)	4 (4)
7	4	(2)	1	(1)	5	(3.5)	5 (3.5)
8	3	(2.5)	2	(1)	5	(4)	3 (2.5)
	$T_1 = 21$		$T_2 = 10$		$T_3 = 24.5$		$T_4 = 24.5$

The value of the test statistic is

$$F_r = \left[\frac{12}{b(k)(k+1)} \sum_{j=1}^{k} T_j^2 \right] - 3b(k+1)$$

$$= \left[\frac{12}{(8)(4)(5)}(21^2 + 10^2 + 24.5^2 + 24.5^2) \right] - 3(8)(5)$$

$$= 10.61$$

 EXCEL

	A	B	C
1	Friedman Test		
2			
3	Group		Rank Sum
4	*Manager1*		21
5	*Manager2*		10
6	*Manager3*		24.5
7	*Manager4*		24.5
8			
9	Fr Stat		10.613
10	df		3
11	p-value		0.014
12	chi-squared Critical		7.8147

COMMANDS

1. Type or import the data into *k* adjacent columns.
2. Click **Tools, Data Analysis Plus**, and **Friedman Test**.
3. Specify the **Input Range**.
4. Click **Labels** if applicable.
5. Specify the value of α (**Alpha**) and click **OK**.

COMMANDS FOR
EXAMPLE 17.6
Open file **Xm17-06**.

A1:D9

.05

MINITAB

Friedman Test: Rating versus Manager, Applicant

```
Friedman test for Rating by Manager blocked by Applican

S = 10.61  DF = 3  P = 0.014
S = 12.86  DF = 3  P = 0.005 (adjusted for ties)

                    Est     Sum of
Manager      N    Median    Ranks
1            8    2.8750     21.0
2            8    2.0000     10.0
3            8    3.0000     24.5
4            8    3.1250     24.5

Grand median  =   2.7500
```

COMMANDS

1. Type or import the data in stacked format. The responses are stored in one column, the treatment codes are stored in another column, and the block codes are stored in a third column.

2. Click **Stat**, **Nonparametrics**, and **Friedman…**.
3. Select the **Response** variable.
4. Select the **Treatment** variable.
5. Select the **Blocks** variable. Click **OK**.

COMMANDS FOR EXAMPLE 17.6

Open file **Xm17-06**. Stack all observations in column 5, put the subscripts in column 6, and type the block codes into column 7.

Ratings or **C5**
Manager or **C6**
Applicant or **C7**

INTERPRET

There appears to be sufficient evidence to indicate that the managers' evaluations differ. The personnel manager should attempt to determine why the evaluations differ. Is there a problem with the way in which the assessment is conducted, or are some managers using different criteria? If it is the latter, those managers may need additional training.

THE FRIEDMAN TEST AND THE SIGN TEST

The relationship between the Friedman and sign tests is the same as the relationship between the Kruskal–Wallis and Wilcoxon rank sum tests. That is, we can use the Friedman test to determine whether two populations differ. The conclusion will be the same as that produced from the sign test. However, we can use the Friedman test only to determine whether a difference exists. If we want to determine whether one population is larger than another, we must use the sign test.

Here is a list of the factors that tell us when to use the Friedman test.

FACTORS THAT IDENTIFY THE FRIEDMAN TEST
1. **Problem objective:** Compare two or more populations.
2. **Data type:** Ordinal or interval but not normal
3. **Experimental design:** Blocked samples

EXERCISES

17.77 Apply the Friedman test to the accompanying table of data to determine whether we can conclude that at least two population locations differ. (Use $\alpha = .10$.)

Block	Treatment 1	2	3	4
1	10	12	15	9
2	8	10	11	6
3	13	14	16	11
4	9	9	12	13
5	7	8	14	10

17.78 The following data were generated from a blocked experiment. Conduct a Friedman test to determine whether at least two population locations differ. (Use $\alpha = .05$.)

Block	Treatment 1	2	3
1	7.3	6.9	8.4
2	8.2	7.0	7.3
3	5.7	6.0	8.1
4	6.1	6.5	9.1
5	5.9	6.1	8.0

17.79 Ten judges were asked to test the sensory quality of four different brands of orange juice. The judges assigned scores using a 5-point scale where 1 = bad, 2 = poor, 3 = average, 4 = good, and 5 = excellent. The results are shown here and stored in file Xr17-79. Can we conclude at the 5% significance level that there are differences in sensory quality between the four brands of orange juice?

Judge	Orange Juice Brand 1	2	3	4
1	3	5	4	3
2	2	3	5	4
3	4	4	3	4
4	3	4	5	2
5	2	4	4	3
6	4	5	5	3
7	3	3	4	4
8	2	3	3	3
9	4	3	5	4
10	2	4	5	3

17.80 The manager of a personnel company is in the process of examining her company's advertising programs. Currently, the company advertises in each of the three local newspapers for a wide variety of positions, including computer programmers, secretaries, and receptionists. The manager has decided that only one newspaper will be used if it can be determined that there are differences between the newspapers in the number of inquiries generated. The following experiment was performed. For 1 week (6 days), six different jobs were advertised in each of the three newspapers. The number of inquiries was counted, and the results appear in the accompanying table.

Job Advertised	Newspaper 1	2	3
Receptionist	14	17	12
Systems analyst	8	9	6
Junior secretary	25	20	23
Computer programmer	12	15	10
Legal secretary	7	10	5
Office manager	5	9	4

a What techniques should be considered to apply in reaching a decision? What are the required conditions? How do we determine whether the conditions are satisfied?

b Assuming that the data are not normally distributed, can we conclude at the 5% significance level that differences exist between the newspapers' abilities to attract potential employees?

Exercises 17.81 to 17.89 require the use of a computer and software. **Use a 5% significance level.**

Developing an Understanding of Statistical Concepts

17.81 A random sample of 30 people was asked to rate each of four different premium brands of coffee. The ratings are

Excellent

Good

Fair

Poor

The responses were assigned numbers 1 through 4, respectively, and stored in file Xr17-81. Can we infer that differences exist between the ratings of the four brands of coffee?

17.82 Refer to Exercise 17.81. Suppose that the codes were 12, 31, 66, and 72, respectively. The data are stored in file Xr17-82. Can we infer that differences exist between the ratings of the four brands of coffee?

17.83 Compare your answers in Exercises 17.81 and 17.82. Why are they identical?

17.84 Refer to Example 17.6. Suppose that the responses were recoded so that the numbers equaled the midpoint of the range of percentiles. That is,

97.5 = The candidate is in the top 5% of applicants.

92.5 = The candidate is in the top 10% of applicants, but not in the top 5%.

82.5 = The candidate is in the top 25% of applicants, but not in the top 10%.

62.5 = The candidate is in the top 50% of applicants, but not in the top 25%.

25 = The candidate is in the bottom 50% of applicants.

The data are stored in file Xr17-84. Can we conclude that differences exist between the ratings assigned by the four managers?

17.85 Compare your answer in Exercise 17.84 with the one obtained in Example 17.6. Are they the same? Explain why.

Applications

Exercises 17.86 to 17.89 may be solved manually. See Appendix A for the sample statistics.

17.86 A well-known soft-drink manufacturer has used the same secret recipe for its product since its introduction over 100 years ago. In response to a decreasing market share, however, the president of the company is contemplating changing the recipe. He has developed two alternative recipes. In a preliminary study, he asked 20 people to taste the original recipe and the two new recipes. He asked each to evaluate the taste of the product on a 5-point scale, where 1 = awful, 2 = poor, 3 = fair, 4 = good, and 5 = wonderful. These data are stored in file Xr17-86. The president decides that unless significant differences exist between evaluations of the products, he will not make any changes. Can we conclude that there are differences in the ratings of the three recipes?

17.87 The manager of a chain of electronic-products retailers is trying to decide on a location for its newest store. After a thorough analysis, the choice has been narrowed to three possibilities. An important factor in the decision is the number of people passing each location. The number of people passing each location per day was counted during 30 days. The data are stored in file Xr17-87.
   a Which techniques should be considered to determine whether the locations differ? What are the required conditions? How do you select a technique?
   b Can management conclude that there are differences in the numbers of people passing the three locations if the number of people passing each location is not normally distributed?

17.88 In recent years, lack of confidence in the Postal Service has led many companies to send all of their correspondence by private courier. A large company is in the process of selecting one of three possible couriers to act as its sole delivery method. To help in making the decision, an experiment was performed whereby letters were sent using each of the three couriers at 12 different times of the day to a delivery point across town. The number of minutes required for delivery was recorded and stored in file Xr17-88. Can we conclude that there are differences in delivery times between the three couriers? (This exercise is identical to Exercise 15.35 except for the data.)

17.89 Many North Americans suffer from high levels of cholesterol, which can lead to heart attacks. For those with very high levels (over 280), doctors prescribe drugs to reduce cholesterol levels. A pharmaceutical company has recently developed four such drugs. To determine whether any differences exist in their benefits, an experiment was organized. The company selected 25 groups of three men, each of whom had levels in excess of 280. In each group, the men were matched according to age and weight. The drugs were administered over a two-month period, and the reduction in cholesterol was recorded. The data are stored in file Xr17-89. Do these results allow the company to conclude that differences exist between the four new drugs? (This exercise is identical to Example 15.2 except for the data.)

17.6 SUMMARY

Nonparametric statistical tests are applied to problems where the data are either ordinal or interval but not normal. The **Wilcoxon rank sum test** is used to compare two populations of ordinal or interval data when the data are generated from independent samples. The **sign test** is used to compare two populations of ordinal data drawn from a matched pairs experiment. The **Wilcoxon signed rank sum test** is employed to compare two populations of nonnormal interval data taken from a matched pairs experiment. When the objective is to compare two or more populations of independently sampled ordinal or interval nonnormal data, the **Kruskal–Wallis test** is employed. The **Friedman** test is used instead of the Kruskal–Wallis test when the samples are blocked.

IMPORTANT TERMS

Nonparametric techniques 559
Distribution-free statistics 559
Population locations 559
Wilcoxon rank sum test 561

Sign test 572
Wilcoxon signed rank sum test 577
Kruskal–Wallis test 585
Friedman test 591

SYMBOLS

Symbol	Pronounced	Represents
T_i	T-sub-i or T-i	Rank sum of sample i ($i = 1, 2, \ldots, k$)
T^+	T-plus	Rank sum of positive differences
T^-	T-minus	Rank sum of negative differences
σ_T	sigma-sub-T or sigma-T	Standard deviation of the sampling distribution of T

FORMULAS

Wilcoxon rank sum test statistic

$$T = T_1$$

$$E(T) = \frac{n_1(n_1 + n_2 + 1)}{2}$$

$$\sigma_T = \sqrt{\frac{n_1 n_2(n_1 + n_2 + 1)}{12}}$$

$$z = \frac{T - E(T)}{\sigma_T}$$

Sign test statistic

$$x = \text{Number of positive differences}$$

$$z = \frac{x - .5n}{.5\sqrt{n}}$$

Wilcoxon signed rank sum test statistic

$$T = T^+$$

$$E(T) = \frac{n(n + 1)}{4}$$

$$\sigma_T = \sqrt{\frac{n(n + 1)(2n + 1)}{24}}$$

$$z = \frac{T - E(T)}{\sigma_T}$$

Kruskal–Wallis test

$$H = \left[\frac{12}{n(n + 1)} \sum_{j=1}^{k} \frac{T_j^2}{n_j} \right] - 3(n + 1)$$

Friedman test

$$F_r = \left[\frac{12}{b(k)(k + 1)} \sum_{j=1}^{k} T_j^2 \right] - 3b(k + 1)$$

COMPUTER OUTPUT AND INSTRUCTIONS

Technique	Excel	Minitab
Wilcoxon rank sum test	566	566
Sign test	575	575
Wilcoxon signed rank sum test	581	581
Kruskal–Wallis test	588	588
Friedman test	593	594

REFERENCES

Conover, W. J., *Practical Nonparametric Statistics*, 2nd edition. New York: John Wiley and Sons, 1980.

Daniel, Wayne W., *Applied Nonparametric Statistics*, 2nd edition. Boston: Duxbury, 1990.

Hollander, M., and D. A. Wolfe, *Nonparametric Statistical Methods*. New York: John Wiley and Sons, 1973.

Lehmann, Erich L., *Nonparametrics: Statistical Methods Based on Ranks*, San Francisco: Holden Day, 1975.

CHAPTER REVIEW EXERCISES

The following exercises require the use of a computer and software.
Use a 5% significance level.

17.90   In a study to determine which of two teaching methods is perceived to be better, two sections of an introductory marketing course were taught in different ways by the same professor. At the course's completion, each student rated the course on a boring/stimulating spectrum, with 1 = very boring, 2 = somewhat boring, 3 = a little boring, 4 = neither boring nor stimulating, 5 = a little stimulating, 6 = somewhat stimulating, and 7 = very stimulating. The results are stored in file Xr17-90. Can we conclude that the ratings of the two teaching methods differ?

17.91   The researchers at a large carpet manufacturer have been experimenting with a new dyeing process in hopes of reducing the streakiness that frequently occurs with the current process. As an experiment, 15 carpets are dyed using the new process, and another 15 are dyed using the existing method. Each carpet is rated on a 5-point scale of streakiness, where 5 is extremely streaky, 4 is quite streaky, 3 is somewhat streaky, 2 is a little streaky, 1 is not streaky at all. The results are stored in file Xr17-91. Is there enough evidence to infer that the new method is better?

17.92   The editor of the student newspaper was in the process of making some major changes in the newspaper's layout. He was also contemplating changing the typeface of the print used. To help make a decision, he set up an experiment in which 20 individuals were asked to read three newspaper pages, with each page printed in a different typeface. If the reading speed differed, the typeface that was read fastest would be used. However, if there was not enough evidence to allow the editor to conclude that such differences exist, the current typeface would be continued. The times (in seconds) to completely read one page were recorded and stored in file Xr17-92. We have determined that the times are not normally distributed. Determine the course of action the editor should follow. (This exercise is identical to Exercise 15.68, except in this exercise, the data are not normally distributed.)

17.93   Large potential profits for pharmaceutical companies exist in the area of hair growth drugs. The head chemist for a large pharmaceutical company is conducting experiments to determine which of two new drugs is more effective in growing hair among balding men. One experiment was conducted as follows. A total of 30 pairs of men—each pair of which was matched according to their degree of baldness—were selected. One man used drug A, and the other used drug B. After 10 weeks, the men's new hair growth was examined, and the new growth was judged using the following ratings:

    0 = no growth
    1 = some growth
    2 = moderate growth

The results are stored in file Xr17-93. Do these data provide sufficient evidence that drug B is more effective?

17.94   Suppose that a precise measuring device for new hair growth has been developed and is used in the experiment described in Exercise 17.93. The percentages of new hair growth for the 30 pairs of men involved in the experiment are stored in file Xr17-94. Do these data allow the chemist to conclude that drug B is more effective?

17.95 The printing department of a publishing company wants to determine whether there are differences in durability between three types of book bindings. Twenty-five books with each type of binding were selected and placed in machines that continually open and close them. The numbers of openings and closings until the pages separate from the binding were recorded and stored in file Xr17-95.

a What techniques should be considered to determine whether differences exist between the types of bindings? What are the required conditions? How do you decide which technique to use?

b If we know that the number of openings and closings is not normally distributed, test to determine whether differences exist between the types of bindings.

17.96 In recent years, consumers have become more safety-conscious, particularly about children's products. A manufacturer of children's pajamas is looking for material that is as nonflammable as possible. In an experiment to compare a new fabric with the kind now being used, 50 pieces of each kind were exposed to an open flame, and the number of seconds until the fabric burst into flames was recorded. The data are stored in file Xr17-96. Because the new material is much more expensive than the current material, the manufacturer will switch only if the new material can be shown to be better. On the basis of these data, what should the manufacturer do?

17.97 Samuel's is a chain of family restaurants. Like many other service companies, Samuel's surveys its customers on a regular basis to monitor their opinions. Two questions (among others) asked in the survey are as follows:

- While you were at Samuel's, did you find the restaurant service

      1 slow   2 moderate   3 fast

- What day was your visit to Samuel's?

The responses of a random sample of 269 customers are stored in file Xr17-97. Can the manager infer that there are differences in customer perceptions of the speed of service between the days of the week?

17.98 An advertising firm wants to determine the relative effectiveness of two recently produced commercials for a car dealership. An important attribute of such commercials is their believability. In order to judge this aspect of the commercials, 60 people were randomly selected. Each watched both commercials and then rated them on a 5-point scale where 1 = not believable, 2 = somewhat believable, 3 = moderately believable, 4 = quite believable, and 5 = very believable. The ratings are stored in file Xr17-98. Do these data provide sufficient evidence to indicate that there are differences in believability between the two commercials?

17.99 Researchers at the U.S. National Institute of Aging in Bethesda, Maryland, have been studying hearing loss. They have hypothesized that as men age, they will lose their hearing faster than comparatively aged women because many more men than women have worked at jobs where noise levels have been excessive. To test their beliefs, the researchers randomly selected one man and one woman aged 45, 46, 47, . . . , 78, 79, 80 and measured the percentage hearing loss for each person. The data are stored in ascending order of age in file Xr17-99. What conclusions can be drawn from these data?

17.100 In a Gallup poll this year, 200 people were asked, "Do you feel that the newspaper you read most does a good job of presenting the news?" The same question was asked of another 200 people 10 years ago. The results of both surveys are stored in file Xr17-100. The possible responses were as follows:

    3 = good job
    2 = fair job
    1 = not a good job

Do these data provide enough evidence to infer that people perceive newspapers as doing a better job 10 years ago than today?

17.101 The increasing number of traveling businesswomen represents a large potential clientele for the hotel industry. Many hotel chains have made changes designed to attract more women. To help direct these changes, a hotel chain commissioned a study to determine whether major differences exist between male and female business travelers. A total of 100 male and 100 female executives were questioned on a variety of topics, one of which was the number of trips they had taken in the previous 12 months. The data are stored in file Xr17-101. We would like to know whether these data provide enough evidence to allow us to conclude that businesswomen and businessmen differ in the number of business trips taken per year.

17.102 To examine the effect that a tough midterm test has on student evaluations of professors, a statistics professor had her class evaluate her teaching effectiveness before the midterm test. The questionnaire asked for opinions on a number of dimensions, but the last question is considered the most important: "How would you rate the overall performance of the instructor?" The possible responses are: 1 = poor, 2 = fair, 3 = good, 4 = excellent. After a difficult test, the evaluation was redone. The evaluation scores before and after the test for each of the 40 students in the class are stored in file Xr17-102. Do the data allow the professor to conclude that the results of the midterm negatively influence student opinion?

17.103 The town of Stratford, Ontario, is very much dependent upon the Shakespearean Festival it holds every summer for its financial well-being. Thousands of people visit

Stratford to attend one or more Shakespearean plays and spend money in hotels, restaurants, and gift shops. As a consequence, any sign that the number of visitors will decrease in the future is cause for concern. Two years ago, a survey of 100 visitors asked how likely it was that they would return within the next 2 years. This year the survey was repeated with another 100 visitors. The likelihood of returning within 2 years was measured as

4 = very likely
3 = somewhat likely
2 = somewhat unlikely
1 = very unlikely

The data are stored in file Xr17-103. Conduct whichever statistical procedures you deem necessary to determine whether the citizens of Stratford should be concerned about the results of the two surveys.

17.104 Scientists have been studying the effects of lead in children's blood, bones, and tissue for a number of years. It is known that lead reduces intelligence and can cause a variety of other problems. A study directed by Dr. Herman Needleman, a psychiatrist at the University of Pittsburgh Medical Center, examined some of these problems. Two hundred boys attending public schools in Pittsburgh were recruited. Each boy was categorized as having low or high levels of lead in his bones. Each boy was then assessed by his teachers on a 4-point scale (1 = low, 2 = moderate, 3 = high, and 4 = extreme) on degrees of aggression. These data are stored in file Xr17-104. Is there evidence to infer that boys with high levels of lead are more aggressive than boys with low levels of lead?

17.105 How does gender affect teaching evaluations? Several researchers addressed this question over the past decade. (See Peter Seldin, "The Use and Abuse of Student Ratings of Professors," *Chronicle of Higher Education*, July 2, 1993.) In one study, several female and male professors in the same department with similar backgrounds were selected. A random sample of 100 female students was drawn. Each student evaluated a female professor and a male professor. A sample of 100 male students was drawn and each also evaluated a female professor and a male professor. The ratings were based on a 4-point scale where 1 = poor, 2 = fair, 3 = good, and 4 = excellent. The evaluations are stored in file Xr17-105 in the following way:

Column 1 = female student
Column 2 = female professor ratings
Column 3 = male professor rating
Column 4 = male student
Column 5 = female professor ratings
Column 6 = male professor rating

a Can we infer that female students rate female professors higher than they rate male professors?

b Can we infer that male students rate male professors higher than they rate female professors?

17.106 It is an unfortunate fact of life that the characteristics that one is born with play a critical role in later life. For example, race is a critical factor in almost all aspects of North American life. Height and weight also determine how friends, teachers, employers, and customers will treat you. And now we may add physical attractiveness to this list. A recent study conducted by economists Jeff Biddle of Michigan State University and Daniel Hamermesh from the University of Texas followed the careers of students from a prestigious U.S. law school. A panel of independent raters examined the graduation yearbook photos of the students and rated their appearance as unattractive, neither attractive nor unattractive, or attractive. The annual incomes in thousands of dollars 5 years after graduation were recorded and stored in file Xr17-106. Assuming that incomes are not normally distributed, can we infer that incomes of lawyers are affected by physical attractiveness?

17.107 According to a CNN news report broadcast on November 26, 1995, 9% of full-time workers telecommute. This means that they do not work in their employers' offices, but instead perform their work at home using a computer and modem. To ascertain whether such workers are more satisfied than their nontelecommuting counterparts, a study was undertaken. A random sample of telecommuters and regular office workers was taken. Each was asked how satisfied they were with their current employment. The responses (1 = very unsatisfied, 2 = somewhat unsatisfied, 3 = somewhat satisfied, 4 = very satisfied) are stored in file Xr17-107. What conclusions can we draw from these data?

17.108 Can you become addicted to exercise? In a study conducted at the University of Wisconsin at Madison, a random sample of dedicated exercisers who usually work out every day was drawn. Each completed a questionnaire that gauged their mood on a 5-point scale, where 5 = very relaxed and happy, 4 = somewhat relaxed and happy, 3 = neutral feeling, 2 = tense and anxious, and 1 = very tense and anxious. The group was then instructed to abstain from all workouts for the next 3 days. Moreover, they were told to be as physically inactive as possible. Each day their mood was measured using the same questionnaire. The data are stored in file Xr17-108. Column 1 stores the code identifying the respondent, and columns 2 through 5 store the measures of mood for the day before the experiment began and for the 3 days of the experiment, respectively.

a Can we infer that for each day the exercisers abstained from physical activity, they were less happy than when they were exercising?

b Do the data indicate that by the third day moods were improving?

c Draw two possible conclusions from your findings.

17.109 How does alcohol affect judgment? To provide some insight, an experiment was conducted. A random sample of customers of an Ohio club was selected. Each respondent was asked to assess the attractiveness of members of the opposite sex who were in the club at the time. The assessment was to be made on a 5-point scale (1 = very unattractive, 2 = unattractive, 3 = neither attractive nor unattractive, 4 = attractive, and 5 = very attractive). The survey was conducted 3 hours before closing and again just before closing using another group of respondents. The data have been stored in file Xr17-109. Can we conclude that the assessments made just before closing are higher than those made 3 hours earlier? If so, what does this imply about the effects of alcohol on judgment? (The survey results were reported in the September 1997 edition of the *Report on Business.*)

◆ CASE 17.1
BANK OF COMMERCE CUSTOMER SURVEY

The concepts and techniques of total quality management have spread to all industries. As a consequence, many firms regularly survey their customers to determine their opinion on a number of issues. The Bank of Commerce is one such company. Each year it undertakes a survey of customers to measure their attitudes about the various services offered by the bank. For example, in addition to questions about the promptness of the service and the adequacy of operating hours, the survey asks the following:

1. How would you rate the overall quality of service you receive from the Bank of Commerce as a whole?
2. How would you rate the overall quality of service at your branch of the Bank of Commerce?

The responses to these questions are rated

1 = extremely poor
2 = very poor
3 = poor
4 = fair
5 = good
6 = very good
7 = extremely good

As part of a more extensive analysis of the survey results, a manager took a random sample of completed surveys at each of three branches. The data are stored in file C17-01 using the following format:

Column 1:   Respondent number from branch 1
Column 2:   Response to question 1
Column 3:   Response to question 2
Column 4:   Respondent number from branch 2
Column 5:   Response to question 1
Column 6:   Response to question 2
Column 7:   Respondent number from branch 3
Column 8:   Response to question 1
Column 9:   Response to question 2

a Do customers at the three branches differ in their assessments of the quality of service at their branch?

b For each branch, do customers have a different opinion of their branch than of the Bank of Commerce as a whole?

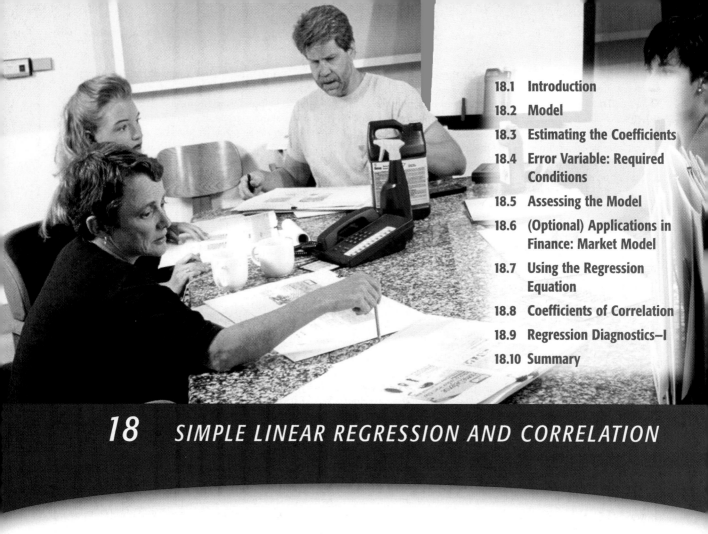

18 SIMPLE LINEAR REGRESSION AND CORRELATION

FOREIGN INDEX FUNDS

Most Americans who invest in the stock market buy stocks that are listed on the New York Stock Exchange or the NASDAQ. Canadians tend to invest in the Toronto Stock Exchange as well as the two American ones. However, restricting equity purchases in these ways likely limits potential profits. It also increases risk because investors are not taking advantage of a potential source of diversification (see Section 7.5).

A certain investor prefers index mutual funds, which are constructed by buying a wide assortment of stocks so that the fund more or less mirrors the entire exchange. Thus, for example, if an investor believes that the NASDAQ will increase rapidly over the next 2 years, but is not confident that he can pick winners among individual stocks, he may instead buy a NASDAQ index fund.

The investor has determined that a foreign index fund is beneficial to him if it is weakly correlated with an American index fund that he owns. He examines a Japanese index constructed by Morgan Stanley Dean Witter, a well-respected financial institution in the United States. The monthly returns on his U.S. index and the Japanese index were computed over a 59-month period. These data* are stored in file Ch18:\Index. He decides that if there is evidence of a linear relationship between the returns on the U.S. and Japanese indexes, he will not buy the Japanese index. What should he do? See page 635 for our answer.

*The authors are grateful to Ariel Aminof for gathering the data. The data were adapted from Morgan Stanley Dean Witter.

18.1 INTRODUCTION

This chapter is the first in a series of three in which the problem objective is to analyze the relationship between interval variables. **Regression analysis** is used to predict the value of one variable on the basis of other variables. This technique may be the most commonly used statistical procedure because, as you can easily appreciate, almost all companies and government institutions forecast variables such as product demand, interest rates, inflation rates, prices of raw materials, and labor costs.

The technique involves developing a mathematical equation that describes the relationship between the variable to be forecast, which is called the **dependent variable**, and variables that the statistics practitioner believes are related to the dependent variable. The dependent variable is denoted y, whereas the related variables are called **independent variables** and are denoted $x_1, x_2, ..., x_k$ (where k is the number of independent variables).

If we are interested only in determining whether a relationship exists, we employ **correlation analysis**, a technique that we have already introduced. In Chapter 2, we presented the graphical method to describe the association between two interval variables—the scatter diagram. We introduced the coefficient of correlation and covariance in Chapter 4.

Because regression analysis involves a number of new techniques and concepts, we divided the presentation into three chapters. In this chapter, we present techniques that allow us to determine the relationship between only two variables. In Chapter 19, we expand our discussion to more than two variables, and in Chapter 20, we discuss how to build regression models.

Here are three illustrations of the use of regression analysis.

Illustration 1 The product manager in charge of a particular brand of children's breakfast cereal would like to predict the demand for the cereal during the next year. In order to use regression analysis, she and her staff list the following variables as likely to affect sales:

Price of the product
Number of children 5 to 12 years of age (the target market)
Prices of competitors' products
Effectiveness of advertising (as measured by advertising exposure)
Annual sales this year
Annual sales in previous years

Illustration 2 A gold speculator is considering a major purchase of gold bullion. He would like to forecast the price of gold 2 years from now (his planning horizon), using regression analysis. In preparation, he produces the following list of independent variables:

Interest rates

Inflation rate

Price of oil

Demand for gold jewelry

Demand for industrial and commercial gold

Dow Jones Industrial Average

Illustration 3 A real estate agent wants to more accurately predict the selling price of houses. She believes that the following variables affect the price of a house:

Size of the house (number of square feet)

Number of bedrooms

Frontage of the lot

Condition

Location

In each of these illustrations, the primary motive for using regression analysis is forecasting. Nonetheless, analyzing the relationship among variables can also be quite useful in managerial decision making. For instance, in the first application, the product manager may want to know how price is related to product demand so that a decision about a prospective change in pricing can be made.

Another application comes from the field of finance. The *market model* analyzes the relationship between the returns of a particular stock and the behavior of a stock index (such as the S&P 500 Index). Its function is not to predict the stock's price but to assess the risk of the stock versus the risk of the stock market in general. (See Section 18.6.)

Regardless of why regression analysis is performed, the next step in the technique is to develop a mathematical equation or model that accurately describes the nature of the relationship that exists between the dependent variable and the independent variables. This stage—which is only a small part of the total process—is described in the next section. In the ensuing sections of this chapter (and in Chapter 19), we will spend considerable time assessing and testing how well the model fits the actual data. Only when we're satisfied with the model do we use it to estimate and forecast.

18.2 MODEL

The job of developing a mathematical equation can be quite complex, because we need to have some idea about the nature of the relationship between each of the independent variables and the dependent variable. For example, the gold speculator mentioned in Illustration 2 needs to know how interest rates affect the price of gold. If he proposes a linear relationship, that may imply that as interest rates rise (or fall), the price of gold will rise (or fall). A quadratic relationship may suggest that the price of gold will increase over a certain range of interest rates but will decrease over a different range. Perhaps certain combinations of values of interest rates and other independent variables influence the price in one way, whereas other combinations influence the price in other ways. The number of different mathematical models that could be proposed is virtually infinite.

You might have encountered various models in previous courses. For instance, the following represent relationships in the natural sciences:

$$E = mc^2, \quad \text{where } E = \text{Energy}, \ m = \text{Mass}, \text{ and } c = \text{Speed of light}$$

$$F = ma, \quad \text{where } F = \text{Force}, \ m = \text{Mass}, \text{ and } a = \text{Acceleration}$$

$$S = at^2/2, \quad \text{where } S = \text{Distance}, \ t = \text{Time}, \text{ and } a = \text{Gravitational acceleration}$$

These are all examples of **deterministic models**, so named because—except for small measurement errors—such equations allow us to determine the value of the dependent variable (on the left side of the equation) from the values of the independent variables. In many practical applications of interest to us, deterministic models are unrealistic. For example, is it reasonable to believe that we can determine the selling price of a house solely on the basis of its size? Unquestionably, the size of a house affects its price, but many other variables (some of which may not be measurable) also influence price. What must be included in most practical models is a method to represent the randomness that is part of a real-life process. Such a model is called a **probabilistic model**.

To create a probabilistic model, we start with a deterministic model that approximates the relationship we want to model. We then add a random term that measures the error of the deterministic component. Suppose that in our earlier Illustration 3, the real estate agent knows that the cost of building a new house is about $75 per square foot and that most lots sell for about $25,000. The approximate selling price would be

$$y = 25,000 + 75x$$

where y = Selling price and x = Size of the house in square feet. A house of 2,000 square feet would therefore be estimated to sell for

$$y = 25,000 + 75(2,000) = 175,000$$

We know, however, that the selling price is not likely to be exactly $175,000. Prices may actually range from $100,000 to $250,000. In other words, the deterministic model is not really suitable. To represent this situation properly, we should use the probabilistic model

$$y = 25,000 + 75x + \varepsilon$$

where ε (the Greek letter epsilon) represents the **random term** (also called the **error variable**)—the difference between the actual selling price and the estimated price based on the size of the house. The random term thus accounts for all the variables, measurable and immeasurable, that are not part of the model. The value of ε will vary from one sale to the next, even if x remains constant. That is, houses of exactly the same size will sell for different prices because of differences in location and number of bedrooms and bathrooms, as well as other variables.

In the three chapters devoted to regression analysis, we will present only probabilistic models. In this chapter we describe only the linear model with one independent variable. This model is called the **first-order linear model**—sometimes called the **simple linear regression model**.

FIRST-ORDER MODEL

$$y = \beta_0 + \beta_1 x + \varepsilon$$

where

y = Dependent variable

x = Independent variable

β_0 = y-intercept

β_1 = Slope of the line (defined as rise/run)

ε = Error variable

The problem objective addressed by the model is to analyze the relationship between two variables, x and y, both of which must be interval. To define the relationship between x and y, we need to know the value of the coefficients of the linear model, β_0 and β_1. However, these coefficients are population parameters, which are almost always unknown. In the next section, we discuss how these parameters are estimated.

18.3 ESTIMATING THE COEFFICIENTS

We estimate the parameters β_0 and β_1 in a way similar to the methods used to estimate all the other parameters discussed in this book. We draw a random sample from the population of interest and calculate the sample statistics we need. However, because β_0 and β_1 represent the coefficients of a straight line, their estimators are based on drawing a straight line through the sample data. The following equation represents the straight line:

$$\hat{y} = b_0 + b_1 x$$

This line is called the **least squares** or **regression line**; b_0 is the y-intercept, b_1 is the slope, and $\hat{y}$ is the predicted or fitted value of y. In Chapter 4 we introduced the least squares method, which produces a straight line that minimizes the sum of the squared differences between the points and the line. That is, the coefficients b_0 and b_1 are calculated so that the sum of squared deviations

$$\sum_{i=1}^{n} (y_i - \hat{y}_i)^2$$

is minimized. The sample coefficients are determined using calculus; details are available in CD Appendix 18.1. The formulas below were first shown in Chapter 4.

LEAST SQUARES LINE COEFFICIENTS

$$b_1 = \frac{\text{cov}(x, y)}{s_x^2}$$

$$b_0 = \bar{y} - b_1\bar{x}$$

where

$$\text{cov}(x, y) = \frac{\sum_{i=1}^{n} (x_i - \bar{x})(y_i - \bar{y})}{n - 1}$$

$$s_x^2 = \frac{\sum_{i=1}^{n} (x_i - \bar{x})^2}{n - 1}$$

$$\bar{x} = \frac{\sum_{i=1}^{n} x_i}{n}$$

$$\bar{y} = \frac{\sum_{i=1}^{n} y_i}{n}$$

In Chapter 4 we provided shortcut formulas for the sample variance (page 103) and the sample covariance (page 117). Combining them provides a shortcut method to manually calculate the slope coefficient.

SHORTCUT FORMULA FOR b_1

$$b_1 = \frac{\text{cov}(x, y)}{s_x^2}$$

$$\text{cov}(x, y) = \frac{1}{n - 1}\left[\sum_{i=1}^{n} x_i y_i - \frac{\sum_{i=1}^{n} x_i \sum_{i=1}^{n} y_i}{n}\right]$$

$$s_x^2 = \frac{1}{n - 1}\left[\sum_{i=1}^{n} x_i^2 - \frac{\left(\sum_{i=1}^{n} x_i\right)^2}{n}\right]$$

Statisticians have shown that b_0 and b_1 are unbiased estimators of β_0 and β_1, respectively. To illustrate how well the least squares method works, consider the following simple example.

EXAMPLE 18.1

Given the following six observations of variables x and y, determine the least squares line.

x	1	2	3	4	5	6
y	6	1	9	5	17	12

SOLUTION To apply the shortcut formula, we need to compute four summations. Using a calculator, we find

$$\sum_{i=1}^{n} x_i = 21$$

$$\sum_{i=1}^{n} y_i = 50$$

$$\sum_{i=1}^{n} x_i y_i = 212$$

$$\sum_{i=1}^{n} x_i^2 = 91$$

The covariance and the variance of x can now be computed:

$$\text{cov}(x, y) = \frac{1}{n-1}\left[\sum_{i=1}^{n} x_i y_i - \frac{\sum_{i=1}^{n} x_i \sum_{i=1}^{n} y_i}{n}\right]$$

$$= \frac{1}{6-1}\left[212 - \frac{(21)(50)}{6}\right] = 7.4$$

$$s_x^2 = \frac{1}{n-1}\left[\sum_{i=1}^{n} x_i^2 - \frac{\left(\sum_{i=1}^{n} x_i\right)^2}{n}\right]$$

$$= \frac{1}{6-1}\left[91 - \frac{(21)^2}{6}\right] = 3.5$$

The sample slope coefficient is calculated next:

$$b_1 = \frac{\text{cov}(x, y)}{s_x^2} = \frac{7.4}{3.5} = 2.114$$

The y-intercept is computed as follows:

$$\bar{x} = \frac{\sum x_i}{n} = \frac{21}{6} = 3.5$$

$$\bar{y} = \frac{\sum y_i}{n} = \frac{50}{6} = 8.333$$

$$b_0 = \bar{y} - b_1\bar{x} = 8.333 - (2.114)(3.5) = .934$$

Thus, the least squares line is

$$\hat{y} = .934 + 2.114x$$

Figure 18.1 depicts the least squares (or regression) line. As you can see, the line fits the data reasonably well. We can measure how well by computing the value of the minimized sum of squared deviations. The deviations between the actual data points and the line are called **residuals,** denoted e_i. That is,

$$e_i = y_i - \hat{y}_i$$

The residuals are observations of the error variable. Consequently, the minimized sum of squared deviations is called the **sum of squares for error**, denoted SSE.

The calculation of the residuals in this example is shown in Figure 18.2. Notice that we compute $\hat{y}_i$ by substituting x_i into the formula of the regression line. The residuals are the differences between the observed values of y_i and the fitted or predicted values of $\hat{y}_i$. Table 18.1 describes these calculations.

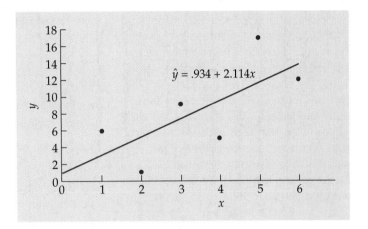

Figure 18.1
Scatter diagram with regression line for Example 18.1

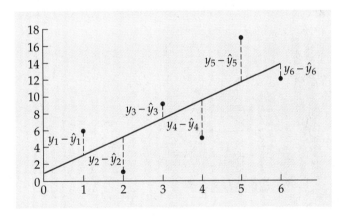

Figure 18.2
Calculation of residuals in Example 18.1

Table 18.1 Calculation of Residuals in Example 18.1

x_i	y_i	$\hat{y}_i = .934 + 2.114x_i$	$y_i - \hat{y}_i$	$(y_i - \hat{y}_i)^2$
1	6	3.048	2.952	8.714
2	1	5.162	−4.162	17.322
3	9	7.276	1.724	2.972
4	5	9.390	−4.390	19.272
5	17	11.504	5.496	30.206
6	12	13.618	−1.618	2.618

$$\sum (y_i - \hat{y}_i)^2 = 81.105$$

Thus, SSE = 81.105. No other straight line will produce a sum of squared deviations as small as 81.105. In that sense, the regression line fits the data best. The sum of squares for error is an important statistic because it is the basis for other statistics that assess how well the linear model fits the data. We will introduce these statistics in Section 18.5.

S e e i n g   S t a t i s t i c s

APPLET 18
FITTING THE REGRESSION LINE

This applet allows you to experiment with the data in Example 18.1. Click or drag the mouse in the graph to change the slope of the line. The errors are measured by the red lines. The squares represent the squared errors. (You can hide or show them by clicking on the "Hide/Show Errors" button.) The error meter on the left keeps track of your progress. The amount of the error that turns green is the proportion of the squared error you eliminate by finding a better regression line. The sum of squared errors is shown at the bottom. The co-efficient of correlation squared (which is the coefficient of determination, explained in Section 18.5) is shown at the top. Change the slope until the sum of squares for error as indicated in the error meter is minimized. If you need help, click the "Find Best Model" button.

Applet Exercises
Change the slope (if necessary) so that the line is horizontal.

18.1 What is the slope of this line?

18.2 What is the y-intercept?

18.3 The y-intercept is equal to $\bar{y}$. What does this tell you about predicting the value of y?

18.4 Drag the mouse to change the slope to 1. What is the sum of squared errors?

18.5 Drag the mouse to change the slope to .5. What is the sum of squared errors?

18.6 Experiment with different lines. What point is common to all the lines?

EXAMPLE 18.2

Car dealers across North America use the *Red Book* to help them determine the value of used cars that their customers trade in when purchasing new cars. The book, which is published monthly, lists the trade-in values for all basic models of cars. It provides alternative values for each car model according to its condition and optional features. The values are determined on the basis of the average paid at recent used-car auctions, the source of supply for many used-car dealers. However, the *Red Book* does not in-dicate the value determined by the odometer reading, despite the fact that a critical factor for used-car buyers is how far the car has been driven. To examine this issue, a used-car dealer randomly selected 100 three-year old Ford Tauruses that were sold at auction during the past month. Each car was in top condition and equipped with auto-matic transmission, AM/FM cassette tape player, and air conditioning. The dealer re-corded the price and the number of miles on the odometer. These data are stored in file Xm18-02; some of the data are listed here. The dealer wants to find the regression line.

Car	Odometer	Price
1	37,388	14,636
2	44,758	14,122
3	45,833	14,016
.	.	.
.	.	.
.	.	.
98	33,190	14,518
99	39,196	14,712
100	36,392	14,266

SOLUTION

IDENTIFY

Notice that the problem objective is to analyze the relationship between two interval variables. Because we believe that the odometer reading affects the selling price, we identify the former as the independent variable, which we label x, and the latter as the dependent variable, which we label y.

COMPUTE

 MANUALLY

From the data set, we find

$$\sum_{i=1}^{n} x_i = 3,600,945$$

$$\sum_{i=1}^{n} y_i = 1,482,282$$

$$\sum_{i=1}^{n} x_i y_i = 53,107,620,968$$

$$\sum_{i=1}^{n} x_i^2 = 133,977,389,207$$

Next we calculate the covariance and the variance of the independent variable x:

$$\text{cov}(x, y) = \frac{1}{n-1}\left[\sum_{i=1}^{n} x_i y_i - \frac{\sum_{i=1}^{n} x_i \sum_{i=1}^{n} y_i}{n}\right]$$

$$= \frac{1}{100-1}\left[53,107,620,968 - \frac{(3,600,945)(1,482,282)}{100}\right] = -2,712,511$$

$$s_x^2 = \frac{1}{n-1}\left[\sum_{i=1}^{n} x_i^2 - \frac{\left(\sum_{i=1}^{n} x_i\right)^2}{n}\right]$$

$$= \frac{1}{100-1}\left[133,977,389,207 - \frac{(3,600,945)^2}{100}\right] = 43,528,690$$

The sample slope coefficient is calculated next:

$$b_1 = \frac{\text{cov}(x, y)}{s_x^2} = \frac{-2,712,511}{43,528,690} = -.0623$$

The y-intercept is computed as follows:

$$\bar{x} = \frac{\sum x_i}{n} = \frac{3{,}600{,}945}{100} = 36{,}009.45$$

$$\bar{y} = \frac{\sum y_i}{n} = \frac{1{,}482{,}282}{100} = 14{,}822.82$$

$$b_0 = \bar{y} - b_1\bar{x} = 14{,}822.82 - (-.0623)(36{,}009.45) = 17{,}067$$

The sample regression line is

$$\hat{y} = 17{,}067 - .0623x$$

EXCEL

	A	B	C	D	E	F
1	SUMMARY OUTPUT					
2						
3	*Regression Statistics*					
4	Multiple R	0.8063				
5	R Square	0.6501				
6	Adjusted R Square	0.6466				
7	Standard Error	303.1				
8	Observations	100				
9						
10	ANOVA					
11		*df*	*SS*	*MS*	*F*	*Significance F*
12	Regression	1	16734111	16734111	182.11	0.0000
13	Residual	98	9005450	91892		
14	Total	99	25739561			
15						
16		*Coefficients*	*Standard Error*	*t Stat*	*P-value*	
17	Intercept	17067	169.0	100.97	0.0000	
18	Odometer	-0.0623	0.0046	-13.49	0.0000	

COMMANDS

1. Type or import the data into two columns.
2. Click **Tools, Data Analysis…**, and **Regression**.
3 Specify the **Input Y Range**.
4 Specify the **Input X Range**.
5 Click **Labels** if appropriate. Click **OK**.

To draw the scatter diagram, click **Line Fit Plots** before clicking **OK**. Alternatively, follow the instructions provided in Chapter 2.

COMMANDS FOR EXAMPLE 18.2

Open file **Xm18-02**.

B1:B101

A1:A101

MINITAB

Regression Analysis: Price versus Odometer

```
The regression equation is
Price = 17067 - 0.0623 Odometer

Predictor        Coef      SE Coef          T        P
Constant      17066.8        169.0     100.97    0.000
Odometer     -0.062315     0.004618     -13.49    0.000

S = 303.1      R-Sq = 65.0%      R-Sq(adj) = 64.7%

Analysis of Variance

Source           DF          SS          MS        F        P
Regression        1    16734111    16734111   182.11    0.000
Residual Error   98     9005450       91892
Total            99    25739561
```

COMMANDS

1. Type or import the data into two columns.
2. Click **Stat, Regression**, and **Regression…**.
3. Select the dependent (**Response**) variable.
4. Select the independent (**Predictors**) variable.
   Click **OK**.

COMMANDS FOR EXAMPLE 18.2

Open file **Xm18-02**.

Price or **C2**

Odometer or **C1**

To draw the scatter diagram, click **Stat, Regression**, and **Fitted Line Plot**. Alternatively, follow the instructions provided in Chapter 2.

The printouts include more statistics than we need right now. However, we will be discussing the rest of the printouts later. We have also included the scatter diagram, which is often a first step in the regression analysis.

> **INTERPRET**

The slope coefficient b_1 is $-.0623$, which means that for each additional mile on the odometer, the price decreases by an average of $.0623$ (6.23 cents).

The intercept is $b_0 = 17,067$. Technically, the intercept is the point at which the regression line and the y-axis intersect. This means that when $x = 0$ (i.e., the car was not driven at all), the selling price is $17,067. However, in this case, the intercept is probably meaningless. Because our sample did not include any cars with zero miles on the odometer, we have no basis for interpreting b_0. As a general rule, we cannot determine the value of $\hat{y}$ for a value of x that is far outside the range of the sample values of x. In this example, the smallest and largest values of x are 19,057 and 49,223, respectively. Because $x = 0$ is not in this interval, we cannot safely interpret the value of $\hat{y}$ when $x = 0$.

It is important to bear in mind that the interpretation of the coefficients pertains only to the sample, which consists of 100 observations. To infer information about the population, we need statistical inference techniques, which are described later in this chapter.

In the sections that follow, we will return to this problem and the computer output to introduce other statistics associated with regression analysis.

EXERCISES

Most of the exercises that follow were created to allow you to see how regression analysis is used to solve realistic problems. As a result, most feature a large number of observations. We anticipate that most students will solve these problems using a computer and statistical software. However, for students without these resources, we have computed the means, variances, and covariances that will permit them to complete the calculations manually. (See Appendix A.)

18.1 The term *regression* was originally used in 1885 by Sir Francis Galton in his analysis of the relationship between the heights of children and parents. He formulated the "law of universal regression," which specifies that "each peculiarity in a man is shared by his kinsmen, but on average in a less degree." (Evidently, people spoke this way in 1885.) In 1903 two statisticians, K. Pearson and A. Lee, took a random sample of 1,078 father–son pairs to examine Galton's law ("On the Laws of Inheritance in Man, I. Inheritance of Physical Characteristics," *Biometrika* 2:457–462). Their sample regression line was

Son's height = $33.73 + .516 \times$ Father's height

a Interpret the coefficients.
b What does the regression line tell you about the heights of sons of tall fathers?
c What does the regression line tell you about the heights of sons of short fathers?

18.2 Suppose that a statistician wanted to update the study described in Exercise 18.1. She collected data on 400 father–son pairs and stored the data (in inches) in file Xr18-02.
a Determine the sample regression line.
b What does the value of b_0 tell you?
c What does the value of b_1 tell you?

Exercises 18.3 and 18.4 feature small data sets. Both problems can be solved manually or by computer.

18.3 Refer to Exercise 2.55. Determine the sample regression line that describes how mortgage rates are related to the number of housing starts. What do the coefficients indicate about this relationship?

18.4 Refer to Exercise 2.61.
a Determine the sample regression line that depicts how the return on common stocks is related to inflation.
b What does the value of b_0 tell you?
c What does the value of b_1 tell you?

18.5 Refer to Exercise 2.66. Find the sample regression line that describes how the amount of work and school performance are related among students who have part-time jobs.

18.6 In television's early years, most commercials were 60 seconds long. Now, however, commercials can be any length. The objective of commercials remains the same—to have as many viewers as possible remember the product in a favorable way and eventually buy it. In an experiment to determine how the length of a commercial is related to people's memory of it, 60 randomly selected people were asked to watch a 1-hour television program. In the middle of the show, a commercial advertising a brand of toothpaste appeared. Some viewers watched a commercial that lasted for 20 seconds, others watched one that lasted for 24 seconds, 28 seconds, . . . , 60 seconds. The essential content of the commercials was the same. After the show, each person was given a test to measure how much he or she remembered about the product. The commercial times and test scores (on a 30-point test) are stored in file Xr18-06.

a Draw a scatter diagram of the data to determine whether a linear model appears to be appropriate.

b Determine the least squares line.

c Interpret the coefficients.

18.7 After several semesters without much success, Pat Statsdud (a student in the lowest quarter of a statistics course) decided to try to improve. Pat needed to know the secret of success for university and college students. After many hours of discussion with other, more successful, students, Pat postulated a rather radical theory: The longer one studied, the better one's grade. To test the theory, Pat took a random sample of 100 students in an economics course and asked each to report the average amount of time he or she studied economics and the final mark (out of 100) received. These data are stored in file Xr18-07.

a Determine the sample regression line.

b Interpret the coefficients.

c Is the sign of the slope logical? If the slope had had the opposite sign, what would that tell you?

APPLICATIONS IN *HUMAN RESOURCES MANAGEMENT*

Retaining workers

Human resource managers are responsible for a variety of tasks within organizations. As we pointed out in the introduction in Chapter 1, personnel/human resource managers are involved with recruiting new workers, determining which applicants are most suitable to hire, and in various aspects of monitoring the workforce, including absenteeism and worker turnover. For many firms, worker turnover is a costly problem. First, there is the cost of recruiting and attracting qualified workers. The firm must advertise vacant positions and make certain that applicants are judged properly. Second, the cost of training hirees can be high, particularly in technical areas. Third,

new employees are often not as productive and efficient as experienced ones. Consequently, it is in the interests of the firm to attract and keep the best workers. Any information that the personnel manager can obtain is likely to be useful. Exercise 18.9 addresses this issue.

18.8 The growing interest in and use of the Internet have forced many companies into considering ways to sell their products on the Web. Therefore, it is of interest to these companies to determine who is using the Web. A statistics practitioner undertook a study to determine how education and Internet use are connected. She took a random sample of 200 adults (20 years of age and older) and asked each to report the years of education they had completed and the number of hours of Internet use in the previous week. These data are stored in file Xr18-08.

a Perform a regression analysis to describe how the two variables are related.

b Interpret the coefficients.

18.9 The human resource manager of a telemarketing firm is concerned about the rapid turnover of the firm's telemarketers. It appears that many telemarketers do not work very long before quitting. There may be a number of reasons, including relatively low pay, personal unsuitability for the work, and the low probability of advancement. Because of the high cost of hiring and training new workers, the manager decided to examine the factors that influence workers to quit. He reviewed the work history of a random sample of workers who have quit in the last year and recorded the number of weeks on the job before quitting and the age of each worker when originally hired. These data are stored in file Xr18-09.

a Use regression analysis to describe how the work period and age are related.

b Briefly discuss what the coefficients tell you.

18.10 The Trans-Alaska Pipeline System carries crude oil from Prudhoe Bay on Alaska's North Slope 800 miles to the port of Valdez, on the southern coast of Alaska. The pipeline carries a mixture of different qualities of oil. Quality of oil is measured in API Gravity degrees—the higher the degrees API, the higher the quality. Because the pipeline mixes oils of different degrees, shippers in Valdez receive oil of different quality than they purchased. To compensate shippers, a "Quality Bank" was established. The owners of the pipeline proposed compensating shippers 15 cents per barrel for every degree below the level to which the shippers agreed. However, a refinery near Fairbanks, which receives 26-degree oil and mixes it with 20-degree oil, objected to the proposal. It suggested a 3.09- to 5.35-cent differential. Because oil carriers are required to establish "just and reasonable" rates, a hearing before an administrative law judge was held. At the hearing, an expert hired by the shippers produced the accompanying table to show the relationship between quality and price per barrel of Mideast oil. (The data are stored in file Xr18-10.) Use regression analysis to determine the appropriate compensation. (*Source:* M. O. Finkelstein and B. Levin, *Statistics for Lawyers* Springer-Verlag, 1990, 338–339)

Mideast oil degrees API	27.0	28.5	30.8	31.3	31.9	34.5	34.0
Price per barrel	12.02	12.04	12.32	12.27	12.49	12.70	12.80

Mideast oil degrees API	34.7	37.0	41.1	41.0	38.8	39.3
Price per barrel	13.00	13.00	13.17	13.19	13.22	13.27

18.11 All Canadians have government-funded health insurance, which pays for any medical care they require. However, when traveling out of the country, Canadians usually acquire supplementary health insurance to cover the difference between the costs incurred for emergency treatment and what the government program pays. In the United States this cost differential can be prohibitive. Until recently, private insurance companies (such as Blue Cross) charged everyone the same weekly rate, regardless of age. However, because of rising costs and the realization that older people frequently incur greater medical emergency expenses, insurers had to change their premium plans. They decided to offer rates that depend on the age of the customer. To help determine the new rates, one insurance company gathered data concerning the age and mean daily medical expenses of a random sample of 1,348 Canadians during the previous 12-month period. The data are stored in file Xr18-11.

a Determine the sample regression line.

b Interpret the coefficients.

c What rate plan would you suggest?

18.12 The four C's—carats, cut, clarity, and color—determine the price of diamonds. Carats refer to the weight of the diamond. One carat equals .2 gram. An advertisement in a Singapore newspaper (*Straits Times*, 29 February, 1992) featured 48 ladies' diamond rings in which the stones varied in weight from .12 carat to .35 carat. The ad listed the weights of the stones together with the nonnegotiable price in Singapore dollars. These data are stored in file Xr18-12.

a Use regression analysis to determine how weight and price are related.

b What do the coefficients tell you?

18.4 ERROR VARIABLE: REQUIRED CONDITIONS

In the previous section, we used the least squares method to estimate the coefficients of the linear regression model. A critical part of this model is the error variable ε. In the next section, we will present an inferential method that determines whether there is a linear relationship. Later we will show how we use the regression equation to estimate and predict. For these methods to be valid, however, four requirements involving the probability distribution of the error variable must be satisfied.

> **REQUIRED CONDITIONS FOR THE ERROR VARIABLE**
> 1. The probability distribution of ε is normal.
> 2. The mean of the distribution is 0; that is, $E(\varepsilon) = 0$.
> 3. The standard deviation of ε is σ_ε, which is a constant regardless of the value of x.
> 4. The value of ε associated with any particular value of y is independent of ε associated with any other value of y.

Requirements 1, 2, and 3 can be interpreted in another way: For each value of x, y is a normally distributed random variable whose mean is

$$E(y) = \beta_0 + \beta_1 x$$

and whose standard deviation is σ_ε. Notice that the mean depends on x. The standard deviation, however, is not influenced by x, because it is a constant over all values of x. Figure 18.3 on page 616 depicts this interpretation. Notice that for each value of x, $E(y)$ changes, but the shape of the distribution of Y remains the same. That is, for each x, y is normally distributed with the same standard deviation.

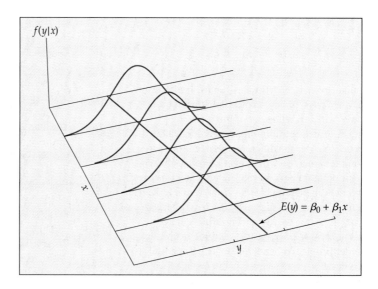

$f(y|x)$

$E(y) = \beta_0 + \beta_1 x$

Figure 18.3
Distribution of _y_ given _x_

In Section 18.9, we will discuss how departures from these required conditions affect the regression analysis and how they are identified.

OBSERVATIONAL AND EXPERIMENTAL DATA

In Chapter 5 and again in Chapter 13 we described the difference between observational and experimental data. We pointed out that statistics practitioners often design controlled experiments to enable them to interpret the results of their analyses more clearly than would be the case after conducting an observational study. Example 18.2 is an illustration of observational data. In that example we merely observed the odometer reading and auction selling price of 100 randomly selected cars.

If you examine Exercise 18.6, you will see experimental data gathered through a controlled experiment. To determine the effect of the length of a television commercial on its viewers' memories of the product advertised, the statistics practitioner arranged for 60 television viewers to watch a commercial of differing lengths and then tested their memories of that commercial. Each viewer was randomly assigned a commercial length. The values of x ranged from 20 to 60 and were set by the statistics practitioner as part of the experiment. For each value of x, the distribution of the memory test scores is assumed to be normally distributed with a constant variance.

We can summarize the difference between the experiment described in Example 18.2 and the one described in Exercise 18.6. In Example 18.2, both the odometer reading and the auction selling price are random variables. We hypothesize that for each possible odometer reading, there is a theoretical population of auction selling prices that are normally distributed with a mean that is a linear function of the odometer reading and a variance that is constant. In Exercise 18.6, the length of commercial is not a random variable but a series of values selected by the statistics practitioner. For each commercial length, the memory test scores are required to be normally distributed with a constant variance.

Regression analysis can be applied to data generated from either observational or controlled experiments. In both cases our objective is to determine how the independent variable is related to the dependent variable. However, observational data can be analyzed in another way. When the data are observational, both variables are random variables. We need not specify that one variable is independent and the other is dependent. We can simply determine _whether_ the two variables are related. The equivalent of the required conditions described above is that the two variables are bivariate normally distributed. (Recall that in Section 7.4 we introduced the bivariate distribution, which describes the joint probability of two variables.) A bivariate normal distribution is described in Figure 18.4. As you can see, it is a three-dimensional bell-shaped curve. The dimensions are the variables x, y, and the joint density function $f(x, y)$.

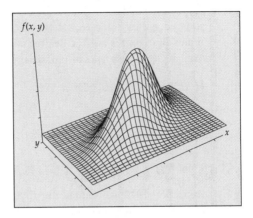

**Figure 18.4
Bivariate normal
distribution**

In Section 18.8 we will discuss the statistical technique that is used when both x and y are random variables and they are bivariate normally distributed. We will also introduce a procedure applied when the normality requirement is not satisfied.

EXERCISES

18.13 Describe what the required conditions mean in Exercise 18.2. Do these requirements seem reasonable?

18.14 If the required conditions are satisfied in Exercise 18.10, what can you say about the distribution of the price per barrel?

18.15 Assuming that the required conditions are satisfied in Exercise 18.11, what does this tell you about the distribution of mean daily expenses?

18.5 ASSESSING THE MODEL

The least squares method produces the best straight line. However, there may in fact be no relationship or perhaps a nonlinear (e.g., quadratic) relationship between the two variables. If so, a linear model is likely to be impractical. Consequently, it is important for us to assess how well the linear model fits the data. If the fit is poor, we should discard the linear model and seek another one.

Several methods are used to evaluate the model. In this section, we present two statistics and one test procedure to determine whether a linear model should be employed. They are the standard error of estimate, the t test of the slope, and the coefficient of determination. All of these methods are based on the sum of squares for error.

SUM OF SQUARES FOR ERROR

The least squares method determines the coefficients that minimize the sum of squared deviations between the points and the line defined by the coefficients. Recall from Section 18.3 that the minimized sum of squared deviations is called the *sum of squares for error*, denoted SSE. In that section we demonstrated the direct method of calculating SSE. For each value of x we compute the value of $\hat{y}$. That is, for $i = 1$ to n, we compute

$$\hat{y}_i = b_0 + b_1 x_i$$

For each point we then compute the difference between the actual value of y and the value calculated at the line, which is the residual. We square each residual and sum the squared values. Table 18.1 shows these calculations for Example 18.1. To calculate SSE manually requires a great deal of arithmetic. Fortunately, there is a shortcut method available that uses the sample variances and the covariance.

> **SHORTCUT CALCULATION OF SSE**
>
> $$\text{SSE} = (n - 1)\left(s_y^2 - \frac{[\text{cov}(x, y)]^2}{s_x^2}\right)$$

STANDARD ERROR OF ESTIMATE

In Section 18.4, we pointed out that the error variable ε is normally distributed with mean 0 and standard deviation σ_ε. If σ_ε is large, some of the errors will be large, which implies that the model's fit is poor. If σ_ε is small, the errors tend to be close to the mean (which is 0), and, as a result, the model fits well. Hence, we could use σ_ε to measure the suitability of using a linear model. Unfortunately, σ_ε is a population parameter and, like most parameters, is unknown. We can, however, estimate σ_ε from the data. The estimate is based on SSE. The unbiased estimator of the variance of the error variable σ_ε^2 is

$$s_\varepsilon^2 = \frac{\text{SSE}}{n - 2}$$

The square root of s_ε^2 is called the *standard error of estimate*.

> **STANDARD ERROR OF ESTIMATE**
>
> $$s_\varepsilon = \sqrt{\frac{\text{SSE}}{n - 2}}$$

EXAMPLE 18.3

Find the standard error of estimate for Example 18.2 and describe what it tells you about the model's fit.

SOLUTION

COMPUTE

 MANUALLY

To compute the standard error of estimate we need to compute SSE, which is calculated from the sample variances and the covariance. We have already determined the covariance and the variance of x. They are −2,712,511 and 43,528,690, respectively. The sample variance of y (applying the shortcut method) is

$$s_y^2 = \frac{1}{n - 1}\left[\sum_{i=1}^{n} y_i^2 - \frac{\left(\sum_{i=1}^{n} y_i\right)^2}{n}\right]$$

$$= \frac{1}{100 - 1}\left[21,997,338,836 - \frac{(1,482,282)^2}{100}\right] = 259,996$$

$$\text{SSE} = (n - 1)\left(s_y^2 - \frac{[\text{cov}(x, y)]^2}{s_x^2}\right)$$

$$= (100 - 1)\left(259,996 - \frac{[-2,712,511]^2}{43,528,690}\right)$$

$$= 9,005,450$$

The standard error of estimate follows:

$$s_\varepsilon = \sqrt{\frac{\text{SSE}}{n - 2}} = \sqrt{\frac{9,005,450}{98}} = 303.1$$

 EXCEL

Standard Error   303.1

This part of the Excel printout was copied from the complete printout on page 612.

 MINITAB

S = 303.1

This part of the Minitab printout was copied from the complete printout on page 612.

INTERPRET

The smallest value that s_ε can assume is 0, which occurs when SSE = 0, that is, when all the points fall on the regression line. Thus, when s_ε is small, the fit is excellent, and the linear model is likely to be an effective analytical and forecasting tool. If s_ε is large, the model is a poor one, and the statistics practitioner should improve it or discard it.

We judge the value of s_ε by comparing it to the values of the dependent variable y or, more specifically, to the sample mean $\bar{y}$. In this example, because $s_\varepsilon = 303.1$ and $\bar{y} = 14,823$, we would have to admit that the standard error of estimate is not very small. On the other hand, it is not a large number. Because there is no predefined upper limit on s_ε, it is difficult to assess the model in this way (except in cases where s_ε is obviously a small number). In general, the standard error of estimate cannot be used as an absolute measure of the model's utility.

Nonetheless, s_ε is useful in comparing models. If the statistics practitioner has several models from which to choose, the one with the smallest value of s_ε should generally be the one used. As you'll see, s_ε is also an important statistic in other procedures associated with regression analysis.

TESTING THE SLOPE

To understand this method of assessing the linear model, consider the consequences of applying the regression technique to two variables that are not at all linearly related. If we could observe the entire population and draw the regression line, we would observe the graph shown in Figure 18.5 on page 620. The line is horizontal, which means that the value of y is not linearly related to the value of x. Recall that a horizontal straight line has a slope of 0; that is, $\beta_1 = 0$.

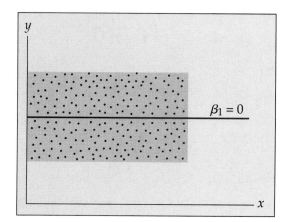

**Figure 18.5
Scatter diagram of
entire population
with $\beta_1 = 0$**

Because we rarely examine complete populations, the parameters are unknown. However, we can draw inferences about the population slope β_1 from the sample slope b_1.

The process of testing hypotheses about β_1 is identical to the process of testing any other parameter. We begin with the hypotheses. The null hypothesis specifies that there is no linear relationship, which means that the slope is 0. Thus, we specify

$$H_0: \quad \beta_1 = 0$$

We can conduct one- or two-tail tests of β_1. Most often we perform a two-tail test to determine whether there is sufficient evidence to infer that a linear relationship exists. We test the alternative hypothesis

$$H_1: \quad \beta_1 \neq 0$$

The test statistic is

$$t = \frac{b_1 - \beta_1}{s_{b_1}}$$

where s_{b_1} is the standard deviation of b_1 (also called the standard error of b_1). It is defined as

$$s_{b_1} = \frac{s_\varepsilon}{\sqrt{(n-1)s_x^2}}$$

If the error variable is normally distributed, the test statistic is Student t distributed with $\nu = n - 2$ degrees of freedom.

EXAMPLE 18.4

Test to determine whether there is enough evidence in Example 18.2 to infer that there is a linear relationship between the auction price and the odometer reading for all 3-year-old Ford Tauruses. Use a 5% significance level.

SOLUTION We test the hypotheses

$$H_0: \quad \beta_1 = 0$$

$$H_1: \quad \beta_1 \neq 0$$

If the null hypothesis is true, no linear relationship exists. If the alternative hypothesis is true, some linear relationship exists between the two variables.

COMPUTE

MANUALLY

To compute the value of the test statistic, we need b_1 and s_{b_1}. In Example 18.2 we found

$$b_1 = -.0623$$

and

$$s_x^2 = 43,528,690$$

Thus,

$$s_{b_1} = \frac{s_\varepsilon}{\sqrt{(n-1)s_x^2}} = \frac{303.1}{\sqrt{(99)(43,528,690)}} = .00462$$

The value of the test statistic is

$$t = \frac{b_1 - \beta_1}{s_{b_1}} = \frac{-.0623 - 0}{.00462} = -13.49$$

The rejection region is

$$t < -t_{\alpha/2,\nu} = -t_{.025,98} \approx -1.984 \quad \text{or} \quad t > t_{\alpha/2,\nu} = t_{.025,98} \approx 1.984$$

EXCEL (See page 612.)

	A	B	C	D	E
16		Coefficients	Standard Error	t Stat	P-value
17	Intercept	17067	169.0	100.97	0.0000
18	Odometer	-0.0623	0.0046	-13.49	0.0000

MINITAB (See page 612.)

```
Predictor      Coef     SE Coef         T         P
Constant    17066.8       169.0    100.97     0.000
Odometer  -0.062315    0.004618    -13.49     0.000
```

INTERPRET

The value of the test statistic is $t = -13.49$, with a p-value of 0. There is overwhelming evidence to infer that a linear relationship exists. What this means is that the odometer reading may affect the auction selling price of the cars. (See the subsection on Cause-and-Effect Relationship on page 625.)

As was the case when we interpreted the y-intercept, the conclusion we draw here is valid only over the range of the values of the independent variable. That is, we can infer that there is a linear relationship between odometer reading and auction price for the 3-year-old Ford Tauruses whose odometer readings lie between 19,057 and 49,223 miles (the minimum and maximum values of x in the sample). Because we have no observations outside this range, we do not know how, or even whether, the two variables are related.

Notice that the printout includes a test for β_0. However, as we pointed out before, interpreting the value of the y-intercept can lead to erroneous, if not ridiculous, conclusions. Consequently, we generally ignore the test of β_0.

COEFFICIENT OF DETERMINATION

The test of β_1 addresses only the question of whether there is enough evidence to infer that a linear relationship exists. In many cases, however, it is also useful to measure the strength of that linear relationship, particularly when we want to compare several different models. The statistic that performs this function is the **coefficient of determination**, which is denoted R^2.

COEFFICIENT OF DETERMINATION

$$R^2 = \frac{[\text{cov}(x, y)]^2}{s_x^2 s_y^2}$$

With a little algebra, statisticians can show that

$$R^2 = 1 - \frac{\text{SSE}}{\sum (y_i - \bar{y})^2}$$

The coefficient of determination is the square of the coefficient of correlation. That is, $R^2 = r^2$. As we pointed out in Chapter 4, except for the values $r = -1$, 0, and 1, we cannot be specific in our interpretation of the coefficient of correlation. However, when we square it we produce a more meaningful statistic.

We'll return to Example 18.1 to learn more about how to interpret the coefficient of determination. In Chapter 15, we partitioned the total sum of squares into two sources of variation. Here, we begin the discussion by observing that the deviation between y_i and $\bar{y}$ can be decomposed into two parts. That is,

$$(y_i - \bar{y}) = (y_i - \hat{y}_i) + (\hat{y}_i - \bar{y})$$

This equation is represented graphically (for $i = 5$) in Figure 18.6.

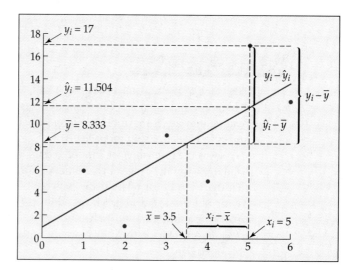

**Figure 18.6
Partitioning the deviation for $i = 5$ in Example 18.1**

Now we ask why the values of y are different from one another. From Figure 18.6, we see that part of the difference between y_i and $\bar{y}$ is the difference between $\hat{y}_i$ and $\bar{y}$, which is accounted for by the difference between x_i and $\bar{x}$. That is, some of the variation in y is explained by the variation in x. The other part of the difference between y_i and $\bar{y}$, however, is accounted for by the difference between y_i and $\hat{y}_i$. This difference is the residual, which to some degree represents variables not otherwise represented by the model. As a result, we say that this part of the difference is *unexplained* by the variation in x.

If we now square both sides of the equation, sum over all sample points, and perform some algebra, we produce

$$\sum (y_i - \bar{y})^2 = \sum (y_i - \hat{y}_i)^2 + \sum (\hat{y}_i - \bar{y})^2$$

The quantity on the left side of this equation is a measure of the variation in the dependent variable y. The first quantity on the right side of the equation is SSE, and the second term is denoted SSR, for *sum of squares for regression*. We can rewrite the equation as

$$\text{Variation in } y = \text{SSE} + \text{SSR}$$

As we did in the analysis of variance, we partition the variation of y into two parts: SSE, which measures the amount of variation in y that remains unexplained; and SSR, which measures the amount of variation in y that is explained by the variation in the independent variable x. We can incorporate this analysis into the definition of R^2.

$$R^2 = 1 - \frac{\text{SSE}}{\sum (y_i - \bar{y})^2} = \frac{\sum (y_i - \bar{y})^2 - \text{SSE}}{\sum (y_i - \bar{y})^2} = \frac{\text{SSR}}{\sum (y_i - \bar{y})^2} = \frac{\text{Explained variation}}{\text{Variation in } y}$$

It follows that R^2 measures the proportion of the variation in y that is explained by the variation in x.

S e e i n g   S t a t i s t i c s

APPLET 19
ANALYSIS OF REGRESSION DEVIATIONS

This applet provides another way to understand the coefficient of determination.

Move the regression line to reduce the sum of squared errors. The vertical line from each point to the horizontal line depicts the deviation from the mean. In regression this is divided into two parts--the green part, which is the deviation that is eliminated by using the regression line, and the red part, which is the deviation remaining. Note that for some points the deviations become larger.

Applet Exercises
Change the slope (if necessary) so that the line is horizontal.

19.1 How much of the variation in y is explained by the variation in x? Why is this so?

Move the line so that it goes through the sixth point ($x = 6$ and $y = 12$).

19.2 What is the value of R^2?

19.3 How much of the variation between y_6 and $\bar{y}$ is explained by the variation between x_6 and $\bar{x}$? Why is this so?

Produce the least squares line. (Click the "Find Best Model" button.)

19.4 How much of the variation in y is explained by the variation in x?

EXAMPLE 18.5

Find the coefficient of determination for Example 18.2 and describe what this statistic tells you about the regression model.

SOLUTION

COMPUTE

 MANUALLY

We have already calculated all the necessary components of this statistic. In Example 18.2 we found

$$\text{cov}(x, y) = -2{,}712{,}511$$

$$s_x^2 = 43{,}528{,}690$$

and from Example 18.3

$$s_y^2 = 259{,}996$$

Thus,

$$R^2 = \frac{[\text{cov}(x, y)]^2}{s_x^2 s_y^2} = \frac{[-2{,}712{,}511]^2}{(43{,}528{,}690)(259{,}996)} = .6501$$

 EXCEL (See page 612.)

R Square   0.6501

 MINITAB (See page 612.)

R-Sq = 65.0%

Both Minitab and Excel print a second R^2 statistic called the *coefficient of determination adjusted for degrees of freedom*. We will define and describe this statistic in Chapter 19.

INTERPRET

We found that R^2 is equal to .6501. This statistic tells us that 65.01% of the variation in the auction selling prices is explained by the variation in the odometer readings. The remaining 34.99% is unexplained. Unlike the value of a test statistic, the coefficient of determination does not have a critical value that enables us to draw conclusions. In general, the higher the value of R^2, the better the model fits the data. From the *t* test of β_1, we know already that there is evidence of a linear relationship. The coefficient of determination merely supplies us with a measure of the strength of that relationship. As you will discover in the next chapter, when we improve the model, the value of R^2 increases.

OTHER PARTS OF THE COMPUTER PRINTOUT

The last part of the printout shown on page 612 relates to our discussion of the interpretation of the value of R^2, when its meaning is derived from the partitioning of the variation in *y*. The values of SSR and SSE are shown in an analysis variance table similar to the tables introduced in Chapter 15. The general form of the table is shown in Table 18.2. The *F* test performed in the ANOVA table will be explained in Chapter 19.

Table 18.2 General Form of the ANOVA Table in the Simple Linear Regression Model

Source	d.f.	Sum of Squares	Mean Square	F Value
Regression	1	SSR	$MSR = SSR/1$	$F = MSR/MSE$
Error	$n-2$	SSE	$MSE = SSE/(n-2)$	
Total	$n-1$	Variation in y		

Note: Excel calls the second source of variation "Residual."

DEVELOPING AN UNDERSTANDING OF STATISTICAL CONCEPTS

Once again, we encounter the concept of explained variation. We first discussed the concept in Chapter 13 when we introduced the matched pairs experiment, where the experiment was designed to reduce the variation among experimental units. This concept was extended in the analysis of variance, where we partitioned the total variation into two or more sources (depending on the experimental design). And now in regression analysis, we use the concept to measure how the dependent variable is related to the independent variable. We partition the variation of the dependent variable into two sources: the variation explained by the variation in the independent variable and the unexplained variation. The greater the explained variation, the better the model is. We often refer to the coefficient of determination as a measure of the explanatory power of the model.

CAUSE-AND-EFFECT RELATIONSHIP

A common mistake is made by many students when they attempt to interpret the results of a regression analysis when there is evidence of a linear relationship. They imply that changes in the independent variable cause changes in the dependent variable. It must be emphasized that we cannot infer a causal relationship from statistics alone. Any inference about the cause of the changes in the dependent variable must be justified by a reasonable theoretical relationship. For example, statistical tests established that the more one smoked, the greater the probability of developing lung cancer. However, this analysis did not prove that smoking causes lung cancer. It only demonstrated that smoking and lung cancer were somehow related. Only when medical investigations established the connection were scientists able to confidently declare that smoking causes lung cancer.

As another illustration, consider Example 18.2, where we showed that the odometer reading is linearly related to the auction price. While it seems reasonable to conclude that decreasing the odometer reading would cause the auction price to rise, the conclusion may not be entirely true. It is theoretically possible that the price is determined by the overall condition of the car and that the condition generally worsens when the car is driven longer. Another analysis would be needed to establish the veracity of this conclusion.

Be cautious about the use of the terms *explained variation* and *explanatory power of the model*. Do not interpret the word *explained* to mean *caused*. We say that the coefficient of determination measures the amount of variation in y that is explained (not caused) by the variation in x. Thus, regression analysis can only show that a statistical relationship exists. We cannot infer that one variable causes another.

EXERCISES

The following exercises require the use of a computer and software. The answers may be calculated manually. See Appendix A for the sample statistics.

18.16 Refer to Exercise 18.2.

a What is the standard error of estimate? Interpret its value.

b Describe how well the heights of the fathers and sons are linearly related.

c Are the heights of fathers and sons linearly related? Test using a 5% significance level.

18.17 Refer to Exercise 18.3. Apply the three methods of assessing the model to determine how well the linear model fits.

18.18 Refer to Exercise 18.4. Are the two variables linearly related? Conduct a test with a 10% significance level.

18.19 Refer to Exercise 18.5. Use two statistics to measure the strength of the linear association. What do these statistics tell you?

18.20 Refer to Exercise 18.6.

a Determine the standard error of estimate and describe what this statistic tells you about the regression model.

b Determine the coefficient of determination. What does this statistic tell you about how well the linear regression model fits?

c Can we infer at the 5% significance level that the length of commercial and memory test score are linearly related?

18.21 Refer to Exercise 18.7.

a Test at the 10% significance level to determine whether there is evidence of a linear relationship between study time and the final mark.

b Determine the coefficient of determination. What does this statistic tell you about the regression line?

18.22 Refer to Exercise 18.8.

a Determine the standard error of estimate, and describe what this statistic tells you about the regression line.

b Can we conclude at the 1% significance level that education and Internet use are linearly related?

c Determine the coefficient of determination and discuss what its value tells you about the two variables.

18.23 Refer to Exercise 18.9. Are work period and age linearly related? (Conduct a statistical test with $\alpha = .05$ to decide.) If so, provide a statistic that measures the strength of the association.

18.24 Refer to Exercise 18.10. Use whatever statistics you think useful to describe the reliability of your suggested compensation plan.

18.25 Refer to Exercise 18.11. Use whatever statistics you think useful to describe the reliability of your insurance premium plan.

18.26 Refer to Exercise 18.12.

a Determine the standard error of estimate and describe what this statistic tells you about the regression model.

b Determine the coefficient of determination. What does this statistic tell you about how well the linear regression model fits?

c Can we infer at the 5% significance level that the weight and price of the diamonds are linearly related?

18.27 An economist wanted to investigate the relationship between office rents and vacancy rates. Accordingly, he took a random sample of monthly office rents and the percentage of vacant office space in 30 different cities. The results were stored in file Xr18-27.

a Determine the regression line.

b Interpret the coefficients.

c Can we conclude at the 5% significance level that higher vacancy rates result in lower rents?

d Measure how well the linear model fits the data. Discuss what this measure tells you.

18.28 Physicians have been recommending more exercise for their patients, particularly those who are overweight. One benefit of regular exercise appears to be a reduction in cholesterol, a substance associated with heart disease. In order to study the relationship more carefully, a physician took a random sample of 50 patients who do not exercise and measured their cholesterol levels. He then started them on regular exercise programs. After 4 months, he asked each patient how many minutes per week (on average) he or she exercised and also measured their cholesterol levels. The results are stored in file Xr18-28 (column 1 = weekly exercise in minutes; column 2 = cholesterol level before exercise program; and column 3 = cholesterol level after exercise program).

a Determine the regression line that relates exercise time with cholesterol reduction.

b Interpret the coefficients.

c Can we conclude at the 5% significance level that the amount of exercise is linearly related to cholesterol reduction?

d Measure how well the linear model fits.

18.29 Although a large number of tasks in the computer industry are robotic, a number of operations require human workers. Some jobs require a great deal of dexterity to properly position components into place. A large North American computer maker routinely tests applicants for these jobs by giving a dexterity test that involves a number of intricate finger and hand movements. The tests are scored on a 100-point scale. Only those who have scored above 70 are hired. To determine whether the tests are valid predictors of job

APPLICATIONS IN *HUMAN RESOURCES MANAGEMENT*

Testing Job Applicants

In our introduction to human resources management in Chapter 1, we noted that the recruitment process at many firms involves tests to determine the suitability of candidates. The tests may be written to determine whether the applicant has sufficient knowledge in his or her area of expertise to perform well on the job. There may be oral tests to determine whether the applicant's personality matches the needs of the job. Manual or technical skills can be tested through a variety of physical tests. The test results contribute to the decision to hire. In some cases, the test result is the only criterion to hire. Consequently, it is vital to ensure that the test is a reliable predictor of job performance. If the tests are poor predictors, they should be discontinued. Statistical analyses allow personnel

managers to examine the link between the test results and job performance.

performance, the personnel manager drew a random sample of 45 workers who were hired 2 months ago. He recorded their test scores and the percentage of nondefective computers they produced in the last week. These data are stored in file Xr18-29. Can the

manager infer at the 5% significance level that the test is a valid predictor? That is, can he infer that higher test results are associated with higher percentages of nondefective units?

18.6 (OPTIONAL) APPLICATIONS IN FINANCE: MARKET MODEL

In this section we describe one of the most important applications of simple linear regression. It is the well-known and often applied *market model*. This model assumes that the rate of return on a stock is linearly related to the rate of return on the overall market. The mathematical description of the model is

$$R = \beta_0 + \beta_1 R_m + \varepsilon$$

where R is the return on a particular stock and R_m is the return on some major stock index, such as the New York Stock Exchange Composite Index.

The coefficient β_1 is called the stock's *beta coefficient*, which measures how sensitive the stock's rate of return is to changes in the level of the overall market. For example, if β_1 is greater than 1, the stock's rate of return is more sensitive to changes in the level of the overall market than is the average stock. To illustrate, suppose that $\beta_1 = 2$. Then a 1% increase in the index results in an average increase of 2% in the stock's return. A 1% decrease in the index produces an average 2% decrease in the stock's return. Thus, a stock with a beta coefficient greater than 1 will tend to be more volatile than the market.

A stock's beta coefficient is determined using the statistical tools described in this chapter. The regression analysis produces b_1, which is an estimate of a stock's beta. The coefficient of determination is also an important part of the financial–statistical analysis.

EXAMPLE 18.6

The monthly rates of return for Northern Telecom (Nortel) stock and for the overall market as measured by the Toronto Stock Exchange (TSE) index over a 5-year period are stored in file Xm18-06. Estimate the market model and analyze the results.

SOLUTION A regression analysis was performed and the Excel and Minitab outputs are shown below.

 EXCEL

	A	B	C	D	E	F
1	SUMMARY OUTPUT					
2						
3	*Regression Statistics*					
4	Multiple R	0.5601				
5	R Square	0.3137				
6	Adjusted R Square	0.3019				
7	Standard Error	0.0631				
8	Observations	60				
9						
10	ANOVA					
11		*df*	*SS*	*MS*	*F*	*Significance F*
12	Regression	1	0.1056	0.1056	26.51	0.0000
13	Residual	58	0.2311	0.0040		
14	Total	59	0.3367			
15						
16		*Coefficients*	*Standard Error*	*t Stat*	*P-value*	
17	Intercept	0.0128	0.0082	1.56	0.1245	
18	TSE	0.8877	0.1724	5.15	0.0000	

 MINITAB

Regression Analysis: Nortel versus TSE

```
The regression equation is
Nortel = 0.0128 + 0.888 TSE

Predictor        Coef      SE Coef          T          P
Constant     0.012818     0.008223       1.56      0.124
TSE            0.8877       0.1724       5.15      0.000

S = 0.06312      R-Sq = 31.4%       R-Sq(adj) = 30.2%

Analysis of Variance

Source           DF           SS           MS          F          P
Regression        1      0.10563      0.10563      26.51      0.000
Residual Error   58      0.23110      0.00398
Total            59      0.33673
```

We can interpret the statistics provided in the printout in the same way we've been doing thus far in this chapter. However, we're especially interested in the financial aspects of this procedure. In particular, the financial analysis focuses on two statistics, b_1 and R^2.

The slope coefficient b_1 is a measure of the stock's *market-related* (or *systematic*) *risk* because it measures the volatility of the stock price that is related to the overall market volatility. We note that the slope coefficient for Nortel is .8877. We interpret this to mean that, in this sample, for each 1% increase in the TSE return, the average increase in Nortel's return is .8877%.

The coefficient of determination measures the proportion of the total risk that is market-related. In this case, we see that 31.37% of Nortel's total risk is market-related. That is, 31.37% of the variation in Nortel's returns are explained by the variation in the TSE's returns. The remaining 68.63% is the proportion of the risk that is associated with events specific to Nortel, rather than the market. A financial analyst (and most everyone else) calls this the *firm-specific* (or *nonsystematic*) *risk*. The firm-specific risk is attributable to variables and events not included in the market model, such as the effectiveness of Nortel's sales force and managers. This is the part of the risk that can be diversified away by creating a portfolio of stocks as discussed in Section 7.5. We cannot, however, diversify away the part of the risk that is market-related.

When a portfolio has been created, we can estimate its beta by averaging the betas of the stocks that compose the portfolio. If an investor believes that the market is likely to rise, a portfolio with a beta coefficient greater than 1 is desirable. Risk-averse investors or ones who believe that the market will fall will seek out portfolios with betas less than 1.

EXERCISES

The following exercises require the use of a computer and software.

Exercises 18.30–18.37 feature real data from the New York Stock Exchange from January 1993 to December 1996. Apply the market model for each stock's returns and the Standard and Poor's Composite Index returns. The data are stored in their respective files. Determine the stock's beta and its coefficient of determination. Briefly describe what these two statistics tell you.

18.30 Stock: Intel

18.31 Stock: Motorola

18.32 Stock: General Motors

18.33 Stock: Gillette

18.34 Stock: General Electric

18.35 Stock: Seagram

18.36 Stock: Coca-Cola

18.37 Stock: McDonald's

18.38 Write a report describing the analyses conducted in Exercises 18.30–18.37. In your report, discuss which stocks are the most and least sensitive to changes in the index. Which stocks' risks can be diversified by creating an appropriate portfolio? Explain.

Exercises 18.39–18.46 feature real data from the Toronto Stock Exchange (TSE) from July 1996 to May 2001. The data are stored in their respective files. Apply the market model for each stock's returns and the TSE Index returns. Determine the stock's beta and its coefficient of determination. Briefly describe what these two statistics tell you.

18.39 Stock: Biomira

18.40 Stock: Lorus Therapeutics

18.41 Stock: Petro Canada

18.42 Stock: Suncor Energy

18.43 Stock: National Bank of Canada

18.44 Stock: Laurentian Bank

18.45 Stock: Bombardier, Class B

18.46 Stock: ATI Technologies

18.47 Write a report describing the analyses conducted in Exercises 18.39–18.46. In your report, discuss which stocks are the most and least sensitive to changes in the index. Which stocks' risks can be diversified by creating an appropriate portfolio? Explain.

18.7 USING THE REGRESSION EQUATION

Using the techniques in Section 18.5, we can assess how well the linear model fits the data. If the model fits satisfactorily, we can use it to forecast and estimate values of the dependent variable. To illustrate, suppose that in Example 18.2, the used-car dealer wanted to predict the selling price of a 3-year-old Ford Taurus with 40,000 miles on the odometer. Using the regression equation, with $x = 40,000$, we get

$$\hat{y} = 17,067 - .0623x = 17,067 - .0623(40,000) = 14,575$$

We call this value the **point prediction**. Thus, the dealer would predict that the car would sell for $14,575.

By itself, however, the point prediction does not provide any information about how closely the value will match the true selling price. To discover that information, we must use an interval. In fact, we can use one of two intervals: the prediction interval of a particular value of y or the confidence interval estimator of the expected value of y.

PREDICTING THE PARTICULAR VALUE OF *y* FOR A GIVEN *x*

The first interval we present is used whenever we want to predict one particular value of the dependent variable, given a specific value of the independent variable. This interval, often called the **prediction interval**, is calculated as follows.

PREDICTION INTERVAL

$$\hat{y} \pm t_{\alpha/2,n-2}s_\varepsilon\sqrt{1 + \frac{1}{n} + \frac{(x_g - \bar{x})^2}{(n-1)s_x^2}}$$

where x_g is the given value of x and

$$\hat{y} = b_0 + b_1 x_g$$

ESTIMATING THE EXPECTED VALUE OF *y* FOR A GIVEN *x*

The conditions described in Section 18.4 imply that for a given value of x, there is a population of values of y whose mean is

$$E(y) = \beta_0 + \beta_1 x$$

To estimate the mean of y, given x, we would use the following interval.

CONFIDENCE INTERVAL ESTIMATOR OF THE EXPECTED VALUE OF *y*

$$\hat{y} \pm t_{\alpha/2,n-2}s_\varepsilon\sqrt{\frac{1}{n} + \frac{(x_g - \bar{x})^2}{(n-1)s_x^2}}$$

Unlike the formula for the prediction interval, this formula does not include the 1 under the square-root sign. As a result, the confidence interval estimate of the expected value of y will be narrower than the prediction interval for the same given value of x and confidence level. This is because there is less error in estimating a mean value as opposed to predicting an individual value.

EXAMPLE 18.7

a A used-car dealer is about to bid on a 3-year-old Ford Taurus equipped with automatic transmission, air conditioner, and AM/FM cassette tape player, and with 40,000 miles on the odometer. To help him decide how much to bid, he needs to predict the selling price.

b The used-car dealer mentioned in part **a** has an opportunity to bid on a lot of cars offered by a rental company. The rental company has 250 Ford Tauruses, all equipped with automatic transmission, air conditioning, and AM/FM cassette tape players. All of the cars in this lot have about 40,000 miles on the odometer. The dealer would like an estimate of the selling price of all the cars in the lot.

SOLUTION

IDENTIFY

a The dealer would like to predict the selling price of a single car. Thus, he needs to employ the prediction interval

$$\hat{y} \pm t_{\alpha/2, n-2} s_\varepsilon \sqrt{1 + \frac{1}{n} + \frac{(x_g - \bar{x})^2}{(n-1)s_x^2}}$$

b The dealer wants to determine the mean price of a large lot of cars, so he needs to calculate the confidence interval estimator of the expected value:

$$\hat{y} \pm t_{\alpha/2, n-2} s_\varepsilon \sqrt{\frac{1}{n} + \frac{(x_g - \bar{x})^2}{(n-1)s_x^2}}$$

Technically, this formula is used for infinitely large populations. However, we can interpret our problem as attempting to determine the average selling price of all Ford Tauruses equipped as described above, all with 40,000 miles on the odometer. The crucial factor in part **b** is the need to estimate the mean price of a number of cars. We arbitrarily select a 95% confidence level.

COMPUTE

 MANUALLY

From previous calculations we have the following:

$$\hat{y} = 17{,}067 - .0623(40{,}000) = 14{,}575$$

$$s_\varepsilon = 303.1$$

$$s_x^2 = 43{,}528{,}690$$

$$\bar{x} = 36{,}009.45$$

From Table 4 in Appendix B, we find

$$t_{\alpha/2} = t_{.025, 98} \approx t_{.025, 100} = 1.984$$

a The 95% prediction interval is

$$\hat{y} \pm t_{\alpha/2, n-2} s_\varepsilon \sqrt{1 + \frac{1}{n} + \frac{(x_g - \bar{x})^2}{(n-1)s_x^2}}$$

$$= 14{,}575 \pm 1.984 \times 303.1 \sqrt{1 + \frac{1}{100} + \frac{(40{,}000 - 36{,}009.45)^2}{(100 - 1)43{,}528{,}690}}$$

$$= 14{,}575 \pm 605$$

The lower and upper limits of the prediction interval are 13,970 and 15,180, respectively.

b The 95% confidence interval estimator of the mean price is

$$\hat{y} \pm t_{\alpha/2, n-2} s_\varepsilon \sqrt{\frac{1}{n} + \frac{(x_g - \bar{x})^2}{(n-1)s_x^2}}$$

$$= 14{,}575 \pm 1.984 \times 303.1\sqrt{\frac{1}{100} + \frac{(40{,}000 - 36{,}009.45)^2}{(100 - 1)43{,}528{,}690}}$$

$$= 14{,}575 \pm 70$$

The lower and upper limits of the confidence interval estimate of the expected value are 14,505 and 14,645, respectively.

EXCEL

	A	B
1	**Prediction Interval**	
2		
3		Price
4		
5	Predicted value	14574
6		
7	Prediction Interval	
8	Lower limit	13968
9	Upper limit	15180
10		
11	Interval Estimate of Expected Value	
12	Lower limit	14504
13	Upper limit	14645

COMMANDS

1. Type or import the data into two columns.
2. Type the given value of x into any cell. We suggest the next available row in the column containing the independent variable.
3. Click **Tools, Data Analysis Plus,** and **Prediction Interval**.
4. Specify the **Input Y Range**.
5. Specify the **Input X Range**.
6. Click **Labels** if appropriate.
7. Specify the **Given X Range**.
8. Specify the **Confidence Level (1-Alpha)**. Click **OK**.

COMMANDS FOR EXAMPLE 18.7

Open file **Xm18-02**.

40000 (in cell A102)

B1:B101
A1:A101

A102
.95

MINITAB

```
Predicted Values for New Observations

New Obs    Fit     SE Fit       95.0% CI             95.0% PI
1       14574.1      35.5   ( 14503.7, 14644.5)  ( 13968.5, 15179.8)

Values of Predictors for New Observations

New Obs   Odometer
1          40000
```

The output includes the predicted value $\hat{y}$ (**Fit**), the standard deviation of $\hat{y}$ (**SE Fit**), the 95% confidence interval estimate of the expected value of y (**CI**), and the 95% prediction interval (**PI**).

COMMANDS

1. Proceed through the first 4 steps of regression analysis described on page 612. Do not click **OK**.
2. Click **Options...**.
3. Specify the given value(s) of x (**Prediction intervals for new observations**).
4. Specify the confidence level. Click **OK**. Click **OK**.

COMMANDS FOR EXAMPLE 18.7

40000

95

> ### INTERPRET

We predict that one car will sell for between $13,968 and $15,180. The average selling price of the population of 3-year-old Ford Tauruses is estimated to lie between $14,504 and $14,645. Because predicting the selling price of one car is more difficult than estimating the mean selling price of all similar cars, the prediction interval is wider than the interval estimate of the expected value.

EFFECT OF THE GIVEN VALUE OF x ON THE INTERVALS

If the two intervals were calculated for various values of x and graphed, Figure 18.7 would be produced. Notice that both intervals are represented by curved lines. This is due to the fact that the farther the given value of x is from $\bar{x}$, the greater the estimated error becomes. This part of the estimated error is measured by

$$\frac{(x_g - \bar{x})^2}{(n - 1)s_x^2}$$

which appears in both the prediction interval and the interval estimate of the expected value.

Figure 18.7
Interval estimates and prediction intervals

EXERCISES

The following exercises require the use of a computer and software. The answers may be calculated manually. See Appendix A for the sample statistics.

18.48 Briefly describe the difference between predicting a value of y and estimating the expected value of y.

18.49 Refer to Exercise 18.2. A statistics practitioner wants to produce a prediction interval of the height of a man whose father is 72 inches tall. What formula should be used? Produce such an interval using a confidence level of 99%.

18.50 Refer to Exercise 18.3. Predict with 95% confidence the number of housing starts when the mortgage rate is 8%.

18.51 Refer to Exercise 18.6.
   a Predict with 95% confidence the memory test score of a viewer who watches a 36-second commercial.
   b Estimate with 95% confidence the mean memory test score of people who watch 36-second commercials.

18.52 Refer to Exercise 18.7.
   a Predict with 90% confidence the final mark of a student who studies for 25 hours.
   b Estimate with 90% confidence the average mark of all students who study for 25 hours.

18.53 Refer to Exercise 18.8. Estimate with 90% confidence the mean amount of time spent on the Internet by people with 15 years of education.

18.54 Refer to Exercise 18.9. The company has just hired a 25-year-old telemarketer. Predict with 95% confidence how long he will stay with the company.

18.55 Refer to Exercise 18.10. Predict with 90% confidence the price of a barrel of oil if the API is 42.0.

18.56 Refer to Exercise 18.11.
  a Predict with 95% confidence the daily emergency medical expense of an average 65-year-old Canadian.
  b Estimate with 95% confidence the mean daily emergency medical expense of all 65-year-old Canadians.

18.57 Refer to Exercise 18.12. Predict with 90% confidence the price of a diamond that weighs .35 carat.

18.58 Refer to Exercise 18.27. Predict with 95% confidence the monthly office rent in a city when the vacancy rate is 10%.

18.59 Refer to Exercise 18.28.
  a Predict with 95% confidence the reduction in cholesterol level of an individual who plans to exercise for 300 minutes per week for a total of 4 months.
  b Suppose that an individual whose cholesterol level is 250 is planning to exercise for 250 minutes per week. Predict with 95% confidence his cholesterol level after 4 months.

18.8 COEFFICIENTS OF CORRELATION

In Section 18.5, we noted that the coefficient of determination is the square of the coefficient of correlation. When we introduced the coefficient of correlation (also called the **Pearson coefficient of correlation**) in Chapter 4, we observed that it is used to measure the strength of association between two variables. Why then do we use the coefficient of determination as our measure of the regression model's fit? The answer: the coefficient of determination is a better measure than the coefficient of correlation because the values of R^2 can be interpreted more precisely. That is, R^2 is defined as the proportion of the variation in y that is explained by the variation in x. Except for $r = -1$, 0, and 1, the coefficient of correlation cannot be interpreted. (When r $= -1$ or 1, every point falls on the regression line, and when $r = 0$, there is no linear pattern.) However, the coefficient of correlation can be useful in another way. We can use it to test for a linear relationship between two variables.

In cases where we're interested in determining how the independent variable is related to the dependent variable, we estimate and test the linear regression model. The t test of the slope presented in Section 18.5 allows us to determine whether a linear relationship actually exists. As we pointed out in Section 18.4, the statistical test requires that for each value of x, there exists a population of values of y that are normally distributed with a constant variance. This condition is required whether the data are experimental or observational.

In many circumstances we're interested in determining only *whether* a linear relationship exists and not the form of the relationship. When the data are observational and the two variables are bivariate normally distributed (see Section 18.4), we can calculate the coefficient of correlation and use it to test for linear association.

As we noted in Chapter 4, the population coefficient of correlation is denoted ρ (the Greek letter *rho*). Because ρ is a population parameter (which is almost always unknown), we must estimate its value from the sample data. Recall that the sample coefficient of correlation is defined as follows.

> *SAMPLE COEFFICIENT OF CORRELATION*
>
> $$r = \frac{\text{cov}(x, y)}{s_x s_y}$$

TESTING THE COEFFICIENT OF CORRELATION

When there is no linear relationship between the two variables, $\rho = 0$. To determine whether we can infer that ρ is 0, we test the hypotheses

H_0: $\rho = 0$

H_1: $\rho \neq 0$

The test statistic is defined in the following way.

TEST STATISTIC FOR TESTING $\rho = 0$

$$t = r\sqrt{\frac{n-2}{1-r^2}}$$

which is Student t distributed with $\nu = n - 2$ degrees of freedom provided that the variables are bivariate normally distributed.

The t test of ρ and the t test of β_1 (where under the null hypothesis both parameters are set equal to 0) produce identical results. If we applied the t test of ρ to Example 18.2, we would produce the same t statistic, p-value, and conclusion (see Exercise 18.63). Hence, practically speaking, it doesn't matter which test we employ. However, conceptually there is a difference between them. The decision about which test to use is based on the type of experiment and the information we seek from the statistical analysis. If we're interested in discovering the relationship between two variables, or if we've conducted an experiment where we controlled the values of the independent variable (as in Exercise 18.6), the t test of β_1 should be applied. If we're interested only in determining *whether* two random variables that are bivariate normally distributed are linearly related, the t test of ρ should be applied. The solution to the chapter opening example illustrates this point.

FOREIGN INDEX FUNDS: SOLUTION

IDENTIFY

The problem objective is to analyze the relationship between two interval variables. Because we're not interested in the form of the linear relationship but only whether a linear relationship exists between the two variables and the data are observational, the parameter of interest is the coefficient of correlation. We test the following hypotheses:

H_0: $\rho = 0$

H_1: $\rho \neq 0$

The test statistic is

$$t = r\sqrt{\frac{n-2}{1-r^2}}$$

COMPUTE

MANUALLY
The rejection region of the test is

$$t < -t_{\alpha/2,\nu} = -t_{.025,57} \approx -2.000 \quad \text{or} \quad t > t_{\alpha/2,\nu} = t_{.025,57} \approx 2.000$$

The value of r is calculated from the covariance and two standard deviations:

$$\text{cov}(x, y) = .001279$$

$$s_x = .0509$$

$$s_y = .0512$$

$$r = \frac{\text{cov}(x, y)}{s_x s_y} = \frac{.001279}{(.0509)(.0512)} = .491$$

The value of the test statistic is

$$t = r\sqrt{\frac{n-2}{1-r^2}} = (.491)\sqrt{\frac{59-2}{1-(.491)^2}} = 4.26$$

(continued)

FOREIGN INDEX FUNDS: SOLUTION *(continued)*

EXCEL

	A	B	C	D
1	Correlation			
2				
3	*US Index and Japanese Index*			
4	Pearson Coefficient of Correlation			0.4911
5	t Stat			4.26
6	df			57
7	P(T<=t) one tail			0
8	t Critical one tail			1.672
9	P(T<=t) two tail			0
10	t Critical two tail			2.0025

COMMANDS

1. Type or import the data into two adjacent columns.
2. Click **Tools, Data Analysis Plus**, and **Correlation (Pearson)**.
3. Specify the **Input Range**.
4. Click **Labels**, if appropriate.
5. Specify a value for α (**Alpha**) and click **OK**.

COMMANDS FOR EXAMPLE

Open file **Index**.

A1:B60

.05

MINITAB

Correlations: US Index, Japanese Index

Pearson correlation of US Index and Japanese Index = 0.491
P-Value = 0.000

COMMANDS

1. Type or import the data into two columns.
2. Click **Stat, Basic Statistics,** and **Correlation....**
3. Select the variables. Click **OK**.

COMMANDS FOR EXAMPLE

Open file **Index**.

US Index
Japanese Index
or **C1 C2**

INTERPRET

The coefficient of correlation is $r = .4911$, the value of the test statistic is $t = 4.26$, which has a p-value of 0. There is overwhelming evidence of a linear relationship between the two indexes. The investor should not buy the Japanese index.

The required condition for the t test of ρ is that the variables are interval and are bivariate normally distributed. We now introduce a technique that can be applied when this condition is not satisfied.

SPEARMAN RANK CORRELATION COEFFICIENT

In the previous sections of this chapter, we have dealt only with interval variables and have assumed that all of the conditions for the validity of the hypothesis tests, prediction intervals, and confidence interval estimates have been met. In many situations, however, one or both variables may be ordinal; or if both variables are interval, the normality requirement may not be satisfied. In such cases, we measure and test to determine whether a relationship exists by employing a nonparametric technique, the **Spearman rank correlation coefficient**.

The Spearman rank correlation coefficient is calculated like all of the previously introduced nonparametric methods by first ranking the data. We then calculate the Pearson correlation coefficient of the ranks. The population Spearman correlation coefficient is labeled ρ_s, and the sample statistic used to estimate its value is labeled r_s.

SAMPLE SPEARMAN RANK CORRELATION COEFFICIENT

$$r_s = \frac{\text{cov}(a, b)}{s_a s_b}$$

where a and b are the ranks of x and y, respectively.

We can test to determine whether a relationship exists between the two variables. The hypotheses to be tested are

$$H_0: \quad \rho_s = 0$$

$$H_1: \quad \rho_s \neq 0$$

(We can also conduct one-tail tests.) The test statistic is r_s. To determine whether the value of r_s is large enough to reject the null hypothesis, we refer to Table 10 in Appendix B, which lists the critical values of the test statistic for one-tail tests. To conduct a two-tail test, the value of α must be doubled. The table lists critical values for $\alpha = .005$, $.01$, $.025$, and $.05$ and for $n = 5$ to 30. When n is greater than 30, r_s is approximately normally distributed with mean 0 and standard deviation $1/\sqrt{n-1}$. Thus, for $n > 30$, the test statistic is as shown in the box.

TEST STATISTIC FOR TESTING $\rho_s = 0$ WHEN $n > 30$

$$z = \frac{r_s - 0}{1/\sqrt{n-1}} = r_s\sqrt{n-1}$$

which is standard normally distributed.

EXAMPLE 18.8

The production manager of a firm wants to examine the relationship between aptitude test scores given prior to hiring of production-line workers and performance ratings received by the employees 3 months after starting work. The results of the study would allow the firm to decide how much weight to give to these aptitude tests relative to other work-history information obtained, including references. The aptitude test results range from 0 to 100. The performance ratings are as follows:

1 = Employee has performed well below average.

2 = Employee has performed somewhat below average.

3 = Employee has performed at the average level.

4 = Employee has performed somewhat above average.

5 = Employee has performed well above average.

A random sample of 20 production workers yielded the results listed below and stored in file Xm18-08. Can the firm's manager infer at the 5% significance level that aptitude test scores are correlated with performance rating?

Employee	Aptitude Test Score	Performance Rating	
1	59	3	
2	47	2	
3	58	4	
4	66	3	
5	77	2	
6	57	4	
7	62	3	*(continued)*

8	68	3
9	69	5
10	36	1
11	48	3
12	65	3
13	51	2
14	61	3
15	40	3
16	67	4
17	60	2
18	56	3
19	76	3
20	71	5

SOLUTION

IDENTIFY

The problem objective is to analyze the relationship between two variables. The aptitude test score is interval, but the performance rating is ordinal. We will treat the aptitude test score as if it were ordinal and calculate the Spearman rank correlation coefficient. To answer the question, we specify the hypotheses as

$$H_0: \quad \rho_s = 0$$

$$H_1: \quad \rho_s \neq 0$$

COMPUTE

 MANUALLY

With $\alpha = .05$ (two-tail) and $n = 20$, the rejection region (from Table 10 in Appendix B) is

$$r_s > .450 \quad \text{or} \quad r_s < -.450$$

We rank each of the variables separately, averaging any ties that we encounter. The original data and ranks are as follows.

Employee	Aptitude Test Score	Rank (a)	Performance Rating	Rank (b)
1	59	9	3	10.5
2	47	3	2	3.5
3	58	8	4	17
4	66	14	3	10.5
5	77	20	2	3.5
6	57	7	4	17
7	62	12	3	10.5
8	68	16	3	10.5
9	69	17	5	19.5
10	36	1	1	1
11	48	4	3	10.5
12	65	13	3	10.5
13	51	5	2	3.5
14	61	11	3	10.5
15	40	2	3	10.5
16	67	15	4	17

(continued)

Employee	Aptitude Test Score	Rank (a)	Performance Rating	Rank (b)
17	60	10	2	3.5
18	56	6	3	10.5
19	76	19	3	10.5
20	71	18	5	19.5

We use the ranks (a) and (b) to compute the Pearson coefficient of correlation. We need to compute s_a, s_b, and $\text{cov}(a, b)$. They are

$$s_a = 5.92$$

$$s_b = 5.50$$

$$\text{cov}(a, b) = 12.34$$

Thus,

$$r_s = \frac{\text{cov}(a, b)}{s_a s_b} = \frac{12.34}{(5.92)(5.50)} = .379$$

EXCEL

	A	B
1	**Spearman Rank Correlation**	
2		
3	*Aptitude and Performance*	
4	Spearman Rank Correlation	0.3792
5	z Stat	1.65
6	P(Z<=z) one tail	0.0492
7	z Critical one tail	1.6449
8	P(Z<=z) two tail	0.0984
9	z Critical two tail	1.96

COMMANDS   COMMANDS FOR EXAMPLE 18.8

1. Type or import the data into two adjacent   Open file **Xm18-08**.
   columns.
2. Click **Tools, Data Analysis Plus,** and
   Correlation (Spearman).
3. Specify the **Input Range**.   **A1:B21**
4. Click **Labels**, if appropriate.
5. Specify a value for α (**Alpha**) and click **OK**.   **.05**

If $n \leq 30$, ignore all values except $r_s = .3792$.

MINITAB

Correlations: Rank apt, Rank Per

```
Pearson correlation of Rank apt and Rank Per = 0.379
```

COMMANDS	COMMANDS FOR EXAMPLE 18.8
1. Type or import the data into two columns.	Open file **Xm18-08**.
2. Click **Manip** and **Rank....**	
3. Specify the first variable.	**Aptitude** or **C1**
4. Specify the column where the ranks are to be stored.	**C3**
5. Repeat steps 2, 3, and 4 for the second variable.	**Performance** or **C2** **C4**
6. Click **Stat, Basic Statistics,** and **Correlation**.	
7. Select the variables representing the ranks.	**C3 C4**
8. If $n > 30$, click **Display p-values** and click **OK**.	

INTERPRET

Because $n \leq 30$, we draw the conclusion based on the rejection region $r_s > .450$ or $r_s < -.450$. There is not enough evidence to believe that the aptitude test scores and performance ratings are related. This conclusion suggests that the aptitude test should be improved to better measure the knowledge and skill required by a production-line worker. If this proves impossible, the aptitude test should be discarded.

EXERCISES

18.60 Given the following data:

x	115	220	86	99	50	110
y	1.0	1.3	.6	.8	.5	.7

a Calculate the Pearson correlation coefficient, and test to determine whether we can infer that a linear relationship exists between the two variables. (Use $\alpha = .05$.)

b Calculate the Spearman rank correlation coefficient, and test to determine whether we can infer that a linear relationship exists between the two variables. (Use $\alpha = .05$.)

18.61 The weekly returns of two stocks are recorded for a 13-week period. These data are stored in file Xr18-61 and listed below.

Week	1	2	3	4	5	6	7	8	9	10	11	12	13
Stock 1	-7	-4	-7	-3	2	-10	-10	5	1	-4	2	6	-13
Stock 2	6	6	-4	9	3	-3	7	-3	4	7	9	5	-7

a Assuming that the returns are normally distributed, can we infer at the 5% significance level that the stock returns are correlated?

b Assuming that the returns are not normally distributed, can we infer at the 5% significance level that the stock returns are correlated?

18.62 The general manager of an engineering firm wants to know whether a draftsman's experience influences the quality of his work. She selects 24 draftsmen at random and records their years of work experience and their quality rating (as assessed by their supervisors). These data are stored in file Xr18-62 (column 1 = work experience in years; column 2 = quality rating, where 5 = excellent, 4 = very good, 3 = average, 2 = fair, and 1 = poor) and listed below. Can we infer from these data that years of work experience is a factor in determining the quality of work performed? Use $\alpha = .10$.

Draftsman	Experience	Rating	Draftsman	Experience	Rating
1	1	1	13	8	2
2	17	4	14	20	5
3	20	4	15	21	3
4	9	5	16	19	2
5	2	2	17	1	1
6	13	4	18	22	3
7	9	3	19	20	4
8	23	5	20	11	3
9	7	2	21	18	5
10	10	5	22	14	4
11	12	5	23	21	3
12	24	2	24	21	1

The following exercises require the use of a computer and software.
Use a 5% significance level.

18.63 Refer to Example 18.2.

    a Conduct the *t* test of ρ to determine whether the odometer reading and the price are linearly related.

    b Compare this result with the test of β_1. What did you discover?

18.64 Refer to Exercise 18.63.

    a What is the required condition for the *t* test of ρ?

    b If the required condition is not satisfied, conduct another more appropriate test to determine whether odometer reading and price are related.

18.65 Refer to Exercise 18.6.

    a Determine the coefficient of correlation.

    b Test the coefficient of correlation to determine whether a linear relationship exists between the length of commercial and memory test score.

    c Assume that the conditions for the test conducted in Exercise 18.6 are not met. Do the data allow us to conclude that the longer the commercial, the higher the memory test score will be?

18.66 Assume that the normality requirement in Exercise 18.7 is not met. Test to determine whether grade and study time are positively related.

18.67 Refer to Exercise 18.8.

    a Determine the coefficient of correlation.

    b Test the coefficient of correlation to determine whether a linear relationship exists between Internet use and education.

    c Assume that the conditions for the test conducted in Exercise 18.8 are not met. Do the data allow us to conclude that people with more education use the Internet more?

18.68 If the normality requirement in Exercise 18.9 has been violated, can we infer that age and work period are related?

18.69 Assume that the price and quality of the oil in Exercise 18.10 are not bivariate normally distributed. Conduct a test to determine whether higher prices are related to higher quality.

18.70 Refer to Exercise 18.11.

    a Determine the coefficient of correlation.

    b Test the coefficient of correlation to determine whether a linear relationship exists between age and average medical expense.

    c Assume that the normality requirement for the test conducted in Exercise 18.11 is not met. Do the data allow us to conclude that older Canadians incur higher medical expenses?

18.71 Refer to Exercise 18.12. If we assume that price and weight are not bivariate normally distributed, can we infer that the two variables are related?

18.72 Refer to the Index example. Assume that the returns are not bivariate normally distributed. Conduct a test to determine whether the returns are related.

18.73 The monthly returns for the period July 1996 to May 2001 for indexes that represent Italian and Hong Kong stocks are stored in file Xr18-73. Is there enough evidence to infer that the returns on the two indexes are linearly related?

18.74 Refer to Exercise 18.73. Assume that the returns are not bivariate normally distributed. Conduct a test to determine whether the returns are related.

18.75 The monthly returns for the period July 1996 to May 2001 for United Kingdom and Australian indexes are stored in file Xr18-75. Is there enough evidence to infer that the returns on the two indexes are linearly related?

18.9 REGRESSION DIAGNOSTICS–I

In Section 18.4, we described the required conditions for the validity of regression analysis. Simply put, the error variable must be normally distributed with a constant variance, and the errors must be independent of each other. In this section, we show how to diagnose violations. Additionally, we discuss how to deal with observations that are unusually large or small. Such observations must be investigated to determine whether an error was made in recording them.

RESIDUAL ANALYSIS

Most departures from required conditions can be diagnosed by examining the residuals, which we discussed in Section 18.5. Most computer packages allow you to output the values of the residuals and apply various graphical and statistical techniques to this variable.

We can also compute the standardized residuals. We standardize residuals in the same way we standardize all variables, by subtracting the mean and dividing by the standard deviation. The mean of the residuals is 0 and because the standard deviation σ_ε is unknown, we must estimate its value. The simplest estimate is the standard error of estimate s_ε. Thus

$$\text{Standardized residual for point } i = \frac{e_i}{s_\varepsilon}$$

EXCEL

Excel calculates the standardized residuals by dividing the residuals by the standard deviation of the residuals. (The difference between the standard error of estimate and the standard deviation of the residuals is that in the formula of the former, the denominator is $n - 2$, whereas in the formula for the latter, the denominator is $n - 1$.)

Part of the printout (we show only the first five and last five values) for Example 18.2 follows.

	A	B	C	D
1	RESIDUAL OUTPUT			
2				
3	Observation	Predicted Price	Residuals	Standard Residuals
4	1	14736.91	-100.91	-0.33
5	2	14277.65	-155.65	-0.52
6	3	14210.66	-194.66	-0.65
7	4	15143.59	446.41	1.48
8	5	15091.05	476.95	1.58
9				
10				
11				
12				
13	96	14808.58	39.42	0.13
14	97	14934.83	-368.83	-1.22
15	98	14998.52	-480.52	-1.59
16	99	14624.25	87.75	0.29
17	100	14798.98	-532.98	-1.77

COMMANDS

Proceed with the first 5 steps of regression analysis described on page 612. Before clicking **OK**, select **Residuals** and **Standardized Residuals**. The predicted values, residuals, and standardized residuals will be printed.

We can also standardize by computing the standard deviation of each residual. Statisticians have determined that the standard deviation of the residual at point i is defined as follows.

STANDARD DEVIATION OF THE iTH RESIDUAL

$$s_{e_i} = s_\varepsilon \sqrt{1 - h_i}$$

where

$$h_i = \frac{1}{n} + \frac{(x_i - \bar{x})^2}{(n - 1)s_x^2}$$

The quantity h_i should look familiar; it was used in the formula for the prediction interval and confidence interval estimate of the expected value of y in Section 18.7. Minitab computes this version of the standardized residuals. Part of the printout (we show only the first five and last five values) for Example 18.2 is shown here.

MINITAB

	C1	C2	C3	C4	C5
	Odometer	Price	RESI1	SRES1	FITS1
1	37388	14636	-100.91	-0.33	14736.9
2	44758	14122	-155.65	-0.52	14277.7
3	45833	14016	-194.66	-0.65	14210.7
4	30862	15590	446.41	1.48	15143.6
5	31705	15568	476.95	1.58	15091.0
6	*	*	*	*	*
7	*	*	*	*	*
8	*	*	*	*	*
9	36238	14848	39.42	0.13	14808.6
10	34212	14566	-368.83	-1.22	14934.8
11	33190	14518	-480.52	-1.59	14998.5
12	39196	14712	87.75	0.29	14624.3
13	36392	14266	-532.98	-1.77	14799.0

COMMANDS
Proceed with the first 4 steps of regression analysis as described on page 612. After specifying the **Response** and **Predictors**, click **Storage. . .**, **Fits**, **Residuals**, and **Standardized residuals**. The residuals (**RESI1**), standardized residuals (**SRES1**), and predicted values (**FITS1**) will be stored in the next three available columns.

An analysis of the residuals will allow us to determine whether the error variable is nonnormal, whether the error variance is constant, and whether the errors are independent. We begin with nonnormality.

NONNORMALITY

As we've done throughout this book, we check for normality by drawing the histogram of the residuals. Excel's version is shown below (Minitab's is similar). As you can see, the histogram is bell shaped, leading us to believe that the error is normally distributed.

Excel histogram of residuals for Example 18.2

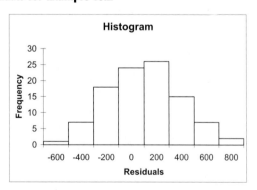

HETEROSCEDASTICITY

The variance of the error variable, σ_ε^2, is required to be constant. When this requirement is violated, the condition is called **heteroscedasticity**. (You can impress friends and relatives by using this term. If you can't pronounce it, try **homoscedasticity**, which refers to the condition where the requirement is satisfied.) One method of diagnosing heteroscedasticity is to plot the residuals against the predicted values of y. We then look for a change in the spread of the plotted points. Figure 18.8 on page 644 describes such a situation. Notice that, in this illustration, σ_ε^2 appears to be small when $\hat{y}$ is small and large when $\hat{y}$ is large. Of course, many other patterns could be used to depict this problem.

Figure 18.9 illustrates a case in which σ_ε^2 is constant. As a result, there is no apparent change in the variation of the residuals.

Figure 18.8
Plot of residuals depicting heteroscedasticity

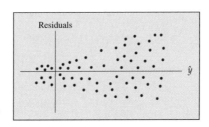

Figure 18.9
Plot of residuals depicting homoscedasticity

Excel's plot of the residuals versus the predicted values of y for Example 18.2 is shown here. There is no sign of heteroscedasticity.

Excel plot of predicted values versus residuals for Example 18.2

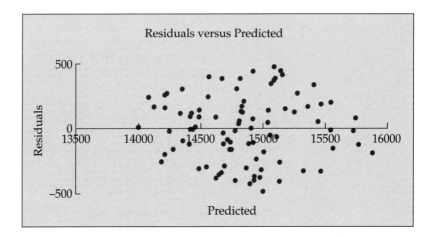

NONINDEPENDENCE OF THE ERROR VARIABLE

In Chapter 2, we briefly described the difference between cross-sectional and time-series data. Cross-sectional data are observations made at approximately the same time, whereas a time series is a set of observations taken at successive points of time. The data in Example 18.2 are cross-sectional because all of the prices and odometer readings were taken at about the same time. If we were to observe the auction price of cars every week for (say) a year, that would constitute a time series.

Condition 4 states that the values of the error variable are independent. When the data are time series, the errors often are correlated. Error terms that are correlated over time are said to be **autocorrelated** or **serially correlated**. For example, suppose that, in an analysis of the relationship between annual gross profits and some independent variable, we observe the gross profits for the years 1981 to 2000. The observed values of y are denoted $y_1, y_2, \ldots, y_{20}$, where y_1 is the gross profit for 1981, y_2 is the gross profit for 1982, and so on. If we label the residuals $e_1, e_2, \ldots, e_{20}$, then—if the independence requirement is satisfied—there should be no relationship between the residuals. However, if the residuals are related, it is likely that autocorrelation exists.

We can often detect autocorrelation by graphing the residuals against the time periods. If a pattern emerges, it is likely that the independence requirement is violated. Figures 18.10 (alternating positive and negative residuals) and 18.11 (increasing residuals) exhibit patterns indicating autocorrelation. (Notice that we joined the points to make it easier to see the patterns.) Figure 18.12 shows no pattern (the residuals appear to be randomly distributed over the time periods), and thus, likely represent the occurrence of independent errors.

In Chapter 19, we introduce the Durbin–Watson test, which is another statistical test to determine whether one form of this problem is present.

Figure 18.10
Plot of residuals versus time indicating autocorrelation (alternating)

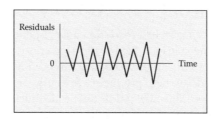

Figure 18.11
Plot of residuals versus time indicating autocorrelation (increasing)

Figure 18.12
Plot of residuals versus time indicating independence

OUTLIERS

An **outlier** is an observation that is unusually small or unusually large. To illustrate, consider Example 18.2, where the range of odometer readings was 19,057 to 49,223 miles. If we had observed a value of 5,000 miles, we would identify that point as an outlier. There are several possibilities that we need to investigate:

1. *There was an error in recording the value.* To detect an error, we would check the point or points in question. In Example 18.2, we could check the car's odometer to determine whether a mistake was made. If so, we would correct it before proceeding with the regression analysis.

2. *The point should not have been included in the sample.* Occasionally, measurements are taken from experimental units that do not belong with the sample. We can check to ensure that the car with the 5,000-mile odometer reading was actually 3 years old. We should also investigate the possibility that the odometer was rolled back. In either case, the outlier should be discarded.

3. *The observation was simply an unusually large or small value that belongs to the sample and that was recorded properly.* In this case we would do nothing to the outlier. It would be judged to be valid.

Outliers can be identified from the scatter diagram. Figure 18.13 depicts a scatter diagram with one outlier. The statistics practitioner should check to determine whether the measurement was recorded accurately and whether the experimental unit should be included in the sample.

The standardized residuals also can be helpful in identifying outliers. Large absolute values of the standardized residuals should be thoroughly investigated. Minitab automatically reports standardized residuals that are less than –2 and greater than 2.

INFLUENTIAL OBSERVATIONS

Occasionally, in a regression analysis, one or more observations have a large influence on the statistics. Figure 18.14 describes such an observation and the resulting least squares line. If the point had not been included, the least squares line in Figure 18.15 would have been produced. Obviously, one point has had an enormous influence on the results. Influential points can be identified by the scatter diagram. The point may be an outlier and as such must be investigated thoroughly. Minitab also identifies influential observations.

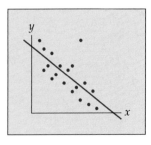

Figure 18.13
Scatter diagram with one outlier

Figure 18.14
Scatter diagram with one influential observation

Figure 18.15
Scatter diagram without the influential observation

PROCEDURE FOR REGRESSION DIAGNOSTICS

The order of the material presented in this chapter is dictated by pedagogical requirements. Consequently, we presented the least squares method, methods of assessing the model's fit, predicting and estimating using the regression equation, coefficients of correlation, and finally, the regression diagnostics. In a practical application, the regression diagnostics would be conducted earlier in the process. It is appropriate to investigate violations of the required conditions when the model is assessed and before using the regression equation to predict and estimate. The following steps describe the entire process. (In Chapter 20, we will discuss model building, for which the following steps represent only a part of the entire procedure.)

1. Develop a model that has a theoretical basis. That is, for the dependent variable in question, find an independent variable that you believe is linearly related to it.

2. Gather data for the two variables. Ideally, conduct a controlled experiment. If that is not possible, collect observational data.

3. Draw the scatter diagram to determine whether a linear model appears to be appropriate. Identify possible outliers.

4. Determine the regression equation.

5. Calculate the residuals and check the required conditions:

    Is the error variable nonnormal?

    Is the variance constant?

    Are the errors independent?

    Check the outliers and influential observations.

6. Assess the model's fit.

    Compute the standard error of estimate.

    Test to determine whether there is a linear relationship. (Test β_1 or ρ.)

    Compute the coefficient of determination.

7. If the model fits the data, use the regression equation to predict a particular value of the dependent variable and/or estimate its mean.

EXERCISES

18.76 Given the following six points.

x	−5	−2	0	3	4	7
y	15	9	7	6	4	1

a Determine the regression equation.

b Use the regression equation to determine the predicted values of y.

c Use the predicted and actual values of y to calculate the residuals.

d Compute the standardized residuals.

e Identify possible outliers.

18.77 Observations of two variables were recorded as shown below.

x	1	2	3	4	5	6	7	8	9
y	5	28	17	14	27	33	39	26	30

a Compute the regression equation.

b Use the regression equation to determine the predicted values of y.

c Use the predicted and actual values of y to calculate the residuals. Compute the standardized residuals.

d Identify possible outliers.

e Plot the residuals against the predicted values of y. Does the variance appear to be constant? Explain.

18.78 Each of the following pairs of values represents an actual value of y and a predicted value of y (based on a simple regression model). Graph the predicted values of y (on the horizontal axis) versus the residuals (on the vertical axis). In each case, determine from the graph whether the requirement that the variance of the error variable be constant is satisfied.

a

y	155	112	163	130	143	182	160	104	125	161	189	102	142	149	180
$\hat{y}$	143	108	180	133	146	193	140	101	126	176	200	97	145	151	158

b

y	10	22	29	15	24	13	17	23	11	27	19	26	20	14
$\hat{y}$	7	21	29	13	25	16	19	22	14	27	17	27	22	11

c

y	46	40	53	60	56	62	44	49	52	59	45	55	47	61	42	57	50
$\hat{y}$	48	43	54	63	54	65	46	47	49	56	41	53	44	57	45	62	51

The following exercises require the use of a computer and software.

18.79 Refer to Exercise 18.6.

a Determine the residuals and the standardized residuals.

b Draw the histogram of the residuals. Does it appear that the errors are normally distributed? Explain.

c Identify possible outliers.

d Plot the residuals versus the predicted values of y. Does it appear that heteroscedasticity is a problem? Explain.

18.80 Refer to Exercise 18.7.

a Does it appear that the errors are normally distributed? Explain.

b Does it appear that heteroscedasticity is a problem? Explain.

18.81 Are the required conditions satisfied in Exercise 18.8?

18.82 Refer to Exercise 18.9.

    a Determine the residuals and the standardized residuals.

    b Draw the histogram of the residuals. Does it appear that the errors are normally distributed? Explain.

c Identify possible outliers.

d Plot the residuals versus the predicted values of y. Does it appear that heteroscedasticity is a problem? Explain.

18.83 Refer to Exercise 18.11. Are the required conditions satisfied?

18.10 SUMMARY

Simple linear regression and **correlation** are techniques for analyzing the relationship between two interval variables. Regression analysis assumes that the two variables are linearly related. The **least squares method** produces estimates of the **intercept** and the **slope** of the regression line. Considerable effort is expended in assessing how well the linear model fits the data. We calculate the **standard error of estimate**, which is an estimate of the standard deviation of the error variable. We test the slope to determine whether there is sufficient evidence of a linear relationship. The strength of the linear association is measured by the **coefficient of determination**. When the model provides a good fit, we can use it to predict the particular value and to estimate the expected value of the dependent variable. We can also use the **Pearson correlation coefficient** to measure and test the relationship between two bivariate normally distributed variables. The **Spearman rank correlation coefficient** analyzes the relationship between two variables, at least one of which is ordinal. It can also be used when the variables are nonnormal. We completed this chapter with a discussion of how to diagnose violations of the required conditions.

IMPORTANT TERMS

Regression analysis 603
Dependent variable 603
Independent variable 603
Deterministic model 605
Probabilistic model 605
First-order linear model 605
Simple linear regression model 605
Error variable 605
Residuals 609
Sum of squares for error 609
Standard error of estimate 618
Coefficient of determination 622
Sum of squares for regression 623

Market model 627
Beta coefficient 627
Market-related (systematic) risk 628
Firm-specific (nonsystematic) risk 628
Point prediction 629
Prediction interval 630
Confidence interval estimate of mean of y 630
Pearson coefficient of correlation 634
Spearman rank correlation coefficient 636
Heteroscedasticity 643
Homoscedasticity 643
Autocorrelation 644

SYMBOLS

Symbol	Pronounced	Represents
β_0	*Beta-sub-zero* or *beta-zero*	y-intercept coefficient
β_1	*Beta-sub-one* or *beta-one*	Slope coefficient
ε	*Epsilon*	Error variable
$\hat{y}$	*y-hat*	Fitted or calculated value of y
b_0	*b-sub-zero* or *b-zero*	Sample y-intercept coefficient
b_1	*b-sub-one* or *b-one*	Sample slope coefficient
σ_ε	*Sigma-sub-epsilon* or *sigma-epsilon*	Standard deviation of error variable
s_ε	*s-sub-epsilon* or *s-epsilon*	Standard error of estimate
s_{b_1}	*s-sub-b-sub-one* or *s-b-one*	Standard error of b_1
R^2	*R-squared*	Coefficient of determination
x_g	*x-sub-g* or *x-g*	Given value of x
ρ	*Rho*	Pearson coefficient of correlation
r		Sample coefficient of correlation
ρ_s	*Rho-sub-S* or *rho-S*	Spearman rank correlation
r_s	*r-sub-S* or *r-S*	Sample Spearman rank correlation
e_i	*e-sub-i* or *e-i*	Residual of ith point

FORMULAS

Sample slope

$$b_1 = \frac{\text{cov}(x, y)}{s_x^2}$$

Sample y-intercept

$$b_0 = \bar{y} - b_1 \bar{x}$$

Sum of squares for error

$$\text{SSE} = \sum_{i=1}^{n} (y_i - \hat{y}_i)^2$$

Standard error of estimate

$$s_\varepsilon = \sqrt{\frac{\text{SSE}}{n - 2}}$$

Test statistic for the slope

$$t = \frac{b_1 - \beta_1}{s_{b_1}}$$

Standard error of b_1

$$s_{b_1} = \frac{s_\varepsilon}{\sqrt{(n - 1)s_x^2}}$$

Coefficient of determination

$$R^2 = \frac{[\text{cov}(x, y)]^2}{s_x^2 s_y^2} = 1 - \frac{\text{SSE}}{\sum (y_i - \bar{y})^2}$$

Prediction interval

$$\hat{y} \pm t_{\alpha/2, n-2} s_\varepsilon \sqrt{1 + \frac{1}{n} + \frac{(x_g - \bar{x})^2}{(n-1)s_x^2}}$$

Confidence interval estimator of the expected value of y

$$\hat{y} \pm t_{\alpha/2, n-2} s_\varepsilon \sqrt{\frac{1}{n} + \frac{(x_g - \bar{x})^2}{(n-1)s_x^2}}$$

Sample coefficient of correlation

$$r = \frac{\text{cov}(x, y)}{s_x s_y}$$

Test statistic for testing $\rho = 0$

$$t = r\sqrt{\frac{n-2}{1-r^2}}$$

Sample Spearman rank correlation coefficient

$$r_s = \frac{\text{cov}(a, b)}{s_a s_b}$$

Test statistic for testing $\rho_s = 0$ when $n > 30$

$$z = \frac{r_s - 0}{1/\sqrt{n-1}} = r_s \sqrt{n-1}$$

COMPUTER OUTPUT AND INSTRUCTIONS

Technique	Excel	Minitab
Regression	612	612
Prediction interval	632	632
Correlation (Pearson)	636	636
Spearman rank correlation	639	639

REFERENCES

Alexander, G. J., W. F. Sharpe, and J. V. Bailey, *Fundamentals of Investing*, 2nd edition. Englewood Cliffs, NJ: Prentice Hall, 1993.

Belsley, David A., Edwin Kuh, and Roy E. Welsch, *Regression Diagnostics: Identifying Influential Data and Sources of Collinearity*. New York: John Wiley & Sons, 1980.

Chatterjee, Samprit, and Bertram Price, *Regression Analysis by Example*, 2nd edition. New York: John Wiley & Sons, 1991.

Conover, W. J., *Practical Nonparametric Statistics*, 2nd edition. New York: John Wiley and Sons, 1980.

Cook, R. Dennis, *Regression Graphics: Ideas for Studying Regressions through Graphics*. New York: John Wiley and Sons, 1998.

Draper, N. R., and H. Smith, *Applied Regression Analysis*, 2nd edition. New York: John Wiley and Sons, 1981.

Graybill, Franklin A., *Theory and Application of the Linear Model.* North Scituate, MA: Duxbury, 1976.

Greene, William, *Econometric Analysis*, 4th edition. Upper Saddle River, NJ: Prentice Hall, 2000.

Kleinbaum, David G., Lawrence I. Kupper, Keith E. Muller, and Azhar Nizam, *Applied Regression Analysis and Multivariable Methods*, 3rd edition. Belmont, CA: Duxbury, 1998.

Neter, John, Michael H. Kutner, Christopher J. Nachtsheim, and William Wasserman, *Applied Linear Statistical Models*, 4th edition. Chicago: Irwin, 1996.

CHAPTER REVIEW EXERCISES

The following exercises require the use of a computer and software. The answers to some of the questions may be calculated manually. See Appendix A for the sample statistics. **Conduct all tests of hypothesis at the 5% significance level.**

18.84 The manager of Colonial Furniture has been reviewing weekly advertising expenditures. During the past 6 months, all advertisements for the store have appeared in the local newspaper. The number of ads per week has varied from one to seven. The store's sales staff has been tracking the number of customers who enter the store each week. The number of ads and the number of customers per week for the past 26 weeks have been stored in the file Xr18-84.

   a Determine the sample regression line.

   b Interpret the coefficients.

   c Can the manager infer that the larger the number of ads, the larger the number of customers?

   d Find and interpret the coefficient of determination.

   e In your opinion, is it a worthwhile exercise to use the regression equation to predict the number of customers who will enter the store, given that Colonial intends to advertise five times in the newspaper? If so, find a 95% prediction interval. If not, explain why not.

18.85 The president of a company that manufactures car seats has been concerned about the number and cost of machine breakdowns. The problem is that the machines are old and becoming quite unreliable. However, the cost of replacing them is quite high, and the president is not certain that the cost can be made up in today's slow economy. To help make a decision about replacement, he gathered data about last month's costs for repairs and the ages (in months) of the plant's 20 welding machines. These data are stored in file Xr18-85.

   a Find the sample regression line.

   b Interpret the coefficients.

   c Determine the coefficient of determination, and discuss what this statistic tells you.

   d Conduct a test to determine whether the age of a machine and its monthly cost of repair are linearly related.

   e Is the fit of the simple linear model good enough to allow the president to predict the monthly repair cost of a welding machine that is 120 months old? If so, find a 95% prediction interval. If not, explain why not.

18.86 Several years ago, Coca-Cola attempted to change its 100-year-old recipe. One reason the company's management thought this was necessary was competition from Pepsi Cola. Respondents of surveys of Pepsi drinkers indicated that they preferred Pepsi because it was sweeter than Coke. As part of the analysis that led to Coke's ill-fated move, the management of Coca-Cola performed extensive surveys wherein consumers tasted various versions of the new Coke. Suppose that a random sample of 200 cola drinkers was given versions of Coke with different amounts of sugar. After tasting the product, each drinker was asked to rate the taste quality. The possible responses were as follows:
5 = excellent, 4 = good, 3 = average, 2 = fair, 1 = poor
The responses and sugar content (percent by volume) of the version tasted were recorded in file Xr18-86. Can management infer that sugar content is related to drinkers' ratings of the cola?

18.87 An agronomist wanted to investigate the factors that determine crop yield. Accordingly, she undertook an experiment wherein a farm was divided into 30 one-acre plots. The amount of fertilizer applied to each plot was varied. Corn was then planted, and the amount of corn harvested at the end of the season was recorded. These data were stored in file Xr18-87.

   a Find the sample regression line, and interpret the coefficients.

   b Can the agronomist conclude that there is a linear relationship between the amount of fertilizer and the crop yield?

   c Find the coefficient of determination, and interpret its value.

   d Does the simple linear model appear to be a useful tool in predicting crop yield from the amount of fertilizer applied? If so, produce a 95% prediction interval of the crop yield when 300 pounds of fertilizer are applied. If not, explain why not.

18.88 Auto manufacturers are required to test their vehicles for a variety of pollutants in the exhaust. The amount of pollutant varies even among identical vehicles, so that several vehicles must be tested. The engineer in charge of testing has collected data (in grams per kilometer driven) on the amounts of two pollutants, carbon monoxide and nitrous oxide, for 50 identical vehicles. These data are stored in file Xr18-88. The engineer believes the company can save money by testing for only one of the pollutants because the two pollutants are closely linked. That is, if a car is emitting a large amount of carbon monoxide, it will also emit a large amount of nitrous oxide. Do the data support the engineer's belief?

18.89 It is doubtful that any sport collects more statistics than baseball. This surfeit of statistics allows fans to conduct a great variety of statistical analyses. For example, fans are always interested in determining which factors lead to successful teams. A statistics practitioner determined the team batting average and the team winning percentage for the 14 American League teams at the end of a recent season. We will assume that these data represent a random sample of the relationship between batting average and winning percentage for all time. These data are stored in file Xr18-89.

  a Find the sample regression line, and interpret the coefficients.

  b Find the standard error of estimate, and describe what this statistic tells you.

  c Do these data provide sufficient evidence to conclude that higher team batting averages lead to higher winning percentages?

  d Find the coefficient of determination, and interpret its value.

  e Predict with 90% confidence the winning percentage of a team whose batting average is .275.

18.90 In an effort to further analyze a baseball team's winning percentage, the statistics practitioner determined each team's earned run average (ERA). (An earned run average is the number of earned runs a baseball team gives up in an average nine-inning game.) These data, together with the team's winning percentage, are stored in file Xr18-90.

  a Find the sample regression line, and interpret the coefficients.

  b Find the standard error of estimate, and describe what this statistic tells you.

  c Do these data provide sufficient evidence to conclude that lower earned run averages lead to higher winning percentages?

  d Find the coefficient of determination, and interpret its value.

  e Predict with 90% confidence the winning percentage of a team whose ERA is 4.00.

18.91 The New York Marathon is run in May when temperatures vary considerably. Because of the enormous strain running more than 26 miles has on the human body, higher temperatures sap the strength of runners and generally result in slower times. To examine the effect of temperature on male runners, the winning times were measured together with the temperature for the years 1978 to 1988. These data are stored in file Xr18-91 (and Xr02-93). Assume that these observations constitute a random sample of the population of times and temperatures. Is there enough evidence to infer that temperatures and winning times for male runners are linearly related?

18.92 Refer to Exercise 18.91. The winning times for female runners (and temperatures) are stored in file Xr18-92 (and Xr02-106). Is there enough evidence to infer that temperatures and winning times for female runners are linearly related?

18.93 In the last decade, society in general and the judicial system in particular have altered their opinions on the seriousness of drunken driving. In most jurisdictions, driving an automobile with a blood alcohol level in excess of .08 is a felony. Because of a number of factors, it is difficult to provide guidelines on when it is safe for someone who has consumed alcohol to drive a car. In an experiment to examine the relationship between blood alcohol level and the weight of a drinker, 50 men of varying weights were each given three beers to drink, and 1 hour later their blood alcohol level was measured. These data are stored in file Xr18-93.

  a If we assume that the two variables are normally distributed, can we conclude that blood alcohol level and weight are related?

  b After examining the data, the statistics practitioner in charge of the experiment concluded that a regression analysis was invalid (because he determined that the error term was nonnormal). What conclusions can you draw from these data about the relationship between blood alcohol level and weight?

18.94 One general belief held by observers of the business world is that taller men earn more money than shorter men. In a University of Pittsburgh study (reported in the *Wall Street Journal*, 30 December 1986), 250 MBA graduates, all about 30 years old, were polled and asked to report their height (in inches) and their annual income (to the nearest $1,000). These data are stored in file Xr18-94.

  a Determine the sample regression line, and interpret the coefficients.

  b Do these data provide sufficient statistical evidence to infer that taller MBA's earn more money than shorter ones?

  c Provide a measure of the strength of the linear relationship between income and height.

  d Do you think that this model is good enough to be used to estimate and predict income on the basis of height? If not, explain why not. If so, estimate with 95% confidence the mean income of all

6-foot men with MBAs and predict with 95% confidence the income of a man 5 feet 10 inches tall with an MBA.

18.95 Every year the United States Federal Trade Commission rates cigarette brands according to their levels of tar and nicotine, substances that are hazardous to smokers' health. Additionally, the commission includes the amount of carbon monoxide, which is a by-product of burning tobacco that seriously affects the heart. A random sample of 25 brands was taken. The data are stored in file Xr18-95.

   a Are the levels of tar and nicotine linearly related?

   b Are the levels of nicotine and carbon monoxide linearly related?

18.96 Some critics of television complain that the amount of violence shown on television contributes to violence in our society. Others point out that television also contributes to the high level of obesity among children. We may have to add financial problems to the list. A sociologist theorized that people who watch television frequently are exposed to many commercials, which in turn leads them to buy more, finally resulting in increasing debt. To test this belief, a sample of 430 families was drawn. For each, the total debt and the number of hours the television is turned on per week were recorded. These data are stored in file Xr18-96. Perform a statistical procedure to help test this theory.

18.97 The analysis the human resources manager performed in Exercise 18.29 indicated that the dexterity test is not a predictor of job performance. However, before discontinuing the test, he decided that the problem is that the statistical analysis was flawed because it examined the relationship between test score and job performance only for those who scored well in the test. (Recall that only those who scored above 70 were hired; applicants who achieved scores below 70 were not hired.) The manager decided to perform another statistical analysis. A sample of 50 job applicants who scored above 50 were hired, and as before, the workers' performance was measured. The test scores and percentages of nondefective computers produced are stored in file Xr18-97. On the basis of these data, should the manager discontinue the dexterity tests?

✦ CASE 18.1
DUXBURY PRESS

The academic book business is different from most other businesses because of the way the purchasing decision is made. The customer, who is usually a student taking a university or college course, buys a specific book because the instructor of the course adopts (chooses to use) that book. Sales representatives of publishers sell their products by persuading instructors to adopt their books. Unfortunately, judging the quality of textbooks is not easy. To help with the decision process, sales representatives give free examination copies to instructors so they can review the book and decide whether to adopt it. In many universities, there are several sections of the same course, and book adoption committees meet to make the adoption decision.

Curt Hinrichs, an editor at Duxbury Press, was examining the latest data on the sales of the three recently published statistics textbooks. He noted that the number of examination copies was quite large, which can be a serious problem given the high cost of producing books. Duxbury distributes review copies only of the books or editions that came out in the current year. He wondered whether his sales representatives were giving away too many free books or perhaps not enough. The data that he is examining contain a code that identifies the sales representative (there is a total of 78 salespeople), the gross revenues

from the sales of the statistics books, and the number of free copies given to professors by that representative. These data are stored in file C18-01. Curt would like to know whether there is a direct link between the number of free copies distributed and the gross revenues from new editions.

Perform an analysis to provide Curt with the information he needs.

✦ CASE 18.2
PREDICTING UNIVERSITY GRADES FROM HIGH SCHOOL GRADES*

Ontario high school students must complete a minimum of six Ontario Academic Credits (OACs) to gain admission to a university in the province. Most students take more than six OACs because universities take the average of the best six in deciding which students to admit. Most programs at universities require high school students to select certain courses. For example, science programs require two of chemistry, biology, and physics. Students applying to engineering must complete at least two mathematics OACs as well as physics. In recent years, one business program began an examination of all aspects of its program, including the criteria used to admit students. Students are required to take English and calculus OACs, and the minimum high school average is about 85%. Strangely enough, even though students are required to complete English and calculus, the marks in these subjects are not included in the average unless they are in the top six courses in a student's transcript. To examine the issue, the registrar took a random sample of students who recently graduated with the BBA (Bachelor of Business Administration) degree. He recorded the university GPA (range 0 to 12), the high school average based on the best six courses, and the high school average using English and calculus and the four next best marks. These data are stored in file C18-02.

a Is there a relationship between university grades and high school average using the best six OACs?

b Is there a relationship between university grades and high school average using the best four OACs plus calculus and English?

c What should the university do about the information provided by this case?

* The authors are grateful to Leslie Grauer for her help in gathering the data for this case.

◈ CASE 18.3
INSURANCE COMPENSATION FOR LOST REVENUES*

In July 1990, a rock-and-roll museum opened in Atlanta, Georgia. The museum was located in a large city block containing a variety of stores. In late July 1992, a fire that started in one of these stores burned the entire block, including the museum. Fortunately, the museum had taken out insurance to cover the cost of rebuilding as well as lost revenue. As a general rule, insurance companies base their payment on how well the company performed in the past. However, the owners of the museum argued that the revenues were increasing, and hence they are entitled to more money under their insurance plan. The argument was based on the revenues and attendance figures of an amusement park that was opened nearby, featuring rides and other similar attractions. The amusement park opened in December 1991. The two entertainment facilities were operating jointly during the last 4 weeks of 1991 and the first 28 weeks of 1992 (the point at which the fire destroyed the museum). In April 1995, the museum reopened with considerably more features than the original one.

The attendance figures for both facilities for December 1991 to October 1995 are listed in columns 1 (museum) and 2 (amusement park) in file C18-03. During the period when the museum was closed, the data show zero attendance.

The owners of the museum argue that the weekly attendance from the 29th week of 1992 to the 16th week of 1995 should be estimated using the most current data (17th to 42nd week of 1995). The insurance company argues that the estimates should be based on the 4 weeks of 1991 and the 28 weeks of 1992, when both facilities were operating and before the museum reopened with more features than the original museum.

a Estimate the coefficients of the simple regression model based on the insurance company's argument. That is, use the attendance figures for the last 4 weeks in 1991 and the next 28 weeks in 1992 to estimate the coefficients. Then, use the model to calculate point predictions for the museum's weekly attendance figures when the museum was closed. Calculate the predicted total attendance.

b Repeat part **a** using the museum's argument. That is, use the attendance figures after the reopening in 1995 to estimate the regression coefficients and use the equation to predict the weekly attendance when the museum was closed. Calculate the total attendance that was lost because of the fire.

c In your opinion, which figure should be used to calculate how much the insurance company should award the museum? How should that compensation be determined?

*The case and the data are real. The names have been changed to preserve anonymity. The authors wish to thank Dr. Kevin Leonard for supplying the problem and the data.

19 · MULTIPLE REGRESSION

MBA PROGRAM ADMISSIONS POLICY–I

The MBA program at a large university is facing a pleasant problem—too many applicants. The current admissions policy requires students to have completed at least 3 years of work experience and an undergraduate degree with a B– average or better. Up to 3 years ago the school admitted any applicant who met these requirements. However, because the program recently converted from a 2-year program (four semesters) to a 1-year program (three semesters), the number of applicants has increased substantially. The dean, who teaches statistics courses, wants to raise the admissions standards by developing a method that more accurately predicts how

well an applicant will perform in the MBA program. She believes that the primary determinants of success are the following:

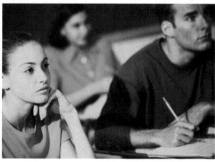

Undergraduate grade point average (GPA)

Graduate Management Admissions Test (GMAT) score

Number of years of work experience

She randomly sampled students who completed the MBA and recorded their MBA program GPA, as well as the three variables listed above. These data are stored in file CH19:\MBA. Develop a plan to decide which applicants to admit.

19.1 INTRODUCTION

In the previous chapter, we employed the simple linear regression model to analyze how one interval variable (the dependent variable y) is related to another interval variable (the independent variable x). The restriction of using only one independent variable was motivated by the need to simplify the introduction to regression analysis. Although there are a number of applications where we purposely develop a model with only one independent variable (see Section 18.6, for example), in general we prefer to include as many independent variables as are believed to affect the dependent variable. Arbitrarily limiting the number of independent variables also limits the usefulness of the model.

In this chapter, we allow for any number of independent variables. In so doing, we expect to develop models that fit the data better than would a simple linear regression model. We proceed in a manner similar to that in Chapter 18. We begin by describing the multiple regression model and listing the required conditions. We let the computer produce the required statistics and use them to assess the model's fit and diagnose violations of the required conditions. We employ the model by interpreting the coefficients, predicting the particular value of the dependent variable, and estimating its expected value.

19.2 MODEL AND REQUIRED CONDITIONS

We now assume that k independent variables are potentially related to the dependent variable. Thus, the model is represented by the following equation:

$$y = \beta_0 + \beta_1 x_1 + \beta_2 x_2 + \cdots + \beta_k x_k + \varepsilon$$

where y is the dependent variable, $x_1, x_2, ..., x_k$ are the independent variables, β_0, $\beta_1, ..., \beta_k$ are the coefficients, and ε is the error variable. The independent variables may actually be functions of other variables. For example, we might define some of the independent variables as follows:

$$x_2 = x_1^2$$

$$x_5 = x_3 x_4$$

$$x_7 = \log(x_6)$$

In Chapter 20, we will discuss how and under what circumstances such functions can be used in regression analysis.

The error variable is retained because, even though we have included additional independent variables, deviations between predicted values of y and actual values of y will still occur. Incidentally, when there is more than one independent variable in the regression model, we refer to the graphical depiction of the equation as a **response surface** rather than as a straight line. Figure 19.1 on page 658 depicts a scatter diagram of a response surface with $k = 2$. (When $k = 2$, the regression equation creates a plane.) Of course, whenever k is greater than 2, we can only imagine the response surface; we cannot draw it.

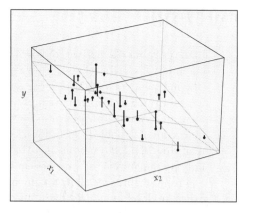

**Figure 19.1
Scatter diagram and
response surface with
k = 2**

An important part of the regression analysis comprises several statistical techniques that evaluate how well the model fits the data. These techniques require the following conditions, which we introduced in the previous chapter.

> **REQUIRED CONDITIONS FOR THE ERROR VARIABLE**
> 1. The probability distribution of the error variable ε is normal.
> 2. The mean of the error variable is 0.
> 3. The standard deviation of ε is σ_ε, which is constant for each value of x.
> 4. The errors are independent.

In Section 18.9, we discussed how to recognize when the requirements are unsatisfied. Those same procedures can be used to detect violations of required conditions in the multiple regression model. We now proceed as we did in Chapter 18: We discuss how the model's coefficients are estimated and how we assess the model's fit. However, there is one major difference between Chapters 18 and 19. In Chapter 18, we allowed for the possibility that some students will perform the calculations manually. The multiple regression model involves so many computations that it is virtually impossible to conduct the analysis without a computer. All analyses in this chapter will be performed by Excel and Minitab. Your job will be to interpret the output.

19.3 ESTIMATING THE COEFFICIENTS AND ASSESSING THE MODEL

The sample regression equation is expressed similarly to the simple regression equation. The general form is

$$\hat{y} = b_0 + b_1 x_1 + b_2 x_2 + \cdots + b_k x_k$$

where k is the number of independent variables.

The procedures introduced in Chapter 18 are extended to the multiple regression model. However, in Chapter 18, we first discussed how to interpret the coefficients and then discussed how to assess the model's fit. In practice, we reverse the process. That is, the first step is to determine how well the model fits. If the model's fit is poor, there is no point in a further analysis of the coefficients of that model. A much higher priority is assigned to the task of improving the model. We will discuss the art and science of model building in Chapter 20. In this chapter, we show how a regression analysis is performed. The steps we use are as follows:

1. Use a computer and software to generate the coefficients and the statistics used to assess the model.

2. Diagnose violations of required conditions. If there are problems, we attempt to remedy them.

3. Assess the model's fit. Three statistics that perform this function are the standard error of estimate, the coefficient of determination, and the F test of the analysis of variance. The first two were introduced in Chapter 18; the third will be introduced here.

4. If we are satisfied with the model's fit and that the required conditions are met, we can interpret the coefficients and test them as we did in Chapter 18. We use the model to predict or estimate the expected value of the dependent variable.

We illustrate these techniques with the following example.

APPLICATIONS IN OPERATIONS MANAGEMENT: *LOCATION ANALYSIS*

Location analysis is one operations management function. As we observed in Chapter 1, deciding where to locate a plant, warehouse, or retail outlet is a crucial decision for any organization. A large number of variables must be considered in this decision problem. For example, a production facility must be located close to suppliers of raw resources and supplies, skilled labor, and transportation to customers. Retail outlets must consider the type and number of potential customers. In the next example, we describe an application of regression analysis to find profitable locations for a motel chain.

EXAMPLE 19.1*

La Quinta Motor Inns is a moderately priced chain of motor inns located across the United States. Its market is the frequent business traveler. The chain recently launched a campaign to increase market share by building new inns. The management of the chain is aware of the difficulty in choosing locations for new motels. Moreover, making decisions without adequate information often results in poor decisions. Consequently, the chain management acquired data on 100 randomly selected inns belonging to La Quinta. The objective was to predict which sites are likely to be profitable.

To measure profitability, La Quinta used *operating margin*, which is the ratio of the sum of profit, depreciation, and interest expenses divided by total revenue. (Although occupancy is often used as a measure of a motel's success, the company statistician concluded that occupancy was too unstable, especially during economic turbulence.) The higher the operating margin, the greater the success of the inn. La Quinta defines profitable inns as those with an operating margin in excess of 50% and unprofitable ones with margins of less than 30%. After a discussion with a number of experienced managers, La Quinta decided to select one or two independent variables from each of the categories: competition, market awareness, demand generators, demographics, and

---

*Adapted from Sheryl E. Kimes and James A. Fitzsimmons, "Selecting Profitable Hotel Sites at La Quinta Motor Inns," *INTERFACES* 20, March–April 1990, pp 12–20.

physical. To measure the degree of competition, they determined the total number of motel and hotel rooms within 3 miles of each La Quinta inn. Market awareness was measured by the number of miles to the closest competing motel. Two variables that represent sources of customers were chosen. The amount of office space and college and university enrollment in the surrounding community are demand generators. Both of these are measures of economic activity. A demographic variable that describes the community is the median household income. Finally, as a measure of the physical qualities of the location, La Quinta chose the distance to the downtown core. These data are stored in file Xm19-01 using the following format:

Column 1: y = Operating margin, in percent

Column 2: x_1 = Total number of motel and hotel rooms within 3 miles of La Quinta inn

Column 3: x_2 = Number of miles to closest competition

Column 4: x_3 = Office space (in thousands of square feet) in surrounding community

Column 5: x_4 = College and university enrollment (in thousands) in nearby university and/or college

Column 6: x_5 = Median household income (in $thousands) in surrounding community

Column 7: x_6 = Distance (in miles) to the downtown core

Some of these data are shown below. Conduct a regression analysis and analyze the results.

Margin	Number	Nearest	Office Space	Enrollment	Income	Distance
55.5	3,203	4.2	549	8	37	2.7
33.8	2,810	2.8	496	17.5	35	14.4
49	2,890	2.4	254	20	35	2.6
⋮	⋮	⋮	⋮	⋮	⋮	⋮
40	3,397	1.6	855	19.5	32	3.1
39.8	3,823	3.6	202	17	38	4.8
35.2	3,251	1.7	275	13	35	4.3

SOLUTION

 EXCEL

	A	B	C	D	E	F
1	SUMMARY OUTPUT					
2						
3	*Regression Statistics*					
4	Multiple R	0.7246				
5	R Square	0.5251				
6	Adjusted R Square	0.4944				
7	Standard Error	5.51				
8	Observations	100				
9						
10	ANOVA					
11		*df*	*SS*	*MS*	*F*	*Significance F*
12	Regression	6	3123.8	520.6	17.14	0.0000
13	Residual	93	2825.6	30.4		
14	Total	99	5949.5			
15						
16		*Coefficients*	*Standard Error*	*t Stat*	*P-value*	
17	Intercept	38.14	6.99	5.45	0.0000	
18	Number	-0.0076	0.0013	-6.07	0.0000	
19	Nearest	1.65	0.63	2.60	0.0108	
20	Office Space	0.020	0.0034	5.80	0.0000	
21	Enrollment	0.21	0.13	1.59	0.1159	
22	Income	0.41	0.14	2.96	0.0039	
23	Distance	-0.23	0.18	-1.26	0.2107	

COMMANDS

1. Type or import the data so that the independent variables are in adjacent columns.
2. Click **Tools, Data Analysis...**, and **Regression**.
3. Specify the **Input Y Range**.
4. Specify the **Input X Range**.
5. Click **Labels** if appropriate and click **OK**.

MINITAB

Regression Analysis: Margin versus Number, Nearest, ...

```
The regression equation is
Margin = 38.1 - 0.00762 Number + 1.65 Nearest + 0.0198 Office Space
            + 0.212 Enrollment + 0.413 Income - 0.225 Distance

Predictor       Coef     SE Coef         T        P
Constant      38.139       6.993      5.45    0.000
Number     -0.007618    0.001255     -6.07    0.000
Nearest       1.6462      0.6328      2.60    0.011
Office S     0.019766    0.003410      5.80    0.000
Enrollme      0.2118      0.1334      1.59    0.116
Income        0.4131      0.1396      2.96    0.004
Distance     -0.2253      0.1787     -1.26    0.211

S = 5.512      R-Sq = 52.5%     R-Sq(adj) = 49.4%

Analysis of Variance

Source            DF          SS         MS         F        P
Regression         6     3123.83     520.64     17.14    0.000
Residual Error    93     2825.63      30.38
Total             99     5949.46
```

COMMANDS

1. Type or import the data.
2. Click **Stat, Regression,** and **Regression....**
3. Specify the dependent variable (**Response**).
4. Specify the independent variables (**Predictors**).

5. Click **OK**.

INTERPRET

The regression model is estimated by

$$\hat{y} = 38.14 - .0076x_1 + 1.65x_2 + .020x_3 + .21x_4 + .41x_5 - .23x_6$$

We assess the model in three ways: the standard error of estimate, the coefficient of determination (both introduced in Chapter 18), and the F test of the analysis of variance (presented below).

STANDARD ERROR OF ESTIMATE

Recall that σ_ε is the standard deviation of the error variable ε and that, because σ_ε is a population parameter, it is necessary to estimate its value by using s_ε. In multiple regression, the standard error of estimate is defined as follows.

> **STANDARD ERROR OF ESTIMATE**
>
> $$s_\varepsilon = \sqrt{\frac{SSE}{n - k - 1}}$$

As we noted in Chapter 18, each of our software packages reports the standard error of estimate in a different way.

EXCEL
Standard Error   5.51

MINITAB
S = 5.512

INTERPRET

Recall that we judge the magnitude of the standard error of estimate relative to the values of the dependent variable, and particularly to the mean of y. In this example, $\bar{y} = 45.739$ (not shown in printouts). It appears that the standard error of estimate is not particularly small.

COEFFICIENT OF DETERMINATION

Recall from Chapter 18 that the coefficient of determination is defined as

$$R^2 = 1 - \frac{SSE}{\sum (y_i - \bar{y})^2}$$

EXCEL
R Square   0.5251

MINITAB
R-Sq = 52.5%

INTERPRET

This means that 52.51% of the variation in operating margin is explained by the six independent variables, while 47.49% remains unexplained.

Notice that Excel and Minitab print a second R^2 statistic, called the **coefficient of determination adjusted for degrees of freedom**, which has been adjusted to take into account the sample size and the number of independent variables. The rationale for this statistic is that, if the number of independent variables k is large relative to the sample size n, the unadjusted R^2 value may be unrealistically high. To understand this point, consider what would happen if the sample size is 2 in a simple linear regression model. The line will fit the data perfectly, resulting in $R^2 = 1$, when, in fact, there may be no linear relationship. To avoid creating a false impression, the adjusted R^2 is often calculated. Its formula follows.

> **COEFFICIENT OF DETERMINATION ADJUSTED FOR DEGREES OF FREEDOM**
>
> $$\text{Adjusted } R^2 = 1 - \frac{\text{SSE}/(n - k - 1)}{\sum (y_i - \bar{y})^2/(n - 1)}$$

If n is considerably larger than k, the actual and adjusted R^2 values will be similar. But if SSE is quite different from 0 and k is large compared to n, the actual and adjusted values of R^2 will differ substantially. If such differences exist, the analyst should be alerted to a potential problem in interpreting the coefficient of determination. In Example 19.1, the adjusted coefficient of determination is 49.44%, indicating that, no matter how we measure the coefficient of determination, the model's fit is moderately good.

TESTING THE VALIDITY OF THE MODEL

In the simple linear regression model, we tested the slope coefficient to determine whether sufficient evidence existed to allow us to conclude that there was a linear relationship between the independent variable and the dependent variable. However, because there is only one independent variable in that model, the t test also tested to determine whether that model is valid. When there is more than one independent variable, we need another method to test the overall validity of the model. The technique is a version of the analysis of variance, which we introduced in Chapter 15.

To test the validity of the regression model, we specify the following hypotheses:

$$H_0: \quad \beta_1 = \beta_2 = \cdots = \beta_k = 0$$

$$H_1: \quad \text{At least one } \beta_i \text{ is not equal to 0.}$$

If the null hypothesis is true, none of the independent variables $x_1, x_2, ..., x_k$ is linearly related to y, and therefore the model is invalid. If at least one β_i is not equal to 0, the model does have some validity.

When we introduced the coefficient of determination in Chapter 18, we noted that the total variation in the dependent variable [measured by $\sum (y_i - \bar{y})^2$] can be decomposed into two parts: the explained variation (measured by SSR) and the unexplained variation (measured by SSE). That is,

Total Variation in y = SSR + SSE

Furthermore, we established that, if SSR is large relative to SSE, the coefficient of determination will be high—signifying a good model. On the other hand, if SSE is large, most of the variation will be unexplained, which indicates that the model provides a poor fit and consequently has little validity.

The test statistic is the same one we encountered in Section 15.2, where we tested for the equivalence of two or more population means. To judge whether SSR is large enough relative to SSE to allow us to infer that at least one coefficient is not equal to 0, we compute the ratio of the two mean squares. (Recall that the mean square is the sum of squares divided by its degrees of freedom; recall, too, that the ratio of two mean squares is F distributed as long as the underlying population is normal—a required condition for this application.) The calculation of the test statistic is summarized in an analysis of variance (ANOVA) table, whose general form appears in Table 19.1 on page 664. The Excel and Minitab ANOVA tables copied from pages 660–661 are shown next.

Table 19.1 Analysis of Variance Table for Regression Analysis

Source of Variation	Degrees of Freedom	Sum of Squares	Mean Square	F Statistic
Regression	k	SSR	MSR = SSR/k	F = MSR/MSE
Residual	$n - k - 1$	SSE	MSE = SSE/(n - k - 1)	
Total	$n - 1$	$\sum (y_i - \bar{y})^2$		

EXCEL

	A	B	C	D	E	F
10	ANOVA					
11		df	SS	MS	F	Significance F
12	Regression	6	3123.8	520.6	17.14	0.0000
13	Residual	93	2825.6	30.4		
14	Total	99	5949.5			

MINITAB

```
Analysis of Variance

Source          DF        SS         MS        F       P
Regression       6   3123.83     520.64    17.14   0.000
Residual Error  93   2825.63      30.38
Total           99   5949.46
```

A large value of F indicates that a significant proportion of the variation in y is explained by the regression equation and that the model is valid. A small value of F indicates that most of the variation in y is unexplained. The rejection region allows us to determine whether F is large enough to justify rejecting the null hypothesis. For this test, the rejection region is

$$F > F_{\alpha, k, n-k-1}$$

In Example 19.1, the rejection region (assuming $\alpha = .05$) is

$$F > F_{\alpha, k, n-k-1} = F_{.05, 6, 93} \approx 2.17$$

As you can see from the printout, $F = 17.14$. The printout also includes the p-value of the test, which is 0. Obviously, there is a great deal of evidence to infer that the model is valid.

Although each assessment measure offers a different perspective, all agree in their assessment of how well the model fits the data, because all are based on the sum of squares for error, SSE. The standard error of estimate is

$$s_\varepsilon = \sqrt{\frac{SSE}{n - k - 1}}$$

and the coefficient of determination is

$$R^2 = 1 - \frac{SSE}{\sum (y_i - \bar{y})^2}$$

When the response surface hits every single point, SSE = 0. Hence $s_\varepsilon = 0$, and $R^2 = 1$.

If the model provides a poor fit, we know that SSE will be large [its maximum value is $\sum (y_i - \bar{y})^2$], s_ε will be large, and [since SSE is close to $\sum (y_i - \bar{y})^2$], R^2 will be close to 0.

The F statistic also depends on SSE. Specifically,

$$F = \frac{[\sum (y_i - \bar{y})^2 - SSE]/k}{SSE/(n - k - 1)}$$

When SSE = 0,

$$F = \frac{\sum (y_i - \bar{y})^2 / k}{0/(n - k - 1)}$$

which is infinitely large. When SSE is large, SSE is close to $\sum (y_i - \bar{y})^2$ and F is quite small. The relationships among s_ε, R^2, and F are summarized in Table 19.2.

Table 19.2 Relationships Among s_ε, R^2, and F

SSE	s_ε	R^2	F	Assessment of Model
0	0	1	∞	Perfect
Small	Small	Close to 1	Large	Good
Large	Large	Close to 0	Small	Poor
$\sum (y_i - \bar{y})^2$	$\sqrt{\dfrac{\sum (y_i - \bar{y})^2}{n - k - 1}}$ *	0	0	Invalid

*When n is large and k is small, this quantity is approximately equal to the standard deviation of y.

If we're satisfied that the model fits the data as well as possible, and that the required conditions are satisfied (see Section 19.4), we can interpret and test the individual coefficients and use the model to predict and estimate.

INTERPRETING THE COEFFICIENTS

Like all statistics, the coefficients b_0, b_1, ..., b_k describe the relationship between each of the independent variables and the dependent variable in the sample. We need to use inferential methods (described below) to draw conclusions about the population. In Example 19.1, the sample consists of the 100 observations. The population is composed of all La Quinta inns.

Intercept

The intercept is $b_0 = 38.14$. This is the predicted operating margin when all of the independent variables are 0. As we observed in Chapter 18, it is often misleading to try to interpret this value, particularly if 0 is outside the range of the values of the independent variables (as is the case here).

Number of motel and hotel rooms

The relationship between operating margin and the number of motel and hotel rooms within 3 miles is described by $b_1 = -.0076$. From this number we learn that, in this model, for each additional room within 3 miles of the La Quinta inn, the operating margin decreases on average by .0076% assuming that the other independent variables in this model are held constant. Changing the units, we can interpret b_1 to say that for each additional 1,000 rooms, the margin decreases by 7.6%.

Distance to nearest competitor

The coefficient $b_2 = 1.65$ specifies that for each additional mile that the nearest competitor is to a La Quinta inn, the average operating margin increases by 1.65%, assuming the constancy of the other independent variables.

The nature of the relationship between operating margin and the number of motel and hotel rooms and between operating margin and the distance to the nearest competitor was expected. The closer the competition, the lower the operating margin.

Office space

The relationship between office space and operating margin is expressed by $b_3 = .020$. Because office space is measured in thousands of square feet, we interpret this number as the average increase in operating margin for each additional thousand square feet of office space, keeping the other independent variables fixed. So, for every extra 100,000 square feet of office space, the operating margin increases on average by 2.0%.

College and university enrollment

The relationship between operating margin and college and university enrollment is described by $b_4 = .21$, which we interpret to mean that for each additional thousand students, the average operating margin increases by .21% when the other variables are constant.

Both office space and enrollment produced positive coefficients, indicating that these measures of economic activity are positively related to the operating margin.

Median household income

The relationship between operating margin and median household income is described by $b_5 = .41$. For each additional thousand-dollar increase in median household income, the average operating margin increases by .41%, holding all other variables constant. This statistic suggests that motels in more affluent communities have higher operating margins.

Distance to downtown core

The last variable in the model is distance to downtown core. Its relationship with operating margin is described by $b_6 = -.23$. This tells us that for each additional mile to the downtown center, the operating margin decreases on average by .23%, keeping the other independent variables constant. It may be that people prefer to stay at motels that are close to the town center.

TESTING THE COEFFICIENTS

In Chapter 18, we described how to test to determine whether there is sufficient evidence to infer that in the simple linear regression model x and y are linearly related. The null and alternative hypotheses were

$$H_0: \quad \beta_1 = 0$$

$$H_1: \quad \beta_1 \neq 0$$

The test statistic was

$$t = \frac{b_1 - \beta_1}{s_{b_1}}$$

which is Student t distributed with $\nu = n - 2$ degrees of freedom.

In the multiple regression model, we have more than one independent variable. For each such variable, we can test to determine whether there is enough evidence of a linear relationship between it and the dependent variable for the entire population.

TESTING THE COEFFICIENTS

$$H_0: \quad \beta_i = 0$$

$$H_1: \quad \beta_i \neq 0$$

(for $i = 1, 2, \ldots, k$); the test statistic is

$$t = \frac{b_i - \beta_i}{s_{b_i}}$$

which is Student t distributed with $\nu = n - k - 1$ degrees of freedom.

To illustrate, we test each of the coefficients in the multiple regression model in Example 19.1. The tests that follow are performed just as all other tests in this book have been performed. We set up the null and alternative hypotheses, identify the test statistic, and use the computer to calculate the value of the test statistic and its p-value. For each independent variable, we test ($i = 1, 2, 3, 4, 5, 6$)

$$H_0: \quad \beta_i = 0$$

$$H_1: \quad \beta_i \neq 0$$

Refer to pages 660–661 and examine the computer output for Example 19.1. The output includes the t tests of β_i. The results of these tests pertain to the entire population of La Quinta inns.

Test of β_1 (Coefficient of the number of motel and hotel rooms)

Value of the test statistic: $t = -6.07$; p-value $= 0$

There is enough evidence to infer that the number of motel and hotel rooms within 3 miles of the La Quinta inn and the operating margin are linearly related.

Test of β_2 (Coefficient of the distance to nearest competitor)

Value of the test statistic: $t = 2.60$; p-value $= .0108$

There is enough evidence to conclude that the distance to the nearest motel and the operating margin of the La Quinta inn are linearly related.

Test of β_3 (Coefficient of office space)

Value of the test statistic: $t = 5.80$; p-value $= 0$

This test allows us to infer that there is a linear relationship between the operating margin and the amount of office space around the inn.

Test of β_4 (Coefficient of college and university enrollment)

Value of the test statistic: $t = 1.59$; p-value $= .1159$

From this statistical test we discover that there is not enough evidence of a linear relationship between college enrollment in the community around the inn and the operating margin.

Test of β_5 (Coefficient of median household income)

Value of the test statistic: $t = 2.96$; p-value $= .0039$

There is enough statistical evidence to indicate that the operating margin and the median household income are linearly related.

Test of β_6 (Coefficient of distance to downtown)

Value of the test statistic: $t = -1.26$; p-value $= .2107$

There is not enough evidence to infer the existence of a linear relationship between the distance to the downtown center and the operating margin of the La Quinta inn.

INTERPRET

We have discovered that in this model the number of hotel and motel rooms, distance to the nearest motel, amount of office space, and median household income are linearly related to the operating margin. Moreover, in this model we found no evidence to infer that college enrollment and distance to downtown center are linearly related to operating margin. The t tests tell La Quinta's management that in choosing the site of a new motel, they should look for locations where there are few other motels nearby, where there is a great deal of office space, and where the surrounding households are relatively affluent.

A CAUTIONARY NOTE ABOUT INTERPRETING THE RESULTS

Care should be taken when interpreting the results of this and other regression analyses. We might find that in one model there is enough evidence to conclude that a particular independent variable is linearly related to the dependent variable, but that in another model no such evidence exists. Consequently, whenever a particular t test is *not* significant, we state that there is not enough evidence to infer that the independent and dependent variable are linearly related *in this model*. The implication is that another model may yield different conclusions.

Furthermore, if one or more of the required conditions are violated, the results may be invalid. In Section 18.9 we introduced the procedures that allow the statistics practitioner to examine the model's requirements. We will add to this discussion in Section 19.4. We also remind you that it is dangerous to extrapolate far outside the range of the observed values of the independent variables.

t TESTS AND THE ANALYSIS OF VARIANCE

The *t* tests of the individual coefficients allow us to determine whether $\beta_i \neq 0$ (for $i = 1, 2, ..., k$), which tells us whether a linear relationship exists between x_i and y. There is a *t* test for each independent variable. Consequently, the computer automatically performs *k* *t*-tests. (It actually conducts $k + 1$ *t*-tests, including the one for the intercept β_0, which we usually ignore.) The *F* test in the analysis of variance combines these *t* tests into a single test. That is, we test all the β_i at one time to determine whether at least one of them is not equal to 0. The question naturally arises, Why do we need the *F* test if it is nothing more than the combination of the previously performed *t* tests? Recall that we addressed this issue before. In Chapter 15, we pointed out that we can replace the analysis of variance by a series of *t* tests of the difference between two means. However, by doing so, we increase the probability of making a Type I error. That means that even when there is no linear relationship between each of the independent variables and the dependent variable, multiple *t* tests will likely show some are significant. As a result, you will conclude erroneously that, since at least one β_i is not equal to 0, the model is valid. The *F* test, on the other hand, is performed only once. Because the probability that a Type I error will occur in a single trial is equal to α, the chance of erroneously concluding that the model is valid is substantially less with the *F* test than with multiple *t* tests.

There is another reason that the *F* test is superior to multiple *t* tests. Because of a commonly occurring problem called *multicollinearity*, the *t* tests may indicate that some independent variables are not linearly related to the dependent variable, when in fact they are. The problem of multicollinearity does not affect the *F* test, nor does it inhibit us from developing a model that fits the data well. Multicollinearity is discussed in Section 19.4.

THE *F* TEST AND THE *t* TEST IN THE SIMPLE LINEAR REGRESSION MODEL

It is useful for you to know that we can use the *F* test to test the validity of the simple linear regression model. However, this test is identical to the *t* test of β_1. The *t* test of β_1 in the simple linear regression model tells us whether that independent variable is linearly related to the dependent variable. However, because there is only one independent variable, the *t* test of β_1 also tells us whether the model is valid, which is the purpose of the *F* test.

The relationship between the *t* test of β_1 and the *F* test can be explained mathematically. Statisticians can show that if we square a *t* statistic with ν degrees of freedom, we produce an *F* statistic with 1 and ν degrees of freedom. (We briefly discussed this relationship in Chapter 15.) To illustrate, consider Example 18.2 on page 610. We found the *t* test of β_1 to be –13.49, with degrees of freedom equal to 98. The *p*-value was 0. The output included the analysis of variance table where $F = 182.11$ and *p*-value = 0. The *t* statistic squared is $t^2 = (-13.49)^2 = 181.98$, which is approximately 182.11. (The difference is due to rounding errors.) Notice that the degrees of freedom of the *F* statistic are 1 and 98. Thus, we can use either test to test the validity of the simple linear regression model.

USING THE REGRESSION EQUATION

As was the case with simple linear regression, we can use the multiple regression equation in two ways: We can produce the prediction interval for a particular value of y, and we can produce the confidence interval estimate of the expected value of y. Like the other calculations associated with multiple regression, we call on the computer to do the work.

Suppose that in Example 19.1 a manager investigated a potential site for a La Quinta inn and found the following characteristics. There are 3,815 rooms within 3 miles of the site ($x_1 = 3,815$) and the closest other hotel or motel is .9 mile away ($x_2 = .9$). The amount of office space is 476,000 square feet ($x_3 = 476$). There is one college and one university nearby with a total enrollment of 24,500 students ($x_4 = 24.5$). From the census the manager learns that the median household income in the area (rounded to the nearest thousand) is $35,000 ($x_5 = 35$). Finally, the distance to the downtown center has been measured at 11.2 miles ($x_6 = 11.2$). The manager wants to predict the operating margin if and when the inn is built.

As you discovered in the previous chapter, both Excel and Minitab output the prediction interval for one inn and interval estimate of the expected (average) operating margin for all sites with the given variables.

EXCEL

	A	B	C
1	**Prediction Interval**		
2			
3			Margin
4			
5	Predicted value		37.1
6			
7	Prediction Interval		
8	Lower limit		25.4
9	Upper limit		48.8
10			
11	Interval Estimate of Expected Value		
12	Lower limit		33.0
13	Upper limit		41.2

COMMANDS

See the commands on page 632. In cells B102 to G102 we input the values **3815, .9, 476, 24.5, 35, 11.2,** respectively. We specified 95% confidence.

MINITAB

```
Predicted Values for New Observations

New Obs     Fit       SE Fit          95.0% CI                95.0% PI
1         37.091      2.076     ( 32.970,  41.213)     ( 25.395,  48.788)
```

COMMANDS

See the commands on page 632. We input the values **3815 .9 476 24.5 35 11.2**, and specified 95% confidence.

INTERPRET

As you can see, we predict that the operating margin will fall between 25.4% and 48.8%. This interval is quite wide, confirming the need to have extremely well-fitting models to make accurate predictions. However, management defines a profitable inn as one with an operating margin greater than 50% and an unprofitable inn as one with an operating margin below 30%. Because the entire prediction interval is below 50% and part of it is below 30%, the management of La Quinta will pass on this site.

The expected operating margin of all sites that fit this category is estimated to be between 33.0% and 41.2%. We interpret this to mean that if we built inns on an infinite number of sites that fit the category described above, the mean operating margin would fall between 33.0% and 41.2%. In other words, the average inn would not be profitable.

MBA PROGRAM ADMISSIONS POLICY: SOLUTION

The model we need to estimate and analyze is

$$y = \beta_0 + \beta_1 x_1 + \beta_2 x_2 + \beta_3 x_3 + \varepsilon$$

where

y = MBA program GPA

x_1 = Undergraduate GPA (range: 0 to 12)

x_2 = GMAT score (range: 200 to 800)

x_3 = Number of years of work experience (minimum = 3)

MINITAB

Regression Analysis: MBA GPA versus UnderGPA, GMAT, Work

```
The regression equation is
MBA GPA = 0.47 + 0.063 UnderGPA + 0.0113 GMAT + 0.0926 Work

Predictor        Coef      SE Coef         T        P
Constant        0.466       1.506       0.31    0.758
UnderGPA       0.0628      0.1199       0.52    0.602
GMAT         0.011281    0.001383       8.16    0.000
Work          0.09259     0.03091       3.00    0.004

S = 0.7879      R-Sq = 46.4%      R-Sq(adj) = 44.5%

Analysis of Variance

Source            DF          SS          MS        F        
Regression         3      45.597      15.199    24.48    0.000
Residual Error    85      52.772       0.621
Total             88      98.369
```

INTERPRET

The coefficient of determination is .4635, which tells the dean that 46.35% of the variation in MBA program GPA is explained by the variation in the independent variables. The test for validity produces a test statistic of $F = 24.48$ with a p-value of 0. The t tests indicate that GMAT score and years of work experience are linearly related to MBA program GPA, but there is no evidence of a linear relationship between undergraduate GPA and MBA program GPA. These results suggest that admissions should be based on the GMAT score as well as the number of years of work experience.

EXCEL

	A	B	C	D	E	F
1	SUMMARY OUTPUT					
2						
3	*Regression Statistics*					
4	Multiple R	0.6808				
5	R Square	0.4635				
6	Adjusted R Square	0.4446				
7	Standard Error	0.788				
8	Observations	89				
9						
10	ANOVA					
11		*df*	*SS*	*MS*	*F*	*Significance F*
12	Regression	3	45.60	15.20	24.48	0.0000
13	Residual	85	52.77	0.62		
14	Total	88	98.37			
15						
16		*Coefficients*	*Standard Error*	*t Stat*	*P-value*	
17	Intercept	0.466	1.51	0.31	0.7576	
18	UnderGPA	0.063	0.120	0.52	0.6017	
19	GMAT	0.011	0.001	8.16	0.0000	
20	Work	0.093	0.031	3.00	0.0036	

EXERCISES

The following exercises require the use of a computer and software. Exercises 19.1 to 19.4 can be solved manually. See Appendix A for the statistics. **Use a 5% significance level.**

19.1 A developer who specializes in summer cottage properties is considering purchasing a large tract of land adjoining a lake. The current owner of the tract has already subdivided the land into separate building lots and has prepared the lots by removing some of the trees. The developer wants to forecast the value of each lot. From previous experience, she knows that the most important factors affecting the price of the lot are size, number of mature trees, and distance to the lake. From a nearby area, she gathers the relevant data for 60 recently sold lots. These data are stored in file Xr19-01.

a Find the regression equation.

b What is the standard error of estimate? Interpret its value.

c What is the coefficient of determination? What does this statistic tell you?

d What is the coefficient of determination, adjusted for degrees of freedom? Why does this value differ from the coefficient of determination? What does this tell you about the model?

e Test the validity of the model. What does the *p*-value of the test statistic tell you?

f Interpret each of the coefficients.

g Test to determine whether each of the independent variables is linearly related to the price of the lot.

19.2 After analyzing the results of Exercise 18.7, Pat decided that a certain amount of studying could actually improve final grades. However, too much studying would not be warranted, since Pat's ambition (if that's what one could call it) was to ultimately graduate with the absolute minimum level of work. Pat was registered in a statistics course, which had only 3 weeks to go before the final exam, and where the final grade was determined in the following way:

Total mark = 20%(Assignment) + 30%(Midterm test) + 50%(Final exam)

In order to determine how much work to do in the remaining 3 weeks, Pat needed to be able to predict the final exam mark on the basis of the assignment mark and the midterm mark. Pat's marks on these were 12/20 and 14/30, respectively. Accordingly, Pat undertook the following analysis. The final exam mark, assignment mark, and midterm test mark for 30 students who took the statistics course last year were collected. These data are stored in file Xr19-02.

a Determine the regression equation.

b What is the standard error of estimate? Briefly describe how you interpret this statistic.

c What is the coefficient of determination? What does this statistic tell you?

d What is the coefficient of determination, adjusted for degrees of freedom? What do this statistic and the one in part **c** tell you about the model?

e Test the validity of the model. What does the *p*-value of the test statistic tell you?

f Interpret each of the coefficients.

g Can Pat infer from these results that the assignment mark is linearly related to the final grade?

h Can Pat infer from these results that the midterm mark is linearly related to the final grade?

19.3 The president of a company that manufactures drywall wants to analyze the variables that affect demand for his product. Drywall is used to construct walls in houses and offices. Consequently, the president decides to develop a regression model in which the dependent variable is monthly sales of drywall (in hundreds of 4 × 8 sheets) and the independent variables are

Number of building permits issued in the county

Five-year mortgage rates (in percentage points)

Vacancy rate in apartments (in percentage points)

Vacancy rate in office buildings (in percentage points)

To estimate a multiple regression model, he took monthly observations from the past 2 years. The data are stored in file Xr19-03.

a Conduct a regression analysis.

b What is the standard error of estimate? Can you use this statistic to assess the model's fit? If so, how?

c What is the coefficient of determination, and what does it tell you about the regression model?

d What is the coefficient of determination, adjusted for degrees of freedom? What do this statistic and the statistic referred to in part **c** tell you about how well this model fits the data?

e Test the validity of the model. What does the *p*-value of the test statistic tell you?

f Interpret each of the coefficients.

g Test to determine whether each of the independent variables is linearly related to drywall demand.

19.4 Suppose that the statistics practitioner who did the analysis described in Exercise 18.2 wanted to investigate other factors that determine heights. As part of the same study, he also recorded the heights of the mothers. These values as well as the data from Exercise 18.2 are stored in file Xr19-04.

a Conduct a regression analysis.

b What is the standard error of estimate, and what does this statistic tell you?

c What is the coefficient of determination? What does this statistic tell you?

d What is the coefficient of determination, adjusted for degrees of freedom? What do this statistic and the one referred to in part **c** tell you about how well the model fits the data?

e Test the validity of the model. What does the test result tell you?

f Interpret each of the coefficients.

g Do these data allow the statistics practitioner to infer that the heights of the sons and the fathers are linearly related?

h Do these data allow the statistics practitioner to infer that the heights of the sons and the mothers are linearly related?

APPLICATIONS IN HUMAN RESOURCES MANAGEMENT: *SEVERANCE PAY*

In most firms, the entire issue of compensation falls into the domain of the human resources manager. The manager must ensure that the method used to determine compensation contributes to the firm's objectives. Moreover, the firm needs to ensure that discrimination or bias of any kind is not a factor. Another function of the personnel manager is to develop severance packages for employees whose services are no longer needed because of downsizing or merger. The size and nature of severance is rarely part of any working agreement and must be determined

by a variety of factors. Regression analysis is often useful in this area.

19.5 When one company buys another company, it is not unusual that some workers are terminated. The severance benefits offered to the laid-off workers are often the subject of dispute. Suppose that the Laurier Company recently bought the Western Company and subsequently terminated 20 of Western's employees. As part of the buyout agreement, it was promised that the severance packages offered to the former Western employees would be equivalent to those offered to Laurier employees who had been terminated in the past year. Thirty-six-year-old Bill Smith, a Western employee for the past 10 years, earning $32,000 per year, was one of those let go. His severance package included an offer of 5 weeks' severance pay. Bill complained that this offer was less than that offered to Laurier's employees when they were laid off, in contravention of the buyout agreement. A statistician was called in to settle the dispute. The statistician was told that severance is determined by three factors: age, length of service with the company, and pay. To determine how generous the severance package had been, a random sample of 50 Laurier ex-employees was taken. For each, the following variables were recorded. (The data are stored in file Xr19-05.)

Number of weeks of severance pay

Age of employee

Number of years with the company

Annual pay (in thousands of dollars)

a Determine the regression equation. Interpret the coefficients.

b Comment on how well the model fits the data.

c Do all the independent variables belong in the equation? Explain.

d Perform an analysis to determine whether Bill is correct in his assessment of the severance package.

19.6 The admissions officer of a university is trying to develop a formal system of deciding which students to admit to the university. She believes that determinants of success include the standard variables—high school grades and SAT scores. However, she also believes that students who have participated in extracurricular activities are more likely to succeed than those who have not. To investigate the issue, she randomly sampled 100 fourth-year students and recorded the following variables:

GPA for the first 3 years at the university (range: 0 to 12)

GPA from high school (range: 0 to 12)

SAT score (range: 200 to 800)

Number of hours on average spent per week in organized extracurricular activities in the last year of high school

The data are stored in file Xr19-06.

a Develop a model that helps the admissions officer decide which students to admit, and use the computer to generate the usual statistics.

b What is the standard error of estimate? What does this statistic tell you?

c What is the coefficient of determination? Interpret its value.

d What is the coefficient of determination, adjusted for degrees of freedom? Interpret its value.

e Test the validity of the model. What does the *p*-value of the test statistic tell you?

f Interpret each of the coefficients.

g Test to determine whether each of the independent variables is linearly related to the dependent variable.

h Predict with 95% confidence the GPA for the first 3 years of university for a student whose high school GPA is 10, whose SAT score is 600, and who worked an average of 2 hours per week on organized extracurricular activities in the last year of high school.

i Estimate with 90% confidence the mean GPA for the first 3 years of university for all students whose high school GPA is 8, whose SAT score is 550, and who worked an average of 10 hours per week on organized extracurricular activities in the last year of high school.

19.7   The marketing manager for a chain of hardware stores needed more information about the effectiveness of the three types of advertising that the chain used. These are localized direct mailing (in which flyers describing sales and featured products are distributed to homes in the area surrounding a store), newspaper advertising, and local television advertisements. To determine which type is most effective, the manager collected one week's data from 25 randomly selected stores. For each store, the following variables were recorded:

>   Weekly gross sales
>
>   Weekly expenditures on direct mailing
>
>   Weekly expenditures on newspaper advertising
>
>   Weekly expenditures on television commercials

All variables were recorded in thousands of dollars and stored in file Xr19-07.

a Find the regression equation.

b What are the coefficient of determination and the coefficient of determination, adjusted for degrees of freedom? What do these statistics tell you about the regression equation?

c What does the standard error of estimate tell you about the regression model?

d Test the validity of the model. What does the *p*-value of the test statistic tell you?

e Which independent variables are linearly related to weekly gross sales? Explain.

f Predict with 95% confidence next week's gross sales if a local store spent $800 on direct mailing, $1,200 on newspaper advertisements, and $2,000 on television commercials.

g Estimate with 95% confidence the mean weekly gross sales for all stores that spend $800 on direct mailing, $1,200 on newspaper advertising, and $2,000 on television commercials.

h Discuss the difference between the two intervals found in parts **f** and **g**.

19.8   In an effort to explain to customers why their electricity bills have been so high lately, and how, specifically, they could save money by reducing the thermostat settings on both space heaters and water heaters, an electric utility company has collected total kilowatt consumption figures for last year's winter months, as well as thermostat settings on space and water heaters, for 100 homes. The data are stored in file Xr19-08.

a Determine the regression equation.

b Determine the standard error of estimate, and comment about what it tells you.

c Determine the coefficient of determination, and comment about what it tells you.

d Test the validity of the model, and describe what this test tells you.

e Predict with 95% confidence the electricity consumption of a house whose space heater thermostat is set at 70 and whose water heater thermostat is set at 130.

f Estimate with 95% confidence the average electricity consumption for houses whose space heater thermostat is set at 70 and whose water heater thermostat is set at 130.

19.9   In Exercise 18.27, a statistics practitioner examined the relationship between office rents and the city's office vacancy rate. The model appears to be quite poor. It was decided to add another variable that measures the state of the economy. The city's unemployment rate was chosen for this purpose. The data are stored in file Xr19-09.

a Determine the regression equation.

b Determine the coefficient of determination and describe what this value means.

c Test the model's validity in explaining office rent.

d Determine which of the two independent variables is linearly related to rents.

e Predict with 95% confidence the office rent in a city whose vacancy rate is 10% and whose unemployment rate is 7%.

19.10   Exercise 18.8 analyzed the relationship between Internet use and education. In an effort to determine whether other variables are linearly related to Internet use, another survey was performed. A random sample of 200 adult Internet users was interviewed. Each person was asked to report his or her age and income. These data are stored in file Xr19-10.

a Determine the regression equation.

b Determine the coefficient of determination and describe what this value means.

c Test the model's validity in explaining Internet use.

d Predict with 90% confidence the Internet use for an individual who is 40 years old and earning $50,000.

e Estimate with 95% confidence the mean Internet use of all individuals who are 30 years old and who earn $35,000.

19.11   Refer to Exercise 19.1.

a Predict with 90% confidence the selling price of a 40,000-square-foot lot that has 50 mature trees and is 25 feet from the lake.

b Estimate with 90% confidence the average selling price of 50,000-square-foot lots that have 10 mature trees and are 75 feet from the lake.

19.12   Refer to Exercise 19.2.

a Predict Pat's final exam mark with 95% confidence.

b Predict Pat's final grade with 95% confidence.

19.13   Refer to Exercise 19.3. Predict next month's drywall sales with 95% confidence if the number of building permits is 50, the 5-year mortgage rate is 9.0%, and the vacancy rates are 3.6% in apartments and 14.3% in office buildings.

19.4 REGRESSION DIAGNOSTICS—II

In Section 18.9, we discussed how to determine whether the required conditions are unsatisfied. The same procedures can be used to diagnose problems in the multiple regression model. Here is a brief summary of the diagnostic procedure we described in Chapter 18.

Calculate the residuals and check the following:

1. *Is the error variable nonnormal?* Draw the histogram of the residuals.

2. *Is the error variance constant?* Plot the residuals versus the predicted values of y.

3. *Are the errors independent (time-series data)?* Plot the residuals versus the time periods.

4. *Are there observations that are inaccurate or do not belong to the target population?* Double-check the accuracy of outliers and influential observations.

If the error is nonnormal and/or the variance is not a constant, several remedies can be attempted. These are described at the end of this section.

Outliers and influential observations are checked by examining the data in question to ensure accuracy.

Nonindependence of a time series can sometimes be detected by graphing the residuals and the time periods and looking for evidence of autocorrelation. In Section 19.5, we introduce the Durbin–Watson test, which tests for one form of autocorrelation. We will offer a corrective measure for nonindependence.

There is another problem that is applicable to multiple regression models only. *Multicollinearity* is a condition wherein the independent variables are highly correlated. Multicollinearity distorts the t tests of the coefficients, making it difficult to determine whether any of the independent variables are linearly related to the dependent variable. It also makes interpreting the coefficients problematic. We will discuss this condition and its remedy next.

MULTICOLLINEARITY

Multicollinearity (also called *collinearity* and *intercorrelation*) is a condition that exists when the independent variables are correlated with one another. The adverse effect of multicollinearity is that the estimated regression coefficients of the independent variables that are correlated tend to have large sampling errors. There are two consequences of multicollinearity. First, because the variability of the coefficients is large, the sample coefficient may be far from the actual population parameter, including the possibility that the statistic and parameter may have opposite signs. Second, when the coefficients are tested the t statistics will be small, which leads to the inference that there is no linear relationship between the affected independent variables and the dependent variable. In some cases, this inference will be wrong. Fortunately, multicollinearity does not affect the F test of the analysis of variance. We will illustrate the effects and remedy with the following example.

EXAMPLE 19.2

A real estate agent wanted to develop a model to predict the selling price of a home. The agent believed that the most important variables in determining the price of a house are its size, number of bedrooms, and lot size. Accordingly, he took a random sample of 100 homes that recently sold and recorded the selling price (y), the number of bedrooms (x_1), the size in square feet (x_2), and the lot size in square feet (x_3). These data are stored in file Xm19-02. Analyze the relationship among the four variables.

The proposed multiple regression model is

$$y = \beta_0 + \beta_1 x_1 + \beta_2 x_2 + \beta_3 x_3 + \varepsilon$$

SOLUTION

 EXCEL

	A	B	C	D	E	F
1	SUMMARY OUTPUT					
2						
3	*Regression Statistics*					
4	Multiple R	0.7483				
5	R Square	0.5600				
6	Adjusted R Square	0.5462				
7	Standard Error	25023				
8	Observations	100				
9						
10	ANOVA					
11		*df*	*SS*	*MS*	*F*	*Significance F*
12	Regression	3	76501718347	25500572782	40.73	0.0000
13	Residual	96	60109046053	626135896		
14	Total	99	136610764400			
15						
16		*Coefficients*	*Standard Error*	*t Stat*	*P-value*	
17	Intercept	37718	14177	2.66	0.0091	
18	Bedrooms	2306	6994	0.33	0.7423	
19	House Size	74.30	52.98	1.40	0.1640	
20	Lot Size	-4.36	17.02	-0.26	0.7982	

MINITAB

Regression Analysis: Price versus Bedrooms, House Size, Lot Size

```
The regression equation is
Price = 37718 + 2306 Bedrooms + 74.3 House Size - 4.4 Lot Size

Predictor      Coef       SE Coef         T        P
Constant      37718         14177      2.66    0.009
Bedrooms       2306          6994      0.33    0.742
House Si      74.30         52.98      1.40    0.164
Lot Size      -4.36         17.02     -0.26    0.798

S = 25023      R-Sq = 56.0%      R-Sq(adj) = 54.6%

Analysis of Variance

Source           DF          SS            MS         F        P
Regression        3 76501718347   25500572782     40.73    0.000
Residual Error   96 60109046053     626135896
Total            99 1.36611E+11
```

INTERPRET

The regression output reveals that none of the independent variables is significantly related to the selling price. (The *p*-values of the *t* tests are .7423, .1640, and .7982, respectively.) However, the *F* test ($F = 40.73$ and *p*-value = 0) indicates that the complete model is valid. Moreover, the coefficient of determination is 56.0%, which tells us that the model's fit is good. How can the model be valid and fit well, when none of the independent variables that make up the model are linearly related to price? To answer this question, we perform a *t* test of the coefficient of correlation between each of the independent variables and the dependent variable.

 EXCEL

	A	B
1	**Correlation**	
2		
3	*Price and Bedrooms*	
4	Pearson Coefficient of Correlation	0.6454
5	t Stat	8.36
6	df	98
7	P(T<=t) one tail	0
8	t Critical one tail	1.6606
9	P(T<=t) two tail	0
10	t Critical two tail	1.9845

	A	B
1	**Correlation**	
2		
3	*Price and House Size*	
4	Pearson Coefficient of Correlation	0.7478
5	t Stat	11.15
6	df	98
7	P(T<=t) one tail	0
8	t Critical one tail	1.6606
9	P(T<=t) two tail	0
10	t Critical two tail	1.9845

	A	B
1	**Correlation**	
2		
3	*Price and Lot Size*	
4	Pearson Coefficient of Correlation	0.7409
5	t Stat	10.92
6	df	98
7	P(T<=t) one tail	0
8	t Critical one tail	1.6606
9	P(T<=t) two tail	0
10	t Critical two tail	1.9845

 MINITAB

Correlations: Price, Bedrooms

```
Pearson correlation of Price and Bedrooms = 0.645
P-Value = 0.000
```

Correlations: Price, House Size

```
Pearson correlation of Price and House Size = 0.748
P-Value = 0.000
```

Correlations: Price, Lot Size

```
Pearson correlation of Price and Lot Size = 0.741
P-Value = 0.000
```

INTERPRET

The *t* tests in the multiple regression model lead to the inference that no independent variable is a factor in determining the selling price. The three *t* tests of the correlation coefficients contradict this conclusion. They tell us that the number of bedrooms, the house size, and the lot size are all linearly related to the price. How do we account for this contradiction? The answer is that the three independent variables are correlated with each other. It is reasonable to believe that larger houses have more bedrooms and are situated on larger lots, and that smaller houses have fewer bedrooms and are located on smaller lots. To confirm this belief, we computed the correlations among the three independent variables.

 EXCEL

	A	B	C	D
1		*Bedrooms*	*House Size*	*Lot Size*
2	Bedrooms	1		
3	House Size	0.846	1	
4	Lot Size	0.837	0.994	1

 MINITAB

Correlations: Bedrooms, H Size, Lot Size

```
            Bedrooms    H Size
H Size       0.846
Lot Size     0.837     0.994

Cell Contents: Pearson correlation
```

INTERPRET

The coefficient of correlation between number of bedrooms and house size is .846; the correlation between number of bedrooms and lot size is .837; the correlation between house size and lot size is .994. In the multiple regression model, multicollinearity affected the *t* tests so that they implied that none of the independent variables is linearly related to price when, in fact, all are.

Another problem caused by multicollinearity is the interpretation of the coefficients. We interpret the coefficients as measuring the change in the dependent variable when the corresponding independent variable increases by 1 unit while all the other independent variables are held constant. This interpretation may be impossible when the independent variables are highly correlated, because when the independent variable increases by 1 unit, some or all of the other independent variables will change. In the multiple regression model in this example, the coefficient of the number of bedrooms is 2,306. Without multicollinearity, we would interpret this coefficient to mean that for each additional bedroom, the average price increases by $2,306, provided that the other variables are held constant. However, since the number of bedrooms is correlated with house size and lot size, it is impossible to increase the number of bedrooms by 1 and hold the other variables constant.

This raises two important questions for the statistics practitioner. First, how do we recognize the problem of multicollinearity when it occurs, and second, how do we avoid or correct it?

Multicollinearity exists in virtually all multiple regression models. In fact, finding two completely uncorrelated variables is rare. The problem becomes serious, however, only when two or more independent variables are highly correlated. Unfortunately, we do not have a critical value that indicates when the correlation between two independent variables is large enough to cause problems. To complicate the issue, multicollinearity also occurs when a combination of several independent variables is correlated with another independent variable or with a combination of other independent variables. Consequently, even with access to all of the correlation coefficients, determining when the multicollinearity problem has reached the serious stage may be extremely difficult. A good indicator of the problem is a large F statistic but small t statistics.

Minimizing the effect of multicollinearity is often easier than correcting it. The statistics practitioner must try to include independent variables that are independent of each other. For example, the real estate agent wanted to include house size, the number of bedrooms, and the lot size, three variables that are clearly related. Rather than developing a model that uses all such variables, the statistics practitioner may choose to include only house size, plus several other variables that measure other aspects of a house's value.

Another alternative is to use a stepwise regression package. *Forward stepwise regression* brings independent variables into the equation one at a time. Only if an independent variable improves the model's fit is it included. If two variables are strongly correlated, the inclusion of one of them in the model makes the second one unnecessary. *Backward stepwise regression* starts with all the independent variables included in the equation and removes variables if they are not strongly related to the dependent variable. Because the stepwise technique excludes redundant variables, it minimizes multicollinearity. Stepwise regression is presented in Chapter 20.

REMEDYING VIOLATIONS OF REQUIRED CONDITIONS

The most commonly used method to remedy nonnormality or heteroscedasticity is to transform the dependent variable. There are several points to note about this procedure. First, the actual form of the transformation depends on which condition is unsatisfied and on the specific nature of the violation. Because there are many different ways to violate the required conditions of the statistical techniques, the list of transformations given here is unavoidably incomplete. Second, these transformations can be useful in improving the model. That is, if the linear model appears to be quite poor, we often can improve the model's fit by transforming y. Third, many computer software systems allow us to make transformations quite easily. You might want to experiment to see the effect these transformations have on your statistical results.

Here is a brief list of the most commonly used transformations.

1. *Log transformation:* $y' = \log y$ (provided $y \geq 0$). The log transformation is used when (a) the variance of the error variable increases as y increases or (b) the distribution of the error variable is positively skewed.

2. *Square transformation:* $y' = y^2$. Use this transformation when (a) the variance is proportional to the expected value of y or (b) the distribution of the error variable is negatively skewed.

3. *Square-root transformation:* $y' = \sqrt{y}$ (provided that $y \geq 0$). The square-root transformation is helpful when the variance is proportional to the expected value of y.

4. *Reciprocal transformation:* $y' = 1/y$. When the variance appears to significantly increase when y increases beyond some critical value, the reciprocal transformation is recommended.

In CD Appendix 19.1, we present an example of how we diagnose a violation of the required condition, its consequences, and how we remedy the problem.

EXERCISES

The following exercises require a computer and software.

19.14 Refer to Exercise 19.1. Compute the residuals and the predicted values.

  a Is the normality requirement violated? Explain.

  b Is the variance of the error variable constant? Explain.

19.15 Refer to Exercise 19.1. Calculate the coefficients of correlation for each pair of independent variables. What do these statistics tell you about the independent variables and the t tests of the coefficients?

19.16 Refer to Exercise 19.2. Determine the coefficient of correlation between the assignment mark and the midterm. What does this statistic tell you about the t tests of the coefficients?

19.17 Refer to Exercise 19.2. Determine the residuals and predicted values.

  a Does it appear that the normality requirement is violated? Explain.

  b Is the variance of the error variable constant? Explain.

19.18 Refer to Exercise 19.4. Find the coefficient of correlation of the heights of fathers and mothers.

  a What does this correlation tell you about the independent variables?

  b What does it say about the t tests of the coefficients?

19.19 Refer to the MBA Program Admissions Policy example. Calculate the coefficients of correlation for each pair of independent variables. What do these statistics tell you about the independent variables and the t tests of the coefficients?

19.20 The observations of variables y, x_1, and x_2 are stored in file Xr19-20.

  a Conduct a regression analysis of these data.

  b Calculate the residuals and standardized residuals. Identify any observations that should be checked.

  c Draw a histogram of the residuals. Is it likely that the normality requirement is violated?

  d Plot the residuals versus the predicted values of y. Is the variance of the error variable constant?

19.21 The observations of variables y, x_1, and x_2 are stored in file Xr19-21.

  a Conduct a regression analysis of these data.

  b Calculate the residuals and standardized residuals. Identify the observations that should be checked for accuracy.

  c Draw a histogram of the residuals. Is it likely that the normality requirement is violated?

  d Plot the residuals versus the predicted values of y. Is the variance of the error variable constant?

19.22 Refer to Exercise 18.6. Conduct an analysis of the residuals to determine whether any of the required conditions are violated.

19.23 Determine whether there are violations of the required conditions in the regression model used in Exercise 18.11.

19.24 Determine whether the required conditions are satisfied in Exercise 18.27.

19.25 Refer to Exercise 19.5.

  a Is multicollinearity a problem? Explain.

  b Determine the residuals and predicted values using the regression equation.

  c Draw a histogram of the residuals. Does it appear that the error variable is normally distributed?

  d Plot the residuals and the predicted values. Is the variance of the error variable constant?

  e Identify observations that should be checked for accuracy.

19.26 Refer to Exercise 19.6.

  a Use whatever techniques you deem necessary to check the normality requirement and for heteroscedasticity.

  b Is multicollinearity a problem? Explain.

  c Identify all observations that should be checked.

19.27 Refer to Exercise 19.7.

  a Use whatever techniques you deem necessary to check the normality requirement and for heteroscedasticity.

  b Is multicollinearity a problem? Explain.

19.28 Refer to Exercise 19.8.

  a Determine whether the required conditions are satisfied.

  b Is multicollinearity a problem?

19.29 Refer to Exercise 19.9. Determine whether the required conditions are satisfied.

19.30 Determine whether the required conditions for the regression analysis conducted in Exercise 19.10 are satisfied.

19.5 REGRESSION DIAGNOSTICS–III (TIME SERIES)

In Chapter 18, we pointed out that, in general, we check to see whether the errors are independent when the data constitute a *times series*—data gathered sequentially over a series of time periods. In Section 18.9, we described the graphical procedure for determining whether the required condition that the errors are independent is violated. We plot the residuals versus the time periods and look for patterns. In this section, we augment that procedure with the **Durbin–Watson test**.

DURBIN–WATSON TEST

The Durbin–Watson test allows the statistics practitioner to determine whether there is evidence of **first-order autocorrelation**—a condition in which a relationship exists between consecutive residuals e_i and e_{i-1}, where i is the time period. The Durbin–Watson statistic is defined as

$$d = \frac{\sum_{i=2}^{n} (e_i - e_{i-1})^2}{\sum_{i=1}^{n} e_i^2}$$

The range of the values of d is

$$0 \leq d \leq 4$$

where small values of d ($d < 2$) indicate a positive first-order autocorrelation and large values of d ($d > 2$) imply a negative first-order autocorrelation. Positive first-order autocorrelation is a common occurrence in business and economic time series. It occurs when consecutive residuals tend to be similar. In that case, $(e_i - e_{i-1})^2$ will be small, producing a small value for d. Negative first-order autocorrelation occurs when consecutive residuals differ widely. For example, if positive and negative residuals generally alternate, $(e_i - e_{i-1})^2$ will be large, and as a result, d will be greater than 2. Figures 19.2 and 19.3 depict positive first-order autocorrelation, whereas Figure 19.4 on page 682 illustrates negative autocorrelation. Notice that in Figure 19.2 the first residual is a small number; the second residual, also a small number, is somewhat larger, and that trend continues. In Figure 19.3, the first residual is large, and in general, succeeding residuals decrease. In both figures, consecutive residuals are similar. In Figure 19.4, the first residual is a positive number and is followed by a negative residual. The remaining residuals follow this pattern (with some exceptions). Consecutive residuals are quite different.

Figure 19.2
Positive first-order autocorrelation

Figure 19.3
Positive first-order autocorrelation

**Figure 19.4
Negative first-order
autocorrelation**

Table 11 in Appendix B is designed to test for positive first-order autocorrelation by providing values of d_L and d_U for a variety of values of n and k and for $\alpha = .01$ and .05. The decision is made in the following way. If $d < d_L$, we conclude that there is enough evidence to show that positive first-order autocorrelation exists. If $d > d_U$, we conclude that there is not enough evidence to show that positive first-order autocorrelation exists. And if $d_L \leq d \leq d_U$, the test is inconclusive. The recommended course of action when the test is inconclusive is to continue testing with more data until a conclusive decision can be made.

For example, to test for positive first-order autocorrelation with $n = 20$, $k = 3$, and $\alpha = .05$, we test the following hypotheses:

H_0:   There is no first-order autocorrelation.

H_1:   There is positive first-order autocorrelation.

The decision is made as follows:

If $d < d_L = 1.00$, reject the null hypothesis in favor of the alternative hypothesis.

If $d > d_U = 1.68$, do not reject the null hypothesis.

If $1.00 \leq d \leq 1.68$, the test is inconclusive.

To test for negative first-order autocorrelation, we change the critical values. If $d > 4 - d_L$, we conclude that negative first-order autocorrelation exists. If $d < 4 - d_U$, we conclude that there is not enough evidence to show that negative first-order autocorrelation exists. If $4 - d_U \leq d \leq 4 - d_L$, the test is inconclusive.

We can also test simply for first-order autocorrelation by combining the two one-tail tests. If $d < d_L$ or $d > 4 - d_L$, we conclude that autocorrelation exists. If $d_U \leq d \leq 4 - d_U$, we conclude that there is no evidence of autocorrelation. If $d_L \leq d \leq d_U$ or $4 - d_U \leq d \leq 4 - d_L$, the test is inconclusive. The significance level will be 2α (where α is the one-tail significance level). Figure 19.5 describes the range of values of d and the conclusion for each interval.

**Figure 19.5
Durbin–Watson test**

For time-series data, we add the Durbin–Watson test to our list of regression diagnostics. That is, we determine whether the error variable is normally distributed with constant variance (as we did in Section 19.4), we identify outliers and (if our software allows it) influential observations that should be verified, and we conduct the Durbin–Watson test.

EXAMPLE 19.3

Christmas week is a critical period for most ski resorts. Because many students and adults are free from other obligations, they are able to spend several days indulging in their favorite pastime, skiing. A large proportion of gross revenue is earned during this period. A ski resort in Vermont wanted to determine the effect that weather had on its sales of lift tickets. The manager of the resort collected data on the number of lift tickets sold during Christmas week (y), the total snowfall in inches (x_1), and the average temperature in degrees Fahrenheit (x_2) for the past 20 years. These data are stored in file Xm19-03. Develop the multiple regression model, and diagnose any violations of the required conditions.

SOLUTION   The model is

$$y = \beta_0 + \beta_1 x_1 + \beta_2 x_2 + \varepsilon$$

 EXCEL

	A	B	C	D	E	F
1	SUMMARY OUTPUT					
2						
3	*Regression Statistics*					
4	Multiple R	0.3465				
5	R Square	0.1200				
6	Adjusted R Square	0.0165				
7	Standard Error	1712				
8	Observations	20				
9						
10	ANOVA					
11		*df*	*SS*	*MS*	*F*	*Significance F*
12	Regression	2	6793798	3396899	1.16	0.3373
13	Residual	17	49807214	2929836		
14	Total	19	56601012			
15						
16		*Coefficients*	*Standard Error*	*t Stat*	*P-value*	
17	Intercept	8308.0	903.7	9.19	0.0000	
18	Snowfall	74.59	51.57	1.45	0.1663	
19	Temperature	-8.75	19.70	-0.44	0.6625	

 MINITAB

Regression Analysis: Tickets versus Snowfall, Temperature

```
The regression equation is
Tickets = 8308 + 74.6 Snowfall - 8.8 Temperature

Predictor      Coef      SE Coef         T        P
Constant      8308.0        903.7      9.19    0.000
Snowfall       74.59        51.57      1.45    0.166
Temperat       -8.75        19.70     -0.44    0.662

S = 1712      R-Sq = 12.0%      R-Sq(adj) = 1.7%

Analysis of Variance

Source          DF          SS         MS        F        P
Regression       2     6793798    3396899     1.16    0.337
Residual Error  17    49807214    2929836
Total           19    56601012
```

INTERPRET

As you can see, the coefficient of determination is small ($R^2 = 12\%$) and the p-value of the F test is .3373, both of which indicate that the model is poor. We used Excel to draw the histogram of the residuals and plot the predicted values of y versus the residuals. Because the observations constitute a time series, we also used Excel to plot the time periods (years) versus the residuals.

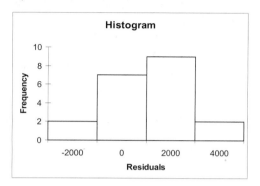

Excel histogram of residuals in Example 19.3

The histogram reveals that the error may be normally distributed.

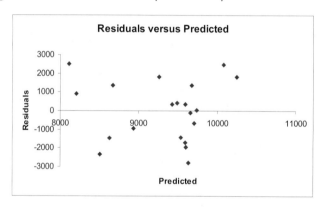

Excel plot of residuals versus predicted values in Example 19.3

There does not appear to be any evidence of heteroscedasticity.

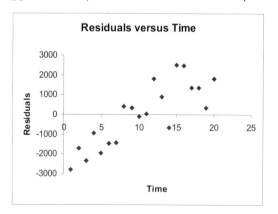

Excel plot of residuals versus time periods in Example 19.3

This graph reveals a serious problem. There is a strong relationship between consecutive values of the residuals, which indicates that the requirement that the errors are independent has been violated. To confirm this diagnosis, we instructed Excel and Minitab to calculate the Durbin–Watson statistic.

EXCEL

	A	B	C
1	**Durbin-Watson Statistic**		
2			
3	d = 0.5931		

COMMANDS
Proceed through the usual steps to conduct a regression analysis and print the residuals (see page 642). Highlight the entire list of residuals and click **Tools, Data Analysis Plus,** and **Durbin-Watson Statistic**.

MINITAB
```
Durbin-Watson statistic = 0.59
```
COMMANDS
Follow steps 1 through 4 on page 612. Before clicking **OK**, click **Options...** and **Durbin-Watson statistic**.

The critical values are determined by noting that $n = 20$ and $k = 2$ (there are two independent variables in the model). If we wish to test for positive first-order autocorrelation with $\alpha = .05$, we find in Table 11(a) in Appendix B

$$d_L = 1.10 \quad \text{and} \quad d_U = 1.54$$

The null and alternative hypotheses are

H_0: There is no first-order autocorrelation.

H_1: There is positive first-order autocorrelation.

The rejection region is $d < d_L = 1.10$. Since $d = .59$, we reject the null hypothesis and conclude that there is enough evidence to infer that positive first-order autocorrelation exists.

Autocorrelation usually indicates that the model needs to include an independent variable that has a time-ordered effect on the dependent variable. The simplest such independent variable represents the time periods. To illustrate, we included a third independent variable that records the number of years since the year the data were gathered. Thus, $x_3 = 1, 2, ..., 20$. The new model is

$$y = \beta_0 + \beta_1 x_1 + \beta_2 x_2 + \beta_3 x_3 + \varepsilon$$

EXCEL

	A	B	C	D	E	F
1	SUMMARY OUTPUT					
2						
3	*Regression Statistics*					
4	Multiple R	0.8608				
5	R Square	0.7410				
6	Adjusted R Square	0.6924				
7	Standard Error	957				
8	Observations	20				
9						
10	ANOVA					
11		*df*	*SS*	*MS*	*F*	*Significance F*
12	Regression	3	41940217	13980072	15.26	0.0001
13	Residual	16	14660795	916300		
14	Total	19	56601012			
15						
16		*Coefficients*	*Standard Error*	*t Stat*	*P-value*	
17	Intercept	5965.6	631.3	9.45	0.0000	
18	Snowfall	70.18	28.85	2.43	0.0271	
19	Temperature	-9.23	11.02	-0.84	0.4145	
20	Time	229.97	37.13	6.19	0.0000	

MINITAB

Regression Analysis: Tickets versus Snowfall, Temperature, Time

```
The regression equation is
Tickets = 5966 + 70.2 Snowfall - 9.2 Temperature + 230 Time

Predictor        Coef      SE Coef         T         P
Constant       5965.6        631.3      9.45     0.000
Snowfall        70.18       28.85       2.43     0.027
Temperat        -9.23       11.02      -0.84     0.414
Time           229.97       37.13       6.19     0.000

S = 957.2      R-Sq = 74.1%     R-Sq(adj) = 69.2%

Analysis of Variance

Source          DF         SS          MS         F        P
Regression       3   41940217    13980072     15.26    0.000
Residual Error  16   14660795      916300
Total           19   56601012
```

As we did before, we calculate the residuals and conduct regression diagnostics using Excel. The results follow.

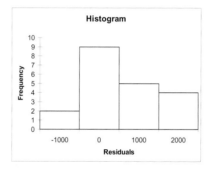

Excel histogram of residuals in Example 19.3 (Time variable included)

The histogram reveals that the error may be normally distributed.

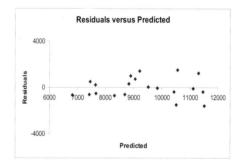

Excel plot of residuals versus predicted values in Example 19.3 (Time variable included)

The error variable variance appears to be constant.

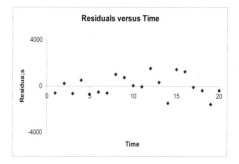

Excel plot of residuals versus time periods in Example 19.3 (Time variable included)

There is no sign of autocorrelation. To confirm our diagnosis we conducted the Durbin–Watson test.

EXCEL

	A	B	C
1	Durbin-Watson Statistic		
2			
3	d = 1.885		

MINITAB

```
Durbin-Watson statistic = 1.88
```

From Table 11(a) in Appendix B, we find the critical values of the Durbin–Watson test. With $k = 3$ and $n = 20$, we find

$$d_L = 1.00 \quad \text{and} \quad d_U = 1.68$$

Since $d > 1.68$, we conclude that there is not enough evidence to infer the presence of positive first-order autocorrelation.

Notice that the model is improved dramatically. The *F* test tells us that the model is valid. The *t* tests tell us that both the amount of snowfall and time are significantly linearly related to the number of lift tickets. This information could prove useful in advertising for the resort. For example, if there has been a recent snowfall, the resort could emphasize that in its advertising. If no new snow has fallen, it may emphasize its snow-making facilities.

DEVELOPING AN UNDERSTANDING OF STATISTICAL CONCEPTS

Notice that the addition of the time variable explained a large proportion of the variation in the number of lift tickets sold. That is, the resort experienced a relatively steady increase in sales over the past 20 years. Once this variable was included in the model, the amount of snowfall became significant because it was able to explain some of the remaining variation in lift ticket sales. Without the time variable, the amount of snowfall and the temperature were unable to explain a significant proportion of the variation in ticket sales. The graph of the residuals versus the time periods and the Durbin–Watson test enabled us to identify the problem and correct it. In overcoming the autocorrelation problem, we improved the model so that we identified the amount of snowfall as an important variable in determining ticket sales. This result is quite common. Correcting a violation of a required condition will frequently improve the model.

EXERCISES

19.31 Given the following information, perform the Durbin–Watson test to determine whether first-order autocorrelation exists.

$$n = 25, \quad k = 5, \quad \alpha = .10, \quad d = .90$$

19.32 Test the following hypotheses with $\alpha = .05$.

H_0: There is no first-order autocorrelation.
H_1: There is positive first-order autocorrelation.
$$n = 50, \quad k = 2, \quad d = 1.38$$

19.33 Test the following hypotheses with $\alpha = .02$.

H_0: There is no first-order autocorrelation.
H_1: There is first-order autocorrelation.
$$n = 90, \quad k = 5, \quad d = 1.60$$

19.34 Test the following hypotheses with $\alpha = .05$.

H_0: There is no first-order autocorrelation.
H_1: There is negative first-order autocorrelation.
$$n = 33, \quad k = 4, \quad d = 2.25$$

The following exercises require software and a computer.

19.35 Observations of variables y, x_1, and x_2 were taken over 100 consecutive time periods. The data are stored in file Xr19-35.

a Conduct a regression analysis of these data.
b Calculate the residuals and standardized residuals.
c Identify observations that should be checked.

d Draw the histogram of the residuals. Does it appear that the normality requirement is satisfied?

e Plot the residuals versus the predicted values of y. Is the error variance constant?

f Perform the Durbin–Watson test. Is there evidence of autocorrelation? Use $\alpha = .10$.

g If autocorrelation was detected in part **f**, propose an alternative regression model to remedy the problem. Use the computer to generate the statistics associated with this model.

h Redo parts **a** through **f**. Compare the two models.

19.36 Weekly sales of a company's product (y) and those of its main competitor (x) were recorded for 1 year. These data are stored in chronological order in file Xr19-36.

a Conduct a regression analysis of these data.

b Calculate the residuals and standardized residuals.

c Identify observations that should be checked.

d Draw the histogram of the residuals. Does it appear that the normality requirement is satisfied?

e Plot the residuals versus the predicted values of y. Is the error variance constant?

f Perform the Durbin–Watson test. Is there evidence of autocorrelation? Use $\alpha = .10$.

g If autocorrelation was detected in part **f**, propose an alternative regression model to remedy the problem. Use the computer to generate the statistics associated with this model.

h Redo parts **a** through **f**. Compare the two models.

19.37 Observations of variables y, x_1, x_2, and x_3 were taken over 80 consecutive time periods. The data are stored in file Xr19-37.

a Conduct a regression analysis of these data.

b Calculate the residuals and standardized residuals.

c Identify observations that should be checked.

d Draw the histogram of the residuals. Does it appear that the normality requirement is satisfied?

e Plot the residuals versus the predicted values of y.

f Perform the Durbin–Watson test. Is there evidence at the 10% significance level of autocorrelation?

g If autocorrelation was detected in part **f**, propose an alternative regression model to remedy the problem. Use the computer to generate the statistics associated with this model.

h Redo parts **a** through **f**. Compare the two models.

19.38 Refer to Exercise 19.3.

a Does it appear that the normality requirement is violated? Explain.

b Is the error variable variance constant? Explain.

19.39 Refer to Exercise 19.3. Compute the correlation coefficients for each pair of independent variables.

a What do these statistics tell you about the independent variables?

b Is it likely that the t tests of the coefficients are meaningful? Explain.

19.40 Refer to Exercise 19.3. Is there evidence of positive first-order autocorrelation? Use $\alpha = .05$.

19.41 Refer to Exercise 18.84. Perform a complete diagnostic analysis of the simple regression model. That is, determine whether the error variable is normal with constant variance and whether the errors are independent. Identify any observations that should be checked for accuracy.

19.42 Refer to Example 18.6.

a Compute the residuals and the standardized residuals.

b Draw the histogram of the residuals. Does it appear that the normality requirement is satisfied?

c Are there observations that should be checked to ensure that they were recorded properly and whether they properly belong in the sample?

d Calculate the predicted values of the dependent variable, and plot them versus the residuals. Does it appear that the variance of the error variable is constant?

e Plot the residuals versus the time periods. Does it appear that the errors are not independent?

f Calculate the Durbin–Watson statistic and test to determine whether first-order autocorrelation exists.

19.43 The manager of a tire store in Minneapolis has been concerned with the high cost of inventory. The current policy is to stock all the snow tires that are predicted to sell over the entire winter at the beginning of the season (end of October). The manager can reduce inventory costs by having suppliers deliver snow tires regularly from October to February. However, he needs to be able to predict weekly sales to avoid stockouts that will ultimately lose sales. To help develop a forecasting model, he records the number of snow tires sold weekly during the last winter and the amount of snowfall (in inches) in each week. These data are stored in file Xr19-43.

a Develop a regression model and use a software package to produce the statistics.

b Perform a complete diagnostic analysis to determine whether the required conditions are satisfied.

c If one or more conditions are unsatisfied, attempt to remedy the problem.

d Use whatever procedures you wish to assess how well the new model fits the data.

e Interpret each of the coefficients.

19.6 SUMMARY

The **multiple regression model** extends the model introduced in Chapter 18. The statistical concepts and techniques are similar to those presented in simple linear regression. We assess the model in three ways: standard error of estimate, the coefficient of determination (and the coefficient of determination adjusted for degrees of freedom), and the F test of the analysis of variance. We can use the t tests of the coefficients to determine whether each of the independent variables is linearly related to the dependent variable. As we did in Chapter 18, we showed how to diagnose violations of the required conditions and to identify other problems. We introduced **multicollinearity** and demonstrated its effect and its remedy. Finally, we presented the **Durbin–Watson test** to detect **first-order autocorrelation**.

IMPORTANT TERMS

Response surface 657
Coefficient of determination adjusted
   for degrees of freedom 662
Multicollinearity 675

Transformations 679
Durbin–Watson test 681
First-order autocorrelation 681

SYMBOLS

Symbol	Pronounced	Represents
β_i	*Beta-sub-i* or *beta-i*	Regression coefficient of ith independent variable
b_i	*b-sub-i* or *b-i*	Sample regression coefficient of ith independent variable
e_i	*e-sub-i* or *e-i*	Residual of the ith point

FORMULAS

Standard error of estimate

$$s_\varepsilon = \sqrt{\frac{\text{SSE}}{n - k - 1}}$$

Test statistic for β_i

$$t = \frac{b_i - \beta_i}{s_{b_i}}$$

Coefficient of determination

$$R^2 - \frac{[\text{cov}(x, y)]^2}{s_x^2 s_y^2} = 1 - \frac{\text{SSE}}{\sum (y_i - \bar{y})^2}$$

Adjusted coefficient of determination

$$\text{Adjusted } R^2 = 1 - \frac{\text{SSE}/(n - k - 1)}{\sum (y_i - \bar{y})^2/(n - 1)}$$

Mean square for error

$$\text{MSE} = \frac{\text{SSE}}{(n - k - 1)}$$

Mean square for regression

$$MSR = \frac{SSR}{k}$$

F statistic

$$F = \frac{MSR}{MSE}$$

Durbin–Watson statistic

$$d = \frac{\sum_{i=2}^{n} (e_i - e_{i-1})^2}{\sum_{i=1}^{n} e_i^2}$$

COMPUTER OUTPUT AND INSTRUCTIONS

Technique	Excel	Minitab
Regression	661	662
Prediction interval	670	670
Durbin–Watson statistic	685	685

REFERENCES

Belsley, David A., Edwin Kuh, and Roy E. Welsch, *Regression Diagnostics: Identifying Influential Data and Sources of Collinearity*. New York: John Wiley & Sons, 1980.

Chatterjee, Samprit, and Bertram Price, *Regression Analysis by Example*, 2nd edition. New York: John Wiley & Sons, 1991.

Cook, R. Dennis, *Regression Graphics: Ideas for Studying Regressions through Graphics*. New York: John Wiley and Sons, 1998.

Draper, N. R., and H. Smith, *Applied Regression Analysis*, 2nd edition. New York: John Wiley and Sons, 1981.

Graybill, Franklin A., *Theory and Application of the Linear Model*. North Scituate, MA: Duxbury, 1976.

Greene, William, *Econometric Analysis*, 4th edition. Upper Saddle River, NJ: Prentice Hall, 2000.

Kleinbaum, David G., Lawrence I. Kupper, Keith E. Muller, and Azhar Nizam, *Applied Regression Analysis and Multivariable Methods*, 3rd edition. Belmont, CA: Duxbury, 1998.

Neter, John, Michael H. Kutner, Christopher J. Nachtsheim, and William Wasserman, *Applied Linear Statistical Models*, 4th edition. Chicago: Irwin, 1996.

CHAPTER REVIEW EXERCISES

The following exercises require the use of a computer and statistical software. **Use a 5% significance level.**

19.44 Refer to the MBA Admissions example. Predict with 95% confidence the MBA program GPA for an applicant whose undergraduate GPA is 8.0, GMAT score is 630, and who has worked for 5 years.

19.45 Refer to the MBA Admissions example. Estimate with 95% confidence the mean MBA program GPA of all students who have an undergraduate GPA of 10.0, GMAT = 500, and who have worked for 10 years.

19.46 Supermarkets frequently price products such as bread and milk to attract customers to the store. A manager of a dairy that supplies milk to a supermarket wanted to know how sales of milk are related to different prices. Consequently, she recorded the weekly sales of milk at one supermarket, the price of a quart of her company's brand (brand A), and the price of a quart of her competitor's brand (brand B). The data for the past 52 weeks are stored in file Xr19-46.

a Develop a regression model, and use a software package to produce the statistics.

b Use whatever procedures you wish to assess how well the model fits the data.

c Interpret each of the coefficients.

d Can we infer that each of the independent variables is linearly related to the weekly sales of milk?

e Test to determine whether the model is valid.

f Predict with 90% confidence the sales of milk when the company's price is 65 cents and the competitor's price is 45 cents.

19.47 Refer to Exercise 19.46.

a Analyze the results and determine whether the required conditions are satisfied.

b Is multicollinearity a problem that affects your answer in part **d**? Explain.

19.48 The general manager of the Cleveland Indians baseball team is in the process of determining which minor-league players to draft. He is aware that his team needs home-run hitters and would like to find a way to predict the number of home runs a player will hit. Being an astute statistician, he gathers a random sample of players and records the number of home runs each player hit in his first two full years as a major-league player, the number of home runs he hit in his last full year in the minor leagues, his age, and the number of years of professional baseball. These data are stored in file Xr19-48.

a Develop a regression model, and use a software package to produce the statistics.

b Interpret each of the coefficients.

c How well does the model fit?

d Test the model's validity.

e Do each of the independent variables belong in the model?

f Predict with 95% confidence the number of home runs in the first two years of a player who is 25 years old, has played professional baseball for 7 years, and hit 22 home runs in his last year in the minor leagues.

g Estimate with 95% confidence the expected number of home runs in the first two years of players who are 27 years old, have played professional baseball for 5 years and hit 18 home runs in their last year in the minors.

19.49 Refer to Exercise 19.48.

a Determine whether the required conditions are satisfied.

b Is multicollinearity a problem? Could we have known about the multicollinearity before the model was created? Explain.

19.50 The agronomist referred to in Exercise 18.87 believed that the amount of rainfall as well as the amount of fertilizer used would affect the crop yield. She redid the experiment in the following way. Thirty greenhouses were rented. In each, the amount of fertilizer and the amount of water were varied. At the end of the growing season, the amount of corn was recorded with the data stored in file Xr19-50.

a Determine the sample regression line, and interpret the coefficients.

b Do these data allow us to infer that there is a linear relationship between the amount of fertilizer and the crop yield?

c Do these data allow us to infer that there is a linear relationship between the amount of water and the crop yield?

d What can you say about the multiple regression model's fit?

e Predict with 95% confidence the crop yield when 100 kilograms of fertilizer and 1,000 liters of water are applied.

19.51 Refer to Exercise 19.50. Perform a complete diagnostic analysis to determine whether the required conditions are satisfied. Which conditions, if any, are unsatisfied? Suggest a way to remedy the problem.

19.52 The administrator of a school board in a large county was analyzing the average mathematics test scores in the schools under her control. She noticed that there were dramatic differences in scores among the schools. In an attempt to improve the scores of all the schools, she attempted to determine the factors that account for the differences. Accordingly, she took a random sample of 40 schools across the county and, for each, determined the mean test score last year, the percentage of teachers in each school who have at least one university degree in mathematics, the mean age, and the mean annual income of the mathematics teachers. These data are stored in file Xr19-52.

a Conduct a regression analysis to develop the equation.

b Is the model valid?

c Are the required conditions satisfied? Explain.

d Is multicollinearity a problem? Explain.

e Interpret and test the coefficients.

f Predict with 95% confidence the test score at a school where 50% of the mathematics teachers have mathematics degrees, the mean age is 43, and the mean annual income is $48,300.

19.53 Life insurance companies are keenly interested in predicting how long their customers will live, because their premiums and profitability depend on such numbers. An actuary for one insurance company gathered data from 100 recently deceased male customers. He recorded the age at death of the customer, the ages at death of his mother and father, the mean ages at death of his grandmothers, and the mean ages at death of his grandfathers. These data are recorded in file Xr19-53.

a Perform a multiple regression analysis on these data.

b Is the model valid?

c Are the required conditions satisfied?

d Is multicollinearity a problem here?

e Interpret and test the coefficients.

f Predict with 95% confidence the longevity of a man whose parents lived to the age of 70, whose grandmothers averaged 80 years, and whose grandfathers averaged 75.

g Estimate with 95% confidence the mean longevity of men whose mothers lived to 75, whose fathers lived to 65, whose grandmothers averaged 85 years, and whose grandfathers averaged 75.

19.54 University students often complain that universities reward professors for research but not for teaching, and argue that professors react to this situation by devoting more time and energy to the publication of their findings and less time and energy to classroom activities. Professors counter that research and teaching go hand in hand; more research makes better teachers. A student organization at one university decided to investigate the issue. They randomly selected 50 economics professors who are employed by a multicampus university. The students recorded the salaries of the professors, their average teaching evaluations (on a 10-point scale), and the total number of journal articles published in their careers. These data are stored in file Xr19-54. Perform a complete analysis (produce the regression equation, assess it, and diagnose it) and report your findings.

19.55 One of the critical factors that determine the success of a catalogue store chain is the availability of products that consumers want to buy. If a store is sold out, future sales to that customer are less likely. Accordingly, delivery trucks operating from a central warehouse regularly resupply stores. In an analysis of a chain's operations, the general manager wanted to determine the factors that are related to how long it takes to unload delivery trucks. A random sample of 50 deliveries to one store was observed. The times (in minutes) to unload the truck, the total number of boxes, and the total weight (in hundreds of pounds) of the boxes were recorded and stored in file Xr19-55.

a Determine the multiple regression equation.

b How well does the model fit the data? Explain.

c Are the required conditions satisfied?

d Is multicollinearity a problem?

e Interpret and test the coefficients. What does this analysis tell you?

f Produce a 95% prediction interval for the amount of time needed to unload a truck with 100 boxes weighing 5,000 pounds.

g Produce a 95% interval estimate of the average amount of time needed to unload trucks with 100 boxes weighing 5,000 pounds.

19.56 Lotteries have become important sources of revenue for governments. Many people have criticized lotteries, however, referring to them as a tax on the poor and uneducated. In an examination of the issue, a random sample of 100 adults was asked how much they spend on lottery tickets and was interviewed about various socioeconomic variables. The purpose of this study is to test the following beliefs:

1. Relatively uneducated people spend more on lotteries than do relatively educated people.

2. Older people buy more lottery tickets than younger people.

3. People with more children spend more on lotteries than people with fewer children.

4. Relatively poor people spend a greater proportion of their income on lotteries than relatively rich people.

The following data were stored in file Xr19-56.

Amount spent on lottery tickets as a percentage of total household income
Number of years of education
Age
Number of children
Personal income (in thousands of dollars)

a Develop the multiple regression equation.

b Is the model valid?

c Are the required conditions satisfied?

d Is multicollinearity a problem?

e Test each of the beliefs. What conclusions can you draw?

✧ CASE 19.1
AN ANALYSIS OF MUTUAL FUND MANAGERS—I*

There are thousands of mutual funds available (see page 158 for a brief introduction to mutual funds). There is no shortage of sources of information about them. Newspapers regularly report the value of each unit, mutual fund companies and brokers advertise extensively, and there are books on the subject. Many of the advertisements imply that individuals should invest in the advertiser's mutual fund because it has performed well in the past. Unfortunately, there is little evidence to infer that past performance is a predictor of the future. However, it may be possible to acquire useful information by examining the managers of mutual funds. Several researchers have studied the issue. One project gathered data concerning the performance of 2,029 funds.

The performance of each fund was measured by its *risk-adjusted excess return*, which is the difference between the return on investment of the fund and a return that is considered a standard. The standard is based on a variety of variables, including the risk-free rate.

There are four variables that describe the fund manager. They are age, tenure (how many years the manager has been in charge), whether the manager has an MBA (1 = yes, 0 = no), and a measure of the quality of the manager's education (the average Scholastic Achievement Test [SAT] score of students at the university where the manager received his or her undergraduate degree). These data are stored in file C19-01.

Conduct an analysis of the data. Discuss how the average SAT score of the manager's alma mater, whether he or she has an MBA, and his or her age and tenure are related to the performance of the fund.

*This case is based on "Are Some Mutual Fund Managers Better Than Others? Cross-Sectional Patterns in Behavior and Performance," by Judith Chevalier and Glenn Ellison, Working Paper 5852, National Bureau of Economic Research.

✧ CASE 19.2
AN ANALYSIS OF MUTUAL FUND MANAGERS—II

In addition to analyzing the relationship between the manager's characteristics and the performance of the fund, researchers wanted to determine whether the same characteristics are related to the behavior of the fund. In particular, they wanted to know whether the risk of the fund and its management expense ratio (MER) are related to the manager's age, tenure, university SAT score, and whether he or she has an MBA.

In Section 18.6 we introduced the market model, wherein we measure

the systematic risk of stocks by the stock's beta. The beta of a portfolio is the average of the betas of the stocks that make up the portfolio. File C19-02a stores the same managers' characteristics as in file C19-01. However, the first column contains the betas of the mutual funds.

To analyze the management expense ratios, it was decided to include a measure of the size of the fund. The logarithm of the fund's assets (in $millions) was recorded with the MER. These data are stored in file C19-02b.

Analyze both sets of data and write a brief report of your findings.

◈ CASE 19.3
QUEBEC REFERENDUM VOTE: WAS THERE ELECTORAL FRAUD?*

As we described in Case 14.2 (page 470), Quebecers have been debating whether to separate from Canada and form an independent nation. A referendum was held on October 30, 1995, in which the people of Quebec voted not to separate. The vote was extremely close, with the "No" side winning by only 52,448 votes. A large number of "No" votes was cast by the non-Francophone (non–French-speaking) people of Quebec, who make up about 20% of the population and who very much want to remain Canadians. The remaining 80% are Francophones, a majority of whom voted "Yes."

After the votes were counted, it became clear that the tallied vote was much closer than it should have been. Supporters of the "No" side charged that poll scrutineers, all of whom were appointed by the proseparatist provincial government, rejected a disproportionate number of ballots in ridings where the percentage of "Yes" votes was low and where there are large numbers of Allophone (people whose first language is neither English nor French) and Anglophone (English-speaking) residents. (Electoral laws require the rejection of ballots that do not appear to be properly marked. They were outraged that in a strong democracy like Canada, votes would be rigged much like in many nondemocratic countries around the world.

If, in ridings where there was a low percentage of "Yes" votes there was a high percentage of rejected ballots, this would be evidence of electoral fraud. Moreover, if in ridings where there were large percentages of Allophone and/or Anglophone voters, there were high percentages of rejected ballots, this too would constitute evidence of fraud on the part of the scrutineers and possibly the government.

In order to determine the veracity of the charges, the following variables were recorded for each riding:

Percentage of rejected ballots in referendum
Percentage of "Yes" votes
Percentage of Allophones
Percentage of Anglophones

These data are stored in file C19-03.
a Perform an analysis to determine how the percentages of "yes" votes, Allophones, and Anglophones are related to the percentage of rejected ballots.
b Can we infer that electoral fraud took place? If so, how did it manifest itself?

---

*This case is based on "Voting Irregularities in the 1995 Referendum on Quebec Sovereignty," by Jason Cawley and Paul Sommers, *Chance*, Vol. 9, No. 4, Fall 1996. We are grateful to Dr. Paul Sommers, Middlebury College, for his assistance in writing this case.

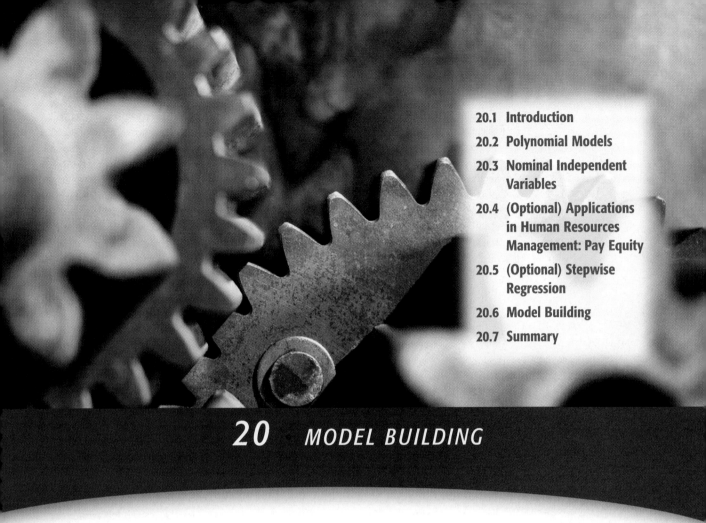

20 MODEL BUILDING

MBA PROGRAM ADMISSIONS POLICY–II

After considering the results of the initial study (see Chapter 19), the dean realized that she may have omitted an important variable—the type of undergraduate degree. She returned to her sample of students and recorded the type of undergraduate degree using the following codes:

1 = BA

2 = BBA (including similar business or management degrees)

3 = BEng or BSc

4 = Other (including no undergraduate degree)

These data plus the data from the original example are stored in file CH20:\MBA-II. Can the dean conclude that the undergraduate degree is a factor in determining how well a student performs in the MBA program? On page 709 we answer this question.

20.1 INTRODUCTION

Chapters 18 and 19 introduced the techniques and concepts of regression analysis. We discussed how the model is developed, interpreted, assessed, and diagnosed for violations of required conditions. However, there is more to regression analysis. In this chapter, we demonstrate why this procedure is one of the most powerful and commonly used techniques in statistics. Regression analysis allows the statistics practitioner to use mathematical models to realistically describe relationships between the dependent variable and independent variables.

In Section 20.2, we introduce models in which the relationship between the dependent variable and the independent variables may not be linear. Section 20.3 introduces indicator variables, which allow us to use nominal independent variables. We describe pay equity, an important human resources management application that employs nominal independent variables, in Section 20.4. In Section 20.5, we introduce stepwise regression, which enables the statistics practitioner to include the independent variables that yield the best-fitting models. Finally, Section 20.6 discusses how to properly use regression analysis in building models.

20.2 POLYNOMIAL MODELS

Chapter 19 introduced the multiple regression model:

$$y = \beta_0 + \beta_1 x_1 + \beta_2 x_2 + \cdots + \beta_k x_k + \varepsilon$$

We included variables $x_1, x_2, \ldots, x_k$ because we believed that these variables were each linearly related to the dependent variable. In this section, we discuss models where the independent variables may be functions of a smaller number of predictor variables. The simplest form of this model is described in the box.

POLYNOMIAL MODEL WITH ONE PREDICTOR VARIABLE

$$y = \beta_0 + \beta_1 x + \beta_2 x^2 + \cdots + \beta_p x^p + \varepsilon$$

Technically, this is a multiple regression model with p independent variables. However, all independent variables are based on only one variable, which we label the **predictor variable**. That is, $x_1 = x, x_2 = x^2, \ldots, x_p = x^p$. In this model, p is the **order** of the equation. For reasons that we discuss later, we rarely propose a model whose order is greater than 3. However, it is worthwhile to devote individual attention to situations where $p = 1, 2,$ and 3.

FIRST-ORDER MODEL

When $p = 1$, we have the now-familiar simple linear regression model introduced in Chapter 18:

$$y = \beta_0 + \beta_1 x + \varepsilon$$

Obviously, this model is chosen when the statistics practitioner believes that there is a straight-line relationship between the dependent and independent variables over the range of the values of x.

SECOND-ORDER MODEL

With $p = 2$, the polynomial model is

$$y = \beta_0 + \beta_1 x + \beta_2 x^2 + \varepsilon$$

When we plot x versus y, the graph is shaped like a parabola, as shown in Figures 20.1 and 20.2. The coefficient β_0 represents the intercept where the response surface intercepts the y-axis. The signs of β_1 and β_2 control the position of the parabola relative to the y-axis. If $\beta_1 = 0$, for example, the parabola is symmetric and centered around $x = 0$. If β_1 and β_2 have the same sign, the parabola shifts to the left. If β_1 and β_2 have opposite signs, the parabola shifts to the right. The coefficient β_2 describes the curvature. If $\beta_2 = 0$, there is no curvature. If β_2 is negative, the graph is concave (as in Figure 20.1). If β_2 is positive, the graph is convex (as in Figure 20.2). The greater the absolute value of β_2, the greater the rate of curvature, as can be seen in Figure 20.3.

Figure 20.1
Second-order model with
$\beta_2 < 0$

Figure 20.2
Second-order model with
$\beta_2 > 0$

Figure 20.3
Second-order model with
various values of β_2

THIRD-ORDER MODEL

By setting $p = 3$, we produce the third-order model

$$y = \beta_0 + \beta_1 x + \beta_2 x^2 + \beta_3 x^3 + \varepsilon$$

Figures 20.4 and 20.5 depict this equation, whose curvature can change twice.

Figure 20.4
Third-order model with
$\beta_3 < 0$

Figure 20.5
Third-order model with
$\beta_3 > 0$

As you can see, when β_3 is negative, y is decreasing over the range of x, and when β_3 is positive, y increases. The other coefficients determine the position of the curvature changes and the point at which the curve intersects the y-axis.

The number of real-life applications of this model is quite small. Statistics practitioners rarely encounter problems involving more than one curvature reversal. Therefore, we will not discuss any higher-order models.

POLYNOMIAL MODELS WITH TWO PREDICTOR VARIABLES

If we believe that two predictor variables influence the dependent variable, we can use one of the following polynomial models. The general form of this model is rather cumbersome, so we will not show it. Instead, we discuss several specific examples.

First-Order Model

The first-order model is represented by

$$y = \beta_0 + \beta_1 x_1 + \beta_2 x_2 + \varepsilon$$

This model is used whenever the statistics practitioner believes that, on average, y is linearly related to each of x_1 and x_2, and the predictor variables do not interact. (Recall that we introduced interaction in Chapter 15.) This means that the effect of one predictor variable on y is independent of the value of the second predictor variable. For example, suppose that the sample regression line of the first-order model is

$$\hat{y} = 5 + 3x_1 + 4x_2$$

If we examine the relationship between y and x_1 for several values of x_2 (say, $x_2 = 1, 2,$ and 3), we produce the following equations.

x_2	$\hat{y} = 5 + 3x_1 + 4x_2$
1	$\hat{y} = 9 + 3x_1$
2	$\hat{y} = 13 + 3x_1$
3	$\hat{y} = 17 + 3x_1$

The only difference in the three equations is the intercept. (See Figure 20.6.) The coefficient of x_1 remains the same, which means that the effect of x_1 on y remains the same no matter what the value of x_2. (We could also have shown that the effect of x_2 on y remains the same no matter what the value of x_1.) As you can see from Figure 20.6, the first-order model with no interaction produces parallel straight lines.

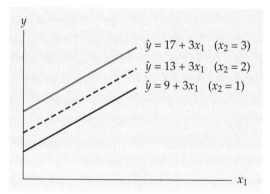

Figure 20.6
First-order model with two independent variables: no interaction

A statistics practitioner who thinks that the effect of one predictor variable on y is influenced by the other predictor variable can use the model described next.

First-Order Model with Two Predictor Variables and Interaction

Interaction means that the effect of x_1 on y is influenced by the value of x_2. (It also means that the effect of x_2 on y is influenced by x_1.)

FIRST-ORDER MODEL WITH INTERACTION

$$y = \beta_0 + \beta_1 x_1 + \beta_2 x_2 + \beta_3 x_1 x_2 + \varepsilon$$

Suppose that the sample regression line is

$$\hat{y} = 5 + 3x_1 + 4x_2 - 2x_1 x_2$$

If we examine the relationship between y and x_1 for $x_2 = 1, 2,$ and 3, we produce the following table of equations.

x_2	$\hat{y} = 5 + 3x_1 + 4x_2 - 2x_1 x_2$
1	$\hat{y} = 9 + x_1$
2	$\hat{y} = 13 - x_1$
3	$\hat{y} = 17 - 3x_1$

As you can see, not only is the intercept different, but the coefficient of x_1 also varies. Obviously, the effect of x_1 on y is influenced by the value of x_2. Figure 20.7 depicts these equations. The straight lines are clearly not parallel.

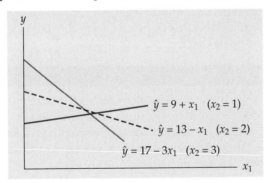

Figure 20.7
First-order model with interaction

Second-Order Model with Interaction

A statistics practitioner who believes that a quadratic relationship exists between y and each of x_1 and x_2, and that the predictor variables interact in their effect on y, can use the following second-order model.

SECOND-ORDER MODEL WITH INTERACTION

$$y = \beta_0 + \beta_1 x_1 + \beta_2 x_2 + \beta_3 x_1^2 + \beta_4 x_2^2 + \beta_5 x_1 x_2 + \varepsilon$$

Figures 20.8 and 20.9 (page 700), respectively, depict this model without and with the interaction term.

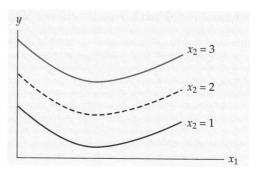

Figure 20.8
Second-order model without interaction ($\beta_5 = 0$)

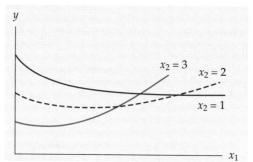

Figure 20.9
Second-order model with interaction

Now that we've introduced several different models, how do we know which model to use? The answer is that we employ a model based on our knowledge of the variables involved and then test that model using the statistical techniques presented in this and the preceding chapters.

EXAMPLE 20.1

In trying to find new locations for their restaurants, fast-food restaurant chains like McDonald's and Wendy's usually consider a number of factors. Suppose that an analyst working for a fast-food restaurant chain has been asked to construct a regression model that will help identify new locations that are likely to be profitable. The analyst knows that this type of restaurant has, as its primary market, middle-income adults and their children, particularly those between the ages of 5 and 12. Which model should the analyst propose?

SOLUTION The dependent variable is gross revenue or net profit. The predictor variables will be mean annual household income and the mean age of children in the restaurant's neighborhood.

The relationship between the dependent variable and each predictor variable is probably quadratic. That is, members of relatively poor or relatively affluent households are less likely to eat at this chain's restaurants, since the restaurants attract mostly middle-income customers. Figure 20.10 depicts the hypothesized relationship.

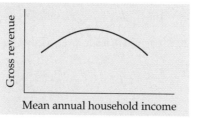

Figure 20.10
Relationship between annual gross revenue and mean annual household income

A similar relationship can be proposed for revenue and age. Neighborhoods where the mean age of children is either quite low or quite high will probably produce lower revenues than in similar areas where the mean age lies in the middle of the 5-to-12 range.

The question of whether or not to include the interaction term is more difficult to answer. When in doubt, it is probably best to include it. Thus, the model to be tested is

$$y = \beta_0 + \beta_1 x_1 + \beta_2 x_2 + \beta_3 x_1^2 + \beta_4 x_2^2 + \beta_5 x_1 x_2 + \varepsilon$$

where

$y =$ Annual gross sales
$x_1 =$ Median annual household income in the neighborhood
$x_2 =$ Mean age of children in the neighborhood

EXAMPLE 20.2

To determine whether the second-order model with interaction is appropriate, the analyst in Example 20.1 selected 25 areas at random. Each area consists of approximately 5,000 households, as well as one of her employer's restaurants and three competing fast-food restaurants. The previous year's annual gross sales, the mean annual household income, and the mean age of children (the latter two figures are available from the latest census) were recorded; some of these data are listed below and stored in file Xm20-02 (which also stores x_1^2, x_2^2, and $x_1 x_2$). What conclusions can be drawn from these data?

Area	Annual Gross Revenue y ($thousands)	Mean Annual Household Income x_1 ($thousands)	Mean Age of Children x_2
1	$1,128	$23.5	10.5
2	1,005	17.6	7.2
3	1,212	26.3	7.6
.	.	.	.
.	.	.	.
.	.	.	.
25	950	17.8	6.1

SOLUTION Both Excel and Minitab were employed to produce the regression analysis shown here.

 EXCEL

	A	B	C	D	E	F
1	SUMMARY OUTPUT					
2						
3	*Regression Statistics*					
4	Multiple R	0.9521				
5	R Square	0.9065				
6	Adjusted R Square	0.8819				
7	Standard Error	44.70				
8	Observations	25				
9						
10	ANOVA					
11		df	SS	MS	F	Significance F
12	Regression	5	368140	73628	36.86	0.0000
13	Residual	19	37956	1998		
14	Total	24	406096			
15						
16		Coefficients	Standard Error	t Stat	P-value	
17	Intercept	-1134	320.0	-3.54	0.0022	
18	Income	173.2	28.20	6.14	0.0000	
19	Age	23.55	32.23	0.73	0.4739	
20	Income sq	-3.73	0.54	-6.87	0.0000	
21	Age sq	-3.87	1.18	-3.28	0.0039	
22	(Income)(Age)	1.97	0.94	2.08	0.0509	

MINITAB

Regression Analysis: Revenue versus Income, Age, ...

```
The regression equation is
Revenue = - 1134 + 173 Income + 23.5 Age - 3.73 Income sq - 3.87 Age sq
          + 1.97 (Income)( Age)

Predictor         Coef      SE Coef         T         P
Constant       -1134.0        320.0     -3.54     0.002
Income          173.20        28.20      6.14     0.000
Age              23.55        32.23      0.73     0.474
Income s        -3.7261       0.5422    -6.87     0.000
Age sq          -3.869        1.179     -3.28     0.004
(Income)         1.9673       0.9441     2.08     0.051

S = 44.70       R-Sq = 90.7%      R-Sq(adj) = 88.2%

Analysis of Variance

Source            DF          SS        MS        F         P
Regression         5      368140     73628    36.86     0.000
Residual Error    19       37956      1998
Total             24      406096
```

INTERPRET

From the computer output, we determine that the value of the coefficient of determination (R^2) is 90.65%, which tells us that the model fits the data quite well. The value of the F statistic is 36.86, which has a p-value of 0. This confirms that the model is valid.

Care must be taken when interpreting the t tests of the coefficients in this type of model. Not surprisingly, each variable will be correlated with its square, and the interaction variable will be correlated with both of its components. As a consequence, multicollinearity distorts the t tests of the coefficients in some cases, making it appear that some of the components should be eliminated from the model. In fact, in Example 20.2, Minitab warns (not shown) the analyst that multicollinearity is a problem. However, in most such applications the objective is to forecast the dependent variable and multicollinearity does not affect the model's fit or forecasting capability.

EXERCISES

20.1 Graph y versus x_1 for $x_2 = 1, 2,$ and 3, for each of the following equations.

  a $y = 1 + 2x_1 + 4x_2$
  b $y = 1 + 2x_1 + 4x_2 - x_1x_2$

20.2 Graph y versus x_1 for $x_2 = 2, 4,$ and 5, for each of the following equations.

  a $y = .5 + 1x_1 - .7x_2 - 1.2x_1^2 + 1.5x_2^2$
  b $y = .5 + 1x_1 - .7x_2 - 1.2x_1^2 + 1.5x_2^2 + 2x_1x_2$

The following exercises require the use of a computer and software. Exercises 20.3 to 20.5 can be solved manually. See Appendix A.

20.3 The general manager of a supermarket chain believes that sales of a product are influenced by the amount of space the product is allotted on shelves. If true, this would have great significance, because the more profitable items could be given more shelf space. The manager realizes that sales volume would likely increase with more space only up to a certain point. Beyond that point, sales would likely flatten and perhaps decrease (because customers often are dismayed by very large exhibits). To test his belief, the manager records the number of boxes of detergent sold during 1 week in 25 stores in the chain. For each store, he records the shelf space (in inches) allotted to the detergent. These data are stored in file Xr20-03.

  a Write the equation that represents the model.
  b Discuss how well the model fits.

APPLICATIONS IN ECONOMICS: *DEMAND CURVE*

The law of supply and demand states that, other things being equal, the higher the price of a product or service, the lower is the quantity demanded. The relationship between quantity and price is called a **demand curve**. Generally such a curve is modeled by a quadratic equation. To estimate the demand curve, we measure the demand at several different prices and then employ regression analysis to calculate the coefficients of the model.

20.4 A fast-food restaurant chain whose menu features hamburgers and chicken sandwiches is about to add a fish sandwich to its menu. There was considerable debate among the executives about the likely demand and what the appropriate price should be. A recently hired economics graduate observed that the demand curve would reveal a great deal about the relationship between price and demand. She convinced the executives to conduct an experiment. A random sample of 20 restaurants was drawn. The restaurants were almost identical in terms of sales and in the demographics of the surrounding area. At each restaurant the fish sandwich was sold at a different price. The number of sandwiches sold over a 7-day period and the price were recorded and stored in file Xr20-04. A first-order model and a second-order model were proposed.

  a Write the equation for each model.

  b Use regression analysis to estimate the coefficients and other statistics for each model.

  c Which model seems to fit better? Explain.

  d Use the better model to calculate the point prediction for weekly sales when the price is $2.95.

APPLICATIONS IN OPERATIONS MANAGEMENT: *LEARNING CURVE*

A well-established phenomenon in operations management is the *learning curve*, which describes how quickly new workers learn to do their jobs. A number of mathematical models are used to describe the relationship between time on the job and productivity. Regression analysis allows the operations manager to select the appropriate model and use it to predict when workers achieve their highest level of productivity.

20.5 A person starting a new job always takes a certain amount of time to adjust fully. In repetitive-task situations, such as on an assembly line, significant productivity gains can occur within a few days. In an experiment to study this phenomenon, the average amount of time required for a new employee to install electronic components in a computer was measured for her first 10 days. These data are shown below (and stored in file Xr20-05).

Day	1	2	3	4	5	6	7	8	9	10
Mean times (minutes)	40	41	36	38	33	32	30	32	29	30

A first-order model and a second-order model were proposed.

  a Write the equation for each model.

  b Analyze both models. Determine whether they are valid.

  c Which model fits better? Explain.

20.6 Refer to the MBA Program Admissions Policy example introduced in Chapter 19. The dean of the school of business wanted to improve the regression model, which was developed to describe the relationship between MBA program GPA and undergraduate GPA, GMAT score, and years of work experience. The dean now believes that there may exist an interaction effect between undergraduate GPA and the GMAT test score.

  a Write the equation that describes the model.

  b Use a computer to generate the regression statistics. Use whatever statistics you deem necessary to assess the model's fit. Is this model valid?

  c Compare your results with those achieved in the original example.

20.7 The manager of the food concession at a major league baseball stadium wanted to be able to predict the attendance of a game 24 hours in advance, in order to prepare the correct amount of food for sale. He believed that the two most important factors were the home team's winning percentage and the visiting team's winning percentage. In order to examine his beliefs, he collected the attendance figures, the home team's winning percentage, and the visiting team's winning percentage for 40 randomly selected games. These data are stored in file Xr20-07.

  a Conduct a regression analysis using a first-order model with interaction.

b Do these results indicate that your model is valid? Explain.

c Should the interaction term be included? Explain.

20.8 The manager of a large hotel on the Riviera in southern France wanted to forecast the monthly vacancy rate (as a percentage) during the peak season. After considering a long list of potential variables, she identified two variables that she believed were most closely related to the vacancy rate: the average daily temperature and the value of the currency in American dollars. She collected data for 25 months and stored them in file Xr20-08.

a Perform a regression analysis using a first-order model with interaction.

b Perform a regression analysis using a second-order model with interaction.

c Which model fits better? Explain.

20.9 The coach and the general manager of a team in the National Hockey League are trying to decide what kinds of players to draft. To help in making their decision, they need to know which variables are most closely related to the goals differential—the difference between the number of goals their team scores and the number of goals scored by their team's opponents. (A positive differential means that their team wins, and a negative differential is a loss.) After some consideration, they decide that there are two important variables: the percentage of face-offs won and the penalty-minutes differential. The latter variable is the difference between the number of penalty minutes

assessed against their team and the number of penalty minutes assessed against their team's opponents. The data from 100 games are stored in file Xr20-09.

a Perform a regression analysis using a first-order model with interaction.

b Is this model valid?

c Should the interaction term be included?

20.10 The production manager of a chemical plant wants to determine the roles that temperature and pressure play in the yield of a particular chemical produced at the plant. From past experience, she believes that when pressure is held constant, lower and higher temperatures tend to reduce the yield. When temperature is held constant, higher and lower pressures tend to increase the yield. She does not have any idea about how the yield is affected by various combinations of pressure and temperature. She observes 80 batches of the chemical in which the pressure and temperature were allowed to vary. These data are stored in file Xr20-10.

a Which model should be used? Explain.

b Conduct a regression analysis using the model you specified in part **a**.

c Assess how well the model fits the data.

20.11 After examining the results of the regression analysis performed on the turnover rate and the age of workers in Exercise 18.9, the personnel manager decided to redo the analysis by proposing a second-order model. Perform the necessary analysis and determine whether this model is better than the first-order model.

20.3 NOMINAL INDEPENDENT VARIABLES

When we introduced regression analysis, we pointed out that all the variables must be interval. But in many real-life cases, one or more independent variables are nominal. For example, suppose that the used-car dealer in Example 18.2 believed that the color of a car is a factor in determining its auction price. Color is clearly a nominal variable. If we assign numbers to each possible color, these numbers will be completely arbitrary, and using them in a regression model will usually be pointless. For example, if the dealer believes the colors that are most popular, white and silver, are likely to lead to higher prices than other colors, he may assign a code of 1 to white cars, a code of 2 to silver cars, and a code of 3 to all other colors. Columns 1 and 2 of file Xm18-02a contain the auction price (y) and the odometer reading (x_1) [identical to file Xm18-02, with the columns reversed]. Column 3 includes codes identifying the color (x_2) of the Ford Tauruses referred to in the original problem. If we now conduct a multiple regression analysis, the following results would be obtained.

EXCEL

	A	B	C	D	E	F
1	SUMMARY OUTPUT					
2						
3	*Regression Statistics*					
4	Multiple R	0.8095				
5	R Square	0.6552				
6	Adjusted R Square	0.6481				
7	Standard Error	302.5				
8	Observations	100				
9						
10	ANOVA					
11		*df*	*SS*	*MS*	*F*	*Significance F*
12	Regression	2	16865053	8432526	92.17	0.0000
13	Residual	97	8874508	91490		
14	Total	99	25739561			
15						
16		*Coefficients*	*Standard Error*	*t Stat*	*P-value*	
17	Intercept	17160	186	92.30	0.0000	
18	Odometer	-0.0626	0.0046	-13.56	0.0000	
19	Color	-43.34	36.23	-1.20	0.2345	

MINITAB

Regression Analysis: Price versus Odometer, Color

```
The regression equation is
Price = 17160 - 0.0626 Odometer - 43.3 Color

Predictor        Coef      SE Coef         T        P
Constant      17160.4        185.9     92.30    0.000
Odometer    -0.062556     0.004612    -13.56    0.000
Color          -43.34        36.23     -1.20    0.234

S = 302.5        R-Sq = 65.5%      R-Sq(adj) = 64.8%

Analysis of Variance

Source            DF           SS           MS         F        P
Regression         2     16865053      8432526     92.17    0.000
Residual Error    97      8874508        91490
Total             99     25739561
```

INTERPRET

The regression equation is

$$\hat{y} = 17{,}160 - .0626x_1 - 43.34x_2$$

Aside from the inclusion of the variable x_2, this equation is very similar to the one we produced in the simple regression model ($\hat{y} = 17{,}067 - .0623x$). An examination of the output above reveals that the variable representing color is not linearly related to price (*t* statistic $= -1.20$, and *p*-value $= .2345$). There are two possible explanations for this result. First, there is no relationship between color and price. Second, color is a factor in determining the car's price, but the way in which the dealer assigned the codes to the colors made detection of that fact impossible. That is, the dealer treated the nominal variable, color, as an interval variable. To further understand why we cannot use nominal data in regression analysis, try to interpret the coefficient of color. Such an effort is similar to attempting to interpret the mean of a sample of nominal data. It is futile. Even though this effort failed, it is possible to include nominal variables in the regression model. This is accomplished through the use of *indicator variables.*

An **indicator variable** (also called a **dummy variable**) is a variable that can assume either one of only two values (usually 0 and 1), where one value represents the existence of a certain condition and the other value indicates that the condition does not hold. In this illustration we would create two indicator variables to represent the color of the car:

$$I_1 = \begin{cases} 1 & \text{if color is white} \\ 0 & \text{if color is not white} \end{cases}$$

and

$$I_2 = \begin{cases} 1 & \text{if color is silver} \\ 0 & \text{if color is not silver} \end{cases}$$

Notice that we need only two indicator variables to represent the three categories. A white car is represented by $I_1 = 1$ and $I_2 = 0$. A silver car is represented by $I_1 = 0$ and $I_2 = 1$. Because cars that are painted some other color are neither white nor silver, they are represented by $I_1 = 0$ and $I_2 = 0$. It should be apparent that we cannot have $I_1 = 1$ and $I_2 = 1$, as long as we assume that no Ford Taurus is two-toned.

The effect of using these two indicator variables is to create three equations, one for each of the three colors. As you're about to discover, we can use the equations to determine how the car's color relates to its auction-selling price.

In general, to represent a nominal variable with m categories, we must create $m - 1$ indicator variables. The last category represented by $I_1 = I_2 = \cdots = I_{m-1} = 0$ is called the **omitted category**.

INTERPRETING AND TESTING THE COEFFICIENTS OF INDICATOR VARIABLES

In columns 3 and 4 of file Xm18-02b, we stored the values of I_1 and I_2. We then performed a multiple regression analysis using the variables odometer reading (x), I_1, and I_2.

EXCEL

	A	B	C	D	E	F
1	SUMMARY OUTPUT					
2						
3	*Regression Statistics*					
4	Multiple R	0.8355				
5	R Square	0.6980				
6	Adjusted R Square	0.6886				
7	Standard Error	284.5				
8	Observations	100				
9						
10	ANOVA					
11		*df*	*SS*	*MS*	*F*	*Significance F*
12	Regression	3	17966997	5988999	73.97	0.0000
13	Residual	96	7772564	80964		
14	Total	99	25739561			
15						
16		*Coefficients*	*Standard Error*	*t Stat*	*P-value*	
17	Intercept	16701	184.3	90.60	0.0000	
18	Odometer	-0.0555	0.0047	-11.72	0.0000	
19	I-1	90.48	68.17	1.33	0.1876	
20	I-2	295.48	76.37	3.87	0.0002	

MINITAB

Regression Analysis: Price versus Odometer, I-1, I-2

```
The regression equation is
Price = 16701 - 0.0555 Odometer + 90.5 I-1 + 295 I-2

Predictor         Coef      SE Coef          T        P
Constant       16700.6        184.3      90.60    0.000
Odometer     -0.055540     0.004737     -11.72    0.000
I-1              90.48        68.17       1.33    0.188
I-2             295.48        76.37       3.87    0.000

S = 284.5        R-Sq = 69.8%      R-Sq(adj) = 68.9%

Analysis of Variance

Source            DF           SS          MS        F        P
Regression         3     17966997     5988999    73.97    0.000
Residual Error    96      7772564       80964
Total             99     25739561
```

INTERPRET

The regression equation is

$$\hat{y} = 16{,}701 - .0555x + 90.48I_1 + 295.48I_2$$

The intercept and the coefficient of odometer reading are interpreted in the usual manner. The intercept ($b_0 = 16{,}701$) is meaningless in the context of this problem. The coefficient of the odometer reading ($b_1 = -.0555$) tells us that for each additional mile on the odometer, the auction price decreases, on average, by 5.55 cents.

Now examine the remaining two coefficients:

$$b_2 = 90.48$$
$$b_3 = 295.48$$

Recall that we interpret the coefficients in a multiple regression model by holding the other variables constant. In this example, we interpret the coefficient of I_1 as follows. In this sample, a white car sells for $90.48 on average more than other colors (nonwhite, nonsilver) with the same odometer reading. A silver car sells for $295.48 on average more than other colors with the same odometer reading. The reason both comparisons are made with other colors is that such cars are represented by $I_1 = I_2 = 0$. Thus, for a nonwhite and nonsilver car, the equation becomes

$$\hat{y} = 16{,}701 - .0555x + 90.48(0) + 295.48(0)$$

which is

$$\hat{y} = 16{,}701 - .0555x$$

For a white car ($I_1 = 1$ and $I_2 = 0$), the regression equation is

$$\hat{y} = 16{,}701 - .0555x + 90.48(1) + 295.48(0)$$

which is

$$\hat{y} = 16{,}791.48 - .0555x$$

Finally, for a silver car ($I_1 = 0$ and $I_2 = 1$), the regression equation is

$$\hat{y} = 16{,}701 - .0555x + 90.48(0) + 295.48(1)$$

which simplifies to

$$\hat{y} = 16{,}996.48 - .0555x$$

Figure 20.11 depicts the graph of price versus odometer reading for the three different color categories. Notice that the three lines are parallel (with slope = .0555) while the intercepts differ.

Figure 20.11
Price versus odometer for three colors

We can also perform t tests on the coefficients of I_1 and I_2. However, because the variables I_1 and I_2 represent different groups (the three color categories), these t tests allow us to draw inferences about the differences in auction selling prices between the groups for the entire population of similar 3-year-old Ford Tauruses.

The test of the coefficient of I_1, which is β_2 is conducted as follows:

$$H_0: \quad \beta_2 = 0$$

$$H_1: \quad \beta_2 \neq 0$$

Test statistic: $\quad t = 1.33, \quad p\text{-value} = .1876$

There is insufficient evidence to infer that in the population, 3-year-old white Tauruses with the same odometer reading have a different selling price than do Tauruses in the other color category.

To determine whether silver-colored Tauruses sell for a different price than Tauruses in the other color category, we test

$$H_0: \quad \beta_3 = 0$$

$$H_1: \quad \beta_3 \neq 0$$

Test statistic: $\quad t = 3.87, \quad p\text{-value} = .0002$

We can conclude that there are differences in auction selling prices between all 3-year-old silver-colored Tauruses and the Tauruses in the other color category with the same odometer readings.

MBA PROGRAM ADMISSIONS POLICY–II: SOLUTION

Because the dean is a statistician, she knows that the codes representing the type of degree are nominal and cannot be used in regression analysis. She creates the following indicator variables (see page 363 to learn how this is done):

$$I_1 = \begin{cases} 1 & \text{if BA} \\ 0 & \text{otherwise} \end{cases}$$

$$I_2 = \begin{cases} 1 & \text{if BBA} \\ 0 & \text{otherwise} \end{cases}$$

$$I_3 = \begin{cases} 1 & \text{if BSc or BEng} \\ 0 & \text{otherwise} \end{cases}$$

EXCEL

	A	B	C	D	E	F
1	SUMMARY OUTPUT					
2						
3	Regression Statistics					
4	Multiple R	0.7461				
5	R Square	0.5566				
6	Adjusted R Square	0.5242				
7	Standard Error	0.729				
8	Observations	89				
9						
10	ANOVA					
11		df	SS	MS	F	Significance F
12	Regression	6	54.75	9.13	17.16	0.0000
13	Residual	82	43.62	0.53		
14	Total	88	98.37			
15						
16		Coefficients	Standard Error	t Stat	P-value	
17	Intercept	0.19	1.41	0.13	0.8930	
18	UnderGPA	-0.0061	0.114	-0.05	0.9577	
19	GMAT	0.0128	0.0014	9.43	0.0000	
20	Work	0.098	0.030	3.24	0.0017	
21	I-1	-0.34	0.22	-1.54	0.1269	
22	I-2	0.71	0.24	2.93	0.0043	
23	I-3	0.035	0.209	0.17	0.8684	

MINITAB

Regression Analysis: MBA GPA versus UnderGPA, GMAT, Work, I-1, I-2, I-

```
The regression equation is
MBA GPA = 0.19 - 0.006 UnderGPA + 0.0128 GMAT + 0.0982 Work - 0.345 I-1
        + 0.706 I-2 + 0.035 I-3

Predictor       Coef      SE Coef         T        P
Constant       0.190       1.407       0.13    0.893
UnderGPA     -0.0061      0.11140      -0.05    0.958
GMAT        0.012793    0.001356       9.43    0.000
Work         0.09818     0.03032       3.24    0.002
I-1          -0.3450      0.2237      -1.54    0.127
I-2           0.7057      0.2405       2.93    0.004
I-3           0.0348      0.2094       0.17    0.868

S = 0.7293    R-Sq = 55.7%    R-Sq(adj) = 52.4%

Analysis of Variance

Source           DF          SS         MS        F       P
Regression        6     54.7518     9.1253    17.16   0.000
Residual Error   82     43.6174     0.5319
Total            88     98.3692
```

INTERPRET

The model has improved somewhat; the coefficient of determination has increased to .5566. The GMAT score and years of work experience continue to be significant variables. The coefficients of the indicator variables are interpreted as follows.

Variable I_1, coefficient $b_4 = -.34$: In this sample the MBA program GPAs of students with a BA degree are on average .34 smaller than the other group, assuming the same undergraduate GPA, GMAT, and number of years of work experience. The t test of β_4 ($t = -1.54$, p-value $= .1269$) indicates that there is no evidence of a difference between otherwise identical students with a BA degree and the other group.

Variable I_2, coefficient $b_5 = .71$: In this sample, the MBA program GPAs of students with a BBA degree are on average .71 larger than the other group, comparing students with the same undergraduate GPA, GMAT score, and years of work experience. The t test of β_5 ($t = 2.93$, p-value $= .0043$) indicates that there is evidence of a difference between otherwise identical students with a BBA degree and the other group.

Variable I_3, coefficient $b_6 = .035$: In this sample, the MBA program GPAs of students with a BSc or BEng degree are on average .035 larger than the other group, once again assuming that the other variables are identical. The t test of β_6 ($t = .17$, p-value $= .8684$) indicates that there is no evidence of a difference between otherwise identical students with a BSc or BEng degree and the other group.

Because of the difference between BBA degree holders and the other group, we can infer that the type of degree is a determinant of success in the MBA program.

EXERCISES

20.12 Create and identify indicator variables to represent the following nominal variables.
   a Religious affiliation (Catholic, Protestant, and others)
   b Working shift (8:00 A.M. to 4:00 P.M., 4:00 P.M. to 12:00 midnight, and 12:00 midnight to 8:00 A.M.)
   c Supervisor (Jack Jones, Mary Brown, George Fosse, and Elaine Smith)

20.13 In a study of computer applications, a survey asked which microcomputer a number of companies used. The following indicator variables were created:

$$I_1 = \begin{cases} 1 & \text{if IBM} \\ 0 & \text{if not} \end{cases}$$

$$I_2 = \begin{cases} 1 & \text{if Macintosh} \\ 0 & \text{if not} \end{cases}$$

What computer is being referred to by each of the following pairs of values?

a $I_1 = 0; I_2 = 1$
b $I_1 = 1; I_2 = 0$
c $I_1 = 0; I_2 = 0$

The following exercises require the use of a computer and software. Exercises 20.15 and 20.16 can be solved manually. See Appendix A. **Use a 5% significance level.**

20.14 Refer to the MBA Program Admissions Policy—II example.
  a Predict with 95% confidence the MBA program GPA of a BEng whose undergraduate GPA was 9.0, whose GMAT score was 700, and who has had 10 years of work experience.
  b Repeat part **a** for a BA student.

20.15 Refer to Exercise 19.53, where a multiple regression analysis was performed to predict men's longevity based on the parents' and grandparents' longevity. Suppose that in addition to these data, the actuary also recorded whether the man was a smoker (1 = yes, 0 = no). These data are stored in column 6 of file Xr20-15. (Columns 1 to 5 are identical to columns 1 to 5 of file Xr19-53.)
  a Use regression analysis to produce the statistics for this model.
  b Compare the equation produced here to that produced in Exercise 19.53. Describe the differences.
  c Are smoking and length of life related? Explain.

20.16 The manager of an amusement park would like to be able to predict daily attendance, in order to develop more accurate plans about how much food to order and how many ride operators to hire. After some consideration, he decided that the following three factors are critical:

Yesterday's attendance

Weekday or weekend

Predicted weather

He then took a random sample of 40 days. For each day, he recorded the attendance, the previous day's attendance, day of the week, and weather forecast. The first independent variable is interval, but the other two are nominal. Accordingly, he created the following sets of indicator variables:

$$I_1 = \begin{cases} 1 & \text{if weekend} \\ 0 & \text{if not} \end{cases}$$

$$I_2 = \begin{cases} 1 & \text{if mostly sunny is predicted} \\ 0 & \text{if not} \end{cases}$$

$$I_3 = \begin{cases} 1 & \text{if rain is predicted} \\ 0 & \text{if not} \end{cases}$$

These data are stored in file Xr20-16.
  a Conduct a regression analysis.
  b Is this model valid? Explain.
  c Can we conclude that weather is a factor in determining attendance?
  d Do these results provide sufficient evidence that weekend attendance is, on average, larger than weekday attendance?

APPLICATIONS IN ACCOUNTING: *FIXED AND VARIABLE COSTS*

Recall that in Chapter 4 (Exercises 4.67 to 4.69) we discussed how the least squares method allows an accountant to estimate the fixed and variable components of costs. In some cases we need to consider other variables in this process.

20.17 Exercise 4.68 considered a firm's investigation into the relationship between direct labor cost and the number of units produced per batch by its sophisticated machines. In Exercise 4.68, you estimated the fixed labor cost and variable cost per unit in a batch. The accountant believes you can improve on your estimates by taking into account the fact that two different products are being produced, and runs producing batches of the more expensive product require longer setup. Conduct a regression to improve upon the previous results. Column 1 of file Xr20-17 stores the labor costs, column 2 stores the number of units per batch, and column 3 stores a 1 to indicate an expensive batch and 0 otherwise.
  a Find the regression equation using the indicator variable.
  b Use the equation to estimate the fixed labor cost and variable cost for each type of batch.

20.18 The real estate agent described in Example 19.2 has become so fascinated by the multiple regression technique that he decided to improve the model. Recall that the agent believed that the most important variables in determining the price of a house are its size, number of bedrooms, and lot size. He took a random sample of 100 houses that were recently sold and recorded the price of the house plus the other three variables. After some consideration, he decided that structure of the house was also a factor. There are four structures: two story, side split, back split, and ranch. Each house was classified. Three indicator variables were created, as follows:

$$I_1 = \begin{cases} 1 & \text{if two story} \\ 0 & \text{if not} \end{cases}$$

$$I_2 = \begin{cases} 1 & \text{if side split} \\ 0 & \text{if not} \end{cases}$$

$$I_3 = \begin{cases} 1 & \text{if back split} \\ 0 & \text{if not} \end{cases}$$

The values of the indicator variables and the data from Xm19-02 are stored in file Xr20-18.

a Perform a multiple regression analysis, and compare your results with those obtained in Example 19.2.

b Interpret and test the coefficients of the indicator variables.

20.19 After reviewing the results of Exercises 18.9 and 20.11, the human resources manager tried one last time to improve the model. He recorded the gender of the worker where 1 = female and 0 = male. These codes were stored in column 3 of file Xr20-20. Columns 1 and 2 are identical to those in file Xr18-09. Can we infer that female telemarketers stay at their jobs longer than male telemarketers?

20.20 Recall Exercise 18.6, where a statistics practitioner analyzed the relationship between the length of a commercial and viewers' memory of the commercial's product. The experiment was repeated, measuring the same two variables. However, in this experiment not only was the length varied but also the type of commercial. There were three types: humorous (1), musical (2), and serious (3). The memory test scores, lengths, and type of commercial (using the codes in parentheses) were recorded in file Xr20-20.

a Perform a regression analysis using the codes provided in the data file.

b Can we infer that the memory test score is related to the type of commercial?

c Create indicator variables to describe the type of commercial and perform another regression analysis.

d Repeat part b using the second model.

e Discuss the reasons for the differences between parts b and d.

20.21 Refer to Exercise 19.55, where the amount of time to unload a truck was analyzed. The manager realized that another variable, the time of day, may affect unloading time. He recorded the following codes: 1 = morning;

2 = early afternoon; 3 = late afternoon. These codes are stored in column 4 of file Xr20-21. (Columns 1 to 3 are identical to columns 1 to 3 of file Xr19-55).

a Run a regression using the codes for time of day.

b Create indicator variables to represent time of day. Perform a regression analysis with these new variables.

c Which model fits better? Explain.

d Is time of day related to time to unload?

20.22 Profitable banks are ones that make good decisions on loan applications. *Credit scoring* is the statistical technique that helps banks make that decision. However, many branches overturn credit scoring recommendations, whereas other banks do not use the technique. In an attempt to determine the factors that affect loan decisions, a statistics practitioner surveyed 100 banks and recorded the percentage of bad loans (any loan that is not completely repaid), the average size of the loan, and whether a scorecard is used, and if so, whether scorecard recommendations are overturned more than 10% of the time. These results are stored in columns 1 (percentage good loans); 2 (average loan); and 3 (code 1 = no scorecard; 2 = scorecard overturned more than 10% of the time; 3 = scorecard overturned less than 10% of the time) in file Xr20-22.

a Create indicator variables to represent the codes.

b Perform a regression analysis.

c How well does the model fit the data?

d Is multicollinearity a problem?

e Interpret the coefficients.

f Predict with 95% confidence the percentage of bad loans for a bank whose average loan is $10,000 and that does not use a scorecard.

20.23 Refer to Exercise 18.85, where a simple linear regression model was used to analyze the relationship between welding machine breakdowns and the age of the machine. The analysis proved to be so useful to company management that they decided to expand the model to include other machines. Data were gathered for two other machines. These data as well as the original data are stored in file Xr20-23 in the following way:

Column 1: Cost of repairs

Column 2: Age of machine

Column 3: Machine (1 = welding machine; 2 = lathe; 3 = stamping machine)

a Develop a multiple regression model.

b Interpret the coefficients.

c Can we conclude that welding machines cost more to repair than other machines?

APPLICATIONS IN HUMAN RESOURCES MANAGEMENT: *PERFORMANCE MEASUREMENT*

Most aspects of workers' performance fall into the domain of the human resources/personnel department. An important performance measurement is the attendance record of each worker. Personnel managers need to know what factors are likely to influence a worker to be absent more frequently than the norm. This can enable the manager to determine whether someone should be hired in the first place. Once hired, the manager needs to be able to influence workers' attitudes and performance.

20.24 Absenteeism is a serious employment problem in most countries. It is estimated that absenteeism reduces potential output by more than 10%. Two economists launched a research project to learn more about the problem. They randomly selected 100 organizations to participate in a 1-year study. For each organization, they recorded the average number of days absent per employee and several variables thought to affect absenteeism. File Xr20-24 contains the following data:

Column 1:   Average employee wage

Column 2:   Percentage of part-time employees

Column 3:   Percentage of unionized employees

Column 4:   Availability of shiftwork (1 = yes; 0 = no)

Column 5:   Union–management relationship (1 = good; 0 = not good)

Column 6:   Average number of days absent per employee

a Conduct a regression analysis.
b Can we infer that the availability of shiftwork is related to absenteeism?
c Is there enough evidence to infer that in organizations where the union–management relationship is good, absenteeism is lower?

(The authors are grateful to James Fong and Diana Mansour for developing this exercise. The data are based on M. Chadhury and I. Ng, "Absenteeism Predictors," *Canadian Journal of Economics,* August 1992.)

20.4 (OPTIONAL) APPLICATIONS IN HUMAN RESOURCES MANAGEMENT: PAY EQUITY

In the history of North America there are many examples of racial, ethnic, and gender discrimination. In the last three decades there have been a number of endeavors designed to eliminate discriminatory practices and to right past wrongs. One of these efforts is pay equity, a program that attempts to correct discrimination in the way workers are paid. Our goal in this section is to describe the statistical component of the pay equity issue.

There are two forms of pay equity. The first is "equal pay for equal work." This form is relatively straightforward, arguing that if two individuals do the same job with similar qualifications and experience, they should be paid the same. In many jurisdictions it is illegal to violate "equal pay for equal work." The second form is "equal pay for work of equal value." This form is controversial for several reasons, including the use of subjectively assigned measures of qualifications and working conditions.

Regression analysis is employed extensively in pay equity cases. However, the methodology used in equal-pay-for-equal-work cases differs from that used for equal-pay-for-work-of-equal-value cases. The following example illustrates how statistical analyses can be utilized for the former.

EXAMPLE 20.3

A large firm employing tens of thousands of workers has been accused of discriminating against its female managers. The accusation is based on a random sample of 100 managers. The mean annual salary of the 38 female managers is $76,189, whereas the mean annual salary of the 62 male managers is $97,832. A statistical analysis reveals that the t test of the difference between two means yields a p-value of less than 1%, which provides overwhelming evidence that male managers, on average, are paid more than female managers. In rebuttal, the president of the firm points out that the company has a strict policy of equal pay for equal work and that the difference may be due to other variables. Accordingly, he found and recorded the number of years of education and the number of years of experience for each of the 100 managers in the sample. Also recorded are the salary and gender (0 = female, 1 = male). All the data are stored in file Xm20-03. The president wanted to know whether a regression analysis would shed some light on the issue.

SOLUTION Using salary as the dependent variable, a multiple regression analysis was performed with the results shown below.

 EXCEL

	A	B	C	D	E	F
1	SUMMARY OUTPUT					
2						
3	*Regression Statistics*					
4	Multiple R	0.8326				
5	R Square	0.6932				
6	Adjusted R Square	0.6836				
7	Standard Error	16274				
8	Observations	100				
9						
10	ANOVA					
11		*df*	*SS*	*MS*	*F*	*Significance F*
12	Regression	3	57434095083	19144698361	72.29	0.0000
13	Residual	96	25424794888	264841613		
14	Total	99	82858889971			
15						
16		*Coefficients*	*Standard Error*	*t Stat*	*P-value*	
17	Intercept	-5835	16083	-0.36	0.7175	
18	Education	2119	1018	2.08	0.0401	
19	Experience	4099	317	12.92	0.0000	
20	Gender	1851	3703	0.50	0.6183	

 MINITAB

Regression Analysis: Salary versus Education, Experience, Gender

```
The regression equation is
Salary = - 5835 + 2119 Education + 4099 Experience + 1851 Gender

Predictor        Coef      SE Coef          T          P
Constant        -5835        16083      -0.36      0.718
Educatio         2119         1018       2.08      0.040
Experien       4099.3        317.2      12.92      0.000
Gender           1851         3703       0.50      0.618

S = 16274      R-Sq = 69.3%      R-Sq(adj) = 68.4%

Analysis of Variance

Source          DF           SS          MS          F          P
Regression       3  57434095083 19144698361      72.29      0.000
Residual Error  96  25424794888   264841613
Total           99  82858889971
```

INTERPRET

The model fits quite well. The coefficient of determination is .6932, which tells the president that 69.32% of the variation in salaries is explained by the model. The F statistic is 72.29, which has a p-value of 0. There is overwhelming evidence to allow us to infer that the model is valid.

The p-values of the t tests to determine whether there is evidence of a linear relationship between salary and each of education, experience, and gender are .0401, 0, and .6183, respectively. Both the number of years of education and the number of years of experience are linearly related to salary. However, the t test of the slope for gender tells us that there is no evidence of a difference between female and male managers. Thus, the result of the t test of the difference between means alluded to in the question is contradicted. A further analysis of the data tells us that the discrepancy in salaries is due to the years of experience. In general, female managers have less experience and hence lower salaries.

REGRESSION ANALYSIS FOR EQUAL-PAY-FOR-WORK-OF-EQUAL-VALUE CASES

Cases involving the issue of equal pay for work of equal value are much more difficult. The issue generally revolves around female-dominated and male-dominated jobs. The former refers to jobs that are generally held by women (e.g., secretaries) and the latter refers to jobs generally held by men (e.g., maintenance workers). Women's groups claim that male-dominated jobs are more highly paid. Here the issue is not underpaying women doing exactly the same job performed by men. Instead, the issue is that women's jobs are undervalued. Thus, it is necessary to evaluate jobs.

Several jurisdictions have enacted laws requiring pay equity for work of equal value. One such jurisdiction is the province of Manitoba. The Manitoba Pay Equity Act is mandatory in the province's civil service, crown corporations, hospitals, and universities. The act defines gender-dominated job classes as ones with at least 10 workers where at least 70% are of the same gender. The act requires that all such jobs be evaluated to determine whether female-dominated jobs are undervalued and underpaid compared to male-dominated jobs.

Although regression analysis is employed, there are major differences between the technique described in Example 20.3 and the one used in this case. Rather than estimate a regression model that explains how several related variables affect pay, we need to develop a job evaluation system (JES). The system is used to assign a score to each job, which is then used as an independent variable in regression where pay is again the dependent variable. The regression analysis can be conducted in several ways. The simple linear regression equation can be estimated using the male-dominated jobs only. The coefficients are then used to calculate the "correct" female-dominated job pay rates. The difference between the "correct" and the actual pay rates represents the degree of underpayment. Alternatively, a regression analysis with both male- and female-dominated jobs can be employed. An indicator variable representing gender is included. The value of the indicator variable's coefficient represents the difference between male- and female-dominated jobs and the degree of underpayment. The following example illustrates the latter type of analysis, which was adapted from the Province of Manitoba Pay Equity Act manuals that describe the law and how it is to be administered.

EXAMPLE 20.4

In a university, a total of eight jobs were identified as gender-dominated. The female-dominated jobs are secretary, cleaner, and workers in the bookstore and cafeteria. The male-dominated jobs are gardener, security guard, maintenance worker, and technician. Perform a pay-equity analysis to determine whether and to what degree female-dominated jobs are undervalued and underpaid.

SOLUTION   The hourly pay rates are as follows.

Job Categories	Pay Rate
Maintenance	13.55
Security	15.65
Gardener	13.80
Technician	19.90
Cleaner	11.85
Secretary	14.75
Bookstore	18.90
Cafeteria	13.30

After some consideration, the following factors were selected as part of the job evaluation system:

Knowledge and training

Responsibility

Mental effort

Physical effort

Working conditions

Each factor is assigned a weight that reflects its importance. The weights (which must sum to 1) are 25%, 23%, 22%, 15%, and 15%, respectively.

A score for each job is determined by assigning a value between 1 and 10 for each of the five factors and then multiplying by the weight. Smaller values represent less demanding requirements or better conditions. The male-dominated jobs are evaluated as follows.

Factors	Weight	Maintenance	Security	Gardener	Technician
Knowledge & training	0.25	1	2	3	9
Responsibility	0.23	2	7	1	7
Mental effort	0.22	2	3	1	8
Physical effort	0.15	7	1	6	4
Working conditions	0.15	7	4	8	1
Total score		3.25	3.52	3.3	6.37

As you can see, the scores assigned to the maintenance workers and gardeners reflect relatively small demands on knowledge, training, and mental effort but high demands on physical effort and poor working conditions. The technician, on the other hand, has excellent working conditions but requires a high level of knowledge and training.

The evaluations of the female dominated jobs are as follows:

Factors	Weight	Cleaner	Secretary	Bookstore	Cafeteria
Knowledge & training	0.25	1	6	4	2
Responsibility	0.23	2	7	7	2
Mental effort	0.22	2	6	7	2
Physical effort	0.15	7	3	2	5
Working conditions	0.15	5	1	1	6
Total score		2.95	5.03	4.6	3.05

As was the case with the male-dominated jobs, the scores for the female-dominated jobs are based on a subjective assessment of the requirements and work that the jobs entail.

The score and an indicator variable are used as independent variables in a regression analysis with pay as the dependent variable. The following data are used in the regression analysis.

Job Categories	Pay Rate	Score	Gender
Maintenance	13.55	3.25	1
Security	15.65	3.52	1
Gardener	13.8	3.3	1
Technician	19.9	6.37	1
Cleaner	11.85	2.95	0
Secretary	14.75	5.03	0
Bookstore	18.9	4.6	0
Cafeteria	13.3	3.05	0

where

$$\text{Gender} = \begin{cases} 1 & \text{if male-dominated job} \\ 0 & \text{if female-dominated job} \end{cases}$$

The results of the regression are shown below.

 EXCEL

	A	B	C	D	E	F
1	SUMMARY OUTPUT					
2						
3	Regression Statistics					
4	Multiple R	0.8515				
5	R Square	0.7251				
6	Adjusted R Square	0.6152				
7	Standard Error	1.750				
8	Observations	8				
9						
10	ANOVA					
11		df	SS	MS	F	Significance F
12	Regression	2	40.388	20.194	6.59	0.0396
13	Residual	5	15.310	3.062		
14	Total	7	55.699			
15						
16		Coefficients	Standard Error	t Stat	P-value	
17	Intercept	7.145	2.309	3.10	0.0270	
18	Score	1.933	0.547	3.54	0.0166	
19	Gender	0.633	1.242	0.51	0.6318	

 MINITAB

Regression Analysis: Pay Rate versus Score, Gender

```
The regression equation is
Pay Rate = 7.15 + 1.93 Score + 0.63 Gender

Predictor        Coef      SE Coef            T        P
Constant        7.145        2.309         3.10    0.027
Score          1.9334       0.5468         3.54    0.017
Gender          0.633        1.242         0.51    0.632

S = 1.750       R-Sq = 72.5%       R-Sq(adj) = 61.5%

Analysis of Variance

Source           DF          SS           MS        F        P
Regression        2      40.388       20.194     6.59    0.040
Residual Error    5      15.310        3.062
Total             7      55.699
```

> **INTERPRET**

We cannot apply the usual statistical inference because the 8 observations represent the entire population under consideration. Instead, we simply use the coefficients of interest. In this case we discover that male-dominated jobs are paid an average of .633 more than female-dominated jobs after adjusting for the value of each job. If we accept the validity of this analysis (see Exercises 20.26 and 20.27), we conclude that the holders of female-dominated jobs need to have their pay rates increased by 63 cents per hour.

EXERCISES

The following exercises require a computer and software.

20.25 Pay equity for men and women has been an ongoing source of conflict for a number of years in North America. Suppose that a statistics practitioner is investigating the factors that affect salary differences between male and female university professors. He believes that the following variables have some impact on a professor's salary:

Number of years since first degree

$$\text{Highest degree} = \begin{cases} 1 & \text{if highest degree is a PhD} \\ 0 & \text{if highest degree is not a PhD} \end{cases}$$

Average score on teaching evaluations

Number of articles published in refereed journals

$$\text{Gender} = \begin{cases} 1 & \text{if professor is male} \\ 0 & \text{if professor is female} \end{cases}$$

A random sample of 100 university professors was taken and the data stored in file Xr20-25.

Column 1: Annual salary
Column 2: Number of years since first degree
Column 3: Highest degree
Column 4: Mean score on teaching evaluation
Column 5: Number of articles published
Column 6: Gender

a Can the statistics practitioner conclude that the model is valid?
b Can the statistics practitioner conclude at the 5% significance level that there is gender discrimination?

*An Excel spreadsheet, **Pay Equity** (stored in the **Excel Workbooks** folder), was created to perform the analysis described in Example 20.4. The jobs, pay rates, job scores, and the values of the indicator variable are shown at the bottom of the sheet. These data were used as inputs in the regression analysis. The worksheet is set up so that any change in the factor scores and/or weights automatically changes the job scores at the bottom of the page.*

20.26 Redo Example 20.4. Change the weights for knowledge and training to 15% and for working conditions to 25%. What effect does this have on the conclusion? Briefly explain why the result was predictable.

20.27 Redo Example 20.4 by assigning your own values to each factor and to the weights. What conclusion did you reach?

20.28 Discuss how the factor values and weights affect the final result. Explain the strengths and weaknesses of the statistical analysis.

20.5 (OPTIONAL) STEPWISE REGRESSION

In Section 19.4 we introduced multicollinearity and described the problems it causes by distorting the *t* tests of the coefficients. If one of the objectives of the regression analysis is to determine whether and how each independent variable is related to the dependent variable, it is necessary to reduce the extent of multicollinearity.

As we discussed in Section 19.4, one of the ways to reduce multicollinearity is to include independent variables that appear to be uncorrelated with each other. A correlation matrix is usually produced to determine the correlation coefficients for each pair of variables. In many cases the correlation matrix will not be able to identify whether multicollinearity is a serious problem because there are many ways for variables to be related. For example, one variable may be a function of several other variables. Consequently, a correlation matrix may not reveal the problem. In this section, we introduce *stepwise regression*, a procedure that eliminates correlated independent variables.

Stepwise regression is an iterative procedure that adds and deletes one independent variable at a time. The decision to add or delete a variable is made on the basis of whether that variable improves the model. Minitab features this and related procedures. Excel does not. However, we created a macro that performs stepwise regression. It should be noted that this macro is different from the ones you have encountered thus far in this book. Specific instructions for its use are provided below.

STEPWISE REGRESSION PROCEDURE

The procedure begins by computing the simple regression model for each independent variable. The independent variable with the largest F statistic (which in a simple regression model is the t statistic squared) or equally, with the smallest p-value, is chosen as the first entering variable. (Minitab uses the F statistic, and the Excel macro can use either the F statistic or the p-value.) The standard is usually set at $F = 4.0$, chosen because the significance level is about 5%. The standard may be changed in both Minitab and Excel. The standard is called the *F-to-enter*. If no independent variable exceeds the *F*-to-enter, the procedure ceases with no regression model produced. If at least one variable exceeds the standard, the procedure continues. It then considers whether the model would be improved by adding a second independent variable. It examines all such models to determine which is best and whether the F statistic of the second variable (with the first variable already in the equation) is greater than the F-to-enter.

If two independent variables are highly correlated, only one of them will enter the equation. Once the first variable is included, the added explanatory power of the second variable will be minimal and its F statistic will not be large enough to enter the model. In this way multicollinearity is reduced.

The procedure continues by deciding whether to add another independent variable at each step. The computer also checks to see whether the inclusion of previously added variables is warranted. At each step the p-values of all variables are computed and compared to the *F-to-remove*. If a variable's F statistic falls below this standard, it is removed from the equation.

These steps are repeated until no more variables are added or removed.

EXAMPLE 20.5

In Exercise 18.89, we examined the relationship between a baseball team's winning percentage and its batting average. Exercise 18.90 looked at the relationship between the winning percentage and the earned run average. In an attempt to learn more about the variables that determine winning and losing, several more variables were recorded. Variables that are believed to be related to scoring runs are batting average, home runs, stolen bases, bases on balls received, and number of strikeouts. Variables related to runs allowed are earned runs, hits, errors, bases on balls allowed, and strikeouts of opposing players. The data from the American League for a recent season are stored in file Xm20-05 and are listed in Tables 20.1 and 20.2.

Table 20.1 shows, for example, that the Baltimore Orioles' winning percentage was .414 (actually 67 wins and 95 losses in the 162-game season); they scored a total of 686 runs and had a team batting average of .254 (1,421 hits in 5,604 at bats) with 170 home runs, 50 stolen bases, 528 bases on balls, and 974 strikeouts. Table 20.2 exhibits defensive statistics. It shows, for example, that Orioles pitchers gave up a total of 796 runs, of which 743 were earned. (An unearned run is a run that is scored because of an error.) Pitchers allowed 1,534 hits, issued 504 bases on balls, and struck out 868 opposing batters. The defense made 91 errors.

Table 20.1 Offensive Statistics

Team	Winning %	Runs	Batting Average	Home Runs	Stolen Bases	Bases on Balls	Strikeouts
Baltimore	.414	686	.254	170	50	528	974
Boston	.519	731	.269	126	59	593	820
California	.500	653	.255	115	94	448	928
Chicago	.537	758	.262	139	134	610	896
Cleveland	.352	576	.254	79	84	449	888
Detroit	.519	817	.247	209	109	699	1,185
Kansas City	.506	727	.264	117	119	523	969
Milwaukee	.512	799	.271	116	106	556	802
Minnesota	.586	776	.280	140	107	526	747
New York	.438	674	.256	147	109	473	861
Oakland	.519	760	.248	159	151	642	981
Seattle	.512	702	.255	126	97	588	811
Texas	.525	829	.270	177	102	596	1,039
Toronto	.562	684	.257	133	148	499	1,043

Table 20.2 Defensive Statistics

Team	Runs	Earned Runs	Hits	Errors	Bases on Balls	Strikeouts
Baltimore	796	743	1,534	91	504	868
Boston	712	642	1,405	116	530	999
California	649	591	1,351	102	543	990
Chicago	681	622	1,302	116	601	923
Cleveland	759	678	1,551	149	441	862
Detroit	794	726	1,570	104	593	739
Kansas City	722	639	1,473	125	529	1,004
Milwaukee	744	674	1,498	118	527	859
Minnesota	652	595	1,402	95	488	876
New York	777	709	1,510	133	506	936
Oakland	776	734	1,425	107	655	892
Seattle	674	616	1,387	110	628	1,003
Texas	814	734	1,486	134	662	1,022
Toronto	622	569	1,301	127	523	971

Source: Creative Statistics Company.

Perform an analysis to determine which variables are related to a team's winning percentage.

SOLUTION Here is an example where we cannot use all the recorded variables in a regression model that attempts to explain the variation in a team's winning percentage. There are two problems. First, when there are few observations relative to the number of variables, the model will almost always appear to fit well, when, in fact, it may not. Consider a simple regression model (one independent variable) with only 3 observations. It is likely that the regression equation will appear to fit well, yet there may be no linear relationship. Thus, to enable us to assess how well each of the variables is related to the winning percentage, it is necessary to reduce the number of variables.

Second, it is likely that some of the independent variables are either correlated directly with each other or correlated with a combination of independent variables. As a result, it will be impossible to determine whether each independent variable is linearly related to the winning percentage.

In fact, the multiple regression model created by using all 12 independent variables was estimated (results shown below). The coefficient of determination was 98.67% (the adjusted coefficient of determination was 82.66%) and the standard error of estimate was quite small (.0252), but the F test was not significant (p-value = .3058) and no t test was significant. (All p-values were at least .4778.) These results are so contradictory that it is impossible to properly interpret them. A large coefficient of determination and a small standard error of estimate indicate a good fit. However, the large p-values for the F test and the t tests indicate that the model is not valid and that none of the independent variables is related to the team's winning percentage.

EXCEL

Output for Example 20.5: Ordinary Multiple Regression

	A	B	C	D	E	F
1	SUMMARY OUTPUT					
2						
3	*Regression Statistics*					
4	Multiple R	0.9933				
5	R Square	0.9867				
6	Adjusted R Square	0.8266				
7	Standard Error	0.0252				
8	Observations	14				
9						
10	ANOVA					
11		*df*	*SS*	*MS*	*F*	*Significance F*
12	Regression	12	0.0471	0.0039	6.17	0.3058
13	Residual	1	0.0006	0.0006		
14	Total	13	0.0478			
15						
16		*Coefficients*	*Standard Error*	*t Stat*	*P-value*	
17	Intercept	-0.1547	0.9048	-0.17	0.8922	
18	Rns_Scrd	0.0006	0.0006	0.95	0.5148	
19	Team_BA	0.8632	3.1020	0.28	0.8272	
20	Team_Hmr	0.0002	0.0006	0.42	0.7450	
21	Team_SB	0.0003	0.0006	0.60	0.6571	
22	Team_Wlk	0.0002	0.0003	0.57	0.6689	
23	Team_SO	0.0001	0.0001	0.40	0.7604	
24	Rns_Alw	-0.0019	0.0020	-0.95	0.5177	
25	Erns_Alw	0.0011	0.0018	0.64	0.6376	
26	Hits_Alw	0.0002	0.0003	0.56	0.6756	
27	Team_Ers	-0.0001	0.0004	-0.32	0.8011	
28	Wlk_Alw	0.0002	0.0002	1.07	0.4778	
29	SO	0.0002	0.0012	0.14	0.9105	

MINITAB
Output for Example 20.5: Ordinary multiple regression

Regression Analysis: Win_Pct versus Rns_Scrd, Team_BA, ...

```
The regression equation is
Win_Pct = - 0.155 +0.000558 Rns_Scrd + 0.86 Team_BA +0.000249 Team_Hmr
          +0.000348 Team_SB +0.000163 Team_Wlk +0.000054 Team_SO
          - 0.00189 Rns_Alw + 0.00115 Erns_Alw +0.000183 Hits_Alw
          -0.000117 Team_Ers +0.000229 Wlk_Alw + 0.00017 SO

Predictor       Coef     SE Coef         T       P
Constant      -0.1547      0.9048     -0.17   0.892
Rns_Scrd    0.0005584   0.0005851      0.95   0.515
Team_BA         0.863       3.102      0.28   0.827
Team_Hmr    0.0002489   0.0005879      0.42   0.745
Team_SB     0.0003479   0.0005822      0.60   0.657
Team_Wlk    0.0001627   0.0002841      0.57   0.669
Team_SO     0.0000541   0.0001370      0.40   0.760
Rns_Alw     -0.001895    0.002003     -0.95   0.518
Erns_Alw     0.001145    0.001789      0.64   0.638
Hits_Alw    0.0001834   0.0003281      0.56   0.676
Team_Ers   -0.0001169   0.0003617     -0.32   0.801
Wlk_Alw     0.0002292   0.0002138      1.07   0.478
SO           0.000169    0.001195      0.14   0.910

S = 0.02524    R-Sq = 98.7%    R-Sq(adj) = 82.7%

Analysis of Variance

Source           DF         SS          MS        F       P
Regression       12  0.0471477   0.0039290     6.17   0.306
Residual Error    1  0.0006372   0.0006372
Total            13  0.0477849
```

We then conducted a stepwise regression analysis. The results are shown below.

EXCEL

Output for Example 20.5: Stepwise regression

	A	B	C	D	E	F	G
1	Results of stepwise regression						
2							
3	Step 1 - Entering variable: Rns_Scrd						
4							
5	Summary measures						
6		Multiple R	0.6792				
7		R-Square	0.4613				
8		Adj R-Square	0.4164				
9		StErr of Est	0.0463				
10							
11	ANOVA Table						
12		Source	df	SS	MS	F	p-value
13		Explained	1	0.0220	0.0220	10.2766	0.0076
14		Unexplained	12	0.0257	0.0021		
15							
16	Regression coefficients						
17			Coefficient	Std Err	t-value	p-value	
18		Constant	0.0716	0.1342	0.5336	0.6034	
19		Rns_Scrd	0.0006	0.0002	3.2057	0.0076	
20							
21	Step 2 - Entering variable: Rns_Alw						
22							
23	Summary measures			Change	% Change		
24		Multiple R	0.9678	0.2886	%42.5		
25		R-Square	0.9367	0.4754	%103.0		
26		Adj R-Square	0.9252	0.5088	%122.2		
27		StErr of Est	0.0166	-0.0297	-%64.2		
28							
29	ANOVA Table						
30		Source	df	SS	MS	F	p-value
31		Explained	2	0.0448	0.0224	81.3769	0.0000
32		Unexplained	11	0.0030	0.0003		
33							
34	Regression coefficients						
35			Coefficient	Std Err	t-value	p-value	
36		Constant	0.4624	0.0645	7.1704	0.0000	
37		Rns_Scrd	0.0007	0.0001	10.9019	0.0000	
38		Rns_Alw	-0.0007	0.0001	-9.0884	0.0000	

COMMANDS

1. Type or import the data according to the instructions below.
2. Click **Tools, Data Analysis Plus,** and **Stepwise Regression**.
3. Specify the dependent variable (**response variable:**).
4. Specify the independent variables (**explanatory variables:**).
5. Select the **Significance option**. Click **OK** to choose **p-values** as the criterion. Click **OK** to accept the default values for **p-to-enter** and **p-to-leave**.
6. Select the **scatterplots** you wish to see. Click **OK**.
7. Select the location of the output. Click **OK**.

COMMANDS FOR EXAMPLE 20.5

Open file **XM20-05**.

Win_Pct

Highlight the entire list.

Special Instructions for Stepwise Regression

Before beginning, place the cursor somewhere in the data set. If you don't, you will be forced to close the macro and repeat.

The macro will ask about missing values. The data sets in this chapter do not have missing values. Simply accept the default and proceed. However, if you have created your own data set that has missing values, click the box to erase the check mark.

Instead of specifying the block coordinates of the data, you simply specify variable names for the dependent and the independent variables. The names must start with a letter or underscore. Do not use names that are the same as cell addresses (e.g., A2), R or C, or names consisting only of numbers (e.g., 55). Do not use symbols other than letters, numbers, and underscores.

The dependent variable must be interval. It cannot be an indicator (dummy) variable. You may use independent indicator variables.

You will be asked to specify the significance options, which refers to the way the stepwise regression decides which variables enter and which variables leave. Until you learn more about these choices, we suggest that you accept the defaults.

The macro will draw several different plots. Specify the ones you want.

The output will be placed on the same worksheet as the data or on a different worksheet. If you choose the latter, the macro will ask you to name the worksheet.

MINITAB
Output for Example 20.5: Stepwise regression

Stepwise Regression: Win_Pct versus Rns_Scrd, Team_BA, ...

```
Forward selection.  Alpha-to-Enter: 0.05

 Response is Win_Pct  on 12 predictors, with N =    14


     Step          1         2
 Constant    0.07162   0.46240

 Rns_Scrd    0.00059   0.00074
 T-Value        3.21     10.90
 P-Value       0.008     0.000

 Rns_Alw                -0.00069
 T-Value                  -9.09
 P-Value                  0.000

 S            0.0463    0.0166
 R-Sq          46.13     93.67
 R-Sq(adj)     41.64     92.52
 C-p            30.4      -3.3
```

COMMANDS	COMMANDS FOR EXAMPLE 20.5
	Open file **XM20-05**.
1. Type or import the data.	
2. Click **Stat, Regression,** and **Stepwise**.	
3. Specify the dependent variable (**Response**).	**Win_Pct** or **C1**
4. Specify the independent variables (**Predictors**).	**C2-C13**
5. Click **Methods** and **Forward selection**.	
6. Specify **Alpha to enter**.	.05
7. Click **OK**. Click **OK**.	

> **INTERPRET**

All one-independent-variable models are proposed, and the one that fits best is chosen. As you can see, in step 1 the variable **Rns_Scrd** was judged to be best. The model is

$$\text{Win\_Pct} = .0716 + .0006 \text{ Rns\_Scrd}$$

Its standard error of estimate is .0463, and the coefficient of determination is 46.13%.

In step 2, each of the remaining independent variables is included in a two-variable model with **Rns_Scrd**. The best two-variable model is selected. Thus, **Rns_Alw** is included with **Rns_Scrd**. At the same time, the new F statistic for **Rns_Scrd** is computed and compared to the F-to-remove. Evidently, it is large enough, and **Rns_Scrd** is retained. The regression equation is

$$\text{Win\_Pct} = .4624 + .0007 \text{ Rns\_Scrd} - .0007 \text{ Rns\_Alw}$$

The standard error of estimate is .0166, and the coefficient of determination is 93.67%.

In step 3, the remaining independent variables are examined. All three-variable models (with **Rns_Scrd** and **Rns_Alw**) are tested. If the new independent variable's F statistic is larger than the F-to-enter, that variable is added to the equation. In this example, the F-statistic of each of the remaining variables was not sufficiently large. No other variables were added to the model. This means that whatever explanatory power is provided by variables such as the number of home runs a team hits or the number of stolen bases it allows, has already been factored into the model with the inclusion of the number of runs scored and the number of runs allowed.

For baseball fans this result is rather obvious (although it was probably not obvious until we pointed this out). The two most important variables in determining a team's winning percentage are the number of runs the team scores and the number of runs the team allows the opponents to score. We don't need sophisticated statistical methods to tell us that. However, stepwise regression could now be useful in identifying which offensive-related variables (Table 20.1) are linearly related to the number of runs a team scores and which defensive variables (Table 20.2) are linearly related to the number of runs a team gives up. (See Exercises 20.33 and 20.34.) In this way, a manager may be able to determine what characteristics of a team are most important in producing a winning team. This information could be most useful in deciding trades, drafts, and free agent signings.

EXERCISES

The following exercises require the use of a computer and statistical software.

20.29 Refer to Exercise 19.5.
  a Use a stepwise regression procedure to produce the regression equation.
  b What differences are there between this printout and the one produced in Exercise 19.5?

20.30 Refer to Exercise 19.6.
  a Use a stepwise regression procedure to produce the regression equation.
  b What differences are there between this printout and the one produced in Exercise 19.6?

20.31 Refer to Exercise 19.7. Use a stepwise regression procedure to produce the regression equation. Why was this result predictable from the analysis performed in Exercise 19.7?

20.32 Refer to Exercise 19.10. Use a stepwise regression procedure to produce the regression equation. Why were both independent variables included in the regression equation?

20.33 Refer to Example 20.5. Use stepwise regression to find which offensive variables (Table 20.1) are linearly related to the number of runs scored.

20.34 Refer to Example 20.5. Use stepwise regression to find which defensive variables (Table 20.2) are linearly related to the number of runs allowed.

20.6 MODEL BUILDING

At this point, we have described several different regression models. You now have the use of nominal independent variables and the tools to describe a variety of nonlinear relationships. In this section, we describe how the statistics practitioner builds a model.

Regression analysis is used either to determine how one or more independent variables are related to a dependent variable or to predict the value of the dependent variable and estimate its expected value. Although the process differs between the two objectives, there are many similarities in the approach.

Here is the procedure that is employed in the building of a model.

Procedure for Building a Model

1. *Identify the dependent variable.* Clearly define the variable that you wish to analyze or predict. For example, if you want to forecast sales, decide whether it is to be the number of units sold, gross revenue, or perhaps net profits. Additionally, decide whether to forecast weekly, monthly, or annual figures.

2. *List potential predictors.* Using your knowledge of the dependent variable, produce a list of predictors that may be related to the dependent variable. Although we cannot establish a causal relationship, we should attempt to include independent variables that cause changes in the dependent variable. Bear in mind the problems caused by multicollinearity and the cost of gathering, storing, and processing data. Be selective in your choices. It is best to use the fewest independent variables that produce a satisfactory model.

3. *Gather the required observations for the potential models.* A general rule is that there should be at least six observations for each independent variable used in the equation.

4. *Identify several possible models.* Once again, use your knowledge of the dependent variable and independent variables to formulate a model. For example, if you believe that an independent variable affects the dependent variable, but you are uncertain about the form of the relationship, formulate first-order and second-order models with and without interaction. It may be helpful to draw a scatter diagram of the dependent variable and each independent variable to discover the nature of the relationship.

5. *Use statistical software to estimate the models.* Use one or more of the variable selection methods described in the previous section to determine which variables to include in the model. If the objective is to determine which independent variables are related to the dependent variable, you will need to ensure that multicollinearity is not a problem. If it is, attempt to reduce the number of independent variables.

6. *Determine whether the required conditions are satisfied.* If not, attempt to correct the problem. At this point, you may have several "equal" models from which to choose.

7. *Use your judgment and the statistical output to select the best model.* This may be the most difficult part of the process. There may be a model that fits best, but another one may be a better predictor, and yet another may feature fewer variables and, thus, be easier to work with. Experience with regression helps. Taking another statistics course is likely your best strategy.

20.7 SUMMARY

This chapter completes our discussion of the regression technique, which began in Chapter 18. We presented several additional models for predicting the value of one variable on the basis of other variables. **Polynomial models** with one and two independent variables were presented. We discussed how **indicator variables** allow us to use nominal variables and we described how indicator variables are used in pay equity discussions. To help choose the model that is best for our purposes, we introduced **stepwise regression**. We completed the chapter by providing some advice on how statisticians build models.

IMPORTANT TERMS

Polynomial model 696
Order 696
First-order model 696
Second-order model 697

Interaction 699
Indicator variable 706
Stepwise regression 718

SYMBOLS

Symbol	Pronounced	Represents
I_i	I-sub-i or I-i	Indicator variable

COMPUTER OUTPUT AND INSTRUCTIONS

Technique	Excel	Minitab
Stepwise regression	722	723

REFERENCES

Draper, N. R., and H. Smith, *Applied Regression Analysis*, 2nd edition. New York: John Wiley and Sons, 1981.

Graybill, Franklin A., *Theory and Application of the Linear Model*. North Scituate, MA: Duxbury, 1976.

Greene, William, *Econometric Analysis*, 4th edition. Upper Saddle River, NJ: Prentice Hall, 2000.

Neter, John, Michael H. Kutner, Christopher J. Nachtsheim, and William Wasserman, *Applied Linear Statistical Models* 4th edition. Chicago: Irwin, 1996.

CHAPTER REVIEW EXERCISES

The following exercises require the use of a computer and statistical software. **Use a 5% significance level.**

20.35 Car designers have been experimenting with ways to improve gas mileage for many years. An important element in this research is the way in which a car's speed affects how quickly fuel is burned. Competitions whose objective is to drive the farthest on the smallest amount of gas have determined that low speeds and high speeds are inefficient. Designers would like to know which speed burns gas most efficiently. As an experiment, 50 identical cars are driven at different speeds and the gas mileage measured. These data are stored in file Xr20-35.

a Write the equation of the model you think is appropriate.

b Perform a regression analysis using your model.

c How well does it fit?

20.36 The number of car accidents on a particular stretch of highway seems to be related to the number of vehicles that travel over it and the speed at which they are traveling. A city alderman has decided to ask the county sheriff to provide him with statistics covering the last few years, with the intention of examining these data statistically so that he can (if possible) introduce new speed laws that will reduce traffic accidents. Using the number of accidents as the dependent variable, he obtains estimates of the number of cars passing along a stretch of road and their average speeds (in miles per hour). The observations for 60 randomly selected days are stored in file Xr20-36.

a Which model should the alderman use?

b Conduct a regression analysis using a first-order model with interaction.

c Is the model valid?

20.37 Refer to Exercise 20.36.

a Estimate a second-order model with interaction.

b Is this model valid?

20.38 After analyzing whether the number of ads is related to the number of customers, the manager in Exercise 18.84 decided to determine whether where he advertised made any difference. As a result, he reorganized the experiment. Each week he advertised several times per week, but in only one of the advertising media. He again recorded the weekly number of customers, the number of ads, and the location of that week's advertisement (1 = newspaper, 2 = radio, 3 = television). These data are stored in file Xr20-38.

a Create indicator variables to describe the advertising medium.

b Conduct a regression analysis. Test to determine whether the model is valid.

c Does the advertising medium make a difference? Explain.

20.39 A baseball fan has been collecting data from a newspaper on the various American League teams. She wants to explain each team's winning percentage as a function of its batting average and its earned run average plus an indicator variable for whether the team fired its manager within the last 12 months (code = 1 if it did, 0 if it did not). The data for 50 randomly selected teams over the last five seasons are stored in file Xr20-39.

a Perform a regression analysis using a first-order model (no interaction).

b Do these data provide sufficient evidence that a team that fired its manager within the last 12 months wins less frequently than a team that did not fire its manager?

20.40 A growing segment of the textile industry in the United States is based on piecework, wherein workers are paid for each unit they produce, instead of receiving an hourly wage. The manager of one such company has observed that inexperienced workers perform quite poorly, but they usually improve quickly. However, very experienced workers do not perform as well as expected. Analysts attribute this phenomenon to boredom. More experienced workers grow weary of the monotonous work and become less productive. In an attempt to learn more about piecework labor, a statistics practitioner took a random sample of workers with varying years of experience and counted the number of units each produced in 8 hours. These data are stored in file Xr20-40.

a Write the equation of the model you think would fit.

b Perform a regression analysis using your model.

c Describe how well the model fits.

20.41 The maintenance of swimming pools is quite costly because of all the chlorine that is needed to keep the water clear and relatively free of germs. A chain of hotels (all with outdoor pools) seeking to reduce costs decided to analyze the factors that determine how much chlorine is needed. They commissioned a chemist to conduct an analysis. It is believed that the speed at which chlorine in a pool is depleted is dependent on the temperature of the water (higher temperature uses chlorine faster); pH level, which is a measure of the acidity of the water (pH ranges from 0 to 14, where 0 is very acidic and 14 is very alkaline; levels around 7.5 use the least chlorine); and weather (sunshine uses up chlorine). The chemist conducted the following experiment. The percentage of chlorine depletion during 8-hour days was recorded under varying conditions of pH level, water temperature, and weather conditions. These data are recorded in file Xr20-41 in the following way:

Column 1: Percentage of chlorine depletion over 8 hours

Column 2: Temperature (degrees Fahrenheit)

Column 3: pH level

Column 4: 1 = mainly cloudy; 2 = sunny; 3 = partly sunny

a Write the equation of the model that you would suggest.

b Use regression analysis to estimate the model's coefficients.

c Test to determine whether the model is valid.

d Can we infer that higher temperatures deplete chlorine more quickly?

e Is there evidence to infer that the belief about the relationship between chlorine depletion and pH level is correct?

f Can we infer that weather is a factor in chlorine depletion?

21 TIME SERIES ANALYSIS AND FORECASTING

HOUSING STARTS

At the end of 1999, a major builder of residential houses in the northeastern United States wanted to predict the number of housing units to be started in 2000. This information would be extremely useful in determining a variety of variables, including housing demand, availability of labor, and the price of building materials. To help develop an accurate forecasting model, an economist collected data on the number of housing starts for the previous 60 months (1995–1999). These data (in thousands of units) are stored in file Ch21:\Housing. Forecast the number of housing starts for

the 12 months of 2000. (*Source*: Standard & Poor's Industry Surveys) On page 751 we show our answer.

21.1 INTRODUCTION

Any variable that is measured over time in sequential order is called a **time series**. Our objective in this chapter is to analyze time series in order to detect patterns that will enable us to forecast future values of the time series. There is an almost unlimited number of such applications in management and economics. Some examples follow.

1. Governments want to know future values of interest rates, unemployment rates, and percentage increases in the cost of living.
2. Housing industry economists must forecast mortgage interest rates, demand for housing, and the cost of building materials.
3. Many companies attempt to predict the demand for their product and their share of the market.
4. Universities and colleges often try to forecast the number of students who will be applying for acceptance at post-secondary-school institutions.

Forecasting is a common practice among managers and government decision-makers. This chapter will focus on time series forecasting, which is forecasting that uses historical time series data to predict future values of variables such as sales or unemployment rates. This entire chapter is an application tool both for economists and for managers in all functional areas of business, because forecasting is such a vital factor in decision making in these areas.

For example, the starting point for aggregate production planning by operations managers is to forecast demand for the company's products. These forecasts will make use of economists' forecasts of macroeconomic variables (such as gross domestic product, disposable income, and housing starts) as well as the marketing managers' internal forecasts of their customers' future needs. Not only are these sales forecasts critical to production planning, but they are the key to accurate pro forma (i.e., forecasted) financial statements, which are produced by the accounting and financial managers to assist in their planning for future financial needs such as borrowing. Likewise, the human resources department will find such forecasts of a company's growth prospects to be invaluable in their planning for future manpower requirements.

There are many different forecasting techniques. Some are based on developing a model that attempts to analyze the relationship between a dependent variable and one or more independent variables. We presented some of these methods in the chapters on regression analysis (Chapters 18, 19, and 20). The forecasting methods to be discussed in this chapter are all based on time series, which we discuss in the next section. In Sections 21.3 and 21.4, we deal with methods for detecting and measuring which components exist. After we uncover this information, we can develop forecasting tools. We will only scratch the surface of this topic. Our objective is to expose you to the concepts of forecasting and to introduce some of the simpler techniques. The level of this text precludes the investigation of more complicated methods.

21.2 TIME SERIES COMPONENTS

A time series can consist of four different components, as described in the box.

> **TIME SERIES COMPONENTS**
> 1. Long-term trend   3. Seasonal variation
> 2. Cyclical variation   4. Random variation

A **trend** (also known as a **secular trend**) is a long-term, relatively smooth pattern or direction exhibited by a series. Its duration is more than 1 year. For example, the population of the United States exhibited a trend of relatively steady growth from 181 million in 1960 to 273 million in 1999. (See Figure 21.1.)

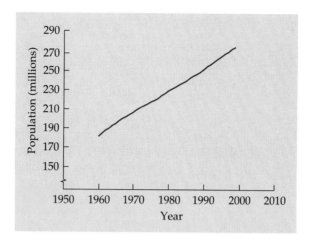

Figure 21.1
U.S. population (in millions), 1960–1999

The trend of a time series is not always linear. For example, Figure 21.2 describes U.S. beer consumption per person (over age 21) from 1970 to 1999. As you can see, per capita consumption grew between 1970 to 1980, leveled off, then decreased until 1993, when it began increasing.

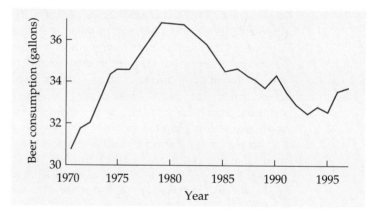

Figure 21.2
U.S. beer consumption per person over 21.
Source: **Standard and Poor's Industry Surveys.**

Cyclical variation is a wavelike pattern describing a long-term trend that is generally apparent over a number of years, resulting in a cyclical effect. By definition, it has duration of more than 1 year. Examples include business cycles that record periods of economic recession and inflation, long-term product demand cycles, and cycles in monetary and financial sectors. However, cyclical patterns that are consistent and predictable are quite rare. For practical purposes, we will ignore this type of variation.

Seasonal variation refers to cycles that occur over short repetitive calendar periods and, by definition, have a duration of less than 1 year. The term "seasonal variation" may refer to the four traditional seasons or to systematic patterns that occur during a month, a week, or even 1 day. Demand for restaurants feature "seasonal" variation throughout the day.

An illustration of seasonal variation is provided in Figure 21.3, which graphs monthly U.S. traffic volume (in billions of miles). It is obvious from the graph that Americans drive more during the summer months than during the winter months.

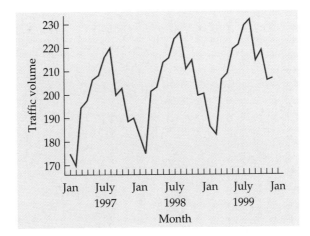

Figure 21.3
Traffic volume in billions of miles.
Source: **Standard and Poor's Industry Surveys.**

Random variation is caused by irregular and unpredictable changes in a time series that are not caused by any other components. It tends to mask the existence of the other more predictable components. Because random variation exists in almost all time series, one of the objectives of this chapter is to introduce ways to reduce the random variation, which will enable statistics practitioners to describe and measure the other components. By doing so, we hope to be able to make accurate predictions of the time series.

21.3 SMOOTHING TECHNIQUES

If we can determine which components actually exist in a time series, we can develop better forecasts. Unfortunately, the existence of random variation often makes the task of identifying components difficult. One of the simplest ways to reduce random variation is to smooth the time series. In this section we introduce two methods: *moving averages* and *exponential smoothing*.

MOVING AVERAGES

A **moving average** for a time period is the arithmetic mean of the values in that time period and those close to it. For example, to compute the three-period moving average for any time period, we would average the time series values in that time period, the previous period, and the following period. We compute the three-period moving averages for all time periods except the first and the last. To calculate the five-period moving average, we average the value in that time period, the values in the two preceding periods, and the two following time periods. We can choose any number of periods with which to calculate the moving averages.

EXAMPLE 21.1

As part of an effort to forecast futures sales, an operator of five independent gas stations recorded the quarterly gasoline sales (in thousands of gallons) for the past 4 years. These data are shown here and stored in file Xm21-01. Calculate the three-quarter and five-quarter moving averages. Draw graphs of the time series and the moving averages.

Time Period	Year	Quarter	Gasoline Sales (thousands of gallons)
1	1	1	39
2		2	37
3		3	61
4		4	58
5	2	1	18
6		2	56
7		3	82
8		4	27
9	3	1	41
10		2	69
11		3	49
12		4	66
13	4	1	54
14		2	42
15		3	90
16		4	66

SOLUTION

COMPUTE

 MANUALLY

To compute the first three-quarter moving average, we group the gasoline sales in periods 1, 2, and 3, and then average them. Thus, the first moving average is

$$\frac{39 + 37 + 61}{3} = \frac{137}{3} = 45.7$$

The second moving average is calculated by dropping the first period's sales (39), adding the fourth period's sales (58), and then computing the new average. Thus, the second moving average is

$$\frac{37 + 61 + 58}{3} = \frac{156}{3} = 52.0$$

The process continues as shown in the following table. Similar calculations are made to produce the five-quarter moving averages (also shown in the table).

Time Period	Gasoline Sales	Three-Quarter Moving Average	Five-Quarter Moving Average
1	39	—	—
2	37	45.7	—
3	61	52.0	42.6
4	58	45.7	46.0
5	18	44.0	55.0
6	56	52.0	48.2
7	82	55.0	44.8
8	27	50.0	55.0
9	41	45.7	53.6
10	69	53.0	50.4
11	49	61.3	55.8
12	66	56.3	56.0
13	54	54.0	60.2
14	42	62.0	63.6
15	90	66.0	—
16	66	—	—

Notice that we place the moving averages in the center of the group of values being averaged. It is for this reason that we prefer to use an odd number of periods in the moving averages. Later in this section, we discuss how to deal with an even number of periods.

EXCEL

COMMANDS	COMMANDS FOR EXAMPLE 21.1

1. Type or import the data into one column
2. Click **Tools, Data Analysis...**, and **Moving Average**.
3. Specify the **Input Range**. Click **Labels in First Row** if appropriate.
4. Specify the number of periods (**Interval**).
5. Specify the **Output Range**.
6. Specify **Chart Output** if you want to graph the time series. Click **OK**.

COMMANDS FOR EXAMPLE 21.1

Open file **Xm21-01.**

A1:A17

3

B2

To modify the table (and hence the graph) so that the moving averages appear in the second period of each group, complete step 7.

7. Use the left button on the mouse and click the first cell containing N/A. Click the right button and click **Delete**. Select **shift cells up** and click **OK**.

MINITAB

COMMANDS

1. Type or import the data into one column.
2. Click **Stat**, **Time Series**, and **Moving Average....**
3. Select the variable.
4. Specify the number of periods (**MA length**).
5. Click **Center the moving averages**.
6. Click **Results...**, **Plot smoothed vs. actual**, and **Summary table**. Click **OK**.
7. Click **Storage...** and **Moving Averages**. Click **OK**.

COMMANDS FOR EXAMPLE 21.1

Open file **Xm21-01.**

Sales or **C1**

3

> **INTERPRET**

To see how the moving averages remove some of the random variation, examine Figures 21.4 and 21.5. Figure 21.4 depicts the quarterly gasoline sales. Discerning any of the time series components is difficult because of the large amount of random variation. Now consider the three-quarter moving average in Figure 21.5. You should be able to detect the seasonal pattern that exhibits peaks in the third quarter of each year (periods 3, 7, 11, and 15) and valleys in the first quarter of the year (periods 5, 9, and 13). There is also a small but discernible long-term trend of increasing sales.

Figure 21.4
Quarterly gasoline sales

Notice also in Figure 21.5 that the five-quarter moving average produces more smoothing than the three-quarter moving average. In general, the longer the time period over which we average, the smoother the series becomes. Unfortunately, in this case we've smoothed too much—the seasonal pattern is no longer apparent in the five-quarter moving average. All we can see is the long-term trend. It is important to realize that our objective is to smooth the time series sufficiently to remove the random variation and to reveal the other components (trend, cycle, and/or season) present. With too little smoothing, the random variation disguises the real pattern. With too much smoothing, however, some or all of the other effects may be eliminated along with the random variation.

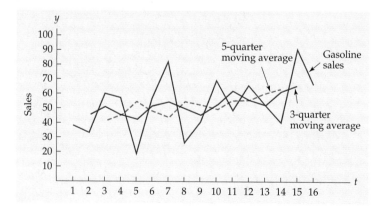

Figure 21.5
Quarterly gasoline sales and the three-quarter and five-quarter moving averages

CENTERED MOVING AVERAGES

Using an even number of periods to calculate the moving averages presents a problem about where to place the moving averages in a graph or table. For example, suppose that we calculate the four-period moving average of the following time series.

Period	Time Series
1	15
2	27
3	20
4	14
5	25
6	11

The first moving average is

$$\frac{15 + 27 + 20 + 14}{4} = 19.0$$

However, because this value represents time periods 1, 2, 3, and 4, we must place it between periods 2 and 3. The next moving average is

$$\frac{27 + 20 + 14 + 25}{4} = 21.5$$

and it must be placed between periods 3 and 4. The moving average that falls between periods 4 and 5 is

$$\frac{20 + 14 + 25 + 11}{4} = 17.5$$

There are several problems that result from placing the moving averages between time periods, including graphing difficulties. Centering the moving average corrects the problem. We do this by computing the two-period moving average of the four-period moving average. Thus, the centered moving average for period 3 is

$$\frac{19.0 + 21.5}{2} = 20.25$$

The centered moving average for period 4 is

$$\frac{21.5 + 17.5}{2} = 19.50$$

The following table summarizes these results.

Period	Time Series	Four-Period Moving Average	Four-Period Centered Moving Average
1	15		—
2	27	—	—
		19.0	
3	20		20.25
		21.5	
4	14		19.50
		17.5	
5	25		—
		—	
6	11		—

Minitab centers the moving averages on command. Excel does not center the moving averages.

EXPONENTIAL SMOOTHING

Two drawbacks are associated with the moving average method of smoothing time series. First, we do not have moving averages for the first and last sets of time periods. If the time series has few observations, the missing values can represent an important loss of information. Second, the moving average "forgets" most of the previous time series values. For example, in the five-quarter moving average described in Example 21.1, the average for quarter 4 reflects quarters 2, 3, 4, 5, and 6 but is not affected by quarter 1. Similarly, the moving average for quarter 5 forgets quarter 1 and 2. Both of these problems are addressed by **exponential smoothing**.

EXPONENTIALLY SMOOTHED TIME SERIES

$$S_t = wy_t + (1 - w)S_{t-1} \qquad \text{for } t \geq 2$$

where

S_t = Exponentially smoothed time series at time period t
y_t = Time series at time period t
S_{t-1} = Exponentially smoothed time series at time period $t-1$
w = Smoothing constant, where $0 \leq w \leq 1$

We begin by setting

$$S_1 = y_1$$

Then

$$
\begin{aligned}
S_2 &= wy_2 + (1 - w)S_1 \\
&= wy_2 + (1 - w)y_1 \\
S_3 &= wy_3 + (1 - w)S_2 \\
&= wy_3 + (1 - w)[wy_2 + (1 - w)y_1] \\
&= wy_3 + w(1 - w)y_2 + (1 - w)^2 y_1
\end{aligned}
$$

and so on. In general, we have

$$S_t = wy_t + w(1 - w)y_{t-1} + w(1 - w)^2 y_{t-2} + \cdots + (1 - w)^{t-1} y_1$$

This formula states that the smoothed time series in period t depends on all the previous observations of the time series.

The smoothing constant w is chosen on the basis of how much smoothing is required. A small value of w produces a great deal of smoothing. A large value of w results in very little smoothing. Figure 21.6 depicts a time series and two exponentially smoothed series with $w = .1$ and $w = .5$.

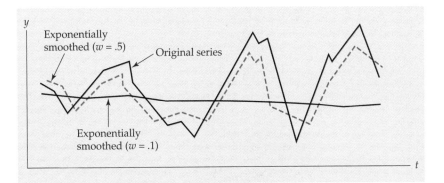

Figure 21.6
Original time series
and two exponentially
smoothed series

EXAMPLE 21.2

Apply the exponential smoothing technique with $w = .2$ and $w = .7$ to the data in Example 21.1, and graph the results.

SOLUTION

COMPUTE

 MANUALLY

The exponentially smoothed values are calculated from the formula

$$S_t = wy_t + (1 - w)S_{t-1}$$

The results with $w = .2$ and $w = .7$ are shown in the following table.

Time Period	Gasoline Sales	Exponentially Smoothed with $w = .2$	Exponentially Smoothed with $w = .7$
1	39	39.0	39.0
2	37	38.6	37.6
3	61	43.1	54.0
4	58	46.1	56.8
5	18	40.5	29.6
6	56	43.6	48.1
7	82	51.2	71.8
8	27	46.4	40.4
9	41	45.3	40.8
10	69	50.1	60.6
11	49	49.8	52.5
12	66	53.1	61.9
13	54	53.3	56.4
14	42	51.0	46.3
15	90	58.8	76.9
16	66	60.2	69.3

EXCEL

COMMANDS

1. Type or import the data into one column.
2. Click **Tools, Data Analysis...**, and **Exponential Smoothing**.
3. Specify the **Input Range**. Click **Labels** if appropriate.
4. Specify the **Damping factor**, which is $1 - w$.
5. Specify the **Output Range**.
6. Specify **Chart Output** if you want to graph the time series. Click **OK**.

To modify the table so that the smoothed values appear the way we calculated manually, complete step 7.

7. Click the cell containing the last smoothed value displayed here (58.8) and drag it to the cell below to reveal the final smoothed value (here 60.2).

COMMANDS FOR EXAMPLE 21.2

Open file **Xm21-01**.

A1:A17
.8
B2

MINITAB

COMMANDS

1. Type or import the data into one column.
2. Click **Stat**, **Time Series**, and **Single Exp Smoothing...**.
3. Select the variable.
4. Specify **Weight to use in Smoothing**, **Use**, and type the value of w.
5. Click **Options...**, **Plot smoothed vs. actual**, and **Summary table**.
6. **Set initial smoothed value** at **1**. Click **OK**.
7. Click **Storage...** and **Smoothed data**. Click **OK**.

COMMANDS FOR EXAMPLE 21.2

Open file **Xm21-01**.

Sales or **C1**

.2

INTERPRET

Figure 21.7 depicts the graph of the original time series and the exponentially smoothed series. As you can see, $w = .7$ results in very little smoothing, whereas $w = .2$ results in perhaps too much smoothing. In both smoothed time series, it is difficult to discern the seasonal pattern that we detected by using moving averages. A different value of w (perhaps $w = .5$) would be likely to produce more satisfactory results.

Figure 21.7
Quarterly gasoline sales and exponentially smoothed sales with $w = .2$ and $w = .7$

Moving averages and exponential smoothing are relatively crude methods of removing the random variation in order to discover the existence of other components. In the next section, we attempt to measure these components more precisely.

EXERCISES

21.1 For the following time series, compute the three-period moving averages.

Period	Time Series	Period	Time Series
1	48	7	43
2	41	8	52
3	37	9	60
4	32	10	48
5	36	11	41
6	31	12	30

21.2 Compute the five-period moving averages for the time series in Exercise 21.1.

21.3 For Exercises 21.1 and 21.2, graph the time series and the two moving averages.

21.4 For the following time series, compute the three-period moving averages.

Period	Time Series	Period	Time Series
1	16	7	24
2	22	8	29
3	19	9	21
4	24	10	23
5	30	11	19
6	26	12	15

21.5 For Exercise 21.4, compute the five-period moving averages.

21.6 For Exercises 21.4 and 21.5, graph the time series and the two moving averages.

21.7 Apply exponential smoothing with $w = .1$ to help detect the components of the following time series.

Period	1	2	3	4	5	6	7	8	9	10
Time series	12	18	16	24	17	16	25	21	23	14

21.8 Repeat Exercise 21.7 with $w = .8$.

21.9 For Exercises 21.7 and 21.8, draw the time series and the two sets of exponentially smoothed values. Does there appear to be a trend component in the times series?

21.10 Apply exponential smoothing with $w = .1$ to help detect the components of the following time series.

Period	1	2	3	4	5	6	7	8	9	10
Time series	38	43	42	45	46	48	50	49	46	45

21.11 Repeat Exercise 21.10 with $w = .8$.

21.12 For Exercises 21.10 and 21.11, draw the time series and the two sets of exponentially smoothed values. Does there appear to be a trend component in the times series?

21.13 The following daily sales figures (in $thousands) have been recorded in a medium-size merchandising firm. (They are also stored in file Xr21-13.)

Day	Week 1	2	3	4
Monday	43	51	40	64
Tuesday	45	41	57	58
Wednesday	22	37	30	33
Thursday	25	22	33	38
Friday	31	25	37	25

a Compute the three-day moving averages.
b Plot the series and the moving averages on a graph.
c Does there appear to be a seasonal (weekly) pattern?

21.14 For Exercise 21.13, compute the five-day moving averages, and superimpose these on the same graph. Does this help you answer part **c** of Exercise 21.13?

21.15 The quarterly sales (in $millions) of a department store chain were recorded for the years 1997–2000.

They are listed below and stored in file Xr21-15.

Quarter	Year 1997	1998	1999	2000
1	18	33	25	41
2	22	20	36	33
3	27	38	44	52
4	31	26	29	45

a Calculate the four-quarter centered moving averages.
b Graph the time series and the moving averages.
c What can you conclude from your time-series smoothing?

21.16 Repeat Exercise 21.15, using exponential smoothing with $w = .4$.

21.17 Repeat Exercise 21.15, using exponential smoothing with $w = .8$.

21.4 TREND AND SEASONAL EFFECTS

In the previous section we described how smoothing a time series can give us a clearer picture of which components are present. In order to forecast, however, we often need more precise measurements of the time series components.

TREND ANALYSIS

A trend can be linear or nonlinear and, indeed, can take on a whole host of functional forms. The easiest way of measuring the long-term trend is by regression analysis, where the independent variable is time. If we believe that the long-term trend is approximately linear, we will use the linear model introduced in Chapter 18:

$$y = \beta_0 + \beta_1 t + \varepsilon$$

If we believe that the trend is nonlinear, we can use one of the polynomial models described in Chapter 20. For example, the quadratic model is

$$y = \beta_0 + \beta_1 t + \beta_2 t^2 + \varepsilon$$

In most realistic applications, the linear model is applied. We will demonstrate how the long-term trend is measured and applied later in this section.

SEASONAL ANALYSIS

Seasonal variation may occur within a year or within shorter intervals, such as a month, week, or day. To measure the seasonal effect, we compute seasonal indexes, which gauge the degree to which the seasons differ from one another. One requirement necessary to calculate seasonal indexes is a time series sufficiently long to allow us to observe the variable over several seasons. For example, if the seasons are defined as the quarters of a year, we need to observe the time series for at least 4 years. The seasonal indexes are computed in the following way.

Procedure for Computing Seasonal Indexes

1. Remove the effect of seasonal and random variation by regression analysis. That is, compute the sample regression line

$$\hat{y}_t = b_0 + b_1 t$$

2. For each time period, compute the ratio

$$\frac{y_t}{\hat{y}_t}$$

This ratio removes most of the trend variation.

3. For each type of season, compute the average of the ratios in step 2. This procedure removes most (but seldom all) of the random variation, leaving a measure of seasonality.

4. Adjust the averages in step 3 so that the average of the the seasons is 1 (if necessary).

EXAMPLE 21.3

The tourist industry is subject to seasonal variation. In most resorts, the spring and summer seasons are considered the "high" seasons. Fall and winter (except for Christmas and New Year) are "low" seasons. A hotel in Bermuda has recorded the occupancy rate for each quarter for the past 5 years. These data are shown below and stored in file Xm21-03. Measure the seasonal variation by computing the seasonal indexes.

Year	Quarter	Occupancy Rate
1996	1	.561
	2	.702
	3	.800
	4	.568
1997	1	.575
	2	.738
	3	.868
	4	.605
1998	1	.594
	2	.738
	3	.729
	4	.600
1999	1	.622
	2	.708
	3	.806
	4	.632
2000	1	.665
	2	.835
	3	.873
	4	.670

SOLUTION

COMPUTE

 MANUALLY

We performed a regression analysis with y = occupancy rate and t = time period 1, 2, ..., 20. The regression equation is

$$\hat{y} = .639368 + .005246t$$

For each time period, we computed the ratio

$$\frac{y_t}{\hat{y}_t}$$

In the next step, we collected the ratios associated with each quarter and computed the average. We then computed the seasonal indexes by adjusting the average ratios so that they summed to 4.0, if necessary. In this example, it was not necessary.

Year	Quarter	t	y_t	$\hat{y} = .639368 + .005246t$	Ratio $\frac{y_t}{\hat{y}_t}$
1996	1	1	.561	.645	.870
	2	2	.702	.650	1.080
	3	3	.800	.655	1.221
	4	4	.568	.660	.860
1997	1	5	.575	.666	.864
	2	6	.738	.671	1.100
	3	7	.868	.676	1.284
	4	8	.605	.681	.888
1998	1	9	.594	.687	.865
	2	10	.738	.692	1.067
	3	11	.729	.697	1.046
	4	12	.600	.702	.854
1999	1	13	.622	.708	.879
	2	14	.708	.713	.993
	3	15	.806	.718	1.122
	4	16	.632	.723	.874
2000	1	17	.665	.729	.913
	2	18	.835	.734	1.138
	3	19	.873	.739	1.181
	4	20	.670	.744	.900

		Quarter		
Year	1	2	3	4
1996	.870	1.080	1.221	.860
1997	.864	1.100	1.284	.888
1998	.865	1.067	1.046	.854
1999	.879	.993	1.122	.874
2000	.913	1.138	1.181	.900
Average	.878	1.076	1.171	.875
Index	.878	1.076	1.171	.875

 EXCEL

	A	B
1	**Seasonal Indexes**	
2		
3	**Season**	**Index**
4	1	0.878
5	2	1.076
6	3	1.171
7	4	0.875

COMMANDS

1. Type or import the time series (in chronological order) into one column and the codes representing the seasons into an adjacent column.

2. Click **Tools**, **Data Analysis Plus**, and **Seasonal Indexes**.
3. Specify the **Input Range**.
4. Click **Labels**, if appropriate, and click **OK**.

COMMANDS FOR EXAMPLE 21.3

Open file **Xm21-03**. Copy the contents of column B into column D.

C1:D21

MINITAB

Time Series Decomposition

```
Data          Rate
Length        20.0000
NMissing      0

Trend Line Equation

Yt = 0.639368 + 5.25E-03*t


Seasonal Indices

Period     Index

    1      0.877012
    2      1.08008
    3      1.17723
    4      0.865681
```

COMMANDS

1. Type or import the data into one column.
2. Click **Stat**, **Time Series**, and **Decomposition....**
3. Select the variable.
4. Specify the **Seasonal length**.
5. Click **Multiplicative** under **Model Type** and **Trend plus seasonality** under **Model Components**.
6. Specify the season of the first observation.
7. Click **Results...**, **Do not display plot**, and **Summary table**. Click **OK**. Click **OK**.

COMMANDS FOR EXAMPLE 21.3

Open file **Xm21-03**.

Rate or **C3**
4

1

INTERPRET

The seasonal indexes tell us that, on average, the occupancy rates in the first and fourth quarters are below the annual average, and the occupancy rates in the second and third quarters are above the annual average. Using Excel's figures (the manually calculated seasonal indexes are the same, but Minitab's indexes differ slightly), we expect the occupancy rate in the first quarter to be 12.2% (100% − 87.8%) below the annual rate. The second and third quarters' rates are expected to be 7.6% and 17.1%, respectively, above the annual rate. The fourth quarter's rate is 12.5% below the annual rate.

Figure 21.8 on page 744 depicts the time series and the regression line.

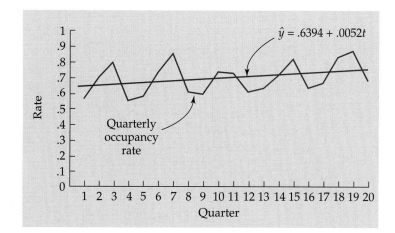

Figure 21.8
Time series and trend for
Example 21.3

DESEASONALIZING A TIME SERIES

One application of seasonal indexes is to remove the seasonal variation in a time series. The process is called **deseasonalizing**, and the result is called a **seasonally adjusted time series**. Often this allows the statistics practitioner to more easily compare the time series across seasons. For example, the unemployment rate varies according to the season. During the winter months, unemployment usually rises; it falls in the spring and summer. The seasonally adjusted unemployment rate allows economists to determine whether unemployment has increased or decreased over the previous months. The process is easy: Simply divide the time series by the seasonal indexes. To illustrate, we have deseasonalized the occupancy rates in Example 21.3 (using the seasonal indexes produced by Excel). The results are shown below.

Year	Quarter	Occupancy Rate y_t	Seasonal Index	Seasonally Adjusted Occupancy rate
1996	1	.561	.878	.639
	2	.702	1.076	.652
	3	.800	1.171	.683
	4	.568	.875	.649
1997	1	.575	.878	.655
	2	.738	1.076	.686
	3	.868	1.171	.741
	4	.605	.875	.691
1998	1	.594	.878	.677
	2	.738	1.076	.686
	3	.729	1.171	.623
	4	.600	.875	.686
1999	1	.622	.878	.708
	2	.708	1.076	.658
	3	.806	1.171	.688
	4	.632	.875	.722
2000	1	.665	.878	.757
	2	.835	1.076	.776
	3	.873	1.171	.746
	4	.670	.875	.766

By removing the seasonality, we can see when there has been a "real" increase or decrease in the occupancy rate. This enables the statistics practitioner to examine the factors that produced the rate change. We can more easily see that there has been an increase in the occupancy rate over the 5-year period.

In the next section we show how to forecast with seasonal indexes.

EXERCISES

21.18 Plot the following time series. Would the linear or quadratic model fit better?

Period	1	2	3	4	5	6	7	8
Time series	.5	.6	1.3	2.7	4.1	6.9	10.8	19.2

21.19 Plot the following time series to determine which of the trend models appears to fit better.

Period	1	2	3	4	5	6	7	8	9	10
Time series	55	57	53	49	47	39	41	33	28	20

21.20 Refer to Exercise 21.18. Use regression analysis to calculate the linear and quadratic trends. Which line fits better?

21.21 Refer to Exercise 21.19. Use regression analysis to calculate the linear and quadratic trends. Which line fits better?

21.22 For the following time series, compute the seasonal (daily) indexes. (The data are also stored in file Xr21-22.) The regression line is

$$\hat{y} = 16.8 + .366t \quad (t = 1, 2, ..., 20)$$

		Week		
Day	1	2	3	4
Monday	12	11	14	17
Tuesday	18	17	16	21
Wednesday	16	19	16	20
Thursday	25	24	28	24
Friday	31	27	25	32

21.23 Given the following time series (stored in file Xr21-23), compute the seasonal indexes. The regression equation is

$$\hat{y} = 47.7 - 1.06t \quad (t = 1, 2, ..., 20)$$

		Year			
Quarter	1	2	3	4	5
1	55	41	43	36	50
2	44	38	39	32	25
3	46	37	39	30	24
4	39	30	35	25	22

Applications

21.24 The quarterly earnings (in $millions) of a large soft-drink manufacturer have been recorded for the years

1997 to 2000. These data are listed below and stored in file Xr21-24. Compute the seasonal indexes given the regression line

$$\hat{y} = 61.75 + 1.18t \quad (t = 1, 2, ..., 16)$$

		Year		
Quarter	1997	1998	1999	2000
1	52	57	60	66
2	67	75	77	82
3	85	90	94	98
4	54	61	63	67

The following exercises require a computer and software.

21.25 College and university enrollment increased sharply during the 1970s and 1980s. However, since then the rate of growth has slowed. To help forecast future enrollments, an economist recorded the total U.S. college and university enrollment from 1990 to 1998. These data (in thousands) are listed below and stored in file Xr21-25.

Year	1990	1991	1992	1993	1994
Enrollment	13,621	14,057	14,035	13,898	15,022

Year	1995	1996	1997	1998
Enrollment	14,715	15,226	15,436	15,546

Source: Statistical Abstract of the United States, 2000, Table 301.

a Plot the time series.
b Use regression analysis to determine the trend.

21.26 Foreign trade is important to the United States. No country exports and imports more. However, there has been a large trade imbalance. To measure the extent of the problem, an economist recorded the difference between exports and imports of merchandise for the years 1980 to 1998. These data (in $ billions) are stored in file Xr21-26. (*Source: Statistical Abstract of the United States, 2000, Table 1084*)

a Plot the trade balance.
b Apply regression analysis to measure the trend.

21.27 The number of cable television subscribers has increased over the past 6 years. The marketing manager for one cable company has recorded the numbers of subscribers for the past 24 quarters. These data are stored in file Xr21-27.

a Plot the numbers.
b Compute the seasonal (quarterly) indexes.

21.28 The owner of a pizzeria wants to forecast the number of pizzas she will sell each day. She recorded the numbers sold daily for the past 4 weeks. These data are stored in file Xr21-28. Calculate the seasonal (daily) indexes.

21.29 A manufacturer of ski equipment is in the process of reviewing his accounts receivable. He noticed that there appears to be a seasonal pattern with the accounts receivable increasing in the winter months and decreasing during the summer. The quarterly accounts receivable (in $millions) are stored in file Xr21-29. Compute the seasonal (quarterly) indexes.

21.5 INTRODUCTION TO FORECASTING

Many different forecasting methods are available for the statistics practitioner. One of the factors to be considered in choosing among them is the type of component that makes up the time series. Even then, however, we have several different methods from which to choose. One way of deciding which method to apply is to select the technique that results in the greatest forecast accuracy. The most commonly used measures of forecast accuracy are **mean absolute deviation (MAD)** and the **sum of squares for forecast errors (SSE)**.

MEAN ABSOLUTE DEVIATION

$$MAD = \frac{\sum_{i=1}^{n} |y_t - F_t|}{n}$$

where

y_t = Actual value of the time series at time period t
F_t = Forecasted value of the time series at time period t
n = Number of time periods

SUM OF SQUARES FOR FORECAST ERROR

$$SSE = \sum_{i=1}^{n} (y_t - F_t)^2$$

MAD averages the absolute differences between the actual and forecast values; SSE is the sum of the squared differences. Which measure to use in judging forecast accuracy depends on the circumstances. If avoiding large errors is important, SSE should be used, because it penalizes large deviations more heavily than does MAD. Otherwise, use MAD.

It is probably best to use some of the observations of the time series to develop several competing forecasting models and then forecast for the remaining time periods. Afterward, compute MAD or SSE for the forecasts. For example, if we have 5 years of monthly observations, use the first 4 years to develop the forecasting models, and then use them to forecast the fifth year. Since we know the actual values in the fifth year, we can choose the technique that results in the most accurate forecast using either MAD or SSE.

EXAMPLE 21.4

Annual data from 1970 to 1996 were used to develop three different forecasting models. Each model was used to forecast the time series for 1997, 1998, 1999, and 2000. The forecasted and actual values for these years are shown below. Use MAD and SSE to determine which model performed best.

Year	Actual Time Series	Forecast Using Method		
		1	2	3
1997	129	136	118	130
1998	142	148	141	146
1999	156	150	158	170
2000	183	175	163	180

SOLUTION   For model 1, we have

$$\text{MAD} = \frac{|129 - 136| + |142 - 148| + |156 - 150| + |183 - 175|}{4}$$

$$= \frac{7 + 6 + 6 + 8}{4} = 6.75$$

$$\text{SSE} = (129 - 136)^2 + (142 - 148)^2 + (156 - 150)^2 + (183 - 175)^2$$

$$= 49 + 36 + 36 + 64 = 185$$

For model 2, we compute

$$\text{MAD} = \frac{|129 - 118| + |142 - 141| + |156 - 158| + |183 - 163|}{4}$$

$$= \frac{11 + 1 + 2 + 20}{4} = 8.5$$

$$\text{SSE} = (129 - 118)^2 + (142 - 141)^2 + (156 - 158)^2 + (183 - 163)^2$$

$$= 121 + 1 + 4 + 400 = 526$$

The measures of forecast accuracy for model 3 are

$$\text{MAD} = \frac{|129 - 130| + |142 - 146| + |156 - 170| + |183 - 180|}{4}$$

$$= \frac{1 + 4 + 14 + 3}{4} = 5.5$$

$$\text{SSE} = (129 - 130)^2 + (142 - 146)^2 + (156 - 170)^2 + (183 - 180)^2$$

$$= 1 + 16 + 196 + 9 = 222$$

Model 2 is inferior to both models 1 and 3, no matter how we measure forecast accuracy. Using MAD, model 3 is best, but using SSE, model 1 is most accurate. The choice between model 1 and model 3 should be made on the basis of whether we prefer a model that consistently produces moderately accurate forecasts (model 1) or one whose forecasts come quite close to most actual values but miss badly in a small number of time periods (model 3).

EXERCISES

21.30   For the actual and forecast values of a time series shown below, calculate MAD and SSE

Period	1	2	3	4	5
Forecast	173	186	192	211	223
Actual value	166	179	195	214	220

21.31   Two forecasting models were used to predict the future values of a time series. These are shown below together with the actual values. Compute MAD and SSE for each model to determine which was more accurate.

Period	1	2	3	4
Forecast (Model 1)	7.5	6.3	5.4	8.2
Forecast (Model 2)	6.3	6.7	7.1	7.5
Actual	6.0	6.6	7.3	9.4

21.32   Calculate MAD and SSE for the forecasts that follow.

Period	1	2	3	4	5
Forecast	63	72	86	71	60
Actual	57	60	70	75	70

21.33   Three forecasting techniques were used to predict the values of a time series. These values are given in the table below. Compute MAD and SSE for each technique to determine which was most accurate.

Period	1	2	3	4	5
Forecast (Model 1)	21	27	29	31	35
Forecast (Model 2)	22	24	26	28	30
Forecast (Model 3)	17	20	25	31	39
Actual	19	24	28	32	38

21.6 FORECASTING MODELS

There is a large number of different forecasting techniques available to statistics practitioners. However, many are beyond the level of this book. At the end of this chapter we provide several references for interested readers. In this section we present three models. Similar to the method of choosing the correct statistical inference technique in Chapters 12 to 20, the choice of model depends on the time series components.

FORECASTING WITH EXPONENTIAL SMOOTHING

If the time series displays a gradual or no trend and no evidence of seasonal variation, exponential smoothing can be effective as a forecasting method. Suppose that t represents the most recent time period and we've computed the exponentially smoothed value S_t. This value is then the forecasted value at time $t + 1$. That is,

$$F_{t+1} = S_t$$

If we wish, we can forecast two or three or any number of periods into the future:

$$F_{t+2} = S_t \quad \text{or} \quad F_{t+3} = S_t$$

It must be understood that the accuracy of the forecast decreases rapidly for predictions more than one time period into the future. However, as long as we're dealing with time series with no cyclical or seasonal variation, we can produce reasonably accurate predictions for the next time period.

FORECASTING WITH SEASONAL INDEXES

If the time series is composed of seasonal variation and long-term trend, we can use seasonal indexes and the regression equation to forecast.

> **FORECAST OF TREND AND SEASONALITY**
> The forecast for time period t is
>
> $$F_t = [b_0 + b_1 t] \times SI_t$$
>
> where
>
> $$F_t = \text{Forecast for period } t$$
> $$b_0 + b_1 t = \text{Regression equation}$$
> $$SI_t = \text{Seasonal index for period } t$$

EXAMPLE 21.5

Forecast hotel occupancy rates for next year in Example 21.3.

SOLUTION   In the process of computing the seasonal indexes, we computed the trend line. It is

$$\hat{y} = .639 + .00525t$$

For $t = 21, 22, 23$, and 24, we calculate the forecasted trend values.

Quarter	t	$\hat{y} = .639 + .00525t$
1	21	$.639 + .00525(21) = .749$
2	22	$.639 + .00525(22) = .755$
3	23	$.639 + .00525(23) = .760$
4	24	$.639 + .00525(24) = .765$

We now multiply the forecasted trend values by the seasonal indexes calculated in Example 21.3. The seasonalized forecasts are as follows.

Quarter	t	Trend Value $\hat{y}_t$	Seasonal Index	Forecast $F_t = \hat{y}_t \times SI_t$
1	21	.749	.878	$.749 \times .878 = .658$
2	22	.755	1.076	$.755 \times 1.076 = .812$
3	23	.760	1.171	$.760 \times 1.171 = .890$
4	24	.765	.875	$.765 \times .875 = .670$

INTERPRET

We forecast that the quarterly occupancy rates during the next year will be .658, .812, .890, and .670.

AUTOREGRESSIVE MODEL

In Chapter 19 we discussed autocorrelation, wherein the errors are not independent of one another. The existence of strong autocorrelation is an indication that the model has been misspecified, which usually means that until we improve the regression model, it will not provide an adequate fit. However, autocorrelation also provides us with an opportunity to develop another forecasting technique. If there is no obvious trend or seasonality and we believe that there is a correlation between consecutive residuals, the autoregressive model may be most effective.

> **AUTOREGRESSIVE FORECASTING MODEL**
>
> $$y_t = \beta_0 + \beta_1 y_{t-1} + \varepsilon$$

The model specifies that consecutive values of the time series are correlated. We estimate the coefficient in the usual way. The estimated regression line is defined as

$$\hat{y}_t = b_0 + b_1 y_{t-1}$$

EXAMPLE 21.6

The Consumer Price Index (CPI) is used as a general measure of inflation. It is an important measure because a high rate of inflation often influences governments to take corrective measures. The table below lists the annual percentage increases in the CPI from 1980 to 1999. The data are stored in file Xm21-06. Forecast next year's change in the CPI.

Year	Percent Increase in CPI (in percent)	Year	Percent Increase in CPI (in percent)
1980	13.5	1990	5.4
1981	10.4	1991	4.2
1982	6.1	1992	3.0
1983	3.2	1993	3.0
1984	4.3	1994	2.6
1985	3.6	1995	2.8
1986	1.9	1996	3.0
1987	3.6	1997	2.3
1988	4.1	1998	1.6
1989	4.8	1999	2.2

Source: Statistical Abstract of the United States, 2000, Table 768.

SOLUTION

 EXCEL

	A	B	C	D	E	F
1	SUMMARY OUTPUT					
2						
3	*Regression Statistics*					
4	Multiple R	0.8748				
5	R Square	0.7653				
6	Adjusted R Square	0.7515				
7	Standard Error	0.9898				
8	Observations	19				
9						
10	ANOVA					
11		*df*	*SS*	*MS*	*F*	*Significance F*
12	Regression	1	54.31	54.31	55.44	0.0000
13	Residual	17	16.66	0.98		
14	Total	18	70.97			
15						
16		*Coefficients*	*Standard Error*	*t Stat*	*P-value*	
17	Intercept	1.20	0.42	2.90	0.0100	
18	CPI (t-1)	0.59	0.08	7.45	0.0000	

 MINITAB

```
Regression Analysis: CPI(t) versus CPI (t-1)


The regression equation is
CPI(t) = 1.20 + 0.590 CPI (t-1)

Predictor        Coef      SE Coef              T        P
Constant       1.2038       0.4155           2.90    0.010
CPI (t-1       0.59025      0.07927          7.45    0.000

S = 0.9898      R-Sq = 76.5%      R-Sq(adj) = 75.2%

Analysis of Variance

Source           DF           SS          MS          F        P
Regression        1       54.314      54.314      55.44    0.000
Residual Error   17       16.655       0.980
Total            18       70.969
```

INTERPRET

The regression line is

$$\hat{y}_t = 1.20 + .59y_{t-1}$$

Because the last CPI change is 2.2%, our forecast for 2000 is

$$\hat{y}_{2000} = 1.20 + .59y_{1999}$$
$$= \hat{y}_t = 1.20 + .59(.022) = 1.21$$

The autoregressive model forecasts a 1.21% increase in the CPI for the year 2000.

HOUSING STARTS: SOLUTION

A preliminary examination of the data reveals that there is an upward trend over the 5-year period. Moreover, the number of housing starts varies by month. The presence of these components suggests that we determine the linear trend and seasonal (monthly) indexes.

EXCEL

With housing starts as the dependent variable and the month as the independent variable, Excel yielded the following regression line:

$$\hat{y} = 9.29 + .0729t \qquad t = 1, 2, ..., 60$$

The seasonal indexes were computed as follows. (See the instructions on page 743.)

	A	B
1	**Seasonal Indexes**	
2		
3	**Season**	**Index**
4	1	0.6402
5	2	0.6587
6	3	0.9634
7	4	1.0686
8	5	1.1603
9	6	1.1993
10	7	1.2018
11	8	1.1482
12	9	1.0739
13	10	1.1269
14	11	0.9788
15	12	0.7799

The regression equation was employed again to predict the number of housing starts based on the linear trend.

$$\hat{y} = 9.29 + .0729t \qquad t = 61, 62, ..., 72$$

These figures were multiplied by the seasonal indexes, which resulted in the following forecasts.

Period t	Month	$\hat{y} = 9.29 + .0729t$	Seasonal Index	Forecasts
61	January	13.74	.6402	8.79
62	February	13.81	.6587	9.10
63	March	13.88	.9634	13.36
64	April	13.96	1.0686	14.91
65	May	14.03	1.1603	16.27
66	June	14.10	1.1993	16.91
67	July	14.17	1.2018	17.03
68	August	14.25	1.1482	16.36
69	September	14.32	1.0739	15.38
70	October	14.39	1.1269	16.22
71	November	14.47	.9788	14.17
72	December	14.54	.7799	11.34

MINITAB

Minitab produces the regression equation, seasonal indexes, and forecasts in one step.

Time Series Decomposition

```
Data          Starts
Length        60.0000
NMissing      0

Trend Line Equation

Yt = 9.28887 + 7.29E-02*t


Seasonal Indices

Period      Index

  1         0.642395
  2         0.670363
  3         0.962759
  4         1.07816
  5         1.12576
  6         1.19492
```

(continued)

HOUSING STARTS: SOLUTION (CONT.)

7	1.17699
8	1.09612
9	1.10712
10	1.22168
11	0.925176
12	0.798571

Accuracy of Model

MAPE:	9.25523
MAD:	1.02025
MSD:	1.75569

Forecasts

Row	Period	Forecast
1	61	8.8229
2	62	9.2559
3	63	13.3633
4	64	15.0436
5	65	15.7899
6	66	16.8470
7	67	16.6800
8	68	15.6138
9	69	15.8511
10	70	17.5804
11	71	13.3811
12	72	11.6081

COMMANDS

Follow the instructions on page 743. Before clicking **Results...** (at step 7), click **Generate forecasts** and specify the **Number of forecasts**. If you leave **Starting from origin** blank, Minitab generates forecasts from the end of the data.

The following table displays the actual and forecasted housing starts (using Excel) for 2000. Figure 21.9 depicts the time series, trend line, and forecasts. (Minitab's Figures differ somewhat.)

Period	Month	Forecasts	Actual
61	January	8.79	9.1
62	February	9.10	9.9
63	March	13.36	12.0
64	April	14.91	12.1
65	May	16.27	14.5
66	June	16.91	14.0
67	July	17.03	14.2
68	August	16.36	13.8
69	September	15.38	13.9
70	October	16.22	16.3
71	November	14.17	12.5
72	December	11.34	12.1

The size of the error was measured by MAD and SSE. They are

$$MAD = 1.61$$
$$SSE = 42.21$$

Figure 21.9
Time series, trend, and forecasts of housing starts

EXERCISES

21.34 The following trend line and seasonal indexes were computed from 10 years of quarterly observations. Forecast the next year's time series.

$$\hat{y} = 150 + 3t \qquad t = 1, 2, ..., 40$$

Quarter	Seasonal Index
1	.7
2	1.2
3	1.5
4	.6

21.35 The following trend line and seasonal indexes were computed from 4 weeks of daily observations.

Forecast the seven values for next week.

$$\hat{y} = 120 + 2.3t \qquad t = 1, 2, ..., 28$$

Day	Seasonal Index
Sunday	1.5
Monday	.4
Tuesday	.5
Wednesday	.6
Thursday	.7
Friday	1.4
Saturday	1.9

21.36 Use the following autoregressive equation to forecast the next value of the time series if the last observed value is 65.

$$\hat{y}_t = 625 - 1.3y_{t-1}$$

21.37 The following autoregressive equation was developed. Forecast the next value if the last observed value was 11.

$$\hat{y}_t = 155 + 21y_{t-1}$$

21.38 Apply exponential smoothing with $w = .4$ to forecast the next four quarters in Exercise 21.16.

21.39 Use the seasonal indexes and trend line to forecast the time series for the next 5 days in Exercise 21.22.

21.40 Refer to Exercise 21.23. Use the seasonal indexes and the trend line to forecast the time series for the next four quarters.

Applications

21.41 Use the seasonal indexes and trend line to forecast the quarterly earnings for the years 2001 and 2002 in Exercise 21.24.

21.42 Refer to Exercise 21.25. Forecast next year's enrollment using the following methods.
  a Autoregressive forecasting model
  b Exponential smoothing method with $w = .5$

21.43 Refer to Exercise 21.26. Forecast next year's merchandise trade balance using the following methods.
  a Autoregressive forecasting model
  b Exponential smoothing method with $w = .7$

21.44 Use the seasonal indexes and trend line from Exercise 21.27 to forecast the number of cable subscribers for the next four quarters.

21.45 Refer to Exercise 21.28. Use the seasonal indexes and trend line to forecast the number of pizzas to be sold for each of the next seven days.

21.46 Apply the trend line and seasonal indexes from Exercise 21.29 to forecast accounts receivable for the next four quarters.

Exercises 21.47–21.52 are based on the following problem.
The revenues (in $millions) of a chain of ice cream stores are listed for each quarter during the previous 5 years. The data are also stored in file Xr21-47.

			Year		
Quarter	1996	1997	1998	1999	2000
1	16	14	17	18	21
2	25	27	31	29	30
3	31	32	40	45	52
4	24	23	27	24	32

21.47 Plot the time series.

21.48 Discuss why exponential smoothing is not recommended as a forecasting tool in this problem.

21.49 Use regression analysis to determine the trend line.

21.50 Determine the seasonal indexes.

21.51 Using the seasonal indexes and trend line, forecast revenues for the next four quarters.

21.7 SUMMARY

In this chapter we discussed the classical **time series** and its decomposition into **trend**, **seasonal**, and **random variation**. **Moving averages** and **exponential smoothing** were used to remove some of the random variation, making it easier to detect trend and seasonality. The long-term trend was measured by regression analysis. Seasonal variation was measured by computing the seasonal indexes. Three forecasting techniques were described in this chapter: **exponential smoothing**, **forecasting with seasonal indexes**, and the **autoregressive model**.

IMPORTANT TERMS

Time series 729
Trend 730
Cyclical variation 730
Seasonal variation 730
Random variation 731
Smoothing 731

Moving average 731
Exponential smoothing 736
Linear model 740
Quadratic model 740
Seasonal indexes 740
Deseasonalizing 744

Mean absolute deviation (MAD) 746
Sum of squares for forecast error (SSE) 746
Autoregressive model 749

SYMBOLS

Symbol	Represents
y_t	Time series
S_t	Exponentially smoothed time series
w	Smoothing constant
F_t	Forecasted time series

FORMULAS

Exponential smoothing

$$S_t = wy_t + (1 - w)S_{t-1}$$

COMPUTER OUTPUT AND INSTRUCTIONS

Technique	Excel	Minitab
Moving averages	733	733
Exponential smoothing	738	738
Seasonal indexes	742	743

REFERENCES

Abraham, B., and J. Ledolter, *Statistical Methods for Forecasting.* New York: John Wiley and Sons, 1983.

Anderson, T. W., *The Statistical Analysis of Time Series.* New York: John Wiley and Sons, 1971.

Bowerman, Bruce L., and Richard T. O'Connell, *Forecasting and Time Series: An Applied Approach,* 3rd edition. Belmont, CA: Duxbury, 1993.

Box, George E. P., Gwilym M. Jenkins, and Gregory C. Reinsel, *Time Series Analysis, Forecasting and Control,* 3rd edition. Englewood Cliffs, NJ: Prentice Hall, 1994.

Brockwell, Peter J., and Richard A. Davis, *Time Series: Theory and Methods,* 2nd edition. New York: Springer Verlag, 1996.

Granger, C. W. J., and P. Newbold, *Forecasting Economic Time Series,* 2nd edition. San Diego: Academic Press, 1986.

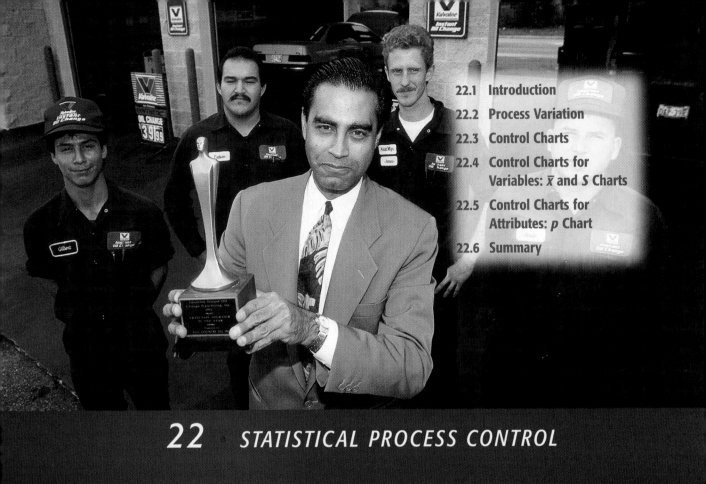

22 · STATISTICAL PROCESS CONTROL

DETECTING THE SOURCE OF DEFECTIVE DISKS

A company that produces 3.5-inch computer disks has been receiving complaints from its customers about the large number of disks that will not store data properly. Company management has decided to institute statistical process control in order to remedy the problem. Every hour, a random sample of 200 disks is taken, and each disk is tested to determine whether it is defective. The results of the first 40 hours are shown below (in chronological order) and stored in file Ch22:\Defectives. Using these data, draw a p chart to monitor the production process. Was the process out of control when the sample results were generated?

```
19,  5, 16, 20,  6, 12, 18,  6, 13, 15,
10,  6,  7, 10, 18, 20, 13,  6,  8,  3,
 8,  7,  4, 19,  3, 19,  9, 10, 10, 18,
15, 16,  5, 14,  3, 10, 19, 13, 19,  9
```

22.1 INTRODUCTION

In the introduction to operations management in Chapter 1, we pointed out that operations managers are responsible for developing and maintaining the production processes that deliver quality products and services. In Section 15.6, we demonstrated an important application of the analysis of variance that is used to investigate sources of variation and determine ways to reduce that variation. The goal is to select the methods, materials, machines, and personnel (manpower) that combine to yield the production process that features the smallest amount of variation at a reasonable cost. Once the production process is operating, it is necessary to constantly monitor it to ensure that it functions the way it was designed. The statistical methods we are about to introduce are the most common application of statistics. At any point in time there are literally thousands of firms applying these methods. This chapter deals with the subject of **statistical process control** or **SPC** (formerly called **quality control**).

There are two general approaches to the management of quality. The first approach is to produce the product and, at the completion of the production process, inspect the unit to determine whether it conforms to specifications; if it doesn't, it is either discarded or repaired. This approach, which is detection oriented, has several drawbacks. Foremost among them is that it is costly to produce substandard products regardless of whether they are later discarded or fixed. In recent years, this approach has been employed by a decreasing number of companies. Instead, many firms have adopted the **prevention approach**. Using the concepts of hypothesis testing, statistics practitioners concentrate on the production process. Rather than inspect the product, they inspect the process to determine when the process starts producing units that do not conform to specifications. This allows them to correct the production process before it creates a large number of defective products.

In the next section, we discuss the problem of process variation and why it is often the key to the management of quality. In Section 22.3, we also introduce the concept and logic of control charts and show why they work. In the rest of the chapter, we introduce three specific control charts.

22.2 PROCESS VARIATION

All production processes result in variation; that is, no product is exactly the same as another. You can see for yourself that this is true by weighing, for example, two boxes of breakfast cereal that are supposed to weigh 16 ounces each. Not only will they not weigh exactly 16 ounces, they will not even have equal weights. All products exhibit some degree of variation. There are two sources of variation. **Chance** or **common variation** is caused by a number of randomly occurring events that are part of the production process and that in general cannot be reduced without changing the process. In effect, chance variation was built into the product when the production process was first set up, perhaps as a result of a statistical analysis that attempted to minimize but not necessarily eliminate such variation. In Section 15.6 we discussed statistical techniques that allow firms to experiment to search for sources of variation and, in so doing, reduce the variation.

Assignable or **special variation** is caused by specific events or factors that are frequently temporary and that can usually be identified and eliminated. To illustrate, consider a paint company that produces and sells paint in 1-gallon cans. The cans are filled by an automatic valve that regulates the amount of paint in each can. The designers of the valve acknowledge that there will be some variation in the amount of paint even when the valve is working as it was designed to do. This is chance variation. Occasionally the valve will malfunction, causing the variation in the amounts delivered to each can to increase. This increase is the assignable variation.

Perhaps the best way to understand what is happening is to consider the volume of paint in each can as a random variable. If the only sources of variation are caused by chance, then each can's volume is drawn from identical distributions. That is, each distribution has the same shape, mean, and standard deviation. Under such circumstances the production process is said to be **under control**. In recognition of the fact that variation in output will occur even when the process is under control and operating properly, most processes are designed so that their products will fall within designated **specification limits** or "specs." For example, the process that fills the paint cans may be designed so that the cans contain between .99 and 1.01 gallons. Inevitably, some event or combination of factors in a production process will cause the process distribution to change. When it does, the process is said to be **out of control**. There are several possible ways for the process to go out of control. Here is a list of the most commonly occurring possibilities and their likely assignable causes.

1. **Level shift**   This is a change in the mean of the process distribution. Assignable causes include machine breakdown, new machine and/or operator, or a change in the environment. In the paint can illustration, a temperature or humidity change may affect the density of the paint, resulting in less paint in each can.

2. **Instability**   This is the name we apply to the process when the standard deviation increases. (As we discuss later, a decrease in the standard deviation is desirable.) This may be caused by a machine in need of repair, defective materials, wear of tools, or an incompetent operator. Suppose, for example, that a part in the valve that controls the amount of paint wears down, causing greater variation than normal.

3. **Trend**   When there is a slow steady shift (either up or down) in the process distribution mean, the result is a trend. This is frequently the result of less-than-regular maintenance, operator fatigue, residue or dirt buildup, or gradual loss of lubricant. If the paint control valve becomes increasingly clogged, we would expect to see a steady decrease in the amount of paint delivered.

4. **Cycle**   This is a repeated series of small observations followed by large observations. Likely assignable causes include environmental changes, worn parts, or operator fatigue. If there are changes in the voltage in the electricity that runs the machines in the paint can example, we might see series of overfilled cans and series of underfilled cans.

The key to quality is to detect when the process goes out of control so that we can correct the malfunction and restore control of the process. The *control chart* is the statistical method that we use to detect problems.

EXERCISES

22.1 What is meant by chance variation?

22.2 Provide two examples of production processes and their associated chance variation.

22.3 What is meant by special variation?

22.4 Your education as a statistics practitioner can be considered a production process overseen by the course instructor. The variable we measure is the grade achieved by each student.

    a Discuss chance variation. That is, describe the sources of variation that the instructor has no control over.

    b Discuss special variation.

22.3 CONTROL CHARTS

A **control chart** is a plot of statistics over time. For example, an $\bar{x}$ **chart** plots a series of sample means taken over a period of time. Each control chart contains a *centerline* and *control limits*. The control limit above the centerline is called the **upper control limit** and that below the centerline is called the **lower control limit**. If, when the sample statistics are plotted, all points are randomly distributed between the control limits, we conclude that the process is under control. If the points are not randomly distributed between the control limits, or if at least one point is outside the control limit, we conclude that the process is out of control.

To illustrate the logic of control charts, let us suppose that in the paint can example described earlier, we want to determine whether the central location of the distribution has changed from one period to another. We will draw our conclusion from an $\bar{x}$ chart. For the moment, let us assume that we know the mean μ and standard deviation σ of the process when it is under control. We can construct the $\bar{x}$ chart, as shown in Figure 22.1. The chart is drawn so that the vertical axis plots the values of $\bar{x}$ that will be calculated and the horizontal axis tracks the samples in the order in which they are drawn. The centerline is the value of μ. The control limits are set at three standard errors from the centerline. Recall that the standard error of $\bar{x}$ is $\sigma / \sqrt{n}$. Hence, we define the control limits as follows:

$$\text{Lower control limit} = \mu - 3\frac{\sigma}{\sqrt{n}}$$

$$\text{Upper control limit} = \mu + 3\frac{\sigma}{\sqrt{n}}$$

Figure 22.1
$\bar{x}$ chart: μ and σ known

After we've constructed the chart by drawing the centerline and control limits, we use it to plot the sample means, which are joined to make it easier to interpret. The principles underlying control charts are identical to the principles of hypothesis testing.

The null and alternative hypotheses are

H_0:   The process is under control.

H_1:   The process is out of control.

For an $\bar{x}$ chart, the test statistic is the sample mean $\bar{x}$. However, because we're dealing with a dynamic process rather than a fixed population, we test a series of sample means. That is, we compute the mean for each of a continuing series of samples taken over time. For each series of samples, we want to determine whether there is sufficient evidence to infer that the process mean has changed. We reject the null hypothesis if at any time the sample mean falls outside the control limits. It is logical to ask why we use 3 standard errors and not 2 or 1.96 or 1.645, as we did when we tested hypotheses about a population mean in Chapter 11. The answer lies in the way in which all tests are conducted. Because test conclusions are based on sample data, there are two possible errors. In statistical process control, a Type I error occurs if we conclude that the process is out of control when in fact it is not. The error can be quite expensive, because the production process must be stopped and the causes of the variation found and repaired. Consequently, we want the probability of a Type I error to be small. With control limits set at 3 standard errors from the mean, the probability of a Type I error for each sample is

$$\alpha = P(|z| > 3) = .0026$$

Recall that a small value of α results in a relatively large value of the probability of a Type II error. A Type II error occurs when at any sample we do not reject a false null hypothesis. This means that, for each sample, we are less likely to recognize when the process goes out of control. However, because we will be performing a series of tests (one for each sample), we will eventually discover that the process is out of control and take steps to rectify the problem.

Suppose that in order to test the production process that fills 1-gallon paint cans, we choose to take a sample of size 4 every hour. Let us also assume that we know the mean and standard deviation of the process distribution of the amount of paint when the process is under control, say, $\mu = 1.001$ and $\sigma = .006$. (This means that when the valve is working the way it was designed, the amount of paint put into each can is a random variable whose mean is 1.001 gallons and whose standard deviation is .006 gallon.) Thus,

Centerline $= \mu = 1.001$

Lower control limit $= \mu - 3\dfrac{\sigma}{\sqrt{n}} = 1.001 - 3\dfrac{.006}{\sqrt{4}} = 1.001 - .009 = .992$

Upper control limit $= \mu + 3\dfrac{\sigma}{\sqrt{n}} = 1.001 + 3\dfrac{.006}{\sqrt{4}} = 1.001 + .009 = 1.010$

Figure 22.2 on page 760 depicts a situation in which the first 15 samples were taken when the process was under control. However, after the 15th sample was drawn, the process went out of control and produced sample means outside the control limits. We conclude that the process distribution has changed, because the data display variability beyond that predicted for a process with the specified mean and standard deviation. This means that the variation is assignable, and that the cause needs to be identified and corrected.

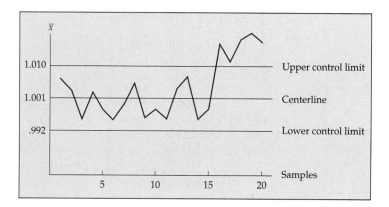

Figure 22.2
$\bar{x}$ chart: Process out of control

As we stated above, SPC is a slightly different form of hypothesis testing. The concept is the same but there are differences that you should be aware of. The most important difference is that when we tested means and proportions in Chapters 11 and 12, we were dealing with fixed but unknown parameters of populations. For instance, in Example 11.1 the population we dealt with was the account balances of the department store customers. The population mean balance was a constant value that we simply did not know. The purpose of the test was to determine whether there was enough statistical evidence to allow us to infer that the mean balance was greater than $170. So we took one sample and based the decision on the sample mean. When dealing with a production process, it's important to realize that the process distribution itself is variable. That is, at any time, the process distribution of the amount of paint fill may change if the valve malfunctions. Consequently, we do not simply take one sample and make the decision. Instead, we plot a number of statistics over time in the control chart. Simply put, in Chapters 11 through 20, we assumed static population distributions with fixed but unknown parameters, whereas in this chapter we assume a dynamic process distribution with parameters subject to possible shifts.

SAMPLE SIZE AND SAMPLING FREQUENCY

In designing a control chart, the statistics practitioner must select a sample size and a sampling frequency. These decisions are based on several factors, including the costs of making Type I and Type II errors, the length of the production run, and the typical change in the process distribution when the process goes out of control. A useful aid in making the decision is the **operating characteristic (OC) curve.**

Operating Characteristic Curve

Recall that in Chapter 11 we drew the operating characteristic curve that plotted the probabilities of Type II errors and population means. Here is how the OC curve for the $\bar{x}$ chart is drawn.

Suppose that when the production process is under control, the mean and standard deviation of the process variable are μ_0 and σ, respectively. For specific values of α and n, we can compute the probability of a Type II error when the process mean changes to $\mu_1 = \mu_0 + k\sigma$. A Type II error occurs when a sample mean falls between the control limits when the process is out of control. In other words, the probability of a Type II error is the probability that the $\bar{x}$ chart will be unable to detect a shift of $k\sigma$ in the process mean on the first sample after the shift has occurred. Figure 22.3 depicts the OC curve for $n = 2, 3, 4,$ and 5. Figure 22.4 is the OC curve for $n = 10, 15, 20,$ and 25. (We drew two curves because one alone would not provide the precision we need.) We can use the OC curves to help determine the sample size we should use.

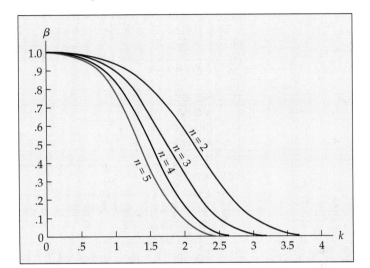

Figure 22.3
Operating characteristic curve for *n* = 2, 3, 4, and 5

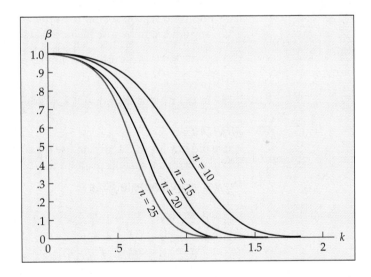

Figure 22.4
Operating characteristic curve for *n* = 10, 15, 20, and 25

Figure 22.3 tells us that for small shifts of 1 standard deviation or less, samples of size 2 to 5 produce probabilities of not detecting the shift that range between .8 and .95 (approximately). To appreciate the effect of large probabilities of Type II errors, consider the paint can illustration. Suppose that when the process goes out of control, it shifts the mean by about one standard deviation. The probability that the first sample after the shift will not detect this shift is approximately .85. The probability that it will not detect the shift for the first m samples after the shift is $.85^m$. Thus for $m = 5$, the probability of not detecting the shift for the first five samples after the shift is .44. If the process fills 1,000 cans per hour, a large proportion of the 5,000 cans filled will be overfilled or underfilled (depending on the direction of the shift). Figure 22.4 suggests that when the shift moves the process mean by 1 standard deviation, samples of size 15 or 20 are recommended. For $n = 15$, the probability that a shift of 1 standard deviation will not be detected by the first sample is approximately .2.

If the typical shift is 2 or more standard deviations, samples of size 4 or 5 will likely suffice. For $n = 5$, the probability of a Type II error is about .07.

USING THE COMPUTER

EXCEL

As we did in Chapter 11, we can use the computer to determine the probability of a Type II error. Here is the printout for $k = 1.5$ and $n = 4$.

	A	B	C	D
1	**Type II Error**			
2				
3	**H0: MU**	0	**Critical values**	-1.51
4	**SIGMA**	1		1.51
5	**Sample size**	4	**Prob(Type II error)**	0.5046
6	**ALPHA**	0.0026	**Power of the test**	0.4954
7	**H1: MU**	1.5		

COMMANDS

1. Open the **Beta-mean** workbook in the **Excel Workbooks** folder. Click the tab to use the **Two-tail Test** worksheet.
2. Type **0** in cell B3.
3. Type **1** in cell B4.
4. Specify the sample size in cell B5.
5. Type **.0026** in cell B6 to set the control limits 3 standard errors from the mean. To set control limits 2 standard errors from the mean, type **.0456**. For any other number use the normal table or type

$$=2^*(1 - \text{normsdist}([\text{Number of standard errors}]))$$

   in cell B6.
6. In cell B7 type the value of k, which describes a shift of $k\sigma$.

MINITAB

As we did in Chapter 11, we can use the computer to determine the probability of a Type II error. Here is the printout for $k = 1.5$ and $n = 4$.

Power and Sample Size

```
1-Sample Z Test

Testing mean = null (versus not = null)
Calculating power for mean = null + difference
Alpha = 0.0026  Sigma = 1

            Sample
Difference    Size    Power
       1.5      4   0.4954
```

COMMANDS

1. Click **Stat, Power and Sample Size,** and **1-Sample Z....**
2. Type the **Sample sizes** (you can specify more than one).
3. Type the **Differences** (you can type more than one), which specifies a shift of $k\sigma$.
4. Specify the standard deviation (**Sigma**) equal to 1.
5. Click **Options,** click **Not equal,** and type the **Significance level: .0026** to set control limits 3 standard errors from the mean or **.0456** to set the control limits 2 standard errors from the mean. To specify any other number use the normal table.
6. Click **OK**. Click **OK**.

Minitab prints the power of the test. Recall that the power of the test is $1 - \beta$.

Average Run Length

The **average run length (ARL)** is the expected number of samples that must be taken before the chart indicates that the process has gone out of control. The ARL is determined by

$$\text{ARL} = \frac{1}{P}$$

where P is the probability that a sample mean falls outside the control limits. Assuming that the control limits are defined as 3 standard errors above and below the centerline, the probability that a sample mean falls outside the control imits when the process is under control is

$$P = P(|z| > .3) = .0026$$

Thus

$$\text{ARL} = \frac{1}{.0026} = 385$$

This means that when the process is under control, the $\bar{x}$ chart will erroneously conclude that it is out of control once every 385 samples on average. If the sampling plan calls for samples to be taken every hour, on average there will be a *false alarm* once every 385 hours.

We can use the OC curve to determine the average run length until the $\bar{x}$ chart detects a process that is out of control. Suppose that when the process goes out of control, it typically shifts the process mean 1.5 standard deviations to the right or left. From Figure 22.3, we can see that for $n = 4$ and $k = 1.5$, the probability of a Type II error is approximately .5. That is, the probability that a mean falls between the control limits, which indicates that the process is under control when there has been a shift of 1.5 standard deviations, is .5. The probability that the sample mean falls outside the control limits is $P = 1 - .5 = .5$. Thus the average run length is

$$\text{ARL} = \frac{1}{.5} = 2$$

This means that the control chart will require two samples on average to detect a shift of 1.5 standard deviations. Suppose that a shift of this magnitude results in an unacceptably high number of nonconforming cans. We can reduce that number in two ways: by sampling more frequently or increasing the sample size. For example, if we take samples of size 4 every half hour then on average it will take 1 hour to detect the shift and make repairs. If we take samples of size 10 every hour, Figure 22.4 indicates that the probability of a Type II error when the shift is 1.5 standard deviations is about .05. Thus $P = 1 - .05 = .95$ and

$$\text{ARL} = \frac{1}{.95} = 1.05$$

This tells us that a sample size of 10 will allow the statistics practitioner to detect a shift of 1.5 standard deviations about twice as quickly as a sample of size 4.

Changing the Control Limits

Another way to decrease the probability of a Type II error is to increase the probability of a Type I error. Thus, we may define the control limits so that they are 2 standard errors above and below the centerline. In order to judge whether this is advisable, it is necessary to draw the operating characteristic curve for this plan.

In our demonstration of the logic of control charts, we resorted to traditional methods of presenting inferential methods; we assumed that the process parameters were known. When the parameters are unknown, we estimate their values from the sample data. In the next two sections, we discuss how to construct and use control charts in more realistic situations. In Section 22.4, we present control charts when the data are interval. In the context of statistical process control, we call these **control charts for variables**. Section 22.5 demonstrates the use of control charts that record whether a unit is defective or nondefective. These are called **control charts for attributes**.

EXERCISES

22.5 If the control limits of an $\bar{x}$ chart are set at 2.5 standard errors from the centerline, what is the probability that on any sample the control chart will indicate that the process is out of control when it is under control?

22.6 Refer to Exercise 22.5 What is the average run length until the $\bar{x}$ chart signals that the process is out of control when it is under control?

22.7 The control limits of an $\bar{x}$ chart are set at 2 standard errors from the centerline. Calculate the probability that on any sample the control chart will indicate that the process is out of control when it is under control.

22.8 Refer to Exercise 22.7. Determine the ARL until the $\bar{x}$ chart signals that the process is out of control when it is under control.

Exercises 22.9–22.15 are based on the following scenario.

A production facility produces 100 units per hour and uses an $\bar{x}$ chart to monitor its quality. The control limits are set at 3 standard errors from the mean. When the process goes out of control, it usually shifts the mean by 1.5 standard deviations. Sampling is conducted once per hour with a sample size of 3.

22.9 On average, how many units will be produced until the control chart signals that the process is out of control when it is under control?

22.10 Refer to Exercise 22.9.
a Find the probability that the $\bar{x}$ chart does not detect a shift of 1.5 standard deviations on the first sample after the shift occurs.
b Compute the probability that the $\bar{x}$ chart will not detect the shift for the first 8 samples after the shift.

22.11 Refer to Exercise 22.10. Find the average run length to detect the shift.

22.12 The operations manager is unsatisfied with the current sampling plan. He changes it to samples of size 2 every half hour. What is the average number of units produced until the chart indicates that the process is out of control when it is not?

22.13 Refer to Exercise 22.12.
a Find the probability that the $\bar{x}$ chart does not detect a shift of 1.5 standard deviations on the first sample after the shift occurs.
b Compute the probability that the $\bar{x}$ chart will not detect the shift for the first 8 samples after the shift.

22.14 Refer to Exercise 22.13. What is the average run length to detect the shift?

22.15 Write a brief report comparing the sampling plans described in Exercises 22.9 and 22.12. Discuss the relative costs of the two plans and the frequency of Type I and Type II errors.

Exercises 22.16–22.22 are based on the following scenario.

A firm that manufactures notebook computers uses statistical process control to monitor all of its production processes. For one component, the company draws samples of size 10 every 30 minutes. The company makes 4,000 of these components per hour. The control limits of the $\bar{x}$ chart are set at 3 standard errors from the mean. When the process goes out of control it usually shifts the mean by .75 standard deviation.

22.16 On average, how many units will be produced until the control chart signals that the process is out of control when it is under control?

22.17 Refer to Exercise 22.16
a Find the probability that the $\bar{x}$ chart does not detect a shift of .75 standard deviation on the first sample after the shift occurs.
b Compute the probability that the $\bar{x}$ chart will not detect the shift for the first 4 samples after the shift.

22.18 Refer to Exercise 22.17. Find the average run length to detect the shift.

22.19 The company is considering changing the sampling plan so that 20 components are sampled every hour.

What is the average number of units produced until the chart indicates that the process is out of control when it is not?

22.20 Refer to Exercise 22.19

  a Find the probability that the $\bar{x}$ chart does not detect a shift of .75 standard deviation on the first sample after the shift occurs.

  b Compute the probability that the $\bar{x}$ chart will not detect the shift for the first 4 samples after the shift.

22.21 Refer to Exercise 22.20. What is the average run length to detect the shift?

22.22 Write a brief report comparing the sampling plans described in Exercises 22.16 and 22.19. Discuss the relative costs of the two plans and the frequency of Type I and Type II errors.

22.4 CONTROL CHARTS FOR VARIABLES: $\bar{x}$ AND S CHARTS

There are several ways to judge whether a change in the process distribution has occurred when the data are interval. To determine whether the distribution means have changed, we employ the $\bar{x}$ chart. To determine whether the process distribution standard deviation has changed, we use the S (which stands for standard deviation) chart or the R (which stands for range) chart.

Throughout this textbook we have used the sample standard deviation to estimate the population standard deviation. However, for a variety of reasons, SPC frequently employs the range instead of the standard deviation. This is primarily because computing the range is simpler than computing the standard deviation. Because many practitioners conducting SPC perform calculations by hand (with the assistance of a calculator), they select the computationally simple range as the method to estimate the process standard deviation. In this section, we will introduce control charts that feature the sample standard deviation. In CD Appendix 22.1 we employ the sample range to construct our charts.

$\bar{x}$ CHART

In Section 22.3 we determined the centerline and control limits of a $\bar{x}$ chart using the mean and standard deviation of the process distribution. However, it is unrealistic to believe that the mean and standard deviation of the process distribution are known. Thus, in order to construct the $\bar{x}$ chart, we need to estimate the relevant parameters from the data.

We begin by drawing samples when the process is under control. The sample size must lie between 2 and 25. We discuss later how to determine that the process is under control. For each sample, we compute the mean and the standard deviation. The estimator of the mean of the distribution is the mean of the sample means (denoted $\bar{\bar{x}}$):

$$\bar{\bar{x}} = \frac{\sum_{j=1}^{k} \bar{x}_j}{k}$$

where $\bar{x}_j$ is the mean of the jth sample and there are k samples.

To estimate the standard deviation of the process distribution, we calculate the sample variance s_j^2 for each sample. We then compute the pooled standard deviation,[*] which we denote S and define as

$$S = \sqrt{\frac{\sum_{j=1}^{k} s_j^2}{k}}$$

[*]This formula requires that the sample size be the same for all samples, a condition that is imposed throughout this chapter.

In the previous section, where we assumed that the process distribution mean and variance were known, the centerline and control limits were defined as

$$\text{Centerline} = \mu$$

$$\text{Lower control limit} = \mu - 3\frac{\sigma}{\sqrt{n}}$$

$$\text{Upper control limit} = \mu + 3\frac{\sigma}{\sqrt{n}}$$

Since the values of μ and σ are unknown, we must use the sample data to estimate them. The estimator of μ is $\bar{\bar{x}}$ and the estimator of σ is S. Therefore the centerline and control limits are as shown in the box.

CENTERLINE AND CONTROL LIMITS FOR $\bar{x}$ CHART

$$\text{Centerline} = \bar{\bar{x}}$$

$$\text{Lower control limit} = \bar{\bar{x}} - 3\frac{S}{\sqrt{n}}$$

$$\text{Upper control limit} = \bar{\bar{x}} + 3\frac{S}{\sqrt{n}}$$

EXAMPLE 22.1*

Lear Seating of Kitchener, Ontario, manufactures seats for Chrysler, Ford, and General Motors cars. Several years ago, Lear instituted statistical process control, which has resulted in improved quality and lower costs. One of the components of a front-seat cushion is a wire spring, produced from 4-mm (millimeter) steel wire. A machine is employed to bend the wire so that the spring's length is 500 mm. If the springs are longer than 500 mm, they will loosen and eventually fall out. If they are too short, they won't easily fit into position. (In fact, in the past, when there were a relatively large number of short springs, workers incurred arm and hand injuries when attempting to install the springs.) To determine whether the process is under control, random samples of four springs are taken every hour. The last 25 samples are shown in Table 22.1 (and stored in file Xm22-01). Construct an $\bar{x}$ chart from these data.

Table 22.1 25 Samples of Springs for Example 22.1

Sample				
1	501.02	501.65	504.34	501.10
2	499.80	498.89	499.47	497.90
3	497.12	498.35	500.34	499.33
4	500.68	501.39	499.74	500.41
5	495.87	500.92	498.00	499.44
6	497.89	499.22	502.10	500.03
7	497.24	501.04	498.74	503.51
8	501.22	504.53	499.06	505.37
9	499.15	501.11	497.96	502.39	*(continued)*

---

*The authors are grateful to Pat Bourke, Barry Cress, Kevin Lewis, and Brian Riehl of Lear Seating Ltd. for their assistance in writing this example and several exercises.

Table 22.1 25 Samples of Springs for Example 22.1 *(continued)*

Sample				
10	498.90	505.99	500.05	499.33
11	497.38	497.80	497.57	500.72
12	499.70	500.99	501.35	496.48
13	501.44	500.46	502.07	500.50
14	498.26	495.54	495.21	501.27
15	497.57	497.00	500.32	501.22
16	500.95	502.07	500.60	500.44
17	499.70	500.56	501.18	502.36
18	501.57	502.09	501.18	504.98
19	504.20	500.92	500.02	501.71
20	498.61	499.63	498.68	501.84
21	499.05	501.82	500.67	497.36
22	497.85	494.08	501.79	501.95
23	501.08	503.12	503.06	503.56
24	500.75	501.18	501.09	502.88
25	502.03	501.44	498.76	499.39

SOLUTION

COMPUTE

 MANUALLY

The means and standard deviations for each sample were computed and listed in Table 22.2 on page 768. We then calculated the mean of the means and the pooled standard deviation:

$$\bar{\bar{x}} = 500.296$$

$$S = 1.971$$

Thus, the centerline and control limits are

$$\text{Centerline} = \bar{\bar{x}} = 500.296$$

$$\text{Lower control limit} = \bar{\bar{x}} - 3\frac{S}{\sqrt{n}} = 500.296 - 3\frac{1.971}{\sqrt{4}} = 497.340$$

$$\text{Upper control limit} = \bar{\bar{x}} + 3\frac{S}{\sqrt{n}} = 500.296 + 3\frac{1.971}{\sqrt{4}} = 503.253$$

The centerline and control limits are drawn and the sample means plotted in the order in which they occurred. The manually drawn chart is identical to the Excel and Minitab versions shown on the following pages.

Table 22.2 Means and Standard Deviations of Samples in Example 21.1

Sample					$\bar{x}_j$	s_j
1	501.02	501.65	504.34	501.10	502.03	1.567
2	499.80	498.89	499.47	497.90	499.02	.833
3	497.12	498.35	500.34	499.33	498.79	1.376
4	500.68	501.39	499.74	500.41	500.56	.683
5	495.87	500.92	498.00	499.44	498.56	2.152
6	497.89	499.22	502.10	500.03	499.81	1.763
7	497.24	501.04	498.74	503.51	500.13	2.741
8	501.22	504.53	499.06	505.37	502.55	2.934
9	499.15	501.11	497.96	502.39	500.15	1.978
10	498.90	505.99	500.05	499.33	501.07	3.316
11	497.38	497.80	497.57	500.72	498.37	1.578
12	499.70	500.99	501.35	496.48	499.63	2.216
13	501.44	500.46	502.07	500.50	501.12	.780
14	498.26	495.54	495.21	501.27	497.57	2.820
15	497.57	497.00	500.32	501.22	499.03	2.059
16	500.95	502.07	500.60	500.44	501.02	.735
17	499.70	500.56	501.18	502.36	500.95	1.119
18	501.57	502.09	501.18	504.98	502.46	1.724
19	504.20	500.92	500.02	501.71	501.71	1.796
20	498.61	499.63	498.68	501.84	499.69	1.507
21	499.05	501.82	500.67	497.36	499.73	1.943
22	497.85	494.08	501.79	501.95	498.92	3.741
23	501.08	503.12	503.06	503.56	502.71	1.106
24	500.75	501.18	501.09	502.88	501.48	.955
25	502.03	501.44	498.76	499.39	500.41	1.576

EXCEL

Statistical Process Control

	Springs
Upper control limit	503.253
Centerline	500.2964
Lower control limit	497.3398

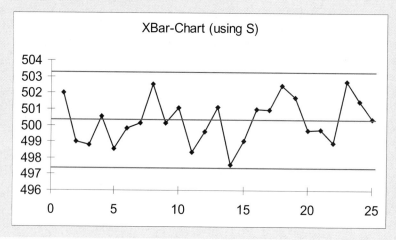

COMMANDS	COMMANDS FOR EXAMPLE 22.1
1. Type or import the data into one column.	Open file **Xm22-01**.
2. Click **Tools, Data Analysis Plus,** and **Statistical Process Control.**	
3. Specify the **Input Range.**	**A1:101**
4. Click **Labels** if appropriate.	
5. Specify the **Sample Size.**	**4**
6. Click **XBAR (Using S)** and click **OK**.	

MINITAB

X-bar Chart for Springs

COMMANDS	COMMANDS FOR EXAMPLE 22.1
1. Type or import the data into one column.	Open file **Xm22-01**.
2. Click **Stat, Control Charts,** and **Xbar....**	
3. Specify **Data are arranged as Single column** and select the variable.	**Springs** or **C1**
4. Type the **Subgroup size.**	**4**
5. Click **Estimate...** and **Pooled standard deviation.**	
6. Click **OK**. Click **OK**.	

INTERPRET

As you can see, no point lies outside the control limits. We conclude that the variation in the lengths of the springs is caused by chance. That is, there is not enough evidence to infer that the process is out of control. No remedial action is called for.

We stress that statistical process control allows us to detect assignable variation only. In Example 22.1, we determined that the process is under control, which means that there are no detectable sources of assignable variation. However, this does not mean that the process is a good one. It may well be that the production process yields a large proportion of defective units because the amount of chance variation is large. Recall that in Section 15.6, we noted that chance variation decreases product quality and increases costs. If the costs of producing defective units are high because of large chance variation, we can improve quality and reduce costs only by changing the process itself.

PATTERN TESTS TO DETERMINE WHEN THE PROCESS IS OUT OF CONTROL

When we tested hypotheses in the other parts of this book, we used only one sample statistic to make a decision. However, in statistical process control, the decision is made from a series of sample statistics. In the $\bar{x}$ chart we make the decision after plotting at least 25 sample means. As a result, we can develop tests that are based on the pattern the sample means make when plotted. To describe them, we need to divide the $\bar{x}$ chart between the control limits into six zones, as shown in Figure 22.5. The C zones represent the area within one standard error of the centerline. The B zones are the regions between one and two standard errors from the centerline. The spaces between two and three standard errors from the centerline are defined as A zones.

Figure 22.5
Zones of $\bar{x}$ charts

The width of the zones is one standard error of $\bar{x}$ $(S/\sqrt{n})$. If the calculations were performed manually, the value of S will be known. However, if a computer was used, the centerline and control limits are the only statistics printed. We can calculate $S/\sqrt{n}$ by finding the differences between the upper and lower control limits and dividing the difference by 6. That is,

$$\frac{S}{\sqrt{n}} = \frac{(\bar{\bar{x}} + 3S/\sqrt{n}) - (\bar{\bar{x}} - 3S/\sqrt{n})}{6} = \frac{503.253 - 497.340}{6} = .9855$$

Figure 22.6 describes the centerline, control limits, and zones for Example 22.1.

Figure 22.6
Zones for $\bar{x}$ chart:
Example 22.1

Several pattern tests can be applied. We list eight tests that are conducted by Minitab and by Data Analysis Plus.

Test 1: One point beyond zone A. This is the method discussed above, where we conclude that the process is out of control if any point is outside the control limits.

Test 2: Nine points in a row in zone C or beyond (on the same side of the centerline).

Test 3: Six increasing or six decreasing points in a row.

Test 4: Fourteen points in a row alternating up and down.

Test 5: Two out of three points in a row in zone A or beyond (on the same side of the centerline).

Test 6: Four out of five points in a row in zone B or beyond (on the same side of the centerline).

Test 7: Fifteen points in a row in zone C (on both sides of the centerline).

Test 8: Eight points in a row beyond zone C (on both sides of the centerline).

In the examples shown in Figure 22.7, each of the eight tests indicates a process out of control.

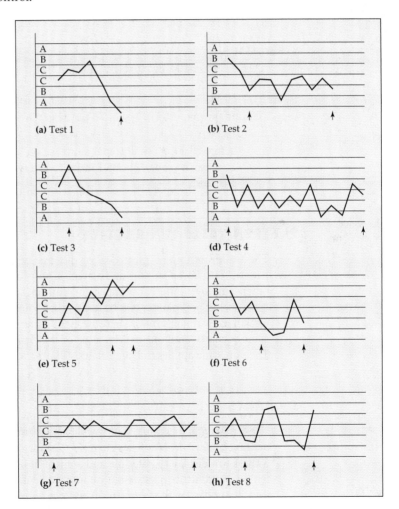

Figure 22.7
Examples of patterns indicating process out of control

All eight tests are based on the same concepts used to test hypotheses throughout this book. That is, each of these patterns is a rare event, unlikely to occur when a process is under control. Thus, when any one of these patterns is recognized, the statistics practitioner has reason to believe that the process is out of control. In fact, it is often possible to identify the cause of the problem from the pattern in the control chart.

Figure 22.8 depicts the zones and the means for Example 22.1. After checking each of the eight pattern tests, we conclude that the process is under control.

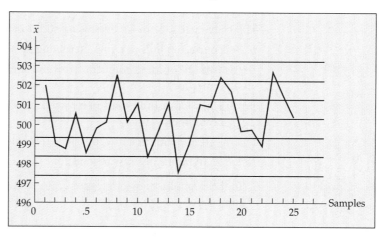

Figure 22.8
$\bar{x}$ chart with zones:
Example 22.1

 EXCEL
Excel automatically performs all eight tests.

 MINITAB
Minitab will perform any or all of the pattern tests and report any that fail.
COMMANDS
Before clicking OK at step 6 above, select **Tests…** and **Perform all eight tests**. To draw the zones, click **S Limits…** and type **1 2 3** in the **Sigma limit positions**.

PATTERN TESTS IN PRACTICE

There appears to be a great deal of disagreement among statisticians with regard to pattern tests. Some authors and statistical software packages apply eight tests, whereas others employ a different number. In addition, some statisticians apply pattern tests to $\bar{x}$ charts, but not to other charts. Rather than joining the debate with our own opinions, we will use Minitab's rules. There are eight pattern tests for $\bar{x}$ charts, no pattern tests for S and R charts, and four pattern tests for the chart presented in Section 22.5 (p charts). The same rule applies to Data Analysis Plus.

S CHARTS

The *S chart* graphs sample standard deviations to determine whether the process distribution standard deviation has changed. The format is similar to that of the $\bar{x}$ chart: The S chart will display a centerline and control limits. However, the formulas for the centerline and control limits are more complicated than those for the $\bar{x}$ chart. Consequently, we will not display the formulas; instead we will let the computer do all the work.

EXAMPLE 22.2

Using the data provided in Example 22.1, determine whether there is evidence to indicate that the process distribution standard deviation has changed over the period when the samples were taken.

SOLUTION

COMPUTE

EXCEL

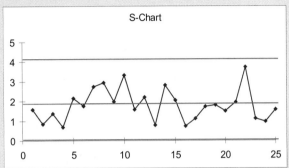

Statistical Process Control

	Springs
Upper control limit	4.1288
Centerline	1.822
Lower control limit	0

COMMANDS

1. Type or import the data into one column.
2. Click **Tools, Data Analysis Plus,** and **Statistical Process Control.**
3. Specify the **Input Range.**
4. Click **Labels** if appropriate.
5. Specify the **Sample Size.**
6. Click **S** and click **OK.**

COMMANDS FOR EXAMPLE 22.2

Open file **Xm22-01.**

A1:101

4

MINITAB

COMMANDS

1. Type or import the data into one column.
2. Click **Stat, Control Charts,** and **S….**
3. Specify **Data are arranged as Single column** and select the variable.
4. Type the **Subgroup size.**
5. Click **Estimate…** and **Pooled standard deviation.**
6. Click **OK.** Click **OK.**

COMMANDS FOR EXAMPLE 22.2

Open file **Xm22-01.**

Springs or **C1**

4

INTERPRET

There are no points outside the control limits. Because we do not apply any of the pattern tests, we conclude that there is no evidence to believe that the standard deviation has changed over this period.

GOOD NEWS AND BAD NEWS ABOUT *S* CHARTS

In analyzing *S* charts, we would conclude that the process distribution has changed if we observe points outside the control limits. Obviously, points above the upper control limit indicate that the process standard deviation has increased—an undesirable situation. Points below the lower control limit also indicate that the process standard deviation has changed. However, cases in which the standard deviation has decreased are welcome occurrences because reducing the variation generally leads to improvements in quality. The operations manager should investigate cases where the sample standard deviations or ranges are small to determine the factors that produced such results. The objective is to determine whether permanent improvements in the production process can be made. Care must be exercised in cases where the *S* chart reveals a decrease in the standard deviation, because this is often caused by improper sampling.

USING THE $\bar{x}$ AND *S* CHARTS

In this section, we have introduced $\bar{x}$ and *S* charts as separate procedures. In actual practice, however, the two charts must be drawn and assessed together. The reason for this is that the $\bar{x}$ chart uses *S* to calculate the control limits and zone boundaries. Consequently, if the *S* chart indicates that the process is out of control, the value of *S* will not lead to an accurate estimate of the standard deviation of the process distribution. The usual procedure is to draw the *S* chart first. If it indicates that the process is under control, we then draw the $\bar{x}$ chart. If the $\bar{x}$ chart also indicates that the process is under control, we are then in a position to use both charts to maintain control. If either chart shows that the process was out of control at some time during the creation of the charts, we can detect and fix the problem, then redraw the charts with new data.

MONITORING THE PRODUCTION PROCESS

When the process is under control we can use the control chart limits and centerline to monitor the process in the fiture. We do so by plotting all future statistics on the control chart.

EXAMPLE 22.3

After determining that the process is under control, the company in Example 22.1 began using the statistics generated in the creation of the $\bar{x}$ and *S* charts to monitor the production process. The sampling plan calls for samples of size 4 every hour. The following table lists the lengths of the springs taken during the first 6 hours.

Sample				
1	502.653	498.354	502.209	500.080
2	501.212	494.454	500.918	501.855
3	500.086	500.826	496.426	503.591
4	502.994	500.481	502.996	503.113
5	500.549	498.780	502.480	499.836
6	500.441	502.666	502.569	503.248

SOLUTION   After each sample is taken, the mean and standard deviation are computed. The standard deviations are plotted on the S chart. The sample means are plotted on the $\bar{x}$ chart and the pattern tests are checked after each point is plotted. The first six samples are shown in Figure 22.9. After the sixth's sample standard deviation and mean are plotted, the technician would stop the production process. The fourth and sixth means combine to indicate that test 5 has failed; there are two out of three points in a row that are in zone A or beyond. It appears that the process mean has shifted upward. Technicians need to find the source of the problem and make repairs. After repairs are completed, production begins and new control charts and their centerlines and control limits are recalculated.

(a) S chart

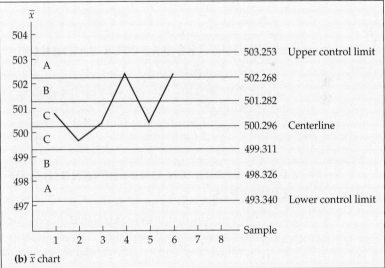

(b) $\bar{x}$ chart

Figure 22.9
S and $\bar{x}$ charts for
Example 22.3

PROCESS CAPABILITY INDEX

In Section 15.6 we discussed the **process capability index**, which measures the capability of the process to produce units whose dimensions fall within the specifications. We defined the index as

$$C_p = \frac{\text{USL} - \text{LSL}}{6\sigma}$$

where USL and LSL are the upper and lower specification limits, respectively. To compute the process capability index, we need to know these limits and the process standard deviation. The standard deviation is a population parameter, which is generally unknown. Thus, C_p measures the theoretical or potential process capability. To produce a measure of the process's actual capability, we need to use statistics computed in the construction of the control chart. Suppose that in Example 22.1 the operations manager determined that the springs will fit provided that their lengths fall between the lower specification limit LSL = 493 and the upper specification limit USL = 507. In Example 22.1 we found $\bar{\bar{x}}$ = 500.296 and S = 1.971.

We define the following:

$$CPL = \frac{\bar{\bar{x}} - LSL}{3S} = \frac{500.296 - 493}{3(1.971)} = 1.23$$

$$CPU = \frac{USL - \bar{\bar{x}}}{3S} = \frac{507 - 500.296}{3(1.971)} = 1.13$$

We define the process capability index as the smaller of these two indexes. That is,

$$C_{pk} = Min(CPL, CPU) = 1.13$$

As is the case with C_p, the larger C_{pk} is, the better the production process meets specifications. By determining this value, operations managers can measure improvements in the production process.

REDUCING THE PROCESS VARIANCE

In Section 15.6 we described how experimentation with the four M's allows statistics practitioners to discover sources of variation and ultimately reduce that variation. Control charts may also contribute to this effort. By examining the results of control charts, we may be able to find additional sources of variation.

DEVELOPING AN UNDERSTANDING OF STATISTICAL CONCEPTS

The concepts that underlie statistical process control are the same as the fundamental principles of hypothesis testing. That is, statistics that are not consistent with the null hypothesis lead us to reject the null hypothesis. However, there are two critical differences between SPC and hypothesis testing. First, in SPC we test processes rather than parameters of populations. That is, we test to determine whether there is evidence that the process distribution has changed. Second, in SPC we test a series of statistics taken over time. From a pedagogical point of view, there is another fundamental difference. Many students of statistics have difficulty identifying the correct hypothesis-testing procedure to employ. However, SPC applications tend to be rather uncomplicated. We use control charts for variables (as in this and the next section) to determine whether the process is under control when the product produced must be measured quantitatively. Identifying the correct technique is seldom difficult and thus does not require technique-identification skills developed throughout this book.

EXERCISES

22.23 Given the following statistics drawn from 30 samples of size 4, calculate the centerline and control limits for the $\bar{x}$ chart.
$$\bar{\bar{x}} = 453.6 \qquad S = 12.5$$

22.24 The mean of the sample means and the pooled standard deviation of 40 samples of size 9 taken from a production process under control are shown below. Compute the centerline, control limits, and zone boundaries for the $\bar{x}$ chart.
$$\bar{\bar{x}} = 181.1 \qquad S = 11.0$$

22.25 Twenty-five samples of size 4 were taken from a production process. The sample means are listed in chronological order below. The mean of the sample means and the pooled standard deviation are $\bar{\bar{x}} = 13.3$ and $S = 3.8$.

14.5 10.3 17.0 9.4 13.2 9.3 17.1 5.5 5.3
16.3 10.5 11.5 8.8 12.6 10.5 16.3 8.7 9.4
11.4 17.6 20.5 21.1 16.3 18.5 20.9

a Find the centerline and control limits for the $\bar{x}$ chart.
b Plot the sample means on the $\bar{x}$ chart.
c Is the process under control? Explain.

The following exercises require a computer and statistical software.

22.26 Thirty samples of size 4 were drawn from a production process. The data were stored in file Xr22-26.
a Construct an S chart.
b Construct an $\bar{x}$ chart.
c Do the charts allow you to conclude that the process is under control?
d If the process went out of control, which of the following is the likely cause: level shift, instability, trend, or cycle?

22.27 The fence of a saw is set so that it automatically cuts 2-by-4's into 96-inch lengths needed to produce prefabricated homes. To ensure that the lumber is cut properly, three pieces of wood are measured after each 100 cuts are made. The measurements in inches for the last 40 samples are stored in file Xr22-27.
a Do these data indicate that the process is out of control?
b If so, when did it go out of control? What is the likely cause: level shift, instability, trend, or cycle?
c Speculate on how the problem could be corrected.

22.28 An Arc Extinguishing Unit (AEU) is used in the high-voltage electrical industry to eliminate the occurrence of electrical flash from one live 25,000-volt switch contact to another. A small but important component of an AEU is a nonconductive sliding bearing called a (ST-90811) pin guide. The dimensional accuracy of this pin guide is critical to the overall operation of the AEU. If any one of its dimensions is "out of spec" (specification), the part will bind within the AEU, causing failure. This would cause the complete destruction of both the AEU and the 25,000 volt-switch contacts, resulting in a

power blackout. A pin guide has a square shape with a circular hole in the center, as shown here with its specified dimensions. The specification limits are LSL = .4370 and USL = .4400.

Due to the critical nature of the dimensions of the pin guide, statistical process control is used during long production runs to check that the production process is under control. Suppose that samples of five pin guides are drawn every hour. The results of the last 25 samples are stored in file Xr22-28. Do these data allow the technician to conclude that the process is out of control?

22.29 Refer to Exercise 22.28. Find the process capability index, C_{pk}.

22.30 KW Paints is a company that manufactures various kinds of paints and sells them in 1- and 4-liter cans. The cans are filled on an assembly line with an automatic valve regulating the amount of paint. If the cans are overfilled, paint and money will be wasted. If the cans are underfilled, customers will complain. To ensure that the proper amount of paint goes into each can, statistical process control is used. Every hour five cans are opened, and the volume of paint is measured. The results from the last 30 hours from the l-liter production line are stored in file Xr22-30. To avoid rounding errors, we recorded the volumes in cubic centimeters (cc) after subtracting 1,000. Thus the file contains the amounts of overfill and underfill. Draw the $\bar{x}$ and S charts to determine whether the process is under control.

22.31 Refer to Exercise 22.30. If the lower and upper specification limits are 998 cc and 1,002 cc, respectively, what is C_{pk}?

22.32 Lear Seating of Kitchener, Ontario, produces seats for Cadillacs and other GM cars and trucks. The Cadillac seat includes a part called the EK headrest. The frame of the headrest is made from steel rods. A machine is used to bend the rod into a U-shape described as shown. The width is critical; if it is too wide or too narrow, it will not fit into the holes drilled into the seat frame. The process is checked by drawing samples of size 3 every 2 hours. The last 20 samples are stored in file Xr22-32.

a What do these data tell you about the process?

b If it went out of control, at what sample did this occur?

c What is the likely assignable cause?

22.33 The degree to which nuts and bolts are tightened in numerous places on a car is often important. For example, in Toyota cars, a nut holds the rear signal light. If the nut is not tightened sufficiently, it will loosen and fall off; if it is too tight, the light may break. The nut is tightened with a torque wrench with a set clutch. The target torque is 8 kgf/cm (kilogram-force per centimeter) with specification limits LSL = 7 kgf/cm and USL = 9 kgf/cm. Statistical process control is employed to constantly check the process. Random samples of size 4 are drawn after every 200 nuts are tightened. The data from the last 25 samples are stored in file Xr22-33. Is the process out of control?

22.34 The seats for the F-150 series Ford trucks are manufactured by Lear Seating. The frames must be 1,496 mm wide with specification limits LSL = 1,494.5 mm and USL = 1,497.5 mm. Frames that are wider than 1,497.5 mm or narrower than 1,494.5 mm result in assembly problems, because seat cushions and/or other parts won't fit. The process is tested by drawing random samples of five frames every 2 hours. The last 25 samples are stored in file Xr22-34. What can we conclude from these data?

22.35 Long Manufacturing produces heat exchangers, primarily for the automotive industry. One such product, a transmission oil cooler, is used in the cooling of bus transmissions. It is composed of a series of copper tubes that are soldered into a header. The header must have a diameter of 4.984 inches with specification limits LSL = 4.981 inches and USL = 4.987 inches. Oversize headers result in fluid mixing and possible failure of the device. For every 100 headers produced the operations manager draws a sample of size 4. The data from the last 25 samples are stored in file Xr22-35. What can we conclude from these data?

22.36 Find the process capability index for Exercise 22.35.

22.37 Refer to Exercise 22.35. Nuts and bolts are used in the assembly of the transmission oil coolers. They are supposed to be tightened by a torque wrench to 7 foot-pounds with specification limits LSL = 6 foot-pounds and USL = 8 foot-pounds. To test the process, three nuts are tested every 3 hours. The results for the last 75 hours are stored in file Xr22-37. Does it appear that the process is under control?

22.38 Motor oil is packaged and sold in plastic bottles. The bottles are often handled quite roughly, either in delivery to the stores (bottles are packed in boxes, which are stacked to conserve truck space), in the stores themselves, or by the consumer. The bottles must be hardy enough to withstand this treatment without leaking. Before leaving the plant, the bottles undergo statistical process control procedures. Five out of every 10,000 bottles are sampled. The burst strength (the pressure required to burst the bottle) is measured in pounds per square inch (psi). The process is designed to produce bottles that can withstand up to 800 psi. The burst strengths of the last 30 samples are stored in file Xr22-38.

a Draw the appropriate control chart(s).

b Does it appear that the process went out of control?

22.39 Almost all computer hardware and software producers offer a toll-free telephone number to solve problems associated with their product. The ability to work quickly to resolve difficulties is critical. One software maker's policy is that all calls must be answered by a software consultant within 120 seconds. (All calls are initially answered by computer and the caller is put on hold until a consultant attends to the caller.) To help maintain the quality of the service, four calls per day are monitored. The amount of time before the consultant responds to the call is recorded. The record of the last 30 days is stored in file Xr22-39.

a Draw the appropriate control chart(s).

b Does it appear that the process went out of control?

22.40 Plastic pipe is used for plumbing in almost all new homes. If the pipes are too narrow or too wide, they will not connect properly with other parts of the plumbing system. A manufacturer of 3-inch diameter pipes employs statistical process control to maintain the quality of its products. The sampling plan is to draw samples of three 10-foot-long pipes every hour and measure the diameters. Twenty hours ago, the production process was shut down for repairs. The results of the first 20 samples taken since are stored in file Xr22-40. Does it appear that the production process is under control?

22.41 If the specification limits for the plastic pipes in Exercise 22.40 are LSL = 2.9 inches and USL = 3.1 inches, determine the process capability index C_{pk}.

22.42 Calculate the process capability index for Exercise 22.34. Does the value of this index indicate that the production process is poor? Explain.

22.5 CONTROL CHARTS FOR ATTRIBUTES: *p* CHART

In this section, we introduce a control chart that is used to monitor a process whose results are categorized as either defective or nondefective. We construct a ***p* chart** to track the proportion of defective units in a series of samples.

p CHART

We draw the p chart in a way similar to the construction of the $\bar{x}$ chart. We draw samples of size n from the process at a minimum of 25 time periods. For each sample, we calculate the sample proportion of defective units, which we label $\hat{p}_j$. We then compute the mean of the sample proportions, which is labeled $\bar{p}$. That is,

$$\bar{p} = \frac{\sum_{j=1}^{k} \hat{p}_j}{k}$$

The centerline and control limits are as follows.

CENTERLINE AND CONTROL LIMITS FOR THE p CHART

$$\text{Centerline} = \bar{p}$$

$$\text{Lower control limit} = \bar{p} - 3\sqrt{\frac{\bar{p}(1 - \bar{p})}{n}}$$

$$\text{Upper control limit} = \bar{p} + 3\sqrt{\frac{\bar{p}(1 - \bar{p})}{n}}$$

If the lower limit is negative, set it equal to 0.

PATTERN TESTS

As we did in the previous sections, we use Minitab's pattern tests. Minitab performs only tests 1 to 4, which are as follows.

Test 1: One point beyond zone A.

Test 2: Nine points in a row in zone C or beyond (on the same side of the centerline).

Test 3: Six increasing or six decreasing points in a row.

Test 4: Fourteen points in a row alternating up and down.

We'll demonstrate this technique using the chapter opening example.

DETECTING THE SOURCE OF DEFECTIVE DISKS: SOLUTION

For each sample, we compute the proportion of defective disks and calculate the mean sample proportion, which is $\bar{p} = .05762$. Thus,

$$\text{Centerline} = \bar{p} = .05762$$

$$\text{Lower control limit} = \bar{p} - 3\sqrt{\frac{\bar{p}(1 - \bar{p})}{n}}$$

$$= .05762 - 3\sqrt{\frac{(.05762)(1 - .05762)}{200}} = .008188$$

$$\text{Upper control limit} = \bar{p} + 3\sqrt{\frac{\bar{p}(1 - \bar{p})}{n}}$$

$$= .05762 + 3\sqrt{\frac{(.05762)(1 - .05762)}{200}} = .1071$$

Because

$$\sqrt{\frac{\bar{p}(1 - \bar{p})}{n}} = \sqrt{\frac{(.05762)(1 - .05762)}{200}} = .01648$$

the boundaries of the zones are as follows:

Zone C: $.05762 \pm .01648 = (.04114, .0741)$
Zone B: $.05762 \pm 2(.01648) = (.02467, .09057)$
Zone A: $.05762 \pm 3(.01648) = (.008188, .1071)$

The output on the next page exhibits this p chart.

DETECTING THE SOURCE OF DEFECTIVE DISKS: SOLUTION *(continued)*

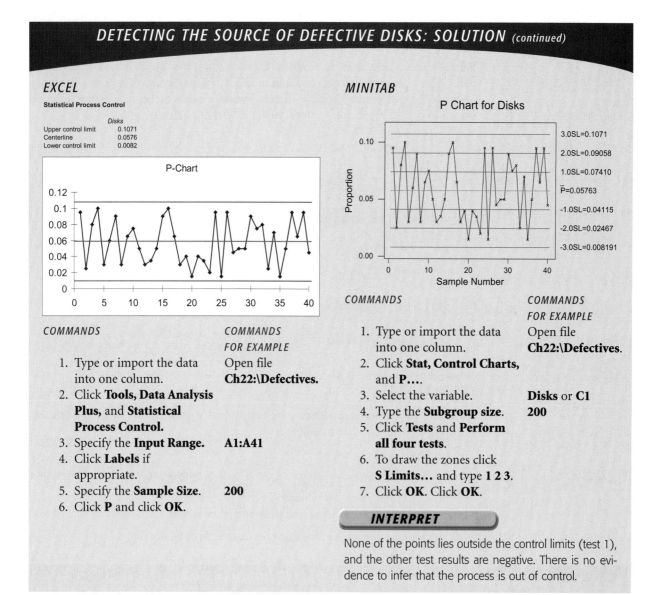

EXCEL

Statistical Process Control

	Disks
Upper control limit	0.1071
Centerline	0.0576
Lower control limit	0.0082

COMMANDS	**COMMANDS FOR EXAMPLE**
1. Type or import the data into one column.	Open file **Ch22:\Defectives.**
2. Click **Tools, Data Analysis Plus,** and **Statistical Process Control.**
3. Specify the **Input Range.**	**A1:A41**
4. Click **Labels** if appropriate.
5. Specify the **Sample Size.**	**200**
6. Click **P** and click **OK.**

MINITAB

P Chart for Disks

COMMANDS	**COMMANDS FOR EXAMPLE**
1. Type or import the data into one column.	Open file **Ch22:\Defectives.**
2. Click **Stat, Control Charts,** and **P….**
3. Select the variable.	**Disks** or **C1**
4. Type the **Subgroup size.**	**200**
5. Click **Tests** and **Perform all four tests.**
6. To draw the zones click **S Limits…** and type **1 2 3.**
7. Click **OK.** Click **OK.**

INTERPRET

None of the points lies outside the control limits (test 1), and the other test results are negative. There is no evidence to infer that the process is out of control.

The comment we made about *S* charts is also valid for *p* charts. That is, sample proportions that are less than the lower control limit indicate a change in the process that we would like to make permanent. We need to investigate the reasons for such a change just as vigorously as we investigate the causes of large proportions of defects.

EXERCISES

22.43 To ensure that a manufacturing process is under control, 40 samples of size 1,000 were drawn and the number of defectives in each sample was counted. The mean sample proportion was .035. Compute the centerline and control limits for the *p* chart.

22.44 Random samples of 200 copier machines were taken on an assembly line every hour for the past 25 hours. The number of defective machines is shown below

and stored in file Xr22-44. Are there any points beyond the control limits? If so, what do they tell you about the production process?

3, 5, 3, 2, 2, 11, 12, 6, 7, 5, 0, 7, 8,
2, 10, 6, 4, 2, 10, 5, 4, 11, 10, 13, 14

22.45 Raytheon of Canada Limited produces printed circuit boards (PCBs), which involve a number of soldering operations. At the end of the process, the PCBs are tested to determine whether they work properly. There are several causes of PCB failure, including bad flux, improper heating, and impurities. A reject rate of less than .80% is considered acceptable. Statistical process control is used by Raytheon to constantly check quality. Every hour, 500 PCBs are tested. The number of defective PCBs for the past 25 hours is shown below and stored in file Xr22-45. Draw a *p* chart and apply the pattern tests to determine whether the process is under control.

3, 1, 2, 2, 1, 2, 3, 3, 3, 2, 3, 0, 0,
0, 2, 0, 0, 2, 4, 1, 1, 1, 4, 1, 3

22.46 A plant produces 1,000 cordless telephones daily. A random sample of 100 telephones is inspected each day. After 30 days, the following numbers of defectives were found. (The data are also stored in file Xr22-46.) Construct a *p* chart to determine whether the process is out of control.

5, 0, 4, 3, 0, 3, 1, 1, 5, 0, 2, 1, 6, 0, 3,
0, 5, 5, 8, 5, 0, 1, 9, 6, 11, 6, 6, 4, 5, 10

22.47 The Woodsworth Publishing Company produces millions of books containing hundred of millions of pages each year. To ensure the quality of the printed page, Woodsworth uses statistical process control. In each production run, 1,000 pages are randomly inspected. The examiners look for print clarity and whether the material is properly centered on the page. The numbers of defective pages in the last 40 production runs are listed below and stored in file Xr22-47. Draw the *p* chart. Using the pattern tests, can we conclude that the production process is under control?

11, 9, 17, 19, 15, 15, 18, 21, 18, 6,
27, 14, 7, 18, 18, 19, 17, 15, 7, 16,
17, 22, 12, 12, 12, 16, 12, 9, 21, 17,
20, 17, 17, 18, 23, 29, 24, 27, 23, 21

The following exercises require the use of a computer and statistical software.

22.48 A company that manufactures batteries employs statistical process control to ensure that its product functions properly. The sampling plan for the D-cell batteries calls for samples of 500 batteries to be taken and tested. The numbers of defective batteries in the last 30 samples are stored in file Xr22-48. Determine whether the process is under control.

22.49 A courier delivery company advertises that it guarantees delivery by noon the following day. The statistical process control plan calls for sampling 2,000 deliveries each day to ensure that the advertisement is reasonable. The numbers of late deliveries for the last 30 days are stored in file Xr22-49. What can we conclude from these data?

22.50 Optical scanners are used in all supermarkets to speed the checkout process. Whenever the scanner fails to read the bar code on the product, the cashier is required to manually punch the code into the register. Obviously, unreadable bar codes slow the checkout process. Statistical process control is used to determine whether the scanner is working properly. Once a day at each checkout counter, a sample of 500 scans is taken and the number of times the scanner is unable to read the bar code is determined. (The sampling process is performed automatically by the cash register.) The results for one checkout counter for the past 25 days are stored in file Xr22-50.

a Draw the appropriate control chart.

b Does it appear that the process went out of control?

22.6 SUMMARY

In this chapter, we introduced **statistical process control** and explained how it contributes to the maintenance of quality. We discussed how **control charts** detect changes in the process distribution and introduced the $\bar{x}$ **chart**, *S* **chart**, and *p* **chart**.

IMPORTANT TERMS

Statistical process control (SPC) 756
Quality control 756
Prevention approach 756
Chance variation 756
Assignable variation 756
Under control 757

Specification limits 757
Out of control 757
Centerline 758
Upper and lower control limits 758
Operating characteristic curve 760
Average run length 763

Control charts for variables 764
Control chart for attributes 764
$\bar{x}$ chart 765
S chart 772
p chart 778

SYMBOLS

Symbol	Pronounced	Represents
S		Pooled standard deviation
s_j	*S-sub-j*	Standard deviation of the *j*th sample
$\hat{p}_j$	*p-hat-sub-j*	Proportion of defectives in *j*th sample
$\bar{p}$	*p-bar*	Mean proportion of defectives

FORMULAS

Centerline and control limits for $\bar{x}$ chart using S

$$\text{Centerline} = \bar{\bar{x}}$$

$$\text{Lower control limit} = \bar{\bar{x}} - 3\frac{S}{\sqrt{n}}$$

$$\text{Upper control limit} = \bar{\bar{x}} + 3\frac{S}{\sqrt{n}}$$

Centerline and control limits for the p chart

$$\text{Centerline} = \bar{p}$$

$$\text{Lower control limit} = \bar{p} - 3\sqrt{\frac{\bar{p}(1 - \bar{p})}{n}}$$

$$\text{Upper control limit} = \bar{p} + 3\sqrt{\frac{\bar{p}(1 - \bar{p})}{n}}$$

COMPUTER OUTPUT AND INSTRUCTIONS

Technique	*Excel*	*Minitab*
$\bar{x}$ chart	768	769
S chart	773	773
p chart	780	780

REFERENCES

Deming, W. Edwards, *Out of the Crisis*, Cambridge, MA: MIT Center for Advanced Engineering Study, 1986.

Duncan, A. J., *Quality Control and Industrial Statistics*, 6th edition. Homewood, IL: Irwin, 1990.

Evans, James R., and William M. Lindsay, *The Management and Control of Quality*, 4th edition. Cincinnati: Southwestern, 1999.

Farnum, Nicholas R., *Modern Statistical Quality Control and Improvement*. Belmont, CA: Duxbury, 1994.

Juran, J. M., and Frank M. Gryna, *Quality Planning and Analysis*, 3rd edition. New York: McGraw Hill, 1993.

Montgomery, D. C., *Introduction to Statistical Quality Control*, 2nd edition. New York: John Wiley and Sons, 1992.

Ryan, T. D., *Statistical Methods for Quality Improvement*. New York: John Wiley and Sons, 1989.

Shewart, Walter A., *Economic Control of Quality of Manufactured Product*. New York: Van Nostrand, 1931.

23 DECISION ANALYSIS

ACCEPTANCE SAMPLING

A factory produces a small but important component used in computers. The factory manufactures the component in 1,000-unit lots. Because of the relatively advanced technology, the manufacturing process results in a large proportion of defective units. In fact, the operations manager has observed that the percentage of defective units per lot has been either 15% or 35%. In the past year, 60% of the lots have had 15% defectives and 40% have had 35% defectives. The present policy of the company

is to send the lot to the customer, replace all defectives, and pay any additional costs. The total cost of replacing a defective unit that has been sent to the customer is $10/unit. Because of the high costs, the company

management is considering inspecting all units and replacing the defective units before shipment. The sampling cost is $2/unit, and the replacement cost is $.50/unit. Each unit sells for $5.

a. Based on the history of the past year, should the company adopt the 100% inspection plan?

b. Is it worthwhile to take a sample of size 2 from the lot before deciding whether to inspect 100%?

23.1 INTRODUCTION

In earlier chapters, we dealt with techniques for summarizing data in order to make decisions about population parameters and population characteristics. Our focus in this chapter is also on decision making, but the types of problems we deal with here differ in several ways. First, the technique for hypothesis testing concludes with either rejecting or not rejecting some hypothesis concerning a dimension of a population. In decision analysis, we deal with the problem of selecting one alternative from a list of several possible decisions. Second, in hypothesis testing the decision is based on the statistical evidence available. In decision analysis, there may be no statistical data, or if there are data, the decision may depend only partly on them. Third, costs (and profits) are only indirectly considered (in the selection of a significance level or in interpreting a *p*-value) in the formulation of a hypothesis test. Decision analysis directly involves profits and losses. Because of these major differences, the only topics covered previously in the text that are required for an understanding of decision analysis are probability (including Bayes' law) and expected value.

23.2 DECISION PROBLEM

You would think that, by this point in the text, we would already have introduced all the necessary concepts and terminology. Unfortunately, because decision analysis is so radically different from statistical inference, several more terms need to be defined. They will be introduced in the following example.

EXAMPLE 23.1

A man wants to invest $1 million for 1 year. After analyzing and eliminating numerous possibilities, he has narrowed his choice to one of three alternatives. These alternatives are referred to as **acts** and are denoted a_i.

a_1:   Invest in a guaranteed income certificate paying 10%.

a_2:   Invest in a bond with a coupon value of 8%.

a_3:   Invest in a well-diversified portfolio of stocks.

He believes that the payoffs associated with the last two acts depend on a number of factors, foremost among which is interest rates. He concludes that there are three possible **states of nature**, denoted s_j:

s_1:   Interest rates increase.

s_2:   Interest rates stay the same.

s_3:   Interest rates decrease.

After further analysis, he determines the amount of profit he will make for each possible combination of an act and a state of nature. Of course, the payoff for the guaranteed income certificate will be $100,000, no matter which state of nature occurs. The profits from each alternative investment are summarized in Table 23.1, in what is called a **payoff table**. Notice that, for example, when the decision is a_2 and the state of nature is s_1, the investor would suffer a $50,000 loss, which is represented by a −$50,000 payoff.

Table 23.1 Payoff Table for Example 23.1

States of Nature	a_1 (GIC)	a_2 (bond)	a_3 (stocks)
s_1 (interest rates increase)	$100,000	−$50,000	$150,000
s_2 (interest rates stay the same)	100,000	80,000	90,000
s_3 (interest rates decrease)	100,000	180,000	40,000

Another way of expressing the consequence of an act involves measuring the *opportunity loss* associated with each combination of an act and a state of nature. An **opportunity loss** is the difference between what the decision maker's profit for an act is and what the profit could have been had the best decision been made. For example, consider the first row of Table 23.1. If s_1 is the state of nature that occurs and the investor chooses act a_1, he makes a profit of $100,000. However, had he chosen act a_3, he would have made a profit of $150,000. The difference between what he could have made ($150,000) and what he actually made ($100,000) is the opportunity loss. Thus, given that s_1 is the state of nature, the opportunity loss of act a_1 is $50,000. The opportunity loss of act a_2 is $200,000, which is the difference between $150,000 and −$50,000. The opportunity loss of act a_3 is 0, because there is no opportunity loss when the best alternative is chosen. In a similar manner, we can compute the remaining opportunity losses for this example (see Table 23.2). Notice that we can never experience a negative opportunity loss.

Table 23.2 Opportunity Loss Table for Example 23.1

States of Nature	a_1 (GIC)	a_2 (bond)	a_3 (stocks)
s_1 (interest rates increase)	$50,000	$200,000	0
s_2 (interest rates stay the same)	0	20,000	10,000
s_3 (interest rates decrease)	80,000	0	140,000

DECISION TREES

Most problems involving a simple choice of alternatives can readily be resolved by using the payoff table (or the opportunity loss table). In other situations, however, the decision maker must choose between sequences of acts. In Section 23.3, we introduce one form of such situations. In these cases, a payoff table will not suffice to determine the best alternative; instead, we require a **decision tree**.

In Chapter 6, we suggested the probability tree as a useful device for computing probabilities. In this type of tree, all the branches represent stages of events. In a decision tree, however, the branches represent both acts and events (states of nature). We distinguish between them in the following way: A square node represents a point where a decision is to be made; a point where a state of nature occurs is represented by a round node. Figure 23.1 on page 786 depicts the decision tree for Example 23.1.

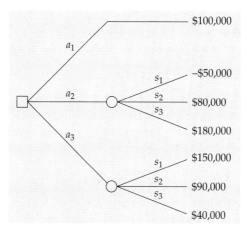

Figure 23.1
Decision tree for
Example 23.1

The tree begins with a square node; that is, we begin by making a choice among a_1, a_2, and a_3. The branches emanating from the square node represent these alternatives. At the ends of branches a_2 and a_3, we reach round nodes representing the occurrence of some state of nature. These are depicted as branches representing s_1, s_2, and s_3. At the end of branch a_1, we don't really have a state of nature, because the payoff is fixed at $100,000, no matter what happens to interest rates.

At the ends of the branches, the payoffs are shown (alternatively, we could have worked with opportunity losses instead of with payoffs). These are, of course, the same values that appear in Table 23.1.

Up to this point, all we have done is set up the problem; we have not made any attempt to determine the decision. It should be noted that in many real-life problems, determining the payoff table or decision tree can be a formidable task in itself. Many managers, however, have observed that this task is often extremely helpful in decision making.

EXPECTED MONETARY VALUE DECISION

In many decision problems, it is possible to assign probabilities to the states of nature. For example, if the decision involves trying to decide whether to draw to an inside straight in the game of poker, the probability of succeeding can easily be determined by the use of simple rules of probability. If we must decide whether to replace a machine that has broken down frequently in the past, we can assign probabilities on the basis of the relative frequency of the breakdowns. In many other instances, however, formal rules and techniques of probability cannot be applied. In Example 23.1, the historical relative frequencies of the ups and downs of interest rates will supply scant useful information to help the investor assign probabilities to the behavior of interest rates during the coming year. In such cases, probabilities must be assigned subjectively. In other words, the determination of the probabilities must be based on the experience, knowledge, and (perhaps) guesswork of the decision maker.

If in Example 23.1 the investor has some knowledge about a number of economic variables, he might have a reasonable guess about what will happen to interest rates in the next year. Suppose, for example, that our investor believes that future interest rates are most likely to remain essentially the same as they are today and that (of the remaining two states of nature) rates are more likely to decrease than to increase. He might then guess the following probabilities:

$$P(s_1) = .2, \quad P(s_2) = .5, \quad P(s_3) = .3$$

Because the probabilities are subjective, we would expect another decision maker to produce a completely different set of probabilities. In fact, if this were not true, we would rarely have buyers and sellers of stocks (or any other investment), because everyone would be a buyer (and there would be no sellers) or everyone would be a seller (with no buyers).

After determining the probabilities of the states of nature, we can address the *expected monetary value decision.* We now calculate what we expect will happen for each decision. Because we generally measure the consequences of each decision in monetary terms, we compute the **expected monetary value (EMV)** of each act. Recall from Section 7.3 that we calculate expected values by multiplying the values of the random variables by their respective probabilities and then summing the products. Thus, in our example, the expected monetary value of alternative a_1 is

$$\text{EMV}(a_1) = .2(100,000) + .5(100,000) + .3(100,000) = \$100,000$$

The expected values of the other decisions are found in the same way:

$$\text{EMV}(a_2) = .2(-50,000) + .5(80,000) + .3(180,000) = \$84,000$$

$$\text{EMV}(a_3) = .2(150,000) + .5(90,000) + .3(40,000) = \$87,000$$

We choose the decision with the largest expected monetary value, which is a_1, and label its expected value EMV*. Hence, EMV* = \$100,000.

In general, the expected monetary values do not represent possible payoffs. For example, the expected monetary value of act a_2 is \$84,000, yet the payoff table indicates that the only possible payoffs from choosing a_2 are −\$50,000, \$80,000, and \$180,000. Of course, the expected monetary value of act a_1 (\$100,000) is possible, because that is the only payoff of the act.

What, then, does the expected monetary value represent? If the investment is made a large number of times, with exactly the same payoffs and probabilities, the expected monetary value is the average payoff per investment. That is, if the investment is repeated an infinite number of times with act a_2, 20% of the investments will result in a \$50,000 loss, 50% will result in an \$80,000 profit, and 30% will result in a \$180,000 profit. The average of all these investments is the expected monetary value, \$84,000. If act a_3 is chosen, the average payoff in the long run will be \$87,000.

An important point is raised by the question of how many investments are going to be made. The answer is one. Even if the investor intends to make the same type of investment annually, the payoffs and the probabilities of the states of nature will undoubtedly change from year to year. Hence, we are faced with having determined the expected monetary value decision on the basis of an infinite number of investments, when there will be only one investment. We can rationalize this apparent contradiction in two ways. First, the expected value decision is the only method that allows us to combine the two most important factors in the decision process—the payoffs and their probabilities. It seems inconceivable that, where both factors are known, the investor would want to ignore either one. (There are processes that make decisions on the basis of the payoffs alone; however, these processes assume no knowledge of the probabilities, which is not the case with our example.) Second, typical decision makers make a large number of decisions over their lifetimes. By using the expected value decision, the decision maker should perform at least as well as anyone else. Thus, despite the problem of interpretation, we advocate the expected monetary value decision.

EXPECTED OPPORTUNITY LOSS DECISION

We can also calculate the **expected opportunity loss (EOL)** of each act. From the opportunity loss table (Table 23.2), we get the following values:

$$EOL\,(a_1) = .2(50{,}000) + .5(0) + .3(80{,}000) = \$34{,}000$$

$$EOL\,(a_2) = .2(200{,}000) + .5(20{,}000) + .3(0) = \$50{,}000$$

$$EOL\,(a_3) = .2(0) + .5(10{,}000) + .3(140{,}000) = \$47{,}000$$

Because we want to minimize losses, we choose the act that produces the smallest expected opportunity loss, which is a_1. We label its expected value EOL*. Observe that the EMV decision is the same as the EOL decision. This is not a coincidence—the opportunity loss table was produced directly from the payoff table.

ROLLBACK TECHNIQUE FOR DECISION TREES

Figure 23.2 presents the decision tree for Example 23.1, with the probabilities of the states of nature included. The process of determining the EMV decision is called the **rollback technique**; it operates as follows. Beginning at the end of the tree (right-hand side), we calculate the expected monetary value at each round node. The numbers above the round nodes in Figure 23.2 specify these expected monetary values.

At each square node, we make a decision by choosing the branch with the largest EMV. In our example, there is only one square node. Our optimal decision is, of course, a_1.

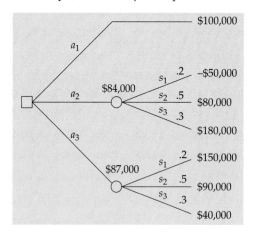

Figure 23.2
Rollback technique for Example 23.1

USING THE COMPUTER

There is yet another Excel add-in called Treeplan that enables Excel to draw the decision tree and produce the optimal solution. Instructions are provided in CD Appendix 23.1.

EXERCISES

23.1 Set up the opportunity loss table from the following payoff table.

	a_1	a_2
s_1	55	26
s_2	43	38
s_3	29	43
s_4	15	51

23.2 Draw the decision tree for Exercise 23.1.

23.3 If we assign the following probabilities to the states of nature in Exercise 23.1, determine the EMV decision.

$$P(s_1) = .4 \qquad P(s_2) = .1 \qquad P(s_3) = .3 \qquad P(s_4) = .2$$

23.4 Given the following payoff table, draw the decision tree.

	a_1	a_2	a_3
s_1	20	5	-1
s_2	8	5	4
s_3	-10	5	10

23.5 Refer to Exercise 23.4. Set up the opportunity loss table.

23.6 If we assign the following probabilities to the states of nature in Exercise 23.5, determine the EOL decision.

$$P(s_1) = .2 \qquad P(s_2) = .6 \qquad P(s_3) = .2$$

Applications

23.7 A baker must decide how many specialty cakes to bake each morning. From past experience, she knows that the daily demand for cakes ranges from 0 to 3. Each cake costs $3.00 to produce and sells for $8.00, and any unsold cakes are thrown into the garbage at the end of the day.
  a Set up a payoff table to help the baker decide how many cakes to bake.
  b Set up the opportunity loss table.
  c Draw the decision tree.

23.8 Refer to Exercise 23.7. Assume that the probability of each value of demand is the same for all possible demands.
  a Determine the EMV decision.
  b Determine the EOL decision.

23.9 The manager of a large shopping center in Buffalo is in the process of deciding on the type of snow-clearing service to hire for his parking lot. Two services are available. The White Christmas Company will clear all snowfalls for a flat fee of $40,000 for the entire winter season. The Weplowem Company charges $18,000 for each snowfall it clears. Set up the payoff table to help the manager decide, assuming that the number of snowfalls per winter season ranges from 0 to 4.

23.10 Refer to Exercise 23.9. Using subjective assessments, the manager has assigned the following probabilities to the number of snowfalls. Determine the optimal decision.

$$p(0) = .05 \qquad p(1) = .15 \qquad p(2) = .30$$
$$p(3) = .40 \qquad p(4) = .10$$

23.11 The owner of a clothing store must decide how many men's shirts to order for the new season. For a particular type of shirt, she must order in quantities of 100 shirts. If she orders 100 shirts, her cost is $10 per shirt; if she orders 200 shirts, her cost is $9 per shirt; and if she orders 300 or more shirts, her cost is $8.50 per shirt. Her selling price for the shirt is $12, but any shirts that remain unsold at the end of the season are sold at her famous "half-price, end-of-season sale." For the sake of simplicity, she is willing to assume that the demand for this type of shirt will be 100, 150, 200, or 250 shirts. Of course, she cannot sell more shirts than she stocks. She is also willing to assume that she will suffer no loss of goodwill among her customers if she understocks and the customers cannot buy all the shirts they want. Furthermore, she must place her order today for the entire season; she cannot wait to see how the demand is running for this type of shirt.
  a Construct the payoff table to help the owner decide how many shirts to order.
  b Set up the opportunity loss table.
  c Draw the decision tree.

23.12 Refer to Exercise 23.11. The owner has assigned the following probabilities.

$$P(\text{Demand} = 100) = .20, \qquad P(\text{Demand} = 150) = .25$$
$$P(\text{Demand} = 200) = .40, \qquad P(\text{Demand} = 250) = .15$$

Find the EMV decision.

23.13 A building contractor must decide how many mountain cabins to build in the ski resort area of Chick-oh-pee. He builds each cabin at a cost of $26,000 and sells each for $33,000. All cabins unsold after 10 months will be sold to a local investor for $20,000. The contractor believes that the demand for cabins follows a Poisson distribution, with a mean of .5. He assumes that any probability less than .01 can be treated as 0. Construct the payoff table and the opportunity loss table for this decision problem.

23.14 The electric company is in the process of building a new power plant. There is some uncertainty regarding the size of the plant to be built. If the community that the plant will service attracts a large number of industries, the demand for electricity will be high. If commercial establishments (offices and retail stores) are attracted, demand will be moderate. If neither industries nor commercial stores locate in the community, the electricity demand will be low. The company can build a small, medium, or large plant, but if the plant is too small, the company will incur extra costs. The total costs (in $millions) of all options are shown in the accompanying table.

| | Size of Plant | | |
Electricity Demand	Small	Medium	Large
Low	220	300	350
Moderate	330	320	350
High	440	390	350

The following probabilities are assigned to the electricity demand.

Demand	P(Demand)
Low	.15
Moderate	.55
High	.30

  a Determine the act with the largest expected monetary value. (*Caution:* All the values in the table are costs.)
  b Draw up an opportunity loss table.
  c Calculate the expected opportunity loss for each decision, and determine the optimal decision.

23.15 A retailer buys bushels of mushrooms for $2 each and sells them for $5 each. The quality of the mushrooms begins to decline after the first day they are offered for sale; therefore, in order to sell the mushrooms for $5/bushel, he must sell them on the first day. Bushels not sold on the first day can be sold to a wholesaler who buys day-old mushrooms at the following rates:

Amount purchased (bushels)	1	2	3	4 or more
Price per bushel	$2.00	$1.75	$1.50	$1.25

A 90-day observation of past demand yields the following information.

Daily demand (bushels)	10	11	12	13
Number of days	9	18	36	27

a Set up a payoff table that could be used by the retailer to decide how many bushels to buy.

b Find the optimal number of bushels the retailer should buy in order to maximize profit.

23.16 An international manufacturer of electronic products is contemplating introducing a new type of compact disk player. After some analysis of the market, the president of the company concludes that, within 2 years, the new product will have a market share of 5%, 10%, or 15%. She assesses the probabilities of these events as .15, .45, and .40, respectively. The vice-president of finance informs her that, if the product captures only a 5% market share, the company will lose $28 million. A 10% market share will produce a $2 million profit, and a 15% market share will produce an $8 million profit. If the company decides not to begin production of the new compact disk player, there will be no profit or loss. Based on the expected value decision, what should the company do?

23.3 ACQUIRING, USING, AND EVALUATING ADDITIONAL INFORMATION

In this section we discuss methods of introducing and incorporating additional information into the decision process. Such information generally has value, but it also has attendant costs; that is, we can acquire useful information from consultants, surveys, or other experiments, but we usually must pay for this information. We can calculate the maximum price that a decision maker should be willing to pay for any information by determining the value of perfect information. We begin by calculating the **expected payoff with perfect information** (EPPI).

If we knew in advance which state of nature would occur, we would certainly make our decisions accordingly. For instance, if the investor in Example 23.1 knew before investing his money what interest rates would do, he would choose the best act to suit that case. Referring to Table 23.1, if he knew that s_1 was going to occur, he would choose act a_3; if s_2 were certain to occur, he'd choose a_1; and if s_3 were certain, he'd choose a_2. Thus, in the long run, his expected payoff from perfect information would be

$$\text{EPPI} = .2(150,000) + .5(100,000) + .3(180,000) = \$134,000$$

Notice that we compute EPPI by multiplying the probability of each state of nature by the largest payoff associated with that state of nature and then summing the products.

This figure, however, does not represent the maximum amount he'd be willing to pay for perfect information. Because the investor could make an expected profit of EMV* = $100,000 without perfect information, we subtract EMV* from EPPI to determine the **expected value of perfect information** (EVPI). That is,

$$\text{EVPI} = \text{EPPI} - \text{EMV}^* = \$134,000 - \$100,000 = \$34,000$$

This means that, if perfect information were available, the investor should be willing to pay up to $34,000 to acquire it.

You may have noticed that the expected value of perfect information (EVPI) equals the smallest expected opportunity loss (EOL*). Again, this is not a coincidence—it will always be the case. In future questions, if the opportunity loss table has been determined, you need only calculate EOL* in order to know EVPI.

DECISION MAKING WITH ADDITIONAL INFORMATION

Suppose the investor in our continuing example wants to improve his decision-making capabilities. He learns about Investment Management Consultants (IMC), who, for a fee of $5,000, will analyze the economic conditions and forecast the behavior of interest rates over the next 12 months. The investor, who is quite shrewd (after all, he does have $1 million to invest), asks for some measure of IMC's past successes. IMC has been forecasting interest rates for many years and so provides him with various conditional probabilities (referred to as **likelihood probabilities**), as shown in Table 23.3. Table 23.3 uses the following notation:

I_1:   IMC predicts that interest rates will increase.

I_2:   IMC predicts that interest rates will stay the same.

I_3:   IMC predicts that interest rates will decrease.

Table 23.3 Likelihood Probabilities $P(I_i|s_j)$

	I_1 (predicts s_1)	I_2 (predicts s_2)	I_3 (predicts s_3)
s_1	$P(I_1|s_1) = .60$	$P(I_2|s_1) = .30$	$P(I_3|s_1) = .10$
s_2	$P(I_1|s_2) = .10$	$P(I_2|s_2) = .80$	$P(I_3|s_2) = .10$
s_3	$P(I_1|s_3) = .10$	$P(I_2|s_3) = .20$	$P(I_3|s_3) = .70$

The I_i terms are referred to as **experimental outcomes**, and the process by which we gather additional information is called the **experiment**.

Examine the first line of Table 23.3. When s_1 actually did occur in the past, IMC correctly predicted s_1 60% of the time; 30% of the time, it predicted s_2; and 10% of the time, it predicted s_3. The second row gives the conditional probabilities of I_1, I_2, and I_3 when s_2 actually occurred. The third row shows the conditional probabilities of I_1, I_2, and I_3 when s_3 actually occurred.

The following question now arises: How is the investor going to use the forecast that IMC produces? One approach is simply to assume that whatever it forecasts will actually take place and to choose the act accordingly. There are several drawbacks to this approach. Foremost among them is that it puts the investor in the position of ignoring whatever knowledge (in the form of subjective probabilities) he had concerning the issue. The optimal way to use the forecast is to incorporate the investor's subjective probabilities with the consultant's forecast. The medium for doing this is Bayes' law, which we introduced in Section 6.5. We'll review Bayes' law in the context of our example.

Suppose that the investor pays IMC the $5,000 fee and IMC forecasts that s_1 will occur. We want to determine the probabilities of the states of nature, given that I_1 is the outcome of the experiment. That is, what are $P(s_1|I_1)$, $P(s_2|I_1)$, and $P(s_3|I_1)$? Before proceeding, let's review some terminology.

Recall from Section 6.5 that the original probabilities, $P(s_1)$, $P(s_2)$, and $P(s_3)$, are called **prior probabilities**, because they were determined prior to the acquisition of any additional information. In this example, they were based on the investor's experience. The set of probabilities we want to compute—$P(s_1|I_1)$, $P(s_2|I_1)$, and $P(s_3|I_1)$—are called **posterior** or **revised probabilities**.

Now we will calculate the posterior probabilities, first by using a probability tree and then by applying a less time-consuming method. Figure 23.3 on page 792 depicts the probability tree. We begin with the branches of the prior probabilities, which are followed by the likelihood probabilities.

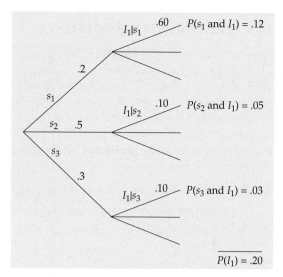

Figure 23.3
Probability tree to compute posterior probabilities

Notice that we label only $P(I_1|s_1)$, $P(I_1|s_2)$, and $P(I_1|s_3)$ because (at this point) we are assuming that I_1 is the experimental outcome. Now recall that conditional probability is defined as

$$P(A|B) = \frac{P(A \text{ and } B)}{P(B)}$$

At the ends of each branch we have the joint probability $P(s_j \text{ and } I_1)$. By summing the joint probabilities $P(s_j \text{ and } I_1)$ for $j = 1$, 2, and 3, we calculate $P(I_1)$. Finally,

$$P(s_j|I_1) = \frac{P(s_j \text{ and } I_1)}{P(I_1)}$$

Table 23.4 performs exactly the same calculations as the probability tree except without the tree.

Table 23.4 Posterior Probabilities for I_1

s_j	$P(s_j)$	$P(I_1|s_j)$	$P(s_j \text{ and } I_1)$	$P(s_j|I_1)$
s_1	.2	.60	(.2)(.60) = .12	.12/.20 = .60
s_2	.5	.10	(.5)(.10) = .05	.05/.20 = .25
s_3	.3	.10	(.3)(.10) = .03	.03/.20 = .15
			$P(I_1)$ = .20	

After the probabilities have been revised, we can use them in exactly the same way we used the prior probabilities. That is, we can calculate the expected monetary value of each act:

$$\text{EMV}(a_1) = .60(100,000) + .25(100,000) + .15(100,000) = \$100,000$$

$$\text{EMV}(a_2) = .60(-50,000) + .25(80,000) + .15(180,000) = \$17,000$$

$$\text{EMV}(a_3) = .60(150,000) + .25(90,000) + .15(40,000) = \$118,500$$

Thus, if IMC forecasts s_1, the optimal act is a_3, and the expected monetary value of the decision is $118,500.

As a further illustration, we now repeat the process for I_2 and I_3 in Tables 23.5 and 23.6, respectively.

Table 23.5 Posterior Probabilities for I_2

s_j	$P(s_j)$	$P(I_2\|s_j)$	$P(s_j \text{ and } I_2)$	$P(s_j\|I_2)$
s_1	.2	.30	(.2)(.30) = .06	.06/.52 = .115
s_2	.5	.80	(.5)(.80) = .40	.40/.52 = .770
s_3	.3	.20	(.3)(.20) = .06	.06/.52 = .115
			$P(I_2) = .52$	

Applying the posterior probabilities for I_2 from Table 23.5 to the payoff table, we find the following:

$$\text{EMV}(a_1) = .115(100,000) + .770(100,000) + .115(100,000) = \$100,000$$

$$\text{EMV}(a_2) = .115(-50,000) + .770(80,000) + .115(180,000) = \$76,550$$

$$\text{EMV}(a_3) = .115(150,000) + .770(90,000) + .115(40,000) = \$91,150$$

As you can see, if IMC predicts that s_2 will occur, the optimal act is a_1, with an expected monetary value of $100,000.

Table 23.6 Posterior Probabilities for I_3

s_j	$P(s_j)$	$P(I_3\|s_j)$	$P(s_j \text{ and } I_3)$	$P(s_j\|I_3)$
s_1	.2	.10	(.2)(.10) = .02	.02/.28 = .071
s_2	.5	.10	(.5)(.10) = .05	.05/.28 = .179
s_3	.3	.70	(.3)(.70) = .21	.21/.28 = .750
			$P(I_3) = .28$	

With the set of posterior probabilities for I_3 from Table 23.6, the expected monetary values are as follows:

$$\text{EMV}(a_1) = .071(100,000) + .179(100,000) + .750(100,000) = \$100,000$$

$$\text{EMV}(a_2) = .071(-50,000) + .179(80,000) + .750(180,000) = \$145,770$$

$$\text{EMV}(a_3) = .071(150,000) + .179(90,000) + .750(40,000) = \$56,760$$

If IMC predicts that s_3 will occur, the optimal act is a_2, with an expected monetary value of $145,770.

At this point, we know the following:

If IMC predicts s_1, then the optimal act is a_3.

If IMC predicts s_2, then the optimal act is a_1.

If IMC predicts s_3, then the optimal act is a_2.

Thus, even before IMC makes its forecast, the investor knows which act is optimal for each of the three possible IMC forecasts. Of course, all these calculations can be performed before paying IMC its $5,000 fee. This leads to an extremely important calculation. By performing the computations just described, the investor can determine *whether* he should hire IMC. That is, he can determine whether the value of IMC's forecast exceeds the cost of its information. Such a determination is called a **preposterior analysis**.

PREPOSTERIOR ANALYSIS

The objective of a preposterior analysis is to determine whether the value of the prediction is greater or less than the cost of the information. *Posterior* refers to the revision of the probabilities, and the *pre* indicates that this calculation is performed before paying the fee.

We begin by finding the expected monetary value of using the additional information. This value is denoted EMV′, which for our example is determined on the basis of the following analysis:

If IMC predicts s_1, then the optimal act is a_3, and the expected payoff is $118,500.

If IMC predicts s_2, then the optimal act is a_1, and the expected payoff is $100,000.

If IMC predicts s_3, then the optimal act is a_2, and the expected payoff is $145,770.

A useful by-product of calculating the posterior probabilities is the set of probabilities of I_1, I_2, and I_3:

$$P(I_1) = .20, \quad P(I_2) = .52, \quad P(I_3) = .28$$

(Notice that these probabilities sum to 1.) Now imagine that the investor seeks the advice of IMC an infinite number of times. (This is the basis for the expected value decision.) The set of probabilities of I_1, I_2, and I_3 indicates the following outcome distribution: 20% of the time, IMC will predict s_1 and the expected monetary value will be $118,500; 52% of the time, IMC will predict s_2 and the expected monetary value will be $100,000; and 28% of the time, IMC will predict s_3 and the expected monetary value will be $145,770.

The expected monetary value with additional information is the weighted average of the expected monetary values, where the weights are $P(I_1)$, $P(I_2)$, and $P(I_3)$. Hence,

$$\text{EMV}' = .20(118,500) + .52(100,000) + .28(145,770) = \$116,516$$

The value of IMC's forecast is the difference between the expected monetary value with additional information (EMV′) and the expected monetary value without additional information (EMV*). This difference is called the **expected value of sample information** and is denoted EVSI. Thus,

$$\text{EVSI} = \text{EMV}' - \text{EMV}^* = \$116,516 - \$100,000 = \$16,516$$

By using IMC's forecast, the investor can make an average additional profit of $16,516, in the long run. Because the cost of the forecast is only $5,000, the investor is advised to hire IMC.

If you review this problem, you'll see that the investor had to make two decisions. The first (chronologically) was whether to hire IMC, and the second was which type of investment to make. A decision tree is quite helpful in describing the acts and states of nature in this question. Figure 23.4 provides the complete tree diagram.

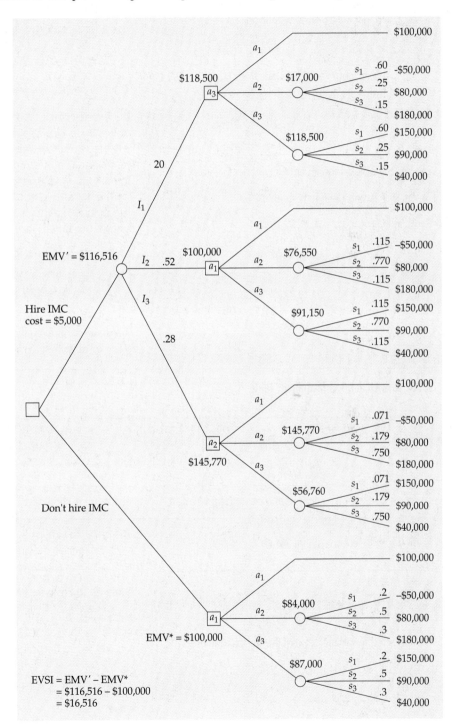

Figure 23.4
Complete decision tree for Example 23.1

ACCEPTANCE SAMPLING: SOLUTION

a. The two alternatives are

a_1:   No inspection (the current policy)

a_2:   100% inspection

The two states of nature are

s_1:   The lot contains 15% defectives.

s_2:   The lot contains 35% defectives.

Based on the past year's historical record,

$$P(s_1) = .60 \quad \text{and} \quad P(s_2) = .40$$

The payoff table is constructed as shown in Table 23.7.

Table 23.7 Payoff table for Example 23.2

a_1	
s_1	$5(1,000) - .15(1,000)(10) = \$3,500$
s_2	$5(1,000) - .35(1,000)(10) = \$1,500$

a_2	
s_1	$5(1,000) - [(1,000)(2) + .15(1,000)(.50)] = \$2,925$
s_2	$5(1,000) - [(1,000)(2) + .35(1,000)(.50)] = \$2,825$

The expected monetary values are

$$EMV(a_1) = .60(3,500) + .40(1,500) = \$2,700$$

$$EMV(a_2) = .60(2,925) + .40(2,825) = \$2,885$$

The optimal act is a_2 with EMV* = $2,885.

b. The cost of the proposed sampling is $4. (The cost of inspecting a single unit is $2.) In order to determine whether we should sample, we need to calculate the expected value of sample information. That is, we need to perform a preposterior analysis.

The first step of the preposterior analysis is to calculate the likelihood probabilities. There are three possible sample outcomes:

I_0:   No defectives in the sample

I_1:   One defective in the sample

I_2:   Two defectives in the sample

Because the sampling process is a binomial experiment, the likelihood probabilities are calculated by using the binomial probability distribution, as summarized in Table 23.8.

Table 23.8 Likelihood probability table

	$P(I_0|s_j)$	$P(I_1|s_j)$	$P(I_2|s_j)$
$s_1 \ (p = .15)$	$P(I_0|s_1) = (.85)^2$ $= .7225$	$P(I_1|s_1) = 2(.15)(.85)$ $= .2550$	$P(I_2|s_1) = (.15)^2$ $= .0225$
$s_2 \ (p = .35)$	$P(I_0|s_2) = (.65)^2$ $= .4225$	$P(I_1|s_2) = 2(.35)(.65)$ $= .4550$	$P(I_2|s_2) = (.35)^2$ $= .1225$

If I_0 is the sample outcome, the posterior probabilities are calculated as shown in Table 23.9.

Table 23.9 Posterior probabilities for I_0

s_j	$P(s_j)$	$P(I_0|s_j)$	$P(s_j \text{ and } I_0)$	$P(s_j|I_0)$
s_1	.60	.7225	(.60)(.7225) = .4335	.4335/.6025 = .720
s_2	.40	.4225	(.40)(.4225) = .1690	.1690/.6025 = .280
			$P(I_0) = .6025$	

The expected monetary values if the sample outcome is I_0

$$EMV(a_1) = .720(3,500) + .280(1,500) = \$2,940$$

$$EMV(a_2) = .720(2,925) + .280(2,825) = \$2,897$$

Therefore, the optimal act is a_1.

If I_1 is the sample outcome, the posterior probabilities are calculated as shown in Table 23.10.

Table 23.10 Posterior probabilities for I_1

s_j	$P(s_j)$	$P(I_1|s_j)$	$P(s_j \text{ and } I_1)$	$P(s_j|I_1)$
s_1	.60	.2550	(.60)(.2550) = .1530	.1530/.3350 = .457
s_2	.40	.4550	(.40)(.4550) = .1820	.1820/.3350 = .543
			$P(I_1) = .3350$	

The expected monetary values if the sample outcome is I_1 are

ACCEPTANCE SAMPLING: SOLUTION

$EMV(a_1) = .457(3,500) + .543(1,500) = \$2,414$

$EMV(a_2) = .457(2,925) + .543(2,825) = \$2,871$

Therefore, the optimal act is a_2.

If I_2 is the sample outcome, the posterior probabilities are calculated as shown in Table 23.11.

Table 23.11 Posterior probabilities for I_2

s_j	$P(s_j)$	$P(I_2\|s_j)$	$P(s_j$ and $I_2)$	$P(s_j\|I_2)$
s_1	.60	.0225	(.60)(.0225) = .0135	.0135/.0625 = .216
s_2	.40	.1225	(.40)(.1225) = .0490	.0490/.0625 = .784
			$P(I_2) = .0625$	

The expected monetary values if the sample outcome is I_2 are

$EMV(a_1) = .216(3,500) + .784(1,500) = \$1,932$

$EMV(a_2) = .457(2,925) + .543(2,825) = \$2,847$

Therefore, the optimal act is a_2.

We can now summarize these results, as shown in Table 23.12.

Table 23.12 Summary of optimal acts

Sample Outcome	Probability	Optimal Act	Expected Monetary Value
I_0	.6025	a_1	$2,940
I_1	.3350	a_2	$2,871
I_2	.0625	a_2	$2,847

The expected monetary value with additional information is

$EMV' = .6025(2,940) + .3350(2,871)$
$\qquad\qquad + .0625(2,847) = \$2,911$

The expected value of sample information is

$EVSI = EMV' - EMV* = 2,911 - 2,885 = \$26$

Because the expected value of sample information is $26 and the sampling cost is $4, the company should take a sample of 2 units before deciding whether to inspect 100%. The optimal sequence is as follows:

1. Take a sample of 2 units.
2. If neither sample unit is defective, continue the current policy of no inspection. If either one or both of the sample units are defective, perform a complete inspection of the lot.

BAYESIAN STATISTICS

In Chapters 10–20 we dealt with inference about unknown parameters. In Chapter 10 we pointed out that when interpreting the confidence interval estimate, we cannot make probability statements about parameters because they are not variables. However, Bayesian statistics specifies that parameters are variables and we can assume various probability distributions. The acceptance sampling example illustrates this concept. The parameter was the proportion p of defective units in the 1,000-unit batch. The example was unrealistic because we allowed the parameter to assume one of only two values, 15% and 35%. We assigned prior probabilities using the relative frequency approach. That is, based on historical records we had

$$P(p = 15\%) = .60 \quad \text{and} \quad P(p = 35\%) = .40$$

To make the problem more realistic, we let p be a continuous random variable rather than a discrete one. That is, p can take on any value between 0 and 100%. We assign a density function also based on historical records. We can express the payoffs as a linear function of p. Then, using calculus, we can determine the optimum decision. We can also revise the prior probabilities based on the outcome of the sampling of 2 units. The technique requires some calculus but the concept is the same as the one developed in this chapter. It should be noted that there is a parallel universe of Bayesian statistics that more or less matches the material in the inference part of this book. Interested readers can learn more about Bayesian statistics from the references at the end of this chapter or from additional courses dedicated to the subject.

EXERCISES

23.17 Find EPPI, EMV*, and EVPI for the accompanying payoff table and probabilities.

	a_1	a_2	a_3
s_1	60	110	75
s_2	40	110	150
s_3	220	120	85
s_4	250	120	130

$P(s_1) = .10, \quad P(s_2) = .25,$
$P(s_3) = .50, \quad P(s_4) = .15$

23.18 For Exercise 23.17, determine the opportunity loss table and compute EOL*. Confirm that EOL* = EVPI.

23.19 Given the following payoff table and probabilities, determine EVPI.

	a_1	a_2	a_3	a_4
s_1	65	20	45	30
s_2	70	110	80	95

$P(s_1) = .5, \quad P(s_2) = .5$

23.20 Redo Exercise 23.19, changing the probabilities to the following values.

a $P(s_1) = .75, \quad P(s_2) = .25$
b $P(s_1) = .95, \quad P(s_2) = .05$

23.21 What conclusion can you draw about the effect of the probabilities on EVPI from Exercises 23.19 and 23.20?

23.22 Determine the posterior probabilities, given the following prior and likelihood probabilities.

Prior Probabilities:

$P(s_1) = .25, \quad P(s_2) = .40, \quad P(s_3) = .35$

Likelihood Probabilities

	I_1	I_2	I_3	I_4
s_1	.40	.30	.20	.10
s_2	.25	.25	.25	.25
s_3	0	.30	.40	.30

23.23 Calculate the posterior probabilities from the prior and likelihood probabilities that follow.

Prior Probabilities:

$P(s_1) = .5, \quad P(s_2) = .5$

Likelihood Probabilities

	I_1	I_2
s_1	.98	.02
s_2	.05	.95

23.24 With the accompanying payoff table and the prior and posterior probabilities computed in Exercise 23.23, calculate the following.
a The optimal act for each experimental outcome
b The expected value of sample information

Payoff Table

	a_1	a_2	a_3
s_1	10	18	23
s_2	22	19	15

23.25 Given the following payoff table, prior probabilities, and likelihood probabilities, find the expected value of sample information.

Payoff Table

	a_1	a_2
s_1	60	90
s_2	90	90
s_3	150	90

Prior Probabilities:

$$P(s_1) = \frac{1}{3}, \quad P(s_2) = \frac{1}{3}, \quad P(s_3) = \frac{1}{3}$$

Likelihood Probabilities

	I_1	I_2
s_1	.7	.3
s_2	.5	.5
s_3	.2	.8

23.26 Repeat Exercise 23.25 with the following prior probabilities:

$P(s_1) = .5, \quad P(s_2) = .4, \quad P(s_3) = .1$

23.27 Repeat Exercise 23.25 with the following prior probabilities.

$P(s_1) = .90, \quad P(s_2) = .05, \quad P(s_3) = .05$

23.28 What conclusions can you draw about the effect of the prior probabilities on EVSI from Exercises 23.25 through 23.27?

Applications

23.29 A sporting-goods storeowner has the opportunity to purchase a lot of 50,000 footballs for $100,000. She believes that she can sell some or all by taking out mail-order advertisements in a magazine. Each football will be sold for $6.00. The advertising cost is $25,000, and the mailing cost per football is $1.00. She believes that the demand distribution is as follows.

Demand	P(Demand)
10,000	.2
30,000	.5
50,000	.3

What is the maximum price the owner should pay for additional information about demand?

23.30 What is the maximum price the electronics product manufacturer should be willing to pay for perfect information regarding the market share in Exercise 23.16?

23.31 In order to improve her decision-making capability, the electronics products manufacturer in Exercise 23.16 performs a survey of potential buyers of compact disk players. She describes the product to 25 individuals, 3 of whom say they would buy it. Using this additional information together with the prior probabilities, determine whether the new product should be produced.

23.32 A radio station currently directing its programming toward middle-age listeners is contemplating switching to rock-and-roll music. After analyzing advertising revenues and operating costs, the owner concludes that, for each percentage point of market share, revenues increase by $100,000 per year. Fixed annual operating costs are $700,000. The owner believes that, with the change, the station will get a 5%, 10%, or 20% market share, with probabilities .4, .4, and .2, respectively. The current annual profit is $285,000.
  a Set up the payoff table.
  b Determine the optimal act.
  c What is the most the owner should be willing to pay to acquire additional information about the market share?

23.33 There is a garbage crisis in North America—too much garbage and no place to put it. As a consequence, the idea of recycling has become quite popular. A waste-management company in a large city is willing to begin recycling newspapers, aluminum cans, and plastic containers. However, it is profitable to do so only if a sufficiently large proportion of households is willing to participate. In this city, 1 million households are potential recyclers. After some analysis it was determined that, for every 1,000 households that participate in the program, the contribution to profit is $500. It was also discovered that fixed costs are

$55,000 per year. It is believed that 50,000, 100,000, 200,000, or 300,000 households will participate, with probabilities .5, .3, .1, and .1, respectively. A preliminary survey was performed wherein 25 households were asked whether they would be willing to be part of this recycling program. Suppose only 3 of the 25 respond affirmatively; incorporate this information into the decision-making process to decide whether the waste-management company should proceed with the recycling venture.

23.34 Repeat Exercise 23.33, given that 12 out of 100 households respond affirmatively.

23.35 Suppose that in Exercise 23.14 a consultant offers to analyze the problem and predict the amount of electricity required by the new community. In order to induce the electric company to hire her, the consultant provides the set of likelihood probabilities given below. Perform a preposterior analysis to determine the expected value of the consultant's sample information.

	I_1 (predict low demand)	I_2 (predict moderate demand)	I_3 (predict high demand)
s_1	.5	.3	.2
s_2	.3	.6	.1
s_3	.2	.2	.6

23.36 In Exercise 23.32, suppose that it is possible to survey radio listeners to determine whether they would tune in to the station if the format changed to rock and roll. What would a survey of size 2 be worth?

23.37 Suppose that in Exercise 23.32 a random sample of 25 radio listeners revealed that 2 people would be regular listeners of the station. What is the optimal decision now?

23.38 The president of an automobile battery company must decide which one of three new types of batteries to produce. The fixed and variable costs of each battery are shown in the accompanying table.

Battery	Fixed Cost	Variable Cost (per unit)
1	$900,000	$20
2	1,150,000	17
3	1,400,000	15

The president believes that demand will be 50,000, 100,000, or 150,000 batteries, with probabilities .3, .3, and .4, respectively. The selling price of the battery will be $40.
  a Determine the payoff table.
  b Determine the opportunity loss table.
  c Find the expected monetary value for each act, and select the optimal one.
  d What is the most the president should be willing to pay for additional information about demand?

23.39 Credibility is often the most effective feature of an advertising campaign. Suppose that, for a particular advertisement, 32% of people surveyed currently believe what the ad claims. A marketing manager believes that for each 1-point increase in that percentage, annual sales will increase by $1 million. For each 1-point decrease, annual sales will decrease by $1 million. The manager believes that a change in the advertising approach can influence the ad's credibility. The probability distribution of the potential percentage changes is listed next.

Percentage Change	Probability
−2	.1
−1	.1
0	.2
+1	.3
+2	.3

If for each dollar of sales the profit contribution is 10 cents and the overall cost of changing the ad is $58,000, should the ad be changed?

23.40 Suppose that in Exercise 23.39 it is possible to perform a survey to determine the percentage of people who believe the ad. What would a sample of size 1 be worth?

23.41 Suppose that in Exercise 23.39 a sample of size 5 showed that only one person believes the new ad. In light of this additional information, what should the manager do?

23.42 Max the Bookie is trying to decide how many telephones to install in his new bookmaking operation. Because of heavy police activity, he cannot increase or decrease the number of telephones once he sets up his operation. He has narrowed the possible choices to three. He can install 25, 50, or 100 telephones. His profit for 1 year (the usual length of time he can remain in business before the police close him down) depends on the average number of calls he receives. The number of calls is Poisson distributed. After some deliberation, he concludes that the average number of calls per minute can be .5, 1.0, or 1.5, with probabilities of .50, .25, and .25, respectively. Max then produces the payoffs given in the accompanying table.

Max's assistant, Lefty (who attended a business school for 2 years), points out that Max may be able to get more information by observing a competitor's similar operation. However, he will be able to watch for only 10 minutes, and doing so will cost him $4,000. Max determines that if he counts fewer than 8 calls, that would be a low number; at least 8 but fewer than 17 would be a medium number; and at least 17 would be a large number of calls. Max also decides that, if the experiment is run, he will record only whether there is a small, medium, or large number of calls. Help Max by performing a preposterior analysis to determine whether the sample should be taken. Conclude by specifying clearly what the optimal strategy is.

Payoff Table

	25 telephones	50 telephones	100 telephones
$s_1 (\mu = .5)$	$50,000	$30,000	$20,000
$s_2 (\mu = 1.0)$	50,000	60,000	40,000
$s_3 (\mu = 1.5)$	50,000	60,000	80,000

23.43 The Megabuck Computer Company is thinking of introducing two new products. The first, Model 101, is a small computer designed specifically for children between the ages of 8 and 16. The second, Model 202, is a medium-size computer suitable for managers. Because of limited production capacity, Megabuck has decided to produce only one of the products.

The profitability of each model depends on the proportion of the potential market that would actually buy the computer. For Model 101, the size of the market is estimated at 10 million, whereas for Model 202, the estimate is 3 million.

After careful analysis, the management of Megabuck has concluded that the percentage of buyers of Model 101 is 5%, 10%, or 15%. The respective profits are given below.

Percentage who Buy Model 101	Net Profits ($millions)
5%	20
10	100
15	210

An expert in probability from the local university estimated the probability of the percentages as $P(5\%) = .2$, $P(10\%) = .4$, and $P(15\%) = .4$.

A similar analysis for Model 202 produced the following table.

Percentage who Buy Model 202	Net Profits ($millions)
30%	70
40	100
50	150

For this model, the expert estimated the probabilities as $P(30\%) = .1$, $P(40\%) = .4$, and $P(50\%) = .5$.

a Based on this information, and with the objective of maximizing expected profit, which model should Megabuck produce?

b In order to make a better decision, Megabuck sampled 10 potential buyers of Model 101 and 20 potential buyers of Model 202. Only 1 of the 10 wished to purchase the Model 101, whereas 9 of the 20 indicated that they would buy Model 202. Given this information, revise the prior probabilities and determine which model should be produced.

23.44 A major movie studio has just completed its latest epic, a musical comedy about the life of Attila the Hun. Because the movie is different (no sex or violence), the studio is uncertain about how to distribute it.

The studio executives must decide whether to release the movie to North American audiences or to sell it to a European distributor and realize a profit of $12 million. If the movie is shown in North America, the studio profit depends on its level of success, which can be classified as excellent, good, or fair. The payoffs and the prior subjective probabilities of the success levels are shown in the accompanying table.

Success Level	Payoff	Probability
Excellent	$33 million	.5
Good	12 million	.3
Fair	−15 million	.2

Another possibility is to have the movie shown to a random sample of North Americans and use their collective judgment to help the studio make a decision. These judgments are categorized as "rave review," "lukewarm response," or "poor response." The cost of the sample is $100,000. The sampling process has been used several times in the past. The likelihood probabilities describing the audience judgments and the movie's success level are shown next. Perform a preposterior analysis to determine what the studio executives should do.

Success Level	Judgment		
	Rave review	Lukewarm response	Poor response
Excellent	.8	.1	.1
Good	.5	.3	.2
Fair	.4	.3	.3

23.4 SUMMARY

The objective of **decision analysis** is to select the optimal act from a list of alternative acts. We define as optimal the act with the largest **expected monetary value** or smallest **expected opportunity loss**. The expected values are calculated after assigning prior probabilities to the states of nature. The acts, states of nature, and their consequences may be presented in a **payoff table**, an **opportunity loss table**, or a **decision tree**. We also discussed a method by which additional information in the form of an experiment can be incorporated in the analysis. This method involves combining **prior** and **likelihood probabilities** to produce **posterior probabilities**. The **preposterior analysis** allows us to decide whether to pay for and acquire the experimental outcome. That decision is based on the **expected value of sample information** and on the sampling cost.

IMPORTANT TERMS

Alternative acts 784
States of nature 784
Payoff table 785
Opportunity loss table 785
Decision tree 785
Expected monetary value 787
Expected opportunity loss 787

Rollback technique 785
Expected payoff with perfect information 790
Expected value of perfect information 790
Likelihood probabilities 791

Experimental outcomes 791
Prior probabilities 791
Posterior probabilities 791
Preposterior analysis 794
Expected value of sample information 794

SYMBOLS

Symbol	Represents
a_i	Acts
s_j	States of nature
I_i	Experimental outcomes
$P(s_j)$	Prior probability
$P(I_i \mid s_j)$	Likelihood probability
$P(s_j \text{ and } I_i)$	Joint probability
$P(s_j \mid I_i)$	Posterior probability

FORMULAS

Expected Value of Perfect Information

$$EVPI = EPPI - EMV*$$

Expected Value of Sample Information

$$EVSI = EMV' - EMV*$$

REFERENCES

Clemen, Robert, *Making Hard Decisions: An Introduction to Decision Analysis,* 2nd edition. Belmont, CA: Duxbury, 1996.

Hammond, John S., Ralph Kenney, and Howard Raiffa, *Smart Choices: A Practical Guide to Making Better Decisions.* Cambridge, MA: Harvard Business School, 1999.

Howard, Ronald, "Heathens, Heretics, and Cults: The Religious Spectrum of Decision Aiding," *Interfaces* 22, No. 6, 1992, 15–27.

Kirkwood, Craig, "An Overview of Methods for Applied Decision Analysis," *Interfaces* 22, No. 6, 1992, 28–39.

Raiffa, Howard, *Decision Analysis: Introductory Lectures on Choices under Uncertainty.* Reading, MA: Addison Wesley, 1968.

Von Neumann, John, and Oskar Morgenstern, *Theory of Games and Economic Behavior.* Princeton, NJ: Princeton University Press, 1944.

Winkler, R. L., *Introduction to Bayesian Inference and Decision.* New York: Holt, Reinhart and Winston, 1972.

24 STATISTICAL INFERENCE: CONCLUSION

24.1 INTRODUCTION

You now have been introduced to about 35 statistical techniques. If you are like most students, you probably understand statistical inference and are capable of interpreting computer output. However, at this point you may not be confident that you can apply statistical techniques in real life. The main problem is that it is difficult to ascertain which statistical procedure to apply. In this chapter, we attempt to calm your fears. We begin by displaying the flowchart that allows statistics practitioners to determine the appropriate technique to apply. As we did in Chapter 14, we provide a guide detailing the test statistics, confidence interval estimators, and required conditions. The flowchart is augmented by an Excel macro that performs the same function. It is described below.

The guide and flowchart apply to the procedures presented in Chapters 12–20. We have omitted time-series analysis and forecasting (Chapter 21), statistical process control (Chapter 22), and decision analysis (Chapter 23) because identifying the appropriate technique is generally not difficult and they represent a different kind of inference.

Use the flowchart and guide to determine how each of the exercises and cases is to be addressed. Because these exercises and cases were drawn from a wide variety of applications and collectively require the use of all the techniques introduced in this book, they provide the same kind of challenge faced by real statistics practitioners. By attempting to solve these problems, you will be getting a realistic exposure to statistical applications. Incidentally, this also provides practice in the approach required to succeed in a statistics course examination.

24.2 IDENTIFYING THE CORRECT TECHNIQUE: SUMMARY OF STATISTICAL INFERENCE

List of Statistical Inference Techniques Introduced in Chapters 12–20

t test and estimator of μ

Chi-squared test and estimator of σ^2

z test and estimator of p

t test and estimator of $\mu_1 - \mu_2$ (equal-variances formulas)

t test and estimator of $\mu_1 - \mu_2$ (unequal-variances formulas)

t test and estimator of μ_D

F test and estimator of σ_1^2/σ_2^2

z test (Cases 1 and 2) and estimator of $p_1 - p_2$

One-way analysis of variance

Two-way (randomized blocks) analysis of variance

Two-factor analysis of variance

LSD multiple comparison method

Tukey's multiple comparison method

Chi-squared goodness-of-fit test

Chi-squared test of a contingency table

Wilcoxon rank sum test

Sign test

Wilcoxon signed rank sum test

Kruskal–Wallis test

Friedman test

Simple linear regression and correlation

Spearman rank correlation

Multiple regression

The following techniques were introduced in Chapters 21 and 22. These techniques are used in analyzing and forecasting time series and production processes.

Time-series analysis and forecasting

> Moving averages

> Exponential smoothing

> Trend analysis

> Measuring seasonal effects

Statistical process control

> Control charts for variables

> Control charts for attributes

Figure 24.1 depicts the flowchart used to identify which technique to employ to solve any problem where we must draw an inference about a population from a sample.

We have also created an Excel add-in that asks the questions that appear in the flowchart. When you supply the answers, Excel identifies the technique. Simply click **Tools, Data Analysis Plus,** and **Technique Identification** and follow instructions.

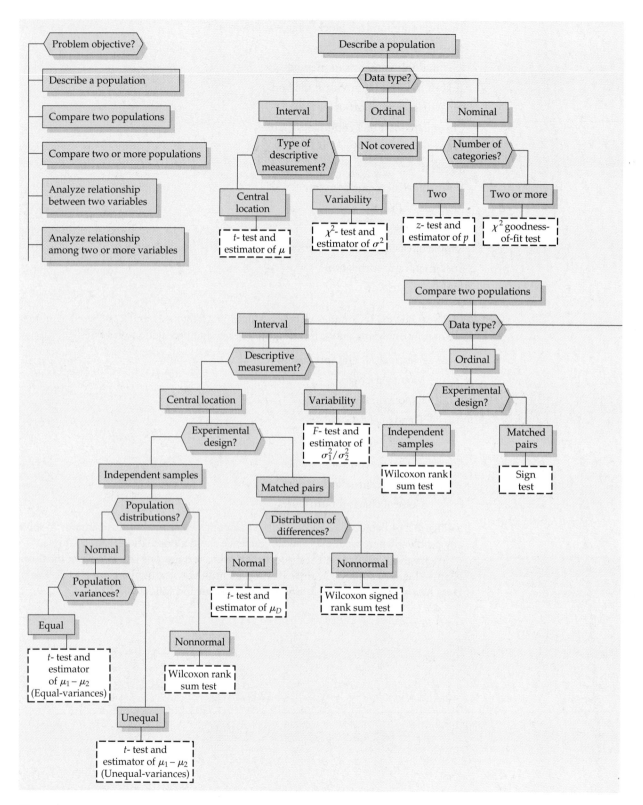

Figure 24.1
Flowchart of techniques:
Statistical inference

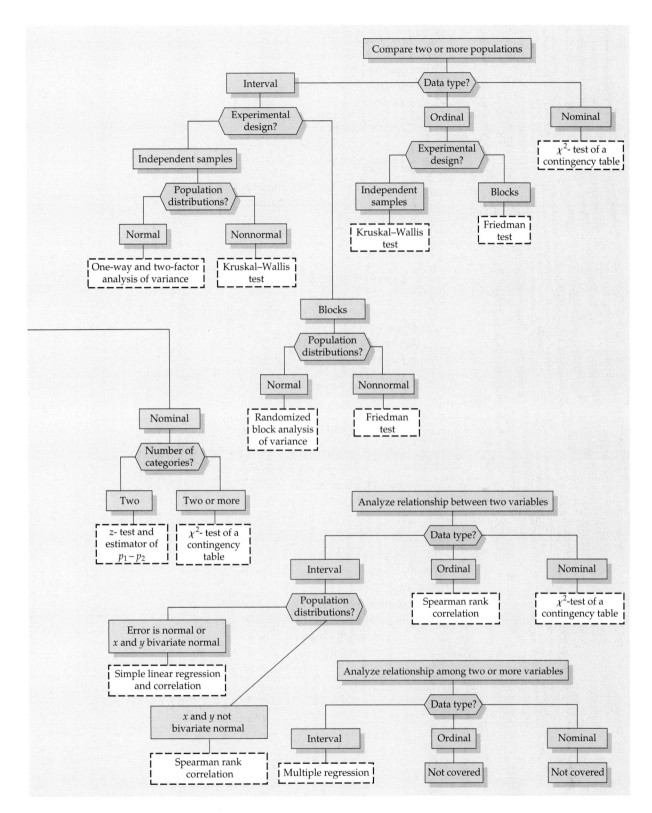

Figure 24.1
Flowchart of techniques
(continued)

Table 24.1 Summary of Statistical Inference Techniques: Chapters 12–20

Problem objective: Describe a population.

   Data type: Interval

      Descriptive measurement: Central location

         Parameter: μ

         Test statistic: $t = \dfrac{\bar{x} - \mu}{s/\sqrt{n}}$

         Interval estimator: $\bar{x} \pm t_{\alpha/2}\dfrac{s}{\sqrt{n}}$

         Required condition: Population is normal.

      Descriptive measurement: Variability

         Parameter: σ^2

         Test statistic: $\chi^2 = \dfrac{(n-1)s^2}{\sigma^2}$

         Interval estimator: $\text{LCL} = \dfrac{(n-1)s^2}{\chi^2_{\alpha/2}} \qquad \text{UCL} = \dfrac{(n-1)s^2}{\chi^2_{1-\alpha/2}}$

         Required condition: Population is normal.

   Data type: Nominal

      Number of categories: Two

         Parameter: p

         Test statistic: $z = \dfrac{\hat{p} - p}{\sqrt{p(1-p)/n}}$

         Interval estimator: $\hat{p} \pm z_{\alpha/2}\sqrt{\dfrac{\hat{p}(1-\hat{p})}{n}}$

         Required condition: $np \geq 5$ and $n(1-p) \geq 5$ (for test)

                                 $n\hat{p} \geq 5$ and $n(1-\hat{p}) \geq 5$ (for estimate)

      Number of categories: Two or more

         Parameters: $p_1, p_2, \ldots, p_k$

         Test statistic: $\chi^2 = \displaystyle\sum_{i=1}^{k} \dfrac{(f_i - e_i)^2}{e_i}$

         Required condition: $e_i \geq 5$

Problem objective: Compare two populations.

   Data type: Interval

      Descriptive measurement: Central location

         Experimental design: Independent samples

             Population variances: $\sigma_1^2 = \sigma_2^2$

             Parameter: $\mu_1 - \mu_2$

             Test statistic: $t = \dfrac{(\bar{x}_1 - \bar{x}_2) - (\mu_1 - \mu_2)}{\sqrt{s_p^2\left(\dfrac{1}{n_1} + \dfrac{1}{n_2}\right)}}$

             Interval estimator: $(\bar{x}_1 - \bar{x}_2) \pm t_{\alpha/2}\sqrt{s_p^2\left(\dfrac{1}{n_1} + \dfrac{1}{n_2}\right)}$

             Required condition: Populations are normal.

             If populations are nonnormal, apply Wilcoxon rank sum test.

            Population variances: $\sigma_1^2 \neq \sigma_2^2$

             Parameter: $\mu_1 - \mu_2$

Test statistic: $t = \dfrac{(\bar{x}_1 - \bar{x}_2) - (\mu_1 - \mu_2)}{\sqrt{\dfrac{s_1^2}{n_1} + \dfrac{s_2^2}{n_2}}}$

$$\nu = \frac{(s_1^2/n_1 + s_2^2/n_2)^2}{\left(\dfrac{(s_1^2/n_1)^2}{n_1 - 1} + \dfrac{(s_2^2/n_2)^2}{n_2 - 1}\right)}$$

Interval estimator: $(\bar{x}_1 - \bar{x}_2) \pm t_{\alpha/2}\sqrt{\dfrac{s_1^2}{n_1} + \dfrac{s_2^2}{n_2}}$

Required condition: Populations are normal.

Experimental design: Matched pairs

Parameter: μ_D

Test statistic: $t = \dfrac{\bar{x}_D - \mu_D}{s_D/\sqrt{n_D}}$

Interval estimator: $\bar{x}_D \pm t_{\alpha/2}\dfrac{s_D}{\sqrt{n_D}}$

Required condition: Differences are normal.

If differences are nonnormal, apply Wilcoxon signed rank sum test.

Nonparametric technique: Wilcoxon signed rank sum test.

Test statistic: $z = \dfrac{T - E(T)}{\sigma_T}$

Required condition: Populations are identical in shape and spread.

Descriptive measurement: Variability

Parameter: σ_1^2/σ_2^2

Test statistic: $F = s_1^2/s_2^2$

Interval estimator: $LCL = \left(\dfrac{s_1^2}{s_2^2}\right)\dfrac{1}{F_{\alpha/2,\nu_1,\nu_2}}$ $UCL = \left(\dfrac{s_1^2}{s_2^2}\right)F_{\alpha/2,\nu_2,\nu_1}$

Required condition: Populations are normal.

Data type: Ordinal

Experimental design: Independent samples

Nonparametric technique: Wilcoxon rank sum test.

Test statistic: $z = \dfrac{T - E(T)}{\sigma_T}$

Required condition: Populations are identical in shape and spread.

Experimental design: Matched pairs

Nonparametric technique: Sign test

Test statistic: $z = \dfrac{x - .5n}{.5\sqrt{n}}$

Required condition: Populations are identical in shaped and spread.

Data type: Nominal

Number of categories: Two

Parameter: $p_1 - p_2$

Test statistic:

Case 1: $H_0: (p_1 - p_2) = 0$

$$z = \frac{(\hat{p}_1 - \hat{p}_2)}{\sqrt{\hat{p}(1 - \hat{p})\left(\dfrac{1}{n_1} + \dfrac{1}{n_2}\right)}}$$

Case 2: H_0: $(p_1 - p_2) = D$ $\qquad (D \neq 0)$

$$z = \frac{(\hat{p}_1 - \hat{p}_2) - (p_1 - p_2)}{\sqrt{\dfrac{\hat{p}_1(1 - \hat{p}_1)}{n_1} + \dfrac{\hat{p}_2(1 - \hat{p}_2)}{n_2}}}$$

Interval estimator: $(\hat{p}_1 - \hat{p}_2) \pm z_{\alpha/2}\sqrt{\dfrac{\hat{p}_1(1 - \hat{p}_1)}{n_1} + \dfrac{\hat{p}_2(1 - \hat{p}_2)}{n_2}}$

Required conditions: $n_1\hat{p}_1$, $n_1(1 - \hat{p}_1)$, $n_2\hat{p}_2$, and $n_2(1 - \hat{p}_2) \geq 5$

Number of categories: Two or more

Statistical technique: Chi-squared test of a contingency table

Test statistic: $\chi^2 = \sum\limits_{i=1}^{k} \dfrac{(f_i - e_i)^2}{e_i}$

Required condition: $e_i \geq 5$

Problem objective: Compare two or more populations.

Data type: Interval

Experimental design: Independent samples (1 and 2 factors)

Parameters: $\mu_1, \mu_2, \ldots, \mu_k$

Test statistic: $F = \dfrac{MST}{MSE}$

Required conditions: Populations are normal with equal variances. If populations are nonnormal, apply Kruskal–Wallis test.

Experimental design: Randomized blocks

Parameters: $\mu_1, \mu_2, \ldots, \mu_k$

Test statistic: $F = \dfrac{MST}{MSE}$

Required conditions: Populations are normal with equal variances. If populations are nonnormal, apply Friedman test.

Data type: Ordinal

Experimental design: Independent samples

Nonparametric technique: Kruskal–Wallis test

Test statistic: $H = \left[\dfrac{12}{n(n + 1)}\sum\limits_{i=1}^{k} \dfrac{T_j^2}{n_j}\right] - 3(n + 1)$

Required condition: Populations are identical in shape and spread and $n_j \geq 5$.

Experimental design: Randomized blocks

Nonparametric technique: Friedman test

Test statistic: $F_r = \left[\dfrac{12}{b(k)(k + 1)}\sum\limits_{j=1}^{k} T_j^2\right] - 3b(k + 1)$

Required condition: Populations are identical in shape and spread and b or $k \geq 5$.

Data type: Nominal

Statistical technique: Chi-squared test of a contingency table

Test statistic: $\chi^2 = \sum\limits_{i=1}^{k} \dfrac{(f_i - e_i)^2}{e_i}$

Required condition: $e_i \geq 5$

Problem objective: Analyze the relationship between two variables.

Data type: Interval

Parameters: β_0, β_1 (simple linear regression), ρ

Test statistic: $t = \dfrac{b_1 - \beta_1}{s_{b_1}}$

Interval estimator: $\hat{y} \pm t_{\alpha/2}s_\varepsilon\sqrt{\dfrac{1}{n} + \dfrac{(x_g - \bar{x})^2}{(n - 1)s_x^2}}$

Prediction interval: $\hat{y} \pm t_{\alpha/2}s_\varepsilon\sqrt{1 + \dfrac{1}{n} + \dfrac{(x_g - \bar{x})^2}{(n - 1)s_x^2}}$

Required conditions: ε is normally distributed with mean 0 and standard deviation σ_ε; ε values are independent.

To test whether two bivariate normally distributed variables are linearly related:

Parameter: ρ

Test statistic: $t = r\sqrt{\dfrac{n-2}{1-r^2}}$

If x and y are not bivariate normally distributed, apply Spearman rank correlation coefficient test.

Data type: Ordinal

Statistical technique: Spearman rank correlation coefficient test

Parameter: ρ_s

Test statistic: $z = r_s \sqrt{n-1}$

Required condition: none

Data type: Nominal

Statistical technique: Chi-squared test of a contingency table

Test statistic: $\chi^2 = \displaystyle\sum_{i=1}^{k} \dfrac{(f_i - e_i)^2}{e_i}$

Required condition: $e_i \geq 5$

Problem objective: Analyze the relationship among two or more variables.

Data type: Interval

$\beta_0, \beta_1, \beta_2, \ldots, \beta_k$ (multiple regression)

Test statistic: $t = \dfrac{b_i - \beta_i}{s_{b_i}}$ $(i = 1, 2, \ldots, k)$

$$F = \dfrac{MSR}{MSE}$$

Required conditions: ε is normally distributed with mean 0 and standard deviation σ_ε; ε values are independent.

We illustrate the use of the guide and flowchart with the following cases.

◈ CASE 24.1
DO BANKS DISCRIMINATE AGAINST WOMEN BUSINESS OWNERS?–I*

Increasingly, more women are becoming owners of small businesses. However, questions concerning how they are treated by banks and other financial institutions have been raised by women's groups. Banks are particularly important to small businesses, since studies show that bank financing represents about one quarter of total debt, and that for medium-size businesses the proportion rises to approximately one half. If women's requests for loans are rejected more frequently than are men's requests, or if women must pay higher interest charges than men do, women have cause for complaint. Banks might then be subject to criminal as well as civil suits. To examine this issue, a research project was launched.

The researchers surveyed a total of 1,165 business owners, of whom 115 were women. The percentage of women in the sample, 9.9%, compares favorably with

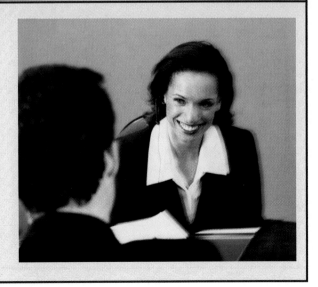

◈ CASE 24.1
DO BANKS DISCRIMINATE AGAINST WOMEN BUSINESS OWNERS?—I* *(continued)*

other sources that indicate that women own about 10% of established small businesses. The survey asked a series of questions to men and women business owners who applied for loans during the previous month. It also determined the nature of the business, its size, and its age. Additionally, the owners were asked about their experiences in dealing with banks. The questions asked in the survey included the following:

1. What is the gender of the owner?
   1 female   2 male
2. Was the loan approved?
   1 no   2 yes
3. If it was approved, what interest rate did you get? How much above the prime rate was your rate?

Of the 115 women who asked for a loan, 14 were turned down. A total of 98 men who asked for a loan were rejected. The rates above prime for all loans that were granted were recorded. These data are stored in file C24-01. What do these data disclose about possible gender bias by the banks?

SOLUTION

IDENTIFY

The problem objective is to compare two populations: small businesses owned by women and those owned by men. We can compare them in two ways: whether their loan applications are denied; and for loans granted, how much above prime they pay in interest. Whether the loans are approved is a nominal variable. There are two possible "values" of this variable: "approve the loan" and "don't approve the loan."

The appropriate technique is the z test of $p_1 - p_2$. To test whether gender bias exists, we test to determine whether the proportions of loans denied is greater for women (p_1) than for men (p_2).

$$H_0: \quad p_1 - p_2 = 0$$

$$H_1: \quad p_1 - p_2 > 0$$

This is an application of the Case 1 test procedure. Thus, the test statistic is

$$z = \frac{(\hat{p}_1 - \hat{p}_2)}{\sqrt{\hat{p}(1 - \hat{p})\left(\dfrac{1}{n_1} + \dfrac{1}{n_2}\right)}}$$

COMPUTE

Both Excel and Minitab can calculate this statistic from the numbers of loans denied and the sample sizes.

🖱 EXCEL

	A	B	C	D	E
1	z-Test of the Difference Between Two Proportions (Case 1)				
2					
3		Sample 1	Sample 2	z Stat	0.9810
4	Sample proportion	0.1217	0.0933	P(Z<=z) one-tail	0.1633
5	Sample size	115	1050	z Critical one-tail	1.6449
6	Alpha	0.05		P(Z<=z) two-tail	0.3266
7				z Critical two-tail	1.9600

🖱 MINITAB

Test and CI for Two Proportions

```
Sample     X      N   Sample p
1         14    115   0.121739
2         98   1050   0.093333

Estimate for p(1) - p(2):  0.0284058
95% lower bound for p(1) - p(2):  -0.0238768
Test for p(1) - p(2) = 0 (vs > 0):  Z = 0.98  P-Value = 0.163
```

INTERPRET

There is not enough evidence to infer that loan requests by women are denied more frequently than loan requests by men.

IDENTIFY

The interest rate is an interval variable, the descriptive measurement is central location, and the samples are independent. A preliminary analysis reveals that the amount above prime may be normally distributed. The histograms (not shown) are bell shaped. The F test of σ_1^2/σ_2^2 (shown below) indicates that there is not enough evidence to believe that the population variances are unequal. Putting all these factors together gives us the equal-variances t test of $\mu_1 - \mu_2$

COMPUTE

We compute the F test of the ratio of two variances to determine which of the two tests of the difference between two means to use.

---

*Adapted from A. L. Riding and C. S. Swift, "Giving Credit Where It's Due: Women Business Owners and Canadian Financial Institutions," Carleton University Working Paper Series WPS 89-07, 1989.

✦ CASE 24.1
DO BANKS DISCRIMINATE AGAINST WOMEN BUSINESS OWNERS?–I* *(continued)*

 EXCEL

	A	B	C
1	F-Test Two-Sample for Variances		
2			
3		W Rate	M Rate
4	Mean	1.545	1.278
5	Variance	0.405	0.446
6	Observations	101	952
7	df	100	951
8	F	0.91	
9	P(F<=f) one-tail	0.2784	
10	F Critical one-tail	0.7713	

The two-tail *p*-value is $2 \times .2784 = .5568$.

 MINITAB

```
F-Test (normal distribution)


Test Statistic: 0.910
P-Value       : 0.557
```

IDENTIFY

For loans granted, we need to know whether there is evidence that the mean interest paid by women (μ_1) is greater than the mean interest paid by men (μ_2).

$$H_0: \quad \mu_1 - \mu_2 = 0$$

$$H_1: \quad \mu_1 - \mu_2 > 0$$

The test statistic is

$$t = \frac{(\bar{x}_1 - \bar{x}_2) - (\mu_1 - \mu_2)}{\sqrt{s_p^2\left(\dfrac{1}{n_1} + \dfrac{1}{n_2}\right)}}$$

 EXCEL

	A	B	C
1	t-Test: Two-Sample Assuming Equal Variances		
2			
3		W Rate	M Rate
4	Mean	1.55	1.28
5	Variance	0.405	0.446
6	Observations	101	952
7	Pooled Variance	0.442	
8	Hypothesized Mean Difference	0	
9	df	1051	
10	t Stat	3.85	
11	P(T<=t) one-tail	0.0001	
12	t Critical one-tail	1.6463	
13	P(T<=t) two-tail	0.0001	
14	t Critical two-tail	1.9622	

 MINITAB

Two-Sample T-Test and CI: W Rate, M Rate

```
Two-sample T for W Rate vs M Rate

            N    Mean   StDev  SE Mean
W Rate    101   1.545   0.637    0.063
M Rate    952   1.278   0.668    0.022

Difference = mu W Rate - mu M Rate
Estimate for difference: 0.2678
95% lower bound for difference: 0.1533
T-Test of difference = 0 (vs >): T-Value = 3.85  P-Value = 0.000  DF = 1051
Both use Pooled StDev = 0.665
```

INTERPRET

There is overwhelming evidence to infer that the mean rate of women's loans is greater than that for men. From this result there appears to be evidence of gender bias by banks.

✦ CASE 24.2
DO BANKS DISCRIMINATE AGAINST WOMEN BUSINESS OWNERS?–II*

To help explain the apparent discrimination against women documented in Case 24.1, researchers performed further analyses. In the original study, the following pieces of information were gathered for each company.

1. Form of business:
   - a Proprietorship
   - b Partnership
   - c Corporation
2. Annual gross sales
3. Age of the firm

✦ CASE 24.2
DO BANKS DISCRIMINATE AGAINST WOMEN BUSINESS OWNERS?—II (continued)

These data, together with the data from Case 24.1, are stored in file C24-02 in the following way:

Column 1:   Rates above prime paid by women

Column 2:   Type of women's business (1 = proprietorship: 2 = partnership; 3 = corporation)

Column 3:   Annual gross sales of women's businesses (in thousands of dollars)

Column 4:   Age of women's businesses

Column 5:   Rates above prime paid by men

Column 6:   Type of men's business (1 = proprietorship; 2 = partnership: 3 = corporation)

Column 7:   Annual gross sales of men's businesses (in thousands of dollars)

Column 8:   Age of men's businesses

What do these data tell you about the alleged discrimination against women by banks?

SOLUTION

IDENTIFY

We are looking for additional reasons to account for the results obtained from Case 24.1. Specifically, we would like to know whether there is a relationship between annual gross sales and interest rates and between age of firm and interest rates. If there are such relationships, we need to know whether men's businesses are older and have higher gross sales. If so, the apparent gender bias shown in Case 24.1 may be explained by banks' legitimate desire to grant favorable terms to more established businesses with higher sales. We can use the data about the type of business to determine whether banks view certain types of businesses more favorably than others, and whether men's businesses tend to be of the types favored by banks. Before we can discuss the consequences of such findings, we need to conduct several tests. We will identify the technique to apply by asking specific questions:

1. Do banks grant lower interest rates to businesses with higher sales?

2. Do banks grant lower interest rates to older businesses?

For each question, we wish to analyze the relationship between two interval variables. An analysis (not shown) indicates that the normality requirement is met. Thus, the appropriate technique is simple linear regression and correlation. Because we want to discover whether a relationship exists (and not the mathematical form of the relationship), we will calculate and test the coefficient of correlation. For each pair of variables, we want to know whether the relationship is negative. We test

$$H_0: \quad \rho = 0$$

$$H_1: \quad \rho < 0$$

The test statistic is

$$t = r\sqrt{\frac{n-2}{1-r^2}}$$

EXCEL

	A	B	C	D
1	Correlation			
2				
3	Rates and Sales			
4	Pearson Coefficient of Correlation			-0.27
5	t Stat			-9.09
6	df			1051
7	P(T<=t) one tail			0
8	t Critical one tail			1.6463
9	P(T<=t) two tail			0
10	t Critical two tail			1.9622

	A	B	C	D
1	Correlation			
2				
3	Rates and Ages			
4	Pearson Coefficient of Correlation			-0.1915
5	t Stat			-6.32
6	df			1051
7	P(T<=t) one tail			0
8	t Critical one tail			1.6463
9	P(T<=t) two tail			0
10	t Critical two tail			1.9622

MINITAB
Correlations: Rates, Sales

```
Pearson correlation of Rates and Sales = -0.270
P-Value = 0.000
```

Correlations: Rates, Ages

```
Pearson correlation of Rates and Ages = -0.191
P-Value = 0.000
```

✦ CASE 24.2
DO BANKS DISCRIMINATE AGAINST WOMEN BUSINESS OWNERS?—II (continued)

INTERPRET

There is overwhelming statistical evidence to infer that banks offer lower rates to businesses with higher sales and to older businesses.

This result presents two additional questions:

3. Do women's businesses have lower gross sales than men's businesses?

4. Are women's businesses younger than men's businesses?

IDENTIFY

The problem objective is to compare two populations of interval data. Using an analysis similar to that employed in Case 24.1, we discover that the appropriate technique for each question is the unequal variances t test of $\mu_1 - \mu_2$. For both questions, we test the following hypotheses [where μ_1 equals the mean (annual gross sales and age) of women's businesses and μ_2 equals the mean (annual gross sales and age) of men's businesses].

$$H_0: \quad \mu_1 - \mu_2 = 0$$

$$H_1: \quad \mu_1 - \mu_2 < 0$$

EXCEL

	A	B	C
1	t-Test: Two-Sample Assuming Unequal Variances		
2			
3		W Sales	M Sales
4	Mean	552	1183
5	Variance	60133	128618
6	Observations	101	952
7	Hypothesized Mean Difference	0	
8	df	150	
9	t Stat	-23.37	
10	P(T<=t) one-tail	0.0000	
11	t Critical one-tail	1.6551	
12	P(T<=t) two-tail	0.0000	
13	t Critical two-tail	1.9759	

	A	B	C
1	t-Test: Two-Sample Assuming Unequal Variances		
2			
3		W Age	M Age
4	Mean	9.24	12.58
5	Variance	15.98	27.05
6	Observations	101	952
7	Hypothesized Mean Difference	0	
8	df	139	
9	t Stat	-7.73	
10	P(T<=t) one-tail	0.0000	
11	t Critical one-tail	1.6559	
12	P(T<=t) two-tail	0.0000	
13	t Critical two-tail	1.9772	

MINITAB

Two-Sample T-Test and CI: W Sales, M Sales

```
Two-sample T for W Sales vs M Sales

             N    Mean   StDev  SE Mean
W Sales    101     552     245       24
M Sales    952    1183     359       12

Difference = mu W Sales - mu M Sales
Estimate for difference:  -631.6
95% upper bound for difference: -586.8
T-Test of difference = 0 (vs <): T-Value = -23.37  P-Value = 0.000  DF = 149
```

Two-Sample T-Test and CI: W Age, M Age

```
Two-sample T for W Age vs M Age

           N    Mean   StDev  SE Mean
W Age    101    9.24    4.00     0.40
M Age    952   12.58    5.20     0.17

Difference = mu W Age - mu M Age
Estimate for difference:  -3.341
95% upper bound for difference: -2.626
T-Test of difference = 0 (vs <): T-Value = -7.73  P-Value = 0.000  DF = 138
```

INTERPRET

There is very strong statistical evidence to infer that men own businesses that are older than women's and that men's businesses have larger gross sales than women's. This result is not surprising, since only in the last 25 years have women become involved in full-time work in large numbers. Until about 1975, ownership of businesses had been a male domain. Moreover, more established businesses tend to have higher gross sales.

There is one more factor that may explain the outcome of Case 24.1. It is the type of business.

5. Do the data allow us to infer that certain types of businesses have different rates of interest?

IDENTIFY

There are three populations of interval data to compare: interest rates for proprietorships, for partnerships, and for corporations. The appropriate technique is the one-way analysis of variance. (We can show that the required conditions are satisfied.)

$$H_0: \quad \mu_1 = \mu_2 = \mu_3$$

$$H_1: \quad \text{At least two means differ}$$

CASE 24.2
DO BANKS DISCRIMINATE AGAINST WOMEN BUSINESS OWNERS?—II (continued)

EXCEL

	A	B	C	D	E	F	G
1	Anova: Single Factor						
2							
3	SUMMARY						
4	Groups	Count	Sum	Average	Variance		
5	Bus 1	193	273.4	1.417	0.411		
6	Bus 2	86	104.2	1.211	0.467		
7	Bus 3	774	994.9	1.285	0.451		
8							
9							
10	ANOVA						
11	Source of Variation	SS	df	MS	F	P-value	F crit
12	Between Groups	3.455	2	1.728	3.88	0.0209	3.00
13	Within Groups	467.4	1050	0.445			
14							
15	Total	470.9	1052				

MINITAB

One-way ANOVA: Bus 1, Bus 2, Bus 3

```
Analysis of Variance
Source    DF        SS        MS       F       P
Factor     2     3.455     1.728    3.88   0.021
Error   1050   467.434     0.445
Total   1052   470.889

                           Individual 95% CIs For Mean
                           Based on Pooled StDev
Level     N     Mean     StDev  -+---------+---------+---------+-----
Bus 1   193   1.4166    0.6415                      (-------*-------)
Bus 2    86   1.2114    0.6830   (-----------*-----------)
Bus 3   774   1.2853    0.6717               (---*---)
                                -+---------+---------+---------+-----
Pooled StDev =   0.6672         1.08      1.20      1.32      1.44
```

INTERPRET

The statistical analysis reveals that there are differences in rates among the three types of businesses.

Finally, we need to know whether men and women own different types of businesses.

6. Is there a relationship between gender and business type?

IDENTIFY

The problem objective is to analyze the relationship between two nominal variables, gender and business type. The appropriate method is the chi-squared test of a contingency table.

H_0:   The two variables are independent.

H_1:   The two variables are dependent.

The test statistic is $\chi^2 = \sum_{i=1}^{k} \dfrac{(f_i - e_i)^2}{e_i}$

EXCEL

	A	B	C	D	E
1	**Contingency Table**				
2					
3		Business			
4	Gender		1	2	TOTAL
5		1	31	162	193
6		2	10	76	86
7		3	60	714	774
8		TOTAL	101	952	1053
9					
10					
11		chi-squared Stat			12.7504
12		df			2
13		p-value			0.0017
14		chi-squared Critical			5.9915

MINITAB

Tabulated Statistics: Business, Gender

```
Rows: Business      Columns: Gender

             1          2         All

  1         31        162         193
  2         10         76          86
  3         60        714         774
All        101        952        1053

Chi-Square = 12.750, DF = 2, P-Value = 0.002
```

INTERPRET

There is a relationship between gender and type of business. The proportion of women's businesses in this study is 9.9%. From the contingency table, you can see that the proportion of proprietorships owned by women is 31/193 = 16.06%. From the analysis of variance printout, we discover that, on average, proprietorships pay the highest interest rates. Apparently, women own businesses that banks view as riskier, resulting in higher rates of interest.

INTERPRETING THE RESULTS OF CASES 24.1 AND 24.2

Cases 24.1 and 24.2 present statistics practitioners with real challenges. The results of the cases are contradictory. One case presents evidence of bias and the other provides evidence to suggest that the apparent bias is actually attributable to other factors. Results such as these have led less-than-competent observers to state that one can prove anything with statistics. Although there are often several different interpretations of data based on different analyses, we can perform further analyses to arrive at the truth. Consider how we can resolve the apparent contradictions in Cases 24.1 and 24.2. It is necessary to consider carefully which data and techniques we should use. You will encounter our answer in Case 24.9.

24.3 THE LAST WORD

We have come to the end of the journey that began with the words, "Statistics is a way to get information from data." You will shortly write the final examination in your statistics course. (We assume that readers of this book are taking a statistics course and not just reading it for fun.) If you believe that this event will be the point where you and statistics part company, you could not be more wrong. In the world into which you are about to graduate, the potential applications of statistical techniques are virtually limitless. However, if you are unable or unwilling to employ statistics, you cannot consider yourself to be competent. Can you imagine a marketing manager who does not fully understand marketing concepts and techniques? Can an accountant who knows little about accounting principles do his or her job? Similarly, you cannot be a competent decision maker without a comprehension of statistical concepts and techniques.

In our experience, we have come across far too many people who display an astonishing ignorance of probability and statistics. In some cases, this is displayed in the way they gamble. (Talk to people in a casino in Las Vegas or Atlantic City and discover how many understand probability; see how many of them lose money.) We have seen managers who regularly make decisions involving millions of dollars who don't understand the fundamental principles that should govern the way decisions are made. The worst may be the managers who have access to vast amounts of information no further away than the nearest computer but don't know how to get it or even that it is there.

This raises the question, "What statistical concepts and techniques will you need for your life after the final exam?" We don't expect students to remember the formulas (or computer commands) that calculate the confidence interval estimates or test statistics. (Statistics reference books are available for that purpose.) However, you must know what you can and cannot do with statistical techniques. You must remember a number of important principles that were covered in this book. To assist you, we have selected the 12 most important concepts and listed them. They are drawn from the "Developing an Understanding of Statistical Concepts" subsections that are scattered throughout the book. We hope that they prove useful to you.

TWELVE STATISTICAL CONCEPTS YOU NEED FOR LIFE AFTER THE STATISTICS FINAL EXAM

1. Statistical techniques are processes that convert data into information. Descriptive techniques describe and summarize; inferential techniques allow us to make estimates and draw conclusions about populations from samples.

2. We need a large number of techniques because there are numerous objectives and types of data. There are three types of data: interval (real numbers), nominal (categories), and ordinal (ratings). Each combination of data type and objective requires specific techniques.

3. We gather data by various sampling plans. However, the validity of any statistical outcome is dependent on the validity of the sampling. "Garbage in–garbage out" very much applies in statistics.

4. The sampling distribution is the source of statistical inference. The confidence interval estimator and the test statistic are derived directly from the sampling distribution. All inferences are actually probability statements based on the sampling distribution.

5. All tests of hypotheses are conducted similarly. We assume that the null hypothesis is true. We then compute the value of the test statistic. If the difference between what we have observed (and calculated) and what we expect to observe is too large, we reject the null hypothesis. The standard that decides what is "too large" is determined by the probability of a Type I error.

6. In any test of hypothesis (and in most decisions) there are two possible errors, Type I and Type II errors. The relationship between the probabilities of these errors helps us decide where to set the standard. If we set the standard so high that the probability of a Type I error is very small, we increase the probability of a Type II error. A procedure designed to decrease the probability of a Type II error must have a relatively large probability of a Type I error.

7. We can improve the exactitude of a confidence interval estimator or decrease the probability of a Type II error by increasing the sample size. More data means more information, which results in narrower intervals or lower probabilities of making mistakes, which produces better decisions.

8. The sampling distributions that are used for interval data are the Student t and the F. These distributions are related so that the various techniques for interval data are themselves related. We can use the analysis of variance in place of the t test of two means. We can use regression analysis with indicator variables in place of the analysis of variance. We often build a model to represent relationships among interval variables, including indicator variables.

9. In analyzing interval data, we attempt to explain as much of the variation as possible. By doing so, we can learn a great deal about whether populations differ and what variables affect the response (dependent) variable.

10. The techniques used on nominal data require that we count the number of times each category occurs. The counts are then used to compute statistics. The sampling distributions we use for nominal data are the standard normal and the chi-squared. These distributions are related, as are the techniques.

11. The techniques used on ordinal data are based on a ranking procedure. We call these techniques nonparametric. Because the requirements for the use of nonparametric techniques are less stringent than those for a parametric procedure, we often use nonparametric techniques in place of parametric ones when the required conditions for the parametric test are not satisfied. To ensure the validity of a statistical technique, we must check the required conditions.

12. We can obtain data through experimentation or by observation. Observational data lend themselves to several conflicting interpretations. Data gathered by an experiment are more likely to lead to a definitive interpretation. In addition to

designing experiments, statistics practitioners can also select particular sample sizes to produce the accuracy and confidence they desire.

We believe that these concepts will serve you well in reading and understanding reports that use statistics. They will also allow you to exploit fully the sets of data that you will encounter in your professional life and apply the appropriate statistical technique that converts the data into information. In so doing, you will be a better decision maker.

EXERCISES

Most of the following exercises require the use of a computer and statistical software. All students should at least attempt to identify the techniques required to answer the questions. Students with the necessary resources should produce the answers and check the required conditions. **Use a 5% significance level.**

24.1 Mutual funds minimize risks by diversifying the investments they make. There are mutual funds that specialize in particular types of investments. For example, the TD Precious Metal Mutual Fund buys shares in gold mining companies. The value of this mutual fund depends on a number of factors related to the companies in which the fund invests as well as on the price of gold. To investigate the relationship between the value of the fund and the price of gold, an MBA student gathered the daily fund price and the daily price of gold for a 28-day period. These data are stored in file Xr24-01. Can we infer from these data that there is a positive linear relationship between the value of the fund and the price of gold? (The authors are grateful to Jim Wheat for writing this exercise.)

24.2 Scientists at the Genetics and IVF Institute, a private fertility center in Virginia, announced the development of a new technique that allows parents to choose the sex of their baby, before conception. A group of women who wanted their babies to be female were impregnated using the new technology. Of the 17 resulting babies, 15 were girls. Does this provide sufficient evidence to infer that the new technology does affect the sex of the baby?

24.3 The widespread use of salt on roads in Canada and the northern United States during the winter and acid precipitation throughout the year combine to cause rust on cars. Car manufacturers and other companies offer rust-proofing services to help purchasers preserve the value of their cars. A consumer protection agency decides to determine whether there are any differences between the rust protection provided by automobile manufacturers and that provided by two competing types of rust-proofing services. As an experiment, 60 identical new cars are selected. Of these, 20 are rust-proofed by the manufacturer.

Another 20 are rust-proofed using a method that applies a liquid to critical areas of the car. The liquid hardens, forming a (supposedly) lifetime bond with the metal. The last 20 are treated with oil and are retreated every 12 months. The cars are then driven under similar conditions in a Minnesota city. The number of months until the first rust appears is recorded and stored in file Xr24-03. Is there sufficient evidence to conclude that at least one rust-proofing method is different from the others?

24.4 In the door-to-door selling of vacuum cleaners, various factors influence sales. The Birk Vacuum Cleaner Company considers its sales pitch and overall package to be extremely important. As a result, it often thinks of new ways to sell its product. Because the company's management develops so many new sales pitches each year, there is a two-stage testing process. In stage 1, a new plan is tested with a relatively small sample. If there is sufficient evidence that the plan increases sales, a second, considerably larger, test is undertaken. In a stage 1 test to determine whether the inclusion of a "free" 10-year service contract increases sales, 100 sales representatives were selected at random from the company's list of several thousand. The monthly sales of these representatives were recorded for 1 month prior to use of the new sales pitch and for 1 month after its introduction. The results are stored in file Xr24-04. Should the company proceed to stage 2?

24.5 Do cell phones cause cancer? This is a multibillion-dollar question. There are currently dozens of lawsuits pending that claim cell phone use has caused cancer. To help shed light on the issue, several scientific research projects have been undertaken. One such project was conducted by Danish researchers. (*Source: Journal of the National Cancer Institute*, 2001) The 13-year study examined 420,000 Danish cell phone users. The scientists determined the percentage of Danes who would be expected to contract various forms of cancer. The percentages are shown on the next page. The actual number of cell phone users who developed each type of cancer is also exhibited.

Cancer	Expected Number	Actual Number
Brain and nervous system	143	135
Salivary glands	9	7
Leukemia	80	77
Pharynx	52	32
Esophagus	57	42
Eye	12	8
Thyroid	13	13

a Can we infer from these data that there is a relationship between cell phone use and cancer?

b Discuss the results, including whether the data are observational or experimental. Provide several interpretations of the statistics. In particular, indicate whether you can infer that cell phone use causes cancer?

24.6 A small but important part of a university library's budget is the amount collected in fines on overdue books. Last year, a library collected $75,652.75 in fine payments; however, the head librarian suspects that some employees are not bothering to collect the fines on overdue books. In an effort to learn more about the situation, she asked a sample of 400 students (out of a total student population of 50,000) how many books they had returned late to the library in the previous 12 months. They were also asked how many days overdue the books had been. The results indicated that the total number of days overdue ranged from 0 to 55 days. The number of days overdue was stored in file Xr24-06.

a Estimate with 95% confidence the average number of days overdue for all 50,000 students at the university.

b If the fine is 25 cents per day, estimate the amount that should be collected annually. Should the librarian conclude that not all the fines were collected?

24.7 The practice of therapeutic touch is used in hospitals all over the world and is taught in some medical and nursing schools. In this therapy, trained practitioners manipulate what they call the "human energy field." The manipulation is carried out without actually touching the patient's body. Practitioners claim that anyone can be trained to feel this energy field. Some researchers say that no reliable evidence exists showing that this technique actually heals patients. James Randi, a professional magician who is also known as a skeptic of some types of alternative medicine, has tried for years to test the practice of therapeutic touch. So far, only one practitioner has agreed to submit to his test, and she did no better than chance in detecting the energy field. Emily Rosa, an 11-year-old Colorado girl working on a science fair project, was more successful in recruiting trained therapists. For her experiment, Emily placed a screen between a practitioner's eyes and hands, and then held her own hand over one of the practitioner's hands. If the human energy field can be felt, then practitioners should be able to identify which of their hands Emily held hers over. Emily conducted 280 tests with the 21 subjects. The results of these tests are stored in file Xr24-07 where 2 = correct location and 1 = incorrect location. What can we infer about touch therapy from these data?

24.8 Alcohol abuse is a serious problem in this country. To examine whether age is a factor in determining who drinks alcohol, the Gallup organization polled 1,054 adults and asked each, "Do you ever use alcoholic beverages such as liquor, wine, or beer?" Respondents were also asked to report their age category. The data are stored in file Xr24-08. (Column 1 records age category: 1 = 18–29, 2 = 30–49, 3 = 50 and over; column 2 records whether the person uses alcohol: 2 = yes, 1 = no.) Can we infer that differences exist among the age categories with respect to alcohol use?

24.9 Despite the increase in the number of working women, it appears that women continue to perform most of the household functions such as cooking and cleaning. Two researchers from the University of Arizona undertook a study to examine how much housework teenagers are performing. The researchers were particularly interested in the differences between boys and girls and between the children of parents where the mother did not go out to work and where both parents worked outside the home. A random sample of teenagers was selected. Each teenager reported the number of hours of housework he or she performs in an average week (column 1), gender (column 2 where 1 = female and 2 = male), and whether the mother works inside or outside the home (column 3 where 1= inside and 2 = outside). The data are stored in file Xr24-09.

a Can we conclude that teenage girls do more housework than teenage boys?

b Can we infer that children whose mothers work outside the home do more housework than children whose mother works inside the home?

24.10 One of the ways in which advertisers measure the value of television commercials is by telephone surveys conducted shortly after commercials are aired. Respondents who watched a certain television station at a given time period during which the commercial appeared are asked whether they can recall the name of the product in the commercial. Suppose an advertiser wants to compare the recall proportions of two commercials. The first commercial is relatively inexpensive. A second commercial shown a week later is quite expensive to produce. The advertiser decides that the second commercial is viable only if its recall proportion is more than 15% higher than the recall proportion of the first commercial. Two surveys of 500 television viewers each were conducted after each commercial was aired. Each person was asked whether he or she remembered the product name. The results are stored in columns 1 (commercial 1) and 2 (commercial 2) (2 = remembered the product name, 1 = did not remember the product name) in file Xr24-10. Can we infer that the second commercial is viable?

24.11 A professor has noted that the exam results of students who write their exams at 1:00 appear to be better than the marks of students who write their exams at 4:00. He forms the belief that the difference is caused by energy levels that are affected by the timing of the most recent meal. In other words, eating a meal before the exam will produce higher grades. To test this belief, he randomly selects 100 students to write a test at 12:30. Half the class is provided lunch and the other half are deprived of lunch. The test scores are recorded in file Xr24-11. Do the data support the professor's belief?

24.12 Refer to Exercise 24.11. The professor would like to know whether the type of meal affects test scores. He randomly selects 200 students; 50 are fed a lunch of pizza, another 50 are fed tuna sandwiches, another 50 are fed hamburgers, and the remaining 50 are provided a salad for lunch. The test scores are stored in file Xr24-12. Do these data indicate that the type of meal affects test scores?

24.13 How consistent are professional athletes? Do they perform at about the same level year in and year out, or do they have great seasons interspersed with bad ones? To answer these questions for hockey players, an MBA student randomly selected 50 National Hockey League players who played in the 1992–1993 and 1993–1994 seasons. For each player, he recorded the average points per game and their plus/minus scores. (Plus/minus scores measure the number of goals their teams score minus the number of goals the opposing team scores while that player is on the ice.) These data are stored in file Xr24-13 in the following way.

Column 1: Player

Column 2: 1993–1994 points per game

Column 3: 1992–1993 points per game

Column 4: 1993–1994 plus/minus

Column 5: 1992–1993 plus/minus

Can we conclude from these data that players' performances differ from one year to the next in terms of points per game and their plus/minus ratio? (The authors are grateful to Gordon Barnett for writing this exercise.)

24.14 Professional athletes in North America are paid very well for their ability to play games that amateurs play for fun. To determine the factors that influence a team to pay a hockey player's salary, an MBA student randomly selected 50 hockey players who played in the 1992–1993 and 1993–1994 seasons. He recorded their salaries at the end of the 1993–1994 season as well as a number of performance measures in the previous two

seasons. The following data were recorded in file Xr24-14.

Columns 1 and 2:	Games played in 1992–1993 and 1993-1994
Columns 3 and 4:	Goals scored in 1992–1993 and 1993-1994
Columns 5 and 6:	Assists recorded in 1992–1993 and 1993-1994
Columns 7 and 8:	Plus/minus score in 1992–1993 and 1993-1994
Columns 9 and 10:	Penalty minutes served in 1992–1993 and 1993–1994
Column 11:	Salary in U.S. dollars

(Plus/minus is the number of goals scored by his team minus the number of goals scored by the opposing team while the player is on the ice.) Develop a model that analyzes the relationship between salary and the performance measures. Describe your findings. (The authors wish to thank Gordon Barnett for writing this exercise.)

24.15 Winter is the influenza season in North America. Each winter, thousands of elderly and sick people die from the flu and its attendant complications. Consequently, many elderly people receive flu shots in the fall. It has generally been accepted that young healthy North Americans need not receive flu shots because although many contract the disease, few die from it. However, there are economic consequences. Sick days cost both the employee and employer. A study published in the *New England Journal of Medicine* reported the results of an experiment to determine whether it is useful for young healthy people to take flu shots. A random sample of working adults was selected. Half received a flu shot in November; the other half received a placebo. The numbers of sick days over the next 6-month period were recorded in columns 1 (flu shot) and 2 (placebo). Columns 3 (flu shot) and 4 (placebo) contain the number of visits to the doctor. All the data are in file Xr24-15.

a Can we conclude that the number of sick days is less for those who take flu shots?

b Can we conclude that those who take flu shots visit their doctors less frequently?

24.16 Sales of a product may depend on its placement in a store. Cigarette manufacturers frequently offer discounts to retailers who display their products more prominently than competing brands. To examine this phenomenon more carefully, a cigarette manufacturer (with the assistance of a national chain of restaurants) planned the following experiment. In 20 restaurants, the manufacturer's brand was displayed behind the cashier's counter with all the other brands (this was called position 1). In another 20 restaurants, the brand was placed separately but close to the other brands (position 2). In a third group of 20 restaurants, the cigarettes were placed in a special display next to the cash register (position 3). The number of cartons sold during 1 week at each restaurant was recorded and stored in file Xr24-16. Is there sufficient evidence to infer that sales of cigarettes differ according to placement?

24.17 After a recent study, researchers reported on the effects of folic acid on the occurrence of spina bifida—a birth defect in which there is incomplete formation of the spine. A sample of 2,000 women who gave birth to children with spina bifida and who were planning another pregnancy was recruited. Before attempting to get pregnant again, half the sample was given regular doses of folic acid, and the other half was given a placebo. After 18 months, researchers recorded the result for each woman: 1 = birth to normal baby, 2 = birth to baby with spina bifida, 3 = not pregnant or no baby yet delivered. The data are stored in file Xr24-17. Can we infer that folic acid reduces the incidence of spina bifida in newborn babies?

24.18 The image of the U.S. Postal Service has suffered in recent years. One reason may be the perception that postal workers are rude in their dealings with the public. In an effort to improve its image, the Postal Service is contemplating the introduction of public relations seminars for all of its inside workers. Because of the substantial costs involved, the Postal Service decided to institute the seminars only if there is more than a 25% reduction in the number of written customer complaints about personnel who took the seminars. As a trial, the employees of 30 large postal centers attended the seminar. The monthly average number of complaints per center (for all centers) was 640 before the trial. The number of complaints in the 30 centers is stored in file Xr24-18. Can we conclude that the seminars should be instituted?

24.19 Discrimination in hiring has been illegal for a number of years. It is illegal to discriminate against any person on the basis of race, gender, or religion. It is also illegal to discriminate because of a person's handicap if it in no way prevents that person from performing that job. In recent years, the definition of "handicap" has widened. Several people have successfully sued companies because they were denied employment for no other reason than that the applicant was overweight. A study was conducted to examine attitudes toward overweight people. The experiment involved showing a number of subjects videotape of an applicant being interviewed for a job. Prior to the interview, the subject was given a description of the job. Following the interview, the subject was asked to score the applicant in terms of how well the applicant was suited for the job. The score was out of 100, where higher scores described greater suitability. (The scores are interval data.) The same procedure was repeated for each subject. However, the gender and weight (average and

overweight) of the applicant varied. The results are stored in file Xr24-19 using the following format:

Column 1:   Score for average-weight males
Column 2:   Score for overweight males
Column 3:   Score for average-weight females
Column 4:   Score for overweight females

a Can we infer that the scores of the four groups of applicants differ?

b Are the differences detected in part **a** due to weight, gender, or some interaction?

24.20 The Scholastic Aptitude Test (SAT), which is organized by the Educational Testing Service (ETS), is important to high school students seeking admission to colleges and universities throughout the United States. A number of companies offer courses to prepare students for the SAT. The Stanley H. Kaplan Educational Center claims that its students gain, on average, more than 110 points by taking its course. ETS, however, insists that preparatory courses can improve a score by no more than 40 points. (The minimum and maximum scores of the SAT are 400 and 1,600, respectively.) Suppose a random sample of 40 students wrote the exam, then took the Kaplan preparatory course, and then wrote the exam again. The results of both tests are stored in file Xr24-20.

a Do these data provide sufficient evidence to refute the ETS claim?

b Do these data provide sufficient evidence to refute Kaplan's claim?

24.21 It is generally believed that salespeople who are paid on a commission basis outperform salespeople who are paid a fixed salary. Some management consultants argue, however, that in certain industries the fixed-salary salesperson may sell more because the consumer will feel less sales pressure and respond to the salesperson less as an antagonist. In an experiment to study this, a random sample of 180 salespeople from a retail clothing chain was selected. Of these, 90 salespeople were paid a fixed salary, and the remaining 90 were paid a commission on each sale. The total dollar amount of 1 month's sales for each was recorded and stored in file Xr24-21. Can we conclude that the commission salesperson outperforms the fixed-salary salesperson?

24.22 Obesity among children in North America is said to be at near-epidemic proportions. Some experts blame television for the problem, citing the statistic that children watch on average about 26 hours per week. During this time, children are not engaged in any physical activity, which results in weight gains. However, the problem may be compounded by a reduction in metabolic rate. In an experiment to address this issue (the study results were published in the February 1993 issue of the medical journal *Pediatrics*), scientists from Memphis State University and the University of Tennessee at Memphis took a random sample of 223 children aged 8 to 12, of whom 41 were obese. Each child's metabolic rate (the amount of calories burned per hour) was measured while at rest and also measured while the child watched a television program ("The Wonder Years"). The differences between the two rates were recorded and are stored in file Xr24-22. (Column 1 contains the numbers representing the decrease in metabolic rate and column 2 codes the children: 1 = obese and 2 = nonobese.)

a Do these data allow us to conclude that there is a decrease in metabolism when children watch television?

b Can we conclude that the decrease in metabolism while watching television is greater among obese children?

24.23 The game of Scrabble is one of the oldest and most popular board games. It is played all over the world, and there is even an annual world championship competition. The game is played by forming words and placing them on the board to obtain the maximum number of points. It is generally believed that a large vocabulary is the only skill required to be successful. However, there is a strategic element to the game that suggests that mathematical skills are just as necessary. To determine which skills are most in demand, a statistician recruited a random sample of fourth-year university English and mathematics majors, and asked them to play the game. A total of 500 games were played by different pairs of English and mathematics majors. The scores in each game are stored in file Xr24-23. (The authors would like to thank Scott Bergen for his assistance in writing this exercise.)

a Can we conclude that mathematics majors win more frequently than do English majors?

b Do these data allow us to infer that the average score obtained by English majors is greater than that for mathematics majors?

c Why are the results of parts **a** and **b** not the same?

24.24 The cost of workplace injuries is high for the individual worker, the company, and for society. It is in everyone's interest to rehabilitate the injured worker as quickly as possible. A statistician working for an insurance company has investigated the problem. He believes that a major determinant in how quickly a worker returns to his or her job after sustaining an injury is the physical condition. To help determine whether he is on the right track, he organized an experiment. He took a random sample of male and female workers who were injured in the last year. He recorded their gender, their physical condition, and the number of working days until they returned to their job. These data are stored in file Xr24-24 in the following way. Columns 1 and 2 store the number of working days until return to work for men and

women, respectively. In each column the first 25 observations relate to those who are physically fit, the next 25 rows relate to individuals who are moderately fit, and the last 25 observations are for those who are in poor physical shape. Can we infer that the six groups differ? If differences exist, determine whether the differences are due to gender, physical fitness, or some combination of gender and physical fitness.

24.25 Some psychologists believe that there are at least three different personality types: Type A is the aggressive workaholic; type B is the relaxed underachiever; type C displays various characteristics of types A and B. The personnel manager of a large insurance company believes that, among life insurance salespersons, there are equal numbers of all three personality types and that their degree of satisfaction and sales ability are not influenced by personality type. In a survey of 150 randomly selected salespersons, he determined the type of personality, measured their job satisfaction on a 7-point scale (where 1 = very dissatisfied and 7 = very satisfied), and determined the total amount of life insurance sold by each during the previous year. The results are stored in file Xr24-25 using the following format:

Column 1: Personality type (A = 1; B = 2; C = 3)

Column 2: Job satisfaction

Column 3: Total amount of life insurance sold (in hundreds of thousands of dollars)

Test all three of the personnel manager's beliefs. That is, test to determine whether there is enough evidence to justify the following conclusions.

i The proportions of each personality type are different.

ii The job satisfaction measures for each personality type are different.

iii The life insurance sales for each personality type are different.

24.26 Simco Inc. is a manufacturer that purchased a new piece of equipment designed to reduce costs. After several months of operation, the results were quite unsatisfactory. The operations manager believes that the problem lies with the machine's operators, who were unable to master the required skills. It was decided to establish a training program to upgrade the skills of those workers with the greatest likelihood of success. To do so, the company needed to know which skills are most needed to run the machine. Experts identified six such skills. They are dexterity, attention to detail, teamwork skills, mathematical ability, problem-solving skills, and technical knowledge. To examine the issue, a random sample of workers was drawn. Workers were measured on each of the six skills through a series of paper-and-pencil tests and through supervisor ratings. Additionally, each worker received a score on the quality of his or her actual work on the machine. These data are stored in columns 1 through 7 of file Xr24-26. (Columns 1 to 6 are the scores on the skill tests, and column 7 stores the quality-of-work scores. All data are interval.) Identify the skills that affect the quality of work. (We are grateful to Scott Bergen for writing this exercise.)

24.27 The high cost of medical care makes it imperative that hospitals operate efficiently and effectively. As part of a larger study, patients leaving a hospital were surveyed. They were asked how satisfied they were with the treatment they received. The responses were recorded with a measure of the degree of severity of their illness (as determined by the admitting physician) and the length of stay. These data are recorded in file Xr24-27 in the following way:

Column 1:   Satisfaction level (1 = very unsatisfied; 2 = somewhat unsatisfied; 3 = neither satisfied nor dissatisfied; 4 = somewhat satisfied; 5 = very satisfied)

Column 2:   Severity of illness (1 = least severe and 10 = most severe)

Column 3:   Number of days in hospital

a Is the satisfaction level affected by the severity of illness?

b Is the satisfaction level higher for patients who stay for shorter periods of time?

24.28 Since germs have been discovered, parents have been telling their children to wash their hands. Common sense tells us that this should help minimize the spread of infectious diseases and lead to better health. A study reported in the *University of California at Berkeley Wellness Letter* (Volume 13, Issue 6, March 1997) may confirm the advice our parents gave us. A study in Michigan tracked a random sample of children, some of whom washed their hands four or more times during the school day. The number of sick days due to colds and flu and the number of sick days due to stomach illness were recorded for the past year and stored in file Xr24-28. Column 1 contains a code representing whether the child washed his or her hands four or more times per school day (1) or not (2). Column 2 stores the number of sick days due to cold and flu, and column 3 contains the number of sick days due to stomach illness.

a Do these data allow us to infer that a child who washed his or her hands four or more times during the school day will have fewer sick days due to cold and flu than other children?

b Repeat part **a** for sick days due to stomach illness.

24.29 The experiment to determine the effect of taking a preparatory course to improve SAT scores in Exercise 24.20 was criticized by other statisticians. They argued that the first test would provide a valuable learning experience that would produce a higher test score from the second exam even without the preparatory course. Consequently, another experiment was performed. Forty students wrote the SAT without taking any preparatory course. At the next scheduled exam (3 months later), these same students took the exam again (again with no preparatory course). The scores for both exams are stored in columns 1 (first test scores) and 2 (second test scores) in file Xr24-29. Can we infer that repeating the SAT produces higher exam scores even without the preparatory course?

24.30 In recent years, North Americans have experienced flooding in various parts of the continent. In an effort to develop flood-forecasting tools, scientists wanted to determine the relationship between river flows and precipitation and evaporation. In one study, scientists gathered annual data for the total discharge of water on the Grand River at Gait, Ontario. They also recorded precipitation (snow and rain) and a measure of potential evaporation (which is a function of temperature, humidity, and wind) for each year between 1914 and 1980 around Galt. These data are stored in columns 1 (potential evaporation), 2 (precipitation in millimeters), and 3 (river flow in cubic decimeters) in file Xr24-30. It is generally believed that flow and precipitation should be positively related, and flow and potential evaporation should be negatively related. Do the data confirm the scientists' beliefs? (This exercise was prepared by Lynette Snelgrove. The data are from *The Impact of Climate Change on the Water in the Grand River Basin, Ontario*, Department of Geography Publication Series No. 40, University of Waterloo.)

24.31 Betting on the results of National Football League games is a popular North American activity. In many states and provinces, it is legal to do so provided that wagers are made through the government-authorized betting organization. In the province of Ontario, Pro-Line serves that function. Bettors can choose any team on which to wager, and Pro-Line sets the odds, which determine the winning payoffs. It is also possible to bet that in any game a tie will be the result. (A tie is defined as a game in which the winning margin is 3 or fewer points. A win occurs when the winning margin is greater than 3.) To assist bettors, Pro-Line lists the favorite for each game and predicts the point spread between the two teams. To judge how well Pro-Line predicts outcomes, the Creative Statistics Company tracked the results of the 1993 season. It recorded whether a team was favored by 3 or fewer points (1); 3.5 to 7 points (2); 7.5 to 11 points (3); or 11.5 or more points (4). It also recorded whether the favored team won (1); lost (2); or tied (3). These data are recorded in columns 1 (Pro-Line's predictions) and 2 (game results) in file Xr24-31. Can we conclude that Pro-Line's forecasts are useful for bettors?

24.32 At the completion of repair work at one of a chain of automotive centers, customers are asked to fill out the following form.

Tell us what you think.

ARE YOU SATISFIED?   GOOD   FAIR   POOR

1 Quality of work performed   ☐   ☐   ☐

2 Fairness of price   ☐   ☐   ☐

3 Explanation of work guarantee   ☐   ☐   ☐

4 Checkout process   ☐   ☐   ☐

5 Will you return in the future?

Comments?

A random sample of 134 responses was drawn. The results were recorded in file Xr24-32. The responses to questions 1 through 4 (1 = poor; 2 = fair; 3 = good) are stored in columns 1 through 4, respectively. Responses to question 5 (2 = yes; 1 = no) are stored in column 5. Column 6 stores a 1 if a positive comment was made, 2 if a negative comment was made, and 3 if no comment was made.

Can we infer that those who say they will return assess each category higher than those who will not return?

24.33 Refer to Exercise 24.32. Is there sufficient evidence to infer that those who make positive comments, negative comments, and no comments differ in their assessment of each category?

24.34 Refer to Exercise 24.32. Suppose that 100 responses from each of three stores in the chain are recorded in file Xr24-34 using the following format:

Columns 1 to 6: Responses to questions 1 to 5 plus comments code

Column 7: Code representing stores 1, 2, and 3

Can we conclude that differences exist among the three stores?

24.35 Several years ago we heard about the "Mommy Track," the phenomenon of women being underpaid in the corporate world because of what is seen as their divided loyalties between home and office. There may also be a "Daddy Differential," which refers to the situation where men whose wives stay at home earn more than men whose wives work. It is argued that the differential occurs because bosses reward their male employees if they come from "traditional families." Linda Stroh of Loyola University of Chicago studied a random sample of 348 male managers employed by 20 *Fortune 500* companies. Each manager reported whether his wife stayed at home to care for their children or worked outside the home, and his annual income. The incomes (in thousands of dollars) are stored in file Xr24-35. The incomes of the managers whose wives stay at home are stored in column 1. Column 2 contains the incomes of managers whose wives work outside the home.

a Can we conclude that men whose wives stay at home earn more than men whose wives work outside the home?

b If your answer in part **a** is affirmative, does this establish a case for discrimination? Can you think of another cause-and-effect scenario? Explain.

24.36 A popular game of chance is craps, which uses two dice. The "shooter" rolls both dice, winning on the first roll if he throws a 7 or 11, and losing if he rolls 2, 3, or 12. If he rolls any other number, he continues to roll the dice until he repeats the number and wins, or throws a 7 and loses. Elementary rules of probability allow even students of probability and statistics to calculate the probability of winning and losing. These probabilities are based on the probability distribution of the total of two fair dice. They are as follows.

Total	2	3	4	5	6	7
Probability	1/36	2/36	3/36	4/36	5/36	6/36
Total	8	9	10	11	12	
Probability	5/36	4/36	3/36	2/36	1/36	

A professor of statistics suspects that the dice are not fairly balanced and records each of 1,000 throws. These data are stored in file Xr24-36.

a Do these data allow us to infer that the dice are not fair?

b Can we conclude that the dice are set up so that the probability of 7 is less than 6/36?

24.37 A programmer for a small software company has almost completed the company's newest network program. He just finished the user interface and was about to perform a routine backup. As a rule, a backup is performed once a day to guard against power, hardware, or software failure. Once the backup has started, the information is unavailable until the backup is completed. The amount of time that the program takes to complete the backup is critical. For systems that are in constant use, a portion of time must be set aside to perform the backup, during which work on that system ceases. The company has developed three different systems of backing up files that are basically equivalent in memory usage. However, because time is critical, the company wanted to determine whether differences existed in the amount of time taken for each to work. A programmer randomly selected 26 different programs and backed up each of them using the three backing systems. The amount of time taken for each was recorded (in minutes) and stored in Xr24-37. Can we infer that the backup times differ among the three systems? (The authors are grateful to James Pong and

Diana Mansour and the Ortech Company for their assistance in this exercise.)

24.38 There are enormous differences between healthcare systems in the United States and Canada. In a study to examine one dimension of these differences, 300 heart attack victims in each country were randomly selected. (Results of the study conducted by Dr. Daniel Mark of Duke University Medical Center, Dr. David Naylor of Sunnybrook Hospital in Toronto, and Dr. Paul Armstrong of the University of Alberta were published in the *Toronto Sun*, 27 October 1994.) Each patient was asked the following questions regarding the effect of his or her treatment:

1. How many days did it take you to return to work?

2. Do you still have chest pain? (This question was asked 1 month, 6 months, and 12 months after the patients' heart attacks.)

The responses are stored in file Xr24-38 in the following way:

Column 1:   Code representing nationality: 1 = U.S.; 2 = Canada

Column 2:   Responses to question 1

Column 3:   Responses to question 2—1 month after heart attack: 2 = yes; 1 = no

Column 4:   Responses to question 2—6 months after heart attack: 2 = yes; 1 = no

Column 5:   Responses to question 2—12 months after heart attack: 2 = yes; 1 = no

Can we conclude that recovery is faster in the United States?

24.39 As all baseball fans know, first base is the only base that the base runner may overrun. At second and third base, the runner may be tagged out if he runs past them. Consequently, on close plays at second and third base, the runner will slide, enabling him to stop at the base. In recent years, however, several players have chosen to slide headfirst when approaching first base, claiming that this is faster than simply running over the base. In an experiment to test this claim, the 25 players on one National League team were recruited. Each player ran to first base with and without sliding, and the times to reach the base were recorded. These data are stored in file Xr24-39. Can we conclude that sliding is slower than not sliding?

24.40 Du Pont is always looking for new ways to improve its products and reduce costs. Researchers in the Teflon coatings laboratory recently uncovered a compound that degrades into two potentially saleable products, which were labeled C and Y. The research team carried out several experiments to determine the factors that affect the production of C and Y. In particular, they examined how the temperature and flow rate deter-

mined the percentage yield of each component. The higher the temperature and flow rate, the more expensive the production becomes. However, this may be offset by greater yields. The experiment used three different flow rates (5, 35, and 80 milliliters per minute) and two temperatures (360°C and 400°C). The experiment was repeated several times for each combination of flow rate and temperature. The percentage yields were recorded and stored in file Xr24-40 using the following format:

Column 1:   Percent yield of C

Column 2:   Percent yield of Y

Column 3:   Flow rate

Column 4:   Temperature

Do the data allow us to conclude that for each of products Y and C

a flow rate affects yield?

b temperature affects yield?

c particular combinations of flow rate and temperature affect yields?

(The authors are grateful to James Fong and Diana Mansour for creating this exercise.)

24.41 How does mental outlook affect a person's health? The answer to this question may allow physicians to care more effectively for their patients. In an experiment to examine the relationship between attitude and physical health, Dr. Daniel Mark, a heart specialist at Duke University, studied 1,719 men and women who recently had undergone a heart catheterization, a procedure that checks for clogged arteries. Patients undergo this procedure when heart disease results in chest pain. All of the patients in the experiment were in about the same condition. In interviews, 14% of the patients doubted that they would recover sufficiently to resume their daily routines. Dr. Mark identified these individuals as pessimists; the others were (by default) optimists. After 1 year, Dr. Mark recorded how many patients were still alive. The data are stored in columns 1 (1 = optimist, 2 = pessimist) and 2 (2 = alive, 1 = dead) in file Xr24-41. Do these data allow us to infer that pessimists are less likely to survive than optimists with similar physical ailments?

24.42 Can music make you smarter? And if so, which kind of music works best? Two University of California at Irvine professors addressed these questions (as reported on "Dateline" in September 1994). A random sample of 135 students was given tests that measured the ability to reason. One-third of the students were then put in a room where rock-and-roll music was played. A second group of 45 students was placed in a room and listened to music composed by Mozart. The last group was placed in a room where no music was played. The students then took another test. The differences (second test score minus first test score) were recorded and stored in file Xr24-42. Can we infer that the type of music affects test results?

24.43 As a follow-up to the experiment described in Exercise 24.42, the students again were placed in their chosen rooms. After leaving their rooms, the students waited 10 minutes before being tested. The differences (third test score minus first test score) were recorded and stored in file Xr24-43. Does it appear that the effects of the music wear off after 10 minutes?

24.44 A study in the journal *Neurology* reported that ibuprofen (sold commercially as Motrin, Advil, and Nuprin) may slow or even prevent the progression of Alzheimer's disease. The study was based on a sample of 1,500 volunteers of varying ages who kept detailed records of what medications they took. Researchers at the Johns Hopkins School of Public Health noticed that those who had taken ibuprofen for at least 2 years showed a 60% lower risk of getting Alzheimer's. Aspirin had a smaller effect, and acetaminophen (the main ingredient in Tylenol) had no effect. Further analysis revealed that almost all of those who had taken ibuprofen for at least 2 years did so to relieve the symptoms of arthritis. Assuming that the 60% reduction in the risk of Alzheimer's seen in the sample is statistically significant, can we infer that taking ibuprofen regularly will reduce the incidence of Alzheimer's? Suggest another way to interpret the results that do not lead to the conclusion about the relationship between ibuprofen and Alzheimer's.

24.45 Researchers in both the business world and the academic world often treat college students as representative of the adult population. This practice reduces sampling costs enormously, but its effectiveness is open to question. An experiment was performed to determine the suitability of using student surrogates in research. The study used two groups of people:

1. The first consisted of 60 adults (18 years of age or older) chosen so that they represented by age and occupation the adult population of a Midwestern state.

2. The second consisted of 60 students enrolled in an introductory marketing course at a public university.

The experiment involved showing each group a 60-second television commercial advertising a financial institution. Each respondent was asked to assess the commercial's believability. The responses were recorded as follows:

4 Very believable

3 Somewhat believable

2 Not very believable

1 Not at all believable

These data are stored in file Xr24-45.

a Can we infer that there are differences among the two groups of respondents?

b What conclusions can you draw regarding the suitability of using students as surrogates in marketing research? (Adapted from R. Kesevan, D. G. Anderson, and O. Mascarenhas, "Students as Surrogates in Advertising Research," *Developments in Marketing Science*, 7 (1984): 438–441.)

24.46 The battle between customers and car dealerships is often intense. Customers want the lowest price and dealers want to extract as much money as possible. One source of conflict is the trade-in car. Most dealers will offer a relatively low trade-in in anticipation of negotiating the final package. In an effort to determine how dealers operate, a consumer organization undertook an experiment. Seventy-two individuals were recruited. Each solicited an offer on "their" 5-year-old Ford Taurus. The exact same car was used throughout the experiment. The only variables were the age and gender of the "owner." The ages were categorized as (1) young, (2) middle, and (3) senior. The cash offers are stored in columns 1 and 2 in file Xr24-46. Column 1 stores the data for female owners, and column 2 contains the offers made to male owners. The first 12 rows in both columns represent the offers made to young people, the next 12 rows represent the middle group, and the last 12 rows represent the elderly owners.

a Can we infer that differences exist among the six groups?

b If differences exist, determine whether the differences are due to gender, age, or some interaction.

24.47 Repeat Cases 24.1 and 24.2, assuming that interest rates, annual gross sales, and ages of businesses are not normally distributed.

CASE 24.3
AMBULANCE AND FIRE DEPARTMENT RESPONSE INTERVAL STUDY*

Every year, thousands of people die of heart attacks, partly because of delays in waiting for emergency medical care to arrive. One form of heart attack is ventricular fibrillation rhythm, which is treated by a defibrillator. However, immediate medical attention is critical. In general, if a patient receives treatment within 8 minutes, he or she is very likely to survive. It is estimated that the probability of survival is reduced by 7–10% for each minute thereafter that defibrillation is delayed.

The region in the Ambulance and Fire Department Response Interval Study is composed of the three cities of Cambridge, Waterloo, and Kitchener. Each city has a fire department, and the region has a 911 emergency telephone system. When a medical-related call is received by the Police Dispatch Center, it is relayed to the Central Ambulance Communication Center (CACC). The CACC dispatches both the ambulance and the fire department to certain calls that match one of several criteria indicating the need for fire department personnel. There are two ambulance services that cover the region: the Cambridge Memorial Hospital Ambulance Service and the Kitchener-Waterloo Regional Ambulance Service. Currently, ambulance personnel

sent to the patient after a 911 call perform all defibrillation. A city counselor recently suggested that, since the fire department has more centers, it is likely that fire department personnel could arrive at the scene more quickly than ambulance personnel. A study was undertaken to determine whether fire department personnel should be trained in the use of defibrillators and sent to treat ventricular fibrillation rhythm.

Between March 1, 1994, and August 31, 1994, all calls that involved both ambulance and fire department personnel were monitored. The times for each service to arrive at the scene were recorded and stored in file C24-03, using the format below:

Column 1:   Call number for Cambridge calls

Column 2:   Time in minutes for the ambulance to arrive

Column 3:   Time for fire truck to arrive

Column 4:   Call number for Kitchener calls

Column 5:   Time in minutes for the ambulance to arrive

Column 6:   Time for fire truck to arrive

Column 7:   Call number for Waterloo calls

Column 8:   Time in minutes for the ambulance to arrive

Column 9:   Time for fire truck to arrive

It has been decided that the training of fire department personnel is warranted only if it can be shown that a fire truck arrives at the scene on average more than 1 minute sooner than an ambulance and that the frequency of arrival within 8 minutes is greater for the fire department.

What conclusions can be drawn from the data?

*The authors are grateful to Bruce Jermyn for supplying this case. The data are real. However, the sample size was reduced to ease disk-storage problems.

◈ CASE 24.4
UNDERPRICING IN INITIAL PUBLIC OFFERINGS*

When a company offers its common shares to the public for the first time, the process is referred to as the company's *initial public offering* (IPO). The company retains an investment banker to establish the price at which the shares will be sold initially. If the price is set too high, there will be insufficient demand to sell all the shares. On the other hand, if the shares are underpriced, the company will receive less money for its shares than the maximum possible.

Studies concerning IPOs in the United States indicate that, on average, "IPOs tend to be underpriced by 11 to 18%." Studies concerning IPOs in Canada, using pre-1970 data, "reported an average degree of underpricing in excess of 40%." The evidence of excessive underpricing has caused the Canadian government to consider direct intervention in the capital markets to reduce this underpricing and thereby encourage entrepreneurs to raise capital through public offerings.

Researchers have suggested that, before the government decides to intervene, it should consider the results of its underpricing study using more recent data. A financial analyst took a sample of 100 Canadian IPOs issued during a recent 12-year period. For each IPO, he computed (for three time intervals) the values of the following underpricing measures:

U_{jt} = the percentage of underpricing of the jth IPO measured from $t = 0$ to day t of public trading (for $t = 1, 3, 5$)

The value of U_{jt} is essentially the percentage price appreciation of the jth IPO, measured from $t = 0$ to day t of public trading. Thus, underpricing is indicated by positive values of U_{jt}.

The observations for $t = 1, 3,$ and 5 are stored in columns 1, 2, and 3, respectively, in file C24-04. The government would be interested in knowing whether there is evidence of (a positive percentage of) underpricing and, also, if this percentage exceeds 5%, in which case the degree of underpricing would be sufficiently high to allow traders to profit from it even after paying brokerage commissions. What conclusions might the government draw from this study?

---

*Adapted from Vijay M. Jog and Allan L. Riding, "Underpricing in Canadian IPOs," *Financial Analysts' Journal* (Nov.–Dec. 1987): 48–55.

◈ CASE 24.5
PC MAGAZINE SURVEY

In general, consumers of personal computers are not particularly brand conscious. Most people decide which brand of computer to buy on the basis of price and features. However, brand-name manufacturers are attempting to win back customers by providing a number of services and high-quality products. To examine whether personal computer users perceive differences among manufacturers, a marketing research consultant undertook a survey of PC users. He asked a random sample of Apple, Compaq, Dell, IBM, and Packard-Bell owners several questions. The questions and possible responses are shown in the next column.

Did you ever call the computer manufacturer to help with a problem?

The following questions were asked only of those who answered "yes."
1. How long approximately (in seconds) did it take to reach a technician?
2. How long approximately (in minutes) did it take to solve the problem?
3. Rate the quality of the technical support.
    1 = poor;   2 = fair;
    3 = average;   4 = good;
    5 = excellent
4. Would you recommend this brand of computer to a friend?
    2 = yes;   1 = no

(The authors are grateful to Alex Eliadis and David Jones for their help in this case. The case is based on an actual survey conducted by Willard Shullman for *PC Magazine*.)

The results are stored in file C24-05. Columns 1 through 4 store the responses to questions 1 to 4, respectively. Column 5 identifies the computer brand (1 = Apple; 2 = Compaq; 3 = Dell; 4 = IBM; 5 = Packard-Bell). For each question, can we infer that differences among the brands exist?

✦ CASE 24.6
WLU GRADUATE SURVEY*

Every year, the graduates of Wilfrid Laurier University are surveyed to determine their employment status and annual income. The university offers undergraduate degrees in Arts and Music, Business Administration, and Science, as well as several master's degrees. The survey asked a random sample of 1994 graduates the following questions.

1. With which degree did you graduate?
   1. Arts and Music
   2. Business Administration—non-accounting
   3. Business Administration—accounting
   4. Science
   5. Master's

2. What is your current employment status?
   1. Completing additional education

   2. Employed
   3. Other
   4. Unemployed

3. If you are employed, what is your annual income?

The data are stored in columns 1 to 7 in file C24-06 in the following way:

   Column 1:   Degree

   Column 2:   Employment status

   Columns 3–7:   Income for those employed with degrees in Arts and Music, Business (non-accounting), Business (accounting), Science, and Master's, respectively.

High school students who are about to choose a university program would like to know the following information.

a Are there differences in the employment rates among the five groups of graduates? (Employment

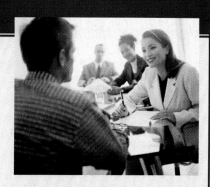

rate is defined as the percentage of graduates who are employed.)

b Are there differences in income among the five groups of graduates?

c Among Business Administration graduates, is there a difference in the employment rates and income between accounting and non-accounting graduates?

---

*Source: "Wilfrid Laurier 1994 Graduate Survey Report," as printed in the *Atrium*, 8 November 1995.

⬧ CASE 24.7
EVALUATION OF A NEW ANTIDEPRESSANT DRUG

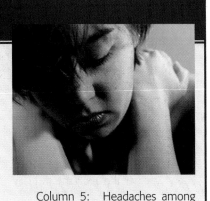

Clinical depression afflicts many people and costs businesses billions of dollars. Fortunately, there are several drugs that effectively treat this disease. Pharmaceutical companies are constantly experimenting to develop new and better drugs. Statistical techniques are used to determine whether and to what degree the new drug is better and whether there are certain people in whom the drug appears to be more effective. Suppose that a random sample of men and women who suffer from moderate depression are given a new antidepressant. Each person is asked to rate its effectiveness by filling out the form below. The form asks people to assess the drug after 7 and 14 days, because antidepressants usually take several days to take effect. Similar drugs often have different effects on men and women.

Consequently, the gender of the patient was recorded. Also recorded is whether the patient suffered from the most common side effect, headaches. *To evaluate your experience with this medication, place a check mark to show how you have felt since you began taking it.*

After Therapy Day   7   14

1. Very much worse
2. Much worse
3. A little worse
4. No change
5. A little better
6. Much better
7. Very much better

The responses are stored in file C24-07 in the following way:

    Columns 1 and 2:   Evaluations for days 7 and 14 for women
    Columns 3 and 4:   Evaluations for days 7 and 14 for men

Column 5: Headaches among women (2 = yes; 1 = no)
Column 6: Headaches among men (2 = yes; 1 = no)

The company wants answers to the following questions.

a Among female patients, is there improvement between days 7 and 14?

b Among male patients, is there improvement between days 7 and 14?

c Does the frequency of headaches differ between men and women?

◈ CASE 24.8
NUTRITION EDUCATION PROGRAMS*

Nutrition education programs, which teach their clients how to lose weight or reduce cholesterol levels through better eating patterns, have been growing in popularity. The nurse in charge of one such program at a local hospital wanted to know whether the programs actually work. A random sample of 33 clients who attended a nutrition education program for those with elevated cholesterol levels was drawn. The study recorded the weight, cholesterol levels, total dietary fat intake per average day, total dietary cholesterol intake per average day, and percent of daily calories from fat. These data were gathered both before and three months after the program. The researchers also determined the gender, age, and height of the clients.

The data are stored in file C24-08 in the following way:

Column 1:   Gender (1 = female; 2 = male)
Column 2:   Age
Column 3:   Height (in meters)
Columns 4 and 5:   Weight, before and after (in kilograms)
Columns 6 and 7:   Cholesterol level, before and after
Columns 8 and 9:   Total dietary fat intake per average day, before and after (in grams)
Columns 10 and 11:   Dietary cholesterol intake per average day, before and after (in milligrams)
Columns 12 and 13:   Percent daily calories from fat, before and after

The nurse would like the following information.

a In terms of each of weight, cholesterol level, fat intake, cholesterol

intake, and calories from fat, is the program a success?

b Does gender affect the amount of reduction in each of weight, cholesterol level, fat intake, cholesterol intake, and calories from fat?

c Does age affect the amount of reduction in weight, cholesterol level, fat intake, cholesterol intake, and calories from fat?

*The authors would like to thank Karen Cavrag for writing this case.

◈ CASE 24.9
DO BANKS DISCRIMINATE AGAINST WOMEN BUSINESS OWNERS?—III

A statistician made a final effort to determine whether banks discriminate against women business owners because of their gender. For each of the women business owners who had received a loan, he attempted to find a male business owner whose characteristics closely matched. The matching was done on the basis of type of business (proprietorship, partnership, or corporation), gross sales, and age of company. A match was made when the type of business was the same, the gross sales were within $10,000 of each other, and the ages were within 1 year of each other. The interest rates (points above prime) for each pair are recorded and stored in columns 2 (women's rates) and 3 (men's rates)—column 1 stores the pair number—in file C24-09. What do these data tell you? Is this analysis definitive? Explain.

Appendix A
Data File Sample Statistics

Chapter 10
10.50 $\bar{x} = 252.38$
10.51 $\bar{x} = 1,810.16$
10.52 $\bar{x} = 12.10$
10.53 $\bar{x} = 10.21$
10.54 $\bar{x} = .510$
10.55 $\bar{x} = 26.81$
10.56 $\bar{x} = 19.28$
10.57 $\bar{x} = 15.00$
10.58 $\bar{x} = 585,063$
10.59 $\bar{x} = 14.98$
10.60 $\bar{x} = 27.19$

Chapter 11
11.45 $\bar{x} = 5,065$
11.46 $\bar{x} = 29,120$
11.47 $\bar{x} = 569$
11.48 $\bar{x} = 19.13$
11.49 $\bar{x} = -1.20$
11.50 $\bar{x} = 55.8$
11.51 $\bar{x} = 5.04$
11.52 $\bar{x} = 19.39$
11.53 $\bar{x} = 105.7$
11.54 $\bar{x} = 4.84$
11.55 $\bar{x} = 5.64$
11.56 $\bar{x} = 29.92$
11.57 $\bar{x} = 231.56$

Chapter 12
12.34 $\bar{x} = 7.15; s = 1.65$
12.35 $\bar{x} = 4.66; s = 2.37$
12.36 $\bar{x} = 63.70; s = 18.94; n = 162$
12.37 $\bar{x} = 53.78; s = 4.05; n = 144$
12.38 $\bar{x} = 2.67; s = 2.50; n = 188$
12.40 $\bar{x} = 62.79; s = 5.32; n = 28$
12.41 $\bar{x} = 29.14; s = 4.62; n = 49$
12.42 $\bar{x} = 13.94; s = 2.16; n = 212$
12.43 $\bar{x} = 15.27; s = 5.72; n = 116$
12.44 $\bar{x} = 3.44; s = 3.33; n = 471$
12.45 $\bar{x} = 89.27; s = 17.30; n = 85$
12.46 $\bar{x} = 2.10; s = .76; n = 100$
12.57 $\chi^2_{.975,143} = 111.787, \chi^2_{.025,143} = 177.998$
12.58 $s^2 = 270.58$
12.60 $\chi^2_{.95,199} = 167.361, \chi^2_{.05,199} = 232.912$

12.61 $s^2 = 22.56, \chi^2_{.10,244} = 272.704$
12.62 $s^2 = 174.47$
12.89 $n(1) = 137; n(2) = 430$
12.90 $n(1) = 153; n(2) = 24$
12.91 $n(1) = 304; n(2) = 418$
12.92 $n(1) = 71; n(2) = 329$
12.93 $n(1) = 119; n(2) = 107$
12.94 $n(1) = 57; n(2) = 35; n(3) = 4;$
$n(4) = 4$
12.96 $n(1) = 226; n(2) = 195; n(3) = 106;$
$n(4) = 328; n(5) = 1,145$
12.97 $n(1) = 355; n(2) = 32$
12.98 $n(1) = 341; n(2) = 59$
12.99 $n(1) = 155; n(2) = 655$
12.100 $n(1) = 518; n(2) = 132$
12.101 $n(1) = 81; n(2) = 47; n(3) = 167;$
$n(4) = 146; n(5) = 34$
12.102 $n(1) = 63; n(2) = 125; n(3) = 45;$
$n(4) = 87$
12.103 $n(1) = 418; n(2) = 536; n(3) = 882$

Chapter 13
13.29 $\bar{x}_1 = 99.30; s_1 = 23.80; n_1 = 165;$
$\bar{x}_2 = 95.77; s_2 = 23.74; n_2 = 217$
13.30 $\bar{x}_1 = 21.51; s_1 = 4.76; n_1 = 121;$
$\bar{x}_2 = 19.76; s_2 = 4.13; n_2 = 84$
13.31 $\bar{x}_1 = 250.4; s_1 = 13.23; n_1 = 40;$
$\bar{x}_2 = 259.8; s_2 = 43.52; n_2 = 40$
13.32 $\bar{x}_1 = 72.93; s_1 = 5.13; n_1 = 400;$
$\bar{x}_2 = 73.99; s_2 = 15.55; n_2 = 400$
13.33 Tastee: $\bar{x}_1 = 36.93; s_1 = 4.23; n_1 = 15;$
Competitor: $\bar{x}_2 = 31.36; s_2 = 3.35; n_2 = 25$
13.34 Supplements: $\bar{x}_1 = 19.02; s_1 = 6.43;$
$n_1 = 48;$ Placebo: $\bar{x}_2 = 21.85; s_2 = 5.05;$
$n_2 = 48$
13.35 18-to-34: $\bar{x}_1 = 58.99; s_1 = 30.77;$
$n_1 = 250;$ 35-to-50: $\bar{x}_2 = 52.96; s_2 = 43.32;$
$n_2 = 250$
13.36 1997: $\bar{x}_1 = 3.19; s_1 = 3.51; n_1 = 124;$
1998: $\bar{x}_2 = 4.35; s_2 = 4.06; n_2 = 98$
13.37 Male: $\bar{x}_1 = 10.23; s_1 = 2.87;$
$n_1 = 100;$ Female: $\bar{x}_2 = 9.66; s_2 = 2.90;$
$n_2 = 100$
13.38 A: $\bar{x}_1 = 115.50; s_1 = 21.69; n_1 = 30;$
B: $\bar{x}_2 = 110.32; s_2 = 22.71; n_2 = 28$
13.39 Exercise: $\bar{x}_1 = 13.52; s_1 = 2.40;$

$n_1 = 25;$ Drug: $\bar{x}_2 = 9.92; s_2 = 3.63;$
$n_2 = 25$
13.40 A: $\bar{x}_1 = 74.91; s_1 = 24.53; n_1 = 23;$ B:
$\bar{x}_2 = 53.40; s_2 = 8.58; n_2 = 15$
13.41 Sucessful: $\bar{x}_1 = 5.02; s_1 = 1.39;$
$n_1 = 200;$ Unsuccessful: $\bar{x}_2 = 7.80;$
$s_2 = 3.09; n_2 = 200$
13.42 Phone: $\bar{x}_1 = .646; s_1 = .045;$
$n_1 = 125;$ Not: $\bar{x}_2 = .601; s_2 = .053;$
$n_2 = 145$
13.43 Chitchat: $\bar{x}_1 = .654; s_1 = .048;$
$n_1 = 95;$ Political: $\bar{x}_2 = .662; s_2 = .045;$
$n_2 = 90$
13.44 Planner: $\bar{x}_1 = 6.18 \; s_1 = 1.59;$
$n_1 = 64;$ Broker: $\bar{x}_2 = 5.94; s_2 = 1.61;$
$n_2 = 81$
13.45 Textbook: $\bar{x}_1 = 63.71; s_1 = 5.90;$
$n_1 = 173;$ No book: $\bar{x}_2 = 66.80; s_2 = 6.85;$
$n_2 = 202$
13.46 Wendy's: $\bar{x}_1 = 149.85; s_1 = 21.82;$
$n_1 = 213;$ McDonald's: $\bar{x}_2 = 154.43;$
$s_2 = 23.64; n_2 = 202$
13.47 General: $\bar{x}_1 = 53.05; s_1 = 3.06;$
$n_1 = 79;$ Pediatrics: $\bar{x}_2 = 51.67; s_2 = 3.64;$
$n_2 = 91$
13.48 Applied: $\bar{x}_1 = 130.93; s_1 = 31.99;$
$n_1 = 100;$ Contacted: $\bar{x}_2 = 126.14;$
$s_2 = 26.00; n_2 = 100$
13.49 New: $\bar{x}_1 = 73.60; s_1 = 15.60; n_1 = 20;$
Existing: $\bar{x}_2 = 69.20; s_2 = 15.06; n_2 = 20$
13.50 British: $\bar{x}_1 = 237.99; s_1 = 12.24;$
$n_1 = 263;$ American: $\bar{x}_2 = 251.99;$
$s_2 = 14.84; n_2 = 279$
13.51 British: $\bar{x}_1 = 6,345; s_1 = 71.3;$
$n_1 = 28;$ American: $\bar{x}_2 = 6,358; s_2 = 55.7;$
$n_2 = 33$
13.52 British: $\bar{x}_1 = 7,137; s_1 = 195.1;$
$n_1 = 28;$ American: $\bar{x}_2 = 9,304; s_2 = 331.9;$
$n_2 = 33$
13.67 $D = X[\text{This year}] - X[\text{5 years ago}]:$
$\bar{x}_D = 12.4; s_D = 99.1; n_D = 150$
13.68 $D = X[\text{Waiter}] - X[\text{Waitress}]:$
$\bar{x}_D = -1.16; s_D = 2.22; n_D = 50$
13.69 $D = X[\text{This year}] - X[\text{Last year}]:$
$\bar{x}_D = 19.75; s_D = 30.63; n_D = 40$
13.70 $D = X[\text{Drug}] - X[\text{Placebo}]:$
$\bar{x}_D = -3.6; s_D = 5.91; n_D = 100$

13.71 $D = X[\text{Men}] - X[\text{Women}]$:
$\bar{x}_D = -42.94$; $s_D = 317.16$; $n_D = 45$

13.72 $D = X[\text{Last year}] - X[\text{Previous year}]$:
$\bar{x}_D = -183.35$; $s_D = 1{,}568.94$; $n_D = 170$

13.73 $D = X[\text{This year}] - X[\text{Last year}]$:
$\bar{x}_D = .0422$; $s_D = .1634$; $n_D = 38$

13.74 $D = X[\text{Company 1}] - X[\text{Company 2}]$:
$\bar{x}_D = 520.85$; $s_D = 1{,}854.92$; $n_D = 55$

13.75 $D = X[\text{New}] - X[\text{Existing}]$:
$\bar{x}_D = 4.55$; $s_D = 7.22$; $n_D = 20$

13.77 $D = X[\text{Finance}] - X[\text{Marketing}]$:
$\bar{x}_D = 4{,}587$; $s_D = 22{,}851$; $n_D = 25$

13.87 $s_1^2 = 15{,}800$; $n_1 = 130$; $s_2^2 = 18{,}734$;
$n_2 = 126$

13.92 Portfolio 1: $s_1^2 = .026$; $n_1 = 52$; Portfolio 2: $s_2^2 = .087$; $n_2 = 52$

13.93 Teller 1: $s_1^2 = 3.35$; $n_1 = 100$; Teller 2: $s_2^2 = 10.95$; $n_2 = 100$

13.108 Source 1: $n_1(1) = 344$; $n_1(2) = 38$; Source 2: $n_2(1) = 275$; $n_2(2) = 41$

13.109 Californians: $n_1(1) = 329$; $n_1(2) = 248$; New Yorkers: $n_2(1) = 387$; $n_2(2) = 221$

13.110 This year: $n_1(1) = 499$; $n_1(2) = 163$; 10 years ago: $n_2(1) = 508$; $n_2(2) = 187$

13.111 Smokers: $n_1(1) = 28$; $n_1(2) = 10$; Nonsmokers: $n_2(1) = 150$; $n_2(2) = 12$

13.112 2 years ago: $n_1(1) = 152$; $n_1(2) = 248$; This year: $n_2(1) = 240$; $n_2(2) = 260$

13.113 This year: $n_1(1) = 306$; $n_1(2) = 171$; 10 years ago: $n_2(1) = 304$; $n_2(2) = 158$

13.114 A: $n_1(1) = 189$; $n_1(2) = 11$; B: $n_2(1) = 178$; $n_2(2) = 22$

13.115 Health conscious: $n_1(1) = 199$; $n_1(2) = 32$; Not health conscious: $n_2(1) = 563$; $n_2(2) = 56$

13.116 Low-income: $n_1(1) = 319$; $n_1(2) = 59$; High-income: $n_2(1) = 138$; $n_2(2) = 14$

13.117 Aspirin: $n_1(1) = 10{,}896$; $n_1(2) = 104$; Placebo: $n_2(1) = 10{,}811$; $n_2(2) = 189$

Chapter 15

15.15

Sample	$\bar{x}_i$	s_i^2	n_i
1	68.83	52.28	20
2	65.08	37.38	26
3	62.01	63.46	16
4	64.64	56.88	19

15.16

Sample	$\bar{x}_i$	s_i^2	n_i
1	90.17	991.52	30
2	95.77	900.87	30
3	106.83	928.70	30
4	111.17	1,023.04	30

15.17

Sample	$\bar{x}_i$	s_i^2	n_i
1	196.83	914.05	41
2	207.78	861.12	73
3	223.38	1,195.44	86
4	232.67	1,079.81	79

15.18

Sample	$\bar{x}_i$	s_i^2	n_i
1	163.96	1,205.61	24
2	185.64	1,719.91	25
3	154.29	1,156.30	24
4	182.60	1,657.83	25
5	178.74	906.02	23

15.19

Sample	$\bar{x}_i$	s_i^2	n_i
1	22.21	121.64	39
2	18.46	90.39	114
3	15.49	85.25	81
4	9.31	65.40	67

15.20

Sample	$\bar{x}_i$	s_i^2	n_i
1	551.50	2,741.95	20
2	576.75	2,641.14	20
3	559.45	3,129.31	20

15.21

Sample	$\bar{x}_i$	s_i^2	n_i
1	5.81	6.22	100
2	5.30	4.05	100
3	5.33	3.90	100

15.22

Sample	$\bar{x}_i$	s_i^2	n_i
1	74.10	249.96	30
2	75.67	184.23	30
3	78.50	233.36	30
4	81.30	242.91	30

15.23 Size

Sample	$\bar{x}_i$	s_i^2	n_i
1	24.97	48.23	50
2	21.65	54.54	50
3	17.84	33.85	50

Nicotine

Sample	$\bar{x}_i$	s_i^2	n_i
1	15.52	3.72	50
2	13.39	3.59	50
3	10.08	3.83	50

15.24a

Sample	$\bar{x}_i$	s_i^2	n_i
1	31.30	28.34	63
2	34.42	23.20	81
3	37.38	31.16	40
4	39.93	72.03	111

b

Sample	$\bar{x}_i$	s_i^2	n_i
1	37.22	39.82	63
2	38.91	40.85	81
3	41.48	61.38	40
4	41.75	46.59	111

c

Sample	$\bar{x}_i$	s_i^2	n_i
1	11.75	3.93	63
2	12.41	3.39	81
3	11.73	4.26	40
4	11.89	4.30	111

15.25

Sample	$\bar{x}_i$	s_i^2	n_i
1	153.60	654.25	20
2	151.50	925.05	20
3	133.25	626.83	20

15.26

Sample	$\bar{x}_i$	s_i^2	n_i
1	18.54	177.95	61
2	19.34	171.42	83
3	20.29	297.50	91

15.27

Sample	$\bar{x}_i$	s_i^2	n_i
1	38.11	71.50	418
2	37.62	70.42	536
3	38.20	71.94	881

15.33 $k = 3$, $b = 10$, SST $= 151.3$, SSB $= 7{,}396.3$, SSE $= 195.4$

15.34 $k = 4$, $b = 25$, SST $= 2{,}127$, SSB $= 35{,}300$, SSE $= 6{,}642$

15.35 $k = 3$, $b = 12$, SST $= 204.2$, SSB $= 1{,}150.2$, SSE $= 495.1$

15.36 $k = 3$, $b = 20$, SST $= 7{,}131$, SSB $= 177{,}465$, SSE $= 1{,}098$

15.37 $k = 3$, $b = 20$, SST $= 10.26$, SSB $= 3{,}020.30$, SSE $= 226.71$

15.38 $k = 4$, $b = 30$, SST $= 4{,}206$, SSB $= 126{,}843$, SSE $= 5{,}764$

15.39 $k = 7$, $b = 200$, SST $= 28{,}674$, SSB $= 209{,}835$, SSE $= 479{,}125$

15.40 $k = 5$, $b = 36$, SST $= 1{,}406.4$, SSB $= 7{,}309.7$, SSE $= 4{,}593.9$

15.41 $k = 4$, $b = 21$, SST $= 563.82$, SSB $= 1{,}327.33$, SSE $= 748.70$

15.65

Sample	$\bar{x}_i$	s_i^2	n_i
1	61.60	80.49	10
2	57.30	70.46	10
3	61.80	22.18	10
4	51.80	75.29	10

15.66

Sample	$\bar{x}_i$	s_i^2	n_i
1	53.17	194.63	30
2	49.37	152.59	30
3	44.33	129.89	30

Chapter 16

16.7 $n(1) = 28$, $n(2) = 17$, $n(3) = 19$, $n(4) = 17$, $n(5) = 19$

16.8 $n(1) = 41$, $n(2) = 107$, $n(3) = 66$, $n(4) = 19$

16.9 $n(1) = 114$, $n(2) = 92$, $n(3) = 84$, $n(4) = 101$, $n(5) = 107$, $n(6) = 102$

16.10 $n(1) = 11$, $n(2) = 32$, $n(3) = 62$, $n(4) = 29$, $n(5) = 16$

16.11 $n(1) = 8$, $n(2) = 4$, $n(3) = 3$, $n(4) = 8$, $n(5) = 2$

16.12 $n(1) = 159$, $n(2) = 28$, $n(3) = 47$, $n(4) = 16$

16.13 $n(1) = 36$, $n(2) = 58$, $n(3) = 74$, $n(4) = 29$

16.14 $n(1) = 408$, $n(2) = 571$, $n(3) = 221$

16.15 $n(1) = 19$, $n(2) = 23$, $n(3) = 14$, $n(4) = 194$

16.16 $n(1) = 63$, $n(2) = 125$, $n(3) = 45$, $n(4) = 87$

16.25

		Thinking		
		1	2	3
Program	1	50	15	8
	2	11	42	25

16.26

		Outcome		
		1	2	3
Drug	1	60	31	12
	2	65	22	13

16.27

		Read		
		1	2	3
Smoker	1	33	24	19
	2	23	17	26
	3	16	27	46
	4	14	38	57

16.28

		Actual	
		1	2
Predicted	1	65	64
	2	39	48

16.29

		Smoker	
		1	2
Education	1	34	23
	2	251	212
	3	159	248
	4	16	57

16.30

		Employment		
		1	2	3
Segment	1	157	44	217
	2	219	53	264
	3	256	102	524

16.31

		Value		
		1	2	3
Segment	1	147	135	136
	2	221	155	160
	3	339	254	289

16.32

		Education			
		1	2	3	4
Group	1	31	62	72	104
	2	55	157	143	129
	3	39	83	74	45
	4	74	107	51	24

16.33

		Degree			
		1	2	3	4
Approach	1	51	8	5	11
	2	24	14	12	8
	3	26	9	19	8

Chapter 17

17.17 $T_1 = 6{,}807$, $n_1 = 82$, $T_2 = 5{,}596$, $n_2 = 75$

17.18 $T_1 = 797$, $n_1 = 30$, $T_2 = 1033$, $n_2 = 30$

17.19 $T_1 = 14{,}873.5$, $n_1 = 125$, $T_2 = 16{,}501.5$, $n_2 = 125$

17.20 $T_1 = 10{,}691$, $n_1 = 100$, $T_2 = 9{,}409$, $n_2 = 100$

17.21 $T_1 = 2{,}810$, $n_1 = 50$, $T_2 = 2{,}240$, $n_2 = 50$

17.22 $T_1 = 383.5$, $n_1 = 15$, $T_2 = 436.5$, $n_2 = 25$

17.23 $T_1 = 439.5$ $n_1 = 20$, $T_2 = 380.5$, $n_2 = 20$

17.24 $T_1 = 13{,}078$ $n_1 = 125$, $T_2 = 18{,}297$, $n_2 = 125$

17.25 $T_1 = 32{,}225.5$ $n_1 = 182$, $T_2 = 27{,}459.5$, $n_2 = 163$

17.48 $T^+ = 378.5$, $T^- = 2{,}249.5$, $n = 72$

17.49 $T^+ = 62$, $T^- = 758$, $n = 40$

17.50 $n(\text{positive}) = 60$, $n(\text{negative}) = 38$

17.51 $T^+ = 40.5$, $T^- = 235.5$, $n = 23$

17.52 $T^+ = 111$, $T^- = 240$, $n = 26$

17.53 $n(\text{positive}) = 30$, $n(\text{negative}) = 8$

17.54 $n(\text{positive}) = 5$, $n(\text{negative}) = 15$

17.55 $T^+ = 190$, $T^- = 135$, $n = 25$

17.56 $n(\text{positive}) = 32$, $n(\text{negative}) = 21$

17.57 $T^+ = 48$, $T^- = 732$, $n = 39$

17.69 $T_1 = 767.5$, $n_1 = 25$, $T_2 = 917$, $n_2 = 25$, $T_3 = 1{,}165.5$, $n_3 = 25$

17.70 $T_1 = 17{,}116.5$, $n_1 = 80$, $T_2 = 16{,}816.5$, $n_2 = 90$, $T_3 = 17{,}277$, $n_3 = 77$, $T_4 = 29{,}391$, $n_4 = 154$

17.71 $T_1 = 2{,}195$, $n_1 = 33$, $T_2 = 1{,}650.5$, $n_2 = 34$, $T_3 = 2{,}830$, $n_3 = 34$, $T_4 = 2{,}102.5$, $n_4 = 31$

17.72 $T_1 = 4{,}180$, $n_1 = 50$, $T_2 = 5{,}262$, $n_2 = 50$, $T_3 = 5{,}653$, $n_3 = 50$, $T_4 = 5{,}005$, $n_4 = 50$

17.73 $T_1 = 1{,}565$, $n_1 = 30$, $T_2 = 1{,}358.5$, $n_2 = 30$, $T_3 = 1{,}171.5$, $n_3 = 30$

17.74 $T_1 = 21{,}246$, $n_1 = 100$, $T_2 = 19{,}784$, $n_2 = 100$, $T_3 = 20{,}976$, $n_3 = 100$, $T_4 = 18{,}194$, $n_4 = 100$

17.75 $T_1 = 28{,}304$, $n_1 = 123$, $T_2 = 21{,}285$, $n_2 = 109$, $T_3 = 21{,}796$, $n_3 = 102$, $T_4 = 20{,}421$, $n_4 = 94$

17.76 $T_1 = 638.5$, $n_1 = 18$, $T_2 = 1{,}233.5$, $n_2 = 14$, $T_3 = 1{,}814.5$, $n_3 = 26$, $T_4 = 3{,}159.5$, $n_4 = 42$, $T_5 = 2{,}065$, $n_5 = 33$

17.86 $T_1 = 33$, $T_2 = 39.5$, $T_3 = 47.5$

17.87 $T_1 = 46$, $T_2 = 72$, $T_3 = 62$

17.88 $T_1 = 28.5$, $T_2 = 22.5$, $T_3 = 21$

17.89 $T_1 = 84.5$, $T_2 = 88.5$, $T_3 = 49$, $T_4 = 78$

Chapter 18

18.2 Fathers: $\bar{x} = 67.14$, $s_x^2 = 16.43$; Sons: $\bar{y} = 68.70$, $s_y^2 = 14.14$; $n = 400$, $\text{cov}(x, y) = 7.87$

18.3 Rate: $\bar{x} = 8.2$, $s_x^2 = .24$; Starts: $\bar{y} = 154.0$, $s_y^2 = 1{,}248.9$; $n = 10$, $\text{cov}(x, y) = -9.40$

18.4 Inflation: $\bar{x} = 3.47$, $s_x^2 = 2.56$; Returns: $\bar{y} = 10.05$, $s_y^2 = 193.06$; $n = 10$, $\text{cov}(x, y) = .121$

18.5 Work: $\bar{x} = 8.18$, $s_x^2 = 10.20$; Mark: $\bar{y} = 67.28$, $s_y^2 = 39.05$; $n = 300$, $\text{cov}(x, y) = -8.27$

18.6 Length: $\bar{x} = 38.00$, $s_x^2 = 193.90$; Test: $\bar{y} = 13.80$, $s_y^2 = 47.96$; $n = 60$, $\text{cov}(x, y) = 51.86$

18.7 Time: $\bar{x} = 27.95$, $s_x^2 = 82.01$; Mark: $\bar{y} = 74.06$, $s_y^2 = 363.94$; $n = 100$, $\text{cov}(x, y) = 153.95$

18.8 Education: $\bar{x} = 11.04$, $s_x^2 = 3.90$; Internet: $\bar{y} = 6.67$, $s_y^2 = 22.16$; $n = 200$, $\text{cov}(x, y) = 3.08$

18.9 Age: $\bar{x} = 37.29$, $s_x^2 = 55.11$; Employment: $\bar{y} = 26.28$, $s_y^2 = 4.00$; $n = 80$, $\text{cov}(x, y) = -6.44$

18.10 Degrees: $\bar{x} = 34.61$, $s_x^2 = 21.39$; Price: $\bar{y} = 12.73$, $s_y^2 = .21$; $n = 13$, $\text{cov}(x, y) = 2.03$

18.11 Age: $\bar{x} = 56.00$, $s_x^2 = 228.26$; Expense: $\bar{y} = 6.67$, $s_y^2 = 179.88$; $n = 1{,}348$, $\text{cov}(x, y) = 51.53$

18.12 Weight: $\bar{x} = .204$, $s_x^2 = .00323$; Price: $\bar{y} = 500.08$, $s_y^2 = 45{,}643$; $n = 48$, $\text{cov}(x, y) = 12.00$

18.27 Vacancy: $\bar{x} = 11.33$, $s_x^2 = 35.47$; Rent: $\bar{y} = 17.20$, $s_y^2 = 11.24$; $n = 30$, $\text{cov}(x, y) = -10.78$

18.28 Exercise: $\bar{x} = 283.14$, $s_x^2 = 13{,}641$; Reduction: $\bar{y} = 27.80$, $s_y^2 = 221.43$; $n = 50$, $\text{cov}(x, y) = 1{,}240.60$

18.29 Test: $\bar{x} = 79.47$, $s_x^2 = 16.07$; Nondefective: $\bar{y} = 93.89$, $s_y^2 = 1.28$; $n = 45$, $\text{cov}(x, y) = .83$

18.84 Ads: $\bar{x} = 4.12$, $s_x^2 = 3.47$; Customers: $\bar{y} = 384.81$, $s_y^2 = 18,552$; $n = 26$, $\text{cov}(x, y) = 74.02$

18.85 Age: $\bar{x} = 113.35$, $s_x^2 = 378.77$; Repairs: $\bar{y} = 395.21$, $s_y^2 = 4,094.79$; $n = 20$, $\text{cov}(x, y) = 936.82$

18.87 Fertilizer: $\bar{x} = 355.00$, $s_x^2 = 7,750.00$; Yield: $\bar{y} = 82.03$, $s_y^2 = 765.93$; $n = 30$, $\text{cov}(x, y) = 469.93$

18.89 Team BA: $\bar{x} = .260$, $s_x^2 = .000091$; Winning %: $\bar{y} = .500$, $s_y^2 = .00368$; $n = 14$, $\text{cov}(x, y) = .000254$

18.90 Team ERA: $\bar{x} = 4.09$, $s_x^2 = .140$; Winning %: $\bar{y} = .500$, $s_y^2 = .00368$; $n = 14$, $\text{cov}(x, y) = -.0112$

18.91 Temperature: $\bar{x} = 63.05$, $s_x^2 = 96.05$; Winning times: $\bar{y} = 130.30$, $s_y^2 = 3.07$; $n = 21$, $\text{cov}(x, y) = 12.43$

18.92 Temperature: $\bar{x} = 63.05$, $s_x^2 = 96.05$; Winning times: $\bar{y} = 147.76$, $s_y^2 = 3.80$; $n = 21$, $\text{cov}(x, y) = 11.44$

18.94 Height: $\bar{x} = 68.95$, $s_x^2 = 9.97$; Income: $\bar{y} = 59.59$, $s_y^2 = 71.95$; $n = 250$, $\text{cov}(x, y) = 6.02$

18.96 Television: $\bar{x} = 30.43$, $s_x^2 = 99.11$; Debt: $\bar{y} = 126,604$, $s_y^2 = 2,152,602,614$; $n = 430$, $\text{cov}(x, y) = 255,877$

18.97 Test: $\bar{x} = 71.92$, $s_x^2 = 90.97$; Nondefective: $\bar{y} = 94.44$, $s_y^2 = 11.84$; $n = 50$, $\text{cov}(x, y) = 13.08$

Chapter 19

19.1 $R^2 = .2425$, $R^2(\text{adjusted}) = .2019$, $s_\varepsilon = 40.24$, $F = 5.97$, p-value $= .0013$

	Coefficients	Standard error	t statistic	p-value
Intercept	51.39	23.52	2.19	.0331
Lot size	.700	.559	1.25	.2156
Trees	.679	.229	2.96	.0045
Distance	−.378	.195	−1.94	.0577

19.2 $R^2 = .7629$, $R^2(\text{adjusted}) = .7453$, $s_\varepsilon = 3.75$, $F = 43.43$, p-value $= 0$

	Coefficients	Standard error	t statistic	p-value
Intercept	13.01	3.53	3.69	.0010
Assignment	.194	.200	.97	.3417
Midterm	1.112	.122	9.12	0

19.3 $R^2 = .8935$, $R^2(\text{adjusted}) = .8711$, $s_\varepsilon = 40.13$, $F = 39.86$, p-value $= 0$

	Coefficients	Standard error	t statistic	p-value
Intercept	−111.8	134.3	−.83	.4155
Permits	4.76	.40	12.06	0
Mortgage	16.99	15.16	1.12	.2764
Apartment vacancy	−10.53	6.39	−1.65	.1161
Office vacancy	1.31	2.79	.47	.6446

19.4 $R^2 = .2672$, $R^2(\text{adjusted}) = .2635$, $s_\varepsilon = 3.23$, $F = 72.37$, p-value $= 0$

	Coefficients	Standard error	t statistic	p-value
Intercept	37.58	3.20	11.73	0
Father	.485	.041	11.78	0
Mother	−.023	.039	−.58	.5615

Chapter 20

20.3 $R^2 = .4068$, $R^2(\text{adjusted}) = .3528$, $s_\varepsilon = 41.15$, $F = 7.54$, p-value $= .0032$

	Coefficients	Standard error	t statistic	p-value
Intercept	−109.0	97.24	−1.12	.2744
Space	33.09	8.59	3.85	.0009
Space^2	−.666	.177	−3.75	.0011

20.4 First-order model $R^2 = .8553$, $R^2(\text{adjusted}) = .8473$, $s_\varepsilon = 13.29$, $F = 106.44$, p-value $= 0$

	Coefficients	Standard error	t statistic	p-value
Intercept	453.6	15.18	29.87	0
Price	−68.91	6.68	−10.32	0

Second-order model $R^2 = .9726$, $R^2(\text{adjusted}) = .9693$, $s_\varepsilon = 5.96$, $F = 301.15$, p-value $= 0$

	Coefficients	Standard error	t statistic	p-value
Intercept	766.9	37.40	20.50	0
Price	−359.1	34.19	−10.50	0
Price^2	64.55	7.58	8.52	0

20.5 First-order model $R^2 = .8504$, $R^2(\text{adjusted}) = .8317$, $s_\varepsilon = 1.79$, $F = 45.48$, p-value $= .0001$

	Coefficients	Standard error	t statistic	p-value
Intercept	41.4	1.22	33.90	0
Day	−1.33	.20	−6.74	.0001

Second-order model $R^2 = .8852$, $R^2(\text{adjusted}) = .8524$, $s_\varepsilon = 1.67$, $F = 26.98$, p-value $= .0005$

	Coefficients	Standard error	t statistic	p-value
Intercept	43.73	1.97	22.21	0
Day	−2.49	.82	−3.03	.0191
Day^2	.106	.073	1.46	.1889

20.15 $R^2 = .8051$, $R^2(\text{adjusted}) = .7947$, $s_\varepsilon = 2.32$, $F = 77.66$, p-value $= 0$

	Coefficients	Standard error	t statistic	p-value
Intercept	23.57	5.98	3.94	.0002
Mother	.31	.05	5.65	0
Father	.30	.05	6.37	0
Gmothers	.032	.058	.55	.5853
Gfathers	.078	.057	1.36	.1777
Smoker	−3.72	.67	−5.56	0

20.16 $R^2 = .7002$, $R^2(\text{adjusted}) = .6659$, $s_\varepsilon = 811$, $F = 20.43$, p-value $= 0$

	Coefficients	Standard error	t statistic	p-value
Intercept	3490	469.16	7.44	0
Yest Att	.37	.078	4.73	0
I1	1623	492.55	3.30	.0023
I2	733.5	394.37	1.86	.0713
I3	−765.5	484.66	−1.58	.1232

Appendix B

Tables

Table 1

Binomial Probabilities

Tabulated values are $P(X \leq k) = \sum_{x=0}^{k} p(x)$. (Values are rounded to three decimal places.)

$n = 5$

k								p							
	.01	.05	.10	.20	.25	.30	.40	.50	.60	.70	.75	.80	.90	.95	.99
0	.951	.774	.590	.328	.237	.168	.078	.031	.010	.002	.001	.000	.000	.000	.000
1	.999	.977	.919	.737	.633	.528	.337	.187	.087	.031	.016	.007	.000	.000	.000
2	1.000	.999	.991	.942	.896	.837	.683	.500	.317	.163	.104	.058	.009	.001	.000
3	1.000	1.000	1.000	.993	.984	.969	.913	.812	.663	.472	.367	.263	.081	.023	.001
4	1.000	1.000	1.000	1.000	.999	.998	.990	.969	.922	.832	.763	.672	.410	.226	.049

$n = 6$

k								p							
	.01	.05	.10	.20	.25	.30	.40	.50	.60	.70	.75	.80	.90	.95	.99
0	.941	.735	.531	.262	.178	.118	.047	.016	.004	.001	.000	.000	.000	.000	.000
1	.999	.967	.886	.655	.534	.420	.233	.109	.041	.011	.005	.002	.000	.000	.000
2	1.000	.998	.984	.901	.831	.744	.544	.344	.179	.070	.038	.017	.001	.000	.000
3	1.000	1.000	.999	.983	.962	.930	.821	.656	.456	.256	.169	.099	.016	.002	.000
4	1.000	1.000	1.000	.998	.995	.989	.959	.891	.767	.580	.466	.345	.114	.033	.001
5	1.000	1.000	1.000	1.000	1.000	.999	.996	.984	.953	.882	.822	.738	.469	.265	.059

$n = 7$

k								p							
	.01	.05	.10	.20	.25	.30	.40	.50	.60	.70	.75	.80	.90	.95	.99
0	.932	.698	.478	.210	.133	.082	.028	.008	.002	.000	.000	.000	.000	.000	.000
1	.998	.956	.850	.577	.445	.329	.159	.063	.019	.004	.001	.000	.000	.000	.000
2	1.000	.996	.974	.852	.756	.647	.420	.227	.096	.029	.013	.005	.000	.000	.000
3	1.000	1.000	.997	.967	.929	.874	.710	.500	.290	.126	.071	.033	.003	.000	.000
4	1.000	1.000	1.000	.995	.987	.971	.904	.773	.580	.353	.244	.148	.026	.004	.000
5	1.000	1.000	1.000	1.000	.999	.996	.981	.937	.841	.671	.555	.423	.150	.044	.002
6	1.000	1.000	1.000	1.000	1.000	1.000	.998	.992	.972	.918	.867	.790	.522	.302	.068

Table 1

continued

n = 8

k	.01	.05	.10	.20	.25	.30	.40	.50	.60	.70	.75	.80	.90	.95	.99
0	.923	.663	.430	.168	.100	.058	.017	.004	.001	.000	.000	.000	.000	.000	.000
1	.997	.943	.813	.503	.367	.255	.106	.035	.009	.001	.000	.000	.000	.000	.000
2	1.000	.994	.962	.797	.679	.552	.315	.145	.050	.011	.004	.001	.000	.000	.000
3	1.000	1.000	.995	.944	.886	.806	.594	.363	.174	.058	.027	.010	.000	.000	.000
4	1.000	1.000	1.000	.990	.973	.942	.826	.637	.406	.194	.114	.056	.005	.000	.000
5	1.000	1.000	1.000	.999	.996	.989	.950	.855	.685	.448	.321	.203	.038	.006	.000
6	1.000	1.000	1.000	1.000	1.000	.999	.991	.965	.894	.745	.633	.497	.187	.057	.003
7	1.000	1.000	1.000	1.000	1.000	1.000	.999	.996	.983	.942	.900	.832	.570	.337	.077

n = 9

k	.01	.05	.10	.20	.25	.30	.40	.50	.60	.70	.75	.80	.90	.95	.99
0	.914	.630	.387	.134	.075	.040	.010	.002	.000	.000	.000	.000	.000	.000	.000
1	.997	.929	.775	.436	.300	.196	.071	.020	.004	.000	.000	.000	.000	.000	.000
2	1.000	.992	.947	.738	.601	.463	.232	.090	.025	.004	.001	.000	.000	.000	.000
3	1.000	.999	.992	.914	.834	.730	.483	.254	.099	.025	.010	.003	.000	.000	.000
4	1.000	1.000	.999	.980	.951	.901	.733	.500	.267	.099	.049	.020	.001	.000	.000
5	1.000	1.000	1.000	.997	.990	.975	.901	.746	.517	.270	.166	.086	.008	.001	.000
6	1.000	1.000	1.000	1.000	.999	.996	.975	.910	.768	.537	.399	.262	.053	.008	.000
7	1.000	1.000	1.000	1.000	1.000	1.000	.996	.980	.929	.804	.700	.564	.225	.071	.003
8	1.000	1.000	1.000	1.000	1.000	1.000	1.000	.998	.990	.960	.925	.866	.613	.370	.086

Table 1

continued

$n = 10$

k	.01	.05	.10	.20	.25	.30	.40	.50	.60	.70	.75	.80	.90	.95	.99
0	.904	.599	.349	.107	.056	.028	.006	.001	.000	.000	.000	.000	.000	.000	.000
1	.996	.914	.736	.376	.244	.149	.046	.011	.002	.000	.000	.000	.000	.000	.000
2	1.000	.988	.930	.678	.526	.383	.167	.055	.012	.002	.000	.000	.000	.000	.000
3	1.000	.999	.987	.879	.776	.650	.382	.172	.055	.011	.004	.001	.000	.000	.000
4	1.000	1.000	.998	.967	.922	.850	.633	.377	.166	.047	.020	.006	.000	.000	.000
5	1.000	1.000	1.000	.994	.980	.953	.834	.623	.367	.150	.078	.033	.002	.000	.000
6	1.000	1.000	1.000	.999	.996	.989	.945	.828	.618	.350	.224	.121	.013	.001	.000
7	1.000	1.000	1.000	1.000	1.000	.998	.988	.945	.833	.617	.474	.322	.070	.012	.000
8	1.000	1.000	1.000	1.000	1.000	1.000	.998	.989	.954	.851	.756	.624	.264	.086	.004
9	1.000	1.000	1.000	1.000	1.000	1.000	1.000	.999	.994	.972	.944	.893	.651	.401	.096

$n = 15$

k	.01	.05	.10	.20	.25	.30	.40	.50	.60	.70	.75	.80	.90	.95	.99
0	.860	.463	.206	.035	.013	.005	.000	.000	.000	.000	.000	.000	.000	.000	.000
1	.990	.829	.549	.167	.080	.035	.005	.000	.000	.000	.000	.000	.000	.000	.000
2	1.000	.964	.816	.398	.236	.127	.027	.004	.000	.000	.000	.000	.000	.000	.000
3	1.000	.995	.944	.648	.461	.297	.091	.018	.002	.000	.000	.000	.000	.000	.000
4	1.000	.999	.987	.836	.686	.515	.217	.059	.009	.001	.000	.000	.000	.000	.000
5	1.000	1.000	.998	.939	.852	.722	.403	.151	.034	.004	.001	.000	.000	.000	.000
6	1.000	1.000	1.000	.982	.943	.869	.610	.304	.095	.015	.004	.001	.000	.000	.000
7	1.000	1.000	1.000	.996	.983	.950	.787	.500	.213	.050	.017	.004	.000	.000	.000
8	1.000	1.000	1.000	.999	.996	.985	.905	.696	.390	.131	.057	.018	.000	.000	.000
9	1.000	1.000	1.000	1.000	.999	.996	.966	.849	.597	.278	.148	.061	.002	.000	.000
10	1.000	1.000	1.000	1.000	1.000	.999	.991	.941	.783	.485	.314	.164	.013	.001	.000
11	1.000	1.000	1.000	1.000	1.000	1.000	.998	.982	.909	.703	.539	.352	.056	.005	.000
12	1.000	1.000	1.000	1.000	1.000	1.000	1.000	.996	.973	.873	.764	.602	.184	.036	.000
13	1.000	1.000	1.000	1.000	1.000	1.000	1.000	1.000	.995	.965	.920	.833	.451	.171	.010
14	1.000	1.000	1.000	1.000	1.000	1.000	1.000	1.000	1.000	.995	.987	.965	.794	.537	.140

Table 1

continued

$n = 20$

								p							
k	.01	.05	.10	.20	.25	.30	.40	.50	.60	.70	.75	.80	.90	.95	.99
0	.818	.358	.122	.012	.003	.001	.000	.000	.000	.000	.000	.000	.000	.000	.000
1	.983	.736	.392	.069	.024	.008	.001	.000	.000	.000	.000	.000	.000	.000	.000
2	.999	.925	.677	.206	.091	.035	.004	.000	.000	.000	.000	.000	.000	.000	.000
3	1.000	.984	.867	.411	.225	.107	.016	.001	.000	.000	.000	.000	.000	.000	.000
4	1.000	.997	.957	.630	.415	.238	.051	.006	.000	.000	.000	.000	.000	.000	.000
5	1.000	1.000	.989	.804	.617	.416	.126	.021	.002	.000	.000	.000	.000	.000	.000
6	1.000	1.000	.998	.913	.786	.608	.250	.058	.006	.000	.000	.000	.000	.000	.000
7	1.000	1.000	1.000	.968	.898	.772	.416	.132	.021	.001	.000	.000	.000	.000	.000
8	1.000	1.000	1.000	.990	.959	.887	.596	.252	.057	.005	.001	.000	.000	.000	.000
9	1.000	1.000	1.000	.997	.986	.952	.755	.412	.128	.017	.004	.001	.000	.000	.000
10	1.000	1.000	1.000	.999	.996	.983	.872	.588	.245	.048	.014	.003	.000	.000	.000
11	1.000	1.000	1.000	1.000	.999	.995	.943	.748	.404	.113	.041	.010	.000	.000	.000
12	1.000	1.000	1.000	1.000	1.000	.999	.979	.868	.584	.228	.102	.032	.000	.000	.000
13	1.000	1.000	1.000	1.000	1.000	1.000	.994	.942	.750	.392	.214	.087	.002	.000	.000
14	1.000	1.000	1.000	1.000	1.000	1.000	.998	.979	.874	.584	.383	.196	.011	.000	.000
15	1.000	1.000	1.000	1.000	1.000	1.000	1.000	.994	.949	.762	.585	.370	.043	.003	.000
16	1.000	1.000	1.000	1.000	1.000	1.000	1.000	.999	.984	.893	.775	.589	.133	.016	.000
17	1.000	1.000	1.000	1.000	1.000	1.000	1.000	1.000	.996	.965	.909	.794	.323	.075	.001
18	1.000	1.000	1.000	1.000	1.000	1.000	1.000	1.000	.999	.992	.976	.931	.608	.264	.017
19	1.000	1.000	1.000	1.000	1.000	1.000	1.000	1.000	1.000	.999	.997	.988	.878	.642	.182

Table 1

continued

$n = 25$

k	.01	.05	.10	.20	.25	.30	.40	.50	.60	.70	.75	.80	.90	.95	.99
								p							
0	.778	.277	.072	.004	.001	.000	.000	.000	.000	.000	.000	.000	.000	.000	.000
1	.974	.642	.271	.027	.007	.002	.000	.000	.000	.000	.000	.000	.000	.000	.000
2	.998	.873	.537	.098	.032	.009	.000	.000	.000	.000	.000	.000	.000	.000	.000
3	1.000	.966	.764	.234	.096	.033	.002	.000	.000	.000	.000	.000	.000	.000	.000
4	1.000	.993	.902	.421	.214	.090	.009	.000	.000	.000	.000	.000	.000	.000	.000
5	1.000	.999	.967	.617	.378	.193	.029	.002	.000	.000	.000	.000	.000	.000	.000
6	1.000	1.000	.991	.780	.561	.341	.074	.007	.000	.000	.000	.000	.000	.000	.000
7	1.000	1.000	.998	.891	.727	.512	.154	.022	.001	.000	.000	.000	.000	.000	.000
8	1.000	1.000	1.000	.953	.851	.677	.274	.054	.004	.000	.000	.000	.000	.000	.000
9	1.000	1.000	1.000	.983	.929	.811	.425	.115	.013	.000	.000	.000	.000	.000	.000
10	1.000	1.000	1.000	.994	.970	.902	.586	.212	.034	.002	.000	.000	.000	.000	.000
11	1.000	1.000	1.000	.998	.989	.956	.732	.345	.078	.006	.001	.000	.000	.000	.000
12	1.000	1.000	1.000	1.000	.997	.983	.846	.500	.154	.017	.003	.000	.000	.000	.000
13	1.000	1.000	1.000	1.000	.999	.994	.922	.655	.268	.044	.011	.002	.000	.000	.000
14	1.000	1.000	1.000	1.000	1.000	.998	.966	.788	.414	.098	.030	.006	.000	.000	.000
15	1.000	1.000	1.000	1.000	1.000	1.000	.987	.885	.575	.189	.071	.017	.000	.000	.000
16	1.000	1.000	1.000	1.000	1.000	1.000	.996	.946	.726	.323	.149	.047	.000	.000	.000
17	1.000	1.000	1.000	1.000	1.000	1.000	.999	.978	.846	.488	.273	.109	.002	.000	.000
18	1.000	1.000	1.000	1.000	1.000	1.000	1.000	.993	.926	.659	.439	.220	.009	.000	.000
19	1.000	1.000	1.000	1.000	1.000	1.000	1.000	.998	.971	.807	.622	.383	.033	.001	.000
20	1.000	1.000	1.000	1.000	1.000	1.000	1.000	1.000	.991	.910	.786	.579	.098	.007	.000
21	1.000	1.000	1.000	1.000	1.000	1.000	1.000	1.000	.998	.967	.904	.766	.236	.034	.000
22	1.000	1.000	1.000	1.000	1.000	1.000	1.000	1.000	1.000	.991	.968	.902	.463	.127	.002
23	1.000	1.000	1.000	1.000	1.000	1.000	1.000	1.000	1.000	.998	.993	.973	.729	.358	.026
24	1.000	1.000	1.000	1.000	1.000	1.000	1.000	1.000	1.000	1.000	.999	.996	.928	.723	.222

Table 2

Poisson Probabilities

Tabulated values are $P(X \leq k) = \sum_{x=0}^{k} p(x)$. (Values are rounded to three decimal places.)

k	.10	.20	.30	.40	.50	1.0	1.5	2.0	2.5	3.0	3.5	4.0	4.5	5.0	5.5	6.0
0	.905	.819	.741	.670	.607	.368	.223	.135	.082	.050	.030	.018	.011	.007	.004	.002
1	.995	.982	.963	.938	.910	.736	.558	.406	.287	.199	.136	.092	.061	.040	.027	.017
2	1.000	.999	.996	.992	.986	.920	.809	.677	.544	.423	.321	.238	.174	.125	.088	.062
3	1.000	1.000	1.000	.999	.998	.981	.934	.857	.758	.647	.537	.433	.342	.265	.202	.151
4	1.000	1.000	1.000	1.000	1.000	.996	.981	.947	.891	.815	.725	.629	.532	.440	.358	.285
5						.999	.996	.983	.958	.916	.858	.785	.703	.616	.529	.446
6						1.000	.999	.995	.986	.966	.935	.889	.831	.762	.686	.606
7							1.000	.999	.996	.988	.973	.949	.913	.867	.809	.744
8								1.000	.999	.996	.990	.979	.960	.932	.894	.847
9									1.000	.999	.997	.992	.983	.968	.946	.916
10										1.000	.999	.997	.993	.986	.975	.957
11											1.000	.999	.998	.995	.989	.980
12												1.000	.999	.998	.996	.991
13													1.000	.999	.998	.996
14														1.000	.999	.999
15															1.000	.999
16																1.000
17																
18																
19																
20																

Table 2

continued

k	6.5	7.0	7.5	8.0	8.5	9.0	μ 9.5	10	11	12	13	14	15
0	.002	.001	.001	.000	.000	.000	.000	.000	.000	.000	.000	.000	.000
1	.011	.007	.005	.003	.002	.001	.001	.000	.000	.000	.000	.000	.000
2	.043	.030	.020	.014	.009	.006	.004	.003	.001	.001	.000	.000	.000
3	.112	.082	.059	.042	.030	.021	.015	.010	.005	.002	.001	.000	.000
4	.224	.173	.132	.100	.074	.055	.040	.029	.015	.008	.004	.002	.001
5	.369	.301	.241	.191	.150	.116	.089	.067	.038	.020	.011	.006	.003
6	.527	.450	.378	.313	.256	.207	.165	.130	.079	.046	.026	.014	.008
7	.673	.599	.525	.453	.386	.324	.269	.220	.143	.090	.054	.032	.018
8	.792	.729	.662	.593	.523	.456	.392	.333	.232	.155	.100	.062	.037
9	.877	.830	.776	.717	.653	.587	.522	.458	.341	.242	.166	.109	.070
10	.933	.901	.862	.816	.763	.706	.645	.583	.460	.347	.252	.176	.118
11	.966	.947	.921	.888	.849	.803	.752	.697	.579	.462	.353	.260	.185
12	.984	.973	.957	.936	.909	.876	.836	.792	.689	.576	.463	.358	.268
13	.993	.987	.978	.966	.949	.926	.898	.864	.781	.682	.573	.464	.363
14	.997	.994	.990	.983	.973	.959	.940	.917	.854	.772	.675	.570	.466
15	.999	.998	.995	.992	.986	.978	.967	.951	.907	.844	.764	.669	.568
16	1.000	.999	.998	.996	.993	.989	.982	.973	.944	.899	.835	.756	.664
17		1.000	.999	.998	.997	.995	.991	.986	.968	.937	.890	.827	.749
18			1.000	.999	.999	.998	.996	.993	.982	.963	.930	.883	.819
19				1.000	.999	.999	.998	.997	.991	.979	.957	.923	.875
20					1.000	1.000	.999	.998	.995	.988	.975	.952	.917
21							1.000	.999	.998	.994	.986	.971	.947
22								1.000	.999	.997	.992	.983	.967
23									1.000	.999	.996	.991	.981
24										.999	.998	.995	.989
25										1.000	.999	.997	.994
26											1.000	.999	.997
27												.999	.998
28												1.000	.999
29													1.000

Table 3

Normal Probabilities

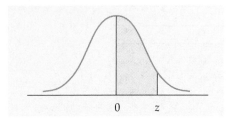

z	.00	.01	.02	.03	.04	.05	.06	.07	.08	.09
0.0	.0000	.0040	.0080	.0120	.0160	.0199	.0239	.0279	.0319	.0359
0.1	.0398	.0438	.0478	.0517	.0557	.0596	.0636	.0675	.0714	.0753
0.2	.0793	.0832	.0871	.0910	.0948	.0987	.1026	.1064	.1103	.1141
0.3	.1179	.1217	.1255	.1293	.1331	.1368	.1406	.1443	.1480	.1517
0.4	.1554	.1591	.1628	.1664	.1700	.1736	.1772	.1808	.1844	.1879
0.5	.1915	.1950	.1985	.2019	.2054	.2088	.2123	.2157	.2190	.2224
0.6	.2257	.2291	.2324	.2357	.2389	.2422	.2454	.2486	.2517	.2549
0.7	.2580	.2611	.2642	.2673	.2704	.2734	.2764	.2794	.2823	.2852
0.8	.2881	.2910	.2939	.2967	.2995	.3023	.3051	.3078	.3106	.3133
0.9	.3159	.3186	.3212	.3238	.3264	.3289	.3315	.3340	.3365	.3389
1.0	.3413	.3438	.3461	.3485	.3508	.3531	.3554	.3577	.3599	.3621
1.1	.3643	.3665	.3686	.3708	.3729	.3749	.3770	.3790	.3810	.3830
1.2	.3849	.3869	.3888	.3907	.3925	.3944	.3962	.3980	.3997	.4015
1.3	.4032	.4049	.4066	.4082	.4099	.4115	.4131	.4147	.4162	.4177
1.4	.4192	.4207	.4222	.4236	.4251	.4265	.4279	.4292	.4306	.4319
1.5	.4332	.4345	.4357	.4370	.4382	.4394	.4406	.4418	.4429	.4441
1.6	.4452	.4463	.4474	.4484	.4495	.4505	.4515	.4525	.4535	.4545
1.7	.4554	.4564	.4573	.4582	.4591	.4599	.4608	.4616	.4625	.4633
1.8	.4641	.4649	.4656	.4664	.4671	.4678	.4686	.4693	.4699	.4706
1.9	.4713	.4719	.4726	.4732	.4738	.4744	.4750	.4756	.4761	.4767
2.0	.4772	.4778	.4783	.4788	.4793	.4798	.4803	.4808	.4812	.4817
2.1	.4821	.4826	.4830	.4834	.4838	.4842	.4846	.4850	.4854	.4857
2.2	.4861	.4864	.4868	.4871	.4875	.4878	.4881	.4884	.4887	.4890
2.3	.4893	.4896	.4898	.4901	.4904	.4906	.4909	.4911	.4913	.4916
2.4	.4918	.4920	.4922	.4925	.4927	.4929	.4931	.4932	.4934	.4936
2.5	.4938	.4940	.4941	.4943	.4945	.4946	.4948	.4949	.4951	.4952
2.6	.4953	.4955	.4956	.4957	.4959	.4960	.4961	.4962	.4963	.4964
2.7	.4965	.4966	.4967	.4968	.4969	.4970	.4971	.4972	.4973	.4974
2.8	.4974	.4975	.4976	.4977	.4977	.4978	.4979	.4979	.4980	.4981
2.9	.4981	.4982	.4982	.4983	.4984	.4984	.4985	.4985	.4986	.4986
3.0	.4987	.4987	.4987	.4988	.4988	.4989	.4989	.4989	.4990	.4990

SOURCE: Abridged from Table 1 of A. Hald, *Statistical Tables and Formulas* (New York: Wiley & Sons, Inc.), 1952. Reproduced by permission of A. Hald and the publisher, John Wiley & Sons, Inc.

DEGREES OF FREEDOM	$t_{.100}$	$t_{.050}$	$t_{.025}$	$t_{.010}$	$t_{.005}$	DEGREES OF FREEDOM	$t_{.100}$	$t_{.050}$	$t_{.025}$	$t_{.010}$	$t_{.005}$
1	3.078	6.314	12.706	31.821	63.657	24	1.318	1.711	2.064	2.492	2.797
2	1.886	2.920	4.303	6.965	9.925	25	1.316	1.708	2.060	2.485	2.787
3	1.638	2.353	3.182	4.541	5.841	26	1.315	1.706	2.056	2.479	2.779
4	1.533	2.132	2.776	3.747	4.604	27	1.314	1.703	2.052	2.473	2.771
5	1.476	2.015	2.571	3.365	4.032	28	1.313	1.701	2.048	2.467	2.763
6	1.440	1.943	2.447	3.143	3.707	29	1.311	1.699	2.045	2.462	2.756
7	1.415	1.895	2.365	2.998	3.499	30	1.310	1.697	2.042	2.457	2.750
8	1.397	1.860	2.306	2.896	3.355	35	1.306	1.690	2.030	2.438	2.724
9	1.383	1.833	2.262	2.821	3.250	40	1.303	1.684	2.021	2.423	2.705
10	1.372	1.812	2.228	2.764	3.169	45	1.301	1.679	2.014	2.412	2.690
11	1.363	1.796	2.201	2.718	3.106	50	1.299	1.676	2.009	2.403	2.678
12	1.356	1.782	2.179	2.681	3.055	60	1.296	1.671	2.000	2.390	2.660
13	1.350	1.771	2.160	2.650	3.012	70	1.294	1.667	1.994	2.381	2.648
14	1.345	1.761	2.145	2.624	2.977	80	1.292	1.664	1.990	2.374	2.639
15	1.341	1.753	2.131	2.602	2.947	90	1.291	1.662	1.987	2.369	2.632
16	1.337	1.746	2.120	2.583	2.921	100	1.290	1.660	1.984	2.364	2.626
17	1.333	1.740	2.110	2.567	2.898	120	1.289	1.658	1.980	2.358	2.617
18	1.330	1.734	2.101	2.552	2.878	140	1.288	1.656	1.977	2.353	2.611
19	1.328	1.729	2.093	2.539	2.861	160	1.287	1.654	1.975	2.350	2.607
20	1.325	1.725	2.086	2.528	2.845	180	1.286	1.653	1.973	2.347	2.603
21	1.323	1.721	2.080	2.518	2.831	200	1.286	1.653	1.972	2.345	2.601
22	1.321	1.717	2.074	2.508	2.819	∞	1.282	1.645	1.960	2.326	2.576
23	1.319	1.714	2.069	2.500	2.807						

SOURCE: From M. Merrington, "Table of Percentage Points of the *t*-Distribution," *Biometrika* 32 (1941): 300. Reproduced by permission of the Biometrika Trustees.

Table 5

Critical Values of χ^2

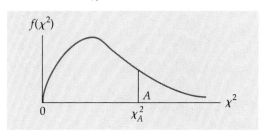

DEGREES OF FREEDOM	$\chi^2_{.995}$	$\chi^2_{.990}$	$\chi^2_{.975}$	$\chi^2_{.950}$	$\chi^2_{.900}$	$\chi^2_{.100}$	$\chi^2_{.050}$	$\chi^2_{.025}$	$\chi^2_{.010}$	$\chi^2_{.005}$
1	0.0000393	0.0001571	0.0009821	0.0039321	0.0157908	2.70554	3.84146	5.02389	6.63490	7.87944
2	0.0100251	0.0201007	0.0506356	0.102587	0.210720	4.60517	5.99147	7.37776	9.21034	10.5966
3	0.0717212	0.114832	0.215795	0.351846	0.584375	6.25139	7.81473	9.34840	11.3449	12.8381
4	0.206990	0.297110	0.484419	0.710721	1.063623	7.77944	9.48773	11.1433	13.2767	14.8602
5	0.411740	0.554300	0.831211	1.145476	1.61031	9.23635	11.0705	12.8325	15.0863	16.7496
6	0.675727	0.872085	1.237347	1.63539	2.20413	10.6446	12.5916	14.4494	16.8119	18.5476
7	0.989265	1.239043	1.68987	2.16735	2.83311	12.0170	14.0671	16.0128	18.4753	20.2777
8	1.344419	1.646482	2.17973	2.73264	3.48954	13.3616	15.5073	17.5346	20.0902	21.9550
9	1.734926	2.087912	2.70039	3.32511	4.16816	14.6837	16.9190	19.0228	21.6660	23.5893
10	2.15585	2.55821	3.24697	3.94030	4.86518	15.9871	18.3070	20.4831	23.2093	25.1882
11	2.60321	3.05347	3.81575	4.57481	5.57779	17.2750	19.6751	21.9200	24.7250	26.7569
12	3.07382	3.57056	4.40379	5.22603	6.30380	18.5494	21.0261	23.3367	26.2170	28.2995
13	3.56503	4.10691	5.00874	5.89186	7.04150	19.8119	22.3621	24.7356	27.6883	29.8194
14	4.07468	4.66043	5.62872	6.57063	7.78953	21.0642	23.6848	26.1190	29.1413	31.3193
15	4.60094	5.22935	6.26214	7.26094	8.54675	22.3072	24.9958	27.4884	30.5779	32.8013
16	5.14224	5.81221	6.90766	7.96164	9.31223	23.5418	26.2962	28.8454	31.9999	34.2672
17	5.69724	6.40776	7.56418	8.67176	10.0852	24.7690	27.5871	30.1910	33.4087	35.7185
18	6.26481	7.01491	8.23075	9.39046	10.8649	25.9894	28.8693	31.5264	34.8053	37.1564
19	6.84398	7.63273	8.90655	10.1170	11.6509	27.2036	30.1435	32.8523	36.1908	38.5822
20	7.43386	8.26040	9.59083	10.8508	12.4426	28.4120	31.4104	34.1696	37.5662	39.9968
21	8.03366	8.89720	10.28293	11.5913	13.2396	29.6151	32.6705	35.4789	38.9321	41.4010
22	8.64272	9.54249	10.9823	12.3380	14.0415	30.8133	33.9244	36.7807	40.2894	42.7956
23	9.26042	10.19567	11.6885	13.0905	14.8479	32.0069	35.1725	38.0757	41.6384	44.1813
24	9.88623	10.8564	12.4011	13.8484	15.6587	33.1963	36.4151	39.3641	42.9798	45.5585
25	10.5197	11.5240	13.1197	14.6114	16.4734	34.3816	37.6525	40.6465	44.3141	46.9278
26	11.1603	12.1981	13.8439	15.3791	17.2919	35.5631	38.8852	41.9232	45.6417	48.2899
27	11.8076	12.8786	14.5733	16.1513	18.1138	36.7412	40.1133	43.1944	46.9630	49.6449
28	12.4613	13.5648	15.3079	16.9279	18.9392	37.9159	41.3372	44.4607	48.2782	50.9933
29	13.1211	14.2565	16.0471	17.7083	19.7677	39.0875	42.5569	45.7222	49.5879	52.3356
30	13.7867	14.9535	16.7908	18.4926	20.5992	40.2560	43.7729	46.9792	50.8922	53.6720
40	20.7065	22.1643	24.4331	26.5093	29.0505	51.8050	55.7585	59.3417	63.6907	66.7659
50	27.9907	29.7067	32.3574	34.7642	37.6886	63.1671	67.5048	71.4202	76.1539	79.4900
60	35.5346	37.4848	40.4817	43.1879	46.4589	74.3970	79.0819	83.2976	88.3794	91.9517
70	43.2752	45.4418	48.7576	51.7393	55.3290	85.5271	90.5312	95.0231	100.425	104.215
80	51.1720	53.5400	57.1532	60.3915	64.2778	96.5782	101.879	106.629	112.329	116.321
90	59.1963	61.7541	65.6466	69.1260	73.2912	107.565	113.145	118.136	124.116	128.299
100	67.3276	70.0648	74.2219	77.9295	82.3581	118.498	124.342	129.561	135.807	140.169

SOURCE: From C. M. Thompson, "Tables of the Percentage Points of the χ^2-Distribution," *Biometrika* 32 (1941): 188–89. Reproduced by permission of the Biometrika Trustees.

Table 6(a)

Critical Values of F, $A = .05$

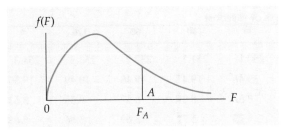

ν_1	NUMERATOR DEGREES OF FREEDOM								
ν_2	1	2	3	4	5	6	7	8	9
1	161.4	199.5	215.7	224.6	230.2	234.0	236.8	238.9	240.5
2	18.51	19.00	19.16	19.25	19.30	19.33	19.35	19.37	19.38
3	10.13	9.55	9.28	9.12	9.01	8.94	8.89	8.85	8.81
4	7.71	6.94	6.59	6.39	6.26	6.16	6.09	6.04	6.00
5	6.61	5.79	5.41	5.19	5.05	4.95	4.88	4.82	4.77
6	5.99	5.14	4.76	4.53	4.39	4.28	4.21	4.15	4.10
7	5.59	4.74	4.35	4.12	3.97	3.87	3.79	3.73	3.68
8	5.32	4.46	4.07	3.84	3.69	3.58	3.50	3.44	3.39
9	5.12	4.26	3.86	3.63	3.48	3.37	3.29	3.23	3.18
10	4.96	4.10	3.71	3.48	3.33	3.22	3.14	3.07	3.02
11	4.84	3.98	3.59	3.36	3.20	3.09	3.01	2.95	2.90
12	4.75	3.89	3.49	3.26	3.11	3.00	2.91	2.85	2.80
13	4.67	3.81	3.41	3.18	3.03	2.92	2.83	2.77	2.71
14	4.60	3.74	3.34	3.11	2.96	2.85	2.76	2.70	2.65
15	4.54	3.68	3.29	3.06	2.90	2.79	2.71	2.64	2.59
16	4.49	3.63	3.24	3.01	2.85	2.74	2.66	2.59	2.54
17	4.45	3.59	3.20	2.96	2.81	2.70	2.61	2.55	2.49
18	4.41	3.55	3.16	2.93	2.77	2.66	2.58	2.51	2.46
19	4.38	3.52	3.13	2.90	2.74	2.63	2.54	2.48	2.42
20	4.35	3.49	3.10	2.87	2.71	2.60	2.51	2.45	2.39
21	4.32	3.47	3.07	2.84	2.68	2.57	2.49	2.42	2.37
22	4.30	3.44	3.05	2.82	2.66	2.55	2.46	2.40	2.34
23	4.28	3.42	3.03	2.80	2.64	2.53	2.44	2.37	2.32
24	4.26	3.40	3.01	2.78	2.62	2.51	2.42	2.36	2.30
25	4.24	3.39	2.99	2.76	2.60	2.49	2.40	2.34	2.28
26	4.23	3.37	2.98	2.74	2.59	2.47	2.39	2.32	2.27
27	4.21	3.35	2.96	2.73	2.57	2.46	2.37	2.31	2.25
28	4.20	3.34	2.95	2.71	2.56	2.45	2.36	2.29	2.24
29	4.18	3.33	2.93	2.70	2.55	2.43	2.35	2.28	2.22
30	4.17	3.32	2.92	2.69	2.53	2.42	2.33	2.27	2.21
40	4.08	3.23	2.84	2.61	2.45	2.34	2.25	2.18	2.12
60	4.00	3.15	2.76	2.53	2.37	2.25	2.17	2.10	2.04
120	3.92	3.07	2.68	2.45	2.29	2.17	2.09	2.02	1.96
∞	3.84	3.00	2.60	2.37	2.21	2.10	2.01	1.94	1.88

DENOMINATOR DEGREES OF FREEDOM

SOURCE: From M. Merrington and C. M. Thompson, "Tables of Percentage Points of the Inverted Beta (F)-Distribution," *Biometrika* 33 (1943): 73–88. Reproduced by permission of the Biometrika Trustees.

Table 6(a)

continued

ν_2 \ ν_1	NUMERATOR DEGREES OF FREEDOM									
	10	12	15	20	24	30	40	60	120	∞
1	241.9	243.9	245.9	248.0	249.1	250.1	251.1	252.2	253.3	254.3
2	19.40	19.41	19.43	19.45	19.45	19.46	19.47	19.48	19.49	19.50
3	8.79	8.74	8.70	8.66	8.64	8.62	8.59	8.57	8.55	8.53
4	5.96	5.91	5.86	5.80	5.77	5.75	5.72	5.69	5.66	5.63
5	4.74	4.68	4.62	4.56	4.53	4.50	4.46	4.43	4.40	4.36
6	4.06	4.00	3.94	3.87	3.84	3.81	3.77	3.74	3.70	3.67
7	3.64	3.57	3.51	3.44	3.41	3.38	3.34	3.30	3.27	3.23
8	3.35	3.28	3.22	3.15	3.12	3.08	3.04	3.01	2.97	2.93
9	3.14	3.07	3.01	2.94	2.90	2.86	2.83	2.79	2.75	2.71
10	2.98	2.91	2.85	2.77	2.74	2.70	2.66	2.62	2.58	2.54
11	2.85	2.79	2.72	2.65	2.61	2.57	2.53	2.49	2.45	2.40
12	2.75	2.69	2.62	2.54	2.51	2.47	2.43	2.38	2.34	2.30
13	2.67	2.60	2.53	2.46	2.42	2.38	2.34	2.30	2.25	2.21
14	2.60	2.53	2.46	2.39	2.35	2.31	2.27	2.22	2.18	2.13
15	2.54	2.48	2.40	2.33	2.29	2.25	2.20	2.16	2.11	2.07
16	2.49	2.42	2.35	2.28	2.24	2.19	2.15	2.11	2.06	2.01
17	2.45	2.38	2.31	2.23	2.19	2.15	2.10	2.06	2.01	1.96
18	2.41	2.34	2.27	2.19	2.15	2.11	2.06	2.02	1.97	1.92
19	2.38	2.31	2.23	2.16	2.11	2.07	2.03	1.98	1.93	1.88
20	2.35	2.28	2.20	2.12	2.08	2.04	1.99	1.95	1.90	1.84
21	2.32	2.25	2.18	2.10	2.05	2.01	1.96	1.92	1.87	1.81
22	2.30	2.23	2.15	2.07	2.03	1.98	1.94	1.89	1.84	1.78
23	2.27	2.20	2.13	2.05	2.01	1.96	1.91	1.86	1.81	1.76
24	2.25	2.18	2.11	2.03	1.98	1.94	1.89	1.84	1.79	1.73
25	2.24	2.16	2.09	2.01	1.96	1.92	1.87	1.82	1.77	1.71
26	2.22	2.15	2.07	1.99	1.95	1.90	1.85	1.80	1.75	1.69
27	2.20	2.13	2.06	1.97	1.93	1.88	1.84	1.79	1.73	1.67
28	2.19	2.12	2.04	1.96	1.91	1.87	1.82	1.77	1.71	1.65
29	2.18	2.10	2.03	1.94	1.90	1.85	1.81	1.75	1.70	1.64
30	2.16	2.09	2.01	1.93	1.89	1.84	1.79	1.74	1.68	1.62
40	2.08	2.00	1.92	1.84	1.79	1.74	1.69	1.64	1.58	1.51
60	1.99	1.92	1.84	1.75	1.70	1.65	1.59	1.53	1.47	1.39
120	1.91	1.83	1.75	1.66	1.61	1.55	1.50	1.43	1.35	1.25
∞	1.83	1.75	1.67	1.57	1.52	1.46	1.39	1.32	1.22	1.00

DENOMINATOR DEGREES OF FREEDOM

Table 6(b)

Critical Values of F: A = .025

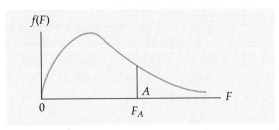

ν_2	\multicolumn{9}{c}{NUMERATOR DEGREES OF FREEDOM ν_1}
	1	2	3	4	5	6	7	8	9
1	647.8	799.5	864.2	899.6	921.8	937.1	948.2	956.7	963.3
2	38.51	39.00	39.17	39.25	39.30	39.33	39.36	39.37	39.39
3	17.44	16.04	15.44	15.10	14.88	14.73	14.62	14.54	14.47
4	12.22	10.65	9.98	9.60	9.36	9.20	9.07	8.98	8.90
5	10.01	8.43	7.76	7.39	7.15	6.98	6.85	6.76	6.68
6	8.81	7.26	6.60	6.23	5.99	5.82	5.70	5.60	5.52
7	8.07	6.54	5.89	5.52	5.29	5.12	4.99	4.90	4.82
8	7.57	6.06	5.42	5.05	4.82	4.65	4.53	4.43	4.36
9	7.21	5.71	5.08	4.72	4.48	4.32	4.20	4.10	4.03
10	6.94	5.46	4.83	4.47	4.24	4.07	3.95	3.85	3.78
11	6.72	5.26	4.63	4.28	4.04	3.88	3.76	3.66	3.59
12	6.55	5.10	4.47	4.12	3.89	3.73	3.61	3.51	3.44
13	6.41	4.97	4.35	4.00	3.77	3.60	3.48	3.39	3.31
14	6.30	4.86	4.24	3.89	3.66	3.50	3.38	3.29	3.21
15	6.20	4.77	4.15	3.80	3.58	3.41	3.29	3.20	3.12
16	6.12	4.69	4.08	3.73	3.50	3.34	3.22	3.12	3.05
17	6.04	4.62	4.01	3.66	3.44	3.28	3.16	3.06	2.98
18	5.98	4.56	3.95	3.61	3.38	3.22	3.10	3.01	2.93
19	5.92	4.51	3.90	3.56	3.33	3.17	3.05	2.96	2.88
20	5.87	4.46	3.86	3.51	3.29	3.13	3.01	2.91	2.84
21	5.83	4.42	3.82	3.48	3.25	3.09	2.97	2.87	2.80
22	5.79	4.38	3.78	3.44	3.22	3.05	2.93	2.84	2.76
23	5.75	4.35	3.75	3.41	3.18	3.02	2.90	2.81	2.73
24	5.72	4.32	3.72	3.38	3.15	2.99	2.87	2.78	2.70
25	5.69	4.29	3.69	3.35	3.13	2.97	2.85	2.75	2.68
26	5.66	4.27	3.67	3.33	3.10	2.94	2.82	2.73	2.65
27	5.63	4.24	3.65	3.31	3.08	2.92	2.80	2.71	2.63
28	5.61	4.22	3.63	3.29	3.06	2.90	2.78	2.69	2.61
29	5.59	4.20	3.61	3.27	3.04	2.88	2.76	2.67	2.59
30	5.57	4.18	3.59	3.25	3.03	2.87	2.75	2.65	2.57
40	5.42	4.05	3.46	3.13	2.90	2.74	2.62	2.53	2.45
60	5.29	3.93	3.34	3.01	2.79	2.63	2.51	2.41	2.33
120	5.15	3.80	3.23	2.89	2.67	2.52	2.39	2.30	2.22
∞	5.02	3.69	3.12	2.79	2.57	2.41	2.29	2.19	2.11

DENOMINATOR DEGREES OF FREEDOM

SOURCE: From M. Merrington and C. M. Thompson, "Tables of Percentage Points of the Inverted Beta (F)-Distribution," *Biometrika* 33 (1943): 73–88. Reproduced by permission of the Biometrika Trustees.

Table 6(b)

continued

ν_2 \ ν_1	NUMERATOR DEGREES OF FREEDOM									
	10	12	15	20	24	30	40	60	120	∞
1	968.6	976.7	984.9	993.1	997.2	1,001	1,006	1,010	1,014	1,018
2	39.40	39.41	39.43	39.45	39.46	39.46	39.47	39.48	39.49	39.50
3	14.42	14.34	14.25	14.17	14.12	14.08	14.04	13.99	13.95	13.90
4	8.84	8.75	8.66	8.56	8.51	8.46	8.41	8.36	8.31	8.26
5	6.62	6.52	6.43	6.33	6.28	6.23	6.18	6.12	6.07	6.02
6	5.46	5.37	5.27	5.17	5.12	5.07	5.01	4.96	4.90	4.85
7	4.76	4.67	4.57	4.47	4.42	4.36	4.31	4.25	4.20	4.14
8	4.30	4.20	4.10	4.00	3.95	3.89	3.84	3.78	3.73	3.67
9	3.96	3.87	3.77	3.67	3.61	3.56	3.51	3.45	3.39	3.33
10	3.72	3.62	3.52	3.42	3.37	3.31	3.26	3.20	3.14	3.08
11	3.53	3.43	3.33	3.23	3.17	3.12	3.06	3.00	2.94	2.88
12	3.37	3.28	3.18	3.07	3.02	2.96	2.91	2.85	2.79	2.72
13	3.25	3.15	3.05	2.95	2.89	2.84	2.78	2.72	2.66	2.60
14	3.15	3.05	2.95	2.84	2.79	2.73	2.67	2.61	2.55	2.49
15	3.06	2.96	2.86	2.76	2.70	2.64	2.59	2.52	2.46	2.40
16	2.99	2.89	2.79	2.68	2.63	2.57	2.51	2.45	2.38	2.32
17	2.92	2.82	2.72	2.62	2.56	2.50	2.44	2.38	2.32	2.25
18	2.87	2.77	2.67	2.56	2.50	2.44	2.38	2.32	2.26	2.19
19	2.82	2.72	2.62	2.51	2.45	2.39	2.33	2.27	2.20	2.13
20	2.77	2.68	2.57	2.46	2.41	2.35	2.29	2.22	2.16	2.09
21	2.73	2.64	2.53	2.42	2.37	2.31	2.25	2.18	2.11	2.04
22	2.70	2.60	2.50	2.39	2.33	2.27	2.21	2.14	2.08	2.00
23	2.67	2.57	2.47	2.36	2.30	2.24	2.18	2.11	2.04	1.97
24	2.64	2.54	2.44	2.33	2.27	2.21	2.15	2.08	2.01	1.94
25	2.61	2.51	2.41	2.30	2.24	2.18	2.12	2.05	1.98	1.91
26	2.59	2.49	2.39	2.28	2.22	2.16	2.09	2.03	1.95	1.88
27	2.57	2.47	2.36	2.25	2.19	2.13	2.07	2.00	1.93	1.85
28	2.55	2.45	2.34	2.23	2.17	2.11	2.05	1.98	1.91	1.83
29	2.53	2.43	2.32	2.21	2.15	2.09	2.03	1.96	1.89	1.81
30	2.51	2.41	2.31	2.20	2.14	2.07	2.01	1.94	1.87	1.79
40	2.39	2.29	2.18	2.07	2.01	1.94	1.88	1.80	1.72	1.64
60	2.27	2.17	2.06	1.94	1.88	1.82	1.74	1.67	1.58	1.48
120	2.16	2.05	1.94	1.82	1.76	1.69	1.61	1.53	1.43	1.31
∞	2.05	1.94	1.83	1.71	1.64	1.57	1.48	1.39	1.27	1.00

DENOMINATOR DEGREES OF FREEDOM

Table 6(c)

Critical Values of F: $A = .01$

ν_1 ν_2	NUMERATOR DEGREES OF FREEDOM								
	1	**2**	**3**	**4**	**5**	**6**	**7**	**8**	**9**
1	4,052	4,999.5	5,403	5,625	5,764	5,859	5,928	5,982	6,022
2	98.50	99.00	99.17	99.25	99.30	99.33	99.36	99.37	99.39
3	34.12	30.82	29.46	28.71	28.24	27.91	27.67	27.49	27.35
4	21.20	18.00	16.69	15.98	15.52	15.21	14.98	14.80	14.66
5	16.26	13.27	12.06	11.39	10.97	10.67	10.46	10.29	10.16
6	13.75	10.92	9.78	9.15	8.75	8.47	8.26	8.10	7.98
7	12.25	9.55	8.45	7.85	7.46	7.19	6.99	6.84	6.72
8	11.26	8.65	7.59	7.01	6.63	6.37	6.18	6.03	5.91
9	10.56	8.02	6.99	6.42	6.06	5.80	5.61	5.47	5.35
10	10.04	7.56	6.55	5.99	5.64	5.39	5.20	5.06	4.94
11	9.65	7.21	6.22	5.67	5.32	5.07	4.89	4.74	4.63
12	9.33	6.93	5.95	5.41	5.06	4.82	4.64	4.50	4.39
13	9.07	6.70	5.74	5.21	4.86	4.62	4.44	4.30	4.19
14	8.86	6.51	5.56	5.04	4.69	4.46	4.28	4.14	4.03
15	8.68	6.36	5.42	4.89	4.56	4.32	4.14	4.00	3.89
16	8.53	6.23	5.29	4.77	4.44	4.20	4.03	3.89	3.78
17	8.40	6.11	5.18	4.67	4.34	4.10	3.93	3.79	3.68
18	8.29	6.01	5.09	4.58	4.25	4.01	3.84	3.71	3.60
19	8.18	5.93	5.01	4.50	4.17	3.94	3.77	3.63	3.52
20	8.10	5.85	4.94	4.43	4.10	3.87	3.70	3.56	3.46
21	8.02	5.78	4.87	4.37	4.04	3.81	3.64	3.51	3.40
22	7.95	5.72	4.82	4.31	3.99	3.76	3.59	3.45	3.35
23	7.88	5.66	4.76	4.26	3.94	3.71	3.54	3.41	3.30
24	7.82	5.61	4.72	4.22	3.90	3.67	3.50	3.36	3.26
25	7.77	5.57	4.68	4.18	3.85	3.63	3.46	3.32	3.22
26	7.72	5.53	4.64	4.14	3.82	3.59	3.42	3.29	3.18
27	7.68	5.49	4.60	4.11	3.78	3.56	3.39	3.26	3.15
28	7.64	5.45	4.57	4.07	3.75	3.53	3.36	3.23	3.12
29	7.60	5.42	4.54	4.04	3.73	3.50	3.33	3.20	3.09
30	7.56	5.39	4.51	4.02	3.70	3.47	3.30	3.17	3.07
40	7.31	5.18	4.31	3.83	3.51	3.29	3.12	2.99	2.89
60	7.08	4.98	4.13	3.65	3.34	3.12	2.95	2.82	2.72
120	6.85	4.79	3.95	3.48	3.17	2.96	2.79	2.66	2.56
∞	6.63	4.61	3.78	3.32	3.02	2.80	2.64	2.51	2.41

(Left vertical label: DENOMINATOR DEGREES OF FREEDOM)

SOURCE: From M. Merrington and C. M. Thompson, "Tables of Percentage Points of the Inverted Beta (F)-Distribution," *Biometrika* 33 (1943): 73–88. Reproduced by permission of the Biometrika Trustees.

Table 6(c)

continued

ν_2 \ ν_1	NUMERATOR DEGREES OF FREEDOM									
	10	**12**	**15**	**20**	**24**	**30**	**40**	**60**	**120**	**∞**
1	6,056	6,106	6,157	6,209	6,235	6,261	6,287	6,313	6,339	6,366
2	99.40	99.42	99.43	99.45	99.46	99.47	99.47	99.48	99.49	99.50
3	27.23	27.05	26.87	26.69	26.60	26.50	26.41	26.32	26.22	26.13
4	14.55	14.37	14.20	14.02	13.93	13.84	13.75	13.65	13.56	13.46
5	10.05	9.89	9.72	9.55	9.47	9.38	9.29	9.20	9.11	9.02
6	7.87	7.72	7.56	7.40	7.31	7.23	7.14	7.06	6.97	6.88
7	6.62	6.47	6.31	6.16	6.07	5.99	5.91	5.82	5.74	5.65
8	5.81	5.67	5.52	5.36	5.28	5.20	5.12	5.03	4.95	4.86
9	5.26	5.11	4.96	4.81	4.73	4.65	4.57	4.48	4.40	4.31
10	4.85	4.71	4.56	4.41	4.33	4.25	4.17	4.08	4.00	3.91
11	4.54	4.40	4.25	4.10	4.02	3.94	3.86	3.78	3.69	3.60
12	4.30	4.16	4.01	3.86	3.78	3.70	3.62	3.54	3.45	3.36
13	4.10	3.96	3.82	3.66	3.59	3.51	3.43	3.34	3.25	3.17
14	3.94	3.80	3.66	3.51	3.43	3.35	3.27	3.18	3.09	3.00
15	3.80	3.67	3.52	3.37	3.29	3.21	3.13	3.05	2.96	2.87
16	3.69	3.55	3.41	3.26	3.18	3.10	3.02	2.93	2.84	2.75
17	3.59	3.46	3.31	3.16	3.08	3.00	2.92	2.83	2.75	2.65
18	3.51	3.37	3.23	3.08	3.00	2.92	2.84	2.75	2.66	2.57
19	3.43	3.30	3.15	3.00	2.92	2.84	2.76	2.67	2.58	2.49
20	3.37	3.23	3.09	2.94	2.86	2.78	2.69	2.61	2.52	2.42
21	3.31	3.17	3.03	2.88	2.80	2.72	2.64	2.55	2.46	2.36
22	3.26	3.12	2.98	2.83	2.75	2.67	2.58	2.50	2.40	2.31
23	3.21	3.07	2.93	2.78	2.70	2.62	2.54	2.45	2.35	2.26
24	3.17	3.03	2.89	2.74	2.66	2.58	2.49	2.40	2.31	2.21
25	3.13	2.99	2.85	2.70	2.62	2.54	2.45	2.36	2.27	2.17
26	3.09	2.96	2.81	2.66	2.58	2.50	2.42	2.33	2.23	2.13
27	3.06	2.93	2.78	2.63	2.55	2.47	2.38	2.29	2.20	2.10
28	3.03	2.90	2.75	2.60	2.52	2.44	2.35	2.26	2.17	2.06
29	3.00	2.87	2.73	2.57	2.49	2.41	2.33	2.23	2.14	2.03
30	2.98	2.84	2.70	2.55	2.47	2.39	2.30	2.21	2.11	2.01
40	2.80	2.66	2.52	2.37	2.29	2.20	2.11	2.02	1.92	1.80
60	2.63	2.50	2.35	2.20	2.12	2.03	1.94	1.84	1.73	1.60
120	2.47	2.34	2.19	2.03	1.95	1.86	1.76	1.66	1.53	1.38
∞	2.32	2.18	2.04	1.88	1.79	1.70	1.59	1.47	1.32	1.00

DENOMINATOR DEGREES OF FREEDOM

Table 7(a)

Critical Values of the Studentized Range, $\alpha = .05$

ν	2	3	4	5	6	7	8	9	10	11	12	13	14	15	16	17	18	19	20
1	18.0	27.0	32.8	37.1	40.4	43.1	45.4	47.4	49.1	50.6	52.0	53.2	54.3	55.4	56.3	57.2	58.0	58.8	59.6
2	6.08	8.33	9.80	10.9	11.7	12.4	13.0	13.5	14.0	14.4	14.7	15.1	15.4	15.7	15.9	16.1	16.4	16.6	16.8
3	4.50	5.91	6.82	7.50	8.04	8.48	8.85	9.18	9.46	9.72	9.95	10.2	10.3	10.5	10.7	10.8	11.0	11.1	11.2
4	3.93	5.04	5.76	6.29	6.71	7.05	7.35	7.60	7.83	8.03	8.21	8.37	8.52	8.66	8.79	8.91	9.03	9.13	9.23
5	3.64	4.60	5.22	5.67	6.03	6.33	6.58	6.80	6.99	7.17	7.32	7.47	7.60	7.72	7.83	7.93	8.03	8.12	8.21
6	3.46	4.34	4.90	5.30	5.63	5.90	6.12	6.32	6.49	6.65	6.79	6.92	7.03	7.14	7.24	7.34	7.43	7.51	7.59
7	3.34	4.16	4.68	5.06	5.36	5.61	5.82	6.00	6.16	6.30	6.43	6.55	6.66	6.76	6.85	6.94	7.02	7.10	7.17
8	3.26	4.04	4.53	4.89	5.17	5.40	5.60	5.77	5.92	6.05	6.18	6.29	6.39	6.48	6.57	6.65	6.73	6.80	6.87
9	3.20	3.95	4.41	4.76	5.02	5.24	5.43	5.59	5.74	5.87	5.98	6.09	6.19	6.28	6.36	6.44	6.51	6.58	6.64
10	3.15	3.88	4.33	4.65	4.91	5.12	5.30	5.46	5.60	5.72	5.83	5.93	6.03	6.11	6.19	6.27	6.34	6.40	6.47
11	3.11	3.82	4.26	4.57	4.82	5.03	5.20	5.35	5.49	5.61	5.71	5.81	5.90	5.98	6.06	6.13	6.20	6.27	6.33
12	3.08	3.77	4.20	4.51	4.75	4.95	5.12	5.27	5.39	5.51	5.61	5.71	5.80	5.88	5.95	6.02	6.09	6.15	6.21
13	3.06	3.73	4.15	4.45	4.69	4.88	5.05	5.19	5.32	5.43	5.53	5.63	5.71	5.79	5.86	5.93	5.99	6.05	6.11
14	3.03	3.70	4.11	4.41	4.64	4.83	4.99	5.13	5.25	5.36	5.46	5.55	5.64	5.71	5.79	5.85	5.91	5.97	6.03
15	3.01	3.67	4.08	4.37	4.59	4.78	4.94	5.08	5.20	5.31	5.40	5.49	5.57	5.65	5.72	5.78	5.85	5.90	5.96
16	3.00	3.65	4.05	4.33	4.56	4.74	4.90	5.03	5.15	5.26	5.35	5.44	5.52	5.59	5.66	5.73	5.79	5.84	5.90
17	2.98	3.63	4.02	4.30	4.52	4.70	4.86	4.99	5.11	5.21	5.31	5.39	5.47	5.54	5.61	5.67	5.73	5.79	5.84
18	2.97	3.61	4.00	4.28	4.49	4.67	4.82	4.96	5.07	5.17	5.27	5.35	5.43	5.50	5.57	5.63	5.69	5.74	5.79
19	2.96	3.59	3.98	4.25	4.47	4.65	4.79	4.92	5.04	5.14	5.23	5.31	5.39	5.46	5.53	5.59	5.65	5.70	5.75
20	2.95	3.58	3.96	4.23	4.45	4.62	4.77	4.90	5.01	5.11	5.20	5.28	5.36	5.43	5.49	5.55	5.61	5.66	5.71
24	2.92	3.53	3.90	4.17	4.37	4.54	4.68	4.81	4.92	5.01	5.10	5.18	5.25	5.32	5.38	5.44	5.49	5.55	5.59
30	2.89	3.49	3.85	4.10	4.30	4.46	4.60	4.72	4.82	4.92	5.00	5.08	5.15	5.21	5.27	5.33	5.38	5.43	5.47
40	2.86	3.44	3.79	4.04	4.23	4.39	4.52	4.63	4.73	4.82	4.90	4.98	5.04	5.11	5.16	5.22	5.27	5.31	5.36
60	2.83	3.40	3.74	3.98	4.16	4.31	4.44	4.55	4.65	4.73	4.81	4.88	4.94	5.00	5.06	5.11	5.15	5.20	5.24
120	2.80	3.36	3.68	3.92	4.10	4.24	4.36	4.47	4.56	4.64	4.71	4.78	4.84	4.90	4.95	5.00	5.04	5.09	5.13
∞	2.77	3.31	3.63	3.86	4.03	4.17	4.29	4.39	4.47	4.55	4.62	4.68	4.74	4.80	4.85	4.89	4.93	4.97	5.01

Table 7(b)

Critical Values of the Studentized Range, $\alpha = .01$

ν	k																		
	2	3	4	5	6	7	8	9	10	11	12	13	14	15	16	17	18	19	20
1	90.0	135	164	186	202	216	227	237	246	253	260	266	272	277	282	286	290	294	298
2	14.0	19.0	22.3	24.7	26.6	28.2	29.5	30.7	31.7	32.6	33.4	34.1	34.8	35.4	36.0	36.5	37.0	37.5	37.9
3	8.26	10.6	12.2	13.3	14.2	15.0	15.6	16.2	16.7	17.1	17.5	17.9	18.2	18.5	18.8	19.1	19.3	19.5	19.8
4	6.51	8.12	9.17	9.96	10.6	11.1	11.5	11.9	12.3	12.6	12.8	13.1	13.3	13.5	13.7	13.9	14.1	14.2	14.4
5	5.70	6.97	7.80	8.42	8.91	9.32	9.67	9.97	10.2	10.5	10.7	10.9	11.1	11.2	11.4	11.6	11.7	11.8	11.9
6	5.24	6.33	7.03	7.56	7.97	8.32	8.61	8.87	9.10	9.30	9.49	9.65	9.81	9.95	10.1	10.2	10.3	10.4	10.5
7	4.95	5.92	6.54	7.01	7.37	7.68	7.94	8.17	8.37	8.55	8.71	8.86	9.00	9.12	9.24	9.35	9.46	9.55	9.65
8	4.74	5.63	6.20	6.63	6.96	7.24	7.47	7.68	7.87	8.03	8.18	8.31	8.44	8.55	8.66	8.76	8.85	8.94	9.03
9	4.60	5.43	5.96	6.35	6.66	6.91	7.13	7.32	7.49	7.65	7.78	7.91	8.03	8.13	8.23	8.32	8.41	8.49	8.57
10	4.48	5.27	5.77	6.14	6.43	6.67	6.87	7.05	7.21	7.36	7.48	7.60	7.71	7.81	7.91	7.99	8.07	8.15	8.22
11	4.39	5.14	5.62	5.97	6.25	6.48	6.67	6.84	6.99	7.13	7.25	7.36	7.46	7.56	7.65	7.73	7.81	7.88	7.95
12	4.32	5.04	5.50	5.84	6.10	6.32	6.51	6.67	6.81	6.94	7.06	7.17	7.26	7.36	7.44	7.52	7.59	7.66	7.73
13	4.26	4.96	5.40	5.73	5.98	6.19	6.37	6.53	6.67	6.79	6.90	7.01	7.10	7.19	7.27	7.34	7.42	7.48	7.55
14	4.21	4.89	5.32	5.63	5.88	6.08	6.26	6.41	6.54	6.66	6.77	6.87	6.96	7.05	7.12	7.20	7.27	7.33	7.39
15	4.17	4.83	5.25	5.56	5.80	5.99	6.16	6.31	6.44	6.55	6.66	6.76	6.84	6.93	7.00	7.07	7.14	7.20	7.26
16	4.13	4.78	5.19	5.49	5.72	5.92	6.08	6.22	6.35	6.46	6.56	6.66	6.74	6.82	6.90	6.97	7.03	7.09	7.15
17	4.10	4.74	5.14	5.43	5.66	5.85	6.01	6.15	6.27	6.38	6.48	6.57	6.66	6.73	6.80	6.87	6.94	7.00	7.05
18	4.07	4.70	5.09	5.38	5.60	5.79	5.94	6.08	6.20	6.31	6.41	6.50	6.58	6.65	6.72	6.79	6.85	6.91	6.96
19	4.05	4.67	5.05	5.33	5.55	5.73	5.89	6.02	6.14	6.25	6.34	6.43	6.51	6.58	6.65	6.72	6.78	6.84	6.89
20	4.02	4.64	5.02	5.29	5.51	5.69	5.84	5.97	6.09	6.19	6.29	6.37	6.45	6.52	6.59	6.65	6.71	6.76	6.82
24	3.96	4.54	4.91	5.17	5.37	5.54	5.69	5.81	5.92	6.02	6.11	6.19	6.26	6.33	6.39	6.45	6.51	6.56	6.61
30	3.89	4.45	4.80	5.05	5.24	5.40	5.54	5.65	5.76	5.85	5.93	6.01	6.08	6.14	6.20	6.26	6.31	6.36	6.41
40	3.82	4.37	4.70	4.93	5.11	5.27	5.39	5.50	5.60	5.69	5.77	5.84	5.90	5.96	6.02	6.07	6.12	6.17	6.21
60	3.76	4.28	4.60	4.82	4.99	5.13	5.25	5.36	5.45	5.53	5.60	5.67	5.73	5.79	5.84	5.89	5.93	5.98	6.02
120	3.70	4.20	4.50	4.71	4.87	5.01	5.12	5.21	5.30	5.38	5.44	5.51	5.56	5.61	5.66	5.71	5.75	5.79	5.83
∞	3.64	4.12	4.40	4.60	4.76	4.88	4.99	5.08	5.16	5.23	5.29	5.35	5.40	5.45	5.49	5.54	5.57	5.61	5.65

SOURCE: From E. S. Pearson and H. O. Hartley, *Biometrika Tables for Statisticians*, 1: 176–77. Reproduced by permission of the Biometrika Trustees.

Table 8   Critical Values for the Wilcoxon Rank Sum Test

n_2 \ n_1	(a) $\alpha = .025$ one-tail; $\alpha = .05$ two-tail															
	3		**4**		**5**		**6**		**7**		**8**		**9**		**10**	
	T_L	T_U	T_L	T_U	T_L	T_U	T_L	T_U	T_L	T_U	T_L	T_U	T_L	T_U	T_L	T_U
4	6	18	11	25	17	33	23	43	31	53	40	64	50	76	61	89
5	6	21	12	28	18	37	25	47	33	58	42	70	52	83	64	96
6	7	23	12	32	19	41	26	52	35	63	44	76	55	89	66	104
7	7	26	13	35	20	45	28	56	37	68	47	81	58	95	70	110
8	8	28	14	38	21	49	29	61	39	73	49	87	60	102	73	117
9	8	31	15	41	22	53	31	65	41	78	51	93	63	108	76	124
10	9	33	16	44	24	56	32	70	43	83	54	98	66	114	79	131

n_2 \ n_1	(b) $\alpha = .05$ one-tail; $\alpha = .10$ two-tail															
	3		**4**		**5**		**6**		**7**		**8**		**9**		**10**	
	T_L	T_U	T_L	T_U	T_L	T_U	T_L	T_U	T_L	T_U	T_L	T_U	T_L	T_U	T_L	T_U
3	6	15	11	21	16	29	23	37	31	46	39	57	49	68	60	80
4	7	17	12	24	18	32	25	41	33	51	42	62	52	74	63	87
5	7	20	13	27	19	36	26	46	35	56	45	67	55	80	66	94
6	8	22	14	30	20	40	28	50	37	61	47	73	57	87	69	101
7	9	24	15	33	22	43	30	54	39	66	49	79	60	93	73	107
8	9	27	16	36	24	46	32	58	41	71	52	84	63	99	76	114
9	10	29	17	39	25	50	33	63	43	76	54	90	66	105	79	121
10	11	31	18	42	26	54	35	67	46	80	57	95	69	111	83	127

SOURCE: From F. Wilcoxon and R.A. Wilcox, "Some Rapid Approximate Statistical Procedures" (1964), p. 28. Reproduced with the permission of American Cyanamid Company.

Table 9   Critical Values for the Wilcoxon Signed Rank Sum Test

n	(a) $\alpha = .025$ one-tail $\alpha = .05$ two-tail T_L	T_U	(b) $\alpha = .05$ one-tail $\alpha = .10$ two-tail T_L	T_U
6	1	20	2	19
7	2	26	4	24
8	4	32	6	30
9	6	39	8	37
10	8	47	11	44
11	11	55	14	52
12	14	64	17	61
13	17	74	21	70
14	21	84	26	79
15	25	95	30	90
16	30	106	36	100
17	35	118	41	112
18	40	131	47	124
19	46	144	54	136
20	52	158	60	150
21	59	172	68	163
22	66	187	75	178
23	73	203	83	193
24	81	219	92	208
25	90	235	101	224
26	98	253	110	241
27	107	271	120	258
28	117	289	130	276
29	127	308	141	294
30	137	328	152	313

Table 10

Critical Values for the Spearman Rank Correlation Coefficient

The α values correspond to a one-tail test of $H_0: \rho_s = 0$. The value should be doubled for two-tail tests.

n	$\alpha = .05$	$\alpha = .025$	$\alpha = .01$	$\alpha = .005$
5	.900	—	—	—
6	.829	.886	.943	—
7	.714	.786	.893	—
8	.643	.738	.833	.881
9	.600	.683	.783	.833
10	.564	.648	.745	.794
11	.523	.623	.736	.818
12	.497	.591	.703	.780
13	.475	.566	.673	.745
14	.457	.545	.646	.716
15	.441	.525	.623	.689
16	.425	.507	.601	.666
17	.412	.490	.582	.645
18	.399	.476	.564	.625
19	.388	.462	.549	.608
20	.377	.450	.534	.591
21	.368	.438	.521	.576
22	.359	.428	.508	.562
23	.351	.418	.496	.549
24	.343	.409	.485	.537
25	.336	.400	.475	.526
26	.329	.392	.465	.515
27	.323	.385	.456	.505
28	.317	.377	.448	.496
29	.311	.370	.440	.487
30	.305	.364	.432	.478

SOURCE: From E. G. Olds, "Distribution of Sums of Squares of Rank Differences for Small Samples," *Annals of Mathematical Statistics* 9 (1938). Reproduced with the permission of the Institute of Mathematical Statistics.

Table 11(a)

Critical Values for the Durbin–Watson Statistic, $\alpha = .05$

n	$k = 1$		$k = 2$		$k = 3$		$k = 4$		$k = 5$	
	d_L	d_U	d_L	d_U	d_L	d_U	d_L	d_U	d_L	d_U
15	1.08	1.36	.95	1.54	.82	1.75	.69	1.97	.56	2.21
16	1.10	1.37	.98	1.54	.86	1.73	.74	1.93	.62	2.15
17	1.13	1.38	1.02	1.54	.90	1.71	.78	1.90	.67	2.10
18	1.16	1.39	1.05	1.53	.93	1.69	.82	1.87	.71	2.06
19	1.18	1.40	1.08	1.53	.97	1.68	.86	1.85	.75	2.02
20	1.20	1.41	1.10	1.54	1.00	1.68	.90	1.83	.79	1.99
21	1.22	1.42	1.13	1.54	1.03	1.67	.93	1.81	.83	1.96
22	1.24	1.43	1.15	1.54	1.05	1.66	.96	1.80	.86	1.94
23	1.26	1.44	1.17	1.54	1.08	1.66	.99	1.79	.90	1.92
24	1.27	1.45	1.19	1.55	1.10	1.66	1.01	1.78	.93	1.90
25	1.29	1.45	1.21	1.55	1.12	1.66	1.04	1.77	.95	1.89
26	1.30	1.46	1.22	1.55	1.14	1.65	1.06	1.76	.98	1.88
27	1.32	1.47	1.24	1.56	1.16	1.65	1.08	1.76	1.01	1.86
28	1.33	1.48	1.26	1.56	1.18	1.65	1.10	1.75	1.03	1.85
29	1.34	1.48	1.27	1.56	1.20	1.65	1.12	1.74	1.05	1.84
30	1.35	1.49	1.28	1.57	1.21	1.65	1.14	1.74	1.07	1.83
31	1.36	1.50	1.30	1.57	1.23	1.65	1.16	1.74	1.09	1.83
32	1.37	1.50	1.31	1.57	1.24	1.65	1.18	1.73	1.11	1.82
33	1.38	1.51	1.32	1.58	1.26	1.65	1.19	1.73	1.13	1.81
34	1.39	1.51	1.33	1.58	1.27	1.65	1.21	1.73	1.15	1.81
35	1.40	1.52	1.34	1.58	1.28	1.65	1.22	1.73	1.16	1.80
36	1.41	1.52	1.35	1.59	1.29	1.65	1.24	1.73	1.18	1.80
37	1.42	1.53	1.36	1.59	1.31	1.66	1.25	1.72	1.19	1.80
38	1.43	1.54	1.37	1.59	1.32	1.66	1.26	1.72	1.21	1.79
39	1.43	1.54	1.38	1.60	1.33	1.66	1.27	1.72	1.22	1.79
40	1.44	1.54	1.39	1.60	1.34	1.66	1.29	1.72	1.23	1.79
45	1.48	1.57	1.43	1.62	1.38	1.67	1.34	1.72	1.29	1.78
50	1.50	1.59	1.46	1.63	1.42	1.67	1.38	1.72	1.34	1.77
55	1.53	1.60	1.49	1.64	1.45	1.68	1.41	1.72	1.38	1.77
60	1.55	1.62	1.51	1.65	1.48	1.69	1.44	1.73	1.41	1.77
65	1.57	1.63	1.54	1.66	1.50	1.70	1.47	1.73	1.44	1.77
70	1.58	1.64	1.55	1.67	1.52	1.70	1.49	1.74	1.46	1.77
75	1.60	1.65	1.57	1.68	1.54	1.71	1.51	1.74	1.49	1.77
80	1.61	1.66	1.59	1.69	1.56	1.72	1.53	1.74	1.51	1.77
85	1.62	1.67	1.60	1.70	1.57	1.72	1.55	1.75	1.52	1.77
90	1.63	1.68	1.61	1.70	1.59	1.73	1.57	1.75	1.54	1.78
95	1.64	1.69	1.62	1.71	1.60	1.73	1.58	1.75	1.56	1.78
100	1.65	1.69	1.63	1.72	1.61	1.74	1.59	1.76	1.57	1.78

SOURCE: From J. Durbin and G. S. Watson, "Testing for Serial Correlation in Least Squares Regression, II," *Biometrika* 30 (1951): 159–78. Reproduced by permission of the Biometrika Trustees.

Table 11(b)

Critical Values for the Durbin–Watson Statistic, $\alpha = .01$

n	$k = 1$ d_L	d_U	$k = 2$ d_L	d_U	$k = 3$ d_L	d_U	$k = 4$ d_L	d_U	$k = 5$ d_L	d_U
15	.81	1.07	.70	1.25	.59	1.46	.49	1.70	.39	1.96
16	.84	1.09	.74	1.25	.63	1.44	.53	1.66	.44	1.90
17	.87	1.10	.77	1.25	.67	1.43	.57	1.63	.48	1.85
18	.90	1.12	.80	1.26	.71	1.42	.61	1.60	.52	1.80
19	.93	1.13	.83	1.26	.74	1.41	.65	1.58	.56	1.77
20	.95	1.15	.86	1.27	.77	1.41	.68	1.57	.60	1.74
21	.97	1.16	.89	1.27	.80	1.41	.72	1.55	.63	1.71
22	1.00	1.17	.91	1.28	.83	1.40	.75	1.54	.66	1.69
23	1.02	1.19	.94	1.29	.86	1.40	.77	1.53	.70	1.67
24	1.04	1.20	.96	1.30	.88	1.41	.80	1.53	.72	1.66
25	1.05	1.21	.98	1.30	.90	1.41	.83	1.52	.75	1.65
26	1.07	1.22	1.00	1.31	.93	1.41	.85	1.52	.78	1.64
27	1.09	1.23	1.02	1.32	.95	1.41	.88	1.51	.81	1.63
28	1.10	1.24	1.04	1.32	.97	1.41	.90	1.51	.83	1.62
29	1.12	1.25	1.05	1.33	.99	1.42	.92	1.51	.85	1.61
30	1.13	1.26	1.07	1.34	1.01	1.42	.94	1.51	.88	1.61
31	1.15	1.27	1.08	1.34	1.02	1.42	.96	1.51	.90	1.60
32	1.16	1.28	1.10	1.35	1.04	1.43	.98	1.51	.92	1.60
33	1.17	1.29	1.11	1.36	1.05	1.43	1.00	1.51	.94	1.59
34	1.18	1.30	1.13	1.36	1.07	1.43	1.01	1.51	.95	1.59
35	1.19	1.31	1.14	1.37	1.08	1.44	1.03	1.51	.97	1.59
36	1.21	1.32	1.15	1.38	1.10	1.44	1.04	1.51	.99	1.59
37	1.22	1.32	1.16	1.38	1.11	1.45	1.06	1.51	1.00	1.59
38	1.23	1.33	1.18	1.39	1.12	1.45	1.07	1.52	1.02	1.58
39	1.24	1.34	1.19	1.39	1.14	1.45	1.09	1.52	1.03	1.58
40	1.25	1.34	1.20	1.40	1.15	1.46	1.10	1.52	1.05	1.58
45	1.29	1.38	1.24	1.42	1.20	1.48	1.16	1.53	1.11	1.58
50	1.32	1.40	1.28	1.45	1.24	1.49	1.20	1.54	1.16	1.59
55	1.36	1.43	1.32	1.47	1.28	1.51	1.25	1.55	1.21	1.59
60	1.38	1.45	1.35	1.48	1.32	1.52	1.28	1.56	1.25	1.60
65	1.41	1.47	1.38	1.50	1.35	1.53	1.31	1.57	1.28	1.61
70	1.43	1.49	1.40	1.52	1.37	1.55	1.34	1.58	1.31	1.61
75	1.45	1.50	1.42	1.53	1.39	1.56	1.37	1.59	1.34	1.62
80	1.47	1.52	1.44	1.54	1.42	1.57	1.39	1.60	1.36	1.62
85	1.48	1.53	1.46	1.55	1.43	1.58	1.41	1.60	1.39	1.63
90	1.50	1.54	1.47	1.56	1.45	1.59	1.43	1.61	1.41	1.64
95	1.51	1.55	1.49	1.57	1.47	1.60	1.45	1.62	1.42	1.64
100	1.52	1.56	1.50	1.58	1.48	1.60	1.46	1.63	1.44	1.65

SOURCE: From J. Durbin and G. S. Watson, "Testing for Serial Correlation in Least Squares Regression, II," *Biometrika* 30 (1951): 159–78. Reproduced by permission of the Biometrika Trustees.

Table 12

Control Chart Constants

SAMPLE SIZE n	A_2	d_2	d_3	D_3	D_4
2	1.880	1.128	.853	.000	3.267
3	1.023	1.693	.888	.000	2.575
4	.729	2.059	.880	.000	2.282
5	.577	2.326	.864	.000	2.115
6	.483	2.534	.848	.000	2.004
7	.419	2.704	.833	.076	1.924
8	.373	2.847	.820	.136	1.864
9	.337	2.970	.808	.184	1.816
10	.308	3.078	.797	.223	1.777
11	.285	3.173	.787	.256	1.744
12	.266	3.258	.778	.284	1.716
13	.249	3.336	.770	.308	1.692
14	.235	3.407	.762	.329	1.671
15	.223	3.472	.755	.348	1.652
16	.212	3.532	.749	.364	1.636
17	.203	3.588	.743	.379	1.621
18	.194	3.640	.738	.392	1.608
19	.187	3.689	.733	.404	1.596
20	.180	3.735	.729	.414	1.586
21	.173	3.778	.724	.425	1.575
22	.167	3.819	.720	.434	1.566
23	.162	3.858	.716	.443	1.557
24	.157	3.895	.712	.452	1.548
25	.153	3.931	.709	.459	1.541

SOURCE: From E. S. Pearson, "The Percentage Limits for the Distribution of Range in Samples from a Normal Population," *Biometrika* 24 (1932): 416. Reproduced by permission of the Biometrika Trustees.

Appendix C
Answers to Selected Even-Numbered Exercises

All answers have been double-checked for accuracy. However, we cannot be absolutely certain that there are no errors. Students should not automatically assume that answers that don't match ours are wrong. When and if we discover mistakes, we will post corrected answers on our Web page. (See page 16 for the address.) If you find any errors, please email the authors (address on Web page). We will be happy to acknowledge you with the discovery.

Chapter 1

1.2 Descriptive statistics summarizes a set of data. Inferential statistics makes inferences about populations from samples.

1.4 a The complete production run **b** 1,000 chips **c** Proportion of the production run that is defective **d** Proportion of sample chips that are defective (7.5%) **e** Parameter **f** Statistic **g** Because the sample proportion is less than 10%, we can conclude that the claim is true.

1.6 a Flip the coin 100 times and count the number of heads and tails. **b** Outcomes of flips **c** Outcomes of the 100 flips **d** Proportion of heads **e** Proportion of heads in the 100 flips

1.8 a The population consists of the fuel mileage of all the taxis in the fleet **b** The owner would like to know the mean mileage **c** The sample consists of the 50 observations **d** The statistic the owner would use is the mean of the 50 observations **e** The statistic would be used to estimate the parameter from which the owner can calculate total costs. We computed the sample mean to be 19.8 mpg.

Chapter 2

2.2 a Interval **b** Interval **c** Nominal **d** Ordinal

2.4 a Nominal **b** Interval **c** Nominal **d** Interval **e** Ordinal

2.6 a Interval **b** Interval **c** Nominal **d** Ordinal **e** Interval

2.8 a Interval **b** Ordinal **c** Nominal **d** Ordinal

2.10 a Ordinal **b** Ordinal **c** Ordinal

2.12 10 or 11

2.14 a 7 to 9 **b** Upper limits: 5.25, 5.40, 5.55, 5.70, 5.85, 6.00, 6.15

2.24 d The histogram is positively skewed, unimodal, and not bell shaped. Most prices lie between $200,000 and $275,000 with a small number of houses selling for more than $275,000.

2.26 a 9 or 10 **c** The histogram is positively skewed. **d** There is more than one modal class. **e** The histogram is not bell shaped.

2.34 d This scorecard is a much better predictor.

2.56 The two bar charts are somewhat similar.

2.58 There is a moderately strong positive relationship between calculus and statistics marks.

2.60 Gender and marital status are unrelated.

2.62 b There is a strong linear relationship between time spent studying and marks.

2.64 b The direction is positive. **c** There does appear to be a linear relationship.

2.66 b There is apparently a weak linear relationship.

2.68 There is some brand loyalty.

2.70 b There is a moderately strong linear relationship between the two variables. Taller MBA graduates earn more on average than shorter ones.

2.78 b There was a large decrease over the first half of the period, but has leveled since.

2.80 b There has been a gradual weekly increase in sales.

2.84 The trend until month 408 was slow but steady. Since then the index has grown exponentially.

2.86 There is a moderately strong positive linear relationship between temperature and the number of tickets.

2.88 Most of the IQs are distributed between 70 and 120. The center of the distribution is about 90.

2.90 There is a strong positive linear relationship between temperature and the number of beers sold.

2.92 Although there are year-to-year fluctuations, the winning time appears to be constant.

2.94 Most students play bridge.

2.102 Most students borrowed no books.

2.104 Most students would not agree.

2.106 There is a moderately strong positive linear relationship between temperature and winning time.

2.108 There is a moderately strong positive linear relationship between the number of occupants and electricity use.

2.110 There is a moderately strong linear relationship between years of education and reading speed.

2.112 The U.S. dollar has steadily increased in value compared to the Canadian dollar.

2.114 The overall impression is poor.

2.116 There is a moderately strong positive linear relationship between education and income.

Chapter 4

4.2 a 6, 5, 5

4.4 a 39.3, 38, all

4.6 .19

4.8 a .106, .10 **b** .102 **c** Geometric mean

4.10 a .20, 0, .25, .33 **b** .195, .225 **c** .188 **d** Geometric mean

4.12 a 24,329, 24,461

4.14 a 152.02, 158

4.16 a 30.53, 31

4.18 a 472.35, 472.5

4.20 1.14

4.22 15.12, 3.89

4.24 a 51.5 **b** 6.5 **c** 174.5

4.26 6, 6, 6, 6, 6

4.28 a About 16% **b** About 97.5% **c** about 16%

4.30 a Nothing **b** At least 75% **c** At least 88.9%

4.32 $s^2 = 40.73$ mph^2, and $s = 6.38$ mph; at least 75% of the speeds lie within 12.76 mph of the mean; at least 88.9% of the speeds lie within 19.14 mph of the mean

4.34 $s^2 = .0858$ cm^2, and $s = .2929$ cm; at least 75% of the lengths lie within .5858 of the mean; at least 88.9% of the rods will lie within .8787 cm of the mean.

4.36 a $s = 15.01$ **b** In approximately 68% of the hours the number of arrivals falls between 83 (rounded from 83.04) and 113; on approximately 95% of the hours the number of arrivals falls between 68 and 128; on approximately 99.7% of the hours the number of arrivals falls between 53 and 143.

4.38 22.3, 30.8

4.40 13.05, 14.7, 15.6

4.42 2.55

4.44 9.25

4.50 The starting salaries of BA and other are the lowest and least variable. Starting salaries for BBA and BSc are higher.

4.52 b The amounts of time taken to complete rounds on the public course are larger and more variable than those on private courses.

4.54 697.19, 804.90, 909.38

4.56 33.19, .1262

4.58 a 43.66 **b** .7788 **c** There is a moderately strong positive linear relationship.

4.60 $r = -.7813$

4.62 a 20.55 **b** .4437

4.64 a $r = -.7501$

b There is a moderately strong negative linear relationship between Internet use and age.

4.66 .6460

4.68 Fixed costs = $315.50, variable costs = $3.30

4.70 $1,448,855

4.72 7.08, 2.93

4.74 3.75, 4, 2.23

4.76 a 12.93

4.78 3.90, 3.81, 1.32

4.80 a 29,913, 30,660 **b** 148,213,791, 12,174

4.82 a $-146,942, -.7409$
b $\hat{y} = 49,337 - 554x$

4.84 a 26.32, 26 **b** 88.57, 9.41

4.86 a 11.60, .6418 **b** $\hat{y} = -8.29 + 3.15x$

4.88 a 1,126.07, .6076 **b** $\hat{y} = 89.54 + .13x$

4.90 a 226.49, 223 **b** 1,934.8, 43.99 **c** 193, 223, and 259

4.92 a $r = .5984$ **b** There is a moderately strong positive linear relationship between the winning times of women and temperatures. **c** They appear to provide the same type of information.

4.94 a $\bar{x} = 12,067$, median = 12,047, mode = 11,621

Chapter 6

6.2 a Subjective approach **b** If all the teams in major league baseball have exactly the same players, the New York Yankees will win 25% of all World Series.

6.4 a Subjective approach **b** The Dow Jones Industrial Index will increase on 60% of the days if economic conditions remain unchanged.

6.6 {Adams wins, Brown wins, Collins wins, Dalton wins}

6.8 a {0, 1, 2, 3, 4, 5} **b** {4, 5} **c** .10 **d** .65 **e** 0

6.10 $\dfrac{2}{6}, \dfrac{3}{6}, \dfrac{1}{6}$

6.12 a .40 **b** .90

6.14 a $P(\text{single}) = .15$, $P(\text{married}) = .50$, $P(\text{divorced}) = .25$, $P(\text{widowed}) = .10$ **b** Relative frequency approach

6.16 $P(A_1) = .3$, $P(A_2) = .4$, $P(A_3) = .3$; $P(B_1) = .6$, $P(B_2) = .4$

6.18 a .5714 **b** .4286 **c** It is not a coincidence.

6.20 The events are not independent.

6.22 The events are independent.

6.24 $P(A_1) = .40$, $P(A_2) = .45$, $P(A_3) = .15$; $P(B_1) = .45$, $P(B_2) = .55$

6.26 a .85 **b** .75 **c** .50

6.28 a .36 **b** .4894 **c** .83

6.30 a .31 **b** .85 **c** .3871 **d** .0435

6.32 a .3898 **b** .66 **c** No

6.34 a .11 **b** .0435 **c** .0909 **d** No

6.36 a .33 **b** .30 **c** Yes, the events are dependent.

6.38 a .507 **b** .441 **c** .588

6.40 a .591 **b** .638 **c** Yes

6.42 a .8309 **b** .5998 **c** .0751

6.44 No

6.46 a .1898 **b** .2131 **c** .3538 **d** No

6.52 a .81 **b** .01 **c** .18 **d** .99

6.54 a .8091 **b** .0091 **c** .1818 **d** .9909

6.56 a .28 **b** .30 **c** .42

6.58 .038

6.60 .335

6.62 .698

6.64 .2520

6.66 .033

6.68 .00000001

6.70 .6125

6.72 a .696 **b** .304 **c** .889 **d** .111

6.74 .526

6.76 .327

6.78 .661

6.80 .2159

6.82 .375

6.84 .757

6.86 .749

6.88 .3439

6.90 a .89 **b** .250 **c** .977 **d** No

6.92 a .49 **b** .44 **c** .449 **d** No

6.94 .2031

6.96 a .2692 **b** .35 **c** No

6.98 a .39 **b** 1

6.100 .5

Chapter 7

7.2 a Any value between 0 and several hundred miles **b** No **c** No **d** Continuous

7.4 a 0, 1, 2, …, 100 **b** Yes **c** Yes, 101 values **d** The variable is discrete.

7.6 $p(x) = 1/6$, for $x = 1, 2, ..., 6$

7.8 a .950 **b** .020 **c** .680

7.10 a .8 **b** .8 **c** .8 **d** .3

7.12 a .48 **b** .52

7.14 a .25 **b** .50 **c** .25 **d** .75

7.16 a .375 **b** .375 **c** .875 **d** .50

7.18 a .06 **b** 0 **c** .35 **d** .65

7.20 a .21 **b** .31 **c** .26

7.22 $\mu = 1.4$, $\sigma^2 = 17.04$, $\sigma = 4.13$

7.28 $\mu = 1.7$, $\sigma = .9$

7.30 $p(.25) = .05$, $p(.50) = .15$, $p(.75) = .15$, $p(1.00) = .25$, $p(1.25) = .20$, $p(1.50) = .10$, $p(1.75) = .10$

7.32 $\mu = 1.025$, $\sigma = .410$

7.34 $\mu = 27.6$, $\sigma^2 = 230.2$, $\sigma = 15.17$

7.36 $\mu = 3.86$, $\sigma = 2.60$

7.38 $E(\text{value of coin}) = \$460$

7.40 $E(\text{profit}) = \$7.40$

7.42 $18

7.44 $\text{COV}(X, Y) = .14$, $\rho = .58$

7.46 a $p(2) = .5$, $p(3) = .2$, $p(4) = .3$ **b** $\mu = 2.8$, $\sigma^2 = .76$ **c** Yes

7.48 $\text{COV}(X, Y) = 0$, $\rho = 0$

7.50 a $p(2) = .28$, $p(3) = .54$, $p(4) = .18$ **b** $\mu = 2.9$, $\sigma^2 = .45$ **c** Yes

7.52

	x		
y	0	1	2
1	.42	.21	.07
2	.18	.09	.03

7.54 a $p(0) = .22$, $p(1) = .49$, $p(2) = .29$ **b** $p(0) = .34$, $p(1) = .39$, $p(2) = .27$ **c** $\mu = 1.07$, $\sigma^2 = .505$ **d** $\mu = .93$, $\sigma^2 = .605$ **e** $\text{COV}(X, Y) = -.045$, $\rho = -.081$

7.56 a .412 **b** .286 **c** .148

7.58 $\mu = 145$, $\sigma^2 = 31$, $\sigma = 5.57$

7.60 $\mu = 168$, $\sigma^2 = 574$, $\sigma = 24.0$

7.62 $E(R_p) = .211$, $V(R_p) = .0114$, $\sigma_{R_p} = .1067$

7.64 The expected value does not change; the standard deviation decreases.

7.66 $E(R_p) = .1060$, $V(R_p) = .0212$

The statistics used in Exercises 7.68 to 7.80 were computed by Excel. The variances were taken from the variance–covariance matrix. As a result, they are the population parameters. To convert to statistics, multiply the variance of the portfolio returns by $n/(n-1)$.

7.68 a Means: .0463, .1293, −.0016; Variances: .0148, .0100, .0039 **b** Invest all your money in stock 2; it has the largest mean return. **c** Invest all your money in stock 3; it has the smallest variance.

7.70 $E(R_p) = .0616$, $V(R_p) = .0060$, $\sigma_{R_p} = .0777$ **b** The mean return on this portfolio is greater than the mean returns on stocks 1 and 3 and the portfolio in Exercise 7.69, but smaller than that of stock 2. The variance of the returns on this portfolio is smaller than that for stocks 1 and 2 and larger than that of stock 3 and the portfolio in Exercise 7.69.

7.72 a $E(R_p) = .0351$, $V(R_p) = .0498$, $\sigma_{R_p} = .2231$ **b** The mean return on the portfolio is greater than the mean returns on stocks 1 and 3, but smaller than that of stock 2. The variance of the returns on the portfolio is smaller than that for the three stocks.

7.74 a Means: .0187, −.0176, .0153, .0495; Variances: .0615, .0232, .0228, .0517 **b** Invest all your money in stock 4; it has the largest mean return. **c** Invest all your money in stock 3; it has the smallest variance.

7.76 $E(R_p) = .0265$, $V(R_p) = .0231$, $\sigma_{R_p} = .1521$ **b** The mean return on this portfolio is greater than the mean return on stocks 1, 2, and 3, and the mean return on the portfolio in Exercise 7.75. It is smaller than the mean return on stock 4. The variance of the returns on this portfolio is smaller than that for stocks 1, 2, and 4, but larger than the variance on the returns of stock 3 and the variance of the returns on the portfolio in Exercise 7.75.

7.82 a .267 **b** .103 **c** .002

7.84 a .0778 **b** .3456 **c** .9130 **d** .6630

7.86 a .07776 **b** .34560 **c** .91296 **d** .66304

7.88 a .17119 **b** .09164 **c** .90953 **d** .81056

7.90 a .4219 **b** .312 **c** .14436

7.92 a .3369 **b** .7576

7.94 a .2990 **b** .91967

7.96 .902

7.98 .970

7.100 .0081

7.102 a .072 **b** .902 **c** .463

7.104 .000001

7.106 a .1353 **b** .1804 **c** .0361

7.108 a .13534 **b** .18045 **c** .03609

7.110 a .607 **b** .303 **c** .076

7.112 a .030 **b** .275 **c** .303

7.114 a .1353 **b** .0663

7.116 .1353

7.118 .6703

7.120 a .442 **b** .151

7.122 a .2231 **b** .703 **c** .577

7.124 a .8 **b** .4457

7.126 a .0993 **b** .809 **c** .888

7.128 .047

7.130 .006

7.132 a .00793 **b** 56 **c** $\sigma = 4.10$

7.134 a .161 **b** .009 **c** .013

7.136 a $\mu = 1.46$, $\sigma^2 = 2.23$, $\sigma = 1.49$ **b** $\mu = 2.22$, $\sigma^2 = 2.11$, $\sigma = 1.45$

7.138 .08755

Chapter 8

8.2 a .0800 **b** .3333 **c** .7533 **d** .1333

8.4 b 0 **c** .25 **d** .005

8.6 a .1667 **b** .3333 **c** 0

8.8 57 minutes

8.10 123 tons

8.12 b .5 **c** .25

8.14 a $f(x) = .10 - .005x$, $0 \leq x \leq 20$ **b** .25 **c** .33

8.16 .4345

8.18 .4441

8.20 .4893

8.22 .9251

8.24 .0475

8.26 .1196

8.28 .0010

8.30 0

8.32 1.70

8.34 .0122

8.36 .4435

8.38 a .6759 **b** .3745 **c** .1469

8.40 .6915

8.42 a .2033 **b** .3372

8.44 a .1056 **b** .1056 **c** .8882

8.46 Top 5%: 34.4675, Bottom 5%: 29.5325

8.48 .1151

8.50 a .1170 **b** .3559 **c** .0162 **d** 4.05 hours

8.52 9,636 pages

8.54 a .3336 **b** .0314 **c** .0436 **d** 32.88

8.56 a .0099 **b** $12.88

8.58 132.80 (rounded to 133)

8.60 246.5 (rounded to 247)

8.62 896.8 (rounded to 897)

8.64 .8621

8.66 .9656

8.68 a .2709 **b** .2177

8.70 a 0 **b** 0 **c** .0475 **d** .6293

8.72 The probability of losing money is greater than that for stock 1 but less than that for stock 2. The probability of returning more than 25% is greater than that for stock 1 but less than that for stock 2.

8.74 a .2327 **b** .3821

The statistics used in Exercises 7.68 to 7.80 were computed by Excel. The variances were taken from the variance–covariance matrix. As a result, they are the population parameters. These values were used in producing the solutions to Exercises 8.76 to 8.79.

8.76 a .1814 **b** .0132

8.78 a .4364 **b** .0505

8.82 a .6065 **b** .8187 **c** .2212 **d** .6321

8.84 a .5488 **b** .6988 **c** .1920 **d** 0

8.86 .1353

8.88 .8647

8.90 .4857

8.92 .1889

8.94 a 2.724 **b** 1.282 **c** 2.132 **d** 2.528

8.96 a 1.6556 **b** 2.6810 **c** 1.9600 **d** 1.6602

8.98 a .1744 **b** .0231 **c** .0251 **d** .0267

8.100 a 17.2919 **b** 50.8922 **c** 2.70554 **d** 53.5400

8.102 a 33.5705 **b** 866.911 **c** 24.3976 **d** 261.058

8.104 a .4881 **b** .9158 **c** .9988 **d** .9077

8.106 a 2.84 **b** 1.93 **c** 3.60 **d** 3.37

8.108 a 1.5204 **b** 1.5943 **c** 2.8397 **d** 1.1670

8.110 a .1050 **b** .1576 **c** .0001 **d** .0044

Chapter 9

9.2 a 5/36 **b** 5/36 **c** 1/36 **d** 1/36

9.4 a .0001286 **b** .0001286

9.8 a .1056 **b** .1587 **c** .0062

9.10 a .4435 **b** .7333 **c** .8185

9.12 a .1191 **b** .2347 **c** .2902

9.16 a .0918 **b** .0104 **c** .00077

9.18 a .3085 **b** 0

9.20 a .0038 **b** It appears to be false.

9.24 .1170

9.26 .0037

9.28 0

9.30 .5

9.32 .0250

9.34 .0035

9.36 .1151; the claim may be true

9.38 0; the claim appears to be false

9.40 a .0071 **b** The claim appears to be false.

9.42 .0066

9.44 The claim appears to be false.

9.46 .0033

9.48 .8413

9.50 .8413

9.52 a .3974 **b** .3050

9.54 1

Chapter 10

10.10 100 ± 5.82

10.14 100 ± 13.86

10.16 100 ± 9.80

10.20 200 ± 6.93

10.22 500 ± 2.79

10.24 500 ± 4.37

10.26 500 ± 2.33

10.30 500 ± 1.40

10.32 100 ± 2.79

10.38 500 ± 3.50

10.41 LCL = 5.79, UCL = 7.99

10.42 LCL = 36.82, UCL = 50.68

10.44 LCL = 6.91, UCL = 12.79

10.46 LCL = 20.71, UCL = 23.29

10.48 LCL = 23.60, UCL = 26.40

10.50 LCL = 249.44, UCL = 255.32

10.52 LCL = 11.86, UCL = 12.34

10.54 LCL = .494, UCL = .526

10.56 LCL = 18.66, UCL = 19.90

10.58 LCL = 579,545, UCL = 590,581

10.60 LCL = 25.62, UCL = 28.76

10.62 271

10.64 17

10.66 166

10.68 97

10.72 150 ± 1

10.74 150 ± 2

10.76 1,537

10.78 500 ± 5

10.82 2,149

10.84 1,083

10.86 217

Chapter 11

11.2 H_0: I will complete the Ph.D.;
H_1: I will not be able to complete the Ph.D.

11.4 H_0: Risky investment is more successful; H_1: Risky investment is not more successful

11.6 O. J. Simpson

11.8 Test statistic: $z = .60$; rejection region: $z > 1.88$; p-value = .2743; there is not enough evidence to infer that $\mu > 50$.

11.10 Test statistic: $z = 0$; rejection region: $z < -1.96$ or $z > 1.96$; p-value = 1.0; there is not enough evidence to infer that $\mu \neq 100$.

11.12 Test statistic: $z = -1.33$; rejection region: $z < -1.645$; p-value = .0918; there is not enough evidence to infer that $\mu < 50$.

11.14 p-value = .0228; there is enough evidence to infer that $\mu > 50$.

11.18 p-value = .3821; there is not enough evidence to infer that $\mu > 50$.

11.20 p-value = .0082; there is enough evidence to infer that $\mu > 50$.

11.24 $z = -.88$, p-value = .1894; there is not enough evidence to infer that $\mu < 100$.

11.28 $z = -.67$, p-value = .2514; there is not enough evidence to infer that $\mu < 100$.

11.30 $z = -2.50$, p-value = .0062; there is enough evidence to infer that $\mu < 100$.

11.34 a $z = 4.57$, p-value = 0. **b** $z = 1.60$, p-value = .0548. The value of the test statistic decreases and the p-value increases.

11.36 a $z = -.62$, p-value = .2676
b $z = -1.38$, p-value = .0838. The value of the test statistic decreases (it becomes more negative) and the p-value decreases.

11.38 p-values: .5, .3121, .1611, .0694, .0239, .0062, .0015, 0, 0

11.40 a $z = 2.30$, p-value = .0214 **b** $z = .46$, p-value = .6456. The value of the test statistic decreases and the p-value increases.

11.42 $z = 3.89$, p-value = 0; yes

11.44 $z = -.44$, p-value = .6600; no

11.46 $z = -2.06$, p-value = .0197; yes

11.48 $z = 1.66$, p-value = .0485; yes

11.50 $z = 2.26$, p-value = .0119; no

11.52 $z = -1.22$, p-value = .1112; no

11.54 $z = 3.34$, p-value = 0; yes

11.56 $z = -3.64$, p-value = 0; there is enough evidence to infer a decrease

11.58 .1492

11.60 .6480

11.64 a .5199 **b** .1170 **c** As μ decreases, β decreases.

11.66 a .0526 **b** .0192 **c** As n increases, β decreases.

11.68 a .2843 **b** .2420 **c** As α increases, β decreases.

11.72 .1949

11.74 .0268

11.78 0

11.80 .0869

11.84 p-value = .9931; there is no evidence to infer that the new system will not be cost effective.

Chapter 12

12.2 510 ± 24.80

12.6 510 ± 21.31

12.8 510 ± 29.63

12.12 $t = 1.05$, p-value = .1597; no

12.16 $t = .67$, p-value = .2552; no

12.18 $t = .50$, p-value = .3125; no

12.22 50 ± 9.30

12.24 $t = -1.41$, p-value = .1001; no

12.28 $15,500 \pm 517.59$

12.30 $t = -.69$, p-value = .2538; no

12.32 $t = .56$, p-value = .2903; no

12.34 LCL = 6.92, UCL = 7.38

12.36 $t = 2.48$, p-value = .0070; yes

12.38 LCL = 2.31, UCL = 3.03

12.40 a LCL = 60.73, UCL = 64.85
b Prices are required to be normally distributed. The histogram (not shown) is bell shaped.

12.42 LCL = 136.5 days, UCL = 142.3 days

12.44 LCL = 3.14, UCL = 3.74

12.46 $t = 1.32$, p-value = .1001; no

12.48 $\chi^2 = 35.93$, p-value = .1643; no. Decreasing the sample size increases the p-value of the test.

12.50 $\chi^2 = 79.20$, p-value = .0714; no. Increasing the sample size decreases the p-value.

12.52 LCL = 8.18, UCL = 19.65. Increasing the sample size narrows the interval.

12.54 $\chi^2 = 6.49$, p-value = .4841; no

12.56 LCL = 1.2533, UCL = 7.2000

12.58 a $\chi^2 = 25.9760$, p-value = .7088; no **b** Demand is required to be normally distributed. **c** The histogram is approximately bell shaped.

12.60 a LCL = 2.3163, UCL = 3.2236
b The histogram is bell shaped.

12.62 $\chi^2 = 86.36$; p-value = .1863; replace bulbs as they burn out.

12.64 $.48 \pm .0692$

12.66 The interval narrows when the sample size increases.

12.68 $.10 \pm .0263$

12.70 $z = .61$, p-value = .2709

12.72 $z = 1.22$, p-value = .1112

12.74 $z = .41$, p-value = .3409

12.78 a $.5 \pm .03$ **b** Yes, because the sample size was chosen to produce this interval.

12.80 564

12.82 a $.92 \pm .0188$ **b** The interval is narrower. **c** Yes, because the interval estimate is better than specified.

12.84 $.84 \pm .0246$

12.86 $z = 1.80$, p-value $= .0359$; yes

12.88 $.0694$

12.90 $z = -1.58$, p-value $= .0571$; no

12.92 $z = 1.13$, p-value $= .1292$; no

12.94 $z = 1.40$, p-value $= .0808$; yes

12.96 LCL $= 8.45$ million, UCL $= 11.05$ million

12.98 $z = 1.69$, p-value $= .0455$; yes

12.100 LCL $= .861$ million, UCL $= 1.17$ million

12.102 LCL $= 7,060,352$, UCL $= 8,681,004$

12.104 a $t = 3.04$, p-value $= .0015$; yes **b** LCL $= 30.68$, UCL $= 33.23$ **c** The costs are required to be normally distributed.

12.106 $\chi^2 = 30.71$, p-value $= .0435$; yes

12.108 a LCL $= 69.03$, UCL $= 74.73$ **b** $t = 2.74$, p-value $= .0043$; yes

12.110 LCL $= .582$, UCL $= .682$

12.112 LCL $= 6.05$, UCL $= 6.65$

12.114 LCL $= .558$, UCL $= .776$

12.116 $z = -1.33$, p-value $= .0912$; yes

12.118 a $t = -2.97$, p-value $= .0018$; yes **b** $\chi^2 = 101.58$, p-value $= .0011$; yes

12.120 LCL $= 49,800$, UCL $= 72,840$

For all exercises in Chapters 13, 14, and 24, we employed the F test of two variances at the 5% significance level to decide which one of the equal–variances or unequal–variances t test and estimator of the difference between two means to use to solve the problem. Additionally, for exercises that compare two populations and are accompanied by data files, our answers were derived by defining the sample from population 1 as the data stored in the first column. The data stored in the second column represent the sample from population 2. Paired differences were defined as the difference between the variable in the first column minus the variable in the second column.

Chapter 13
13.2 55 ± 160.35

13.4 55 ± 37.69

13.6 $t = .44$, p-value $= .6617$; no

13.14 3 ± 10.38

13.16 3 ± 3.22

13.18 $t = .62$, p-value $= .2689$; no

13.28 $t = -.38$, p-value $= .7089$; no

13.30 a $t = 2.72$, p-value $= .0036$; yes **b** LCL $= .69$, UCL $= 2.81$ **c** The two populations must be normally distributed.

d The histograms are bell shaped.

13.32 $t = -1.30$, p-value $= .0974$; yes

13.34 $t = -2.40$, p-value $= .0092$; yes

13.36 $t = -2.27$, p-value $= .0122$; yes

13.38 $t = .89$, p-value $= .1891$; switch to supplier B.

13.40 a $t = 3.86$, p-value $= .0006$; yes **b** LCL $= 10.11$, UCL $= 32.92$ **c** The amount of time is required to be normally distributed. **d** The histograms are somewhat bell shaped.

13.42 $t = 7.44$, p-value $= 0$; yes

13.44 $t = .87$, p-value $= .1917$; no

13.46 $t = -2.05$, p-value $= .0407$; yes

13.48 $t = 1.16$, p-value $= .2467$; no

13.50 $t = -12.00$, p-value $= 0$; yes

13.52 $t = -31.61$, p-value $= 0$; yes

13.60 $t = 2.73$, p-value $= .0263$; no

13.62 a LCL $= -3.39$, UCL $= -.81$

13.64 a $t = -.32$, p-value $= .7646$; no **b** The variable used to match the pairs was not strongly related to the variable being tested. As a consequence, the matched pairs experiment did not reduce the variation. The smaller number of degrees of freedom produced a larger p-value.

13.66 a $t = 1.81$, p-value $= .0484$; yes **b** LCL $= -.66$, UCL $= 6.82$ **c** Yes, because medical expenses will vary by the month of the year.

13.68 $t = -3.70$, p-value $= .0006$; yes

13.70 $t = -6.09$, p-value $= 0$; yes

13.72 $t = -1.52$, p-value $= .0647$; no

13.74 $t = 2.08$, p-value $= .0210$; yes

13.76 The matched pairs experiment reduced the variation caused by different drivers.

13.78 $F = .50$, p-value $= .0669$; no

13.82 LCL $= .649$, UCL $= 3.35$

13.84 $F = 2.40$, p-value $= .0318$; yes

13.86 $F = .70$, p-value $= .6068$; no

13.88 LCL $= .590$, UCL $= 1.21$

13.90 $F = .71$, p-value $= .1214$; correct method used

13.92 $F = .30$, p-value $= 0$; yes

13.94 $z = .72$, p-value $= .4716$

13.102 $-.040 \pm .116$

13.104 $z = .71$, p-value $= .2389$; no

13.106 $z = -2.85$, p-value $= .0022$; yes

13.108 $z = -1.26$, p-value $= .2076$; no

13.110 $z = -.96$, p-value $= .1685$; no

13.112 a $z = 3.01$, p-value $= .0013$; yes **b** LCL $= .0457$, UCL $= .1543$

13.114 $z = -1.28$, p-value $= .1003$; choose machine B

13.116 $z = 1.93$, p-value $= .0268$; yes

13.118 $t = 1.56$, p-value $= .1204$; no

13.120 $t = 2.65$, p-value $= .0059$; yes

13.122 $t = -8.73$, p-value $= 0$; yes

13.124 $t = -1.29$, p-value $= .1993$; no

13.126 a $t = -2.02$, p-value $= .0218$; yes **b** The histograms are bell shaped.

13.128 a $t = -1.13$, p-value $= .2710$; no **b** A large variation within each gender group was expected. **c** The histogram of the differences is somewhat bell shaped.

13.130 $t = 1.75$, p-value $= .0433$; yes

13.132 Dry cleaner: $t = .96$, p-value $= .1780$; no. Doughnut shop: $t = 3.24$, p-value $= .0032$; yes. Convenience store: $t = 7.34$, p-value $= 0$; yes.

13.134 a $z = 2.33$, p-value $= .0100$; yes **b** No, we cannot establish a causal relationship.

13.136 $t = -1.14$, p-value $= .1288$; no

13.138 $z = 2.13$, p-value $= .0166$; yes

13.140 $t = -11.21$, p-value $= 0$; yes

13.142 $z = 1.26$, p-value $= .1037$; no

13.144 $t = 2.28$, p-value $= .0115$; yes

Chapter 14
14.2 a $z = 2.83$, p-value $= .0024$; yes **b** $t = .90$, p-value $= .1853$; no **c** LCL $= .3423$, UCL $= .5250$ **d** LCL $= \$90.22$, UCL $= \$194.55$

14.4 a $z = 1.54$, p-value $= .0619$; no **b** $z = 3.02$, p-value $= .0013$; yes

14.6 Speeds: $t = 1.07$, p-value $= .1424$; no. Proper stops: $t = -.84$, p-value $= .2021$; no.

14.8 $t = 3.73$, p-value $= .0002$; yes

14.10 $t = .96$, p-value $= .1711$; no

14.12 $z = 1.48$, p-value $= .0694$; no

14.14 $t = 14.06$, p-value $= 0$; yes

14.16 Overall conclusion: p-values are .0008, .0000, .5637, and .2163. There is overwhelming evidence to indicate that bridge players score higher on memory and reasoning tests. There is no evidence of a difference in reaction time or vocabulary between players and nonplayers.

14.18 LCL $= .204$, UCL $= .436$. Number of service calls: LCL $= 204$, UCL $= 436$.

14.20 $t = -3.27$, p-value $= .0011$; yes

14.22 a $z = 1.74$, p-value $= .0406$; yes **b** $z = 1.07$, p-value $= .1417$; no

14.24 a $t = -6.00$, p-value $= 0$; yes **b** $z = -.29$, p-value $= .3867$; no

Chapter 15
15.14 $F = 7.68$; evidence of differences

15.16 a $F = 2.94$, p-value $= .0363$; there is evidence of differences **b** The times must be normally distributed with the same variance. **c** Yes

15.18 a $F = 3.25$, p-value $= .0144$; no **b** The times until first sign of corrosion for each lacquer must be normally distributed with a common variance. **c** Yes

15.20 $F = 1.17$, p-value $= .3162$; no

15.22 $F = 1.33$, p-value $= .2675$; no

15.24 $F = 25.60$, p-value $= 0$ **b** $F = 7.37$, p-value $= .0001$ **c** $F = 1.82$, p-value $= .1428$ **d** Using the F tests and the descriptive statistics, we see that the mean ages and mean household incomes are in ascending order. For example, Sugar Smacks buyers are younger and earn less than the buyers of the other three cereals. Cheerios purchasers are older and earn the most.

15.26 $F = .26$, p-value $= .7730$; no

15.28 a $F = 24.04$; evidence that the treatment means differ **b** $F = 4.00$; evidence that the block means differ

15.30 a $F = 7.98$; yes **b** $F = 6.05$; yes

15.32 a $F = 9.73$; yes **b** $F = 6.82$; yes

15.34 a $F = 7.68$, p-value $= .0002$; yes **b** $F = 15.94$, p-value $= 0$; yes **c** The response is required to be normally distributed with a common variance. **d** Yes

15.36 a $F = 123.36$, p-value $= 0$; yes **b** $F = 323.16$, p-value $= 0$; yes

15.38 a $F = 21.16$, p-value $= 0$; yes **b** $F = 66.02$, p-value $= 0$; randomized block design is best.

15.40 a $F = 10.72$, p-value $= 0$; yes **b** $F = 6.36$, p-value $= 0$; yes, blocking by age was appropriate

15.42 a $F = 5.85$; evidence of differences between the levels of factor A **b** $F = 7.20$; evidence of differences between the levels of factor B **c** $F = 9.50$; evidence that factors A and B interact

15.44 a $F = .31$; no evidence that factors A and B interact **b** $F = 1.23$; no evidence of differences between the levels of factor A **c** $F = 13.01$; evidence of differences between the levels of factor B

15.46 a Factor A is the drug mixture and factor B is the schedule. **b** Improvement index **c** There are $a = 4$ drug mixtures and $b = 2$ schedules. **d** $F = .57$, p-value $= .4548$; no **e** $F = 7.71$, p-value $= .0005$; yes **f** $F = 7.27$, p-value $= .0007$; evidence that the schedules and drug mixtures interact

15.48 a There are 12 treatments. **b** There are two factors—tax form and income group. **c** There are $a = 4$ forms and $b = 3$ income groups. **d** $F = 2.56$, p-value $= .0586$; no **e** $F = 4.11$, p-value $= .0190$; yes **f** $F = 1.04$, p-value $= .4030$; no

15.50 The p-values for machines, alloys, and interaction are .0173, .0005, and .8814, respectively. Both machines and alloys are sources of variation.

15.52 The p-values for methods, skills, and interaction are .7348, 0, and .9874. The only source of variation is skill level.

15.54 μ_2 and μ_3 differ.

15.56 The following pairs of means differ: μ_1 and μ_2, μ_1 and μ_4, μ_1 and μ_5, μ_2 and μ_4, μ_3 and μ_4, μ_3 and μ_5, and μ_4 and μ_5.

15.58 The following pairs of means differ: μ_1 and μ_2, μ_1 and μ_5, μ_2 and μ_4, μ_3 and μ_4, and μ_4 and μ_5.

15.60 The mean grades from high schools A and C differ.

15.62 No means differ.

15.64 The means of lacquers 2 and 3, and 3 and 4 differ.

15.66 a $F = 3.70$, p-value $= .0286$; yes **b** Answer (v) is correct.

15.68 $F = 13.79$, p-value $= 0$; use the typeface that was read the fastest.

15.70 a $F = 7.67$, p-value $= .0001$; yes **b** Companies that offered extensive training have productivity levels different from the other companies.

15.72 a There are 4 levels of ranks and 4 levels of faculties for a total of 16 treatments. **b** $F = 2.84$, p-value $= .0019$; evidence that at least two treatment means differ. **c** Factor A is the faculty. The levels are business, engineering, arts, and science. Factor B is the rank. The levels are professor, associate professor, assistant professor, and lecturer. **d** $F = .61$, p-value $= .6109$; no **e** $F = 4.49$, p-value $= .0064$; yes **f** $F = 3.04$, p-value $= .0044$; yes

15.74 $F = 6.69$, p-value $= .0143$; yes

15.76 Age groups: $F = 58.78$, p-value $= 0$; evidence of differences between the three age groups. Gender: $F = 3.66$, p-value $= .0576$; not enough evidence of differences between males and females. Interaction: $F = .44$, p-value $= .6418$; no evidence that age and gender interact.

15.78 a $F = 9.54$, p-value $= .0002$; yes **b** The mean time of the Mozart group differs from the mean times of white noise and the Glass groups.

15.80 $F = 10.26$, p-value $= 0$; yes

15.82 $F = 9.17$, p-value $= 0$; yes

Chapter 16

16.2 $\chi^2 = 2.27$, p-value $= .6868$; not enough evidence that at least one p_i is not equal to its specified value.

16.6 $\chi^2 = 9.96$, p-value $= .0189$; evidence that at least one p_i is not equal to its specified value.

16.8 $\chi^2 = 6.85$, p-value $= .0769$; not enough evidence that at least one p_i is not equal to its specified value.

16.10 $\chi^2 = 14.07$, p-value $= .0071$; yes

16.12 $\chi^2 = 33.85$, p-value $= 0$; yes

16.14 $\chi^2 = 6.35$, p-value $= .0419$; yes

16.16 $\chi^2 = 5.70$, p-value $= .1272$; no

16.18 $\chi^2 = 9.56$, p-value $= .0020$; evidence of a relationship

16.22 $\chi^2 = 2.27$, p-value $= .3221$; no

16.24 $\chi^2 = 70.675$, p-value $= 0$; yes

16.26 $\chi^2 = 1.7243$, p-value $= .4222$; no

16.28 a $\chi^2 = .6434$, p-value $= .4225$; no **b** Ignore what the other investors are doing.

16.30 $\chi^2 = 23.0946$, p-value $= .0001$; yes

16.32 $\chi^2 = 108.9699$, p-value $= 0$; yes

16.34 $\chi^2 = 8.71$, p-value $= .0128$; yes

16.36 $\chi^2 = 16.6238$, p-value $= .0002$; evidence that the amount of time at part-time jobs is not normally distributed.

16.38 Successful firms: $\chi^2 = 3.0288$, p-value $= .2199$; not enough evidence to infer that productivity in successful firms is not normally distributed. Unsuccessful firms: $\chi^2 = 1.1347$, p-value $= .5670$; not enough evidence that productivity in unsuccessful firms is not normally distributed.

16.40 $\chi^2 = 3.2$, p-value $= .2019$; no

16.42 $\chi^2 = 4.77$, p-value $= .3119$; no

16.44 $\chi^2 = 74.47$, p-value $= 0$; yes

16.46 $\chi^2 = .5803$, p-value $= .9009$; no

16.48 a $\chi^2 = 38.22$, p-value $= .8427$; no

16.50 $\chi^2 = 4.13$, p-value $= .5310$; no

16.52 $\chi^2 = 20.9881$, p-value $= 0$; yes

16.54 $\chi^2 = 35.6322$, p-value $= 0$; yes

Chapter 17

17.2 $z = 1.76$, p-value $= .0784$

17.4 $z = 1.66$, p-value $= .0485$

17.6 The value of the test statistic decreases and the p-value increases.

17.8 $T = 118$, no evidence that the population locations differ

17.12 $z = 3.61$, p-value $= .0004$; yes

17.18 $z = -1.75$, p-value $= .0401$; yes

17.20 $z = 1.57$, p-value $= .0582$; yes

17.22 $z = 2.12$, p-value $= .0170$; yes

17.24 $z = -4.56$, p-value $= 0$; yes

17.26 $z = -2.24$, p-value $= .0250$; evidence that the population locations differ

17.28 $z = 1.10$, p-value $= .1357$; no

17.30 $z = -.92$, p-value $= .3576$; not enough evidence that the population locations differ

17.32 $T = 19.5$; evidence that the population locations differ

17.34 $z = 1.84$, p-value $= .0332$; yes

17.40 $z = 2.71$, p-value $= .0034$; yes

17.42 $z = -2.06$, p-value $= .0396$; evidence that the population locations differ

17.46 $z = -2.91$, p-value $= .0036$; evidence that the population locations differ

17.48 $z = -5.25$, p-value $= 0$; yes

17.50 $z = 2.22$, p-value $= .0132$; yes

17.52 $z = -1.64$, p-value $= .0505$; no

17.54 $z = -2.24$, p-value $= .0125$; no

17.56 $z = 1.51$, p-value $= .0655$; no

17.58 $H = 1.56$; not enough evidence that the population locations differ

17.60 $H = 6.30$; evidence that the population locations differ

17.62 $H = 4.46$, p-value $= .1075$; not enough evidence that the population locations differ

17.64 $H = .899$, p-value $= .8257$; no

17.70 $H = 6.65$, p-value $= .0838$; no

17.72 a The one-way analysis of variance and the Kruskal–Wallis test should be considered. **b** $H = 6.96$, p-value $= .0733$; no

17.74 $H = 4.34$, p-value $= .2269$; no

17.76 $H = 18.73$, p-value $= .0009$; yes

17.78 $F_r = 4.80$, p-value $= .0907$; not enough evidence that the population locations differ

17.80 a The randomized block experimental design of the analysis of variance and the Friedman test **b** $F_r = 7.00$, p-value $= .0302$; yes

17.84 $F_r = 10.613$, p-value $= .0140$; yes

17.86 $F_r = 5.28$, p-value $= .0715$; no

17.88 $F_r = 2.63$, p-value $= .2691$; no

17.90 $z = 2.65$, p-value $= .0082$; yes

17.92 $F_r = 12.615$, p-value $= .0055$; yes

17.94 $z = -3.68$, p-value $= .0001$; yes

17.96 $z = 1.53$, p-value $= .0630$; no

17.98 $z = -1.00$, p-value $= .3174$; no

17.100 $z = -2.23$, p-value $= .0130$; yes

17.102 $z = 2.86$, p-value $= .0021$; yes

17.104 $z = -2.43$, p-value $= .0075$; yes

17.106 $H = 42.59$, p-value $= 0$; yes

17.108 Day 1 versus Before: $z = 8.19$, p-value $= 0$; Day 2 versus Before: $z = 7.68$, p-value $= 0$; Day 3 versus Before: $z = 5.92$, p-value $= 0$. There is enough evidence to infer that exercisers who abstain from physical activity are less happy than when they are

exercising. **b** $z = -5.38$, p-value $= 0$; yes **c** 1. Exercisers who abstained were adjusting to their inactivity by the third day. 2. By the third day, exercisers realized that they were closer to the end of their inactivity.

Chapter 18

18.2 a $\hat{y} = 36.54 + .479x$ **b** Nothing **c** For each additional inch of father's height, the son's height increases on average by .479 inch.

18.4 a $\hat{y} = 9.88 - .048x$ **b** Nothing **c** For each one-point increase in the inflation rate, the return on common stocks increases on average by .048.

18.6 b $\hat{y} = 3.64 + .267x$ **c** For each additional second of commercial, the memory test score increases on average by .267.

18.8 a $\hat{y} = -2.03 + .788x$ **b** For each additional year of education, Internet use increases on average by .788 hour.

18.10 $\hat{y} = 9.44 + .0949x$; the appropriate compensation is 9.49 cents per degree API

18.12 a $\hat{y} = -259.6 + 3{,}721x$ **b** For each additional carat of weight, the price increases on average by $3,721.

18.16 a $s_\varepsilon = 3.22$; this statistic is an estimate of the standard deviation of the error variable. **b** $R^2 = .2665$ **c** $t = 12.03$, p-value $= 0$; yes

18.18 $t = .02$, p-value $= .9880$; no

18.20 a $s_\varepsilon = 5.89$; this statistic is an estimate of the standard deviation of the error variable. **b** $R^2 = .2893$; 28.93% of the variation in memory test scores is explained by the variation in commercial lengths. **c** $t = 4.86$, p-value $= 0$; evidence that the length of commercial and memory test score are linearly related.

18.22 a $s_\varepsilon = 4.45$; this statistic is an estimate of the standard deviation of the error variable. **b** $t = 4.93$, p-value $= 0$; yes

18.24 $t = 11.48$, p-value $= 0$; evidence that oil quality and price are linearly related. $R^2 = .9229$

18.26 a $s_\varepsilon = 31.84$; this statistic is an estimate of the standard deviation of the error variable. **b** $R^2 = .9783$; 97.83% of the variation in price is explained by the variation in weight. **c** $t = 45.50$, p-value $= 0$; yes

18.28 a $\hat{y} = 2.05 + .0909x$ **b** For each additional minute of exercise, cholesterol is reduced on average by .0909. **c** $t = 7.06$, p-value $= 0$; yes **d** $R^2 = .5095$; the model fits moderately well.

18.30 $b_1 = 1.47$, $R^2 = .1480$

18.32 $b_1 = .843$, $R^2 = .1280$

18.34 $b_1 = 1.09$, $R^2 = .4049$

18.36 $b_1 = .506$, $R^2 = .0962$

18.40 $b_1 = 1.69$, $R^2 = .1145$

18.42 $b_1 = .326$, $R^2 = .0575$

18.44 $b_1 = .485$, $R^2 = .1293$

18.46 $b_1 = 1.19$, $R^2 = .1541$

18.50 Lower prediction limit $= 85.07$, upper prediction limit $= 238.60$

18.52 a Lower prediction limit $= 54.00$, upper prediction limit $= 83.05$ **b** Lower confidence limit $= 67.00$, upper confidence limit $= 70.04$

18.54 Lower prediction limit $= 24.02$, upper prediction limit $= 31.40$

18.56 a Lower prediction limit $= 0$, upper prediction limit $= 34.17$ **b** Lower confidence limit $= 7.90$, upper confidence limit $= 9.51$

18.58 Lower prediction limit $= 11.61$, upper prediction limit $= 23.59$

18.60 a $r = .9375$, $t = 5.39$, p-value $= .0058$; evidence of a linear relationship **b** $r_s = .9429$, $z = 2.11$, p-value $= .0350$; evidence of a linear relationship.

18.62 $z = 1.12$, p-value $= .2626$; no

18.64 a The required condition is that odometer reading and price are bivariate normally distributed. **b** $z = -8.00$, p-value $= 0$; evidence that odometer reading and price are related.

18.66 $z = 7.85$, p-value $= 0$; evidence that marks and study times are positively related.

18.68 $z = -4.14$, p-value $= 0$; yes

18.70 a $r = .2543$ **b** $t = 9.65$, p-value $= 0$; evidence that there is a linear relationship between age and medical expense **c** $z = 6.78$, p-value $= 0$; yes

18.72 $z = 3.20$, p-value $= .0014$; evidence that the returns are linearly related

18.74 $z = 1.89$, p-value $= .0584$; no

18.76 a $\hat{y} = 8.24 - 1.07x$

18.84 a $\hat{y} = 296.92 + 21.36x$ **b** On average, each ad generates 21.36 customers. **c** $t = 1.50$, p-value $= .0740$; yes **d** $R^2 = .0852$; 8.52% of the variation in the number of customers is explained by the variation in the number of ads. **e** The poor fit of the model precludes its use for prediction.

18.86 $z = 11.28$, p-value $= 0$; yes

18.88 Assuming normality: $t = 13.62$, p-value $= 0$; yes

18.90 $\hat{y} = .83 - .080x$. For each additional point increase in ERA, the team's winning percentage decreases on average by .080 point. **b** $s_\varepsilon = .0549$. This statistic is large relative to the average winning percentage, .500. The model is poor. **c** $t = -1.96$, p-value $= .0367$; yes **d** $R^2 = .2431$; 24.31% of the variation in winning percentage is explained by the variation in ERA. **e** Lower prediction limit = .406, upper prediction limit = .609

18.92 $t = 3.26$, p-value = .0042; yes

18.94 a $\hat{y} = 17.93 + .60x$. For each additional inch of height, annual income increases on average by .60 thousand dollars ($600). **b** $t = 3.63$, p-value = .0002; yes **c** $R^2 = .0505$; 5.05% of the variation in incomes is explained by the variation in heights. **d** The model is too poor to be used to predict and estimate.

18.96 $t = 13.77$, p-value = 0; evidence of a positive linear relationship

Chapter 19

19.2 a $\hat{y} = 13.01 + .194x_1 + 1.112x_2$. **b** 3.75 **c** .7629 **d** .7453 **e** $F = 43.43$, p-value = 0; evidence that the model is valid **f** For each additional mark on assignments, the final exam mark on average increases by .194. For each additional midterm mark, the final exam mark on average increases by 1.112. **g** $t = .97$, p-value = .3417; no **h** $t = 9.12$, p-value = 0; yes

19.4 b 3.23 **c** .2672 **d** .2635 **e** $F = 72.37$, p-value = 0; evidence that the model is valid **f** For each additional inch of height of mothers, the son's height decreases on average by .0229 inch. For each additional inch of height of fathers, the son's height increases on average by .4849 inch. **g** $t = 11.78$, p-value = 0; yes **h** $t = -.58$, p-value = .5615; no

19.6 b 2.03 **c** .2882 **d** .2660 **e** $F = 12.96$, p-value = 0; evidence that the model is valid **f** For each additional point of high school GPA, university GPA increases on average by .611. For each additional point of SAT, university GPA increases on average by .0027. For each additional hour of activities, university GPA increases on average by .046. **g** High school GPA: $t = 6.06$, p-value = 0; SAT: $t = .94$, p-value = .3482; Activities: $t = .72$, p-value = .4720. Only high school GPA is linearly related to university GPA. **h** Lower prediction limit = 4.45, upper prediction limit = 12.00 (maximum) **i** LCL = 6.90, UCL = 8.22

19.8 a $\hat{y} = 576.8 + 90.61x_1 + 9.66x_2$. **b** 213.7 **c** $R^2 = .7081$, R^2(adjusted) = .7021 **d** $F = 117.64$, p-value = 0; evidence that the model is valid **e** Lower prediction limit = 7,748, upper prediction limit = 8,601 **f** LCL = 8,127, UCL = 8,222

19.10 a $\hat{y} = 13.03 - .279x_1 + .094x_2$. **b** .1985 **c** $F = 24.39$, p-value = 0; evidence that the model is valid **d** Lower prediction limit = 0 (minimum), upper prediction limit = 13.50 **e** LCL = 6.27, UCL = 9.61

19.12 a Lower prediction limit = 23, upper prediction limit = 38.8 **b** Lower prediction limit = 49, upper prediction limit = 64.8

19.16 The two variables are very weakly correlated. The two t tests are valid.

19.20 a $\hat{y} = -103.1 + 5.82x_1 + 8.56x_2$. **b** Observations 63, 81, 82, and 97 should be checked. **c** The histogram is bell shaped. The error variable is normally distributed. **d** The variance of the error variable grows as $\hat{y}$ increases. It appears that the error variable's variance is not constant.

19.34. There is no evidence of negative first-order autocorrelation.

19.36 a The regression equation is $\hat{y} = 2{,}260 + .423x$. **c** Check observation 4. **d** The histogram is bell shaped; the errors are normal. **e** The error variable variance appears to be constant. **f** $d = .7859$. There is evidence of first-order autocorrelation. **g** The model is $y = \beta_0 + \beta_1 x + \beta_2 t + \varepsilon$. The regression equation is $\hat{y} = 446.2 + 1.10x + 38.92t$. **h** First model: $s_\varepsilon = 709.7$ and $R^2 = .0146$. Second model: $s_\varepsilon = 413.7$ and $R^2 = .6718$. The second model fits better.

19.40 $d = 1.755$; $d_L = 1.01$, $d_U = 1.78$, $4 - d_U = 2.22$, $4 - d_L = 2.99$. The test is inconclusive.

19.42 The histogram is bell shaped; apparently the errors are normally distributed. **c** Check observations 1, 11, 25, 28, and 46. **d** The error variable variance appears to be constant. **e** The errors appear to be independent. **f** $d = 1.9547$; $d_L = 1.55$, $d_U = 1.62$, $4 - d_U = 2.38$, $4 - d_L = 2.54$. There is no evidence of first-order autocorrelation.

19.44 Lower prediction limit = 6.87, upper prediction limit = 10.20

19.46 b $s_\varepsilon = 558.7$ and $R^2 = .4933$; the model's fit is only moderately good. **c** For each one cent increase in the price of milk, sales decrease on average by 46.77. For each one cent increase in the competitor's price of milk, sales increase on average by 58.52. **d** Company's price: $t = -4.32$, p-value = .0001; Competitor's price: $t = 5.59$, p-value = 0. Both prices are linearly related to sales. **e** $F = 23.85$, p-value = 0; evidence that the model is valid. **f** Lower prediction limit = 2,341, upper prediction limit = 4,284

19.48 b For each additional minor league home run, the number of major league home runs increases on average by .67. For each additional year of age, the number of major league home runs increases on average by .14. For each additional year as a professional, the number of major league home runs increases on average by 1.18. **c** $s_\varepsilon = 6.99$ and $R^2 = .3511$; the model's fit

is not very good. **d** $F = 22.01$, p-value = 0; evidence that the model is valid **e** Minor league home runs: $t = 7.64$, p-value = 0; Age: $t = .26$, p-value = .7961; Years professional: $t = 1.75$, p-value = .0819. Only the number of minor league home runs is linearly related to the number of major league home runs. **f** Lower prediction limit = 9.86 (rounded to 10), upper prediction limit = 38.76 (rounded to 39) **g** LCL = 14.66, UCL = 24.47

19.50 a $\hat{y} = 194.84 + .12x_1 + .025x_2$ **b** $t = 1.66$, p-value = .1088; no **c** $t = 4.06$, p-value = .0004; yes **d** $s_\varepsilon = 57.29$ and $R^2 = .4157$; the model's fit is not very good. **e** Lower prediction limit = 104.7, upper prediction limit = 359.2

19.52 a $\hat{y} = 35.68 + .25x_1 + .24x_2 + .13x_3$ **b** $F = 6.66$, p-value = .0011; evidence that the model is valid **c** The error variable appears to be normal. The variance of the errors appears to be constant. **d** The correlation between income and age is high enough to distort the t tests. **e** For each one-percentage-point increase in the proportion of teachers with mathematics degrees, the test score increases on average by .25. For each one-year increase in mean age, test score increases on average by .24. For each one-thousand-dollar increase in salary, test score increases on average by .13. Proportion of teachers with at least one mathematics degree: $t = 3.54$, p-value = .0011; Age: $t = 1.32$, p-value = .1945; Income: $t = .87$, p-value = .3889. The proportion of teachers with at least one mathematics degree is linearly related to test scores. The other two variables may be related to test scores but the multicollinearity makes it difficult to discern. **f** Lower prediction limit = 49.02, upper prediction limit = 81.02

19.54 Diagnosing violations: The error variable appears to be normal. The error variable's variance appears to be constant. The required conditions are satisfied. Assessing the model: $s_\varepsilon = 7.01$ and $R^2 = .7209$; the model fits well. Testing the validity of the model: $F = 60.70$, p-value = 0; evidence that the model is valid. Drawing inferences about the independent variables: Evaluations: $t = .60$, p-value = .5529; Articles: $t = 8.08$, p-value = 0. The number of articles a professor publishes is linearly related to salary. Teaching evaluations are not.

19.56 b $F = 18.17$, p-value = 0; evidence that the model is valid **c** The errors appear to be normally distributed. The variance of the errors is not constant. **d** There is a strong correlation between income and education. The t tests of these two coefficients may be distorted. **e** Belief 1: $t = -3.26$, p-

value = .0008; Belief 2: $t = 1.16$, p-value = .1251; Belief 3: $t = .42$, p-value = .3390; Belief 4: $t = -2.69$, p-value = .0043. Despite multicollinearity, there is enough evidence to support beliefs 1 and 4. There is no evidence to support beliefs 2 and 3.

Chapter 20

20.4 a First-order model: Demand = $\beta_0 + \beta_1$ Price + ε; Second-order model: Demand = $\beta_0 + \beta_1$ Price + β_2 Price^2 + ε **c** The second-order model fits better because its standard error of estimate is 5.96, whereas that of the first-order model is 13.29.

20.6 a MBA GPA= $\beta_0 + \beta_1$ UnderGPA + β_2 GMAT + β_3 Work + β_4 UnderGPA $\times$ GMAT + ε **b** $s_\varepsilon = .790$ and $R^2 = .4674$. The model's fit is relatively poor. **c** MBA example $s_\varepsilon = .788$ and $R^2 = .4635$. There is little difference between the fits of the two models.

20.10 a Yield = $\beta_0 + \beta_1$ Pressure + β_2 Temperature + β_3 Pressure^2 + β_4 Temperature^2 + β_5 Pressure $\times$ Temperature + ε **c** $s_\varepsilon = 512$ and $R^2 = .6872$. The model's fit is good.

20.14 Lower prediction limit = 8.55, upper prediction limit = 11.67 **b** Lower prediction limit = 8.15, upper prediction limit = 11.31

20.16 b $F = 20.43$, p-value = 0; evidence that the model is valid **c** I_2: $t = 1.86$, p-value = .0713; I_3: $t = -1.58$, p-value = .1232. Weather is not a factor in attendance. **d** $t = 3.30$, p-value =.0012; yes

20.18 b On average, two-story houses sell for \$20,487 more than other houses with the same number of bedrooms, square footage, and lot size; on average, side-split houses sell for \$12,795 more than other houses with the same number of bedrooms, square footage, and lot size; on average, back-split houses sell for \$19,512 more than other houses with the same number of bedrooms, square footage, and lot size. I_1: $t = 2.93$, p-value = .0043; I_2: $t = 1.76$, p-value = .0812; I_3: $t = 2.45$, p-value = .0162. We can infer that two-story and back-split houses sell for more than other.

20.20 b $t = -1.43$, p-value = .1589; no **c** Let

$$I_1 = \begin{cases} 1 \text{ if humorous} \\ 0 \text{ otherwise} \end{cases}$$

$$I_2 = \begin{cases} 1 \text{ if musical} \\ 0 \text{ otherwise} \end{cases}$$

d I_1: $t = 1.61$, p-value = .1130; I_2: $t = 3.01$, p-value = .0039. There is enough evidence to infer that there is a difference in memory test scores between watchers of humorous

and serious commercials. **e** The variable type of commercial in parts (a) and (b) is nominal.

20.22 a Let

$$I_1 = \begin{cases} 1 \text{ if no scorecard} \\ 0 \text{ otherwise} \end{cases}$$

$$I_2 = \begin{cases} 1 \text{ if scorecard overturned} \\ \quad \text{more than } 10\% \text{ of the time} \\ 0 \text{ otherwise} \end{cases}$$

c $s_\varepsilon = 4.20$ and $R^2 = .5327$. The model's fit is mediocre. **d** There is a high correlation between I_1 and I_2 that may distort the t tests. **e** For each additional dollar lent, the default rate increases by .00012; banks that don't use scorecards on average have default rates 4.08 percentage points higher than banks that overturn their scorecards less than 10% of the time; banks that overturn their scorecards more than 10% of the time on average have default rates 10.18 percentage points higher than banks that overturn their scorecards less than 10% of the time. Banks are advised to use scorecards and not overturn them. **e** Lower prediction limit = 1.39, upper prediction limit = 18.49

20.24 b $t = 3.11$, p-value = .0025; yes **c** $t = -5.36$, p-value = 0; yes

20.36 a Apply a first-order model with interaction. **c** $F = 54.14$, p-value = 0; evidence that the model is valid

20.38 a Let

$$I_1 = \begin{cases} 1 \text{ if ad was in newspaper} \\ 0 \text{ otherwise} \end{cases}$$

$$I_2 = \begin{cases} 1 \text{ if ad was on radio} \\ 0 \text{ otherwise} \end{cases}$$

c I_1: $t = -1.48$, p-value = .1467; I_2: $t = -2.83$, p-value = .0067. There is enough evidence to infer that the advertising medium makes a difference.

20.40 a Units = $\beta_0 + \beta_1$ Years + β_2 Years^2 + ε **c** $s_\varepsilon = 87.98$ and $R^2 = .1893$. The model fits poorly.

Chapter 21

21.2 38.8, 35.4, 35.8, 38.8, 44.4, 46.8, 48.8, 46.2

21.4 19.00, 21.67, 24.33, 26.67, 26.67, 26.33, 24.67, 24.33, 21.00, 19.00

21.8 12.00, 16.80, 16.16, 22.43, 18.09, 16.42, 23.28, 21.46, 22.69, 15.74

21.10 38.00, 38.50, 38.85, 39.47, 40.12, 40.91, 41.82, 42.53, 42.88, 43.09

21.14 33.20, 34.80, 34.00, 37.00, 36.40, 35.20, 33.00, 36.20, 34.80, 37.00, 39.40, 44.20, 44.40, 45.00, 46.00, 43.60

21.16 18.00, 19.60, 22.56, 25.94, 28.76, 25.26, 30.35, 28.61, 27.17, 30.70, 36.02, 33.21, 36.33, 35.00, 41.80, 43.08

21.18 The quadratic model would appear to be the best model.

21.20 Linear model: $\hat{y} = -4.96 + 2.38t$ ($R^2 = .81$). Quadratic model: $\hat{y} = 3.14 - 2.48t + .54t^2$ ($R^2 = .98$). The quadratic trend line fits better.

21.22 .675, .892, .864, 1.212, 1.357

21.24 .839, 1.058, 1.270, .833

21.26 b $\hat{y} = 16,204 - 8.21$Year

21.28 1.404, .517, .515, .621, .675, 1.145, 2.123

21.30 MAD = 4.60, SSE = 125

21.32 MAD = 9.6, SSE = 552

21.34 191.1, 331.2, 418.5, 169.2

21.36 540.5

21.38 43.08

21.40 30.71, 23.38, 22.67, 19.21

21.42 a 15,532 **b** 15,359

21.44 349.20, 323.16, 318.28, 367.60

21.46 136.47, 121.44, 88.60, 164.81

21.48 The only component appears to be seasonality.

21.50 .6464, 1.0450, 1.4050, .9037

Chapter 22

22.6 81

22.8 22

22.10 a .6604 **b** .0362

22.12 19,250

22.14 5.36

22.16 770,000

22.18 3.83

22.19 1,540,000

22.20 a .3660 **b** .0179

22.26 c The process is out of control at samples 29 and 30. **d** A level shift occurred.

22.28 The process is under control.

22.30 The process is under control.

22.32 a The process is out of control. **b** The process is out of control at sample 19. **c** The width became too small.

22.34 The process is out of control at sample 23.

22.36 .90

22.38 The process went out of control at sample 29.

22.40 The process is under control.

22.42 .07. The value of the index is low because the statistics used to calculate the control limits were taken when the process was out of control.

22.44 Centerline = .0324; control limits: 0, .06996. The process is out of control at sample 25.

22.46 Centerline = .0383; control limits: 0, .0959. The process is out of control at samples 25 and 30.

22.48 The process is out of control at sample 28.

22.50 The process is out of control at sample 24.

Chapter 23

23.6 a $EOL(a_1) = 4.0$, $EOL(a_2) = 5.8$, $EOL(a_3) = 6.6$

23.8 a & **b** Bake 2 cakes.

23.10 Pay flat fee.

23.12 Order 200 shirts.

23.14 a & **b** Build a medium-size plant.

23.16 Don't produce.

23.18 32.5

23.20 a 10 **b** 2

23.22 I_1: .50, .50, 0. I_2: .268, .357, .375. I_3: .172, .345, .483. I_4: .109, .435, .456.

23.24 a I_1: a_3; I_2: a_1 **b** 3.191

23.26 .30

23.28 As the prior probabilities become more diverse, EVSI decreases.

23.30 4.1 million

23.32 b Switch to rock and roll. **c** 194,000

23.34 Don't proceed with recycling venture.

23.36 38,104

23.38 c Produce Battery 2. **d** 50,000

23.40 315

23.42 Sample. Small number: Install 25. Medium number: Install 50. Large number: Install 100.

23.44 Sample. Rave review: Release in North America. Lukewarm response: Sell to European distributor, Poor response: Sell to European distributor.

Chapter 24

24.2 $z = 3.15$, p-value = .0016; yes

24.4 $t = -2.29$, p-value = .0121; yes

24.6 b LCL = $80,033, UCL = $97,155; it does appear that not all fines are collected.

24.8 $\chi^2 = 25.0273$, p-value = 0; yes

24.10 $z = -2.28$, p-value = .0114; yes

24.12 $F = 1.37$, p-value = .2543; no

24.14 Stepwise regression result: The only independent variables that are linearly related to salary are assists in 1992–93 and goals in 1992–93.

24.16 $F = 1.09$, p-value = .3441; no

24.18 $t = -1.31$, p-value = .0994; no

24.20 a $t = 2.98$, p-value = .0024; yes **b** $t = -3.39$, p-value = .0008; yes

24.22 a $t = 20.61$, p-value = 0; yes **b** $z = 3.10$, p-value = .0010; yes

24.24 Gender: $F = 3.77$, p-value = .0541. Fitness: $F = 39.97$, p-value = 0. Interaction: $F = 1.66$, p-value = .1935. There are differences between fitness levels.

24.26 Only problem-solving skill (p-value = 0) and technical knowledge (p-value = 0) are linearly related to quality.

24.28 a $t = -3.71$, p-value = .0001; yes **b** $z = -6.03$, p-value = 0; yes

24.30 Neither variable appears to be related to flow.

22.32 Question 1: $z = -4.95$, p-value = 0; yes. Question 2: $z = -1.56$, p-value = .0589; no. Question 3: $z = -.56$, p-value = .2888; no. Question 4: $z = -1.65$, p-value = .0490; yes.

22.34 Question 1: $H = 2.6349$, p-value = .2678; no. Question 2: $H = 5.2525$, p-value = .0723; no. Question 3: $H = .3716$, p-value = .8304; no. Question 4: $H = 1.2542$, p-value = .5341; no. Question 5: $\chi^2 = 2.4777$, p-value = .2897; no. Comments: $\chi^2 = 30.9799$, p-value = 0; yes

22.36 a p-value = .4943; no **b** $z = -.48$, p-value = .3143; no

24.38 Question 1: $t = -4.00$, p-value = 0; yes. Question 2: $z = -1.55$, p-value = .0609; no. 6 months after heart attack: $z = .43$, p-value = .6646; no. 12 months after heart attack: $z = .26$, p-value = .6016; no.

24.40 Product C: Flow: $F = 3.69$, p-value = .0315; yes. Temperature: $F = 14.06$, p-value = .0004; yes. Interaction: $F = 1.03$, p-value = .3628; no. Product Y: flow: $F = 67.85$, p-value = 0; yes. Temperature: $F = 32.05$, p-value = 0; yes. Interaction: $F = 14.03$, p-value = 0; yes.

24.42 $F = 34.35$, p-value = 0; yes

24.44 The data are observational. There may be a link between arthritis and Alzheimer's disease that explains the statistical result.

24.46 Age: $F = 6.37$, p-value = .0030; gender: $F = 7.98$, p-value = .0062; interaction: $F = .72$, p-value = .4927. Differences are due to age and gender.

Credits

Index

Index of Computer Output and Instructions